Third Edition

ESSENTIALS OF INVESTMENTS

SERIES IN FINANCE, INSURANCE AND REAL ESTATE
Stephen A. Ross
Sterling Professor of Economics and Finance
Yale University
Consulting Editor

FINANCIAL MANAGEMENT

Benninga and Sarig
Corporate Finance: A Valuation Approach

Block and Hirt
Foundations of Financial Management
Eighth Edition

Brealey and Myers
Principles of Corporate Finance
Fifth Edition

Brealey, Myers and Marcus
Fundamentals of Corporate Finance

Brooks
PC FinGame: The Financial Management Decision Game
Version 2.0 - DOS and Windows

Bruner
Case Studies in Finance: Managing for Corporate Value Creation
Second Edition

Chew
The New Corporate Finance: Where Theory Meets Practice

Grinblatt and Titman
Financial Markets and Corporate Strategy

Helfert
Techniques of Financial Analysis: A Modern Approach
Ninth Edition

Higgins
Analysis for Financial Management
Fifth Edition

Hite
A Programmed Learning Guide to Finance

Kester, Fruhan, Piper and Ruback
Case Problems in Finance
Eleventh Edition

Nunnally and Plath
Cases in Finance
Second Edition

Parker and Beaver
Risk Management: Challenges and Solutions

Ross, Westerfield and Jaffe
Corporate Finance
Fourth Edition

Ross, Westerfield and Jordan
Essentials of Corporate Finance

Ross, Westerfield and Jordan
Fundamentals of Corporate Finance
Fourth Edition

Smith
The Modern Theory of Corporate Finance
Second Edition

White
Financial Analysis with an Electronic Calculator
Third Edition

INVESTMENTS

Ball and Kothari
Financial Statement Analysis

Bodie, Kane and Marcus
Essentials of Investments
Third Edition

Bodie, Kane and Marcus
Investments
Third Edition

Cohen, Zinbarg and Zeikel
Investment Analysis and Portfolio Management
Fifth Edition

Farrell
Portfolio Management: Theory and Applications
Second Edition

Gibson
Option Valuation

Hirt and Block
Fundamentals of Investment Management
Fifth Edition

Jarrow
Modeling Fixed Income Securities and Interest Rate Options

Lorie, Dodd and Kimpton
The Stock Market: Theories and Evidence
Second Edition

Morningstar, Inc. and Remaley
U.S. Equities On Floppy Educational Version
Annual Edition

Shimko
The Innovative Investor
Version 2.0 - Lotus and Excel

FINANCIAL INSTITUTIONS AND MARKETS

Flannery and Flood
Flannery and Flood's ProBanker: A Financial Services Simulation

James and Smith
Studies in Financial Institutions: Non-Bank Intermediaries

Rose
Commercial Bank Management: Producing and Selling Financial Services
Third Edition

Rose
Money and Capital Markets: Financial Institutions and Instruments in a Global Marketplace
Sixth Edition

Third Edition

ESSENTIALS OF INVESTMENTS

ZVI BODIE
Boston University

ALEX KANE
University of California, San Diego

ALAN J. MARCUS
Boston College

Boston, Massachusetts   Burr Ridge, Illinois   Dubuque, Iowa   Madison, Wisconsin
New York, New York   San Francisco, California   St. Louis, Missouri

To our families with love and gratitude.

Irwin/McGraw-Hill

A Division of The McGraw·Hill Companies

Essentials of Investments

Copyright © 1998 by The McGraw-Hill Companies, Inc. All rights reserved. Previous editions © 1992 and 1995 by Richard D. Irwin, a Times Mirror Higher Education Group, Inc., company. Printed in the United States of America. Except as permitted under the United States Copyright Act of 1976, no part of this publication may be reproduced or distributed in any form or by any means, or stored in a database or retrieval system, without the prior written permission of the publisher.

This book is printed on acid-free paper.

3 4 5 7 8 9 0 VH/VH 9 0 9

ISBN 0-256-16459-2

Vice President and Editorial Director: *Michael W. Junior*
Publisher: *Gary Burke*
Associate editor: *Shelley Kronzek*
Developmental editor: *Michele Janicek*
Senior marketing manager: *Katie M. Rose Matthews*
Project manager: *Robert A. Preskill and Jean Lou Hess*
Production supervisor: *Lori Koetters*
Senior designer: *Crispin Prebys*
Designer: *Maureen McCutchean*
Compositor: *Shepard Poorman Communications*
Typeface: *10/12 Times Roman*
Printer: *Von Hoffmann Press, Inc.*

Library of Congress Cataloging-in-Publication Data

Bodie, Zvi.
    Essentials of investments / Zvi Bodie, Alex Kane, Alan J. Marcus.
  — 3rd ed.
      p. cm. — (The Irwin series in finance)
    Includes bibliographical references and indexes.
    ISBN 0-256-16459-2. — ISBN 0-256-27134-8 (Wall Street Journal ed.)
    1. Investments. I. Kane, Alex. II. Marcus, Alan J. III. Title.
  IV. Series.
  HG4521.B563   1998
  332.6—dc21   97-13806

INTERNATIONAL EDITION
Copyright © 1998. Exclusive rights by The McGraw-Hill Companies, Inc. for manufacture and export. This
  book cannot be re-exported from the country to which it is consigned by McGraw-Hill.
The International edition is not available in North America.

When ordering the title, use ISBN 0-07-115428-0.

http://www.mhhe.com

About the Authors

ZVI BODIE
Boston University

Zvi Bodie is professor of finance at Boston University School of Management. He holds a PhD from the Massachusetts Institute of Technology and has served on the finance faculty at Harvard University and at MIT. He currently serves as a member of the Global Financial System Group at Harvard University and the Pension Research Council at the University of Pennsylvania.

He has published widely on pension finance, the management of financial guarantees in both the private and public sector, and investment strategy in an inflationary environment. He has coedited several books on pensions, including *Securing Employer Pensions: An International Perspective; Pensions and the Economy: Sources, Uses and Limitations of Data. Pensions in the U.S. Economy; Issues in Pension Economics;* and *Financial Aspects of the U.S. Pension System.*

Professor Bodie's research on pensions has focused on the funding and investment policies of private pension plans and on public policies such as the provision of government pension insurance. He has consulted on pension policy for the U.S. Department of Labor, the Pension Benefit Guaranty Corporation, and the State of Israel.

ALEX KANE
University of California, San Diego

Alex Kane is professor of finance and economics at the Graduate School of International Relations and Pacific Studies at the University of California, San Diego. He was visiting professor at the Faculty of Economics, University of Tokyo; Graduate School of Business, Harvard; Kennedy School of Government, Harvard; and research associate, National Bureau of Economic Research. An author of many articles in finance and management journals, Professor Kane's research is mainly in corporate finance, portfolio management, and capital markets, most recently in the measurement of market volatility and the pricing of options. Professor Kane is the developer of the *International Simulation Laboratory (ISL)* for training and experimental research in executive decision making.

ALAN J. MARCUS
Boston College

Alan Marcus is professor of finance and chairman of the finance department in the Wallace E. Carroll School of Management at Boston College. He received his PhD in Economics from MIT in 1981. Professor Marcus recently has been a visiting professor at the Athens Laboratory of Business Administration and at MIT's Sloan School of Management and has served as a research associate at the National Bureau of Economic Research. He also established the Chartered Financial Analysts Review Program at Boston College. Professor Marcus has published widely in the fields of capital markets and portfolio management, with an emphasis on applications of futures and options pricing models. His consulting work has ranged from new product development to provision of expert testimony in utility rate proceedings. He also spent two years at the Federal Home Loan Mortgage Corporation (Freddie Mac), where he developed models of mortgage pricing and credit risk, and he currently serves on the Advisory Council for the Currency Risk Management Alliance of State Street Bank and Windham Capital Management Boston.

Preface

In no other field is the transfer of theory to real-world practice as rapid as it is now in the financial industry. New securities and trading strategies derived from financial theory emerge continually. As a result, the line between finance practitioners and theorists has become increasingly fuzzy. A solid grounding in principles is required for all those who participate in the markets and work with the instruments now commonly traded.

Essentials of Investments, Third Edition, is intended as a textbook on investment analysis most applicable for the undergraduate student's first course in investments. Our focus on investment analysis allows us to present financial theory as well as highlight its use in the practical world and convey insights of practical value. We have eliminated unnecessary mathematical detail and instead concentrated on the intuition and insights that will be useful to practitioners throughout their careers as new ideas and challenges emerge from the financial marketplace.

In our effort to link theory to practice, we also have attempted to make our approach consistent with that of the Institute of Chartered Financial Analysts (ICFA), a subsidiary of the Association of Investment Management and Research (AIMR). In addition to fostering research in finance, the AIMR and ICFA administer an education and certification program to candidates seeking the title of Chartered Financial Analyst (CFA). The CFA curriculum represents the consensus of a committee of distinguished scholars and practitioners regarding the core of knowledge required by the investment professional.

There are many features of this text that make it consistent with and relevant to the CFA curriculum. The end-of-chapter problem sets contain questions from past CFA exams, and, for students who will be taking the exam, Appendix D is a useful tool that lists each CFA question in the text and the exam from which it has been taken. Chapter 3 includes excerpts from the "Code of Ethics and Standards of Professional Conduct" of the ICFA, and Chapter 5, which discusses investors and the investment process and is modeled after the ICFA outline, includes guidelines on "How to Become a Chartered Financial Analyst."

UNDERLYING PHILOSOPHY

Legend has it that a student once approached a renowned traditional scholar and asked to be taught the entire Bible while standing on one foot. The angry scholar kicked the fresh would-be student out the door. The student then approached the best-known liberal scholar of the day with the same request. "This is quite simple," the wise man told the boy. "Thou shalt love thy neighbor as thyself." "Is this all?" gasped the fellow in disbelief. "Oh yes," said the old man. "All else is explanation."

Like the liberal scholar, we believe that attention to a few important principles can simplify the study of otherwise difficult material and that fundamental principles should organize and motivate all study. These principles are crucial to understanding the securities already traded in financial markets and in understanding new securities that will be introduced in the future. For this reason, we have made this book thematic, meaning we never offer rules of thumb without reference to the central tenets of the modern approach to finance.

The common theme unifying this book is that *security markets are nearly efficient*, meaning most securities are usually priced appropriately given their risk and return attributes. There are few free lunches found in markets as competitive as the financial market. This simple observation is, nevertheless, remarkably powerful in its implications for the design of investment strategies; as a result, our discussions of strategy are always guided by the implications of the efficient markets hypothesis. While the degree of market efficiency is, and always will be, a matter of debate, we hope our discussions throughout the book convey a good dose of healthy criticism concerning much conventional wisdom.

DISTINCTIVE THEMES

This edition of *Essentials of Investments* has three distinctive themes:

1. First is the thematic organization of the text around a central core of consistent principles. The central theme is the near-informational-efficiency of well-developed security markets, such as those in the U.S. Other themes are the centrality of the risk-return trade-off in developing investment strategy and the general awareness that competitive markets do not offer "free lunches" to participants.

2. This text places greater emphasis on **asset allocation** than most of its competitors. We prefer this emphasis for two important reasons. First, it corresponds to the procedure that most individuals actually follow. Typically, you start with all of your money in a bank account, only then considering how much to invest in something riskier that might offer a higher expected return. The logical step at this point is to consider other risky asset classes, such as stock, bonds, or real estate. This is an asset allocation decision. Second, in most cases, the asset allocation choice is far more important in determining overall investment performance than is the set of security selection decisions. Asset allocation is the primary determinant of the risk-return profile of the investment portfolio, and so it deserves primary attention in a study of investment policy.

3. This text offers a much broader and deeper treatment of futures, options, and other derivative security markets than most investments texts. These markets have become both crucial and integral to the financial universe and are the major sources of innovation in that universe. Your only choice is to become conversant in these markets—whether you are to be a finance professional or simply a sophisticated individual investor.

NEW IN THE THIRD EDITION

Following is a summary of the content changes in the Third Edition:

Market Structure (Chapter 3)

We have updated our treatment of market microstructure in Chapter 3 with an additional discussion of the recent controversy over trading practices in the Nasdaq market. This discussion brings students up to date on trading practices in various security markets and provides an overview of the advantages and disadvantages of various forms of market organization.

New Chapter on Mutual Funds and Other Investment Companies (Chapter 4)

Chapter 4 provides considerable detail on the organization of funds, reviews the costs and benefits associated with investing via mutual funds, examines empirical evidence on the investment performance of funds, and discusses how to find and interpret information on funds such as that presented in *Morningstar's* guide. This chapter thus provides the background necessary to understand this increasingly important market.

Expanded Discussion of Historical Rates of Return (Chapter 6)

In Chapter 6 of this edition, we have added tables of historical data regarding the performance of several asset classes, as well as detailed discussions of various measures of historical rates of return. The new rate of return series give a richer set of benchmarks by which to evaluate investment performance. The expanded discussion of rate of return facilitates the interpretation of these data.

Efficient Markets (Chapter 9)

Chapter 9's review of the empirical literature on the efficient markets hypothesis has been thoroughly updated. The new coverage highlights important new anomalies and attempts to provide balanced interpretations of them.

Fixed Income Management (Chapter 11)

A new discussion of convexity has been added to Chapter 11 of this edition. The new material highlights some of the problems encountered in fixed-income risk management and provides an introduction to more advanced techniques. The discussion appears in a modular format that can be easily skipped if the instructor views the material as too advanced.

Equity Markets (Chapter 13)

Chapter 13, which covers equity valuation, contains an expanded discussion of P/E ratios. These ratios are crucial to security analysis and the new coverage provides additional insight into how they may be interpreted.

Increased International Coverage

This edition contains new coverage of the organization of international equity markets in Chapter 3 as well as new data on the historical performance of major stock indexes in Chapter 20. These additions allow the student to place the organization and historical performance of U.S. markets in a wider context by allowing for international comparisons.

In addition to these changes, we have updated and edited our treatment of topics wherever it was possible to improve exposition or coverage.

ORGANIZATION AND CONTENT

The Third Edition of *Essentials of Investments* is composed of six sections that are fairly independent and may be studied in a variety of sequences. Since there is enough material in the book for a two-semester course, clearly a one-semester course will require the instructor to decide which parts to include. The Instructor's Manual that accompanies the text offers several alternative syllabi for a one- or two-course sequence in Investments.

Part One is introductory and contains important institutional material focusing on the financial environment. We discuss the major players in the financial markets, provide an overview of the types of securities traded in those markets, and explain how and where securities are traded. We also discuss in depth mutual funds and other investment companies, which have become an increasingly important means of investing for individual investors. Part One also lays out the general framework for the investment process in a nontechnical manner, modeled after the approach presented in CFA study materials.

The material presented in Part One should make it possible for instructors to assign term projects early in the course. These projects might require the student to analyze in detail a particular group of securities. Many instructors like to involve their students in some sort of investment game and the material in these chapters will facilitate this process.

Part Two contains the core of modern portfolio theory. We start with a general discussion of risk and return and the lessons of capital market history, and then we proceed to asset allocation and portfolio optimization. After our treatment of modern portfolio theory, we investigate its implications for the equilibrium structure of expected rates of return on risky assets, covering both the capital asset pricing model and arbitrage pricing theory. We complete Part Two with a chapter on the efficient market hypothesis, including its rationale as well as the evidence for and against it.

Part Three is the first of three parts on security valuation. The chapters in this part focus on fixed-income securities—bond pricing, term structure relationships, and risk management. The next two parts deal with equity securities and derivative securities. For a course emphasizing security analysis and excluding portfolio theory, an instructor may proceed directly from Part One to Part Three with no loss in continuity.

Part Four is devoted to equity securities. We proceed in a "top-down" manner, starting with the broad macroeconomic environment and then moving on to equity valuation, fundamental analysis, including financial statement analysis, and finally technical analysis.

Part Five covers derivative assets such as options, futures, swaps, and callable and convertible securities. It contains two chapters on options and one on futures.

Finally, Part Six presents extensions of previous material. Topics covered in this part include the evaluation of portfolio performance, portfolio management in an international setting, and an overview of active portfolio management.

PEDAGOGICAL FEATURES

Opening Vignettes

Each part of the Third Edition begins with an opening vignette. These openers provide a broad and high-interest introduction to the material that is to follow. The vignettes often cite high-profile cases from current events to illustrate the importance of the material to real-world practice.

Chapter Objectives

Each chapter begins with a statement of the objectives of the chapter and describes the material to be covered, providing students with an overview of the concepts they will understand after reading the chapter.

Boxed Readings

Current articles from financial publications, such as *The Wall Street Journal*, *Business Week*, and *The Economist*, are featured as boxed readings. Each box is discussed in the narrative of the text, and, therefore, its real-world relevance to the chapter material is clearly defined for the students. For instructors who do not have time to cover these boxes, the text references provide a sufficient guide for students. For instructors who do wish to discuss the boxes in class, each reading is included in the presentation of chapter material in the Instructor's Manual, and the Test Bank includes at least one test question per article, making it easy for instructors to incorporate these current events articles into their classroom discussions.

Concept Checks

Strategically placed throughout each chapter, self-test questions and problems enable the student to determine whether he or she has understood the preceding material and to reinforce that understanding before reading further. Detailed solutions to these questions are found at the end of each chapter.

Key Terms

Key terms are indicated in boldface within the narrative and are defined in the margin the first time they are used. The terms also are listed at the end of the chapter, with page references for easy review.

Numbered Equations

Key equations are called out in the text and identified by equation numbers. Equations that are frequently used are also featured on the text's back endsheets for convenient reference.

Numbered Examples

Separate numbered and titled examples are integrated in the chapters and indicated by a colored sidebar. Using the worked-out solutions to these examples as models, students can learn how to solve particular problems in a step-by-step manner as well as gain insight into general principles by seeing how they are applied to answer concrete questions.

END-OF-CHAPTER FEATURES

Summary

This bulleted feature helps students review the key points and provides closure to the chapter.

List of Key Terms

To facilitate students' review of the chapter's key concepts, a list of key terms, including page references, appears at the end of each chapter.

Problem Sets

The end-of-chapter problems for each chapter progress from the simple to the complex. We strongly believe that practice in solving problems is a critical part of learning investments, so we provide a good variety of problems.

CFA Questions

We provide numerous CFA questions in applicable chapters. These questions represent the kinds of questions that professionals in the field believe are relevant to the practicing money manager. These problems are identified by an icon in the text margin. Appendix D lists each CFA question and the level and year of the CFA exam it was included in, for easy reference when studying for the exam.

IEM Applications

This new section includes questions and projects to accompany the Iowa Electronic Markets (IEM), a real-time/real-money, on-line futures market. (See IEM under "Ancillary Materials" below for information on how to access this product.) This feature allows students to take their understanding of the chapter material and apply it to a real-world situation. Solutions and tips relevant to these questions are included in the Solutions Manual, available to instructors and students, which allows students to use IEM without instructor guidance. In addition, the questions and solutions are reprinted in the Instructor's Manual, along with additional questions for instructors who require IEM for their class and want related homework assignments.

ANCILLARY MATERIALS

For the Instructor:

Instructor's Manual

Prepared by Richard D. Johnson, Colorado State University, this instructional tool provides an integrated learning approach. Each chapter includes a Chapter Overview, Learning Objectives, and Presentation of Chapter Material, which outlines the material and organizes it around the Transparency Masters/PowerPoint Presentation Software. Transparency Masters are located at the end of each chapter. The boxed readings also are summarized, with tips on how to incorporate them into your classroom discussion.

Also included in the Instructor's Manual is a section that includes questions and projects for the Iowa Electronic Markets. Please see the *"For the Student"* section below for more information on this product.

New! PowerPoint Presentation Software

These presentation slides, also developed by Richard D. Johnson, provide the instructor with an electronic format of the Transparency Masters. These slides follow the order of the chapters, but if you have PowerPoint software, you may customize the program to fit your lecture presentation.

Test Bank

Prepared by David Louton, Bryant College, the Test Bank has been expanded to include more than 1,000 questions. Each question is ranked by level of difficulty (easy, medium, hard), which allows greater flexibility in creating a test. For instructors who like to cover the boxed readings, there is at least one test question per article included. Detailed solutions to the problems also are included. The Test Bank also is available in a computerized format for DOS, Windows, and Macintosh.

For the Student:

New! The Wall Street Journal Edition

Available through a unique arrangement with Dow Jones & Company, *The Wall Street Journal* Edition of *Essentials of Investments* includes a free 10-week subscription to *The Wall Street Journal* included in the price of the book. Instructors should contact their sales representative about ordering this special edition.

Solutions Manual

The Solutions Manual, prepared by the authors, provides detailed solutions to the end-of-chapter problems. The authors' involvement in the Solutions Manual ensures consistency between the solution approaches shown in the examples in the text and those presented in the solutions manual.

New! Ready Notes

This note-taking supplement contains a reduced copy of every image from the Transparency Masters and PowerPoint Presentation Software packages. There is room to take notes next to each image, allowing students a more complete and organized method for recording lecture notes.

The Innovative Investor, Version 2.0

Prepared by David Shimko, this software is available in Lotus and a new Excel version. These templates are designed to provide students with quick access to difficult calculations associated with the analysis of securities such as stocks, bonds, callable and convertible securities, options, and futures, as well as to facilitate the analytics underlying asset allocation, performance evaluation, and other applications. All spreadsheets come complete with comprehensive "What-if" analysis, in addition to automatic graphing and printing capabilities. These user-friendly capsules are designed to solve many problems a student of investments might encounter, beginning with problems available in the User's Manual, but extending as well to problems you may encounter in a career as a financial analyst or sophisticated investor. Together with the text, the software enables students not only to process calculations, but to ask questions and build upon the intuition established in the text.

New! Iowa Electronic Markets (IEM)

The IEM is an on-line, real-time and real-money electronic futures market, sponsored by the University of Iowa and Irwin/McGraw-Hill. Students use real money accounts to trade contracts with payoffs based upon real-world events, such as political outcomes, companies' earnings per share, and stock price returns. The markets run continuously, with new sets of contracts opening at least once a month. Participating in IEM provides students with real incentives to learn about markets and follow economic, financial, and political news.

This edition of *Essentials of Investments* includes questions and projects for this supplement under the heading of "IEM Applications" in the end-of-chapter material. These questions help students apply the material they have learned in the text to real-world situations. The solutions are available in the Solutions Manual. All questions and solutions are reprinted in the Instructor's Manual, and additional questions are provided to assign as projects if the instructor desires.

Students can sign up and use IEM individually, without an instructor's guidance, or instructors can engage their class in a term-long project. For more information on IEM, go to http://www.mhhe.com/irwin/iem. For information on how to use IEM in the classroom, with sample syllabi and projects, go to http://biz.uiowa.edu/iem and click on "Classroom IEM." If you have additional questions, please contact your Irwin/McGraw-Hill sales representative.

ACKNOWLEDGMENTS

We received help from many people as we prepared this book. An insightful group of reviewers commented on this and previous editions of this text. Their comments and suggestions improved the exposition of the material considerably. These reviewers all deserve special thanks for their contributions.

Randall S. Billingsley
Virginia Polytechnic Institute and State University

Howard Bohnen
St. Cloud State University

Paul Bolster
Northeastern University

Alyce R. Campbell
University of Oregon

Greg Chaudoin
Loyola University

Ji Chen
University of Colorado at Denver

Mustafa Chowdhury
Louisiana State University

Diane Del Guercio
University of Oregon

David C. Distad
University of California at Berkeley

Gary R. Dokes
University of San Diego

Peter D. Ekman
Kansas State University

James F. Feller
Middle Tennessee State University

Deborah Gunthorpe
University of Tennessee

Thomas Hamilton
St. Mary's University

Gay Hatfield
University of Mississippi

Larry C. Holland
Oklahoma State University

Ron E. Hutchins
Eastern Michigan University

Richard Johnson
Colorado State University

Donald Kummer
University of Missouri, St. Louis

John Loughlin
St. Louis University

David Louton
Bryant College

David Loy
Illinois State University

Laurian Casson Lytle
University of Wisconsin at Whitewater

Leo Mahoney
Bryant College

Steven V. Mann
University of South Carolina

Jeffrey A. Manzi
Ohio University

James Marchand
Westminster College

Robert J. Martel
Bentley College

Linda J. Martin
Arizona State University

Edward Miller
University of New Orleans

Majed Muhtaseb
California State Polytechnic University

Mike Murray
Winona State University

Raj Padmaraj
Bowling Green University

John C. Park
Frostburg State University

Rose Prasad
Central Michigan University

Elias A. Raad
Ithaca College

Craig Ruff
Georgia State University

Edwin Stuart
Southeastern Oklahoma State University

George S. Swales
Southwest Missouri State University

Bruce Swensen
Adelphi University

Glenn Tanner
University of Hawaii

Donald J. Thompson
Georgia State University

Steven Thorley
Brigham Young University

Joe Walker
University of Alabama at Birmingham

Andrew L. Whitaker
North Central College

Howard Whitney
Franklin University

Michael E. Williams
University of Texas at Austin

Tony Wingler
University of North Carolina

Annie Wong
Western Connecticut State University

Richard H. Yanow
North Adams State College

Thomas J. Zwirlein
University of Colorado at Colorado Springs

For granting us permission to include many of its examination questions in the text, we are grateful to the Institute of Chartered Financial Analysts.

Much credit also is due to the development and production team: our special thanks goes to Michele Janicek, development editor; Mike Junior, editorial director; Robert Preskill, project manager; and Crispin Prebys, senior designer.

Finally, once again, our most important debts are to Judy, Hava, and Sheryl for their unflagging support.

Zvi Bodie
Alex Kane
Alan J. Marcus

Brief Contents

Contents

Part One

ELEMENTS OF INVESTMENTS

Even a cursory glance at *The Wall Street Journal* reveals a bewildering collection of securities, markets, and financial institutions. Although it may appear so, the financial environment is not chaotic: There is a rhyme and reason behind the vast array of financial instruments and the markets in which they trade.

These introductory chapters provide a bird's-eye view of the investing environment. We will give you a tour of the major types of markets in which securities trade, the trading process, and the major players in these arenas. You will see that both markets and securities have evolved to meet the changing and complex needs of different participants in the financial system.

Markets innovate and compete with each other for traders' business just as vigorously as competitors in other industries. The competition between the National Association of Securities Dealers Automatic Quotation System (Nasdaq) and the New York Stock Exchange (NYSE) for claim to the title "Market for the 21st Century" is fierce and public.

Trading practices and the way they differ across exchanges can mean big money to investors. Allegations of price-fixing on the Nasdaq market resulted in an antitrust investigation by the Department of Justice, private law suits that are still pending, as well as new directives by the Securities and Exchange Commission for dramatic reforms in the way that prices are quoted for stocks listed on Nasdaq. These rules can affect dealers' profits (and the cost of trading) by many millions of dollars.

These chapters will give you a good foundation with which to understand the basic types of securities and financial markets as well as how trading in those markets is conducted.

Chapter 1

INVESTMENTS:
BACKGROUND AND ISSUES

AFTER STUDYING THIS CHAPTER YOU SHOULD BE ABLE TO:

- Define an investment.

- Distinguish between real assets and financial assets.

- Describe the major steps in the construction of an investment portfolio.

- Identify major participants in financial markets.

- Identify types of financial markets and recent trends in those markets.

investment

Commitment of current resources in the expectation of deriving greater resources in the future.

An **investment** is the *current* commitment of money or other resources in the expectation of reaping *future* benefits. For example, an individual might purchase shares of stock anticipating that the future proceeds from the shares will justify both the time that her money is tied up as well as the risk of the investment. The time you will spend studying this text (not to mention its cost) also is an investment. You are forgoing either current leisure or the income you could be earning at a job in the expectation that your future career will be sufficiently enhanced to justify this commitment of time and effort. While these two investments differ in many ways, they share one key attribute that is central to all investments: You sacrifice something of value now, expecting to benefit from that sacrifice later.

This text can help you become an informed practitioner of investments. We will focus on investments in securities such as stocks, bonds, or options and futures contracts, but much of what we discuss will be useful in the analysis of any type of investment. The text will provide you with background in the organization of various securities markets, will survey the valuation and risk-management principles useful in particular markets, such as those for bonds or stocks, and will introduce you to the principles of portfolio construction.

Broadly speaking, this chapter addresses three topics that will provide a useful perspective for the material that is to come later. First, before delving into the topic of "investments," we consider the role of financial assets in the economy. We discuss the relationship between securities and the "real" assets that actually produce goods and services for consumers, and we consider why financial assets are important to the functioning of a developed economy. Given this background, we then take a first look at the types of decisions that confront investors as they assemble a portfolio of assets. These investment decisions are made in an environment where higher returns usually can be obtained only at the price of greater risk, and in which it is rare to find assets that are so mispriced as to be obvious bargains. These themes—the risk-return trade-off and the efficient pricing of financial assets—are central to the investment process, so it is worth pausing for a brief discussion of their implications as we begin the text. These implications will be fleshed out in much greater detail in later chapters. Finally, we conclude the chapter with an introduction to the organization of security markets, the various players that participate in those markets, and a brief overview of some of the more important changes in those markets in recent years. Together, these various topics should give you a feel for who the major participants are in the securities markets as well as the setting in which they act. We close the chapter with an overview of the remainder of the text.

1.1 REAL ASSETS VERSUS FINANCIAL ASSETS

real assets
Assets used to produce goods and services.

The material wealth of a society is ultimately determined by the productive capacity of its economy, that is, the goods and services its members can create. This capacity is a function of the **real assets** of the economy: the land, buildings, machines, and knowledge that can be used to produce goods and services.

financial assets
Claims on real assets or the income generated by them.

In contrast to such real assets are **financial assets,** such as stocks and bonds. Such securities are no more than sheets of paper (or entries in a computer!) and do not contribute directly to the productive capacity of the economy. Instead, these assets are the means by which individuals in well-developed economies hold their claims on real assets. Financial assets are claims to the income generated by real assets (or claims on income from the government). If we cannot own our own auto plant, we can still buy shares in General Motors or Toyota and, thereby, share in the income derived from the production of automobiles.

While real assets generate net income to the economy, financial assets simply define the allocation of income or wealth among investors. Individuals can choose between consuming their wealth today or investing for the future. If they choose to invest, they may place their wealth in financial assets by purchasing various securities. When investors buy these securities from companies, the firms use the money so raised to pay for real assets, such as plant, equipment, technology, or inventory. So investors' returns on securities ultimately come from the income produced by the real assets that were financed by the issuance of those securities.

The distinction between real and financial assets is apparent when we compare the balance sheet of U.S. households, shown in Table 1.1, with the composition of national wealth in the United States, shown in Table 1.2. Household wealth includes financial assets such as bank accounts, corporate stock, or bonds. However, these securities, which are financial assets of households, are *liabilities* of the issuers of the securities. For example, a bond that you treat as an asset because it gives you a claim on interest income and repayment of principal from General Motors is a liability of General Motors, which is obligated to make these payments to you. Your asset is GM's liability. Therefore, when we aggregate over all balance sheets, these claims cancel out, leaving only real assets as the net wealth of the economy. National wealth consists of structures, equipment, inventories of goods, and land.

We will focus almost exclusively on financial assets. But you shouldn't lose sight of the fact that the successes or failures of the financial assets we choose to purchase ultimately depend on the performance of the underlying real assets.

Concept Check

1. Are the following assets real or financial?
   a. Patents
   b. Lease obligations
   c. Customer goodwill
   d. A college education
   e. A $5 bill

TABLE 1.1   Balance Sheet of U.S. Households*

Assets	$ Billion	% Total	Liabilities & Net Worth	$ Billion	% Total
Tangible assets					
Houses	$ 4,518	15.8%	Mortgages	$ 3,163	11.1%
Land	3,015	10.6	Consumer credit	984	3.4
Durables	2,491	8.7	Bank & other loans	173	0.6
Other	520	1.8	Other	506	1.8
Total tangibles	$10,544	36.9%	Total liabilities	$ 4,826	16.9%
Financial assets					
Deposits	$ 3,102	10.9%			
Life insurance reserves	488	1.7			
Pension reserves	5,010	17.6			
Corporate equity	2,886	10.1			
Equity in noncorporate business	2,511	8.8			
Mutual fund shares	1,067	3.7			
Personal trusts	670	2.3			
Debt securities	1,873	6.6			
Other	388	1.4			
Total financial assets	17,995	63.1	Net worth	23,713	83.1
Total	$28,539	100.0%	Total	$28,539	100.0%

*Column sums subject to rounding error.

Source: *Balance Sheets for the U.S. Economy, 1945–94*, Board of Governors of the Federal Reserve System, June 1995.

TABLE 1.2
Domestic Net Worth*

Source: *Balance Sheets for the U.S. Economy, 1945–94*, Board of Governors of the Federal Reserve System, June 1995.

Assets	$ Billion
Residential structures	$ 5,856
Plant and equipment	6,061
Inventories	1,221
Consumer durables	2,491
Land	4,364
Gold and SDRs	21
Total	$20,014

*Column sums subject to rounding error.

1.2 A TAXONOMY OF FINANCIAL ASSETS

fixed-income securities
Pay a specified cash flow over a specific period.

It is common to distinguish among three broad types of financial assets: fixed income, equity, and derivatives. **Fixed-income securities** promise either a fixed stream of income or a stream of income that is determined according to a specified formula. For example, a corporate bond typically would promise that the bondholder will receive a fixed amount of interest each year. Other so-called floating-rate bonds promise payments that depend on current interest rates. For example, a bond may pay an interest rate that is fixed at three percentage points above the rate paid on U.S. Treasury bills. Unless the borrower is declared bankrupt, the payments on these securities are either fixed or determined by formula. For this reason, the investment performance of fixed-income securities typically is least closely tied to the financial condition of the issuer.

Nevertheless, fixed-income securities come in a tremendous variety of maturities and payment provisions. At one extreme, the *money market* refers to fixed-income securities that are short term, highly marketable, and generally of very low risk. Examples of money market securities are U.S. Treasury bills or bank certificates of deposit (CDs). In contrast, the fixed-income *capital market* includes long-term securities such as Treasury bonds, as well as bonds issued by federal agencies, state and local municipalities, and corporations. These bonds range from very safe in terms of default risk (for example, Treasury securities) to relatively risky (for example, high yield or "junk" bonds). They also are designed with extremely diverse provisions regarding payments provided to the investor, and protection against the bankruptcy of the issuer. We will take a first look at these securities in Chapter 2 and undertake a more detailed analysis of the fixed-income market in Part Three.

equity
An ownership share in a corporation.

Unlike fixed-income securities, common stock, or **equity,** in a firm represents an ownership share in the corporation. Equity holders are not promised any particular payment. They receive any dividends the firm may pay and have prorated ownership in the real assets of the firm. If the firm is successful, the value of equity will increase; if not, it will decrease. The performance of equity investments, therefore, is tied directly to the success of the firm and its real assets. For this reason, equity investments tend to be riskier than investments in fixed-income securities. Equity markets and equity valuation are the topics of Part Four.

derivative securities
Securities providing payoffs that depend on the values of other assets.

Finally, **derivative securities** such as options and futures contracts provide payoffs that are determined by the prices of *other* assets such as bond or stock prices. For example, a call option on a share of Du Pont stock might turn out to be worthless if Du Pont's share price remains below a threshold or "exercise" price such as $80 a share, but it can be quite valuable if the stock price rises above that level.[1] Derivative securities are so named because their values derive from the prices of other assets. For example, the value of the call option will depend on the price of Du Pont stock. Other important derivative securities are futures and swap contracts. We will treat these in Part Five.

Derivatives have become an integral part of the investment environment. One use of derivatives, perhaps the primary use, is to hedge risks or transfer them to other parties. This is done successfully every day, and the use of these securities for risk management is so commonplace that the multitrillion dollar market in derivative assets is routinely taken for granted. Derivatives also can be used to take highly speculative positions, however. Moreover, when complex derivatives are misunderstood, firms that believe they are hedging might in fact be increasing their exposure to various sources of risk. This seemed to be the case in 1994 when several firms lost large sums on their derivatives positions. Among the more spectacular losses were those of Procter & Gamble, which took a $157 million pretax charge on two interest-rate related derivative products, and Piper Jaffray Companies, a financial services firm which suffered a loss of $700 million in its fixed-income portfolios, many of which were believed by clients to be very conservatively invested. While these losses attracted considerable attention, they were in fact the exception to the more common use of such securities as risk management tools. Derivatives will continue to play an important role in portfolio construction and the financial system. We will return to this topic later in the text. For the time being, however, we direct you to the primer on derivatives in the nearby box.

In addition to these financial assets, individuals might invest directly in some real assets. For example, real estate or commodities such as precious metals or agricultural products are real assets that might form part of an investment portfolio.

1.3 FINANCIAL MARKETS AND THE ECONOMY

We stated earlier that real assets determine the wealth of an economy, while financial assets merely represent claims on real assets. Nevertheless, financial assets and the markets in which they are traded play several crucial roles in developed economies. Financial assets allow us to make the most of the economy's real assets.

---

[1]A call option is the right to buy a share of stock at a given exercise price on or before the option's maturity date. If the market price of Du Pont remains below $80 a share, the right to buy for $80 will turn out to be valueless. If the share price rises above $80 before the option matures, however, the option can be exercised to obtain the share for only $80.

Understanding the Complex World of Derivatives

What are derivatives anyway, and why are people saying such terrible things about them?

Some critics see the derivatives market as a multi-trillion-dollar house of cards composed of interlocking, highly leveraged transactions. They fear that the default of a single large player could stun the world financial system.

But others, including Federal Reserve Chairman Alan Greenspan, say the risk of such a meltdown is negligible. Proponents stress that the market's hazards are more than outweighed by the benefits derivatives provide in helping banks, corporations, and investors manage their risks.

Because the science of derivatives is relatively new, there's no easy way to gauge the ultimate impact these instruments will have. There are now more than 1,200 different kinds of derivatives on the market, most of which require a computer program to figure out. Surveying this complex subject, dozens of derivatives experts offered these insights:

Q: What is the broadest definition of derivatives?

A: Derivatives are financial arrangements between two parties whose payments are based on, or "derived" from, the performance of some agreed-upon benchmark. Derivatives can be issued based on currencies, commodities, government or corporate debt, home mortgages, stocks, interest rates, or any combination.

Company stock options, for instance, allow employees and executives to profit from changes in a company's stock price without actually owning shares. Without knowing it, homeowners frequently use a type of privately traded "forward" contract when they apply for a mortgage and lock in a borrowing rate for their house closing, typically for as many as 60 days in the future.

Q: What are the most common forms of derivatives?

A: Derivatives come in two basic categories—option-type contracts and forward-type contracts. These may be exchange-listed, such as futures and stock options, or they may be privately traded.

Options give buyers the right, but not the obligation, to buy or sell an asset at a preset price over a specific period. The option's price is usually a small percentage of the underlying asset's value.

Forward-type contracts, which include forwards, futures, and swaps, commit the buyer and the seller to trade a given asset at a set price on a future date. These are "price fixing" agreements that saddle the buyer with the same price risks as actually owning the asset. But normally, no money changes hands until the delivery date, when the contract is often settled in cash rather than by exchanging the asset.

Q: In business, what are they used for?

A: While derivatives can be powerful speculative instruments, businesses most often use them to hedge. For instance, companies often use forwards and exchange-listed futures to protect against fluctuations in currency or commodity prices, thereby helping to manage import and raw-materials costs. Options can serve a similar purpose; interest-rate options such as caps and floors help companies control financing costs in much the same way that caps on adjustable-rate mortgages do for homeowners.

Q: Why are derivatives potentially dangerous?

A: Because these contracts expose the two parties to market moves with little or no money actually changing hands, they involve leverage. And that leverage may be vastly increased by the terms of a particular contract. In the derivatives that hurt P&G, for instance, a given move in U.S. or German interest rates was multiplied 10 times or more.

When things go well, that leverage provides a big return, compared with the amount of capital at risk. But it also causes equally big losses when markets move the wrong way. Even companies that use derivatives to hedge, rather than speculate, may be at risk, since their operation would rarely produce perfectly offsetting gains.

Q: If they are so dangerous, why are so many businesses using derivatives?

A: They are among the cheapest and most readily available means at companies' disposal to buffer themselves against shocks in currency values, commodity prices, and interest rates. Donald Nicoliasen, a Price Waterhouse expert on derivatives, says derivatives "are a new tool in everybody's bag to better manage business returns and risks."

Source: Lee Berton. "Understanding the Complex World of Derivatives," *The Wall Street Journal*, June 14, 1994. Excerpted by permission of *The Wall Street Journal* © 1994 Dow Jones & Company, Inc. All Rights Reserved Worldwide.

Consumption Timing

Some individuals in an economy are earning more than they currently wish to spend. Others, for example, retirees, spend more than they currently earn. How can you shift your purchasing power from high-earnings periods to low-earnings periods of life? One way is to "store" your wealth in financial assets. In high-earnings periods, you can invest your savings in financial assets such as stocks and bonds. In low-earnings periods, you can sell these assets to provide funds for your consumption needs. By so doing, you can "shift" your consumption over the course of your lifetime, thereby allocating your consumption to periods that provide the greatest satisfaction. Thus, financial markets allow individuals to separate decisions concerning current consumption from constraints that otherwise would be imposed by current earnings.

Allocation of Risk

Virtually all real assets involve some risk. When GM builds its auto plants, for example, it cannot know for sure what cash flows those plants will generate. Financial markets and the diverse financial instruments traded in those markets allow investors with the greatest taste for risk to bear that risk, while other, less risk-tolerant individuals can, to a greater extent, stay on the sidelines. For example, if GM raises the funds to build its auto plant by selling both stocks and bonds to the public, the more optimistic or risk-tolerant investors can buy shares of stock in GM, while the more conservative ones can buy GM bonds. Because the bonds promise to provide a fixed payment, the stockholders bear most of the business risk. Thus, capital markets allow the risk that is inherent to all investments to be borne by the investors most willing to bear that risk.

This allocation of risk also benefits the firms that need to raise capital to finance their investments. When investors are able to select security types with the risk-return characteristics that best suit their preferences, each security can be sold for the best possible price. This facilitates the process of building the economy's stock of real assets.

Separation of Ownership and Management

Many businesses are owned and managed by the same individual. This simple organization is well-suited to small businesses and, in fact, was the most common form of business organization before the Industrial Revolution. Today, however, with global markets and large-scale production, the size and capital requirements of firms have skyrocketed. For example, General Electric has assets worth over $33 billion. Corporations of such size simply cannot exist as owner-operated firms. G.E. actually has about one-half million stockholders with an ownership stake in the firm proportional to their holdings of shares.

Such a large group of individuals obviously cannot actively participate in the day-to-day management of the firm. Instead, they elect a board of directors which in turn hires and supervises the management of the firm. This structure means that the owners and managers of the firm are different parties. This gives the firm a stability that the owner-managed firm cannot achieve. For example, if some stockholders decide they no longer wish to hold shares in the firm, they can sell their shares to another investor, with no impact on the management of the firm. Thus, financial assets and the ability to buy and sell those assets in the financial markets allow for easy separation of ownership and management.

How can all of the disparate owners of the firm, ranging from large pension funds holding hundreds of thousands of shares to small investors who may hold only a single share, agree on the objectives of the firm? Again, the financial markets provide some guidance. All may agree that the firm's management should pursue strategies that enhance the value of their shares. Such policies will make all shareholders wealthier and allow them all to better pursue their personal goals, whatever those goals might be.

1.4 THE INVESTMENT PROCESS

An investor's *portfolio* is simply his collection of investment assets. Once the portfolio is established, it is updated or "rebalanced" by selling existing securities and using the proceeds to buy new securities, by investing additional funds to increase the overall size of the portfolio, or by selling securities to decrease the size of the portfolio.

asset allocation
Allocation of investment portfolio across broad asset classes.

Investment assets can be categorized into broad asset classes, such as stocks, bonds, real estate, commodities, and so on. Investors make two types of decisions in constructing their portfolios. The **asset allocation** decision is the choice among broad asset classes, while the **security selection** decision is the choice of which particular securities to hold *within* each asset class.

security selection
Choice of specific securities within each asset class.

"Top-down" portfolio construction starts with asset allocation. For example, an individual who currently holds all of his money in a bank account would first decide what proportion of the overall portfolio ought to be moved into stocks, bonds, and so on. In this way, the broad features of the portfolio are established. Only after the asset allocation decision is made would the investor turn to the particular securities to be held.

security analysis
Analysis of the value of securities.

Security analysis involves the valuation of particular securities that might be included in the portfolio. For example, an investor might ask whether Merck or Pfizer is more attractively priced. Both bonds and stocks must be evaluated for investment attractiveness, but valuation is far more difficult for stocks because a stock's performance usually is far more sensitive to the condition of the issuing firm.

In contrast to top-down portfolio management is the "bottom-up" strategy. In this process, the portfolio is constructed from the securities that seem attractively priced without as much concern for the resultant asset allocation. Such a technique can result in unintended bets on one or another sector of the economy. For example, it might turn out that the portfolio ends up with a very heavy representation of firms in one industry, from one part of the country, or with exposure to one source of uncertainty. However, a bottom-up strategy does focus the portfolio on the assets that seem to offer the most attractive investment opportunities.

1.5 MARKETS ARE COMPETITIVE

Financial markets are highly competitive. Thousands of intelligent and well-backed analysts constantly scour the securities markets searching for the best buys. This competition means that we should expect to find few, if any, "free lunches," securities that are so underpriced that they represent obvious bargains. There are several implications of this no-free-lunch proposition. Let's examine two.

The Risk-Return Trade-Off

Investors invest for anticipated future returns, but those returns rarely can be predicted precisely. There will almost always be risk associated with investments. Actual or realized returns will almost always deviate from the expected return anticipated at the start of the investment period. For example, since 1926 the rate of return on common stocks of large firms has averaged about 12% per year. But actual returns have varied widely around this average value. In 1931 (the worst calendar year for the market since 1926), the stock market lost 43% of its value. In 1933 (the best year), the stock market gained 54%. You can be sure that investors did not anticipate such extreme performance at the start of either of these years. While the expected rate of return at the start of any year may be in the neighborhood of 12%, investors know the actual returns might not be even close to 12%.

Naturally, if all else could be held equal, investors would prefer investments with the highest expected return.[2] However, the no-free-lunch rule tells us that all else cannot be held equal. If you want higher expected returns, you will have to pay a price in terms of accepting higher investment risk. If higher expected return can be achieved without bearing extra risk, there will be a rush to buy the high-return assets, with the result that their prices will be driven up. Individuals considering investing in the asset at the now-higher price will find the investment less attractive: If you buy at a higher price, your expected rate of return (that is, profit per dollar invested) is lower. The asset will be considered attractive and its price will continue to rise until its expected return is no more than commensurate with risk. At this point, investors can anticipate a "fair" return relative to the asset's risk, but no more. Similarly, if returns are independent of risk, there will be a rush to sell high-risk assets. Their prices will fall (and their expected future rates of return will rise) until they eventually become attractive enough to be included again in investor portfolios. We conclude that there should be a **risk-return trade-off** in the securities markets, with higher-risk assets priced to offer higher expected returns than lower-risk assets.

risk-return trade-off
Assets with higher expected returns have greater risk.

Of course, this discussion leaves several important questions unanswered. How should one measure the risk of an asset? What should be the quantitative trade-off between risk (properly measured) and expected return? One would think that risk would have something to do with the volatility of an asset's returns, but this guess turns out to be only partly correct. When we mix assets into diversified portfolios, we need to consider the interplay among assets and the effect of diversification on the risk of the entire portfolio. *Diversification* means that many assets are held in the portfolio so that the exposure to any particular asset is limited. The effect of diversification on portfolio risk, the implications for the proper measurement of risk, and the risk-return relationship are the topics of Part Two. These topics are the subject of what has come to be known as *modern portfolio theory*. The development of this theory brought two of its pioneers, Harry Markowitz and William Sharpe, Nobel Prizes.

Efficient Markets

Another implication of the no-free-lunch proposition is that we should rarely expect to find bargains in the security markets. We will spend all of Chapter 9 examining the theory and evidence concerning the hypothesis that financial markets process all relevant information about securities quickly and efficiently, that is, that the security price usually reflects all the information available to investors concerning the value of the security. According to this hypothesis, as new information about a security becomes available, the price of the security quickly adjusts so that at any time, the security price equals the market consensus estimate of the value of the security. If this were so, there would be neither underpriced nor overpriced securities.

One interesting implication of this "efficient market hypothesis" concerns the choice between active and passive investment-management strategies. **Passive management** calls for holding highly diversified portfolios without spending effort or other resources attempting to improve investment performance through security analysis. **Active management** is the attempt to improve performance either by identifying mispriced securities or by timing the performance of broad asset classes, for example, increasing one's commitment to stocks when one is bullish on the stock market. If markets are efficient and prices reflect all relevant information, perhaps it is better to follow passive strategies instead of spending resources in a futile attempt to outguess your competitors in the financial markets.

passive management
Buying and holding a diversified portfolio without attempting to identify mispriced securities.

active management
Attempting to identify mispriced securities or to forecast broad market trends.

If the efficient market hypothesis were taken to the extreme, there would be no point in active security analysis; only fools would actively analyze securities. Without ongoing

---

[2]The "expected" return is not the return investors believe they necessarily will earn, or even their most likely return. It is instead the result of averaging across all possible outcomes, recognizing that some outcomes are more likely than others. It is the average rate of return across possible economic scenarios.

security analysis, however, prices eventually would depart from "correct" values, creating new incentives for experts to move in. Therefore, even in environments as competitive as the financial markets, we may observe only *near*-efficiency, and profit opportunities may exist for especially diligent and creative investors. This motivates our discussion of active portfolio management in Part Six. More importantly, our discussions of security analysis and portfolio construction generally must account for the likelihood of nearly efficient markets.

1.6 THE PLAYERS

From a birds's-eye view, there would appear to be three major players in the financial markets:

1. Firms are net borrowers. They raise capital now to pay for investments in plant and equipment. The income generated by those real assets provides the returns to investors who purchase the securities issued by the firm.
2. Households typically are net savers. They purchase the securities issued by firms that need to raise funds.
3. Governments can be borrowers or lenders, depending on the relationship between tax revenue and government expenditures. In the past two decades, however, the U.S. government systematically has run budget deficits, meaning that its tax receipts have been less than its expenditures. The government, therefore, has had to borrow funds to cover its budget deficit. Issuance of Treasury bills, notes, and bonds is the major way that the government borrows funds from the public.

Corporations and governments do not sell all or even most of their securities directly to individuals. For example, about half of all stock is held by large financial institutions such as pension funds, mutual funds, insurance companies, and banks. These financial institutions stand between the security issuer (the firm) and the ultimate owner of the security (the individual investor). For this reason, they are called *financial intermediaries*. Similarly, corporations do not market their own securities to the public. Instead, they hire agents, called investment bankers, to represent them to the investing public. Let's examine the roles of these intermediaries.

Financial Intermediaries

Households want desirable investments for their savings, yet the small (financial) size of most households makes direct investment difficult. A small investor seeking to lend money to businesses that need to finance investments doesn't advertise in the local newspaper to find a willing and desirable borrower. Moreover, an individual lender would not be able to diversify across borrowers to reduce risk. Finally, an individual lender is not equipped to assess and monitor the credit risk of borrowers.

financial intermediaries
Institutions that "connect" borrowers and lenders by accepting funds from lenders and loaning funds to borrowers.

For these reasons, **financial intermediaries** have evolved to bring lenders and borrowers together. These financial intermediaries include banks, investment companies, insurance companies, and credit unions. Financial intermediaries issue their own securities to raise funds to purchase the securities of other corporations.

For example, a bank raises funds by borrowing (taking deposits) and lending that money to other borrowers. The interest spread between the rates paid to depositors and the rates charged to borrowers is the source of the bank's profit. In this way, lenders and borrowers do not need to contact each other directly. Instead, each goes to the bank, which acts as an intermediary between the two. The problem of matching lenders with borrowers is solved when each comes independently to the common intermediary.

Financial intermediaries are distinguished from other businesses in that both their assets and their liabilities are overwhelmingly financial. Table 1.3 shows that the balance sheets of

TABLE 1.3 Balance Sheet of Financial Institutions*

Assets	$ Billion	% Total	Liabilities and Net Worth	$ Billion	% Total
Tangible assets			Liabilities		
Equipment and structures	$ 528	3.1%	Deposits	$ 3,462	20.1%
Land	99	0.6	Mutual fund shares	1,564	9.1
Total tangibles	$ 628	3.6%	Life insurance reserves	478	2.8
			Pension reserves	4,651	27.0
			Money market securities	1,150	6.7
			Bonds and mortgages	1,589	9.2
Financial assets			Other	3,078	17.8
Deposits and cash	$ 364	2.1%	Total liabilities	$15,971	92.6%
Government securities	3,548	20.6			
Corporate bonds	1,924	11.2			
Mortgages	2,311	13.4			
Consumer credit	894	5.2			
Other loans	1,803	10.4			
Corporate equity	3,310	19.2			
Other	2,471	14.3			
Total financial assets	16,625	96.4	Net worth	1,281	7.4
Total	$17,252	100.0%	Total	$17,252	100.0%

*Column sums subject to rounding error.

Source: *Balance Sheets for the U.S. Economy, 1945–94*,
    Board of Governors of the Federal Reserve System, June 1995.

TABLE 1.4 Balance Sheet of Nonfinancial U.S. Business*

Assets	$ Billion	% Total	Liabilities and Net Worth	$ Billion	% Total
Tangible assets			Liabilities		
Equipment and structures	$4,023	49.7%	Bonds and mortgages	$1,522	18.8%
Land	141	1.7	Bank loans	563	6.9
Inventories	1,066	13.2	Other loans	457	5.6
Total tangibles	$5,230	64.6%	Trade debt	800	9.9
			Other	811	10.0
Financial assets			Total liabilities	$4,152	51.3%
Deposits and cash	$ 298	3.7%			
Marketable securities	559	6.9			
Consumer credit	90	1.1			
Trade credit	942	11.6			
Other	978	12.1			
Total financial assets	2,867	35.4	Net worth	3,945	48.7
Total	$8,097	100.0%	Total	$8,097	100.0%

*Column sums subject to rounding error.

Source: *Balance Sheets for the U.S. Economy, 1945–94*,
    Board of Governors of the Federal Reserve System, June 1995.

financial institutions include very small amounts of tangible assets. Compare Table 1.3 to the aggregated balance sheet of the nonfinancial corporate sector in Table 1.4. The contrast arises because intermediaries simply move funds from one sector to another. In fact, the primary social function of such intermediaries is to channel household savings to the business sector.

Other examples of financial intermediaries are investment companies, insurance companies, and credit unions. All these firms offer similar advantages in their intermediary role. First, by pooling the resources of many small investors, they are able to lend considerable sums to large borrowers. Second, by lending to many borrowers, intermediaries achieve significant diversification, so they can accept loans that individually might be too risky. Third, intermediaries build expertise through the volume of business they do and can use economies of scale and scope to assess and monitor risk.

investment companies
Firms managing funds for
investors. An investment
company may manage
several mutual funds.

Investment companies, which pool and manage the money of many investors, also arise out of economies of scale. Here, the problem is that most household portfolios are not large enough to be spread among a wide variety of securities. It is very expensive in terms of brokerage fees and research costs to purchase one or two shares of many different firms. Mutual funds have the advantage of large-scale trading and portfolio management, while participating investors are assigned a prorated share of the total funds according to the size of their investment. This system gives small investors advantages they are willing to pay for via a management fee to the mutual fund operator.

Investment companies also can design portfolios specifically for large investors with particular goals. In contrast, mutual funds are sold in the retail market, and their investment philosophies are differentiated mainly by strategies that are likely to attract a large number of clients.

Economies of scale also explain the proliferation of analytic services available to investors. Newsletters, databases, and brokerage house research services all engage in research to be sold to a large client base. This setup arises naturally. Investors clearly want information, but with small portfolios to manage, they do not find it economical to personally gather all of it. Hence, a profit opportunity emerges: A firm can perform this service for many clients and charge for it.

Concept Check

2. Computer networks have made it much cheaper and easier for small investors to trade for their own accounts and perform their own security analysis. What will be the likely effect on financial intermediation?

Investment Bankers

Just as economies of scale and specialization create profit opportunities for financial intermediaries, so too do these economies create niches for firms that perform specialized services for businesses. Firms raise much of their capital by selling securities such as stocks and bonds to the public. Because these firms do not do so frequently, however, investment banking firms that specialize in such activities can offer their services at a cost below that of maintaining an in-house security issuance division.

investment bankers
Firms specializing in the
sale of new securities to
the public, typically by
underwriting the issue.

Investment bankers such as Goldman Sachs, Merrill Lynch, or Salomon Brothers advise the issuing corporation on the prices it can charge for the securities issued, appropriate interest rates, and so forth. Ultimately, the investment banking firm handles the marketing of the security issue to the public.

Investment bankers can provide more than just expertise to security issuers. Because investment bankers are constantly in the market, assisting one firm or another in issuing securities, the public knows that it is in the banker's own interest to protect and maintain its reputation for honesty. The investment banker will suffer along with investors if the securities it underwrites are marketed to the public with overly optimistic or exaggerated claims, for the public will not be so trusting the next time that investment banker participates in a security sale. The investment banker's effectiveness and ability to command future business thus depend on the reputation it has established over time. Obviously, the economic incentives to maintain a trustworthy reputation are not nearly as strong for firms that plan to go to the securities markets only once or very infrequently. Therefore, investment bankers can provide a certification role— a "seal of approval"—to security issuers. Their investment in reputation is another type of scale economy that arises from frequent participation in the capital markets.

1.7 MARKETS AND MARKET STRUCTURE

Just as securities and financial institutions are born and evolve in response to investor demands, financial markets also develop to meet the needs of particular traders. Consider what would happen if organized markets did not exist. Any household wishing to invest in some type of financial asset would have to find others wishing to sell.

This is how financial markets evolved. Meeting places established for buyers and sellers of financial assets became a financial market. A pub in old London called Lloyd's launched the maritime insurance industry. A Manhattan curb on Wall Street became synonymous with the financial world.

We can differentiate four types of markets: direct search markets, brokered markets, dealer markets, and auction markets.

Direct Search Markets

A *direct search market* is the least organized market. Buyers and sellers must seek each other out directly. An example of a transaction in such a market is the sale of a used refrigerator where the seller advertises for buyers in a local newspaper. Such markets are characterized by sporadic participation and low-priced and nonstandard goods. It does not pay most people or firms to seek profits by specializing in such an environment.

Brokered Markets

The next level of organization is a *brokered market.* In markets where trading in a good is active, brokers find it profitable to offer search services to buyers and sellers. A good example is the real estate market, where economies of scale in searches for available homes and for prospective buyers make it worthwhile for participants to pay brokers to conduct the searches. Brokers in particular markets develop specialized knowledge on valuing assets traded in that market.

primary market
A market in which new issues of securities are offered to the public.

An important brokered investment market is the so-called **primary market,** where new issues of securities are offered to the public. In the primary market, investment bankers who market a firm's securities to the public act as brokers; they seek investors to purchase securities directly from the issuing corporation.

Another brokered market is that for large block transactions, in which very large blocks of stock are bought or sold. These blocks are so large (technically more than 10,000 shares but usually much larger) that brokers or "block houses" often are engaged to search directly for other large traders, rather than bring the trade directly to the stock exchange where relatively smaller investors trade.

Dealer Markets

dealer markets
Markets in which traders specializing in particular assets buy and sell for their own accounts.

When trading activity in a particular type of asset increases, **dealer markets** arise. Dealers specialize in various assets, purchase these assets for their own accounts, and later sell them for a profit from their inventory. The spreads between dealers' buy (or "bid") prices and sell (or "ask") prices are a source of profit. Dealer markets save traders on search costs because market participants can easily look up the prices at which they can buy from or sell to dealers. A fair amount of market activity is required before dealing in a market is an attractive source of income. The over-the-counter (OTC) market is one example of a dealer market.

secondary markets
Already existing securities are bought and sold on the exchanges or in the OTC market.

Trading among investors of already-issued securities is said to take place in **secondary markets**. Therefore, the over-the-counter market is one example of a secondary market. Trading in secondary markets does not affect the outstanding amount of securities; ownership is simply transferred from one investor to another.

Auction Markets

auction market
A market where all traders in a good meet at one place to buy or sell an asset.

The most integrated market is an **auction market,** in which all traders converge at one place to buy or sell an asset. The New York Stock Exchange (NYSE) is an example of an auction market. An advantage of auction markets over dealer markets is that one need not search across dealers to find the best price for a good. If all participants converge, they can arrive at mutually agreeable prices and save the bid-ask spread.

Continuous auction markets (as opposed to periodic auctions, such as in the art world) require very heavy and frequent trading to cover the expense of maintaining the market. For this reason, the NYSE and other exchanges set up listing requirements, which limit the stocks traded on the exchange to those of firms in which sufficient trading interest is likely to exist.

The organized stock exchanges are also secondary markets. They are organized for investors to trade existing securities among themselves.

Concept Check

3. Many assets trade in more than one type of market. What types of markets do the following trade in? *a.* Used cars; *b.* Paintings; *c.* Rare coins.

1.8 RECENT TRENDS

Three important trends have changed the contemporary investment environment: (1) globalization, (2) securitization, and (3) financial engineering.

Globalization

If a wider range of investment choices can benefit investors, why should we limit ourselves to purely domestic assets? Increasingly efficient communication technology and the dismantling of regulatory constraints have encouraged **globalization** in recent years.

globalization
Tendency toward a worldwide investment environment, and the integration of national capital markets.

U.S. investors commonly can participate in foreign investment opportunities in several ways: (1) purchase foreign securities using American Depository Receipts (ADRs), which are domestically traded securities that represent claims to shares of foreign stocks; (2) purchase foreign securities that are offered in dollars; (3) buy mutual funds that invest internationally; and (4) buy derivative securities with payoffs that depend on prices in foreign security markets.

Once upon a time, a U.S. investor who wished to hold a French stock had to engage in four transactions: (1) purchase French francs, (2) purchase the stock on the French Bourse, (3) sell the stock in France, and (4) sell the French francs for dollars. Today, the same investor can purchase ADRs of this stock.

Brokers who act as intermediaries for these transactions purchase an inventory of stock from some foreign issuer. The broker then issues an American Depository Receipt that represents a claim to some number of those foreign shares held in inventory. The ADR is denominated in dollars and can be traded on U.S. stock exchanges but is in essence no more than a claim on a foreign stock. Thus, from the investor's point of view, there is no more difference between buying a French versus a U.S. stock than there is in holding a Massachusetts-based company compared with a California-based one. Of course, the investment implication may differ: ADRs still expose investors to exchange-rate risk.

Many foreign firms are so eager to lure U.S. investors that they will save these investors the expense of paying the higher commissions associated with the ADRs. Figure 1.1 shows an example. Cadbury Schweppes is a United Kingdom–based corporation that has marketed its stock directly to U.S. investors in ADRs. Each ADR represents a claim to 10 shares of Cadbury Schweppes stock.

An example of how far globalization has progressed appears in Figure 1.2. Here, Walt Disney is selling debt claims denominated in European currency units (ECUs), an index of a basket of European currency values.

pass-through securities
Pools of loans (such as home mortgage loans) sold in one package. Owners of pass-throughs receive all of the principal and interest payments made by the borrowers.

Securitization

In 1970, mortgage **pass-through securities** were introduced by the Government National Mortgage Association (GNMA, or Ginnie Mae). These securities aggregate individual home mortgages into relatively homogeneous pools. Each pool acts as backing for a GNMA

FIGURE 1.1

Globalization and American Depository Receipts

Source: Cadbury Schweppes p.l.c., September 1984.

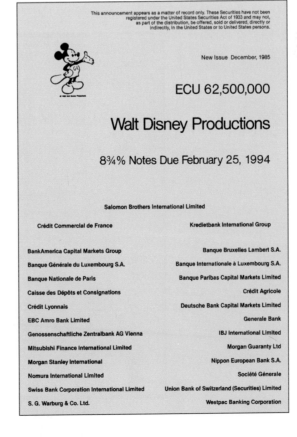

This announcement is neither an offer to sell nor a solicitation of an offer to buy any of these Securities. This offer is made only by the Prospectus.

Cadbury Schweppes p.l.c.

6,000,000 American Depositary Shares

Representing

60,000,000 Ordinary Shares

Price $17 an American Depositary Share

Copies of the Prospectus may be obtained in any State from only such of the undersigned as may legally offer these Securities in compliance with the securities laws of such State.

MORGAN STANLEY & CO.
Incorporated

LEHMAN BROTHERS
Shearson Lehman American Express Inc.

KLEINWORT, BENSON
Incorporated

BEAR, STEARNS & CO.   THE FIRST BOSTON CORPORATION   ALEX. BROWN & SONS
                                                                    Incorporated
DILLON, READ & CO. INC.   DONALDSON, LUFKIN & JENRETTE
                                                        Securities Corporation
DREXEL BURNHAM LAMBERT   GOLDMAN, SACHS & CO.   HAMBRECHT & QUIST
       Incorporated   Incorporated
HOARE GOVETT LTD.   E. F. HUTTON & COMPANY INC.   KIDDER, PEABODY & CO.
                                                                    Incorporated
LAZARD FRERES & CO.   MERRILL LYNCH CAPITAL MARKETS   SAMUEL MONTAGU & CO.
                                                                        Limited
PAINE WEBBER   PRUDENTIAL-BACHE   ROBERTSON, COLMAN & STEPHENS
   Incorporated   Securities
L. F. ROTHSCHILD, UNTERBERG, TOWBIN   SALOMON BROTHERS INC.

SMITH BARNEY, HARRIS UPHAM & CO.   WERTHEIM & CO., INC.   DEAN WITTER REYNOLDS INC.
       Incorporated

September 12, 1984

FIGURE 1.2

Globalization: A Debt Issue Denominated in European Currency Units

Source: Walt Disney Productions, December 1985.

This announcement appears as a matter of record only. These Securities have not been registered under the United States Securities Act of 1933 and may not, as part of the distribution, be offered, sold or delivered, directly or indirectly, in the United States or to United States persons.

New Issue December, 1985

ECU 62,500,000

Walt Disney Productions

8¾% Notes Due February 25, 1994

Salomon Brothers International Limited

Crédit Commercial de France   Kredietbank International Group

BankAmerica Capital Markets Group   Banque Bruxelles Lambert S.A.

Banque Générale du Luxembourg S.A.   Banque Internationale à Luxembourg S.A.

Banque Nationale de Paris   Banque Paribas Capital Markets Limited

Caisse des Dépôts et Consignations   Crédit Agricole

Crédit Lyonnais   Deutsche Bank Capital Markets Limited

EBC Amro Bank Limited   Generale Bank

Genossenschaftliche Zentralbank AG Vienna   IBJ International Limited

Mitsubishi Finance International Limited   Morgan Guaranty Ltd

Morgan Stanley International   Nippon European Bank S.A.

Nomura International Limited   Société Génerale

Swiss Bank Corporation International Limited   Union Bank of Switzerland (Securities) Limited

S. G. Warburg & Co. Ltd.   Westpac Banking Corporation

pass-through security. Investors who buy GNMA securities receive prorated shares of all the principal and interest payments made on the underlying mortgage pool.

For example, the pool might total $100 million of 12%, 30-year conventional mortgages. The rights to the cash flows could then be sold as 5,000 units, each worth $20,000. Each unit holder would then receive 1/5,000 of all monthly interest and principal payments made on the pool. The banks that originated the mortgages continue to service them (receiving fee-for-service), but they no longer own the mortgage investment; the investment has been passed through to the GNMA security holders.

Pass-through securities represent a tremendous innovation in mortgage markets. The **securitization** of mortgages means mortgages can be traded just like other securities. Availability of funds to homebuyers no longer depends on local credit conditions and is no longer subject to local banks' potential monopoly powers; with mortgage pass-throughs trading in national markets, mortgage funds can flow from any region (literally worldwide) to wherever demand is greatest.

Securitization also expands the menu of choices for the investor. Whereas it would have been impossible before 1970 for investors to invest in mortgages directly, they now can purchase mortgage pass-through securities or invest in mutual funds that offer portfolios of such securities.

Today, the majority of home mortgages are pooled into mortgage-backed securities. The two biggest players in the market are the Federal National Mortgage Association (FNMA, or Fannie Mae) and the Federal Home Loan Mortgage Corporation (FHLMC, or Freddie Mac). Over $1.5 trillion of mortgage-backed securities are outstanding, making this market larger than the market for corporate bonds.

Another example of securitization is the collateralized automobile receivable (CAR), a pass-through arrangement for car loans. Figure 1.3 shows an example of such a note. The loan originator passes the loan payments through to the holder of the CAR.

securitization
Pooling loans into standardized securities backed by those loans, which can then be traded like any other security.

FIGURE 1.3
Securitization of Automobile Loans

Source: The First Boston Corporation, March 1985.

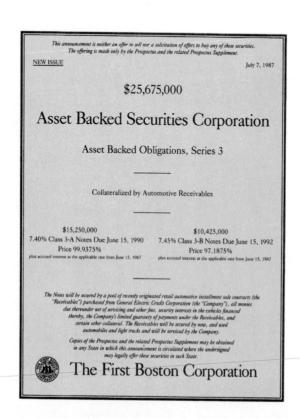

This announcement is neither an offer to sell nor a solicitation of offers to buy any of these securities. The offering is made only by the Prospectus and the related Prospectus Supplement.

NEW ISSUE   July 7, 1987

$25,675,000

Asset Backed Securities Corporation

Asset Backed Obligations, Series 3

Collateralized by Automotive Receivables

$15,250,000
7.40% Class 3-A Notes Due June 15, 1990
Price 99.9375%
plus accrued interest at the applicable rate from June 15, 1987

$10,425,000
7.45% Class 3-B Notes Due June 15, 1992
Price 97.1875%
plus accrued interest at the applicable rate from June 15, 1987

The Notes will be secured by a pool of recently originated retail automotive installment sale contracts (the "Receivables") purchased from General Electric Credit Corporation (the "Company"), all monies due thereunder net of servicing and other fees, security interests in the vehicles financed thereby, the Company's limited guaranty of payments under the Receivables, and certain other collateral. The Receivables will be secured by new, and used automobiles and light trucks and will be serviced by the Company.

Copies of the Prospectus and the related Prospectus Supplement may be obtained in any State in which this announcement is circulated where the undersigned may legally offer these securities in such State.

The First Boston Corporation

Securitization also has been used to allow U.S. banks to unload their portfolios of shaky loans to developing nations. So-called *Brady bonds* (named after former Secretary of Treasury Nicholas Brady) are formed by securitizing bank loans to several countries in shaky fiscal condition. The U.S. banks exchange their loans to developing nations for bonds backed by those loans. The payments that the borrowing nation would otherwise make to the lending bank are directed instead to the holder of the bond. These bonds are traded in capital markets. Therefore, if they choose, banks can remove these loans from their portfolios simply by selling the bonds. In addition, the U.S. in many cases has enhanced the credit quality of these bonds by designating a quantity of Treasury bonds to serve as partial collateral for the loans. In the event of a foreign default, the holders of the Brady bonds have claim to the collateral.

Concept Check

4. When mortgages are pooled into securities, the pass-through agencies (Freddie Mac and Fannie Mae) typically guarantee the underlying mortgage loans. If the homeowner defaults on the loan, the pass-through agency makes good on the loan; the investor in the mortgage-backed security does not bear the credit risk.
   a. Why does the allocation of risk to the pass-through agency rather than the security holder make economic sense?
   b. Why is the allocation of credit risk less of an issue for Brady bonds?

bundling, unbundling
Creation of new securities either by combining primitive and derivative securities into one composite hybrid or by separating returns on an asset into classes.

Financial Engineering

Financial engineering refers to the creation of new securities by **unbundling**—breaking up and allocating the cash flows from one security to create several new securities—or by **bundling**—combining more than one security into a composite security. Such creative engineering of new investment products allows one to design securities with custom-tailored risk attributes. An example of bundling appears in Figure 1.4.

FIGURE 1.4
Bundling Creates a Complex Security

Source: Goldman, Sachs & Co. July 1967.

3,000,000 Shares
The Chubb Corporation
$4.25 Convertible Exchangeable Preferred Stock
(Stated Value $50 Per Share)

The $4.25 Convertible Exchangeable Preferred Stock (the "Preferred Stock"), $1.00 par value, of The Chubb Corporation (the "Corporation") offered hereby is convertible at the option of the holder at any time, unless previously redeemed, into Common Stock, $1.00 par value, of the Corporation (the "Common Stock") at the rate of .722 shares of Common Stock for each share of Preferred Stock (equivalent to a conversion price of $69.25 per share), subject to adjustment under certain conditions. On March 25, 1985, the last reported sale price of the Common Stock on the New York Stock Exchange was $57¼ per share.

The Preferred Stock also is exchangeable in whole at the sole option of the Corporation on any dividend payment date beginning April 15, 1988 for the Corporation's 8½% Convertible Subordinated Debentures due April 15, 2010 (the "Debentures") at the rate of $50 principal amount of Debentures for each share of Preferred Stock. See "Description of Debentures".

The Preferred Stock is redeemable for cash at any time, in whole or in part, at the option of the Corporation at redemption prices declining to $50 on April 15, 1995, plus accrued and unpaid dividends to the redemption date. However, the Preferred Stock is not redeemable prior to April 15, 1988 unless the closing price of the Common Stock on the New York Stock Exchange shall have equaled or exceeded 140% of the then effective conversion price per share for at least 20 consecutive trading days ending within 5 days prior to the notice of redemption. Dividends on the Preferred Stock will be cumulative and are payable quarterly on January 15, April 15, July 15 and October 15. The initial dividend will be payable on July 15, 1985 and will accrue from the date of issuance. See "Description of Preferred Stock".

Application will be made to list the Preferred Stock on the New York Stock Exchange.

THESE SECURITIES HAVE NOT BEEN APPROVED OR DISAPPROVED BY THE SECURITIES AND EXCHANGE COMMISSION NOR HAS THE COMMISSION PASSED UPON THE ACCURACY OR ADEQUACY OF THIS PROSPECTUS. ANY REPRESENTATION TO THE CONTRARY IS A CRIMINAL OFFENSE.

	Initial Public Offering Price	Underwriting Discount	Proceeds to Corporation(1)
Per Share	$50.00	$1.375	$48.625
Total	$150,000,000	$4,125,000	$145,875,000

(1) Before deducting expenses payable by the Corporation estimated at $500,000.

The shares of Preferred Stock are offered severally by the Underwriters, as specified herein, subject to receipt and acceptance by them and subject to their right to reject any order in whole or in part. It is expected that certificates for the shares of Preferred Stock will be ready for delivery at the offices of Goldman, Sachs & Co., New York, New York on or about April 2, 1985.

Goldman, Sachs & Co.

The date of this Prospectus is March 26, 1985.

FIGURE 1.5
Unbundling of
Mortgages into
Principal- and Interest-
Only Securities

Source: Goldman, Sachs &
Co. March 1985.

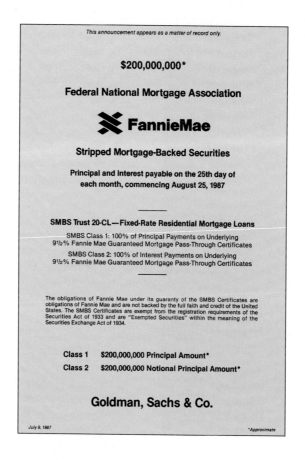

The Chubb Corporation, with the aid of Goldman Sachs, has combined three primitive securities—stocks, bonds, and preferred stock—into one hybrid security.

Chubb is issuing preferred stock that is convertible into common stock at the option of the holder and is exchangeable into convertible bonds at the option of the firm. Hence this security is a bundling of preferred stock with several options.

Often, creating a security that appears to be attractive requires the unbundling of an asset. An example is given in Figure 1.5. There, a mortgage pass-through certificate is unbundled into classes. Class 1 receives only principal payments from the mortgage pool, whereas Class 2 receives only interest payments.

financial engineering
The process of creating and designing securities with custom-tailored characteristics.

The process of bundling and unbundling is called **financial engineering,** which refers to the creation and design of securities with custom-tailored characteristics, often regarding exposures to various sources of risk. Financial engineers view securities as bundles of (possible risky) cash flows that may be carved up and rearranged according to the needs or desires of traders in the security markets. Many of the derivative securities discussed earlier in this chapter are products of financial engineering.

1.9 OUTLINE OF THE TEXT

The text has six parts, which are fairly independent and may be studied in a variety of sequences. Part One is an introduction to financial markets, instruments, and trading of securities. This part also describes the investment process. It shows how different investors' objectives and constraints can lead to a variety of investment policies.

Part Two is a fairly detailed presentation of "modern portfolio theory." This part of the text treats the effect of diversification on portfolio risk, the efficient diversification of investor portfolios, the choice of portfolios that strike an attractive balance between risk and return, and the trade-off between risk and expected return.

Parts Three through Five cover security analysis and valuation. Part Three is devoted to fixed-income markets and Part Four to equity markets. Part Five covers derivative assets, such as options and futures contracts.

Part Six is an introduction to active investment management. It discusses the role of such management in nearly efficient markets and considers how one should evaluate the performance of managers who pursue active strategies. It also shows how the principles of portfolio construction can be extended to the international setting.

Summary

- Real assets represent wealth. Financial assets represent claims to parts or all of that wealth. Financial assets determine how the ownership of real assets is distributed among investors.
- Financial assets can be categorized as fixed income, equity, or derivative instruments. Top-down portfolio construction techniques start with the asset allocation decision—the allocation of funds across broad asset classes—and then progress to more specific security-selection decisions.
- Competition in financial markets leads to a risk-return trade-off, in which securities that offer higher expected rates of return also impose greater risks on investors. The presence of risk, however, implies that actual returns can differ considerably from expected returns at the beginning of the investment period. Competition among security analysts also results in financial markets that are nearly informationally efficient, meaning that prices reflect all available information concerning the value of the security. Passive investment strategies may make sense in nearly efficient markets.
- Financial intermediaries pool investor funds and invest them. Their services are in demand because small investors cannot efficiently gather information, diversify, and monitor portfolios. The financial intermediary sells its own securities to the small investors. The intermediary invests the funds thus raised, uses the proceeds to pay back the small investors, and profits from the difference (the spread).
- Investment banking brings efficiency to corporate fund-raising. Investment bankers develop expertise in pricing new issues and in marketing them to investors.
- There are four types of financial markets. Direct search markets are the least efficient and sophisticated, where each transactor must find a counterpart. In brokered markets, brokers specialize in advising and finding counterparts for fee-paying traders. Dealers provide a step up in convenience. They keep an inventory of the asset and stand ready to buy or sell on demand, profiting from the bid-ask spread. Auction markets allow a trader to benefit from direct competition. All interested parties bid for the goods or services.
- Recent trends in financial markets include globalization, securitization, and financial engineering of assets.

Key Terms

active management, *9*	financial intermediaries, *10*	primary market, *13*
asset allocation, *8*	fixed-income securities, *4*	real assets, *3*
auction market, *13*	globalization, *14*	risk-return trade-off, *9*
bundling, *17*	investment, *2*	secondary markets, *13*
dealer markets, *13*	investment bankers, *12*	securitization, *16*
derivative securities, *5*	investment companies, *12*	security analysis, *8*
equity, *5*	passive management, *9*	security selection, *8*
financial assets, *3*	pass-through securities, *14*	unbundling, *17*
financial engineering, *18*		

Problem Sets

1. Suppose you discover a treasure chest of $10 billion in cash.
   a. Is this a real or financial asset?
   b. Is society any richer for the discovery?
   c. Are you wealthier?
   d. Can you reconcile your answers to (b) and (c)? Is anyone worse off as a result of the discovery?

2. Lanni Products is a start-up computer software development firm. It currently owns computer equipment worth $30,000 and has cash on hand of $20,000 contributed by Lanni's owners. For each of the following transactions, identify the real and/or financial assets that trade hands. Are any financial assets created or destroyed in the transaction?
   a. Lanni takes out a bank loan. It receives $50,000 in cash and signs a note promising to pay back the loan over three years.
   b. Lanni uses the cash from the bank plus $20,000 of its own funds to finance the development of new financial planning software.
   c. Lanni sells the software product to Microsoft, which will market it to the public under the Microsoft name. Lanni accepts payment in the form of 1,500 shares of Microsoft stock.
   d. Lanni sells the shares of stock for $80 per share and uses part of the proceeds to pay off the bank loan.

3. Reconsider Lanni Products from Problem 2.
   a. Prepare its balance sheet just after it gets the bank loan. What is the ratio of real assets to total assets?
   b. Prepare the balance sheet after Lanni spends the $70,000 to develop its software product. What is the ratio of real assets to total assets?
   c. Prepare the balance sheet after Lanni accepts the payment of shares from Microsoft. What is the ratio of real assets to total assets?

4. Financial engineering has been disparaged as nothing more than paper shuffling. Critics argue that resources used for *rearranging* wealth (that is, bundling and unbundling financial assets) might be better spent on *creating* wealth (that is, creating real assets). Evaluate this criticism. Are any benefits realized by creating an array of derivative securities from various primary securities?

5. Examine the balance sheet of the financial sector in Table 1.3. What is the ratio of tangible assets to total assets? What is that ratio for nonfinancial firms (Table 1.4)? Why should this difference be expected?

6. Consider Figure 1.6, below, which describes an issue of American gold certificates.
   a. Is this issue a primary or secondary market transaction?
   b. Are the certificates primitive or derivative assets?
   c. What market niche is filled by this offering?

7. Why would you expect securitization to take place only in highly developed capital markets?

8. What is the relationship between securitization and the role of financial intermediaries in the economy? What happens to financial intermediaries as securitization progresses?

9. Although we stated that real assets comprise the true productive capacity of an economy, it is hard to conceive of a modern economy without well-developed financial markets and security types. How would the productive capacity of the U.S. economy be affected if there were no markets in which one could trade financial assets?

FIGURE 1.6
A Gold-Backed Security

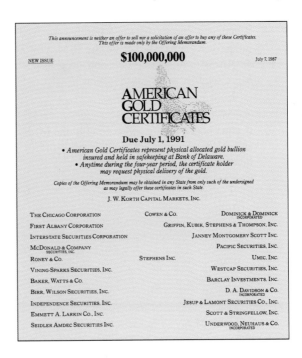

10. The rate of return on investments in stocks has outpaced that on investments in Treasury bills by an average of about 8.5% since 1926. Why, then, does anyone invest in Treasury bills?

11. What are some advantages and disadvantages of top-down versus bottom-up investing styles?

12. You see an advertisement for a book that claims to show how you can make $1 million with no risk and with no money down. Will you buy the book?

IEM Applications

For the IEM Applications throughout the text, please keep the following in mind (go to http://www.mhhe.com/irwin/iem for information on IEM):

The letter "m" designates the contract month with "a" representing January, "b" representing February, etc. The notation "xxx" designates a cutoff price level for the stock.

1. What kind of assets are traded on the IEM?
   a. Real, Derivative
   b. Financial, Derivative
   c. Real, Fixed Income
   d. Financial, Equity

2. What kind of market is the IEM?
   a. Primary and Continuous
   b. Secondary and Periodic
   c. Primary, Secondary, and Continuous
   d. Primary and Periodic

3. When you choose between putting cash in an IEM account or in your bank account, you are engaging in:
   a. An asset allocation decision
   b. A security selection decision
   c. Both
   d. Neither

4. When you choose between purchasing AAPLm and IBMm contracts in the Computer Industry Returns Market on the IEM, you are engaging in:
   a. An asset allocation decision
   b. A security selection decision
   c. Both
   d. Neither

5. If you choose to buy MSxxxmH in the MSFT (Microsoft) Price Level Market in the IEM and hold this contract until it pays off in the IEM, you are following what kind of investment strategy:
   a. Passive
   b. Active
   c. Both
   d. Neither

Solutions to Concept Checks

1. a. Real
   b. Financial
   c. Real
   d. Real
   e. Financial

2. If the new technology enables investors to trade and perform research for themselves, the need for financial intermediaries will decline. Part of the service intermediaries now offer is a lower-cost method for individuals to participate in securities markets. This part of the intermediaries' service would be less sought after.

3. a. Used cars trade in dealer markets (used-car lots or auto dealerships) and in direct search markets when individuals advertise in local newspapers.
   b. Paintings trade in broker markets when clients commission brokers to buy or sell art for them, in dealer markets at art galleries, and in auction markets.
   c. Rare coins trade mostly in dealer markets in coin shops, but they also trade in auctions and in direct search markets when individuals advertise they want to buy or sell coins.

4. a. The pass-through agencies are far better equipped to evaluate the credit risk associated with the pool of mortgages. They are constantly in the market, have ongoing relationships with the originators of the loans, and find it economical to set up "quality control" departments to monitor the credit risk of the mortgage pools. Therefore, the pass-through agencies are better able to incur the risk; they charge for this "service" via a "guarantee fee." Investors might not find it worthwhile to purchase these securities if they must assess the credit risk of these loans for themselves. It is far cheaper for them to allow the agencies to collect the guarantee fee.
   b. In contrast to mortgage-backed securities, which are backed by large numbers of mortgages, Brady bonds are backed by large government loans. It is more feasible for the investor to evaluate the credit quality of a few governments than it is to evaluate dozens or hundreds of individual mortgages.

Chapter 2

FINANCIAL MARKETS AND INSTRUMENTS

AFTER STUDYING THIS CHAPTER YOU SHOULD BE ABLE TO:

- Distinguish among the major assets that trade in money markets and in capital markets.

- Describe the construction of stock market indexes.

- Calculate the profit or loss on investments in options and futures contracts.

This chapter covers a range of financial securities and the markets in which they trade. Our goal is to introduce you to the features of various security types. This foundation will be necessary to understand the more analytic material that follows in later chapters.

We first describe money market instruments and how to measure their yield. We then move on to fixed-income and equity securities. We explain the structure of various stock market indexes in this chapter because market benchmark portfolios play an important role in portfolio construction and evaluation. Finally, we survey the derivative security markets for options and futures contracts. A summary of the markets, instruments, and indexes covered in this chapter appears in Table 2.1.

2.1 THE MONEY MARKET

money markets
Includes short-term, highly liquid, and relatively low-risk debt instruments.

capital markets
Includes longer-term, relatively riskier securities.

Financial markets are traditionally segmented into **money markets** and **capital markets.** Money market instruments include short-term, marketable, liquid, low-risk debt securities. Money market instruments sometimes are called *cash equivalents*, or just *cash* for short. Capital markets, in contrast, include longer-term and riskier securities. Securities in the capital market are much more diverse than those found within the money market. For this reason, we will subdivide the capital market into four segments: longer-term fixed-income markets, equity markets, and the derivative markets for options and futures.

The money market is a subsector of the fixed-income market. It consists of very short-term debt securities that are highly marketable. Many of these securities trade in large denominations and so are out of the reach of individual investors. Money market mutual funds, however, are easily accessible to small investors. These mutual funds pool the resources of many investors and purchase a wide variety of money market securities on their behalf.

TABLE 2.1
Financial Markets and
Indexes

The Money Market	The Fixed-Income Capital Market
Treasury bills	Treasury bonds and notes
Certificates of deposit	Federal agency debt
Commercial paper	Municipal bonds
Bankers' acceptances	Corporate bonds
Eurodollars	Mortgage-backed securities
Repos and reverses	
Federal funds	**Equity Markets**
Brokers' calls	Common stocks
	Preferred stocks
Indexes	
Dow Jones averages	**Derivative Markets**
Standard & Poor's	Options
indexes	Futures and Forwards
Bond market indicators	
International indexes	

Figure 2.1 is a reprint of a money rates listing from *The Wall Street Journal*. It includes the various instruments of the money market that we describe in detail below. Table 2.2 lists outstanding volume in 1995 of the major instruments of the money market.

Treasury Bills

Treasury bills
Short-term government
securities issued at a
discount from face value
and returning the face
amount at maturity.

U.S. **Treasury bills** (T-bills, or just bills, for short) are the most marketable of all money market instruments. T-bills represent the simplest form of borrowing. The government raises money by selling bills to the public. Investors buy the bills at a discount from the stated maturity value. At the bill's maturity, the holder receives from the government a payment equal to the face value of the bill. The difference between the purchase price and the ultimate maturity value represents the investor's earnings.

T-bills with initial maturities of 91 and 182 days are issued weekly. Offerings of 52-week bills are made monthly. Sales are conducted by an auction where investors can submit competitive or noncompetitive bids.

A competitive bid is an order for a given quantity of bills at a specific offered price. The order is filled only if the bid is high enough relative to other bids to be accepted. If the bid is high enough to be accepted, the bidder gets the order at the bid price. Thus, the bidder risks paying one of the highest prices for the same bill (bidding at the top), against the hope of bidding "at the tail," that is, making the cutoff at the lowest price.

A noncompetitive bid is an unconditional offer to purchase bills at the average price of the successful competitive bids. The Treasury ranks bids by offering price and accepts bids in order of descending price until the entire issue is absorbed by the competitive plus noncompetitive bids. Competitive bidders face two dangers: They may bid too high and overpay for the bills or bid too low and be shut out of the auction. Noncompetitive bidders, by contrast, pay the average price for the issue, and all noncompetitive bids are accepted up to a maximum of $1 million per bid. In recent years, noncompetitive bids have absorbed between 10 and 25% of the total auction.

Individuals can purchase T-bills directly at the auction or on the secondary market from a government securities dealer. T-bills are highly liquid; that is, they are easily converted to cash and sold at low transaction cost and with little price risk. Unlike most other money market instruments, which sell in minimum denominations of $100,000, T-bills sell in minimum denominations of only $10,000. While the income earned on T-bills is taxable at the Federal level, it is exempt from all state and local taxes, another characteristic distinguishing T-bills from other money market instruments.

Bank Discount Yields

T-bill yields are not quoted as effective annual interest rates. To illustrate, consider a $10,000 par value T-bill sold at $9,600 with a maturity of one-half year. The $9,600 investment provides $400 in earnings. The rate of return on the investment is defined as dollars earned per dollar invested, in this case,

$$\frac{\text{Dollars earned}}{\text{Dollars invested}} = \frac{\$400}{\$9,600} = .0417 \text{ per six-month period, or } 4.17\% \text{ semiannually}$$

FIGURE 2.1

Rates on Money Market Securities

Source: From *The Wall Street Journal*, June 7, 1996. Reprinted by permission of *The Wall Street Journal*, ©1996 Dow Jones & Company, Inc. All Rights Reserved Worldwide.

MONEY RATES

Thursday, June 6, 1996

The key U.S. and foreign annual interest rates below are a guide to general levels but don't always represent actual transactions.

PRIME RATE: 8.25% (effective 2/01/96). The base rate on corporate loans posted by at least 75% of the nation's 30 largest banks.

DISCOUNT RATE: 5%. The charge on loans to depository institutions by the Federal Reserve Banks.

FEDERAL FUNDS: 5 3/8% high, 5 1/4% low, 5 1/4% near closing bid, 5 5/16% offered. Reserves traded among commercial banks for overnight use in amounts of $1 million or more. Source: Prebon Yamane (U.S.A.) Inc.

CALL MONEY: 7%. The charge on loans to brokers on stock exchange collateral. Source: Dow Jones Telerate Inc.

COMMERCIAL PAPER placed directly by General Electric Capital Corp.: 5.30% 30 to 44 days; 5.31% 45 to 119 days; 5.36% 120 to 149 days; 5.38% 150 to 179 days; 5.35% 180 to 244 days; 5.50% 245 to 270 days.

COMMERCIAL PAPER: High-grade unsecured notes sold through dealers by major corporations: 5.40% 30 days; 5.40% 60 days; 5.40% 90 days.

CERTIFICATES OF DEPOSIT: 4.68% one month; 4.75% two months; 4.85% three months; 5.08% six months; 5.38% one year. Average of top rates paid by major New York banks on primary new issues of negotiable C.D.s, usually on amounts of $1 million and more. The minimum unit is $100,000. Typical rates in the secondary market: 5.36% one month; 5.43% three months; 5.58% six months.

BANKERS ACCEPTANCES: 5.27% 30 days; 5.27% 60 days; 5.28% 90 days; 5.32% 120 days; 5.35% 150 days; 5.37% 180 days. Offered rates of negotiable, bank-backed business credit instruments typically financing an import order.

LONDON LATE EURODOLLARS: 5 7/16% - 5 5/16% one month; 5 1/2% - 5 3/8% two months; 5 1/2% - 5 3/8% three months; 5 9/16% - 5 7/16% four months; 5 5/8% - 5 1/2% five months; 5 5/8% - 5 1/2% six months.

LONDON INTERBANK OFFERED RATES (LIBOR): 5 15/32% one month; 5 17/32% three months; 5 11/16% six months; 6 1/16% one year. The average of interbank offered rates for dollar deposits in the London market based on quotations at five major banks. Effective rate for contracts entered into two days from date appearing at top of this column.

FOREIGN PRIME RATES: Canada 6.50%; Germany 3.35%; Japan 1.625%; Switzerland 4.75%; Britain 5.75%. These rate indications aren't directly comparable; lending practices vary widely by location.

TREASURY BILLS: Results of the Monday, June 3, 1996, auction of short-term U.S. government bills, sold at a discount from face value in units of $10,000 to $1 million: 5.09% 13 weeks; 5.21% 26 weeks.

OVERNIGHT REPURCHASE RATE: 5.27%. Dealer financing rate for overnight sale and repurchase of Treasury securities. Source: Dow Jones Telerate Inc.

FEDERAL HOME LOAN MORTGAGE CORP. (Freddie Mac): Posted yields on 30-year mortgage commitments. Delivery within 30 days 8.21%, 60 days 8.29%, standard conventional fixed-rate mortgages; 5.375%, 2% rate capped one-year adjustable rate mortgages. Source: Dow Jones Telerate Inc.

FEDERAL NATIONAL MORTGAGE ASSOCIATION (Fannie Mae): Posted yields on 30 year mortgage commitments (priced at par) for delivery within 30 days 8.18%, 60 days 8.24%, standard conventional fixed rate-mortgages; 6.80%, 6/2 rate capped one-year adjustable rate mortgages. Source: Dow Jones Telerate Inc.

MERRILL LYNCH READY ASSETS TRUST: 4.78%. Annualized average rate of return after expenses for the past 30 days; not a forecast of future returns.

TABLE 2.2

Components of the Money Market (November 1995)

Source: Data from *Economic Report of the President*, U.S. Government Printing Office, 1996.

	$ Billion
Overnight repurchase agreements*	116.3
Term repurchase agreements	111.6
Small-denomination time deposits†	932.6
Large-denomination time deposits‡	416.8
Term Eurodollars	61.1
Short-term Treasury securities	465.0
Bankers' acceptances	13.1
Commercial paper	435.6
Money market deposit accounts	1131.3

*Includes overnight Eurodollars.

†Less than $100,000 denomination.

‡More than $100,000 denomination.

Invested funds increase over the six-month period by a factor of 1.0417. If one continues to earn this rate of return over an entire year, then invested funds grow by a factor of 1.0417 in each six-month period; by year-end, each dollar invested grows with compound interest to $1 \times (1.0417)^2 = \$1.0851$. Therefore, we say that the **effective annual rate** on the bill is 8.51%. The effective annual rate is thus defined as the total growth of funds after a year if all funds are reinvested at the same rate they earn during the actual investment period. This approach to annualizing returns is designed to account for compound interest.

effective annual rate
Annualized interest rate on a security computed using compound interest techniques.

Unfortunately, T-bill yields in the financial pages are quoted using the **bank discount method.** In this approach, the bill's discount from par value, \$400, is "annualized" based on a 360-day year. The \$400 discount is annualized as follows: $\$400 \times (360/182) = \$791.21$. This figure is divided by the \$10,000 par value of the bill to obtain a bank discount yield of 7.912%.

bank discount method
An annualized interest rate assuming simple interest, a 360-day year, and using the face value of the security rather than the purchase price to compute return per dollar invested.

We can highlight the source of the discrepancy between the bank discount yield and the effective annual yield by examining the bank discount formula.

$$r_{BD} = \frac{10,000 - P}{10,000} \times \frac{360}{n} \tag{2.1}$$

where P is the bond price, n is the maturity of the bill in days, and r_{BD} is the bank discount yield. Actually, because of the convention of skip-day settlement, two business days are subtracted from n because the T-bill sale is consummated, that is, cash has to be disbursed, two business days after the date on which the price is quoted. For example, Figure 2.2, which reports prices on May 29, 1996, shows only six days to maturity for the first bill despite the fact that eight days remain until maturity.

The bank discount formula thus takes the bill's discount from par as a fraction of par value and then annualizes by the factor $360/n$. There are three problems with this technique, and they all combine to reduce the bank discount yield compared with the effective annual yield. First, the bank discount yield is annualized using a 360-day year rather than a 365-day year. Second, the annualization technique uses simple interest rather than compound interest. Multiplication by $360/n$ does not account for the ability to earn interest on interest, which is the essence of compounding. Finally, the denominator in the first term in Equation 2.1 is the

FIGURE 2.2
Treasury Bill Listing

TREASURY BILLS					
Maturity	Days to Mat.	Bid	Asked	Chg.	Ask Yld.
Jun 06 '96	6	5.03	4.93	− 0.03	5.02
Jun 13 '96	13	5.06	4.96	....	5.05
Jun 20 '96	20	5.06	4.96	....	5.06
Jun 27 '96	27	4.99	4.89	− 0.04	4.99
Jul 05 '96	35	4.99	4.95	− 0.03	5.06
Jul 11 '96	41	4.97	4.93	− 0.03	5.04
Jul 18 '96	48	4.76	4.72	− 0.04	4.83
Jul 25 '96	55	4.96	4.92	− 0.04	5.04
Aug 01 '96	62	5.00	4.98	− 0.02	5.11
Aug 08 '96	69	5.03	5.01	....	5.14
Aug 15 '96	76	5.04	5.02	+ 0.01	5.16
Aug 22 '96	83	5.05	5.03	+ 0.01	5.17
Aug 29 '96	90	5.04	5.02	+ 0.02	5.17
Sep 05 '96	97	5.03	5.01	....	5.15
Sep 12 '96	104	5.03	5.01	+ 0.01	5.15
Sep 19 '96	111	5.05	5.03	+ 0.02	5.19
Sep 26 '96	118	5.04	5.02	+ 0.01	5.17
Oct 03 '96	125	5.07	5.05	+ 0.01	5.21
Oct 10 '96	132	5.08	5.06	+ 0.02	5.23
Oct 17 '96	139	5.10	5.08	+ 0.02	5.27
Oct 24 '96	146	5.09	5.07	+ 0.01	5.25
Oct 31 '96	153	5.11	5.09	+ 0.02	5.27
Nov 07 '96	160	5.13	5.11	+ 0.02	5.30
Nov 14 '96	167	5.14	5.12	+ 0.01	5.33
Nov 21 '96	174	5.13	5.11	+ 0.01	5.31
Nov 29 '96	182	5.15	5.13	+ 0.01	5.34
Dec 12 '96	195	5.16	5.14	+ 0.03	5.37
Jan 09 '97	223	5.21	5.19	+ 0.04	5.43
Feb 06 '97	251	5.23	5.21	+ 0.05	5.46
Mar 06 '97	279	5.26	5.24	+ 0.05	5.49
Apr 03 '97	307	5.31	5.29	+ 0.07	5.55
May 01 '97	335	5.35	5.33	+ 0.07	5.61
May 29 '97	363	5.39	5.37	+ 0.06	5.68

par value, $10,000, rather than the purchase price of the bill, *P*. We really want an interest rate to tell us the rate that we can earn per dollar invested, but dollars invested here are *P*, not $10,000. Less than $10,000 is required to purchase the bill.

Figure 2.2 shows Treasury bill listings from *The Wall Street Journal* for May 30, 1996. The discount yield on the bill maturing on August 29 is 5.04% based on the bid price of the bond and 5.02% based on the ask price. (The bid price is the price at which a customer can sell the bill to a dealer in the security, while the ask price is the price at which the customer can buy a security from a dealer. The difference in bid and ask prices is a source of profit to the dealer.)

To determine the bill's true market price, we must solve Equation 2.1 for *P*. Rearranging 2.1, we obtain

$$P = 10,000 \times [1 - r_{BD} \times (n/360)] \tag{2.2}$$

Equation 2.2 in effect first "deannualizes" the bank discount yield to obtain the actual proportional discount from par, then finds the fraction of par for which the bond sells (which is the expression in brackets), and finally multiplies the result by par value, or $10,000. In the case at hand, there are 92 days between May 29, the date on which the price was observed, and August 29, the maturity date of the T-bill. Subtracting two days for skip-day settlement gives us the 90 days to maturity reported in *The Wall Street Journal*. The discount yield based on the ask price is 5.02%, or .0502, so the ask price of the bill is found to be

$$\$10,000 \times [1 - .0502 \times (90/360)] = \$9,874.50$$

bond equivalent yield
Bond yield calculated using simple rather than compound interest.

The "yield" column in Figure 2.2 is the **bond equivalent yield** of the T-bill. This is a simple interest measure of the bill's annualized rate of return, assuming it is purchased for the asking price. The bond equivalent yield is the return on the bill over the period corresponding to its remaining maturity multiplied by the number of such periods in a year. Because 1996 is a leap year, we compute the bond equivalent yield using a 366-day year as:

$$r_{BEY} = \frac{10,000 - P}{P} \times \frac{366}{n} \tag{2.3}$$

In Equation 2.3 the 90-day rate of return of the bill is computed in the first term on the right-hand side as the price increase of the bill if held until maturity per dollar paid for the bill. The second term annualizes that return. Note that the bond equivalent yield correctly uses the price of the bill in the denominator of the first term and uses a 365-day year in the second term to annualize. (In a leap year, as in this example, we use a 366-day year in Equation 2.3.) It still, however, uses a simple interest procedure known as **annual percentage rate,** or APR, to annualize so problems still remain in comparing yields on bills with different maturities. Nevertheless, yields on most securities with less than a year to maturity are annualized using a simple interest approach.

annual percentage rate
Rate is annualized assuming simple interest.

Thus, for our demonstration bill,

$$r_{BEY} = \frac{10,000 - 9,874.50}{9,874.50} \times \frac{366}{90} = .0517$$

or 5.17%, as reported in *The Wall Street Journal*.

A convenient formula relating the bond equivalent yield to the bank discount yield is

$$r_{BEY} = \frac{365 \times r_{BD}}{360 - (n \times r_{BD})}$$

Here, r_{BD} = .0502, and we use a 366-day year, so that

$$r_{BEY} = \frac{366 \times .0502}{360 - (90 \times .0502)} = .0517$$

Finally, the effective annual yield on the bill based on the ask price, $9,874.50, is obtained from a compound interest calculation. The 90-day return equals

$$(10,000 - 9,874.50)/9,874.50 = .0127, \text{ or } 1.27\%$$

Annualizing, we find that funds invested at this rate would grow over the course of a year by the factor $(1.0127)^{366/90} = 1.0527$, implying an effective annual yield of 5.27%.

This example illustrates the general rule that the bank discount yield is less than the bond equivalent yield, which in turn is less than the effective annual yield.

Concept Check

1. Find the bid price of the August 29 maturity bill based on the bank discount yield at bid.

Certificates of Deposit

certificate of deposit
A bank time deposit.

A **certificate of deposit** (CD) is a time deposit with a bank. Time deposits may not be withdrawn on demand. The bank pays interest and principal to the depositor only at the end of the fixed term of the CD. CDs issued in denominations larger than $100,000 are usually negotiable, however; that is, they can be sold to another investor if the owner needs to cash in the certificate before its maturity date. Short-term CDs are highly marketable, although the market significantly thins out for maturities of six months or more. CDs are treated as bank deposits by the Federal Deposit Insurance Corporation, so they are insured for up to $100,000 in the event of a bank insolvency.

Commercial Paper

commercial paper
Short-term unsecured debt issued by large corporations.

The typical corporation is a net borrower of both long-term funds (for capital investments) and short-term funds (for working capital). Large, well-known companies often issue their own short-term unsecured debt notes directly to the public, rather than borrowing from banks. These notes are called **commercial paper** (CP). Sometimes, CP is backed by a bank line of credit, which gives the borrower access to cash that can be used if needed to pay off the paper at maturity.

CP maturities range up to 270 days; longer maturities require registration with the Securities and Exchange Commission and so are almost never issued. CP most commonly is issued with maturities of less than one or two months in denominations of multiples of $100,000. Therefore, small investors can invest in commercial paper only indirectly, through money market mutual funds.

CP is considered to be a fairly safe asset, given that a firm's condition presumably can be monitored and predicted over a term as short as one month. It is worth noting, though, that many firms issue commercial paper intending to roll it over at maturity, that is, issue new paper to obtain the funds necessary to retire the old paper. If lenders become complacent about monitoring a firm's prospects and grant rollovers willy-nilly, they can suffer big losses. When Penn Central defaulted in 1970, it had $82 million of commercial paper outstanding—the only major default on commercial paper in the past 40 years.

CP trades in secondary markets and so is quite liquid. Most issues are rated by at least one agency such as Standard & Poor's. The yield on CP depends on the time to maturity and the credit rating.

Bankers' Acceptances

bankers' acceptance
An order to a bank by a customer to pay a sum of money at a future date.

A **bankers' acceptance** starts as an order to a bank by a bank's customer to pay a sum of money at a future date, typically within six months. At this stage, it is like a postdated check. When the bank endorses the order for payment as "accepted," it assumes responsibility for ultimate payment to the holder of the acceptance. At this point, the acceptance may be traded in secondary markets much like any other claim on the bank. Bankers' acceptances are considered very safe assets, as they allow traders to substitute the bank's credit standing for their own. They are used widely in foreign trade where the creditworthiness of one trader is unknown to the trading partner. Acceptances sell at a discount from the face value of the payment order, just as T-bills sell at a discount from par value.

Eurodollars

Eurodollars
Dollar-denominated deposits at foreign banks or foreign branches of American banks.

Eurodollars are dollar-denominated deposits at foreign banks or foreign branches of American banks. By locating outside the United States, these banks escape regulation by the Federal Reserve Board. Despite the tag "Euro," these accounts need not be in European banks, although that is where the practice of accepting dollar-denominated deposits outside the United States began.

Most Eurodollar deposits are for large sums, and most are time deposits of less than six months' maturity. A variation on the Eurodollar time deposit is the Eurodollar certificate of deposit. A Eurodollar CD resembles a domestic bank CD except it is the liability of a non-U.S branch of a bank, typically a London branch. The advantage of Eurodollar CDs over Eurodollar time deposits is that the holder can sell the asset to realize its cash value before maturity. Eurodollar CDs are considered less liquid and riskier than domestic CDs, however, and so offer higher yields. Firms also issue Eurodollar bonds, that is, dollar-denominated bonds in Europe, although such bonds are not a money market investment by virtue of their long maturities.

Repos and Reverses

repurchase agreements (repos)
Short-term sales of government securities with an agreement to repurchase the securities at a higher price.

Dealers in government securities use **repurchase agreements,** also called repos, or RPs, as a form of short-term, usually overnight, borrowing. The dealer sells securities to an investor on an overnight basis, with an agreement to buy back those securities the next day at a slightly higher price. The increase in the price is the overnight interest. The dealer thus takes out a one-day loan from the investor. The securities serve as collateral for the loan.

A *term repo* is essentially an identical transaction, except the term of the implicit loan can be 30 days or more. Repos are considered very safe in terms of credit risk because the loans are backed by the government securities. A *reverse repo* is the mirror image of a repo. Here, the dealer finds an investor holding government securities and buys them with an agreement to resell them at a specified higher price on a future date.

The repo market was upset by several failures of government security dealers in 1985. In these cases, the dealers had entered into the typical repo arrangements with investors, pledging government securities as collateral. The investors did not take physical possession of the securities as they could have under the purchase and resale arrangement. Some of the dealers, unfortunately, fraudulently pledged the same securities as collateral in different repos; when the dealers went under, the investors found they could not collect the securities they had "purchased" in the first leg of the repo transaction. In the wake of the scandal, repo rates for nonprimary dealers increased, while rates for some well-capitalized firms fell as investors became more sensitive to credit risk. Investors can best protect themselves by taking delivery of the securities, either directly or through an agent such as a bank custodian.

Brokers' Calls

Individuals who buy stocks on margin borrow part of the funds to pay for the stocks from their broker. The broker in turn may borrow the funds from a bank, agreeing to repay the bank immediately (on call) if the bank requests it. The rate paid on such loans is usually about one percentage point higher than the rate on short-term T-bills.

Federal Funds

Federal funds
Funds in the accounts of commercial banks at the Federal Reserve Bank.

Just as most of us maintain deposits at banks, banks maintain deposits of their own at the Federal Reserve Bank, or the Fed. Each member bank of the Federal Reserve System is required to maintain a minimum balance in a reserve account with the Fed. The required balance depends on the total deposits of the bank's customers. Funds in the bank's reserve account are called **Federal funds** or *Fed funds*. At any time, some banks have more funds than required at the Fed. Other banks, primarily big New York and other financial center banks, tend to have a shortage of Federal funds. In the Federal funds market, banks with excess funds lend to those with a shortage. These loans, which are usually overnight transactions, are arranged at a rate of interest called the Federal funds rate.

While the Fed funds rate is not directly relevant to investors, it is used as one of the barometers of the money market and so is widely watched by them.

The LIBOR Market

LIBOR
Lending rate among banks in the London market.

The **London Interbank Offer Rate (LIBOR)** is the rate at which large banks in London are willing to lend money among themselves. This rate has become the premier short-term interest rate quoted in the European money market and serves as a reference rate for a wide range of transactions. A corporation might borrow at a rate equal to LIBOR plus 2 percentage points, for example. Like the Fed funds rate, LIBOR is a statistic widely followed by investors.

Yields on Money Market Instruments

Although most money market securities are of low risk, they are not risk free. As we noted earlier, the commercial paper market was rocked by the Penn Central bankruptcy, which precipitated a default on $82 million of commercial paper. Money market investments became more sensitive to creditworthiness after this episode, and the yield spread between low- and high-quality paper widened.

The securities of the money market do promise yields greater than those on default-free T-bills, at least in part because of greater relative riskiness. Investors who require more liquidity also will accept lower yields on securities, such as T-bills, that can be more quickly and cheaply sold for cash. Figure 2.3 shows that bank CDs, for example, consistently have paid a risk premium over T-bills. Moreover, that risk premium increases with economic crises such as

FIGURE 2.3

Spread between Three-Month CDs and T-Bills

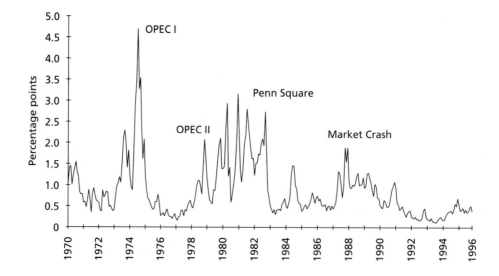

the energy price shocks associated with the Organization of Petroleum Exporting Countries (OPEC) disturbances, the failure of Penn Square Bank, or the stock market crash in 1987.

2.2 THE FIXED-INCOME CAPITAL MARKET

The fixed-income capital market is composed of longer-term borrowing instruments than those that trade in the money market. This market includes Treasury notes and bonds, corporate bonds, municipal bonds, mortgage securities, and federal agency debt.

The title "fixed-income" is given to these securities because most of them promise either a fixed stream of income or a stream of income that is determined according to a specified formula. Payments are administered by the issuer or a banking agent on the issuer's behalf. These payments are fixed unless the issuer is declared bankrupt.

Treasury Notes and Bonds

Treasury notes or bonds
Debt obligations of the federal government that make semiannual payments and are sold at or near par value in denominations of $1,000 or more.

The U.S. government borrows funds in large part by selling **Treasury notes** and **bonds.** T-note maturities range up to 10 years, while T-bonds are issued with maturities ranging from 10 to 30 years. Both are issued in denominations of $1,000 or more. Both make semiannual interest payments called *coupon payments*, so named because in precomputer days, investors would literally clip a coupon attached to the bond and present it to an agent of the issuing firm to receive the interest payment. Aside from their differing maturities at issuance, the only major distinction between T-notes and T-bonds is that T-bonds may be callable during a given period, usually the last five years of the bond's life. The call provision gives the Treasury the right to repurchase the bond at par value. While callable T-bonds still are outstanding, the Treasury no longer issues callable bonds.

Figure 2.4 is an excerpt from a listing of Treasury issues in *The Wall Street Journal*. The highlighted bond matures in July 2000. The coupon income or interest paid by the bond is 6⅛ percent of par value, meaning that for a $1,000 face value bond, $61.25 in annual interest payments will be made in two semiannual installments of $30.625 each. The numbers to the right of the colon in the bid and ask prices represent units of $\frac{1}{32}$ of a point.

The bid price of the highlighted bond is 98%₃₂, or 98.28125. The ask price is 98¹¹/₃₂ or 98.34375. Although bonds are sold in denominations of $1,000 par value, the prices are quoted as a percentage of par value. Thus, the ask price of 98.34375 should be interpreted as 98.34375% of par or $983.4375 for the $1,000 par value bond. Similarly, the bond could be sold to a dealer for $982.8125. The − 2 change means the closing price on this day fell ²⁄₃₂ (as a percentage of par value) from the previous day's closing price. Finally, the yield to maturity on the bond based on the ask price is 6.60%.

The yield to maturity reported in the last column is a measure of the annualized rate of return to an investor who buys the bond and holds it until maturity. It is calculated by determining the semiannual yield and then doubling it, rather than compounding it for two half-year periods. This use of a simple interest technique to annualize means that the yield is quoted on an annual percentage rate (APR) basis rather than as an effective annual yield. The APR method in this context is also called the bond equivalent yield. We discuss the yield to maturity in detail in Chapter 10.

You can pick out the callable bonds in Figure 2.4 because a range of years appears in the maturity date column. These are the years during which the bond is callable. Yields on premium bonds (bonds selling above par value) are calculated as though the bonds will be redeemed on the first call date; this is because at prices above par value, the government will find it advantageous to call the bonds for par value as soon as it is allowed. Conversely, yields on bonds selling at prices below par value are calculated as though the bonds will remain outstanding until maturity, since there would be no reason for the government to call bonds for par when the market price of the bonds is less than par.

FIGURE 2.4

Listing of Treasury
Issues

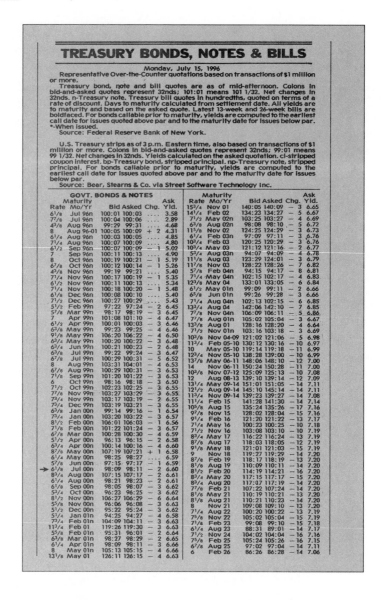

Concept Check

2. This rule for calculating yield to maturity assumes that the government makes a binding decision now as to whether it will call the bonds early. In fact, the government need not decide now whether it will call the bonds at a later date. It can wait to observe bond prices as the call date approaches. When is this flexibility most likely to be important in terms of valuing the bonds?

Federal Agency Debt

Some government agencies issue their own securities to finance their activities. These agencies usually are formed for public policy reasons to channel credit to a particular sector of the economy that Congress believes is not receiving adequate credit through normal private sources. Figure 2.5 reproduces listings of some of these securities from *The Wall Street Journal*. The majority of the debt is issued in support of home mortgages and farm credit.

The major mortgage-related agencies are the Federal Home Loan Bank (FHLB), the Federal National Mortgage Association (FNMA, or Fannie Mae), the Government National Mortgage Association (GNMA, or Ginnie Mae), and the Federal Home Loan Mortgage Corporation (FHLMC, or Freddie Mac).

FIGURE 2.5

Listing of Government
Agency Securities

Source: From *The Wall Street
Journal*, July 16, 1996.
Reprinted by permission of
The Wall Street Journal.
©1996 Dow Jones &
Company, Inc. All Rights
Reserved Worldwide.

The FHLB borrows money by issuing securities and relends this money to savings and loan institutions to be lent to individuals borrowing for home mortgages.

Freddie Mac, Fannie Mae, and Ginnie Mae were organized to provide liquidity to the mortgage market. Until establishment of the pass-through securities sponsored by these government agencies, the lack of a secondary market in mortgages hampered the flow of investment funds into mortgages and made mortgage markets dependent on local, rather than national, credit availability. The pass-through financing initiated by these agencies represents one of the most important financial innovations of the 1980s.

The farm credit agencies are 12 district Banks for Cooperatives that make seasonal loans to farm cooperatives, 12 Federal Land Banks that make mortgage loans on farm properties, and 12 Federal Intermediate Credit Banks that provide short-term financing for production and marketing of crops and livestock.

Although the debt of federal agencies is not explicitly insured by the federal government, it is assumed the government will assist an agency nearing default. Thus, these securities are considered extremely safe assets, and their yield spread over Treasury securities is usually small.

Concept Check

3. Using Figures 2.4 and 2.5, compare the yield to maturity on one of the agency bonds with that of the T-bond with the nearest maturity date.

Municipal Bonds

municipal bonds
Tax-exempt bonds issued
by state and local
governments.

Municipal bonds ("munis") are issued by state and local governments. They are similar to Treasury and corporate bonds, except their interest income is exempt from federal income taxation. The interest income also is exempt from state and local taxation in the issuing state.

Capital gains taxes, however, must be paid on munis if the bonds mature or are sold for more than the investor's purchase price.

There are basically two types of municipal bonds. These are *general obligation bonds*, which are backed by the "full faith and credit" (i.e., the taxing power) of the issuer, and *revenue bonds*, which are issued to finance particular projects and are backed either by the revenues from that project or by the municipal agency operating the project. Typical issuers of revenue bonds are airports, hospitals, and turnpike or port authorities. Revenue bonds are riskier in terms of default than general obligation bonds.

A particular type of revenue bond is the industrial development bond, which is issued to finance commercial enterprises, such as the construction of a factory that can be operated by a private firm. In effect, this device gives the firm access to the municipality's ability to borrow at tax-exempt rates.

Like Treasury bonds, municipal bonds vary widely in maturity. A good deal of the debt issued is in the form of short-term tax anticipation notes that raise funds to pay for expenses before actual collection of taxes. Other municipal debt may be long term and used to fund large capital investments. Maturities range up to 30 years.

The key feature of municipal bonds is their tax-exempt status. Because investors pay neither federal nor state taxes on the interest proceeds, they are willing to accept lower yields on these securities. This represents a huge savings to state and local governments. Correspondingly, it is huge drain of potential tax revenue from the federal government, which has shown some dismay over the explosive increase in the use of industrial development bonds.

Because of concern that these bonds were being used to take advantage of the tax-exempt feature of municipal bonds rather than as a source of funds for publicly desirable investments, the Tax Reform Act of 1986 restricted their use. A state is now allowed to issue mortgage revenue and private purpose tax-exempt bonds only up to a limit of $50 per capita or $150 million, whichever is larger. In fact, the outstanding amount of industrial revenue bonds stopped growing after 1986, as evidenced in Figure 2.6.

An investor choosing between taxable and tax-exempt bonds needs to compare after-tax returns on each bond. An exact comparison requires the computation of after-tax rates of

FIGURE 2.6

Outstanding Tax-Exempt Debt

Source: Balance Sheets for the U.S. Economy, 1945–94. Board of Governors of the Federal Reserve System, 1995.

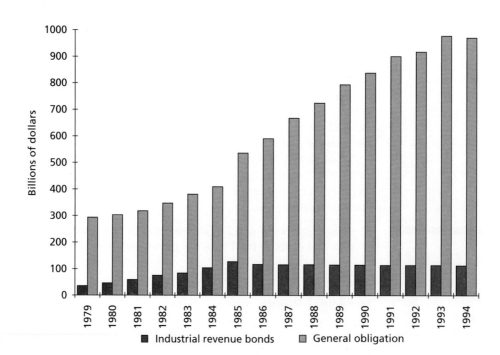

TABLE 2.3

Equivalent Taxable
Yields Corresponding
to Various Tax-Exempt
Yields

Marginal Tax Rate	Tax-Exempt Yield				
	4%	6%	8%	10%	12%
20%	5.0	7.5	10.0	12.5	15.0
30%	5.7	8.6	11.4	14.3	17.1
40%	6.7	10.0	13.3	16.7	20.0
50%	8.0	12.0	16.0	20.0	24.0

return with explicit recognition of taxes on income and realized capital gains. In practice, there is a simpler rule of thumb. If we let t denote the investor's federal plus local marginal tax rate and r denote the total before-tax rate of return available on taxable bonds, then $r(1 - t)$ is the after-tax rate available on those securities. If this value exceeds the rate on municipal bonds, r_m, the investor does better holding the taxable bonds. Otherwise, the tax-exempt municipals provide higher after-tax returns.

One way of comparing bonds is to determine the interest rate on taxable bonds that would be necessary to provide an after-tax return equal to that of municipals. To derive this value, we set after-tax yields equal and solve for the *equivalent taxable yield* of the tax-exempt bond. This is the rate a taxable bond would need to offer in order to match the after-tax yield on the tax-free municipal.

$$r(1 - t) = r_m \qquad (2.4)$$

or

$$r = \frac{r_m}{1 - t} \qquad (2.5)$$

Thus, the equivalent taxable yield is simply the tax-free rate divided by $1 - t$. Table 2.3 presents equivalent taxable yields for several municipal yields and tax rates.

This table frequently appears in the marketing literature for tax-exempt mutual bond funds because it demonstrates to high tax-bracket investors that municipal bonds offer highly attractive equivalent taxable yields. Each entry is calculated from Equation 2.5. If the equivalent taxable yield exceeds the actual yields offered on taxable bonds, after taxes the investor is better off holding municipal bonds. The equivalent taxable interest rate increases with the investor's tax bracket; the higher the bracket, the more valuable the tax-exempt feature of municipals. Thus, high-bracket individuals tend to hold municipals.

We also can use Equations 2.4 or 2.5 to find the tax bracket at which investors are indifferent between taxable and tax-exempt bonds. The cutoff tax bracket is given by solving Equation 2.4 for the tax bracket at which after-tax yields are equal. Doing so, we find

$$t = 1 - \frac{r_m}{r} \qquad (2.6)$$

Thus, the yield ratio r_m/r is a key determinant of the attractiveness of municipal bonds. The higher the yield ratio, the lower the cutoff tax bracket, and the more individuals will prefer to hold municipal debt.

Figure 2.7 graphs the yield ratio since 1960. In recent years, the ratio has hovered at about .73, implying that investors in tax brackets (federal plus local) greater than 27% derive greater after-tax yields from municipals. Note, however, that it is difficult to control precisely for differences in the risks of these bonds, so the cutoff tax bracket must be taken as approximate.

Concept Check

4. Suppose your tax bracket is 28%. Would you prefer to earn a 6% taxable return or a 4% tax-free yield? What is the equivalent taxable yield of the 4% tax-free yield?

FIGURE 2.7

Ratio of Yields on Tax-
Exempt to Taxable
Bonds, 1960–1995

Source: Data from Moody's
Investor Service, 1996.

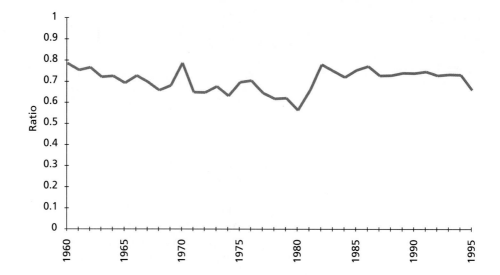

Corporate Bonds

corporate bonds
Long-term debt issued by
private corporations
typically paying
semiannual coupons and
returning the face value of
the bond at maturity.

Corporate bonds are the means by which private firms borrow money directly from the public. These bonds are structured much like Treasury issues in that they typically pay semiannual coupons over their lives and return the face value to the bondholder at maturity. Where they differ most importantly from Treasury bonds is in risk.

Default risk is a real consideration in the purchase of corporate bonds. We treat this issue in considerable detail in Chapter 10. For now, we distinguish only among secured bonds, which have specific collateral backing them in the event of firm bankruptcy; unsecured bonds, called debentures, which have no collateral; and subordinated debentures, which have a lower priority claim to the firm's assets in the event of bankruptcy.

Corporate bonds usually come with options attached. Callable bonds give the firm the option to repurchase the bond from the holder at a stipulated call price. Convertible bonds give the bondholder the option to convert each bond into a stipulated number of shares of stock. These options are treated in more detail in Part Three.

Figure 2.8 is a partial listing of corporate bond prices from *The Wall Street Journal*. The listings are similar to those for Treasury bonds. The highlighted IBM bond has a coupon rate of 7¼ percent and a maturity date of 2002. Its current yield, defined as annual coupon income divided by price, is 7.1%. (Note that current yield is a different measure from yield to maturity. The differences are explored in Part Three.)

Only 95 IBM bonds traded on this day. The closing price of the bond was 101¾ percent of par, or $1,017.50, which was up ¾ of a point from the previous day's close. In contrast to Treasury bonds, price quotes on corporate bonds use explicit fractions.

Mortgages and Mortgage-Backed Securities

Thirty years ago, your investments text probably would not have included a section on mortgage loans, for investors could not invest in these loans. Now, because of the explosion in mortgage-backed securities, almost anyone can invest in a portfolio of mortgage loans, and these securities have become a major component of the fixed-income market.

Until the 1970s, almost all home mortgages were written for a long term (15- to 30-year maturity), with a fixed interest rate over the life of the loan, and with equal, fixed monthly payments. These so-called conventional mortgages are still the most popular, but a diverse set of alternative mortgage designs have appeared.

FIGURE 2.8
Listing of Corporate Bond Prices

Source: From *The Wall Street Journal*, June 7, 1996. Reprinted by permission of *The Wall Street Journal*, ©1996 Dow Jones & Company, Inc. All Rights Reserved Worldwide.

NEW YORK EXCHANGE BONDS

Bonds	Cur Yld	Vol	Close	Net Chg.
GMA zr12	...	51	285⅛	+ 2⅝
GMA zr15	...	97	246⅛	+ 1¼
Genesc 10⅜03	10.4	40	99⅜	− 1½
GenesisH 9¾05	9.5	95	102½	− ¼
Genrad 7¼11	cv	47	116	− ½
GaPw 6⅛99	6.2	25	98⅛	...
Gerrity 11¾04	11.1	154	105½	+ 1⅝
Grancre 6½03	6.9	17	94	− ½
Gulfrd 6s12	cv	2	98	− ½
GlfMo 5s56f rg	8.6	1	58⅛	− 4⅜
HFS 4¾03	cv	7	115¾	+ ¾
Hallwd na13½09	...	1	67	− ⅜
Hollngr 9¼06	9.9	10	93	...
vjHuntIR 9⅞04f	...	2	1¼	− ½
ICN Ph 8½99	cv	27	127	− 1½
IllPwr 8s23	8.1	55	99	+ 1
IBM 6⅜97	6.4	297	100⅛	+ ⅛
IBM 6⅜00	6.4	134	99	+ ⅜
→ IBM 7¼02	7.1	95	101¾	+ ¾
IBM 8⅜19	7.8	115	108	+ ¼
IntShip 9s03	9.4	10	96	...
JCP 7½23	8.0	3	94	+ 2
KaufB 10⅜99	10.1	10	103	...
KaufB 9⅜03	9.3	105	101	...
Kroger 9s99	9.0	25	100½	...
LaFrg 7s13	cv	25	108	+ ⅝
PacTT 7¼08	7.3	20	99½	+ 1
ParCm 7s03A	7.8	30	89⅞	+ ¾
ParkElc 5½06	cv	46	86½	− ¼
PaylCsh 9⅛03	11.3	64	81⅛	+ ¼
PennTr 9⅝05	12.5	1287	76⅞	− 2⅛
Pennzl 4¾03	4.5	37	105½	− 1½
PepBoys 4s99	cv	30	104½	+ ½
Pepsic 7⅝98	7.4	20	102¾	− ½
PhilEl 7¾23	8.0	10	96¾	+ 1
PhilPt 7.2s03	8.0	17	90	+ ⅝
PhilPt 7.92s23	8.0	10	98¾	+ 1¾
Pier1 6⅞02	cv	5	143	+ 1
PogoP 8s05	cv	1	104½	− 1
PotEl 7s18	cv	11	101½	...
Primark 8¾00	8.8	127	99⅜	− ¼
PrmHsp 7s02	cv	1	144	...
PrmHsp 9¼06	9.5	20	97¼	− 1
PSEG 6⅞97	6.8	70	101½	+ 1⅜
PSEG 8¾99	...	5	104½	− 2⅜
PSEG 7½23	7.8	15	96⅛	+ 1
Quanx 6.88s07	cv	5	97¾	+ ½
RJR Nb 8s01	8.0	5	99½	+ ⅜
RJR Nb 8⅝02	8.6	17	100⅝	+ ⅛
RJR Nb 7⅝03	8.0	116	94⅞	+ ⅜
RJR Nb 8¾05	8.8	45	99⅛	− ⅜
RJR Nb 8¾07	8.8	35	99¼	+ ⅞

Fixed-rate mortgages have created considerable difficulties for banks in years of increasing interest rates. Because banks commonly issue short-term liabilities (the deposits of their customers) and hold long-term assets, such as fixed-rate mortgages, they suffer losses when interest rates increase. The rates they pay on deposits increase, while their mortgage income remains fixed.

A relatively recent introduction is the adjustable-rate mortgage. These mortgages require the borrower to pay an interest rate that varies with some measure of the current market interest rate. The interest rate, for example, might be set at two points above the current rate on one-year Treasury bills and might be adjusted once a year. Often, a contract limits the maximum interest rate change within a year and over the life of the contract. The adjustable-rate contract shifts the risk of fluctuations in interest rates from the bank to the borrower.

Because of the shifting of interest rate risk to their customers, banks are willing to offer lower rates on adjustable-rate mortgages than on conventional fixed-rate mortgages. This has encouraged borrowers during periods of high interest rates, such as in the early 1980s. But as interest rates have fallen, conventional mortgages appear to have regained popularity. While adjustable-rate mortgages accounted for about half of all mortgage lending at year-end 1983, that figure has since fallen to one-quarter.

A *mortgage-backed security* is either an ownership claim in a pool of mortgages or an obligation that is secured by such a pool. These claims represent securitization of mortgage loans. Mortgage lenders originate loans and then sell packages of these loans in the secondary market. Specifically, they sell their claim to the cash inflows from the mortgages as those loans are paid off. The mortgage originator continues to service the loan, collecting principal and interest payments, and passes these payments along to the purchaser of the mortgage. For this reason, these mortgage-backed securities are called *pass-throughs*.

Mortgage-backed pass-through securities were introduced by the Government National Mortgage Association (GNMA, or Ginnie Mae) in 1970. GNMA pass-throughs carry a guarantee from the U.S. government that ensures timely payment of principal and interest, even if the borrower defaults on the mortgage. This guarantee increases the marketability of the pass-through. Thus, investors can buy and sell GNMA securities like any other bond.

Other mortgage pass-throughs have since become popular. These are sponsored by FNMA (Fannie Mae) and FHLMC (Freddie Mac). By the end of 1995, more than $1.5

FIGURE 2.9
Mortgage-Backed
Securities Outstanding,
1979–1996

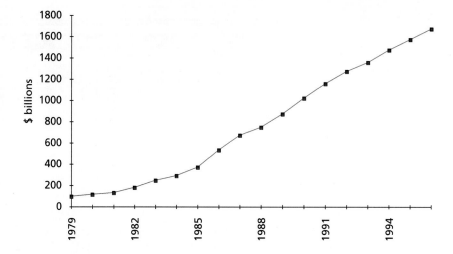

trillion of outstanding mortgages were securitized into mortgage-backed securities, making the mortgage-backed securities market larger than the corporate bond market. Figure 2.9 illustrates the explosive growth of these securities since 1979.

The success of mortgage-backed pass-throughs has encouraged the introduction of pass-through securities backed by other assets. For example, the Student Loan Marketing Association (SLMA, or Sallie Mae) sponsors pass-throughs backed by loans originated under the Guaranteed Student Loan Program and by other loans granted under various federal programs for higher education.

2.3 EQUITY SECURITIES

Common Stock as Ownership Shares

common stocks
Ownership shares in a publicly held corporation. Shareholders have voting rights and may receive dividends.

Common stocks, also known as equity securities, or equities, represent ownership shares in a corporation. Each share of common stock entitles its owners to one vote on any matters of corporate governance put to a vote at the corporation's annual meeting and to a share in the financial benefits of ownership[1] (e.g., the right to any dividends that the corporation may wish to distribute).

A corporation is controlled by a board of directors elected by the shareholders.[2] The board, which meets only a few times each year, selects managers who run the corporation on a day-to-day basis. Managers have the authority to make most business decisions without the board's approval. The board's mandate is to oversee the management to ensure that it acts in the best interests of shareholders.

The members of the board are elected at the annual meeting. Shareholders who do not attend the annual meeting can vote by proxy, empowering another party to vote in their name. Management usually solicits the proxies of shareholders and normally gets a vast majority of these proxy votes. Occasionally, however, a group of shareholders intent on unseating the current management or altering its policies will wage a proxy fight to gain the voting rights of shareholders not attending the annual meeting. Thus, while management usually has considerable discretion to run the firm as it sees fit, without daily oversight from

---

[1]Sometimes a corporation issues two classes of common stock, one bearing the right to vote, the other not. Because of its restricted rights, the nonvoting stocks sell for a lower price, reflecting the value of control.
[2]The voting system specified in the corporate articles determines the chances of affecting the elections to specific directorship seats. In a majority voting system, each shareholder can cast one vote per share for each seat. A cumulative voting system allows shareholders to concentrate all their votes on one seat, enabling minority shareholders to gain representation.

the equity holders who actually own the firm, both oversight from the board and the possibility of a proxy fight serve as checks on management's jurisdiction.

In practice, where ownership is greatly diffused in widely held corporations, management controls are less stringent than in theory. In proxy fights, management defends its board member allies at corporate expense, while the outsiders must finance the fight from their own pockets. A typical proxy fight costs millions, and about three-fourths of the attempts have historically failed—statistics that send chills down the spines of would-be proxy fighters.

The most effective check on management's discretion may be the possibility of a corporate takeover; that is, an outside investor who believes the firm is mismanaged will attempt to acquire the firm. Usually, this is accomplished with a *tender offer*, which is an offer made to stockholders to purchase their shares at a stipulated price, usually substantially above the current market price. If the tender is successful, the acquiring investor can purchase enough shares to obtain control of the firm and can replace its management.

The common stock of most large corporations can be bought or sold freely on one or more of the stock exchanges. A corporation whose stock is not publicly traded is said to be closely held. In most closely held corporations, the owners of the firm also take an active role in its management. Takeovers generally are not an issue.

Thus, while there is substantial separation of the ownership and the control of large corporations, there are at least some implicit controls on management that encourage it to act in the best interest of the shareholders.

Characteristics of Common Stock

The two most important characteristics of common stock as an investment are its residual claim and its limited liability features.

Residual claim means stockholders are the last in line of all those who have a claim on the assets and income of the corporation. In a liquidation of the firm's assets, the shareholders have claim to what is left after paying all other claimants, such as the tax authorities, employees, suppliers, bondholders, and other creditors. In a going concern, shareholders have claim to the part of operating income left after interest and income taxes have been paid. Management either can pay this residual as cash dividends to shareholders or reinvest it in the business to increase the value of the shares.

Limited liability means that the most shareholders can lose in event of the failure of the corporation is their original investment. Shareholders are not like owners of unincorporated businesses, whose creditors can lay claim to the personal assets of the owner—such as houses, cars, and furniture. In the event of the firm's bankruptcy, corporate stockholders at worst have worthless stock. They are not personally liable for the firm's obligations: Their liability is limited.

Concept Check

5. *a.* If you buy 100 shares of IBM common stock, to what are you entitled?
    b. What is the most money you can make over the next year?
    c. If you pay $50 per share, what is the most money you could lose over the year?

Stock Market Listings

Figure 2.10 is a partial listing from *The Wall Street Journal* of stocks traded on the New York Stock Exchange. The NYSE is one of several markets in which investors may buy or sell shares of stock. We will examine issues of trading in these markets in the next chapter.

To interpret the information provided for each traded stock, consider the listing for Baltimore Gas and Electric, BaltimrGE. The first two columns provide the highest and lowest price at which the stock has traded in the last 52 weeks, $29½ and $23⅞, respectively.

FIGURE 2.10
Listing of Stocks Traded on the New York Stock Exchange

Source: From *The Wall Street Journal*, June 7, 1996. Reprinted by permission of *The Wall Street Journal*, © 1996 Dow Jones & Company, Inc. All Rights Reserved Worldwide.

NEW YORK STOCK EXCHANGE COMPOSITE TRANSACTIONS

	52 Weeks Hi	52 Weeks Lo	Stock	Sym	Div	Yld %	PE	Vol 100s	Hi	Lo	Close	Net Chg
s	47½	32¾	AvonPdts	AVP	1.16	2.5	24	3344	46¾	45⅝	45¾	– ¼
n▼	**38**	**20⅞**	**AVX Cp**	**AVX**	**.22f**	**1.1**	**...**	**2656**	**21⅝**	**20⅝**	**20⅝**	**–1⅛**
	19⅜	12⅞	Aydin	AYD		...	21	67	15⅛	14⅞	15	– ⅛
▲	12¼	6⅞	AztarCp	AZR		...	dd	11236	12½	12	12⅛	+ ⅛
			-B-B-B-									
	48¾	17½	BBN	BBN		...	dd	615	26	24⅝	24⅞	–1⅛
▲	40¼	30⅜	BCE Inc g	BCE	2.72	...	...	1053	40⅜	40	40¼	+ ¼
	38¾	25¾	Ball Cp	BLL	.60	2.2	dd	1629	27⅞	27½	27½	– ⅛
	20⅝	11⅜	♣ BallrdMed	BMP	.08	.4	24	784	20¼	19⅜	19⅜	–1
▲	**26¼**	**9⅛**	**BallyEntmt**	**BLY**		**...**	**26**	**60346**	**29**	**26⅞**	**27⅝**	**+1½**
n▲	24¾	10¾	BallyEntmt prides		.89	3.4	...	19801	27⅛	25	25⅞	+1⅛
→ x	29½	23⅞	BaltimrGE	BGE	1.60f	5.8	12	986	27½	27¼	27⅜	+ ¼
s	38½	27⅞	♣ BancOne	ONE	1.36b	3.7	11	9609	37¾	36⅞	36⅞	– ¾
	29	26⅜	BancoBilV pf		2.44	8.6	...	67	28¼	28	28¼	– ⅛
	26¼	23⅜	BancoBil pfC		2.00	7.8	...	171	25½	25 13/64	25½	+ ¼
	40½	28⅜	BancoBilV	BBV	1.61e	4.3	...	35	37⅜	37¼	37⅜	+ ¼

	52 Weeks Hi	52 Weeks Lo	Stock	Sym	Div	Yld %	PE	Vol 100s	Hi	Lo	Close	Net Chg
	25¾	23⅝	BearStearns EPICS		2.00	8.2	...	54	24½	24¼	24⅜	...
s	33¾	20⅛	♣ Bearings	BER	.56	2.0	16	1141	28⅞	28½	28½	– ⅛
	21	14⅞	BeazerHm	BZH		...	11	36	18⅜	18⅛	18⅜	+ ⅛
n	31⅞	23¾	BeazerHm pfA		2.00	7.0	...	27	28½	28¼	28½	+ ⅝
	41⅛	26⅞	♣ BeckmanInstr	BEC	.52	1.4	20	933	37	36¼	36¼	– ¼
	89⅛	55⅝	BectonDksn	BDX	.92	1.1	21	1314	85½	84⅛	84⅜	– ⅝
s	16	10¾	BedfdPrpty	BED	.96	7.3	31	260	13½	13⅛	13⅛	– ¼
n	30⅞	21⅝	BelcoOG	BOG		...	...	171	27⅞	27½	27⅞	+ ⅛
	38000	22125	BerkHathwy A	BRKA		...	17	z110	32800	32400	32400	–200
n	1220	990	BerkHathwy B	BRKB		...	...	z1840	1100	1085	1085	–8
	11⅛	9¼	BrkshreRlty	BRI	.90	8.2	31	433	11⅛	11	11	...
	¾	5/16	BrkshreRlty wt			...	...	53	¾	11/16	11/16	...
	19½	14	Berlitz	BTZ		...	63	5	19½	19½	19½	+ ⅛
	12½	8¾	BerryPete	BRY	.40	3.8	17	247	11	10⅝	10⅝	– ¼
	46⅞	27	BestBuyCap pf		3.25	8.2	...	136	39⅞	39⅜	39⅞	...
	30¼	12	BestBuy	BBY		...	22	11591	25⅛	24½	24⅞	– ⅛
▼	18¼	12⅜	BethSteel	BS		...	16	17605	12½	12¼	12¼	– ¼

The 1.60 figure means that the last quarter's dividend was \$.40 per share, which is consistent with annual dividend payments of $\$.40 \times 4 = \$1.60$.

This value corresponds to a dividend yield of 5.8%: Since BaltimrGE stock is selling at 27⅜ (the last recorded, or "close," price in the next-to-last column), the dividend yield is $1.60/27.375 = .058$, or 5.8%.

The stock listings show that dividend yields vary widely among firms. High dividend-yield stocks are not necessarily better investments than low-yield stocks. Total return to an investor comes from both dividends and capital gains, or appreciation in the value of the stock. Low dividend-yield firms presumably offer greater prospects for capital gains, or else investors would not be willing to hold the low-yield firms in their portfolios.

The P/E ratio, or price-to-earnings ratio, is the ratio of the current stock price to last year's earnings. The P/E ratio tells us how much stock purchasers must pay per dollar of earnings the firm generates for each share. The P/E ratio also varies widely across firms. Where the dividend yield and P/E ratio are not reported in Figure 2.10, the firms have zero dividends, or zero or negative earnings. We shall have much to say about P/E ratios in Part Four.

The sales column ("Vol") shows that 986 hundred shares of BaltimrGE were traded on June 6, 1996. Shares commonly are traded in round lots of 100 shares each. Investors who wish to trade in smaller "odd lots" generally must pay higher commissions to their stockbrokers. The highest price and lowest price per share at which the stock traded on June 6 were \$27½ and \$27¼, respectively. The last, or closing, price of \$27⅜ was up \$¼ from the closing price of the previous day.

Preferred Stock

preferred stock
Nonvoting shares in a corporation, usually paying a fixed stream of dividends.

Preferred stock has features similar to both equity and debt. Like a bond, it promises to pay to its holder a fixed stream of income each year. In this sense, preferred stock is similar to an infinite-maturity bond, that is, a perpetuity. It also resembles a bond in that it does not give the holder voting power regarding the firm's management.

Preferred stock is an equity investment, however. The firm retains discretion to make the dividend payments to the preferred stockholders: It has no contractual obligation to pay those dividends. Instead, preferred dividends are usually *cumulative*; that is, unpaid dividends cumulate and must be paid in full before any dividends may be paid to holders of common stock. In contrast, the firm does have a contractual obligation to make the interest payments on the debt. Failure to make these payments sets off corporate bankruptcy proceedings.

Preferred stock also differs from bonds in terms of its tax treatment for the firm. Because preferred stock payments are treated as dividends rather than as interest on debt, they are not tax-deductible expenses for the firm. This disadvantage is largely offset by the fact that corporations may exclude 70% of dividends received from domestic corporations in the computation of their taxable income. Preferred stocks, therefore, make desirable fixed-income investments for some corporations.

Even though preferred stock ranks after bonds in terms of the priority of its claim to the assets of the firm in the event of corporate bankruptcy, preferred stock often sells at lower yields than corporate bonds. Presumably this reflects the value of the dividend exclusion, for risk considerations alone indicate that preferred stock ought to offer higher yields than bonds. Individual investors, who cannot use the 70% exclusion, generally will find preferred stock yields unattractive relative to those on other available assets.

Corporations issue preferred stock in variations similar to those of corporate bonds. Preferred stock can be callable by the issuing firm, in which case it is said to be *redeemable*. It also can be convertible into common stock at some specified conversion ratio. A relatively recent innovation in the market is adjustable-rate preferred stock, which, like adjustable-rate mortgages, ties the dividend rate to current market interest rates.

2.4 STOCK AND BOND MARKET INDEXES

Stock Market Indexes

The daily performance of the Dow Jones Industrial Average is a staple portion of the evening news report. While the Dow is the best-known measure of the performance of the stock market, it is only one of several indicators. Other more broadly based indexes are computed and published daily. In addition, several indexes of bond market performance are widely available. The nearby box on page 42 describes the Dow Jones Industrial Average, gives a bit of its history, and discusses some of its strengths and shortcomings.

The ever-increasing role of international trade and investments has made indexes of foreign financial markets part of the general news. Thus, foreign stock exchange indexes such as the Nikkei Average of Tokyo and the *Financial Times* index of London are fast becoming household names.

Dow Jones Averages

The Dow Jones Industrial Average (DJIA) of 30 large, "blue-chip" corporations has been computed since 1896. Its long history probably accounts for its preeminence in the public mind. (The average covered only 20 stocks until 1928.)

Originally, the DJIA was calculated as the simple average of the stocks included in the index. So, if there were 30 stocks in the index, one would add up the value of the 30 stocks and divide by 30. The percentage change in the DJIA would then be the percentage change in the average price of the 30 shares.

This procedure means that the percentage change in the DJIA measures the return on a portfolio that invests one share in each of the 30 stocks in the index. The value of such a portfolio (holding one share of each stock in the index) is the sum of the 30 prices. Because the percentage change in the *average* of the 30 prices is the same as the percentage change in the *sum* of the 30 prices, the index and the portfolio have the same percentage change each day.

To illustrate, consider the data in Table 2.4 for a hypothetical two-stock version of the Dow Jones Average. Stock ABC sells initially at $25 a share, while XYZ sells for $100. Therefore, the initial value of the index would be $(25 + 100)/2 = 62.5$. The final share prices are $30 for stock ABC and $90 for XYZ, so the average falls by 2.5 to $(30 + 90)/2 = 60$. The 2.5 point drop in the index is a 4% decrease: $2.5/62.5 = .04$. Similarly, a portfolio holding

What, How, Why: So What Is the Dow Jones Industrial Average, Anyway?

Quick. How did the market do yesterday? If you're like most people, you'd probably answer by saying that the Dow Jones Industrial Average rose or fell.

At 100 years old, the Dow Jones Industrial Average has acquired a unique place in the collective consciousness of investors. It is the number quoted on the nightly news, and remembered when the market takes a dive.

But enough with the blandishments. What *is* the Dow, exactly, and what does it do?

The first part is easy: The Dow is an average of 30 blue-chip U.S. stocks. As for what it does, perhaps the simplest explanation is this: It's a tool by which the general public can measure the overall performance of the U.S. stock market.

INDUSTRY BELLWETHERS

Even though the industrial average consists of only 30 stocks, the theory is that each one represents a particular sector of the economy and serves as a reliable bellwether for that industry. Thus, the Dow Jones roster is made up of giants such as **International Business Machines** Corp., **J.P. Morgan** & Co., and **AT&T** Corp. Together, the 30 stocks reflect the market as a whole.

Initially, the industrial average comprised 12 companies. Only one, **General Electric** Co., remains in the average under its original name. Many of the others are extinct today, while some have mutated into companies that are still active. But a century ago, these were the corporate titans of the time. On October 1, 1928, a year before the crash, the Dow was expanded to a 30-stock average.

MARCHING HIGHER

As times have changed, so have the makeup and mechanics of the Dow. Back in 1896, all Charles Dow needed was a pencil and paper to compute the industrial average: He simply added up the prices of the 12 stocks and then divided by 12.

Today, the first step in calculating the Dow is still totaling the prices of the component stocks. But the rest of the math isn't so easy anymore, because the divisor is continually being adjusted. The reason? To preserve historical continuity. In the past 100 years, there have been many stock splits, spinoffs, and stock substitutions that, without adjustment, would distort the value of the Dow.

To understand how the formula works, consider a stock split. Say three stocks are trading at $15, $20, and $25; the average of the three is $20. But if the company with the $20 stock has a 2-for-1 split, its shares suddenly are priced at half of their previous level. That's not to say the value of the investment has changed; rather, the $20 stock simply sells for $10, with twice as many shares available. The

average of the three stocks, meanwhile, falls to $16.66. So, the Dow divisor is adjusted to keep the average at $20 and reflect the continuing value of the investment represented by the gauge.

MINIMAL CHANGE

Over time, the divisor has been adjusted several times, mostly downward (it now stands at .31143932). This explains why the average can be reported as, say, 7000, though no single stock in the average is close to that price.

Since Charles Dow's time, several stock market indexes have challenged the Dow Jones Industrial Average. In 1928, Standard & Poor's Corp. developed the S&P 90, which by the 1950s evolved into the S&P 500, a benchmark widely used today by professional money managers. And now indexes abound. Wilshire Associates in Santa Monica, California, for example, uses computers to compile an index of nearly 7,000 stocks.

Nevertheless, the Dow remains unique. For one, it isn't market-weighted like other indicators, which means it isn't adjusted to reflect the market capitalization of the component stocks. Because of that, the Dow gives more emphasis to higher-priced stocks than to lower-priced stocks.

So, a stock such as **United Technologies** Corp. constitutes only 0.26% of the S&P 500. Yet it accounts for a whopping 5.5% of the Dow Jones industrials, because it is one of the most expensive stocks in the Dow.

Despite the weighting difference, the Dow, by and large, closely tracks other major market indexes. That's because, for one, the stocks in the industrial average do an adequate job of representing their industries.

"There are only 30 stocks in the Dow and 500 stocks in the S&P, but it is the weighting that makes them track closely," says Mr. Dickey of Dain Bosworth. Since the S&P 500 is weighted by market capitalization, "a large part of the movement is determined by the biggest companies," he explains. And these big companies that drive the S&P are invariably also found in the Dow.

In the end, while some indexes may be more closely watched by professionals, the Dow Jones Industrial Average has retained its position as the most popular measure, if for no other reason than that it has stood the test of time. As the oldest continuing barometer of the U.S. stock market, it tells us where we came from, which helps us understand where we are.

Source: From Anita Raghavan and Nancy Ann Jeffrey, "What, How, Why: So What Is the Dow Jones Industrial Average, Anyway?" *The Wall Street Journal*, May 28, 1996, p. R30. Reprinted by permission of *The Wall Street Journal*, © 1996 Dow Jones & Company, Inc. All Rights Reserved Worldwide.

TABLE 2.4

Data to Construct Stock Price Indexes

Stock	Initial Price	Final Price	Shares (Million)	Initial Value of Outstanding Stock ($ Million)	Final Value of Outstanding Stock ($ Million)
ABC	25	30	20	500	600
XYZ	100	90	1	100	90
Total				600	690

TABLE 2.5

Data to Construct Stock Price Indexes After a Stock Split

Stock	Initial Price	Final Price	Shares (Million)	Initial Value of Outstanding Stock ($ Million)	Final Value of Outstanding Stock ($ Million)
ABC	25	30	20	500	600
XYZ	50	45	2	100	90
Total				600	690

one share of each stock would have an initial value of $25 + $100 = $125 and a final value of $30 + $90 = $120, for an identical 4% decrease.

Because the Dow measures the return on a portfolio that holds one share of each stock, it is called a **price-weighted average.** The amount of money invested in each company represented in the portfolio is proportional to that company's share price.

price-weighted average
An average computed by adding the prices of the stocks and dividing by a "divisor."

Price-weighted averages give higher-priced shares more weight in determining the performance of the index. For example, although ABC increased by 20% while XYZ fell by only 10%, the index dropped in value. This is because the 20% increase in ABC represented a smaller price gain ($5 per share) than the 10% decrease in XYZ ($10 per share). The "Dow portfolio" has four times as much invested in XYZ as in ABC because XYZ's price is four times that of ABC. Therefore, XYZ dominates the average.

You might wonder why the DJIA is now (in mid-1997) at a level of about 7,000 if it is supposed to be the average price of the 30 stocks in the index. The DJIA no longer equals the average price of the 30 stocks because the averaging procedure is adjusted whenever a stock splits, pays a stock dividend of more than 10%, or when one company in the group of 30 industrial firms is replaced by another. When these events occur, the divisor used to compute the "average price" is adjusted so as to leave the index unaffected by the event.

For example, if XYZ were to split two for one and its share price to fall to $50, we would not want the average to fall, as that would incorrectly indicate a fall in the general level of market prices. Following a split, the divisor must be reduced to a value that leaves the average unaffected by the split. Table 2.5 illustrates this point. The initial share price of XYZ, which was $100 in Table 2.4, falls to $50 if the stock splits at the beginning of the period. Notice that the number of shares outstanding doubles, leaving the market value of the total shares unaffected. The divisor, d, which originally was 2.0 when the two-stock average was initiated, must be reset to a value that leaves the "average" unchanged. Because the sum of the postsplit stock prices is 75, while the presplit average price was 62.5, we calculate the new value of d by solving $75/d = 62.5$. The value of d, therefore, falls from its original value of 2.0 to $75/62.5 = 1.20$, and the initial value of the average is unaffected by the split: $75/1.20 = 62.5$.

At period-end, ABC will sell for $30, while XYZ will sell for $45, representing the same negative 10% return it was assumed to earn in Table 2.4. The new value of the price-weighted average is $(30 + 45)/1.20 = 62.5$. The index is unchanged, so the rate of return is zero, rather than the -4% return that would be calculated in the absence of a split. This return is greater than that calculated in the absence of a split. The relative weight of XYZ, which is the poorer-performing stock, is reduced by a split because its price is lower; so the

How the 30 Stocks in the Dow Jones Industrial Average Have Changed Since October 1, 1928

Oct. 1, 1928	1929	1930s	1940s	1950s	1960s	1970s	1980s	May 6, 1991	March 12, 1997
Allied Chemical & Dye							AlliedSignal*('85)		AlliedSignal
Wright Aeronautical	Curtiss-Wright ('29)	Hudson Motor ('30) Coca-Cola ('32) National Steel ('35)		Aluminum Co. of America ('59)					Aluminum Co. of America
North American		Johns-Manville ('30)					Amer. Express ('82)		American Express
Victor Talking Machine	Natl Cash Register ('29)	IBM ('32) AT&T ('39)							AT&T
International Nickel						Inco Ltd.*('76)	Boeing ('87)		Boeing
International Harvester							Navistar*('86)	Caterpillar	Caterpillar
Goodrich		Standard Oil (Calif.) ('30)					Chevron*('84)		Chevron
Texas Gulf Sulphur		Intl. Shoe ('32) United Aircraft ('33) National Distillers ('34)		Owens-Illinois('59)			Coca-Cola ('87)		Coca-Cola
U.S. Steel							USX Corp.*('86)	Walt Disney	Walt Disney
American Sugar		Borden ('30) DuPont ('35)							DuPont
American Tobacco (B)		Eastman Kodak ('30)							Eastman Kodak
Standard Oil (N.J.)						Exxon*('72)			Exxon
General Electric									General Electric
General Motors									General Motors
Atlantic Refining		Goodyear ('30)							Goodyear
Texas Corp.				Texaco*('59)					Hewlett-Packard
Chrysler						IBM ('79)			IBM
Paramount Publix		Loew's ('32)		Intl. Paper ('56)					International Paper
Bethlehem Steel									Johnson & Johnson
General Railway Signal		Liggett & Myers ('30) Amer. Tobacco ('32)					McDonald's ('85)		McDonald's
Mack Trucks		Drug Inc. ('32) Corn Products ('33)		Swift & Co. ('59)		Esmark*('73) Merck ('79)			Merck
American Smelting				Anaconda ('59)		Minn. Mining ('76)			Minn. Mining
American Can							Primerica*('87)	J.P. Morgan	J.P. Morgan
Postum Inc.	General Foods*('29)						Philip Morris ('85)		Philip Morris
Nash Motors		United Air Trans. ('30) Procter & Gamble ('32)							Procter & Gamble
Sears Roebuck									Sears Roebuck
Westinghouse Electric									Travelers Group
Union Carbide									Union Carbide
Radio Corp.		Nash Motors ('32) United Aircraft ('39)				United Tech.*('75)			United Technologies
Woolworth									Wal-Mart Stores

Source: Data from *Economic Report of the President*, U.S. Government Printing Office, 1996.
*Includes overnight Eurodollars.
†Less than $100,000 denomination.
‡More than $100,000 denomination.

Note: Year of change shown in ( ); *denotes name change, in some cases following a takeover or merger. To track changes in the components, begin in the column for 1928 and work across. For instance, American Sugar was replaced by Borden in 1930, which in turn was replaced by Du Pont in 1935.

Source: From *The Wall Street Journal*, March 13, 1997. Reprinted by permission of *The Wall Street Journal* © 1997 Dow Jones & Company, Inc. All Rights Reserved Worldwide.

performance of the average is higher. This example illustrates that the implicit weighting scheme of a price-weighted average is somewhat arbitrary, being determined by the prices rather than by the outstanding market values (price per share times number of shares) of the shares in the average.

Because the Dow Jones averages are based on small numbers of firms, care must be taken to ensure that they are representative of the broad market. As a result, the composition of the average is changed every so often to reflect changes in the economy. The last change took place on March 12, 1997, when Hewlett-Packard, Johnson & Johnson, Travelers Group, and Wal-Mart were added to the index and Texaco, Bethlehem Steel, Westinghouse, and Woolworth were dropped. The nearby box on page 44 presents the history of the firms in the index since 1928. The fate of many companies once considered "the bluest of the blue chips" is striking evidence of the changes in the U.S. economy in the last 68 years.

In the same way that the divisor is updated for stock splits, if one firm is dropped from the average and another firm with a different price is added, the divisor has to be updated to leave the average unchanged by the substitution. By now, the divisor for the Dow Jones Industrial Average has fallen to a value of about .311.

<table>
<tr><td>

Concept Check

</td><td>

6. Suppose XYZ's final price in Table 2.4 increases in price to $110, while ABC falls to $20. Find the percentage change in the price-weighted average of these two stocks. Compare that to the percentage return of a portfolio that holds one share in each company.

</td></tr>
</table>

Dow Jones & Company also computes a Transportation Average of 20 airline, trucking, and railroad stocks; a Public Utility Average of 15 electric and natural gas utilities; and a Composite Average combining the 65 firms of the three separate averages. Each is a price-weighted average and thus overweights the performance of high-priced stocks.

Figure 2.11 reproduces some of the data reported on the Dow Jones averages from *The Wall Street Journal* (which is owned by Dow Jones & Company). The bars show the range of values assumed by the average on each day. The crosshatch indicates the closing value of the average.

Standard & Poor's Indexes

The Standard & Poor's Composite 500 (S&P 500) stock index represents an improvement over the Dow Jones averages in two ways. First, it is a more broadly based index of 500 firms. Secondly, it is a **market value-weighted index.** In the case of the firms XYZ and ABC discussed above, the S&P 500 would give ABC five times the weight given to XYZ because the market value of its outstanding equity is five times larger, $500 million versus $100 million.

market value-weighted index
Computed by calculating a weighted average of the returns of each security in the index, with weights proportional to outstanding market value.

The S&P 500 is computed by calculating the total market value of the 500 firms in the index and the total market value of those firms on the previous day of trading. The percentage increase in the total market value from one day to the next represents the increase in the index. The rate of return of the index equals the rate of return that would be earned by an investor holding a portfolio of all 500 firms in the index in proportion to their market value, except that the index does not reflect cash dividends paid by those firms.

To illustrate, look again at Table 2.4. If the initial level of a market value-weighted index of stocks ABC and XYZ were set equal to an arbitrarily chosen starting value such as 100, the index value at year-end would be $100 \times (690/600) = 115$. The increase in the index reflects the 15% return earned on a portfolio consisting of those two stocks held in proportion to outstanding market values.

Unlike the price-weighted index, the value-weighted index gives more weight to ABC. Whereas the price-weighted index fell because it was dominated by higher-price XYZ, the value-weighted index rises because it gives more weight to ABC, the stock with the higher total market value.

FIGURE 2.11
The Dow Jones
Industrial Average

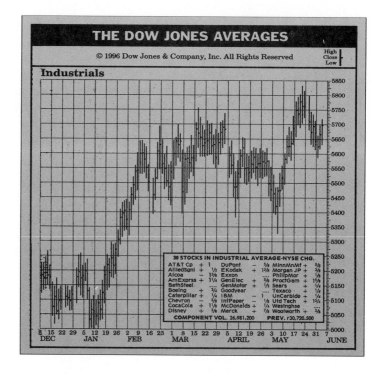

Note also from Tables 2.4 and 2.5 that market value-weighted indexes are unaffected by stock splits. The total market value of the outstanding XYZ stock increases from $100 million to $110 million regardless of the stock split, thereby rendering the split irrelevant to the performance of the index.

A nice feature of both market value-weighted and price-weighted indexes is that they reflect the returns to straightforward portfolio strategies. If one were to buy each share in the index in proportion to its outstanding market value, the value-weighted index would perfectly track capital gains on the underlying portfolio. Similarly, a price-weighted index tracks the returns on a portfolio comprised of equal shares of each firm.

Investors today can purchase shares in mutual funds that hold shares in proportion to their representation in the S&P 500 as well as other stock indexes. These *index funds* yield a return equal to that of the particular index and so provide a low-cost passive investment strategy for equity investors.

Standard & Poor's also publishes a 400-stock Industrial Index, a 20-stock Transportation Index, a 40-stock Utility Index, and a 40-stock Financial Index.

Concept Check

7. Reconsider companies XYZ and ABC from Question 6. Calculate the percentage change in the market value-weighted index. Compare that to the rate of return of a portfolio that holds $500 of ABC stock for every $100 of XYZ stock (i.e., an index portfolio).

Other Market Value Indexes

The New York Stock Exchange publishes a market value-weighted composite index of all NYSE-listed stocks, in addition to subindexes for industrial, utility, transportation, and financial stocks. The American Stock Exchange, or Amex, also computes a market value-weighted index of its stocks. These indexes are even more broadly based than the S&P 500. The National Association of Securities Dealers publishes an index of nearly 3,000 OTC firms using the National Association of Securities Dealers Automatic Quotations (Nasdaq) service.

The ultimate U.S. equity index so far computed is the Wilshire 5000 index of the market value of all NYSE and Amex stocks plus actively traded OTC stocks. Despite its name, the

FIGURE 2.12

Listing of Stock Index Performance

Source: From *The Wall Street Journal*, June 11, 1996. Reprinted by permission of *The Wall Street Journal*, © 1996 Dow Jones & Company, Inc. All Rights Reserved Worldwide.

STOCK MARKET DATA BANK   6/10/96

MAJOR INDEXES

365 DAY HIGH	LOW		DAILY HIGH	LOW	CLOSE	NET CHG	% CHG	†365 DAY CHG	% CHG	FROM 12/31	% CHG
DOW JONES AVERAGES											
5778.00	4446.46	30 Industrials	5703.02	5663.86	5687.87	− 9.24	− 0.16	+1241.41	+27.92	+ 570.75	+11.15
2296.20	1663.22	20 Transportation	2238.84	2228.14	x2231.70	− 5.71	− 0.26	+ 568.48	+34.18	+ 250.70	+12.66
234.00	200.76	15 Utilities	209.54	207.87	208.50	− 0.97	− 0.46	+ 5.23	+ 2.57	− 16.90	− 7.50
1890.51	1463.91	65 Composite	1854.78	1844.58	x1850.33	− 4.17	− 0.22	+ 386.42	+26.40	+ 157.12	+ 9.28
641.65	501.14	Equity Mkt. Index	637.17	634.19	635.93	− 0.96	− 0.15	+ 134.79	+26.90	+ 54.50	+ 9.37
NEW YORK STOCK EXCHANGE											
363.74	285.56	Composite	360.82	359.34	360.17	− 0.44	− 0.12	+ 74.61	+26.13	+ 30.66	+ 9.30
464.47	362.06	Industrials	462.14	460.09	461.49	− 0.38	− 0.08	+ 99.43	+27.46	+ 48.20	+11.66
266.69	213.48	Utilities	248.00	247.00	247.30	− 0.53	− 0.21	+ 33.82	+15.84	− 5.60	− 2.21
341.99	252.91	Transportation	334.62	333.97	334.13	− 0.34	− 0.10	+ 81.22	+32.11	+ 32.17	+10.65
299.57	232.00	Finance	295.41	294.50	294.55	− 0.69	− 0.23	+ 62.55	+26.96	+ 20.30	+ 7.40
STANDARD & POOR'S INDEXES											
678.51	530.88	500 Index	673.61	670.15	672.16	− 1.15	− 0.17	+ 141.28	+26.61	+ 56.23	+ 9.13
807.88	632.08	Industrials	803.89	799.59	802.47	− 1.06	− 0.13	+ 170.39	+26.96	+ 81.28	+11.27
213.83	165.23	Utilities	191.12	190.21	190.83	− 0.12	− 0.06	+ 25.60	+15.49	− 11.75	− 5.80
242.42	192.44	400 MidCap	240.29	239.66	240.08	+ 0.40	+ 0.17	+ 47.64	+24.76	+ 22.24	+10.21
140.61	104.72	600 SmallCap	138.96	138.51	138.61	− 0.03	− 0.02	+ 33.89	+32.36	+ 17.51	+14.46
147.25	115.17	1500 Index	146.12	145.46	145.85	− 0.19	− 0.13	+ 30.68	+26.64	+ 12.61	+ 9.46
NASDAQ											
1249.15	887.98	Composite	1233.66	1228.95	1230.04	+ 0.28	+ 0.02	+ 342.06	+38.52	+ 177.91	+16.91
1193.13	850.14	Industrials	1164.93	1161.33	1162.67	+ 1.22	+ 0.11	+ 312.53	+36.76	+ 197.99	+20.52
1344.70	1050.93	Insurance	1308.64	1301.00	1302.75	− 3.21	− 0.25	+ 228.23	+21.24	+ 10.11	+ 0.78
1074.89	824.29	Banks	1072.16	1068.20	1069.17	− 1.74	− 0.16	+ 244.88	+29.71	+ 58.76	+ 5.92
559.09	397.25	Nat. Mkt. Comp.	552.01	549.87	550.45	+ 0.18	+ 0.03	+ 153.20	+38.57	+ 79.28	+16.83
486.92	346.42	Nat. Mkt. Indus.	474.48	472.97	473.68	+ 0.68	+ 0.14	+ 127.26	+36.74	+ 80.38	+20.44
OTHERS											
614.99	489.11	Amex	599.88	597.16	599.48	+ 0.17	+ 0.03	+ 110.16	+22.51	+ 51.25	+ 9.35
362.23	281.81	Russell 1000	359.40	357.78	358.72	− 0.46	− 0.13	+ 76.91	+27.29	+ 29.83	+ 9.07
364.61	276.45	Russell 2000	360.00	358.84	359.75	+ 0.91	+ 0.25	+ 83.30	+30.13	+ 43.78	+13.86
389.31	302.17	Russell 3000	386.13	384.52	385.48	− 0.35	− 0.09	+ 83.31	+27.57	+ 33.57	+ 9.54
364.96	305.37	Value-Line(geom.)	360.33	359.57	359.97	− 0.08	− 0.02	+ 54.60	+17.88	+ 28.93	+ 8.74
6758.69	5204.07	Wilshire 5000	...		6686.03	− 8.11	− 0.12	+1481.96	+28.48	+ 628.82	+10.28

†Based on comparable trading day in preceding year.

TABLE 2.6

MSCI Stock Indexes

Source: Morgan Stanley Capital International Perspective III '90 Geneva Switzerland.

International Indexes
The World Index
North America
EAFE
Europe 13
Nordic Countries
Pacific
Far East

Special Areas
The World Index ex USA
Kokusai Index (World ex Japan)
EASEA Index (EAFE ex Japan)
Pacific ex Japan
The World Index ex The UK
EAFE ex The UK
Europe 13 ex The UK

National Indexes
Spain
Sweden
Switzerland
United Kingdom
Italy

Japan
Hong Kong
New Zealand
France
United States

Australia
Singapore/Malaysia
Belgium
Netherlands
Denmark

Norway
Canada
Germany
Austria
Finland

index actually includes about 7,000 stocks. Figure 2.12 reproduces a *Wall Street Journal* listing of stock index performance. Vanguard offers a mutual fund to small investors, the Total Stock Market Portfolio, that enables them to match the performance of the Wilshire 5000 index.

More recently, market value-weighted indexes of non-U.S. stock markets have been developed and disseminated. A leader in this field has been Morgan Stanley Capital International (MSCI). Table 2.6 presents many of the MSCI indexes.

FIGURE 2.13

Listing of Foreign Stock Market Indexes

Source: From *The Wall Street Journal*, June 11, 1996. Reprinted by permission of *The Wall Street Journal*, © 1996 Dow Jones & Company, Inc. All Rights Reserved Worldwide.

DOW JONES WORLD STOCK INDEX

REGION/COUNTRY	DJ EQUITY MARKET INDEX, LOCAL CURRENCY		PCT. CHG.	5:30 P.M. INDEX	CHG.		PCT. CHG.	
Americas				157.11	− 0.24	−	0.15	
Canada	137.40	− 0.07		116.43	− 0.01	−	0.01	
Mexico	230.58	− 0.50		93.68	− 1.04	−	1.10	
U.S.	635.93	− 0.15		635.93	− 0.96	−	0.15	
Europe/Africa				142.01	+ 0.79	+	0.56	
Austria	114.96	+ 0.12		113.77	− 0.40	−	0.35	
Belgium	148.07	+ 0.70		147.17	+ 1.21	+	0.83	
Denmark	115.00	+ 0.05		114.84	+ 0.10	+	0.09	
Finland	244.93	+ 0.85		215.73	+ 2.12	+	0.99	
France	130.97	+ 0.72		130.47	+ 1.04	+	0.80	
Germany	145.05	+ 0.03		143.10	+ 0.22	+	0.15	
Ireland	205.28	+ 0.16		168.57	+ 0.12	+	0.07	
Italy	141.08	− 0.01		112.32	+ 0.10	+	0.09	
Netherlands	187.59	+ 0.45		183.76	+ 0.86	+	0.47	
Norway	156.05	+ 1.97		142.44	+ 3.02	+	2.17	
South Africa	210.03	+ 0.10		132.30	+ 0.44	+	0.33	
Spain	165.05	+ 0.93		123.61	+ 0.87	+	0.71	
Sweden	225.74	+ 1.61		185.60	+ 3.01	+	1.65	
Switzerland	214.06	+ 0.70		228.96	+ 1.96	+	0.86	
United Kingdom	153.46	+ 0.56		126.01	+ 0.58	+	0.46	
Europe/Africa (ex. South Africa)				142.36	+ 0.81	+	0.57	
Europe/Africa (ex. U.K. & S. Africa)				154.81	+ 0.95	+	0.62	
Asia/Pacific				120.69	+ 0.04	+	0.03	
Australia	closed			136.48	+ 0.29	+	0.21	
Hong Kong	247.09	− 0.36		248.06	− 0.96	−	0.39	
Indonesia	224.64	− 0.05		191.66	− 0.15	−	0.08	
Japan	98.37	− 0.11		112.57	+ 0.09	+	0.08	
Malaysia	228.77	− 0.44		249.05	− 1.31	−	0.52	
New Zealand	134.84	+ 0.43		167.72	+ 1.37	+	0.82	
Philippines	364.92	+ 0.18		362.05	+ 0.65	+	0.18	
Singapore	176.52	+ 0.50		203.09	+ 0.89	+	0.44	
South Korea	143.69	− 0.97		137.83	− 1.85	−	1.32	
Taiwan	153.37	− 0.67		142.82	− 0.64	−	0.45	
Thailand	closed			198.75	− 0.11	−	0.06	
Asia/Pacific (ex. Japan)				188.34	− 0.27	−	0.14	
World (ex. U.S.)				128.00	+ 0.32	+	0.25	
DJ WORLD STOCK INDEX				140.40	+ 0.11	+	0.08	

Indexes based on 6/30/82=100 for U.S., 12/31/91=100 for World.

Equally Weighted Indexes

Market performance is sometimes measured by an equally weighted average of the returns of each stock in an index. Such an averaging technique, by placing equal weight on each return, calls for a portfolio strategy that places equal dollar values in each stock. This is in contrast to both price weighting, which requires equal numbers of shares of each stock, and market value weighting, which requires investments in proportion to outstanding value.

equally weighted index
An index computed from a simple average of returns.

Unlike price- or market value-weighted indexes, **equally weighted indexes** do not correspond to buy-and-hold portfolio strategies. Suppose you start with equal dollar investments in the two stocks of Table 2.4, ABC and XYZ. Because ABC increases in value by 20% over the year, while XYZ decreases by 10%, your portfolio is no longer equally weighted but is now more heavily invested in ABC. To reset the portfolio to equal weights, you would need to rebalance: Either sell some ABC stock and/or purchase more XYZ stock. Such rebalancing would be necessary to align the return on your portfolio with that on the equally weighted index.

Foreign and International Stock Market Indexes

Development in financial markets worldwide includes the construction of indexes for these markets. The most important are the Nikkei, FTSE (pronounced "footsie"), and DAX. The Nikkei 225 is a price-weighted average of the largest Tokyo Stock Exchange (TSE) stocks. The Nikkei 300 is a value-weighted index. FTSE is published by the *Financial Times* of London and is a value-weighted index of 100 of the largest London Stock Exchange corporations. The DAX index is the premier German stock index.

Figure 2.13 shows the list of foreign stock exchange indexes published by *The Wall Street Journal*. The indexes are used to measure the return of the stock markets in each country in both local currencies as well as in U.S. dollars, accounting for the effect of exchange rate movements. The range of countries for which stock indexes are regularly computed gives a sense of how pervasive the use of this approach to measuring market conditions has become. Other indexes, such as Morgan Stanley's (see Table 2.6), provide a rich picture of international indexes for professional investors.

TABLE 2.7

The U.S. Fixed-Income
Market and Its Indexes

Source: Panel A: *Flow of
Funds Accounts, Flows and
Outstandings.* Board of
Governors of the Federal
Reserve System. March 8,
1996. Panel B: Frank K.
Reilly, G. Wenchi Kao, and
David J. Wright, "Alternative
Bond Market Indexes."
Financial Analysts Journal
(May–June 1992), pp. 44–58.

A. The Fixed-Income Market

Sector	Size ($ Billions)	Percentage of Market
Treasury	$3,637	41.8%
Federal agency	809	9.3
Corporate	1,328	15.3
Tax-exempt*	1,056	12.2
Mortgage-backed	1,573	18.1
Asset-backed	287	3.3
Total	$8,690	100.0%

Note: *Includes private purpose tax-exempt debt.

B. Profile of Bond Indexes

	Lehman Brothers	Merrill Lynch	Salomon Brothers
Number of issues	Over 6,500	Over 5,000	Over 5,000
Maturity of included bonds	≥ 1 year	≥ 1 year	≥ 1 year
Excluded issues	Junk bonds Convertibles Flower bonds Floating rate	Junk bonds Convertibles Flower bonds	Junk bonds Convertibles Floating rate bonds
Weighting	Market value	Market value	Market value
Reinvestment of intramonth cash flows	No	Yes (in specific bond)	Yes (at one-month T-bill rate)
Daily availability	Yes	Yes	Yes

Bond Market Indicators

Just as stock market indexes provide guidance concerning the performance of the overall stock market, several bond market indicators measure the performance of various categories of bonds. The three most well-known groups of indexes are those of Merrill Lynch, Lehman Brothers, and Salomon Brothers.

Table 2.7, Panel A, lists the components of the fixed-income market at the beginning of 1996. Panel B presents a profile of the characteristics of the three major bond indexes.

The major problem with these indexes is that true rates of return on many bonds are difficult to compute because bonds trade infrequently, which makes it hard to get reliable, up-to-date prices. In practice, some prices must be estimated from bond valuation models. These so-called matrix prices may differ from true market values.

2.5 DERIVATIVE MARKETS

A significant development in financial markets in recent years has been the growth of futures and options markets. Futures and options provide payoffs that depend on the values of other assets, such as commodity prices, bond and stock prices, or market index values. For this reason, these instruments sometimes are called **derivative assets** or **contingent claims.** Their values derive from or are contingent on the values of other assets. We discuss derivative assets in detail in Part Five.

**derivative asset or
contingent claim**
A security with a payoff
that depends on the
prices of other securities.

Options

A **call option** gives its holder the right to purchase an asset for a specified price, called the *exercise* or *strike price*, on or before some specified expiration date. An October call option on Exxon stock with exercise price $85, for example, entitles its owner to purchase Exxon stock for a price of $85 at any time up to and including the option's expiration date in October. Each option contract is for the purchase of 100 shares, with quotations made on a

call option
The right to buy an asset
at a specified price on or
before a specified
expiration date.

FIGURE 2.14

Listing of Stock Option Quotations

Source: From *The Wall Street Journal*, June 7, 1996. Reprinted by permission of *The Wall Street Journal*, ©1996 Dow Jones & Company, Inc. All Rights Reserved Worldwide.

LISTED OPTIONS QUOTATIONS

Option/Strike		Exp.	Call Vol.	Call Last	Put Vol.	Put Last	Option/Strike		Exp.	Call Vol.	Call Last	Put Vol.	Put Last
30	35	Jun	78	11/16	...	...	InputO	40	Jul	100	1 5/8	...	...
EgyCnv	30	Jul	65	11/16	...	...	IntgDv	12 1/2	Jun	113	1/2	42	9/16
EnglhCp	25	Jun	180	3/8	...	...	12 1/4	12 1/2	Aug	28	1 1/8	663	1 1/4
24 1/8	25	Oct	110	1 11/16	...	...	12 1/4	15	Aug	76	9/16	14	2 7/8
EnzoBi	15	Oct	15	4	75	1 3/8	12 1/4	15	Nov	81	1 1/16	...	...
17 1/8	17 1/2	Jun	120	1/2	...	...	IntgSilS	12 1/2	Jul	60	1 13/16	...	...
17 1/8	17 1/2	Jan	...	...	75	3 1/4	13 7/8	15	Jun	74	1/4	5	1 3/8
Epitpe	15	Jul	137	4 5/8	...	...	13 7/8	20	Sep	51	1/2	...	...
19 1/2	20	Jun	220	1 1/16	20	1 1/8	Intel	45	Jan	...	...	100	9/16
19 1/2	20	Jul	70	1 1/8	10	1 11/16	75 1/4	55	Jan	6	23 1/8	1000	3/4
19 1/2	22 1/2	Jul	52	1/2	...	...	75 1/4	60	Jun	27	15 7/8	1006	1/16
EricTel	22 1/2	Jul	50	1 9/16	...	...	75 1/4	60	Jul	144	15 7/8	48	3/16
EsteeL	40	Jun	110	1 1/8	5	1 9/16	75 1/4	60	Jan	90	18 3/4	3	1 1/8
Exide	20	Aug	10	3 3/4	135	1 3/16	75 1/4	65	Jun	75	10 5/8	10	1/16
22 5/8	25	Jun	10	5/16	50	2 3/4	75 1/4	65	Jul	120	10 7/8	170	3/8
22 5/8	25	Jul	60	3/4	60	3 1/8	75 1/4	65	Oct	27	13 1/2	110	1 7/16
22 5/8	25	Aug	12	1 3/16	60	3 5/8	75 1/4	70	Jun	506	5 1/2	643	5/16
22 5/8	25	Nov	...	...	375	4 3/8	75 1/4	70	Jul	383	7	832	1 1/8
22 5/8	30	Aug	50	5/16	...	...	75 1/4	70	Oct	77	9 1/4	75	2 3/4
22 5/8	30	Nov	3	1	375	8	75 1/4	75	Jun	1245	1 7/8	565	1 5/8
Exxon	85	Jun	110	1	90	1 3/4	75 1/4	75	Jul	520	3 5/8	1035	2 7/8
84 7/8	85	Jul	56	2 1/8	...	...	75 1/4	75	Oct	89	6 3/4	72	4 3/4
84 3/8	85	Oct	6	3 7/8	171	3 3/4	75 1/4	75	Jan	222	8 1/2	1122	6
84 3/8	90	Oct	64	1 11/16	5	7	75 1/4	80	Jun	529	3/8	551	5 1/8
84 3/8	90	Jan	60	3	5	7 5/8	75 1/4	80	Jul	1138	1 5/8	10	5 1/2
FHLB	85	Jul	200	2 11/16	10	2 9/16	75 1/4	80	Oct	180	4 1/8	11	7 3/4
FNM	27 1/2	Sep	150	5 3/8	10	7/16	75 1/4	80	Jan	119	6 1/8	2	8 5/8
32	30	Jun	220	2 5/16	14	3/16	75 1/4	85	Oct	69	2 3/4	...	...
32	30	Jul	110	3 1/8	188	9/16	75 1/4	90	Jan	136	3	...	...
32	30	Sep	102	3 1/2	...	...	IntelEl	10	Jun	70	5/8	...	...

per share basis. The holder of the call need not exercise the option; it will be profitable to exercise only if the market value of the asset that may be purchased exceeds the exercise price.

When the market price exceeds the exercise price, the option holder may "call away" the asset for the exercise price and reap a profit equal to the difference between the stock price and the exercise price. Otherwise, the option will be left unexercised. If not exercised before the expiration date, the option expires and no longer has value. Calls, therefore, provide greater profits when stock prices increase and so represent bullish investment vehicles.

put option

The right to sell an asset at a specified exercise price on or before a specified expiration date.

A **put option** gives its holder the right to sell an asset for a specified exercise price on or before a specified expiration date. An October put on Exxon with exercise price $85 entitles its owner to sell Exxon stock to the put writer at a price of $85 at any time before expiration in October even if the market price of Exxon is lower than $85. While profits on call options increase when the asset increases in value, profits on put options increase when the asset value falls. The put is exercised only if its holder can deliver an asset worth less than the exercise price in return for the exercise price.

Figure 2.14 presents stock option quotations from *The Wall Street Journal*. The highlighted options are for Exxon. The repeated number below the name of the firm is the current price of Exxon shares, $84⅜. The two columns to the right of the firm name give the exercise price and expiration month of each option. Thus, we see listings for call and put options on Exxon with exercise prices of $85 and $90, and with expiration dates in June, July, October, and the following January.

The next four columns provide the trading volume and closing prices of each option. For example, six contracts traded on the October expiration call with an exercise price of $85. The last trade was at $3⅞, meaning that an option to purchase one share of Exxon at an exercise price of $85 sold for $3.875. Each option *contract* (on 100 shares of stock), therefore, costs $3.875 × 100 = $387.50.

Notice that the prices of call options decrease as the exercise price increases. For example, the October 1996 maturity call with exercise price $90 costs only $1¹¹/₁₆. This makes sense, as the right to purchase a share at a higher exercise price is less valuable. Conversely, put prices increase with the exercise price. The right to sell a share of Exxon at a price of $85 costs $3¾ while the right to sell at $90 costs $7.

8. What would be the profit or loss per share of stock to an investor who bought the October maturity Exxon call option with exercise price $85, if the stock price at the expiration of the option is $93? What about a purchaser of the put option with the same exercise price and maturity?

Futures Contracts

futures contract
Obliges traders to purchase or sell an asset at an agreed-upon price at a specified future date.

A **futures contract** calls for delivery of an asset (or in some cases, its cash value) at a specified delivery or maturity date, for an agreed-upon price, called the *futures price*, to be paid at contract maturity. The long position is held by the trader who commits to purchasing the commodity on the delivery date. The trader who takes the short position commits to delivering the commodity at contract maturity.

Figure 2.15 illustrates the listing of several futures contracts for trading on June 6, 1996, as they appeared in *The Wall Street Journal*. The top line in boldface type gives the contract name, the exchange on which the futures contract is traded (in parentheses), and the contract size. Thus, the first contract listed is for corn traded on the Chicago Board of Trade (CBT). Each contract calls for delivery of 5,000 bushels of corn.

The next several rows detail prices for contracts expiring on various dates. The July 1996 maturity contract opened during the day at a futures price of $4.35 per bushel. The highest futures price during the day was $4.47, the lowest was $4.34, and the settlement price (a representative trading price during the last few minutes of trading) was $4.47. The settlement price increased by $.12 from the previous trading day. The highest and lowest futures prices over the contract's life to date have been $5.135 and $2.54, respectively. Finally, open interest, or the number of outstanding contracts, was 105,681. Corresponding information is given for each maturity date.

The trader holding the long position profits from price increases. Suppose that at expiration, corn is selling for $4.67 per bushel. The long position trader who entered the contract at the futures price of $4.47 on June 6 would pay the previously agreed-upon $4.47 for each unit of the index, which at contract maturity would be worth $4.67.

Because each contract calls for delivery of 5,000 bushels, the profit to the long position, ignoring brokerage fees, would equal $5,000 \times (\$4.67 - \$4.47) = \$1,000$. Conversely, the short position must deliver 5,000 bushels for the previously agreed-upon futures price. The short position's loss equals the long position's profit.

The distinction between the *right* to purchase and the *obligation* to purchase the asset is the difference between a call option and a long position in a futures contract. A futures contract *obliges* the long position to purchase the asset at the futures price; the call option merely *conveys the right* to purchase the asset at the exercise price. The purchase will be made only if it yields a profit.

Clearly, the holder of a call has a better position than the holder of a long position on a futures contract with a futures price equal to the option's exercise price. This advantage, of course, comes only at a price. Call options must be purchased; futures investments are contracts only. The purchase price of an option is called the *premium*. It represents the compensation the purchaser of the call must pay for the ability to exercise the option only when it is profitable to do so. Similarly, the difference between a put option and a short futures position is the right, as opposed to the obligation, to sell an asset at an agreed-upon price.

FIGURE 2.15

Listing of Commodity Futures Contracts

Source: From *The Wall Street Journal*, June 7, 1996. Reprinted by permission of *The Wall Street Journal*, ©1996 Dow Jones & Company, Inc. All Rights Reserved Worldwide.

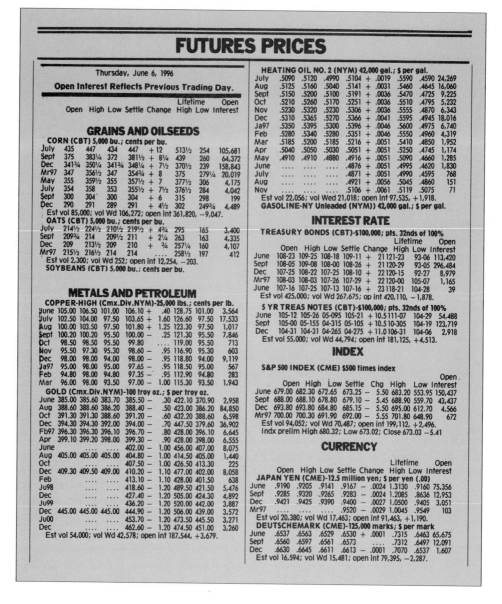

Summary

- Money market securities are very short-term debt obligations. They are usually highly marketable and have relatively low credit risk. Their low maturities and low credit risk ensure minimal capital gains or losses. These securities trade in large denominations, but they may be purchased indirectly through money market funds.
- Much of U.S. government borrowing is in the form of Treasury bonds and notes. These are coupon-paying bonds usually issued at or near par value. Treasury bonds are similar in design to coupon-paying corporate bonds.
- Municipal bonds are distinguished largely by their tax-exempt status. Interest payments (but not capital gains) on these securities are exempt from income taxes.
- Mortgage pass-through securities are pools of mortgages sold in one package. Owners of pass-throughs receive all principal and interest payments made by the borrower. The firm that originally issued the mortgage merely services the mortgage, simply "passing

through" the payments to the purchasers of the mortgage. The pass-through agency usually guarantees the payment of interest and principal on mortgages pooled into these pass-through securities.

- Common stock is an ownership share in a corporation. Each share entitles its owner to one vote on matters of corporate governance and to a prorated share of the dividends paid to shareholders. Stock, or equity, owners are the residual claimants on the income earned by the firm.

- Preferred stock usually pays a fixed stream of dividends for the life of the firm: It is a perpetuity. A firm's failure to pay the dividend due on preferred stock, however, does not set off corporate bankruptcy. Instead, unpaid dividends simply cumulate. New varieties of preferred stock include convertible and adjustable-rate issues.

- Many stock market indexes measure the performance of the overall market. The Dow Jones averages, the oldest and best-known indicators, are price-weighted indexes. Today, many broad-based, market value-weighted indexes are computed daily. These include the Standard & Poor's composite 500 stock index, the NYSE and Amex indexes, the Nasdaq index, the Wilshire 5000 index, and several international indexes.

- A call option is a right to purchase an asset at a stipulated exercise price on or before a maturity date. A put option is the right to sell an asset at some exercise price. Calls increase in value, while puts decrease in value as the value of the underlying asset increases.

- A futures contract is an obligation to buy or sell an asset at a stipulated futures price on a maturity date. The long position, which commits to purchasing, gains if the asset value increases, while the short position, which commits to delivering the asset, loses.

Key Terms

annual percentage rate, *27*	derivative asset/contingent claim, *49*	money markets, *23*
bank discount method, *26*		municipal bonds, *33*
bankers' acceptance, *28*	effective annual rate, *26*	preferred stock, *40*
bond equivalent yield, *27*	equally weighted index, *48*	price-weighted average, *43*
call option, *49*	Eurodollars, *29*	put option, *50*
capital markets, *23*	Federal funds, *30*	repurchase agreements, *29*
certificate of deposit, *28*	futures contract, *51*	Treasury bills, *24*
commercial paper, *28*	LIBOR, *30*	Treasury bonds, *31*
common stocks, *38*	market value-weighted index, *45*	Treasury notes, *31*
corporate bonds, *36*		

Problem Sets

1. The following multiple-choice problems are based on questions that appeared in past CFA exams.
   a. Preferred stock
      (1) Is actually a form of equity.
      (2) Pays dividends not fully taxable to U.S. corporations.
      (3) Is normally considered a fixed-income security.
      (4) All of the above.
   b. Straight preferred stock yields often are lower than yields on straight bonds of the same quality because of
      (1) Marketability
      (2) Risk
      (3) Taxation
      (4) Call protection

2. The investment manager of a corporate pension fund has purchased a U.S. Treasury bill with 180 days to maturity at a price of $9,600 per $10,000 face value. The manager has computed the bank discount yield at 8%.

a. Calculate the bond equivalent yield for the Treasury bill. Show calculations. (Ignore skip-day settlement and assume this is not a leap year.)

b. Briefly state two reasons why a Treasury bill's bond equivalent yield is always different from the discount yield.

3. A bill has a bank discount yield of 6.81% based on the ask price and 6.90% based on the bid price. The maturity of the bill (already accounting for skip-day settlement) is 60 days. Find the bid and ask prices of the bill.

4. Reconsider the T-bill in problem 3. Calculate its bond equivalent yield and effective annual yield based on the ask price. Confirm that these yields exceed the discount yield.

5. *a.* Which security offers a higher effective annual yield?

    (1) A three-month bill selling at $9,764.

    (2) A six-month bill selling at $9,539.

  b. Calculate the bank discount yield on each bill.

6. Find the after-tax return to a corporation that buys a share of preferred stock at $40, sells it at year-end at $40, and receives a $4 year-end dividend. The firm is in the 30% tax bracket.

7. Consider the three stocks in the following table. P_t represents price at time t, and Q_t represents shares outstanding at time t. Stock C splits two-for-one in the last period.

	P_0	Q_0	P_1	Q_1	P_2	Q_2
A	90	100	95	100	95	100
B	50	200	45	200	45	200
C	100	200	110	200	55	400

a. Calculate the rate of return on a price-weighted index of the three stocks for the first period ($t = 0$ to $t = 1$).

b. What must happen to the divisor for the price-weighted index in year 2?

c. Calculate the price-weighted index for the second period ($t = 1$ to $t = 2$).

8. Using the data in problem 7, calculate the first period rates of return on the following indexes of the three stocks:

a. a market value-weighted index.

b. an equally weighted index.

9. An investor is in a 28% tax bracket. If corporate bonds offer 9% yields, what must municipals offer for the investor to prefer them to corporate bonds?

10. Suppose that short-term municipal bonds currently offer yields of 4%, while comparable taxable bonds pay 5%. Which gives you the higher after-tax yield if your tax bracket is:

a. Zero

b. 10%

c. 20%

d. 30%

11. Find the equivalent taxable yield of the municipal bond in the previous question for tax brackets of zero, 10%, 20%, and 30%.

12. Which security should sell at a greater price?

a. A 10-year Treasury bond with a 9% coupon rate or a 10-year T-bond with a 10% coupon.

b. A three-month maturity call option with an exercise price of $40 or a three-month call on the same stock with an exercise price of $35.

c. A put option on a stock selling at $50 or a put option on another stock selling at $60. (All other relevant features of the stocks and options are assumed to be identical.)

    d. A three-month T-bill with a discount yield of 6.1% or a three-month bill with a discount yield of 6.2%.

13. Why do call options with exercise prices higher than the price of the underlying stock sell for positive prices?

14. Both a call and a put currently are traded on stock XYZ; both have strike prices of $50 and maturities of six months. What will be the profit to an investor who buys the call for $4 in the following scenarios for stock prices in six months? (*a*) $40; (*b*) $45; (*c*) $50; (*d*) $55; (*e*) $60. What will be the profit in each scenario to an investor who buys the put for $6?

15. Explain the difference between a put option and a short position in a futures contract.

16. Explain the difference between a call option and a long position in a futures contract.

17. What would you expect to happen to the spread between yields on commercial paper and Treasury bills if the economy were to enter a steep recession?

18. Examine the first 25 stocks listed in Figure 2.10. For how many of these stocks is the 52-week high price at least 50% greater than the 52-week low price? What do you conclude about the volatility of prices on individual stocks?

⬛ IEM
Applications

1. What kind of market is the IEM?
   - *a.* A stock market
   - *b.* A bond market
   - *c.* A contingent claim market
   - *d.* All of the above
   - *e.* None of the above

2. The IEM contract SP500m is based on the return on the S&P 500 index. What kind of index is the S&P 500?
   - *a.* Market value weighted
   - *b.* Price weighted
   - *c.* Both
   - *d.* Neither

3. Connect to the IEM and look at the market "F"undamental information under the "I"nformation menu in the Computer Industry Returns Market. What have the monthly returns to the S&P 500 been over the last year? What was the high return? What was the low return? Why do returns vary from month to month?

4. How would you go about constructing a price-weighted index for the computer industry using Apple, IBM, and Microsoft stock? How would you go about constructing a market value-weighted index for the computer industry using the same stocks? What other stocks might you want to include in your index?

Solutions to
Concept Checks

1. The discount yield at bid is 5.04%, so its bid price must be

$$P = 10,000[1 - .0504 \times (90/360)] = \$9,874.00$$

compared with the ask price of $9,874.50.

2. The option the government retains to buy back the bond for par value gives it the right to wait to decide whether that action will be desirable. The ability to wait conveyed by this (and other) options is most important when there is a great deal of uncertainty as to whether that action will in fact turn out to be profitable. In this particular case, this is when the bond is selling at a price near par value, or when bond prices are particularly volatile. If there is little uncertainty regarding the ultimate action, the option to decide later is less important: If the ultimate decision is obvious, the government could precommit to that decision now without harming itself.

3. Compare the 7.26% yield on the Tennessee Valley Authority bond maturing in 8-02 (August 2002) with the 6.72% yield on the August 02 T-bond. The differential can be attributed largely to the difference in default risk.

4. A 6% taxable return is equivalent to an after-tax return of $6(1 - .28) = 4.32\%$. Therefore, you would be better off in the taxable bond. The equivalent taxable yield of the tax-free bond is $4/(1 - .28) = 5.55\%$. So a taxable bond would have to pay a 5.55% yield to provide the same after-tax return as a tax-free bond offering a 4% yield.

5. *a.* You are entitled to a prorated share of IBM's dividend payments and to vote in any of IBM's stockholder meetings.
   b. Your potential gain is unlimited because IBM's stock price has no upper bound.
   c. Your outlay was $50 \times 100 = \$5,000$. Because of limited liability, this is the most you can lose.

6. The price-weighted index increases from 62.5 [$= (100 + 25)/2$] to 65 [$= (110 + 20)/2$], a gain of 4%. An investment of one share in each company requires an outlay of $125 that would increase in value to $130, for a return of 4% (5/125), which equals the return to the price-weighted index.

7. The market value-weighted index return is calculated by computing the increase in value of the stock portfolio. The portfolio of the two stocks starts with an initial value of $100 million + $500 million = $600 million and falls in value to $110 million + $400 million = $510 million, a loss of 90/600 = .15, or 15%. The index portfolio return is a weighted average of the returns on each stock with weights of ⅙ on XYZ and ⅚ on ABC (weights proportional to relative investments). Because the return on XYZ is 10%, while that on ABC is − 20%, the index portfolio return is (⅙)10 + (⅚) (− 20) = − 15%, equal to the return on the market value-weighted index.

8. The payoff to the call option is $8. The call cost $3.875. The profit is $4.125 per share. The put will pay off zero—it expires worthless since the stock price exceeds the exercise price. The loss is the cost of the put, $3.75.

Chapter 3

HOW SECURITIES ARE TRADED

AFTER STUDYING THIS CHAPTER YOU SHOULD BE ABLE TO:

- Describe the role of investment bankers in primary issues.

- Identify the various security markets.

- Compare trading practices in stock exchanges with those in dealer markets.

- Describe the role of brokers.

The first time a security trades is when it is issued. Therefore, we begin our examination of trading with a look at how securities are first marketed to the public by investment bankers, the midwives of securities. Then, we turn to the various exchanges where already-issued securities can be traded among investors. We examine the competition among the New York Stock Exchange, the American Stock Exchange, the regional exchanges, and the over-the-counter market for the patronage of security traders.

Next, we turn to the mechanics of trading in these various markets. We describe the role of the specialist in exchange markets and the dealer in over-the-counter markets. We also touch briefly on block trading and the SuperDot system of the NYSE for electronically routing orders to the floor of the exchange. We discuss the costs of trading and describe the recent debate between the NYSE and its competitors over which market provides the lowest-cost trading arena.

Finally, we describe the essentials of specific transactions, such as buying on margin and selling stock short and discuss relevant regulations governing security trading. In the process, we will see that some regulations, such as those governing insider trading, can be difficult to interpret in practice.

3.1 HOW FIRMS ISSUE SECURITIES

primary market
Market for new issues of securities.

When firms need to raise capital they may choose to sell or *float* securities. These new issues of stocks, bonds, or other securities typically are marketed to the public by investment bankers in what is called the **primary market.** Purchase and sale of already-issued securities among investors occur in the **secondary market.**

FIGURE 3.1

Relationship among a
Firm Issuing Securities,
the Underwriters, and
the Public

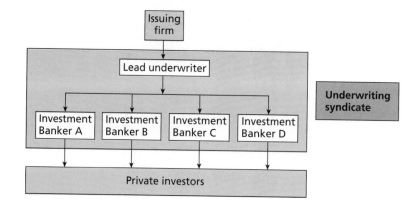

There are two types of primary market issues of common stock. **Initial public offerings** or **IPOs,** are stocks issued by a formerly privately owned company that is going public, that is, selling stock to the public for the first time. *Seasoned* new issues are offered by companies that already have floated equity. For example, a sale by IBM of new shares of stock would constitute a seasoned new issue.

In the case of bonds, we also distinguish between two types of primary market issues, a *public offering* and a *private placement*. The former refers to an issue of bonds sold to the general investing public that can then be traded on the secondary market. The latter refers to an issue that usually is sold to one or a few institutional investors and is generally held to maturity.

Investment Banking

Public offerings of both stocks and bonds typically are marketed by investment bankers who in this role are called **underwriters.** More than one investment banker usually markets the securities. A lead firm forms an underwriting syndicate of other investment bankers to share the responsibility for the stock issue.

Investment bankers advise the firm regarding the terms on which it should attempt to sell the securities. A preliminary registration statement must be filed with the Securities and Exchange Commission (SEC), describing the issue and the prospects of the company. This preliminary prospectus is known as a *red herring* because it includes a statement printed in red, stating the company is not attempting to sell the security before the registration is approved. When the statement is in final form, and approved by the SEC, it is called the **prospectus.** At this point, the price at which the securities will be offered to the public is announced.

In a typical underwriting arrangement, the investment bankers purchase the securities from the issuing company and then resell them to the public. The issuing firm sells the securities to the underwriting syndicate for the public offering price less a spread that serves as compensation to the underwriters. This procedure is called a *firm commitment*; the underwriters receive the issue and assume the full risk that the shares cannot be sold to the public at the stipulated offering price. Figure 3.1 depicts the relationships among the firm issuing the security, the lead underwriter, the underwriting syndicate, and the public.

An alternative to the firm commitment is the *best-efforts* agreement. In this case, the investment banker does not actually purchase the securities but agrees to help the firm sell the issue to the public. The banker simply acts as an intermediary between the public and the firm and does not bear the risk of not being able to resell purchased securities at the offering price. The best-efforts procedure is more common for initial public offerings of common stock, where the appropriate share price is less certain.

Corporations engage investment bankers either by negotiation or competitive bidding, although negotiation is far more common. In addition to the compensation resulting from the spread between the purchase price and the public offering price, an investment banker may receive shares of common stock or other securities of the firm.

In the case of competitive bidding, a firm may announce its intent to issue securities and invite investment bankers to submit bids for the underwriting. Such a bidding process may reduce the cost of the issue; it might also bring fewer services from the investment banker. Many public utilities are required to solicit competitive bids from underwriters.

Shelf Registration

An important innovation in the issuing of securities was introduced in 1982 when the SEC approved Rule 415, which allows firms to register securities and gradually sell them to the public for two years following the initial registration. Because the securities are already registered, they can be sold on short notice, with little additional paperwork. Moreover, they can be sold in small amounts without incurring substantial flotation costs. The securities are "on the shelf," ready to be issued, which has given rise to the term *shelf registration*.

1. Why does it make sense for shelf registration to be limited in time?

Concept Check

Initial Public Offerings

Investment bankers manage the issuance of new securities to the public. Once the SEC has commented on the registration statement and a preliminary prospectus has been distributed to interested investors, the investment bankers organize *road shows* in which they travel around the country to publicize the imminent offering. These road shows serve two purposes. First, they generate interest among potential investors and provide information about the offering. Second, they also provide information to the issuing firm and its underwriters about the price at which they will be able to market the securities. Large investors communicate their interest in purchasing shares of the IPO to the underwriters; these indications of interest are called a *book* and the process of polling potential investors is called *bookbuilding*. These indications of interest provide valuable information to the issuing firm because institutional investors often will have useful insights about both the market demand for the security as well as the prospects of the firm and its competitors. It is common for investment bankers to revise both their initial estimates of the offering price of a security and the number of shares offered based on feedback from the investing community.

Why do investors truthfully reveal their interest in an offering to the investment banker? Might they be better off expressing little interest, in the hope that this will drive down the offering price? Truth is the better policy in this case because truth telling is rewarded. Shares of IPOs are allocated across investors in part based on the strength of each investor's expressed interest in the offering. If a firm wishes to get a large allocation when it is optimistic about the security, it needs to reveal its optimism. In turn, the underwriter needs to offer the security at a bargain price to these investors to induce them to participate in bookbuilding and share their information. Thus, IPOs commonly are underpriced compared to the price at which they could be marketed. Such underpricing is reflected in price jumps that occur on the date when the shares are first traded in public security markets.

For example, a dramatic case of underpricing took place on August 8, 1995, when Netscape stock was issued at $28 a share and closed at $58¼ on the first day of trading. Investors who bought at the issue price earned a *one-day* return of 108%. This degree of underpricing is far more dramatic than is common, but underpricing seems to be a universal phenomenon. Figure 3.2 presents average first-day returns on IPOs of stocks across the world. The results consistently indicate that IPOs are marketed to investors at attractive prices.

Underpricing of IPOs makes them appealing to all investors, yet institutional investors are allocated the bulk of a typical new issue. Some view this as unfair discrimination against small investors. However, this analysis suggests that the apparent discounts on IPOs may be no more than fair payments for a valuable service, specifically, the information contributed

FIGURE 3.2

Average Initial Returns
for IPOs in Various
Countries

Source: Tim Loughran, Jay
Ritter, and Kristian Rydquist,
"Initial Public Offerings:
International Insights,"
Pacific-Basin Finance Journal
2 (1994), 165–199.

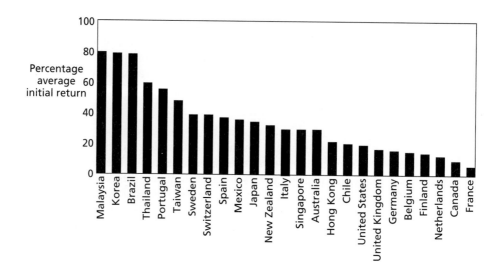

FIGURE 3.3

Long-Term Relative
Performance of Initial
Public Offerings

Source: Tim Loughran and Jay
R. Ritter, "The New Issues
Puzzle," *The Journal
of Finance* 50 (March 1995),
pp. 23–51.

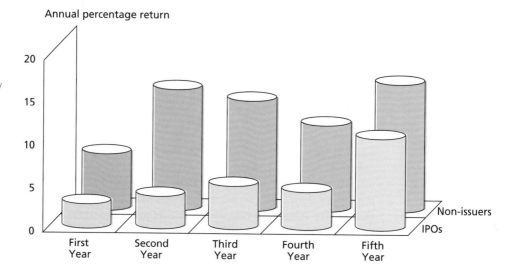

by the institutional investors. The right to allocate shares in this way may contribute to efficiency by promoting the collection and dissemination of such information.[1]

Pricing of IPOs is not trivial and not all IPOs turn out to be underpriced. Some do poorly after issue and others cannot even be fully sold to the market. Underwriters left with unmarketable securities are forced to sell them at a loss on the secondary market. Therefore, the investment banker bears the price risk of an underwritten issue.

Interestingly, despite their dramatic initial investment performance, IPOs have been poor long-term investments. Figure 3.3 compares the stock price performance of IPOs with shares of other firms of the same size for each of the five years after issue of the IPO. The year-by-year underperformance of the IPOs is dramatic, suggesting that, on average, the investing public may be too optimistic about the prospects of these firms.

Very small firms may find initial public offerings using underwriters too expensive. The nearby box (page 61) discusses how one firm has used the Internet to do an IPO on its own, thereby avoiding underwriting fees. The article also discusses the growing feasibility of stock trading over the Internet.

---

[1]An elaboration of this point and a more complete discussion of the bookbuilding process is provided in "Going by the Book," by Lawrence Benveniste and William Wilhelm. See the References appendix at the end of the text for a complete citation.

SEC Says Brewery May Use Internet to Offer Its Stock

Confronting the first real-world collision of free markets and cyberspace, the Securities and Exchange Commission gave a cautious blessing to a New York brewery that has been using the Internet to underwrite and sell its own stock.

The company, Spring Street Brewing Co., faced a classic fund-raising problem of the small company—too small to interest Wall Street underwriters but reluctant to sell itself to venture capitalists. So it came up with a new approach. It posted a page on the World Wide Web to let people interested in buying and selling its stock meet and do deals. It called the system Wit-Trade, after the Wit beer it brews. And it launched an initial public offering, raising $1.6 million without paying a penny to underwriters.

The episode is extraordinary in several respects. For one, it shows the power of the Internet to free companies from their traditional market limitations, says Spring Street President and Chief Executive Andrew Klein.

"We've proved that there is a demand from small investors for illiquid, high-risk, high-potential securities," he says. "My phone's been ringing off the hook from companies that want to know how they can sell a piece of their companies to the public using this technology, without paying underwriters or brokers and without having to give the company away to venture capitalists."

Robert Colby, deputy director of the SEC's market-regulation division, says it's not uncommon for a small company to keep a list of shareholders that want to buy its stock. "What's unusual here," Mr. Colby says, "is that [Mr. Klein] put this list up on the Internet. And he added new elements, such as receiving buyers' funds and holding them."

That, indeed, is how the Wit-Trade system was working before Spring Street suspended it. On its web site, the company posted contracts that buyers and sellers filled out us-ing their home computers. The buyer then mailed a check to Spring Street, which processed the trade as a Wall Street firm would and sent the seller's stock certificate back to the buyer.

That's where the SEC came in. "As you are not a registered broker-dealer, we suggest you modify your system to eliminate the company's control over these funds," the SEC's letter prodded. It asked the company to arrange for the trades to be processed by a bank or escrow agent, which Spring Street plans to do, Mr. Klein says.

While novel, the use of the Internet to trade and underwrite securities is going to increase quickly, says Daniel Weaver, a finance professor at Marquette University. "It's a natural place for small companies," he says. "I think small companies are getting dissatisfied with the service they get from underwriters." He notes that discount brokerage Charles Schwab Corp. plans an Internet trading system and predicts that other brokerage firms will follow suit, allowing companies to market more or less directly to the public.

All the same, the potential explosion of Internet trading is a daunting one for the SEC. So-called self-regulating organizations like the New York Stock Exchange and the National Association of Securities Dealers now take responsibility for policing much of the trading on more conventional securities markets. If trading on the Internet increases, there isn't anyone to monitor it—at least at the moment—except the SEC.

Source: From Jeffrey Taylor, "SEC Says Brewery May Use Internet to Offer Its Stock," *The Wall Street Journal*, March 26, 1996. Reprinted by permission of *The Wall Street Journal*, © 1996 Dow Jones & Company, Inc. All Rights Reserved Worldwide.

Concept Check

2. Your broker just called. You can buy 200 shares of Good Time Inc.'s IPO at the initial offering price. What should you do? (Hint: Why is the broker calling *you*?)

3.2 WHERE SECURITIES ARE TRADED

Once securities are issued to the public, investors may trade them among themselves. Purchase and sale of already-issued securities occur in the secondary markets, which include (1) national and local securities exchanges, (2) the over-the-counter market, and (3) direct trading between two parties.

The Secondary Markets

stock exchanges
Secondary markets where already-issued securities are bought and sold by members.

There are several **stock exchanges** in the United States. Two of these, the New York Stock Exchange (NYSE, or the Big Board) and the American Stock Exchange (Amex), are national in scope and are located in New York City. The others, such as the Boston or Pacific

TABLE 3.1

Seat Prices on the
NYSE

Source: From the New York
Stock Exchange *Fact Book*,
1995.

Year	High	Low
1875	$ 6,800	$ 4,300
1905	85,000	72,000
1935	140,000	65,000
1965	250,000	190,000
1975	138,000	55,000
1980	275,000	175,000
1985	480,000	310,000
1990	430,000	250,000
1992	600,000	410,000
1995	1,050,000	785,000

TABLE 3.2

Trading in Various
Stock Markets, 1995

Source: The Nasdaq Stock
Market 1996 *Fact Book &
Company Directory.*

	Trading Volume during the Year (Billions of Shares)	% Total	Dollar Volume of Trading ($ Billions)	% Total
Exchange Trading				
New York	104.64	87.2%	$4,063.7	89.6%
American	5.63	4.7	91.3	2.1
Regional Exchanges*	9.79	8.1	380.3	7.9
Total	120.06	100.0%	$4,535.5	100.0%
Dealer Market				
Nasdaq	145.60	100.0%	$3,592.5	100.0%

*Regional exchanges include the Boston, Chicago, Pacific, and Philadelphia stock exchanges.

stock exchanges, are to a considerable extent regional exchanges, which tend to list firms located in a particular geographic area. There also are several exchanges for the trading of options and futures contracts, which we will discuss later in the options and futures chapters.

An exchange provides a facility for its members to trade securities, and only members of the exchange may trade there. Therefore, memberships or *seats* on the exchange are valuable assets. The majority of seats are *commission broker* seats, most of which are owned by the large full-service brokerage firms. The seat entitles the firm to place one of its brokers on the floor of the exchange where he or she can execute trades. The exchange member charges investors for executing trades on their behalf. The commissions that members can earn through this activity determine the market value of a seat. A seat on the NYSE has sold over the years for as little as $4,000 (in 1878) and as much as $1,150,000 (in 1987). See Table 3.1 for a history of seat prices since 1875.

The NYSE is by far the largest single exchange. The shares of approximately 2,600 firms trade there, and more than 3,000 stock issues (common plus preferred stock) are listed. Daily trading volume on the NYSE averaged 400 million shares in 1996. Table 3.2 shows the trading activity of securities listed on the various stock exchanges as of the end of 1995. The table documents that the NYSE accounts for about 85–90% of the trading that takes place on stock exchanges.

The American Stock Exchange also is national in scope, but it focuses on listing smaller and younger firms than the NYSE. The national exchanges are willing to list a stock (allow trading in that stock on the exchange) only if the firm meets certain criteria of size and stability. Regional exchanges provide a market for the trading of shares of local firms that do not meet the listing requirements of the national exchanges.

Table 3.3 gives the initial listing requirements for the NYSE. These requirements ensure that firms are of significant trading interest before the NYSE will allocate facilities for it to be traded on the floor of the exchange. If a listed company suffers a decline and fails to meet the criteria in Table 3.3, it may be delisted.

TABLE 3.3

Initial Listing
Requirements for
the NYSE

Source: Data from the New
York Stock Exchange *Fact
Book*, 1995.

Pretax income in last year	$ 2,500,000
Average annual pretax income in previous two years	$ 2,000,000
Net tangible assets	$40,000,000
Market value of publicly held stock	$40,000,000
Shares publicly held	1,100,000
Number of holders of 100 shares or more	2,000

TABLE 3.4

Listing Requirements
for the American Stock
Exchange and Nasdaq

Source: Amex and Nasdaq
Fact Books, 1996.

	Amex Entry Standards	Nasdaq Entry Standards
Total assets	None	$4 million
Stockholders' equity	$4 million	None
Number of shares in public hands	500,000 shares	500,000 shares
Market value of shares	$3 million	$3 million
Price of stock	$3	$5
Pretax income	$750,000	$750,000

Regional exchanges also sponsor trading of some firms that are traded on national exchanges. This dual listing enables local brokerage firms to trade in shares of large firms without purchasing a membership on the NYSE.

The NYSE recently has lost market share to the regional exchanges and, far more dramatically, to the over-the-counter market. Today, approximately two-thirds of the trades in stocks listed on the NYSE are actually executed on the NYSE. In contrast, about 80% of the trades in NYSE-listed shares were executed on the exchange in the early 1980s. The loss is attributed to lower commissions charged on other exchanges, although, as we will see below, the NYSE believes that a more comprehensive treatment of trading costs would show that it is the most cost-effective trading arena. In any case, many of these non-NYSE trades were for relatively small transactions. The NYSE is still by far the preferred exchange for large traders, and its market share of exchange-listed companies—when measured in share volume rather than number of trades—is still a bit above 80%.

The over-the-counter Nasdaq market (described in detail shortly) has posed a bigger competitive challenge to the NYSE. Its share of trading volume in NYSE-listed firms has increased from 2.5% in 1983 to about 9% in 1996. Moreover, many large firms that would be eligible to list their shares on the NYSE now choose instead to list on Nasdaq. Some of the well-known firms currently trading on Nasdaq are Microsoft, Intel, Apple Computer, Netscape, Sun Microsystems, and MCI Communications. Total trading volume in over-the-counter stocks on the computerized Nasdaq system has increased six-fold in the last decade, rising from about 50 million shares per day in 1984 to 400 million shares per day in 1996. Share volume on Nasdaq actually surpasses that on the NYSE. However, because Nasdaq-listed firms tend to be smaller firms that also sell at lower prices, the dollar value of Nasdaq trades is still only about 75% that of NYSE trades. Table 3.4 presents listing requirements for Amex and Nasdaq. Notice that these requirements are less demanding than those for the NYSE.

Other new sources of competition to the NYSE have come from abroad. For example, the London Stock Exchange is preferred by some traders because it offers greater anonymity. In addition, new restrictions introduced by the NYSE to limit price volatility in the wake of the market crash of 1987 are viewed by some traders as another reason to trade abroad. These so-called circuit breakers are discussed below.

While most common stocks are traded on the exchanges, the reverse is true for bonds and other fixed-income securities. Corporate bonds are traded both on the exchanges and over the counter, but all federal and municipal government bonds are traded over the counter.

The Over-the-Counter Market

over-the-counter (OTC) market
An informal network of brokers and dealers who negotiate sales of securities.

Roughly 35,000 issues are traded on the **over-the-counter (OTC) market,** which allows any security to be traded there, but the OTC market is not a formal exchange. There are no membership requirements for trading or listing requirements for securities (although there are requirements to be listed on Nasdaq, the computer-linked network for trading securities of larger OTC firms). Thousands of brokers register with the SEC as dealers in OTC securities. Security dealers quote prices at which they are willing to buy or sell securities. A broker then executes a trade by contacting the dealer listing an attractive quote.

Before 1971, all OTC quotations of stock were recorded manually and published daily. The so-called pink sheets were the means by which dealers communicated their interest in trading at various prices. This was a cumbersome and inefficient technique, and published quotes were a day out of date. In 1971, the National Association of Securities Dealers Automatic Quotation System, or **NASDAQ,** was developed to offer via a computer-linked system immediate information on bid and ask prices for stocks offered by various dealers. The **bid price** is the price at which a dealer is willing to purchase a security; the **ask price** is the one at which the dealer will sell a security. Hence, the ask price is always higher than the bid price, and the difference, the *bid-ask spread*, makes up the dealer's profit. The system allows a broker who receives a buy or sell order from an investor to examine all current quotes, call the dealer with the best quote, and execute a trade. The securities of more than 5,000 firms are quoted on the system, which now is called the Nasdaq Stock Market and is no longer treated as an acronym. Nasdaq listing requirements are presented in Table 3.4.

Nasdaq
The computer-linked price quotation system for the OTC market.

bid price
The price at which a dealer is willing to purchase a security.

ask price
The price at which a dealer will sell a security.

Nasdaq has three levels of subscribers. The highest, level 3 subscribers, are for firms dealing, or "making markets," in OTC securities. These market makers maintain inventories of a security and constantly stand ready to buy or sell these shares from or to the public at the quoted bid and ask prices. They earn profits from the spread between the bid and ask prices.

Level 3 subscribers may enter the bid and ask prices at which they are willing to buy or sell stocks into the computer network and may update these quotes as desired.

Level 2 subscribers receive all bid and ask quotes, but they cannot enter their own quotes. These subscribers tend to be brokerage firms that execute trades for clients but do not actively deal in the stocks on their own account. Brokers attempting to buy or sell shares call the market maker (a level 3 subscriber) with the best quote in order to executive a trade. Notice that Nasdaq is a price quotation, rather than a trading, system. While bid and ask prices can be obtained from the Nasdaq computer network, the actual trade still requires direct negotiation (usually over the phone) between the broker and the dealer in the security.

Level 1 subscribers receive only the "inside quotes" (i.e., the highest bid and lowest ask prices on each stock). Level 1 subscribers are investors who are not actively buying and selling securities but want information on current prices.

For bonds, the over-the-counter market is a loosely organized network of dealers linked by a computer quotation system. In practice, the corporate bond market often is quite "thin," in that there may be few investors interested in trading a given bond at any particular time. As a result, the bond market is subject to a type of liquidity risk, for it can be difficult to sell one's holdings quickly if the need arises.

The Third and Fourth Markets

third market
Trading of exchange-listed securities on the OTC market.

The **third market** refers to trading of exchange-listed securities on the over-the-counter market. In the past, members of an exchange were required to execute all their trades of exchange-listed securities on the exchange and to charge commissions according to a fixed schedule. This procedure was disadvantageous to large traders when it prevented them from realizing economies of scale on large trades. Because of this restriction, brokerage firms that were not members of the NYSE and so not bound by its rules, established trading in the

OTC market of large NYSE-listed stocks. These trades could be accomplished at lower commissions than would have been charged on the NYSE, and the third market grew dramatically until 1972, when the NYSE allowed negotiated commissions on orders exceeding $300,000. On May 1, 1975, frequently referred to as "May Day," commissions on all NYSE orders became negotiable, and they have been ever since.

fourth market
Direct trading in exchange-listed securities between one investor and another without the benefit of a broker.

The **fourth market** refers to direct trading between investors in exchange-listed securities without the benefit of a broker. Large institutions that wish to avoid brokerage fees may engage in direct trading. The fourth market has grown dramatically in recent years as big institutional investors have begun using electronic trading networks to step around brokers. Networks such as Instinet or Posit allow traders to trade stocks directly without ever going through a broker or an exchange. Posit allows for trades in both single stocks and stock portfolios. Both networks allow for much greater anonymity than does exchange trading.

The National Market System

The Securities Act Amendments of 1975 directed the Securities and Exchange Commission to implement a national competitive securities market. Such a market would entail centralized reporting of transactions and a centralized quotation system, with the aim of enhanced competition among market makers.

In 1975, Consolidated Tape began reporting trades on the NYSE, Amex, and major regional exchanges, as well as trades of Nasdaq-listed stocks. In 1977, the Consolidated Quotations Service began providing on-line bid and ask quotes for NYSE securities also traded on various other exchanges. This has enhanced competition by allowing market participants, including brokers or dealers who are at different locations, to interact and for orders to be directed to the market in which the best price can be obtained. In 1978, the Intermarket Trading System was implemented to link seven exchanges by computer (NYSE, Amex, Boston, Cincinnati, Midwest, Pacific, and Philadelphia). Brokers and market makers now can display quotes on all markets and execute cross-market trades.

The final step in integrating securities markets would be the establishment of a central *limit order* book. Such an electronic "book" would contain all orders conditional on both prices and dates. All markets would be linked and all traders could compete for all orders. Such a system has not yet been implemented, however, and does not appear to be imminent.

3.3 TRADING ON EXCHANGES

Most of the information in this section applies to all securities traded on exchanges. Some of it, however, applies just to stocks, and in such cases we use the specific words, *stocks* or *shares*.

The Participants

We begin our discussion of the mechanics of exchange trading with a brief description of the potential parties to a trade. When an investor instructs a broker to buy or sell securities, a number of players must act to consummate the deal.

The investor places an order with a broker. The brokerage firm for which the broker works, and which owns a seat on the exchange, contacts its *commission broker*, who is on the floor of the exchange, to execute the order. When the firm's commission brokers are overloaded and have too many orders to handle, they will use the services of *floor brokers*, who are independent members of the exchange (and own seats), to execute orders.

Registered traders are frequent traders who perform no public function but instead use their membership to execute trades for their own accounts. By trading directly, they avoid the commissions that would be incurred if they had to trade through a broker. There are relatively few registered traders.

The *specialist* is central to the trading process. All trading in a given stock takes place at one location on the floor of the exchange called the specialist's post. At the specialist's post is a monitor that presents all the current offers from interested traders to buy or sell shares at various prices as well as the number of shares these quotes are good for. The specialist manages the trading in the stock. The market making responsibility for each stock is assigned by the NYSE to one specialist firm. There is only one specialist per stock but most firms will have responsibility for trading in several stocks. The specialist firm also may act as a dealer in the stock, trading for its own account. We will examine the role of the specialist in more detail shortly.

Types of Orders

Market orders are simply buy or sell orders that are to be executed immediately at current market prices. For example, an investor might call his broker and ask for the market price of Exxon. The retail broker will wire this request to the commission broker on the floor of the exchange, who will approach the specialist's post and ask the specialist for best current quotes. Finding that the current quotes are $98 per share bid, and $98¼ asked, the investor might direct the broker to buy 100 shares "at market," meaning that he is willing to pay $98¼ per share for an immediate transaction. Similarly, an order to "sell at market" will result in stock sales at $98 per share. When a trade is executed, the specialist's clerk will fill out an order card that reports the time, price, and quantity of shares traded and the transaction will be reported on the exchange's ticker tape.

There are two potential complications to this simple scenario, however. First, as noted earlier, the posted quotes of $98 and $98¼ actually represent commitments to trade up to a specified number of shares. If the market order is for more than this number of shares, the order may be filled at multiple prices. For example, if the asked price is good for orders up to 600 shares and the investor wishes to purchase 1,000 shares, it may be necessary to pay a slightly higher price for the last 400 shares than the quoted asked price.

The second complication arises from the possibility of trading "inside the quoted spread." If the broker who has received a market buy order for Exxon meets another broker who has received a market sell order for Exxon, they can agree to trade with each other at a price of $98⅛ per share. By meeting in the middle of the quoted spread, both the buyer and the seller obtain "price improvements," that is, transaction prices better than the best quoted prices. Such "meetings" of brokers are more than accidental. Because all trading takes place at the specialist's post, floor brokers know where to look for counterparties to take the other side of a trade. A study by Ross, Shapiro, and Smith (1996) finds that when the spread between the quoted bid and asked price is $¼ or greater, approximately one-half of trades on the NYSE will actually be executed "inside the quotes."

Investors also may choose to place a *limit offer*, where they specify prices at which they are willing to buy or sell a security. If Exxon is selling at $98 bid, $98¼ asked, for example, a limit buy order may instruct the broker to buy the stock if and when the share price falls *below* $95. Correspondingly, a limit sell order instructs the broker to sell as soon as the stock price goes *above* the specified limit.

What happens if a limit order is placed in between the quoted bid and ask prices? For example, suppose you have instructed your broker to buy Exxon at a price of $98⅛ or better. The order may not be executed immediately, since the quoted asked price for the shares is $98¼, which is more than you are willing to pay. However, your willingness to buy at $98⅛ is better than the quoted bid price of $98 per share. Therefore, you may find that there are traders who were unwilling to sell their shares at the $98 bid price but are happy to sell shares to you at your higher bid price of $98⅛.

Orders also can be limited by a time period. Day orders, for example, expire at the close of the trading day. If it is not executed on that day, the order is canceled. Open or good-till-

FIGURE 3.4
Limit Orders

Condition

	Price below the limit	Price above the limit
Action Buy	Limit buy order	Stop-buy order
Sell	Stop-loss order	Limit sell order

canceled orders, in contrast, remain in force for up to six months, unless canceled by the customer.

Stop-loss orders are similar to limit orders in that the trade is not to be executed unless the stock hits a price limit. Here, however, the stock is to be *sold* if its price falls *below* a stipulated level. As the name suggests, the order lets the stock be sold to stop further losses from accumulating. Similarly, stop-buy orders specify that a stock should be bought when its price rises above a limit. These trades often accompany *short sales* (sales of securities you don't own but have borrowed from your broker) and are used to limit potential losses from the short position. Short sales are discussed in greater detail later in this chapter. Figure 3.4 organizes these types of trades in a convenient matrix.

Specialists and the Execution of Trades

specialist
A trader who makes a market in the shares of one or more firms and who maintains a "fair and orderly market" by dealing personally in the market.

A **specialist** "makes a market" in the shares of one or more firms. This task may require the specialist to act as either a broker or a dealer. The specialist's role as a broker is simply to execute the orders of other brokers. Specialists also may buy or sell shares of stock for their own portfolios. When no other broker can be found to take the other side of a trade, specialists will do so even if it means they must buy for or sell from their own accounts. The NYSE commissions these companies to perform this service and monitors their performance.

Part of the specialist's job as a broker is simply clerical. The specialist maintains a "book" listing all outstanding unexecuted limit orders entered by brokers on behalf of clients. Actually, the book is now a computer console. When limit orders can be executed at market prices, the specialist executes, or "crosses," the trade.

The specialist is required to use the highest outstanding offered purchase price and the lowest outstanding offered selling price when matching trades. Therefore, the specialist system results in an auction market, meaning all buy and all sell orders come to one location, and the best orders "win" the trades. In this role, the specialist acts merely as a facilitator.

The more interesting function of the specialist is to maintain a "fair and orderly market" by acting as a dealer in the stock. In return for the exclusive right to make the market in a specific stock on the exchange, the specialist is required by the exchange to maintain an orderly market by buying and selling shares from inventory. Specialists maintain their own portfolios of stock and quoted bid and ask prices at which they are obligated to meet at least a limited amount of market orders. If market buy orders come in, specialists must sell shares from their own accounts at the ask price; if sell orders come in, they must stand willing to buy at the listed bid price.[2]

Ordinarily, however, in an active market, specialists can match buy and sell orders without using their own accounts. That is, the specialist's own inventory of securities need not be

---

[2]The specialist's published quotes are valid only for a given number of shares. If a buy or sell order is placed for more shares than the quotation size, the specialist has the right to revise the quote.

the primary means of order execution. Sometimes, the specialist's bid and ask prices are better than those offered by any other market participant. Therefore, at any point, the effective ask price in the market is the lower of either the specialist's ask price or the lowest of the unfilled limit-sell orders. Similarly, the effective bid price is the highest of the unfilled limit buy orders or the specialist's bid. These procedures ensure that the specialist provides liquidity to the market. In practice, specialists participate in approximately 10% to 20% of the transactions on the NYSE.

By standing ready to trade at quoted bid and ask prices, the specialist is exposed to exploitation by other traders. Larger traders with ready access to superior information will trade with specialists when the specialist's quotes are temporarily out of line with assessments of value based on that information. Specialists who cannot match the information resources of large traders will be at a disadvantage when their quoted prices offer profit opportunities to more advantaged traders.

You might wonder why specialists do not protect their interests by setting a low bid price and a high ask price. Specialists using that strategy would protect themselves from losses in a period of dramatic movements in the stock price. In contrast, specialists who offer a narrow spread between the bid and ask price have little leeway for error and must constantly monitor market conditions to avoid offering other investors advantageous terms.

Large bid-ask spreads are not viable options for the specialist for two reasons. First, one source of the specialist's income is frequent trading at the bid and ask prices, with the spread as a trading profit. A too-large spread would make the specialist's quotes uncompetitive with the limit orders placed by other traders. If the specialist's bid and asked quotes are consistently worse than those of public traders, it will not participate in any trades and will lose the ability to profit from the bid-ask spread. Another reason specialists cannot use large bid-ask spreads to protect their interests is that they are obligated to provide *price continuity* to the market.

To illustrate the principle of price continuity, suppose the highest limit buy order for a stock is $30, while the lowest limit sell order is $32. When a market buy order comes in, it is matched to the best limit sell at $32. A market sell order would be matched to the best limit buy at $30. As market buys and sells come to the floor randomly, the stock price would fluctuate between $30 and $32. The exchange authorities would consider this excessive volatility, and the specialist would be expected to step in with bid and/or ask prices between these values to reduce the bid-ask spread to an acceptable level, such as a quarter or a half point.

Specialists earn income both from commissions for acting as brokers for orders and from the spreads at which they buy and sell securities. Some believe specialists' access to their "book" of limit orders gives them unique knowledge about the probable direction of price movement over short periods of time. However, these days, interested floor traders also have access to the consoles of outstanding limit orders.

For example, suppose the specialist sees that a stock now selling for $45 has limit buy orders for over 100,000 shares at prices ranging from $44.50 to $44.75. This latent buying demand provides a cushion of support, in that it is unlikely that enough sell pressure will come in during the next few hours to cause the price to drop below $44.50. If there are very few limit sell orders above $45, in contrast, some transient buying demand could raise the price substantially.

The specialist in such circumstances realizes that a position in the stock offers little downside risk and substantial upside potential. Such access to the trading intentions of other market participants seems to allow a specialist and agile floor traders to earn profits on personal transactions and for selected clients. One can easily overestimate such advantages because ever more of the large orders are negotiated "upstairs," that is, as fourth-market deals.

TABLE 3.5

Transactions on the New York Stock Exchange

Source: Data from the New York Stock Exchange *Fact Book*, 1995.

Year	Shares (Thousands)	% Reported Volume	Average Number of Block Transactions per Day
1965	48,262	3.1%	9
1970	450,908	15.4	68
1975	778,540	16.6	136
1980	3,311,132	29.2	528
1985	14,222,272	51.7	2,139
1990	19,681,849	49.6	3,333
1991	22,474,383	49.6	3,878
1992	26,069,383	50.7	4,468
1993	35,959,117	53.7	5,841
1994	40,757,770	55.5	6,565
1995	49,736,912	57.0	7,793

Block Sales

block transactions
Large transactions in which at least 10,000 shares of stock are bought or sold.

Institutional investors frequently trade blocks of tens of thousands of shares of stock. Table 3.5 shows that **block transactions** of over 10,000 shares now account for more than half of all trading. The larger block transactions are often too large for specialists to handle, as they do not wish to hold such large blocks of stock in their inventory. For example, the largest block transaction in terms of dollar value in 1995 was for $600 million worth of ITT Corporation stock.

"Block houses" have evolved to aid in the placement of block trades. Block houses are brokerage firms that specialize in matching block buyers and sellers. Once a buyer and a seller have been matched, the block is sent to the exchange floor where specialists execute the trade. If a buyer cannot be found, the block house might purchase all or part of a block sale for its own account. The block house then can resell the shares to the public.

The DOT System

A relatively recent innovation is the Designated Order Turnaround (DOT) system and its technically improved successor, SuperDot. SuperDot enables exchange members to send orders directly to the specialist over computer lines. The largest market order that can be handled is 30,099 shares. In 1995, SuperDot processed an average of 304,000 orders per day, with an average execution time of less than 24 seconds.

program trade
Coordinated sale or purchase of a portfolio of stocks.

SuperDot is especially useful to program traders. A **program trade** is a coordinated purchase or sale of an entire portfolio of stocks. Many trading strategies (such as index arbitrage, a topic we will study in Chapter 18) require that an entire portfolio of stocks be purchased or sold simultaneously in a coordinated program. SuperDot is the tool that enables the many trading orders to be sent out at once and executed almost simultaneously.

Approximately 85% of all orders are submitted through SuperDot. However, these tend to be smaller orders and account for only one-third of total share volume.

Settlement

Until June 1995, an order executed on the exchange had to be settled within five working days. Today, settlement is required within 3 days; this requirement is often called T + 3, for trade date plus three days. The purchaser must deliver the cash, and the seller must deliver the stock to the broker, who in turn delivers it to the buyer's broker. Frequently, a firm's clients keep their securities in *street name*, which means the broker holds the shares registered in the firm's own name on behalf of the client. This convention can speed security transfer. T + 3 settlement has made such arrangements more important: It can be quite difficult for a seller of a security to complete delivery to the purchaser within the 3-day period if the stock is kept in a safe deposit box.

Settlement is simplified further by the existence of a clearinghouse. The trades of all exchange members are recorded each day, with members' transactions netted out, so that each member need transfer or receive only the net number of shares sold or bought that day. An exchange member then settles with the clearinghouse instead of individually with every firm with which it made trades.

3.4 TRADING ON THE OTC MARKET

On the exchanges, all trading occurs through a specialist. On the over-the-counter (OTC) market, however, trades are negotiated directly through dealers who maintain an inventory of selected securities. Dealers sell from their inventories at ask prices and buy for them at bid prices.

An investor who wishes to purchase or sell shares OTC engages a broker who tries to locate the dealer offering the best deal on the security. This is in contrast to exchange trading, where all buy or sell orders are negotiated through the specialist, who arranges for the best bids to get the trade. In the OTC market, brokers must search the offers of dealers directly to find the best trading opportunity.

Because this system does not use a specialist, OTC trades do not require a centralized trading floor as do exchange-listed stocks. Dealers can be located anywhere they can communicate effectively with other buyers and sellers.

One disadvantage of the decentralized dealer market is that the investing public is vulnerable to *trading through*, which refers to the possibility that dealers can trade with the public at their quoted bid or asked prices even if other customers have offered to trade at better prices. For example, a dealer who posts $20 bid and $20½ asked prices for a stock may continue to fill market buy orders at the ask price and fill market sell orders at the bid price—even if there are limit orders by public customers "inside the spread," for example, limit orders to buy at $20⅛ or limit orders to sell at $20⅜. This practice harms the investor whose limit order is not filled (is "traded through") as well as the investor whose market buy or sell order is not filled at the best available price.

Trading through on Nasdaq sometimes results from imperfect coordination among dealers. A limit order placed with one broker may not be seen by brokers for other traders because computer systems are not linked and only the broker's own bid and asked prices are posted on the Nasdaq system. In contrast, trading through is strictly forbidden on the NYSE or Amex, where "price priority" requires that the specialist fill the best-priced order first. Moreover, because all traders in an exchange market must trade through the specialist, the exchange provides true *price discovery*, meaning that market prices reflect the prices at which *all* participants at that moment are willing to trade. This is the advantage of a centralized auction market.

In October 1994, the Justice Department announced an investigation of the Nasdaq Stock Market regarding possible collusion among market makers to maintain spreads at artificially high levels. The probe was encouraged by the observation that Nasdaq stocks rarely trade at bid-ask spreads of odd eighths, that is, ⅛, ⅜, ⅝, or ⅞. Even for the biggest and most active shares trading on Nasdaq, the vast majority of trades seem to be executed at quarter- or half-point spreads. Cooperation among Nasdaq dealers to increase their profits by maintaining wide spreads would be a violation of antitrust laws. In addition to the Justice Department investigation, the controversy over spreads in the Nasdaq market generated an SEC investigation as well as private lawsuits alleging that traders suffered losses from excessive spreads maintained through collusion among Nasdaq market makers.

In July 1996, the Justice Department settled with the Nasdaq dealers accused of colluding to maintain wide spreads. While none of the dealer firms had to pay penalties, they agreed to refrain from pressuring any other market maker to maintain wide spreads and from refusing to deal with other traders who try to undercut an existing spread. In addition, the firms agreed to randomly monitor phone conversations among dealers to ensure that the terms of the settlement are adhered to.

FIGURE 3.5

Dollar Volume of Equity Trading in Major World Markets, 1995

Source: The Nasdaq Stock Market 1996 *Fact Book & Company Directory*.

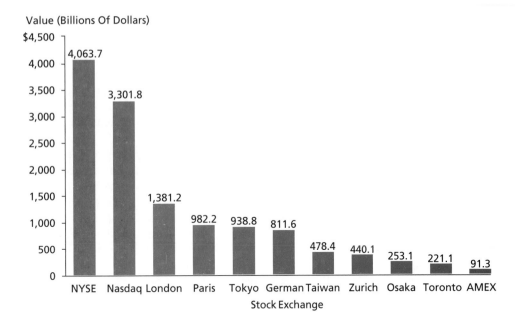

In August 1996, the SEC settled with the National Association of Securities Dealers (NASD) as well as with the Nasdaq Stock Market. The SEC concluded that NASD had failed to adequately monitor trading on the Nasdaq market. The settlement called for NASD to spend up to $100 million over five years to improve its surveillance of the Nasdaq market and to take specific steps to prohibit market makers from either colluding on spreads or intimidating and harassing other dealers that quote narrow spreads. Much of the $100 million will be spent to improve NASD's ability to create an audit trail to track how dealers execute investor's trades.

Market Structure in Other Countries

The structure of security markets varies considerably from one country to another. A full cross-country comparison is far beyond the scope of this text. Therefore, we will instead briefly review the two biggest non-U.S. stock markets: the London and Tokyo exchanges. Figure 3.5 shows the volume of trading in major world markets.

London   The London Stock Exchange is conveniently located between the world's two largest financial markets, those of the U.S. and Japan. The trading day in London overlaps with Tokyo in the morning and New York in the afternoon. Trading arrangements on the London Stock Exchange resemble those on Nasdaq. Competing dealers who wish to make a market in a stock enter bid and ask prices into the Stock Exchange Automated Quotations (SEAQ) computer system. Markets orders then can be matched against those quotes. However, negotiation among institutional traders results in more trades being executed "inside the published quotes" than is true of Nasdaq. As in the U.S., London security firms are allowed to act both as dealers and as brokerage firms, that is, both making a market in securities and executing trades for their clients.

The London Stock Exchange is attractive to some traders because it offers greater anonymity than U.S. markets, primarily because records of trades are not published for a period of time until after they are completed. Therefore, it is harder for market participants to observe or infer a trading program of another investor until after that investor has completed the program. This anonymity can be quite attractive to institutional traders that wish to buy or sell large quantities of stock over a period of time.

Tokyo   The Tokyo Stock Exchange (TSE) is the largest stock exchange in Japan, accounting for about 80% of total trading. There is no specialist system on the TSE. Instead, a *saitori* maintains a public limit order book, matches market and limit orders, and is obliged to follow certain actions to slow down price movements when simple matching of orders would result in price changes greater than exchange-prescribed minimums. In their clerical role of matching orders, *saitoris* are somewhat similar to specialists on the NYSE. However, *saitoris* do not trade for their own accounts, and therefore they are quite different from either dealers or specialists in the U.S.

Because the *saitori* performs an essentially clerical role, there are no market making services or liquidity provided to the market by dealers or specialists. The limit order book is the primary provider of liquidity. In this regard, the TSE bears some resemblance to the fourth market in the U.S., in which buyers and sellers trade directly via networks such as Instinet or Posit. On the TSE, however, if order imbalances result in price movements across sequential trades that are considered too extreme by the exchange, the *saitori* may temporarily halt trading and advertise the imbalance in the hope of attracting additional trading interest to the "weak" side of the market.

The TSE organizes stocks into two categories. The First Section consists of about 1,200 of the most actively traded stocks. The Second Section is for about 400 of the less actively traded stocks. Trading in the larger First Section stocks occurs on the floor of the exchange. The remaining securities in the First Section and the Second Section trade electronically.

3.5   TRADING COSTS

Part of the cost of trading a security is obvious and explicit. Your broker must be paid a commission. Individuals may choose from two kinds of brokers: full-service or discount brokers. Full-service brokers who provide a variety of services often are referred to as account executives or financial consultants.

Besides carrying out the basic services of executing orders, holding securities for safekeeping, extending margin loans, and facilitating short sales, brokers routinely provide information and advice relating to investment alternatives.

Full-service brokers usually depend on a research staff that prepares analyses and forecasts of general economic as well as industry and company conditions and often makes specific buy or sell recommendations. Some customers take the ultimate leap of faith and allow a full-service broker to make buy and sell decisions for them by establishing a *discretionary account*. In this account, the broker can buy and sell prespecified securities whenever deemed fit. The broker cannot withdraw any funds, though. This action requires an unusual degree of trust on the part of the customer, for an unscrupulous broker can "churn" an account, that is, trade securities excessively with the sole purpose of generating commissions.

Discount brokers, on the other hand, provide "no-frills" services. They buy and sell securities, hold them for safekeeping, offer margin loans, and facilitate short sales, and that is all. The only information they provide about the securities they handle is price quotations.

Discount brokerage services have become increasingly available in recent years. Many banks, thrift institutions, and mutual fund management companies now offer such services to the investing public as part of a general trend toward the creation of one-stop "financial supermarkets."

One important service most full-service and discount brokers offer their customers is an automatic cash management feature. Cash generated from the sale of securities or the receipt of dividends and interest is automatically invested in a money market fund. This ensures that cash will not be idle and will always earn interest.

bid-ask spread
The difference between a dealer's bid and asked price.

In addition to the explicit part of trading costs—the broker's commission—there is an implicit part—the dealer's **bid-ask spread.** Sometimes the broker is a dealer in the security

TABLE 3.6

Commission Schedule
Quoted by a Large
Discount Brokerage
Firm

Value of Shares	Fixed Charge	plus	Variable Charge (% of purchase or sale)
$0–$2,500	$ 25		1.60%
$2,501–$5,000	35		0.84
$5,001–$15,000	50		0.40
$15,001–$50,000	60		0.30
$50,001–$250,000	100		0.125
Above $250,000	125		0.11

Note: Minimum commission = $36.25, or $.0275 per share, whichever is greater.
Maximum commission = $.48 per share.

being traded and charges no commission but instead collects the fee entirely in the form of the bid-ask spread.

Another implicit cost of trading that some observers would distinguish is the price concession an investor may be forced to make for trading in any quantity that exceeds the quantity the dealer is willing to trade at the posted bid or asked price.

The commission for trading common stocks is generally around 2% of the value of the transaction, but it can vary significantly. Before 1975 the schedule of commissions was fixed, but in today's environment of negotiated commissions there is substantial flexibility. On some trades, full-service brokers will offer even lower commissions than will discount brokers. In general, it pays the investor to shop around. Table 3.6 presents the commission schedule for one prominent discount broker, which is fairly representative of the industry. Notice that there is a minimum charge regardless of trade size, and that cost as a fraction of the value of traded shares falls as trade size increases.

Total trading costs consisting of the commission, the dealer bid-asked spread, and the price concession can be substantial. According to one study (Loeb, 1987), the round-trip costs (costs of purchase and resale) of trading large blocks of stocks of small companies can be as high as 30%. However, in most cases, costs of trades are far smaller. The commissions can be as low as 0.25% of the value of stocks traded for large transactions made through discount houses.

An ongoing controversy between the NYSE and its competitors is the extent to which better execution on the NYSE offsets the generally lower explicit costs of trading in other markets. Execution refers to the size of the effective bid-ask spread and the amount of price impact in a market. The NYSE believes that many investors focus too intently on the costs they can see, despite the fact that quality of execution can be a far more important determinant of total costs. When the specialist's spread is greater than an eighth of a point, more than one-half of NYSE trades are executed at a price inside the spread. This can happen because floor brokers at the specialist's post can bid above or sell below the specialist's quote. In this way, two public orders can cross without incurring the specialist's spread.

In contrast, in a dealer market, all trades go through the dealer, and all trades, therefore, are subject to a bid-ask spread. The client never sees the spread as an explicit cost, however. The price at which the trade is executed incorporates the dealer's spread, but this part of the price is never reported to the investor. Similarly, regional markets are disadvantaged in terms of execution because their lower trading volume means that fewer brokers congregate at a specialist's post, resulting in a lower probability of two public orders crossing.

A controversial practice related to the bid-ask spread and the quality of trade execution is "paying for order flow." This entails paying a broker a rebate for directing the trade to a particular dealer rather than to the NYSE. By bringing the trade to a dealer instead of to the exchange, however, the broker eliminates the possibility that the trade could have been executed without incurring a spread. Moreover, a broker that is paid for order flow might direct a trade to a dealer that does not even offer the most competitive price. (Indeed, the fact that dealers can afford to pay for order flow suggests that they are able to lay off the trade at better prices elsewhere, and possibly, that the broker also could have found a better price with some additional effort.)

Such practices raise serious ethical questions, because the broker's primary obligation is to obtain the best deal for the client. Payment for order flow might be justified if the rebate is passed along to the client either directly or through lower commissions, but it is not clear that such rebates are passed through.

3.6 BUYING ON MARGIN

When purchasing securities, investors have easy access to a source of debt financing called *broker's call loans*. The act of taking advantage of broker's call loans is called *buying on margin*.

margin

Describes securities purchased with money borrowed in part from a broker.

Purchasing stocks on **margin** means the investor borrows part of the purchase price of the stock from a broker. The brokers in turn borrow money from banks at the call money rate to finance these purchases; they then charge their clients that rate (defined in Chapter 2), plus a service charge for the loan. All securities purchased on margin must be maintained with the brokerage firm in street name, for the securities are collateral for the loan.

The Board of Governors of the Federal Reserve System limits the extent to which stock purchases can be financed using margin loans. The current initial margin requirement is 50%, meaning that at least 50% of the purchase price must be paid for in cash, with the rest borrowed.

The percentage margin is defined as the ratio of the net worth, or the "equity value," of the account to the market value of the securities. To demonstrate, suppose an investor initially pays $6,000 toward the purchase of $10,000 worth of stock (100 shares at $100 per share), borrowing the remaining $4,000 from a broker. The balance sheet looks like this:

Assets		Liabilities and Owners' Equity	
Value of stock	$10,000	Loan from broker	$4,000
		Equity	$6,000

The initial percentage margin is

$$\text{Margin} = \frac{\text{Equity in account}}{\text{Value of stock}} = \frac{\$6,000}{\$10,000} = .60, \text{ or } 60\%$$

If the stock's price declines to $70 per share, the account balance becomes:

Assets		Liabilities and Owners' Equity	
Value of stock	$7,000	Loan from broker	$4,000
		Equity	$3,000

The assets in the account fall by the full decrease in the stock value, as does the equity. The percentage margin is now

$$\text{Margin} = \frac{\text{Equity in account}}{\text{Value of stock}} = \frac{\$3,000}{\$7,000} = .43, \text{ or } 43\%$$

If the stock value were to fall below $4,000, owners' equity would become negative, meaning the value of the stock is no longer sufficient collateral to cover the loan from the broker. To guard against this possibility, the broker sets a *maintenance margin*. If the percentage margin falls below the maintenance level, the broker will issue a *margin call*, which requires the investor to add new cash or securities to the margin account. If the investor does not act, the broker may sell the securities from the account to pay off enough of the loan to restore the percentage margin to an acceptable level.

An example will show how maintenance margin works. Suppose the maintenance margin is 30%. How far could the stock price fall before the investor would get a margin call? Answering this question requires some algebra.

Let P be the price of the stock. The value of the investor's 100 shares is then $100P$, and the equity in the account is $100P - \$4,000$. The percentage margin is $(100P - \$4,000)/100P$. The price at which the percentage margin equals the maintenance margin of .3 is found by solving the equation

$$\frac{100P - 4,000}{100P} = .3$$

which implies that $P = \$57.14$. If the price of the stock were to fall below $57.14 per share, the investor would get a margin call.

Concept Check

3. Suppose the maintenance margin in the above example was 40%. How far can the stock price fall before the investor gets a margin call?

Why do investors buy securities on margin? They do so when they wish to invest an amount greater than their own money allows. Thus, they can achieve greater upside potential, but they also expose themselves to greater downside risk.

To see how, let's suppose an investor is bullish on IBM stock, which is selling for $100 per share. An investor with $10,000 to invest expects IBM to go up in price by 30% during the next year. Ignoring any dividends, the expected rate of return would be 30% if the investor invested $10,000 to buy 100 shares.

But now assume the investor borrows another $10,000 from the broker and invests it in IBM, too. The total investment in IBM would be $20,000 (for 200 shares). Assuming an interest rate on the margin loan of 9% per year, what will the investor's rate of return be now (again ignoring dividends) if IBM stock goes up 30% by year's end?

The 200 shares will be worth $26,000. Paying off $10,900 of principal and interest on the margin loan leaves $15,100 (i.e., $26,000 - $10,900). The rate of return in this case will be

$$\frac{\$15,100 - \$10,000}{\$10,000} = 51\%$$

The investor has parlayed a 30% rise in the stock's price into a 51% rate of return on the $10,000 investment.

Doing so, however, magnifies the downside risk. Suppose that, instead of going up by 30%, the price of IBM stock goes down by 30% to $70 per share. In that case, the 200 shares will be worth $14,000, and the investor is left with $3,100 after paying off the $10,900 of principal and interest on the loan. The result is a disastrous return of

$$\frac{3,100 - 10,000}{10,000} = -69\%$$

Table 3.7 summarizes the possible results of these hypothetical transactions. If there is no change in IBM's stock price, the investor loses 9%, the cost of the loan.

TABLE 3.7
Illustration of Buying
Stock on Margin

Change in Stock Price	End of Year Value of Shares	Repayment of Principal and Interest*	Investor's Rate of Return
30% increase	$26,000	$10,900	51%
No change	20,000	10,900	−9
30% decrease	14,000	10,900	−69

Note: *Assuming the investor buys $20,000 worth of stock by borrowing $10,000 at an interest rate of 9% per year.

Concept Check

4. Suppose that in the previous example, the investor borrows only $5,000 at the same interest rate of 9% per year. What will the rate of return be if the price of IBM goes up by 30%? If it goes down by 30%? If it remains unchanged?

3.7 SHORT SALES

Normally, an investor would first buy a stock and later sell it. With a short sale, the order is reversed. First, you sell and then you buy the shares. In both cases, you begin and end with no shares.

short sale
The sale of shares not owned by the investor but borrowed through a broker and later purchased to replace the loan.

A **short sale** allows investors to profit from a decline in a security's price. An investor borrows a share of stock from a broker and sells it. Later, the short-seller must purchase a share of the same stock in the market in order to replace the share that was borrowed. This is called *covering the short position*. Table 3.8 compares stock purchases to short sales.

The short-seller anticipates the stock price will fall, so that the share can be purchased at a lower price than it initially sold for; if so, the short-seller will reap a profit. Short-sellers must not only replace the shares but also pay the lender of the security any dividends paid during the short sale.

In practice, the shares loaned out for a short sale are typically provided by the short-seller's brokerage firm, which holds a wide variety of securities of its other investors in street name. The owner of the shares need not know that the shares have been lent to the short-seller. If the owner wishes to sell the shares, the brokerage firm will simply borrow shares from another investor. Therefore, the short sale may have an indefinite term. However, if the brokerage firm cannot locate new shares to replace the ones sold, the short-seller will need to repay the loan immediately by purchasing shares in the market and turning them over to the brokerage house to close out the loan.

Exchange rules permit short sales only after an *uptick*, that is, only when the last recorded change in the stock price is positive. This rule apparently is meant to prevent waves of speculation against the stock. In essence, the votes of "no confidence" in the stock that short sales represent may be entered only after a price increase.

Finally, exchange rules require that proceeds from a short sale must be kept on account with the broker. The short-seller cannot invest these funds to generate income, although large institutional investors typically will receive some income from the proceeds of a short sale being held with the broker. Short-sellers also are required to post margin (cash or collateral) with the broker to cover losses should the stock price rise during the short sale.

To illustrate the mechanics of short-selling, suppose you are bearish (pessimistic) on Xerox stock, and that its market price is $100 per share. You tell your broker to sell short

TABLE 3.8
Cash Flows from Purchasing versus Short-Selling Shares of Stock

Purchase of Stock

Time	Action	Cash Flow
0	Buy share	− Initial price
1	Receive dividend, sell share	Ending price + Dividend

Profit = (Ending price + Dividend) − Initial price
Note: A negative cash flow implies a cash *outflow*.

Short Sale of Stock

Time	Action	Cash Flow
0	Borrow share: sell it	+ Initial price
1	Repay dividend and buy share to replace the share originally borrowed	− (Ending price + Dividend)

Profit = Initial price − (Ending price + Dividend)

1,000 shares. The broker borrows 1,000 shares either from another customer's account or from another broker.

The $100,000 cash proceeds from the short sale are credited to your account. Suppose the broker has a 50% margin requirement on short sales. This means you must have other cash or securities in your account worth at least $50,000 that can serve as margin on the short sale. Let's say that you have $50,000 in Treasury bills. Your account with the broker after the short sale will then be:

Assets		Liabilities and Owner's Equity	
Cash	$100,000	Short position in Xerox stock (1,000 shares owed)	$100,000
T-bills	50,000	Equity	50,000

Your initial percentage margin is the ratio of the equity in the account, $50,000, to the current value of the shares you have borrowed and eventually must return, $100,000:

$$\text{Percentage margin} = \frac{\text{Equity}}{\text{Value of stock owed}} = \frac{\$50,000}{\$100,000} = .50$$

Suppose you are right and Xerox falls to $70 per share. You can now close out your position at a profit. To cover the short sale, you buy 1,000 shares to replace the ones you borrowed. Because the shares now sell for $70, the purchase costs only $70,000. Because your account was credited for $100,000 when the shares were borrowed and sold, your profit is $30,000: The profit equals the decline in the share price times the number of shares sold short. On the other hand, if the price of Xerox goes up unexpectedly while you are short, you may get a margin call from your broker.

Suppose the broker has a maintenance margin of 30% on short sales. This means the equity in your account must be at least 30% of the value of your short position at all times. How far can the price of Xerox stock go up before you get a margin call?

Let P be the price of Xerox stock. Then the value of your short position is $1,000P$, and the equity in your account is $\$150,000 - 1,000P$. Your short position margin ratio is equity/value of stock $= (150,000 - 1,000P)/1,000P$. The critical value of P is thus

$$\frac{\text{Equity}}{\text{Value of shares owed}} = \frac{150,000 - 1,000P}{1,000P} = .3$$

which implies that $P = \$115.38$ per share. If Xerox stock should *rise* above $115.38 per share, you will get a margin call, and you will either have to put up additional cash or cover your short position by buying shares to replace the ones borrowed.

Concept Check

5. *a.* Construct the balance sheet if Xerox goes up to $110.
   b. If the short position maintenance margin in the Xerox example is 40%, how far can the stock price rise before the investor gets a margin call?

3.8 REGULATION OF SECURITIES MARKETS

Trading in securities markets in the United States is regulated by a myriad of laws. The major governing legislation includes the Securities Act of 1933 and the Securities Exchange Act of 1934. The 1933 Act requires full disclosure of relevant information relating to the issue of new securities. This is the act that requires registration of new securities and issuance of a prospectus that details the financial prospects of the firm. SEC approval of a prospectus or financial report is not an endorsement of the security as a good investment. The SEC cares only that the relevant facts are disclosed; investors must make their own evaluation of the security's value.

The 1934 Act established the Securities and Exchange Commission to administer the provisions of the 1933 Act. It also extended the disclosure principle of the 1933 Act by requiring periodic disclosure of relevant financial information by firms with already-issued securities on secondary exchanges.

The 1934 Act also empowers the SEC to register and regulate securities exchanges, OTC trading, brokers, and dealers. While the SEC is the administrative agency, responsible for broad oversight of the securities markets, it shares responsibility with other regulatory agencies. The Commodity Futures Trading Commission (CFTC) regulates trading in futures markets, while the Federal Reserve has broad responsibility for the health of the U.S. financial system. In this role, the Fed sets margin requirements on stocks and stock options and regulates bank lending to securities markets participants.

The Securities Investor Protection Act of 1970 established the Securities Investor Protection Corporation (SIPC) to protect investors from losses if their brokerage firms fail. Just as the Federal Deposit Insurance Corporation provides depositors with federal protection against bank failure, the SIPC ensures that investors will receive securities held for their account in street name by a failed brokerage firm up to a limit of $500,000 per customer. The SIPC is financed by levying an "insurance premium" on its participating, or member, brokerage firms. It also may borrow money from the SEC if its own funds are insufficient to meet its obligations.

In addition to federal regulations, security trading is subject to state laws, known generally as *blue sky laws* because they are intended to give investors a clearer view of the investment prospects. State laws to outlaw fraud in security sales existed before the Securities Act of 1933. Varying state laws were somewhat unified when many states adopted portions of the Uniform Securities Act, which was enacted in 1956.

Self-Regulation and Circuit Breakers

Much of the securities industry relies on self-regulation. The SEC delegates to secondary exchanges such as the NYSE much of the responsibility for day-to-day oversight of trading. Similarly, the national Association of Securities Dealers oversees trading of OTC securities. The Institute of Chartered Financial Analysts' Code of Ethics and Professional Conduct sets out principles that govern the behavior of CFAs. The nearby box on page 79 presents a brief outline of those principles.

The market collapse of October 19, 1987, prompted several suggestions for regulatory change. Among these was a call for "circuit breakers" to slow or stop trading during periods of extreme volatility. In response, the NYSE initially instituted the following rules:

- **Trading halts**. When the Dow Jones Industrial Average declines by 250 points from its previous day's close, trading is halted for one-half hour. If the Average falls by 400 points from its previous day's close, trading is halted for two hours.

- **Sidecars**. If the S&P 500 futures contract falls by 12 points from its previous day's close, all program trades executed through SuperDot must sit unexecuted for five minutes. (In addition, a 12-point drop will trigger the Chicago Mercantile Exchange to halt trading in the S&P 500 futures contract for one hour.)

- **Collars**. When the Dow moves 50 points in either direction from the previous day's close, Rule 80A of the NYSE requires that index arbitrage orders pass a "tick test." In a falling market, sell orders may be executed only at a plus tick or zero-plus tick, meaning that the trade may be done at a higher price than the last trade (a plus tick) or at the last price if the last recorded change in the stock price is positive (a zero-plus tick). The rule remains in effect for the rest of the day unless the Dow returns to within 25 points of the previous day's close.

Excerpts from AIMR Standards of Professional Conduct

Standard I: Fundamental Responsibilities
Members shall maintain knowledge of and comply with all applicable laws, rules, and regulations including AIMR's Code of Ethics and Standards of Professional Conduct.

Standard II: Responsibilities to the Profession

- *Professional misconduct.* Members shall not engage in any professional conduct involving dishonesty, fraud, deceit, or misrepresentation,
- *Prohibition against plagiarism.*

Standard III: Responsibilities to the Employer

- *Obligation to inform employer of code and standards.* Members shall inform their employer that they are obligated to comply with these Code and Standards.
- *Disclosure of additional compensation arrangements.* Members shall disclose to their employer all benefits that they receive in addition to compensation from that employer.

Standard IV: Responsibilities to Clients and Prospects

- *Investment process and research reports.* Members shall exercise diligence and thoroughness in making investment recommendations . . . distinguish between facts and opinions in research reports . . . and use reasonable care to maintain objectivity.
- *Interactions with clients and prospects.* Members must place their clients' interests before their own.

- *Portfolio investment recommendations.* Members shall make a reasonable inquiry into a client's financial situation, investment experience, and investment objectives prior to making appropriate investment recommendations . . .
- *Priority of transactions.* Transactions for clients and employers shall have priority over transactions for the benefit of a member.
- *Disclosure of conflicts to clients and prospects.* Members shall disclose to their clients and prospects all matters, including ownership of securities or other investments, that reasonably could be expected to impair the member's ability to make objective recommendations.

Standard V: Responsibilities to the Public

- *Prohibition against use of material nonpublic [inside] information.* Members who possess material nonpublic information related to the value of a security shall not trade in that security.
- *Performance presentation.* Members shall not make any statements that misrepresent the investment performance that they have accomplished or can reasonably be expected to achieve.

Source: Abridged from *The Standards of Professional Conduct* of the AIMR.

The idea behind circuit breakers is that a temporary halt in trading during periods of very high volatility can help mitigate informational problems that might contribute to excessive price swings. For example, even if a trader is unaware of any specific adverse economic news, if he sees the market plummeting, he will suspect that there might be a good reason for the price drop and will become unwilling to buy shares. In fact, he might decide to sell shares to avoid losses. Thus, feedback from price swings to trading behavior can exacerbate market movements. Circuit breakers give participants a chance to assess market fundamentals while prices are temporarily frozen. In this way, they have a chance to decide whether price movements are warranted while the market is closed.

Of course, circuit breakers have no bearing on trading in non-U.S. markets. It is quite possible that they simply have induced those who engage in program trading to move their operations into foreign exchanges.

The NYSE recently modified its policies concerning circuit breakers. When the rules were put into place in late 1988, the Dow Jones Industrial Index was at a level of about 2000, and a 250-point decline would have represented a 12% drop in the market. In late 1996, with the Dow at about 6500, such a decline would represent a drop of less than 4%, which does not seem severe enough to most observers to warrant a trading halt.

In December 1996, the NYSE reduced the duration of the trading halt from one hour to one-half hour. It later increased the point decline in the Dow necessary to trigger trading halts from 250 to 350. If the Dow were to decline by 550 points, trading would cease for an additional hour. Some have suggested tying circuit breakers to percentage rather than point movements in the index.

Insider Trading

Inside information
Nonpublic knowledge about a corporation possessed by corporate officers, major owners, or other individuals with privileged access to information about the firm.

Regulations also prohibit insider trading. It is illegal for anyone to transact in securities to profit from **inside information,** that is, private information held by officers, directors, or major stockholders that has not yet been divulged to the public. But the definition of insiders can be ambiguous. While it is obvious that the chief financial officer of a firm is an insider, it is less clear whether the firm's biggest supplier can be considered an insider. Yet a supplier may deduce the firm's near-term prospects from significant changes in orders. This gives the supplier a unique form of private information, yet the supplier is not technically an insider.

These ambiguities plague security analysts, whose job is to uncover as much information as possible concerning the firm's expected prospects. The distinction between legal private information and illegal inside information can be fuzzy (see accompanying box on page 81).

The SEC requires officers, directors, and major stockholders to report all transactions in their firm's stock. A compendium of insider trades is published monthly in the SEC's *Official Summary of Securities Transactions and Holdings.* The idea is to inform the public of any implicit vote of confidence or no confidence made by insiders.

Insiders *do* exploit their knowledge. Three forms of evidence support this conclusion. First, there have been well-publicized convictions of principals in insider trading schemes.

Second, there is considerable evidence of "leakage" of useful information to some traders before any public announcement of that information. For example, share prices of firms announcing dividend increases (which the market interprets as good news concerning the firm's prospects) commonly increase in value a few days *before* the public announcement of the increase. Clearly, some investors are acting on the good news before it is released to the public. Similarly, share prices tend to increase a few days before the public announcement of above-trend earnings growth. Share prices still rise substantially on the day of the public release of good news, however, indicating that insiders, or their associates, have not fully bid up the price of the stock to the level commensurate with the news.

A third form of evidence on insider trading has to do with returns earned on trades by insiders. Researchers have examined the SEC's summary of insider trading to measure the performance of insiders. In one of the best known of these studies, Jaffee (1974) examined the abnormal return of stocks over the months following purchases or sales by insiders. For months in which insider purchasers of a stock exceeded insider sellers of the stock by three or more, the stock had an abnormal return in the following eight months of about 5%. Moreover, when insider sellers exceeded insider buyers, the stock tended to perform poorly.

Restriction of the use of inside information is not universal. Japan has no such prohibition. An argument in favor of free use of inside information is that investors are not misled to believe that the financial market is a level playing field for all. At the same time, free use of inside information means that such information will more quickly be reflected in stock prices.

Most Americans believe, however, that it is valuable as well as virtuous to take the moral high ground and outlaw such advantage, even if less-than-perfect enforcement may leave the door open for some profitable violation of the law.

Cloudy Cases: Insider-Trading Law Leads to an Array of Interpretations

You go to a party and meet a lawyer who advises Rupert Omnivore, a notorious corporate raider. The lawyer gives you a tip: Mr. Omnivore will soon "make a run at" Deadwood Industries Inc. You promptly buy stock in Deadwood. A week later, its share price surges as Mr. Omnivore goes public with his intentions.

Are you guilty of insider trading?

That sort of hypothetical question has legal experts, investment bankers, and stock market investors tied up in knots these days.

Some practices clearly are illegal, but there are plenty of gray areas in insider-trading law. In fact, the Securities and Exchange Commission says it has resisted efforts to spell out precise guidelines, partly because it worries that shrewd market players may find ways to evade the spirit of the law, while just barely complying with the letter.

Here are some examples of what legal experts say are ambiguous areas that ordinary investors may have to worry about—along with some sense of how the law currently stands.

THE RAIDER'S TIP

To some top lawyers, the example at the start of this story looks like a big loophole in current law. Raiders may be perfectly willing to have intermediaries tip off other investors about their next move. That's because such leaks can help move shares into "sympathetic hands," aiding raiders in later stages of a battle for corporate control.

A critical issue is whether a tender offer is involved, says John Coffee, a securities law professor at Stanford University. If so, Rule 14e-3 under the Securities Exchange Act strictly limits trading by interested parties. But if a raider hasn't yet decided how to wage a fight, Rule 14e-3 might not apply, lawyers say.

THE CHAIN

You're an officer of Ennui Enterprises, and you're about to report disappointing quarterly earnings. You know not to sell before the news, but you tell your college roommate. He tells his daughter, who's married to a stockbroker. The broker tells his clients. They dump their stock in Ennui— hours before the earnings are reported and the stock falls.

Have the clients done anything wrong? Have you?

Lawyers say the critical question for recipients of such tips is whether they knew, or had reason to know, that any of the sources were breaching a fiduciary duty in leaking information. If so, tip recipients shouldn't trade on the information.

In practical terms, the longer the chain, the less likely regulators are to pursue the case. Law enforcement officials do pursue some chains, however, and the original leaker can face heavy sanctions.

EARLY WORD OF NEWS STORIES

It could involve television, the business press, or a medical journal. But you know in advance about a news report that should boost a company's stock. Is it legal to trade on this information?

The law is still in flux here, says Stanford's Professor Coffee. A former *Wall Street Journal* reporter, R. Foster Winans, was convicted of securities fraud for leaking information about future *Journal* articles. His case is due to be reviewed by the Supreme Court.

An important test here is how such traders learned of the future news reports, says Professor Coffee. If they misappropriated information from their employer, in violation of company policy, they would seem to be guilty of insider trading under the current Winans ruling. But it's questionable whether any insider-trading offense would occur if the investor didn't have a fiduciary duty to the news organization.

THE OVERHEARD TIP

Tired of your duties at Ennui Enterprises, you take off for the golf course instead. You can't help overhearing another group talking about their corporate acquisition plans. You buy the stock they mention. Sure enough, their bid comes a week later, bringing you big profits.

Have the other executives done anything wrong? Have you?

If the leak really was inadvertent, despite sensible precautions to avoid it, the overheard executives face little legal risk, experts say. They add that accidental tip recipients are probably in the clear, too, as long as they haven't taken unusual steps to glean the information.

But enforcement officials may ask a lot of questions before they're convinced that a leak was an accident. And Bevis Lonstretlh, currently a partner in the New York law firm of Debevoise & Plimpton, says investors should think a little about their conscience, as well as the law.

"For all the talk about gray areas, my clients can sense what's all right and what isn't," he says. "They don't call me and say: 'Where's the line, so I can stay just barely on the safe side of it.' "

Summary

- Firms issue securities to raise the capital necessary to finance their investments. Investment bankers market these securities to the public on the primary market. Investment bankers generally act as underwriters who purchase the securities from the firm and resell them to the public at a markup. Before the securities may be sold to the public, the firm must publish an SEC-approved prospectus that provides information on the firm's prospects.

- Already-issued securities are traded on the secondary market, that is, on organized stock exchanges. Securities also trade on the over-the-counter market and, for large trades, through direct negotiation. Only members of exchanges may trade on the exchange. Brokerage firms holding seats on the exchange sell their services to individuals, charging commissions for executing trades on their behalf. The NYSE and, to a lesser extent, the Amex have fairly strict listing requirements. Regional exchanges provide listing opportunities for local firms that do not meet the requirements of the national exchanges.

- Trading of common stocks on exchanges occurs through specialists. The specialist acts to maintain an orderly market in the shares of one or more firms. The specialist maintains "books" of limit buy and sell orders and matches trades at mutually acceptable prices. Specialists also will accept market orders by selling from or buying for their own inventory of stocks when there is an imbalance of buy and sell orders.

- The over-the-counter market is not a formal exchange but an informal network of brokers and dealers who negotiate sales of securities. The Nasdaq system provides on-line computer quotes offered by dealers in the stock. When an individual wishes to purchase or sell a share, the broker can search the listing of bid and ask prices, call the dealer with the best quote, and execute the trade.

- Block transactions are a fast-growing segment of the securities market that currently accounts for more than half of trading volume. These trades often are too large to be handled readily by specialists and so have given rise to block houses that specialize in identifying potential trading partners for their clients.

- Buying on margin means borrowing money from a broker in order to buy more securities than can be purchased with one's own money alone. By buying securities on a margin, an investor magnifies both the upside potential and the downside risk. If the equity in a margin account falls below the required maintenance level, the investor will get a margin call from the broker.

- Short-selling is the practice of selling securities that the seller does not own. The short-seller borrows the securities sold through a broker and may be required to cover the short position at any time on demand. The cash proceeds of a short sale are always kept in escrow by the broker, and the broker usually requires that the short-seller deposit additional cash or securities to serve as margin (collateral) for the short sale.

- Securities trading is regulated by the Securities and Exchange Commission as well as by self-regulation of the exchanges. Many of the important regulations have to do with full disclosure of relevant information concerning the securities in question. Insider trading rules also prohibit traders from attempting to profit from inside information.

- In addition to providing the basic services of executing buy and sell orders, holding securities for safekeeping, making margin loans, and facilitating short sales, full-service brokers offer investors information, advice, and even investment decisions. Discount brokers offer only the basic brokerage services but usually charge less. Total trading costs consist of commissions, the dealer's bid-ask spread, and price concessions.

Key Terms

ask price, *64*
bid-ask spread, *72*
bid price, *64*

block transactions, *69*
fourth market, *65*

initial public offerings
(IPOs), *58*
inside information, *80*

margin, *74*
Nasdaq, *64*
over-the-counter (OTC)
  market, *64*
primary market, *57*

program trade, *69*
prospectus, *58*
secondary market, *57*
short sale, *76*

specialist, *67*
stock exchanges, *61*
third market, *64*
underwriters, *58*

Problem Sets

CFA

1. FBN, Inc., has just sold 100,000 shares in an initial public offering. The underwriter's explicit fees were $70,000. The offering price for the shares was $50, but immediately upon issue, the share price jumped to $53.
   a. What is your best guess as to the total cost to FBN of the equity issue?
   b. Is the entire cost of the underwriting a source of profit to the underwriters?

2. Suppose you short-sell 100 shares of IBM, now selling at $120 per share.
   a. What is your maximum possible loss?
   b. What happens to the maximum loss if you simultaneously place a stop-buy order at $128?

3. An expiring put will be exercised and the stock sold if the stock price is below the exercise price. A stop-loss order causes a stock sale when the stock price falls below some limit. Compare and contrast the two strategies of purchasing put options versus issuing a stop-loss order.

4. Compare call options and stop-buy orders.

5. Do you think it is possible to replace market-making specialists with a fully automated, computerized trade-matching system?

6. Consider the following limit order book of a specialist. The last trade in the stock occurred at a price of $50.

Limit Buy Orders		Limit Sell Orders	
Price	Shares	Price	Shares
$49.75	500	$50.25	100
49.50	800	51.50	100
49.25	500	54.75	300
49.00	200	58.25	100
48.50	600		

   a. If a market buy order for 100 shares comes in, at what price will it be filled?
   b. At what price would the next market buy order be filled?
   c. If you were the specialist, would you want to increase or decrease your inventory of this stock?

7. You are bullish on AT&T stock. The current market price is $50 per share, and you have $5,000 of your own to invest. You borrow an additional $5,000 from your broker at an interest rate of 8% per year and invest $10,000 in the stock.
   a. What will be your rate of return if the price of AT&T stock goes up by 10% during the next year? (Ignore the expected dividend.)
   b. How far does the price of AT&T stock have to fall for you to get a margin call if the maintenance margin is 30%?

8. You are bearish on AT&T and decide to sell short 100 shares at the current market price of $50 per share.
   a. How much in cash or securities must you put into your brokerage account if the broker's initial margin requirement is 50% of the value of the short position?
   b. How high can the price of the stock go before you get a margin call if the maintenance margin is 30% of the value of the short position?

9. Suppose that Intel currently is selling at $80 per share. You buy 250 shares by using $15,000 of your own money and borrowing the remainder of the purchase price from your broker. The rate on the margin loan is 8%.

   a. What is the percentage increase in the net worth of your brokerage account if the price of Intel *immediately* changes to: (i) $88; (ii) $80; (iii) $72? What is the relationship between your percentage return and the percentage change in the price of Intel?

   b. If the maintenance margin is 25%, how low can Intel's price fall before you get a margin call?

   c. How would your answer to (b) change if you had financed the initial purchase with only $10,000 of your own money?

   d. What is the rate of return on your margined position (assuming again that you invest $15,000 of your own money) if Intel is selling *after one year* at: (i) $88; (ii) $80; (iii) $72? What is the relationship between your percentage return and the percentage change in the price of Intel? Assume that Intel pays no dividends.

   e. Continue to assume that a year has passed. How low can Intel's price fall before you get a margin call?

10. Suppose that you sell short 250 shares of Intel, currently selling for $80 per share, and give your broker $15,000 to establish your margin account.

   a. If you earn no interest on the funds in your margin account, what will be your rate of return after one year if Intel stock is selling at: (i) $88; (ii) $80; (iii) $72? Assume that Intel pays no dividends.

   b. If the maintenance margin is 25%, how high can Intel's price rise before you get a margin call?

   c. Redo parts (a) and (b), assuming that Intel's dividend (paid at year end) is $2 per share.

11. Call one full-service broker and one discount broker and find out the transaction costs of implementing the following strategies:

   a. Buying 100 shares of IBM now and selling them six months from now.

   b. Investing an equivalent amount in six-month at-the-money call options on IBM stock now and selling them six months from now.

12. Here is some price information on Marriott:

	Bid	Asked
Marriott	37¼	38⅛

You have placed a stop-loss order to sell at $38. What are you telling your broker? Given market prices, will your order be executed?

13. Here is some price information on Fincorp stock. Suppose first that Fincorp trades in a dealer market such as Nasdaq.

Bid	Asked
55¼	55½

   a. Suppose you have submitted an order to your broker to buy at market. At what price will your trade be executed?

   b. Suppose you have submitted an order to sell at market. At what price will your trade be executed?

   c. Suppose you have submitted a limit order to sell at $55⅝. What will happen?

   d. Suppose you have submitted a limit order to buy at $55⅜. What will happen?

14. Now reconsider problem 13 assuming that Fincorp sells in an exchange market like the NYSE.
    a. Is there any chance for price improvement in the market orders considered in parts (a) and (b)?
    b. Is there any chance of an immediate trade at $55⅜ for the limit buy order in part (d)?

15. What purpose does the SuperDot system serve on the New York Stock Exchange?

16. Who sets the bid and asked price for a stock traded over the counter? Would you expect the spread to be higher on actively or inactively traded stocks?

17. Consider the following data concerning the NYSE:

Year	Average Daily Trading Volume (Thousands of Shares)	Annual High Price of an Exchange Membership
1985	109,169	$ 480,000
1986	141,028	600,000
1987	188,938	1,150,000
1988	161,461	820,000
1989	165,470	675,000
1990	156,777	430,000
1991	178,917	440,000
1992	202,266	600,000
1993	264,519	775,000
1994	291,351	830,000
1995	346,101	1,050,000

    a. What do you conclude about the short-run relationship between trading activity and the value of a seat?
    b. Based on these data, what do you think has happened to the average commission charged to traders in the last decade?

18. On January 1, you sold short one round lot (that is, 100 shares) of Zenith stock at $14 per share. On March 1, a dividend of $2 per share was paid. On April 1, you covered the short sale by buying the stock at a price of $9 per share. You paid 50 cents per share in commissions for each transaction. What is the value of your account on April 1?

The following questions are from past CFA examinations.

CFA

19. If you place a stop-loss order to sell 100 shares of stock at $55 when the current price is $62, how much will you receive for each share if the price drops to $50?
    a. $50.
    b. $55.
    c. $54⅞.
    d. Cannot tell from the information given.

20. You wish to sell short 100 shares of XYZ Corporation stock. If the last two transactions were at 34⅛ followed by 34¼, you can sell short on the next transaction only at a price of
    a. 34⅛ or higher
    b. 34¼ or higher
    c. 34¼ or lower
    d. 34⅛ or lower

21. Specialists on the New York Stock Exchange do all of the following *except*:
    a. Act as dealers for their own accounts.
    b. Execute limit orders.
    c. Help provide liquidity to the marketplace.
    d. Act as odd-lot dealers.

1. What kind of market is the IEM?
   a. Direct search
   b. Over the counter
   c. Exchange
   d. All of the above
   e. None of the above

2. Describe the process through which securities are created on the IEM. (Hint: Suppose you were the first trader on the IEM and there were no asks outstanding for securities, how would you obtain securities?)

3. How are secondary transactions carried out on the IEM? (Hint: How do traders buy and sell securities from each other?)

4. Look up the prospectuses for the Computer Industry Returns Market and the MSFT (Microsoft) Price Level Market on the IEM. (These can be found in the "N"ews windows of the market "I"nformation menu.) Describe the important features of the contracts traded in these markets.

5. Look up and record the current bid and ask for MSFTm on the Computer Industry Returns Market. What does this bid mean? What does this ask mean? What is the bid-ask spread and what does it mean?

6. Using the IEM, how would you:
   a. Submit a market order buy SP500m?
   b. Submit a market order to sell MSxxxmH?
   c. Submit a limit order to buy MSxxxmL for $0.646?
   d. Submit a limit order to sell AAPLm for $0.745?

**Solutions to
Concept Checks**

1. Limited time shelf registration was introduced because of its favorable trade-off of saving issue cost against mandated disclosure. Allowing unlimited shelf registration would circumvent "blue sky" laws that ensure proper disclosure.

2. Run for the hills! If the issue were underpriced, it most likely would be oversubscribed by institutional traders. The fact that the underwriters need to actively market the shares to the general public may indicate that better-informed investors view the issue as overpriced.

3. Solving

$$\frac{100P - \$4,000}{100P} = .4$$

yields $P = \$66.67$ per share.

4. The investor will purchase 150 shares, with a rate of return as follows:

Year-End Change in Price	Year-End Value of Shares	Repayment of Principal and Interest	Investor's Rate of Return
30%	$19,500	$5,450	40.5%
No change	15,000	5,450	−4.5
−30%	10,500	5,450	−49.5

5. *a.* Once Xerox stock goes up to \$110, your balance sheet will be:

Assets		Liabilities and Owner's Equity	
Cash	\$100,000	Short position in Xerox	\$110,000
T-bills	50,000	Equity	40,000

b. Solving

$$\frac{\$150,000 - 1,000P}{1,000P} = .4$$

yields $P = \$107.14$ per share.

Chapter 4

MUTUAL FUNDS AND OTHER INVESTMENT COMPANIES

AFTER STUDYING THIS CHAPTER YOU SHOULD BE ABLE TO:

- Cite advantages and disadvantages of investing with an investment company rather than buying securities directly.

- Contrast open-end mutual funds with closed-end funds and unit investment trusts.

- Define net asset value and measure the rate of return on a mutual fund.

- Classify mutual funds according to investment style.

- Demonstrate the impact of expenses and turnover on mutual fund investment performance.

The previous chapter provided an introduction to the mechanics of trading securities and the structure of the markets in which securities trade. Increasingly, however, individual investors are choosing not to trade securities directly for their own accounts. Instead, they direct their funds to investment companies that purchase securities on their behalf. The most important of these financial intermediaries are mutual funds, to which we will devote most of this chapter. However, we also will touch briefly on other types of investment companies, such as unit investment trusts and closed-end funds.

We begin the chapter by describing and comparing the various types of investment companies available to investors—unit investment trusts, closed-end investment companies, and open-end investment companies, more commonly known as mutual funds. We devote most of our attention to mutual funds, examining the functions of such funds, their investment styles and policies, and the costs of investing in these funds.

Next, we take a first look at the investment performance of these funds. We consider the impact of expenses and turnover on net performance and examine the extent to which performance is consistent from one period to the next. In other words, will the mutual funds that were the best *past* performers be the best *future* performers? Finally, we discuss sources of information on mutual funds and consider in detail the information provided in the most comprehensive guide, Morningstar's *Mutual Fund Sourcebook*.

4.1 INVESTMENT COMPANIES

investment companies
Financial intermediaries
that invest the funds of
individual investors in
securities or other assets.

Investment companies are financial intermediaries that collect funds from individual investors and invest those funds in a potentially wide range of securities or other assets. Pooling of assets is the key idea behind investment companies. Each investor has a claim to the portfolio established by the investment company in proportion to the amount invested. These companies thus provide a mechanism for small investors to "team up" to obtain the benefits of large-scale investing.

Investment companies perform several important functions for their investors:

1. *Record keeping and administration.* Investment companies issue periodic status reports, in which they report capital gain distributions, dividends, investments, and redemptions. They also may reinvest dividend and interest income for shareholders.

2. *Diversification and divisibility.* By pooling their money, investment companies enable investors to hold fractional shares of many different securities. They can act as large investors even if any individual shareholder cannot.

3. *Professional management.* Most, but not all, investment companies have full-time staffs of security analysts and portfolio managers who attempt to achieve superior investment results for their investors.

4. *Lower transaction costs.* Because they trade large blocks of securities, investment companies can achieve substantial savings on brokerage fees and commissions.

While all investment companies pool the assets of individual investors, they also need to divide claims to those assets among those investors. Investors buy shares in investment companies, and ownership is proportional to the number of shares purchased. The value of each share is called the **net asset value,** or **NAV.** Net asset value equals assets minus liabilities expressed on a per share basis:

net asset value (NAV)
Assets minus liabilities
expressed on a per share
basis.

$$\text{Net asset value} = \frac{\text{Market value of assets minus liabilities}}{\text{Shares outstanding}}$$

As an example, consider a mutual fund that manages a portfolio of securities worth $120 million. Suppose the fund owes $4 million to its investment advisors and owes another $1 million to various suppliers of office products. The fund has 5 million shareholders. Then

$$\text{Net asset value} = \frac{\$120 \text{ million} - \$5 \text{ million}}{5 \text{ million shares}} = \$23 \text{ per share}$$

Concept Check

1. Consider these data from the December 31, 1995, balance sheet of the Index Trust 500 Portfolio mutual fund sponsored by the Vanguard Group. What was the net asset value of the portfolio?

Assets:	$17,442,229,000
Liabilities:	70,394,000
Shares:	301,573,850

4.2 TYPES OF INVESTMENT COMPANIES

In the United States, investment companies are classified by the Investment Company Act of 1940 as either unit investment trusts or managed investment companies. The portfolios of unit investment trusts are essentially fixed and thus are called *unmanaged*. In contrast, managed companies are so named because securities in their investment portfolios are continually bought and sold: The portfolios are *managed*. Managed companies are further classified as either closed-end or open-end. Open-end companies are what we commonly call mutual funds.

Unit Investment Trusts

Unit investment trusts are pools of money invested in a portfolio that is fixed for the life of the fund. To form a unit investment trust, a sponsor, typically a brokerage firm, buys a portfolio of securities that are deposited into a trust. It then sells to the public shares or "units" in the trust called *redeemable trust certificates*. All income and payments of principal from the portfolio are paid out by the fund's trustees (a bank or trust company) to the shareholders. Most unit trusts hold fixed-income securities and expire at their maturity, which may be as short as several months, if the trust invests in short-term securities like money market instruments, or many years, if the trust holds long-term assets like fixed-income securities. The fixed life of fixed-income securities makes them a good fit for fixed-life unit investment trusts. In fact, about 90% of all unit investment trusts are invested in fixed-income portfolios, and about 90% of fixed-income unit investment trusts are invested in tax-exempt debt.

There is little active management of a unit investment trust because, once established, the portfolio composition is fixed; hence these trusts are referred to as unmanaged. Trusts tend to invest in relatively uniform types of assets; for example, one trust may invest in municipal bonds, another in corporate bonds, and so on. The uniformity of the portfolio is consistent with the lack of active management. The trust provides investors a vehicle to purchase a bundle of one particular type of asset, which can be included in an overall portfolio as desired. The lack of active management of the portfolio implies that management fees can be quite low.

Sponsors of unit investment trusts earn their profit by selling shares in the trust at a premium to the cost of acquiring the underlying assets. For example, a trust that has purchased $5 million of assets may sell 5,000 shares to the public at a price of $1,030 per share, which (assuming the trust has no liabilities) represents a 3% premium over the net asset value of the securities held by the trust. The 3% premium over net asset value is the trustee's fee for establishing the trust.

Investors who wish to liquidate their holdings of a unit investment trust may sell the shares back to the trustee for net asset value. The trustees either can sell enough securities from the asset portfolio to obtain the cash necessary to pay the investor, or they may instead sell the shares to a new investor (again at a slight premium to net asset value).

Managed Investment Companies

There are two types of managed companies: closed-end and open-end. In both cases, the fund's board of directors, which is elected by shareholders, will hire a management company to manage the portfolio for an annual management fee that typically ranges from 0.2% to 1.5% of assets. In many cases, the management company is the firm that organized the fund. For example, Fidelity Management and Research Corporation sponsors many Fidelity mutual funds and is responsible for managing the portfolios. It assesses a management fee on each Fidelity fund. In other cases, a mutual fund will hire an outside portfolio manager. For example, Vanguard has hired Wellington Management as the investment advisor for its Wellington fund. Most management companies have contracts to manage several funds.

Open-end funds stand ready to redeem or issue shares at their net asset value (although both purchases and sales may involve sales commissions). When investors in open-end funds wish to "cash out" their shares, they sell them back to the fund at NAV. In contrast, closed-end funds do not redeem or issue shares. Investors in closed-end funds who wish to cash out must sell their shares to other investors. Shares of closed-end funds are traded on organized exchanges and can be purchased through brokers just like other common stock; their prices therefore can differ from NAV.

Figure 4.1 is a listing of closed-end funds from *The Wall Street Journal*. The first column after the name of the fund indicates the exchange on which the shares trade (A: Amex;

FIGURE 4.1
Closed-End Funds

Source: *The Wall Street Journal*, July 1, 1996. Reprinted by permission of *The Wall Street Journal*, © 1996 Dow Jones & Company, Inc. All Rights Reserved Worldwide.

CLOSED-END FUNDS

Friday, June 28 1996

Closed-end funds sell a limited number of shares and invest the proceeds in securities. Unlike open-funds, closed-ends generally do not buy their shares back from investors who wish to cash in their holdings. Instead, fund shares trade on a stock exchange. The following list, provided by Lipper Analytical Services, shows the exchange where each fund trades (A: American; C: Chicago; N: NYSE; O: Nasdaq; T: Toronto; z: does not trade on an exchange). The data also include the fund's most recent net asset value, its closing share price on the day NAV was calculated, and the percentage difference between the market price and the NAV (often called the premium or discount). For equity funds, the final column provides 52-week returns based on market prices plus dividends. For bond funds, the final column shows the past 12 months' income distributions as a percentage of the current market price. Footnotes appear after a fund's name. a: the NAV and market price are ex dividend. b: the NAV is fully diluted. c: NAV, market price and premium or discount are as of Thursday's close. d: NAV, market price and premium or discount are as of Wednesday's close. e: NAV assumes rights offering is fully subscribed. v: NAV is converted at the commercial Rand rate. w: Convertible Note-NAV (not market) conversion value. y: NAV and market price are in Canadian dollars. All other footnotes refer to unusual circumstances; explanations for those that appear can be found at the bottom of this list. N/A signifies that the information is not available or not applicable.

Fund Name	Stock Exch	NAV	Market Price	Prem /Disc	52 week Market Return
General Equity Funds					
Adams Express	N	22.94	19 1/8	– 16.6	20.5
Alliance All-Mkt -a	N	22.57	19	– 15.8	17.1
Avalon Capital	O	10.77	9 3/4	– 9.5	N/A
Baker Fentress	A	23.88	19 1/8	– 19.9	29.2
Bergstrom Cap	A	133.84	116 1/2	– 13.0	31.7
Blue Chip Value	N	9.46	8 1/2	– 10.1	34.5
Central Secs	A	22.67	24	+ 5.9	25.8
Corp Renaissance -c	O	10.36	8 3/8	– 19.2	–9.5
Engex	A	16.25	12 3/4	– 21.5	36.0
Equus II	A	21.18	14 5/8	– 30.9	19.3
Gabelli Equity	N	10.10	9 5/8	– 4.7	8.3
General American	N	26.42	22	– 16.7	23.7
Inefficient Mkt	A	13.44	11 3/8	– 15.4	32.5
Librty Allstr Eq	N	11.55	10 3/4	– 6.9	18.9
Librty Allstr Gr	N	11.31	9 5/8	– 14.9	13.6
MicroCap Fund	O	N/A	6	0.0	26.3
Morgan FunShares -c	O	10.50	8 7/8	– 15.5	21.0
Morgan Gr Sm Cap -h	N	12.72	10 3/8	– 18.4	30.8
NAIC Growth -c	C	16.93	17 1/2	+ 3.4	59.4
Royce Value	N	14.52	12 3/8	– 14.8	14.9
Royce,5.75 '04Cv -w	N	109.18	101 1/4	– 7.3	1.8
Salomon SBF	N	16.67	14 1/4	– 14.5	33.7
Source Capital	N	44.53	41 1/4	– 7.4	10.9
Trl-Continental	N	29.57	24	– 18.8	18.1
Zweig	N	11.02	11 1/8	+ 1.0	10.0
Specialized Equity Funds					
Alliance Gl Env	N	16.73	13 1/8	– 21.5	44.1
C&S Realty	A	9.03	9 1/4	+ 2.4	7.4
C&S Total Rtn	N	13.97	13 1/2	– 3.4	15.7
Cemrl Fd Canada -c	A	4.74	4 3/4	+ 0.2	–1.1
Counsellors Tand	N	19.40	18 1/4	– 5.9	27.4
India Fund	N	9.73	9 1/4	– 4.9	–9.8
India Growth -d	N	13.74	14 5/8	+ 6.4	–16.3
Indonesia	N	9.90	11 1/8	+ 12.4	0.0
Irish Inv	N	16.17	13 1/8	– 18.8	21.8
Italy	N	10.67	8 7/8	– 16.8	14.8
Jakarta Growth	N	9.16	8 3/4	– 4.5	–1.6
Japan Equity	N	11.94	12 5/8	+ 5.7	–8.5
Japan OTC Equity	N	9.14	8 5/8	– 5.6	–2.8
Jardine Fl China	N	12.08	10 3/8	– 14.1	–5.1
Jardine Fl India -c	N	9.80	9 1/4	– 5.6	–20.3
Korea	N	18.52	21 1/8	+ 14.1	9.8
Korea Equity	N	8.17	8 1/2	+ 4.0	6.5
Korean Inv	N	10.30	9 7/8	– 4.1	–5.4
Latin Amer Disc	N	14.60	12 5/8	– 13.5	17.2
Latin Amer Eq	N	17.41	15 1/8	– 13.1	9.8
Latin Amer Growth	N	12.74	10 1/2	– 17.6	2.1
Latin Amer Inv	N	19.71	16 3/4	– 15.0	5.9
Malaysia	N	21.54	18 3/4	– 13.0	1.1
Mexico -ac	N	17.90	15	– 16.2	–1.0
Mexico Eqty&Inc -c	N	12.19	9 7/8	– 19.0	–5.7
Morgan St Africa	N	16.06	12 5/8	– 21.4	20.6
Morgan St Asia	N	13.45	12	– 10.8	17.2
Morgan St Em	N	17.44	16 7/8	– 3.2	11.6
Morgan St India	N	11.06	11 1/4	+ 1.7	9.8
New South Africa	N	17.57	13 3/4	– 21.7	1.2
New World Inv	z	N/A	N/A	0.0	N/A
Pakistan Inv	N	7.15	6 3/4	– 5.6	0.1
Portugal	N	15.27	12 1/2	– 18.1	–6.1
ROC Taiwan	N	10.77	11 3/8	+ 5.6	3.0
Schroder Asian	N	14.27	13 1/8	– 8.0	18.0
Scudder New Asia	N	16.06	14 5/8	– 8.9	0.1
Scudder New Eur	N	15.99	12 5/8	– 21.0	23.7
Singapore -c	N	12.91	12 3/4	– 1.2	–8.9
Southern Africa	N	20.84	16 3/4	– 19.6	29.2
Spain	N	12.24	9 7/8	– 19.3	14.8
Swiss Helvetia	N	25.56	21 1/4	– 16.9	8.6
TCW/DW Emer Mkts	N	13.53	11	– 18.7	9.3
Taiwan -c	N	22.74	24	+ 5.5	9.8
Taiwan Equity -c	N	11.23	10 7/8	– 3.2	2.4
Templeton China -c	N	13.33	11 1/8	– 16.5	11.8
Templeton Dragon	N	16.01	13 1/4	– 17.2	13.8
Templeton Em App -c	N	13.99	12 1/2	– 10.7	10.4
Templeton Em Mkt	N	17.52	19	+ 8.4	7.1
Templeton Russia -c	N	22.41	26 1/4	+ 17.1	N/A
Templeton Vietnm	N	13.85	11 1/4	– 18.8	–4.7
Thal	N	24.60	23 5/8	– 4.0	2.3
Thai Capital	N	14.62	13 1/4	– 9.4	–7.2
Third Canadian -cy	T	15.02	14 1/4	– 5.1	17.6
Turkish Inv	N	5.83	6	+ 2.9	–4.0
United Corps Ltd -cy	T	52.03	35 1/2	– 31.8	11.2
United Kingdom -a	N	15.86	12 5/8	– 20.4	17.9
Worldwide Value	N	25.53	21 1/2	– 15.8	42.6
Z-Seven	O	19.38	20	+ 3.2	19.7

Fund Name	Stock Exch	NAV	Market Price	Prem /Disc	12 Mo Yield 5/31/96
U.S. Gov't. Bond Funds					
ACM Govt Inc	N	9.33	9 7/8	+ 5.8	8.5

C: Chicago; N: NYSE; O: Nasdaq; T: Toronto; z: does not trade on an exchange). The next three columns give the fund's most recent net asset value, the closing share price, and the percentage difference between the two: (Price – NAV)/NAV. Notice that there are more funds selling at discounts to NAV (indicated by negative differences) than premiums. Finally, the 52-week return based on the percentage change in share price plus dividend income is presented in the last column.

The common divergence of price from net asset value, often by wide margins, is a puzzle that has yet to be fully explained. To see why this is a puzzle, consider a closed-end fund that is selling at a discount from net asset value. If the fund were to sell all the assets in the portfolio, it would realize proceeds equal to net asset value. The difference between the market price of the fund and the fund's NAV would represent the per share increase in the wealth of the fund's investors. Despite this apparent profit opportunity, sizeable discounts seem to persist for long periods of time.

Interestingly, while many closed-end funds sell at a discount from net asset value, the prices of these funds when originally issued are typically above NAV. This is a further puzzle, as it is hard to explain why investors would purchase these newly issued funds at a premium to NAV when the shares tend to fall to a discount shortly after issue.

Many investors consider closed-end funds selling at a discount to NAV to be a bargain. Even if the market price never rises to the level of NAV, the dividend yield on an investment in the fund at this price would exceed the dividend yield on the same securities held outside the fund. To see this, imagine a fund with an NAV of $10 per share holding a portfolio that pays an annual dividend of $1 per share; that is, the dividend yield to investors that hold this portfolio directly is 10%. Now suppose that the market price of a share of this closed-end fund is $9. If management pays out dividends received from the shares as they come in, then the dividend yield to those that hold the same portfolio through the closed-end fund will be $1/$9, or 11.1%.

interval closed-end fund
A type of closed-end fund that can purchase from 5 to 25% of outstanding shares from investors at intervals of 3, 6, or 12 months.

Recent variations on closed-end funds are **interval closed-end funds** and **discretionary closed-end funds.** Interval closed-end funds may purchase from 5% to 25% of outstanding shares from investors at intervals of 3, 6, or 12 months. Discretionary closed-end funds may purchase any or all of outstanding shares from investors, but not more frequently than once every two years. The repurchase of shares for either of these funds takes place at net asset value plus a repurchase fee that may not exceed 2%.

discretionary closed-end fund
A type of closed-end fund that can purchase any or all of outstanding shares from investors, but no more than once every two years.

In contrast to closed-end funds, the price of open-end funds cannot fall below NAV, because these funds stand ready to redeem shares at NAV. The purchase price will exceed NAV, however, if the fund carries a **load.** A load is, in effect, a sales commission, which is paid to the seller. Load funds are sold by security brokers, many insurance brokers, and others.

load
A sales commission charged on a mutual fund.

Unlike closed-end funds, open-end mutual funds do not trade on organized exchanges. Instead, investors simply buy shares from or sell shares to the investment company at net asset value. Thus, the number of outstanding shares of these funds changes daily.

Other Investment Organizations

There are intermediaries not formally organized or regulated as investment companies that nevertheless serve similar functions as investment companies. Two of the more important are commingled funds and real estate investment trusts.

commingled funds
Partnerships of investors that pool their funds.

Commingled Funds   **Commingled funds** are partnerships of investors that pool their funds. The management firm that organizes the partnership, for example, a bank or insurance company, manages the funds for a fee. Typical partners in a commingled fund might be trust or retirement accounts, which have portfolios that are much larger than those of most individual investors but are still too small to warrant managing on a separate basis.

Commingled funds are similar in form to open-end mutual funds. Instead of shares, though, the fund offers "units" that are bought and sold at net asset value. A bank or insurance company may offer an array of different commingled funds from which trust or retirement accounts can choose. Examples are a money market fund, a bond fund, and a common stock fund.

real estate investment trust (REIT)
An intermediary that invests in real estate or loans secured by real estate.

Real Estate Investment Trusts   A **real estate investment trust (REIT)** is similar to a closed-end fund. REITs invest in real estate or loans secured by real estate. Besides issuing shares, they raise capital by borrowing from banks and issuing bonds or mortgages. Most of them are highly leveraged, with a typical debt ratio of 70%.

There are two principal kinds of REITs. *Equity trusts* invest in real estate directly, while *mortgage trusts* invest primarily in mortgage and construction loans. REITs generally are established by banks, insurance companies, or mortgage companies, which then serve as investment managers to earn a fee.

REITs are exempt from taxes as long as at least 95% of their taxable income is distributed to shareholders. For shareholders, however, the dividends are taxable as personal income.

4.3 MUTUAL FUNDS

Mutual funds are the common name for open-end investment companies. This is the dominant version of investment company today, accounting for roughly 90% of investment company assets. Assets under management in the mutual fund industry surpassed $3 trillion in March 1996.

Investment Policies

Each mutual fund has a specified investment policy, which is described in the fund's prospectus. For example, money market mutual funds hold the short-term, low-risk instruments of the money market (see Chapter 2 for a review of these securities), while bond funds hold fixed-income securities. Some funds have even more narrowly defined mandates. For example, some fixed-income funds will hold primarily Treasury bonds, while others will hold primarily mortgage-backed securities.

Management companies manage a family or "complex" of mutual funds. They organize an entire collection of funds and then collect a management fee for operating them. By managing a collection of funds under one umbrella, these companies make it easy for investors to allocate assets across market sectors and switch assets across funds, but they still benefit from centralized record keeping. Some of the most well-known management companies are Fidelity, Vanguard, Dreyfus, and Putnum. Each offers an array of open-end mutual funds with different investment policies. Thus, while there were about 9,000 mutual funds at the end of 1996, these funds were offered by only 400 fund complexes.

Some of the more important fund types, classified by investment policy, are as follows:

- **Money market funds.** These funds invest in money market securities. They usually offer check-writing features, and net asset value is fixed at $1 per share, so that there are no tax implications such as capital gains or losses associated with the redemption of shares.

- **Equity funds.** Equity funds invest primarily in stock, although, at the portfolio manager's discretion, they may also hold fixed-income or other types of securities. Funds commonly will hold at least some money market securities to provide the liquidity necessary to meet potential redemption of shares.

  The *Investment Companies* manual published by Wiesenberger (an investment service company) classifies common stock funds according to the following objectives: (1) maximum capital gain; (2) growth; (3) growth and income; (4) income; and (5) income and security. The objectives are arranged "in descending order of emphasis on capital appreciation and, consequently, in ascending order of the importance placed on current income and relative price stability."

- **Fixed income funds.** As the name suggests, these funds specialize in the fixed-income sector. Within that sector, however, there is considerable room for specialization. For example, various funds will concentrate on corporate bonds, Treasury bonds, mortgage-backed securities, or municipal (tax-free) bonds. Indeed, some of the municipal bond funds will invest only in bonds of a particular state in order to satisfy the investment desires of residents of that state who wish to avoid state as well as federal taxes on the interest paid on the bonds. Many funds also will specialize by the maturity of the securities, ranging from short-term to intermediate to long-term, or by the credit risk of the issuer, ranging from very safe to high-yield or "junk" bonds.

- **Balanced and income funds.** Some funds are designed to be candidates for an individual's entire investment portfolio. Therefore, they hold both equities and fixed-income securities in relatively stable proportions. Wiesenberger's manual classifies such funds as *income* or *balanced funds*. Income funds "provide as liberal a current income from investments as possible," while balanced funds "minimize investment risks so far as this is possible without unduly sacrificing possibilities for long-term growth and current income."

- **Asset allocation funds.** These funds are similar to balanced funds in that they hold both stocks and bonds. However, asset allocation funds may dramatically vary the proportions allocated to each market in accord with the portfolio manager's forecast of the relative performance of each sector. Hence, these funds are engaged in market timing and are not designed to be low-risk investment vehicles.

- **Index funds.** An index fund tries to match the performance of a broad market index. The fund buys shares in securities included in a particular index in proportion to the security's representation in that index. For example, Vanguard Index Trust 500 Portfolio is a mutual fund that replicates the composition of the Standard & Poor's 500 stock price index. Because the S&P 500 is a value-weighted index, the fund buys shares in each S&P 500 company in proportion to the market value of that company's outstanding equity. Investment in an index fund is a low-cost way for small investors to pursue a passive investment strategy. Of course, index funds can be tied to nonequity indexes as well. For example, Vanguard offers a bond-index fund and a real-estate index fund.

- **Specialized sector funds.** Some funds concentrate on a particular industry. For example, Fidelity markets over 30 different Select Funds, each of which invests in specific industries such as biotechnology, utilities, precious metals, or telecommunications. Other funds specialize in securities of particular countries.

Table 4.1 breaks down the number of mutual funds by investment orientation as of the end of 1996.

Figure 4.2 shows part of the listings for mutual funds from *The Wall Street Journal*. Notice that the funds are organized by the fund family. For example, the funds sponsored by the Vanguard Group appear at the right of the figure. The first two columns after the name of each fund present the net asset value of the fund and the change in NAV from the previous day. The last column is the year-to-date return on the fund.

Often the fund name describes its investment policy. For example, Vanguard's GNMA fund invests in mortgage-backed securities; its municipal intermediate fund (MuInt) invests in intermediate-term municipal bonds; and its high-yield corporate bond fund (HYCorp) invests in large part in speculative grade or "junk" bonds with high yields. You can see that Vanguard offers more than a dozen index funds, including portfolios indexed to the bond market (IdxTotB), the Wilshire 5000 index (IdxTot), the Russell 2000 Index of small firms (IdxSmC), as well as European and Pacific Basin indexed portfolios (IdxEur and IdxPac). However, names of common stock funds often give little or no guidance as to their investment policies. Examples are Vanguard's Windsor and Wellington funds.

How Funds Are Sold

Most mutual funds have an underwriter that has exclusive rights to distribute shares to investors. Mutual funds generally are marketed to the public either directly from the fund company or indirectly through brokers acting on behalf of the underwriter. Direct market funds are sold through the mail, at local offices of the fund, over the phone, and very recently, over the Internet. Investors contact the fund directly to purchase shares. For example, if you look at the financial pages of your local newspaper, you will see several advertisements for funds, along with toll-free phone numbers that you can call to receive a fund's

TABLE 4.1
Classification of Mutual
Funds (as of
December 31, 1996)*

Source: *Intestment Companies*
1997. CDA Wiesenberger
Investment Companies

Type of Fund	Number of Funds	Assets ($ Million)	% of Total
Common Stock			
Maximum capital gain	180	$ 68,395	2.1
Small company growth	491	109,590	3.4
International equity	995	257,959	8.0
Long-term growth	1153	509,004	15.8
Growth and current income	618	416,826	12.9
Equity income	189	73,895	2.3
	3,626	$1,435,669	44.6
Bond Funds			
Flexible income	90	$ 69,915	2.2
Corporate bond	685	137,218	4.3
Corporate high yield	190	79,867	2.5
Government mortgage-backed	165	43,681	1.4
Government securities	540	86,601	2.7
Municipal bonds	502	110,577	3.4
Municipal high yield	67	30,659	1.0
Municipal single state	1302	113,142	3.5
International bond	264	26,208	0.8
	3,805	$ 697,859	21.7
Specialized			
Energy/natural resources	42	$ 6,043	0.2
Financial services	21	7,300	0.2
Gold and precious metals	50	4,890	0.2
Health care	28	9,344	0.2
Other	56	7,421	0.2
Technology	53	17,486	0.5
Utilities	101	24,544	0.8
	250	$ 52,464	1.6
Money Market			
Taxable	736	$ 761,799	23.7
Tax-free	396	140,046	4.3
	1132	$ 901,845	28.4
Mixed Asset Classes			
Balanced	320	$ 68,235	2.1
Asset allocation	178	40,105	1.2
Total	9,412	$3,220,721	100.0

*Column sums subject to rounding error.

prospectus and an application to open an account with the fund. Close to 40% of stock and bond fund sales in 1995 were distributed directly to investors.

About half of fund sales in 1995 were distributed through a sales force. Brokers or financial advisors receive a commission for selling shares to investors. (Ultimately, the commission is paid by the investor. More on this shortly.) In some cases, funds use a "captive" sales force that sells shares only in funds of the mutual fund management company. The trend today, however, is toward "financial supermarkets" that can sell shares in funds of many complexes.

4.4 COSTS OF INVESTING IN MUTUAL FUNDS

Fee Structure

An individual investor choosing a mutual fund should consider not only the fund's stated investment policy, but also its management fees and other expenses. Comparative data on virtually all important aspects of mutual funds are available in the annual volumes prepared by Wiesenberger Investment Companies Service or in Morningstar's *Sourcebook*, both of

FIGURE 4.2

Mutual Fund
Quotations

Source: *The Wall Street Journal*, July 1, 1996.
Reprinted by permission of *the Wall Street JOURNAL, © 1996 Dow Jones & Company, Inc. All Rights Reserved Worldwide.*

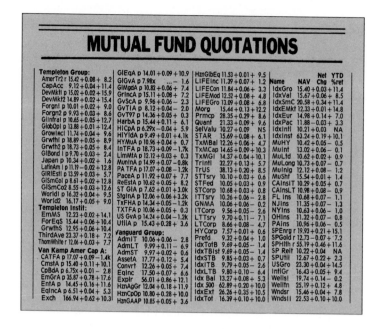

which can be found in many academic and public libraries. You should be aware of four general classes of fees.

- **Front-end load.** A front-end load is a commission or sales charge paid when you purchase the shares. These charges, which are used to pay the brokers who sell the funds, may not exceed 8.5%. *Low-load funds* have loads that range from 1 to 3% of invested funds. No-load funds have no front-end sales charges. Loads effectively reduce the funds being invested. For example, each $1,000 paid for a fund with an 8.5% load results in a sales charge of $85, and a portfolio that starts at only $915. You need cumulative returns of 9.3% of your net investment (85/915 = .093) just to break even.

- **Back-end load.** A back-end load is a redemption or "exit" fee incurred when you sell your shares. Typically, funds that impose back-end loads start them at 5 or 6% and reduce them by 1 percentage point for every year the funds are left invested. Thus, an exit fee that starts at 6% would fall to 4% by the start of your third year. These charges are known more formally as "contingent deferred sales charges."

- **Operating expenses.** Operating expenses are the costs incurred by the mutual fund in operating the portfolio, including administrative expenses and advisory fees paid to the investment manager. These expenses usually are expressed as a percentage of total assets under management and may range from 0.2 to 2%. Shareholders do not receive an explicit bill for these operating expenses; however, the expenses periodically are deducted from the assets of the fund. These charges reduce the value of the portfolio, so, in effect, shareholders do pay for these expenses.

- **12b-1 charges.** The Securities and Exchange Commission (SEC) allows the managers of so-called 12b-1 funds to use fund assets to pay for distribution costs such as advertising, promotional literature (including annual reports and prospectuses), and most importantly, commissions paid to brokers who sell the fund to investors. These 12b-1 fees are named after the SEC rule that permits use of these plans. Funds may use 12b-1 charges instead of, or in addition to, loads to generate the fees with which to pay brokers. As with operating expenses, investors are not explicitly billed for 12b-1 charges. Instead, the fees are deducted from the assets of the fund. Therefore, 12b-1 fees (if any) must be added to operating expenses to obtain the true annual expense ratio of the fund. The SEC now requires that all funds include in the prospectus a consolidated expense table that summarizes all relevant fees. 12b-1 fees are limited to 1% of a fund's average net assets per year.[1]

A recent innovation in the fee structure of mutual funds is the creation of different "classes" that represent ownership in the same portfolio of securities but impose different combinations of fees. For example, Class A shares typically are sold with front-end loads of 4 to 5%. Class B shares instead impose 12b-1 charges and back-end loads. Because Class B shares pay 12b-1 fees while Class A shares do not, the rate of return on the B shares will be less than that of the A shares despite the fact that they represent holdings in the same portfolio. Class C shares do not impose back-end redemption fees, but they impose 12b-1 fees higher than those in Class B, often as high as 1% annually. Obviously, other classes and combinations of fees can be devised by mutual fund companies. For example, Merrill Lynch introduced Class D shares of some of its funds in 1994, which included front-end loads and 12b-1 charges of 0.25%.

Each investor must choose the best combination of fees. Obviously, no-load no-fee funds distributed directly from the mutual fund are the cheapest alternative, and these will often make the most sense for knowledgeable investors. However, many investors are willing to pay for financial advice, and the commissions paid to advisors who sell these funds are the most common form of payment. Alternatively, investors may choose to hire a fee-only financial manager who charges directly for services and does not accept commissions. These advisors can help investors select portfolios of low- or no-load funds (as well as provide other financial advice). Independent financial planners have become increasingly important distribution channels for funds in recent years.

If you do buy a fund through a broker, the choice between paying a load versus 12b-1 fees will depend primarily on your expected time horizon. Loads are paid only once, while 12b-1 fees are paid annually. Thus, if you plan to hold your fund for a long time, a one-time load may be preferable to recurring 12b-1 charges.

You can identify the various charges of funds by the letters that follow the fund name in the listing of mutual funds in the financial pages. For example, *r* denotes redemption or exit fees; *p* denotes 12b-1 fees; and *t* denotes both redemption and 12b-1 fees. The listings do not allow you to identify funds that involve front-end loads, however; while NAV for each fund is presented, the price at which the fund can be purchased, which may include a load, is not.

Fees and Mutual Fund Returns

The rate of return on an investment in a mutual fund is measured as the increase or decrease in net asset value plus income distributions such as dividends or distributions of capital gains expressed as a fraction of net asset value at the beginning of the investment period. If we denote the net asset value at the start and end of the period as NAV_0 and NAV_1 respectively, then

$$\text{Rate of return} = \frac{NAV_1 - NAV_0 + \text{Income and capital gain distributions}}{NAV_0}$$

For example, if a fund has an initial NAV of $20 at the start of the month, makes income distributions of $.15 and capital gain distributions of $.05, and ends the month with NAV of $20.10, the monthly rate of return is computed as:

$$\text{Rate of return} = \frac{\$20.10 - \$20.00 + \$.15 + \$.05}{\$20.00} = .015, \text{ or } 1.5\%$$

---

[1]The maximum 12b-1 charge for the sale of the fund is 0.75%. However, an additional service fee of 0.25% of the fund's assets also is allowed for personal service and/or maintenance of shareholder accounts.

TABLE 4.2

Impact of Costs on
Investment
Performance

	Cumulative Proceeds (All Dividends Reinvested)		
	Fund A	**Fund B**	**Fund C**
Initial investment*	$10,000	$10,000	$9,200
5 years	17,234	16,474	15,225
10 years	29,699	27,141	25,196
15 years	51,183	44,713	41,698
20 years	88,206	73,662	69,006

*After front-end load, if any.

Notes:

1. Fund A is no load, with 0.5% expense ratio.

2. Fund B is no load, with 1.5% expense ratio.

3. Fund C has an 8% load on purchases and reinvested dividends, with a 1% expense ratio. The dividend yield on the fund is 5%. (Thus, the 8% load on reinvested dividends reduces net returns by .08 × 5% = 0.4%.)

4. Gross return on all funds is 12% per year before expenses.

Notice that this measure of the rate of return ignores any commissions such as front-end loads paid to purchase the fund.

On the other hand, the rate of return is affected by the fund's expenses and 12b-1 fees. This is because such charges are periodically deducted from the portfolio, which reduces net asset value. Thus, the rate of return on the fund equals the gross return on the underlying portfolio minus the total expense ratio.

EXAMPLE 4.1
Rate of Return
for Mutual Funds

Consider a fund with $100 million in assets at the start of the year and with 10 million shares outstanding. The fund invests in a portfolio of stocks that provides no income but that increases in value by 10%. The expense ratio, including 12b-1 fees, is 1%. What is the rate of return for an investor in the fund?

The initial NAV equals $100 million/10 million shares = $10 per share. In the absence of expenses, fund assets would grow to $110 million and NAV would grow to $11 per share, for a 10% rate of return. However, the expense ratio of the fund is 1%. Therefore, $1 million will be deducted from the fund to pay these fees, leaving the portfolio worth only $109 million, and NAV equal to $10.90. The rate of return on the fund is only 9%, which equals the gross return on the underlying portfolio minus the total expense ratio.

Fees can have a big effect on performance. Table 4.2 considers an investor who starts with $10,000 and can choose among three funds that all earn an annual 12% return on investment before fees, but that all have different fee structures. The table shows the cumulative amount in each fund after several investment horizons. Fund A has total operating expenses of 0.5%, no load, and no 12b-1 charges. This might represent a low-cost producer like Vanguard. Fund B has no load but has 1% in management expenses and 0.5% in 12b-1 fees. This level of charges is fairly typical of actively managed equity funds. Finally, Fund C has 1% in management expenses, no 12b-1 charges, but assesses an 8% front-end load on purchases as well as reinvested dividends. We assume the dividend yield on the fund is 5%.

Note the substantial return advantage of low-cost Fund A. Moreover, that differential is greater for longer investment horizons.

Although expenses can have a big impact on net investment performance, it is sometimes difficult for the investor in a mutual fund to measure true expenses accurately. This is because of the common practice of paying for some expenses in *soft dollars*. A portfolio manager earns soft dollar credits with a stockbroker by directing the fund's trades to that broker. Based on those credits, the broker will pay for some of the mutual fund's expenses, such as for databases, computer hardware, or stock-quotation systems. The soft dollar arrangement means that the stockbroker effectively returns part of the trading commission to the fund. The advantage to the mutual fund is that purchases made with soft dollars are not included in the fund's expenses, so the fund can advertise an unrealistically low expense ratio to the public. Although the fund may have paid the broker needlessly high commissions to obtain the soft dollar "rebate," trading costs are not included in the fund's expenses. The impact of the higher trading commission shows up instead in net investment performance. Soft dollar arrangements make it difficult for investors to compare fund expenses and periodically come under attack. The nearby box on page 100 explores some of these issues.

Concept Check

2. The Equity Fund sells Class A shares with a front-end load of 6% and Class B shares with 12b-1 fees of 1.0% annually as well as redemption fees that start at 5% and fall by 1% for each full year the investor holds the portfolio (until the fifth year). Assume the rate of return on the fund portfolio net of operating expenses is 10% annually. What will be the value of a $10,000 investment in Class A and Class B shares if the shares are sold after (a) 1 year, (b) 4 years, (c) 8 years? Which fee structure provides higher net proceeds at the end of each investment horizon?

4.5 TAXATION OF MUTUAL FUND INCOME

Investment returns of mutual funds are granted "pass-through status" under the U.S. tax code, meaning that taxes are paid only by the investor in the mutual fund, not by the fund itself. The income is treated as passed through to the investor as long as the fund meets several requirements, most notably that at least 90% of all income is distributed to shareholders. In addition, the fund must receive less than 30% of its gross income from the sale of securities held for less than three months, and the fund must satisfy some diversification criteria. Actually, the earnings pass-through requirements can be even more stringent than 90%, since to avoid a separate excise tax, a fund must distribute at least 98% of income in the calendar year that it is earned.

A fund's short-term capital gains, long-term capital gains, and dividends are passed through to investors as though the investor earned the income directly. The investor then pays taxes at the appropriate rate, depending upon the type of income as well as the investor's own tax bracket.

The pass through of investment income has one important disadvantage for individual investors. When you manage your own portfolio, you can decide when to realize capital gains and losses on any security; therefore, you can time those realizations to efficiently manage your tax liabilities. When you invest through a mutual fund, however, the timing of the sale of securities from the portfolio is out of your control, which reduces your ability to engage in tax management. Of course, if the mutual fund is held in a tax-sheltered retirement account such as an individual retirement account (IRA) or 401(k) account, these tax management issues are irrelevant.

A fund with a high portfolio turnover rate can be particularly "tax inefficient." **Turnover** is the ratio of the trading activity of a portfolio to the assets of the portfolio. It measures the fraction of the portfolio that is "replaced" each year. For example, a $100 million portfolio with $50 million in sales of some securities with purchases of other securities would have a turnover rate of 50%. High turnover means that capital gains or losses are being realized constantly and, therefore, that the investor cannot time the realizations to manage his or her overall tax obligation.

turnover
The ratio of the trading activity of a portfolio to the assets of the portfolio.

Concept Check

3. An investor's portfolio currently is worth $1 million. During the year, the investor sells 1,000 shares of Microsoft at a price of $80 per share and 2,000 shares of Ford at a price of $40 per share. The proceeds are used to buy 1,600 shares of IBM at $100 per share.
   a. What was the portfolio turnover rate?
   b. If the shares in Microsoft originally were purchased for $70 each and those in Ford were purchased for $35, and if the investor's tax rate on capital gains income is 28%, how much extra will the investor owe on this year's taxes as a result of these transactions?

Use of 'Soft Dollars' Makes a Hard Task for Investors Comparing Fund Costs

Savvy investors have learned that mutual funds with lean expenses can produce better returns. But can you find out what a fund's expenses really are?

Probably not, because fund managers can, and do, hide much of their actual costs by paying for research, computers, stock-quote systems, and even phone calls and newspaper subscriptions with so-called soft dollars instead of cash.

It works like this: Say a fund manager needs a new laptop computer. Instead of buying the laptop and putting it down as a fund expense, the manager pays a slightly higher-than-necessary commission to a stockbroker—hence the term soft dollars—and the broker buys the laptop for him. Or, the fund manager might buy the computer himself and send the bill to the broker. In general, a fund's expenses cover management fees and general operating costs, but not commissions.

The more a fund manager can use soft dollars to pay expenses, the less expensive it appears that it is to run the fund—because soft dollars aren't included in calculating a fund's annual expenses. The consumer reading a prospectus is none the wiser.

RAISING TRADING COSTS
Soft dollars can also result in higher trading costs for the fund. That can occur if a fund group's trading desk improperly steers stock and bond trades to certain soft-dollar brokers despite higher commissions charged by those brokers.

Despite their resemblance to kickbacks, soft dollars are legal in most instances. And they are nothing new. They originated way back when the Securities and Exchange Commission required brokerage firms to charge customers fixed commission rates. Soft dollars became a popular incentive for brokers to offer customers, and when the SEC deregulated commissions in 1975, it allowed the practice to continue.

But that may change. In August the SEC proposed new measures that would bring to light at least a small portion of soft-dollar use. And in September the agency's chairman, Arthur Levitt, denounced soft dollars in a speech, advising fund directors "to stay on top of issues" raised by their use.

The August proposal would require fund managers to include expenses such as custodial fees, printing, and legal fees in calculating a fund's expense ratio, fee table, and current yield. But it wouldn't include such major expenses as research, software, and databases.

CALLS FOR TOUGHER RULES
Some regulators think the proposal should go further. One senior SEC official, who insisted on anonymity, calls the plan a "cowardly" attempt at reform, which would miss about 90% of soft-dollar business. "Funds know expenses are important and they all want to underreport," says the official. For consumers, "it's much more important over the long run to contain expenses than to chase winners," says the official, who estimates that, on average, soft-dollar use adds a hidden 5% to the annual cost of running a fund. And the cost of running a fund comes out of investors' pockets.

The limited disclosure proposed so far by the SEC is supported by many in the fund industry, including its biggest trade group, the Investment Company Institute. "Those who appear to have artificially low expense ratios will no longer be able to compete based on expense ratios that are lower than they should be," says Dan Maclean, general counsel at Dreyfus Mutual Funds in New York.

But the ICI, Dreyfus, and many other fund groups don't want the SEC to force funds to tell how much research or research-related service they buy with soft dollars. It would be too difficult for a fund group to break up its research costs and allocate them to individual funds, they say. Research on a broad topic, such as the direction of interest rates, often influences the investment decisions of several funds in a group.

INFORMING THE INVESTORS
But Harold Bradley, head trader for Twentieth Century Mutual Funds, disagrees. "How will disclosure kill anything that is right and good for the shareholders? Wouldn't they like to know their money is being well-stewarded?" he asks.

Mr. Bradley says the SEC ought to lift the lid so consumers can see where their real dollars are going and what they are getting in return. The Twentieth Century group favors including soft-dollar expenses in calculating a fund's expense ratio and yield. "We're not saying put an end to the practice," says Mr. Bradley. "We're saying, let's put some rules in place."

4.6 MUTUAL FUND INVESTMENT PERFORMANCE: A FIRST LOOK

We noted earlier that one of the benefits of mutual funds for the individual investor is the ability to delegate management of the portfolio to investment professionals. The investor retains control over the broad features of the overall portfolio through the asset allocation decision: Each individual chooses the fraction of the portfolio to invest in bond funds versus equity funds versus money market funds, and so forth, but can leave the specific security selection decisions within each market to the managers of each fund. It is hoped that these portfolio managers can achieve better investment performance than the shareholders could obtain on their own.

What is the investment record of the mutual fund industry? This question seems straightforward, but it is deceptively difficult to answer because we need a standard against which to evaluate performance. For example, we clearly would not want to compare the investment performance of an equity fund to the rate of return available in the money market. The vast differences in the risk of these two markets dictate that year-by-year as well as average performance will differ considerably. We would expect to find that equity funds outperform money market funds (on average) as compensation to investors for the extra risk incurred in equity markets. This is no more than the risk-return trade-off we mentioned in Chapter 1. How then can we determine whether mutual fund portfolio managers are performing up to par *given* the level of risk they incur? In other words, what is the proper benchmark against which investment performance ought to be evaluated?

Measuring portfolio risk properly and using such measures to choose an appropriate benchmark is an extremely difficult task. We devote all of Parts Two and Three of the text to issues surrounding the proper measurement of portfolio risk and the trade-off between risk and return. In this chapter, therefore, we will satisfy ourselves with a first look at the question of fund performance by using only very simple performance benchmarks and ignoring the more subtle issues of risk differences across funds. However, we will return to this topic in Chapter 9, where we take a closer look at mutual fund performance after controlling for differences in the exposures of portfolios to various sources of risk.

Here, we will use as a benchmark for the performance of equity fund managers the rate of return on the Wilshire 5000 index. Recall from Chapter 2 that this is a value-weighted index of about 7,000 stocks that trade on the NYSE, Nasdaq, and Amex stock markets. It is the most inclusive index of the performance of U.S. equities. The performance of the Wilshire 5000 is a useful benchmark with which to evaluate professional managers because it corresponds to a simple passive investment strategy: Buy all the shares in the index in proportion to their outstanding market value.[2] Moreover, this is a feasible strategy for even small investors, because the Vanguard Group offers an index fund (its Total Stock Market Portfolio) designed to replicate the performance of the Wilshire 5000 index. The expense ratio of the fund is extremely small by the standards of other equity funds, only 0.25% per year. Using the Wilshire 5000 index as a benchmark, we may pose the problem of evaluating the performance of mutual fund portfolio managers this way: How does the typical performance of actively managed equity mutual funds compare to the performance of a passively managed portfolio that simply replicates the composition of a broad index of the stock market?

By using the Wilshire 5000 as a benchmark, we compare apples with apples: We use a well-diversified equity index to evaluate the performance of managers of diversified equity

---

[2]Recall from Chapter 1, Section 1.5, that active managers attempt to predict which securities will be the best performers. Passive managers follow a simpler and lower cost strategy of buying a well-diversified portfolio usually indexed to some index of the broad market. They do not expend resources in an attempt to beat the market. The question for investors choosing between actively versus passively managed funds is whether the resources expended by active managers improve performance enough to pay for the extra costs associated with such management.

FIGURE 4.3

Percent of Equity
Mutual Funds
Outperformed by
Wilshire 5000 Index

Source: The Vanguard Group.

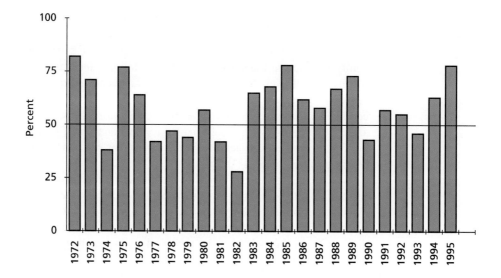

FIGURE 4.4

Growth of $1 Invested
in Wilshire 5000 Index
versus Average General
Equity Fund

Source: The Vanguard Group.

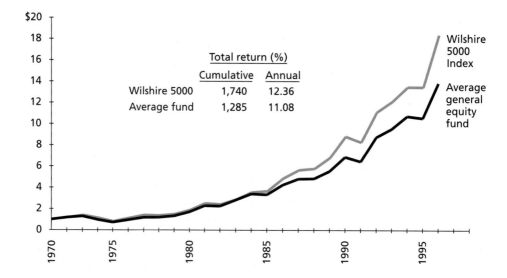

funds. Nevertheless, as noted earlier, this is only an imperfect comparison, as the risk of the Wilshire 5000 portfolio need not be comparable to that of any particular fund.

Casual comparisons of the performance of the Wilshire 5000 index versus that of professionally managed mutual fund portfolios show disappointing results for most fund managers. Figure 4.3 shows the percent of mutual fund managers whose performance was inferior in each year to the Wilshire 5000. In more years than not, the index has outperformed the median manager. Figure 4.4 shows the cumulative return since 1971 of the Wilshire 5000 compared to the Lipper General Equity Fund Average. The annualized return of the Wilshire 5000 was 12.36% versus 11.08% for the average fund. The 1.28% margin is substantial.

To some extent, however, this comparison is unfair. Real funds incur expenses that reduce the rate of return of the portfolio, as well as trading costs such as commissions and bid-ask spreads that also reduce returns. John Bogle, former chairman of the Vanguard Group, has estimated that operating expenses reduce the return of typical managed portfolios by about 1% and that transaction fees associated with trading reduce returns by an additional 0.7%. In

TABLE 4.3
Consistency of
Investment Results

Sources: Panel A: William N. Goetzmann and Roger G. Ibbotson, "Do Winners Repeat?" *Journal of Portfolio Management*, Winter 1994, pp. 9–18. Panels B and C: Burton G. Malkiel, "Returns from Investing in Equity Mutual Funds, 1971–1991," *Journal of Finance* 50 (June 1995), pp. 549–572.

A. Goetzmann and Ibbotson Study

Initial Period Performance	Successive Period Performance	
	Top Half	Bottom Half
Top half	62.0%	38.0%
Bottom half	36.6%	63.4%

B. Malkiel Study, 1970s

Initial Period Performance	Successive Period Performance	
	Top Half	Bottom Half
Top half	65.1%	34.9%
Bottom half	35.5%	64.5%

C. Malkiel Study, 1980s

Initial Period Performance	Successive Period Performance	
	Top Half	Bottom Half
Top half	51.7%	48.3%
Bottom half	47.5%	52.5%

contrast, the return to the Wilshire index is calculated as though investors can costlessly buy or sell the index with reinvested dividends.

These considerations suggest that a better benchmark for the performance of actively managed funds is the performance of index funds, rather than the performance of the indexes themselves. Vanguard's Wilshire 5000 fund was established only recently, and so it has a short track record. However, because it is passively managed, its expense ratio is quite low, about 0.25%, and because index funds need to engage in very little trading, its turnover rate also is extremely low, about 3% per year. If we reduce the rate of return on the index by about 0.30%, we ought to obtain a good estimate of the rate of return achievable by a low-cost indexed portfolio. This procedure reduces the average margin of superiority of the index strategy over the average mutual fund from 1.28% to 0.98% and still suggests that, over the past two decades, passively managed (indexed) equity funds would have outperformed the typical actively managed fund.

This result may seem surprising to you. After all, it is not unreasonable to expect that professional money managers should be able to outperform a very simple rule such as "hold an indexed portfolio." As it turns out, however, there may be good reasons to expect such a result. We will explore these reasons in detail in Chapter 9, "The Efficient Market Hypothesis."

Of course, one might argue that there are good managers and bad managers, and that the good managers can, in fact, consistently outperform the index. To test this notion, we examine whether managers with good performance in one year are likely to repeat that performance in a following year. In other words, is superior performance in any particular year due to luck, and therefore random, or is it due to skill, and therefore persistent?

In a recent study, Goetzmann and Ibbotson (1994) examined the performance of a large sample of equity mutual fund portfolios over the 1976–1985 period. Dividing the funds into two groups based on total investment return for different subperiods, they posed the question: "Do funds with investment returns in the top half of the sample in one two-year period continue to perform well in the subsequent two-year period?"

Panel A of Table 4.3 presents a summary of their results. The table shows the fraction of "winners" (i.e., top-half performers) in the initial period that turn out to be winners or losers in the following two-year period. If performance were purely random from one period to the next, there would be entries of 50% in each cell of the table, as top- or bottom-half performers would be equally likely to perform in either the top or bottom half of the sample in the following period. On the other hand, if performance were due entirely to skill, with no randomness, we would expect to see entries of 100% on the diagonals and entries of 0% on the off-diagonals: All top-half performers would remain in the top half while all bottom-half performers would remain in the bottom half. In fact, the table shows that 62% of initial top-half performers fall in the top half of the sample in the following period, while 63.4% of initial bottom-half performers fall in the bottom half in the following period. This evidence is consistent with the notion that at least part of a fund's performance is a function of skill as opposed to luck, so that relative performance tends to persist from one period to the next.

On the other hand, this relationship does not seem stable across different sample periods. Malkiel (1995) uses a larger sample but a similar methodology (except that he uses one-year instead of two-year investment returns) to examine performance consistency. He finds that while initial year performance predicts subsequent year performance in the 1970s (see Table 4.3, Panel B), the pattern of persistence in performance virtually disappears in the 1980s (Panel C).

To summarize, the evidence that performance is consistent from one period to the next is suggestive, but inconclusive. In the 1970s, top-half funds in one year were twice as likely in the following year to be in the top half rather than the bottom half of funds. In the 1980s, the odds that a top-half fund would fall in the top half in the following year were essentially equivalent to those of a coin flip.

Other studies suggest that bad performance is more likely to persist than good performance. This makes some sense: It is easy to identify fund characteristics that will predictably lead to consistently poor investment performance, notably high expense ratios and high turnover ratios with associated trading costs. It is far harder to identify the secrets of successful stock picking. (If it were easy, we all would be rich!) Thus, the consistency we do observe in fund performance may be due in large part to the poor performers. This suggests that the real value of past performance data is the ability it gives to avoid truly poor funds, even if identifying the future top performers is still a daunting task.

Concept Check

4. Suppose you observe the investment performance of 200 portfolio managers and rank them by investment returns during the year. Of the managers in the top half of the sample, 40% are truly skilled, but the other 60% fall in the top half purely because of good luck. What fraction of these top-half managers would you expect to be top-half performers next year?

4.7 INFORMATION ON MUTUAL FUNDS

The first place to find information on a mutual fund is in its prospectus. The Securities and Exchange Commission (SEC) requires that the prospectus describe the fund's investment objectives and policies in a concise "Statement of Investment Objectives" as well as in lengthy discussions of investment policies and risks. The fund's investment advisor and its portfolio manager also are described therein. The prospectus also presents the costs associated with purchasing shares in the fund in a fee table that details sales charges, such as front-end and back-end loads, as well as annual operating expenses, such as management fees and 12b-1 fees.

Despite this useful information, there is widespread agreement that most prospectuses are difficult to read and laden with legalese. Several mutual fund complexes currently are experimenting with a simplified, plain-English pamphlet that can be distributed with the formal prospectus. The pamphlets present fees and expenses very clearly and use simple bar charts to present historical returns. It is expected that these simplified profiles, or some variant of them, will be made mandatory in the near future.

Funds provide information about themselves in two other sources. The "Statement of Additional Information," also known as Part B of the prospectus, includes a list of the securities in the portfolio at the end of the fiscal year, audited financial statements, and a list of the directors and officers of the fund. The fund's annual report, which generally is issued semiannually, also includes portfolio composition and financial statements, as well as a discussion of the factors that influenced fund performance over the last reporting period.

With over 7,000 mutual funds to choose from, it can be difficult to find and select the fund that is best suited for a particular need. Several publications now offer "encyclopedias" of mutual fund information to help in the search process. Two prominent sources are Wiesenberger's *Investment Companies* and Morningstar's *Mutual Fund Sourcebook*. The Investment Company Institute, the national association of mutual funds, closed-end funds, and unit investment trusts, also publishes an annual *Directory of Mutual Funds* that includes information on fees as well as phone numbers to contact funds. To illustrate the range of information available about funds, we will consider Morningstar's report on Vanguard's Windsor Fund, reproduced in Figure 4.5.

Some of Morningstar's analysis is qualitative. The box on the top left-hand side of the page provides a short description of the fund, in particular the types of securities in which the fund tends to invest and a short biography of the current portfolio manager. The box on the bottom left ("Analysis") is a more detailed discussion of the fund's income strategy. The short statement of the fund's investment policy is in the top right-hand corner: Windsor is a growth and income equity fund.

The table on the left-hand side of the page labeled "Performance" reports on the fund's returns over the last few years and over longer periods up to 15 years. Comparisons of returns to relevant indexes, in this case the S&P 500 and the Wilshire 5000 indexes, are provided to serve as a benchmark in evaluating the performance of the fund. (Morningstar uses the Lehman Brothers Aggregate Bond Index as the benchmark for fixed-income funds.) The values under this column give the performance of the fund relative to the index. For example, Windsor's return was 4.07% below the S&P 500 over the last three months, but 1.17% per year better than the S&P over the past 15 years. The returns reported for the fund are calculated net of expenses, 12b-1 fees, and any other fees automatically deducted from fund assets, but they do not account for any sales charges such as front-end loads or redemption charges. Next appear the percentile ranks of the fund compared to all other funds (see the column headed by "All") and to all funds with the same investment objective (see the column headed by "Obj"). A rank of 1 means the fund is a top performer. A rank of 80 would mean that it was beaten by 80% of the funds in the comparison group. You can see from the table that Windsor has had a very poor year compared to other growth and income funds, but that its longer-term performance, for example over the past five years, has been excellent—better than all but 17% of the funds in the growth and income category. Finally, growth of $10,000 invested in the fund over various periods ranging from the past three months to the past 15 years is given in the last column.

More data on the performance of the fund are provided in the graph at the top of the figure. The graph shows how $10,000 invested in 1985 in either Windsor (dotted line) or the S&P 500 (solid line) with all dividends reinvested would have grown through 1996. Below the graph is a box for each year that depicts the relative performance of the fund for that year. The shaded area on the graph shows the quartile in which the fund's performance falls relative to other funds with the same objective. If the shaded band is at the top of the box, the firm was a top quartile performer in that period, and so on.

The table below and to the right of the graph presents historical data on characteristics of the fund. These data include return; return relative to appropriate benchmark indexes, such as the S&P 500; the component of returns due to income (dividends) or capital gains; the percentile rank of the fund compared to all funds and funds in its objective class (where again, 1% is the best performer, and 99% would mean that the fund was outperformed by 99% of its comparison group); the expense ratio; and the turnover rate of the portfolio.

FIGURE 4.5   Morningstar Report

Vanguard/Windsor

	Ticker	Load	NAV	Yield	SEC Yield	Assets	Objective
	VWNDX	Closed	$14.92	2.8%	2.79%	$13997.0 mil	Growth/Inc.

Vanguard/Windsor Fund seeks long-term growth of capital and income; current income is a secondary consideration.

The fund invests primarily in common stocks. Management typically selects securities that it believes have relatively low P/E ratios and meaningful income yields. The fund may also invest in preferred stocks, fixed-income securities, convertible securities, and money-market instruments.

On April 17, 1991, Vanguard High-Yield Stock Fund merged into this fund. Prior to May 17, 1993, the fund was named Windsor Fund.

Portfolio Manager(s)

Charles Freeman. Since 12-95. BS'66 U. of Pennsylvania; MBA'69 Wharton School of Finance. Freeman is partner and senior vice president with Wellington Management Co., his employer since 1969. Previously, he was a senior accountant with Peat Marwick & Mitchell from 1966 to 1968. Prior to becoming manager of Vanguard/Windsor, he served as an assistant on the fund for 26 years.

Performance 02-29-96

	1st Qtr	2nd Qtr	3rd Qtr	4th Qtr	Total
1991	18.25	0.74	5.59	2.20	28.55
1992	4.27	5.55	-2.62	8.70	16.50
1993	8.87	1.40	7.36	0.72	19.37
1994	-1.80	3.79	1.14	-3.15	-0.15
1995	8.50	11.35	7.93	-0.19	30.15

Trailing	Total Return %	+/- S&P500	+/- Wil 5000	% Rank All	Obj	Growth of $10,000
3 Mo	2.30	-4.07	-3.88	49	98	10,230
6 Mo	3.07	-12.24	-10.68	89	99	10,307
1 Yr	24.91	-9.76	-9.29	29	90	12,491
3 Yr Avg	14.27	-1.85	-1.70	23	51	14,921
5 Yr Avg	15.51	0.52	0.05	15	17	20,561
10 Yr Avg	12.87	-1.61	-0.88	23	35	33,552
15 Yr Avg	16.48	1.17	1.78	6	6	98,549

Most Similar Funds in MMF

Davis NY Venture A	Fair Fit
Fidelity Select Financial Services	Weak Fit
John Hancock Growth & Income A	Weak Fit

Tax Analysis

	Tax-Adj Return %	% Pretax Return
3 Yr Avg	10.63	74.5
5 Yr Avg	12.03	77.6
10 Yr Avg	8.70	67.6
Potential Capital Gain Exposure		14% of assets

Analysis by Paul Reis 03-15-96

Vanguard/Windsor Fund has passed the torch.

Legendary value investor John Neff retired from this fund as of the new year, ending his 31-year reign. His successor, Charles Freeman, is hardly a newcomer to the fund, though. He served a quarter-century apprenticeship under Neff, and is therefore uniquely qualified to continue the fund's scrappy, contrarian approach to investing.

Freeman inherits a portfolio that is vintage Neff. As usual, the fund's price/earnings and price/book ratios are among the lowest in the growth-and-income group. These multiples show management's unadulterated commitment to Graham-and-Dodd-style value investing, an approach Freeman will carry on.

The fund's concentrated sector weightings are also par for the course. Neff described these as "neck out" positions in a recent shareholder report, and Freeman seems willing to take similar risks. Recently, for example, Freeman has added to the fund's

aluminum and chemical holdings, industries that investors fled because of recessionary fears. With these additions, economically sensitive stocks, such as industrial cyclicals and consumer durables, claim more than 46.5% of holdings. If a recession should develop, this fund could take it on the chin.

Of course, the fund has taken some bad hits in the past and gone on to prosper. In 1990, Neff's collection of cyclical and financial stocks imploded, and the fund posted an ugly 15.5% loss. Neff stuck by his style and his picks, however, and enjoyed strong returns in 1992 and 1993. Over the long-term, the fund has posted some of the best returns in its group, even if its risk scores are a tad high by staid growth-and-income standards.

Neff's willingness to ride out rough times was as much a matter of character as investment style. Freeman clearly shares the same style. Investors will now want to see if he shares the same insight, tenacity, and grit.

Address	Vanguard Financial Ctr. P.O. Box 2600 Valley Forge, PA 19482
Telephone	800-662-7447 / 610-669-1000.
Advisor	Wellington Management
Subadvisor	None
Distributor	Vanguard Group
States Available	All plus PR,VI,GU
Report Grade	B
Income Distrib	Semiannually

Minimum Purchase	Closed	Add: $100	IRA: ---
Min Auto Inv Plan	Closed	Systematic Inv: $50	
Date of Inception	10-23-58		

Expenses & Fees

Sales Fees	No-load
Management Fee	0.35% max./0.15% min.+(-)0.10%P
Actual Fees	Mgt: 0.24% Dist: ---
Expense Projections	3Yr: $14 5Yr: $25 10Yr: $57
Annual Brokerage Cost	0.08%

Historical Profile

Return	Average
Risk	Average
Rating	★★★ Neutral

83%	87%	73%	77%	78%	87%	85%	80%

Investment Style History
Equity
Average Stock %

Growth of $10,000
- Investment Value ($000) of Fund
- Investment Value ($000) S&P 500
- ▼ Manager Change
- ▽ Partial Manager Change
- ► Mgr Unknown After
- ◄ Mgr Unknown Before

Performance Quartile (Within Objective)

History

	1985	1986	1987	1988	1989	1990	1991	1992	1993	1994	1995	02-96	History
	14.50	13.95	11.11	13.07	13.41	10.30	11.72	12.74	13.91	12.59	14.53	14.92	NAV
	28.03	20.27	1.23	28.70	15.03	-15.50	28.55	16.50	19.37	-0.15	30.15		Total Return %
	-3.71	1.60	-4.03	12.09	-16.66	-12.38	-1.93	8.88	9.31	-1.46	-7.39	-1.68	+/- S&P 500
	-4.54	4.18	-1.14	10.76	-14.15	-9.32	-5.66	7.53	8.09	-0.08	-6.30	-1.79	+/- Wilshire 5000
	6.49	5.94	6.77	5.62	5.71	5.79	5.34	4.27	2.84	3.28	3.30	0.00	Income Return %
	21.54	14.33	-5.54	23.07	9.31	-21.29	23.21	12.23	16.53	-3.43	26.84	2.68	Capital Return %
	34	19	49	4	47	93	30	8	18	22	19	36	Total Rtn %Rank All
	45	20	57	4	87	96	49	6	8	46	69	89	Total Rtn %Rank Obj
	0.79	0.85	0.87	0.63	0.75	0.74	0.57	0.49	0.37	0.44	0.46	0.00	Income $
	0.74	2.59	2.21	0.55	0.85	0.32	0.84	0.38	0.89	0.86	1.38	0.00	Capital Gains $
	0.53	0.52	0.43	0.46	0.41	0.37	0.30	0.26	0.40	0.45	0.43	---	Expense Ratio %
	6.19	5.28	4.86	5.08	5.07	5.82	4.84	3.89	2.68	3.11	3.01	---	Income Ratio %
	23	51	46	24	34	21	36	32	25	34	32	---	Turnover Rate %
	3814.3	4893.8	4565.2	5826.1	8062.6	6523.8	7822.3	8832.6	10610.8	10672.9	13646.3	13997.0	Net Assets ($mil)

Risk Analysis

Time Period	Load-Adj Return %	Risk %Rank[1] All	Obj	Mstar Score Return	Risk	Morningstar Risk-Adj Rating
1 Yr	24.91					
3 Yr	14.27	76	87	1.02	0.86	★★★
5 Yr	15.51	73	81	1.24	0.81	★★★★
10 Yr	12.87	74	92	1.09	0.94	★★★
Average Historical Rating (123 months)					4.2	★s

[1]1=low, 100=high

Other Measures		Standard Index S&P 500	Best Fit Index S&P 500
Standard Deviation	9.88	Alpha	-1.2	-1.2
Mean	13.90	Beta	0.98	0.98
Sharpe Ratio	0.97	R-Squared	66	66

Portfolio Analysis 12-31-95

Share Chg (10-95) 000	Amount 000	Total Stocks: 89 Total Fixed-Income: 0	Value $000	% Net Assets
0	14785	Chrysler	818730	6.00
150	23617	Ford Motor	684899	5.02
0	9551	Citicorp	642318	4.71
1599	9010	Georgia-Pacific	618277	4.53
-143	4447	Atlantic Richfield	492505	3.61
0	12455	Burlington Resources	488859	3.58
0	24027	USX-Marathon Group	468530	3.43
0	6178	Reynolds Metals	349818	2.56
509	6940	Union Camp	330518	2.42
-74	5764	Golden West Financial	318450	2.33
-2350	5080	First Union	282553	2.07
-548	3792	NationsBank	263997	1.93
-1411	10243	Great Western Financial	261189	1.91
5700	5700	Champion International	239400	1.75
-1254	8516	HF Ahmanson	225683	1.65
-380	2146	CIGNA	221605	1.62
-600	3189	BankAmerica	206491	1.51
0	3542	ALCOA	187299	1.37
0	7375	Lyondell Petrochemical	168703	1.24
-2774	3996	Allstate	164340	1.20
0	10881	Bethlehem Steel	152328	1.12
-1119	4139	KeyCorp	150054	1.10
1500	9010	Advanced Micro Devices	148672	1.09
-520	3190	Owens-Corning	143133	1.05
0	3310	Pennzoil	139826	1.02

Investment Style

Style: Value Blend Growth
Size: Large Med Small

	Stock Portfolio Avg	Rel S&P 500	Rel Objective
Price/Earnings Ratio	12.3	0.56	0.59
Price/Book Ratio	2.1	0.46	0.52
5 Yr Earnings Gr %	12.1	0.99	1.02
Return on Assets %	5.0	0.61	0.67
Debt % Total Cap	48.6	1.56	1.50
Med Mkt Cap ($mil)	5317	0.28	0.46

Special Securities % of assets 10-31-95

○ Private/Illiquid Securities	0
○ Structured Notes	0
○ Emerging-Markets Secs	0
○ Options/Futures/Warrants	No

Composition % of assets 12-31-95

		Index Allocation % of stocks	
Cash	20.0	S&P 500	84.0
Stocks	80.0	S&P Mid	6.1
Bonds	0.0	US Sm Cap	7.9
Other	0.0	Foreign	2.0

Sector Weightings

	% of Stocks	Rel S&P
Utilities	0.9	0.08
Energy	19.7	2.17
Financials	27.2	2.05
Industrial Cyclicals	31.7	1.87
Consumer Durables	14.8	3.60
Consumer Staples	0.0	0.00
Services	1.1	0.11
Retail	0.3	0.06
Health	0.5	0.04
Technology	3.8	0.42

MORNINGSTAR   Mutual Funds   603

Below this table of historical data is a table entitled "Portfolio Analysis" that presents the 25 largest holdings of the portfolio and the change in the holding of each of these securities over the past quarter. Investors thus can get a quick look at the manager's biggest bets.

Below the portfolio analysis table is a box labeled "Investment Style." In this box, Morningstar evaluates style along two dimensions: One dimension is the size of the firms held in the portfolio, as measured by the market value of outstanding equity; the other dimension is a value/growth continuum. Morningstar defines *value stocks* as those with low ratios of market price per share to earnings per share or book value per share. These are called value stocks because they have a low price relative to these two measures of value. In contrast, *growth stocks* have high ratios, suggesting that investors in these firms must believe that the firm will experience high rapid growth to justify the prices at which the stocks sell. The shaded box for Windsor shows that the portfolio tends to hold larger firms (top row) and value stocks (left column). A year-by-year history of Windsor's investment style is presented in the sequence of such boxes at the top of the figure.

The table in the center of the figure, labeled "Risk Analysis," is one of the more complicated but interesting facets of Morningstar's analysis. The column labeled "Load-Adj Return" rates a fund's return compared to other funds with the same investment policy. Returns for periods ranging from 1 to 10 years are calculated with all loads and redemption fees applicable to that investment period subtracted from total income. The return is then divided by the average return for the comparison group of funds to obtain the "Morningstar Return"; therefore, a value of 1.0 in the column "MStar Return" would indicate average performance while a value of 1.10 would indicate returns 10% above the average for the comparison group (e.g., 11% return for the fund versus 10% for the comparison group).

The risk measure indicates the portfolio's exposure to poor performance, that is, the "downside risk" of the fund. Morningstar focuses on periods in which the fund's return is less than that of risk-free T-bills. The total underperformance compared to T-bills in those months with poor portfolio performance divided by total months sampled is the measure of downside risk. This measure also is scaled by dividing by the average downside risk measure for all firms with the same investment objective. Therefore, the average value in the "MStar Risk" column is 1.0.

The two columns to the left of the Morningstar risk and return columns are the percentile scores of risk and return for each fund. The risk-adjusted rating, ranging from 1 to 5 stars, is based on the Morningstar return score minus the risk score.

The "Tax Analysis" table on the left-hand side of the figure provides some evidence on the tax efficiency of the fund, by comparing pretax and after-tax returns. The after-tax return, given in the first column, is computed based on the dividends paid to the portfolio as well as realized capital gains, assuming the investor is in the maximum tax bracket at the time of the distribution. State and local taxes are ignored. The "tax efficiency" of the fund is defined as the ratio of after-tax to pretax returns, and it is presented in the second column, labeled "% Pretax Return." Tax efficiency will be lower when turnover is higher because capital gains are taxed as they are realized.

At the bottom of the figure, Morningstar provides information on the expenses and loads associated with investments in the fund, as well as information on the fund's investment advisor. Thus, Morningstar provides a considerable amount of the information you would need to decide among several competing funds. Still, as the nearby box on page 108 suggests, choosing a fund involves fairly sophisticated analysis. The box provides some reasonable pointers for investors confronting this decision.

If You're Betting on Managed Funds, Here Are Tips to Pick the Right Pony

Hope springs eternal.

Folks keep buying lottery tickets. They keep stuffing quarters into slot machines. And yes, they keep buying actively managed stock funds.

The grim truth, however, is that most actively managed funds fail to beat the market. That is why I am such a big fan of index funds, which simply purchase the stocks in an index in an effort to match the index's performance.

But there is an undeniable allure to buying actively managed stock funds. If you're going to engage in this dubious endeavor, how can you stack the odds in your favor? Here are some pointers from the pros:

GO LONG

Mutual fund analysts do just what the rest of us do. They start by looking for managers with long and venerable track records, preferably extending back 10 or 15 years. "You want people who have created happiness for long periods, and you hope the experience will continue," says Michael Stolper, publisher of Mutual Fund Monthly, a San Diego newsletter.

INVEST IN STYLE

But while an impressive record is nice, it is only a starting point. Analysts also want some sense that the record is repeatable. They look for consistency of performance and ignore those whose long-term record is built on one or two years of outsized returns.

Analysts also tend to be leery of market-timing and sector-rotating managers, who aim to bail out of stocks at the right time or astutely switch among stock market sectors. How come? These managers may have built their entire record on just four or five good calls, so it is difficult to know if they are tremendously skillful, or very lucky. Instead, analysts favor managers with a stellar history of careful stock selection, because such a record typically involves making the right decision on hundreds of different securities.

For instance, you might try to find the best stock-pickers in six fund categories: large-company value, small-company value, large-company growth, small-company growth, de-veloped foreign markets, and emerging markets. Value funds look for stocks that are cheap based on market yardsticks such as dividends and earnings, while growth funds hunt for companies with rapid revenue and profit growth.

The trouble is, how do you know if a manager really has stuck to his discipline? My suggestion: See if your local library carries Morningstar Mutual Funds. This newsletter gives detailed information on 1,500 funds, including historical style boxes, which provide a year-by-year look at whether a fund held, say, large-company value stocks or midsize growth stocks. If a fund consistently falls in or near a particular style box, it is a sign that the fund has stuck to its knitting.

THINK SMALL

If you identify a manager who has put together a sparkling record by mining a single part of the stock market, you are unlikely to be alone in this discovery. "The great managers attract money really quickly," says Kenneth Gregory, editor of the No-Load Fund Analyst, a San Francisco newsletter. "It's a real dilemma."

He says there are still a few highly regarded managers who haven't been inundated with money. But these are the exception. What to do? Be prepared to compromise, by buying smaller funds with shorter track records, and don't ignore new offerings.

PINCH PENNIES

The more a fund charges, the tougher it is for the manager to beat the market, so pay careful attention to cost.

Don Phillips, president of Morningstar Inc., which publishes Morningstar Mutual Funds, advises sticking with funds that charge annual expenses of less than 1%, and certainly not more than 1.5%. "And that's especially the case if you're retaining an investment advisor, who is charging a fee on top of that," Mr. Phillips says.

Source: Jonathan Clements, "If You're Betting on Managed Funds, Here Are Tips to Pick the Right Pony," *The Wall Street Journal*, July 2, 1996.

Summary

- Unit investment trusts, closed-end management companies, and open-end management companies are all classified and regulated as investment companies. Unit investment trusts essentially are unmanaged in the sense that the portfolio, once established, is fixed. Managed investment companies, in contrast, may change the composition of the portfolio as deemed fit by the portfolio manager. Closed-end funds are traded like other securities; they do not redeem shares for their investors. Open-end funds will redeem shares for net asset value at the request of the investor.

- Net asset value equals the market value of assets held by a fund minus the liabilities of the fund divided by the shares outstanding.
- Mutual funds free the individual from many of the administrative burdens of owning individual securities and offer professional management of the portfolio. They also offer advantages that are available only to large-scale investors, such as lower trading costs. On the other hand, funds are assessed management fees and incur other expenses, which reduce the investor's rate of return. They also remove some of the control over the timing of capital gains realizations from the investor.
- Mutual funds often are categorized by investment policy. Major policy groups include: money market funds; equity funds, which are further grouped according to emphasis on income versus growth; fixed-income funds; balanced and income funds; asset allocation funds; index funds; and specialized sector funds.
- Costs of investing in mutual funds include front-end loads, which are sales commissions; back-end loads, which are redemption fees; fund operating expenses; and 12b-1 charges, which are recurring fees used to pay for the expenses of marketing the fund to the public.
- Income earned on mutual fund portfolios is not taxed at the level of the fund. Instead, as long as the fund meets certain requirements for pass-through status, the income is treated as being earned by the investors in the fund.
- The average rate of return of the average equity mutual fund in the last 25 years has been below that of a passive index fund holding a portfolio that replicates a broad-based index like the S&P 500 or the Wilshire 5000. Some of the reasons for this disappointing record are the costs incurred by actively managed funds: the expense of conducting the research to guide stock-picking activities and trading costs due to higher portfolio turnover. The record on the consistency of fund performance is mixed. In some sample periods, the better-performing funds continue to perform well in the following periods; in other sample periods, they do not.

Key Terms

commingled funds, *92*
discretionary closed-end funds, *92*
interval closed-end funds, *92*

investment companies, *89*
load, *92*
net asset value (NAV), *89*

real estate investment trust (REIT), *92*
turnover, *99*

Problem Sets

1. Would you expect a typical open-end fixed-income mutual fund to have higher or lower operating expenses than a fixed-income unit investment trust? Why?

2. An open-end fund has a net asset value of $10.70 per share. It is sold with a front-end load of 6%. What is the offer price?

3. If the offer price of an open-end fund is $12.30 per share and the fund is sold with a front-end load of 5%, what is its net asset value?

4. The composition of the Fingroup Fund portfolio is as follows:

Stock	Shares	Price
A	200,000	$35
B	300,000	40
C	400,000	20
D	600,000	25

The fund has not borrowed any funds, but its accrued management fee with the portfolio manager currently totals $30,000. There are 4 million shares outstanding. What is the net asset value of the fund?

5. Reconsider the Fingroup Fund in problem 4. If during the year the portfolio manager sells all of the holdings of Stock D and replaces it with 200,000 shares of Stock E at

$50 per share and 200,000 shares of Stock F at $25 per share, what is the portfolio turnover rate?

6. The Closed Fund is a closed-end investment company with a portfolio currently worth $200 million. It has liabilities of $3 million and 5 million shares outstanding.
   a. What is the NAV of the fund?
   b. If the fund sells for $36 per share, what is the percentage premium or discount that will appear in the listings in the financial pages?

7. Corporate Fund started the year with a net asset value of $12.50. By year end, its NAV equaled $12.10. The fund paid year-end distributions of income and capital gains of $1.50. What was the rate of return to an investor in the fund?

8. A closed-end fund starts the year with a net asset value of $12.00. By year end, its NAV equals $12.10. At the beginning of the year, the fund is selling at a 2% premium to NAV. By the end of the year, the fund is selling at a 7% discount to NAV. The fund pays year-end distributions of income and capital gains of $1.50.
   a. What is the rate of return to an investor in the fund during the year?
   b. What would have been the rate of return to an investor who held the same securities as the fund manager during the year?

9. What are some comparative advantages of investing your assets in the following choices?
   a. Unit investment trusts.
   b. Open-end mutual funds.
   c. Individual stocks and bonds that you choose for yourself.

10. Open-end equity mutual funds find it necessary to keep a significant fraction of total investments, typically around 5% of the portfolio, in very liquid money-market assets. Closed-end funds do not have to maintain such a position in "cash-equivalent" securities. What difference between open-end and closed-end funds might account for their differing policies?

11. Both balanced funds and asset allocation funds invest in both the stock and bond markets. What is the difference between these types of funds?

12. a. Impressive Fund had excellent investment performance last year, with portfolio returns that placed it in the top 10% of all funds with the same investment policy. Do you expect it to be a top performer next year? Why or why not?
    b. Suppose instead that Impressive Fund was among the poorest performers in its comparison group. Would you be more or less likely to believe its relative performance will persist into the following year. Why?

13. Consider a mutual fund with $200 million in assets at the start of the year and 10 million shares outstanding. The fund invests in a portfolio of stocks that provides dividend income at the end of the year of $2 million. The stocks included in the fund's portfolio increase in price by 8%, but no securities are sold, and there are no capital gains distributions. The fund charges 12b-1 fees of 1%, which are deducted from portfolio assets at year-end. What is the fund's net asset value at the start and end of the year? What is the rate of return for an investor in the fund?

14. The Investments Fund sells Class A shares with a front-end load of 6% and Class B shares with 12b-1 fees of 0.5% annually as well as redemption fees that start at 5% and fall by 1% for each full year the investor holds the portfolio (until the fifth year). Assume the portfolio rate of return net of operating expenses is 10% annually. If you plan to sell the fund after four years, are Class A or Class B shares the better choice for you? What if you plan to sell after 15 years?

15. Suppose you observe the investment performance of 350 portfolio managers for five years and rank them by investment returns during each year. After five years, you find

that 11 of the funds have investment returns that place the fund in the top half of the sample in each and every year of your sample. Such consistency of performance indicates to you that these must be the funds whose managers are in fact skilled, and you invest your money in these funds. Is your conclusion warranted?

16. You are considering an investment in a mutual fund with a 4% load and an expense ratio of 0.5%. An alternative investment is a bank CD paying 6% interest.
    a. If you plan to invest for two years, what annual rate of return must the fund portfolio earn for you to be better off in the fund than in the CD? Use annual compounding.
    b. How does your answer change if you plan to invest for six years? Why does your answer change?
    c. Now suppose that instead of a front-end load the fund assesses a 12b-1 fee of 0.75% per year. What annual rate of return must the fund portfolio earn for you to be better off in the fund than in the CD? Does your answer in this case depend on your time horizon?

17. Suppose that every time a fund manager trades stock, transaction costs such as commissions and bid-ask spreads amount to 0.4% of the value of the trade. If the portfolio turnover rate is 50%, by how much is the total return of the portfolio reduced by trading costs?

18. You expect a tax-free municipal bond portfolio to provide a rate of return of 4%. Management fees of the fund are 0.6%. What fraction of portfolio income is given up to fees? If management fees for an equity fund also are 0.6%, but you expect a portfolio return of 12%, what fraction of portfolio income is given up to fees? Why might management fees be a bigger factor in your investment decision for bond funds than for stock funds? Can your conclusion help explain why unmanaged unit investment trusts tend to focus on the fixed-income market?

Solutions to Concept Checks

1. $NAV = \dfrac{\$17,442,229,000 - \$70,394,000}{301,573,850} = \$57.60$

2. The net investment in the Class A shares after the 6% commission is $9,400. If the fund earns a 10% return, the investment will grow after n years to $\$9,400 \times (1.10)^n$. The Class B shares have no front-end load. However, the net return to the investor after 12b-1 fees will be only 9%. In addition, there is a back-end load that reduces the sales proceeds by a percentage equal to (5 − Years until sale) until the fifth year, when the back-end load expires.

Horizon, n	Class A Shares $\$9,400 \times (1.10)^n$	Class B Shares $\$10,000 \times (1.09)^n \times (1 - \text{Percentage exit fee})$
1 year	$10,340.00	$10,000 \times (1.09) \times (1 - .04) = \$10,464.00$
4 years	$13,762.54	$10,000 \times (1.09)^4 \times (1 - .01) = \$13,974.66$
8 years	$20,149.73	$10,000 \times (1.09)^8 = \$19,925.63$

For short investment horizons, the Class B shares provide the higher proceeds. For longer horizons, the Class A shares, which impose a one-time commission, are better.

3. a. Turnover = $160,000 in trades per $1 million of portfolio value = 16%.
   b. Realized capital gains are $10 × 1,000 = $10,000 on Microsoft and $5 × 2,000 = $10,000 on Ford. The tax owed on the capital gains is therefore 0.28 × $20,000 = $5,600.

4. Out of the 100 top-half managers, 40 are skilled and will certainly repeat their performance next year. The other 60 were just lucky, but we should expect half of them to be lucky again next year, meaning that 30 of the lucky managers will be in the top half next year. Therefore, we should expect a total of 70 managers, or 70% of the sample, to repeat their top-half performance.

Chapter 5

INVESTORS AND THE INVESTMENT PROCESS

AFTER STUDYING THIS CHAPTER YOU SHOULD BE ABLE TO:

- Specify investment objectives of individual and institutional investors.
- Identify constraints on individual and institutional investors.
- Compare and contrast major types of investment policies.

Translating the aspirations and circumstances of diverse households into appropriate investment decisions is a daunting task. The task is equally difficult for institutions, most of which have many stakeholders and often are regulated by various authorities. The investment process is not easily reduced to a simple or mechanical algorithm.

While many principles of investments are quite general and apply to virtually all investors, some issues are peculiar to the specific investor. For example, tax bracket, age, risk tolerance, wealth, and job prospects and uncertainties make each investor's circumstances somewhat unique. In this chapter we focus on the process by which investors systematically review their objectives, constraints, and circumstances. Along the way, we survey some of the major classes of institutional investors and examine the special issues they must confront.

There is of course no unique "correct" investment process. However, some approaches are better than others, and it can be helpful to take one high-quality approach as a useful case study. For this reason, we will examine the systematic approach suggested by the Association for Investment Management and Research (AIMR). Among other things, the AIMR administers examinations to certify investment professionals as Chartered Financial Analysts. Therefore, the approach we outline is also one that a highly respected professional group endorses through the curriculum that it requires investment practitioners to master. The nearby box on page 113 describes how to become a Chartered Financial Analyst.

The basic framework involves dividing the investment process into four stages: specifying objectives, specifying constraints, formulating policy, and monitoring and updating the portfolio as needed. We will treat each of these activities in turn. We start with a description of the major types of investors, both individual and institutional, as well as their special objectives. We turn next to the constraints or circumstances peculiar to each investor class, and we consider some of the investment policies that each can choose.

How to Become a Chartered Financial Analyst

The Association for Investment Management and Research (AIMR) is a nonprofit international organization with a mission of serving investors by educating and examining investment professionals. The AIMR also has established a *Code of Ethics and Standards of Professional Conduct* that establishes guidelines of practice for investment professionals.

The AIMR was established in January 1990 through the combination of the previously-existing Financial Analysts Federation and the Institute of Chartered Financial Analysts. The AIMR, through the ICFA, administers the program through which an investment professional can be designated as a Chartered Financial Analyst (CFA). This designation has become a progressively more important requirement for a career in institutional money management. About 24,000 investment professionals have been awarded the charter since it was first established in 1963; in 1996 alone, more than 33,000 candidates sat for the CFA examination.

To become a CFA, you must pass a series of three annual examinations that demonstrate knowledge of:

- Valuation principles for fixed income, equity, and derivative securities
- Financial statement analysis and corporate finance
- Industry and company analysis
- Microeconomic and macroeconomic theory
- Quantitative methods
- Principles of portfolio construction and management
- Capital market theory
- Financial markets and instruments
- The ICFA Code of Ethics and Standards of Professional Conduct

Beyond these exams, the candidate must have three years of work experience in money management and must be a member of a local Society of the Financial Analysts Federation.

For more information, you can contact the Association of Investment Management and Research at P.O. Box 3668, Charlottesville, VA 22903, or visit the AIMR Web site at http://www.aimr.org.

5.1 INVESTORS AND OBJECTIVES

Most investors would agree with the notion that they want to earn as much money on their investments as possible. But while the concept "earn money" is simple enough *after the fact*, since you simply count the profits on your investments, it is vague when applied to an investment *before the fact*, since you rarely will know for sure what your earnings will be. Almost all investments entail uncertainty. Thus, while investors all wish to earn the highest rate of return possible, they also seek to avoid risk. It is not surprising that ultimately, then, investments that offer higher expected returns will impose greater risk. This is the risk-return trade-off.

The concepts "risk" and "expected rate of return" can be quite difficult to define and measure precisely, but they are usually intuitively understood. In Chapter 6 we will define and quantify these concepts more precisely; here we need only the qualitative insight you already possess about these concepts. Investors must consider a large set of investment assets because each asset carries with it a unique set of risk and return characteristics.

risk tolerance
The investor's willingness to accept higher risk to attain higher expected returns.

Investors will differ in their choice of investments because they differ in their willingness to trade off expected return against risk. We describe the willingness to accept higher risk to attain higher expected returns the investor's **risk tolerance;** equivalently, we describe attitudes toward risk using the concept of the investor's **risk aversion,** or reluctance to accept risk. The nearby box on page 114 explores these concepts and shows that while they seem straightforward, real-life behavior can be difficult to characterize so neatly.

risk aversion
The investor's reluctance to accept risk.

These terms describe behavior: If we could observe an investor making many choices among assets whose return and risk were well understood, we could measure an investor's risk aversion (or risk tolerance) by observing his or her willingness to invest in various portfolios with differing risk and return attributes. With no access to such data, and without

Are You Irrational or Thrill-Seeking When It Comes to Risky Investments?

If stocks stumbled, would you stick with them or become unstuck?

Your stomach for market gyrations should be a key factor when deciding how to divvy up your money among stocks, bonds, and cash investments like money market funds and certificates of deposit. Yet it's extraordinarily difficult to nail down how much risk an investor really can tolerate. Here's why:

JUST FOR KICKS

When experts discuss risk, usually they are referring to a security's likely price swings and the chance that returns will be lower than expected. But when regular investors "talk about risk, they are often talking about thrill-seeking behavior," says Meir Statman, a finance professor at Santa Clara University. "They talk about people who watch the tape and jump in and out of stocks. But these people's portfolios may be no riskier than mine. They may have 90% of their portfolio in money market funds and only 10% in stocks."

ON THE OTHER HAND

Not only do investors have different definitions of risk, but also they can be both conservative and aggressive at the same time. "People who insist on owning money funds that hold only Treasury bills are also buying initial public offerings," Mr. Statman notes.

Irrational behavior? Yes and no. Investors may divide their investments into different mental accounts, with some money designated as "conservative" and some as "aggressive," to make it easier to handle market downdrafts.

"The main purpose of these mental accounts is to deal with self-control problems," says Richard Thaler, an economics professor at the University of Chicago. "Suppose you think a young person should be putting most of his money into equities, as I do. You may think that strategy is too frightening in the face of a market downturn, but a somewhat more conservative strategy will help him stay the course. If you put 20% into fixed income, maybe that will let him put the rest into stocks."

TRUTH OR DARE

Many investment advisors use questionnaires to assess their clients' risk tolerance. But the responses given depend a lot on how the questions are asked, and different questions often elicit contradictory answers.

When filling out questionnaires or talking to investment advisors, investors often "treat it as a test," notes Scott Lummer, a managing director with Ibbotson Associates, a Chicago research firm. "They know they should be more in stocks. They try to say what's right, rather than what they can handle emotionally."

But the reality is, most folks are risk-averse. They get far more pain from losses than pleasure from gains, according to experts in behavioral finance.

WHAT GOES UP

Judging risk tolerance is further complicated because "people's risk tolerance isn't stable," says Michael Roszkowski, an associate professor of psychology at the American College, which educates financial planners and insurance agents. "When you get a market like this one, people's risk tolerance goes up. But if the market goes down, we'll get a shake-out and we'll find out who the real risk-takers are."

So what should you do? Your best bet may be to analyze your own investment history, especially how you reacted to market drops and what prompted you to sell securities.

"If you look at your investment behavior in the past, what you've bought and sold and when you've bought and sold, it can tell you a great deal," says Eleanor Blayney, a financial planner in McLean, Virginia. "If investors want to know what sort of investor they are, they should look back and see what sort of investor they've been."

Source: Jonathan Clements, "Are You Irrational or Thrill-Seeking When It Comes to Risky Investments?" *The Wall Street Journal*, June 4, 1996.

---

perfect insight into the risk-return characteristics of investments, we can only surmise an investor's risk aversion. Note that, explicitly or implicitly, many professional investors do exactly that (although, obviously they do more than just that); by choosing investments on behalf of their clients, they make the risk-return choice for their clients.

A natural place to begin a study of the investment process, therefore, is to specify the investor's objectives with two indicators: *return requirement* and *risk tolerance*. The investor then must reconcile these objectives with what is feasible, since any investor faces several constraints. This means that the objective cannot be set as a hard number, but rather as a set of guidelines as to the choice of assets.

TABLE 5.1

Amount of Risk
Investors Said They
Were Willing to Take
by Age

Source: From Market Facts,
Inc., Chicago, IL.

	Under 25	35–54	55 and Over
No risk	54%	57%	71%
A little risk	30	30	21
Some risk	14	18	8
A lot of risk	2	1	1

Investor objectives arise from a number of factors. Understanding these factors helps investors determine appropriate objectives. It also makes it easier for professional investors to derive appropriate policies for their clients.

Individual Investors

The basic factors affecting an individual investor usually arise from that investor's stage in the life cycle. The first significant investment decision for most individuals concerns education, which is an investment in "human capital." The major asset most people have during their early working years is the earning power derived from their skills. For these people, the financial risk due to illness or injury is far greater than that associated with the rate of return on their portfolios of financial assets. At this point in the life cycle, the most important financial decisions concern insurance against the possibility of disability or death.

The first major economic asset many people acquire is their own house. One can view the purchase of a house as a hedge[1] against two types of risk. The first is the risk of increases in rental rates. If you "pay rent to yourself," you do not need to be concerned with increases in the cost of housing. The second kind of risk is that the particular house or apartment where you live may not always be available to you. By buying, you guarantee its availability.

As one ages and accumulates savings to provide for consumption during retirement, the composition of wealth shifts from human capital toward financial capital. At this point, portfolio choices become progressively more important. In middle age, most investors will be willing to take on a meaningful amount of portfolio risk in order to increase their expected rates of return. As retirement draws near, however, risk tolerance seems to diminish.

The evidence in Table 5.1 supports the life-cycle view of investment behavior. Questionnaire results suggest that attitudes shift away from risk tolerance and toward risk aversion as investors near retirement age. With age, individuals lose the potential to recover from a disastrous investment performance. When they are young, investors can respond to a loss by working harder and saving more of their income. But as retirement approaches, investors realize there will be less time to recover, hence, the shift to safe assets.

The task of life-cycle financial planning is a formidable one for most people. It is not surprising that a whole industry has sprung up to provide personal financial advice.

Professional Investors

Professional investors provide investment management services for a fee. Some are employed directly by wealthy individual investors. Most professional investors, however, either pool many individual investor funds and manage them or serve institutional investors.

---

[1]To hedge means to mitigate a financial risk, a possible loss from a decline in the value of an asset. The return on a hedging asset will be higher when losses from the risk in question are greater. In other words, the return on the hedge asset offsets the risk in question—its returns are inversely related to the exposure from that risk. The greater the negative correlation between the returns on the hedge asset and the risk, the better the hedge. For example, an insurance policy against a specified risk is a perfect hedge, since it is designed precisely to cover a potential loss; its correlation is perfectly negative.

personal trust
An interest in an asset held by a trustee for the benefit of another person.

Personal Trusts   A **personal trust** is established when an individual confers legal title to property to another person or institution, who then manages that property for one or more beneficiaries. The holder of the title is called the *trustee*. The trustee is usually a bank, a lawyer, or an investment professional. Investment of a trust is subject to state trust laws and prudent man rules that limit the types of allowable trust investment.

The objectives of personal trusts normally are more limited in scope than those of the individual investor. Because of their fiduciary responsibility, personal trust managers typically are expected to invest with more risk aversion than individual investors. Certain asset classes, such as options and futures contracts for example, and strategies, such as short-selling (betting the price of a security will fall) or buying on margin (borrowing up to 50% of the purchase price), are ruled out. Short sales and margin purchases were discussed in Chapter 3.

mutual fund
A firm pooling and managing funds of investors.

Mutual Funds   **Mutual funds** are firms that manage pools of individual investor money. They invest in accordance with their objectives and issue shares that entitle investors to a pro rata portion of the income generated by the funds.

A mutual fund's objectives are spelled out in its prospectus. We discussed mutual funds in detail in Chapter 4.

Pension Funds

There are two basic types of pension plans: *defined contribution* and *defined benefit*. Defined contribution plans are in effect savings accounts established by the firm for its employees. The employer contributes funds to the plan, but the employee bears all the risk of the fund's investment performance. These plans are called defined contribution because the firm's only obligation is to make the stipulated contributions to the employee's retirement account. The employee is responsible for directing the management of the assets, usually by selecting among several investment funds in which the assets can be placed. Investment earnings in these retirement plans are not taxed until the funds are withdrawn, usually after retirement.

In defined benefit plans, by contrast, the employer has an obligation to provide a specified annual retirement benefit. That benefit is defined by a formula that typically takes into account years of service and the level of salary or wages. For example, the employer may pay the retired employee a yearly amount equal to 2% of the employee's final annual salary for each year of service. A 30-year employee would then receive an annual benefit equal to 60% of his or her final salary. The payments are an obligation of the employer, and the assets in the pension fund provide collateral for the promised benefits. If the investment performance of the assets is poor, the firm is obligated to make up the shortfall by contributing additional assets to the fund. In contrast to defined contribution plans, the risk surrounding investment performance in defined benefit plans is borne by the firm.

A pension actuary makes an assumption about the rate of return that will be earned on the plan's assets and uses this assumed rate to compute the amount the firm must contribute regularly to fund the plan's liabilities. For example, if the actuary assumes a rate of return of 10%, then the firm must contribute $385.54 now to fund $1,000 of pension liabilities that will arise in 10 years, because $385.54 \times 1.10^{10} = \$1,000$.

If a pension fund's *actual* rate of return exceeds the actuarial *assumed* rate, then the firm's shareholders reap an unanticipated gain, because the excess return can be used to reduce future contributions. If the plan's actual rate of return falls short of the assumed rate, however, the firm will have to increase future contributions. Because the sponsoring firm's shareholders bear the risk in a defined benefit pension plan, the objective of the plan will be consistent with the objective of the firm's shareholders.

Many pension plans view their assumed actuarial rate of return as their target rate of return and have little tolerance for earning less than that. Hence, they will take only as much risk as necessary to earn the actuarial rate.

Life Insurance Companies

Life insurance companies generally invest so as to hedge their liabilities, which are defined by the policies they write. The company can reduce its risk by investing in assets that will return more in the event the insurance policy coverage becomes more expensive.

For example, if the company writes a policy that pays a death benefit linked to the consumer price index, then the company is subject to inflation risk. It might search for assets expected to return more when the rate of inflation rises, thus hedging the price-index linkage of the policy.

There are as many objectives as there are distinct types of insurance policies. Until the 1970s, only two types of life insurance policies were available for individuals: whole-life and term.

A *whole-life insurance policy* combines a death benefit with a kind of savings plan that provides for a gradual buildup of cash value that the policyholder can withdraw later in life, usually at age 65.

Term insurance, on the other hand, provides death benefits only, with no buildup of cash value.

The interest rate imbedded in the schedule of cash value accumulation promised under the whole-life policy is a fixed rate. One way life insurance companies try to hedge this liability is by investing in long-term bonds. Often the insured individual has the right to borrow at a prespecified fixed interest rate against the cash value of the policy.

Insurance companies have seen considerable change in policyholder behavior in recent decades. During the high-interest-rate years of the 1970s and early 1980s, many older whole-life policies allowed policyholders to borrow at rates as low as 4 or 5% per year; some holders borrowed heavily against the cash value to invest in assets paying double-digit yields. Other actual and potential policyholders abandoned whole-life policies and took out term insurance, which accounted for more than half the volume of new sales of individual life policies.

In response to these developments, the insurance industry came up with two new policy types: variable life and universal life. A *variable life policy* entitles the insured to a fixed death benefit plus a cash value that can be invested in the policyholder's choice of mutual funds. A universal life policy allows policyholders to increase or reduce either the insurance premium (the annual fee paid on the policy) or the death benefit (the cash amount paid to beneficiaries in the event of death) according to their changing needs. Furthermore, the interest rate on the cash value component changes with market interest rates.

The great advantage of variable and universal life insurance policies is that earnings on the cash value are not taxed until the money is withdrawn. These policies are one of the few tax-advantaged investments left following the Tax Reform Act of 1986.

Nonlife Insurance Companies

Nonlife insurance companies such as property and casualty insurers have investable funds primarily because they pay claims *after* they collect policy premiums. Typically, they are conservative in their attitude toward risk.

A common thread in the objectives of pension plans and insurance companies is the need to hedge predictable long-term liabilities. Investment strategies typically call for hedging these liabilities with bonds of various maturities.

Banks

Most bank investments are loans to businesses and consumers, and most of their liabilities are accounts of depositors. As investors, banks try to match the risk of assets to liabilities while earning a profitable spread between the lending and borrowing rates. The difference between the interest charged to a borrower and the interest rate that banks pay on their liabilities is called the bank interest rate spread.

Most liabilities of banks and thrift institutions are checking accounts, time or saving deposits, and certificates of deposit (CDs). Checking account funds may be withdrawn at any time, so they are of the shortest maturity. Time or saving deposits are of various maturities. Some time deposits may extend as long as seven years, but, on average, they are of fairly short maturity. CDs are bonds of various maturities that the bank issues to investors. While the range of maturities is from 90 days to 10 years, the average is about one year.

Traditionally, a large part of the loan portfolio of saving and loan (S&L) institutions was in collateralized real estate loans, better known as mortgages. Typically, mortgages are of 15 to 30 years, significantly longer than the maturity of the average liability. Thus, profits were exposed to interest rate risk. When rates rose, thrifts had to pay higher rates to depositors, while the income from their longer-term investments was relatively fixed. This problem probably was a contributing factor in the S&L debacle of the 1980s. When interest rates rose throughout the 1970s, the financial condition of many banks and thrift institutions deterio- rated, making them more willing to assume greater risk in order to achieve higher returns. The greater risk of the loan portfolios was of little concern to depositors because deposits were insured by the Federal Deposit Insurance Corporation (FDIC) or the now-defunct Federal Savings and Loan Insurance Corporation (FSLIC).

As we noted in Chapter 2, most long-term fixed-rate mortgages today are securitized into pass-through certificates and held as securities in the portfolios of mutual funds, pension funds, and other institutional investors. Mortgage originators typically sell the mortgages they originate to pass-through agencies like Fannie Mae or Freddie Mac rather than holding them in a portfolio. They earn their profits on mortgage origination and servicing fees. The trend away from maintaining portfolio holdings of long-term mortgages also has reduced interest-rate risk.

Endowment Funds

endowment funds
Portfolios operated for the benefit of a nonprofit entity.

Endowment funds are held by organizations chartered to use their money for specific nonprofit purposes. They are financed by gifts from one or more sponsors and are typically managed by educational, cultural, and charitable organizations or by independent founda- tions established solely to carry out the fund's specific purposes. Generally, the investment objectives of an endowment fund are to produce a steady flow of income subject to only a moderate degree of risk. Trustees of an endowment fund, however, can specify other objec- tives as circumstances dictate.

Concept Check

1. Describe several distinguishing characteristics of endowment funds that differentiate them from pension funds.

5.2 INVESTOR CONSTRAINTS

Even with identical attitudes toward risk, different households and institutions might choose different investment portfolios because of their differing circumstances. These circum- stances include tax status, requirements for liquidity or a flow of income from the portfolio, or various regulatory restrictions. These circumstances impose *constraints* on investor choice. Together, objectives and constraints determine appropriate investment policy.

As noted, constraints usually have to do with investor circumstances. For example, if a family has children about to enter college, there will be a high demand for liquidity since cash will be needed to pay tuition bills. Other times, however, constraints are imposed externally. For example, banks and trusts are subject to legal limitations on the types of assets they may hold in their portfolios. Finally, some constraints are self-imposed. For example, "social investing" means that investors will not hold shares of firms involved in ethically objectionable activities. Some criteria that have been used to judge firms as ineligible for a portfolio are: involvement in nuclear power generation; production of tobacco or alcohol; participation in polluting activities; or, until recently, involvement in the South African economy.

Five common types of constraints are described below.

Liquidity

liquidity
Liquidity refers to the speed and ease with which an asset can be converted to cash.

Liquidity is the speed and ease with which an asset can be sold and still fetch a fair price. It is a relationship between the time dimension (how long it will take to sell) and the price dimension (the discount from fair market price) of an investment asset.

When an actual concrete measure of liquidity is necessary, one thinks of the discount when an immediate sale is unavoidable.[2] Cash and money market instruments such as Treasury bills and commercial paper, where the bid-ask spread is a fraction of 1%, are the most liquid assets, and real estate is among the least liquid. Office buildings and manufacturing structures in extreme cases can suffer a 50% liquidity discount.

Both individual and institutional investors must consider how likely they are to require cash at short notice. From this likelihood, they establish the minimum level of liquid assets they need in the investment portfolio.

Investment Horizon

investment horizon
The planned liquidation date.

This is the *planned* liquidation date of the investment. Examples of an individual's **investment horizon** could be the time to fund a college education or the retirement date for a wage earner. For a university endowment, an investment horizon could relate to the time to fund a major campus construction project. Horizon dates must be considered when investors choose between assets of various maturities. For example, the maturity date of a bond might make it a more attractive investment if it coincides with a date on which cash is needed.

Regulations

prudent man law
The fiduciary responsibility of a professional investor.

Only professional and institutional investors are constrained by regulations. First and foremost is the **prudent man law**. That is, professional investors who manage other people's money have a fiduciary responsibility to restrict investment to assets that would have been approved by a prudent investor. The law is purposefully nonspecific. Every professional investor must stand ready to defend an investment policy in a court of law, and interpretation may differ according to the standards of the times.

Also, specific regulations apply to various institutional investors. For instance, U.S. mutual funds may not hold more than 5% of the shares of any publicly traded corporation.

Sometimes, "self-imposed" regulations also affect the investment choice. We have noted several times, for example, that mutual funds describe their investment policies in a prospectus. These policy guidelines amount to constraints on the ability to choose portfolios freely. The nearby box on page 120 notes that while such constraints used to be treated a bit casually, there is a growing trend today for investment companies to enforce these constraints more vigorously.

---

[2]In most cases, it is impossible to know the liquidity of an asset with certainty until it is put up for sale. In dealer markets (described in Chapter 3), however, the liquidity of the traded assets can be observed from the bid-ask spread that is quoted by the dealers, that is, the difference between the "bid" quote (the lower price the dealer will pay the owner) and the "ask" quote (the higher price a buyer would have to pay the dealer).

Just What the Patient Ordered

Compared with most financial concepts, tax-exempt mutual funds seem fairly uncomplicated. They are mutual funds that invest in bonds exempt from America's income tax, such as those issued by local governments. That is not exactly brain surgery. Yet the managers of such funds appear to find this definition hard to understand. Last year, many of them chose to invest a portion of their clients' money in instruments that were subject to (you guessed) income tax. Why did they do it? For their customers—of course.

They were not alone. Managers of mutual funds frequently choose to abandon their stated objectives in the scramble for higher returns. When such bets pay off, they tend to go unnoticed. Many American small-company funds, for example, have chosen recently to pour their money into big-company stocks, judging them to be a better bet. In the fourth quarter of 1996, that gamble paid off, and few complained. But when fund managers stray from their investment guidelines and guess wrong, investors are predictably outraged.

Consider the plight of the Magellan Fund, flagship of the Fidelity mutual fund group. Most of Magellan's investors thought it was an equity fund. But last year it turned out that the fund's star manager, Jeffrey Vinik, had invested heavily in bonds and cash, thereby depressing returns in a booming stock market. Mr. Vinik was forced to resign, and the fund's investors have been leaving in droves. In 1995, the villains were managers of American money market funds, many of whom were caught out by Mexico's peso crisis at the end of 1994. Investors had thought their money was safely tucked away in short-term domestic paper, not peso-denominated bonds. They were not impressed.

Investors, of course, can punish wayward managers by removing their money. But except in the most publicized cases, it is hard to know how closely a manager is adhering to his guidelines. Most customers invest in a variety of funds, making it time-consuming to monitor each of them personally. And although several fund-tracking companies publish tables which measure each fund relative to others in its class, those boundaries are notoriously fuzzy: In many cases, a fund can invest up to a third of its assets outside its category without violating the guidelines.

PHYSICIAN, RESTRAIN THYSELF

Now, however, small investors are finally gaining some power, as they rely increasingly on big intermediaries to deal with fund managers on their behalf. The most influential are financial-advisory companies, which help retail investors to assess their financial needs and then allocate their money for them.

Consider, for example, the approach of Linsco/Private Ledger, an advisory firm based in San Diego. Linsco maintains a centralized research unit that tracks each fund's behavior and lets its advisors know which ones are hewing most closely to their objectives.

In America, administrators of 401(k) plans are beginning to play a similar role. These plans, which are now the main pension scheme for many workers, let the employee decide in which funds to invest his retirement savings, and force him to bear the investment risk. The employer deals with funds on its employees' behalf, deciding which to include as options and monitoring the behavior of each fund. Since they are already passing off risks to their employees, 401(k) administrators are keen to avoid surprises.

Such shifts are changing the role of fund managers in the investment process. Many are finding that they may not roam so far afield as they pick which stocks and bonds to buy, and, of course, they resent the demotion.

And what if a fund's investment objective falls from favor? Investors can rearrange their own fund portfolios, rather than leaving their fund managers to do the rearranging. In America, most owners of mutual fund shares can pick up the telephone whenever they like and shift money from, say, a small-company fund into a big-company fund. If fund managers tried to do it for them, they would only be undoing their customers' decisions.

Source: *The Economist*, January 18, 1997.

Tax Considerations

Tax consequences are central to investment decisions. The performance of any investment strategy should be measured by its rate of return *after* taxes. For household and institutional investors who face significant tax rates, tax sheltering and deferral of tax obligations may be pivotal in their investment strategy.

Unique Needs

Virtually every investor faces special circumstances. Imagine husband-and-wife aeronautical engineers holding high-paying jobs in the same aerospace corporation. The entire human capital of that household is tied to a single player in a rather cyclical industry. This couple

TABLE 5.2
Determination of
Portfolio Policies

Objectives	Constraints
Return requirements	Liquidity
Risk tolerance	Horizon
	Regulations
	Taxes
	Unique needs, such as:
	• Ethical concerns
	• Specific hedging needs
	• Age
	• Wealth

would need to hedge the risk of a deterioration in the economic well-being of the aerospace industry.

Similar issues would confront an executive on Wall Street who owns an apartment near work. Because the value of the home in that part of Manhattan probably depends on the vitality of the securities industry, the individual is doubly exposed to the vagaries of the stock market. Because both job and home already depend on the fortunes of Wall Street, the purchase of a typical diversified stock portfolio would actually increase the exposure to the stock market.

These examples illustrate that the job is often the primary "investment" of an individual, and the unique risk profile that results from employment can play a big role in determining a suitable investment portfolio.

Other unique needs of individuals often center around their stage in the life cycle, as discussed above. Retirement, housing, and children's education constitute three major demands for funds, and investment policy will depend in part on the proximity of these expenditures.

Institutional investors also face unique needs. For example, pension funds will differ in their investment policy, depending on the average age of plan participants. Another example of a unique need for an institutional investor would be a university whose trustees allow the administration to use only cash income from the endowment fund. This constraint would translate into a preference for high-dividend-paying assets.

Table 5.2 summarizes the types of objectives and constraints that investors must face as they form their investment portfolios. We turn next to an examination of the specific objectives and constraints of the major investor types.

5.3 OBJECTIVES AND CONSTRAINTS OF VARIOUS INVESTORS

We are now in a position to compare investors on the basis of their objectives and constraints. The next two tables will show how we can apply the objective/constraint approach to the formation of policies.

Objectives

Table 5.3 presents a matrix of objectives for various investors. For mutual funds, the return requirement and risk tolerance are said to be variable because mutual funds segment the investor market. Various funds appeal to distinct investor groups and will adopt a return requirement and risk tolerance that fit an entire spectrum of market niches. For example, "high-income" funds cater to the conservative investor, while "high-growth" funds seek out the more risk-tolerant ones. Tax-free bond funds segment the market by tax obligation.

Pension funds must meet the actuarial rate; otherwise, the corporation sponsoring the plan will need to make additional contributions. Once a pension fund's actuarial rate is set, it establishes the fund return requirement, and additional risk tolerance becomes very low.

Endowment funds are classified as having "conservative" risk tolerance on the basis of observation, although individual institutions can differ in investment policy.

TABLE 5.3
Matrix of Objectives

Type of Investor	Return Requirement	Risk Tolerance
Individual and personal trusts	Life cycle (education, children, retirement)	Life cycle (younger are more risk tolerant)
Mutual funds	Variable	Variable
Pension funds	Assumed actuarial rate	Depends on proximity of payouts
Endowment funds	Determined by current income needs and need for asset growth to maintain real value	Generally conservative
Life insurance companies	Should exceed new money rate by sufficient margin to meet expenses and profit objectives; also actuarial rates important	Conservative
Nonlife insurance companies	No minimum	Conservative
Banks	Interest spread	Variable

TABLE 5.4
Matrix of Constraints

Type of Investor	Liquidity	Horizon	Regulatory	Taxes
Individuals and personal trusts	Variable	Life cycle	Prudent man laws (for trusts)	Variable
Mutual funds	Low	Short	Little	None
Pension funds	Young, low; mature, high	Long	ERISA	None
Endowment funds	Little	Long	Little	None
Life insurance companies	Low	Long	Complex	Yes
Nonlife insurance companies	High	Short	Little	Yes
Banks	Low	Short	Changing	Yes

Life insurance companies have obligations to whole-life policyholders that are similar to those of pension funds. These obligations require them to earn a minimum rate (analogous to the pension fund's actuarial rate), if the company is to meet its liabilities.

Banks earn profit from the interest rate spread between loans extended (the bank's assets) and deposits and CDs (the bank's liabilities), as well as from fees for services. Managing bank assets calls for balancing the loan portfolio with the portfolio of deposits and CDs. A bank can increase the interest rate spread by lending to riskier borrowers and by increasing the proportion of longer-term loans. Both policies threaten bank solvency though, so their deployment must match the risk tolerance of the bank shareholders. In addition, bank capital regulations now are risk based, so higher-risk strategies will elicit higher capital requirements as well as the possibility of greater regulatory interference in the bank's affairs.

Constraints

Table 5.4 presents a matrix of constraints for various investors. As you would expect, liquidity and tax constraints for individuals are variable because of wealth and age differentials.

A particular constraint for mutual funds arises from investor response to the fund performance. When a mutual fund earns an unsatisfactory rate of return, investors often redeem their shares—they withdraw money from the fund. The mutual fund then contracts. The reverse happens when a mutual fund earns an unusually high return: It can become popular with investors overnight, and its asset base will grow dramatically.

Pension funds are heavily regulated by the Employee Retirement Income Security Act of 1974 (ERISA). This law revolutionized savings for retirement in the United States and remains a major piece of social legislation. Thus, for pension funds, regulatory constraints are relatively important. Also, mature pension funds are required to pay out more than young funds and hence need more liquidity.

Endowment funds, on the other hand, usually do not need to liquidate assets, or even use dividend income, to finance payouts. Contributions are expected to exceed payouts and increase the real value of the endowment fund, so liquidity is not an overriding concern.

Life insurance companies are subject to complex regulation. The corporate tax rate, which today is 35% for large firms, also applies to insurance company investment income, so taxes an important concern.

Property and casualty insurance, like term life insurance, is written on a short-term basis. Most policies must be renewed annually, which means property and casualty insurance companies are subject to short-term horizon constraints.

The short horizon constraint for banks comes from the interest rate risk component of the interest rate spread (i.e., the risk of interest rate increases that banks face when financing long-term assets with short-term liabilities).

Concept Check

2. *a.* Think about the financial circumstances of your closest relative in your parents' generation (for example, your parents' household if you are fortunate enough to have them around). Write down the objectives and constraints for their investment decisions.

   b. Now consider the financial situation of your closest relative who is in his or her 30s. Write down the objectives and constraints that would fit his or her investment decision.

   c. How much of the difference between the two statements is due to the age of the investors?

5.4 INVESTMENT POLICIES

Once objectives and constraints are determined, an investment policy that suits the investor can be formulated. That policy must reflect an appropriate risk-return profile as well as needs for liquidity, income generation, and tax positioning. For example, the most important portfolio decision an investor makes is the proportion of the total investment fund allocated to risky as opposed to safe assets such as money market securities, usually called cash equivalents or simply cash. This choice is the most fundamental means of controlling investment risk.

It follows that the first decision an investor must make is the asset allocation decision. Asset allocation refers to the allocation of the portfolio across major asset categories such as:

1. Money market assets (cash equivalents).
2. Fixed-income securities (primarily bonds).
3. Stocks.
4. Non-U.S. stocks and bonds.
5. Real estate.
6. Precious metals and other commodities.

Only after the broad asset classes to be held in the portfolio are determined can one sensibly choose the specific securities to purchase.

Investors who have relatively high degrees of risk tolerance will choose asset allocations more concentrated in higher-risk investment classes, such as equity, to obtain higher expected rates of return. More conservative investors will choose asset allocations with a greater weight in bonds and cash equivalents. The nearby box (page 124) on Vanguard's asset allocation recommendations illustrates this principle.

Asset Allocation for Strength and Balance

There is one decision about your investments that will have more impact on your returns than any other: the allocation of your assets among stocks, bonds, and cash reserves.

Far more than any particular mutual funds you may select, your portfolio's asset allocation will govern not only the long-term returns you may receive, but the level of short-term risk you will assume, too. A portfolio of stock funds should provide a higher total return over time than one that concentrates on bond or money market funds. However, the latter portfolio offers a higher degree of stability plus the comfort of regular income. A balanced approach has characteristics of both portfolios, plus the benefit of diversification across asset classes. Drawing on these strengths, a balanced portfolio is well suited to withstand the financial markets' ups and downs.

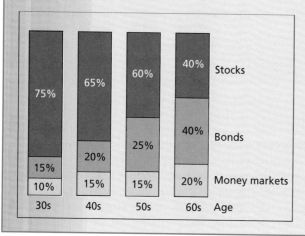

THE LIFE CYCLE APPROACH

In your early years, your goal is to accumulate capital for retirement. Later, conserving and spending capital take precedence. Logically, your investment strategy should be tailored to these life stages.

When you are in your 20s, 30s, and 40s, emphasize stocks for their potentially higher long-term returns. You have the time to recover from spasmodic short-term declines that grip equity markets with varying degrees of severity. A portfolio mix of 65–75% stocks and 25–35% bonds and money market investments would seem reasonable. As you move into your 50s, reduce risk and increase income by trimming stocks (perhaps to 50%) and raising bond and money market investments.

Once you retire, your emphasis shifts to receiving income. The majority (some 60%) of your portfolio should be allocated to bonds and money market funds. As an inflation hedge, maintain a significant stock position (40% is a good starting point), particularly early in your retirement years.

REBALANCING YOUR PORTFOLIO

Whichever approach you choose will require fortitude to make necessary rebalancing decisions. Moving assets from high-performing funds to those that may be lagging (on a relative basis) is not easy—but it is at the heart of a balanced investment strategy.

Source: Abridged from "Asset Allocation for Strength and Balance," *In the Vanguard*, Summer 1993, courtesy of The Vanguard Group.

Top-Down Policies for Institutional Investors

Individual investors need not concern themselves with organizational efficiency. But professional investors with large amounts to invest must structure asset allocation activities to decentralize some of the decision making.

A common feature of large organizations is the investment committee and the asset universe. The investment committee includes top management officers, senior portfolio managers, and senior security analysts. The committee determines investment policies and verifies that portfolio managers and security analysts are operating within the bounds of specified policies. A major responsibility of the investment committee is to translate the objectives and constraints of the company into an **asset universe,** an approved list of assets for each of the company's portfolios.

asset universe
Approved list of assets in which portfolio manager may invest.

Thus, the investment committee has responsibility for broad asset allocation. While the investment manager might have some leeway to tilt the portfolio toward or away from one or another asset class, the investment committee establishes the benchmark allocation that largely determines the risk characteristics of the portfolio. The task of choosing specific securities from the approved universe is more fully delegated to the investment manager.

FIGURE 5.1   Asset Allocation and Security Selection for Palatial

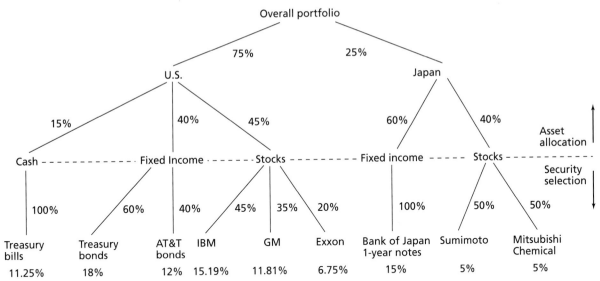

Figure 5.1 illustrates the stages of the portfolio choice process for Palatial Investments, a hypothetical firm that invests internationally. The first two stages are asset allocation choices. The broadest choice is in the weighting of the portfolio between U.S. and Japanese securities. Palatial has chosen a weight of 75% in the U.S. and 25% in Japan. The allocation of the portfolio across asset classes may now be determined. For example, 15% of the U.S. portfolio is invested in cash equivalents, 40% in fixed income, and 45% in equity. The asset-class weights are, in general, a policy decision of the investment committee, although the investment manager might have some authority to alter the asset allocation to limited degrees based on her expectations concerning the investment performance of various asset classes. Finally, security selection within each country is determined by the portfolio manager from the approved universe. For example, 45% of funds held in the U.S. equity market will be placed in IBM, 35% in GM, and 20% in Exxon. (We show only three securities in the figure because of space limitations. Obviously a $1 billion fund will hold securities of many more firms.)

These ever-finer decisions determine the proportion of each individual security in the overall portfolio. As an example, consider the determination of the proportion of Palatial's portfolio invested in Exxon, 6.75%. This fraction results from the following decisions. First, the United States receives a weight of 75% of the overall portfolio, and equities comprise 45% of the U.S. component of the portfolio. These are asset allocation choices. Exxon comprises 20% of the U.S. equity component of the portfolio. This is a security selection choice. Therefore, Exxon's weight in the overall portfolio is $0.75 \times 0.45 \times 0.20 = .0675$, or 6.75%. If the entire portfolio is $1 billion, $67,500,000 will be invested in Exxon. If Exxon is selling for $60 a share, 1,125,000 shares must be purchased. The bottom line in Figure 5.1 shows the percentage of the overall portfolio held in each asset.

This example illustrates a top-down approach that is consistent with the needs of large organizations. The top managers set the overall policy of the portfolio by specifying asset allocation guidelines. Lower-level portfolio managers fill in the details with their security selection decisions.

Active versus Passive Policies

One choice that must be confronted by all investors, individual as well as institutional, is the degree to which the portfolio will be actively versus passively managed. Recall that passive management is based on the belief that security prices usually are at close to "fair" levels.

Instead of spending time and other resources attempting to "beat the market," that is, to find mispriced securities with unusually attractive risk-return characteristics, the investor simply assumes that she will be fairly compensated for the risk she is willing to take on and selects a portfolio consistent with her risk tolerance.[3]

Passive management styles can be applied to both the security selection and the asset allocation decisions. With regard to asset allocation, passive management simply means that the manager does not depart from his or her "normal" asset-class weightings in response to changing expectations about the performance of different markets. Those "normal" weights are based on the investor's risk and return objectives, as discussed earlier. For example, we saw in an earlier box that Vanguard's asset allocation recommendation for a 45-year-old investor was 65% equity, 20% bonds, and 15% cash equivalents. A purely passive manager would not depart from these weights in response to forecasts of market performances. The weighting scheme would be adjusted only in response to changes in risk tolerance as age and wealth change over time.

Next consider passive security selection. Imagine that you must choose a portfolio of stocks without access to any special information about security values. This would be the case if you believed that anything you know about a stock is already known by the rest of the investors in the market and therefore is already reflected in the stock price. If you cannot predict which stocks will be winners, you should broadly diversify your portfolio to avoid putting all your eggs in one basket. A natural course of action for such an investor would be to choose a portfolio with "a little bit of everything."

This reasoning leads one to look for a portfolio that is invested across the entire security market. We saw in Chapter 2 that some mutual fund operators have established index funds that follow just such a strategy. These funds hold each stock or bond in proportion to its representation in a particular index, such as the Standard & Poor's 500 stock price index or the Lehman Brothers bond index. Holding an indexed portfolio represents purely passive security selection since the investor's return simply duplicates the return of the overall market without making a bet on one or another stock or sector of the market.

In contrast to passive strategies, active management assumes an ability to outguess the other investors in the market and to identify either securities or asset classes that will shine in the near future. Active security selection for institutional investors typically requires two layers: security analysis and portfolio choice. Security analysts specialize in particular industries and companies and prepare assessments of their particular market niches. The portfolio managers then sift through the reports of many analysts. They use forecasts of market conditions to make asset allocation decisions and use the security analysts' recommendations to choose the particular securities to include within each asset class.

The choice between active and passive strategies need not be all-or-nothing. One can pursue both active security selection and passive asset allocation, for example. In this case, the manager would maintain fixed asset allocation targets but would actively choose the securities within each asset class. Or one can pursue active asset allocation and passive security selection. In this case, the manager might actively shift the allocation between equity and bond components of the portfolio but hold indexed portfolios within each sector. Another mixed approach is called a *passive core* strategy. In this case, the manager indexes *part* of the portfolio, the passive core, and actively manages the rest of the portfolio.

Is active or passive management the better approach? It might seem at first blush that active managers have the edge because active management is necessary to achieve outstanding performance. But remember that active managers start out with some disadvantages as well. They incur significant costs when preparing their analyses of markets and securities and incur heavier trading costs from the more rapid turnover of their portfolios. If they don't

---

[3]We spend all of Chapter 9 discussing the argument for passive management. For now, therefore, we simply present an overview of the issues.

uncover information or insights currently unavailable to other investors, then all of this costly activity will be wasted, and they will underperform a passive strategy. In fact, low-cost passive strategies have performed surprisingly well in the last few decades. We will discuss this issue in detail in Chapter 9.

3. Identify the following conditions according to where each fits in the objective-constraints-policies framework.
    a. Invest 5% in bonds and 95% in stocks.
    b. Do not invest more than 10% of the budget in any one security.
    c. Shoot for an average rate of return of 11%.
    d. Make sure there is $95,000 in cash in the account on December 31, 2002.
    e. If the market is bearish, reduce the investment in stocks to 80%.
    f. As of next year, we will be in a higher tax bracket.
    g. Our new president believes pension plans should take no risk whatsoever with the pension fund.
    h. Our acquisition plan will require large sums of cash to be available at any time.

5.5 TAXES AND INVESTMENT STRATEGY

So far, we have ignored income taxes in discussing asset allocation. Of course, to the extent that investments are tax-exempt, as is the case for pension funds, or the portfolio is invested in a tax-sheltered account, such as an individual retirement account (IRA), taxes are irrelevant to your portfolio decisions.

But suppose at least some of your investment income is subject to income taxes. You would be interested in the *after-tax* rate of return on your portfolio. At first glance, it might appear to be a simple matter to figure out after-tax returns on stocks, bonds, and cash if you know the before-tax returns, but there are several complicating factors.

The first (and easiest) issue is that you can choose between tax-exempt and taxable bonds. You will choose to invest in tax-exempt bonds if your personal tax rate is high enough that the after-tax rate of interest on taxable bonds is less than the interest rate on tax-exempt bonds. We discussed this in Chapter 2. All you need to do is choose the investment with the higher equivalent taxable yield.

The second complication is not as easy to deal with. Part of your return will be in the form of a capital gain or loss. Under the current tax system, you pay income taxes on a capital gain only if you *realize* it by selling the asset during the holding period. This applies to bonds as well as stocks and makes the after-tax rate of return for any investment period a function of whether the security will actually be sold by the end of that period. Sophisticated investors time the sale of securities and the realization of capital gains or losses to maximize their tax advantage. This often calls for selling securities that are losing money at the end of the tax year and holding on to those that are making money.

Furthermore, because cash dividends on stocks are fully taxable while capital gains taxes can be deferred by not selling stocks that appreciate in value, the after-tax rate of return on stocks will depend on the dividend payout policy of the corporations that issue the stock.

Tax-Shelter Options

Four important tax-sheltering options can radically affect optimal asset allocation for individual investors. The first is the tax-deferral option, which arises because you pay tax on a capital gain only when you realize the gain. The second option is tax-deferred retirement plans, such as individual retirement accounts. The third is tax-deferred annuities offered by life insurance companies. The last option is investing in tax-exempt instruments.

The next two sections provide numerical examples of the first two options: tax deferral and the tax-deferred retirement plan.

The Tax-Deferral Option   A fundamental feature of the U.S. tax code is that the tax on a capital gain on an asset is payable only when the asset is sold.[4] This results in a *tax-deferral option*. The investor can control the timing of the tax payment.

To see how this option can be valuable, compare investments in GM stock versus GM bonds. Suppose that both offer an expected total pretax return of 15%. The stock has a dividend yield of 5% and an expected appreciation in price of 10%. The dividend payment is an immediately taxable part of the annual return on the stock. The GM stockholder pays tax only on the 5% dividend and defers paying tax on capital gains until the stock is sold. The bond pays an interest or "coupon" rate of 15%, and the bond investor must pay tax on the bond's interest in the year it is earned.

Suppose you invest $5,000 for five years and are in a 28% tax bracket. An investment in the bond will earn an after-tax return of 10.8% per year: $(1 - \text{Tax rate}) \times (\text{Rate of return}) = (1 - 0.28) \times 15\% = 10.8\%$. We assume for simplicity that the after-tax interest is reinvested in GM bonds that continue to yield 15% before taxes throughout the five years. The after-tax value of the investment fund at the end of five years is

$$\$5,000 \times 1.108^5 = \$8,349.66$$

For the stock, the dividend yield after taxes will be 3.6% [because $(1 - .28) \times 5\% = 3.6\%$], and we assume dividends are reinvested in GM stock that continues to yield 5% in dividends and 10% in capital gains throughout the five years. Because no taxes are paid on the capital gain until the fifth year, the return before paying the capital gains tax will be

$$\$5,000 \times [1 + \text{After-tax dividend yield} + \text{Capital gains rate}]^5$$
$$= \$5,000 \times (1 + .036 + .10)^5$$
$$= \$5,000 \times (1.136)^5 = \$9,459.36$$

In the fifth year, the capital gain is equal to the full value of the investment less the invested funds, which include the original principal of $5,000 plus the reinvested after-tax dividends (at the 3.6% rate)

$$\$9,459.36 - 5,000 \times (1.036)^5 = 9,459.36 - 5,967.18 = \$3,492.18$$

Taxes due are $0.28 \times 3,492.18 = \$977.81$, leaving a net after-tax value of $9,459.36 - \$977.81 = \$8,481.55$. This is $131.89 more than the bond investment terminal value. Deferral of the capital gains tax allows the investment to compound at a faster rate until the tax is actually paid.

The more an investor's total return is in the form of price appreciation, the greater the value of the tax-deferral option.

Tax-Deferred Retirement Plans and the Value of Tax Deferral   Recent years have seen the establishment of a number of *tax-deferred* retirement plans, where investors can choose how to allocate assets. Individual retirement accounts (IRAs) and 401(k) retirement plans are two examples. In all these plans, neither contributions nor earnings are subject to federal income tax until the individual withdraws them as benefits.

Suppose you have saved $10,000 from after-tax wages over the past year. You are in the 28% tax bracket and expect to remain in the same bracket until you retire in 20 years. For simplicity, we assume that you will withdraw the entire amount on retirement. (If you withdraw the retirement funds over a protracted period, then the tax-deferral benefits will be even greater.) Assume that the annual, before-tax rate of return on savings will be 10% until retirement.

---

[4]The major exception to this rule occurs in futures investing, where a gain is treated as taxable in the year it occurs regardless of whether the investor closes the position.

Case 1: Without any tax sheltering, your money will grow at an after-tax rate of $(1 - 0.28) \times 10\% = 7.2\%$. Therefore, the terminal value of the $10,000 savings will be

$$\$10,000 \times (1.072)^{20} = \$40,169.43$$

Case 2: If the contribution itself is not sheltered, but income on it is tax deferred, the before-tax terminal value will be

$$\$10,000 \times (1 + .10)^{20} = \$67,275.00$$

of which all but the original investment of $10,000 is taxable income at 28%. The after-tax terminal value in this case will be

$$\$67,275.00 - 0.28 \times (\$67,275.00 - \$10,000) = \$51,238.00$$

The value of the tax deferral of income is the difference in proceeds between Case 1 and Case 2: $51,238.00 − $40,169.43 = $11,068.57. Another way to look at this is that the deferral of income tax produces an after-tax rate of return of 8.5%, compared with 7.2% without shelter.

Case 3: Suppose contributions also are tax deferred, as they are for many individuals' contributions to retirement plans. A contribution of $13,888.89 therefore reduces after-tax income by only $10,000, because $13,888.89 × .72 = $10,000. Therefore, you actually can invest $13,888.89 and your after-tax income will fall by the same $10,000 without shelter. The before-tax terminal value is

$$\$13,888.89 \times (1.10)^{20} = \$93,437.51$$

This entire amount is subject to taxes, however, because the original contribution as well as the interest earnings were originally sheltered from taxes. Hence, the after-tax terminal value becomes

$$\$93,437.51 \times .72 = \$67,275.00$$

Thus, the benefit attributable to sheltering the contribution is the difference between Case 3 and Case 2 proceeds:

$$\$67,275.00 - \$51,238.00 = \$16,037$$

and the *total* value of tax deferral equals the difference between Case 3 and Case 1 proceeds, which amounts to a hefty $27,105.57.

Another way to express this value is that it is equivalent to an after-tax rate of 10%, compared to the 7.2% without any shelter.

Concept Check

4. *a.* How would the benefits of deferral of income and contributions to an IRA change if you were in the 33% tax bracket?
   b. How would the benefits change if you plan to retire in 10 years?

5.6 MONITORING AND REVISING INVESTMENT PORTFOLIOS

Choosing the investment portfolio requires the investor to set objectives, acknowledge constraints, determine asset-class proportions, and perform security analysis. Is the process ever finished and behind us? By the time we have completed all of these steps, many of the inputs we have used will be out of date. Moreover, our circumstances as well as our objectives change over time. Therefore, the investment process requires that we continually monitor and update our portfolios.

Moreover, even if our circumstances do not change, our portfolios necessarily will. For example, suppose you currently hold 1,000 shares of Exxon, selling at $65 a share, and 1,000 shares of Microsoft, selling at $80 a share. If the price of Exxon falls to $50 a share, while that of Microsoft rises to $90 a share, the fractions of your portfolio allocated to each security change without your taking any direct action. The value of your investment in Exxon is now lower, and the value of the Microsoft investment is higher. Unless you are happy with this reallocation of investment proportions, you will need to take some action to restore the portfolio weights to desired levels.

Asset allocation also will change over time, as the investment performance of different asset classes diverge. If the stock market outperforms the bond market, the proportion of your portfolio invested in stocks will increase, while the proportion invested in bonds will decrease. If you are uncomfortable with this shift in the asset mix, you must rebalance the portfolio by selling some of the stocks and purchasing bonds.

Therefore, investing is a *dynamic* process, meaning that you must continually update and reevaluate your decisions over time.

Summary

- The Association for Investment Management and Research developed a systematic framework for the translation of investor goals to investment strategy. Its three main parts are: objectives, constraints, and policy. Investor objectives include the return requirement and risk tolerance, articulating the overriding concern of investment with the risk-return trade-off. Investor constraints include liquidity requirements, investment horizon, regulatory concerns, tax obligations, and the unique needs of various investors. Investment policies specify the degree of involvement in market timing, asset allocation, and security selection decisions.

- Major institutional investors include pension funds, mutual funds, life insurance companies, nonlife insurance companies, banks, and endowment funds. For individual investors, life-cycle concerns are the most important factor in setting objectives, constraints, and policies.

- Major asset classes include: cash (money market assets), fixed-income securities (bonds), stocks, real estate, precious metals, and collectibles. Asset allocation refers to the decision made as to the investment proportion to be allocated to each asset class. An active asset allocation strategy calls for the production of frequent market forecasts and the adjustment of asset allocation according to these forecasts.

- Active security selection requires security analysis and portfolio choice. Analysis of individual securities is required to choose securities that will make up a coherent portfolio and outperform a passive benchmark.

- Investors have four important tax-sheltering options: tax deferral through the timing of the realization of capital gains and losses, tax-deferred retirement plans, tax-deferred annuities (issued by insurance companies), and tax-exempt securities.

- Perhaps the most important feature of the investment process is that it is dynamic. Portfolios must be continually monitored and updated. The frequency and timing of various decisions are in themselves important decisions. Successful investment management requires management of these dynamic aspects.

Key Terms

asset universe, *124*	liquidity, *119*	prudent man law, *119*
endowment funds, *118*	mutual funds, *116*	risk aversion, *113*
investment horizon, *119*	personal trust, *116*	risk tolerance, *113*

Problem Set

CFA

1. Your client says, "With the unrealized gains in my portfolio, I have almost saved enough money for my daughter to go to college in eight years, but educational costs keep going up." Based on this statement alone, which one of the following appears to be least important to your client's investment policy?

   a. Time horizon.

   b. Purchasing power risk.

    c. Liquidity.

    d. Taxes.

2. The aspect least likely to be included in the portfolio management process is

    a. Identifying an investor's objectives, constraints, and preferences.

    b. Organizing the management process itself.

    c. Implementing strategies regarding the choice of assets to be used.

    d. Monitoring market conditions, relative values, and investor circumstances.

3. A clearly written investment policy statement is critical for

    a. Mutual funds

    b. Individuals

    c. Pension funds

    d. All investors

4. The investment policy statement of an institution must be concerned with all of the following *except*:

    a. Its obligations to its clients.

    b. The level of the market.

    c. Legal regulations.

    d. Taxation.

5. You are a portfolio manager and senior executive vice president of Advisory Securities Selection, Inc. Your firm has been invited to meet with the trustees of the Wood Museum Endowment Funds. Wood Museum is a privately endowed charitable institution that is dependent on the investment return from a $25 million endowment fund to balance the budget. The treasurer of the museum has recently completed the budget that indicates a need for cash flow of $3 million in 1998, $3.2 million in 1999, and $3.5 million in 2000 from the endowment fund to balance the budget in those years. Currently, the entire endowment portfolio is invested in Treasury bills and money market funds because the trustees fear a financial crisis. The trustees do not anticipate any further capital contributions to the fund.

    The trustees are all successful businesspeople, and they have been critical of the fund's previous investment advisors because they did not follow a logical decision-making process. In fact, several previous managers have been dismissed because of their inability to communicate with the trustees and their preoccupation with the fund's relative performance rather than the cash flow needs.

    Advisory Securities Selection, Inc., has been contacted by the trustees because of its reputation for understanding and relating to the client's needs. The trustees have asked you, as a prospective portfolio manager for the Wood Museum Endowment Fund, to prepare a written report in response to the following questions. Your report will be circulated to the trustees before the initial interview on June 15, 1998.

    Explain in detail how each of the following relates to the determination of either investor objectives or investor constraints that can be used to determine the portfolio policies for this three-year period for the Wood Museum Endowment Fund.

    a. Liquidity requirements.

    b. Return requirements.

    c. Risk tolerance.

    d. Time horizon.

    e. Tax considerations.

    f. Regulatory and legal considerations.

    g. Unique needs and circumstances.

6. Mrs. Mary Atkins, age 66, has been your firm's client for five years, since the death of her husband, Dr. Charles Atkins. Dr. Atkins had built a successful newspaper business that he sold two years before his death to Merit Enterprises, a publishing and broadcasting conglomerate, in exchange for Merit common stock. The Atkinses have no children,

and their wills provide that upon their deaths the remaining assets shall be used to create a fund for the benefit of Good Samaritan Hospital, to be called the Atkins Endowment Fund.

Good Samaritan is a 180-bed, not-for-profit hospital with an annual operating budget of $12.5 million. In the past, the hospital's operating revenues have often been sufficient to meet operating expenses and occasionally even generate a small surplus. In recent years, however, rising costs and declining occupancy rates have caused Good Samaritan to run a deficit. The operating deficit has averaged $300,000 to $400,000 annually over the last several years. Existing endowment assets (that is, excluding the Atkins's estate) of $7.5 million currently generate approximately $375,000 of annual income, up from less than $200,000 five years ago. This increased income has been the result of somewhat higher interest rates, as well as a shift in asset mix toward more bonds. To offset operating deficits, the Good Samaritan Board of Governors has determined that the endowment's current income should be increased to approximately 6% of total assets (up from 5% currently). The hospital has not received any significant additions to its endowment assets in the past five years.

Identify and describe an appropriate set of investment objectives and constraints for the Atkins Endowment Fund to be created after Mrs. Atkins's death.

7. Several discussion meetings have provided the following information about one of your firm's new advisory clients, a charitable endowment fund recently created by means of a one-time $10 million gift:

Objectives

Return requirement. Planning is based on a minimum total return of 8% per year, including an initial current income component of $500,000 (5% on beginning capital). Realizing this current income target is the endowment fund's primary return goal. (See "unique needs" following.)

Constraints

Time horizon. Perpetuity, except for requirement to make an $8,500,000 cash distribution on June 30, 1999. (See "unique needs.")

Liquidity needs. None of a day-to-day nature until 1999. Income is distributed annually after year-end. (See "unique needs" below.)

Tax considerations. None; this endowment fund is exempt from taxes.

Legal and regulatory considerations. Minimal, but the prudent man rule applies to all investment actions.

Unique needs, circumstances, and preferences. The endowment fund must pay out to another tax-exempt entity the sum of $8,500,000 in cash on June 30, 1999. The assets remaining after this distribution will be retained by the fund in perpetuity. The endowment fund has adopted a "spending rule" requiring a first-year current income payout of $500,000; thereafter, the annual payout is to rise by 3% in real terms. Until 1999, annual income in excess of that required by the spending rule is to be reinvested. After 1999, the spending rate will be reset at 5% of the then-existing capital.

With this information and information found in this chapter, do the following:

a. Formulate an appropriate investment policy statement for the endowment fund.

b. Identify and briefly explain three major ways in which your firm's initial asset allocation decisions for the endowment fund will be affected by the circumstances of the account.

8. You have been named as investment advisor to a foundation established by Dr. Walter Jones with an original contribution consisting entirely of the common stock of Jomedco, Inc. Founded by Dr. Jones, Jomedco manufactures and markets medical devices invented by the doctor and collects royalties on other patented innovations.

All of the shares that made up the initial contribution to the foundation were sold at a public offering of Jomedco common stock, and the $5 million proceeds will be delivered to the foundation within the next week. At the same time, Mrs. Jones will receive $5 million in proceeds from the sale of her stock in Jomedco.

Dr. Jones's purpose in establishing the Jones Foundation was to "offset the effect of inflation on medical school tuition for the maximum number of worthy students."

You are preparing for a meeting with the foundation trustees to discuss investment policy and asset allocation.

a. Define and give examples that show the differences between an investment objective, an investment constraint, and investment policy.

b. Identify and describe an appropriate set of investment objectives and investment constraints for the Jones Foundation.

c. Based on the investment objectives and investment constraints identified in part **b**, prepare a comprehensive instrument policy statement for the Jones Foundation to be recommended for adoption by the trustees.

9. You are P. J. Walter, CFA, a managing partner of a prestigious investment counseling firm that specializes in individual rather than institutional accounts. The firm has developed a national reputation for its ability to blend modern portfolio theory and traditional portfolio methods. You have written a number of articles on portfolio management. You are an authority on the subject of establishing investment policies and programs for individual clients, tailored to their particular circumstances and needs.

Dr. and Mrs. A. J. Mason have been referred to your firm and to you in particular. At your first meeting on June 2, 1997, Dr. Mason explained that he is an electrical engineer and long-time professor at the Essex Institute. He is also an inventor and, after 30 years of teaching, the rights to one of his patented inventions, the "inverse thermothrocle valve," has just been acquired by a new electronics company, ACS, Inc.

In anticipation of the potential value of his invention, Dr. Mason had followed his accountant's advice and established a private corporation, wholly owned by the Masons, to hold the title to the inverse thermothrocle valve patent. It was this corporation that ACS acquired from the Masons for $1 million in cash, payable at the closing on June 7, 1997. In addition, ACS has agreed to pay royalties to Dr. Mason or his heirs, based on its sales of systems that utilize the inverse thermothrocle valve.

Since ACS has no operating record, it is difficult for either the company or Dr. Mason to forecast future sales and royalties. While all parties are optimistic about prospects for success, they are also mindful of the risks associated with any new firm, especially those exposed to the technological obsolescence of the electronics industry. The management of ACS has indicated to Dr. Mason that he might expect royalties of as much as $100,000 in the first year of production and maximum royalties of as much as $500,000 annually thereafter.

During your counseling meeting, Mrs. Mason expressed concern for the proper investment of the $1,000,000 initial payment. She pointed out that Dr. Mason has invested all of their savings in his inventions. Thus, they will have only their Social Security retirement benefits and a small pension from the Essex Institute to provide for their retirement. Dr. Mason will be 65 in 2001. His salary from the Essex Institute is $55,000 per year. Additionally, he expects to continue earning $10,000–$25,000 annually from consulting and speaking engagements.

The Masons have two daughters and a son, all of whom are married and have families of their own. Dr. and Mrs. Mason are interested in helping with the education of their grandchildren and have provided in their wills for their estate to be divided among their children and grandchildren.

In the event that the royalty payments from ACS meet the projections cited above, Mrs. Mason is interested in providing a scholarship fund in the name of Dr. Mason for the benefit of enterprising young engineers attending the Essex Institute. The scholarship fund ranks third behind the provision for the Masons' retirement and for the education of their grandchildren.

In your discussions with Dr. and Mrs. Mason, you have stressed the importance of identifying investment objectives and constraints and having an appropriate investment policy. Identify and describe an appropriate set of investment objectives and investment constraints for Dr. and Mrs. Mason, and prepare a comprehensive investment policy statement based on these investment objectives and constraints.

10. You are being interviewed for a job as a portfolio manager at an investment counseling partnership. As part of the interview, you are asked to demonstrate your ability to develop investment portfolio policy statements for the clients listed below:

   a. A pension fund that is described as a mature defined benefit plan; with the work force having an average age of 54; no unfunded pension liabilities; and wage cost increases forecast at 9% annually.

   b. A university endowment fund that is described as conservative; with investment returns being utilized along with gifts and donations received to meet current expenses, the spending rate is 5% per year; and inflation in costs is expected at 8% annually.

   c. A life insurance company that is described as specializing in annuities; policy premium rates are based on a minimum annual accumulation rate of 14% in the first year of the policy and a 10% minimum annual accumulation rate in the next five years.

List and discuss separately for *each* client described above the objectives and constraints that will determine the portfolio policy you would recommend for that client.

◼ IEM Applications

1. Describe your IEM investment objective and trading strategy. Are you an active investor or a passive investor? Why?

Solutions to Concept Checks

1. A convenient and effective way to organize the answer to this question is to cast it in the context of the investment policy statement framework.

   Risk: Endowment funds have no "safety nets" such as pension funds enjoy in the event of difficulty, either in the form of corporate assets to fall back on or a call on public assistance, such as from the Pension Benefit Guaranty Corporation. Moreover, endowment fund cash flows may be highly erratic due to the uncertain timing of income from gifts and/or bequests, while pension fund cash flows tend to be very predictable and steady. These differences suggest the typical endowment fund will adopt a more conservative risk-bearing posture than will the typical pension fund, both as to asset-class exposures and to the type of security content of such exposures.

   Return: Because investment-related spending usually is limited to "yield," endowment funds often focus their return goals on the matter of current spendable income; pension funds, on the other hand, tend to adopt total return approaches, at least until a plan matures. Although inflation protection is of great importance to both types of funds, endowment funds appear to be less concerned with real return production than are pension funds, perhaps because of their common emphasis on "income now" in setting return goals.

   Time horizon: Theoretically, an endowment fund is a perpetuity while a pension fund may well have a finite life span. Therefore, an endowment fund should operate with a very long-term view of investment. However, such funds in practice tend to adopt shorter horizons than are typical of pension funds (just as they typically assume less risk). Their tendency to emphasize income production in the near term is the probable reason for this common occurrence.

   Liquidity: Endowment funds, particularly those that use gifts and bequests to supplement their investment income, often have fairly large liquidity reserves—both to protect against fluctuations in their cash flows and reflecting their generally conservative outlooks—while, except for very mature plans, pension funds tend to require minimum liquidity reserves. Endowment funds also frequently maintain substantial liquid holdings to provide for known future cash payout requirements, such as for new buildings.

Taxes: Here, although differing in detail, the situation of the two forms of institutions are very much the same. In the United States, tax considerations are normally of minimal importance in both cases.

Regulatory/Legal: Endowment fund investment is carried out under state governance, while pension fund investment, in the United States, is carried out under federal law, specifically under ERISA. The difference is significant. Endowment funds operate under the prudent man rule, where each investment must be judged on its own merits apart from any other portfolio holdings, while pension plans operate under a broader context for investment—each security being judged in terms of the portfolio as a whole—and an ERISA-mandated diversification requirement that often leads to wider asset-class exposures. In a pragmatic sense, the prudent man rule is aimed at risk *reduction*, while the prudent expert provision of ERISA is aimed at risk *management*.

Unique circumstances: Endowment funds often are faced with unique situations that infrequently affect pension fund management, including the scrutiny of such special-interest groups as trustees, alumni, faculty, student organizations, local community pressure groups, etc., each with separate and often incomparable complaints and goals that may need to be accommodated in policy setting and/or in investment content. Similarly, endowment funds often are subjected to severe "social pressures" that, as in the case of tobacco firm divestment, can have an important investment impact by restricting the available universe of investment securities, mandating participation or nonparticipation in certain industries, sectors, or countries, or otherwise changing investment action from what it would otherwise have been. In pension fund investment, ERISA requires that no other interests be put ahead of the interests of the beneficiaries in determining investment actions.

2. Identify the elements that are life-cycle driven in the two schemes of objectives and constraints.

3. *a.* Policy, asset allocation.
   b. Constraint, regulation.
   c. Objective, return requirement.
   d. Constraint, horizon.
   e. Policy, market timing.
   f. Constraint, taxes.
   g. Objectives, risk tolerance.
   h. Constraint, liquidity.

4. *a.* Without any tax sheltering, the terminal value of the $10,000 savings is

$$\$10,000 \times [1 + (1 - 0.33)0.10]^{20} = \$36,583.76$$

When the contribution itself is not sheltered, but income on it is tax deferred, the before-tax terminal value is as before

$$\$10,000 \times (1 + 0.10)^{20} = \$67,275.00$$

of which all but $10,000 is taxable at 33%. The after-tax terminal value in this case is: $67,275 − 0.33(67,275 − 10,000) = $48,374.25. The value of tax deferral of income is: $48,374.25 − 36,583.76 = $11,790.49.

When the contribution tax is deferred, the before-tax contribution with an after-tax value of $10,000 is $10,000/0.67 = $14,925.37. The terminal value is

$$\$14,925.37(1 + 0.10)^{20} (1 - 0.33) = \$67,275.00$$

and the value of the tax deferral of the contribution is: $67,275.00 − 48,374.25 = $18,900.75.

b. When retiring in 10 years, the unsheltered terminal value is $19,126.88. When income is sheltered (tax deferred), the after-tax terminal value is $20,678.07. When contribution is sheltered, too, the after-tax terminal value is $25,937.42.

Part Two

PORTFOLIO THEORY

Suppose you believe that investments in stock offer an expected rate of return of 12% while the expected rate of return on bonds is only 8%. Would you invest all of your money in stock? Probably not: putting all of your eggs in one basket in such a manner would violate even the most basic notion of diversification. But what is the optimal combination of these two asset classes? And how will the opportunity to invest in other asset classes—for example, real estate, foreign stocks, precious metals, and so on—affect your decision? In short, is there a "best" solution to your asset allocation problem?

These questions are the focus of the first chapters of Part II, which address what has come to be known as Modern Portfolio Theory, or MPT. In large part, MPT addresses the question of "efficient diversification," how to achieve the best trade-off between portfolio risk and reward.

This analysis quickly leads to other questions. For example, how should one measure the risk of an individual asset held as part of a diversified portfolio? You will probably be surprised at the answer. Once we have an acceptable measure of risk, what precisely should be the relation between risk and return? And what is the minimally acceptable rate of return for an investment to be considered attractive? These questions also are addressed in this Part of the text.

Finally, we come to one of the most controversial topics in investment management, the question of whether portfolio managers—amateur or professional—can outperform simple investment strategies such as "buy a market index fund." The evidence will at least make you pause before pursuing active strategies.

You will come to appreciate how good active managers must be to outperform their passive counterparts.

Chapter 6

RISK AND RETURN:
PAST AND PROLOGUE

AFTER STUDYING THIS CHAPTER YOU SHOULD BE ABLE TO:

- Use data on the past performance of stocks and bonds to characterize the risk and return features of these investments.
- Determine the expected return and risk of portfolios that are constructed by combining risky assets with risk-free investments in Treasury bills.
- Evaluate the performance of a passive strategy.

What constitutes a satisfactory investment portfolio? Until the early 1970s, a reasonable answer would have been a bank savings account (a risk-free asset) plus a risky portfolio of U.S. stocks. Nowadays, investors have access to a vastly wider array of assets and may contemplate complex portfolio strategies that may include foreign stocks and bonds, real estate, precious metals, and collectibles. Even more complex strategies may include futures and options to insure portfolios against unacceptable losses. How might such portfolios be constructed?

Clearly, every individual security must be judged on its contributions to both the expected return and the risk of the entire portfolio. But these contributions must be evaluated in the context of the expected performance of the overall portfolio. To guide us in forming reasonable expectations for portfolio performance, we will start this chapter with an examination of various conventions for measuring and reporting rates of return. Given these measures, we turn to the historical performance of several broadly diversified investment portfolios. In doing so, we use a risk-free portfolio of Treasury bills as a benchmark to evaluate the historical performance of diversified stock and bond portfolios.

We then proceed to consider the trade-offs investors face when they practice the simplest form of risk control: choosing the fraction of the portfolio invested in virtually risk-free money market securities versus risky securities such as stocks. We show how to calculate the performance one may reasonably expect from various allocations between a risk-free asset and a risky portfolio and discuss the considerations that determine the mix that would best suit different investors. With this background, we can evaluate a passive strategy that will serve as a benchmark for the active strategies considered in the next chapter.

6.1 RATES OF RETURN

holding-period return
Rate of return over a
given investment period.

A key measure of investors' success is the rate at which their funds have grown during the investment period. The total **holding-period return (HPR)** of a share of stock depends on the increase (or decrease) in the price of the share over the investment period as well as on any dividend income the share has provided. The rate of return is defined as dollars earned over the investment period (price appreciation as well as dividends) per dollar invested.

$$HPR = \frac{\text{Ending price} - \text{Beginning price} + \text{Cash dividend}}{\text{Beginning price}}$$

This definition of the HPR assumes that the dividend is paid at the end of the holding period. To the extent that dividends are received earlier, the definition ignores reinvestment income between the receipt of the dividend and the end of the holding period. Recall also that the percentage return from dividends is called the dividend yield, and so the dividend yield plus the capital gains yield equals the HPR.

While we are assuming for now that the investor is holding stocks and receiving dividend income, the definition of holding return is easy to modify for other types of investments. For example, the HPR on a bond would be calculated using the same formula, except that the bond's interest or coupon payments would take the place of the stock's dividend payments.

EXAMPLE 6.1
Holding-Period
Return

Suppose you are considering investing some of your money, now all invested in a bank account, in a stock-market index fund. The price of a share in the fund is currently $100, and your time horizon is one year. You expect the cash dividend during the year to be $4, so your expected dividend yield is 4%.

Your HPR will depend on the price one year from now. Suppose your best guess is that it will be $110 per share. Then your *capital gain* will be $10, so your capital gains yield is $10/$100 = .10, or 10%. The total holding period rate of return is the sum of the dividend yield plus the capital gain yield, 4% + 10% = 14%.

$$HPR = \frac{\$110 - \$100 + \$4}{\$100} = .14, \text{ or } 14\%$$

Measuring Investment Returns over Multiple Periods

The holding period return is a simple and unambiguous measure of investment return over a single period. But often you will be interested in average returns over longer periods of time. For example, you might want to measure how well a mutual fund has performed over the preceding five-year period. In this case, return measurement is more ambiguous.

Consider, for example, a mutual fund that starts with $1 million under management at the beginning of the year. The fund receives additional funds to invest from new and existing shareholders, and also receives requests for redemptions from existing shareholders. Its net cash inflow can be positive or negative. Suppose its quarterly results are as given in the table below, with negative numbers reported in parentheses.

	1st Quarter	2nd Quarter	3rd Quarter	4th Quarter
Assets under management at start of quarter ($ million)	1.0	1.2	2.0	0.8
Holding period return (%)	10.0	25.0	(20.0)	25.0
Total assets before net inflows	1.1	1.5	1.6	1.0
Net inflow ($ million)[a]	0.1	0.5	(0.8)	0.0
Assets under managment at end of quarter ($ million)	1.2	2.0	0.8	1.0

[a]New investment less redemptions and distributions, all assumed to occur at the end of each quarter.

The story behind these numbers is that when the firm does well (i.e., reports a good HPR), it attracts new funds; otherwise it may suffer a net outflow. For example, the 10% return in the first quarter by itself increased assets under management by $0.10 \times \$1$ million = $100,000; it also elicited new investments of $100,000, thus bringing assets under management to $1.2 million by the end of the quarter. An even better HPR in the second quarter elicited a larger net inflow, and the second quarter ended with $2 million under management. However, HPR in the third quarter was negative, and net inflows were negative.

How would we characterize fund performance over the year, given that the fund experienced both cash inflows and outflows? There are several candidate measures of average performance, each with its own advantages and shortcomings. These are the *arithmetic average*, the *geometric average*, and the *dollar-weighted return*. These measures may vary considerably, so it is important to understand their differences.

arithmetic average
The sum of returns in each period divided by the number of periods.

Arithmetic Average   The **arithmetic average** of the quarterly returns is just the sum of the quarterly returns divided by the number of quarters; in the above example: $(10 + 25 - 20 + 25)/4 = 10\%$. Since this statistic ignores compounding, it does not represent an equivalent, single quarterly rate for the year. The arithmetic average is useful, though, because it is the best forecast of performance in future quarters, using this particular sample of historic returns. (Whether the sample is large enough or representative enough to make accurate forecasts is, of course, another question.)

geometric average
The single per-period return that gives the same cumulative performance as the sequence of actual returns.

Geometric Average   The **geometric average** of the quarterly returns is equal to the single per-period return that would give the same cumulative performance as the sequence of actual returns. We calculate the geometric average by compounding the actual period-by-period returns and then finding the equivalent single per-period return. In this case, the geometric average quarterly return, r_G, is defined by:

$$(1 + 0.10) \times (1 + 0.25) \times (1 - 0.20) \times (1 + 0.25) = (1 + r_G)^4$$

so that

$$r_G = [(1 + 0.10) \times (1 + 0.25) \times (1 - 0.20) \times (1 + 0.25)]^{1/4} - 1 = .0829, \text{ or } 8.29\%$$

The geometric return also is called a *time-weighted average return* because it ignores the quarter-to-quarter variation in funds under management. In fact, an investor will obtain a larger cumulative return if high returns are earned in those periods when additional sums have been invested, while the lower returns are realized when less money is at risk. Here, the highest returns (25%) were achieved in quarters 2 and 4, when the fund managed $1,200,000 and $800,000, respectively. The worst returns (−20% and 10%) occurred when the fund managed $2,000,000 and $1,000,000, respectively. In this case, better returns were earned when *less* money was under management—an unfavorable combination.

The appeal of the time-weighted return is that in some cases we *wish* to ignore variation in money under management. For example, published data on past returns earned by mutual funds actually are *required* to be time-weighted returns. The rationale for this practice is that since the fund manager does not have full control over assets under management, we should not weight returns in one period more heavily than those in other periods when assessing "typical" past performance.

Dollar-Weighted Return   When we wish to account for the varying amounts under management, we treat the fund cash flows to investors as we would a capital budgeting problem in corporate finance. The initial value of $1 million and the net cash inflows are treated as the cash flows associated with an investment "project." The final "liquidation value" of the project is the ending value of the portfolio. In this case, therefore, investor net cash flows are as follows:

	Time				
	0	**1**	**2**	**3**	**4**
Net cash flow ($ million)	−1.0	−0.1	−0.5	0.8	1.0

The entry for time 0 reflects the starting contribution of $1 million, while the entries for times 1, 2, and 3 represent net inflows at the end of the first three quarters. Finally, the entry for time 4 represents the value of the portfolio at the end of the fourth quarter. This is the value for which the portfolio could have been liquidated by year end based on the initial investment and net additional investments earlier in the year.

dollar-weighted average return
The internal rate of return on an investment.

The **dollar-weighted average return** is the internal rate of return (IRR) of the project, which is 4.17%. The IRR is the interest rate that sets the present value of the cash flows realized on the portfolio (including the $1 million for which the portfolio can be liquidated at the end of the year) equal to the initial cost of establishing the portfolio. It therefore is the interest rate that satisfies the following equation:

$$1.0 = \frac{-0.1}{1 + \text{IRR}} + \frac{-0.5}{(1 + \text{IRR})^2} + \frac{0.8}{(1 + \text{IRR})^3} + \frac{1.0}{(1 + \text{IRR})^4}$$

The dollar-weighted return is less than the time-weighted return of 8.29% because, as we noted, the portfolio returns were higher when less money was under management. The difference between the dollar- and time-weighted average return in this case is quite large.

Are time- and dollar-weighted averages to be preferred? It depends on whether amounts under management do affect performance.

Concept Check

1. A fund begins with $10 million and reports the following three-month results (with negative figures in parentheses):

	Month		
	1	**2**	**3**
Net inflows (End of month, $ million)	3	5	0
HPR (%)	2	8	(4)

Compute the arithmetic, time-weighted, and dollar-weighted average returns.

Conventions for Quoting Rates of Return

We've seen that there are several ways to compute average rates of return. There also is some variation in how the mutual fund in our example might annualize its quarterly returns.

Returns on assets with regular cash flows, such as mortgages (with monthly payments) and bonds (with semiannual coupons), usually are quoted as annual percentage rates, or APRs, which annualize per-period rates using a simple interest approach, ignoring compound interest. The APR can be translated to an effective annual rate (EAR) by remembering that

$$\text{APR} = \text{Per period rate} \times \text{Periods per year}$$

Therefore, to obtain the EAR if there are n compounding periods in the year, we first recover the rate per period as APR/n and then compound that rate for the number of periods in a year. (For example, $n = 12$ for mortgages and $n = 2$ for bonds making payments semiannually).

$$1 + \text{EAR} = (1 + \text{Rate per period})^n = \left(1 + \frac{\text{APR}}{n}\right)^n$$

Rearranging,

$$\text{APR} = [(1 + \text{EAR})^{1/n} - 1] \times n \tag{6.1}$$

The formula assumes that you can earn the APR each period. Therefore, after one year (when n periods have passed), your cumulative return would be $(1 + \frac{APR}{n})^n$. Note that one needs to know the holding period when given an APR in order to convert it to an effective rate.

The EAR diverges from the APR as n becomes larger (i.e., as we compound cash flows more often). In the limit, we can envision continuous compounding; that is, we assume extremely large n in Equation 6.1. With continuous compounding, the relationship between the APR and EAR becomes

$$EAR = e^{APR} - 1$$

or equivalently,

$$APR = \log(1 + EAR) \tag{6.2}$$

EXAMPLE 6.2 **Annualizing** **Treasury-Bill** **Returns**	Suppose you buy a Treasury bill maturing in one month for $9,900. On the bill's maturity date, you collect the face value of $10,000. Since there are no other interest payments, the holding period return for this one-month investment is:

$$HPR = \frac{\text{Cash income} + \text{Price change}}{\text{Initial price}} = \frac{\$100}{\$9,900} = 0.0101 = 1.01\%$$

The APR on this investment is therefore $1.01\% \times 12 = 12.12\%$. The effective annual rate is higher:

$$1 + EAR = (1.0101)^{12} = 1.1282$$

which implies that $EAR = .1282 = 12.82\%$

The considerable difficulty with interpreting rates of return over time does not end here. Two thorny issues remain: the uncertainty surrounding the investment in question, and the effect of inflation.

6.2 RISK AND RISK PREMIUMS

Any investment involves some degree of uncertainty about future holding period returns, and in most cases that uncertainty is considerable. Sources of investment risk range from macroeconomic fluctuations, to the changing fortunes of various industries, to asset-specific unexpected developments. Analysis of these multiple sources of risk is presented in Part Four.

scenario analysis
Process of devising a list of possible economic scenarios and specifying the likelihood of each one, as well as the HPR that will be realized in each case.

probability distribution
List of possible outcomes with associated probabilities.

expected return
The "reward" from an investment.

Scenario Analysis and Probability Distributions

When we attempt to quantify risk, we begin with the question: "What HPRs are possible, and how likely are they?" A good way to approach this question is to devise a list of possible economic outcomes, or *scenarios*, and specify both the likelihood (i.e., the probability) of each scenario and the HPR the asset will realize in that scenario. Therefore, this approach is called **scenario analysis.** The list of possible HPRs with associated probabilities is called the **probability distribution** of HPRs. Consider an investment in a broad portfolio of stocks, say an index fund, which we will refer to as the "stock market." A very simple scenario analysis for the stock market (assuming only three possible scenarios) is illustrated in Table 6.1.

The probability distribution lets us derive measurements for both the reward and the risk of the investment. The reward from the investment is its **expected return,** which you can think of as the average HPR you would earn if you were to repeat an investment in the asset

TABLE 6.1

Probability Distribution of HPR on the Stock Market

State of the Economy	Scenario, s	Probability, p(s)	HPR
Boom	1	0.25	44%
Normal growth	2	0.50	14
Recession	3	0.25	−16

many times. The expected return also is called the mean of the distribution of HPRs, and often is referred to as the *mean return*.

To compute the expected return from the data provided, we label scenarios by s and denote the HPR in each scenario as $r(s)$, with probability $p(s)$. The expected return, denoted $E(r)$, is then the weighted average of returns in all possible scenarios, with weights equal to the probability of that particular scenario.

$$E(r) = \sum_s p(s)r(s) \tag{6.3}$$

We show in Example 6.3, which follows shortly, that the data in Table 6.1 imply $E(r) = 14\%$.

Of course, there is risk to the investment, and the actual return may be more or less than 14%. If a "boom" materializes, the return will be better, 44%, but in a recession, the return will be only −16%. How can we quantify the uncertainty of the investment?

The "surprise" return on the investment in any scenario is the difference between the actual return and the expected return. For example, in a boom (scenario 1) the surprise is 30%: $r(1) − E(r) = 44\% − 14\% = 30\%$. In a recession (scenario 3), the surprise is −30%: $r(3) − E(r) = −16\% − 14\% = −30\%$.

variance
The expected value of the squared deviation from the mean.

Uncertainty surrounding the investment is a function of the magnitudes of the possible surprises. To summarize risk with a single number we first define the **variance** as the expected value of the *squared* deviation from the mean (i.e., the expected value of the squared "surprise" across scenarios).

$$\text{Var}(r) \equiv \sigma^2 = \sum_s p(s)[r(s) − E(r)]^2 \tag{6.4}$$

We first square the deviations because if we did not, negative deviations would offset positive deviations, with the result that the expected deviation from the mean return would necessarily be zero. Squared deviations are necessarily positive. Of course, squaring is a nonlinear transformation that exaggerates large (positive or negative) deviations and deemphasizes small deviations.

Another result of squaring deviations is that the variance has a dimension of percent squared. To give the measure of risk the same dimension as expected return (%), we use the **standard deviation,** defined as the square root of the variance:

standard deviation
The square root of the variance.

$$SD(r) \equiv \sigma = \sqrt{\text{Var}(r)} = \{\sum_s p(s)[r(s) − E(r)]^2\}^{1/2} \tag{6.5}$$

A potential drawback to the use of standard deviation as a measure of risk is that it treats positive deviations and negative deviations from the expected return symmetrically. In practice, of course, we know that investors welcome positive surprises, and a natural measure of risk would focus only on bad outcomes. However, if the distribution of returns is symmetric (meaning that the likelihood of negative surprises is roughly equal to the probability of positive surprises of the same magnitude), then standard deviation will approximate risk measures that concentrate solely on negative deviations. In the special case that the distribution of returns is approximately normal—represented by the well-known bell-shaped curve—the standard deviation will be perfectly adequate to measure risk. The evidence shows that for fairly short holding periods, the returns of most diversified portfolios are reasonably close to a normal distribution.

EXAMPLE 6.3
Expected Return
and Standard
Deviation

Applying Equation 6.3 to the data in Table 6.1, we find that the expected rate of return on the stock index fund is

$$E(r) = 0.25 \times 44\% + 0.50 \times 14\% + 0.25 \times (-16\%) = 14\%$$

We use Equation 6.4 to find the variance. First we take the difference between the holding period return in each scenario and the mean return, then we square that difference, and finally we multiply by the probability of each scenario to find the average of the squared deviations. The result is

$$\sigma^2 = 0.25(44 - 14)^2 + 0.50(14 - 14)^2 + 0.25(-16 - 14)^2 = 450$$

and so the standard deviation is

$$\sigma = \sqrt{450} = 21.21\%$$

How much, if anything, should you invest in an index stock fund such as the one described in Table 6.1? First, you must ask how much of an expected reward is offered to compensate for the risk involved in investing money in stocks.

risk-free rate
The rate of return that can be earned with certainty.

risk premium
An expected return in excess of that on risk-free securities.

risk aversion
Reluctance to accept risk.

We measure the "reward" as the difference between the expected HPR on the index stock fund and the **risk-free rate,** that is, the rate you can earn by leaving money in risk-free assets such as T-bills, money market funds, or the bank. We call this difference the **risk premium** on common stocks. For example, if the risk-free rate in the example is 6% per year, and the expected index fund return is 14%, then the risk premium on stocks is 8% per year.

The degree to which investors are willing to commit funds to stocks depends on **risk aversion**. It seems obvious that investors are risk averse in the sense that, if the risk premium were zero, people would not be willing to invest any money in stocks. In theory then, there must always be a positive risk premium on stocks in order to induce risk-averse investors to hold the existing supply of stocks instead of placing all their money in risk-free assets.

In fact, the risk premium is what distinguishes gambling from speculation. Investors who are willing to take on risk because they expect to earn a risk premium are speculating. Speculation is undertaken *despite* the risk because the speculator sees a favorable risk-return trade-off. In contrast, gambling is the assumption of risk for no purpose beyond the enjoyment of the risk itself. Gamblers take on risk even without the prospect of a risk premium.[1]

Although our simple scenario analysis illustrates the concepts behind the quantification of risk and return, you still may wonder how to get a more realistic estimate of the expected return and volatility of common stocks and other types of securities. Here history has insights to offer.

Concept Check

2. A share of stock of A-Star Inc. is now selling for $23.50. A financial analyst summarizes the uncertainty about the rate of return on the stock by specifying three possible scenarios:

Business Conditions	Scenario, s	Probability, p	End-of-Year Price	Annual Dividend
High growth	1	0.35	$35	$4.40
Normal growth	2	0.30	27	4.00
No growth	3	0.35	15	4.00

What are the holding period returns for a one-year investment in the stock of A-Star Inc. for each of the three scenarios? Calculate the expected HPR and standard deviation of the HPR.

---

[1]Sometimes a gamble might *seem* like speculation to the participants. If two investors have different views about the future, they might take opposite positions in a security, and both may have an expectation of earning a positive risk premium. In such cases, only one party can, in fact, be correct.

TABLE 6.2

Rates of Return
1926–1996

Source: Inflation data: Bureau
of Labor Statistics
Security return data for 1926–
1995: Center for Research in
Security Prices
Security return data for 1996:
Returns on appropriate index
portfolios

Year	Small Stocks	Large Stocks	Long-Term T-Bonds	Intermediate-term T-Bonds	T-Bills	Inflation
1926	−8.91	12.21	4.54	4.96	3.19	−1.12
1927	32.23	35.99	8.11	3.34	3.12	−2.26
1928	45.02	39.29	−0.93	0.96	3.21	−1.16
1929	−50.81	−7.66	4.41	5.89	4.74	0.58
1930	−45.69	−25.90	6.22	5.51	2.35	−6.40
1931	−49.17	−45.56	−5.31	−5.81	0.96	−9.32
1932	10.95	−9.14	11.89	8.44	1.16	−10.27
1933	187.82	54.56	1.03	0.35	0.07	0.76
1934	25.13	−2.32	10.15	9.00	0.60	1.52
1935	68.44	45.67	4.98	7.01	−1.59	2.99
1936	84.47	33.55	6.52	3.77	−0.95	1.45
1937	−52.71	−36.03	0.43	1.56	0.35	2.86
1938	24.69	29.42	5.25	5.64	0.09	−2.78
1939	−0.10	−1.06	5.90	4.52	0.02	0.00
1940	−11.81	−9.65	6.54	2.03	0.00	0.71
1941	−13.08	−11.20	0.99	−0.59	0.06	9.93
1942	51.01	20.80	5.39	1.81	0.26	9.03
1943	99.79	26.54	4.87	2.78	0.35	2.96
1944	60.53	20.96	3.59	1.98	−0.07	2.30
1945	82.24	36.11	6.84	3.60	0.33	2.25
1946	−12.80	−9.26	0.15	0.69	0.37	18.13
1947	−3.09	4.88	−1.19	0.32	0.50	8.84
1948	−6.15	5.29	3.07	2.21	0.81	2.99
1949	21.56	18.24	6.03	2.22	1.10	−2.07
1950	45.48	32.68	−0.96	0.25	1.20	5.93
1951	9.41	23.47	−1.95	0.36	1.49	6.00
1952	6.36	18.91	1.93	1.63	1.66	0.75
1953	−5.68	−1.74	3.83	3.63	1.82	0.75
1954	65.13	52.55	4.88	1.73	0.86	−0.74
1955	21.84	31.44	−1.34	−0.52	1.57	0.37
1956	3.82	6.45	−5.12	−0.90	2.46	2.99
1957	−15.03	−11.14	9.46	7.84	3.14	2.90
1958	70.63	43.78	−3.71	−1.29	1.54	1.76
1959	17.82	12.95	−3.55	−1.26	2.95	1.73
1960	−5.16	0.19	13.78	11.98	2.66	1.36
1961	30.48	27.63	0.19	2.23	2.13	0.67
1962	−16.41	−8.79	6.81	7.38	2.72	1.33
1963	12.20	22.63	−0.49	1.79	3.12	1.64
1964	18.75	16.67	4.51	4.45	3.54	0.97
1965	37.67	12.50	−0.27	1.27	3.94	1.92
1966	−8.08	−10.25	3.70	5.14	4.77	3.46
1967	103.39	24.11	−7.41	0.16	4.24	3.04
1968	50.61	11.00	−1.20	2.48	5.24	4.72
1969	−32.27	−8.33	−6.52	−2.10	6.59	6.20
1970	−16.54	4.10	12.69	13.93	6.50	5.57
1971	18.44	14.17	17.47	8.71	4.34	3.27
1972	−0.62	19.14	5.55	3.80	3.81	3.41
1973	−40.54	−14.75	1.40	2.90	6.91	8.71
1974	−29.74	−26.40	5.53	6.03	7.93	12.34
1975	69.54	37.26	8.50	6.79	5.80	6.94
1976	54.81	23.98	11.07	14.20	5.06	4.86
1977	22.02	−7.26	0.90	1.12	5.10	6.70
1978	22.29	6.50	−4.16	0.32	7.15	9.02
1979	43.99	18.77	9.02	4.29	10.45	13.29
1980	35.34	32.48	13.17	0.83	11.57	12.52
1981	7.79	−4.98	3.61	6.09	14.95	8.92
1982	27.44	22.09	6.52	33.39	10.71	3.83
1983	34.49	22.37	−0.53	5.44	8.85	3.79
1984	−14.02	6.46	15.29	14.46	10.02	3.95
1985	28.21	32.00	32.68	23.65	7.83	3.80
1986	3.40	18.40	23.96	17.22	6.18	1.10
1987	−13.95	5.34	−2.65	1.68	5.50	4.43
1988	21.72	16.86	8.40	6.63	6.44	4.42
1989	8.37	31.34	19.49	14.82	8.32	4.65
1990	−27.08	−3.20	7.13	9.05	7.86	6.11
1991	50.24	30.66	18.39	16.67	5.65	3.06
1992	27.84	7.71	7.79	7.25	3.54	2.90
1993	20.30	9.87	15.48	12.02	2.97	2.75
1994	−3.34	1.29	−7.18	−4.42	3.91	2.67
1995	33.21	37.71	31.67	18.07	5.58	2.54
1996	16.50	23.00	0.10	2.70	5.20	3.32
Average	19.02	12.50	5.31	5.16	3.76	3.22
Standard Deviation	40.44	20.39	7.96	6.47	3.35	4.54
Minimum	−52.71	−45.56	−7.41	−5.81	−1.59	−10.27
Maximum	187.82	54.56	32.68	33.39	14.95	18.13

6.3 THE HISTORICAL RECORD

Bills, Bonds, and Stocks, 1926–1996

The record of past rates of return is one possible source of information about risk premiums and standard deviations. We can estimate the historical risk premium by taking an average of the past differences between the HPRs on an asset class and the risk-free rate. Table 6.2 presents the annual HPRs on five asset classes for the period 1926–1996.

"Large Stocks" in Table 6.2 refer to Standard & Poor's market value-weighted portfolio of 500 U.S. common stocks with the largest market capitalization. "Small Company Stocks" represent the value-weighted portfolio of the lowest-capitalization quintile (that is, the firms in the bottom 20% of all companies traded on the NYSE when ranked by market capitalization). Since 1982, this portfolio has included smaller stocks listed on the Amex and Nasdaq markets as well. The portfolio contains approximately 2,000 stocks with average capitalization of $100 million, and it is tilted toward smaller companies.

"Long-Term T-Bonds" are represented by a government bond with at least a 20-year maturity and approximately current-level coupon rate.[2] "Intermediate-Term T-Bonds" Have at least a seven-year maturity with a current-level coupon rate.

"T-Bills" in Table 6.2 are of approximately 30-day maturity, and the one-year HPR represents a policy of "rolling over" the bills as they mature. Because T-bill rates can change from month to month, the total rate of return on these T-bills is riskless only for 30-day holding periods.[3] The last column gives the annual inflation rate as measured by the rate of change in the Consumer Price Index.

Figure 6.1 summarizes some of the data in Table 6.2. The first column gives the geometric averages of the historical rates of return on each asset class; this figure thus represents the compound rate of growth in the value of an investment in these assets. The second column shows the arithmetic averages that, absent additional information, might serve as forecasts of the future HPRs for these assets. The last column is the variability of asset returns, as measured by standard deviation. The historical results are consistent with the risk-return trade-off: Riskier assets have provided higher expected returns, and historical risk premiums are considerable.

FIGURE 6.1

Frequency Distribution of Annual HPRs, 1926 to 1996

Source: Prepared from data in Table 6.2.

Series	Geometric Mean	Arithmetic Mean	Standard Deviation	Distribution
Large company stocks	10.5%	12.5%	20.4%	
Small company stocks	12.6	19.0	40.4	*
Long-term gov't bonds	5.0	5.3	8.0	
U.S. Treasury bills	3.7	3.8	3.3	
Inflation	3.1	3.2	4.5	

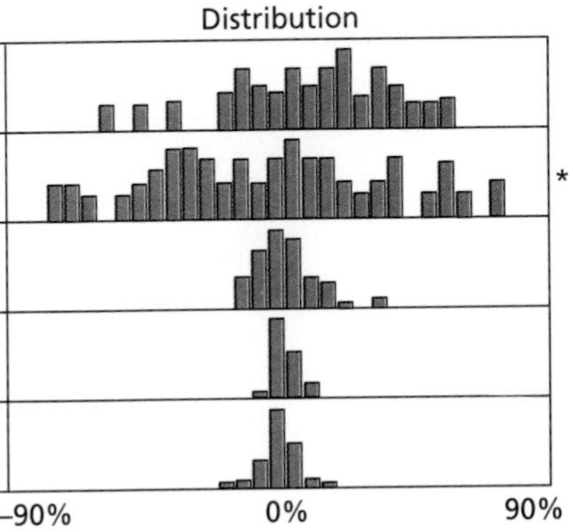

−90%   0%   90%

*The 1933 small company stock total return was 187.8%.

---

[2] The importance of the coupon rate when comparing returns on bonds is discussed in Part Three.

[3] The few negative returns in this column, all dating from before World War II, reflect periods where, in the absence of T-bills, returns on government securities with about 30-day maturity have been used. However, these securities included options to be exchanged for other securities, thus increasing their price and lowering their yield relative to what a simple T-bill would have offered.

**EXAMPLE 6.4
The Risk
Premium and
Growth of
Wealth**

The dollar import of the risk premiums suggested by Table 6.2 can be illustrated with a simple example. Consider two investors with $1,000 as of December 31, 1986. One invests in the small-stock portfolio, and the other in T-bills. Both investors reinvest all income from their portfolios and liquidate their investments on December 31, 1996. Using the rates from Table 6.2 we have:

Year	r(Small Stocks) %	r(T-Bills) %
1987	−13.95	5.50
1988	21.72	6.44
1989	8.37	8.32
1990	−27.08	7.86
1991	50.24	5.65
1992	27.84	3.54
1993	20.30	2.97
1994	−3.34	3.91
1995	33.21	5.58
1996	16.50	5.20
Final value of portfolio	$2,869	$1,706

The final value of the portfolio is obtained by multiplying the initial $1,000 investment by 1 plus the rate of return (expressed as a decimal) for each year. The results show an increase of 186.9% in the value of the small-stock portfolio and an increase of 70.6% for T-bills.

We also can calculate the geometric average return over this period. For small stocks, the geometric average, r_G, over this 10-year period is defined by:

$$(1 + r_G)^{10} = 2.869$$

$$1 + r_G = (2.869)^{1/10} = 1.1112$$

$$r_G = .1112 = 11.12\%$$

You can confirm that the geometric average return for bills was 5.49%. This tells us that the 10-year period between 1987–1996 was less favorable to small stocks than the 1926–1996 period (during which the geometric average return was 12.6%), and more favorable to T-bills (with long-run geometric average return of 3.7%). Nevertheless, even in this period there was a considerable reward to the risky investment.

The third statistic reported in Figure 6.1 is the standard deviation. The higher the standard deviation, the more volatile the HPR. The standard deviation reported in Figure 6.1, however, is based on historical data rather than forecasts of future scenarios, as in Equation 6.5. To calculate standard deviation from historical data, we treat each year's outcome as one possible scenario in a scenario analysis. Each historical outcome is taken as equally likely and given a "probability" of $1/n$.

The formula for historical variance is thus similar to Equation 6.5, but instead of using deviations of returns around *mean* returns based on the scenario analysis, we use deviations from *average* returns during the sample period. This procedure results in one minor complication. When we use the sample average return $\bar{r}$ in place of the mean return, $E(r)$, we must modify the average of the squared deviations for what statisticians call a "lost degree of freedom." The modification is easy: Multiply the average value of the squared deviations by $\frac{n}{n-1}$. The formula for variance based on historical data is thus:

$$\sigma^2 = \frac{n}{n-1} \times \text{Sample average of squared deviations from average return}$$

$$= \frac{n}{n-1} \times \sum_{t=1}^{n} \frac{(r_t - \bar{r})^2}{n} \tag{6.6}$$

When you are using large samples and n is large, the modification is unimportant, since $n/(n-1)$ is close to 1.0.

EXAMPLE 6.5
Historical Means and Standard Deviations

To illustrate how to calculate the mean returns and standard deviations from historical data, let's compute these statistics for the returns on the S&P 500 portfolio using the five years of data in Table 6.2 from 1988–1992. The average return is 16.7%, computed by dividing the sum of column (1), below, by the number of observations. In column (2), we take the deviation of each year's return from the 16.7% average return. In column (3), we calculate the squared deviation. The variance is the average squared deviation multiplied by $5/(5-1) = 5/4$. The standard deviation is the square root of the variance.

Year	(1) Rate of Return	(2) Deviation from Average Return	(3) Squared Deviation
1988	16.9%	0.2%	0.0
1989	31.3	14.6	213.2
1990	−3.2	−19.9	396.0
1991	30.7	14.0	196.0
1992	7.7	−9.0	81.0
Total	83.4%		886.2

Average rate of return = 83.4/5 = 16.7

$$\text{Variance} = \frac{5}{4} \times \frac{886.2}{5} = 221.6$$

$$\text{Standard deviation} = \sqrt{221.6} = 14.9\%$$

Figure 6.2 gives a graphic representation of the relative variabilities of the annual HPR for three different asset classes: large stocks, long-term T-bonds, and T-bills. We have plotted the three time series on the same set of axes, each in a different color. The graph shows very clearly that the annual HPR on stocks is the most variable series. The standard deviation of large-stock returns has been 20.4% compared to 7.96% for long-term government bonds and 3.76% for bills. Here is evidence of the risk-return trade-off that characterizes security markets: The markets with the highest average returns are also the most volatile.

An all-stock portfolio with a standard deviation of 20.4% would represent a very volatile investment. For example, if stock returns are normally distributed with a standard deviation of 20.4% and an expected rate of return of 12.5% (the historical average), then in roughly

FIGURE 6.2

Rates of Return on Stocks, Bonds, and Treasury Bills, 1926–1996.

Source: Prepared from data in Table 6.2.

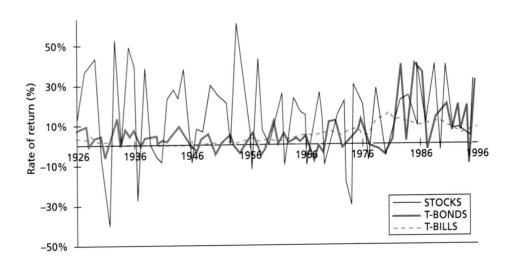

FIGURE 6.3
The Normal
Distribution

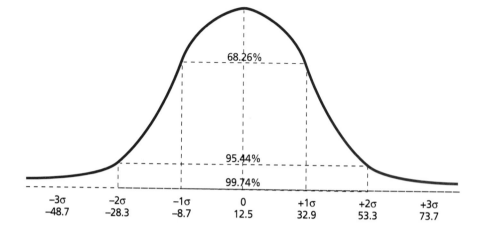

Decile	Geometric Mean	Arithmetic Mean	Standard Deviation
1-Largest	9.8%	11.6%	18.9%
2	11.1	13.5	22.4
3	11.5	14.1	24.2
4	11.6	14.8	26.7
5	12.2	15.6	27.5
6	11.8	15.6	28.5
7	11.9	16.1	31.0
8	12.2	17.3	34.8
9	12.3	18.0	37.3
10-Smallest	13.8	21.9	46.5
Mid-cap, deciles 3-5	11.7	14.6	25.4
Low-cap, deciles 6-8	12.0	16.1	30.4
Micro-cap, deciles 9-10	12.8	19.0	39.6
NYSE total value-weighted index	10.4	12.3	20.2

TABLE 6.3
Summary of Annual
Returns on Size-Decile
Portfolios of the NYSE,
1926–1996

one year out of three, returns will be less than −7.9% (12.5 − 20.4), or greater than 32.9% (12.5 + 20.4).

Figure 6.3 is a graph of the normal curve with mean 12.5% and standard deviation 20.4%. The graph shows the theoretical probability of rates of return within various ranges given these parameters. Now observe the frequency distributions in Figure 6.1. The resemblance to the normal distribution is quite clear, and the variation in the dispersion of the frequency distributions across the different asset classes vividly illustrates the difference in standard deviation and its implication for risk.

The performance of the small stock portfolio documented in the preceding figures and tables is striking. Table 6.3 shows average returns and standard deviation for NYSE portfolios arranged by firm size. Average returns generally are higher as firm size declines. The data clearly suggest that small firms have earned a substantial risk premium and therefore that firm size seems to be an important proxy for risk. In later chapters we will further explore this phenomenon and will see that the size effect can be further explained by other attributes of the firm.

We would stress that variability of HPR in the past sometimes can be an unreliable guide to risk, at least in the case of the risk-free asset. For an investor with a holding period of one year, for example, a one-year T-bill is a riskless investment, at least in terms of its nominal return, which is known with certainty. However, the standard deviation of the one-year T-bill rate estimated from historical data is not zero: This reflects variation in expected returns rather than fluctuations of actual returns around prior expectations.

Concept Check

3. Compute the average excess return on large company stocks (over the T-bill rate) and the standard deviation for the years 1926–1934.

6.4 INFLATION AND REAL RATES OF RETURN

The historical rates of return we reviewed in the previous section were measured in dollars. A 10% annual rate of return, for example, means that your investment was worth 10% more at the end of the year than it was at the beginning of the year. This does not necessarily mean, however, that you could have bought 10% more goods and services with that money, for it is possible that in the course of the year prices of goods also increased. If prices have changed, the increase in your purchasing power will not equal the increase in your dollar wealth.

At any time, the prices of some goods may rise while the prices of other goods may fall; the *general* trend in prices is measured by examining changes in the consumer price index, or CPI. The CPI measures the cost of purchasing a bundle of goods that is considered representative of the "consumption basket" of a typical urban family of four. Increases in the cost of this standardized consumption basket are indicative of a general trend toward higher prices. The **inflation rate,** or the rate at which prices are rising, is measured as the rate of increase of the CPI.

inflation rate
The rate at which prices are rising, measured as the rate of increase of the CPI.

Suppose the rate of inflation (the percentage change in the CPI, denoted by i) for the last year amounted to $i = 6\%$. This tells you the purchasing power of money is reduced by 6% a year. The value of each dollar depreciates by 6% a year in terms of the goods it can buy. Therefore, part of your interest earnings are offset by the reduction in the purchasing power of the dollars you will receive at the end of the year. With a 10% interest rate, after you net out the 6% reduction in the purchasing power of money, you are left with a net increase in purchasing power of about 4%. Thus, we need to distinguish between a **nominal interest rate**—the growth rate of your money—and a **real interest rate**—the growth rate of your purchasing power. If we call R the nominal rate, r the real rate, and i the inflation rate, then we conclude

nominal interest rate
The interest rate in terms of nominal (not adjusted for purchasing power) dollars.

$$r \approx R - i$$

real interest rate
The excess of the interest rate over the inflation rate. The growth rate of purchasing power derived from an investment.

In words, the real rate of interest is the nominal rate reduced by the loss of purchasing power resulting from inflation.

In fact, the exact relationship between the real and nominal interest rate is given by

$$1 + r = \frac{1 + R}{1 + i}$$

In words, the growth factor of your purchasing power, $1 + r$, equals the growth factor of your money, $1 + R$, divided by the new price level that is $1 + i$ times its value in the previous period. The exact relationship can be rearranged to

$$r = \frac{R - i}{1 + i}$$

which shows that the approximation rule overstates the real rate by the factor $1 + i$.

For example, if the interest rate on a one-year CD is 8%, and you expect inflation to be 5% over the coming year, then using the approximation formula, you expect the real rate to be $r = 8\% - 5\% = 3\%$. Using the exact formula, the real rate is $r = \frac{.08 - .05}{1 + .05}$ = .0286, or 2.86%. Therefore, the approximation rule overstates the expected real rate by only 0.14 percentage points. The approximation rule is more accurate for small inflation rates and is perfectly exact for continuously compounded rates.

To summarize, in interpreting the historical returns on various asset classes presented in Table 6.2, we must recognize that to obtain the real returns on these assets, we must reduce the nominal returns by the inflation rate presented in the last column of the table. In fact, while the return on a U.S. Treasury bill usually is considered to be riskless, this is true only with regard to its nominal return. To infer the expected real rate of return on a Treasury bill, you must subtract your estimate of the inflation rate over the coming period.

It is always possible to calculate the real rate after the fact. The inflation rate is published by the Bureau of Labor Statistics. The *future* real rate, however, is unknown, and one has to rely on expectations. In other words, because future inflation is risky, the real rate of return is risky even if the nominal rate is risk free.

The Equilibrium Nominal Rate of Interest

We've seen that the real rate of return on an asset is approximately equal to the nominal rate minus the inflation rate. Because investors should be concerned with their real returns—the increase in their purchasing power—we would expect that as the inflation rate increases, investors will demand higher nominal rates of return on their investments. This higher rate is necessary to maintain the expected real return offered by an investment.

Irving Fisher (1930) argued that the nominal rate ought to increase one for one with increases in the expected inflation rate. If we use the notation $E(i)$ to denote the current expectation of the inflation rate that will prevail over the coming period, then we can state the so-called Fisher equation formally as

$$R = r + E(i)$$

Suppose the real rate of interest is 2%, and the inflation rate is 4%, so that the nominal interest rate is about 6%. If the rate of inflation increases to 5%, the nominal rate should climb to roughly 7%. The increase in the nominal rate offsets the increase in the inflation rate, giving investors an unchanged growth of purchasing power at a 2% real rate. The evidence for the Fisher equation is that periods of high inflation and high nominal rates generally coincide, although taxes may complicate the relationship. Figure 6.4 illustrates this fact.

Concept Check

4. *a.* Suppose the real interest rate is 3% per year, and the expected inflation rate is 8%. What is the nominal interest rate?

   b. Suppose the expected inflation rate rises to 10%, but the real rate is unchanged. What happens to the nominal interest rate?

FIGURE 6.4

Interest and Inflation Rates, 1953–1995

Source: Economic Report of the President, 1996.

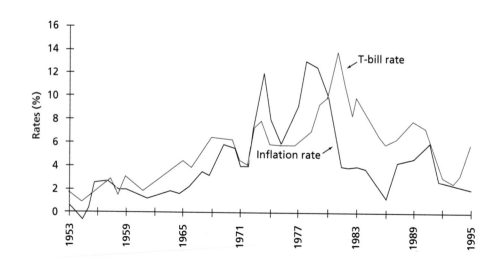

6.5 ASSET ALLOCATION ACROSS RISKY AND RISK-FREE PORTFOLIOS

History shows us that long-term bonds have been riskier investments than investments in Treasury bills and that stock investments have been riskier still. On the other hand, the riskier investments have offered higher average returns. Investors, of course, do not make all-or-nothing choices from these investment classes. They can and do construct their portfolios using securities from all asset classes. Some of the portfolio may be in risk-free Treasury bills and some in high-risk stocks.

asset allocation
Portfolio choice among
broad investment classes.

The most straightforward way to control the risk of the portfolio is through the fraction of the portfolio invested in Treasury bills and other safe money market securities versus risky assets. This is an example of an **asset allocation** choice—a choice among broad investment classes, rather than among the specific securities within each asset class. Most investment professionals consider asset allocation the most important part of portfolio construction. Consider this statement by John Bogle, the chairman of the Vanguard Group of Investment Companies:

> The most fundamental decision of investing is the allocation of your assets: How much should you own in stock? How much should you own in bonds? How much should you own in cash reserves? . . . That decision [has been shown to account] for an astonishing 94% of the differences in total returns achieved by institutionally managed pension funds . . . There is no reason to believe that the same relationship does not also hold true for individual investors.[4]

Therefore, we start our discussion of the risk-return trade-off available to investors by examining the most basic asset allocation choice: the choice of how much of the portfolio to place in risk-free money market securities versus other risky asset classes.

We will denote the investor's portfolio of risky assets as P, and the risk-free asset as F. We will assume for the sake of illustration that the risky component of the investor's overall portfolio is comprised of two mutual funds: one invested in stocks and the other invested in long-term bonds. For now, we take the composition of the risky portfolio as given and focus only on the allocation between it and risk-free securities. In the next chapter, we turn to asset allocation and security selection across risky assets.

The Risky Asset

When we shift wealth from the risky portfolio (P) to the risk-free asset, we do not change the relative proportions of the various risky assets within the risky portfolio. Rather, we reduce the relative weight of the risky portfolio as a whole in favor of risk-free assets.

A simple example demonstrates the procedure. Assume the total market value of an initial portfolio is $300,000. Of that, $90,000 is invested in the Ready Assets money market fund, a risk-free asset. The remaining $210,000 is in risky securities, say $113,400 in the Vanguard S&P 500 index fund (called the Index Trust 500 Portfolio) and $96,600 in Fidelity's Investment Grade Bond Fund.

The Vanguard fund (V) is a passive equity fund that replicates the S&P 500 portfolio. The Fidelity Investment Grade Bond Fund (IG) invests primarily in corporate bonds with high safety ratings and also in Treasury bonds. We choose these two funds for the risky portfolio in the spirit of a low-cost, well-diversified portfolio. While in the next chapter we discuss portfolio optimization, here we simply assume the investor considers the given weighting of V and IG to be optimal.

The holdings in Vanguard and Fidelity make up the risky portfolio, with 54% in V and 46% in IG.

$$w_V = 113,400/210,000 = 0.54 \text{ (Vanguard)}$$
$$w_{IG} = 96,600/210,000 = 0.46 \text{ (Fidelity)}$$

---

[4]John C. Bogle, *Bogle on Mutual Funds* (Burr Ridge, IL: Irwin Professional Publishing, 1994), p. 235.

complete portfolio
The entire portfolio including risky and risk-free assets.

The weight of the risky portfolio, P, in the **complete portfolio,** *including* risk-free as well as risky investments, is denoted by y, and so the weight of the money market fund in P is $1 - y$.

$$y = 210,000/300,000 = 0.7 \text{ (risky assets, portfolio } P)$$
$$1 - y = 90,000/300,000 = 0.3 \text{ (risk-free assets)}$$

The weights of the individual assets in the complete portfolio (C) are:

Vanguard	113,400/300,000 = 0.378
Fidelity	96,600/300,000 = 0.322
Portfolio P	210,000/300,000 = 0.700
Ready Assets F	90,000/300,000 = 0.300
Portfolio C	300,000/300,000 = 1.000

Suppose the investor decides to decrease risk by reducing the exposure to the risky portfolio from $y = 0.7$ to $y = 0.56$. The risky portfolio would total only $0.56 \times 300,000 = \$168,000$, requiring the sale of $\$42,000$ of the original $\$210,000$ risky holdings, with the proceeds used to purchase more shares in Ready Assets. Total holdings in the risk-free asset will increase to $300,000 (1 - 0.56) = \$132,000$ (the original holdings plus the new contribution to the money market fund: $90,000 + 42,000 = \$132,000$).

The key point is that we leave the proportion of each asset in the risky portfolio unchanged. Because the weights of Vanguard and Fidelity in the risky portfolio are 0.54 and 0.46, respectively, we sell $0.54 \times 42,000 = \$22,680$ of Vanguard and $0.46 \times 42,000 = \$19,320$ of Fidelity. After the sale, the proportions of each fund in the risky portfolio are unchanged.

$$w_V = \frac{113,400 - 22,680}{210,000 - 42,000} = 0.54 \text{ (Vanguard)}$$

$$w_{IG} = \frac{96,600 - 19,320}{210,000 - 42,000} = 0.46 \text{ (Fidelity)}$$

This procedure shows that rather than thinking of our risky holdings as Vanguard and Fidelity separately, we may view our holdings as if they are in a single fund holding Vanguard and Fidelity in fixed proportions. In this sense, we may treat the risky fund as a single risky asset, that asset being a particular bundle of securities. As we shift in and out of safe assets, we simply alter our holdings of that bundle of securities commensurately.

Given this simplification, we now can turn to the desirability of reducing risk by changing the risky/risk-free asset mix, that is, reducing risk by decreasing the proportion y. Because we do not alter the weights of each asset within the risky portfolio, the probability distribution of the rate of return on the *risky portfolio* remains unchanged by the asset reallocation. What will change is the probability distribution of the rate of return on the *complete portfolio* that is made up of the risky and risk-free assets.

Concept Check

5. What will be the dollar value of your position in Vanguard and its proportion in your complete portfolio if you decide to hold 50% of your investment budget in Ready Assets?

The Risk-Free Asset

The power to tax and to control the money supply lets the government, and only government, issue default-free bonds. The default-free guarantee by itself is not sufficient to make the bonds risk-free in real terms, since inflation affects the purchasing power of the proceeds from an investment in T-bills. The only risk-free asset in real terms would be a perfectly price-indexed bond. Even then, a default-free, perfectly indexed bond offers a guaranteed

FIGURE 6.5

Spread between 3-Month CDs and T-bills

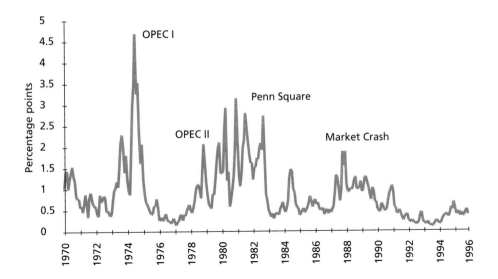

real rate to an investor only if the maturity of the bond is identical to the investor's desired holding period.

These qualifications notwithstanding, it is common to view Treasury bills as *the* risk-free asset. Because they are short-term investments, they are relatively insensitive to interest rate fluctuations. An investor can lock in a short-term nominal return by buying a bill and holding it to maturity. Any inflation uncertainty over the course of a few weeks, or even months, is negligible compared to the uncertainty of stock market returns.

In practice, most investors use a broader range of money market instruments as a risk-free asset. All the money market instruments are virtually immune to interest rate risk (unexpected fluctuations in the price of a bond due to changes in market interest rates) because of their short maturities, and all are fairly safe in terms of default or credit risk.

Money market funds hold, for the most part, three types of securities: Treasury bills, bank certificates of deposit (CDs), and commercial paper. The instruments differ slightly in their default risk. The yields to maturity on CDs and commercial paper, for identical maturities, are always slightly higher than those of T-bills. A history of this yield spread for 90-day CDs is shown in Figure 6.5.

Money market funds have changed their relative holdings of these securities over time, but by and large, T-bills make up only about 15% of their portfolios. Nevertheless, the risk of such blue-chip, short-term investments as CDs and commercial paper is minuscule compared to that of most other assets, such as long-term corporate bonds, common stocks, or real estate. Hence, we treat money market funds as representing the most easily accessible risk-free asset for most investors.

Portfolio Expected Return and Risk

Now that we have specified the risky portfolio and the risk-free asset, we can examine the risk-return combinations that result from various investment allocations between these two assets. Finding the available combinations of risk and return is the "technical" part of asset allocation; it deals only with the opportunities available to investors given the features of the asset markets in which they can invest. In the next section, we address the "personal" part of the problem, the specific individual's choice of the best risk-return combination from the set of feasible combinations, given his or her level of risk aversion.

Since we assume the composition of the optimal risky portfolio (*P*) already has been determined, the concern here is with the proportion of the investment budget (*y*) to be

FIGURE 6.6

The Investment
Opportunity Set with a
Risky Asset and a Risk-
Free Asset

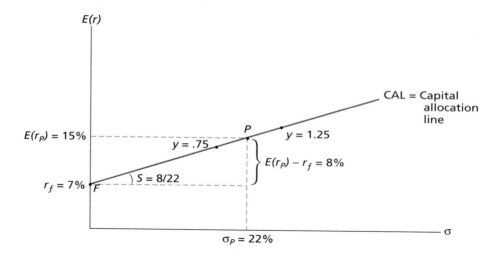

allocated to the risky portfolio. The remaining proportion $(1 - y)$ is to be invested in the risk-free asset (F).

We denote the risky rate of return by r_P, the expected rate of return on P by $E(r_P)$, and its standard deviation by σ_P. The rate of return on the risk-free asset is denoted as r_f. In the numerical example, we assume $E(r_P) = 15\%$, $\sigma_P = 22\%$, and $r_f = 7\%$. Thus, the risk premium on the risky asset is $E(r_P) - r_f = 8\%$.

Let's start with two extreme cases. If you invest all of your funds in the risky asset, that is, if you choose $y = 1.0$, the expected return of your complete portfolio will be 15% and the standard deviation will be 22%. This combination of risk and return is plotted as point P in Figure 6.6. At the other extreme, you might put all of your funds into the risk-free asset, that is, you choose $y = 0$. In this case, your portfolio would behave just as the risk-free asset, and you would earn a riskless return of 7%. (This choice is plotted as point F in Figure 6.6.)

Now consider more moderate choices. For example, if you allocate equal amounts of your overall or *complete portfolio*, C, to the risky and risk-free assets, that is, if you choose $y = 0.5$, the expected return on the complete portfolio will be an average of the expected return on portfolios F and P. Therefore, $E(r_C) = 0.5 \times 7\% + 0.5 \times 15\% = 11\%$. The risk premium of the complete portfolio is therefore $11\% - 7\% = 4\%$, which is half of the risk premium of P. The standard deviation of the portfolio also is one-half of P's, that is, 11%. When you reduce the fraction of the complete portfolio allocated to the risky asset by half, you reduce both the risk and the risk premium by half.

To generalize, the risk premium of the complete portfolio, C, will equal the risk premium of the risky asset times the fraction of the portfolio invested in the risky asset.

$$E(r_C) - r_f = y[E(r_P) - r_f] \tag{6.7}$$

The standard deviation of the complete portfolio will equal the standard deviation of the risky asset times the fraction of the portfolio invested in the risky asset.

$$\sigma_C = y\sigma_P \tag{6.8}$$

In sum, both the risk premium and the standard deviation of the complete portfolio increase in proportion to the investment in the risky portfolio. Therefore, the points that describe the risk and return of the complete portfolio for various asset allocations, that is, for various choices of y, all plot on the straight line connecting F and P, as shown in Figure 6.6, with an intercept of r_f and slope (rise/run) of

$$S = \frac{E(r_P) - r_f}{\sigma_P} = \frac{15 - 7}{22} = 0.36 \tag{6.9}$$

6. What are the expected return, risk premium, standard deviation, and ratio of risk premium to standard deviation for a complete portfolio with $y = 0.75$?

The Capital Allocation Line

capital allocation line
Plot of risk-return combinations available by varying portfolio allocation between a risk-free asset and a risky portfolio.

The line plotted in Figure 6.6 depicts the risk-return combinations available by varying asset allocation, that is, by choosing different values of y. For this reason, it is called the **capital allocation line,** or **CAL.** The slope, S, of the CAL equals the increase in expected return that an investor can obtain per unit of additional standard deviation. In other words, it shows extra return per extra risk. For this reason, the slope also is called the **reward-to-variability ratio.**

reward-to-variability ratio
Ratio of risk premium to standard deviation.

Notice that the reward-to-variability ratio is the same for risky portfolio P and the complete portfolio that was formed by mixing portfolio P and the risk-free asset in equal proportions.

	Expected Return	Risk Premium	Standard Deviation	Reward-to-Variability Ratio
Portfolio P:	15%	8%	22%	$\frac{8}{22} = 0.36$
Portfolio C:	11%	4%	11%	$\frac{4}{11} = 0.36$

In fact, the reward-to-variability ratio is the same for all complete portfolios that plot on the capital allocation line. While the risk-return combinations differ, the *ratio* of reward to risk is constant.

What about points on the line to the right of portfolio P in the investment opportunity set? If investors can borrow at the (risk-free) rate of $r_f = 7\%$, they can construct complete portfolios that plot on the CAL to the right of P. They simply choose values of y greater than 1.0.

EXAMPLE 6.6
Levered Complete Portfolios

Suppose the investment budget is $300,000, and our investor borrows an additional $120,000, investing the $420,000 in the risky asset. This is a levered position in the risky asset, which is financed in part by borrowing. In that case

$$y = \frac{420,000}{300,000} = 1.4$$

and $1 - y = 1 - 1.4 = -0.4$, reflecting a short position in the risk-free asset, or a borrowing position. Rather than lending at a 7% interest rate, the investor borrows at 7%. The portfolio rate of return still exhibits the same reward-to-variability ratio because

$$E(r_C) = 7 + (1.4 \times 8) = 18.2$$

$$\sigma_C = 1.4 \times 22 = 30.8$$

$$S = \frac{E(r_C) - r_f}{\sigma_C} = \frac{11.2}{30.8} = 0.36$$

As you might expect, the levered portfolio has both a higher expected return and a higher standard deviation than an unlevered position in the risky asset.

Of course, nongovernment investors cannot borrow at the risk-free rate. The risk of a borrower's default leads lenders to demand higher interest rates on loans. Therefore, the nongovernment investor's borrowing cost will exceed the lending rate of $r_f = 7\%$.

Suppose the borrowing rate is $r_B = 9\%$. Then, for y greater than 1.0 (the borrowing range), the reward-to-variability ratio (the slope of the CAL) will be: $[E(r_P) - r_B]/\sigma_P = 6/22 = 0.27$.

FIGURE 6.7

The Opportunity Set
with Differential
Borrowing and Lending
Rates

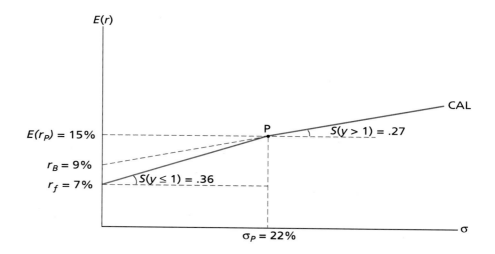

Here, the borrowing rate (r_B) replaces the lending rate (r_f), reducing the "reward" (numerator) in the reward-to-variability ratio. The CAL will be "kinked" at point P as in Figure 6.7. To the left of P, where $y < 1$, the investor is lending at 7% and the slope of the CAL is 0.36. To the right of P, where $y > 1$, the investor is borrowing (at a higher than risk-free rate) to finance extra investments in the risky asset, and the slope is 0.27.

In practice, borrowing to invest in the risky portfolio is easy and straightforward if you have a margin account with a broker. All you have to do is tell your broker you want to buy "on margin." Margin purchases may not exceed 50% of the purchase value. Therefore, if your net worth in the account is $300,000, the broker is allowed to lend you up to $300,000 to purchase additional stock. You would then have $600,000 on the asset side of your account and $300,000 on the liability side, resulting in $y = 2.0$.

Concept Check

7. Suppose there is a shift upward in the expected rate of return on the risky asset, from 15% to 17%. If all other parameters remain unchanged, what will be the slope of the CAL for $y \le 1$ and $y > 1$?

Risk Tolerance and Asset Allocation

We have developed the CAL, the graph of all feasible risk-return combinations available from allocating the complete portfolio between a risky portfolio and a risk-free asset. The investor confronting the CAL now must choose one optimal combination from the set of feasible choices. This choice entails a trade-off between risk and return. Individual investors with different levels of risk aversion, given an identical capital allocation line, will choose different positions in the risky asset. Specifically, the more risk-averse investors will choose to hold *less* of the risky asset and *more* of the risk-free asset.

Graphically, more risk-averse investors will choose portfolios near point F on the capital allocation line plotted in Figure 6.6. More risk-tolerant investors will choose points closer to P, with higher expected return and higher risk. The most risk-tolerant investors will choose portfolios to the right of point P. These levered portfolios provide even higher expected returns, but even greater risk.

The nearby box on page 157 contains a further discussion of this risk-return trade-off, which sometimes is characterized as a decision to "eat well," versus "sleep well." You will eat well if you earn a high expected rate of return on your portfolio. However, this requires that you accept a large risk premium and, therefore, a large amount of risk. Unfortunately, this risk may make it difficult to sleep well.

The investor's asset allocation choice also will depend on the trade-off between risk and return. If the reward-to-variability ratio increases, then investors might well decide to take on riskier positions. For example, suppose an investor reevaluates the probability distribu-

The Right Mix: Fine-Tuning a Portfolio to Make Money and Still Sleep Soundly

Plunged into doubt?

Amid the recent market turmoil, maybe you are wondering whether you really have the right mix of investments. Here are a few thoughts to keep in mind:

TAKING STOCK

If you are a bond investor who is petrified of stocks, the wild price swings of the past few weeks have probably confirmed all of your worst suspicions. But the truth is, adding stocks to your bond portfolio could bolster your returns, without boosting your portfolio's overall gyrations.

How can that be? While stocks and bonds often move up and down in tandem, this isn't always the case, and sometimes stocks rise when bonds are tumbling.

Indeed, Chicago researchers Ibbotson Associates figures a portfolio that's 100% in longer-term government bonds has the same risk profile as a mix that includes 83% in longer-term government bonds and 17% in the blue-chip stocks that constitute Standard & Poor's 500 stock index.

The bottom line? Everybody should own some stocks. Even cowards.

PADDING THE MATTRESS

On the other hand, maybe you're a committed stock market investor, but you would like to add a calming influence to your portfolio. What's your best bet?

When investors look to mellow their stock portfolios, they usually turn to bonds. Indeed, the traditional balanced portfolio, which typically includes 60% stocks and 40% bonds, remains a firm favorite with many investment experts.

A balanced portfolio isn't a bad bet. But if you want to calm your stock portfolio, I would skip bonds and instead add cash investments such as Treasury bills and money market funds. Ibbotson calculates that, over the past 25 years, a mix of 75% stocks and 25% Treasury bills would have performed about as well as a mix of 60% stocks and 40% longer-term government bonds, and with a similar level of portfolio price gyrations.

Moreover, the stock–cash mix offers more certainty, because you know that even if your stocks fall in value, your cash never will. By contrast, both the stocks and bonds in a balanced portfolio can get hammered at the same time.

PATIENCE HAS ITS REWARDS, SOMETIMES

Stocks are capable of generating miserable short-run results. During the past 50 years, the worst five-calendar-year stretch for stocks left investors with an annualized loss of 2.4%.

But while any investment can disappoint in the short run, stocks do at least sparkle over the long haul. As a long-term investor, your goal is to fend off the dual threats of inflation and taxes and make your money grow. And on that score, stocks are supreme.

According to Ibbotson Associates, over the past 50 years, stocks gained 5.5% a year after inflation and an assumed 28% tax rate. By contrast, longer-term government bonds waddled along at just 0.8% a year and Treasury bills returned a mere 0.3%.

Source: Jonathan Clements, "The Right Mix: Fine-Tuning a Portfolio to Make Money and Still Sleep Soundly," *The Wall Street Journal*, July 23, 1996.

tion of the risky portfolio and now perceives a greater expected return without an accompanying increase in the standard deviation. This amounts to an increase in the reward-to-variability ratio or, equivalently, an increase in the slope of the CAL. As a result, this investor will choose a higher y, that is, a greater position in the risky portfolio.

One role of a professional financial advisor is to present investment opportunity alternatives to clients, obtain an assessment of the client's risk tolerance, and help determine the appropriate complete portfolio.[5]

6.6 PASSIVE STRATEGIES AND THE CAPITAL MARKET LINE

The capital allocation line shows the risk-return trade-offs available by mixing risk-free assets with the investor's risky portfolio. Investors can choose the assets included in the

---

[5]As noted in Chapter 5, "risk tolerance" is simply the flip side of "risk aversion." Either term is a reasonable way to describe attitudes toward risk. We generally find it easier to talk about risk aversion, but practitioners often use the term risk tolerance.

Riding Wall St. on Autopilot: Investors Rush to Index Funds

Time was when most American investors chose their own stocks, one at a time. More recently they asked mutual fund managers to do the picking for them.

Now, cocky as the longest bull market in history continues without a substantial decline, many are deciding that they no longer need an expert to find the best investments. Instead, they are investing in mutual funds whose sole purpose is to mimic the performance of the stock market.

Known as index funds, these funds simply hold shares in all the companies that make up a popular stock market index—for example, the 500 stocks in the Standard & Poor's 500 index, which, after the Dow Jones Industrial Average, is the most widely followed market barometer. In essence, these funds run on autopilot, giving up the chance to do any better than the market average but also guaranteeing that except for the nominal cost of running the fund, they will do no worse.

Index funds have been growing in popularity far faster than even the mutual fund business as a whole. Over the last decade, the amount of mutual fund money invested in the most widely held stock index funds has risen more than a hundredfold, to $65 billion—a growth rate 18 times that of the rapidly expanding fund industry overall. And much of that money found its way to index funds in just the last two years.

The growth of index funds has created a broader challenge for the mutual fund industry as a whole. Index funds, by their very nature, undermine the central tenet of the mutual fund business—that individual investors who do not have the time to manage their own money should put their trust in a financial professional trading on their behalf.

But if index funds, which are much less profitable for the industry than traditional mutual funds, can consistently outperform professional stock pickers, investors are likely to demand better results to justify the higher fees that most mutual funds charge. Indeed, it is not clear that the industry's giants will be able to maintain the elaborate marketing and management structure they have built up if much of what they do is put on automatic pilot.

Investors are clearly pouring more and more money into index funds. A decade ago, index funds that tracked the S&P 500 had only $556 million in assets, less than half of 1% of the $146 billion in United States equity funds. Last year, though, assets in those funds topped $65 billion, or 4.4% of the $1.5 trillion in domestic equity funds. And of the $165 billion in new cash that flowed into American stock funds in the first 11 months of last year, index funds took in $15.2 billion, or more than 9 percent—triple the portion of just two years before, according to Lipper Analytical Services.

Institutions, too, have been increasing the portion of their portfolios they devote to indexing. According to Greenwich Associates, a Connecticut investment research company, American pension funds last year devoted nearly 16% of their total assets, a larger portion than ever before, to stock index funds. Those assets accounted for one-third of the funds' holdings of American stocks.

While novices in the market may have misconceptions, certainly most investors understand that if the stock market as a whole goes down, so will their index fund. And some of them vow to keep on investing through the inevitable bumps in the road.

But few neophyte fund investors recall a period like the five years that ended in 1982, when more than 80% of actively managed portfolios performed better than the S&P 500. That was clear to Mr. Brennan of Vanguard this month. After he spent a few days hearing comments from callers to Vanguard, he ordered that a special article be prepared for this month's newsletter for investors.

Under the heading "Remarkable returns may raise unrealistic expectations," the article also warned "Indexing isn't invulnerable."

Source: Abridged from Edward Wyatt, "Riding Wall St. on Autopilot: Investors Rush to Index Funds," *New York Times*, January 28, 1997, p. A1.

---

passive strategy
Investment policy that avoids security analysis.

risky portfolio using either passive or active strategies. A **passive strategy** is based on the premise that securities are fairly priced and avoids the costs involved in undertaking security analysis. Such a strategy might at first blush appear to be naive. However, we will see in Chapter 9 that intense competition among professional money managers might indeed force security prices to levels at which further security analysis is unlikely to turn up significant profit opportunities. Passive investment strategies may make sense for many investors.

To avoid the costs of acquiring information on any individual stock or group of stocks, we may follow a "neutral" diversification approach. A natural strategy is to select a diversified portfolio of common stocks that mirrors the corporate sector of the U.S. economy. This

TABLE 6.4

Average Rates of Return, Standard Deviations, and the Reward-to-Variability Ratio of the Risk Premiums of Common Stocks (S&P 500) over One-Month Bills over 1926–1996 and Various Subperiods

Source: Data in Table 6.2.

| | Risk Premium | | |
	Mean	Standard Deviation	Reward-to-Variability Ratio
1926–1942	6.20	29.86	0.2075
1943–1959	17.06	17.72	0.9627
1960–1977	2.96	18.18	0.1626
1978–1996	9.07	13.37	0.6781
1926–1996	8.74	20.82	0.4201

results in a value-weighted portfolio, which, for example, invests a proportion in GM stock that equals the ratio of GM's market value to the market value of all listed stocks.

Such strategies are called *indexing*. The investor chooses a portfolio with all the stocks in a broad market index such as the Standard & Poor's 500 index. The rate of return on the portfolio then replicates the return on the index. Indexing has become an extremely popular strategy for passive investors. The nearby box (page 158) reviews the remarkable growth of indexing in the 1990s.

capital market line
The capital allocation line using the market index portfolio as the risky asset.

We call the capital allocation line provided by one-month T-bills and a broad index of common stocks the **capital market line** (CML). That is, a passive strategy based on stocks and bills generates an investment opportunity set that is represented by the CML.

Historical Evidence on the Capital Market Line

Can we use past data to help forecast the risk-return trade-off offered by the CML? The notion that one can use historical returns to forecast the future seems straightforward but actually is somewhat problematic. On one hand, you wish to use all available data to obtain a large sample. But when using long time series, old data may no longer be representative of future circumstances. Another reason for weeding out subperiods is that some past events simply may be too improbable to be given equal weight with results from other periods. Do the data we have pose this problem?

Table 6.4 breaks the 71-year period, 1926–1996, into four subperiods and shows each subperiod risk premium, standard deviation, and reward-to-variability ratio. That ratio is the slope of the CML based on the subperiod data. Indeed, the differences across subperiods are quite striking. What might be the reasons behind them?

One explanation is that the subperiods were characterized by different profit opportunities for the corporations. Perhaps we might view the period 1926–1942 as dominated by the Great Depression; 1943–1959 as dominated by World War II and the Korean War; and 1960–1977 as dominated by the Vietnam War. If so, there may be "good" and "bad" wars when it comes to profit opportunities. Finally, 1978–1996 was dominated by peace, one short recession, and the end of the Cold War. These explanations are admittedly superficial, and surely they can be improved; but even with improvements, can such explanations be used to select subperiods that are better for forecasting, without additional insight into the future? We doubt it. *After* the fact, there is always a good story to explain returns, but such explanations are of questionable use for the future.

Another possible, but also unconvincing, explanation is that variation in average returns across subperiods reflects rapidly changing risk premiums due to changing risk aversion among investors. Perhaps the standard deviation can be predicted from past returns, and then expected returns can be predicted from the forecasted standard deviation. Improved statistical methods have increased our insight into the manner in which the standard deviation of market returns changes over time. Even so, volatility seems to be relatively predictable only over the short run, and, as with other social phenomena, long-run predictions are unreliable.

Moreover, even if we could make such predictions, the evidence for rapidly changing risk aversion has no empirical support.

The most plausible explanation for the variation in subperiod returns is based on the observation that the standard deviation of returns is quite large in all subperiods. If we take the 71-year standard deviation of 20.9% as representative and assume that returns in one year are nearly uncorrelated with those in other years (the evidence suggests that any correlation across years is small), then the standard deviation of our estimate of the mean return in any of our 18-year subperiods will be $20.9/\sqrt{18} = 4.9\%$, which is fairly large. This means that in approximately one out of three cases, an 18-year average will deviate by 5% or more from the true mean. Applying this insight to the data in Table 6.4 tells us that we cannot reject with any confidence the possibility that the true mean is similar in all subperiods! In other words, the "noise" in the data is so large that we simply cannot make reliable inferences from average returns in any subperiod. The variation in returns across subperiods may simply reflect statistical variation, and we have to reconcile ourselves to the fact that the market return and the reward-to-variability ratio for passive (as well as active!) strategies is simply very hard to predict.

Costs and Benefits of Passive Investing

How reasonable is it for an investor to pursue a passive strategy? We cannot answer such a question definitively without comparing passive strategy results to the costs and benefits accruing to an active portfolio strategy. Some issues are worth considering, however.

First, the alternative active strategy entails costs. Whether you choose to invest your own valuable time to acquire the information needed to generate an optimal active portfolio of risky assets or whether you delegate the task to a professional who will charge a fee, constructing an active portfolio is more expensive than constructing a passive one. The passive portfolio requires only small commissions on purchases of U.S. T-bills (or zero commissions if you purchase bills directly from the government) and management fees to a mutual fund company that offers a market index fund to the public. An index fund has the lowest operating expenses of all mutual stock funds because it requires minimum effort.

A second argument supporting a passive strategy is the free-rider benefit. If you assume there are many active, knowledgeable investors who quickly bid up prices of undervalued assets and offer down overvalued assets (by selling), you have to conclude that most of the time most assets will be fairly priced. Therefore, a well-diversified portfolio of common stock will be a reasonably fair buy, and the passive strategy may not be inferior to that of the average active investor. We will expand on this insight and provide a more comprehensive analysis of the relative success of passive strategies in Chapter 9.

To summarize, a passive strategy involves investment in two passive portfolios: virtually risk-free short-term T-bills (or a money market fund) and a fund of common stocks that mimics a broad market index. Recall that the capital allocation line representing such a strategy is called the *capital market line*. Using Table 6.4, we see that using 1926 to 1996 data, the passive risky portfolio has offered an average risk premium of 8.74% and a standard deviation of 20.82%, resulting in a reward-to-variability ratio of 0.42.

Summary

- Investors face a trade-off between risk and expected return. Historical data confirm our intuition that assets with low degrees of risk provide lower returns on average than do those of higher risk.
- Shifting funds from the risky portfolio to the risk-free asset is the simplest way to reduce risk. Another method involves diversification of the risky portfolio. We take up diversification in later chapters.
- U.S. T-bills provide a perfectly risk-free asset in nominal terms only. Nevertheless, the standard deviation of real rates on short-term T-bills is small compared to that of assets

such as long-term bonds and common stocks, so for the purpose of our analysis, we consider T-bills the risk-free asset. Besides T-bills, money market funds hold short-term, safe obligations such as commercial paper and CDs. These entail some default risk but relatively little compared to most other risky assets. For convenience, we often refer to money market funds as risk-free assets.

- A risky investment portfolio (referred to here as the risky asset) can be characterized by its reward-to-variability ratio. This ratio is the slope of the capital allocation line (CAL), the line that goes from the risk-free asset through the risky asset. All combinations of the risky and risk-free asset lie on this line. Investors would prefer a steeper sloping CAL, because that means higher expected returns for any level of risk. If the borrowing rate is greater than the lending rate, the CAL will be "kinked" at the point corresponding to investment of 100% of the complete portfolio in the risky asset.
- An investor's preferred choice among the portfolios on the capital allocation line will depend on risk aversion. Risk-averse investors will weight their complete portfolios more heavily toward Treasury bills. Risk-tolerant investors will hold higher proportions of their complete portfolios in the risky asset.
- The capital market line is the capital allocation line that results from using a passive investment strategy that treats a market index portfolio, such as the Standard & Poor's 500, as the risky asset. Passive strategies are low-cost ways of obtaining well-diversified portfolios with performance that will reflect that of the broad stock market.

Key Terms

arithmetic average, *139*
asset allocation, *151*
capital allocation line, *155*
capital market line, *159*
complete portfolio, *152*
dollar-weighted average
  return, *140*
expected return, *141*
geometric average, *139*

holding-period return, *138*
inflation rate, *149*
nominal interest rate, *149*
passive strategy, *158*
probability distribution, *141*
real interest rate, *149*
reward-to-variability
  ratio, *155*

risk aversion, *143*
risk-free rate, *143*
risk premium, *143*
scenario analysis, *141*
standard deviation, *142*
variance, *142*

Problem Sets

1. Look at Table 6.1 in the text. Suppose you now revise your expectations regarding the stock market as follows:

State of the Economy	Probability	HPR
Boom	0.3	44%
Normal growth	0.4	14
Recession	0.3	−16

Use Equations 6.3–6.5 to compute the mean and standard deviation of the HPR on stocks. Compare your revised parameters with the ones in the text.

2. The stock of Business Adventures sells for $40 a share. Its likely dividend payout and end-of-year price depend on the state of the economy by the end of the year as follows:

	Dividend	Stock Price
Boom	$2.00	$50
Normal Economy	1.00	43
Recession	.50	34

   a. Calculate the expected holding-period return and standard deviation of the holding-period return. All three scenarios are equally likely.

    b. Calculate the expected return and standard deviation of a portfolio half invested in Business Adventures and half in Treasury bills. The return on bills is 4%.

3. XYZ stock price and dividend history are as follows:

Year	Beginning of Year Price	Dividend Pair at Year-End
1996	$100	$4
1997	$110	$4
1998	$90	$4
1998	$95	$4

An investor buys three shares of XYZ at the beginning of 1996 buys another two shares at the beginning of 1997, sells one share at the beginning of 1998, and sells all four remaining shares at the beginning of 1999.

    a. What are the arithemtic and geometric average time-weighted rates of return for the investor?

    b. What is the dollar-weighted rate of return. Hint: Carefully prepare a chart of cash flows for the *four* dates corresponding to the turns of the year for January 1, 1996 to January 1, 1999. If your calculator cannot calculate internal rate of return, you will have to use that trial and error.

4. Based on current dividend yields and expected capital gains, the expected rates of return on portfolio A and B are 0.11 and 0.14, respectively. The beta of A is 0.8 while that of B is 1.5. The T-bill rate is currently 0.06, while the expected rate of return of the S&P 500 index is 0.12. The standard deviation of portfolio A is 0.10 annually, while that of B is 0.31, and that of the index is .20.

    a. If you currently hold a market index portfolio, would you choose to add either of these portfolios to your holdings? Explain.

    b. If instead you could invest *only* in bills and one of these portfolios, which would you choose?

5. Using the historical risk premiums as your guide, what is your estimate of the expected annual HPR on the S&P 500 stock portfolio if the current risk-free interest rate is 5%?

6. Compute the means and standard deviations of the annual HPR listed in Table 6.2 of the text using only the 30 years 1967–1996. How do these statistics compare with those computed from the data for the period 1926–1942? Which do you think are the most relevant statistics to use for projecting into the future?

7. What has been the historical average *real* rate of return on stocks, Treasury bonds, and Treasury notes?

8. Consider a risky portfolio. The end-of-year cash flow derived from the portfolio will be either $50,000 or $150,000, with equal probabilities of 0.5. The alternative riskless investment in T-bills pays 5%.

    a. If you require a risk premium of 10%, how much will you be willing to pay for the portfolio?

    b. Suppose the portfolio can be purchased for the amount you found in (*a*). What will the expected rate of return on the portfolio be?

    c. Now suppose you require a risk premium of 15%. What is the price you will be willing to pay now?

    d. Comparing your answers to (*a*) and (*c*), what do you conclude about the relationship between the required risk premium on a portfolio and the price at which the portfolio will sell?

    For problems 9–13, assume that you manage a risky portfolio with an expected rate of return of 17% and a standard deviation of 27%. The T-bill rate is 7%.

TABLE 6.5   Compound Annual Rates of Return by Decade

	1920s*	1930s	1940s	1950s	1960s	1970s	1980s	1990s**	1987–96
Large company	6.98%	−1.25%	9.11%	19.41%	7.84%	5.90%	17.60%	14.42%	15.30%
Small company	−1.51	7.28	20.63	19.01	13.72	8.75	12.46	14.16	11.11
Long-term government	1.57	4.60	3.59	−0.26	1.14	6.63	11.50	9.86	9.31
Inter. term government	1.49	3.91	1.70	1.11	3.41	6.11	12.01	8.51	8.23
Treasury bills	1.41	0.30	0.37	1.87	3.89	6.29	9.00	4.95	5.48
Inflation	−0.40	−2.04	5.36	2.22	2.52	7.36	5.10	3.33	3.68

*Based on the period 1926–1929.
**Based on the period 1990–1996.
Source: Data in Table 6.2.

9. *a.* Your client chooses to invest 70% of a portfolio in your fund and 30% in a T-bill money market fund. What is the expected return and standard deviation of your client's portfolio?

b. Suppose your risky portfolio includes the following investments in the given proportions:

Stock A	27%
Stock B	33%
Stock C	40%

What are the investment proportions of your client's overall portfolio, including the position in T-bills?

c. What is the reward-to-variability ratio (S) of your risky portfolio and your client's overall portfolio?

d. Draw the CAL of your portfolio on an expected return–standard deviation diagram. What is the slope of the CAL? Show the position of your client on your fund's CAL.

10. Suppose the same client in problem 9 decides to invest in your risky portfolio a proportion (y) of his total investment budget so that his overall portfolio will have an expected rate of return of 15%.

a. What is the proportion y?

b. What are your client's investment proportions in your three stocks and the T-bill fund?

c. What is the standard deviation of the rate of return on your client's portfolio?

11. Suppose the same client in problem 9 prefers to invest in your portfolio a proportion (y) that maximizes the expected return on the overall portfolio subject to the constraint that the overall portfolio's standard deviation will not exceed 20%.

a. What is the investment proportion, y?

b. What is the expected rate of return on the overall portfolio?

12. You estimate that a passive portfolio invested to mimic the S&P 500 stock index yields an expected rate of return of 13% with a standard deviation of 25%. Draw the CML and your fund's CAL on an expected return–standard deviation diagram.

a. What is the slope of the CML?

b. Characterize in one short paragraph the advantage of your fund over the passive fund.

13. Your client (see problem 9) wonders whether to switch the 70% that is invested in your fund to the passive portfolio.

a. Explain to your client the disadvantage of the switch.

b. Show your client the maximum fee you could charge (as a percent of the investment in your fund deducted at the end of the year) that would still leave him at least as well off investing in your fund as in the passive one. (Hint: The fee will lower the slope of your client's CAL by reducing the expected return net of the fee.)

14. What do you think would happen to the expected return on stocks if investors perceived an increase in the volatility of stocks?

15. Input the data in Table 6.5 into a spreadsheet. Compute the serial correlation in decade returns for each asset class and for inflation. Also find the correlation between the returns of various asset classes. What do the data indicate?

16. Convert the asset returns by decade presented in Table 6.5 into real rates. Repeat the analysis of problem 15 for the real rates of return.

▣IEM
Applications

1. Look up the last price for the IBMm contract in the Computer Industry Returns Market. Suppose you purchased this contract at this price and held it until maturity. Based on this information, answer questions *a*, *b*, and *c*.
   a. What is your holding period return if the IBMm contract pays off $1?
   b. What is your holding period return if the IEMm contract pays off $0?
   c. Financial theory predicts that the price should approximate the probability that IBMm will pay off $1. If this is true, calculate your expected return, its variance and its standard deviation.

2. How do you construct a risk-free portfolio on the IEM?

3. How do you take a risky portfolio position on the IEM?

Solutions to Concept Checks

1. *a.* The arithmetic average is $(2 + 8 - 4)/3 = 2\%$ per month.
   b. The time-weighted (geometric) average is
   $[(1 + .02) \times (1 + .08) \times (1 - .04)]^{1/3} = .0188 = 1.88\%$ per month
   c. We compute the dollar-weighted average (IRR) from the cash flow sequence (in $ millions):

	Month		
	1	**2**	**3**
Assets under management at beginning of month	10.0	13.2	19.256
Investment profits during month (HPR × Assets)	0.2	1.056	(0.77)
Net inflows during month	3.0	5.0	0.0
Assets under management at end of month	13.2	19.256	18.486

	Time			
	0	**1**	**2**	**3**
Net cash flow*	−10	−3.0	−5.0	+18.486

*Time 0 is today. Time 1 is the end of the first month. Time 3 is the end of the third month, when net cash flow equals the ending value (potential liquidation value) of the portfolio.

The IRR of the sequence of net cash flows is 1.17% per month.
The dollar-weighted average is lower than the time-weighted average because the negative return was realized when the fund had the most money under management.

2. Computing the HPR for each scenario we convert the price and dividend data to rate of return data:

Business Conditions	Probability	HPR
High growth	0.35	67.66% = (4.40 + 35 − 23.50)/23.50
Normal growth	0.30	31.91% = (4.00 + 27 − 23.50)/23.50
No growth	0.35	−19.15% = (4.00 + 15 − 23.50)/23.50

Using equations 6.1 and 6.2 we obtain

$E(r) = 0.35 \times 67.66 + 0.30 \times 31.91 + 0.35 \times (-19.15) = 26.55\%$

$\sigma^2 = 0.35 \times (67.66 - 26.55)^2 + 0.30 \times (31.91 - 26.55)^2 + 0.35 \times (-19.15 - 26.55)^2$

$\quad = 1331$

and $\sigma = \sqrt{1331} = 36.5\%$

3. The mean excess return for the period 1926–1934 is 3.56% (below the historical average), and the standard deviation (using $n - 1$ degrees of freedom) is 32.69% (above the historical average). These results reflect the severe downturn of the great crash and the unusually high volatility of stock returns in this period.

4. *a.* Solving

$$1 + R = (1 + r)(1 + i) = (1.03)(1.08) = 1.1124$$
$$R = 11.24\%$$

b. Solving

$$1 + R = (1.03)(1.10) = 1.133$$
$$R = 13.3\%$$

5. Holding 50% of your invested capital in Ready Assets means your investment proportion in the risky portfolio is reduced from 70% to 50%.

   Your risky portfolio is constructed to invest 54% in Vanguard and 46% in Fidelity. Thus, the proportion of Vanguard in your overall portfolio is $0.5 \times 54\% = 27\%$, and the dollar value of your position in Vanguard is $300,000 \times 0.27 = \$81,000$.

6. $$E(r) = 7 + 0.75 \times 8\% = 13\%$$
   $$\sigma = 0.75 \times 22\% = 16.5\%$$

   Risk premium $= 6\%$

   $$\frac{\text{Risk premium}}{\text{Standard deviation}} = \frac{13-7}{16.5} = .36$$

7. The lending and borrowing rates are unchanged at $r_f = 7\%$ and $r_B = 9\%$. The standard deviation of the risky portfolio is still 22%, but its expected rate of return shifts from 15% to 17%. The slope of the kinked CAL is

$$\frac{E(r_P) - r_f}{\sigma_P} \text{ for the lending range}$$

$$\frac{E(r_P) - r_B}{\sigma_P} \text{ for the borrowing range}$$

   Thus, in both cases, the slope increases: from 8/22 to 10/22 for the lending range, and from 6/22 to 8/22 for the borrowing range.

Chapter 7

EFFICIENT DIVERSIFICATION

AFTER STUDYING THIS CHAPTER YOU SHOULD BE ABLE TO:

- Show how covariance and correlation affect the power of diversification to reduce portfolio risk.
- Construct efficient portfolios.
- Calculate the composition of the optimal risky portfolio.
- Use factor models to analyze the risk characteristics of securities and portfolios.

In this chapter we describe how investors can construct the best possible risky portfolio. The key concept is efficient diversification.

The notion of diversification is age old. The adage "don't put all your eggs in one basket" obviously predates economic theory. However, a formal model showing how to make the most of the power of diversification was not devised until 1952, a feat for which Harry Markowitz eventually won the Nobel Prize in economics. This chapter is largely developed from his work, as well as from later insights that built on his work.

We start with a bird's-eye view of how diversification reduces the variability of portfolio returns. We then turn to the construction of optimal risky portfolios. We follow a top-down approach, starting with asset allocation across a small set of broad asset classes, such as stocks, bonds, and money market securities. Then we show how the principles of optimal asset allocation can easily be generalized to solve the problem of security selection among many risky assets. We discuss the efficient set of risky portfolios and show how it leads us to the best attainable capital allocation. Finally, we show how factor models of security returns can simplify the search for efficient portfolios and the interpretation of the risk characteristics of individual securities.

An appendix examines the common fallacy that long-term investment horizons mitigate the effect of asset risk. We argue that the common belief in "time diversification" is in fact an illusion and is not real diversification.

7.1 DIVERSIFICATION AND PORTFOLIO RISK

Suppose you have in your risky portfolio only one stock, say, Digital Equipment Corporation. What are the sources of risk affecting this "portfolio"?

We can identify two broad sources of uncertainty. The first is the risk that has to do with general economic conditions, such as the business cycle, the inflation rate, interest rates, exchange rates, and so forth. None of these macroeconomic factors can be predicted with certainty, and all affect the rate of return Digital stock eventually will provide. Then you must add to these macro factors firm-specific influences, such as Digital's success in research and development, its management style and philosophy, and so on. Firm-specific factors are those that affect Digital without noticeably affecting other firms.

Now consider a naive diversification strategy, adding another security to the risky portfolio. If you invest half of your risky portfolio in Exxon, leaving the other half in Digital, what happens to portfolio risk? Because the firm-specific influences on the two stocks differ (statistically speaking, the influences are independent), this strategy should reduce portfolio risk. For example, when oil prices fall, hurting Exxon, computer prices might rise, helping Digital. The two effects are offsetting, which stabilizes portfolio return.

But why stop at only two stocks? Diversifying into many more securities continues to minimize exposure to firm-specific factors, so portfolio volatility should continue to fall. Ultimately, however, even with a large number of risky securities in a portfolio, there is no way to avoid all risk. To the extent that virtually all securities are affected by common (risky) macroeconomic factors, we cannot eliminate our exposure to general economic risk, no matter how many stocks we hold.

Figure 7.1 illustrates these concepts. When all risk is firm-specific, as in Figure 7.1A, diversification can reduce risk to low levels. With all risk sources independent, and with investment spread across many securities, exposure to any particular source of risk is negligible. This is just an application of the law of averages. The reduction of risk to very low levels because of independent risk sources is sometimes called the *insurance principle*.

When common sources of risk affect all firms, however, even extensive diversification cannot eliminate risk. In Figure 7.1B, portfolio standard deviation falls as the number of securities increases, but it is not reduced to zero. The risk that remains even after diversification is called **market risk,** risk that is attributable to marketwide risk sources. Other names are **systematic risk** or **nondiversifiable risk.** The risk that *can* be eliminated by diversification is called **unique risk, firm-specific risk, nonsystematic risk,** or **diversifiable risk.**

This analysis is borne out by empirical studies. Figure 7.2 shows the effect of portfolio diversification, using data on NYSE stocks. The figure shows the average standard devia-

market risk, systematic risk, nondiversifiable risk
Risk factors common to the whole economy.

unique risk, firm-specific risk, nonsystematic risk, diversifiable risk,
Risk that can be eliminated by diversification.

FIGURE 7.1
Portfolio Risk as a Function of the Number of Stocks in the Portfolio

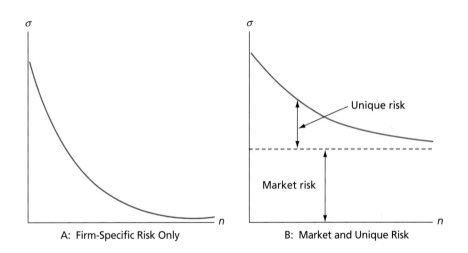

A: Firm-Specific Risk Only   B: Market and Unique Risk

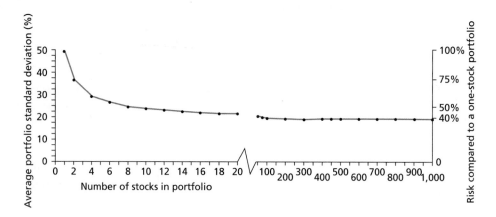

tions of equally weighted portfolios constructed by selecting stocks at random as a function of the number of stocks in the portfolio. On average, portfolio risk does fall with diversification, but the power of diversification to reduce risk is limited by common sources of risk.

7.2 ASSET ALLOCATION WITH TWO RISKY ASSETS

In the last chapter we examined the simplest asset allocation decision, that involving the choice of how much of the portfolio to place in risk-free money market securities versus in a risky portfolio. We simply assumed that the risky portfolio was comprised of a stock and a bond fund in given proportions. Of course, investors need to decide on the proportion of their portfolios to allocate to the stock versus the bond market. This, too, is an asset allocation decision. As the nearby box (page 169) emphasizes, most investment professionals recognize that "the really critical decision is how to divvy up your money among stocks, bonds, and supersafe investments such as Treasury bills."

We examined capital allocation between risky and risk-free assets in the last chapter. We turn now to asset allocation between two risky assets, which we will continue to assume are two mutual funds, one a bond fund and the other a stock fund. After we understand the properties of portfolios formed by mixing two risky assets, we will reintroduce the choice of the third, risk-free portfolio. This will allow us to complete the basic problem of asset allocation across the three key asset classes: stocks, bonds, and risk-free money market securities. Once you understand this case, it will be easy to see how portfolios of many risky securities might best be constructed.

Covariance and Correlation

Because we now envision forming a risky portfolio from two risky assets, we need to understand how the uncertainties of asset returns interact. It turns out that an important determinant of portfolio risk is the extent to which the returns on the two assets tend to vary either in tandem or in opposition. Portfolio risk depends on the *correlation* between the returns of the assets in the portfolio. We can see why using a simple scenario analysis.

Suppose there are three equally likely scenarios for the economy: a recession, normal growth, and a boom. The performance of stock funds tends to follow the performance of the broad economy. So suppose that in a recession, the stock fund will have a rate of return of −7%, in a normal period it will have a rate of return of 12%, and in a boom period it will have a rate of return of 28%. In contrast, bond funds often do better when the economy is weak. This is because interest rates fall in a recession, which means that bond prices rise. Suppose that a bond fund will provide a rate of return of 17% in a recession, 7% in a normal period, and −3% in a boom. These assumptions are summarized in Table 7.1.

Recipe for Successful Investing: First, Mix Assets Well

First things first.

If you want dazzling investment results, don't start your day foraging for hot stocks and stellar mutual funds. Instead, say investment advisors, the really critical decision is how to divvy up your money among stocks, bonds, and supersafe investments such as Treasury bills.

In Wall Street lingo, this mix of investments is called your asset allocation. "The asset-allocation choice is the first and most important decision," says William Droms, a finance professor at Georgetown University. "How much you have in [the stock market] really drives your results."

"You cannot get [stock market] returns from a bond portfolio, no matter how good your security selection is or how good the bond managers you use," says William John Mikus, a managing director of Financial Design, a Los Angeles investment advisor.

For proof, Mr. Mikus cites studies such as the 1991 analysis done by Gary Brinson, Brian Singer, and Gilbert Beebower. That study, which looked at the 10-year results for 82 large pension plans, found that a plan's asset-allocation policy explained 91.5% of the return earned.

DESIGNING A PORTFOLIO

Because your asset mix is so important, some mutual fund companies now offer free services to help investors design their portfolios. Dreyfus Corp., Fidelity Investments, T. Rowe Price Associates, and SteinRoe Mutual Funds will either suggest an asset allocation if you fill out a questionnaire or provide a worksheet that allows you to figure out your own mix.

Gerald Perritt, editor of the Mutual Fund Letter, a Chicago newsletter, says you should vary your mix of assets depending on how long you plan to invest. The further you are from your investment goal, the more you should have in stocks. The closer you get, the more you should lean toward bonds and money market instruments, such as Treasury bills. Bonds and money market instruments may generate lower returns than stocks. But for those who need money in the near future, conservative investments make more sense, because there's less chance of suffering a devastating short-term loss.

SUMMARIZING YOUR ASSETS

"One of the most important things people can do is summarize all their assets on one piece of paper and figure out their asset allocation," says Mr. Pond.

Once you've settled on a mix of stocks and bonds, you should seek to maintain the target percentages, says Mr. Pond. To do that, he advises figuring out your asset allocation once every six months. Because of a stock market plunge, you could find that stocks are now a far smaller part of your portfolio than you envisaged. At such a time, you should put more into stocks and lighten up on bonds.

When devising portfolios, some investment advisors consider gold and real estate in addition to the usual trio of stocks, bonds, and money market instruments. Gold and real estate give "you a hedge against hyperinflation," says Mr. Droms. "But real estate is better than gold, because you'll get better long-run returns."

Source: Jonathan Clements, "Recipe for Successful Investing: First, Mix Assets Well," *The Wall Street Journal*, October 6, 1993. Reprinted by permission of *The Wall Street Journal*, © 1993 Dow Jones & Company, Inc. All Rights Reserved Worldwide.

Because all three scenarios are equally likely, the expected return on each fund equals the average of the outcomes in the three scenarios. The expected return of the stock fund is 11%, and that of the bond fund is 7%. As we discussed in the last chapter, the variance is the average across all scenarios of the squared deviation between the actual return of the fund and its expected return; the standard deviation is the square root of the variance. These values are computed in Table 7.2.

What about the risk and return characteristics of a portfolio made up from the stock and bond funds? The portfolio return is the weighted average of the returns on each fund with

TABLE 7.1

Rate of Return Assumptions for Stock and Bond Funds

Scenario	Probability	Rate of Return	
		Stock Fund	**Bond Fund**
Recession	1/3	− 7%	+17%
Normal	1/3	+12	+ 7
Boom	1/3	+28	− 3

TABLE 7.2

Expected Return and
Volatility for Two Funds

Scenario	Stock Fund			Bond Fund		
	Rate of Return	Deviation from Expected Return	Squared Deviation	Rate of Return	Deviation from Expected Return	Squared Deviation
Recession	− 7%	−18%	324	+17%	+10%	100
Normal	+12	+ 1	1	+ 7	+ 0	0
Boom	+28	+17	289	− 3	−10	100
Expected return	$\frac{1}{3}(-7 + 12 + 28) = 11\%$			$\frac{1}{3}(+17 + 7 - 3) = 7\%$		
Variance	$\frac{1}{3}(324 + 1 + 289) = 204.7$			$\frac{1}{3}(100 + 0 + 100) = 66.7$		
Standard deviation	$\sqrt{204.7} = 14.3\%$			$\sqrt{66.7} = 8.2\%$		

TABLE 7.3

Rate of Return for Two
Funds and the Portfolio

Scenario	Probability	Rate of Return		Portfolio Return
		Stock Fund	Bond Fund	
Recession	1/3	− 7%	+17%	+ 5.0%
Normal	1/3	+12	+ 7	+ 9.5
Boom	1/3	+28	− 3	+12.5
Expected return		11%	7%	9%
Variance		204.7	66.7	9.5
Standard deviation		14.3%	8.2%	3.1%

weights equal to the proportion of the portfolio invested in each fund. Suppose we form an equally weighted portfolio, meaning that 50% of the risky portfolio is invested in the stock fund and 50% is in the bond fund. Then the portfolio return in each scenario is just the average of the returns on the two funds. For example

$$\text{Portfolio return in recession} = 0.50 \times (-7\%) + 0.50 \times 17\%$$
$$= 5\%$$

Table 7.3 shows the rate of return of the equally weighted portfolio in each scenario, as well as the portfolio's expected return, variance, and standard deviation. Notice that while the portfolio's expected return is just the average of the expected return of the two assets, the standard deviation is actually less than that of *either* asset.

The low risk of the portfolio is due to the inverse relationship between the performance of the two funds. In a recession, stocks fare poorly, but this is offset by the good performance of the bond fund. Conversely, in a boom scenario, bonds fall, but stocks do well. Therefore, the portfolio of the two risky assets is less risky than either asset individually. Portfolio risk is reduced most when the returns of the two assets most reliably offset each other.

The natural question investors should ask, therefore, is how one can measure the tendency of the returns on two assets to vary either in tandem or in opposition to each other. The statistics that provide this measure are the covariance and the correlation coefficient.

The covariance is calculated in a manner similar to the variance. Instead of measuring the typical difference of an asset return from its expected value, however, we wish to measure the extent to which the uncertainties of the returns on the two assets tend to reinforce or offset each other.

We start in Table 7.4 with the deviation of the return on each fund from its expected or mean value. For each scenario, we multiply the deviation of the stock fund return from its mean by the deviation of the bond fund return from its mean. The product will be positive if both asset returns exceed their respective means in that scenario or if both fall short of their respective means. The product will be negative if one asset exceeds its mean return, while

TABLE 7.4

The Covariance between the Returns of the Stock and Bond Funds

	Stock Fund		Bond Fund		
Scenario	Rate of Return	Deviation from Expected Return	Rate of Return	Deviation from Expected Return	Product of Deviations
Recession	− 7%	−18%	+17%	+10%	−180
Normal	+12	+ 1	+ 7	+ 0	0
Boom	+28	+17	− 3	−10	−170

Covariance = Average of product of deviations = $\frac{1}{3} \times (-180 + 0 - 170) = -116.7$

the other falls short of its mean return. For example, Table 7.4 shows that the stock fund return in the recession falls short of its expected value by 18%, while the bond fund return exceeds its mean by 10%. Therefore, the product of the two deviations in the recession is $-18 \times 10 = -180$, as reported in the last column. The product of deviations is negative if one asset performs well when the other is performing poorly. It is positive if both assets perform well or poorly in the same scenarios.

If we average these products across all scenarios, we obtain a measure of the *average* tendency of the asset returns to vary in tandem. Since this is a measure of the extent to which the returns tend to vary with each other, that is, to co-vary, it is called the *covariance*. The covariance of the stock and bond funds is computed in the last line of the Table 7.4. The negative value for the covariance indicates that the two assets vary inversely, that is, when one asset performs well, the other tends to perform poorly.

Unfortunately, it is difficult to interpret the magnitude of the covariance. For instance, does the covariance of − 116.7 indicate that the inverse relationship between the returns on stock and bond funds is strong or weak? It's hard to say. An easier statistic to interpret is the *correlation coefficient*, which is simply the covariance divided by the product of the standard deviations of the returns on each fund. We denote the correlation coefficient by the Greek letter rho, ρ.

$$\text{Correlation coefficient} = \rho = \frac{\text{Covariance}}{\sigma_{\text{stock}} \times \sigma_{\text{bond}}}$$

$$= \frac{-116.7}{14.3 \times 8.2} = -0.99$$

Correlations can range from values of − 1 to + 1. Values of − 1 indicate perfect negative correlation, that is, the strongest possible tendency for two returns to vary inversely. Values of + 1 indicate perfect positive correlation. Correlations of zero indicate that the returns on the two assets are unrelated to each other. The correlation coefficient of − 0.99 confirms the overwhelming tendency of the returns on the stock and bond funds to vary inversely in this scenario analysis.

We are now in a position to derive the risk and return features of portfolios of risky assets.

Concept Check

1. Suppose the rates of return of the bond portfolio in the three scenarios are 10% in a recession, 7% in a normal period, and − 2% in a boom. What would be the covariance and correlation coefficient between the rates of return on the stock and bond portfolios?

The Three Rules of Two-Risky-Asset Portfolios

Suppose a proportion denoted by w_B is invested in the bond fund, and the remainder $1 - w_B$, denoted by w_S, is invested in the stock fund. The properties of the portfolio are determined by the following three rules, which apply the rules of statistics governing combinations of random variables:

Rule 1. The rate of return on the portfolio is a weighted average of the returns on the component securities, with the investment proportions as weights.

$$r_P = w_B r_B + w_S r_S \tag{7.1}$$

Rule 2. The *expected* rate of return on the portfolio is a weighted average of the *expected* returns on the component securities, with the same portfolio proportions as weights. In symbols, the expectation of Equation 7.1 is

$$E(r_P) = w_B E(r_B) + w_S E(r_S) \tag{7.2}$$

The first two rules are simple linear expressions. This is not so in the case of the portfolio variance, as the third rule shows.

Rule 3. The variance of the rate of return on the two-risky-asset portfolio is

$$\sigma_P^2 = (w_B \sigma_B)^2 + (w_S \sigma_S)^2 + 2(w_B \sigma_B)(w_S \sigma_S)\rho_{BS} \tag{7.3}$$

where ρ_{BS} is the correlation coefficient between the returns on the stock and bond funds.

The variance of the portfolio is a *sum* of the contributions of the component security variances *plus* a term that involves the correlation coefficient between the returns on the component securities. We know from the last section why this last term arises. If the correlation between the component securities is small or negative, then there will be a greater tendency for the variability in the returns on the two assets to offset each other. This will reduce portfolio risk. Notice in Equation 7.3 that portfolio variance is lower when the correlation coefficient is lower.

The formula describing portfolio variance is more complicated than that describing portfolio return. This complication has a virtue, however: namely, the tremendous potential for gains from diversification.

The Risk-Return Trade-Off with Two-Risky-Asset Portfolios

Suppose now that the standard deviation of bonds is 12% and that of stocks is 25%, and assume that there is zero correlation between the return on the bond fund and the return on the stock fund. A correlation coefficient of zero means that stock and bond returns vary independently of each other.

Say we start out with a position of 100% in bonds, and we now consider a shift: Invest 50% in bonds and 50% in stocks. We can compute the portfolio variance from Equation 7.3.

Input data:

$$\sigma_B = 12\%; \ \sigma_S = 25\%; \ \rho_{BS} = 0; \ w_B = 0.5; \ w_S = 0.5$$

Portfolio variance:

$$\sigma_P^2 = (0.5 \times 12)^2 + (0.5 \times 25)^2 + 2(0.5 \times 12) \times (0.5 \times 25) \times 0$$
$$= 192.25$$

The standard deviation of the portfolio (the square root of the variance, 192.25) is 13.87%. Had we mistakenly calculated portfolio risk by averaging the two standard deviations [(25 + 12)/2], we would have predicted incorrectly an increase in the portfolio standard deviation by a full 6.50 percentage points, to 18.5%. Instead, the portfolio variance equation shows that the addition of stocks to the formerly all-bond portfolio actually increases the portfolio standard deviation by only 1.87 percentage points. So the gain from diversification can be seen as a full 4.63%.

This gain is cost-free in the sense that diversification allows us to experience the full contribution of the stock's higher expected return, while keeping the portfolio standard deviation below the average of the component standard deviations. As Equation 7.2 shows, the portfolio expected return is the weighted average of expected returns of the component securities. If the expected return on bonds is 10% and the expected return on stocks is 17%, then shifting from 0% to 50% investment in stocks will increase our expected return from 10% to 13.5%.

FIGURE 7.3
Investment Opportunity
Set for Bond and Stock
Funds

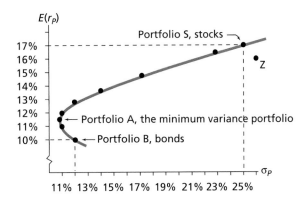

**EXAMPLE 7.1
Benefits from
Diversification**

Suppose we invest 75% in bonds and only 25% in stocks. We can construct a portfolio with an expected return higher than bonds $(0.75 \times 10) + (0.25 \times 17) = 11.75\%$ and, at the same time, a standard deviation that is less than bonds. Using Equation 7.3 again, we find that the portfolio variance is

$$(0.75 \times 12)^2 + (0.25 \times 25)^2 + 2(0.75 \times 12)(0.25 \times 25) \times 0 = 120$$

and, accordingly, the portfolio standard deviation is $\sqrt{120} = 10.96\%$, which is less than the standard deviation of either bonds or stocks alone. Taking on a more volatile asset (stocks) actually reduces portfolio risk! Such is the power of diversification.

We can find investment proportions that will reduce portfolio risk even further. The risk-minimizing proportions will be 81.27% in bonds and 18.73% in stocks.[1] With these proportions, the lowest risk portfolio standard deviation will be 10.82%, and the portfolio's expected return will be 11.31%.

Is this portfolio preferable to the one with 25% in the stock fund? That depends on investor preferences, because the portfolio with the lower variance also has a lower expected return.

investment opportunity set
Set of available portfolio risk-return combinations.

What the analyst can and must do, however, is to show investors the entire **investment opportunity set** as we do in Figure 7.3. This is the set of all attainable combinations of risk and return offered by portfolios formed using the available assets in differing proportions.

Points on the investment opportunity set of Figure 7.3 can be found by varying the investment proportions and computing the resulting expected returns and standard deviations from Equations 7.2 and 7.3. We can feed the input data and the two equations into a personal computer and let it draw the graph. With the aid of the computer, we can easily find the portfolio composition corresponding to any point on the opportunity set. Table 7.5 shows the investment proportions and the mean and standard deviation for a few portfolios.

The Mean-Variance Criterion

Investors desire portfolios that lie to the "northwest" in Figure 7.3. These are portfolios with high expected returns (toward the "north" of the figure) and low volatility (to the "west"). These preferences mean that we can compare portfolios using a *mean-variance criterion* in the following way. Portfolio A is said to dominate portfolio B if all investors prefer A over B. This will be the case if it has higher mean return and lower variance:

$$E(r_A) \geq E(r_B) \text{ and } \sigma_A \leq \sigma_B$$

Graphically, portfolio A will lie to the northwest of B in Figure 7.3. Given a choice between portfolios A and B, *all* investors will choose A. For example, the stock fund in Figure 7.3 dominates portfolio Z; the stock fund has higher expected return and lower volatility.

---

[1]With a zero correlation coefficient, the variance-minimizing proportion in the bond fund is given by the expression: $\sigma_S^2/(\sigma_B^2 + \sigma_S^2)$.

TABLE 7.5

Investment Opportunity
Set for Bond and Stock
Funds

Investment Proportions		Expected Return (%) $E(r_P)$	Standard Deviation (%) σ_P
w_B	w_S		
0.0	1.0	17.0	25.0
0.2	0.8	15.6	20.14
0.4	0.6	14.2	15.75
0.5	0.5	13.5	13.87
0.6	0.4	12.8	12.32
0.8	0.2	11.4	10.824
0.8127*	0.1873*	11.31	10.822
1.0	0.0	10.0	12.0

Input data: $E(r_B) = 10\%$ $E(r_S) = 17\%$ $\sigma_B = 12\%$ $\sigma_S = 25\%$ $\rho_{BS} = 0$

*Minimum variance portfolio.

Portfolios that lie below the minimum-variance portfolio in the figure (portfolio A) can therefore be rejected out of hand as inefficient. Any portfolio on the downward sloping portion of the curve is "dominated" by the portfolio that lies directly above it on the upward sloping portion of the curve since that portfolio has higher expected return and equal standard deviation. The best choice among the portfolios on the upward sloping portion of the curve is not as obvious, because in this region higher expected return is accompanied by higher risk. The best choice will depend on the investor's willingness to trade off risk against expected return.

So far we have assumed a correlation of zero between stock and bond returns. We know that low correlations aid diversification and that a higher correlation coefficient between stocks and bonds results in a reduced effect of diversification. What are the implications of perfect positive correlation between bonds and stocks?

Assuming the correlation coefficient is 1.0 simplifies Equation 7.3 for portfolio variance. Looking at it again, you will see that substitution of $\rho_{BS} = 1$ in Equation 7.3 means we can "complete the square" of the quantities $w_B\sigma_B$ and $w_S\sigma_S$ to obtain

$$\sigma_P^2 = (w_B\sigma_B + w_S\sigma_S)^2$$

and, therefore,

$$\sigma_P = w_B\sigma_B + w_S\sigma_S$$

The portfolio standard deviation is a weighted average of the component security standard deviations only in the special case of perfect positive correlation. In this circumstance, there are no gains to be had from diversification. Whatever the proportions of stocks and bonds, both the portfolio mean and the standard deviation are simply weighted averages. Figure 7.4 shows the opportunity set with perfect positive correlation—a straight line through the component securities. No portfolio can be discarded as inefficient in this case, and the choice among portfolios simply depends on risk preference. Diversification in the case of perfect positive correlation is not effective.

Perfect positive correlation is the *only* case in which there is no benefit from diversification. Whenever $\rho < 1$, the portfolio standard deviation is less than the weighted average of the standard deviations of the component securities. Therefore, *there are benefits to diversification whenever asset returns are less than perfectly correlated.*

Our analysis has ranged from very attractive diversification benefits ($\rho_{BS} < 0$) to no benefits at all ($\rho_{BS} = 1.0$). For ρ_{BS} within this range, the benefits will be somewhere in between. As Figure 7.4 illustrates, $\rho_{BS} = 0.5$ is a lot better for diversification than perfect positive correlation and quite a bit worse than zero correlation.

A realistic correlation coefficient between stocks and bonds based on historical experience actually is 0.20. The expected returns and standard deviations that we have so far assumed also reflect historical experience, which is why we include a graph for $\rho_{BS} = 0.2$ in Figure 7.4. Table 7.6 enumerates some of the points on the various opportunity sets in Figure 7.4.

FIGURE 7.4

Investment Opportunity Sets for Bonds and Stocks with Various Correlation Coefficients

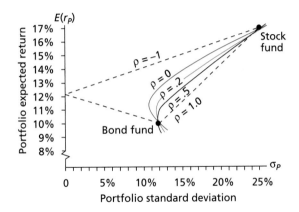

Negative correlation between a pair of assets is also possible. Where negative correlation is present, there will be even greater diversification benefits. Again, let us start with an extreme. With perfect negative correlation, we substitute $\rho_{BS} = -1.0$ in Equation 7.3 and simplify it in the same way as with positive perfect correlation. Here, too, we can complete the square, this time, however, with different results

$$\sigma_P^2 = (w_B\sigma_B - w_S\sigma_S)^2$$

and, therefore

$$\sigma_P = ABS[w_B\sigma_B - w_S\sigma_S] \tag{7.4}$$

The right-hand side of Equation (7.4) is the absolute value of $w_B\sigma_B - w_S\sigma_S$. The solution involves the absolute value because standard deviation is always positive.

With perfect negative correlation, the benefits from diversification stretch to the limit. Equation 7.4 points to the proportions that will reduce the portfolio standard deviation all the way to zero.[2] With our data, this will happen when $w_B = 67.57\%$. While exposing us to zero risk, investing 32.43% in stocks (rather than placing all funds in bonds) will still increase the portfolio expected return to 12.27%. Of course, we can hardly expect results like this in reality.

TABLE 7.6

Investment Opportunity Sets for Bonds and Stocks with Various Correlation Coefficients

		Portfolio Standard Deviation (%) for Given Correlation				
w_S	$E(r_P)$	$\rho = -1.0$	$\rho = 0$	$\rho = 0.2$	$\rho = 0.5$	$\rho = 1.0$
0.0	17.0	25.0	25.0	25.0	25.0	25.0
0.2	15.6	17.6	20.1	20.6	21.3	22.4
0.4	14.2	10.2	15.8	16.6	17.9	19.8
0.6	12.8	2.8	12.3	13.4	15.0	17.2
0.8	11.4	4.6	10.8	11.7	12.9	14.6
1.0	10.0	12.0	12.0	12.0	12.0	12.0
		Minimum Variance Portfolio				
$w_B(min)*$		0.6757	0.8127	0.8706	1.0128	1.00
$E(r_P)$		12.27%	11.31%	10.91%	9.81%	10%
σ_P		0	10.82%	11.54%	11.83%	12%

$*w_B \text{ (min)} = \dfrac{\sigma_S^2 - \sigma_B\sigma_S\rho_{BS}}{\sigma_B^2 + \sigma_S^2 - 2\sigma_B\sigma_S\rho_{BS}}$ is the proportion in bonds that minimizes portfolio variance.

---

[2]The proportion in bonds that will get the standard deviation to zero when $\rho = -1$ is:

$$w_B = \frac{\sigma_S}{\sigma_B + \sigma_S}$$

Compare this formula to the formula in footnote 1 for the variance-minimizing proportions when $\rho = 0$.

Concept Check

2. Suppose that for some reason you are *required* to invest 50% of your portfolio in bonds and 50% in stocks.

   a. If the standard deviation of your portfolio is 15%, what must be the correlation coefficient between stock and bond returns?

   b. What is the expected rate of return on your portfolio?

   c. Now suppose that the correlation between stock and bond returns is 0.22 but that you are free to choose whatever portfolio proportions you desire. Are you likely to be better or worse off than you were in part (*a*)?

Using Historical Data

We've seen that portfolio risk and return depend on the means and variances of the component securities, as well as on the covariance between their returns. One way to obtain these inputs is a scenario analysis, such as the simple one we presented in Tables 7.1–7.4. As we noted in Chapter 6, however, a common alternative approach to produce these inputs is to make use of historical data.

In this approach, we use realized returns to estimate mean returns and volatility as well as the tendency for security returns to co-vary. The estimate of the mean return for each security is its average value in the sample period; the estimate of variance is the average value of the squared deviations around the sample average; the estimate of the covariance is the average value of the cross-product of deviations. As we noted in Chapter 6, Example 6.5, the averages used to compute variance and covariance are adjusted by the ratio $n/(n-1)$ to account for the "lost degree of freedom" when using the sample average in place of the true mean return, $E(r)$.

Notice that, as in scenario analysis, the focus for risk and return analysis is on average returns and the deviations of returns from their average value. Here, however, instead of using mean returns based on the scenario analysis, we use average returns during the sample period.

We can illustrate this approach with a simple example.

EXAMPLE 7.2
Using Historical Data to Estimate Means, Variances, and Covariances

Consider the five-year return history of stocks ABC and XYZ shown in the first two columns of Table 7.7. We can use these historical data to compute average returns, variances, standard deviations, and the correlation of returns. These calculations are detailed in the next columns of Table 7.7; they can be easily programmed into any spreadsheet.

TABLE 7.7   Estimation of Risk and Return Statistics

Year	Rate of Return		Deviations from Average Return		Squared Deviation		Product of Deviations ABC × XYZ
	ABC	XYZ	ABC	XYZ	ABC	XYZ	
1	11.34	23.57	2.05	1.70	4.20	2.89	3.49
2	−17.64	51.95	−26.93	30.08	725.22	904.81	−810.05
3	−5.38	−20.45	−14.67	−42.32	215.21	1790.98	620.83
4	44.72	48.12	35.43	26.25	1255.28	688.06	930.04
5	13.39	6.17	4.10	−15.70	16.81	246.49	−64.37
Average	9.29	21.87			443.34	726.65	135.99
Variance or covariance estimate[a]:					554.18	908.31	169.99
					↑	↑	↑
					Estimates of variance		Estimate of covariance
Standard deviation					23.54	30.14	
Correlation coefficient[b]							0.24

[a]Variances are estimated as $n/(n-1)$ times the average of the squared deviations from the average, where n is the number of observations; in this case $n = 5$. Similarly the covariance estimate is the average of the cross-product of the deviations (see the last column), also multiplied by $n/(n-1)$.

[b]Correlation $= \dfrac{\text{Cov}(r_{ABC}, r_{XYZ})}{\sigma_{ABC} \times \sigma_{XYZ}} = \dfrac{169.99}{23.54 \times 30.14}$

Given the estimates of mean returns, standard deviations, and the correlation coefficient derived in Table 7.7, we can apply Equations 7.1–7.3 to estimate the means and standard deviations for various portfolios composed of ABC and XYZ. These are presented in Table 7.8. The bottom line of that table describes the minimum variance portfolio.

TABLE 7.8   Means and Standard Deviations of Portfolios Composed of Various Combinations of Stocks ABC and XYZ

Portfolio Proportions		Portfolio Characteristics		
ABC	**XYZ**	**Mean**	**Standard Deviation**	
0.00	1.00	21.87	30.14	
0.20	0.80	19.35	25.11	
0.40	0.60	16.84	21.37	
0.60	0.40	14.32	19.64	
0.80	0.20	11.80	20.45	
1.00	0.00	9.29	23.54	
0.66	0.34	13.59	19.61	←Minimum variance portfolio

7.3 THE OPTIMAL RISKY PORTFOLIO WITH A RISK-FREE ASSET

Now we can expand the asset allocation problem to include a risk-free asset. Let us continue to use the input data from Table 7.5, but now assume a realistic correlation coefficient between stocks and bonds of 0.20. Suppose then that we are still confined to the risky bond and stock funds, but now can also invest in risk-free T-bills yielding 8%. Figure 7.5 shows the opportunity set generated from the bond and stock funds. This is the same opportunity set as graphed in Figure 7.4 with $\rho_{BS} = 0.20$.

Two possible capital allocation lines (CALs) are drawn from the risk-free rate ($r_f = 8\%$) to two feasible portfolios. The first possible CAL is drawn through the variance-minimizing portfolio (A), which invests 87.06% in bonds and 12.94% in stocks. Portfolio A's expected return is 10.91% and its standard deviation is 11.54%. With a T-bill rate (r_f) of 8%, the

FIGURE 7.5
The Opportunity Set Using Bonds and Stocks and Two Capital Allocation Lines

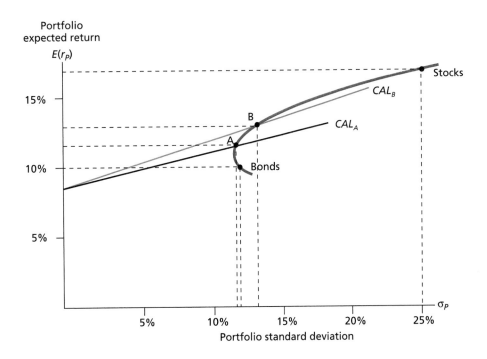

reward-to-variability ratio of portfolio *A* (which is also the slope of the CAL that combines T-bills with portfolio *A*) is

$$S_A = \frac{E(r_A) - r_f}{\sigma_A}$$

$$= \frac{10.91 - 8}{11.54} = 0.25$$

Now consider the CAL that uses portfolio *B* instead of *A*. Portfolio *B* invests 65% in bonds and 35% in stocks, providing an expected return of 12.45% with a standard deviation of 12.83%. Thus, the reward-to-variability ratio of any portfolio on the CAL of *B* is

$$S_B = \frac{4.45}{12.83} = 0.35$$

This is significantly higher than the reward-to-variability ratio of the CAL of the variance-minimizing portfolio *A*.

The difference in the reward-to-variability ratios is $S_B - S_A = 0.10$. This implies that portfolio *B* provides 10 extra basis points (0.10%) of expected return for every percentage point increase in standard deviation.

The higher reward-to-variability ratio of portfolio *B* means that its capital allocation line is steeper than that of *A*. Therefore, CAL_B plots above CAL_A in Figure 7.5. In other words, combinations of portfolio *B* and the risk-free asset provide a higher expected return for any level of risk (standard deviation) than combinations of portfolio *A* and the risk-free asset. Therefore, all risk-averse investors would prefer to form their complete portfolio using the risk-free asset with portfolio *B* rather than with portfolio *A*. In this sense, portfolio *B* dominates *A*.

But why stop at portfolio *B*? We can continue to ratchet the CAL upward until it reaches the ultimate point of tangency with the investment opportunity set. This must yield the CAL with the highest feasible reward-to-variability ratio. Therefore, the tangency portfolio (*O*) in

optimal risky portfolio
The best combination of risky assets to be mixed with safe assets to form the complete portfolio.

Figure 7.6 is the **optimal risky portfolio** to mix with T-bills, which may be defined as the risky portfolio resulting in the highest possible CAL. We can read the expected return and standard deviation of portfolio *O* (for "optimal") off the graph in Figure 7.6 as

$$E(r_O) = 14.36\%$$

$$\sigma_O = 17.07\%$$

FIGURE 7.6

The Optimal Capital Allocation Line with Bonds, Stocks, and T-Bills

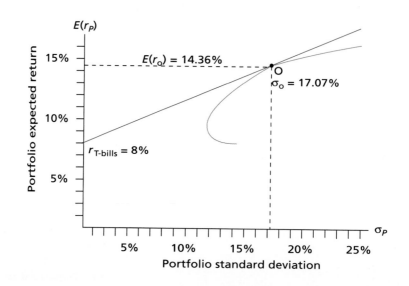

FIGURE 7.7

The Complete Portfolio

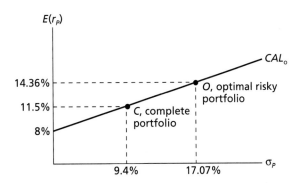

which can be identified as the portfolio that invests 37.65% in bonds and 62.35% in stocks.[3] We can obtain a numerical solution to this problem using a computer program.

The CAL with our optimal portfolio has a slope of

$$S_O = \frac{14.36 - 8}{17.07} = 0.37$$

which is the reward-to-variability ratio of portfolio O. This slope exceeds the slope of any other feasible portfolio, as it must if it is to be the slope of the best feasible CAL.

In the last chapter we saw that the preferred *complete* portfolio formed from a risky portfolio and a risk-free asset depends on the investor's risk aversion. More risk-averse investors will prefer low-risk portfolios despite the lower expected return, while more risk-tolerant investors will choose higher-risk, higher-return portfolios. Both investors, however, will choose portfolio O as their risky portfolio since that portfolio results in the highest return per unit of risk, that is, the steepest capital allocation line. Investors will differ only in their allocation of investment funds between portfolio O and the risk-free asset.

Figure 7.7 shows one possible choice for the preferred complete portfolio, C. The investor places 55% of wealth in portfolio O and 45% in Treasury bills. The rate of return and volatility of the portfolio are

$$E(r_C) = 8 + 0.55 \times (14.36 - 8) = 11.5\%$$

$$\sigma_C = 0.55 \times 17.07 = 9.4\%$$

In turn, we found above that portfolio O is formed by mixing the bond fund and stock fund with weights of 37.65% and 62.35%. Therefore, the overall asset allocation of the complete portfolio is as follows:

Weight in risk-free asset		45.0%
Weight in bond fund	$0.3765 \times 55\% =$	20.7
Weight in stock fund	$0.6235 \times 55\% =$	34.3
Total		100.0%

Figure 7.8 depicts the overall asset allocation. The allocation reflects considerations of both efficient diversification (the construction of the optimal risky portfolio, O) and risk aversion (the allocation of funds between the risk-free asset and the risky portfolio O to form the complete portfolio, C).

---

[3]The proportion of portfolio O invested in bonds is:

$$w_B = \frac{[E(r_B) - r_f]\sigma_S^2 - [E(r_S) - r_f]\sigma_B\sigma_S\,\rho_{BS}}{[E(r_B) - r_f]\sigma_S^2 + [E(r_S) - r_f]\sigma_B^2 - [E(r_B) - r_f + E(r_S) - r_f]\sigma_B\sigma_S\rho_{BS}}$$

FIGURE 7.8

The Composition of the Complete Portfolio: The Solution to the Asset Allocation Problem

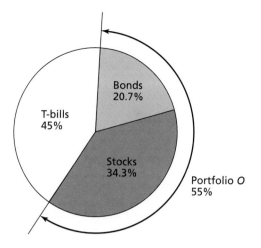

3. A universe of securities includes a risky stock (X), a stock index fund (S), and T-bills. The data for the universe are:

	Expected Return	Standard Deviation
X	25%	60%
S	20	30
T-bills	5	0

The correlation coefficient between X and S is -0.2.

a. Draw the opportunity set of securities X and S.
b. Find the optimal risky portfolio (O) and its expected return and standard deviation.
c. Find the slope of the CAL supported by T-bills and portfolio O.
d. Suppose an investor places 2/9 (i.e., 22.22%) of the complete portfolio in the risky portfolio O and the remainder in T-bills. Calculate the composition of the complete portfolio.

7.4 EFFICIENT DIVERSIFICATION WITH MANY RISKY ASSETS

We can extend this portfolio construction methodology to cover the case of many risky assets and a risk-free asset. First, we offer an overview. As in the two-risky-assets example, the problem has three separate steps. To begin, we identify the best possible or most *efficient* risk-return combinations available from the universe of risky assets. Next we determine the optimal portfolio of risky assets by finding the portfolio that supports the steepest CAL. Finally, we choose an appropriate complete portfolio based on the investor's risk aversion by mixing the risk-free asset with the optimal risky portfolio.

The Efficient Frontier of Risky Assets

The techniques used to devise efficient combinations of risky assets were developed and published by Harry Markowitz at the University of Chicago in 1951 and ultimately earned him the Nobel Prize in economics. We will sketch his approach here.

First, we determine the risk-return opportunity set. The aim is to construct the northwestern-most portfolios in terms of expected return and standard deviation from the universe of securities. The inputs are the expected returns and standard deviations of each asset in the universe, along with the correlation coefficients between each pair of assets. These data come from security analysis, to be discussed in Part Four. The graph that connects all the northwestern-most portfolios is called the **efficient frontier** of risky assets. It represents the

efficient frontier
Graph representing a set of portfolios that maximizes expected return at each level of portfolio risk.

FIGURE 7.9

The Efficient Frontier of Risky Assets and Individual Assets

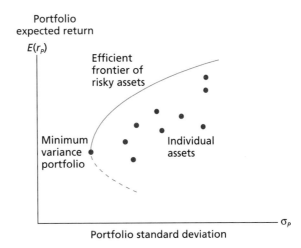

set of portfolios that offers the highest possible expected rate of return for each level of portfolio standard deviation. These portfolios may be viewed as efficiently diversified. One such frontier is shown in Figure 7.9.

Expected return–standard deviation combinations for any *individual* asset end up inside the efficient frontier, because single-asset portfolios are inefficient—as they are not efficiently diversified.

When we choose among portfolios on the efficient frontier, we can immediately discard portfolios below the minimum-variance portfolio. These are dominated by portfolios on the upper half of the frontier with equal risk but higher expected returns. Therefore, the real choice is among portfolios on the efficient frontier above the minimum-variance portfolio.

Various constraints may preclude a particular investor from choosing portfolios on the efficient frontier, however. If an institution is prohibited by law from taking short positions in any asset, for example, the portfolio manager must add constraints to the computer-optimization program that rule out negative (short) positions.

Short sale restrictions are only one possible constraint. Some clients may want to assume a minimum level of expected *dividend* yield. In this case, data input must include a set of expected dividend yields. The optimization program is made to include a constraint to ensure the expected *portfolio* dividend yield will equal or exceed the desired level. Another popular constraint forbids investments in companies engaged in "undesirable social activity."

In principle, portfolio managers can tailor an efficient frontier to meet any particular objective. Of course, satisfying constraints carries a price tag. An efficient frontier subject to a number of constraints will offer a lower reward-to-variability ratio than a less constrained one. Clients should be aware of this cost and may want to think twice about constraints that are not mandated by law.

Deriving the efficient frontier may be quite difficult conceptually, but computing and graphing it with any number of assets and any set of constraints is quite straightforward. For a small number of assets, and in the absence of constraints beyond the obvious one that portfolio proportions must sum to 1.0, the efficient frontier can be computed and graphed with a spreadsheet program.

Choosing the Optimal Risky Portfolio

The second step of the optimization plan involves the risk-free asset. Using the current risk-free rate, we search for the capital allocation line with the highest reward-to-variability ratio (the steepest slope), as shown in Figures 7.5 and 7.6.

The CAL formed from the optimal risky portfolio (*O*) will be tangent to the efficient frontier of risky assets discussed above. This CAL dominates all alternative feasible lines (the dashed lines that are drawn through the frontier). Portfolio *O*, therefore, is the optimal risky portfolio.

The Preferred Complete Portfolio and the Separation Property

Finally, in the third step, the investor chooses the appropriate mix between the optimal risky portfolio (*O*) and T-bills, exactly as in Figure 7.7.

A portfolio manager will offer the same risky portfolio (*O*) to all clients, no matter what their degree of risk aversion. Risk aversion comes into play only when clients select their desired point on the CAL. More risk-averse clients will invest more in the risk-free asset and less in the optimal risky portfolio *O* than less risk-averse clients, but both will use portfolio *O* as the optimal risky investment vehicle.

separation property
The property that portfolio choice can be separated into two independent tasks: (1) determination of the optimal risky portfolio, which is a purely technical problem, and (2) the personal choice of the best mix of the risky portfolio and the risk-free asset.

This result is called a **separation property,** introduced by James Tobin (1958), the 1983 Nobel Laureate for economics: It implies that portfolio choice can be separated into two independent tasks. The first task, which includes steps one and two, determination of the optimal risky portfolio (*O*), is purely technical. Given the particular input data, the best risky portfolio is the same for all clients regardless of risk aversion. The second task, construction of the complete portfolio from bills and portfolio *O*, however, depends on personal preference. Here the client is the decision maker.

Of course, the optimal risky portfolio for different clients may vary because of portfolio constraints such as dividend yield requirements, tax considerations, or other client preferences. Our analysis, though, suggests that a few portfolios may be sufficient to serve the demands of a wide range of investors. We see here the theoretical basis of the mutual fund industry.

If the optimal portfolio is the same for all clients, professional management is more efficient and less costly. One management firm can serve a number of clients with relatively small incremental administrative costs.

The (computerized) optimization technique is the easiest part of portfolio construction. If different managers use different input data to develop different efficient frontiers, they will offer different "optimal" portfolios. Therefore, the real arena of the competition among portfolio managers is in the sophisticated security analysis that underlies their choices. The rule of GIGO (garbage in–garbage out) applies fully to portfolio selection. If the quality of the security analysis is poor, a passive portfolio such as a market index fund can yield better results than an active portfolio tilted toward *seemingly* favorable securities.

Concept Check

4. Two portfolio managers work for competing investment management houses. Each employs security analysts to prepare input data for the construction of the optimal portfolio. When all is completed, the efficient frontier obtained by Manager A dominates that of manager B in that A's optimal risky portfolio lies northwest of B's. Is the more attractive efficient frontier asserted by manager A evidence that she really employs better security analysts?

7.5 A SINGLE-FACTOR ASSET MARKET

We started this chapter with the distinction between systematic and firm-specific risk. Systematic risk is largely macroeconomic, affecting all securities, while firm-specific risk factors affect only one particular firm or, perhaps, its industry. **Factor models** are statistical models designed to estimate these two components of risk for a particular security or portfolio. The first to use a factor model to explain the benefits of diversification was another Nobel Prize winner, William S. Sharpe (1963). We will introduce his major work (the capital asset pricing model) in the next chapter.

factor model
Statistical model to measure the firm-specific versus systematic risk of a stock's rate of return.

excess return
Rate of return in excess of the risk-free rate.

Let us use R_i to denote the **excess return** on a security, that is, the rate of return in excess of the risk-free rate: $R_i = r_i - r_f$. Then we can express the distinction between macroeconomic and firm-specific factors by decomposing this excess return in some holding period into three components

$$R_i = E(R_i) + \beta_i M + e_i \tag{7.5}$$

In Equation 7.5, $E(R_i)$ is the *expected* excess holding-period return (HPR) at the start of the holding period. The next two terms reflect the impact of two sources of uncertainty. *M* quantifies the market or macroeconomic surprises (with zero meaning that there is "no surprise") during the holding period. β_i is the sensitivity of the security to the macroeconomic factor. Finally, e_i is the impact of unanticipated firm-specific events.

Both M and e_i have zero expected values because each represents the impact of unanticipated events, which by definition must average out to zero. The **beta** (β_i) denotes the responsiveness of security i to macroeconomic events; this sensitivity will be different for different securities.

As an example of a factor model, suppose that the excess return on Digital stock is *expected* to be 9% in the coming holding period. However, on average, for every unanticipated increase of 1% in the vitality of the general economy, which we take as the macroeconomic factor M, Digital's stock return will be enhanced by 1.2%. Digital's β is therefore 1.2. Finally, Digital is affected by firm-specific surprises as well. Therefore, we can write the realized excess return on Digital stock as follows

$$R_D = 9\% + 1.2\,M + e_i$$

If the economy outperforms expectations by 2%, then we would revise upward our expectations of Digital's excess return by $1.2 \times 2\%$, or 2.4%, resulting in a new expected excess return of 11.4%. Finally, the effects of Digital's firm-specific news during the holding period must be added to arrive at the actual holding-period return on Digital stock.

Equation 7.5 describes a factor model for stock returns. This is a simplification of reality; a more realistic decomposition of security returns would require more than one factor in Equation 7.5. We treat this issue in the next chapter, but for now, let us examine the single-factor case.

Specification of a Single-Index Model of Security Returns

A factor model description of security returns is of little use if we cannot specify a way to measure the factor that we say affects security returns. One reasonable approach is to use the rate of return on a broad index of securities, such as the S&P 500, as a proxy for the common macro factor. With this assumption, we can use the excess return on the market index, R_M, to measure the direction of macro shocks in any period.

The **index model** separates the realized rate of return on a security into macro (systematic) and micro (firm-specific) components much like Equation 7.5. The excess rate of return on each security is the sum of three components:

	Symbol
1. The stock's excess return if the market factor is neutral, that is, if the market's excess return is zero.	α_i
2. The component of return due to movements in the overall market (as represented by the index R_M); β_i is the security's responsiveness to the market.	$\beta_i R_M$
3. The component attributable to unexpected events that are relevant only to this security (firm-specific).	e_i

The excess return on the stock now can be stated as

$$R_i = \alpha_i + \beta_i R_M + e_i \tag{7.6}$$

Equation 7.6 specifies the two sources of security risk: market or systematic risk ($\beta_i R_M$), attributable to the security's sensitivity (as measured by beta) to movements in the overall market, and firm-specific risk (e_i), which is the part of uncertainty independent of the market factor. Because the firm-specific component of the firm's return is uncorrelated with the market return, we can write the variance of the excess return of the stock as[4]

---

[4]Notice that because α_i is a constant, it has no bearing on the variance of R_i.

beta
The sensitivity of a security's returns to the systematic or market factor.

index model
A model of stock returns using a market index such as the S&P 500 to represent common or systematic risk factors.

$$\begin{aligned}
\text{Variance } (R_i) &= \text{Variance } (\alpha_i + \beta_i R_M + e_i) \\
&= \text{Variance } (\beta_i R_M) + \text{Variance } (e_i) \\
&= \beta_i^2\, \sigma_M^2 \qquad\qquad + \sigma^2(e_i) \\
&= \text{Systematic risk } + \text{Firm-specific risk}
\end{aligned}$$

(7.7)

Therefore, the total variability of the rate of return of each security depends on two components:

1. The variance attributable to the uncertainty common to the entire market. This systematic risk is attributable to the uncertainty in R_M. Notice that the systematic risk of each stock depends on both the volatility in R_M (that is, σ_M^2) *and* the sensitivity of the stock to fluctuations in R_M. That sensitivity is measured by β_i.
2. The variance attributable to firm-specific risk factors, the effects of which are measured by e_i. This is the variance in the part of the stock's return that is independent of market performance.

This single-index model is convenient. It relates security returns to a market index that investors follow. Moreover, as we soon shall see, its usefulness goes beyond mere convenience.

Statistical and Graphical Representation of the Single-Index Model

Equation 7.6, $R_i = \alpha_i + \beta_i R_M + e_i$, may be interpreted as a single-variable *regression equation* of R_i on the market excess return R_M. The excess return on the security (R_i) is the dependent variable that is to be explained by the regression. On the right-hand side of the equation are the intercept α_i; the regression (or slope) coefficient beta, β_i, multiplying the independent (or explanatory) variable R_M; and the security residual (unexplained) return, e_i. We can plot this regression relationship as in Figure 7.10, which shows a scatter diagram for Digital Equipment Corporation (DEC) excess return against the excess return of the market index.

The horizontal axis of the scatter diagram measures the explanatory variable, here the market excess return, R_M. The vertical axis measures the dependent variable, here DEC's excess return, R_D. Each point on the scatter diagram represents a sample pair of returns (R_M, R_D) that might be observed for a particular holding period. Point T, for instance, describes a holding period when the excess return was 17% on the market index and 27% on DEC.

Regression analysis lets us use the sample of historical returns to estimate a relationship between the dependent variable and the explanatory variable. The regression line in Figure 7.10 is drawn so as to minimize the sum of all the squared deviations around it. Hence, we

FIGURE 7.10

Scatter Diagram for DEC

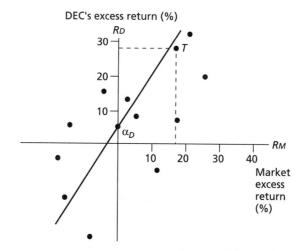

say the regression line "best fits" the data in the scatter diagram. The line is called the *security characteristic line*.

The regression intercept (α_D) is measured from the origin to the intersection of the regression line with the vertical axis. Any point on the vertical axis represents zero market excess return, so the intercept gives us the *expected* excess return on DEC during the sample period when market performance was neutral. The intercept in Figure 7.10 is about 4.5%.

The slope of the regression line can be measured by dividing the rise of the line by its run. It also is expressed by the number multiplying the explanatory variable, which is called the regression coefficient or the slope coefficient or simply the beta. The regression beta is a natural measure of systematic risk since it measures the typical response of the security return to market fluctuations.

The regression line does not represent the *actual* returns: that is, the points on the scatter diagram almost never lie on the regression line, although the actual returns are used to calculate the regression coefficients. Rather, the line represents average tendencies; it shows the effect of the index return on our *expectation* of R_D. The algebraic representation of the regression line is

$$E(R_D \mid R_M) = \alpha_D + \beta_D R_M \tag{7.8}$$

which reads: The expectation of R_D *given* a value of R_M equals the intercept plus the slope coefficient times the given value of R_M.

Because the regression line represents expectations, and because these expectations may not be realized in any or all of the actual returns (as the scatter diagram shows), the *actual* security returns also include a residual, the firm-specific surprise, e_i. This surprise (at point T, for example) is measured by the vertical distance between the point of the scatter diagram and the regression line. For example, the expected return on DEC, given a market return of 17%, would have been 4.5% + 1.4 × 17% = 28.3%. The actual return was only 27%, so point T falls below the regression line by 1.3%.

Equation 7.7 shows that the greater the beta of the security, that is, the greater the slope of the regression, the greater the security's systematic risk ($\beta_D^2 \sigma_M^2$), as well as its total variance (σ_D^2). The *average security* has a slope coefficient (beta) of 1.0: Because the market is composed of all securities, the typical response to a market movement must be one for one. An "aggressive" investment will have a beta higher than 1.0; that is, the security has above-average market risk. In Figure 7.10, DEC's beta is 1.4. Conversely, securities with betas lower than 1.0 are called defensive.[5]

A security may have a negative beta. Its regression line will then slope downward, meaning that, for more favorable macro events (higher R_M), we would expect a *lower* return, and vice versa. The latter means that when the macro economy goes bad (negative R_M) and securities with positive beta are expected to have negative excess returns, the negative-beta security will shine. The result is that a negative-beta security has *negative* systematic risk, that is, it provides a hedge against systematic risk.

The dispersion of the scatter of actual returns about the regression line is determined by the residual variance $\sigma^2(e_D)$, which measures the effects of firm-specific events. The magnitude of firm-specific risk varies across securities. One way to measure the relative

---

[5]Note that the average beta of all securities will be 1.0 only when we compute a *weighted* average of betas (using market values as weights), since the stock market index is value weighted. We know from Chapter 5 that the distribution of securities by market value is not symmetric: There are relatively few large corporations and many more smaller ones. Thus, if you were to take a randomly selected sample of stocks, you should expect smaller companies to dominate. As a result, the simple average of the betas of individual securities, when computed against a value-weighted index such as the S&P 500, will be greater than 1.0, pushed up by the tendency for stocks of low-capitalization companies to have betas greater than 1.0.

FIGURE 7.11
Various Scatter
Diagrams

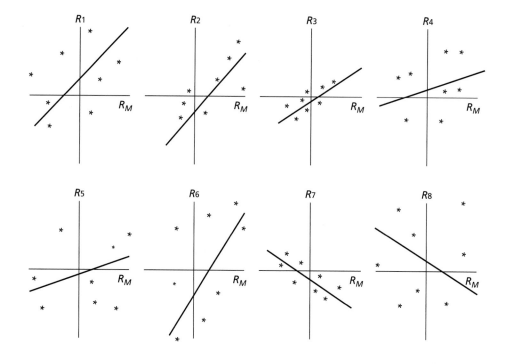

importance of systematic risk is to measure the ratio of systematic variance to total variance.

$$\rho^2 = \frac{\text{Systematic or explained variance}}{\text{Total variance}}$$

$$= \frac{\beta_D^2 \sigma_M^2}{\sigma_D^2} = \frac{\beta_D^2 \sigma_M^2}{\beta_D^2 \sigma_M^2 + \sigma^2(e_D)}$$

(7.9)

where ρ is the correlation coefficient between R_D and R_M. Its square measures the ratio of explained variance to total variance, that is, the proportion of total variance that can be attributed to market fluctuations. But if beta is negative, so is the correlation coefficient, an indication that the explanatory and dependent variables are expected to move in opposite directions.

At the extreme, when the correlation coefficient is either 1.0 or − 1.0, the security return is fully explained by the market return, that is, there are no firm-specific effects. All the points of the scatter diagram will lie exactly on the line. This is called perfect correlation (either positive or negative); the return on the security is perfectly predictable from the market return. A large correlation coefficient (in absolute value terms) means systematic variance dominates the total variance; that is, firm-specific variance is relatively unimportant. When the correlation coefficient is small (in absolute value terms), the market factor plays a relatively unimportant part in explaining the variance of the asset, and firm-specific factors predominate.

5. Interpret the eight scatter diagrams of Figure 7.11 in terms of systematic risk, diversifiable risk, and the intercept.

Concept Check

EXAMPLE 7.3
Estimating the
Index Model
Using Historical
Data

Table 7.9 reproduces the data presented in Table 7.7 with the addition of a risk-free rate and the market index portfolio.

TABLE 7.9   Rates of Return on Various Securities

	Rate of Return (%)			
Year	**ABC**	**XYZ**	**Market Index**	**Risk-Free Asset**
1	11.34	23.57	14.40	5.23%
2	−17.64	51.95	−0.24	4.76
3	−5.38	−20.45	−9.15	6.22
4	44.72	48.12	45.57	3.78
5	13.39	6.17	11.59	4.43

Entering the raw data in Table 7.9 into a spreadsheet, we calculate the excess returns of the individual securities and the market index. Table 7.10 presents the excess returns.

TABLE 7.10   Excess Returns on Securities and Market Index

	Excess Returns (%)		
Year	**ABC**	**XYZ**	**Index**
1	6.11	18.34	9.17
2	−22.40	47.19	−5.00
3	−11.60	−26.67	−15.37
4	40.94	44.34	41.79
5	8.96	1.74	7.16
Average	4.40	16.99	7.55

The easiest route to estimate the parameters of the security characteristic line (i.e., the regression line described by Equation 7.6) is to use the regression function of your spreadsheet, regressing the excess return of each security against that of the market index. We show the actual calculations in Table 7.11 using standard formulas for regression slope and intercept. We use the following regression-equation relationships:

$$\text{Slope coefficient for ABC: } \beta_{ABC} = \frac{\text{Cov}(R_{ABC}, R_{Index})}{\text{Var}(R_{Index})} \tag{7.10}$$

$$\text{Intercept for ABC: } \alpha_{ABC} = \text{Average }(R_{ABC}) - \beta_{ABC} \times \text{Average }(R_{Index}) \tag{7.11}$$

The calculations in Table 7.11 show that the security characteristic line of ABC is described by $R_{ABC} = -3.53 + 1.05\, R_{Index}$

TABLE 7.11   ABC's Security Characteristic Line

	Excess Return		Deviations from Average Excess Return		Squared Deviation		Product of Deviations
Year	**ABC**	**Index**	**ABC**	**Index**	**ABC**	**Index**	**ABC × Index**
1	6.11	9.17	1.71	1.62	2.92	2.62	2.77
2	−22.40	−5.00	−26.80	−12.55	718.24	157.50	336.34
3	−11.60	−15.37	−16.00	−22.92	256.00	525.33	366.72
4	40.94	41.79	36.54	34.24	1335.17	1172.38	1251.13
5	8.96	7.16	4.56	−0.39	20.79	0.15	−1.78
Average	4.40	7.55			466.62	371.60	391.04
Variance or covariance estimate[a]					583.28	464.50	488.80
					↑	↑	↑
					Estimates of variance		Estimate of covariance

[a]Variances are estimated as $n/(n-1)$ times the average of the squared deviations from the average, where n is the number of observations; in this case $n = 5$. Similarly the covariance estimate is the average of the cross-product of the deviations (see the last column), also multiplied by $n/(n-1)$.

$$\text{Slope coefficient for ABC: } \beta_{ABC} = \frac{\text{Cov}(R_{ABC}, R_{Index})}{\text{Var}(R_{Index})} = \frac{488.80}{464.50} = 1.05$$

$$\text{Intercept for ABC: } \alpha_{ABC} = \text{Average }(R_{ABC}) - \beta_{ABC} \times \text{Average }(R_{Index})$$
$$= 4.40 - 1.05 \times 7.55 = -3.53$$

Diversification in a Single-Factor Security Market

Imagine a portfolio that is divided equally among securities whose returns are given by the single-index model in Equation 7.6. What are the systematic and nonsystematic (firm-specific) variances of this portfolio?

The beta of the portfolio is the simple average of the individual security betas, which we denote β. Hence, the systematic variance equals $\beta_P^2 \sigma_M^2$. This is the level of market risk in Figure 7.1B. The market variance (σ_M^2) and the market sensitivity of the portfolio (β_P) determine the market risk of the portfolio.

The systematic part of each security return, $\beta_i R_M$, is fully determined by the market factor and therefore is perfectly correlated with the systematic part of any other security return. Hence, there are no diversification effects on systematic risk no matter how many securities are involved. As far as *market risk* goes, a single-security portfolio with a small beta will result in a low market-risk portfolio. The number of securities makes no difference.

It is quite different with firm-specific or unique risk. If you choose securities with small residual variances for a portfolio, it, too, will have low unique risk. But you can do even better simply by holding more securities, even if each has a large residual variance. Because the firm-specific effects are independent of each other, their risk effects are offsetting. This is the insurance principle applied to the firm-specific component of risk. The portfolio ends up with a negligible level of nonsystematic risk.

In sum, when we control the systematic risk of the portfolio by manipulating the average beta of the component securities, the number of securities is of no consequence. But in the case of *nonsystematic* risk, the number of securities involved is more important than the firm-specific variance of the securities. Sufficient diversification can virtually eliminate firm-specific risk. Understanding this distinction is essential to understanding the role of diversification in portfolio construction.

We have just seen that when forming highly diversified portfolios, firm-specific risk becomes *irrelevant*. Only systematic risk remains. We conclude that in measuring security risk for diversified investors, we should focus our attention on the security's systematic risk. This means that for diversified investors, the relevant risk measure for a security will be the security's beta, β, since firms with higher β have greater sensitivity to broad market disturbances. As Equation 7.7 makes clear, systematic risk will be determined both by market volatility, σ_M^2, and the firm's sensitivity to the market, β.

Summary

- The expected rate of return of a portfolio is the weighted average of the component asset expected returns with the investment proportions as weights.
- The variance of a portfolio is a sum of the contributions of the component-security variances *plus* terms involving the correlation among assets.
- Even if correlations are positive, the portfolio standard deviation will be less than the weighted average of the component standard deviations, as long as the assets are not *perfectly* positively correlated. Thus, portfolio diversification is of value as long as assets are less than perfectly correlated.
- The contribution of an asset to portfolio variance depends on its correlation with the other assets in the portfolio, as well as on its own variance. An asset that is perfectly negatively correlated with a portfolio can be used to reduce the portfolio variance to zero. Thus, it can serve as a perfect hedge.
- The efficient frontier of risky assets is the graphical representation of the set of portfolios that maximizes portfolio expected return for a given level of portfolio standard deviation. Rational investors will choose a portfolio on the efficient frontier.

- A portfolio manager identifies the efficient frontier by first establishing estimates for the expected returns and standard deviations and determining the correlations among them. The input data are then fed into an optimization program that produces the investment proportions, expected returns, and standard deviations of the portfolios on the efficient frontier.

- In general, portfolio managers will identify different efficient portfolios because of differences in the methods and quality of security analysis. Managers compete on the quality of their security analysis relative to their management fees.

- If a risk-free asset is available and input data are identical, all investors will choose the same portfolio on the efficient frontier, the one that is tangent to the CAL. All investors with identical input data will hold the identical risky portfolio, differing only in how much each allocates to this optimal portfolio and to the risk-free asset. This result is characterized as the separation principle of portfolio selection.

- The single-index representation of a single-factor security market expresses the excess rate of return on a security as a function of the market excess return: $R_i = \alpha_i + \beta_i R_M + e_i$. This equation also can be interpreted as a regression of the security excess return on the market-index excess return. The regression line has intercept α_i and slope β_i and is called the security characteristic line.

- In a single-index model, the variance of the rate of return on a security or portfolio can be decomposed into systematic and firm-specific risk. The systematic component of variance equals β^2 times the variance of the market excess return. The firm-specific component is the variance of the residual term in the index model equation.

- The beta of a portfolio is the weighted average of the betas of the component securities. A security with negative beta reduces the portfolio beta, thereby reducing exposure to market volatility. The unique risk of a portfolio approaches zero as the portfolio becomes more highly diversified.

Key Terms

beta, *183*
diversifiable risk, *167*
efficient frontier, *180*
excess return, *182*
factor model, *182*
firm-specific risk, *167*

index model, *183*
investment opportunity
  set, *173*
market risk, *167*
nondiversifiable risk, *167*

nonsystematic risk, *167*
optimal risky portfolio, *178*
separation property, *182*
systematic risk, *167*
unique risk, *167*

Problem Sets

1. Suppose that the returns on the stock fund presented in Table 7.1 were − 9%, 12%, and + 30% in the three scenarios.

   a. Would you expect the mean return and variance of the stock fund to be more than, less than, or equal to the values computed in Table 7.2? Why?

   b. Calculate the new values of mean return and variance for the stock fund using a format similar to Table 7.2. Confirm your intuition from part (*a*).

   c. Calculate the new value of the covariance between the stock and bond funds using a format similar to Table 7.4. Explain intuitively why covariance has increased.

2. Use the rate of return data for the stock and bond funds presented in Table 7.1, but now assume that the probability of each scenario is: Recession: 0.4; Normal: 0.2; Boom: 0.4.

   a. Would you expect the mean return and variance of the stock fund to be more than, less than, or equal to the values computed in Table 7.2? Why?

   b. Calculate the new values of mean return and variance for the stock fund using a format similar to Table 7.2. Confirm your intuition from part (*a*).

   c. Calculate the new value of the covariance between the stock and bond funds using a format similar to Table 7.4. Explain intuitively why covariance has increased.

The following data apply to problems 3–7.

A pension fund manager is considering three mutual funds. The first is a stock fund, the second is a long-term government and corporate bond fund, and the third is a T-bill money market fund that yields a sure rate of 9%. The probability distributions of the risky funds are:

	Expected Return	Standard Deviation
Stock fund (S)	22%	32%
Bond fund (B)	13	23

The correlation between the fund returns is 0.15.

3. Tabulate and draw the investment opportunity set of the two risky funds. Use investment proportions for the stock fund of 0 to 100% in increments of 20%. What expected return and standard deviation does your graph show for the minimum variance portfolio?

4. Draw a tangent from the risk-free rate to the opportunity set. What does your graph show for the expected return and standard deviation of the optimal risky portfolio?

5. What is the reward-to-variability ratio of the best feasible CAL?

6. Suppose now that your portfolio must yield an expected return of 15% and be efficient, that is, on the best feasible CAL.
   a. What is the standard deviation of your portfolio?
   b. What is the proportion invested in the T-bill fund and each of the two risky funds?

7. If you were to use the two risky funds and still require an expected return of 15%, what would be the investment proportions of your portfolio? Compare its standard deviation to that of the optimal portfolio in problem 6. What do you conclude?

8. Stocks offer an expected rate of return of 18% with a standard deviation of 22% and gold offers an expected return of 10% with a standard deviation of 30%.
   a. In light of the apparent inferiority of gold to stocks with respect to both mean return and volatility, would anyone hold gold? If so, demonstrate graphically why one would do so.
   b. How would you answer (a) if the correlation coefficient between gold and stocks were 1.0? Draw a graph illustrating why one would or would not hold gold. Could these expected returns, standard deviations, and correlation represent an equilibrium for the security market?

9. Suppose that many stocks are traded in the market and that it is possible to borrow at the risk-free rate, r_f. The characteristics of two of the stocks are as follows:

Stock	Expected Return	Standard Deviation
A	8%	40%
B	13	60
Correlation = – 1		

Could the equilibrium r_f be greater than 10%?

10. Assume expected returns and standard deviations for all securities, as well as the risk-free rate for lending and borrowing, are known. Will investors arrive at the same optimal risky portfolio? Explain.

11. What is the relationship of the portfolio standard deviation to the weighted average of the standard deviations of the component assets?

12. A project has a 0.7 chance of doubling your investment in a year and a 0.3 chance of halving your investment in a year. What is the standard deviation of the rate of return on this investment?

13. Investors expect the market rate of return this year to be 10%. The expected rate of return on a stock with a beta of 1.2 is currently 12%. If the market return this year turns out to be 8%, how would you revise your expectation of the rate of return on the stock?

14. The following figure shows plots of monthly rates of return and the stock market for two stocks.

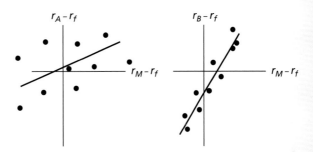

   a. Which stock is riskiest to an investor currently holding her portfolio in a diversified portfolio of common stock?
   b. Which stock is riskiest to an undiversified investor who puts all of his funds in only one of these stocks?

15. Here are rates of return for six months for Generic Risk, Inc. What is Generic's beta? (Hint: Find the answer by plotting the scatter diagram.)

Month	Market Return	Generic Return
1	0%	+2%
2	0	0
3	−1	0
4	−1	−2
5	+1	+4.0
6	+1	+2.0

The following data apply to problems 16–18:

   Hennessy & Associates manages a $30 million equity portfolio for the multimanager Wilstead Pension Fund. Jason Jones, financial vice president of Wilstead, noted that Hennessy had rather consistently achieved the best record among the Wilstead's six equity managers. Performance of the Hennessy portfolio had been clearly superior to that of the S&P 500 in four of the past five years. In the one less favorable year, the shortfall was trivial.

   Hennessy is a "bottom-up" manager. The firm largely avoids any attempt to "time the market." It also focuses on selection of individual stocks, rather than the weighting of favored industries.

   There is no apparent conformity of style among the six equity managers. The five managers, other than Hennessy, manage portfolios aggregating $250 million made up of more than 150 individual issues.

   Jones is convinced that Hennessy is able to apply superior skill to stock selection, but the favorable results are limited by the high degree of diversification in the portfolio. Over the years, the portfolio generally held 40–50 stocks, with about 2% to 3% of total funds committed to each issue. The reason Hennessy seemed to do well most years was because the firm was able to identify each year 10 or 12 issues that registered particularly large gains.

Based on this overview, Jones outlined the following plan to the Wilstead pension committee:

> Let's tell Hennessy to limit the portfolio to no more than 20 stocks. Hennessy will double the commitments to the stocks that it really favors and eliminate the remainder. Except for this one new restriction, Hennessy should be free to manage the portfolio exactly as before.

All the members of the pension committee generally supported Jones's proposal, because all agreed that Hennessy had seemed to demonstrate superior skill in selecting stocks. Yet, the proposal was a considerable departure from previous practice, and several committee members raised questions.

16. Answer the following:
    a. Will the limitation of 20 stocks likely increase or decrease the risk of the portfolio? Explain.
    b. Is there any way Hennessy could reduce the number of issues from 40 to 20 without significantly affecting risk? Explain.

17. One committee member was particularly enthusiastic concerning Jones's proposal. He suggested that Hennessy's performance might benefit further from reduction in the number of issues to 10. If the reduction to 20 could be expected to be advantageous, explain why reduction to 10 might be less likely to be advantageous. (Assume that Wilstead will evaluate the Hennessy portfolio independently of the other portfolios in the fund.)

18. Another committee member suggested that, rather than evaluate each managed portfolio independently of other portfolios, it might be better to consider the effects of a change in the Hennessy portfolio on the total fund. Explain how this broader point of view could affect the committee decision to limit the holdings in the Hennessy portfolio to either 10 or 20 issues.

19. Assume security returns are generated by the single index model

$$R_i = \alpha_i + \beta_i R_M + e_i$$

where R_i is the excess return for security i, and R_M is the market's excess return. Suppose also that there are three securities (A, B, and C) characterized by the following data.

Security	β	E(R)	$\sigma^2(e)$
A	0.8	10	5
B	1.0	12	1
C	1.2	14	10

   a. If $\sigma_M^2 = 4$, calculate the variance of returns of securities A, B, and C.
   b. Now assume there are an infinite number of assets with return characteristics identical to those of A, B, and C, respectively. If one forms a well-diversified portfolio of type A securities, what will be the mean and variance of the portfolio's excess return? What about portfolios composed only of type B or C stocks?
   c. Is there an arbitrage opportunity in this market? Analyze the opportunity using a graph.

20. Use the data in Table 7.9 and a spreadsheet to compute the security characteristic line of XYZ stock.

IEM
Applications

1. In the IEM, there are two ways to hold risk-free investment:
   a. Hold cash in your trading account.
   b. Hold a complete unit portfolio (e.g., one share each of AAPLm, IBMm, MSFTm, and SP500m or one share each of MSxxxmH and MSxxxmL).
   Given this, what should the return to holding a unit portfolio be? Given that you can purchase a unit portfolio from the IEM at any time for $1 (using the contract name $1m), what will the return to holding a unit portfolio actually be?

2. Suppose you purchase one share each of MSxxxmH and MSxxmL in the MSFT (Microsoft) Price Level Market. Suppose further that the prices were $0.400 and $0.600, respectively. Finally, suppose the price of each contract is the probability that it will pay off $1. What is the unique risk to MSxxxmH? What is the unique risk to MSxxxmL? What is the portfolio risk? What is the systematic risk to MSxxxmH and MSxxxmL? What is the correlation between the returns on MSxxxmH and MSxxxmL?

3. Suppose you purchase one share each of MSFTm and SP500m in the Computer Industry Returns Market. Suppose further that the prices were $0.200 and $0.300, respectively. Suppose the price of each contract is the probability that it will pay off $1. Finally, suppose that the correlation coefficient between these returns is -0.3273. What is the unique risk to MSFTm? What is the unique risk to SP500m? What is the portfolio risk? What happens to the portfolio risk as the correlation coefficient varies between -1, 0, and 1? Compare the portfolio risk to the risk of an IEM contract with a price of $0.500.

Solutions to Concept Checks

1.

	Stock Fund			Bond Fund		
Scenario	Rate of Return	Deviation from Expected Return	Squared Deviation	Rate of Return	Deviation from Expected Return	Squared Deviation
Recession	− 7%	−18%	324	+10%	+5%	25
Normal	+12	+ 1	1	+ 7	+2	4
Boom	+28	+17	289	− 2	−7	49

Expected return $\frac{1}{3}(-7 + 12 + 28) = 11\%$ $\frac{1}{3}(+10 + 7 - 2) = 5\%$

Variance $\frac{1}{3}(324 + 1 + 289) = 204.7$ $\frac{1}{3}(25 + 4 + 49) = 26$

Standard deviation $\sqrt{204.7} = 14.3\%$ $\sqrt{26} = 5.1\%$

Covariance = Average of product of deviations

$$= \frac{1}{3} \times \{(-18 \times 5) + (1 \times 2) + [17 \times (-7)]\}$$

$$= -69$$

Correlation coefficient $= \dfrac{\text{Covariance}}{\sigma_{\text{stocks}} \times \sigma_{\text{bonds}}} = \dfrac{-69}{14.3 \times 5.1} = -.946$

2. a. Using Equation 7.3 with the data: $\sigma_B = 12$; $\sigma_S = 25$; $w_B = 0.5$; and $w_S = 1 - w_B = 0.5$, we obtain the equation

$$\sigma_P^2 = 15^2 = (w_B\sigma_B)^2 + (w_S\sigma_S)^2 + 2(w_B\sigma_B)(w_S\,\sigma_S)\rho_{BS}$$

$$= (0.5 \times 12)^2 + (0.5 \times 25)^2 + 2\,(0.5 \times 12)(0.5 \times 25)\rho_{BS}$$

which yields $\rho = 0.2183$.

   b. Using Equation 7.2 and the additional data: $E(r_B) = 10$; $E(r_S) = 17$, we obtain

$$E(r_P) = w_BE(r_B) + w_SE(r_S) = (0.5 \times 10) + (0.5 \times 17) = 13.5\%$$

c. On the one hand, you should be happier with a correlation of 0.2148 than one of 0.22 since the lower correlation implies greater benefits from diversification and means that, for any level of expected return, there will be lower risk. On the other hand, the constraint that you must hold 50% of the portfolio in bonds represents a cost to you since it prevents you from choosing the risk-return trade-off most suited to your tastes. Unless you would choose to hold about 50% of the portfolio in bonds anyway, you are better off with the slightly higher correlation but with the ability to choose your own portfolio weights.

3. a. Using Equations 7.2 and 7.3, we generate the data shown in the following table:

Data	X	S	T-Bills
Mean	25%	12%	5%
Standard deviation	60	30	0
Correlation coefficient	0.50		

Portfolio Opportunity Set

	Weight in X	Weight in S	Portfolio Mean (%)	Portfolio Standard Deviation (%)
	−1.00	2.00	−1.00	60.00
	−0.90	1.90	0.30	55.56
	−0.80	1.80	1.60	51.26
	−0.70	1.70	2.90	47.15
	−0.60	1.60	4.20	43.27
	−0.50	1.50	5.50	39.69
	−0.40	1.40	6.80	36.50
	−0.30	1.30	8.10	33.81
	−0.20	1.20	9.40	31.75
	−0.10	1.10	10.70	30.45
	0.00	1.00	12.00	30.00
	0.10	0.90	13.30	30.45
	0.20	0.80	14.60	31.75
	0.30	0.70	15.90	33.81
	0.40	0.60	17.20	36.50
	0.50	0.50	18.50	39.69
	0.60	0.40	19.80	43.27
	0.70	0.30	21.10	47.15
	0.80	0.20	22.40	51.26
	0.90	0.10	23.70	55.56
	1.00	0.00	25.00	60.00
	1.10	−0.10	26.30	64.55
	1.20	−0.20	27.60	69.20
	1.30	−0.30	28.90	73.91
	1.40	−0.40	30.20	78.69
	1.50	−0.50	31.50	83.52
	1.60	−0.60	32.80	88.39
	1.70	−0.70	34.10	93.29
	1.80	−0.80	35.40	98.22
	1.90	−0.90	36.70	103.18
	2.00	−1.00	38.00	108.17
Optimal portfolio	0.619	0.381	20.05	43.99

b. From the above table, we can draw the opportunity set of risky assets as in the following diagram.

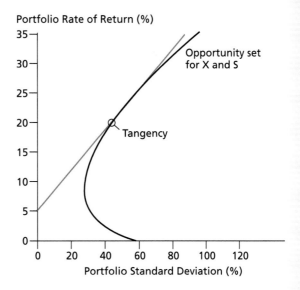

Portfolio Rate of Return (%)

If you draw a ray from the T-bill rate (on the vertical axis) that is tangent to the opportunity set, the point of tangency (portfolio O) is approximately at the mean of 20% and standard deviation of 45%, close to the portfolio with 60% in stock X and 40% in the index fund. Using the formula in footnote 3, you can compute the exact proportion of O in X as 61.90% and 38.10% in the index fund. Using the formulas for mean and standard deviation again, we find that the mean of O is 20.05% and its standard deviation is 43.99%.

c. The slope of the CAL (its reward-to-variability ratio) is computed by

$$S_O = [E(r_O) - r_f]/\sigma_O = (20.05 - 5)/43.99 = .3421$$

d. If we propose the optimal position in portfolio O for an individual investor as $y = 22.22\%$, then this investor will hold 77.78% in T-bills, $0.2222 \times 0.6190 = 13.75\%$ in X, and $0.2222 \times 0.3810 = 8.47\%$ in the index fund.

4. Efficient frontiers derived by portfolio managers depend on forecasts of the rates of return on various securities and estimates of risk, that is, standard deviations and correlation coefficients. The forecasts themselves do not control outcomes. Thus, to prefer a manager with a rosier forecast (northwesterly frontier) is tantamount to rewarding the bearers of good news and punishing the bearers of bad news. What the investor wants is to reward bearers of *accurate* news. Investors should monitor forecasts of portfolio managers on a regular basis to develop a track record of their forecasting accuracy. Portfolio choices of the more accurate forecasters will, in the long run, outperform the field.

5. a. Beta, the slope coefficient of the security on the factor: Securities R_1–R_6 have a positive beta. These securities move, on average, in the same direction as the market (R_M). R_1, R_2, R_6 have large betas, so they are "aggressive" in that they carry more systematic risk than R_3, R_4, R_5, which are "defensive." R_7 and R_8 have a negative beta. These are hedge assets that carry negative systematic risk.

b. Intercept, the expected return when the market is neutral: The estimates show that R_1, R_4, R_8 have a positive intercept, while R_2, R_3, R_5, R_6, R_7 have negative intercepts. To the extent that one believes these intercepts will persist, a positive value is preferred.

c. Residual variance, the nonsystematic risk: R_2, R_3, R_7 have a relatively low residual variance. With diversification, residual risk eventually will be eliminated, and hence, the difference in the residual variance is of little economic significance.

d. Total variance, the sum of systematic and nonsystematic risk: R_3 has a low beta and low residual variance, so its total variance will be low. R_1, R_6 have high betas and high residual variance, so their total variance will be high. But R_4 has a low beta and high residual variance, while R_2 has a high beta with a low residual variance. In sum, total variance often will misrepresent systematic risk, which is the part that counts.

Appendix:

THE FALLACY OF TIME DIVERSIFICATION

There is a common misunderstanding of the rationale behind the insurance industry. Many people believe risk pooling is at the heart of the industry, yet risk sharing is what attracts investors to become insurers. When insurers hold a small share of their portfolios in any given policy, then any risk, no matter how unique and "unpooled," will be tolerable. Of course, insurers have to worry about correlation among insured risks, lest the entire portfolio collapse from one shock and its ripple effect.

The root of the misconception lies in comparing portfolios of different sizes. Pooling risks means the portfolio grows in total size. Each additional life insurance policy that a company sells increases the dollar value of the entire portfolio, hence the dollar risk always goes up with risk pooling. Thus, while the properties of the larger pie may be better, it may still be too large to swallow. Risk sharing, on the other hand, means we take a given pie and split it into ever smaller parts, making each palatable for a small mouth. We take each life insurance policy and sell a small portion of it to many investors. In this way, the size of the pie that each investor holds can be made small enough.

A parallel version of this misconception is "time diversification." Consider the case of Mr. Frier. Planning to retire in five years makes him an investor with a five-year horizon. Confronted with the fact that the standard deviation of stock returns exceeds 20% per year, Mr. Frier has become aware of his acute risk aversion and is keeping most of his retirement portfolio in money market assets.

Recently, Mr. Frier has learned of the large potential gains from diversification. He wonders whether investing for as long as five years might not take the standard deviation sting out of stocks while keeping the expected return honey.

Mr. Mavin, a highly recommended financial advisor, argues that the time factor is all important. He cites academic research showing that asset rates of return over successive holding periods are nearly independent. Therefore, he argues that over a five-year period, returns in good years and bad years will cancel out, making the average rate of return on the portfolio over the investment period less risky than would appear from an analysis of single-year volatility. Because returns in each year are nearly independent, Mr. Mavin tells Mr. Frier a five-year investment is equivalent to a portfolio of five equally weighted, independent assets.

Mr. Frier is convinced and intends to transfer his funds to a stock fund right away. Is his conviction warranted? Does Mr. Mavin's time diversification really reduce risk?

It is true that the standard deviation of the *average* annual rate of return over the five years will be smaller than the one-year standard deviations, as Mr. Mavin claims. But what about the volatility of Mr. Frier's total retirement fund?

Mr. Mavin is wrong: Time diversification does not reduce risk. While it is true that the per year *average* rate of return has a smaller standard deviation for a longer time horizon, it is also true that the uncertainty compounds over a greater number of years. Unfortunately, this latter effect dominates; that is, the total T-year return becomes more uncertain the longer the investment horizon (T years).

Investing for more than one holding period means the amount at risk is growing. This is analogous to an insurer taking on more insurance policies. The fact that these policies are independent does not offset the effect of placing more funds at risk. Focus on the standard deviation of the *average* rate of return should never obscure the more proper emphasis on the ultimate dollar value of a portfolio strategy.

There may in fact be good reasons for the commonly accepted belief that younger investors with longer investment horizons should invest higher fractions of their portfolios in risky assets with higher expected returns, such as stocks. For example, if things go wrong, there is more time to spread out the burden and recover from the loss. But the rationale for these investors to direct their funds to the stock market should not be that the stock market is less risky if one's investment horizon is longer.

Chapter 8

CAPITAL ASSET PRICING AND ARBITRAGE PRICING THEORY

AFTER STUDYING THIS CHAPTER YOU SHOULD BE ABLE TO:

- Use the implications of capital market theory to compute security risk premiums.
- Construct and use the security market line.
- Take advantage of an arbitrage opportunity with a portfolio that includes mispriced securities.
- Use arbitrage pricing theory with more than one factor to identify mispriced securities.

The capital asset pricing model, almost always referred to as the CAPM, is a centerpiece of modern financial economics. It was first proposed by William F. Sharpe, who was awarded the 1990 Nobel Prize for economics.

The CAPM provides a precise prediction of the relationship we should observe between the risk of an asset and its expected return. This relationship serves two vital functions.

First, it provides a benchmark rate of return for evaluating possible investments. For example, a security analyst might want to know whether the expected return she forecasts for a stock is more or less than its "fair" return given risk. Second, the model helps us make an educated guess as to the expected return on assets that have not yet been traded in the marketplace. For example, how do we price an initial public offering of stock? How will a major new investment project affect the return investors require on a company's stock? Although the CAPM does not fully withstand empirical tests, it is widely used because of the insight it offers and because its accuracy suffices for many important applications.

The exploitation of security mispricing to earn risk-free economic profits is called *arbitrage*. It typically involves the simultaneous purchase and sale of equivalent securities (often in different markets) in order to profit from discrepancies in their price relationship.

The most basic principle of capital market theory is that equilibrium market prices should rule out arbitrage opportunities. If actual security prices allow for arbitrage, the resulting opportunities for profitable trading will lead to strong pressure on security prices that will persist until equilibrium is restored. Only a few investors need be aware of arbitrage opportunities to bring about a large volume of trades, and these trades will bring prices back into alignment. Therefore, no-arbitrage restrictions on security prices are extremely powerful.

The implications of no-arbitrage principles for financial economics were first explored by Modigliani and Miller, both Nobel Laureates (1985 and 1990).

The Arbitrage Pricing Theory (APT) developed by Stephen Ross uses a no-arbitrage argument to derive the same relationship between expected return and risk as the CAPM. We explore the risk-return relationship using well-diversified portfolios and discuss the similarities and differences between the APT and the CAPM.

8.1 THE CAPITAL ASSET PRICING MODEL

capital asset pricing model (CAPM)
A model that relates the required rate of return for a security to its risk as measured by beta.

The **capital asset pricing model,** or **CAPM,** predicts the relationship between the risk and equilibrium expected returns on risky assets. We will approach the CAPM in a simplified setting. Thinking about an admittedly unrealistic world allows a relatively easy leap to the solution. With this accomplished, we can add complexity to the environment, one step at a time, and see how the theory must be amended. This process allows us to develop a reasonably realistic and comprehensible model.

A number of simplifying assumptions lead to the basic version of the CAPM. The fundamental idea is that individuals are as alike as possible, with the notable exceptions of initial wealth and risk aversion. The list of assumptions that describes the necessary conformity of investors follows:

1. Investors cannot affect prices by their individual trades. This means that there are many investors, each with an endowment that is small compared with the total endowment of all investors. This assumption is analogous to the perfect competition assumption of microeconomics.
2. All investors plan for one identical holding period.
3. Investors form portfolios from a universe of publicly traded financial assets, such as stocks and bonds, and have access to unlimited risk-free borrowing or lending opportunities.
4. Investors pay neither taxes on returns nor transaction costs (commissions and service charges) on trades in securities. In such a simple world, investors will not care about the difference between returns from capital gains and those from dividends.
5. All investors attempt to construct efficient frontier portfolios; that is, they are rational mean-variance optimizers.
6. All investors analyze securities in the same way and share the same economic view of the world. Hence, they all end with identical estimates of the probability distribution of future cash flows from investing in the available securities. This means that, given a set of security prices and the risk-free interest rate, all investors use the same expected returns, standard deviations, and correlations to generate the efficient frontier and the unique optimal risky portfolio. This assumption is often called *homogeneous expectations*.

Obviously, these assumptions ignore many real-world complexities. However, they lead to some powerful insights into the nature of equilibrium in security markets.

Given these assumptions, we summarize the equilibrium that will prevail in this hypothetical world of securities and investors. We elaborate on these implications in the following sections.

market portfolio
The portfolio for which each security is held in proportion to its market value.

1. All investors will choose to hold the **market portfolio** (*M*), which includes all assets of the security universe. For simplicity, we shall refer to all assets as stocks. The proportion of each stock in the market portfolio equals the market value of the stock (price per share times the number of shares outstanding) divided by the total market value of all stocks.
2. The market portfolio will be on the efficient frontier. Moreover, it will be the optimal risky portfolio, the tangency point of the capital allocation line (CAL) to the efficient frontier. As a result, the capital market line (CML), the line from the risk-free rate through the market portfolio, *M*, is also the best attainable capital allocation line. All investors hold *M* as their optimal risky portfolio, differing only in the amount invested in it as compared to investment in the risk-free asset.

3. The risk premium on the market portfolio will be proportional to the variance of the market portfolio and investors' typical degree of risk aversion. Mathematically

$$E(r_M) - r_f = A^*\sigma_M^2 \tag{8.1}$$

where σ_M is the standard deviation of the return on the market portfolio and A^* is a scale factor representing the degree of risk aversion of the average investor.

4. The risk premium on individual assets will be proportional to the risk premium on the market portfolio (M) and to the *beta coefficient* of the security on the market portfolio. This implies that the rate of return on the market portfolio is the single factor of the security market. The beta measures the extent to which returns on the stock respond to the returns of the market portfolio. Formally, beta is the regression (slope) coefficient of the security return on the market portfolio return, representing the sensitivity of the stock return to fluctuations in the overall security market.

Why All Investors Would Hold the Market Portfolio

Given all our assumptions, it is easy to see why all investors hold identical risky portfolios. If all investors use identical mean-variance analysis (assumption 5), apply it to the same universe of securities (assumption 3), with an identical time horizon (assumption 2), use the same security analysis (assumption 6), and experience identical tax consequences (assumption 4), they all must arrive at the same determination of the optimal risky portfolio. That is, they all derive identical efficient frontiers and find the same tangency portfolio for the capital allocation line (CAL) from T-bills (risk-free rate, zero standard deviation) to that frontier, as in Figure 8.1.

With everyone choosing to hold the same risky portfolio, stocks will be represented in the aggregate risky portfolio in the same proportion as they are in each investor's (common) risky portfolio. If GM represents 1% in each common risky portfolio, GM will be 1% of the aggregate risky portfolio. This in fact is the market portfolio since the market is no more than the aggregate of all individual portfolios. Because each investor uses the market portfolio for the optimal risky portfolio, the CAL in this case is called the capital market line, or CML, as in Figure 8.1.

Suppose the optimal portfolio of our investors does not include the stock of some company, say, Delta Air Lines. When no investor is willing to hold Delta stock, the demand is zero, and the stock price will take a free fall. As Delta stock gets progressively cheaper, it begins to look more attractive, while all other stocks look (relatively) less attractive. Ultimately, Delta will reach a price where it is desirable to include it in the optimal stock portfolio, and investors will buy.

This price adjustment process guarantees that all stocks will be included in the optimal portfolio. The only issue is the price. At a given price level, investors will be willing to buy

FIGURE 8.1

The Efficient Frontier and the Capital Market Line

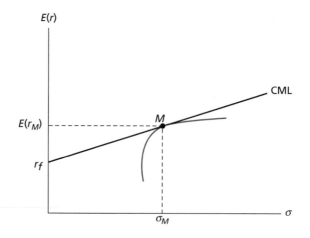

a stock; at another price, they will not. The bottom line is this: If all investors hold an *identical* risky portfolio, this portfolio must be the *market* portfolio.

The Passive Strategy Is Efficient

A passive strategy, using the CML as the optimal CAL, is a powerful alternative to an active strategy. The market portfolio proportions are a result of profit-oriented "buy" and "sell" orders that cease only when there is no more profit to be made. And in the simple world of the CAPM, all investors use precious resources in security analysis. A passive investor who takes a free ride by simply investing in the market portfolio benefits from the efficiency of that portfolio. In fact, an active investor who chooses any other portfolio will end on a CAL that is less efficient than the CML used by passive investors.

mutual fund theorem
States that all investors desire the same portfolio of risky assets and can be satisfied by a single mutual fund composed of that portfolio.

We sometimes call this result a **mutual fund theorem** because it implies that only one mutual fund of risky assets—the market portfolio—is sufficient to satisfy the investment demands of all investors. The mutual fund theorem is another incarnation of the separation property discussed in Chapter 7. Assuming all investors choose to hold a market index mutual fund, we can separate portfolio selection into two components: (1) a technical side, in which an efficient mutual fund is created by professional management; and (2) a personal side, in which an investor's risk aversion determines the allocation of the complete portfolio between the mutual fund and the risk-free asset. Here, all investors agree that the mutual fund they would like to hold is the market portfolio.

While different investment managers do create risky portfolios that differ from the market index, we attribute this in part to the use of different estimates of risk and expected return. Still, a passive investor may view the market index as a reasonable first approximation to an efficient risky portfolio.

The logical inconsistency of the CAPM is this: If a passive strategy is costless *and* efficient, why would anyone follow an active strategy? But if no one does any security analysis, what brings about the efficiency of the market portfolio?

We have acknowledged from the outset that the CAPM simplifies the real world in its search for a tractable solution. Its applicability to the real world depends on whether its predictions are accurate enough. The model's use is some indication that its predictions are reasonable. We discuss this issue in Section 8.3 and in greater depth in Chapter 9.

Concept Check

1. If only some investors perform security analysis while all others hold the market portfolio (*M*), would the CML still be the efficient CAL for investors who do not engage in security analysis? Explain.

The Risk Premium of the Market Portfolio

In Chapters 6 and 7 we showed how individual investors decide how much to invest in the risky portfolio when they can include a risk-free asset in the investment budget. Returning now to the decision of how much to invest in the market portfolio M and how much in the risk-free asset, what can we deduce about the equilibrium risk premium of portfolio M?

We asserted earlier that the equilibrium risk premium of the market portfolio, $E(r_M) - r_f$, will be proportional to the degree of risk aversion of the average investor and to the risk of the market portfolio, σ_M^2. Now we can explain this result.

When investors purchase stocks, their demand drives up prices, thereby lowering expected rates of return and risk premiums. But if risk premiums fall, then relatively more risk-averse investors will pull their funds out of the risky market portfolio, placing them instead in the risk-free asset. In equilibrium, of course, the risk premium on the market portfolio must be just high enough to induce investors to hold the available supply of stocks. If the risk premium is too high compared to the average degree of risk aversion, there will be excess demand for securities, and prices will rise; if it is too low, investors will not hold enough stock to absorb the supply, and prices will fall. The *equilibrium* risk premium of the market portfolio is therefore proportional to both the risk of the market, as measured by the variance of its returns, and to the degree of risk aversion of the average investor, denoted by $A*$ in Equation 8.1.

EXAMPLE 8.1
Market Risk, the
Risk Premium,
and Risk
Aversion

Suppose the risk-free rate is 5%, the average investor has a risk aversion coefficient of $A* = 2$, and the standard deviation of the market portfolio is 20%. Then, from Equation 8.1, we estimate the equilibrium value of the market risk premium[1] as $2 \times 0.20^2 = 0.08$. So the expected rate of return on the market must be

$$E(r_M) = r_f + \text{Equilibrium risk premium}$$
$$= 0.05 + 0.08 = 0.13 = 13\%$$

If investors were more risk averse, it would take a higher risk premium to induce them to hold shares. For example, if the average degree of risk aversion were 3, the market risk premium would be $3 \times 0.20^2 = 0.12$, or 12%, and the expected return would be 17%.

Concept Check

2. Historical data for the S&P 500 index show an average excess return over Treasury bills of about 8.5% with standard deviation of about 20%. To the extent that these averages approximate investor expectations for the sample period, what must have been the coefficient of risk aversion of the average investor? If the coefficient of risk aversion were 3.5, what risk premium would have been consistent with the market's historical standard deviation?

Expected Returns on Individual Securities

The CAPM is built on the insight that the appropriate risk premium on an asset will be determined by its contribution to the risk of investors' overall portfolios. Portfolio risk is what matters to investors, and portfolio risk is what governs the risk premiums they demand.

We know that nonsystematic risk can be reduced to an arbitrarily low level through diversification; therefore, investors do not require a risk premium as compensation for bearing nonsystematic risk. They need to be compensated only for bearing systematic risk, which cannot be diversified. We know also that the contribution of a single security to the risk of a large diversified portfolio depends only on the systematic risk of the security as measured by its beta.[2] Therefore, it should not be surprising that the risk premium of an asset is proportional to its beta; for example, if you double a security's systematic risk, you must double its risk premium for investors still to be willing to hold the security. Thus, the ratio of risk premium to beta should be the same for any two securities or portfolios.

For example, if we were to compare the ratio of risk premium to systematic risk for the market portfolio, which has a beta of 1.0, with the corresponding ratio for DEC stock, we would conclude that

$$\frac{E(r_M) - r_f}{1} = \frac{E(r_D) - r_f}{\beta_D}$$

expected return–beta relationship
Implication of the CAPM that security risk premiums (expected excess returns) will be proportional to beta.

Rearranging this relationship results in the CAPM's **expected return–beta relationship**

$$E(r_D) = r_f + \beta_D[E(r_M) - r_f] \tag{8.2}$$

In words, the rate of return on any asset exceeds the risk-free rate by a risk premium equal to the asset's systematic risk measure (its beta) times the risk premium of the (bench-

---

[1]To use Equation 8.1, we must express returns in decimal form rather than as percentages.
[2]This is literally true with a sufficient number of securities so that all nonsystematic risk is diversified away. In a market as diversified as the U.S. stock market, this would be true for all practical purposes.

mark) market portfolio. This expected return–beta relationship is the most familiar expression of the CAPM.

The expected return–beta relationship of the CAPM makes a powerful economic statement. It implies, for example, that a security with a high variance but a relatively low beta of 0.5 will carry one-third the risk premium of a low-variance security with a beta of 1.5. Thus, Equation 8.2 quantifies the conclusion we reached in Chapter 7 that only systematic risk matters to investors who can diversify, and that systematic risk is measured by the beta of the security.

EXAMPLE 8.2
Expected Returns and Risk Premiums

Suppose the risk premium of the market portfolio is 9%, and we estimate the beta of DEC as $\beta_D = 1.3$. The risk premium predicted for the stock is therefore 1.3 times the market risk premium, or $1.3 \times 9\% = 11.7\%$. The expected rate of return on DEC is the risk-free rate plus the risk premium. For example, if the T-bill rate were 5%, the expected rate of return would be $5\% + 11.7\% = 16.7\%$, or using Equation 8.2 directly,

$$E(r_D) = r_f + \beta_D[\text{Market risk premium}]$$
$$= 5\% + 1.3 \times 9\% = 16.7\%$$

If the estimate of the beta of DEC were only 1.2, the required risk premium for DEC would fall to 10.8%. Similarly, if the market risk premium were only 8% and $\beta_D = 1.3$, DEC's risk premium would be only 10.4%.

The fact that few real-life investors actually hold the market portfolio does not necessarily invalidate the CAPM. Recall from Chapter 7 that reasonably well-diversified portfolios shed (for practical purposes) firm-specific risk and are subject only to systematic or market risk. Even if one does not hold the precise market portfolio, a well-diversified portfolio will be so highly correlated with the market that a stock's beta relative to the market still will be a useful risk measure.

In fact, several researchers have shown that modified versions of the CAPM will hold despite differences among individuals that may cause them to hold different portfolios. A study by Brennan (1970) examines the impact of differences in investors' personal tax rates on market equilibrium. Another study by Mayers (1972) looks at the impact of nontraded assets such as human capital (earning power). Both find that while the market portfolio is no longer each investor's optimal risky portfolio, a modified version of the expected return–beta relationship still holds.

If the expected return–beta relationship holds for any individual asset, it must hold for any combination of assets. The beta of a portfolio is simply the weighted average of the betas of the stocks in the portfolio, using as weights the portfolio proportions. This beta also predicts the portfolio's risk premium in accordance with Equation 8.2.

EXAMPLE 8.3
Portfolio Beta and Risk Premium

Consider the following portfolio:

Asset	Beta	Risk Premium	Portfolio Weight
Microsoft	1.2	9.0%	0.5
Con Edison	0.8	6.0	0.3
Gold	0.0	0.0	0.2
Portfolio	0.84	?	1.0

If the market risk premium is 7.5%, the CAPM predicts that the risk premium on the portfolio is $0.84 \times 7.5\% = 6.3\%$. This is the same result that is obtained by taking the weighted average of the risk premiums of the individual stocks. (Verify this for yourself.)

A word of caution: We often hear that well-managed firms will provide high rates of return. We agree this is true if one measures the *firm's* return on investments in plant and equipment. The CAPM, however, predicts returns on investments in the *securities* of the firm.

Say that everyone knows a firm is well run. Its stock price should, therefore, be bid up, and returns to stockholders who buy at those high prices will not be extreme. Security *prices* reflect public information about a firm's prospects, but only the risk of the company (as measured by beta in the context of the CAPM) should affect *expected returns*. In a rational market, investors receive high expected returns only if they are willing to bear risk.

Concept Check

3. Suppose the risk premium on the market portfolio is estimated at 8% with a standard deviation of 22%. What is the risk premium on a portfolio invested 25% in GM with a beta of 1.15 and 75% in Ford with a beta of 1.25?

The Security Market Line

We can view the expected return–beta relationship as a reward-risk equation. The beta of a security is the appropriate measure of its risk because beta is proportional to the risk the security contributes to the optimal risky portfolio.

Risk-averse investors measure the risk of the optimal risky portfolio by its standard deviation. In this world, we would expect the reward, or the risk premium on individual assets, to depend on the risk an individual asset contributes to the overall portfolio. Because the beta of a stock measures the stock's contribution to the standard deviation of the market portfolio, we expect the required risk premium to be a function of beta. The CAPM confirms this intuition, stating further that the security's risk premium is directly proportional to both the beta and the risk premium of the market portfolio; that is, the risk premium equals $\beta[E(r_M) - r_f]$.

security market line (SML)
Graphical representation of the expected return–beta relationship of the CAPM.

The expected return–beta relationship is graphed as the **security market line (SML)** in Figure 8.2. Its slope is the risk premium of the market portfolio. At the point where $\beta = 1.0$ (which is the beta of the market portfolio) on the horizontal axis, we can read off the vertical axis the expected return on the market portfolio.

It is useful to compare the security market line to the capital market line. The CML graphs the risk premiums of efficient portfolios (that is, complete portfolios made up of the risky market portfolio and the risk-free asset) as a function of portfolio standard deviation. This is appropriate because standard deviation is a valid measure of risk for portfolios that are candidates for an investor's complete (overall) portfolio.

FIGURE 8.2
The Security Market Line and a Positive-Alpha Stock

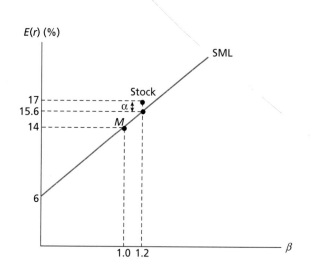

The SML, in contrast, graphs *individual asset* risk premiums as a function of asset risk. The relevant measure of risk for individual assets (which are held as parts of a well-diversified portfolio) is not the asset's standard deviation; it is, instead, the contribution of the asset to the portfolio standard deviation as measured by the asset's beta. The SML is valid both for portfolios and individual assets.

The security market line provides a benchmark for evaluation of investment performance. Given the risk of an investment as measured by its beta, the SML provides the required rate of return that will compensate investors for the risk of that investment, as well as for the time value of money.

Because the security market line is the graphical representation of the expected return–beta relationship, "fairly priced" assets plot exactly on the SML. The expected returns of such assets are commensurate with their risk. Whenever the CAPM holds, all securities must lie on the SML in market equilibrium. Underpriced stocks plot above the SML: Given their betas, their expected returns are greater than is indicated by the CAPM. Overpriced stocks plot below the SML. The difference between the fair and actually expected rate of return on a stock is called the stock's **alpha,** denoted α.

alpha
The abnormal rate of return on a security in excess of what would be predicted by an equilibrium model such as the CAPM or APT.

EXAMPLE 8.4
The Alpha of a Security

Suppose the return on the market is expected to be 14%, a stock has a beta of 1.2, and the T-bill rate is 6%. The SML would predict an expected return on the stock of

$$E(r) = r_f + \beta [E(r_M) - r_f]$$
$$= 6 + 1.2 \, (14 - 6) = 15.6\%$$

If one believes the stock will provide instead a return of 17%, its implied alpha would be 1.4%, as shown in Figure 8.2.

Applications of the CAPM

One place the CAPM may be used is in the investment management industry. Suppose the SML is taken as a benchmark to assess the *fair* expected return on a risky asset. Then an analyst calculates the return he or she actually expects. Notice that we depart here from the simple CAPM world in that some investors apply their own analysis to derive an "input list" that may differ from their competitors'. If a stock is perceived to be a good buy, or underpriced, it will provide a positive alpha, that is, an expected return in excess of the fair return stipulated by the SML.

The CAPM also is useful in capital budgeting decisions. If a firm is considering a new project, the CAPM can provide the return the project needs to yield to be acceptable to investors. Managers can use the CAPM to obtain this cutoff internal rate of return (IRR) or "hurdle rate" for the project.

EXAMPLE 8.5
The CAPM and Capital Budgeting

Suppose Silverado Springs Inc. is considering a new spring-water bottling plant. The business plan forecasts an internal rate of return of 14% on the investment. Research shows the beta of similar products is 1.3. Thus, if the risk-free rate is 4%, and the market excess return is estimated at 8%, the hurdle rate for the project should be $4 + 1.3 \times 8 = 14.4\%$. Because the IRR is less than the risk-adjusted discount or hurdle rate, the project has a negative net present value and ought to be rejected.

Yet another use of the CAPM is in utility rate-making cases. Here the issue is the rate of return a regulated utility should be allowed to earn on its investment in plant and equipment.

EXAMPLE 8.6
The CAPM and Regulation

Suppose equity holders' investment in the firm is $100 million, and the beta of the equity is 0.6. If the T-bill rate is 6%, and the market risk premium is 8%, then a fair annual profit will be $6 + (0.6 \times 8) = 10.8\%$ of $100 million, or $10.8 million. Since regulators accept the CAPM, they will allow the utility to set prices at a level expected to generate these profits.

4. *a.* Stock XYZ has an expected return of 12% and risk of $\beta = 1.0$. Stock ABC is expected to return 13% with a beta of 1.5. The market's expected return is 11% and $r_f = 5\%$. According to the CAPM, which stock is a better buy? What is the alpha of each stock? Plot the SML and the two stocks and show the alphas on the graph.

b. The risk-free rate is 8% and the expected return on the market portfolio is 16%. A firm considers a project with an estimated beta of 1.3. What is the required rate of return on the project? If the IRR of the project is 19%, what is the project α?

8.2 THE CAPM AND INDEX MODELS

The CAPM has two limitations: It relies on the theoretical market portfolio, which includes *all* assets (such as real estate, foreign stocks, etc.), and it deals with *expected* as opposed to actual returns. To implement the CAPM, we cast it in the form of an *index model* and use realized, not expected, returns.

An index model uses actual portfolios, such as the S&P 500, rather than the theoretical market portfolio to represent the relevant factors in the economy. The important advantage of index models is that the composition and rate of return of the index is easily measured and unambiguous.

In contrast to an index model, the CAPM revolves around the "market portfolio." However, because many assets are not traded, investors would not have full access to the market portfolio even if they could exactly identify it. Thus, the theory behind the CAPM rests on a shaky real-world foundation. But, as in all science, a theory may be viewed as legitimate if its predictions approximate real-world outcomes with a sufficient degree of accuracy. In particular, the reliance on the market portfolio shouldn't faze us if we can verify that the predictions of the CAPM are sufficiently accurate when the index portfolio is substituted for the market.

We can start with one central prediction of the CAPM: The market portfolio is mean-variance efficient. An index model can be used to test this hypothesis by verifying that an index chosen to be representative of the full market is a mean-variance efficient portfolio.

Another aspect of the CAPM is that it predicts relationships among *expected* returns, while all we can observe are realized (historical) holding-period returns; actual returns in a particular holding period seldom, if ever, match our initial expectations. To test the mean-variance efficiency of an index portfolio, we would have to show that the reward-to-variability ratio of the index is not surpassed by any other portfolio. The reward-to-variability ratio, however, is set in terms of expectations, and we can measure it only in terms of realizations.

The Index Model, Realized Returns, and the Expected Return–Beta Relationship

To move from a model cast in expectations to a realized-return framework, we start with a form of the single-index regression equation in realized excess returns, similar to that of Equation 7.6 in Chapter 7:

$$r_i - r_f = \alpha_i + \beta_i(r_M - r_f) + e_i \tag{8.3}$$

where r_i is the holding-period return (HPR) on asset i, and α_i and β_i are the intercept and slope of the line that relates asset i's realized excess return to the realized excess return of the index. We denote the index returns by r_M to emphasize that the index portfolio is proxying for the market. The e_i measures firm-specific effects during the holding period; it is the deviation of security i's realized HPR from the regression line, that is, the deviation from the forecast that accounts for the index's HPR. We set the relationship in terms of *excess* returns (over the risk-free rate, r_f), for consistency with the CAPM's logic of risk premiums.

Given that the CAPM is a statement about the expectation of asset returns, we look at the expected return of security i predicted by Equation 8.3. Recall that the expectation of e_i is zero (the firm-specific surprise is expected to average zero over time), so the relationship expressed in terms of expectations is

$$E(r_i) - r_f = \alpha_i + \beta_i[E(r_M) - r_f] \tag{8.4}$$

Comparing this relationship to the expected return–beta relationship (Equation 8.2) of the CAPM reveals that the CAPM predicts $\alpha_i = 0$. Thus, we have converted the CAPM prediction about unobserved expectations of security returns relative to an unobserved market portfolio into a prediction about the intercept in a regression of observed variables: realized excess returns of a security relative to those of a specified index.

Operationalizing the CAPM in the form of an index model has a drawback, however. If intercepts of regressions of returns on an index differ substantially from zero, you will not be able to tell whether it is because you chose a bad index to proxy for the market or because the theory is not useful.

In actuality, few instances of persistent, positive significant alpha values have been identified; these will be discussed in Chapter 9. Among these are: (1) small versus large stocks; (2) stocks of companies that have recently announced unexpectedly good earnings; (3) stocks with high ratios of book value to market value; and (4) stocks that have experienced recent sharp price declines. In general, however, future alphas are practically impossible to predict from past values. The result is that index models are widely used to operationalize capital asset pricing theory.

Estimating the Index Model

Equation 8.3 also suggests how we might go about actually measuring market and firm-specific risk. Suppose that we observe the excess return on the market index and a specific asset over a number of holding periods. We use as an example monthly excess returns on the S&P 500 index and GM stock for a particular year. We can summarize the results for a sample period in a scatter diagram, as illustrated in Figure 8.3.

The horizontal axis in Figure 8.3 measures the excess return (over the risk-free rate) on the market index; the vertical axis measures the excess return on the asset in question (GM stock in our example). A pair of excess returns (one for the market index, one for GM stock) over a holding period constitutes one point on this scatter diagram. The points are numbered 1 through 12, representing excess returns for the S&P 500 and GM for each month from January through December. The single-index model states that the relationship between the excess returns on GM and the S&P 500 is given by

$$R_{GMt} = \alpha_{GM} + \beta_{GM}R_{Mt} + e_{GMt}$$

We have noted the resemblance of this relationship to a regression equation.

In a single-variable linear regression equation, the dependent variable plots around a straight line with an intercept α and a slope β. The deviations from the line, e_i, are assumed to be mutually independent and independent of the right-hand side variable. Because these assumptions are identical to those of the index model, we can look at the index model as a regression model. The sensitivity of GM to the market, measured by β_{GM}, is the slope of the regression line. The intercept of the regression line is α (which represents the average firm-specific return), and deviations of particular observations from the regression line are denoted e. These *residuals* are the differences between the actual stock return and the return that would be predicted from the regression equation describing the usual relationship between the stock and the market; therefore, they measure the impact of firm-specific events

FIGURE 8.3
Characteristic Line for
GM

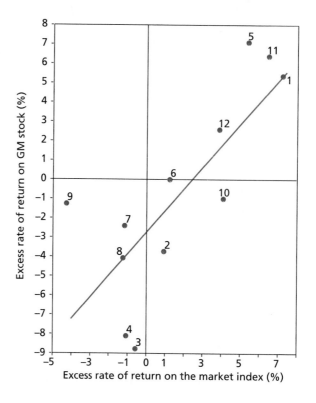

during the particular month. The parameters of interest, α, β, and Var(e), can be estimated using standard regression techniques.

security characteristic line (SCL)
A plot of a security's expected excess return over the risk-free rate as a function of the excess return on the market.

Estimating the regression equation of the single-index model gives us the **security characteristic line (SCL),** which is plotted in Figure 8.3. (The regression results and raw data appear in Table 8.1.) The SCL is a plot of the typical excess return on a security over the risk-free rate as a function of the excess return on the market.

This sample of 12 monthly holding-period returns is, of course, too small to yield reliable statistics. We use it only for demonstration. For this sample period, we find that the beta coefficient of GM stock, as estimated by the slope of the regression line, is 1.1357, and that the intercept for this SCL is −2.59% per month.

For each month, our estimate of the residual, e, which is the deviation of GM's excess return from the prediction of the SCL, equals

$$\text{Residual} = \text{Actual} - \text{Predicted return}$$

$$e_{GMt} = R_{GMt} - (\beta_{GM}R_{Mt} + \alpha_{GM})$$

These residuals are estimates of the monthly unexpected *firm-specific* component of the rate of return on GM stock. Hence we can estimate the firm-specific variance by[3]

$$\sigma^2(e_{GM}) = \frac{1}{10}\sum_{t=1}^{12} e_t^2 = 12.60$$

Therefore, the standard deviation of the firm-specific component of GM's return, $\sigma(e_{GM})$, equals 3.55% per month.

---

[3]Because the mean of e_t is zero, e_t^2 is the squared deviation from its mean. The average value of e_t^2 is therefore the estimate of the variance of the firm-specific component. We divide the sum of squared residuals by the degrees of freedom of the regression, $n - 2 = 12 - 2 = 10$, to obtain an unbiased estimate of $\sigma^2(e)$.

TABLE 8.1

Characteristic Line for GM Stock

Month	GM Return	Market Return	Monthly T-Bill Rate	Excess GM Return	Excess Market Return
January	6.06	7.89	0.65	5.41	7.24
February	−2.86	1.51	0.58	−3.44	0.93
March	−8.18	0.23	0.62	−8.79	−0.39
April	−7.36	−0.29	0.72	−8.08	−1.01
May	7.76	5.58	0.66	7.10	4.92
June	0.52	1.73	0.55	−0.03	1.18
July	−1.74	−0.21	0.62	−2.36	−0.83
August	−3.00	−0.36	0.55	−3.55	−0.91
September	−0.56	−3.58	0.60	−1.16	−4.18
October	−0.37	4.62	0.65	−1.02	3.97
November	6.93	6.85	0.61	6.32	6.24
December	3.08	4.55	0.65	2.43	3.90
Mean	0.02	2.38	0.62	−0.60	1.76
Standard deviation	4.97	3.33	0.05	4.97	3.32

Regression results
$$r_{GM} - r_t = \alpha + \beta(r_M - r_f)$$

	α	β
Estimated coefficient	−2.590	1.1357
Standard error of estimate	(1.547)	(0.309)

Variance of residuals = 12.601
Standard deviation of residuals = 3.550
R-SQR = 0.575

TABLE 8.2

True Parameters of Securities

A. Market Index
Expected excess return over T-bill rate, $E(R_M) = 8\%$
Standard deviation of excess return, $\sigma(R_M) = 20\%$

B. Individual Stocks

	Beta	Standard Deviation of Residual, $\sigma(e)$	Total Standard Deviation of Returns[a]
Stock A	1.30	54.07%	60%
Stock B	0.70	37.47	40

[a]Standard deviation = $[\beta^2\sigma_M^2 + \sigma^2(e)]^{1/2}$
  Stock A: $[1.3^2 \times 20^2 + 54.07^2]^{1/2}$
  Stock B: $[0.7^2 \times 20^2 + 37.47^2]^{1/2}$

C. T-Bills
Average value in sample period = 5%
Month-to-month variation results in a standard deviation across months of 1.5%

The CAPM and the Index Model

We have introduced the CAPM and shown how the model can be made operational and how beta can be estimated with the additional simplification of the index model of security returns. Of course, when we estimate the statistical properties of security returns (e.g., betas or variances) using historical data, we are subject to sampling error. Regression parameters are only estimates and necessarily are subject to some imprecision.

In this section, we put together much of the preceding material in an extended example. We show how historical data can be used in conjunction with the CAPM, but we also highlight some pitfalls to be avoided.

Suppose that the *true* parameters for two stocks, A and B, and the market index portfolio are given in Table 8.2. However, investors cannot observe this information directly. They must estimate these parameters using historical returns.

To illustrate the investor's problem, we first produce 24 possible observations for the risk-free rate and the market index. Using the random number generator from a spreadsheet

TABLE 8.3

Simulated Data for
Estimation of Security
Characteristic Line
(Raw Data from
Random Number
Generator)

	T-Bill Rate	Excess Return on Index	Residuals for Each Stock		Excess Returns	
			Stock A	Stock B	Stock A	Stock B
	5.97	−3.75	7.52	44.13	2.64	41.50
	4.45	−9.46	26.14	−38.79	13.85	−45.41
	3.24	26.33	18.09	−65.43	52.32	−46.99
	5.70	6.06	−0.88	69.24	7.00	73.49
	3.89	38.97	48.37	61.51	99.03	88.78
	5.56	−1.35	−30.80	26.25	−32.56	25.30
	5.03	−24.18	−10.74	0.93	−42.18	−16.00
	2.70	15.20	68.91	−18.53	88.66	−7.89
	5.57	39.52	−14.09	16.80	37.29	44.46
	5.94	−2.84	0.43	−36.15	−3.26	−38.14
	4.41	−0.97	73.75	−20.33	72.48	−21.01
	4.43	29.82	25.31	68.88	64.08	89.76
	2.88	0.73	−83.07	−10.82	−82.13	−10.31
	5.77	16.54	−33.45	43.85	−11.95	55.43
	2.85	−39.43	60.21	−11.82	8.95	−39.42
	5.11	−4.94	3.84	2.95	−2.59	−0.51
	5.89	3.01	47.37	12.80	51.29	14.91
	7.96	36.98	−32.91	−30.88	15.16	−4.99
	7.13	42.22	−58.15	−58.68	−3.26	−29.12
	3.46	24.67	77.05	3.89	109.11	21.15
	4.72	−11.64	−51.49	−16.87	−66.62	−25.02
	4.21	19.15	14.06	−18.79	38.95	−5.39
	5.27	−19.13	−80.44	59.07	−105.31	45.69
	6.05	5.05	−91.90	−67.83	−85.33	−64.29
True mean	5.00	8.00	0.00	0.00	10.40	5.60
True standard deviation	1.50	20.00	54.07	37.47	60.00	40.00
Sample average	4.93	7.77	−0.70	0.64	9.40	6.08
Sample standard deviation	1.34	21.56	50.02	41.48	58.31	43.95

package (e.g., you can use "data analysis tools" in Microsoft Excel), we draw 24 observations from a normal distribution. These random numbers capture the phenomenon that actual returns will differ from expected returns: This is the "statistical noise" that accompanies all real-world return data. For the risk-free rate we set a mean of 5% and a standard deviation of 1.5% and record the results in the first column of Table 8.3. We then generate 24 observations for excess returns of the market index, using a mean of 8% and a standard deviation of 20%. We record these observations in the second column of Table 8.3.

The bottom four rows in Table 8.3 show the true values for the means and standard deviations as well as the actual sample averages and standard deviations. As you would expect, the sample averages and standard deviations are close but not precisely equal to the true parameters of the probability distribution. This is a reflection of the statistical variation that gives rise to sampling error.

In the next step we wish to generate excess returns for stocks A and B that are consistent with the CAPM. According to the CAPM, the rate of return on any security is given by

$$r - r_f = \beta(r_M - r_f) + e$$

or using capital letters to denote excess returns,

$$R = \beta R_M + e$$

Therefore, the CAPM hypothesizes an alpha of zero in Equation 8.3. Given the values of β and R_M, we need only random residuals, e, to generate a simulated sample of returns on each stock. Using the random number generator once again, we generate 24 observations for the residuals of stock A from a normal distribution with a mean of zero and a standard deviation of 54.07%. These observations are recorded in the third column of Table 8.3. Similarly, the

TABLE 8.4

Regression Analysis for
Stock *A*

	Coefficients	Standard Error	*t* Stat
Alpha-Stock *A*	−0.46	11.12	−0.04
Beta - Stock *A*	1.27	0.50	2.52

Residual Output - Stock *A*

Observation	Predicted *A*	Residuals	Actual Returns
1	−5.22	7.86	2.64
2	−12.45	26.29	13.85
3	32.93	19.40	52.32
4	7.23	−0.23	7.00
5	48.94	50.08	99.03
6	−2.17	−30.38	−32.56
7	−31.12	−11.05	−42.18
8	4.86	69.50	74.36
9	49.65	−12.36	37.29
10	−4.06	0.80	−3.26
11	−1.69	74.17	72.48
12	37.35	26.73	64.08
13	0.46	−82.59	−82.13
14	20.51	−32.46	−11.95
15	−50.45	59.40	8.95
16	−6.73	4.14	−2.59
17	3.36	47.92	51.29
18	46.43	−31.27	15.16
19	53.08	−56.33	−3.26
20	30.82	78.30	109.11
21	−15.22	−51.40	−66.62
22	23.81	15.13	38.95
23	−15.83	−80.38	−96.21
24	5.95	−91.28	−85.33

randomly generated residuals for stock *B* use a standard deviation of 37.47% and are recorded in the fourth column of Table 8.3.

The excess rates of return of stocks *A* and *B* are computed by multiplying the excess return on the market index by beta and adding the residual. The results appear in the last two columns of Table 8.3. Thus, the first two and last two columns of Table 8.3 correspond to the type of historical data that we might observe if the CAPM adequately describes capital market equilibrium. The numbers come from probability distributions consistent with the CAPM, but, because of the residuals, the CAPM will not hold exactly due to sampling error.

We now use a regression program (again, from the "data analysis" menu of our spreadsheet) to regress the excess return of each stock against the excess return of the index. The regression routine allows us to save the predicted return for each stock, based on the market return in that period, as well as the regression residuals. These values, and the regression statistics, are presented in Table 8.4 for stock *A* and Table 8.5 for stock *B*.

Observe from the regression statistics in Tables 8.4 and 8.5 that the beta of stock *A* is estimated at 1.27 (versus the true value of 1.3), and the beta of stock *B* is estimated at 0.73 (versus the true value of 0.7). The regression also shows estimates of alpha as − 0.46% for *A* and 0.39% for *B* (versus a true value of zero for both stocks), but the standard error of these estimates is large and their *t*-values are low, indicating that these are not statistically significant. The regression residuals allow us to plot the security characteristic line (SCL) for both stocks, shown in Figure 8.4 for stock *A* and Figure 8.5 for stock *B*.

The CAPM representation of the securities is shown in Figures 8.6 and 8.7. Figure 8.6 shows the security market line (SML) supported by the risk-free rate and the market index. Stock *A* has a negative estimated alpha and is therefore below the line. Not knowing that the true value of alpha is zero, these data might lead us to believe that stock *A* is overpriced, that is, its expected return is below that which can be obtained with efficient portfolios and the

TABLE 8.5

Regression Analysis for Stock *B*

	Coefficients	Standard Error	*t* Stat
Alpha-Stock *B*	0.39	9.22	0.04
Beta - Stock *B*	0.73	0.42	1.76

Residual Output - Stock *B*

Observation	Predicted *B*	Residuals	Actual Returns
1	−2.36	43.87	41.50
2	−6.55	−38.86	−45.41
3	19.70	−66.69	−46.99
4	4.83	68.65	73.49
5	28.96	59.82	88.78
6	−0.60	25.91	25.30
7	−17.35	1.35	−16.00
8	3.46	−19.05	−15.59
9	29.37	15.09	44.46
10	−1.70	−36.45	−38.14
11	−0.33	−20.68	−21.01
12	22.25	67.50	89.76
13	0.92	−11.23	−10.31
14	12.52	42.91	55.43
15	−28.52	−10.90	−39.42
16	−3.24	2.72	−0.51
17	2.60	12.31	14.91
18	27.51	−32.50	−4.99
19	31.35	−60.47	−29.12
20	18.48	2.68	21.15
21	−8.15	−16.87	−25.02
22	14.43	−19.82	−5.39
23	−8.50	59.09	50.59
24	4.09	−68.38	−64.29

risk-free rate. The negative estimated alpha is due to the effect of the firm-specific residuals. Similarly, stock *B* plots above the SML. Here, not knowing the true value of alpha, we might be led to believe that stock *B* is underpriced and has an expected return above that which can be obtained with the market index and the risk-free asset (given by the SML).

Figure 8.7 shows the capital market line (CML) that is supported by the risk-free rate and the market index. The efficient frontier is generated by the Markowitz algorithm applied to the means, standard deviations, and correlation coefficients of the full set of risky assets in the

FIGURE 8.4

Security Characteristic Line for Stock *A*

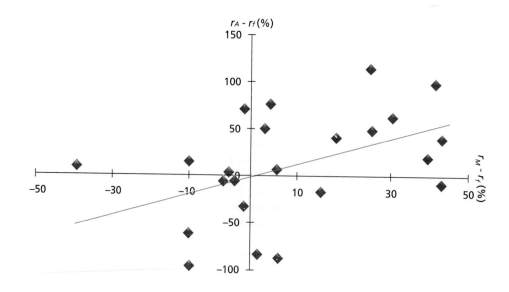

FIGURE 8.5

Security Characteristic
Line for Stock *B*

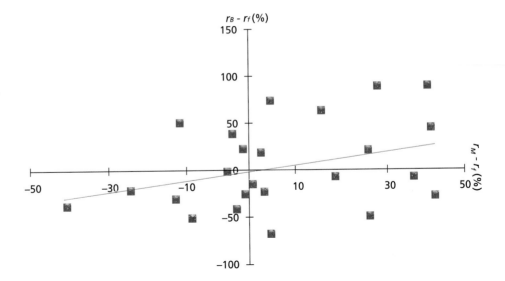

FIGURE 8.6

Security Market Line

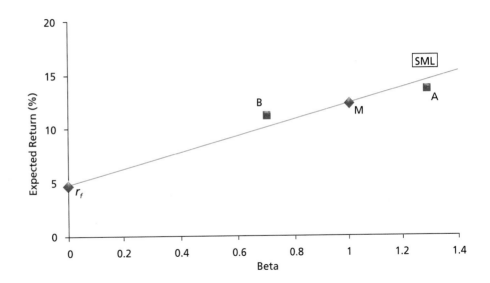

universe of securities. (This additional information is not shown here.) Stocks *A* and *B* plot far below the CML and below the efficient frontier, demonstrating that undiversified individual securities are dominated by efficiently diversified portfolios.

Predicting Betas

Even if a single-index model representation is not fully consistent with the CAPM, the concept of systematic versus diversifiable risk is still useful. Systematic risk is well approximated by the regression equation beta and nonsystematic risk by the residual variance of the regression.

Often, we estimate betas in order to forecast the rate of return of an asset. The beta from the regression equation is an estimate based on past history; it will not reveal possible changes in future beta. As an empirical rule, it appears that betas exhibit a statistical property called "regression toward the mean." This means that high β (that is, $\beta > 1$) securities in one period tend to exhibit a lower β in the future, while low β (that is, $\beta < 1$) securities exhibit a higher β in future periods. Researchers who desire predictions of future betas often

FIGURE 8.7
Capital Market Line

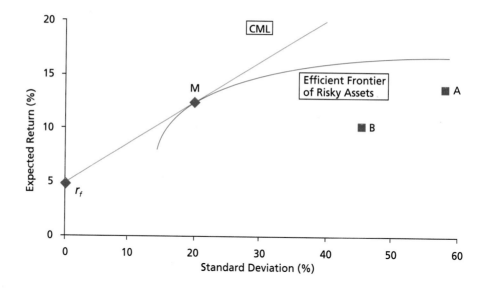

adjust beta estimates derived from historical data to account for regression toward the mean. For this reason, it is necessary to verify whether the estimates are already "adjusted betas."

A simple way to account for the tendency of future betas to "regress" toward the average value of 1.0 is to use as your forecast of beta a weighted average of the sample estimate with the value 1.0.

EXAMPLE 8.7
Forecast of Beta

Suppose that past data yield a beta estimate of 0.65. A common weighting scheme is ⅔ on the sample estimate and ⅓ on the value 1.0. Thus, the final forecast of beta will be

$$\text{Adjusted beta} = \tfrac{2}{3} \times 0.65 + \tfrac{1}{3} \times 1.0 = 0.77$$

The final forecast of beta is in fact closer to 1.0 than the sample estimate.

A more sophisticated technique would base the weight assigned to the sample estimate of beta on its statistical reliability. That is, if we have a more precise estimate of beta from historical data, we increase the weight placed on the sample estimate.

However, obtaining a precise statistical estimate of beta from past data on individual stocks is a formidable task, because the volatility of rates of return is so large. In other words, there is a lot of "noise" in the data due to the impact of firm-specific events. The problem is less severe with diversified portfolios because diversification reduces the effect of firm-specific events.

One might hope that more precise estimates of beta could be obtained by using more data, that is, by using a long time series of the returns on the stock. Unfortunately, this is not a solution, because regression analysis presumes that the regression coefficient (the beta) is constant over the sample period. Since betas change over time, we would be defeating the purpose using a very long time series. More complicated regression techniques that allow for time-varying coefficients also have not proved to be very successful.

One promising avenue is an application of a technique that goes by the name of ARCH models.[4] An ARCH model posits that changes in stock volatility, and covariance with other

---

[4]ARCH stands for autoregressive conditional heteroskedasticity. This is a fancy way of saying that the volatility (and covolatility) of stocks changes over time in ways that can be at least partially predicted from past levels of volatility.

stocks, are partially predictable and analyzes recent levels and trends in volatility and co-variance. This technique has penetrated the industry only recently and so has not yet produced truly reliable betas. Thus, the problem of estimating the critical parameters of the CAPM and index models has been a stick in the wheels of testing and applying the theory.

8.3 THE CAPM AND THE REAL WORLD

In limited ways, portfolio theory and the CAPM have become accepted tools in the practitioner community. Many investment professionals think about the distinction between firm-specific and systematic risk and are comfortable with the use of beta to measure systematic risk. Still, the nuances of the CAPM are not nearly as well established in the community. For example, the compensation of portfolio managers is not based on alphas calculated relative to the security market line. What can we make of this?

New ways of thinking about the world (that is, new models or theories) displace old ones when the old models become either intolerably inconsistent with data, or when the new model is demonstrably more consistent with available data. For example, when Copernicus overthrew the age-old belief that the earth is fixed in the center of the universe and that the stars orbit about it in circular motions, it took many years before astronomers and navigators replaced old astronomical tables with superior ones based on his theory. The old tools fit the data available from astronomical observation with sufficient precision to suffice for the needs of the time. To some extent, the slowness with which the CAPM has permeated daily practice in the money management industry also has to do with its precision in fitting data, that is, in precisely explaining variation in rates of return across assets. Let's review some of the evidence on this score.

The CAPM was first published by Sharpe in the *Journal of Finance* (the official journal of the American Finance Association) in 1964 and took the world of finance by storm. Douglas (1969) was the first to cast doubt on the empirical content of the model.

Douglas found damning evidence on two counts. First, contrary to the predictions of the theory, nonsystematic risk did seem to explain average returns. Second, the estimated security market line was too shallow, that is, its intercept was greater than the risk-free rate, implying that defensive stocks ($\beta < 1$) tended to have positive alphas, while aggressive stocks (with $\beta > 1$) tended to have negative alphas.

Four years later, Miller and Scholes (1972) published a paper demonstrating formidable statistical problems that hinder a straightforward test like that of Douglas. They estimated the potential error that may have resulted from each step of Douglas's procedure and, sure enough, they were able to rationalize his findings.

But Miller and Scholes's explanation does not in itself provide *positive* evidence that the CAPM is valid. Later studies, most notably those of Black, Jensen, and Scholes (1972), and Fama and MacBeth (1973), used procedures designed to address the various econometric problems. The most important of these was to test the CAPM using cleverly constructed portfolios to diminish the statistical noise resulting from firm-specific risk. But even these efforts could not establish the validity of the CAPM.

While all this accumulating evidence against the CAPM remained largely within the ivory towers of academia, Roll's (1977) paper entitled "A Critique of Capital Asset Pricing Tests" shook the practitioner world as well. Roll argued that since the true market portfolio can never be observed, the CAPM is *necessarily* untestable.

The publicity of the now classic "Roll's critique" resulted in popular articles such as "Is Beta Dead?" that effectively slowed the permeation of portfolio theory through the world of finance.[5] This is quite ironic since, although Roll is absolutely correct on theoretical

---

[5]A. Wallace, "Is Beta Dead?" *Institutional Investor* 14 (July 1980), pp. 22–30.

Beta Beaten

A battle between some of the top names in financial economics is attracting attention on Wall Street. Under attack is the famous capital asset pricing model (CAPM), widely used to assess risk and return. A new paper by two Chicago economists, Eugene Fama and Kenneth French, explodes that model by showing that its key analytical tool does not explain why returns on shares differ.

According to the CAPM, returns reflect risk. The model uses a measure called beta—shorthand for relative volatility—to compare the riskiness of one share with that of the whole market, on the basis of past price changes. A share with a beta of one is just as risky as the market; one with a beta of 0.5 is less risky. Because investors need to earn more on riskier investments, share prices will reflect the requirement for higher-than-average returns on shares with higher betas.

Whether beta does predict returns has long been debated. Studies have found that market capitalization, price/earnings ratios, leverage and book-to-market ratios do just as well. Messrs Fama and French are clear: Beta is not a good guide.

The two economists look at all nonfinancial shares traded on the NYSE, Amex and Nasdaq between 1963 and 1990. The shares were grouped into portfolios. When grouped solely on the basis of size (that is, market capitalization), the CAPM worked—but each portfolio contained a wide range of betas. So the authors grouped shares of similar beta and size. Betas now were a bad guide to returns.

Instead of beta, say Messrs Fama and French, differences in firm size and in the ratio of book value to market value explain differences in returns—especially the latter. When shares were grouped by book-to-market ratios, the gap in returns between the portfolio with the lowest ratio and that with the highest was far wider than when shares were grouped by size.

So should analysts stop using the CAPM? Probably not. Although Mr. Fama and Mr. French have produced intriguing results, they lack a theory to explain them. Their best hope is that size and book-to-market ratios are proxies for other fundamentals. For instance, a high book-to-market ratio may indicate a firm in trouble; its earnings prospects might thus be especially sensitive to economic conditions, so its shares would need to earn a higher return than its beta suggested.

Advocates of CAPM—including Fischer Black, of Goldman Sachs, an investment bank, and William Sharpe of Stanford University, who won the Nobel Prize for economics in 1990—reckon the results of the new study can be explained without discarding beta. Investors may irrationally favor big firms. Or they may lack the cash to buy enough shares to spread risk completely, so that risk and return are not perfectly matched in the market.

Those looking for a theoretical alternative to CAPM will find little satisfaction, however. Voguish rivals, such as the "arbitrage pricing theory," are no better than CAPM and betas at explaining actual share returns. Which leaves Wall Street with an awkward choice: Believe the Fama–French evidence, despite its theoretical vacuum, and use size and the book-to-market ratios as a guide to returns; or stick with a theory that, despite the data, is built on impeccable logic.

Source: "Beta Beaten," *The Economist*, March 7, 1992, p. 87, based on Eugene Fama and Kenneth French, "The Cross-Section of Expected Stock Returns," University of Chicago Center for Research in Security Prices, 1991.

grounds, some tests suggest that the error introduced by using a broad market index as proxy for the true, unobserved market portfolio is perhaps the lesser of the problems involved in testing the CAPM.

Fama and French (1992) published a study that dealt the CAPM an even harsher blow. It claimed that once you control for a set of widely followed characteristics of the firm, such as the size of the firm and its ratio of market value to book value, the firm's beta (that is, its systematic risk) does not contribute anything to the prediction of future returns. This time, the piece was picked up by *The Economist* and the *New York Times* (see box on this page) even before it was published in the *Journal of Finance*.

Fama and French and several others have published many follow-up studies of this topic. We will review some of this literature in the next chapter. However, it seems clear from these studies that beta does not tell the whole story of risk. There seem to be risk factors that affect security returns beyond beta's one-dimensional measurement of market sensitivity. In fact, in the next section of this chapter, we will introduce a theory of risk premiums that explicitly allows for multiple risk factors.

Nevertheless, beta is not dead. Other research shows that when we use a more inclusive proxy for the market portfolio than the S&P 500 (specifically, an index that includes human capital) and allow for the fact that beta changes over time, the performance of beta in explaining security returns is considerably enhanced (Jagannathan and Wang, 1996). We know that the CAPM is not a perfect model and that ultimately, it will be far from the last word on security pricing. Still, the logic of the model is compelling, and more sophisticated models of security pricing all rely on the key distinction between systematic versus diversifiable risk. The CAPM therefore provides a useful framework for thinking rigorously about the relationship between security risk and return. This is as much as Copernicus had when he was shown the prepublication version of his book just before he passed away.

8.4 ARBITRAGE PRICING THEORY

In the 1970s, as researchers were working on test methodologies for variants of the CAPM, Stephen Ross (1976) stunned the world of finance with the arbitrage pricing theory (APT). Moving away from construction of mean-variance efficient portfolios, Ross instead calculated relations among expected rates of return that would rule out riskless profits by any investor in well-functioning capital markets. This generated a theory of risk and return similar to the CAPM.

Arbitrage Opportunities and Profits

arbitrage
Creation of riskless profits made possible by relative mispricing among securities.

To explain the APT, we begin with the concept of **arbitrage,** which is the exploitation of relative mispricing among two or more securities to earn risk-free economic profits.

A riskless arbitrage opportunity arises when an investor can construct a **zero-investment portfolio** that will yield a sure profit. Zero investment means investors need not use any of their own money. To construct a zero-investment portfolio, one has to be able to sell short at least one asset and use the proceeds to purchase (go long) one or more assets. Even a small investor, using borrowed money in this fashion, can take a large position in such a portfolio.

zero-investment portfolio
A portfolio of zero net value, established by buying and shorting component securities, usually in the context of an arbitrage strategy.

An obvious case of an arbitrage opportunity arises in the violation of the law of one price: When an asset is trading at different prices in two markets (and the price differential exceeds transaction costs), a simultaneous trade in the two markets will produce a sure profit (the net price differential) without any net investment. One simply sells short the asset in the high-priced market and buys it in the low-priced market. The net proceeds are positive, and there is no risk because the long and short positions offset each other.

In modern markets with electronic communications and instantaneous execution, such opportunities have become rare but not extinct. The same technology that enables the market to absorb new information quickly also enables fast operators to make large profits by trading huge volumes at the instant an arbitrage opportunity opens. This is the essence of program trading and index arbitrage, to be discussed in Part Five.

From the simple case of a violation of the law of one price, let us proceed to a less obvious (yet just as profitable) arbitrage opportunity. Imagine that four stocks are traded in an economy with only four possible scenarios. The rates of return on the four stocks for each inflation-interest rate scenario appear in Table 8.6. The current prices of the stocks and rate of return statistics are shown in Table 8.7.

The rate of return data give no immediate clue to any arbitrage opportunity lurking in this set of investments. The expected returns, standard deviations, and correlations do not reveal any abnormality to the naked eye.

Consider, however, an equally weighted portfolio of the first three stocks (Apex, Bull, and Crush), and contrast its possible future rates of return with those of the fourth stock, Dreck. We do this in Table 8.8.

TABLE 8.6
Rate of Return
Projections

	High Real Interest Rates		Low Real Interest Rates	
	High Inflation	**Low Inflation**	**High Inflation**	**Low Inflation**
Probability:	0.25	0.25	0.25	0.25
Stock				
Apex (*A*)	−20	20	40	60
Bull (*B*)	0	70	30	−20
Crush (*C*)	90	−20	−10	70
Dreck (*D*)	15	23	15	36

TABLE 8.7
Rate of Return
Statistics

				Correlation Matrix			
Stock	**Current Price**	**Expected Return (%)**	**Standard Deviation (%)**	**A**	**B**	**C**	**D**
A	$10	25.0%	29.58%	1.00	−0.15	−0.29	0.68
B	10	20.0	33.91	−0.15	1.00	−0.87	−0.38
C	10	32.5	48.15	−0.29	−0.87	1.00	0.22
D	10	22.25	8.58	0.68	−0.38	0.22	1.00

TABLE 8.8
Rate of Return
Projections

	High Real Interest Rates		Low Real Interest Rates	
	Rate of Inflation		Rate of Inflation	
	High	**Low**	**High**	**Low**
Equally weighted portfolio: *A*, *B*, and *C*	23.33	23.33	20.00	36.67
Dreck (*D*)	15.00	23.00	15.00	36.00

Table 8.8 reveals that in all scenarios, the equally weighted portfolio will outperform Dreck. The rate of return statistics of the two alternatives are

	Mean	Standard Deviation	Correlation
Three-stock portfolio	25.83	6.40	
			0.94
Dreck	22.25	8.58	

The two investments are not perfectly correlated and are not perfect substitutes. Nevertheless, the equally weighted portfolio will fare better under *any* circumstances. Any investor, no matter how risk averse, can take advantage of this dominance by taking a short position in Dreck and using the proceeds to purchase the equally weighted portfolio. Let us see how it would work.

Suppose we sell short 300,000 shares of Dreck and use the $3 million proceeds to buy 100,000 shares each of Apex, Bull, and Crush. The dollar profits in each of the four scenarios will be as follows.

		High Real Interest Rates		Low Real Interest Rates	
		Inflation Rate		Inflation Rate	
Stock	**Dollar Investment**	**High**	**Low**	**High**	**Low**
Apex	$ 1,000,000	$−200,000	$ 200,000	$ 400,000	$ 600,000
Bull	1,000,000	0	700,000	300,000	−200,000
Crush	1,000,000	900,000	−200,000	−100,000	700,000
Dreck	−3,000,000	−450,000	−690,000	−450,000	−1,080,000
Portfolio	$ 0	$ 250,000	$ 10,000	$ 150,000	$ 20,000

The first column verifies that the net investment in our portfolio is zero. Yet this portfolio yields a positive profit in all scenarios. It is therefore a money machine. Investors will want to take an infinite position in such a portfolio, for larger positions entail no risk of losses yet yield ever-growing profits.[6] In principle, even a single investor would take such large positions that the market would react to the buying and selling pressure: The price of Dreck would come down, and/or the prices of Apex, Bull, and Crush would go up. The pressure would persist until the arbitrage opportunity was eliminated.

Concept Check

5. Suppose Dreck's price starts falling without any change in its per share dollar payoffs. How far must the price fall before arbitrage between Dreck and the equally weighted portfolio is no longer possible? (Hint: Account for the amount of the equally weighted portfolio that can be purchased with the proceeds of the short sale as Dreck's price falls.)

The critical property of an arbitrage portfolio is that any investor, regardless of risk aversion or wealth, will want to take an infinite position in it so that profits will be driven to an infinite level. Because those large positions will force some prices up and/or some down until the opportunity vanishes, we can derive restrictions on security prices that satisfy the condition that no arbitrage opportunities are left in the marketplace.

The idea that equilibrium market prices ought to be rational in the sense that they rule out arbitrage opportunities is perhaps the most fundamental concept in capital market theory. Violation of this principle would indicate the grossest form of market irrationality.

There is an important distinction between arbitrage and CAPM risk-versus-return dominance arguments in support of equilibrium price relationships. A dominance argument, as in the CAPM, holds that when an equilibrium price relationship is violated, many investors will make portfolio changes. Each individual investor will make a limited change, though, depending on wealth and degree of risk aversion. Aggregation of these limited portfolio changes over many investors is required to create a large volume of buying and selling, which restores equilibrium prices.

When arbitrage opportunities exist, by contrast, each investor wants to take as large a position as possible; in this case, it will not take many investors to bring about the price pressures necessary to restore equilibrium. Implications derived from the no-arbitrage argument, therefore, are stronger than implications derived from a risk-versus-return dominance argument, because they do not depend on a large, well-educated population of investors.

The CAPM argues that all investors hold mean-variance efficient portfolios. When a security (or a bundle of securities) is mispriced, investors will tilt their portfolios toward the underpriced and away from the overpriced securities. The resulting pressure on prices comes from many investors shifting their portfolios, each by a relatively small dollar amount. The assumption that a large number of investors are mean-variance optimizers, is critical; in contrast, even few arbitrageurs will mobilize large dollar amounts to take advantage of an arbitrage opportunity.

Well-Diversified Portfolios and the Arbitrage Pricing Theory

The arbitrage opportunity described in the previous section is further obscured by the fact that it is almost always impossible to construct a precise scenario analysis for individual stocks that would uncover an event of such straightforward mispricing.

---

[6]We have described pure arbitrage: the search for a costless sure profit. Practitioners often use the terms *arbitrage* and *arbitrageurs* more loosely. An arbitrageur may be a professional searching for mispriced securities in specific areas such as merger-target stocks, rather than one looking for strict (risk-free) arbitrage opportunities in the sense that no loss is possible. The search for mispriced securities is called risk arbitrage to distinguish it from pure arbitrage.

arbitrage pricing theory (APT)
A theory of risk-return relationships derived from no-arbitrage considerations in large capital markets.

Using the concept of well-diversified portfolios, the **arbitrage pricing theory,** or **APT,** resorts to statistical modeling to attack the problem more systematically. By showing that mispriced portfolios would give rise to arbitrage opportunities, the APT arrives at an expected return–beta relationship for portfolios identical to that of the CAPM. In the next section, we will compare and contrast the two theories.

In its simple form, just like the CAPM, the APT posits a single-factor security market. Thus, the excess rate of return on each security, $R_i = r_i - r_f$, can be represented by

$$R_i = \alpha_i + \beta_i R_M + e \tag{8.5}$$

where alpha, α_i, and beta, β_i, are known, and where we treat R_M as the single factor.

Suppose now that we construct a highly diversified portfolio with a given beta. If we use enough securities to form the portfolio, the resulting diversification will strip the portfolio of nonsystematic risk. Because such a **well-diversified portfolio** has for all practical purposes zero firm-specific risk, we can write its returns as

well-diversified portfolio
A portfolio sufficiently diversified that nonsystematic risk is negligible.

$$R_P = \alpha_P + \beta_P R_M \tag{8.6}$$

(This portfolio is risky, however, because the excess return on the index, R_M, is random.)

Figure 8.8 illustrates the difference between a single security with a beta of 1.0 and a well-diversified portfolio with the same beta. For the portfolio (Panel A), all the returns plot exactly on the security characteristic line. There is no dispersion around the line, as in Panel B, because the effects of firm-specific events are eliminated by diversification. Therefore, in Equation 8.6, there is no residual term, e.

Notice that Equation 8.6 implies that if the portfolio beta is zero, then $R_P = \alpha_P$. This implies a riskless rate of return: There is no firm-specific risk because of diversification and no factor risk because beta is zero. Remember, however, that capital R denotes excess returns. So the equation implies that a portfolio with a beta of zero has a riskless *excess* return of α_P, that is, a return higher than the risk-free rate by the amount α_P. But this implies that α_P must equal zero, or else an immediate arbitrage opportunity opens up. For example, if α_P is greater than zero, you can borrow at the risk-free rate and use the proceeds to buy the well-diversified zero-beta portfolio. You borrow risklessly at rate r_f and invest risklessly at rate $r_f + \alpha_P$, clearing the riskless differential of α_P.

**EXAMPLE 8.8
Arbitrage with a Zero-Beta Portfolio**

Suppose that the risk-free rate is 6%, and a well-diversified zero-beta portfolio earns (a sure) rate of return of 7%, that is, an excess return of 1%. Then borrow at 6% and invest in the zero-beta portfolio to earn 7%. You will earn a sure profit of 1% of the invested funds without putting up any of your own money. If the zero-beta portfolio earns 5%, then you can sell it short and lend at 6% with the same result.

FIGURE 8.8
Security Characteristic Lines

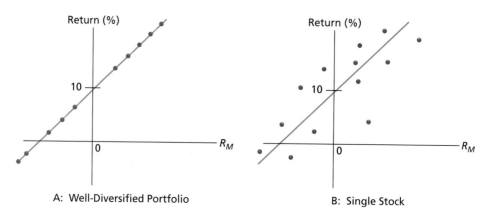

A: Well-Diversified Portfolio   B: Single Stock

In fact, we can go further and show that the alpha of *any* well-diversified portfolio in Equation 8.6 must be zero, even if the beta is not zero. The proof is similar to the easy zero-beta case. If the alphas were not zero, then we could combine two of these portfolios into a zero-beta riskless portfolio with a rate of return not equal to the risk-free rate. But this, as we have just seen, would be an arbitrage opportunity.

To see how the arbitrage strategy would work, suppose that portfolio V has a beta of β_v and an alpha of α_v. Similarly, suppose portfolio U has a beta of β_u and an alpha of α_u.

Taking advantage of any arbitrage opportunity involves buying and selling assets in proportions that create a risk-free profit on a costless position. To eliminate risk, we buy portfolio V and sell portfolio U in proportions chosen so that the combination portfolio $(V + U)$ will have a beta of zero. The portfolio weights that satisfy this condition are

$$w_v = \frac{-\beta_u}{\beta_v - \beta_u} \qquad w_u = \frac{\beta_v}{\beta_v - \beta_u}$$

Note that w_v plus w_u add up to 1.0 and that the beta of the combination is in fact zero:

$$\text{Beta}(V + U) = \beta_v \frac{-\beta_u}{\beta_v - \beta_u} + \beta_u \frac{\beta_v}{\beta_v - \beta_u} = 0$$

Therefore, the portfolio is riskless: It has no sensitivity to the factor. But the excess return of the portfolio is not zero unless α_v and α_u equal zero.

$$R(V + U) = \alpha_v \frac{-\beta_u}{\beta_v - \beta_u} + \alpha_u \frac{\beta_v}{\beta_v - \beta_u} \neq 0$$

Therefore, unless α_v and α_u equal zero, the zero-beta portfolio has a certain rate of return that differs from the risk-free rate (its excess return is different from zero): We have seen that this gives rise to an arbitrage opportunity.

**EXAMPLE 8.9
Arbitrage with
Mispriced
Portfolios**

Suppose that the risk-free rate is 7% and a well-diversified portfolio, V, with beta of 1.3 has an alpha of 2% and another well-diversified portfolio, U, with beta of 0.8 has an alpha of 1%. We go long on V and short on U with proportions

$$w_v = \frac{-0.8}{1.3 - 0.8} = -1.6 \qquad w_u = \frac{1.3}{1.3 - 0.8} = 2.6$$

These proportions add up to 1.0 and result in a portfolio with beta $= -1.6 \times 1.3 + 2.6 \times 0.8 = 0$. The alpha of the portfolio is: $-1.6 \times 2 + 2.6 \times 1 = -0.6\%$. This means that the riskless portfolio will earn a rate of return that is less than the risk-free rate by 6%. We now complete the arbitrage by selling (or going short on) the combination portfolio and investing the proceeds at 7%, risklessly profiting by the 60 basis point differential in returns.

We conclude that the only value for alpha that rules out arbitrage opportunities is zero. Therefore, rewrite Equation 8.6 setting alpha equal to zero

$$R_P = \beta_P R_M$$

$$r_P - r_f = \beta_P(r_M - r_f)$$

$$E(r_P) = r_f + \beta_P[E(r_M) - r_f]$$

Hence, we arrive at the same expected return–beta relationship as the CAPM without any assumption about either investor preferences or access to the all-inclusive (and elusive) market portfolio.

The APT and the CAPM

Why did we need so many restrictive assumptions to derive the CAPM when the APT seems to arrive at the expected return–beta relationship with seemingly fewer and less objectionable assumptions? The answer is simple: The APT applies only to well-diversified portfolios. Absence of riskless arbitrage alone cannot guarantee that, in equilibrium, the expected return–beta relationship will hold for any and all assets.

With additional effort, however, one can use the APT to show that the relationship must hold approximately even for individual assets. The essence of the proof is that if the expected return–beta relationship were violated by many individual securities, it would be virtually impossible for all well-diversified portfolios to satisfy the relationship. So the relationship must *almost* surely hold true for individual securities.

We say "almost" because, according to the APT, there is no guarantee that all individual assets will lie on the SML. If only a few securities violated the SML, their effect on well-diversified portfolios could conceivably be offsetting. In this sense, it is possible that the SML relationship is violated for single securities. If many securities violate the expected return–beta relationship, however, the relationship will no longer hold for well-diversified portfolios comprised of these securities, and arbitrage opportunities will be available.

The APT serves many of the same functions as the CAPM. It gives us a benchmark for fair rates of return that can be used for capital budgeting, security evaluation, or investment performance evaluation. Moreover, the APT highlights the crucial distinction between nondiversifiable risk (systematic or factor risk) that requires a reward in the form of a risk premium and diversifiable risk that does not.

The bottom line is that neither of these theories dominates the other. The APT is more general in that it gets us to the expected return–beta relationship without requiring many of the unrealistic assumptions of the CAPM, particularly the reliance on the market portfolio. The latter improves the prospects for testing the APT. But the CAPM is more general in that it applies to all assets without reservation. The good news is that both theories agree on the expected return–beta relationship.

It is worth noting that because past tests of the expected return–beta relationship examined the rates of return on highly diversified portfolios, they actually came closer to testing the APT than the CAPM. Thus, it appears that econometric concerns, too, favor the APT.

Multifactor Generalization of the APT and CAPM

We've assumed all along that there is only one systematic factor affecting stock returns. This assumption may be too simplistic. It is easy to think of several factors that might affect stock returns: business cycles, interest rate fluctuations, inflation rates, oil prices, and so on. Presumably, exposure to any of these factors singly or together will affect a stock's perceived riskiness and appropriate expected rate of return. We can use a multifactor version of the APT to accommodate these multiple sources of risk.

Suppose we generalize the single-factor model expressed in Equation 8.5 to a two-factor model:

$$R_i = \alpha_i + \beta_{i1}R_{M1} + \beta_{i2}R_{M2} + e_i \tag{8.7}$$

factor portfolio
A well-diversified portfolio constructed to have a beta of 1.0 on one factor and a beta of zero on any other factor.

where R_{M1} and R_{M2} are the excess returns on portfolios that represent the two systematic factors. Factor 1 might be, for example, unanticipated changes in industrial production, while factor 2 might represent unanticipated changes in short-term interest rates. We assume again that there are many securities available with any combination of betas. This implies that we can form well-diversified **factor portfolios,** that is, portfolios that have a beta of 1.0 on one factor and a beta of zero on all others. Thus, a factor portfolio with a beta of 1.0 on the first factor will have a rate of return of R_{M1}; a factor portfolio with a beta of 1.0 on the second factor will have a rate of return of R_{M2}; and so on. Factor portfolios can serve as the benchmark portfolios for a multifactor generalization of the security market line relationship.

Suppose the two-factor portfolios, here called portfolios 1 and 2, have expected returns $E(r_1) = 10\%$ and $E(r_2) = 12\%$. Suppose further that the risk-free rate is 4%. The risk premium on the first factor portfolio becomes 6%, while that on the second factor portfolio is 8%.

Now consider an arbitrary well-diversified portfolio (A), with beta on the first factor, $\beta_{A1} = 0.5$, and on the second factor, $\beta_{A2} = 0.75$. The multifactor APT states that the portfolio risk premium required as compensation to investors for each source of systematic risk must equal the sum of the risk premiums required as compensation to investors for each source of systematic risk. The risk premium attributable to risk factor 1 is the portfolio's exposure to factor 1, β_{A1}, times the risk premium earned on the first factor portfolio, $E(r_1) - r_f$. Therefore, the portion of portfolio A's risk premium that is compensation for its exposure to the first risk factor is $\beta_{A1}[E(r_1) - r_f] = 0.5\,(10\% - 4\%) = 3\%$, while the risk premium attributable to risk factor 2 is $\beta_{A2}\,[E(r_2) - r_f] = 0.75\,(12\% - 4\%) = 6\%$. The total risk premium on the portfolio, therefore, should be $3 + 6 = 9\%$, and the total return on the portfolio should be 13%.

4%	Risk-free rate
+ 3%	Risk premium for exposure to factor 1
+ 6%	Risk premium for exposure to factor 2
13%	Total expected return

To see why the expected return on the portfolio must be 13%, consider the following argument. Suppose the expected return on portfolio A is 12% rather than 13%. This return would give rise to an arbitrage opportunity. Form a portfolio from the factor portfolios with the same betas as portfolio A. This requires weights of 0.5 on the first factor portfolio, 0.75 on the second portfolio, and -0.25 on the risk-free asset. This portfolio has exactly the same factor betas as portfolio A: a beta of 0.5 on the first factor because of its 0.5 weight on the first factor portfolio and a beta of 0.75 on the second factor.

In contrast to portfolio A's 12% expected return, however, this portfolio's expected return is $(0.5 \times 10) + (0.75 \times 12) - (0.25 \times 4) = 13\%$. A long position in this portfolio and a short position in portfolio A would yield an arbitrage profit. The total proceeds per dollar long or short in each position would be

$0.13 + 0.5\,R_{M1} + 0.75\,R_{M2}$	Long position in factor portfolios
$-(0.12 + 0.5\,R_{M1} + 0.75\,R_{M2})$	Short position in portfolio A
.01	

for a positive risk-free return on a zero net investment position.

To generalize this argument, note that the factor exposure of any portfolio P is given by its betas, β_{P1} and β_{P2}. A competing portfolio, Q, can be formed from factor portfolios with the following weights: β_{P1} in the first factor portfolio; β_{P2} in the second factor portfolio; and $1 - \beta_{P2} - \beta_{P2}$ in T-bills. By construction, Q will have betas equal to those of portfolio P and an expected return of

$$E(r_Q) = \beta_{P1}E(r_1) + \beta_{P2}E(r_2) + (1 - \beta_{P1} - \beta_{P2})r_f$$
$$= r_f + \beta_{P1}[E(r_1) - r_f] + \beta_{P2}[E(r_2) - r_f] \tag{8.8}$$

Hence, any well-diversified portfolio with betas β_{P1} and β_{P2} must have the return given in Equation 8.8 if arbitrage opportunities are to be ruled out. A comparison of Equations 8.2 and 8.8 shows that 8.8 is simply a generalization of the one-factor SML.

Finally, extension of the multifactor SML of Equation 8.8 to individual assets is precisely the same as for the one-factor APT. Equation 8.8 cannot be satisfied by every well-diversified portfolio unless it is satisfied by virtually every security taken individually. Equation 8.8 thus represents the multifactor SML for an economy with multiple sources of risk.

The generalized APT must be qualified with respect to individual assets just as in the single-factor case. A multifactor CAPM would, at the cost of additional assumptions, apply to any and all individual assets. As we have seen, the result will be a security market equation (a multidimensional SML) that is identical to that of the multifactor APT.

Concept Check

6. Using the factor portfolios just considered, find the fair rate of return on a security with $\beta_1 = 0.2$ and $\beta_2 = 1.4$.

Summary

- The CAPM assumes investors are rational, single-period planners who agree on a common input list from security analysis and seek mean-variance optimal portfolios.
- The CAPM assumes ideal security markets in the sense that: (a) markets are large, and investors are price takers, (b) there are no taxes or transaction costs, (c) all risky assets are publicly traded, and (d) any amount can be borrowed and lent at a fixed, risk-free rate.
- These assumptions mean that all investors will hold identical risky portfolios. The CAPM implies that, in equilibrium, the market portfolio is the unique mean-variance efficient tangency portfolio, which indicates that a passive strategy is efficient.
- The market portfolio is a value-weighted portfolio. Each security is held in a proportion equal to its market value divided by the total market value of all securities. The risk premium on the market portfolio is proportional to its variance, σ_M^2, and to the risk aversion of the average investor.
- The CAPM implies that the risk premium on any individual asset or portfolio is the product of the risk premium of the market portfolio and the asset's beta.
- In a single-index security market, once an index is specified, any security beta can be estimated from a regression of the security's excess return on the index's excess return. This regression line is called the security characteristic line (SCL). The intercept of the SCL, called alpha, represents the average excess return on the security when the index excess return is zero. The CAPM implies that alphas should be zero.
- Estimates of beta from past data often are adjusted when used to assess required future returns.
- An arbitrage opportunity arises when the disparity between two or more security prices enables investors to construct a zero net investment portfolio that will yield a sure profit. Rational investors will want to take infinitely large positions in arbitrage portfolios regardless of their degree of risk aversion.
- The presence of arbitrage opportunities and the resulting volume of trades will create pressure on security prices that will persist until prices reach levels that preclude arbitrage. Only a few investors need to become aware of arbitrage opportunities to trigger this process because of the large volume of trades in which they will engage.
- When securities are priced so that there are no arbitrage opportunities, the market satisfies the no-arbitrage condition. Price relationships that satisfy the no-arbitrage condition are important because we expect them to hold in real-world markets.
- Portfolios are called *well diversified* if they include a large number of securities in such proportions that the residual or diversifiable risk of the portfolio is negligible.
- In a single-factor security market, all well-diversified portfolios must satisfy the expected return–beta relationship of the SML in order to satisfy the no-arbitrage condition.
- If all well-diversified portfolios satisfy the expected return–beta relationship, then all but a small number of securities also must satisfy this relationship.
- The APT implies the same expected return–beta relationship as the CAPM yet does not require that all investors be mean-variance optimizers. The price of this generality is that the APT does not guarantee this relationship for all securities at all times.

- A multifactor APT generalizes the single-factor model to accommodate several sources of systematic risk.

Key Terms

alpha, *205*
arbitrage, *217*
arbitrage pricing theory
  (APT), *220*
capital asset pricing model
  (CAPM), *199*

expected return–beta
  relationship, *202*
factor portfolio, *222*
market portfolio, *199*
mutual fund theorem, *201*
security characteristic line
  (SCL), *208*

security market line
  (SML), *204*
well-diversified
  portfolio, *220*
zero-investment
  portfolio, *217*

Problem Sets

1. What is the beta of a portfolio with $E(r_P) = 20\%$, if $r_f = 5\%$ and $E(r_M) = 15\%$?

2. The market price of a security is $40. Its expected rate of return is 13%. The risk-free rate is 7%, and the market risk premium is 8%. What will the market price of the security be if its beta doubles (and all other variables remain unchanged)? Assume the stock is expected to pay a constant dividend in perpetuity.

3. You are a consultant to a large manufacturing corporation considering a project with the following net after-tax cash flows (in millions of dollars)

Years from Now	After-Tax CF
0	−20
1–9	10
10	20

The project's beta is 1.7. Assuming $r_f = 9\%$ and $E(r_M) = 19\%$, what is the net present value of the project? What is the highest possible beta estimate for the project before its NPV becomes negative?

4. Are the following statements true or false? Explain.
   a. Stocks with a beta of zero offer an expected rate of return of zero.
   b. The CAPM implies that investors require a higher return to hold highly volatile securities.
   c. You can construct a portfolio with a beta of 0.75 by investing 0.75 of the budget in T-bills and the remainder in the market portfolio.

5. Consider the following table, which gives a security analyst's expected return on two stocks for two particular market returns:

Market Return	Aggressive Stock	Defensive Stock
5%	2%	3.5%
20	32	14

   a. What are the betas of the two stocks?
   b. What is the expected rate of return on each stock if the market return is equally likely to be 5% or 20%?
   c. If the T-bill rate is 8%, and the market return is equally likely to be 5% or 20%, draw the SML for this economy.
   d. Plot the two securities on the SML graph. What are the alphas of each?
   e. What hurdle rate should be used by the management of the aggressive firm for a project with the risk characteristics of the defensive firm's stock?

If the simple CAPM is valid, which of the situations in problems 6–12 below are possible? Explain. Consider each situation independently.

6.

Portfolio	Expected Return	Beta
A	20%	1.4
B	25	1.2

7.

Portfolio	Expected Return	Standard Deviation
A	30%	0.35%
B	40	0.25

8.

Portfolio	Expected Return	Standard Deviation
Risk-free	10%	0%
Market	18	24
A	16	12

9.

Portfolio	Expected Return	Standard Deviation
Risk-free	10%	0%
Market	18	24
A	20	22

10.

Portfolio	Expected Return	Beta
Risk-free	10%	0
Market	18	1.0
A	16	1.5

11.

Portfolio	Expected Return	Beta
Risk-free	10%	0
Market	18	1.0
A	16	.9

12.

Portfolio	Expected Return	Standard Deviation
Risk-free	10%	0%
Market	18	24
A	16	22

In problems 13–15 below, assume the risk-free rate is 8% and the expected rate of return on the market is 18%.

13. A share of stock is now selling for $100. It will pay a dividend of $9 per share at the end of the year. Its beta is 1.0. What do investors expect the stock to sell for at the end of the year?

14. I am buying a firm with an expected perpetual cash flow of $1,000 but am unsure of its risk. If I think the beta of the firm is zero, when the beta is really 1.0, how much *more* will I offer for the firm than it is truly worth?

15. A stock has an expected return of 6%. What is its beta?

16. Two investment advisors are comparing performance. One averaged a 19% return and the other a 16% return. However, the beta of the first advisor was 1.5, while that of the second was 1.0.
    a. Can you tell which advisor was a better selector of individual stocks (aside from the issue of general movements in the market)?
    b. If the T-bill rate were 6%, and the market return during the period were 14%, which advisor would be the superior stock selector?
    c. What if the T-bill rate were 3% and the market return 15%?

17. In 1997, the yield on sort-term government securities (perceived to be risk-free) was about 5%. Suppose the expected return required by the market for a portfolio with a beta of 1.0 is 12%. According to the capital asset pricing model:
    a. What is the expected return on the market portfolio?
    b. What would be the expected return on a zero-beta stock?
    c. Suppose you consider buying a share of stock at a price of $40. The stock is expected to pay a dividend of $3 next year and to sell then for $41. The stock risk has been evaluated at $\beta = -0.5$. Is the stock overpriced or underpriced?

18. Consider the following data for a one-factor economy. All portfolios are well diversified.

Portfolio	E(r)	Beta
A	10%	1.0
F	4	0

Suppose another portfolio E is well diversified with a beta of ⅔ and expected return of 9%. Would an arbitrage opportunity exist? If so, what would the arbitrage strategy be?

19. Following is a scenario for three stocks constructed by the security analysts of PF Inc.

		Scenario Rate of Return (%)		
Stock	Price ($)	Recession	Average	Boom
A	10	−15	20	30
B	15	25	10	−10
C	50	12	15	12

    a. Construct an arbitrage portfolio using these stocks.
    b. How might these prices change when equilibrium is restored? Give an example where a change in stock C's price is sufficient to restore equilibrium, assuming the dollar payoffs to stock C remain the same.

20. Assume both portfolios A and B are well diversified, that $E(r_A) = 14\%$ and $E(r_B) = 14.8\%$. If the economy has only one factor, and $\beta_A = 1.0$ while $\beta_B = 1.1$, what must be the risk-free rate?

21. Assume a market index represents the common factor, and all stocks in the economy have a beta of 1.0. Firm-specific returns all have a standard deviation of 30%.

   Suppose an analyst studies 20 stocks and finds that one-half have an alpha of 3%, and one-half have an alpha of − 3%. The analyst then buys $1 million of an equally weighted portfolio of the positive alpha stocks and sells short $1 million of an equally weighted portfolio of the negative alpha stocks.

   a. What is the expected profit (in dollars), and what is the standard deviation of the analyst's profit?

   b. How does your answer change if the analyst examines 50 stocks instead of 20? 100 stocks?

22. If the APT is to be a useful theory, the number of systematic factors in the economy must be small. Why?

23. The APT itself does not provide information on the factors that one might expect to determine risk premiums. How should researchers decide which factors to investigate? Is industrial production a reasonable factor to test for a risk premium? Why or why not?

24. Suppose two factors are identified for the U.S. economy: the growth rate of industrial production, IP, and the inflation rate, IR. IP is expected to be 4% and IR 6%. A stock with a beta of 1.0 on IP and 0.4 on IR currently is expected to provide a rate of return of 14%. If industrial production actually grows by 5%, while the inflation rate turns out to be 7%, what is your best guess for the rate of return on the stock?

25. Suppose there are two independent economic factors, M_1 and M_2. The risk-free rate is 7%, and all stocks have independent firm-specific components with a standard deviation of 50%. The following are well-diversified portfolios.

Portfolio	Beta on M_1	Beta on M_2	Expected Return (%)
A	1.8	2.1	40
B	2.0	−0.5	10

What is the expected return–beta relationship in this economy?

◆IEM
Applications

1. What is the market portfolio in the IEM Computer Industry Returns Market? What should the return on this portfolio be? Should there be risk premiums in the IEM?

2. Suppose the following bids and asks exist in the MSFT (Microsoft) Price Level Market:

Contract	Bid	Ask
MSxxxmH	0.463	0.472
MSxxxmL	0.546	0.550

An arbitrage opportunity exists! Describe how you exploit it to make a certain profit.

3. Find and record betas for the common stock of each company traded on the IEM Computer Industry Returns Market. Betas can be found from the following sources, among others:

   1. Value Line Investment Survey or Value Screen
   2. Standard & Poor's Reports
   3. S&P Stock Market Encyclopedia
   4. Bloomberg Information Services
   5. From various sources on the WWW. (See the IEM web pages at http://www.biz.uiowa.edu/iem for current links to sources of betas.)

Compare these betas from those you estimate using a regression and the data from the IEM's Computer Industry Returns Market, "F"undamental Information page under the "I"nformation menu.

4. Given the betas you estimate from IEM data in Question 3, calculate the one-month CAPM expected return for each company according to the following rates:
   1. The current one-month T-bill return from the WSJ.
   2. The average one-month return for the S&P 500 from the IEM data.

Solutions to Concept Checks

1. The CML would still represent efficient investments. We can characterize the entire population by two representative investors. One is the "uninformed" investor, who does not engage in security analysis and holds the market portfolio, while the other optimizes using the Markowitz algorithm with input from security analysis. The uninformed investor does not know what input the informed investor uses to make portfolio purchases. The uninformed investor knows, however, that if the other investor is informed, the market portfolio proportions will be optimal. Therefore, to depart from these proportions would constitute an uninformed bet, which will, on average, reduce the efficiency of diversification with no compensating improvement in expected returns.

2. Substituting the historical mean and standard deviation in Equation 8.1 yields a coefficient of risk aversion of

$$A^* = \frac{E(r_M) - r_f}{\sigma_M^2} = \frac{.085}{0.20^2} = 2.1$$

This relationship also tells us that for the historical standard deviation and a coefficient of risk aversion of 3.5, the risk premium would be

$$E(r_M) - r_f = A^*\sigma_M^2 = 3.5 \times 0.20^2 = 0.14 \; (14\%)$$

3. $\beta_{Ford} = 1.25$, $\beta_{GM} = 1.15$. Therefore, given the investment proportions, the portfolio beta is

$$\beta_P = w_{Ford}\beta_{Ford} + w_{GM}\beta_{GM} = (0.75 \times 1.25) + (0.25 \times 1.15) = 1.225$$

and the risk premium of the portfolio will be

$$E(r_P) - r_f = \beta_P[E(r_M) - r_f] = 1.225 \times 8\% = 9.8\%$$

4. *a.* The alpha of a stock is its expected return in excess of that required by the CAPM.

$$\alpha = E(r) - \{r_f + \beta[E(r_M) - r_f]\}$$
$$\alpha_{XYZ} = 12 - [5 + 1.0(11 - 5)] = 1$$
$$\alpha_{ABC} = 13 - [5 + 1.5(11 - 5)] = -1\%$$

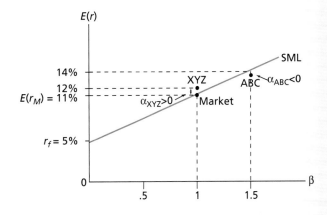

b. The project-specific required rate of return is determined by the project beta coupled with the market risk premium and the risk-free rate. The CAPM tells us an acceptable expected rate of return for the project is

$$E(r_f) + \beta[E(r_M) - r_f] = 8 + 1.3(16 - 8) = 18.4\%$$

which becomes the project's hurdle rate. If the IRR of the project is 19%, then it is desirable. Any project (of similar beta) with an IRR equal to or less than 18.4% should be rejected.

5. The least profitable scenario currently yields a profit of $10,000 and gross proceeds from the equally weighted portfolio of $700,000. As the price of Dreck falls, less of the equally weighted portfolio can be purchased from the proceeds of the short sale. When Dreck's price falls by more than a factor of 10,000/700,000, arbitrage no longer will be feasible, because the profits in the worst state will be driven below zero.

To see this, suppose Dreck's price falls to $10 × (1 − 1/70). The short sale of 300,000 shares now yields $2,957,142, which allows dollar investments of only $985,714 in each of the other shares. In the high real interest rate, low inflation scenario, profits will be driven to zero.

Stock	Dollar Investment	Rate of Return (%)	Dollar Return
Apex	$ 985,714	20	$ 197,143
Bull	985,714	70	690,000
Crush	985,714	−20	−197,143
Dreck	− 2,957,142	NA	−690,000
Total	$ 0		$ 0

*The dollar return on Dreck is assumed to be held fixed as its price falls. Therefore, Dreck's rate of return will depend on the price to which its stock price falls, but in any case the rate of return is not necessary to answer the question.

At any price for Dreck stock below $10 × (1 − 1/70) = $9.857, profits will be negative, which means the arbitrage opportunity is eliminated. Note: $9.857 is not the equilibrium price of Dreck. It is simply the upper bound on Dreck's price that rules out the simple arbitrage opportunity.

6. Using Equation 8.8, the expected return is

$$4 + (0.2 \times 6) + (1.4 \times 8) = 16.4\%$$

Chapter 9

THE EFFICIENT
MARKET HYPOTHESIS

AFTER STUDYING THIS CHAPTER YOU SHOULD BE ABLE TO:

- Demonstrate why security price movements should be essentially unpredictable.

- Cite evidence that supports and contradicts the efficient market hypothesis.

- Formulate investment strategies that make sense in informationally efficient markets.

One of the early applications of computers in economics in the 1950s was to analyze economic time series. Business cycle theorists believed tracing the evolution of several economic variables over time would clarify and predict the progress of the economy through boom and bust periods. A natural candidate for analysis was the behavior of stock market prices over time. Assuming stock prices reflect the prospects of the firm, recurring patterns of peaks and troughs in economic performance ought to show up in those prices.

Maurice Kendall (1953) was one of the first to examine this proposition. He found to his great surprise that he could identify *no* predictable patterns in stock prices. Prices seemed to evolve randomly. They were as likely to go up as they were to go down on any particular day regardless of past performance. The data provided no way to predict price movements.

At first blush, Kendall's results disturbed some financial economists. They seemed to imply that the stock market is dominated by erratic market psychology, or "animal spirits," and that it follows no logical rules. In short, the results appeared to confirm the irrationality of the market. On further reflection, however, economists reversed their interpretation of Kendall's study.

It soon became apparent that random price movements indicated a well-functioning or efficient market, not an irrational one. In this chapter, we will explore the reasoning behind what may seem to be a surprising conclusion. We show how competition among analysts leads naturally to market efficiency, and we examine the implications of the efficient market hypothesis for investment policy. We also consider empirical evidence that supports and contradicts the notion of market efficiency.

9.1 RANDOM WALKS AND THE EFFICIENT MARKET HYPOTHESIS

Suppose Kendall had discovered that stock prices are predictable. Imagine the gold mine for investors! If they could use Kendall's equations to predict stock prices, investors would reap unending profits simply by purchasing stocks the computer model implied were about to increase in price and selling those stocks about to fall in price.

A moment's reflection should be enough to convince you that this situation could not persist for long. For example, suppose the model predicts with great confidence that XYZ's stock price, currently at $100 per share, will rise dramatically in three days to $110. All investors with access to the model's prediction would place a great wave of immediate buy orders to cash in on the prospective increase in stock price. No one in the know holding XYZ, however, would be willing to sell, and the net effect would be an *immediate* jump in the stock price to $110. The forecast of a future price increase leads instead to an immediate price increase. Another way of putting this is that the stock price will immediately reflect the "good news" implicit in the model's forecast.

This simple example illustrates why Kendall's attempts to find recurring patterns in stock price movements were in vain. A forecast about favorable *future* performance leads instead to favorable *current* performance, as market participants all try to get in on the action before the price jump.

More generally, one could say that any publicly available information that might be used to predict stock performance, including information on the macroeconomy, the firm's industry, and its operations, plans, and management, should already be reflected in stock prices. As soon as there is any information indicating a stock is underpriced and offers a profit opportunity, investors flock to buy the stock and immediately bid up its price to a fair level, where again only ordinary rates of return can be expected. These "ordinary rates" are simply rates of return commensurate with the risk of the stock.

But if prices are bid immediately to fair levels, given all available information, it must be that prices increase or decrease only in response to new information. New information, by definition, must be unpredictable; if it could be predicted, then that prediction would be part of today's information! Thus, stock prices that change in response to new (unpredictable) information also must move unpredictably.

random walk
The notion that stock price changes are random and unpredictable.

This is the essence of the argument that stock prices should follow a **random walk,** that is, that price changes should be random and unpredictable. Far from being a proof of market irrationality, randomly evolving stock prices are the necessary consequence of intelligent investors competing to discover relevant information before the rest of the market becomes aware of that information.

Don't confuse randomness in price *changes* with irrationality in the *level* of prices. If prices are determined rationally, then only new information will cause them to change. Therefore, a random walk would be the natural consequence of prices that always reflect all current knowledge.

efficient market hypothesis
The hypothesis that prices of securities fully reflect available information about securities.

Indeed, if stock price movements were predictable, that would be damning evidence of stock market *inefficiency*, because the ability to predict prices would indicate that all available information was not already impounded in stock prices. Therefore, the notion that stocks already reflect all available information is referred to as the **efficient market hypothesis** (EMH).

Competition as the Source of Efficiency

Why should we expect stock prices to reflect all available information? After all, if you were to spend time and money gathering information, you would hope to turn up something that had been overlooked by the rest of the investment community. When information costs you money to uncover and analyze, you expect your investment analysis to result in an increased expected return.

Investors will have an incentive to spend time and resources to analyze and uncover new information only if such activity is likely to generate higher investment returns. Therefore, in market equilibrium, efficient informational gathering activity should be fruitful.[1] Moreover, it would not be surprising to find that the degree of efficiency across various markets may differ. For example, emerging markets, which are less intensively analyzed than U.S. markets and in which information is harder to come by, may be less efficient than U.S. markets. Small stocks, which receive less coverage by Wall Street analysts, may be less efficiently priced than large ones. Still, while we would not go so far as to say you absolutely cannot come up with new information, it still makes sense to consider and respect your competition.

Assume an investment management firm is managing a $5 billion portfolio. Suppose the fund manager can devise a research program that could increase the portfolio rate of return by one-tenth of 1% per year, a seemingly modest amount. This program would increase the dollar return to the portfolio by $5 billion × .001, or $5 million. Therefore, the fund is presumably willing to spend up to $5 million per year on research to increase stock returns by a mere one-tenth of 1% per year.

With such large rewards for such small increases in investment performance, is it any surprise that professional portfolio managers are willing to spend large sums on industry analysts, computer support, and research effort? With so many well-backed analysts willing to spend considerable resources on research, there cannot be many easy pickings in the market. Moreover, the incremental rates of return on research activity are likely to be so small that only managers of the largest portfolios will find them worth pursuing.

While it may not literally be true that *all* relevant information will be uncovered, it is virtually certain there are many investigators hot on the trail of any leads that seem likely to improve investment performance. Competition among these many well-backed, highly paid, aggressive analysts ensures that, as a general rule, stock prices ought to reflect available information regarding their proper levels.

Versions of the Efficient Market Hypothesis

It is common to distinguish among three versions of the EMH: the weak, the semistrong, and the strong forms of the hypothesis. These versions differ according to their notions of what is meant by the term *all available information.*

weak-form EMH
The assertion that stock prices already reflect all information contained in the history of past trading.

The **weak-form EMH** asserts that stock prices already reflect all information that can be derived by examining market trading data such as the history of past prices, trading volume, or short interest. This version of the hypothesis implies that trend analysis is fruitless. Past stock price data are publicly available and virtually costless to obtain. The weak-form hypothesis holds that if such data ever conveyed reliable signals about future performance, all investors would have learned long since to exploit the signals. Ultimately, the signals lose their value as they become widely known, because a buy signal, for instance, would result in an immediate price increase.

semistrong-form EMH
The assertion that stock prices already reflect all publicly available information.

The **semistrong-form EMH** states that all publicly available information regarding the prospects of a firm must be reflected already in the stock price. Such information includes, in addition to past prices, fundamental data on the firm's product line, quality of management, balance sheet composition, patents held, earnings forecasts, accounting practices, and so

---

[1]A challenging and insightful discussion of this point may be found in Sanford J. Grossman and Joseph E. Stiglitz, "On the Impossibility of Informationally Efficient Markets," *American Economic Review* 70 (June 1980).

strong-form EMH
The assertion that stock prices reflect all relevant information, including inside information.

forth. Again, if any investor has access to such information from publicly available sources, one would expect it to be reflected in stock prices.

Finally, the **strong-form EMH** states that stock prices reflect all information relevant to the firm, even including information available only to company insiders. This version of the hypothesis is quite extreme. Few would argue with the proposition that corporate officers have access to pertinent information long enough before public release to enable them to profit from trading on that information. Indeed, much of the activity of the Securities and Exchange Commission (SEC) is directed toward preventing insiders from profiting by exploiting their privileged situation. Rule 10b-5 of the Security Exchange Act of 1934 limits trading by corporate officers, directors, and substantial owners, requiring them to report trades to the SEC. Anyone trading on information supplied by insiders is considered in violation of the law.

Defining insider trading is not always easy, however. After all, stock analysts are in the business of uncovering information not already widely known to market participants. As we saw in Chapter 3, the distinction between private and inside information is sometimes murky.

Concept Check

1. If the weak form of the efficient market hypothesis is valid, must the strong form also hold? Conversely, does strong-form efficiency imply weak-form efficiency?

9.2 IMPLICATIONS OF THE EMH FOR INVESTMENT POLICY

Technical Analysis

technical analysis
Research on recurrent and predictable stock price patterns and on proxies for buy or sell pressure in the market.

Technical analysis is essentially the search for recurring and predictable patterns in stock prices. Although technicians recognize the value of information that has to do with future economic prospects of the firm, they believe such information is not necessary for a successful trading strategy. Whatever the fundamental reason for a change in stock price, if the stock price responds slowly enough, the analyst will be able to identify a trend that can be exploited during the adjustment period. Technical analysis assumes a sluggish response of stock prices to fundamental supply and demand factors. This assumption is diametrically opposed to the notion of an efficient market.

Technical analysts sometimes are called *chartists* because they study records or charts of past stock prices, hoping to find patterns they can exploit to make a profit. As an example of technical analysis, consider the *relative strength* approach. The chartist compares stock performance over a recent period to performance of the market or other stocks in the same industry. A simple version of relative strength takes the ratio of the stock price to a market indicator such as the S&P 500 index. If the ratio increases over time, the stock is said to exhibit relative strength, because its price performance is better than that of the broad market. Such strength presumably may continue for a long enough period to offer profit opportunities.

The efficient market hypothesis predicts that technical analysis is without merit. The past history of prices and trading volume is publicly available at minimal cost. Therefore, any information that was ever available from analyzing past prices has already been reflected in stock prices. As investors compete to exploit their common knowledge of a stock's price history, they necessarily drive stock prices to levels where expected rates of return are commensurate with risk. At those levels, stocks are neither bad nor good buys. They are just fairly priced, meaning one should not expect abnormal returns.

Despite these theoretical considerations, some technically oriented trading strategies would have generated abnormal profits in the past. We will consider these strategies, and technical analysis more generally, in Chapter 15.

Fundamental Analysis

fundamental analysis
Research on determinants of stock value, such as earnings and dividends prospects, expectations for future interest rates, and risk of the firm.

Fundamental analysis uses earnings and dividend prospects of the firm, expectations of future interest rates, and risk evaluation of the firm to determine proper stock prices. Ultimately, it represents an attempt to determine the present discounted value of all the payments a stockholder will receive from each share of stock. If that value exceeds the stock price, the fundamental analyst would recommend purchasing the stock.

Fundamental analysts usually start with a study of past earnings and an examination of company balance sheets. They supplement this analysis with further detailed economic analysis, ordinarily including an evaluation of the quality of the firm's management, the firm's standing within its industry, and the prospects for the industry as a whole. The hope is to attain some insight into the future performance of the firm that is not yet recognized by the rest of the market. Chapters 12 to 14 provide a detailed discussion of the types of analyses that underlie fundamental analysis.

Once again, the efficient market hypothesis predicts that *most* fundamental analysis adds little value. If analysts rely on publicly available earnings and industry information, one analyst's evaluation of the firm's prospects is not likely to be significantly more accurate than another's. There are many well-informed, well-financed firms conducting such market research, and in the face of such competition, it will be difficult to uncover data not also available to other analysts. Only analysts with a unique insight will be rewarded.

Fundamental analysis is much more difficult than merely identifying well-run firms with good prospects. Discovery of good firms does an investor no good in and of itself if the rest of the market also knows those firms are good. If the knowledge is already public, the investor will be forced to pay a high price for those firms and will not realize a superior rate of return.

The trick is not to identify firms that are good, but to find firms that are *better* than everyone else's estimate. Similarly, poorly run firms can be great bargains if they are not quite as bad as their stock prices suggest.

This is why fundamental analysis is difficult. It is not enough to do a good analysis of a firm; you can make money only if your analysis is better than that of your competitors because the market price is expected to already reflect all commonly available information.

Active versus Passive Portfolio Management

Casual efforts to pick stocks are not likely to pay off. Competition among investors ensures that any easily implemented stock evaluation technique will be used widely enough so that any insights derived will be reflected in stock prices. Only serious analysis and uncommon techniques are likely to generate the *differential* insight necessary to generate trading profits.

Moreover, these techniques are economically feasible only for managers of large portfolios. If you have only $100,000 to invest, even a 1% per year improvement in performance generates only $1,000 per year, hardly enough to justify herculean efforts. The billion-dollar manager, however, would reap extra income of $10 million annually for the same 1% increment.

If small investors are not in a favored position to conduct active portfolio management, what are their choices? The small investor probably is better off placing funds in a mutual fund. By pooling resources in this way, small investors can obtain the advantages of large size.

More difficult decisions remain, though. Can investors be sure that even large mutual funds have the ability or resources to uncover mispriced stocks? Further, will any mispricing uncovered be sufficiently large to repay the costs entailed in active portfolio management?

passive investment strategy
Buying a well-diversified portfolio without attempting to search out mispriced securities.

Proponents of the efficient market hypothesis believe active management is largely wasted effort and unlikely to justify the expenses incurred. Therefore, they advocate a **passive investment strategy** that makes no attempt to outsmart the market. A passive strategy aims only at establishing a well-diversified portfolio of securities without attempting to find under- or overvalued stocks. Passive management usually is characterized by a buy-and-hold strategy. Because the efficient market theory indicates stock prices are at fair levels, given all available information, it makes no sense to buy and sell securities frequently, as transactions generate large trading costs without increasing expected performance.

index fund
A mutual fund holding shares in proportion to their representation in a market index such as the S&P 500.

One common strategy for passive management is to create an **index fund,** which is a fund designed to replicate the performance of a broad-based index of stocks. For example, in 1976, the Vanguard Group of mutual funds introduced a mutual fund called the Index 500 Portfolio that holds stocks in direct proportion to their weight in the Standard & Poor's 500 stock price index. The performance of the Index 500 fund replicates the performance of the S&P 500. Investors in this fund obtain broad diversification with relatively low management fees. The fees can be kept to a minimum because Vanguard does not need to pay analysts to assess stock prospects and does not incur transaction costs from high portfolio turnover. While the typical annual expense ratio for an actively managed fund is over 1% of assets, Vanguard charges only about 0.2% for the Index 500 Portfolio.

Indexing has grown in appeal considerably since 1976. Vanguard's Index 500 Portfolio was the third-largest mutual fund by the end of 1996, with over $30 billion in assets. Several other firms have introduced S&P 500 index funds but Vanguard still dominates the retail market for indexing. Moreover, corporate pension plans now place more than one-fourth of their equity investments in index funds. Including pension funds and mutual funds, approximately $500 billion was indexed to the S&P 500 by the end of 1996. Many institutional investors now hold indexed bond portfolios as well as indexed stock portfolios.

Mutual funds now offer indexed portfolios that match a wide variety of market indexes. For example, some of the funds offered by the Vanguard Group track the S&P 500 index, the Wilshire 5000 index, the Salomon Brothers Broad Investment Grade Bond Index, the Russell 2000 index of small capitalization companies, the European equity market, and the Pacific Basin equity market.

Concept Check

2. What would happen to market efficiency if *all* investors attempted to follow a passive strategy?

The Role of Portfolio Management in an Efficient Market

If the market is efficient, why not throw darts at *The Wall Street Journal* instead of trying to choose a stock portfolio rationally? It's tempting to draw this sort of conclusion from the notion that security prices are fairly set, but it's a far too simple one. There is a role for rational portfolio management, even in perfectly efficient markets.

A basic principle in portfolio selection is diversification. Even if all stocks are priced fairly, each still poses firm-specific risk that can be eliminated through diversification. Therefore, rational security selection, even in an efficient market, calls for the selection of a carefully diversified portfolio. Moreover, that portfolio should provide the systematic risk level the investor wants. Even in an efficient market, investors must choose the risk-return profiles they deem appropriate.

Rational investment policy also requires that investors take tax considerations into account in security choice. If you are in a high tax bracket, you generally will not want the same securities that low-bracket investors find favorable. At an obvious level, high-bracket investors find it advantageous to buy tax-exempt municipal bonds despite their relatively low pretax yields, while those same bonds are unattractive to low-bracket investors. At a more subtle level, high-bracket investors might want to tilt or specialize their portfolios toward securities that provide capital gains as opposed to dividend or interest income, because the option to defer the realization of capital gains income is more valuable, the higher the investor's current tax bracket. High tax bracket investors also will be more attracted to investment opportunities where returns are sensitive to tax benefits, such as real estate ventures.

A third argument for rational portfolio management relates to the particular risk profile of the investor. For example, a General Motors executive whose annual bonus depends on GM's profits generally should not invest additional amounts in auto stocks. To the extent that his or her compensation already depends on GM's well-being, the executive is over-invested in GM now and should not exacerbate the lack of diversification.

Investors of varying ages also might warrant different portfolio policies with regard to risk bearing. For example, older investors who are essentially living off savings might avoid long-term bonds, whose market values fluctuate dramatically with changes in interest rates. Because these investors rely on accumulated savings, they require conservation of principal. In contrast, younger investors might be more inclined toward long-term bonds. The steady flow of income over long periods that is locked in with long-term bonds can be more important than preservation of principal to those with long life expectancies.

In short, there is a role for portfolio management even in an efficient market. Investors' optimal positions will vary according to factors such as age, tax bracket, risk aversion, and employment. The role of the portfolio manager in an efficient market is to tailor the portfolio to these needs, rather than to attempt to beat the market.

9.3 ARE MARKETS EFFICIENT?

The Issues

Not surprisingly, the efficient market hypothesis is not universally hailed by professional port-folio managers. It implies that a great deal of the activity of portfolio managers—the search for undervalued securities—is at best wasted effort and possibly harmful to clients because it costs money and leads to imperfectly diversified portfolios. Consequently, the EMH has never been widely accepted on Wall Street, and debate continues today on the degree to which security analysis can improve investment performance. Before discussing empirical tests of the hypoth-esis, we want to note three factors that together imply the debate probably never will be settled: the *magnitude issue*, the *selection bias issue*, and the *lucky event issue*.

The Magnitude Issue   Consider an investment manager overseeing a $2 billion portfolio. If she can improve performance by only one-tenth of 1% per year, that effort will be worth .001 × $2 billion = $2 million annually. This manager clearly would be worth her salary! Yet we, as observers, probably cannot statistically measure her contribution. A one-tenth of 1% contribution would be swamped by the yearly volatility of the market. Remember, the annual standard deviation of the well-diversified S&P 500 index has been more than 20% per year. Against these fluctuations, a small increase in performance would be hard to detect. Nevertheless, $2 million remains an extremely valuable improvement in performance.

All might agree that stock prices are very close to fair values, and that only managers of large portfolios can earn enough trading profits to make the exploitation of minor mispricing worth the effort. According to this view, the actions of intelligent investment managers are the driving force behind the constant evolution of market prices to fair levels. Rather than ask the qualitative question "Are markets efficient?" we ought instead to ask the more quantitative question "How efficient are markets?"

The Selection Bias Issue   Suppose you discover an investment scheme that could really make money. You have two choices: Either publish your technique in *The Wall Street Journal* to win fleeting fame, or keep your technique secret and use it to earn millions of dollars. Most investors would choose the latter option, which presents us with a conundrum. Only investors who find that an investment scheme cannot generate abnormal returns will be willing to report their findings to the whole world. Hence, opponents of the efficient mar-ket's view of the world always can use evidence that various techniques do not provide investment rewards as proof that the techniques that do work simply are not being reported

How to Guarantee a Successful Market Newsletter

Suppose you want to make your fortune publishing a market newsletter. You need first to convince potential subscribers that you have talent worth paying for. But what if you have no market prediction talent? The solution is simple: Start eight market newsletters.

In year one, let four of your newsletters predict an up market and four a down market. In year two, let half of the originally optimistic group of newsletters continue to predict an up market and the other half a down market. Do the same for the originally pessimistic group. Continue in this manner to obtain the following pattern of predictions (U = prediction of an up market, D = prediction of a down market.)

After three years, no matter what has happened to the market, one of the newsletters would have had a perfect

prediction record. This is because after three years, there are $2^3 = 8$ outcomes for the market, and we've covered all eight possibilities with the eight letters. Now, we simply slough off the seven unsuccessful newsletters and market the eighth letter based on its perfect track record. If we want to establish a letter with a perfect track record over a four-year period, we need $2^4 = 16$ newsletters. A five-year period requires 32 newsletters, and so on.

After the fact, the one newsletter that was always right will attract attention for your uncanny foresight and investors will rush to pay large fees for its advice. Your fortune is made, and you never even researched the market!

WARNING: This scheme is illegal! The point, however, is that with hundreds of market newsletters, you can find one that has stumbled onto an apparently remarkable string of successful predictions without any real degree of skill. After the fact, *someone's* prediction history can seem to imply great forecasting skill. This person is the one we will read about in *The Wall Street Journal*; the others will be forgotten.

	Newsletter Predictions							
Year	1	2	3	4	5	6	7	8
1	U	U	U	U	D	D	D	D
2	U	U	D	D	U	U	D	D
3	U	D	U	D	U	D	U	D

to the public. This is a problem in *selection bias*; the outcomes we are able to observe have been preselected in favor of failed attempts. Therefore, we cannot fairly evaluate the true ability of portfolio managers to generate winning stock market strategies.

The Lucky Event Issue   In virtually any month, it seems we read an article in *The Wall Street Journal* about some investor or investment company with a fantastic investment performance over the recent past. Surely the superior records of such investors disprove the efficient market hypothesis.

This conclusion is far from obvious, however. As an analogy to the "contest" among portfolio managers, consider a contest to flip the most heads out of 50 trials using a fair coin. The expected outcome for any person is 50% heads and 50% tails. If 10,000 people, however, compete in this contest, it would not be surprising if at least one or two contestants flipped more than 75% heads. In fact, elementary statistics tells us that the expected number of contestants flipping 75% or more heads would be two. It would be silly, though, to crown these people the head-flipping champions of the world. They are simply the contestants who happened to get lucky on the day of the event (See the box on this page).

The analogy to efficient markets is clear. Under the hypothesis that any stock is fairly priced given all available information, any bet on a stock is simply a coin toss. There is equal likelihood of winning or losing the bet. Yet, if many investors using a variety of schemes make fair bets, statistically speaking, *some* of those investors will be lucky and win a great majority of bets. For every big winner, there may be many big losers, but we never hear of these managers. The winners, though, turn up in *The Wall Street Journal* as the latest stock market gurus; then they can make a fortune publishing market newsletters.

Our point is that after the fact there will have been at least one successful investment scheme. A doubter will call the results luck; the successful investor will call it skill. The proper test would be to see whether the successful investors can repeat their performance in another period, yet this approach is rarely taken.

With these caveats in mind, we now turn to some of the empirical tests of the efficient market hypothesis.

Concept Check

3. Fidelity's Magellan Fund outperformed the S&P 500 in 11 of the 13 years that Peter Lynch managed the fund, resulting in an average annual return for this period more than 10% better than that of the index. Is Lynch's performance sufficient to cause you to doubt the efficient markets theory? If not, would *any* performance record be sufficient to dissuade you?

Tests of Predictability in Stock Market Returns

Returns over Short Horizons   Early tests of efficient markets were tests of the weak form. Could speculators find trends in past prices that would enable them to earn abnormal profits? This is essentially a test of the efficacy of technical analysis.

The already-cited work of Kendall and of Roberts (1959), both of whom analyzed the possible existence of patterns in stock prices, suggest that such patterns are not to be found. One way of discerning trends in stock prices is by measuring the *serial correlation* of stock market returns. Serial correlation refers to the tendency for stock returns to be related to past returns. Positive serial correlation means that positive returns tend to follow positive returns (a momentum type of property). Negative serial correlation means that positive returns tend to be followed by negative returns (a reversal or "correction" property).

Both Conrad and Kaul (1988) and Lo and MacKinlay (1988) examine weekly returns of NYSE stocks and find positive serial correlation over short horizons. However, the correlation coefficients of weekly returns tend to be fairly small, at least for large stocks for which price data are the most reliably up-to-date. Thus, while these studies demonstrate price trends over short periods, the evidence does not clearly suggest the existence of trading opportunities.

filter rule
A rule for buying or selling stock according to recent price movements.

A more sophisticated version of trend analysis is a **filter rule.** A filter technique gives a rule for buying or selling a stock depending on past price movements. One rule, for example, might be: "Buy if the last two trades each resulted in a stock price increase." A more conventional one might be: "Buy a security if its price increased by 1%, and hold it until its price falls by more than 1% from the subsequent high." Alexander (1964) and Fama and Blume (1966) found that such filter rules generally could not generate trading profits.

These very short-horizon studies offer the suggestion of momentum in stock market prices, albeit of a magnitude that may be too small to exploit. However, in an investigation of intermediate horizon stock price behavior (using 3- to 12-month holding periods), Jegadeesh and Titman (1993) found that stocks exhibit a momentum property in which good or bad recent performance continues. They conclude that while the performance of individual stocks is highly unpredictable, *portfolios* of the best-performing stocks in the recent past appear to outperform other stocks with enough reliability to offer profit opportunities.

Returns over Long Horizons   While studies of short-horizon returns have detected minor positive serial correlation in stock market prices, more recent tests[2] of long-horizon returns (that is, returns over multiyear periods) have found suggestions of pronounced negative long-term serial correlation. The latter result has given rise to a "fads hypothesis," which asserts that stock prices might overreact to relevant news. Such overreaction leads to positive serial correlation (momentum) over short time horizons. Subsequent correction of the overreaction leads to poor performance following good performance and vice versa. The corrections mean that a run of positive returns eventually will tend to be followed by negative returns, leading to negative serial correlation over longer horizons. These episodes

---

[2]Eugene F. Fama and Kenneth R. French, "Permanent and Temporary Components of Stock Prices," *Journal of Political Economy* 96 (April 1988), pp. 246–73; James Poterba and Lawrence Summers, "Mean Reversion in Stock Prices: Evidence and Implications," *Journal of Financial Economics* 22 (October 1988), pp. 27–59.

of apparent overshooting followed by correction give stock prices the appearance of fluctuating around their fair values and suggest that market prices exhibit excessive volatility compared to intrinsic value.[3]

These long-horizon results are dramatic, but the studies offer far from conclusive evidence regarding efficient markets. First, the study results need not be interpreted as evidence for stock market fads. An alternative interpretation of these results holds that they indicate only that market risk premiums vary over time: The response of market prices to variation in the risk premium can lead one to incorrectly infer the presence of mean reversion and excess volatility in prices. For example, when the risk premium and the required return on the market rises, stock prices will fall. When the market then rises (on average) at this higher rate of return, the data convey the impression of a stock price recovery. The impression of overshooting and correction is in fact no more than a rational response of market prices to changes in discount rates.

Second, these studies suffer from statistical problems. Because they rely on returns measured over long time periods, these tests of necessity are based on few observations of long-horizon returns. Moreover, it appears that much of the statistical support for mean reversion in stock market prices derives from returns during the Great Depression. Other periods do not provide strong support for the fads hypothesis.[4]

Predictors of Broad Market Movements

Several studies have documented the ability of easily observed variables to predict market returns. For example, Fama and French (1988) show that the return on the aggregate stock market tends to be higher when the dividend/price ratio, the dividend yield, is high. Campbell and Shiller (1988) find that the earnings yield can predict market returns. Keim and Stambaugh (1986) show that bond market data such as the spread between yields on high- and low-grade corporate bonds also help predict broad market returns.

Again, the interpretation of these results is difficult. On the one hand, they may imply that stock returns can be predicted, in violation of the efficient market hypothesis. More probably, however, these variables are proxying for variation in the market risk premium. For example, given a level of dividends or earnings, stock prices will be lower and dividend and earnings yields will be higher when the risk premium (and therefore the expected market return) is larger. Thus, a high dividend or earnings yield will be associated with higher market returns. This does not indicate a violation of market efficiency. The predictability of market returns is due to predictability in the risk premium, not in risk-adjusted abnormal returns.

Fama and French (1989) show that the yield spread between high- and low-grade bonds has greater predictive power for returns on low-grade bonds than for returns on high-grade bonds, and greater predictive power for stock returns than for bond returns, suggesting that the predictability in returns is in fact a risk premium rather than evidence of market inefficiency. Similarly, the fact that the dividend yield on stocks helps to predict bond market returns suggests that the yield captures a risk premium common to both markets rather than mispricing in the equity market.

Portfolio Strategies and Market Anomalies

Fundamental analysis calls on a much wider range of information to create portfolios than does technical analysis, and tests of the value of fundamental analysis, therefore, are correspondingly more difficult to evaluate. They have, however, revealed a number of so-called

---

[3]The fads debate started as a controversy over whether stock prices exhibit excess volatility. See Robert J. Shiller, "Do Stock Prices Move Too Much to Be Justified by Subsequent Changes in Dividends?" *American Economic Review* 71 (June 1971), pp. 421–36. However, it is now apparent that excess volatility and fads are essentially different ways of describing the same phenomenon.

[4]Myung J. Kim, Charles R. Nelson, and Richard Startz, "Mean Reversion in Stock Prices? A Reappraisal of the Empirical Evidence," National Bureau of Economic Research Working Paper No. 2795, December 1988.

anomalies, that is, evidence that seems inconsistent with the efficient market hypothesis. We will review several such anomalies in the following pages.

One major problem with these tests is that most require risk adjustments to portfolio performance, and most tests use the CAPM to make the risk adjustments. We know that even if beta is a relevant descriptor of stock risk, the empirically measured quantitative trade-off between risk as measured by beta and expected return differs from the predictions of the CAPM. If we use the CAPM to adjust portfolio returns for risk, inappropriate adjustments might lead to the incorrect conclusion that various portfolio strategies can generate superior returns.

Tests of risk-adjusted returns are *joint tests* of the efficient market hypothesis *and* the risk adjustment procedure. If it appears that a portfolio strategy can generate superior returns, we then must choose between rejecting the EMH or rejecting the risk adjustment technique. Usually, the risk adjustment technique is based on more questionable assumptions than the EMH; if we reject the procedure, we are left with no conclusion about market efficiency.

P/E effect
Portfolios of low P/E stocks have exhibited higher average risk-adjusted returns than high P/E stocks.

An example of this problem is the discovery by Basu (1977, 1983) that portfolios of low price/earnings ratio stocks have higher average returns than high P/E portfolios. The **P/E effect** holds up even if returns are adjusted for portfolio beta. Is this a confirmation that the market systematically misprices stocks according to the P/E ratio?

This would be a surprising and, to us, disturbing conclusion, because analysis of P/E ratios is such a simple procedure. While it may be possible to earn superior returns using hard work and much insight, it hardly seems likely that following such a basic technique is enough to generate abnormal returns.

One possible interpretation of these results is that the model of capital market equilibrium is at fault in that the returns are not properly adjusted for risk.

This makes sense, since if two firms have the same expected earnings, then the riskier stock will sell at a lower price and lower P/E ratio. Because of its higher risk, the low P/E stock also will have higher expected returns. Therefore, unless the CAPM beta fully adjusts for risk, P/E will act as a useful additional descriptor of risk and will be associated with abnormal returns if the CAPM is used to establish benchmark performance.

small-firm effect
Stocks of small firms have earned abnormal returns, primarily in the month of January.

The Small-Firm-in-January Effect   One of the most frequently cited anomalies with respect to the efficient market hypothesis is the so-called size or **small-firm effect,** originally documented by Banz (1981). Banz found that both total and risk-adjusted rates of return tend to fall with increases in the relative size of the firm, as measured by the market value of the firm's outstanding equity. Dividing all NYSE stocks into quintiles according to firm size, Banz found that the average annual return of firms in the smallest size quintile was 19.8% greater than the average return of firms in the largest size quintile.

This is a huge premium; imagine earning an extra return of this amount on a billion-dollar portfolio. Yet it is remarkable that following a simple (even simplistic) rule such as "invest in low capitalization stocks" should enable an investor to earn excess returns. After all, any investor can measure firm size costlessly. One would not expect such minimal effort to yield such large rewards.

Later studies (Keim [1983], Reinganum [1983], and Blume and Stambaugh [1983]) showed that the small-firm effect occurs virtually entirely in the first two weeks of January. The size effect is in fact a small-firm-in-January effect.

Figure 9.1 illustrates the January effect. Keim ranked firms in order of increasing size as measured by market value of equity and then divided them into 10 portfolios grouped by the size of each firm. In each month of the year, he calculated the difference in the average excess return of firms in the smallest-firm portfolio and largest-firm portfolio. The average monthly differences over the years 1963–1979 appear in Figure 9.1. January clearly stands out as an exceptional month for small firms, with an average small firm premium of 0.714% (an annualized premium of 8.9%).

FIGURE 9.1

Average Difference between Daily Excess Returns (in Percentages) of Lowest-Firm-Size and Highest-Firm-Size Deciles by Month

Source: Data from Donald B. Keim "Size Related Anomalies and Stock Return Seasonality: Further Empirical Evidence," *Journal of Financial Economics* 12 (June 1983).

FIGURE 9.2

Average Daily Returns of Small Firms in January for Securities in the Upper Quartile and Bottom Quartile of the Tax-Loss Selling Distribution

Source: Marc R. Reinganum, "The Anomalous Stock Market Behavior of Small Firms in January: Empirical Tests for Tax-Loss Effects," *Journal of Financial Economics* 12 (June 1983).

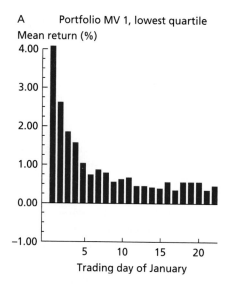

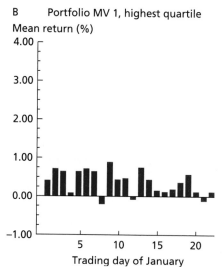

Some researchers believe the January effect is tied to tax-loss selling at the end of the year. The hypothesis is that many people sell stocks that have declined in price during the previous months to realize their capital losses before the end of the tax year. Such investors do not put the proceeds from these sales back into the stock market until after the turn of the year. At that point, the rush of demand for stock places an upward pressure on prices that results in the January effect. Finally, the January effect is said to show up most dramatically for the smallest firms because the small-firm group includes, as an empirical matter, stocks with the greatest variability of prices during the year. The group, therefore, includes a relatively large number of firms that have declined sufficiently to induce tax-loss selling.

Some empirical evidence supports the belief that the January effect is connected to tax-loss selling. For example, Ritter (1988) shows that the ratio of stock purchases to sales by individual investors is below normal in late December and above normal in early January. This is consistent with tax-loss rebalancing.

Reinganum (1983) found that within size class, firms that had declined more severely in price had larger January returns. This pattern is illustrated in Figure 9.2. Reinganum divided firms into quartiles based on the extent to which stock prices had declined during the year. Big price declines would be expected to generate big January returns if these firms tend to be unloaded in December and enjoy demand pressure in January. The figure shows that the lowest quartile (biggest tax loss) portfolios within the smallest size group show the greatest January effect.

TABLE 9.1
January Effect by
Degree of Neglect

Source: From Avner Arbel, "Generic Stocks: An Old Product in a New Package," *Journal of Portfolio Management*, Summer 1985, pp. 4–13.

	Average January Return (%)	Average January Return minus Average Return during Rest of Year (%)	Average January Return after Adjusting for Systematic Risk (%)
S&P 500 Companies			
Highly researched	2.48	1.63	−1.44
Moderately researched	4.95	4.19	1.69
Neglected	7.62	6.87	5.03
Non-S&P 500 Companies			
Neglected	11.32	10.72	7.71

The fundamental question is why market participants do not exploit the January effect and thereby ultimately eliminate it by bidding stock prices to appropriate levels. One possible explanation lies in segmentation of the market into two groups: institutional investors who invest primarily in large firms, and individual investors who invest disproportionately in smaller firms. According to this view, managers of large institutional portfolios are the moving force behind efficient markets. It is professionals who seek out profit opportunities and bid prices to their appropriate levels. Institutional investors do not seem to buy at the small-size end of the market, perhaps because of limits on allowed portfolio positions, so the small-firm anomaly persists without the force of their participation.

Concept Check

4. Does this market segmentation theory get the efficient market hypothesis off the hook, or are there still market mechanisms that, in theory, ought to eliminate the small-firm anomaly?

The Neglected-Firm Effect and Liquidity Effects   Arbel and Strebel (1983) give another interpretation of the small-firm effect. Because small firms tend to be neglected by large institutional traders, information about such firms is less available. This information deficiency makes smaller firms riskier investments that command higher returns. "Brand-name" firms, after all, are subject to considerable monitoring from institutional investors that assures high-quality information, and presumably investors do not purchase "generic" stocks without the prospect of greater returns.

neglected-firm effect
The tendency of investments in stock of less well-known firms to generate abnormal returns.

As evidence for the **neglected-firm effect,** Arbel (1985) measures the information deficiency of firms using the coefficient of variation of analysts' forecasts of earnings. (The coefficient of variation is the ratio of standard deviation to mean and measures the dispersion of forecasts. It is a "noise-to-signal" ratio.) The correlation coefficient between the coefficient of variation and total return was 0.676, quite high, and statistically significant. In a related test, Arbel divided firms into highly researched, moderately researched, and neglected groups based on the number of institutions holding the stock. Table 9.1 shows that the January effect was largest for the neglected firms.

Research by Amihud and Mendelson (1991) on the effect of liquidity on stock returns might be related to both the small-firm and neglected-firm effects. They argue that investors will demand a rate-of-return premium to invest in less liquid stocks that entail higher trading costs. Indeed, spreads for the least liquid stocks easily can be more than 5% of stock value. In accord with their hypothesis, Amihud and Mendelson show that these stocks show a strong tendency to exhibit abnormally high risk-adjusted rates of return. Because small and less-analyzed stocks as a rule are less liquid, the liquidity effect might be a partial explanation of their abnormal returns. However, this theory does not explain why the abnormal returns of small firms should be concentrated in January. In any case, exploiting these effects

FIGURE 9.3

Average Rate of Return
as a Function of the
Book-to-Market Ratio

Source: Eugene F. Fama and
Kenneth R. French, "The
Cross Section of Expected
Stock Returns," *Journal of
Finance* 47 (1992),
pp. 427–65.

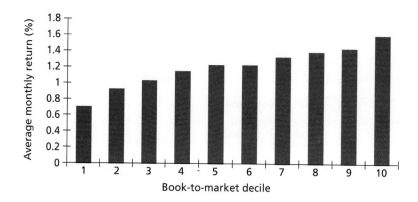

can be more difficult than it would appear. The effect of trading costs on small stocks can easily wipe out any apparent abnormal profit opportunity.

Book-to-Market Ratios   Fama and French (1992) and Reinganum (1988) show that a seemingly powerful predictor of returns across securities is the ratio of the book value of the firm's equity to the market value of equity. Fama and French stratify firms into 10 groups according to book-to-market ratios and examine the average monthly rate of return of each of the 10 groups during the period July 1963 through December 1990. The decile with the highest book-to-market ratio had an average monthly return of 1.65%, while the lowest-ratio decile averaged only 0.72% per month. Figure 9.3 shows the pattern of returns across deciles. The dramatic dependence of returns on book-to-market ratio is independent of beta, suggesting either that high book-to-market ratio firms are relatively underpriced, or that the book-to-market ratio is serving as a proxy for a risk factor that affects equilibrium expected returns.

In fact, Fama and French found that after controlling for the size and book-to-market effects, beta seemed to have no power to explain average security returns.[5] This finding is an important challenge to the notion of rational markets, since it seems to imply that a factor that should affect returns—systematic risk—seems not to matter, while a factor that should not matter—the book-to-market ratio—seems capable of predicting future returns. We will return to the interpretation of this anomaly below.

Reversals   While some of the studies cited above suggest momentum in stock market prices over short horizons (of less than one year), many other studies suggest that over longer horizons, extreme stock market performance tends to reverse itself: The stocks that have performed best in the recent past seem to underperform the rest of the market in following periods, while the worst past performers tend to offer above-average future performance. DeBondt and Thaler (1985) and Chopra, Lakonishok, and Ritter (1992) find strong tendencies for poorly performing stocks in one period to experience sizable reversals over the subsequent period, while the best-performing stocks in a given period tend to follow with poor performance in the following period.

For example, the DeBondt and Thaler study found that if one were to rank order the performance of stocks over a five-year period and then group stocks into portfolios based on investment performance, the base-period "loser" portfolio (defined as the 35 stocks with the worst investment performance) would outperform the "winner" portfolio (the top 35 stocks) by an average of 25% (cumulative return) in the following three-year period. This

---

[5]In a recent study, Kothari, Shanken, and Sloan (1995) found that when betas are estimated using annual rather than monthly returns, securities with high beta values do in fact have higher average returns. Moreover, they found a book-to-market effect that is attenuated compared to the results in Fama and French and furthermore is inconsistent across different samples of securities. They conclude that the empirical case for the importance of the book-to-market ratio may be somewhat weaker than the Fama–French study would suggest.

reversal effect
The tendency of poorly performing stocks and well-performing stocks in one period to experience reversals in the following period.

reversal effect, in which losers rebound and winners fade back, seems to suggest that the stock market overreacts to relevant news. After the overreaction is recognized, extreme investment performance is reversed. This phenomenon would imply that a *contrarian* investment strategy—investing in recent losers and avoiding recent winners—should be profitable. Moreover, these returns seem pronounced enough to be exploited profitably.

Risk Premiums or Inefficiencies?   The small-firm, book-to-market, and reversal effects are currently among the most puzzling phenomena in empirical finance. There are several interpretations of these effects. First note that, to some extent, these three phenomena may be related. The feature that small firms, high book-to-market firms, and recent stock market "losers" seem to have in common is a stock price that has fallen considerably in recent months or years. Indeed, a firm can become a small firm, or can become a high book-to-market firm, by suffering a sharp drop in price. These groups therefore may contain a relatively high proportion of distressed firms that have suffered recent difficulties.

Fama and French (1993) argue that these anomalies can be explained as manifestations of risk premiums. Using an arbitrage pricing approach,[6] they show that stocks with greater sensitivity to size or book-to-market factors have higher average returns and interpret these returns as evidence of a risk premium associated with these factors. Fama and French argue that a so-called *three-factor model*, in which risk is determined by the sensitivity of a stock to (1) the market portfolio, (2) a portfolio that reflects the relative returns of small versus large firms, and (3) a portfolio that reflects the relative returns of firms with high versus low ratios of book value to market value, does a good job in explaining security returns. While size or book-to-market ratios per se are obviously not risk factors, they perhaps might act as proxies for more fundamental determinants of risk. Fama and French argue that these patterns of returns may therefore be consistent with an efficient market in which expected returns are consistent with risk.

The opposite interpretation is offered by Lakonishok, Shleifer, and Vishney (1995), who argue that these phenomena are evidence of inefficient markets—more specifically, of systematic errors in the forecasts of stock market analysts. They present evidence that analysts extrapolate past performance too far into the future and therefore overprice firms with recent good performance and underprice firms with recent poor performance. Ultimately, when market participants recognize their errors, prices reverse. This explanation is obviously consistent with the reversal effect and also, to a degree, with the small firm and book-to-market effects because firms with sharp price drops may tend be small or have high book-to-market ratios.

If Lakonishok, Shleifer, and Vishney are correct, we ought to find that analysts systematically err when forecasting returns of recent "winner" versus "loser" firms. A recent study by La Porta (1996) is consistent with this pattern. He finds that the equity of firms for which analysts predict low earnings growth actually perform better than those with high predicted earnings growth. Analysts seem overly pessimistic about firms with low growth prospects, and overly optimistic about firms with high growth prospects. When those too-extreme expectations are "corrected," the low-expected-growth firms outperform the high-expected-growth firms.

Inside Information   It would not be surprising if insiders were able to make superior profits trading in their firm's stock. The ability of insiders to trade profitability in their own stock has been documented in studies by Jaffee (1974), Seyhun (1986), Givoly and Palmon (1985), and others. Jaffee's was one of the earliest studies to show the tendency for stock prices to rise after insiders intensively bought shares and to fall after intensive insider sales.

To level the playing field, the Securities and Exchange Commission requires all insiders to register all their trading activity, and it publishes these trades in an *Official Summary of Insider*

---

[6]We discussed arbitrage pricing models in Chapter 8, Section 8.4.

Trading. Once the *Official Summary* is published, the trades become public information. At that point, if markets are efficient, fully and immediately processing the information released, an investor should no longer be able to profit from following the pattern of those trades.

Surprisingly, early studies like Jaffee's seemed to indicate that following insider transactions, that is, buying after inside purchases were reported in the *Official Summary* and selling after insider sales, could offer substantial abnormal returns to an outside investor. This would be a clear violation of market efficiency, as the data in the *Official Summary* are publicly available. Work since then by Seyhun, who carefully tracked the public release dates of the *Official Summary*, found that following insider transactions would be to no avail. While there is some tendency for stock prices to increase even after the *Official Summary* reports insider buying, the abnormal returns are not of sufficient magnitude to overcome transaction costs.

Postearnings Announcement Price Drift   A fundamental principle of efficient markets is that any new information ought to be reflected in stock prices very rapidly. When good news is made public, for example, the stock price should jump immediately. A puzzling anomaly, therefore, is the apparently sluggish response of stock prices to firms' earnings announcements.

The "news content" of an earnings announcement can be evaluated by comparing the announcement of actual earnings to the value previously expected by market participants. The difference is the "earnings surprise." (Market expectations of earnings can be roughly measured by averaging the published earnings forecasts of Wall Street analysts or by applying trend analysis to past earnings.) Foster, Olsen, and Shevlin (1984) have examined the impact of earnings announcements on stock returns.

Each earnings announcement for a large sample of firms was placed in 1 of 10 deciles ranked by the magnitude of the earnings surprise, and the abnormal returns of the stock in each decile were calculated. The abnormal return in a period is the return of a portfolio of all stocks in a given decile after adjusting for both the market return in that period and the portfolio beta. It measures return over and above what would be expected given market conditions in that period. Figure 9.4 is a graph of the cumulative abnormal returns for each decile.

FIGURE 9.4

Cumulative Abnormal Returns in Response to Earnings Announcements

Source: Foster, George; Chris Olsen; and Terry Shevlin. "Earnings Releases, Anomalies, and the Behavior of Security Returns," *The Accounting Review* 59 (October 1984).

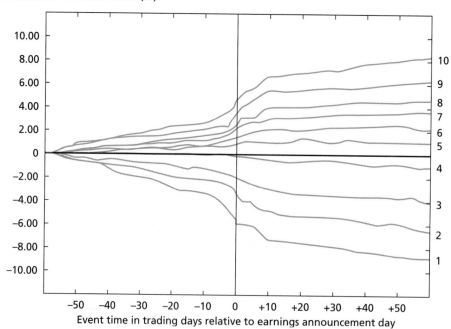

Cumulative abnormal return (%)

Event time in trading days relative to earnings announcement day

The results of this study are dramatic. The correlation between ranking by earnings surprise and abnormal returns across deciles is as predicted. There is a large abnormal return (a large increase in cumulative abnormal return) on the earnings announcement day (time 0). The abnormal return is positive for positive-surprise firms and negative for negative-surprise firms.

The more remarkable, and interesting, result of the study concerns stock price movements *after* the announcement date. The cumulative abnormal returns of positive-surprise stocks continue to grow even after the earnings information becomes public, while the negative-surprise firms continue to suffer negative abnormal returns. The market appears to adjust to the earnings information only gradually, resulting in a sustained period of abnormal returns.

Evidently, one could have earned abnormal profits simply by waiting for earnings announcements and purchasing a stock portfolio of positive earnings-surprise companies. These are precisely the types of predictable continuing trends that ought to be impossible in an efficient market.

Some research suggests that the postannouncement drift in security prices might be related in part to trading costs. Bernard and Thomas (1989) find that postannouncement abnormal returns increase with the magnitude of the earnings surprise until it becomes fairly large. Beyond this point, they speculate, the change in the perceived value of the firm due to the earnings announcement is so large that transaction costs no longer impede trading and prices change more rapidly. They also point out that postannouncement abnormal returns are larger for smaller firms, for which trading costs are higher. Still, these results do not satisfactorily explain the postannouncement drift anomaly. First, while trading costs may explain the existence of postannouncement drift, they do not explain why the total *postannouncement* abnormal return is higher for firms with higher earnings surprises. Second, Bernard and Thomas show that firms with positive earnings surprises in one quarter exhibit positive abnormal returns at the earnings announcement in the *following* quarter, suggesting that the market does not fully account for the implications of current earnings announcements when it revises its expectations for future earnings. This suggests informational inefficiency, leaving this phenomenon a topic for future research.

The Value Line Enigma　The Value Line Investment Survey is an investment advisory service that ranks securities on a timeliness scale of one (best buy) to five (sell). Ranks are based on relative earnings and price performance across securities, price momentum, quarterly earnings momentum, and a measure of unexpected earnings in the most recent quarter. The Value Line technique is discussed in more detail in Chapter 15 on technical analysis.

Several studies have examined the predictive value of the Value Line recommendations. Black (1971) found that Portfolio 1 (the "buy" portfolio) had a risk-adjusted excess rate of return of 10%, while Portfolio 5 (the "sell" portfolio) had an abnormal return of − 10%. These results imply a fantastic potential value to the Value Line forecasts. Copeland and Mayers (1982) performed a similar study using a more sophisticated risk-adjustment technique, which found that the difference in the risk-adjusted performance of Portfolios 1 and 5 was much smaller: Portfolio 1 earned an abnormal six-month rate of return of 1.52%, while Portfolio 5 earned an abnormal return of − 2.97%. Even this smaller difference, however, seems to be a substantial deviation from the prediction of the efficient market hypothesis, although it is an open question as to whether the abnormal returns present profit opportunities after accounting for bid-ask spreads and transaction costs.

Of course, we should note that the Value Line effect is not wholly independent of other anomalies. Notice that two of Value Line's criteria are earnings momentum and unexpected earnings. Therefore, a good part of the effect may be a manifestation of post-earnings announcement drift.

The Market Crash of October 1987　The market crash of October 1987 seems to be a glaring counterexample to the efficient market hypothesis. If prices reflect market fundamentals, then defenders of the EMH must look for news on the 19th of that month that was

The 'Efficient Market' Was a Good Idea—and Then Came the Crash

IT LAUNCHED A REVOLUTION, BUT THE THEORY CAN'T EXPLAIN WHY INVESTORS PANICKED ON OCTOBER 19

The October 19 stock market collapse crushed more than $500 billion in investor wealth. It also struck a blow against one of the most powerful ideas in finance—the efficient market theory (EMT).

That theory bucked the popular view that stocks move on the latest fad or the speculative fever of the crowd. Well-informed investors could make a bundle, went the conventional wisdom. Not so, says the EMT. The stock market is an efficient information processing machine. Investors act rationally, and stock prices reflect whatever information people have about the fundamentals, such as present and future earnings. Stock prices change only on fresh news—and that doesn't include crowd psychology.

HERD INSTINCT

The theory had few believers back in the early 1960s. But the EMT ended up launching a market revolution. Finance professors and math whizzes built careers on Wall Street exploiting its insights. For instance, the theory says that you can't consistently outperform the market averages, since only unexpected news moves prices. Did the EMT catch on with big money? You bet. Many pension-fund sponsors turned their backs on money managers who claimed that they could beat the market and bought some $175 billion in index funds that track the market.

Then came Bloody Monday. Efficient market theory is useless in explaining the biggest stock market calamity in 58 years. What new information jarred investors into slashing their estimate of the value of corporate America's assets by some 23% in the 6½ hours the New York Stock Exchange was open? Hardly enough news came out that day, or over the weekend, to account for the plunge.

Indeed, a survey by Yale University's Robert Shiller of nearly 1,000 big and small investors showed that the reason for selling was not a change in the fundamentals. Rather, it was the declines that took place in the market itself the Thursday and Friday before, as well as the sharp sell-off on the morning of October 19. "Lots of nervous people came to believe the price drops themselves signaled a crash, and everyone tried to be the first out the door," says Shiller. Investors panicked because the market was falling like a stone. There was no rationality, only herd instinct.

The rout of the efficient market theory holds important implications not only for investors but also for the idea that the market is the best possible way to channel capital to its most productive uses. According to this belief, investors allowed to choose in a competitive market will funnel money to those companies with the best prospects. It's no coincidence that the EMT was mainly developed at the University of Chicago, a laissez-faire bastion. Moreover, the so-called derivative securities—stock index futures and options—were conceived in the Windy City and traded on the Chicago exchanges largely because of the impetus from the university's free market theorists, who argued that the new instruments would make the stock market even more efficient.

REASON TO BELIEVE

But if crowd psychology, not rationality, rules stock prices, investors and policymakers might be getting the wrong signals from the market. Money might flow to unproductive businesses, such as junk-bond-financed leveraged buyouts. Meanwhile, companies spending a lot on future products

---

consistent with the 20% one-day decline in stock prices. Yet no events of such importance seem to have transpired on that date. The fantastic price swing is hard to reconcile with market fundamentals. The accompanying box (page 248) offers an assessment of efficient market theory in light of the crash.

Concept Check

5. Some say that continued worry concerning the U.S. trade deficit brought down the market on October 19. Is this explanation consistent with the EMH?

Mutual Fund Performance   We have documented some of the apparent chinks in the armor of efficient market proponents. Ultimately, however, from the perspective of portfolio management, the issue of market efficiency boils down to whether skilled investors can make consistent abnormal trading profits. The best test is simply to look at the performance of market professionals and see if their performance is superior to that of a passive index fund that buys and holds the market.

concluded

and cultivating markets could starve for cheap capital. Even Chicago's pioneering efficient-market theorist Eugene Fama admits the EMT is "a matter of belief" to him. If prices are not being set the way the theory assumes, then the free market system is not allocating resources efficiently, says Fama.

Signs that the EMT doesn't work began to show up in the stock market well before Bloody Monday. The crash is only the latest, most dramatic, instance of the theory's failure. A cottage industry has sprung up in academe documenting market "anomalies" inconsistent with the EMT. Take the "January effect." Small-capitalization stocks repeatedly show large returns during the first five trading days of the year. According to the EMT, the January effect shouldn't persist. Sophisticated investors, anticipating the easy gains, should have bid up prices well before the beginning of the year.

Other economists believe they have found further instances of investor irrationality. A study by economists Richard Thaler and Werner DeBondt shows that a stock portfolio made up of the 35 worst-performing NYSE issues consistently outperformed the market by an average of 19.6% over a period of three years. The reason, explains Thaler, is that investors overreacted to the bad news and drove the dogs way down—far below what they were really worth. Stocks again and again overshoot the fundamentals, a finding that doesn't square with the EMT.

NEVER SAY DIE

The EMT is far from dead, however. Yale University's Stephen Ross challenges the view that there was little news to

account for the crash. He says volatility rose as investors became nervous about the market weeks before October 19. Under the circumstances, "only a small change in news can start an avalanche," says Ross.

The market should have been able to hold back the avalanche, says the EMT theorist, but the exchanges simply broke down. The Brady report pointed out that many NYSE specialists buckled under pressure on Oct. 19 and 20 and were selling, not buying. At the same time, the Big Board computers could not handle he volume. The institutions that make up the market failed, not the EMT.

Still, there is evidence that the stock market is not as competitive as the efficient market theorists believe. the Brady report said that a handful of mutual and pension funds unleashed enormous selling pressure at the opening of the market on Bloody Monday, swamping the system. For the EMT to work, no one seller should be able to influence the market very much. More telling, four months after the crash, the Dow Jones industrial average is still some 800 points below its peak in August. What changes in U.S. business prospects can account for such a downgrading?

The arguments over the EMT are likely to continue. But the theory's apparent failure to explain the greatest stock market crash in history may suggest to policymakers and to the exchanges that the "market" is not all that it was cracked up to be.

Source: "The 'Efficient Market' Was a Good Idea—Then Came the Crash," by Christopher Farrell, BUSINESS WEEK magazine, 22 February 1988, pp. 140–141.

As we pointed out in Chapter 4, casual evidence does not support the claim that professionally managed portfolios can consistently beat the market. Figures 4.3 and 4.4 in that chapter demonstrated that between 1972 and 1995, a passive portfolio indexed to the Wilshire 5000 typically would have better returns than the average equity fund. On the other hand, there was some (admittedly inconsistent) evidence (see Table 4.3) of persistence in performance, meaning that the better managers in one period tended to be better managers in following periods. Such a pattern would suggest that the better managers can with some consistency outperform their competitors and would be inconsistent with the notion that market prices already reflect all relevant information.

On the other hand, the analyses in Chapter 4 were based on total returns unadjusted for exposure to systematic risk factors. In this section, we will revisit the question of mutual fund performance, paying more attention to the benchmark against which performance ought to be evaluated.

As a first pass, we can examine the risk-adjusted returns (i.e., the alpha, or return in excess of required return based on beta and the market return in each period) of a large sample of mutual funds. Malkiel (1995) computes these abnormal returns for a large sample of mutual funds between 1972 and 1991. His results, which appear in Figure 9.5, show that

FIGURE 9.5

Estimates of Individual Mutual Fund Alphas, 1972 to 1991

Source: Burton G. Malkiel, "Returns from Investing in Equity Mutual Funds 1971–1991," *Journal of Finance* 50 (June 1995), 549–572.

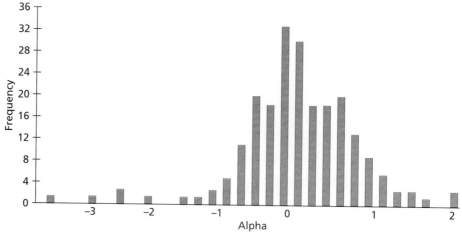

Note: The frequency distribution of estimated alphas for all equity mutual funds with 10-year continuous records.

the distribution of alphas is roughly bell shaped, with a mean that is slightly negative but statistically indistinguishable from zero.

One problem in interpreting these alphas is that the S&P 500 may not be an adequate benchmark against which to evaluate mutual fund returns. Because mutual funds tend to maintain considerable holdings in the equity of small firms, while the S&P 500 is exclusively comprised of large firms, mutual funds as a whole will tend to outperform the index when small firms outperform large ones, and underperform when small firms fare worse. Thus, a better benchmark for the performance of funds would be an index that incorporates the stock market performance of smaller firms.

The importance of the benchmark can be illustrated by examining the returns on small stocks in various subperiods.[7] In the 20-year period between 1945 and 1964, a small stock index underperformed the S&P 500 by about 4% per year on a risk-adjusted basis. In the more recent 20-year period between 1965 and 1984, small stocks outperformed the S&P index by 10%. Thus, if one were to examine mutual fund returns in the earlier period, they would tend to look poor, not necessarily because small fund managers were poor stock pickers, but simply because mutual funds as a group tend to hold more small stocks than are represented in the S&P 500. In the later period, funds would look better on a risk-adjusted basis relative to the S&P 500 because small funds performed better. The "style choice" (i.e., the exposure to small stocks, which is an asset allocation decision) would dominate the evaluation of performance even though it has little to do with managers' stock-picking ability.[8]

Elton, Gruber, Das, and Hlavka (1993) attempt to control for the impact of non-S&P assets on mutual fund performance. They calculate mutual fund alphas controlling for both the effects of firm size and interest rate movements. Some of their results are presented in Table 9.2, which shows that average alphas are negative for each type of equity fund, although generally not of statistically significant magnitude. They conclude that after controlling for the relative performance of these three asset classes—large stocks, small stocks, and bonds—mutual fund managers as a group do not demonstrate an ability to beat passive strategies that would simply mix index funds from among these asset classes. They also find that mutual fund performance is worse for firms that have higher expense ratios and higher turnover ratios. Thus, it appears that funds with higher fees do not increase gross returns by enough to justify those fees.

---

[7]This illustration and the statistics cited are based on a paper by Elton, Gruber, Das, and Hlavka (1993).
[8]Remember from Chapter 1 that the asset allocation decision is usually in the hands of the individual investor. Investors allocate their investment portfolios to mutual funds with holdings in asset classes they desire and can reasonably expect only that portfolio managers will choose stocks advantageously *within* those asset classes.

TABLE 9.2

Performance of Mutual
Funds Based on the
Three-Index Model

Source: E. J. Elton, M. J.
Gruber, S. Das, and M.
Hlavka, "Efficiency with
Costly Information: A
Reinterpretation of Evidence
from Managed Portfolios,"
Review of Financial Studies 6
(1993), pp. 1–22.

Type of Fund (Wiesenberger Classification)	Number of Funds	Alpha	*t*-Statistic for Alpha
Equity Funds			
Maximum capital gain	12	−4.59	−1.87
Growth	33	−1.55	−1.23
Growth and income	40	−0.68	−1.65
Balanced Funds	**31**	**−1.27**	**−2.73**

Note: The three-index model calculates the alpha of each fund as the intercept of the following regression:

$$r - r_f = \alpha + \beta_M(r_M - r_f) + \beta_S(r_S - r_f) + \beta_D(r_D - r_f) + e$$

where r is the return on the fund, r_f is the risk-free rate, r_M is the return on the S&P 500 index, r_S is the return on a non-S&P small stock index, r_D is the return on a bond index, e is the fund's residual return, and the betas measure the sensitivity of fund returns to the various indexes.

Carhart (1994) reexamines the issue of consistency in mutual fund performance controlling for non-S&P factors in a manner similar to Elton, Gruber, Das, and Hlavka. He finds that there is persistence in relative performance across managers but that much of the persistence seems due to expenses and transaction costs rather than gross investment returns. This last point is important: While there can be no consistently superior performers in a fully efficient market, there *can* be consistently inferior performers. Repeated weak performance would not be due to a tendency to pick bad stocks consistently (that would be impossible in an efficient market!), but it could result from a consistently high expense ratio or high portfolio turnover with the resulting trading costs. Carhart also finds that the evidence of persistence is concentrated at the two extremes of the best and worst performers. This suggests that there may be a small group of exceptional managers who can with some consistency outperform a passive strategy, but that for the majority of managers, over- or underperformance in any period is largely a matter of chance.

Thus, the evidence on the risk-adjusted performance of professional managers is mixed at best. We conclude that the performance of professional managers is broadly consistent with market efficiency. The amounts by which professional managers as a group beat or are beaten by the market fall within the margin of statistical uncertainty. In any event, it is quite clear that performance superior to passive strategies is far from routine. Studies show either that most managers cannot outperform passive strategies, or that if there is a margin of superiority, it is small.

On the other hand, a small number of investment superstars—Peter Lynch (formerly of Fidelity's Magellan Fund), Warren Buffet (of Berkshire Hathaway), John Templeton (of Templeton Funds), and George Soros (of the Quantum Fund), among them—have compiled career records that show a consistency of superior performance hard to reconcile with absolutely efficient markets. A "pantheon of great investors" appears in the nearby box (page 252). Nobel Prize winner Paul Samuelson (1989) reviews this investment hall of fame but points out that the records of the vast majority of professional money managers offer convincing evidence that there are no easy strategies to guarantee success in the securities markets.

Scientific and Computing Power in Search of Abnormal Returns

Reviewing the evidence on market efficiency, you must have noticed the increasing abundance of data, sophistication of statistical methods, and, most of all, computing power that is brought to bear on the analysis. Add to this the vast increase in funds under professional management and the corresponding increase in research budgets, and you may be convinced that markets should become ever more efficient over time.

This phenomenon illustrates that market efficiency is a dynamic process. Profit opportunities occasionally arise as market participants devise as-yet-unexploited trading strategies.

Who's Number One?

Is Warren Buffett the greatest investor of all time? That question can never be settled, any more than baseball fans can settle the question of whether Babe Ruth was greater than Hank Aaron. But a good case can be made for Mr. Buffett.

The table lists a few of the most successful investors in history. A couple of them—George Soros and Peter Lynch—show higher compound average annual returns than Mr. Buffett's. But that doesn't truly settle the debate.

Mr. Lynch, for example, compiled a sparkling 29% annual return as manager of the Fidelity Magellan Fund. At first blush, that seems to top Mr. Buffet's 27% annual return. However, during the 13-year stretch when Mr. Lynch was burning up the track, Mr. Buffett did even better: up 39% a year, according to Morningstar Inc.

Mr. Soros, manager of Quantum Fund, also has a higher annual return than Mr. Buffett. But Mr. Buffett has maintained his performance for a longer time. Also, notes Edward Macheski, a money manager in Chatham, N.Y., Mr. Buffett racked up his king-sized returns without much use of leverage, or debt, to magnify investment results. Hedge funds, such as those run by Mr. Soros, Michael Steinhardt, and Julian Robertson, often use heavy leverage.

The Buffett record shown in the table is a composite. From 1957 to 1969, his main investment vehicle was Buffett Partnership Ltd. In 1965, the partnership acquired a controlling interest in Berkshire, which became Mr. Buffett's main vehicle in 1970.

A Pantheon of Great Investors
Financial professionals consider these people among the greast investors of all time. Even in this select group, Warren Buffett stands out.

Name	Main Affiliation	Estimated Returns (1)	Comments
Warren Buffett	Berkshire Hathaway	Up 27% a year since 1957	Wants to invest in "wonderful businesses." Favorite holding period: forever.
Benjamin Graham	Graham-Newman	Up 17% a year, 1929–56	Considered the father of value investing. Liked stocks that are cheap relative to earnings or book value.
John Maynard Keynes	National Mutual Life Assurance Society (Britain)	Up most years during treacherous 1930s markets	Famous economist was also an avid and serious investor. Posted big losses but even bigger gains.
Peter Lynch	Fidelity Magellan Fund	Up 29% a year, May 1977– May 1990	Bought dozens of stocks in industries he favored. Workaholic until his surprise "retirement."
Julian Robertson	Tiger Fund	Up 27% a year since September 1980	Names hedge funds after big cats—"Tiger," "Puma," "Jaguar." Big player in Latin America, Japan, etc.
George Soros	Quantum Fund	Up 34% a year since 1969	Huge bets on international currencies and bonds; uses major leverage.
Michael Steinhardt	Steinhardt Partners	Up 21% a year since 1968	Hunch player, bold trader in both U.S. and foreign markets.
John Templeton	Templeton Growth Fund	Up 18% a year, Nov. 1954– March 1987	Bargain hunter worldwide; a pioneer of international investing.

Note: Estimated compound annual returns, after fees. With certain funds, publicly available results for foreign clients are used to approximate results for U.S. clients.

Sources: Morningstar Inc.; U.S. Offshore Funds Directory; "Benjamin Graham on Value Investing," by Janet Lowe; Wall Street Journal research.

Source: John R. Dorfman, "Who's Number One?" *The Wall Street Journal*, August 18, 1995, p. C1.

However, as those opportunities are exploited and security prices respond to the trading activity, the trading rule becomes less valuable. The true test of market efficiency is whether a trading rule based on a novel trading strategy will continue to succeed once market participants are aware of it.

As an example, consider neural networks, a recent technique to penetrate the field of investments. *Neural networks* are computer programs that are designed to recognize patterns. By identifying patterns in data that might not be obvious without computer analysis, neural networks enable traders to make money from these price relationships. Of course, once such a tool becomes available, one would predict a surge of demand, and this in fact has materialized. Even before one study had appeared in a scholarly journal, neural network software promising fantastic profits was widely offered to individuals and institutions.

In the *Journal of Portfolio Management*, Trippi and Desieno (1992) use six neural network models to arrive at a daily trading decision on the S&P 500 futures contract. They use data from 1986 to 1990 to estimate the parameters of each model and the first 106 days of 1991 to determine the optimal trading rules. These rules were used over the subsequent eight weeks of 1991, and the authors report profits equivalent to an annualized rate of return of 100%, with a standard deviation of 20%.

These developments demonstrate the process by which markets become ever more efficient. Because the market cannot be efficient with respect to information and information-processing techniques that are not yet available, there is always an incentive to apply new and more powerful techniques to the search for profit opportunities. In the process of extracting their honey, however, these bees increase the breadth and depth of market efficiency. The search for still-better techniques then begins anew.

So, Are Markets Efficient?

There is a telling joke about two economists walking down the street. They spot a $20 bill on the sidewalk. One starts to pick it up, but the other one says, "Don't bother; if the bill were real someone would have picked it up already."

The lesson here is clear. An overly doctrinaire belief in efficient markets can paralyze the investor and make it appear that no research effort can be justified. This extreme view is probably unwarranted. There are enough anomalies in the empirical evidence to justify the search for underpriced securities that clearly goes on.

The bulk of the evidence suggests that any supposedly superior investment strategy should be taken with many grains of salt. The market is competitive *enough* that only differentially superior information or insight will earn money; the easy pickings have been picked. In the end, it is likely that the margin of superiority that any professional manager can add is so slight that the statistician will not be able to detect it.

We conclude that markets are very efficient, but rewards to the especially diligent, intelligent, or creative may be waiting.

Summary

- Statistical research has shown that stock prices seem to follow a random walk with no discernible predictable patterns that investors can exploit. Such findings now are taken to be evidence of market efficiency, that is, of evidence that market prices reflect all currently available information. Only new information will move stock prices, and this information is equally likely to be good news or bad news.

- Market participants distinguish among three forms of the efficient market hypothesis. The weak form asserts that all information to be derived from past stock prices already is reflected in stock prices. The semistrong form claims that all publicly available information is already reflected. The strong form, usually taken only as a straw man, asserts that all information, including inside information, is reflected in prices.

- Technical analysis focuses on stock price patterns and on proxies for buy or sell pressure in the market. Fundamental analysis focuses on the determinants of the underlying value of the firm, such as current profitability and growth prospects. As both types of analysis are based on public information, neither should generate excess profits if markets are operating efficiently.

- Proponents of the efficient market hypothesis often advocate passive as opposed to active investment strategies. The policy of passive investors is to buy and hold a broad-based market index. They expend resources neither on market research nor on frequent purchase and sale of stocks. Passive strategies may be tailored to meet individual investor requirements.

- Empirical studies of technical analysis generally do not support the hypothesis that such analysis can generate trading profits. Only very short-term filters seem to offer any hope for profits, yet these are extremely expensive in terms of trading costs. These costs exceed potential profits even in the case of floor traders.

- Several anomalies regarding fundamental analysis have been uncovered. These include the P/E effect, the small-firm effect, the neglected-firm effect, and the book-to-market effect.

- By and large, the performance record of professionally managed funds lends little credence to claims that professionals can consistently beat the market.

Key Terms

efficient market
  hypothesis, *232*
filter rule, *239*
fundamental analysis, *235*
index fund, *236*
neglected-firm effect, *243*

passive investment
  strategy, *235*
P/E effect, *241*
random walk, *232*
reversal effect, *245*

semistrong-form EMH, *233*
small-firm effect, *241*
strong-form EMH, *234*
technical analysis, *234*
weak-form EMH, *233*

Problem Set

1. If markets are efficient, what should be the correlation coefficient between stock returns for two nonoverlapping time periods?

2. Which of the following most appears to contradict the proposition that the stock market is *weakly* efficient? Explain.
   a. Over 25% of mutual funds outperform the market on average.
   b. Insiders earn abnormal trading profits.
   c. Every January, the stock market earns above normal returns.

3. Suppose, after conducting an analysis of past stock prices, you come up with the following observations. Which would appear to *contradict* the *weak* form of the efficient market hypothesis? Explain.
   a. The average rate of return is significantly greater than zero.
   b. The correlation between the market return one week and the return the following week is zero.
   c. One could have made superior returns by buying stock after a 10% rise in price and selling after a 10% fall.
   d. One could have made higher than average capital gains by holding stock with low dividend yields.

4. Which of the following statements are true if the efficient market hypothesis holds?
   a. It implies perfect forecasting ability.
   b. It implies prices reflect all available information.
   c. It implies that the market is irrational.
   d. It implies prices do not fluctuate.

5. Which of the following observations would provide evidence *against* the *semistrong form* of the efficient market theory? Explain.

    a. Mutual fund managers do not on average make superior returns.

    b. You cannot make superior profits by buying (or selling) stocks after the announcement of an abnormal rise in earnings.

    c. Low P/E stocks tend to provide abnormal risk-adjusted returns.

    d. In any year, approximately 50% of pension funds outperform the market.

6. A successful firm like Wal-Mart has consistently generated large profits for years. Is this a violation of the EMH?

7. Prices of stocks before stock *splits* show on average consistently positive abnormal returns. Is this a violation of the EMH?

8. "If the business cycle is predictable, and a stock has a positive beta, the stock's returns also must be predictable." Respond.

9. "The expected return on all securities must be equal if markets are efficient." Comment.

10. We know the market should respond positively to good news, and good news events such as the coming end of a recession can be predicted with at least some accuracy. Why, then, can we not predict that the market will go up as the economy recovers?

11. If prices are as likely to increase or decrease, why do investors earn positive returns from the market on average?

12. You know that firm XYZ is very poorly run. On a management scale of 1 (worst) to 10 (best), you would give it a score of 3. The market consensus evaluation is that the management score is only 2. Should you buy or sell the stock?

13. Some scholars contend that professional managers are incapable of outperforming the market. Others come to an opposite conclusion. Compare and contrast the assumptions about the stock market that support (*a*) passive portfolio management, and (*b*) active portfolio management.

14. You are a portfolio manager meeting a client. During the conversation that followed your formal review of her account, your client asked the following question:

> "My grandson, who is studying investments, tells me that one of the best ways to make money in the stock market is to buy the stocks of small-capitalization firms late in December and to sell the stocks one month later. What is he talking about?

    a. Identify the apparent market anomalies that would justify the proposed strategy.

    b. Explain why you believe such a strategy might or might not work in the future.

15. Which of the following phenomena would be either consistent with or in violation of the efficient market hypothesis? Explain briefly.

    a. Nearly half of all professionally managed mutual funds are able to outperform the S&P 500 in a typical year.

    b. Money managers that outperform the market (on a risk-adjusted basis) in one year are likely to outperform the market in the following year.

    c. Stock prices tend to be predictably more volatile in January than in other months.

    d. Stock prices of companies that announce increased earnings in January tend to outperform the market in February.

    e. Stocks that perform well in one week perform poorly in the following week.

16. Dollar-cost averaging means that you buy equal dollar amounts of a stock every period, for example, $500 per month. The strategy is based on the idea that when the stock price is low, your fixed monthly purchase will buy more shares, and when the price is high, fewer shares. Averaging over time, you will end up buying more shares when the stock is cheaper and fewer when it is relatively expensive. Therefore, by design, you will exhibit good market timing. Evaluate this strategy.

17. Steady Growth Industries has never missed a dividend payment in its 94-year history. Does this make it more attractive to you as a possible purchase for your stock portfolio?

18. Good News, Inc., just announced an increase in its annual earnings, yet its stock price fell. Is there a rational explanation for this phenomenon?

Use the following information to solve problems 19 and 20:

As director of research for a medium-sized investment firm, Jeff Cheney was concerned about the mediocre investment results experienced by the firm in recent years. He met with his two senior equity analysts to consider alternatives to the stock selection techniques employed in the past.

One of the analysts suggested that the current literature has examined the relationship between price-earnings ratios (P/E) and securities returns. A number of studies had concluded that high P/E stocks tended to have higher betas and lower risk-adjusted returns than stocks with low P/E ratios.

The analyst also referred to recent studies analyzing the relationship between security returns and company size as measured by equity capitalization. The studies concluded that when compared to the S&P 500 index, small-capitalization stocks tended to provide above-average risk-adjusted returns, while large-capitalization stocks tended to provide below-average risk-adjusted returns. It was further noted that little correlation was found to exist between a company's P/E ratio and the size of its equity capitalization.

Jeff's firm has employed a strategy of complete diversification and the use of beta as a measure of portfolio risk. He and his analysts were intrigued as to how these recent studies might be applied to their stock selection techniques and thereby improve their performance. Given the results of the studies indicated above:

19. Explain how the results of these studies might be used in the stock selection and portfolio management process. Briefly discuss the effects on the objectives of diversification and on the measurement of portfolio risk.

20. List the reasons and briefly discuss why this firm might *not* want to adopt a new strategy based on these studies in place of its current strategy of complete diversification and the use of beta as a measure of portfolio risk.

21. Use data from MarketBase-E to rank firms based on:
    a. Price-earnings ratio
    b. Price–book value ratio

    Examine the data for the five firms at the top and the five firms at the bottom of each list. What caused the values of the ratios to be so high (low)? Of the two portfolios from each list, which would you prefer? Explain. Give your opinion on the following investment advice: "Each quarter, using updated information, rank all firms by their P/E ratio and invest an equal dollar amount in the 20 firms with the lowest P/E ratios."

22. Divide the firms into 10 groups based on their ranking for the price-earnings ratio. Calculate the average beta for each group. Assuming the P/E effect exists, what, if anything, might the results imply about beta?

23. Form a portfolio that uses two criteria simultaneously. Find the portfolio of stocks that are both in the lowest decile of P/E ratios and the lowest decile of price–book value ratios. From this group select all the firms that have had positive earnings for each of the past five years and whose earnings have increased over the past full year. Rank by dividend yield and comment on the top five companies on the list.

Applications

1. What are the implications for IEM prices of:
   a. Weak-form efficiency?
   b. Semistrong-form efficiency?
   c. Strong-form efficiency?

2. According to each form of efficiency, which of the following activities should be profitable for you as an IEM trader:
   a. Looking up current AAPL, IBM, MSFT, and S&P 500 prices in the newspaper to see which IEM contract is most likely to pay off.
   b. Statistical analysis of past IEM prices to look for trends, patterns, etc.
   c. An in-depth analysis of Apple, IBM, and Microsoft annual reports to look for company strengths and weaknesses.
   d. Calling a friend at MSFT and getting the inside scoop on the next product that they are planning to release.
3. Suppose everyone believes that the IEM is so efficient that none of the activities in Question 2 will prove profitable and no one undertakes any of these activities. Do you expect that the IEM prices will still be efficient? Will they still reflect the relative probabilities that each contract will pay off $1? How do you explain this paradox?

Solutions to Concept Checks

1. The information sets that pertain to the weak, semistrong, and strong form of the EMH can be described by:

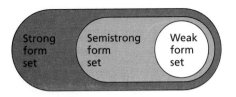

The weak-form information set includes only the history of prices and trading. The semistrong-form set includes the weak-form set *plus* all other publicly available information. In turn, the strong-form set includes the semistrong set *plus* inside information. The direction of *valid* implication is

Strong-form EMH ⇒ semistrong-form EMH ⇒ weak-form EMH

The reverse direction implication is *not* valid. For example, stock prices may reflect all past price data (weak-form efficiency) but may not reflect relevant fundamental data (semistrong-form inefficiency).

2. If *everyone* follows a passive strategy, sooner or later prices will fail to reflect new information. At this point, there are profit opportunities for active investors who uncover mispriced securities. As they buy and sell these assets, prices again will be driven to fair levels.

3. The answer depends on your prior beliefs about market efficiency. Magellan's record was incredibly strong. On the other hand, with so many funds in existence, it is less surprising that *some* fund would appear to be consistently superior after the fact. In fact, Magellan's record was so good that even accounting for its selection after the fact as the "winner" of an investment "contest," it still appears to be too good to be attributed to chance. For further analysis and discussion of Magellan's performance, refer to the articles by Marcus and Samuelson in Appendix B.

4. If profit opportunities can be made, one would expect mutual funds specializing in small stocks to spring into existence. Moreover, one wonders why buyers of small stocks don't compete for those stocks in December and bid up their prices before the January rise.

5. Concern over the deficit was an ongoing issue in 1987. No significant *new* information concerning the deficit was released October 19. Hence, this explanation for the crash is not consistent with the EMH.

Part Three

FIXED-INCOME SECURITIES

Fixed-income markets used to be a sedate arena for risk-averse investors who wanted worry-free investments with modest but stable returns. They are no longer so quiet. Annual trading in U.S. government bonds alone is about 10 times the total amount of national debt. The market in mortgage-backed securities alone is now about $2 trillion.

Higher trading activity is not the only reason these markets are more interesting than they once were. These markets are no longer free of risk. Interest rates in the last decade or so have become more volatile than anyone in 1965 would have dreamed possible. Volatility means that investors have great opportunities for gain, but also for losses, and we have seen dramatic examples of both in recent years. A single trader at Merrill Lynch lost $250 hundred million in less than a month trading mortgage-backed securities in 1987. Procter & Gamble lost about $100 million in interest rate swaps in 1994. Of course, there were traders on the other side of these transactions who did quite well in these instances.

The chapters in Part Three provide an introduction to fixed-income markets and securities. We will show you how to value such securities and why their values change with interest rates. We will see what features determine the sensitivity of bond prices to interest rates, and how investors measure and manage interest rate risk.

Chapter 10

BOND PRICES AND YIELDS

AFTER STUDYING THIS CHAPTER YOU SHOULD BE ABLE TO:

- Compute a bond's price given its yield to maturity, and compute its yield to maturity given its price.
- Calculate how bond prices will change over time for a given interest rate projection.
- Identify the determinants of bond safety and rating.
- Analyze how call, convertibility, and sinking fund provisions will affect a bond's equilibrium yield to maturity.
- Analyze the factors likely to affect the shape of the yield curve at any time.

In the previous chapters on risk and return relationships, we have treated securities at a high level of abstraction. We have assumed implicitly that a prior, detailed analysis of each security already has been performed, and that its risk and return features have been assessed.

We turn now to specific analyses of particular security markets. We examine valuation principles, determinants of risk and return, and portfolio strategies commonly used within and across the various markets.

fixed-income security
A security such as a bond that pays a specified cash flow over a specific period.

We begin by analyzing **fixed-income securities.** A fixed-income security is a claim on a specified periodic stream of income. Fixed-income securities have the advantage of being relatively easy to understand because the level of payments is specified in advance. Uncertainty surrounding cash flows paid to the security holder is minimal as long as the issuer of the security is sufficiently creditworthy. That makes these securities a convenient starting point for our analysis of the universe of potential investment vehicles.

The bond is the basic fixed-income security, and this chapter reviews the principles of bond pricing. We show how bond prices are set in accordance with market interest rates, and why bond prices change with those rates. After examining the Treasury bond market, where default risk may be ignored, we move to the corporate bond sector. Here, we look at the determinants of credit risk and the default premium built into bond yields. We examine the impact of call and convertibility provisions on prices and yields. Finally, we take a look at the yield curve, the relationship between bond maturity and bond yield.

10.1 BOND CHARACTERISTICS

bond
A security that obligates the issuer to make specified payments to the holder over a period of time.

A **bond** is a security that is issued in connection with a borrowing arrangement. The borrower issues (i.e., sells) a bond to the lender for some amount of cash; the bond is in essence the "IOU" of the borrower. The arrangement obligates the issuer to make specified payments to the bondholder on specified dates. A typical coupon bond obligates the issuer to make semiannual payments of interest, called *coupon payments*, to the bondholder for the life of the bond. These are called coupon payments because in precomputer days, most bonds had coupons that investors would clip off and mail to the issuer of the bond to claim the interest payment. When the bond matures, the issuer repays the debt by paying the bondholder the bond's **par value** (or equivalently, its **face value**). The **coupon rate** of the bond serves to determine the interest payment: The annual payment equals the coupon rate times the bond's par value. The coupon rate, maturity date, and par value of the bond are part of the *bond indenture*, which is the contract between the issuer and the bondholder.

face value, par value
The payment to the bondholder at the maturity of the bond.

coupon rate
A bond's annual interest payment per dollar of par value.

To illustrate, a bond with a par value of $1,000 and a coupon rate of 8% might be sold to a buyer for $1,000. The issuer then pays the bondholder 8% of $1,000, or $80 per year, for the stated life of the bond, say 30 years. The $80 payment typically comes in two semiannual installments of $40 each. At the end of the 30-year life of the bond, the issuer also pays the $1,000 par value to the bondholder.

zero-coupon bond
A bond paying no coupons that sells at a discount and provides only a payment of par value at maturity.

Bonds usually are issued with coupon rates set high enough to induce investors to pay par value to buy the bond. Sometimes, however, **zero-coupon bonds** are issued that make no coupon payments. In this case, investors receive par value at the maturity date, but receive no interest payments until then: The bond has a coupon rate of zero. These bonds are issued at prices considerably below par value, and the investor's return comes solely from the difference between issue price and the payment of par value at maturity. We will return to these bonds below.

Treasury Bonds and Notes

Figure 10.1 is an excerpt from the listing of Treasury issues in *The Wall Street Journal*. Treasury note maturities range up to 10 years, while Treasury bonds are issued with maturities ranging from 10 to 30 years. Both are issued in denominations of $1,000 or more. Both make semiannual coupon payments. Aside from their differing maturities at issue date, the only major distinction between T-notes and T-bonds is that in the past, some T-bonds were **callable** for a given period, usually during the last five years of the bond's life. The call provision gives the Treasury the right to repurchase the bond at par value during the call period. The Treasury no longer issues callable bonds, but several previously issued callable bonds still are outstanding.

callable bonds
Bonds that may be repurchased by the issuer at a specified call price during the call period.

The callable bonds are easily identified in Figure 10.1 because a range of years appears in the maturity date column. The first date is the time at which the bond is first callable. The second date is the maturity date of the bond. The bond may be called by the Treasury at any coupon date in the call period, but must be retired by the maturity date.

The highlighted bond in Figure 10.1 matures in July 2000. Its coupon rate is 6⅛%. Par value is $1,000; thus, the bond pays interest of $61.25 per year in two semiannual payments of $30.625. Payments are made in January and July of each year. The bid and ask prices[1] are quoted in points plus fractions of $1/32$ of a point (the numbers after the colons are the fractions of a point). Although bonds are sold in denominations of $1,000 par value, the prices are quoted as a percentage of par value. Therefore, the bid price of the bond is 98:02 = 98²/₃₂ = 98.0625% of par value or $980.625, while the ask price is 98⁴/₃₂ percent of par, or $981.25.

---

[1]Recall that the bid price is the price at which you can sell the bond to a dealer. The ask price, which is slightly higher, is the price at which you can buy the bond from a dealer.

FIGURE 10.1

Listing of Treasury Issues

Source: *The Wall Street Journal*. Reprinted by permission of *The Wall Street Journal*, © 1995 Dow Jones & Company. All Rights Reserved Worldwide.

TREASURY BONDS, NOTES & BILLS

Thursday, September 5, 1996

Representative Over-the-Counter quotations based on transactions of $1 million or more.

Treasury bond, note and bill quotes are as of mid-afternoon. Colons in bid-and-asked quotes represent 32nds; 101:01 means 101 1/32. Net changes in 32nds. n-Treasury note. Treasury bill quotes in hundredths, quoted on terms of a rate of discount. Days to maturity calculated from settlement date. All yields are to maturity and based on the asked quote. Latest 13-week and 26-week bills are boldfaced. For bonds callable prior to maturity, yields are computed to the earliest call date for issues quoted above par and to the maturity date for issues below par. *-When issued.

Source: Federal Reserve Bank of New York.

U.S. Treasury strips as of 3 p.m. Eastern time, also based on transactions of $1 million or more. Colons in bid-and-asked quotes represent 32nds; 99:01 means 99 1/32. Net changes in 32nds. Yields calculated on the asked quotation. ci-stripped coupon interest. bp-Treasury bond, stripped principal. np-Treasury note, stripped principal. For bonds callable prior to maturity, yields are computed to the earliest call date for issues quoted above par and to the maturity date for issues below par.

Source: Bear, Stearns & Co. via Street Software Technology Inc.

GOVT. BONDS & NOTES

Rate	Maturity Mo/Yr	Bid	Asked	Chg.	Ask Yld.
6 1/2	Sep 96n	100:03	100:05	+ 1	3.67
7	Sep 96n	100:03	100:05	....	4.14
8	Oct 96n	100:09	100:11	....	4.35
8 1/2	Jul 97n	102:02	102:04	− 1	5.90
5 1/2	Jul 97n	99:19	99:21	....	5.90
5 7/8	Jul 97n	99:29	99:31	....	5.91
6 1/2	Aug 97n	100:13	100:15	− 1	5.98
8 5/8	Aug 97n	102:11	102:13	− 1	5.94
5 5/8	Aug 97n	99:19	99:21	− 1	5.99
6	Aug 97n	99:30	100:00	....	6.00
5 1/2	Sep 97n	99:14	99:16	− 1	5.99
5 3/4	Sep 97n	99:22	99:24	....	6.00
8 3/4	Oct 97n	102:25	102:27	− 1	6.04
5 5/8	Oct 97n	99:15	99:17	....	6.06
5 3/4	Oct 97n	99:19	99:21	− 1	6.07
7 3/8	Nov 97n	101:11	101:13	....	6.13
8 7/8	Nov 97n	103:02	103:04	− 1	6.10
5 3/8	Nov 97n	99:01	99:03	− 1	6.15
6	Nov 97n	99:25	99:27	− 1	6.13
5 1/4	Dec 97n	98:26	98:28	− 1	6.16
6	Dec 97n	99:25	99:27	− 1	6.13
7 7/8	Jan 98n	102:04	102:06	− 1	6.16
5 1/4	Jul 98n	98:02	98:04	− 1	6.32
6 1/4	Jul 98n	99:25	99:27	− 2	6.34
5 7/8	Aug 98n	99:02	99:04	− 2	6.36
9 1/4	Aug 98n	105:04	105:06	− 3	6.36
4 3/4	Aug 98n	97:01	97:03	− 1	6.34
6 1/8	Aug 98n	99:17	99:19	....	6.35
4 3/4	Sep 98n	96:29	96:31	− 1	6.34
7 1/8	Oct 98n	101:14	101:16	− 2	6.35
4 3/4	Oct 98n	96:23	96:25	− 1	6.38
3 1/2	Nov 98	97:22	98:22	....	4.13
5 1/2	Nov 98n	98:04	98:06	− 1	6.40
8 7/8	Nov 98n	104:29	104:31	− 2	6.40
5 1/8	Nov 98n	97:10	97:12	− 2	6.41
5 1/8	Dec 98n	97:08	97:10	− 1	6.40
6 3/8	Jan 99n	99:27	99:29	− 1	6.42
5	Jan 99n	96:25	96:27	− 1	6.44
5	Feb 99n	96:23	96:25	− 1	6.45
8 7/8	Feb 99n	105:09	105:11	− 2	6.47
5 1/2	Feb 99n	97:25	97:27	− 1	6.46
5 7/8	Mar 99n	98:18	98:20	− 2	6.47
7	Apr 99n	101:05	101:07	− 2	6.48
6 1/2	Apr 99n	99:31	100:01	− 1	6.49
6 3/8	May 99n	99:19	99:21	− 2	6.52
9 1/8	May 99n	106:09	106:11	− 2	6.51
6 3/4	May 99n	100:16	100:18	− 2	6.52
6 3/4	Jun 99n	100:17	100:19	− 2	6.52
6 3/8	Jul 99n	99:20	99:22	− 1	6.50
6 7/8	Jul 99n	100:25	100:27	− 1	6.55
6	Aug 99n	98:17	98:19	....	6.53
8	Aug 99n	103:23	103:25	− 2	6.56
6 7/8	Aug 99n	100:26	100:28	− 1	6.55
7 1/8	Sep 99n	101:15	101:17	− 2	6.56
6	Oct 99n	98:15	98:17	− 1	6.53
7 1/2	Oct 99n	102:17	102:19	....	6.57
7 7/8	Nov 99n	103:18	103:20	− 2	6.59
7 3/4	Nov 99n	103:08	103:10	− 2	6.59
7 3/4	Dec 99n	103:10	103:12	− 2	6.60
6 3/8	Jan 00n	99:09	99:11	− 1	6.60
7 3/4	Jan 00n	103:10	103:12	− 2	6.62
8 1/2	Feb 00n	105:20	105:22	− 2	6.62
7 1/8	Feb 00n	101:15	101:17	− 1	6.62
6 7/8	Mar 00n	100:22	100:24	− 2	6.63
5 1/2	Apr 00n	96:10	96:12	− 2	6.65
6 3/4	Apr 00n	100:08	100:10	− 2	6.65
8 7/8	May 00n	107:04	107:06	− 3	6.64
6 1/4	May 00n	98:19	98:21	− 3	6.66
5 7/8	Jun 00n	97:10	97:12	− 3	6.67
→ 6 1/8	Jul 00n	98:02	98:04	− 2	6.68
8 3/4	Aug 00n	107:00	107:02	− 3	6.68
6 1/4	Aug 00n	98:14	98:16	− 3	6.69
6 1/8	Sep 00n	97:30	98:00	− 2	6.70
5 3/4	Oct 00n	96:18	96:20	− 2	6.70
8 1/2	Nov 00n	106:13	106:15	− 3	6.70
5 5/8	Nov 00n	96:00	96:02	− 2	6.71
5 1/2	Dec 00n	95:15	95:17	− 2	6.71
5 1/4	Jan 01n	94:23	94:25	− 2	6.64
7 3/4	Feb 01n	103:27	103:29	− 3	6.72
11 3/4	Feb 01	119:00	119:04	− 3	6.69
10 3/4	Feb 03	119:31	120:03	− 6	6.84
10 3/4	May 03	120:14	120:18	− 5	6.86
5 3/4	Aug 03n	93:28	93:30	− 4	6.86
11 1/8	Aug 03	123:02	123:06	− 4	6.87
11 7/8	Nov 03	127:23	127:27	− 5	6.90
11 3/4	Feb 05-10	129:16	129:20	−12	7.03
10	May 05-10	118:26	118:30	−12	7.05
12 3/4	Nov 05-10	137:25	137:29	−13	7.07
13 7/8	May 06-11	146:30	147:02	−15	7.08
14	Nov 06-11	149:18	149:22	−13	7.07
10 3/8	Nov 07-12	124:08	124:12	−14	7.17
12	Aug 08-13	138:03	138:07	−14	7.18
13 1/4	May 09-14	149:24	149:28	−14	7.19
12 1/2	Aug 09-14	144:03	144:07	−15	7.19
11 3/4	Nov 09-14	138:16	138:20	−13	7.17
11 1/4	Feb 15	140:11	140:13	−21	7.24
10 5/8	Aug 15	134:09	134:11	−20	7.26
9 7/8	Nov 15	126:22	126:24	−19	7.27
9 1/4	Feb 16	120:08	120:10	−19	7.28
7 1/4	May 16	99:19	99:21	−15	7.28
7 1/2	Nov 16	102:04	102:06	−15	7.29
8 3/4	May 17	115:12	115:14	−17	7.29
8 7/8	Aug 17	116:25	116:27	−17	7.29
7 5/8	Feb 25	104:15	104:17	−16	7.25
6	Feb 26	85:18	85:20	−15	7.18
6 3/4	Aug 26	95:04	95:06	−17	7.14

U.S. TREASURY STRIPS

Mat.	Type	Bid	Asked	Chg.	Ask Yld.
Nov 96	ci	99:01	99:01	+ 4	5.31
Nov 96	np	99:01	99:01	+ 2	5.31
Feb 97	ci	97:24	97:24	+ 1	5.31
May 97	ci	96:05	96:05	+ 2	5.82
May 97	np	96:04	96:04	+ 1	5.87
Aug 97	ci	94:23	94:24	+ 1	5.86
Aug 97	np	94:20	94:21	+ 1	5.98
Nov 97	ci	93:01	93:02	+ 1	6.17
Nov 97	np	93:01	93:02	+ 1	6.18
Jan 98	ci	92:01	92:02	+ 1	6.23
Feb 98	ci	91:17	91:18	+ 1	6.25
Feb 98	np	91:16	91:17	+ 1	6.28
May 98	ci	90:02	90:03	+ 1	6.29
May 98	np	90:02	90:04	+ 1	6.29
Aug 98	ci	88:19	88:21	+ 1	6.34
Aug 98	np	88:17	88:18	+ 1	6.38
Nov 98	ci	87:02	87:04	....	6.41
Nov 98	np	87:02	87:04	....	6.42
Feb 99	ci	85:19	85:21	....	6.47
Feb 99	np	85:18	85:20	....	6.49
May 99	ci	84:02	84:04	....	6.55
May 99	np	84:01	84:03	− 1	6.56
Aug 99	ci	82:21	82:23	− 1	6.58
Aug 99	np	82:19	82:21	− 1	6.60
Nov 99	ci	81:06	81:09	− 1	6.62
Nov 99	np	81:05	81:08	− 1	6.64
Feb 00	ci	79:26	79:28	− 1	6.65
Feb 00	np	79:24	79:26	− 1	6.68
May 00	ci	78:15	78:18	− 1	6.66
May 00	np	78:14	78:17	− 1	6.68
Jul 00	ci	77:17	77:20	− 1	6.70
Aug 00	ci	77:04	77:07	− 1	6.69
Aug 00	np	77:01	77:04	− 1	6.72
Nov 00	ci	75:26	75:29	− 2	6.71
Nov 00	np	75:23	75:26	− 2	6.74
Jan 01	ci	74:29	75:00	− 3	6.73
Feb 01	ci	74:16	74:19	− 3	6.72
Feb 01	np	74:12	74:16	− 3	6.76
May 01	ci	73:07	73:10	− 2	6.74
May 01	np	73:04	73:07	− 2	6.77
Jul 01	ci	72:10	72:14	− 2	6.77
Aug 01	ci	71:30	72:02	− 2	6.76
Aug 01	np	71:27	71:30	− 2	6.79
Nov 01	ci	70:23	70:26	− 2	6.77
Nov 01	np	70:19	70:22	− 2	6.81
Jan 02	ci	69:27	69:30	− 3	6.80
Feb 02	ci	69:15	69:19	− 3	6.79
May 02	ci	68:07	68:10	− 3	6.82
May 02	np	68:08	68:11	− 3	6.81
Jul 02	ci	67:13	67:16	− 3	6.83
Aug 02	ci	67:02	67:05	− 3	6.82
Aug 02	np	67:00	67:03	− 3	6.84
Nov 04	bp	56:19	56:23	− 6	7.05
Nov 04	np	56:26	56:30	− 6	7.00
Jan 05	ci	55:31	56:03	− 6	7.05
Feb 05	ci	55:20	55:24	− 6	7.05
Feb 05	np	55:26	55:31	− 4	7.01
May 05	ci	54:18	54:23	− 6	7.07
May 05	bp	54:16	54:20	− 7	7.09
May 05	np	54:30	55:02	− 4	6.99
Jul 05	ci	53:29	54:01	− 6	7.08
Aug 05	ci	53:18	53:23	− 6	7.08
Aug 05	bp	53:17	53:21	− 6	7.09
Aug 05	np	53:28	54:01	− 6	7.01
Nov 05	ci	52:19	52:24	− 6	7.09
Nov 05	bp	53:02	53:06	− 3	6.99
Jan 06	ci	51:30	52:03	− 6	7.10
Feb 06	ci	51:20	51:24	− 6	7.11
Feb 06	bp	52:02	52:06	− 8	7.01
May 06	ci	50:21	50:25	− 6	7.12
Jul 06	ci	50:01	50:05	− 7	7.13
Aug 06	ci	49:23	49:27	− 7	7.13
Nov 06	ci	48:26	48:30	− 7	7.14
Feb 07	ci	47:28	48:00	− 7	7.16
May 07	ci	46:31	47:04	− 7	7.17
Aug 07	ci	46:03	46:08	− 7	7.18
Nov 07	ci	45:08	45:12	− 7	7.19
Feb 08	ci	44:11	44:16	− 7	7.21
Feb 14	ci	27:28	28:01	− 9	7.43
May 14	ci	27:12	27:16	− 9	7.44
Aug 14	ci	26:27	26:31	− 9	7.44
Nov 14	ci	26:11	26:15	− 9	7.45
Feb 15	ci	25:26	25:31	− 9	7.45
Feb 15	bp	26:00	26:04	− 10	7.41
May 15	ci	25:11	25:15	− 9	7.45
Aug 15	ci	24:28	25:00	− 9	7.46
Aug 15	bp	24:31	25:04	− 10	7.43
Nov 15	ci	24:12	24:17	− 9	7.46
Nov 15	bp	24:16	24:20	− 10	7.44
Feb 16	ci	23:30	24:02	− 9	7.46
Feb 16	bp	24:00	24:04	− 10	7.45
May 16	ci	23:15	23:20	− 9	7.47
May 16	bp	23:22	23:26	− 9	7.42
Aug 16	ci	23:01	23:06	− 9	7.47
Nov 16	ci	22:20	22:24	− 9	7.47
Nov 16	bp	22:25	22:29	− 9	7.44
Feb 17	ci	22:06	22:10	− 9	7.48
Feb 20	ci	17:25	17:29	− 8	7.48
Feb 20	bp	17:27	17:30	− 8	7.47
May 20	ci	17:15	17:19	− 7	7.48
May 20	bp	17:16	17:20	− 8	7.47
Aug 20	ci	17:05	17:09	− 7	7.47
Aug 20	bp	17:06	17:10	− 7	7.47
Nov 20	ci	16:29	17:00	− 7	7.46
Feb 21	ci	16:21	16:24	− 7	7.45
Feb 21	bp	16:21	16:25	− 7	7.44
May 21	ci	16:10	16:14	− 7	7.45
May 21	bp	16:11	16:15	− 7	7.44
Aug 21	ci	16:02	16:06	− 7	7.44
Aug 21	bp	16:02	16:06	− 7	7.44
Nov 21	ci	15:26	15:29	− 7	7.43
Nov 21	bp	15:26	15:30	− 7	7.43
Feb 22	ci	15:18	15:22	− 7	7.42
May 22	ci	15:10	15:13	− 7	7.41
Aug 22	ci	15:02	15:05	− 7	7.41
Aug 22	bp	15:03	15:07	− 7	7.40
Nov 22	ci	14:24	14:28	− 7	7.41
Nov 22	bp	14:27	14:31	− 7	7.39
Feb 23	ci	14:21	14:25	− 7	7.37
Feb 23	bp	14:21	14:25	− 7	7.37
May 23	ci	14:13	14:17	− 7	7.36
Aug 23	ci	14:06	14:10	− 7	7.35
Aug 23	bp	14:09	14:13	− 7	7.33
Nov 23	ci	14:00	14:04	− 7	7.33
Feb 24	ci	13:26	13:29	− 7	7.32
May 24	ci	13:19	13:23	− 7	7.31
Aug 24	ci	13:13	13:16	− 7	7.30
Nov 24	ci	13:06	13:10	− 7	7.29
Nov 24	bp	13:06	13:10	− 7	7.29
Feb 25	ci	13:03	13:06	− 7	7.25
Feb 25	bp	13:04	13:07	− 7	7.24
Aug 25	ci	12:30	13:02	− 7	7.16
Aug 25	bp	12:30	13:02	− 7	7.16
Feb 26	ci	12:30	13:01	− 7	7.04
Feb. 26	bp	12:29	13:00	− 7	7.05

TREASURY BILLS

Maturity	Days to Mat.	Bid	Asked	Chg.	Ask Yld.
Sep 12 '96	3	5.10	5.00	−0.05	5.07
Sep 17 '96	8	5.23	5.13	+0.01	5.21
Sep 19 '96	10	5.13	5.03	−0.04	5.12
Sep 26 '96	17	4.89	4.79	+0.01	4.87
Oct 03 '96	24	5.03	4.93	−0.02	5.01
Oct 10 '96	31	5.03	4.99	−0.02	5.08
Oct 17 '96	38	5.03	4.99	−0.01	5.10
Oct 24 '96	45	5.06	5.02	+0.01	5.12
Oct 31 '96	52	5.04	5.00	−0.05	5.11
Nov 07 '96	59	5.12	5.10	....	5.21
Nov 14 '96	66	5.15	5.13	+0.01	5.27
Nov 21 '96	73	5.16	5.14	+0.01	5.27
Nov 29 '96	81	5.19	5.17	+0.01	5.30
Dec 05 '96	**87**	**5.20**	**5.18**	**+0.02**	**5.32**
Dec 12 '96	94	5.21	5.19	+0.02	5.35

The last column, labeled "Ask Yld," is the yield to maturity on the bond based on the ask price. The yield to maturity is often interpreted as a measure of the average rate of return to an investor who purchases the bond for the ask price and holds it until its maturity date. We will have much to say about yield to maturity below.

Accrued Interest and Quoted Bond Prices   The bond prices that you see quoted in the financial pages are not actually the prices that investors pay for the bond. This is because the quoted price does not include the interest that accrues between coupon payment dates.

If a bond is purchased between coupon payments, the buyer must pay the seller for accrued interest, the prorated share of the upcoming semiannual coupon. For example, if 40 days have passed since the last coupon payment, and there are 182 days in the semiannual coupon period, the seller is entitled to a payment of accrued interest of 40/182 of the semiannual coupon. The sale, or *invoice price* of the bond, which is the amount the buyer actually pays, would equal the stated price plus the accrued interest.

EXAMPLE 10.1 **Accrued Interest**

Suppose that the coupon rate is 8%. Then the semiannual coupon payment is $40. Because 40 days have passed since the last coupon payment, the accrued interest on the bond is $40 × (40/182) = $8.79. If the quoted price of the bond is $990, then the invoice price will be $990 + $8.79 = $998.79.

The practice of quoting bond prices net of accrued interest explains why the price of a maturing bond is listed at $1,000 rather than $1,000 plus one coupon payment. A purchaser of an 8% coupon bond one day before the bond's maturity would receive $1,040 on the following day and so should be willing to pay a total price of $1,040 for the bond. In fact, $40 of that total payment constitutes the accrued interest for the preceding half-year period. The bond price is quoted net of accrued interest in the financial pages and thus appears as $1,000.

Corporate Bonds

Like the government, corporations borrow money by issuing bonds. Figure 10.2 is a sample of corporate bond listings in *The Wall Street Journal*. The data presented here differ only slightly from U.S. Treasury bond listings. For example, the highlighted AT&T bond pays a coupon rate of 7% and matures in 2005. Unlike Treasury bonds, corporate bonds trade in increments of 1/8 point. AT&T's *current yield* is 7.2%, which is simply the annual coupon payment divided by the bond price ($70/$976.25). Note that current yield measures only the annual interest income the bondholder receives as a percentage of the price paid for the bond. It ignores the fact that an investor who buys the bond for $976.25 will be able to redeem it for $1,000 on the maturity date. Prospective price appreciation or depreciation does not enter the computation of the current yield. The trading volume column shows that 189 bonds traded on that day. The change from yesterday's closing price is given in the last column. Like government bonds, corporate bonds sell in units of $1,000 par value but are quoted as a percentage of par value.

Although the bonds listed in Figure 10.2 trade on a formal exchange operated by the New York Stock Exchange, most bonds are traded over the counter in a loosely organized network of bond dealers linked by a computer quotation system. (See Chapter 3 for a comparison of exchange versus OTC trading.) In practice, the bond market can be quite "thin," in that there are few investors interested in trading a particular bond at any particular time. Figure 10.2 shows that trading volume of many bonds on the New York exchange is quite low. On any day, it could be difficult to find a buyer or seller for a particular issue, which introduces some "liquidity risk" into the bond market. It may be difficult to sell bond holdings quickly if the need arises.

Bonds issued in the United States today are *registered*, meaning that the issuing firm keeps records of the owner of the bond and can mail interest checks to the owner. Registration of bonds is helpful to tax authorities in the enforcement of tax collection. *Bearer bonds*

FIGURE 10.2
Listing of Corporate Bonds

From *The Wall Street Journal*, July 9, 1996. Reprinted by permission of *The Wall Street Journal*, © 1996 Dow Jones & Company, Inc. All Rights Reserved Worldwide.

NEW YORK EXCHANGE BONDS

CORPORATION BONDS
Volume, $21,718,000

Bonds	Cur Yld	Vol	Close	Net Chg.
AMR 9s16	8.6	25	105	− 1⅛
ATT 4⅝99	4.7	55	94	+ ⅜
ATT 6s00	6.2	99	97⅛	+ ⅛
ATT 5⅛01	5.6	8	92⅜	− ⅜
ATT 7⅛02	7.2	62	99½	− ⅞
ATT 6¾04	7.0	119	96⅞	− 1⅝
ATT 7s05	7.2	189	97⅝	− 1½
ATT 7½06	7.5	5	100⅝	− ⅞
ATT 8⅛22	8.0	415	102	− ½
ATT 8⅛24	7.9	53	102¾	+ 1
ATT 8.35s25	8.1	45	103½	+ ½
ATT 8⅝31	8.3	125	104⅜	− 1⅛
Advst 9s08	cv	5	102½	− ½
AirbF 6¾01	cv	3	99	− ½
AlskAr 6⅞14	cv	40	97	− ½
AlldC zr97	...	20	93	− 1
AlldC zr03	...	5	60	− 1
AlldC zr09	...	25	37	− ½

Bonds	Cur Yld	Vol	Close	Net Chg.
Lilly 8⅛01	7.7	15	105⅝	+ 1¾
Lilly 8¾06	7.8	5	107	− 1
LglsLt 7.3s99	7.6	13	96⅝	− ½
LglsLt 7.05s03	8.0	20	88½	− 1⅛
LglsLt 8⅝04	8.8	89	97⅞	− ⅝
LglsLt 8½06	8.9	20	95½	− 1
LglsLt 7½07	8.8	30	85⅛	− ⅝
LglsLt 8.9s19	9.8	105	90⅝	− ⅜
LglsLt 9¾21	9.8	25	100	+ ¾
LglsLt 9s22	9.8	286	91⅝	− ½
LglsLt 8.2s23	9.5	5	86	− 1
LglsLt 9⅝24	9.7	100	99½	− ¼
MGM Grd 11¾99	11.2	100	105⅛	− ¼
MGM Grd 12s02	11.1	34	108½	− ⅜
MarO 7s02	7.2	52	97¾	+ ¼
MarO 8.5s06	8.4	23	101¼	− ⅛
Masco 5¼12	cv	42	91	− 1
Mascotch 03	cv	10	77¾	− 2¼
Maxus 8½08	9.1	22	93½	+ ½
McDnl 6¾03	6.9	10	97⅜	− 1¾
McDnl 8 11	7.9	40	112⅜	− ⅝

are those traded without any record of ownership. The investor's physical possession of the bond certificate is the only evidence of ownership. These are now rare in the United States, but less rare in Europe.

Call Provisions on Corporate Bonds While we have seen that the Treasury no longer issues callable bonds, almost all corporate bonds are issued with call provisions. The call provision allows the issuer to repurchase the bond at a specified *call price* before the maturity date. For example, if a company issues a bond with a high coupon rate when market interest rates are high, and interest rates later fall, the firm might like to retire the high-coupon debt and issue new bonds at a lower coupon rate to reduce interest payments. The proceeds from the new bond issue are used to pay for the repurchase of the existing higher coupon bonds at the call price. This is calling *refunding*.

The call price of a bond is commonly set at an initial level near par value plus one annual coupon payment. The call price falls as time passes, gradually approaching par value.

Callable bonds typically come with a period of call protection, an initial time during which the bonds are not callable. Such bonds are referred to as *deferred* callable bonds.

The option to call the bond is valuable to the firm, allowing it to buy back the bonds and refinance at lower interest rates when market rates fall. Of course, the firm's benefit is the bondholder's burden. Holders of called bonds forfeit their bonds for the call price, thereby giving up the prospect of an attractive rate of interest on their original investment. To compensate investors for this risk, callable bonds are issued with higher coupons and promised yields to maturity than noncallable bonds.

Concept Check

1. Suppose that General Motors issues two bonds with identical coupon rates and maturity dates. One bond is callable, however, while the other is not. Which bond will sell at a higher price?

convertible bond
A bond with an option allowing the bondholder to exchange the bond for a specified number of shares of common stock in the firm.

Convertible Bonds **Convertible bonds** give bondholders an option to exchange each bond for a specified number of shares of common stock of the firm. The *conversion ratio* gives the number of shares for which each bond may be exchanged. To see the value of this right, suppose a convertible bond that is issued at par value of $1,000 is convertible into 40 shares of a firm's stock. The current stock price is $20 per share, so the option to convert is not profitable now. Should the stock price later rise to $30, however, each bond may be converted profitably into $1,200 worth of stock. The *market conversion value* is the current value of the shares for which the bonds may be exchanged. At the $20 stock price, for example, the bond's conversion value is $800. The *conversion premium* is the excess of the bond value over its conversion value. If the bond were selling currently for $950, its premium would be $150.

Convertible bonds give their holders the ability to share in price appreciation of the company's stock. Again, this benefit comes at a price; convertible bonds offer lower coupon rates and stated or promised yields to maturity than nonconvertible bonds. At the same time, the actual return on the convertible bond may exceed the stated yield to maturity if the option to convert becomes profitable.

We discuss convertible and callable bonds further in Chapter 17.

put bond
A bond that the holder may choose either to exchange for par value at some date or to extend for a given number of years.

Puttable Bonds   A relatively new development is the **put bond** or extendable bond. While the callable bond gives the issuer the option to extend or retire the bond at the call date, the put bond gives this option to the bondholder. If the bond's coupon rate exceeds current market yields, for instance, the bondholder will choose to extend the bond's life. If the bond's coupon rate is too low, it will be optimal not to extend; the bondholder instead reclaims principal, which can be invested at current yields.

floating-rate bonds
Bonds with coupon rates periodically reset according to a specified market rate.

Floating-Rate Bonds   **Floating-rate bonds** make interest payments that are tied to some measure of current market rates. For example, the rate might be adjusted annually to the current T-bill rate plus 2%. If the one-year T-bill rate at the adjustment date is 4%, the bond's coupon rate over the next year would then be 6%. This arrangement means that the bond always pays approximately current market rates.

The major risk involved in floaters has to do with changing credit conditions. The yield spread is fixed over the life of the security, which may be many years. If the financial health of the firm deteriorates, then a greater yield premium would be required than is offered by the security. In this case, the price of the bond would fall. While the coupon rate on floaters adjusts to changes in the general level of market interest rates, it does not adjust to changes in the financial condition of the firm.

Preferred Stock

Although preferred stock strictly speaking is considered to be equity, it often is included in the fixed-income universe. This is because, like bonds, preferred stock promises to pay a specified stream of dividends. However, unlike bonds, the failure to pay the promised dividend does not result in corporate bankruptcy. Instead, the dividends owed simply cumulate, and the common stockholders may not receive any dividends until the preferred stockholders have been paid in full. In the event of bankruptcy, the claim of preferred stockholders to the firm's assets has lower priority than that of bondholders, but higher priority than that of common stockholders.

Most preferred stock pays a fixed dividend. Therefore, it is in effect a perpetuity, providing a level cash flow indefinitely. In the last few years, however, adjustable or floating-rate preferred stock has become popular. Floating-rate preferred stock is much like floating-rate bonds. The dividend rate is linked to a measure of current market interest rates and is adjusted at regular intervals.

Unlike interest payments on bonds, dividends on preferred stock are not considered tax-deductible expenses to the firm. This reduces their attractiveness as a source of capital to issuing firms. On the other hand, there is an offsetting tax advantage to preferred stock. When one corporation buys the preferred stock of another corporation, it pays taxes on only 30% of the dividends received. For example, if the firm's tax bracket is 35%, and it receives $10,000 in preferred dividend payments, it will pay taxes on only $3,000 of that income: Total taxes owed on the income will be $0.35 \times \$3,000 = \$1,050$. The firm's effective tax rate on preferred dividends is therefore only $0.30 \times 35\% = 10.5\%$. Given this tax rule, it is not surprising that most preferred stock is held by corporations.

Preferred stock rarely gives its holders full voting privileges in the firm. However, if the preferred dividend is skipped, the preferred stockholders will then be provided some voting power.

Other Domestic Issuers

There are, of course, several issuers of bonds in addition to the Treasury and private corporations. For example, state and local governments issue municipal bonds. The outstanding feature of these is that interest payments are tax-free. We examined municipal bonds and the value of the tax exemption in Chapter 2.

Government agencies, such as the Federal Home Loan Bank Board, the Farm Credit agencies, and the mortgage pass-through agencies Ginnie Mae, Fannie Mae, and Freddie Mac, also issue considerable amounts of bonds. These too were reviewed in Chapter 2.

International Bonds

International bonds are commonly divided into two categories: *foreign bonds* and *Eurobonds*. Foreign bonds are issued by a borrower from a country other than the one in which the bond is sold. The bond is denominated in the currency of the country in which it is marketed. For example, if a German firm sells a dollar-denominated bond in the U.S., the bond is considered a foreign bond. These bonds are given colorful names based on the countries in which they are marketed. For example, foreign bonds sold in the U.S. are called *Yankee bonds*. Like other bonds sold in the U.S., they are registered with the Securities and Exchange Commission. Yen-denominated bonds sold in Japan by non-Japanese issuers are called *Samurai bonds*. British pound-denominated foreign bonds sold in the U.K. are called *bulldog bonds*.

In contrast to foreign bonds, Eurobonds are bonds issued in the currency of one country but sold in other national markets. For example, the Eurodollar market refers to dollar-denominated bonds sold outside the U.S. (not just in Europe), although London is the largest market for Eurodollar bonds. Because the Eurodollar market falls outside of U.S. jurisdiction, these bonds are not regulated by U.S. federal agencies. Similarly, Euroyen bonds are yen-denominated bonds selling outside of Japan, Eurosterling bonds are pound-denominated Eurobonds selling outside of the U.K., and so on.

Innovation in the Bond Market

Issuers constantly develop innovative bonds with unusual features; these issues illustrate that bond design can be extremely flexible. For example, issuers of *pay in kind* bonds may choose to pay interest either in cash or in additional bonds with the same face value. If the issuer is short on cash, it will likely choose to pay with new bonds rather than scarce cash. *Reverse floaters* are similar to the floating rate bonds we described above, except that the coupon rate on these bonds *falls* when the general level of interest rates rises.

Even more unusual bonds may be designed. Walt Disney has issued bonds with coupon rates tied to the financial performance of several of its films. Electrolux once issued a bond with a final payment that depended on whether there has been an earthquake in Japan. The box on page 266 discusses so-called disaster bonds further.

Indexed bonds make payments that are tied to a general price index or the price of a particular commodity. For example, Mexico has issued 20-year bonds with payments that depend on the price of oil. Bonds tied to the general price level have been common in countries experiencing high inflation. Although Great Britain is not a country experiencing such extreme inflation, about 20% of its government bonds issued in the last decade have been inflation-indexed. The United States Treasury started issuing such inflation-indexed bonds in January 1997. They are called Treasury Inflation Protected Securities (TIPS). By tying the par value of the bond to the general level of prices, coupon payments, as well as the final repayment of par value, on these bonds will increase in direct proportion to the consumer price index. Therefore, the interest rate on these bonds is a risk-free real rate.

To illustrate how TIPS work, consider one that is maturing in one year. Assume that it offers a risk-free real coupon rate of 3% per year. The *nominal* rate of return is not known with certainty in advance because it depends on the rate of inflation. If the inflation rate turns out to be only 2%, then the realized dollar rate of return will be approximately 5%; if,

Disaster Bonds Have Investors "Rolling the Dice With God"

The next few weeks could determine whether "disaster" bonds become the hottest new offering dreamed up by the wizards of the fixed-income markets.

"There is no reason that, given 10 years or so, this couldn't develop into a $50 billion-plus market," James Tilley, managing director of Morgan Stanley & Co., says of the burgeoning interest in passing along insurance-related risks of natural disasters to bond market investors.

With hurricanes and earthquakes increasingly wreaking not only physical but also financial havoc, the prospect of having to shell out billions of dollars in claims has sent insurance and reinsurance companies in quest of new ways to protect themselves. The latest twist is to offer bond market investors a chance to bet against the likelihood of such catastrophes occurring.

Over the next month or so, Merrill Lynch & Co. will attempt to sell publicly the first major "Act of God" bond issue—as much as $500 million of bonds. Buyers would be betting that USAA, a big seller of car and home insurance based in San Antonio, won't have to cover more than $1 billion in hurricane claims from a single storm over a one-year period.

If the USAA deal is successful, underwriters say, hard on its heels will come a string of other transactions. One megadeal is on the horizon: $3.35 billion of securities to be sold to fund a proposed California Earthquake Authority, a public agency whose creation is pushed by state Insurance Commissioner Charles Quackenbush to alleviate a growing home-insurance availability crunch in that state.

"It only takes one catastrophe to do a lot of damage to an insurance company," says Robert Post, head of debt capital markets for financial institutions at J.P. Morgan & Co. "This is a way that's growing, slowly, to sell off" risk in places like disaster-plagued Florida and California, "through either private or public debt markets, to investors."

But these bonds also could do some heavy damage to holders, too. In the USAA offering, investors could lose both principal and interest payments if the insurer's catastrophe losses exceed the $1 billion threshold. Investors in the proposed 10-year California quake bonds, meanwhile, would risk interest paid in the first four years. "It's like rolling the dice with God," says Jeanne Dunleavy, an assistant vice president with A.M. Best Co., an insurance rating firm.

Source: Suzanne McGre and Leslie Scism, "Disaster Bonds Have Investors 'Rolling the Dice with God,' " *The Wall Street Journal*, August 15, 1996.

---

however, the rate of inflation turns out to be 10%, then the realized dollar rate of return will be approximately 13%, consisting of the 3% coupon plus a 10% increase in the dollar value of the bond, from $1,000 to $1,100. In early 1997, TIPS bonds were trading at a real yield to maturity a shade below 3.5%.

10.2 DEFAULT RISK

Although bonds generally *promise* a fixed flow of income, that income stream is not riskless unless the investor can be sure the issuer will not default on the obligation. While U.S. government bonds may be treated as free of default risk, this is not true of corporate bonds. If the company goes bankrupt, the bondholders will not receive all the payments they have been promised. Therefore, the actual payments on these bonds are uncertain, for they depend to some degree on the ultimate financial status of the firm.

investment grade bond
A bond rated BBB and above by Standard & Poor's, or Baa and above by Moody's.

Bond default risk is measured by Moody's Investor Services, Standard & Poor's Corporation, Duff and Phelps, and Fitch Investors Service, all of which provide financial information on firms as well as quality ratings of large corporate and municipal bond issues. Each firm assigns letter grades to the bonds of corporations and municipalities to reflect their assessment of the safety of the bond issue. The top rating is AAA or Aaa. Moody's modifies each rating class with a 1, 2, or 3 suffix (e.g., Aaa1, Aaa2, Aaa3) to provide a finer gradation of ratings. The other agencies use a + or − modification.

speculative grade or junk bond
A bond rated BB or lower by Standard & Poor's, Ba or lower by Moody's, or an unrated bond.

Those rated BBB or above (S&P, Duff and Phelps, Fitch) or Baa and above (Moody's) are considered **investment grade bonds,** while lower rated bonds are classified as **speculative grade** or **junk bonds.** Certain regulated institutional investors such as insurance companies have not always been allowed to invest in speculative grade bonds.

FIGURE 10.3

Definitions of Each
Bond Rating Class

Source: From Stephen A. Ross
and Randolph W. Westerfield,
Corporate Finance (St. Louis:
Times Mirror/Mosby College
Publishing, 1988). Data from
various editions of *Standard &
Poor's Bond Guide* and
Moody's Bond Guide.

	Bond Ratings			
	Very High Quality	**High Quality**	**Speculative**	**Very Poor**
Standard & Poor's	AAA AA	A BBB	BB B	CCC D
Moody's	Aaa Aa	A Baa	Ba B	Caa C

At times both Moody's and Standard & Poor's have used adjustments to these ratings.
S&P uses plus and minus signs: A+ is the strongest A rating and A − the weakest.
Moody's uses a 1, 2, or 3 designation—with 1 indicating the strongest.

Moody's	S&P	
Aaa	AAA	Debt rated Aaa and AAA has the highest rating. Capacity to pay interest and principal is extremely strong.
Aa	AA	Debt rated Aa and AA has a very strong capacity to pay interest and repay principal. Together with the highest rating, this group comprises the high-grade bond class.
A	A	Debt rated A has a strong capacity to pay interest and repay principal, although it is somewhat more susceptible to the adverse effects of changes in circumstances and economic conditions than debt in higher rated categories.
Baa	BBB	Debt rated Baa and BBB is regarded as having an adequate capacity to pay interest and repay principal. Whereas it normally exhibits adequate protection parameters, adverse economic conditions or changing circumstances are more likely to lead to a weakened capacity to pay interest and repay principal for debt in this category than in higher rated categories. These bonds are medium grade obligations.
Ba B Caa Ca	BB B CCC CC	Debt rated in these categories is regarded, on balance, as predominantly speculative with respect to capacity to pay interest and repay principal in accordance with the terms of the obligation. BB and Ba indicate the lowest degree of speculation, and CC and Ca the highest degree of speculation. Although such debt will likely have some quality and protective characteristics, these are outweighed by large uncertainties or major risk exposures to adverse conditions. Some issues may be in default.
C	C	This rating is reserved for income bonds on which no interest is being paid.
D	D	Debt rated D is in default, and payment of interest and/or repayment of principal is in arrears.

Figure 10.3 provides the definitions of each bond rating classification.

Junk Bonds

Junk bonds are nothing more than speculative grade (low-rated or unrated) bonds. Before 1977, almost all junk bonds were "fallen angels," that is, bonds issued by firms that originally had investment grade ratings but that had since been downgraded. In 1977, however, firms began to issue "original-issue junk."

Much of the credit for this innovation is given to Drexel Burnham Lambert, and especially its trader, Michael Milken. Drexel had long enjoyed a niche as a junk bond trader and had established a network of potential investors in junk bonds. Its reasoning for marketing original-issue junk, so-called emerging credits, lay in the belief that default rates on these bonds did not justify the large yield spreads commonly exhibited in the marketplace. Firms not able to muster an investment grade rating were happy to have Drexel (and other investment bankers) market their bonds directly to the public, as this opened up a new source of financing. Junk issues were a lower cost financing alternative than borrowing from banks.

Junk bonds gained considerable notoriety in the 1980s when they were used as financing vehicles in leveraged buyouts and hostile takeover attempts. Shortly thereafter, however, the legal difficulties of Drexel and Michael Milken in connection with Wall Street's insider trading scandals of the late 1980s tainted the junk bond market. Drexel agreed to pay $650 million in fines and plead guilty to six felony charges to avoid racketeering charges. Milken was indicted on racketeering and security fraud charges, resigned from Drexel, and eventually agreed in a plea bargain to plead guilty to six felony charges and to pay $600 million in fines. Moreover, as the junk bond market tumbled in late 1989, Drexel suffered large losses in its own billion-dollar portfolio of junk bonds. In February 1990, Drexel filed for bankruptcy.

At the height of Drexel's difficulties, the high-yield bond market nearly dried up. New issues of high-yield bonds fell from approximately $30 billion per year in 1988 and 1989 to about $1 billion in 1990, and prices on these issues fell so severely that their yields exceeded Treasury yields by about 7.5 percentage points, the largest margin in history. Since then, however, the market has rebounded. New issues in 1993 were a record-breaking $55 billion, and issues in 1995 were a still-strong $30 billion. However, it is worth noting that the average credit quality of high-yield debt issued today is higher than the average quality in the boom years of the 1980s.

Determinants of Bond Safety

Bond rating agencies base their quality ratings largely on an analysis of the level and trend of some of the issuer's financial ratios. The key ratios used to evaluate safety are:

1. *Coverage ratios.* Ratios of company earnings to fixed costs. For example, the *times-interest-earned ratio* is the ratio of earnings before interest payments and taxes to interest obligations. The *fixed-charge coverage ratio* adds lease payments and sinking fund payments to interest obligations to arrive at the ratio of earnings to all fixed cash obligations. Low or falling coverage ratios signal possible cash flow difficulties.

2. *Leverage ratio.* Debt to equity ratio. A too-high leverage ratio indicates excessive indebtedness, signaling the possibility the firm will be unable to earn enough to satisfy the obligations on its bonds.

3. *Liquidity ratios.* The two common liquidity ratios are the *current ratio* (current assets/current liabilities) and the *quick ratio* (current assets excluding inventories/current liabilities). These ratios measure the firm's ability to pay bills coming due with cash currently being collected.

4. *Profitability ratios.* Measures of rates of return on assets or equity. Profitability ratios are indicators of a firm's overall financial health. The *return on assets* (earnings before interest and taxes divided by total assets) is the most popular of these measures. Firms with higher return on assets should be better able to raise money in security markets because they offer prospects for better returns on the firm's investments.

5. *Cash flow to debt ratio.* This is the ratio of total cash flow to outstanding debt.

Standard & Poor's periodically computes median values of selected ratios for firms in each of the four investment grade classes, which we present in Table 10.1. Of course, ratios must be evaluated in the context of industry standards, and analysts differ in the weights they place on particular ratios. Nevertheless, Table 10.1 demonstrates the tendency of ratios to improve along with the firm's rating class.

TABLE 10.1

Rating Classes and Median Financial Ratios, 1991–1993

Source: Standard & Poor's *Debt Rating Guide*, 1994. Reprinted by permission of Standard & Poor's Ratings Group.

Rating Category	Fixed-Charge Coverage Ratio	Cash Flow to Total Debt	Return on Capital (%)	Long-Term Debt to Capital (%)
AAA	6.34	0.49	24.2	11.7
AA	4.48	0.32	18.4	19.1
A	2.93	0.17	13.5	29.4
BBB	1.82	0.04	9.7	39.6
BB	1.33	0.01	9.1	51.1
B	0.78	(0.02)	6.3	61.8

Bond Indentures

indenture
The document defining the contract between the bond issuer and the bondholder.

In addition to specifying a payment schedule, the bond **indenture,** which is the contract between the issuer and the bondholder, also specifies a set of restrictions on the issuer to protect the rights of the bondholders. Such restrictions include provisions relating to collateral, sinking funds, dividend policy, and further borrowing. The issuing firm agrees to these so-called *protective covenants* in order to market its bonds to investors concerned about the safety of the bond issue.

sinking fund
A bond indenture that calls for the issuer to periodically repurchase some proportion of the outstanding bonds prior to maturity.

Sinking Funds   Bonds call for the payment of par value at the end of the bond's life. This payment constitutes a large cash commitment for the issuer. To help ensure the commitment does not create a cash flow crisis, the firm agrees to establish a **sinking fund** to spread the payment burden over several years. The fund may operate in one of two ways:

1. The firm may repurchase a fraction of the outstanding bonds in the open market each year.
2. The firm may purchase a fraction of outstanding bonds at a special call price associated with the sinking fund provision. The firm has an option to purchase the bonds at either the market price or the sinking fund price, whichever is lower. To allocate the burden of the sinking fund call fairly among bondholders, the bonds chosen for the call are selected at random based on serial number.[2]

The sinking fund call differs from a conventional bond call in two important ways. First, the firm can repurchase only a limited fraction of the bond issue at the sinking fund call price. At best, some indentures allow firms to use a *doubling option*, which allows repurchase of double the required number of bonds at the sinking fund call price. Second, the sinking fund call price generally is lower than the call price established by other call provisions in the indenture. The sinking fund call price usually is set at the bond's par value.

Although sinking funds ostensibly protect bondholders by making principal repayment more likely, they can hurt the investor. If interest rates fall and bond prices rise, firms will benefit from the sinking fund provision that enables them to repurchase their bonds at below-market prices. In these circumstances, the firm's gain is the bondholder's loss.

One bond issue that does not require a sinking fund is a *serial bond* issue. In a serial bond issue, the firm sells bonds with staggered maturity dates. As bonds mature sequentially, the principal repayment burden for the firm is spread over time just as it is with a sinking fund. Serial bonds do not include call provisions. Unlike sinking fund bonds, serial bonds do not confront security holders with the risk that a particular bond may be called for the sinking fund. The disadvantage of serial bonds, however, is that the bonds of each maturity date are different bonds, which reduces the liquidity of the issue. Trading these bonds, therefore, is more expensive.

subordination clauses
Restrictions on additional borrowing that stipulate that senior bondholders will be paid first in the event of bankruptcy.

Subordination of Further Debt   One of the factors determining bond safety is the total outstanding debt of the issuer. If you bought a bond today, you would be understandably distressed to see the firm tripling its outstanding debt tomorrow. Your bond would be of lower quality than it appeared when you bought it. To prevent firms from harming bondholders in this manner, **subordination clauses** restrict the amount of their additional borrowing. Additional debt might be required to be subordinated in priority to existing debt; that is, in the event of bankruptcy, *subordinated* or *junior* debtholders will not be paid unless and until the prior senior debt is fully paid off. For this reason, subordination is sometimes called a

---

[2]While it is uncommon, the sinking fund provision also may call for periodic payments to a trustee, with the payments invested so that the accumulated sum can be used for retirement of the entire issue at maturity.

"me-first rule," meaning the senior (earlier) bondholders are to be paid first in the event of bankruptcy.

Dividend Restrictions   Covenants also limit firms in the amount of dividends they are allowed to pay. These limitations protect the bondholders because they force the firm to retain assets rather than paying them out to stockholders. A typical restriction disallows payments of dividends if cumulative dividends paid since the firm's inception exceed cumulative net income plus proceeds from sales of stock.

collateral
A specific asset pledged against possible default on a bond.

Collateral   Some bonds are issued with specific collateral behind them. **Collateral** can take several forms, but it represents a particular asset of the firm that the bondholders receive if the firm defaults on the bond. If the collateral is property, the bond is called a *mortgage bond*. If the collateral takes the form of other securities held by the firm, the bond is a *collateral trust bond*. In the case of equipment, the bond is known as an *equipment obligation bond*. This last form of collateral is used most commonly by firms such as railroads, where the equipment is fairly standard and can be easily sold to another firm should the firm default and the bondholders acquire the collateral.

Because of the specific collateral that backs them, collateralized bonds generally are considered the safest variety of corporate bonds. General **debenture** bonds by contrast do not provide for specific collateral; they are *unsecured* bonds. The bondholder relies solely on the general earning power of the firm for the bond's safety. If the firm defaults, debenture owners become general creditors of the firm. Because they are safer, collateralized bonds generally offer lower yields than general debentures.

debenture
A bond not backed by specific collateral.

Figure 10.4 shows the terms of a bond issued by Mobil as described in *Moody's Industrial Manual*. The terms of the bond are typical and illustrate many of the indenture provisions we have mentioned. The bond is registered and listed on the NYSE. Although it was issued in 1991, it is not callable until 2002. Although the call price started at 105.007% of par value, it falls gradually until it reaches par after 2020.

10.3 BOND PRICING

Because a bond's coupon and principal repayments all occur months or years in the future, the price an investor would be willing to pay for a claim to those payments depends on the value of dollars to be received in the future compared to dollars in hand today. This "present value" calculation depends in turn on market interest rates. As we saw in Chapter 6, the nominal risk-free interest rate equals the sum of (1) a real risk-free rate of return, and (2) a premium above the real rate to compensate for expected inflation. In addition, because most bonds are not riskless, the discount rate will embody an additional premium that reflects bond-specific characteristics such as default risk, liquidity, tax attributes, call risk, and so on.

We simplify for now by assuming there is one interest rate that is appropriate for discounting cash flows of any maturity, but we can relax this assumption easily. In practice, there may be different discount rates for cash flows accruing in different periods. For the time being, however, we ignore this refinement.

To value a security, we discount its expected cash flows by the appropriate discount rate. The cash flows from a bond consist of coupon payments until the maturity date plus the final payment of par value. Therefore

Bond value = Present value of coupons + Present value of par value

If we call the maturity date T and call the discount rate r, the bond value can be written as

FIGURE 10.4

Callable Bond Issued
by Mobil

Source: *Moody's Industrial
Manual*, Moody's Investor
Services, 1994.

& Mobil Corp. debenture 8s, due 2032:
Rating — Aa2
AUTH — $250,000,000.
OUTSTG — Dec. 31, 1993, $250,000,000.
DATED — Oct. 30, 1991.
INTEREST — F&A 12.
TRUSTEE — Chemical Bank.
DENOMINATION — Fully registered, $1,000 and
integral multiples thereof. Transferable and
exchangeable without service charge.
CALLABLE — As a whole or in part, at any time,
on or after Aug. 12, 2002, at the option of Co. on
at least 30 but not more than 60 days' notice to
each Aug. 11 as follows:

2003	105.007	2004	104.756	2005	104.506
2006	104.256	2007	104.005	2008	103.755
2009	103.505	2010	103.254	2011	103.004
2012	102.754	2013	102.503	2014	102.253
2015	102.003	2016	101.752	2017	101.502
2018	101.252	2019	101.001	2020	100.751
2021	100.501	2022	100.250		

and thereafter at 100 plus accrued interest.
SECURITY — Not secured. Ranks equally with all
other unsecured and unsubordinated indebtedness
of Co. Co. nor any Affiliate will not incurr any
indebtedness; provided that Co. will not create as
security for any indebtedness for borrowed money,
any mortgage, pledge, security interest or lien on
any stock or indebtedness is directly owned by
Co., without effectively providing that the debt
securities shall be secured equally and ratably with
such indebtedness, so long as such indebtedness
shall be so secured.
INDENTURE   MODIFICATION — Indenture
may be modified, except as provided with, consent
of 66⅔% of debs. outstg.
RIGHTS ON DEFAULT — Trustee, or 25% of
debs. outstg., may declare principal dua nad payable (30 days' grace for payment of interest).
LISTED — On New York Stock Exchange.
PURPOSE — Proceeds used for general corporate
purposes.
OFFERED — ($250,000,000) at 99.51 plus accrued
interest (proceeds to Co., 99.11) on Aug. 5, 1992
thru Merrill Lynch & Co., Donaldson, Lufkin &
Jenrette Securities Corp., PaineWebber Inc., Prudential Securities Inc., Smith Barney, Harris
Upham & Co. Inc. and associates.

$$\text{Bond value} = \sum_{t=1}^{T} \frac{\text{Coupon}}{(1+r)^t} + \frac{\text{Par value}}{(1+r)^T} \qquad (10.1)$$

The summation sign in Equation 10.1 directs us to add the present value of each coupon payment; each coupon is discounted based on the time until it will be paid. The first term on the right-hand side of Equation 10.1 is the present value of an annuity. The second term is the present value of a single amount, the final payment of the bond's par value.

EXAMPLE 10.2
Bond Pricing

We discussed earlier an 8% coupon, 30-year maturity bond with par value of $1,000 paying 60 semiannual coupon payments of $40 each. Suppose that the interest rate is 8% annually, or 4% per six-month period. Then the value of the bond can be written as

$$\text{Price} = \sum_{t=1}^{60} \frac{\$40}{(1.04)^t} + \frac{\$1,000}{(1.04)^{60}}$$

For notational simplicity, we can rewrite this equation as

$$\text{Price} = \$40 \times \text{Annuity factor } (4\%, 60) + \$1,000 \times \text{PV factor } (4\%, 60)$$

where Annuity factor (4%, 60) represents the present value of an annuity of $1 when the interest rate is 4% and the annuity lasts for 60 periods, and PV factor (4%, 60) is the present value of a single payment of $1 to be received in 60 periods.

It is easy to confirm that the present value of the bond's 60 semiannual coupon payments of $40 each is $904.94, while the $1,000 final payment of par value has a present value of $95.06, for a total bond value of

$1,000. You can perform these calculations on any financial calculator or use a set of present value tables such as those in Appendix C at the end of the text.

In this example, the coupon rate equals yield to maturity, and the bond price equals par value. If the interest rate were not equal to the bond's coupon rate, the bond would not sell at par value. For example, if the interest rate were to rise to 10% (5% per six months), the bond's price would fall by $189.29, to $810.71, as follows

$$\$40 \times \text{Annuity factor } (5\%, 60) + \$1,000 \times \text{PV factor } (5\%, 60)$$
$$= \$757.17 + \$53.54$$
$$= \$810.71$$

At a higher interest rate, the present value of the payments to be received by the bondholder is lower. Therefore, the bond price will fall as market interest rates rise. This illustrates a crucial general rule in bond valuation. When interest rates rise, bond prices must fall be-cause the present value of the bond's payments are obtained by discounting at a higher interest rate.

Figure 10.5 shows the price of the 30-year, 8% coupon bond for a range of interest rates. The negative slope illustrates the inverse relationship between prices and yields. Note also from the figure (and from Table 10.2) that the shape of the curve implies that an increase in the interest rate results in a price decline that is smaller than the price gain resulting from a decrease of equal magnitude in the interest rate. This property of bond prices is called *convexity* because of the convex shape of the bond price curve. This curvature reflects the fact that progressive increases in the interest rate result in progressively smaller reductions in the bond price.[3] Therefore, the price curve becomes flatter at higher interest rates. We will return to the issue of convexity in the next chapter.

FIGURE 10.5

The Inverse Relationship between Bond Prices and Yields

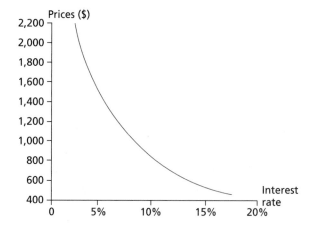

TABLE 10.2

Bond Prices at Different Interest Rates (8% Coupon Bond, Coupons Paid Semiannually)

| | Bond Price at Given Market Interest Rate | | | | |
Time to Maturity	4%	6%	8%	10%	12%
1 year	$1,038.83	$1,019.13	$1,000.00	$981.41	$963.33
10 years	1,327.03	1,148.77	1,000.00	875.38	770.60
20 years	1,547.11	1,231.15	1,000.00	828.41	699.07
30 years	1,695.22	1,276.76	1,000.00	810.71	676.77

[3]The progressively smaller impact of interest rate increases results from the fact that at higher rates the bond is worth less. Therefore, an additional increase in rates operates on a smaller initial base, resulting in a smaller price reduction.

Concept Check

2. Calculate the price of the bond for a market interest rate of 3% per half year. Compare the capital gains for the interest rate decline to the losses incurred when the rate increases to 5%.

Corporate bonds typically are issued at par value. This means the underwriters of the bond issue (the firms that market the bonds to the public for the issuing corporation) must choose a coupon rate that very closely approximates market yields. In a primary issue of bonds, the underwriters attempt to sell the newly issued bonds directly to their customers. If the coupon rate is inadequate, investors will not pay par value for the bonds.

After the bonds are issued, bondholders may buy or sell bonds in secondary markets, such as the one operated by the New York Stock Exchange or the over-the-counter market, where most bonds trade. In these secondary markets, bond prices move in accordance with market forces. The bond prices fluctuate inversely with the market interest rate.

The inverse relationship between price and yield is a central feature of fixed-income securities. Interest rate fluctuations represent the main source of risk in the fixed-income market, and we devote considerable attention in the next chapter to assessing the sensitivity of bond prices to market yields. For now, however, it is sufficient to highlight one key factor that determines that sensitivity, namely, the maturity of the bond.

A general rule in evaluating bond price risk is that, keeping all other factors the same, the longer the maturity of the bond, the greater the sensitivity of its price to fluctuations in the interest rate. For example, consider Table 10.2, which presents the price of an 8% coupon bond at different market yields and times to maturity. For any departure of the interest rate from 8% (the rate at which the bond sells at par value), the change in the bond price is smaller for shorter times to maturity.

This makes sense. If you buy the bond at par with an 8% coupon rate, and market rates subsequently rise, then you suffer a loss: You have tied up your money earning 8% when alternative investments offer higher returns. This is reflected in a capital loss on the bond—a fall in its market price. The longer the period for which your money is tied up, the greater the loss and, correspondingly, the greater the drop in the bond price. In Table 10.2, the row for one-year maturity bonds shows little price sensitivity—that is, with only one year's earnings at stake, changes in interest rates are not too threatening. But for 30-year maturity bonds, interest rate swings have a large impact on bond prices.

This is why short-term Treasury securities such as T-bills are considered to be the safest. They are free not only of default risk, but also largely of price risk attributable to interest rate volatility.

10.4 BOND YIELDS

We have noted that the current yield of a bond measures only the cash income provided by the bond as a percentage of bond price and ignores any prospective capital gains or losses. We would like a measure of rate of return that accounts for both current income as well as the price increase or decrease over the bond's life. The yield to maturity is the standard measure of the total rate of return of the bond over its life. However, it is far from a perfect measure, and we will explore several variations of this statistic.

Yield to Maturity

yield to maturity (YTM)
The discount rate that makes the present value of a bond's payments equal to its price.

In practice, an investor considering the purchase of a bond is not quoted a promised rate of return. Instead, the investor must use the bond price, maturity date, and coupon payments to infer the return offered by the bond over its life. The **yield to maturity** (YTM) is defined as the discount rate that makes the present value of a bond's payments equal to its price. This rate is often viewed as a measure of the average rate of return that will be earned on a bond if it is bought now and held until maturity. To calculate the yield to maturity, we solve the bond price equation for the interest rate given the bond's price.

For example, suppose an 8% coupon, 30-year bond is selling at $1,276.76. What average rate of return would be earned by an investor purchasing the bond at this price? To answer this question, we find the interest rate at which the present value of the remaining bond payments equals the bond price. This is the rate that is consistent with the observed price of the bond. Therefore, we solve for r in the following equation

$$\$1,276.76 = \sum_{t=1}^{60} \frac{\$40}{(1+r)^t} + \frac{\$1,000}{(1+r)^{60}}$$

or, equivalently

$$1,276.76 = 40 \times \text{Annuity factor } (r, 60) + 1,000 \times \text{PV factor } (r, 60)$$

These equations have only one unknown variable, the interest rate, r. You can use a financial calculator to confirm that the solution to the equation is $r = .03$, or 3% per half year.[4] This is considered the bond's yield to maturity, as the bond would be fairly priced at $1,276.76 if the fair market rate of return on the bond over its entire life were 3% per half year.

The financial press reports yields on an annualized basis, however, and annualizes the bond's semiannual yield using simple interest techniques, resulting in an annual percentage rate or APR. Yields annualized using simple interest are also called "bond equivalent yields." Therefore, the semiannual yield would be doubled and reported in the newspaper as a bond equivalent yield of 6%. The *effective* annual yield of the bond, however, accounts for compound interest. If one earns 3% interest every six months, then after one year, each dollar invested grows with interest to $1 \times (1.03)^2 = 1.0609$, and the effective annual interest rate on the bond is 6.09%.

The bond's yield to maturity is the internal rate of return on an investment in the bond. The yield to maturity can be interpreted as the compound rate of return over the life of the bond under the assumption that all bond coupons can be reinvested at an interest rate equal to the bond's yield to maturity.[5] Yield to maturity therefore is widely accepted as a proxy for average return.

Yield to maturity can be difficult to calculate without a financial calculator. However, it is easy to calculate with one. Financial calculators are designed with present value and future value formulas already programmed. The basic financial calculator uses five keys that correspond to the inputs for time value of money problems such as bond pricing:

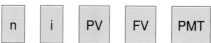

- n is the number of time periods. In the case of a bond, n equals the number of periods until the bond matures. If the bond makes semiannual payments, n is the number of half-year periods or, equivalently, the number of semiannual coupon payments. For example, if the bond has 10 years until maturity, you would enter 20 for n, since each payment period is one-half year.

- i is the interest rate per period, expressed as a percentage (not a decimal). For example, if the interest rate is 6%, you would enter 6, not 0.06.

---

[4]Without a financial calculator, you still could solve the equation, but you would need to use a trial-and-error approach.
[5]If the reinvestment rate does not equal the bond's yield to maturity, the compound rate of return will differ from YTM. This is demonstrated below in Example 10.6.

- *PV* is the present value. Many calculators will require that *PV* be entered as a negative number, in recognition of the fact that purchase of the bond is a cash *outflow*, while the receipt of coupon payments and face value are cash *inflows*.
- *FV* is the future value or face value of the bond. In general, *FV* is interpreted as a one-time future payment of a cash flow, which, for bonds, is the face (i.e., par) value.
- *PMT* is the amount of any recurring payment. For coupon bonds, *PMT* is the coupon payment; for zero-coupon bonds, *PMT* will be zero.

Given any four of these inputs, the calculator will solve for the fifth. We can illustrate with several examples.

EXAMPLE 10.3
Bond Valuation
Using a Financial
Calculator

Consider the yield to maturity problem that we just solved. We would enter the following inputs (in any order):

n	60	[The bond has a maturity of 30 years, so it makes 60 semiannual payments.]
PMT	40	[Each semiannual coupon payment is $40.]
PV	(−)1,276.76	[The bond can be purchased for $1,276.76, which on some calculators must be entered as a negative number as it is a cash outflow.]
FV	1,000	[The bond will provide a one-time cash flow of $1,000 when it matures.]

Given these inputs, you now use the calculator to find the interest rate at which the *PV* of $1,276.76 actually equals the present value of the 60 payments of $40 each plus the one-time payment of $1,000 at maturity. On most calculators, you first punch the "compute" key (labeled *COMP* or *CPT*) and then enter *i* to have the interest rate computed. If you do so, you will find that *i* = 3, or 3% semiannually, as we claimed. (Notice that just as the cash flows are paid semiannually, the computed interest rate is a rate per semiannual time period.)

You can also find bond prices given a yield to maturity. For example, we saw in Example 10.2 that if the yield to maturity is 5% semiannually, the bond price will be $810.71. You can confirm this with the following inputs on your calculator:

$$n = 60; \ i = 5; \ FV = 1,000; \ PMT = 40$$

and then computing *PV* to find that *PV* = 810.71. Once again, your calculator may report the result as −810.71.

current yield
Annual coupon divided by bond price.

Yield to maturity is different from the **current yield** of a bond, which is the bond's annual coupon payment divided by the bond price. For example, for the 8%, 30-year bond currently selling at $1,276.76, the current yield would be $80/$1,276.76 = 0.0627, or 6.27% per year. In contrast, recall that the effective annual yield to maturity is 6.09%. For this bond, which is selling at a premium over par value ($1,276 rather than $1,000), the coupon rate (8%) exceeds the current yield (6.27%), which exceeds the yield to maturity (6.09%). The coupon rate exceeds current yield because the coupon rate divides the coupon payments by par value ($1,000) rather than by the bond price ($1,276). In turn, the current yield exceeds yield to maturity because the yield to maturity accounts for the built-in capital loss on the bond; the bond bought today for $1,276 will eventually fall in value to $1,000 at maturity.

Concept Check

3. What will be the relationship among coupon rate, current yield, and yield to maturity for bonds selling at discounts from par?

Yield to Call

Yield to maturity is calculated on the assumption that the bond will be held until maturity. What if the bond is callable, however, and may be retired prior to the maturity date? How should we measure average rate of return for bonds subject to a call provision?

FIGURE 10.6

Bond Prices: Callable
and Straight Debt

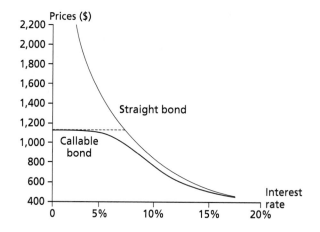

Figure 10.6 illustrates the risk of call to the bondholder. The colored line is the value at various market interest rates of a "straight" (that is, noncallable) bond with par value $1,000, an 8% coupon rate, and a 30-year time to maturity. If interest rates fall, the bond price, which equals the present value of the promised payments, can rise substantially. Now consider a bond that has the same coupon rate and maturity date but is callable at 110% of par value, or $1,100. When interest rates fall, the present value of the bond's *scheduled* payments rises, but the call provision allows the issuer to repurchase the bond at the call price. If the call price is less than the present value of the scheduled payments, the issuer can call the bond at the expense of the bondholder.

The black line in Figure 10.6 is the value of the callable bond. At high interest rates, the risk of call is negligible, and the values of the straight and callable bonds converge. At lower rates, however, the values of the bonds begin to diverge, with the difference reflecting the value of the firm's option to reclaim the callable bond at the call price. At very low rates, the bond is called, and its value is simply the call price, $1,100.

This analysis suggests that bond market analysts might be more interested in a bond's yield to call rather than its yield to maturity if the bond is especially vulnerable to being called. The yield to call is calculated just like the yield to maturity except that the time until call replaces time until maturity, and the call price replaces the par value. This computation is sometimes called "yield to first call," as it assumes the bond will be called as soon as it is first callable.

EXAMPLE 10.4
Yield to Call

Suppose the 8% coupon, 30-year maturity bond sells for $1,150 and is callable in 10 years at a call price of $1,100. Its yield to maturity and yield to call would be calculated using the following inputs:

	Yield to Call	Yield to Maturity
Coupon payment	$40	$40
Number of semiannual periods	20 periods	60 periods
Final payment	$1,100	$1,000
Price	$1,150	$1,150

Yield to call is then 6.64% [to confirm this on your calculator, input $n = 20$; $PV = (-)1,150$; $FV = 1,100$; $PMT = 40$; compute i], while yield to maturity is 6.82% [to confirm, input $n = 60$; $PV = (-)1,150$; $FV = 1,000$; $PMT = 40$; compute i].

We have noted that most callable bonds are issued with an initial period of call protection. In addition, an implicit form of call protection operates for bonds selling at deep discounts from their call prices. Even if interest rates fall a bit, deep-discount bonds still will sell below the call price and thus will not be subject to a call.

Premium bonds that might be selling near their call prices, however, are especially apt to be called if rates fall further. If interest rates fall, a callable premium bond is likely to provide a lower return than could be earned on a discount bond whose potential price appreciation is not limited by the likelihood of a call. Investors in premium bonds often are more interested in the bond's yield to call rather than yield to maturity as a consequence, because it may appear to them that the bond will be retired at the call date.

In fact, the yield reported for callable Treasury bonds in the financial pages of the newspaper (see Figure 10.1) is the yield to *call* for premium bonds and the yield to *maturity* for discount bonds. This is because the call price on Treasury issues is simply par value. If the bond is selling at a premium, it is more likely that the Treasury will find it advantageous to call the bond when it enters the call period. If the bond is selling at a discount from par, the Treasury will not find it advantageous to exercise its option to call.

Concept Check

4. A 20-year maturity 9% coupon bond paying coupons semiannually is callable in five years at a call price of $1,050. The bond currently sells at a yield to maturity of 8% (bond equivalent yield). What is the yield to call?

Yield to Maturity and Default Risk

Because corporate bonds are subject to default risk, we must distinguish between the bond's promised yield to maturity and its expected yield. The promised or stated yield will be realized only if the firm meets the obligations of the bond issue. Therefore, the stated yield is the *maximum possible* yield to maturity of the bond. The expected yield to maturity must take into account the possibility of a default.

For example, in August 1993, Wang Laboratories, Inc., was in bankruptcy proceedings, and its bonds due in 2009 were selling at about 35% of par value, resulting in a yield to maturity of over 26%. Investors did not really expect these bonds to provide a 26% rate of return. They recognized that bondholders were very unlikely to receive all the payments promised in the bond contract, and that the yield based on *expected* cash flows was far less than the yield based on *promised* cash flows.

**EXAMPLE 10.5
Expected versus
Promised Yield**

Suppose a firm issued a 9% coupon bond 20 years ago. The bond now has 10 years left until its maturity date but the firm is having financial difficulties. Investors believe that the firm will be able to make good on the remaining interest payments, but that at the maturity date, the firm will be forced into bankruptcy, and bondholders will receive only 70% of par value. The bond is selling at $750.

Yield to maturity (YTM) would then be calculated using the following inputs:

	Expected YTM	Stated YTM
Coupon payment	$45	$45
Number of semiannual periods	20 periods	20 periods
Final payment	$700	$1,000
Price	$750	$750

The yield to maturity based on promised payments is 13.7%. Based on the expected payment of $700 at maturity, however, the yield would be only 11.6%. The stated yield to maturity is greater than the yield investors actually expect to receive.

Concept Check

5. What is the expected yield to maturity if the firm is in even worse condition and investors expect a final payment of only $600?

To compensate for the possibility of default, corporate bonds must offer a **default premium.** The default premium is the difference between the promised yield on a corporate

default premium
The increment to promised yield that compensates the investor for default risk.

bond and the yield of an otherwise identical government bond that is riskless in terms of default. If the firm remains solvent and actually pays the investor all of the promised cash flows, the investor will realize a higher yield to maturity than would be realized from the government bond. If, however, the firm goes bankrupt, the corporate bond is likely to provide a lower return than the government bond. The corporate bond has the potential for both better and worse performance than the default-free Treasury bond. In other words, it is riskier.

The pattern of default premiums offered on risky bonds is sometimes called the *risk structure of interest rates*. The greater the default risk, the higher the default premium. Figure 10.7 shows the yield to maturity of bonds of different risk classes since 1954 and the yields on junk bonds since 1984. You can see here clear evidence of default-risk premiums on promised yields.

Realized Compound Yield versus Yield to Maturity

We have noted that yield to maturity will equal the rate of return realized over the life of the bond if all coupons are reinvested at an interest rate equal to the bond's yield to maturity. Consider for example, a two-year bond selling at par value paying a 10% coupon once a year. The yield to maturity is 10%. If the $100 coupon payment is reinvested at an interest rate of 10%, the $1,000 investment in the bond will grow after two years to $1,210, as illustrated in Figure 10.8, Panel A. The coupon paid in the first year is reinvested and grows with interest to a second-year value of $110, which, together with the second coupon payment and payment of par value in the second year, results in a total value of $1,210. The compound growth rate of invested funds, therefore, is calculated from

$$\$1,000 \ (1 + y_{\text{realized}})^2 = \$1,210$$
$$y_{\text{realized}} = 0.10 = 10\%$$

With a reinvestment rate equal to the 10% yield to maturity, the *realized* compound yield equals yield to maturity.

But what if the reinvestment rate is not 10%? If the coupon can be invested at more than 10%, funds will grow to more than $1,210, and the realized compound return will exceed 10%. If the reinvestment rate is less than 10%, so will be the realized compound return. Consider the following example.

FIGURE 10.7

Yields on Long-term Bonds

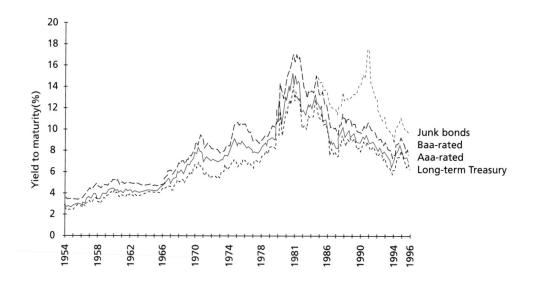

EXAMPLE 10.6
Realized
Compound Yield

If the interest rate earned on the first coupon is less than 10%, the final value of the investment will be less than $1,210, and the realized compound yield will be less than 10%. Suppose the interest rate at which the coupon can be invested equals 8%. The following calculations are illustrated in Panel B of Figure 10.8.

Future value of first coupon payment with interest earnings	$100 \times 1.08 = $108
Cash payment in second year (final coupon plus par value)	$1,100
Total value of investment with reinvested coupons	$1,208

The realized compound yield is computed by calculating the compound rate of growth of invested funds, assuming that all coupon payments are reinvested. The investor purchased the bond for par at $1,000, and this investment grew to $1,208.

$$\$1,000 \ (1 + y_{\text{realized}})^2 = \$1,208$$
$$y_{\text{realized}} = 0.0991 = 9.91\%$$

Example 10.6 highlights the problem with conventional yield to maturity when reinvestment rates can change over time. However, in an economy with future interest rate uncertainty, the rates at which interim coupons will be reinvested are not yet known. Therefore, while realized compound yield can be computed *after* the investment period ends, it cannot be computed in advance without a forecast of future reinvestment rates. This reduces much of the attraction of the realized yield measure.

Yield to Maturity versus Holding-Period Return

You should not confuse the rate of return on a bond over any particular holding period with the bond's yield to maturity. The yield to maturity is defined as the single discount rate at which the present value of the payments provided by the bond equals its price. The yield to maturity is a measure of the average rate of return over the bond's life if it is held until maturity. In contrast, the holding-period return equals income earned over a period (includ-

FIGURE 10.8
Growth of Invested
Funds

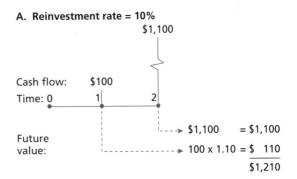

ing capital gains or losses) as a percentage of the bond price at the start of the period. The holding-period return can be calculated for any holding period based on the income generated over that period.

For example, if a 30-year bond paying an annual coupon of $80 is purchased for $1,000, its yield to maturity is 8%. If the bond price increases to $1,050 by year end, its yield to maturity will fall below 8% (the bond is now selling above par value, so yield to maturity must be less than the 8% coupon rate), but the holding-period return for the year is greater than 8%:

$$\text{Holding-period return} = \frac{\$80 + (\$1,050 - \$1,000)}{\$1,000} = 0.13, \text{ or } 13\%$$

10.5 BOND PRICES OVER TIME

As we noted earlier, a bond will sell at par value when its coupon rate equals the market interest rate. In these circumstances, the investor receives fair compensation for the time value of money in the form of the recurring interest payments. No further capital gain is necessary to provide fair compensation.

When the coupon rate is lower than the market interest rate, the coupon payments alone will not provide investors as high a return as they could earn elsewhere in the market. To receive a fair return on such an investment, investors also need to earn price appreciation on their bonds. The bonds, therefore, would have to sell below par value to provide a "built-in" capital gain on the investment.

To illustrate this point, suppose a bond was issued several years ago when the interest rate was 7%. The bond's annual coupon rate was thus set at 7%. (We will suppose for simplicity that the bond pays its coupon annually.) Now, with three years left in the bond's life, the interest rate is 8% per year. The bond's fair market price is the present value of the remaining annual coupons plus payment of par value. That present value is

$$\$70 \times \text{Annuity factor (8\%, 3)} + \$1,000 \times \text{PV factor (8\%, 3)} = \$974.23$$

which is less than par value.

In another year, after the next coupon is paid, the bond would sell at

$$\$70 \times \text{Annuity factor (8\%, 2)} + \$1,000 \times \text{PV factor (8\%, 2)} = \$982.17$$

thereby yielding a capital gain over the year of $7.94. If an investor had purchased the bond at $974.23, the total return over the year would equal the coupon payment plus capital gain, or $70 + $7.94 = $77.94. This represents a rate of return of $77.94/$974.23, or 8%, exactly the current rate of return available elsewhere in the market.

Concept Check

6. What will the bond price be in yet another year, when only one year remains until maturity? What is the rate of return to an investor who purchases the bond at $982.17 and sells it one year hence?

When bond prices are set according to the present value formula, any discount from par value provides an anticipated capital gain that will augment a below-market coupon rate just sufficiently to provide a fair total rate of return. Conversely, if the coupon rate exceeds the market interest rate, the interest income by itself is greater than that available elsewhere in the market. Investors will bid up the price of these bonds above their par values. As the bonds approach maturity, they will fall in value because fewer of these above-market coupon payments remain. The resulting capital losses offset the large coupon payments so that the bondholder again receives only a fair rate of return.

FIGURE 10.9

Price Paths of Coupon Bonds

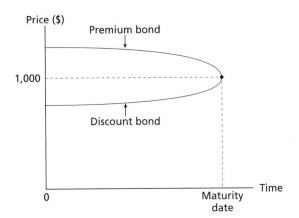

Problem 8 at the end of the chapter asks you to work through the case of the high coupon bond. Figure 10.9 traces out the price paths of high and low coupon bonds (net of accrued interest) as time to maturity approaches. The low coupon bond enjoys capital gains, while the high coupon bond suffers capital losses.

We use these examples to show that each bond offers investors the same total rate of return. Although the capital gain versus income components differ, the price of each bond is set to provide competitive rates, as we should expect in well-functioning capital markets. Security returns all should be comparable on an after-tax risk-adjusted basis. If they are not, investors will try to sell low-return securities, thereby driving down the prices until the total return at the now lower price is competitive with other securities. Prices should continue to adjust until all securities are fairly priced in that expected returns are appropriate (given necessary risk and tax adjustments).

Zero-Coupon Bonds

Original issue discount bonds are less common than coupon bonds issued at par. These are bonds that are issued intentionally with low coupon rates that cause the bond to sell at a discount from par value. An extreme example of this type of bond is the *zero-coupon bond*, which carries no coupons and must provide all its return in the form of price appreciation. Zeros provide only one cash flow to their owners, and that is on the maturity date of the bond.

U.S. Treasury bills are examples of short-term zero-coupon instruments. The Treasury issues or sells a bill for some amount less than $10,000, agreeing to repay $10,000 at the bill's maturity. All of the investor's return comes in the form of price appreciation over time.

Longer term zero-coupon bonds are commonly created from coupon-bearing notes and bonds with the help of the U.S. Treasury. A broker that purchases a Treasury coupon bond may ask the Treasury to break down the cash flows to be paid by the bond into a series of independent securities, where each security is a claim to one of the payments of the original bond. For example, a 10-year coupon bond would be "stripped" of its 20 semiannual coupons and each coupon payment would be treated as a stand-alone zero-coupon bond. The maturities of these bonds would thus range from 6 months to 20 years. The final payment of principal would be treated as another stand-alone zero-coupon security. Each of the payments would then be treated as an independent security and assigned its own CUSIP number, the security identifier that allows for electronic trading over the Fedwire system. The payments are still considered obligations of the U.S. Treasury. The Treasury program under which coupon stripping is performed is called STRIPS (Separate Trading of Registered Interest and Principal of Securities), and these zero-coupon securities are called *Treasury strips*. See Figure 10.1 for a listing of these bonds in *The Wall Street Journal*.

FIGURE 10.10

The Price of a 30-Year Zero-Coupon Bond over Time (Price Equals $1000/(1.10)^T$ Where T is Time until Maturity

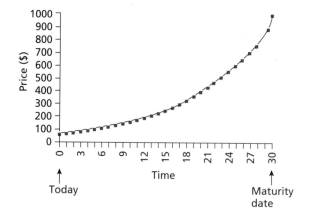

What should happen to prices of zeros as time passes? On their maturity dates, zeros must sell for par value. Before maturity, however, they should sell at discounts from par, because of the time value of money. As time passes, price should approach par value. In fact, if the interest rate is constant, a zero's price will increase at exactly the rate of interest.

To illustrate this property, consider a zero with 30 years until maturity, and suppose the market interest rate is 10% per year. The price of the bond today will be $\$1{,}000/(1.10)^{30} = \$57.31$. Next year, with only 29 years until maturity, the price will be $\$1{,}000/(1.10)^{29} = \$63.04$, a 10% increase over its previous-year value. Because the par value of the bond is now discounted for one fewer year, its price has increased by the one-year discount factor.

Figure 10.10 presents the price path of a 10-year zero-coupon bond until its maturity date for an annual market interest rate of 10%. The bond's price rises exponentially, not linearly, until its maturity.

After-Tax Returns

The tax authorities recognize that the "built-in" price appreciation on original-issue discount (OID) bonds such as zero-coupon bonds represents an implicit interest payment to the holder of the security. The Internal Revenue Service (IRS), therefore, calculates a price appreciation schedule to impute taxable interest income for the built-in appreciation during a tax year, even if the asset is not sold or does not mature until a future year. Any additional gains or losses that arise from changes in market interest rates are treated as capital gains or losses if the OID bond is sold during the tax year.

EXAMPLE 10.7
Taxation of OID Bonds

If the interest rate originally is 10%, the 30-year zero would be issued at a price of $\$1{,}000/(1.10)^{30} = \$57.31$. The following year, the IRS calculates what the bond price would be if the yield remains at 10%. This is $\$1{,}000/(1.10)^{29} = \$63.04$. Therefore, the IRS imputes interest income of $\$63.04 - \$57.31 = \$5.73$. This amount is subject to tax. Notice that the imputed interest income is based on a "constant yield method" that ignores any changes in market interest rates.

If interest rates actually fall, let's say to 9.9%, the bond price actually will be $\$1{,}000/(1.099)^{29} = \$64.72$. If the bond is sold, then the difference between $64.72 and $63.04 will be treated as capital gains income and taxed at the capital gains tax rate. If the bond is not sold, then the price difference is an unrealized capital gain and does not result in taxes in that year. In either case, the investor must pay taxes on the $5.73 of imputed interest at the ordinary income tax rate.

The procedure illustrated in Example 10.7 is applied to the taxation of other original issue discount bonds, even if they are not zero-coupon bonds. Consider, as another example, a 30-year maturity bond that is issued with a coupon rate of 4% and a yield to maturity of 8%. For simplicity, we will assume that the bond pays coupons once annually. Because of the low coupon rate, the bond will be issued at a price far below par value, specifically at a price of $549.69. (Confirm this for yourself.) If the bond's yield to maturity remains at 8%, then its price in one year will rise to $553.66. (Confirm this also.) This provides a pretax holding-period return of exactly 8%:

$$HPR = \frac{\$40 + (\$553.66 - \$549.69)}{\$549.69} = 0.08$$

The increase in the bond price based on a constant yield, however, is treated as interest income, so the investor is required to pay taxes on imputed interest income of $553.66 − $549.69 = $3.97, as well as on the explicit coupon income of $40. If the bond's yield actually changes during the year, the difference between the bond's price and the "constant yield value" of $553.66 would be treated as capital gains income if the bond were sold at year-end.

Concept Check

7. Suppose that the yield to maturity of the 4% coupon, 30-year maturity bond actually falls to 7% by the end of the first year, and that the investor sells the bond after the first year. If the investor's tax rate on interest income is 36% and the tax rate on capital gains is 28%, what is the investor's after-tax rate of return?

10.6 THE YIELD CURVE

yield curve
A graph of yield to maturity as a function of term to maturity.

term structure of interest rates
The relationship between yields to maturity and terms to maturity across bonds.

Return to Figure 10.1, and you will see that while yields to maturity on bonds of various maturities are reasonably similar, yields do differ. Bonds with shorter maturities generally offer lower yields to maturity than longer-term bonds. The graphical relationship between the yield to maturity and the term to maturity is called the **yield curve.** The relationship also is called the **term structure of interest rates** because it relates yields to maturity to the term (maturity) of each bond. The yield curve is published regularly in *The Wall Street Journal*; three such sets of curves are reproduced in Figure 10.11. The yield curve is said to be "flat" if yields on bonds of different maturities are approximately equal. This is the case in Figure 10.11C. A "rising" yield curve is illustrated in 10.11A, in which longer term bonds generally have higher yields. A "hump-shaped" curve is illustrated in 10.11B, in which yields first rise but then fall as maturity increases. For maturities beyond two years, the curve in Figure 10.11B is "inverted," meaning that yields tend to fall with longer maturities. Rising yield curves are most commonly observed. We will see why momentarily.

Why should bonds of differing maturity offer different yields? The two most plausible possibilities have to do with expectations of future rates and risk premiums. We will consider each of these arguments in turn.

The Expectations Theory

Suppose everyone in the market believes firmly that while the current one-year interest rate is 8%, the interest rate on one-year bonds next year will rise to 10%. What would this belief imply about the proper yield to maturity on two-year bonds issued today?

It is easy to see that an investor who buys the one-year bond and rolls the proceeds into another one-year bond in the following year will earn, on average, about 9% per year. This value is just the average of the 8% earned this year and the 10% earned next year. More precisely, the investment will grow by a factor of 1.08 in the first year and 1.10 in the second year, for a total two-year growth factor of 1.08 × 1.10 = 1.188. This corresponds to an annual growth rate of 8.995% (because $1.188^{1/2} = 1.08995$).

For investments in two-year bonds to be competitive with the strategy of rolling over one-year bonds, they too must offer an average annual return of 8.995% over the two-year holding period. Hence, the yield curve will be upward sloping; while one-year bonds offer an 8% yield to maturity, two-year bonds must offer a 8.995% yield.

FIGURE 10.11
Treasury Yield Curves

Source: From various editions
of *The Wall Street Journal*
Reprinted by permission of
The Wall Street Journal ©
Dow Jones & Company, Inc.
All Rights Reserved
Worldwide.

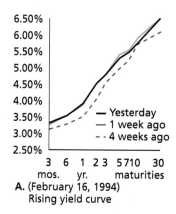

Treasury Yield Curve
Yield as of 4:30 p.m. Eastern time

— Yesterday
— 1 week ago
- - 4 weeks ago

3 6   1 2 5 7 10   30
mos.   yr.   maturities

A. (February 16, 1994)
Rising yield curve

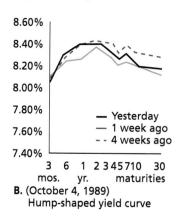

Treasury Yield Curve
Yield as of 4:30 p.m. Eastern time

— Yesterday
— 1 week ago
- - 4 weeks ago

3 6   1 2 3 4 5 7 10   30
mos.   yr.   maturities

B. (October 4, 1989)
Hump-shaped yield curve

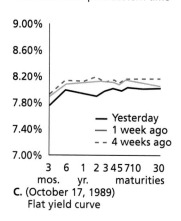

Treasury Yield Curve
Yield as of 4:30 p.m. Eastern time

— Yesterday
— 1 week ago
- - 4 weeks ago

3 6   1 2 3 4 5 7 10   30
mos.   yr.   maturities

C. (October 17, 1989)
Flat yield curve

expectations hypothesis
The theory that yields to
maturity are determined
solely by expectations of
future short-term interest
rates.

This notion is the essence of the **expectations hypothesis** of the yield curve, which asserts that the slope of the yield curve is attributable to expectations of changes in short-term rates. Relatively high yields on long-term bonds are attributed to expectations of future increases in rates, while relatively low yields on long-term bonds (a downward-sloping or inverted yield curve) are attributed to expectations of falling short-term rates.

While many factors can influence expectations of future rates, one of the most important is inflation. Increases in expected inflation, for example, increase expected future nominal interest rates and can result in a rising yield curve. For this reason, some investors view the yield curve as a means to infer the market consensus prognosis for future inflation.

One of the implications of the expectations hypothesis is that expected holding-period returns on bonds of all maturities ought to be about equal. Even if the yield curve is upward sloping (so that two-year bonds offer higher yields to maturity than one-year bonds), this does not necessarily mean investors expect higher rates of return on the two-year bonds. As we've seen, the higher initial yield to maturity on the two-year bond is necessary to compensate investors for the fact that interest rates next year will be even higher. Over the two-year period, and indeed over any holding period, this theory predicts that holding-period returns will be equalized across bonds of all maturities.

In fact, advocates of the expectations hypothesis commonly invert the theory to arrive at an estimate of the market's expectation of the future short-term interest rate. For example, if one-year bonds offer an 8% return while two-year bonds have a 8.995% yield to maturity, then, according to the expectations hypothesis, the market's expectations of next year's one-year rate must be 10%. At this level, the sequence of two one-year investments will provide a cumulative return of 18.8% (8% followed by 10%), while the two-year investment also will return 18.8% (two years at an average return of 8.995%). The future short-term rate that makes expected returns to these two investment strategies equal is called the **forward rate** of interest.

forward rate
The inferred short-term rate of interest for a future period that makes the expected total return of a long-term bond equal to that of rolling over short-term bonds.

EXAMPLE 10.8
Forward Rates

Suppose that two-year maturity bonds offer yields to maturity of 6%, and three-year bonds have yields of 7%. What is the forward rate for the third year? Ignoring compound interest, we could compare these two strategies as follows:

1. Buy a three-year bond. Total proceeds per dollar invested will be

$$\$1 \times (1.07)^3 = \$1.2250$$

2. Buy a two-year bond. Reinvest all proceeds in a one-year bond in the third year, which will provide a return in that year of r_3. Total proceeds per dollar invested will be the result of two years' growth of invested funds at 6% plus the final year's growth at rate r_3:

$$\$1 \times (1.06)^2 \times (1 + r_3) = \$1.1236 \times (1 + r_3)$$

If the two strategies are equally attractive, then

$$1.2250 = 1.1236 \times (1 + r_3)$$

We conclude that the forward rate for the third year satisfies $(1 + r_3) = 1.0902$, so that r_3 is 9.02%.

The Liquidity Preference Theory

We have seen that longer term bonds are subject to greater interest rate risk than short-term bonds. As a result, investors in long-term bonds might require a risk premium to compensate them for tying up money longer. In this case, the yield curve will be upward sloping even in the absence of any expectations of future increases in rates. The source of the upward slope in the curve is investor demand for higher expected returns on assets that are perceived as riskier.

liquidity preference theory
The theory that investors demand a risk premium on long-term bonds.

This viewpoint is called the **liquidity preference theory** of the term structure. Its name derives from the fact that shorter term bonds have more "liquidity" than longer term bonds, in the sense that they offer greater price certainty and trade in more active markets with lower bid-ask spreads. The preference of investors for greater liquidity makes them willing to hold these shorter term bonds even if they do not offer expected returns as high as those of longer term bonds.

liquidity premium
The extra expected return demanded by investors as compensation for the greater risk of longer term bonds.

The risk premium required to hold longer term bonds is called a **liquidity premium.** It is the extra expected return demanded by investors as compensation for the lower liquidity of longer term bonds.

Advocates of the liquidity preference theory also note that issuers of bonds seem to prefer to issue long-term bonds. This allows them to lock in an interest rate on their borrowing for long periods. If issuers do prefer to issue long-term bonds, they will be willing to pay higher yields on these issues as a way of eliminating interest rate risk. In sum, borrowers demand higher rates on longer term bonds, and issuers are willing to pay higher rates on longer term bonds. The conjunction of these two preferences means longer term bonds typically should offer higher expected rates of return to investors than shorter term bonds. These expectations will show up in an upward-sloping yield curve.

One application of this principle arises in the practice of *riding the yield curve*. This strategy is used by many investors in the short-term money market. When the yield curve is upward sloping, investors will increase the maturity of their investments, say from one month to two months, in order to earn the liquidity premium. A study of Grieves and Marcus (1992) shows that this strategy has proven to be effective.

If the liquidity preference theory is valid, the forward rate of interest is not a good estimate of market expectations of future interest rates. Even if rates are expected to remain unchanged, for example, the yield curve will slope upward because of the liquidity premium. That upward slope would be mistakenly attributed to expectations of rising rates if one were to use the pure expectations hypothesis to interpret the yield curve.

Market Segmentation Theory

Both the liquidity premium and expectations hypothesis theories of the term structure implicitly view bonds of different maturities as some sort of substitute for each other. That is, investors considering holding bonds of one maturity might be attracted instead into holding bonds of another maturity by the prospect of earning a risk premium. In this sense, markets for bonds of all maturities are inextricably linked, and yields on short- and long-term bonds are determined jointly in market equilibrium. Forward rates cannot differ from expected short-term rates by more than a fair risk premium, or investors will reallocate their fixed-income portfolios to exploit what they perceive as abnormal profit opportunities.

In contrast, the *market segmentation* or *preferred habitat* theory holds that long- and short-term maturity bonds are traded in essentially distinct or segmented markets, each of which finds its own equilibrium independently. The activities of long-term borrowers and lenders determine rates on long-term bonds. Similarly, short-term traders set short-term rates independently of long-term expectations. The term structure of interest rates, in this view, is determined by the equilibrium rates set in the various maturity markets.

This view of the market is not common today. Both borrowers and lenders seem to compare long- and short-term rates as well as expectations of future rates before deciding whether to borrow or lend long or short term. That they make these comparisons, and are willing to move into a particular maturity if it seems sufficiently profitable to do so, indicates that all maturity bonds compete with each other for investors' attention, which implies the rate on a bond of any given maturity is determined with an eye toward rates on competing bonds. Markets are not so segmented that an appropriate term premium cannot attract an investor preferring one investment horizon to consider a different one.

A Synthesis

Of course, it is silly to treat theories of the term structure as requiring an either/or choice between expectations and risk premiums. Both of these factors can influence the yield curve, and both should be considered in interpreting the curve.

Figure 10.12 shows two possible yield curves. In Figure 10.12A, rates are expected to rise over time. This fact, together with a liquidity premium, makes the yield curve steeply upward sloping. In Figure 10.12B, rates are expected to fall, which tends to make the yield curve slope downward, even though the liquidity premium lends something of an upward slope. The net effect of these two opposing factors is a "hump-shaped" curve.

These two examples make it clear that the combination of varying expectations and risk or liquidity premiums can result in a wide array of yield-curve profiles. For example, an upward-sloping curve does not in and of itself imply expectations of higher future interest rates, because the slope can result either from expectations or from risk premiums. A curve

FIGURE 10.12

Illustrative Yield Curves

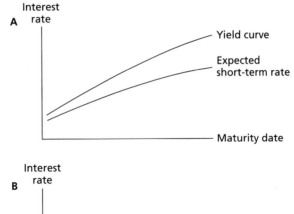

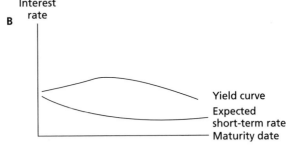

FIGURE 10.13

Price Volatility of Long-Term Treasury Bonds

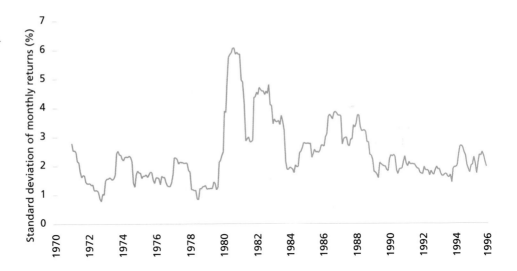

that is more steeply sloped than usual might signal expectations of higher rates, but even this inference is perilous.

Figure 10.13 shows the variability of prices on long-term Treasury bonds over a 25-year period during which interest rate risk fluctuated dramatically. So might we expect risk premiums on various maturity bonds to fluctuate, meaning the slope of the yield curve can vary because of varying risk as well as varying expected future rates.

Figure 10.14 presents yield spreads between short-term and long-term bonds since 1970. The figure shows that the yield curve is generally upward sloping in that the longer term bonds usually offer higher yields to maturity, despite the fact that rates could not have been expected to increase throughout the entire period. This tendency is the empirical basis for the liquidity premium doctrine that at least part of the upward slope in the yield curve must be because of a risk premium.

FIGURE 10.14

Term Spread,
1970–1996

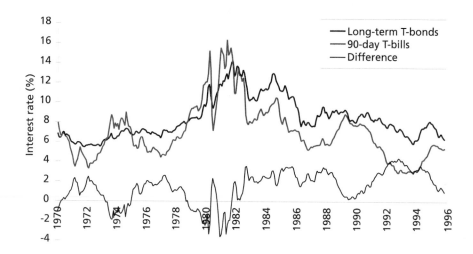

Summary

- Fixed-income securities are distinguished by their promise to pay a fixed or specified stream of income to their holders. The coupon bond is a typical fixed-income security.
- Treasury notes and bonds have original maturities greater than one year. They are issued at or near par value, with their prices quoted net of accrued interest. T-bonds may be callable during their last five years of life.
- When bonds are subject to potential default, the stated yield to maturity is the maximum possible yield to maturity that can be realized by the bondholder. In the event of default, however, that promised yield will not be realized. To compensate bond investors for default risk, bonds must offer default premiums, that is, promised yields in excess of those offered by default-free government securities. If the firm remains healthy, its bonds will provide higher returns than government bonds. Otherwise, the returns may be lower.
- Bond safety often is measured using financial ratio analysis. Bond indentures are another safeguard to protect the claims of bondholders. Common indentures specify sinking fund requirements, collateralization of the loan, dividend restrictions, and subordination of future debt.
- Callable bonds should offer higher promised yields to maturity to compensate investors for the fact that they will not realize full capital gains should the interest rate fall and the bonds be called away from them at the stipulated call price. Bonds often are issued with a period of call protection. In addition, discount bonds selling significantly below their call price offer implicit call protection.
- Put bonds give the bondholder rather than the issuer the option to terminate or extend the life of the bond.
- Convertible bonds may be exchanged, at the bondholder's discretion, for a specified number of shares of stock. Convertible bondholders "pay" for this option by accepting a lower coupon rate on the security.
- Floating-rate bonds pay a fixed premium over a reference short-term interest rate. Risk is limited because the rate paid is tied to current market conditions.
- The yield to maturity is the single interest rate that equates the present value of a security's cash flows to its price. Bond prices and yields are inversely related. For premium bonds, the coupon rate is greater than the current yield, which is greater than the yield to maturity. The order of these inequalities is reversed for discount bonds.
- The yield to maturity often is interpreted as an estimate of the average rate of return to an investor who purchases a bond and holds it until maturity. This interpretation is subject to

error, however. Related measures are yield to call, realized compound yield, and expected (versus promised) yield to maturity.

- Treasury bills are U.S. government-issued zero-coupon bonds with original maturities of up to one year. Prices of zero-coupon bonds rise exponentially over time, providing a rate of appreciation equal to the interest rate. The IRS treats this price appreciation as imputed taxable interest income to the investor.

Key Terms

bond, *260*
callable bonds, *260*
collateral, *270*
convertible bonds, *263*
coupon rate, *260*
current yield, *275*
debenture, *270*
default premium, *277*
expectations
  hypothesis, *284*
face value, *260*

fixed-income securities, *259*
floating-rate bonds, *264*
forward rate, *285*
indenture, *269*
investment grade
  bonds, *266*
liquidity preference
  theory, *285*
liquidity premium, *285*
par value, *260*

put bond, *264*
sinking fund, *269*
speculative grade or junk
  bonds, *266*
subordination clauses, *269*
term structure of interest
  rates, *283*
yield curve, *283*
yield to maturity, *273*
zero-coupon bond, *260*

Problem Sets

1. Which security has a higher *effective* annual interest rate?
   a. A three-month T-bill selling at $97,645.
   b. A coupon bond selling at par and paying a 10% coupon semiannually.

2. Treasury bonds paying an 8% coupon rate with *semiannual* payments currently sell at par value. What coupon rate would they have to pay in order to sell at par if they paid their coupons *annually*?

3. Two bonds have identical times to maturity and coupon rates. One is callable at 105, the other at 110. Which should have the higher yield to maturity? Why?

4. Consider a bond with a 10% coupon and with yield to maturity = 8%. If the bond's YTM remains constant, then in one year, will the bond price be higher, lower, or unchanged? Why?

5. Under the expectations hypothesis, if the yield curve is upward sloping, the market must expect an increase in short-term interest rates. True/false/uncertain? Why?

6. Under the liquidity preference theory, if inflation is expected to be falling over the next few years, long-term interest rates will be higher than short-term rates. True/false/uncertain? Why?

7. The yield curve is upward sloping. Can you conclude that investors expect short-term interest rates to rise? Why or why not?

8. Consider a bond paying a coupon rate of 10% per year semiannually when the market interest rate is only 4% per half year. The bond has three years until maturity.
   a. Find the bond's price today and six months from now after the next coupon is paid.
   b. What is the total rate of return on the bond?

9. A 20-year maturity bond with par value $1,000 makes semiannual coupon payments at a coupon rate of 8%. Find the bond equivalent and effective annual yield to maturity of the bond if the bond price is:
   a. $950
   b. $1,000
   c. $1,050

10. Redo problem 9 using the same data, but assume that the bond makes its coupon payments annually. Why are the yields you compute lower in this case?

11. Fill in the table below for the following zero-coupon bonds, all of which have par values of $1,000.

Price	Maturity (Years)	Bond-Equivalent Yield to Maturity
$400	20	?
$500	20	?
$500	10	?
?	10	10%
?	10	8%
$400	?	8%

12. Assume you have a one-year investment horizon and are trying to choose among three bonds. All have the same degree of default risk and mature in 10 years. The first is a zero-coupon bond that pays $1,000 at maturity. The second has an 8% coupon rate and pays the $80 coupon once per year. The third has a 10% coupon rate and pays the $100 coupon once per year.

    a. If all three bonds are now priced to yield 8% to maturity, what are their prices?

    b. If you expect their yields to maturity to be 8% at the beginning of next year, what will their prices be then? What is your rate of return on each bond during the one-year holding period?

13. A bond with a coupon rate of 7% makes semiannual coupon payments on January 15 and July 15 of each year. *The Wall Street Journal* reports the ask price for the bond on January 30 at 100:02. What is the invoice price of the bond? The coupon period has 182 days.

14. A bond has a current yield of 9% and a yield to maturity of 10%. Is the bond selling above or below par value? Explain.

15. Is the coupon rate of the bond in the previous problem more or less than 9%?

16. A newly issued 20-year maturity, zero-coupon bond is issued with a yield to maturity of 8% and face value $1,000. Find the imputed interest income in the first, second, and last year of the bond's life.

17. A newly issued 10-year maturity, 4% coupon bond making *annual* coupon payments is sold to the public at a price of $800. What will be an investor's taxable income from the bond over the coming year? The bond will not be sold at the end of the year. The bond is treated as an original issue discount bond.

18. A newly issued bond pays its coupons once annually. Its coupon rate is 5%, its maturity is 20 years, and its yield to maturity is 8%.

    a. Find the holding-period return for a one-year investment period if the bond is selling at a yield to maturity of 7% by the end of the year.

    b. If you sell the bond after one year when its yield is 7%, what taxes will you owe if the tax rate on interest income is 40% and the tax rate on capital gains income is 30%? The bond is subject to original-issue discount (OID) tax treatment.

    c. What is the after-tax holding-period return on the bond?

    d. Find the realized compound yield *before taxes* for a two-year holding period, assuming that (*i*) you sell the bond after two years, (*ii*) the bond yield is 7% at the end of the second year, and (*iii*) the coupon can be reinvested for one year at a 3% interest rate.

    e. Use the tax rates in part (*b*) to compute the *after-tax* two-year realized compound yield. Remember to take account of OID tax rules.

19. A 30-year maturity, 8% coupon bond paying coupons semiannually is callable in five years at a call price of $1,100. The bond currently sells at a yield to maturity of 7% (3.5% per half year).

    a. What is the yield to call?

    b. What is the yield to call if the call price is only $1,050?

    c. What is the yield to call if the call price is $1,100, but the bond can be called in two years instead of five years?

20. A 10-year bond of a firm in severe financial distress has a coupon rate of 14% and sells for $900. The firm is currently renegotiating the debt, and it appears that the lenders will allow the firm to reduce coupon payments on the bond to one-half the originally contracted amount. The firm can handle these lower payments. What are the stated and expected yields to maturity of the bonds? The bond makes its coupon payments annually.

21. A two-year bond with par value $1,000 making annual coupon payments of $100 is priced at $1,000. What is the yield to maturity of the bond? What will be the realized compound yield to maturity if the one-year interest rate next year turns out to be (*a*) 8%, (*b*) 10%, (*c*) 12%?

22. The stated yield to maturity and realized compound yield to maturity of a (default-free) zero-coupon bond will always be equal. Why?

23. Suppose that today's date is April 15. A bond with a 10% coupon paid semiannually every January 15 and July 15 is listed in *The Wall Street Journal* as selling at an ask price of 101:04. If you buy the bond from a dealer today, what price will you pay for it?

24. Assume two firms PG and CLX were concurrently to undertake private debt placements with the following contractual details:

	PG	CLX
Issue size	$1 billion	$100 million
Issue price	100	100
Maturity	2003*	2013
Coupon	10%	11%
Collateral	First mortgage	Unsecured
First call date	2008	2005
Call price	111	106
Sinking fund—beginning	nil	2003
—amount	nil	$5 million/year

*Extendable at the option of the holder for an additional 10 years (to 2013) with no change in coupon rate.

Ignoring credit quality, identify four features of these issues that might account for the lower coupon on the PG debt. Explain.

25. A large forest products manufacturer has outstanding two Baa-rated, $150 million par amount, intermediate-term debt issues:

	10.10% Notes	Floating-Rate Notes
Maturity	2005	2002
Issue date	6-12-95	9-27-94
Callable (beginning on)	6-15-01	10-01-99
Callable at	100	100
Sinking fund	None	None
Current coupon	10.10%	9.9%
Coupon changes	Fixed	Every 6 months
Rate adjusts to	—	1% above 6-month T-bill rate
Range since issued	—	12.9%–8.3%
Current price	73 3/8	97
Current yield	13.77%	10.3%
Yield to maturity	15.87%	—
Price range since issue	100–72	102–93

Given these data:

a. State the minimum coupon rate of interest at which the firm could sell a fixed-rate issue at par due in 2005. Assume the same indenture provisions as the 10.10% notes and disregard any tax considerations.
b. Give two reasons why the floating-rate notes are not selling at par (offering price).
c. State and justify whether the risk of call is high, moderate, or low for the fixed-rate issue.
d. Assuming a decline in interest rates is anticipated, identify and justify which issue would be most appropriate for an actively managed bond portfolio where total return is the primary objective.
e. Explain why yield to maturity is not valid for the floating-rate note.

26. You have the following information about a convertible bond issue:

Burroughs Corp. 7¼% Due 8/1/2010	
Agency rating (Moody's/S&P)	A3/A-
Conversion ratio	12.882
Market price of convertible	$102.00
Market price of common stock	$ 66.00
Dividend per share—common	$ 2.60
Call price (first call—8/1/1990)	$106.00
Estimated floor price	$ 66.50

Using this information, calculate the following values and show calculations.
a. Market conversion value.
b. Conversion premium per common share.
c. Current yield—convertible.
d. Dividend yield—common.

27. As the portfolio manager for a large pension fund, you are offered the following bonds:

	Coupon	Maturity	Price	Call Price	Yield to Maturity
Edgar Corp. (new issue)	14.00%	2005	$101 3/4	$114	13.75%
Edgar Corp. (new issue)	6.00	2005	48 1/8	103	13.60

Assuming you expect a decline in interest rates over the next three years, identify which of the bonds you would select. Justify your answer.

28. The yield to maturity on one-year zero-coupon bonds is 8%. The yield to maturity on two-year zero-coupon bonds is 9%.
a. What is the forward rate of interest for the second year?
b. If you believe in the expectations hypothesis, what is your best guess as to the expected value of the short-term interest rate next year?
c. If you believe in the liquidity preference theory, is your best guess as to next year's short-term interest rate higher or lower than in (b)?

29. The following multiple-choice problems are based on questions that appeared in past CFA examinations.
a. Which bond probably has the highest credit quality?
(1) Sumter, South Carolina, Water and Sewer Revenue Bond.
(2) Riley County, Kansas, General Obligation Bond.
(3) University of Kansas Medical Center Refunding Revenue Bonds (insured by American Municipal Bond Assurance Corporation).
(4) Euless, Texas, General Obligation Bond (refunded and secured by the U.S. government in escrow to maturity).

   b. The spread between Treasury and Baa corporate bond yields widens when:
   (1) Interest rates are low.
   (2) There is economic uncertainty.
   (3) There is a "flight from quality."
   (4) All of the above.
   c. The market risk of an AAA-rated preferred stock relative to an AAA-rated bond is:
   (1) Lower
   (2) Higher
   (3) Equal
   (4) Unknown
   d. A bond with a call feature:
   (1) Is attractive because the immediate receipt of principal plus premium produces a high return.
   (2) Is more apt to be called when interest rates are high because the interest saving will be greater.
   (3) Will usually have a higher yield than a similar noncallable bond.
   (4) None of the above.
   e. The yield to maturity on a bond is:
   (1) Below the coupon rate when the bond sells at a discount, and above the coupon rate when the bond sells at a premium.
   (2) The discount rate that will set the present value of the payments equal to the bond price.
   (3) The current yield plus the average annual capital gains rate.
   (4) Based on the assumption that any payments received are reinvested at the coupon rate.
   f. A particular bond has a yield to maturity on an APR basis of 12.00% but makes equal quarterly payments. What is the effective annual yield to maturity?
   (1) 11.45%
   (2) 12.00%
   (3) 12.55%
   (4) 37.35%
   g. In which *one* of the following cases is the bond selling at a discount?
   (1) Coupon rate is greater than current yield, which is greater than yield to maturity.
   (2) Coupon rate, current yield, and yield to maturity are all the same.
   (3) Coupon rate is less than current yield, which is less than yield to maturity.
   (4) Coupon rate is less than current yield, which is greater than yield to maturity.
   h. Consider a five-year bond with a 10% coupon that has a present yield to maturity of 8%. If interest rates remain constant, one year from now the price of this bond will be:
   (1) Higher
   (2) Lower
   (3) The same
   (4) Par
   i. A revenue bond is distinguished from a general obligation bond in that revenue bonds:
   (1) Are issued by counties, special districts, cities, towns, and state-controlled authorities; whereas general obligation bonds are only issued by the states themselves.
   (2) Are typically secured by limited taxing power; whereas general obligation bonds are secured by unlimited taxing power.
   (3) Are issued to finance specific projects and are secured by the revenues of the project being financed.
   (4) Have first claim to any revenue increase of the tax authority issuing the bonds.

   j. Serial obligation bonds differ from *most* other bonds because:
   (1) They are secured by the assets and taxing power of the issuer.
   (2) Their par value is usually well below $1,000.
   (3) Their term to maturity is usually very long (30 years or more).
   (4) They possess multiple maturity dates.

   k. Which *one* of the following is *not* an advantage of convertible bonds for the investor?
   (1) The yield on the convertible typically will be higher than the yield on the underlying common stock.
   (2) The convertible bond will likely participate in a major upward move in the price of the underlying common stock.
   (3) Convertible bonds typically are secured by specific assets of the issuing company.
   (4) Investors normally may convert to the underlying common stock.

   l. The call feature of a bond means the:
   (1) Investor can call for payment on demand.
   (2) Investor can only call if the firm defaults on an interest payment.
   (3) Issuer can call the bond issue before the maturity date.
   (4) Issuer can call the issue during the first three years.

   m. The annual interest paid on a bond relative to its prevailing market price is called its:
   (1) Promised yield
   (2) Yield to maturity
   (3) Coupon rate
   (4) Current yield

   n. Which of the following statements is *true*?
   (1) The expectations hypothesis indicates a flat yield curve if anticipated future short-term rates exceed current short-term rates.
   (2) The basic conclusion of the expectations hypothesis is that the long-term rate is equal to the anticipated short-term rate.
   (3) The liquidity hypothesis indicates that, all other things being equal, longer maturities will have lower yields.
   (4) The segmentation hypothesis contends that borrowers and lenders are constrained to particular segments of the yield curve.

   o. Which theory explains the shape of the yield curve by considering the relative demands for various maturities?
   (1) Relative strength theory
   (2) Segmentation theory
   (3) Unbiased expectations theory
   (4) Liquidity premium theory

◼ IEM
Applications

1. In the IEM, some traders buy particular contracts (e.g., IBMm and MSFTm) and hold them until they pay off regardless of prices. This would lead to a market characterized by:
   a. Expectations theory
   b. Liquidity preference theory
   c. Market segmentation theory
   d. All of the above
   e. None of the above

2. What are the implications of this kind of behavior for IEM market prices?

Solutions to
Concept Checks

1. The callable bond will sell at the *lower* price. Investors will not be willing to pay as much if they know that the firm retains a valuable option to reclaim the bond for the call price if interest rates fall.

2. At a semiannual interest rate of 3%, the bond is worth $40 × Annuity factor (3%, 60) + $1,000 × PV factor (3%, 60) = $1,276.75, which results in a capital gain of $276.75. This exceeds the capital loss of $189.29 ($1,000 − $810.71) when the interest rate increased to 5%.

3. Yield to maturity exceeds current yield, which exceeds coupon rate. Take as an example the 8% coupon bond with a yield to maturity of 10% per year (5% per half year). Its price is $810.71, and therefore its current yield is 80/810.77 = 0.0987, or 9.87%, which is higher than the coupon rate but lower than the yield to maturity.

4. The current price of the bond can be derived from the yield to maturity. Using your calculator, set: n = 40 (semiannual periods); *PMT* = $45 per period; *FV* = $1,000; i = 4% per semiannual period. Calculate present value as $1,098.96. Now we can calculate yield to call. The time to call is five years, or 10 semiannual periods. The price at which the bond will be called is $1,050. To find yield to call, we set: n = 10 (semiannual periods); *PMT* = $45 per period; *FV* = $1,050; *PV* = $1,098.96. Calculate the semiannual yield to call as 3.72%.

5. The coupon payment is $45. There are 20 semiannual periods. The final payment is assumed to be $600. The present value of expected cash flows is $750. The yield to maturity is 5.42% semiannual, or 10.8% as an annualized bond equivalent yield.

6. Price = $70 × Annuity factor (8%, 1) + $1,000 × PV factor (8%, 1) = $990.74

$$\text{Rate of return to investor} = \frac{\$70 + (\$990.74 - \$982.17)}{\$982.17} = 0.080$$

$$= 8\%$$

7. At the lower yield, the bond price will be $631.67 [$n$ = 29, i = 7%, *FV* = $1,000, *PMT* = $40]. Therefore, total after-tax income is

Coupon	$40 × (1 − 0.36) =	$25.60
Imputed interest ($553.66 − $549.69) × (1 − 0.36) =		2.54
Capital gains	($631.67 − $553.66) × (1 − 0.28) =	56.17
Total income after taxes:		$84.31

Rate of return = 84.31/549.69 = .153 = 15.3%

Chapter 11

MANAGING FIXED-INCOME INVESTMENTS

AFTER STUDYING THIS CHAPTER YOU SHOULD BE ABLE TO:

- Analyze the features of a bond that affect the sensitivity of its price to interest rates.
- Compute the duration of bonds.
- Formulate fixed-income immunization strategies for various investment horizons.
- Analyze the choices to be made in an actively managed fixed-income portfolio.
- Determine how swaps can be used to mitigate interest rate risk.

In this chapter, we turn to various strategies that fixed-income portfolio managers can pursue, making a distinction between passive and active strategies. A *passive investment strategy* takes market prices of securities as fairly set. Rather than attempting to beat the market by exploiting superior information or insight, passive managers act to maintain an appropriate risk-return balance given market opportunities. One special case of passive management is an immunization strategy that attempts to insulate the portfolio from interest rate risk.

An *active investment strategy* attempts to achieve returns that are more than commensurate with the risk borne. In the context of fixed-income management, this style of management can take two forms. Active managers either use interest rate forecasts to predict movements in the entire fixed-income market, or they employ some form of intramarket analysis to identify particular sectors of the fixed-income market (or particular securities) that are relatively mispriced.

We begin our discussion with an analysis of the sensitivity of bond prices to interest rate fluctuations. The concept of duration, which measures interest rate sensitivity, is basic to formulating both active and passive fixed-income strategies. We then turn to passive strategies and show how duration-matching strategies can be used to immunize the holding-period return of a fixed-income portfolio from interest rate risk. Finally, we explore a variety of active strategies, including intramarket analysis, interest rate forecasting, and interest rate swaps.

11.1 INTEREST RATE RISK

You know already that there is an inverse relationship between bond prices and yields and that interest rates can fluctuate substantially. As interest rates rise and fall, bondholders experience capital losses and gains. It is these gains or losses that make fixed-income investments risky, even if the coupon and principal payments are guaranteed, as in the case of Treasury obligations.

Why do bond prices respond to interest rate fluctuations? In a competitive market, all securities must offer investors fair expected rates of return. If a bond is issued with an 8% coupon when competitive yields are 8%, then it will sell at par value. If the market rate rises to 9%, however, who would purchase an 8% coupon bond at par value? The bond price must fall until its expected return increases to the competitive level of 9%. Conversely, if the market rate falls to 7%, the 8% coupon on the bond is attractive compared to yields on alternative investments. Investors eager for that return will respond by bidding the bond price above its par value until the total rate of return falls to the market rate.

Interest Rate Sensitivity

The sensitivity of bond prices to changes in market rates is obviously of great concern to investors. The determinants of that sensitivity have been described by Malkiel (1962) in five well-known bond-pricing relationships. The five bond-pricing relationships identified by Malkiel are as follows:

1. Bond prices and yields are inversely related: As yields increase, bond prices fall; as yields fall, bond prices rise.
2. An increase in a bond's yield to maturity results in a smaller price decline than the price gain associated with a decrease of equal magnitude in yield.
3. Prices of long-term bonds tend to be more sensitive to interest rate changes than prices of short-term bonds.
4. Interest rate risk increases at a decreasing rate as maturity increases. In other words, bond-price sensitivity to changes in yields increases less than proportionally to increases in the maturity of the bond.
5. Interest rate risk is inversely related to the bond's coupon rate. Prices of high-coupon bonds are less sensitive to changes in interest rates than prices of low-coupon bonds.

In addition, a sixth bond-pricing relationship has been demonstrated by Homer and Liebowitz (1972):

6. Bond prices are more sensitive to changes in yields when the bond is selling at a lower initial yield to maturity.

These six relationships are illustrated in Figure 11.1, which presents the percentage change in price corresponding to changes in yield to maturity for four bonds that differ according to coupon rate, initial yield to maturity, and time to maturity. All four bonds illustrate relationships (1) and (2): Prices increase when yields fall, and the price curve is convex, meaning that decreases in yields have bigger impacts on price than increases in yields of equal magnitude. Comparing bonds A and B illustrates the third relationship: The price of bond B, which has a longer maturity than bond A, exhibits greater sensitivity to interest rate changes. In addition, the graph shows that while bond B has six times the maturity of bond A, it has less than six times the interest rate sensitivity. This is consistent with Malkiel's fourth point that interest rate sensitivity increases less than proportionally as bond maturity increases. Bonds B and C, which are alike in all respects except for coupon rate, illustrate the fifth relationship. The lower coupon bond exhibits greater sensitivity to changes in interest rates. Finally, bonds C and D are alike except for the yield to maturity at

FIGURE 11.1   Change in Bond Price as a Function of Change in Yield to Maturity

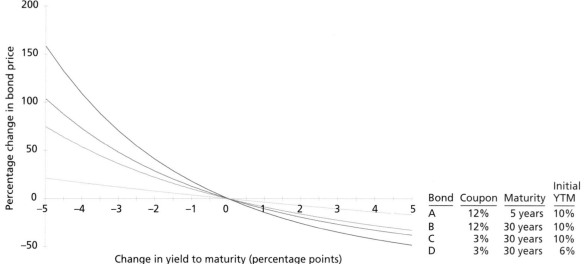

Bond	Coupon	Maturity	Initial YTM
A	12%	5 years	10%
B	12%	30 years	10%
C	3%	30 years	10%
D	3%	30 years	6%

which the bonds currently sell. Consistent with the sixth relationship, the bond with the lower yield is indeed more sensitive to changes in the interest rate.

Malkiel's relationships confirm that maturity is a major determinant of interest rate risk. However, they also show that maturity alone is not sufficient to measure interest rate sensitivity. For example, bonds *B* and *C* in Figure 11.1 have the same maturity, but the higher coupon bond has less price sensitivity to interest rate changes. Obviously, we need to know more than a bond's maturity to quantify its interest rate risk.

To see why bond characteristics such as coupon rate or yield to maturity affect interest rate sensitivity, let's start with a simple numerical example.

Table 11.1 gives bond prices for 8% annual coupon bonds at different yields to maturity and times to maturity. (For simplicity, we assume coupons are paid once a year rather than semiannually.) The shortest term bond falls in value by less than 1% when the interest rate increases from 8% to 9%. The 10-year bond falls by 6.4% and the 20-year bond by more than 9%.

Let us now look at a similar computation using a zero-coupon bond rather than the 8% coupon bond. The results are shown in Table 11.2.

TABLE 11.1
Prices of 8% Annual
Coupon Bonds

Bond's Yield to Maturity	*T* = 1 Year	*T* = 10 Years	*T* = 20 Years
8%	1,000	1,000	1,000
9%	990.83	935.82	908.71
Percent change in price*	−0.92%	−6.42%	−9.13%

*Equals value of bond at a 9% yield to maturity minus value of bond at (the original) 8% yield, divided by the value at 8% yield.

TABLE 11.2
Prices of Zero-Coupon
Bonds

Bond's Yield to Maturity	*T* = 1 Year	*T* = 10 Years	*T* = 20 Years
8%	925.93	463.19	214.55
9%	917.43	422.41	178.43
Percent change in price*	−0.92%	−8.80%	−16.84%

*Equals value of bond at a 9% yield to maturity minus value of bond at (the original) 8% yield, divided by the value at 8% yield.

For both maturities beyond one year, the price of the zero-coupon bond falls by a greater proportional amount than the price of the 8% coupon bond. The observation that long-term bonds are more sensitive to interest rate movements than short-term bonds suggests that in some sense a zero-coupon bond represents a longer term investment than an equal-time-to-maturity coupon bond. In fact, this insight about effective maturity is a useful one that we can make mathematically precise.

To start, note that the times to maturity of the two bonds in this example are not perfect measures of the long- or short-term nature of the bonds. The 8% bond makes many coupon payments, most of which come years before the bond's maturity date. Each payment may be considered to have its own "maturity date," which suggests that the *effective* maturity of the bond should be measured as some sort of average of the maturities of *all* the cash flows paid out by the bond. The zero-coupon bond, by contrast, makes only one payment at maturity. Its time to maturity is a well-defined concept.

Duration

duration
A measure of the effective maturity of a bond, defined as the weighted average of the times until each payment, with weights proportional to the present value of the payment.

To deal with the concept of the "maturity" of a bond that makes many payments, we need a measure of the average maturity of the bond's promised cash flows to serve as a summary statistic of the effective maturity of the bond. This measure also should give us some information on the sensitivity of a bond to interest rate changes because we have noted that price sensitivity tends to increase with time to maturity.

Frederick Macaulay (1938) called the effective maturity concept the **duration** of the bond; he suggested that duration be computed as the weighted average of the times to each coupon or principal payment made by the bond. He recommended further that the weight applied to each time to payment be related to the "importance" of that payment to the value of the bond, specifically, that the weight for each payment time be the proportion of the total value of the bond accounted for by that payment. This proportion is just the present value of the payment divided by the bond price.

Therefore, the weight, denoted w_t, associated with the cash flow made at time t (denoted CF_t) would be

$$w_t = \frac{CF_t/(1 + y)^t}{\text{Bond price}}$$

where y is the bond's yield to maturity. The numerator on the right-hand side of this equation is the present value of the cash flow occurring at time t, while the denominator is the value of all the payments forthcoming from the bond. These weights sum to 1.0 because the sum of the cash flows discounted at the yield to maturity equals the bond price.

Using these values to calculate the weighted average of the times until the receipt of each of the bond's payments, we obtain Macaulay's formula for duration, denoted D.

$$D = \sum_{t=1}^{T} t \times w_t \tag{11.1}$$

If we write out each term in the summation sign, we can express duration in the following equivalent equation

$$D = w_1 + \quad 2w_2 + \quad 3w_3 + \quad 4w_4 + \quad \ldots + \quad Tw_T$$

time until weight time until weight of
2nd cash of 2nd 4th CF 4th CF
flow CF

TABLE 11.3

Calculation of the
Duration of Two Bonds

	(1) Time until Payment (in years)	(2) Payment	(3) Payment Discounted at 10% (YTM)	(4) Weight*	(5) Column (1) Times Column (4)
A. 8% bond	1	$ 80	$ 72.727	0.0765	0.0765
	2	80	66.116	0.0690	0.1392
	3	1,080	811.420	0.8539	2.5617
Sum:			$950.263	1.0000	2.7774
B. Zero-coupon bond	1–2	$ 0	$ 0	0	0
	3	1,000	751.31	1.0	3
Sum:			$ 751.31	1.0	3

*Weight = Present value of each payment (column [3]) divided by the bond price: $950.26 for bond *A* and $751.31 for bond *B*.

An example of how to apply Equation 11.1 appears in Table 11.3, where we derive the durations of an 8% coupon and zero-coupon bond each with three years to maturity. We assume that the yield to maturity on each bond is 10%.

The numbers in column (5) are the products of time to payment and payment weight. Each of these products corresponds to one of the terms in Equation 11.1. According to that equation, we can calculate the duration of each bond by adding the numbers in column (5).

The duration of the zero-coupon bond is exactly equal to its time to maturity, three years. This makes sense for, with only one payment, the average time until payment must be the bond's maturity. The three-year coupon bond, in contrast, has a shorter duration of 2.7774 years.

Duration is a key concept in fixed-income portfolio management for at least three reasons. First, it is a simple summary statistic of the effective average maturity of the portfolio. Second, it turns out to be an essential tool in immunizing portfolios from interest rate risk. We will explore this application in the next section. Third, duration is a measure of the interest rate sensitivity of a bond portfolio, which we explore here.

We have already noted that long-term bonds are more sensitive to interest rate movements than short-term bonds. The duration measure enables us to quantify this relationship. It turns out that, when interest rates change, the percentage change in a bond's price is proportional to its duration. Specifically, the proportional change in a bond's price can be related to the change in its yield to maturity, y, according to the rule

$$\frac{\Delta P}{P} = - D \times \left[\frac{\Delta(1 + y)}{1 + y} \right] \tag{11.2}$$

The proportional price change equals the proportional change in (1 plus the bond's yield) times the bond's duration. Therefore, bond price volatility is proportional to the bond's duration, and duration becomes a natural measure of interest rate exposure.[1] This relationship is key to interest rate risk management.

Practitioners commonly use Equation 11.2 in a slightly different form. They define "modified duration" as $D^* = D/(1 + y)$ and rewrite Equation 11.2 as

$$\Delta P/P = - D^* \, \Delta y \tag{11.2'}$$

The percentage change in bond price is just the product of modified duration and the change in the bond's yield to maturity. Because the percentage change in the bond price is proportional to modified duration, modified duration is a natural measure of the bond's exposure to interest rate volatility.

---

[1]Actually, Equation 11.2 is only approximately valid for large changes in the bond's yield. The approximation becomes exact as one considers smaller, or localized, changes in yields.

**EXAMPLE 11.1
Duration and
Interest Rate
Risk**

A bond with maturity of 30 years has a coupon rate of 8% (paid annually) and a yield to maturity of 9%. Its price is $897.26, and its duration is 11.37 years. What will happen to the bond price if the bond's yield to maturity increases to 9.1%?

Equation 11.2′ tells us that an increase of 0.1% in the bond's yield to maturity ($\Delta y = .001$ in decimal terms) will result in a price change of

$$\Delta P = -(D^* \ \Delta y) \times P$$

$$= -\frac{11.37}{1.09} \times 0.001 \times \$897.26$$

$$= -\$9.36$$

To confirm the relationship between duration and the sensitivity of bond price to interest rate changes, let's compare the price sensitivity of the three-year coupon bond in Table 11.3, which has a duration of 2.7774 years, to the sensitivity of a zero-coupon bond with maturity and duration of 2.7774 years. Both should have equal interest rate exposure if duration is a useful measure of price sensitivity.

The three-year bond sells for $950.263 at the initial interest rate of 10%. If the bond's yield increases by 1 basis point (1/100 of a percent) to 10.01%, its price will fall to $950.0231, a percentage decline of 0.0252%. The zero-coupon bond has a maturity of 2.7774 years. At the initial interest rate of 10%, it sells at a price of $767.425 ($1,000/$1.10^{2.7774}$). Its price falls to $767.2313 ($1,000/1.1001^{2.7774}$) when the interest rate increases, for an identical 0.0252% capital loss. We conclude, therefore, that equal-duration assets are equally sensitive to interest rate movements.

Incidentally, this example confirms the validity of Equation 11.2. The equation predicts that the proportional price change of the two bonds should have been $-2.7774 \times 0.0001/1.10 = 0.000252$, or 0.0252%, just as we found from direct computation.

Concept Check

1. *a.* Calculate as in Table 11.3 the price and duration of a two-year maturity, 9% coupon bond when the market interest rate is 10%.
   b. Now suppose the interest rate increases to 10.05%. Calculate the new value of the bond and the percentage change in the bond's price.
   c. Calculate the percentage change in the bond's price predicted by the duration formula in Equation 11.2 or 11.2′. Compare this value to your answer for (*b*).

What Determines Duration?

The sensitivity of a bond's price to changes in market interest rates is influenced by three key factors: time to maturity, coupon rate, and yield to maturity. These determinants of price sensitivity are important to fixed-income portfolio management. Therefore, we summarize some of the important relationships in the following five rules. These rules are also illustrated in Figure 11.2, which contains plots of durations of bonds of various coupon rates, yields to maturity, and times to maturity.

We have already established:

> *Rule 1: The duration of a zero-coupon bond equals its time to maturity.*

We also have seen that the three-year coupon bond has a lower duration than the three-year zero because coupons early in the bond's life lower the bond's weighted average time until payments. This illustrates another general property:

> *Rule 2: Holding time to maturity and yield to maturity constant, a bond's duration and interest rate sensitivity are higher when the coupon rate is lower.*

FIGURE 11.2

Duration as a Function of Maturity

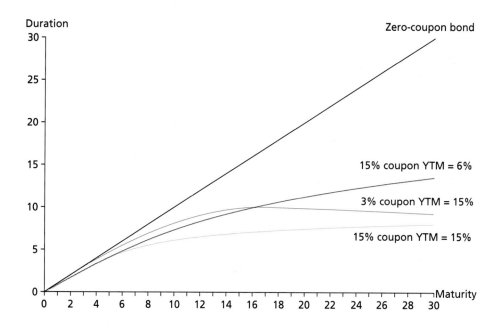

This property corresponds to Malkiel's fifth relationship, and is attributable to the impact of early coupons on the average maturity of a bond's payments. The lower these coupons, the less weight these early payments have on the weighted average maturity of all the bond's payments. Compare the plots in Figure 11.2 of the durations of the 3% coupon and 15% coupon bonds, each with identical yields of 15%. The plot of the duration of the 15% coupon bond lies below the corresponding plot for the 3% coupon bond.

> *Rule 3: Holding the coupon rate constant, a bond's duration and interest rate sensitivity generally increase with time to maturity. Duration always increases with maturity for bonds selling at par or at a premium to par.*

This property of duration corresponds to Malkiel's third relationship, and is fairly intuitive. What is surprising is that duration need not always increase with time to maturity. For some deep discount bonds, such as the 3% coupon bond selling to yield 15% in Figure 11.2, duration may eventually fall with increases in maturity. For virtually all traded bonds, however, it is safe to assume that duration increases with maturity.

Notice in Figure 11.2 that for the zero-coupon bond, maturity and duration are equal. For all the coupon bonds, however, duration increases by less than a year for each year's increase in maturity. The slope of the duration graph is less than one, and duration is always less than maturity for positive-coupon bonds.

While long-maturity bonds generally will be high-duration bonds, duration is a better measure of the long-term nature of the bond because it also accounts for coupon payments. Only when the bond pays no coupons is time to maturity an adequate measure; then maturity and duration are equal.

Notice also in Figure 11.2 that the two 15% coupon bonds have different durations when they sell at different yields to maturity. The lower yield bond has longer duration. This makes sense, because at lower yields the more distant payments have relatively greater present values and thereby account for a greater share of the bond's total value. Thus, in the weighted-average calculation of duration, the distant payments receive greater weights, which results in a higher duration measure. This establishes

> *Rule 4: Holding other factors constant, the duration and interest rate sensitivity of a coupon bond are higher when the bond's yield to maturity is lower.*

TABLE 11.4
Durations of Annual
Coupon Bonds (Initial
Bond Yield = 8%)

Years to Maturity	Coupon Rates (% per year)			
	6	8	10	12
1	1.000	1.000	1.000	1.000
5	4.439	4.312	4.204	4.110
10	7.615	7.247	6.996	6.744
20	11.231	10.604	10.182	9.880
Infinite (perpetuity)	13.500	13.500	13.500	13.500

Rule 4, which is the sixth bond-pricing relationship noted above, applies to coupon bonds. For zeros, duration equals time to maturity, regardless of the yield to maturity.

Finally, we present an algebraic rule for the duration of a perpetuity. This rule is derived from and is consistent with the formula for duration given in Equation 11.1, but it is far easier to use for infinitely lived bonds.

> *Rule 5: The duration of a level perpetuity is (1 + y)/y. For example, at a 15% yield, the duration of a perpetuity that pays $100 once a year forever will equal 1.15/0.15 = 7.67 years, while at an 8% yield, it will equal 1.08/0.08 = 13.5 years.*

Rule 5 makes it obvious that maturity and duration can differ substantially. The maturity of the perpetuity is infinite, while the duration of the instrument at a 15% yield is only 7.67 years. The present-value-weighted cash flows early on in the life of the perpetuity dominate the computation of duration. Notice from Figure 11.2 that as their maturities become ever longer, the durations of the two coupon bonds with yields of 15% both converge to the duration of the perpetuity with the same yield, 7.67 years.

Concept Check

2. Show that the duration of a perpetuity increases as the interest rate decreases, in accordance with Rule 4.

Durations can vary widely among traded bonds. Table 11.4 presents durations for several bonds all assumed to pay annual coupons and to yield 8% per year. Duration decreases as coupon rates increase and gradually increases with time to maturity. According to Table 11.4 and Equation 11.2, if the interest rate were to increase from 8% to 8.1%, the 6% coupon, 20-year bond would fall in value by about 1.04% (= 11.231 × 0.1%/1.08) while the 10% coupon, one-year bond would fall by only 0.093% (= 1 × 0.1%/1.08). Notice also from Table 11.4 that duration is independent of coupon rate only for the perpetual bond.

11.2 PASSIVE BOND MANAGEMENT

Passive managers take bond prices as fairly set and seek to control only the risk of their fixed-income portfolio. Generally, there are two ways of viewing this risk, depending on the investor's circumstances. Some institutions, such as banks, are concerned with protecting the portfolio's current net worth or net market value against interest rate fluctuations. Risk-based capital guidelines for commercial banks and thrift institutions require the setting aside of additional capital as a buffer against potential losses in market value incurred from interest rate fluctuations. The amount of capital required is directly related to the losses that may be incurred under various changes in market interest rates. Other investors, such as pension funds, may have an investment goal to be reached after a given number of years. These investors are more concerned with protecting the future values of their portfolios.

What is common to the bank and pension fund, however, is interest rate risk. The net worth of the firm and its ability to meet future obligations fluctuate with interest rates. If

immunization
A strategy to shield net worth from interest rate movements.

they adjust the maturity structure of their portfolios, these institutions can shed their interest rate risk. **Immunization** and dedication techniques refer to strategies that investors use to shield their net worth from exposure to interest rate fluctuations.

Net Worth Immunization

Many banks and thrift institutions have a natural mismatch between the maturities of assets and liabilities. Liabilities are primarily the deposits owed to customers, most of which are short-term in nature and consequently of low duration. Assets are comprised largely of commercial and consumer loans or mortgages. These assets are of longer duration than deposits, which means their values are correspondingly more sensitive than deposits to interest rate fluctuations. When interest rates increase unexpectedly, banks can suffer serious decreases in net worth—their assets fall in value by more than their liabilities.

The watchword in bank portfolio strategy has become asset and liability management. Techniques called *gap* management limit the disparity between asset and liability durations. Adjustable-rate mortgages are one example. Conventional mortgages fall in value when market interest rates rise, but adjustable-rate mortgages do not because the rates they pay are tied to an index of the current market rate. Even if the indexing is imperfect or entails lags, indexing greatly diminishes the sensitivity of the mortgage value to interest rate fluctuations. On the other side of the balance sheet, bank certificates of deposit with fixed terms to maturity lengthen the duration of bank liabilities, also reducing the duration gap.

In this way, banks attempt to protect their overall position by immunizing themselves against interest rate movements. As long as bank assets and liabilities are roughly equal in size, any change in interest rates will affect the value of assets and liabilities equally, if their durations are also equal. Interest rates will not affect net worth, in other words. Therefore, banks, which typically have roughly equal assets and liabilities, can shed interest rate risk by equating the durations of their assets and liabilities.

Target Date Immunization

Pension funds are different from banks. They think more in terms of future commitments than current net worth. Pension funds have an obligation to provide workers with a flow of income on retirement, and they must have sufficient funds available to meet such commitments. As interest rates fluctuate, both the value of the fund's assets and the rate at which those assets generate income fluctuate. The pension fund manager, therefore, may want to protect or "immunize" the fund's future accumulated value at the target date against interest rate movements.

The box on page 305 illustrates the dangers that pension funds face when they neglect the interest rate exposure of *both* assets and liabilities. The article points out that when interest rates change, the present value of the fund's liabilities change. For example, pension funds lost ground in 1995 despite the fact that they enjoyed excellent investment returns. This is because, as interest rates fell, the value of the funds' liabilities grew even faster than the value of their assets. The article concludes that funds should match the interest rate exposure of assets and liabilities so that the value of assets will track the value of liabilities whether rates rise or fall.

Pension funds are not alone in this concern. Any institution with a future fixed obligation might consider immunization a reasonable risk management policy. Insurance companies, for example, also pursue immunization strategies. The notion of immunization was introduced by F. M. Redington (1952), an actuary for a life insurance company. The idea behind immunization is that duration-matched assets and liabilities let the asset portfolio meet the firm's obligations despite interest rate movements.

Consider, for example, an insurance company that issues a guaranteed investment contract, or GIC, for $10,000. (GICs are essentially zero-coupon bonds issued by the insurance company to its customers. They are popular products for individuals' retirement-saving

How Pension Funds Lost in Market Boom

In one of the happiest reports to come out of Detroit lately, **General Motors** proclaimed Tuesday that its U.S. pension funds are now "fully funded on an economic basis." Less noticed was GM's admission that, in accounting terms, it is still a few cents—well, $3 billion—shy of the mark.

Wait a minute. If GM's pension plans were $9.3 billion in the hole when 1995 began, and if the company, to its credit, shoveled in $10.4 billion more during the year, how come its pension deficit wasn't wiped out in full?

We'll get to that, but the real news here is broader than GM. According to experts, most pension funds actually *lost* ground in 1995, even though, as you may recall, it was a rather good year for stocks and bonds.

True, pension-fund assets did have a banner year. But as is sometimes overlooked, pension funds also have liabilities (their obligations to retirees). And at most funds, liabilities grew at a rate that put asset growth to shame. At the margin, that means more companies' pension plans will be "underfunded." And down the road, assuming no reversal in the trend, more companies will have to pony up more cash.

What's to blame? The sharp decline in interest rates that brought joy to everyone else. As rates fall, pension funds have to set aside more money today to pay off a fixed obligation tomorrow. In accounting-speak, this "discounted present value" of their liabilities rises.

By now, maybe you sense that pension liabilities swing more, in either direction, than assets. How come? In a phrase, most funds are "mismatched," meaning their liabilities are longer-lived than their investments. The longer an obligation, the more its current value reacts to changes in rates. And at a typical pension fund, even though the average obligation is 15 years away, the average duration of its bond portfolio is roughly five years.

If this seems to defy common sense, it does. No sensible family puts its grocery money (a short-term obligation) into common stocks (a long-term asset). And a college sophomore is unlikely to put his retirement savings into two-year bonds. Ordinary Joes and Janes grasp the principle of "matching" without even thinking about it.

But fund managers—the pros—insist on shorter, unmatching bond portfolios for a simple, stupefying reason. They are graded—usually by consultants—according to how they perform against standard (and shorter term) bond indexes. Thus, rather than invest to keep up with liabilities, managers are investing so as to avoid lagging behind the popular index in any year. A gutsy exception is AMR (average bond duration: 26 years). Its assets will get hammered if rates rise, but they should track liabilities either way.

Source: Roger Lowenstein, "How Pension Funds Lost in Market Boom," *The Wall Street Journal*, February 1, 1996.

---

accounts.) If the GIC has a five-year maturity and a guaranteed interest rate of 8%, the insurance company is obligated to pay $10,000 \times (1.08)^5 = $14,693.28 in five years.

Suppose that the insurance company chooses to fund its obligation with $10,000 of 8% *annual* coupon bonds, selling at par value, with six years to maturity. As long as the market interest rate stays at 8%, the company has fully funded the obligation, as the present value of the obligation exactly equals the value of the bonds.

Table 11.5A shows that if interest rates remain at 8%, the accumulated funds from the bond will grow to exactly the $14,693.28 obligation. Over the five-year period, the year-end coupon income of $800 is reinvested at the prevailing 8% market interest rate. At the end of the period, the bonds can be sold for $10,000; they still will sell at par value because the coupon rate still equals the market interest rate. Total income after five years from reinvested coupons and the sale of the bond is precisely $14,693.28.

If interest rates change, however, two offsetting influences will affect the ability of the fund to grow to the targeted value of $14,693.28. If interest rates rise, the fund will suffer a capital loss, impairing its ability to satisfy the obligation. The bonds will be worth less in five years than if interest rates had remained at 8%. However, at a higher interest rate, reinvested coupons will grow at a faster rate, offsetting the capital loss. In other words, fixed-income investors face two offsetting types of interest rate risk: *price risk* and *reinvestment rate risk*. Increases in interest rates cause capital losses but at the same time increase the rate at which reinvested income will grow. If the portfolio duration is chosen appropriately, these two effects will cancel out exactly. When the portfolio duration is set equal to the investor's horizon date, the accumulated value of the investment fund at the horizon date

TABLE 11.5

Terminal Value of a
Bond Portfolio after
Five Years (All
Proceeds Reinvested)

Payment Number	Years Remaining until Obligation	Accumulated Value of Invested Payment
A. Rates Remain at 8%		
1	4	$800 \times (1.08)^4 =$ 1,088.39
2	3	$800 \times (1.08)^3 =$ 1,007.77
3	2	$800 \times (1.08)^2 =$ 933.12
4	1	$800 \times (1.08)^1 =$ 864.00
5	0	$800 \times (1.08)^0 =$ 800.00
Sale of bond	0	10,800/1.08 = 10,000.00
		14,693.28
B. Rates Fall to 7%		
1	4	$800 \times (1.07)^4 =$ 1,048.64
2	3	$800 \times (1.07)^3 =$ 980.03
3	2	$800 \times (1.07)^2 =$ 915.92
4	1	$800 \times (1.07)^1 =$ 856.00
5	0	$800 \times (1.07)^0 =$ 800.00
Sale of bond	0	10,800/1.07 = 10,093.46
		14,694.05
C. Rates Increase to 9%		
1	4	$800 \times (1.09)^4 =$ 1,129.27
2	3	$800 \times (1.09)^3 =$ 1,036.02
3	2	$800 \times (1.09)^2 =$ 950.48
4	1	$800 \times (1.09)^1 =$ 872.00
5	0	$800 \times (1.09)^0 =$ 800.00
Sale of bond	0	10,800/1.09 = 9,908.26
		14,696.02

Note: The sale price of the bond portfolio equals the portfolio's final payment ($10,800) divided by
$1 + r$, because the time to maturity of the bonds will be one year at the time of sale.

will be unaffected by interest rate fluctuations. *For a horizon equal to the portfolio's duration, price risk and reinvestment risk exactly cancel out.* The obligation is immunized.

In the example we are discussing, the duration of the six-year maturity bonds used to
fund the GIC is five years. You can confirm this following the procedure in Table 11.3. The
duration of the (zero-coupon) GIC is also five years. Because the fully funded plan has equal
duration for its assets and liabilities, the insurance company should be immunized against
interest rate fluctuations. To confirm that this is the case, let us now investigate whether the
bond can generate enough income to pay off the obligation five years from now regardless
of interest rate movements.

Tables 11.5B and C consider two possible interest rate scenarios: Rates either fall to 7%
or increase to 9%. In both cases, the annual coupon payments from the bond are reinvested
at the new interest rate, which is assumed to change before the first coupon payment, and the
bond is sold in year 5 to help satisfy the obligation of the GIC.

Table 11.5B shows that if interest rates fall to 7%, the total funds will accumulate to
$14,694.05, providing a small surplus of $0.77. If rates increase to 9% as in Table 11.5C, the
fund accumulates to $14,696.02, providing a small surplus of $2.74.

Several points are worth highlighting. First, duration matching balances the difference
between the accumulated value of the coupon payments (reinvestment rate risk) and the sale
value of the bond (price risk). That is, when interest rates fall, the coupons grow less than in
the base case, but the gain on the sale of the bond offsets this. When interest rates rise, the
resale value of the bond falls, but the coupons more than make up for this loss because they
are reinvested at the higher rate. Figure 11.3 illustrates this case. The solid curve traces out
the accumulated value of the bonds if interest rates remain at 8%. The dashed curve shows
that value if interest rates happen to increase. The initial impact is a capital loss, but this loss
eventually is offset by the now-faster growth rate of reinvested funds. At the five-year

FIGURE 11.3
Growth of Invested
Funds

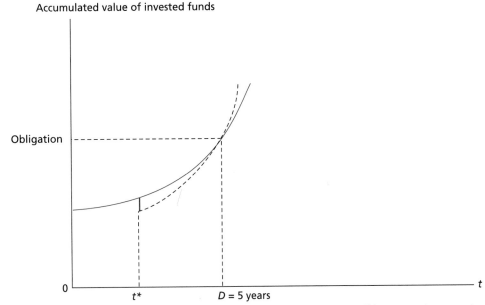

Accumulated value of invested funds

Obligation

0   t^* D = 5 years t

Note: The solid curve represents the growth of portfolio value at the original interest rate. If interest rates increase at time t^* the portfolio value falls but increases thereafter at the faster rate represented by the broken curve. At time D (duration) the curves cross.

FIGURE 11.4
Market Value Balance
Sheets

A. Interest Rate = 8%			
Assets		**Liabilities**	
Bonds	$10,000	Obligation	$10,000

B. Interest Rate = 7%			
Assets		**Liabilities**	
Bonds	$10,476.65	Obligation	$10,476.11

C. Interest Rate = 9%			
Assets		**Liabilities**	
Bonds	$9,551.41	Obligation	$9,549.62

Notes:

Value of bonds = 800 × Annuity factor $(r, 6)$ + 10,000 × PV factor$(r, 6)$

Value of obligation = $\dfrac{14,693.28}{(1 + r)^5}$ = 14,693.28 × PV factor$(r, 5)$

horizon date, the two effects just cancel, leaving the company able to satisfy its obligation with the accumulated proceeds from the bond.

We can also analyze immunization in terms of present as opposed to future values. Figure 11.4A shows the initial balance sheet for the insurance company's GIC account. Both assets and the obligation have market values of $10,000, so that the plan is just fully funded. Figures 11.4B and C show that whether the interest rates increases or decreases, the value of the bonds funding the GIC and the present value of the company's obligation change by virtually identical amounts. Regardless of the interest rate change, the plan remains fully funded, with the surplus in Figures 11.4B and C just about zero. The duration-matching strategy has ensured that both assets and liabilities react equally to interest rate fluctuations.

Figure 11.5 is a graph of the present values of the bond and the single-payment obligation as a function of the interest rate. At the current rate of 8%, the values are equal, and the obligation is fully funded by the bond. Moreover, the two present value curves are tangent at y = 8%. As interest rates change, the change in value of both the asset and the obligation are

FIGURE 11.5
Immunization

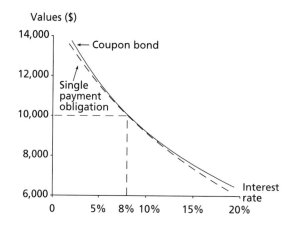

equal, so the obligation remains fully funded. For greater changes in the interest rate, however, the present value curves diverge. This reflects the fact that the fund actually shows a small surplus at market interest rates other than 8%.

Why is there any surplus in the fund? After all, we claimed that a duration-matched asset and liability mix would make the investor indifferent to interest rate shifts. Actually, such a claim is valid only for *small* changes in the interest rate, because as bond yields change, so too does duration. (Recall Rule 4 for duration.) In fact, while the duration of the bond in this example is equal to five years at a yield to maturity of 8%, the duration rises to 5.02 years when the bond yield falls to 7% and drops to 4.97 years at $y = 9\%$. That is, the bond and the obligation were not duration-matched *across* the interest rate shift, so the position was not fully immunized.

rebalancing
Realigning the proportions of assets in a portfolio as needed.

This example demonstrates the need for **rebalancing** immunized portfolios. As interest rates and asset durations continually change, managers must rebalance, that is, change the composition of, the portfolio of fixed-income assets to realign its duration with the duration of the obligation. Moreover, even if interest rates do not change, asset durations *will* change solely because of the passage of time. Recall from Figure 11.2 that duration generally decreases less rapidly than maturity as time passes, so even if an obligation is immunized at the outset, the durations of the asset and liability will fall at different rates. Without portfolio rebalancing, durations will become unmatched and the goals of immunization will not be realized. Therefore, immunization is a passive strategy only in the sense that it does not involve attempts to identify undervalued securities. Immunization managers still actively update and monitor their positions.

**EXAMPLE 11.2
Constructing an Immunized Portfolio**

An insurance company must make a payment of $19,487 in seven years. The market interest rate is 10%, so the obligation has a present value of $10,000. The company's portfolio manager wishes to fund the obligation using three-year zero-coupon bonds and perpetuities paying annual coupons. (We focus on zeros and perpetuities to keep the algebra simple.) How can the manager immunize the obligation?

Immunization requires that the duration of the portfolio of assets equal the duration of the liability. We can proceed in four steps:

Step 1. Calculate the duration of the liability. In this case, the liability duration is simple to compute. It is a single-payment obligation with duration of seven years.

Step 2. Calculate the duration of the asset portfolio. The portfolio duration is the weighted average of duration of each component asset, with weights proportional to the funds placed in each asset. The duration of the zero-coupon bond is simply its maturity, three years. The duration of the perpetuity is $1.10/0.10 = 11$ years. Therefore, if the fraction of the portfolio invested in the zero is called w, and the fraction invested in the perpetuity is $(1 - w)$, the portfolio duration will be

Asset duration = $w \times 3$ years + $(1 - w) \times 11$ years

Step 3. Find the asset mix that sets the duration of assets equal to the seven-year duration of liabilities. This requires us to solve for w in the following equation

$$w \times 3 \text{ years} + (1 - w) \times 11 \text{ years} = 7 \text{ years}$$

This implies that $w = 1/2$. The manager should invest half the portfolio in the zero and half in the perpetuity. This will result in an asset duration of seven years.

Step 4. Fully fund the obligation. Since the obligation has a present value of $10,000, and the fund will be invested equally in the zero and the perpetuity, the manager must purchase $5,000 of the zero-coupon bond and $5,000 of the perpetuity.

Even if a position is immunized, however, the portfolio manager still cannot rest. This is because of the need for rebalancing in response to changes in interest rates. Moreover, even if rates do not change, the passage of time also will affect duration and require rebalancing. Let us continue Example 11.2 and see how the portfolio manager can maintain an immunized position.

EXAMPLE 11.3
Rebalancing

Suppose that one year has passed, and the interest rate remains at 10%. The portfolio manager of Example 11.2 needs to reexamine her position. Is the position still fully funded? Is it still immunized? If not, what actions are required?

First, examine funding. The present value of the obligation will have grown to $11,000, as it is one year closer to maturity. The manager's funds also have grown to $11,000: The zero-coupon bonds have increased in value from $5,000 to $5,500 with the passage of time, while the perpetuity has paid its annual $500 coupons and remains worth $5,000. Therefore, the obligation is still fully funded.

The portfolio weights must be changed, however. The zero-coupon bond now will have a duration of two years, while the perpetuity duration remains at 11 years. The obligation is now due in six years. The weights must now satisfy the equation

$$w \times 2 + (1 - w) \times 11 = 6$$

which implies that $w = 5/9$. To rebalance the portfolio and maintain the duration match, the manager now must invest a total of $11,000 \times 5/9 = $6,111.11 in the zero-coupon bond. This requires that the entire $500 coupon payment be invested in the zero, with an additional $111.11 of the perpetuity sold and invested in the zero-coupon bond.

Of course, rebalancing of the portfolio entails transaction costs as assets are bought or sold, so continuous rebalancing is not feasible. In practice, managers strike some compromise between the desire for perfect immunization, which requires continual rebalancing, and the need to control trading costs, which dictates less frequent rebalancing.

3. What would be the immunizing weights in the second year if the interest rate were to fall to 8%?

Cash Flow Matching and Dedication

The problems associated with immunization seem to have a simple solution. Why not simply buy a zero-coupon bond that provides a payment in an amount exactly sufficient to cover the projected cash outlay? This is **cash flow matching**, which automatically immunizes a portfolio from interest rate movements because the cash flow from the bond and the obligation exactly offset each other.

Cash flow matching on a multiperiod basis is referred to as a **dedication strategy**. In this case, the manager selects either zero-coupon or coupon bonds that provide total cash flows

cash flow matching
Matching cash flows from a fixed-income portfolio with an obligation.

dedication strategy
Refers to multiperiod cash flow matching.

in each period that match a series of obligations. The advantage of dedication is that it is a once-and-for-all approach to eliminating interest rate risk. Once the cash flows are matched, there is no need for rebalancing. The dedicated portfolio provides the cash necessary to pay the firm's liabilities regardless of the eventual path of interest rates.

Cash flow matching is not widely pursued, however, probably because of the constraints it imposes on bond selection. Immunization/dedication strategies are appealing to firms that do not wish to bet on general movements in interest rates, yet these firms may want to immunize using bonds they believe are undervalued. Cash flow matching places enough constraints on bond selection that it can make it impossible to pursue a dedication strategy using only "underpriced" bonds. Firms looking for underpriced bonds exchange exact and easy dedication for the possibility of achieving superior returns from their bond portfolios.

Sometimes, cash flow matching is not even possible. To cash flow match for a pension fund that is obligated to pay out a perpetual flow of income to current and future retirees, the pension fund would need to purchase fixed-income securities with maturities ranging up to hundreds of years. Such securities do not exist, making exact dedication infeasible. Immunization is easy, however. If the interest rate is 8%, for example, the duration of the pension fund obligation is 1.08/0.08 = 13.5 years (see Rule 5 above). Therefore, the fund can immunize its obligation by purchasing zero-coupon bonds with maturity of 13.5 years and a market value equal to that of the pension liabilities.

Concept Check

4. *a.* Suppose that this pension fund is obligated to pay out $800,000 per year in perpetuity. What should be the maturity and face value of the zero-coupon bond it purchases to immunize its obligation?
   b. Now suppose the interest rate immediately increases to 8.1%. How should the fund rebalance in order to remain immunized against further interest rate shocks? Ignore transaction costs.
5. How would an increase in trading costs affect the attractiveness of dedication versus immunization?

11.3 CONVEXITY

Duration clearly is a key tool in fixed-income portfolio management. Yet, the duration rule for the impact of interest rates on bond prices is only an approximation. Equation 11.2′, which we repeat here, states that the percentage change in the value of a bond approximately equals the product of modified duration times the change in the bond's yield:

$$\frac{\Delta P}{P} = -D^* \, \Delta y \qquad\qquad (11.2')$$

This rule asserts that the percentage price change is directly proportional to the change in the bond's yield. If this were *exactly* so, however, a graph of the percentage change in bond price as a function of the change in its yield would plot as a straight line, with slope equal to $-D^*$. Yet we know from Figure 11.1, and more generally from Malkiel's five bond-pricing relationships (specifically relationship 2), that the relationship between bond prices and yields is *not* linear. The duration rule is a good approximation for small changes in bond yield, but it is less accurate for larger changes.

Figure 11.6 illustrates this point. Like Figure 11.1, this figure presents the percentage change in bond price in response to a change in the bond's yield to maturity. The curved line is the percentage price change for a 30-year maturity, 8% coupon bond, selling at an initial yield to maturity of 8%. The straight line is the percentage price change predicted by the duration rule: The modified duration of the bond at its initial yield is 11.26 years, so the straight line is a plot of $-D^*\Delta y = -11.26 \times \Delta y$. Notice that the two plots are tangent at the initial yield. Thus, for small changes in the bond's yield to maturity, the duration rule is quite accurate. However, for larger changes in yield, there is progressively more "daylight"

FIGURE 11.6
Bond Price Convexity

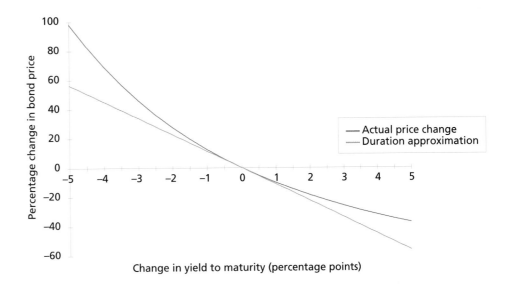

FIGURE 11.7
Convexity of Two
Bonds

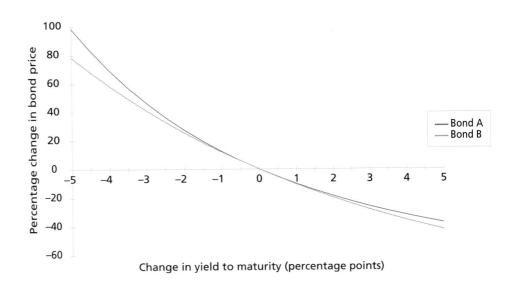

between the two plots, demonstrating that the duration rule becomes progressively less accurate.

Notice from Figure 11.6 that the duration approximation (the straight line) always understates the value of the bond; it underestimates the increase in bond price when the yield falls, and it overestimates the decline in price when the yield rises. This is due to the curvature of the true price-yield relationship. Curves with shapes such as that of the price-yield relationship are said to be convex, and the curvature of the price-yield curve is called the **convexity** of the bond. Convexity is generally considered a desirable trait in bonds: Prices of bonds with greater curvature will increase more when yields decrease and fall less when yields increase. For example, in Figure 11.7, bonds *A* and *B* have the same duration at the initial yield: The plots of their proportional price changes as a function of interest rate changes are tangent, meaning that their sensitivities to changes in yields are equal, at least for small changes in yields. However, bond *A* is more convex than bond *B*. It enjoys greater price increases and smaller price declines when rates change by larger amounts. Of course, if convexity is desirable, it will not be available for free: Investors may have to pay more and accept lower yields to maturity on more convex bonds.

convexity
The curvature of the price-yield relationship of a bond.

Convexity means that the bond price-yield curve becomes flatter at higher yields: Its slope is less negative. Therefore, we can quantify convexity as the rate of change of the slope of the price-yield curve, expressed as a fraction of the bond price.[2] As a practical rule, you can view bonds with higher convexity as exhibiting higher curvature in the price-yield relationship. The convexity of noncallable bonds, such as that in Figure 11.6, is positive: The slope increases (i.e., becomes less negative) at higher yields.

Convexity allows us to improve the duration approximation for bond price changes. Accounting for convexity, Equation 11.2′ can be modified as follows:

$$\frac{\Delta P}{P} = -D^* \Delta y + \frac{1}{2} \times \text{Convexity} \times (\Delta y)^2 \tag{11.3}$$

The first term on the right-hand side is the same as the duration rule, Equation 11.2′. The second term is the modification for convexity. Notice that for a bond with positive convexity, the second term is positive, regardless of whether the yield rises or falls. This insight corresponds to the fact noted just above that the duration rule always underestimates the new value of a bond following a change in its yield. The more accurate Equation 11.3, which accounts for convexity, always predicts a higher bond price than Equation 11.2′. Of course, if the change in yield is small, the convexity term, which is multiplied by $(\Delta y)^2$ in Equation 11.3, will be extremely small and will add little to the approximation. In this case, the linear approximation given by the duration rule will be sufficiently accurate. Thus, convexity is more important as a practical matter when potential interest rate changes are large.

Convexity is the reason that the immunization examples we considered above resulted in small errors. For example, if you turn back to Figures 11.4 and 11.5, you will see that the single payment obligation that was funded with a coupon bond of the same duration was well immunized for small changes in yields. However, for larger yield changes, the two pricing curves diverged a bit, implying that such changes in yields would result in small surpluses. This is due to the greater convexity of the coupon bond.

EXAMPLE 11.4
Convexity

The bond in Figure 11.6 has a 30-year maturity, an 8% coupon, and sells at an initial yield to maturity of 8%. Because the coupon rate equals yield to maturity, the bond sells at par value, or $1,000. The modified duration of the bond at its initial yield is 11.26 years, and its convexity is 212.4. (Convexity can be calculated using the formula in footnote 2.) If the bond's yield increases from 8% to 10%, the bond price will fall to $811.46, a decline of 18.85%. The duration rule, Equation 11.2′, would predict a price decline of

$$\frac{\Delta P}{P} = -D^* \, \Delta y = -11.26 \times 0.02 = -0.2252 = -22.52\%$$

which is considerably more than the bond price actually falls. The duration-with-convexity rule, Equation 11.3, is more accurate.[3]

$$\frac{\Delta P}{P} = -D^* \, \Delta y + \frac{1}{2} \times \text{Convexity} \times (\Delta y)^2$$

$$= -11.26 \times 0.02 + \frac{1}{2} \times 212.4 \times (0.02)^2 = -0.1827 = -18.27\%$$

---

[2]If you have taken a calculus class, you will recognize that Equation 11.2′ for modified duration can be written as $dP/P = -D^* \, dy$. Thus, $-D^* = 1/P \times dP/dy$ is the slope of the price-yield curve expressed as a fraction of the bond price. Similarly, the convexity of a bond equals the second derivative (the rate of change of the slope) of the price-yield curve divided by bond price: $1/P \times d^2P/dy^2$. The formula for the convexity of a bond with a maturity of n years making annual coupon payments is:

$$\text{Convexity} = \frac{1}{P \times (1 + y)^2} \sum_{t=1}^{n} \left[\frac{CF_t}{(1 + y)^t} (t^2 + t) \right]$$

where CF_t is the cash flow paid to the bondholder at date t; CF_t represents either a coupon payment before maturity or final coupon plus par value at the maturity date.
[3]To use the convexity rule, you must express interest rates as decimals rather than percentages.

which is far closer to the exact change in bond price.

Notice that if the change in yield were smaller, say 0.1%, convexity would matter less. The price of the bond actually would fall to $988.85, a decline of 1.115%. Without accounting for convexity, we would predict a price decline of:

$$\frac{\Delta P}{P} = -D^* \, \Delta y = -11.26 \times 0.001 = 0.01126 = 1.126\%$$

Accounting for convexity, we get almost the precisely correct answer:

$$\frac{\Delta P}{P} = -11.26 \times 0.001 + \frac{1}{2} \times 212.4 \times (0.001)^2 = 0.01115 = 1.115\%$$

Nevertheless, the duration rule is quite accurate in this case, even without accounting for convexity.

11.4 ACTIVE BOND MANAGEMENT

Sources of Potential Profit

Broadly speaking, there are two sources of potential value in active bond management. The first is interest rate forecasting; that is, anticipating movements across the entire spectrum of the fixed-income market. If interest rate declines are forecast, managers will increase portfolio duration; if increases seem likely, they will shorten duration. The second source of potential profit is identification of relative mispricing within the fixed-income market. An analyst might believe, for example, that the default premium on one bond is unnecessarily large and the bond is underpriced.

These techniques will generate abnormal returns only if the analyst's information or insight is superior to that of the market. There is no way of profiting from knowledge that rates are about to fall if everyone else in the market is on to this. In that case, the anticipated lower future rates are built into bond prices in the sense that long-duration bonds are already selling at higher prices that reflect the anticipated fall in future short rates. If the analyst does not have information before the market does, it will be too late to act on that information—prices will have responded already to the news. You know this from our discussion of market efficiency.

For now we simply repeat that valuable information is differential information. And it is worth noting that interest rate forecasters have a notoriously poor track record.

Homer and Leibowitz have developed a popular taxonomy of active bond portfolio strategies. They characterize portfolio rebalancing activities as one of four types of *bond swaps*. In the first two swaps, the investor typically believes the yield relationship between bonds or sectors is only temporarily out of alignment. Until the aberration is eliminated, gains can be realized on the underpriced bond during a period of realignment called the *workout period*.

substitution swap
Exchange of one bond for a bond with similar attributes but more attractively priced.

1. The **substitution swap** is an exchange of one bond for a nearly identical substitute. The substituted bonds should be of essentially equal coupon, maturity, quality, call features, sinking fund provisions, and so on. A substitution swap would be motivated by a belief that the market has temporarily mispriced the two bonds, with a discrepancy representing a profit opportunity.

An example of a substitution swap would be a sale of a 20-year maturity, 9% coupon Ford Motor Company bond callable after five years at $1,050 that is priced to provide a yield to maturity of 9.05% coupled with a purchase of a 9% coupon Chrysler bond with the same call provisions and time to maturity that yields 9.15%. If the bonds have about the same credit rating, there is no apparent reason for the Chrysler bonds to provide a higher yield. Therefore, the higher yield actually available in the market makes the Chrysler bond seem relatively attractive. Of course, the equality of credit risk is an important condition. If the Chrysler bond is in fact riskier, then its higher yield does not represent a bargain.

intermarket spread swap
Switching from one segment of the bond market to another.

2. The **intermarket spread swap** is an exchange of two bonds from different sectors of the bond market. It is pursued when an investor believes the yield spread between two sectors of the bond market is temporarily out of line.

For example, if the yield spread between 20-year Treasury bonds and 20-year Baa-rated corporate bonds is now 3%, and the historical spread has been only 2%, an investor might consider selling holdings of Treasury bonds and replacing them with corporates. If the yield spread eventually narrows, the Baa-rated corporate bonds will outperform the Treasury bonds.

Of course, the investor must consider carefully whether there is a good reason that the yield spread seems out of alignment. For example, the default premium on corporate bonds might have increased because the market is expecting a severe recession. In this case, the wider spread would not represent attractive pricing of corporates relative to Treasuries, but would simply be an adjustment for a perceived increase in credit risk.

rate anticipation swap
A switch made in response to forecasts of interest rate changes.

3. The **rate anticipation swap** is an exchange of bonds with different maturities. It is pegged to interest rate forecasting. Investors who believe rates will fall will swap into bonds of greater duration. For example, the investor might sell a five-year maturity Treasury bond, replacing it with a 25-year maturity Treasury bond. The new bond has the same lack of credit risk as the old one, but it has longer duration.

pure yield pickup swap
Moving to higher yield bonds, usually with longer maturities.

4. The **pure yield pickup swap** is an exchange of a shorter duration bond for a longer duration bond. This swap is pursued not in response to perceived mispricing but as a means of increasing return by holding higher yielding, longer maturity bonds. The investor is willing to bear the interest rate risk this strategy entails. Riding the yield curve, discussed in the previous chapter, is an example of a pure yield pickup strategy.

A yield pickup swap can be illustrated using the Treasury bond listings in Figure 10.1 from the last chapter. You can see from that table that a Treasury note maturing in November 1998 yields 6.4%, while one maturing in February 2025 yields 7.25%. The investor who swaps the shorter term bond for the longer one will earn a higher rate of return as long as the yield curve does not shift upward during the holding period. Of course, if it does, the longer duration bond will suffer a greater capital loss.

tax swap
Swapping two similar bonds to receive a tax benefit.

We can add a fifth swap, called a **tax swap** to this list. This simply refers to a swap to exploit some tax advantage. For example, an investor may swap from one bond that has decreased in price to another similar bond if realization of capital losses is advantageous for tax purposes.

Investors and analysts commonly use this classification of strategies, if only implicitly. Consider these quotations from the Merrill Lynch "Fixed-Income Strategy" booklet.

> Projected returns at alternative settings of the funds rate strongly favor ownership of short-term notes. At almost every [projected] setting of the [federal] funds rate, returns from both 10-year notes and 30-year bonds would be negative . . . In a rising interest rate environment, where yields rise by 35 basis points for two-year notes and 25 basis points for three-year notes, the two-year is projected to outperform by approximately 50 basis points. . . .

This analysis has to do with rate anticipation, which follows from Merrill Lynch's overall macroeconomic analysis. Given Merrill Lynch's belief in rising rates, it recommends short asset durations.

Following this general analysis comes a sector-oriented intermarket spread analysis that expresses Merrill Lynch's view that yield relationships across two fixed-income submarkets are temporarily out of line. The history of 1982–1984 leads Merrill Lynch to believe that corporate yields will fall relative to Treasury yields, making corporates attractive relative to Treasuries:

> Corporate/Treasury yield ratios are unusually high for both intermediate and long-term securities. These ratios are now [April 1986] almost as high as those that emerged late in 1982, following a sharp drop in bond yields. The respective yield ratios for new-issue long-term AA utilities and AA industrials were 1.17 and 1.13 at the end of this past quarter, compared with 1.22 and 1.15 in

December 1982. By mid-1983, these ratios had declined to 1.10 and 1.08, respectively. By July 1984, they had declined further, to 1.08 and 1.05. Yield ratios for intermediate corporates display a similar pattern. This record suggests that corporate/Treasury yield ratios are likely to fall in the months ahead if, as we expect, the Treasury yield curve steepens (page 16).

Finally, we see an example of a yield pickup recommendation:

Although the slope of the corporate yield curve is 30 to 50 basis points steeper than that of the Treasury curve, it has flattened by approximately the same degree. Thus, any steepening in the Treasury curve would probably spark a similar response in corporates, hurting the long corporate market much more than the short and intermediate coupons. Consequently, the 2- to 10-year maturity sector performs far better in the total return simulations [than longer-term issues]. Moreover, since this is the steepest area of the yield curve, it offers investors the opportunity to capture more than 90% of the yield on long bonds while owning 10-year rather than 30-year maturities (page 17).

The Merrill Lynch strategy book is devoted to broad sectors of the fixed-income market and so does not include any examples of substitution swaps.

Horizon Analysis

horizon analysis
Forecast of bond returns based largely on a prediction of the yield curve at the end of the investment horizon.

One form of interest rate forecasting is called **horizon analysis**. The analyst selects a particular investment period and predicts bond yields at the end of that period. Given the predicted yield to maturity at the end of the investment period, the bond price can be calculated. The coupon income earned over the period is then added to the predicted capital gain or loss to obtain a forecast of the total return on the bond over the holding period.

EXAMPLE 11.5
Horizon Analysis

A 20-year maturity bond with a 10% coupon rate (paid annually) currently sells at a yield to maturity of 9%. A portfolio manager with a two-year horizon needs to forecast the total return on the bond over the coming two years. In two years, the bond will have an 18-year maturity. The analyst forecasts that two years from now, 18-year bonds will sell at yields to maturity of 8%, and that coupon payments can be reinvested in short-term securities over the coming two years at a rate of 7%.

To calculate the two-year return on the bond, the analyst would perform the following calculations:

1. Current price = $100 × Annuity factor (9%, 20 years) + $1,000 × PV factor (9%, 20 years)
   = $1,091.29
2. Forecast price = $100 × Annuity factor (8%, 18 years) + $1,000 × PV factor (8%, 18 years)
   = $1,187.44
3. The future value of reinvested coupons will be ($100 × 1.07) + $100 = $207
4. The two-year return is $\dfrac{\$207 + (\$1,187.44 - \$1,091.29)}{\$1,091.29} = 0.278$, or 27.8%

The annualized rate of return over the two-year period would then be $(1.278)^{1/2} - 1 = 0.13$, or 13%.

Concept Check

6. What will be the rate of return if the manager forecasts that in two years the yield to maturity on 18-year maturity bonds will be 10% and that the reinvestment rate for coupons will be 8%?

Contingent Immunization

Some investment styles fall within the spectrum of active versus passive strategies. An example is a technique called **contingent immunization**, first suggested by Liebowitz and Weinberger (1982). The idea is to allow the fixed-income manager to manage the portfolio actively unless and until poor performance endangers the prospect of achieving a minimum

contingent immunization
A strategy that immunizes a portfolio if necessary to guarantee a minimum acceptable return but otherwise allows active management.

acceptable portfolio return. At that point, the portfolio is immunized, providing a guaranteed rate of return over the remaining portion of the investment period.

To illustrate, suppose a manager with a two-year horizon is responsible for a $10 million portfolio. The manager wishes to provide a two-year cumulative return of at least 10%, that is, the minimum acceptable final value of the portfolio is $11 million. If the interest rate currently is 10%, only $9.09 million would be necessary to guarantee a terminal value of $11 million, because $9.09 million invested in an immunized portfolio would grow after two years to $9.09 × (1.10)² = $11 million. Since the manager starts with $10 million, she can afford to risk some losses at the outset and might therefore start out with an active strategy rather than immediately immunizing.

How much can the manager risk losing? If the interest rate at any time is r, and T is the time left until the horizon date, the amount needed to achieve a terminal value of $11 million is simply the present value of $11 million, or $11 million$/(1 + r)^T$. A portfolio of this size, if immunized, will grow risk-free to $11 million by the horizon date. This value becomes a trigger point: If and when the actual portfolio value dips to the trigger point, active management will cease. *Contingent* upon reaching the trigger point, an immunization strategy is initiated.

Figure 11.8 illustrates two possible outcomes in a contingent immunization strategy. In Figure 11.8A, the portfolio falls in value and hits the trigger at time t^*. At that point, immunization is pursued, and the portfolio rises smoothly to the $11 million value. In Figure 11.8B, the portfolio does well, never reaches the trigger point, and is worth more than $11 million at the horizon date.

Concept Check

7. What is the trigger point if the manager has a three-year horizon, the interest rate is 8%, and the minimum acceptable terminal value is $10 million?

An Example of a Fixed-Income Investment Strategy

To demonstrate a reasonable, active fixed-income portfolio strategy, we discuss here the policies of Sanford Bernstein & Co., as explained in a speech by its manager of fixed-income investments, Francis Trainer. The company believes big bets on general marketwide interest movements are unwise. Instead, it concentrates on exploiting numerous instances of perceived *relative* minor pricing misalignments *within* the fixed-income sector. The firm takes as a risk benchmark the Lehman Brothers Government/Corporate Bond Index, which includes the vast majority of publicly traded bonds with maturities greater than one year. Any deviation from this passive or neutral position must be justified by active analysis. Bernstein considers a neutral portfolio duration to be equal to that of the index.

The firm is willing to make only limited bets on interest rate movements. As Francis Trainer puts it in his speech:

> If we set duration of our portfolios at a level equal to the index and never allow them to vary, this would imply that we are perpetually neutral on the direction of interest rates. However, as those of you who have followed our economic forecasts are aware, this is rarely the case. We believe the utilization of these forecasts will add value and, therefore, we incorporate our economic forecast into the bond management process by altering the durations of our portfolios.
>
> However, in order to prevent fixed-income performance from being dominated by the accuracy of just a single aspect of our research effort, we limit the degree to which we are willing to alter our interest rate exposure. Under the vast majority of circumstances, we will not permit the duration of our portfolios to differ from that of the Shearson Lehman Index [now the Lehman Brothers Index] by more than one year.

The company expends most of its effort in exploiting numerous but minor inefficiencies in bond prices that result from lack of attention by its competitors. Its analysts follow about

FIGURE 11.8
Contingent
Immunization

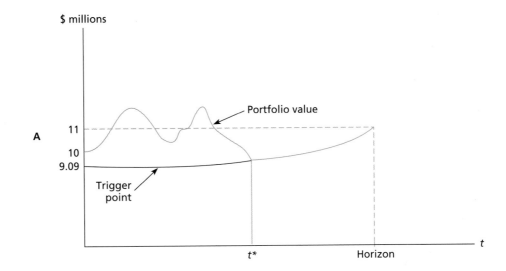

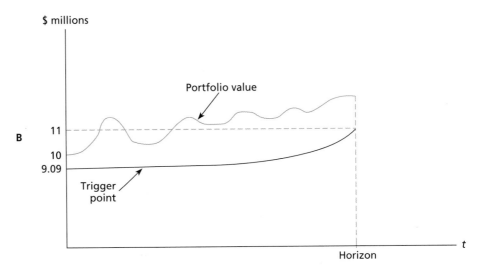

1,000 securities, attempting to "identify specific securities that are attractive or unattractive as well as identify trends in the richness or cheapness of industries and sectors." These two activities would be characterized as substitution swaps and intermarket spread swaps in the Homer–Leibowitz scheme.

Sanford Bernstein & Co. realizes that market opportunities will arise, if at all, only in sectors of the bond market that present the least competition from other analysts. For this reason, it tends to avoid recently issued bonds because "most of the attention that is focused on the bond market is concentrated on those securities that have been recently issued." Similarly, it tends to focus on relatively more complicated bond issues in the belief that extensive research efforts give the firm a comparative advantage in that sector. Finally, the company does not take unnecessary risks. If there do not appear to be enough seemingly attractive bonds, funds are placed in Treasury securities as a "neutral" parking space until new opportunities are identified.

To summarize the key features of this sort of strategy, we can make the following observations:

1. A firm like Bernstein has a respect for market prices. It believes that only minor mispricing usually can be detected. It works toward meaningful abnormal returns by combining numerous *small* profit opportunities, not by hoping for the success of one big bet.

2. To have value, information cannot be reflected already in market prices. A large research staff must focus on market niches that appear to be neglected by others.
3. Interest rate movements are extremely hard to predict, and attempts to time the market can wipe out all the profits of intramarket analysis.

11.5 INTEREST RATE SWAPS

interest rate swaps
Contracts between two parties to trade the cash flows corresponding to different securities without actually exchanging the securities directly.

Interest rate swaps have emerged as an important tool for fixed-income managers. An interest rate swap is a contract between two parties to exchange a series of cash flows similar to those that would result if the parties instead were to exchange equal dollar values of different types of bonds. Swaps arose originally as a means of managing interest rate risk. The volume of swaps has increased from virtually zero in 1980 to over $5 trillion today. (Interest rate swaps do not have anything to do with the Homer–Leibowitz bond swap taxonomy set out earlier.)

To illustrate how swaps work, consider the manager of a large portfolio that currently includes $100 million par value of long-term bonds paying an average coupon rate of 7%. The manager believes that interest rates are about to rise. As a result, he would like to sell the bonds and replace them with either short-term or floating-rate issues. However, it would be exceedingly expensive in terms of transaction costs to replace the portfolio every time the forecast for interest rates is updated. A cheaper and more flexible way to modify the portfolio is for the manager to "swap" the $7 million a year in interest income the portfolio currently generates for an amount of money that is tied to the short-term interest rate. That way, if rates do rise, so will the portfolio's interest income.

A swap dealer might advertise its willingness to exchange or "swap" a cash flow based on the six-month LIBOR rate for one based on a fixed rate of 7%. (The LIBOR, or London Interbank Offer Rate, is the interest rate at which banks borrow from each other in the Eurodollar market. It is the most commonly used short-term interest rate in the swap market.) The portfolio manager would then enter into a swap agreement with the dealer to *pay* 7% on **notional principal** of $100 million and *receive* payment of the LIBOR rate on that amount of notional principal.[4] In other words, the manager swaps a payment of 0.07 × $100 million for a payment of LIBOR × $100 million. The manager's *net* cash flow from the swap agreement is therefore (LIBOR − 0.07) × $100 million.

notional principal
Principal amount used to calculate swap payments.

Now consider the net cash flow to the manager's portfolio in three interest rate scenarios:

	LIBOR Rate		
	6.5%	**7.0%**	**7.5%**
Interest income from bond portfolio (= 7% of $100 million bond portfolio)	$7,000,000	$7,000,000	$7,000,000
Cash flow from swap [= (LIBOR − 7%) × notional principal of $100 million]	(500,000)	0	500,000
Total (= LIBOR × $100 million)	$6,500,000	$7,000,000	$7,500,000

Notice that the total income on the overall position—bonds plus swap agreement—is now equal to the LIBOR rate in each scenario times $100 million. The manager has in effect converted a fixed-rate bond portfolio into a synthetic floating-rate portfolio.

You can see now that swaps can be immensely useful for firms in a variety of applications. For example, a corporation that has issued fixed-rate debt can convert it into synthetic

---

[4]The participants to the swap do not loan each other money. They agree only to exchange a fixed cash flow for a variable cash flow that depends on the short-term interest rate. This is why the principal is described as *notional*. The notional principal is simply a way to describe the size of the swap agreement. In this example, the parties to the swap exchange a 7% fixed rate for the LIBOR rate; the difference between LIBOR and 7% is multiplied by notional principal to determine the cash flow exchanged by the parties.

FIGURE 11.9 Interest Rate Swap

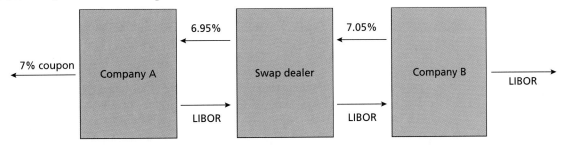

Company B pays a fixed rate of 7.05% to the swap dealer in return for LIBOR.
Company A receives 6.95% from the dealer in return for LIBOR. The swap dealer
realizes a cash flow each period equal to .1% of notional principal.

floating-rate debt by entering a swap to receive a fixed interest rate (offsetting its fixed-rate coupon obligation) and pay a floating rate. Or, a bank that pays current market interest rates to its depositors might enter a swap to receive a floating rate and pay a fixed rate on some amount of notional principal. This swap position, added to its floating rate deposit liability, would result in a net liability of a fixed stream of cash. The bank might then be able to invest in long-term fixed-rate loans without encountering interest rate risk.

What about the swap dealer? Why is the dealer, which is typically a financial intermediary such as a bank, willing to take on the opposite side of the swaps desired by these participants?

Consider a dealer who takes on one side of a swap, let's say paying LIBOR and receiving a fixed rate. The dealer will search for another trader in the swap market who wishes to receive a fixed rate and pay LIBOR. For example, company *A* may have issued a 7% coupon fixed-rate bond that it wishes to convert into synthetic floating-rate debt, while company *B* may have issued a floating-rate bond tied to LIBOR that it wishes to convert into synthetic fixed-rate debt. The dealer will enter a swap with company *A* in which it pays a fixed rate and receives LIBOR, and it will enter another swap with company *B* in which it pays LIBOR and receives a fixed rate. When the two swaps are combined, the dealer's position is effectively neutral on interest rates, paying LIBOR on one swap, and receiving it on another. Similarly, the dealer pays a fixed rate on one swap and receives it on another. The dealer becomes little more than an intermediary, funneling payments from one party to the other.[5] The dealer finds this activity profitable because he or she will charge a bid-ask spread on the transaction.

This arrangement is illustrated in Figure 11.9. Company *A* has issued 7% fixed-rate debt (the left-most arrow in the figure) but enters a swap to pay the dealer LIBOR and receive a 6.95% fixed rate. Therefore, the company's net payment is 7% + (LIBOR − 6.95%) = LIBOR + 0.05%. It has thus transformed its fixed-rate debt into synthetic floating-rate debt. Conversely, company *B* has issued floating-rate debt paying LIBOR (the right-most arrow), but enters a swap to pay a 7.05% fixed rate in return for LIBOR. Therefore, its net payment is LIBOR + (7.05% − LIBOR) = 7.05%. It has thus transformed its floating-rate debt into synthetic fixed-rate debt. The bid-ask spread in the example illustrated in Figure 11.9 is 0.1% of notional principal each year.

---

[5]Actually, things are a bit more complicated. The dealer is more than just an intermediary because he or she bears the credit risk that one or the other of the parties to the swap might default on the obligation. Referring to Figure 11.9, if company *A* defaults on its obligation, for example, the swap dealer still must maintain its commitment to company *B*. In this sense, the dealer does more than simply pass through cash flows to the other swap participants.

Concept Check

8. A pension fund holds a portfolio of money market securities that the manager believes are paying excellent yields compared to other comparable-risk short-term securities. However, the manager believes that interest rates are about to fall. What type of swap will allow the fund to continue to hold its portfolio of short-term securities while at the same time benefiting from a decline in rates?

Interest rate swaps create an interesting problem for financial statement analysis. Firms are not required to disclose them in corporate financial statements unless the swaps have a "material impact" on the firm and, even then, they appear only in the footnotes. This means the firm's true net obligations may be quite different from its apparent or presented debt structure.

Summary

- Even default-free bonds such as Treasury issues are subject to interest rate risk. Longer term bonds generally are more sensitive to interest rate shifts than short-term bonds. A measure of the average life of a bond is Macaulay's duration, defined as the weighted average of the times until each payment made by the security, with weights proportional to the present value of the payment.
- Duration is a direct measure of the sensitivity of a bond's price to a change in its yield. The proportional change in a bond's price approximately equals the negative of duration times the proportional change in $1 + y$.
- Immunization strategies are characteristic of passive fixed-income portfolio management. Such strategies attempt to render the individual or firm immune from movements in interest rates. This may take the form of immunizing net worth or, instead, immunizing the future accumulated value of a fixed-income portfolio.
- Convexity refers to the curvature of a bond's price-yield relationship. Accounting for convexity can substantially improve on the accuracy of the duration approximation for bond-price sensitivity to changes in yields.
- Immunization of a fully funded plan is accomplished by matching the durations of assets and liabilities. To maintain an immunized position as time passes and interest rates change, the portfolio must be periodically rebalanced.
- A more direct form of immunization is dedication or cash flow matching. If a portfolio is perfectly matched in cash flow with projected liabilities, rebalancing will be unnecessary.
- Active bond management can be decomposed into interest rate forecasting techniques and intermarket spread analysis. One popular taxonomy classifies active strategies as substitution swaps, intermarket spread swaps, rate anticipation swaps, or pure yield pickup swaps.
- Interest rate swaps are important instruments in the fixed-income market. In these arrangements, parties trade the cash flows of different securities without actually exchanging any securities directly. This can be a useful tool to manage the duration of a portfolio.

Key Terms

cash flow matching, *309*	horizon analysis, *315*	pure yield pickup
contingent	immunization, *304*	swap, *314*
immunization, *315*	interest rate swaps, *318*	rate anticipation swap, *314*
convexity, *311*	intermarket spread	rebalancing, *308*
dedication strategy, *309*	swap, *314*	substitution swap, *313*
duration, *299*	notional principal, *318*	tax swap, *314*

Problem Set

1. A nine-year bond has a yield of 10% and a duration of 7.194 years. If the bond's yield changes by 50 basis points, what is the percentage change in the bond's price?

2. Find the duration of a 6% coupon bond making *annual* coupon payments if it has three years until maturity and a yield to maturity of 6%. What is the duration if the yield to maturity is 10%?

3. A pension plan is obligated to make disbursements of $1 million, $2 million, and $1 million at the end of each of the next three years, respectively. Find the duration of the plan's obligations if the interest rate is 10% annually.

4. If the plan in problem 3 wants to fully fund and immunize its position, how much of its portfolio should it allocate to one-year zero-coupon bonds and perpetuities, respectively, if these are the only two assets funding the plan?

5. You own a fixed-income asset with a duration of five years. If the level of interest rates, which is currently 8%, goes down by 10 basis points, how much do you expect the price of the asset to go up (in percentage terms)?

6. Rank the interest-rate sensitivity of the following pairs of bonds.
   a. Bond *A* is an 8% coupon bond, with 20-year time to maturity selling at par value. Bond *B* is an 8% coupon, 20-year maturity bond selling below par value.
   b. Bond *A* is a 20-year, noncallable coupon bond with a coupon rate of 8%, selling at par.
      Bond *B* is a 20-year, callable bond with a coupon rate of 9%, also selling at par.

7. Rank the following bonds in order of descending duration.

Bond	Coupon	Time to Maturity	Yield to Maturity
A	15%	20 years	10%
B	15	15	10
C	0	20	10
D	8	20	10
E	15	15	15

8. You will be paying $10,000 a year in tuition expenses at the end of the next two years. Bonds currently yield 8%.
   a. What is the present value and duration of your obligation?
   b. What maturity zero-coupon bond would immunize your obligation?
   c. Suppose you buy a zero-coupon bond with value and duration equal to your obligation. Now suppose that rates immediately increase to 9%. What happens to your net position, that is, to the difference between the value of the bond and that of your tuition obligation? What if rates fall to 7%?

9. Pension funds pay lifetime annuities to recipients. If a firm remains in business indefinitely, the pension obligation will resemble a perpetuity. Suppose, therefore, that you are managing a pension fund with obligations to make perpetual payments of $2 million per year to beneficiaries. The yield to maturity on all bonds is 16%.
   a. If the duration of five-year maturity bonds with coupon rates of 12% (paid annually) is four years and the duration of 20-year maturity bonds with coupon rates of 6% (paid annually) is 11 years, how much of each of these coupon bonds (in market value) will you want to hold to both fully fund and immunize your obligation?
   b. What will be the *par value* of your holdings in the 20-year coupon bond?

10. You are managing a portfolio of $1 million. Your target duration is 10 years, and you can choose from two bonds: a zero-coupon bond with maturity five years, and a perpetuity, each currently yielding 5%.
    a. How much of each bond will you hold in your portfolio?
    b. How will these fractions change *next year* if target duration is now nine years?

11. You manage a pension fund that will provide retired workers with lifetime annuities. You determine that the payouts of the fund are essentially going to resemble level

perpetuities of $1 million per year. The interest rate is 10%. You plan to fully fund the obligation using 5-year and 20-year maturity zero-coupon bonds.

   a. How much *market value* of each of the zeros will be necessary to fund the plan if you desire an immunized position?

   b. What must be the *face value* of the two zeros to fund the plan?

12. Your client is concerned about the apparent inconsistency between the following two statements.

   • Short-term interest rates are more volatile than long-term rates.

   • The rates of return of long-term bonds are more volatile than returns on short-term securities.

   Discuss why these two statements are not necessarily inconsistent.

13. A 30-year maturity bond making annual coupon payments with a coupon rate of 12% has duration of 11.54 years and convexity of 192.4. The bond currently sells at a yield to maturity of 8%. Use a financial calculator to find the price of the bond if its yield to maturity falls to 7% or rises to 9%. What prices for the bond at these new yields would be predicted by the duration rule and the duration-with-convexity rule? What is the percent error for each rule? What do you conclude about the accuracy of the two rules?

14. A 12.75-year maturity zero-coupon bond selling at a yield to maturity of 8% (effective annual yield) has convexity of 150.3 and modified duration of 11.81 years. A 30-year maturity 6% coupon bond making annual coupon payments also selling at a yield to maturity of 8% has nearly identical duration—11.79 years—but considerably higher convexity of 231.2.

   a. Suppose the yield to maturity on both bonds increases to 9%. What will be the actual percentage capital loss on each bond? What percentage capital loss would be predicted by the duration-with-convexity rule?

   b. Repeat part (*a*), but this time assume the yield to maturity decreases to 7%.

   c. Compare the performance of the two bonds in the two scenarios, one involving an increase in rates, the other a decrease. Based on their comparative investment performance, explain the attraction of convexity.

   d. In view of your answer to (*c*), do you think it would be possible for two bonds with equal duration, but different convexity, to be priced initially at the same yield to maturity if the yields on both bonds always increased or decreased by equal amounts, as in this example? Would anyone be willing to buy the bond with lower convexity under these circumstances?

15. The following questions appeared in past CFA examinations.

   a. Which set of conditions will result in a bond with the greatest price volatility?
      (1) A high coupon and a short maturity.
      (2) A high coupon and a long maturity.
      (3) A low coupon and a short maturity.
      (4) A low coupon and a long maturity.

   b. An investor who expects declining interest rates would be likely to purchase a bond that has a _____ coupon and a _____ term to maturity.
      (1) Low, long
      (2) High, short
      (3) High, long
      (4) Zero, long

   c. With a zero-coupon bond:
      (1) Duration equals the weighted average term to maturity.
      (2) Term to maturity equals duration.

(3) Weighted average term to maturity equals the term to maturity.

(4) All of the above.

 d. As compared with bonds selling at par, deep discount bonds will have:

  (1) Greater reinvestment risk.

  (2) Greater price volatility.

  (3) Less call protection.

  (4) None of the above.

16. The ability to *immunize* a bond portfolio is very desirable for bond portfolio managers in some instances.

 a. Discuss the components of interest rate risk—that is, assuming a change in interest rates over time, explain the two risks faced by the holder of a bond.

 b. Define immunization and discuss why a bond manager would immunize his or her portfolio.

 c. Explain why a duration-matching strategy is a superior technique to a maturity-matching strategy for the minimization of interest rate risk.

 d. Explain in specific terms how you would use a zero-coupon bond to immunize a bond portfolio. Discuss why a zero-coupon bond is an ideal instrument in this regard.

 e. Explain how contingent immunization, another bond portfolio management technique, differs from conventional immunization. Discuss why a bond portfolio manager would engage in contingent immunization.

17. You are the manager for the bond portfolio of a pension fund. The policies of the fund allow for the use of active strategies in managing the bond portfolio.

 It appears that the economic cycle is beginning to mature, inflation is expected to accelerate, and, in an effort to contain the economic expansion, central bank policy is moving toward constraint. For each of the situations below, *state* which one of the two bonds you would prefer. *Briefly justify* your answer in each case.

 a. Government of Canada (Canadian pay), 10% due in 1998 and priced at 98.75 to yield 10.50% to maturity;

  or

  Government of Canada (Canadian pay), 10% due in 2008 and priced at 91.75 to yield 11.19% to maturity.

 b. Texas Power and Light Co., 7½% due in 2005, rated AAA, and priced at 85 to yield 10.1% to maturity;

  or

  Arizona Public Service Co., 7.45% due in 2005, rated A–, and priced at 75 to yield 12.1% to maturity.

 c. Commonwealth Edison, 2¾% due in 2005, rated Baa, and priced at 61 to yield 12.2% to maturity;

  or

  Commonwealth Edison, 15⅜% due in 2006, rated Baa, and priced at 114 to yield 12.2% to maturity.

 d. Shell Oil Co., 8¾% sinking fund debentures due in 2015, rated AAA (sinking fund begins in 2005 at par), and priced at 69 to yield 11.91% to maturity;

  or

  Warner-Lambert, 8⅞% sinking fund debentures due in 2015, rated AAA (sinking fund begins in 2009 at par), and priced at 75 to yield 11.31% to maturity.

 e. Bank of Montreal (Canadian pay), 12% certificates of deposit due in 1997, rated AAA, and priced at 100 to yield 12% to maturity;

  or

Bank of Montreal (Canadian pay), floating-rate notes due in 2003, rated AAA. Coupon currently set at 10.65% and priced at 100 (coupon adjusted semiannually to 0.5% above the three-month Government of Canada Treasury bill rate).

18. The following bond swaps could have been made in recent years as investors attempted to increase the total return on their portfolio.

   From the information presented below, identify the reason(s) investors may have made each swap.

Action			Call	Price	YTM (%)
a.	Sell	Baa1 Electric Pwr. 1st mtg. 10⅝% due 2003	108.24	95⅝	11.71
	Buy	Baa1 Electric Pwr. 1st mtg. 6⅜% due 2004	105.20	79⅛	11.39
b.	Sell	Aaa Phone Co. notes 8½% due 2004	101.50	90⅛	10.02
	Buy	U.S. Treasury notes 9½% due 2004	NC	97.15	9.78
c.	Sell	Aa1 Apex Bank zero coupon due 2005	NC	35¼	10.51
	Buy	Aa1 Apex Bank float rate notes due 2022	103.90	90¼	—
d.	Sell	A1 Commonwealth Oil & Gas 1st mtg. 7½% due 2010	105.75	72	11.09
	Buy	U.S. Treasury bond 7½% due 2018	NC	80.60	9.40
e.	Sell	A1 Z mart convertible deb. 3% due 2012	103.90	62¾	6.92
	Buy	A2 Lucky Ducks deb. 7¾% due 2018	109.86	65	12.43

19. Long-term Treasury bonds currently are selling at yields to maturity of nearly 8%. You expect interest rates to fall. The rest of the market thinks that they will remain unchanged over the coming year. In each question, choose the bond that will provide the higher capital gain if you are correct. *Briefly* explain your answer.
   a. i. A Baa-rated bond with coupon rate 8% and time to maturity 20 years.
      ii. An Aaa-rated bond with coupon rate 8% and time to maturity 20 years.
   b. i. An A-rated bond with coupon rate 4% and maturity 20 years, callable at 105.
      ii. An A-rated bond with coupon rate 8% and maturity 20 years, callable at 105.
   c. i. A 6% coupon noncallable T-bond with maturity 20 years and YTM = 8%.
      ii. A 9% coupon noncallable T-bond with maturity 20 years and YTM = 8%.

20. Currently, the term structure is as follows: one-year bonds yield 7%, two-year bonds yield 8%, three-year bonds and greater maturity bonds all yield 9%. An investor is choosing between one-, two-, and three-year maturity bonds all paying *annual* coupons of 8%, once a year. Which bond should you buy if you strongly believe that at year-end the yield curve will be flat at 9%?

21. A fixed income portfolio manager is unwilling to realize a rate of return of less than 3% annually over a five-year investment period on a portfolio currently valued at $1 million. Three years later, the interest rate is 8%. What is the trigger point of the portfolio at this time, that is, how low can the value of the portfolio fall before the manager will be forced to immunize to be assured of achieving the minimum acceptable return?

22. What type of interest rate swap would be appropriate for a corporation holding long-term assets that it funded with floating-rate bonds?

23. What type of interest rate swap would be appropriate for a speculator who believes interest rates soon will fall?

24. A corporation has issued a $10 million issue of floating-rate bonds on which it pays an interest rate 1% over the LIBOR rate. The bonds are selling at par value. The firm is worried that rates are about to rise, and it would like to lock in a fixed interest rate on its borrowings. The firm sees that dealers in the swap market are offering swaps of LIBOR for 7%. What swap arrangement will convert the firm's borrowings to a

synthetic fixed-rate loan? What interest rate will it pay on that synthetic fixed-rate loan?

25. A 30-year maturity bond has a 7% coupon rate, paid annually. It sells today for $867.42. A 20-year maturity bond has a 6.5% coupon rate, also paid annually. It sells today for $879.50. A bond market analyst forecasts that in five years, 25-year maturity bonds will sell at yields to maturity of 8% and that 15-year maturity bonds will sell at yields of 7.5%. Because the yield curve is upward sloping, the analyst believes that coupons will be invested in short-term securities at a rate of 6%. Which bond offers the higher expected rate of return over the five-year period?

Solutions to Concept Checks

1. *a.*

(1) Time until Payment	(2) Payment	(3) Payment Discounted at 10%	(4) Weight	(5) Column (1) × Column (4)
1	$ 90	$ 81.8182	0.0833	0.0833
2	1,090	900.8264	0.9167	1.8334
		$982.6446	1.0	1.9167

Duration is 1.9167 years. Price is $982.6446.

b. At an interest rate of 10.05%, the bond's price is

90 × Annuity factor (10.05%, 2) + 1,000 PV factor (10.05%, 2) = 981.7891

The percentage change in price is −0.087%.

c. The duration formula would predict a price change of

$$-\frac{1.9167}{1.10} \times 0.0005 = -0.00087 = -0.087\%$$

which is the same answer that we obtained from direct computation in (*b*).

2. The duration of a level perpetuity is $(1 + y)/y$ or $1 + 1/y$, which clearly falls as y increases. Tabulating duration as a function of y we get:

y	D
0.01 (i.e., 1%)	101 years
0.02	51
0.05	21
0.10	11
0.20	6
0.25	5
0.40	3.5

3. The perpetuity's duration now would be 1.08/0.08 = 13.5. We need to solve the following equation for w

$$w \times 2 + (1 - w) \times 13.5 = 6$$

Therefore, $w = 0.6522$.

4. *a.* The present value of the fund's obligation is $800,000/0.08 = $10 million. The duration is 13.5 years. Therefore, the fund should invest $10 million in zeros with a 13.5 year maturity. The face value of the zeros will be $10,000,000 × 1.08^{13.5} = $28,263,159.

b. When the interest rate increases to 8.1%, the present value of the fund's obligation drops to 800,000/0.081 = $9,876,543. The value of the zero-coupon bond falls by roughly the same amount, to $28,263,159/1.081^{13.5} = $9,875,835. The duration of the perpetual obligation falls to 1.081/0.081 = 13.346 years. The fund should sell the zero it currently holds and purchase $9,876,543 in zero-coupon bonds with maturity of 13.346 years.

5. Dedication would be more attractive. Cash flow matching eliminates the need for rebalancing and, thus, saves transaction costs.

6. Current price = $1,091.29

   Forecast price = $100 × Annuity factor (10%, 18 years) + $1,000 × PV factor (10%, 18 years) = $1,000

   The future value of reinvested coupons will be ($100 × 1.08) + $100 = $208

$$\text{The two-year return is } \frac{\$208 + (\$1,000 - \$1,091.29)}{\$1,091.29} = 0.107, \text{ or } 10.7\%$$

   The annualized rate of return over the two-year period would then be $(1.107)^{1/2} - 1 = .052$, or 5.2%.

7. The trigger point is the present value of the minimum acceptable terminal value: $10 million/$(1.08)^3$ = $7.94 million

8. The manager would like to hold on to the money market securities because of their attractive relative pricing compared to other short-term assets. However, there is an expectation that rates will fall. The manager can hold this *particular* portfolio of short-term assets and still benefit from the drop in interest rates by entering a swap to pay a short-term interest rate and receive a fixed interest rate. The resulting synthetic fixed-rate portfolio will increase in value if rates do fall.

Part Four

SECURITY ANALYSIS

Tell your friends or relatives that you are studying Investments and they will ask you, "What stocks should I buy?" This is the question at the heart of security analysis. How do analysts choose the stocks and other securities to hold in their portfolios?

Security analysis requires a wide mix of skills. You need to be a decent economist with a good grasp of both macroeconomics and microeconomics, the former to help you form forecasts of the general direction of the market and the latter to help you assess the relative position of particular industries or firms. You need a good sense of demographic and social trends to help identify industries with bright prospects. You need to be a quick study of the ins and outs of particular industries in order to choose the firms that will succeed within each industry. You need a good accounting background to analyze the financial statements that firms provide to the public. You also need to have mastered corporate finance, since security analysis at its core is the ability to value a firm. In short, a good security analyst will be a generalist, with a grasp of the widest range of financial issues. This is where there is the biggest premium on "putting it all together."

The chapters in Part Four are an introduction to security analysis. We will provide you with a "top-down" approach to the subject, starting with an overview of international, macroeconomic, and industry issues, and only then progressing to the analysis of particular firms. Our treatment of firm valuation is primarily focused on fundamental analysis, but we also devote a chapter to technical analysis. After reading these chapters, you will have a good sense of the various techniques used to analyze stocks and the stock market.

Chapter 12

MACROECONOMIC AND INDUSTRY ANALYSIS

AFTER STUDYING THIS CHAPTER YOU SHOULD BE ABLE TO:

- Predict the effect of monetary and fiscal policies on key macroeconomic variables such as gross domestic product, interest rates, and the inflation rate.
- Use leading, coincident, and lagging economic indicators to describe and predict the economy's path through the business cycle.
- Predict which industries will be more or less sensitive to business cycle fluctuations.
- Analyze the effect of industry life cycles and structure on industry earnings prospects over time.

fundamental analysis
The analysis of determinants of firm value, such as prospects for earnings and dividends.

To determine a proper price for a firm's stock, the security analyst must forecast the dividends and earnings that can be expected from the firm. This is the heart of **fundamental analysis,** that is, the analysis of determinants of value such as earnings prospects. Ultimately, the business success of the firm determines the dividends it can pay to shareholders and the price it will command in the stock market. Because the prospects of the firm are tied to those of the broader economy, however, valuation analyses must consider the business environment in which the firm operates. For some firms, macroeconomic and industry circumstances might have a greater influence on profits than the firm's relative performance within its industry.

In analyzing a firm's prospects it often makes sense to start with the broad economic environment, examining the state of the aggregate economy and even the international economy. From there, one considers the implications of the outside environment on the industry in which the firm operates. Finally, the firm's position within the industry is examined.

This chapter examines the broad-based aspects of fundamental analysis—macroeconomic and industry analysis. The two chapters following cover firm-specific analysis. We begin with a discussion of international factors relevant to firm performance and move on to an overview of the significance of the key variables usually used to summarize the state of the economy. We then discuss government macroeconomic policy and the determination of interest rates. We conclude the analysis of the macroeconomic environment with a discus-

TABLE 12.1

Economic Performance in Selected Emerging Markets

Source: *The Economist*, December 23, 1995–January 5, 1996.

Country	Growth in Real Gross Domestic Product, 1995	Stock Market Return in 1995	
		Local Currency	$ Terms
China	+8.9	− 8.0	− 6.5
Hong Kong	+4.5	+19.7	+19.8
India	+5.0	−22.5	−30.4
Indonesia	+6.8	+ 5.1	+ 1.0
Malaysia	+8.8	+ 1.3	+ 1.7
Philippines	+5.7	−10.5	−16.7
Singapore	+9.0	− 1.7	+ 1.4
South Korea	+9.0	−15.6	−13.8
Taiwan	+6.0	−28.1	−30.9
Thailand	+8.5	− 7.3	− 7.5
Argentina	−4.6	+ 5.7	+ 5.7
Brazil	+1.2	− 6.8	−20.0
Chile	+8.4	+ 5.3	+ 3.7
Mexico	−9.6	+11.8	−28.7
Venezuela	−3.3	+54.5	−19.3
Greece	+1.5	+ 2.5	+ 4.1
Israel	+8.8	+19.7	+15.9
Portugal	+0.1	−14.0	− 8.9
South Africa	+3.3	+ 6.4	+18.4
Turkey	+9.5	+48.5	+ 1.3
Czech Republic	+4.1	−17.6	−13.8
Hungary	+2.9	+ 3.8	−14.9
Poland	+5.2	+ 4.7	+ 1.0
Russia	−4.0	−10.2	−31.1

sion of business cycles. Next, we move to industry analysis, treating issues concerning the sensitivity of the firm to the business cycle, the typical life cycle of an industry, and strategic issues that affect industry performance.

12.1 THE GLOBAL ECONOMY

A top-down analysis of a firm's prospects must start with the global economy. The international economy might affect a firm's export prospects, the price competition it faces from foreign competitors, or the profits it makes on investments abroad. Certainly, despite the fact that the economies of most countries are linked in a global macroeconomy, there is considerable variation in the economic performance across countries at any time. Consider, for example, Table 12.1, which presents data on several so-called "emerging" economies. The table documents striking variation in growth rates of economic output in 1995. For example, while the Chinese economy grew by 8.9% in 1995, Mexican output fell by 9.6%. Similarly, there has been considerable variation in stock market returns in these countries in recent years.

These data illustrate that the national economic environment can be a crucial determinant of industry performance. It is far harder for businesses to succeed in a contracting economy than in an expanding one.

In addition, the global environment presents political risks of far greater magnitude than are typically encountered in U.S.-based investments. For example, the Hong Kong stock market was extremely sensitive to political developments leading up to the transfer of governance to China in 1997. In 1992 and 1993, the Mexican stock market responded dramatically to changing assessments regarding the prospect of the passage of the North American Free Trade Agreement by the U.S. Congress. The presence of these political considerations adds a dimension of risk to foreign investments beyond the purely economic.

Of course, political developments can be positive, as well. For example, the end of apartheid in South Africa and the resultant end of the economic embargo portended great growth for that economy. These political developments (and the bumps along the way) offer significant opportunities to make or lose money.

Other political issues that are less sensational but still extremely important to economic growth and investment returns include issues of protectionism and trade policy, the free flow of capital, and the status of a nation's work force.

One obvious factor that affects the international competitiveness of a country's industries is the exchange rate between that country's currency and other currencies. The **exchange rate** is the rate at which domestic currency can be converted into foreign currency. For example, in July 1996, it took about 108 Japanese yen to purchase one U.S. dollar. We would say that the exchange rate is ¥108 per dollar, or equivalently, $0.0092 per yen.

exchange rate
The rate at which domestic currency can be converted into foreign currency.

As exchange rates fluctuate, the dollar value of goods priced in foreign currency similarly fluctuates. For example, in 1980, the dollar–yen exchange rate was about $0.0045 per yen. Since the exchange rate in 1996 was $0.0092 per yen, a U.S. citizen would have needed about twice as many dollars in 1996 to buy a product selling for ¥10,000 as would have been required in 1980. If the Japanese producer were to maintain a fixed yen price for its product, the price expressed in U.S. dollars would have to double. This would make Japanese products more expensive to U.S. consumers, however, and result in lost sales. Obviously, appreciation of the yen creates a problem for Japanese producers like auto makers that must compete with U.S. producers.

Figure 12.1 shows the change in the purchasing power of the U.S. dollar relative to the purchasing power of the currencies of several major industrial countries in the decade ending in 1995. The ratio of purchasing powers is called the "real" or inflation-adjusted exchange rate. The change in the real exchange rate measures how much more or less expensive foreign goods have become to U.S. citizens, accounting for both exchange rate fluctuations and inflation differentials across countries. A positive value in Figure 12.1 means that the dollar has gained purchasing power relative to another currency; a negative number indicates a depreciating dollar. Therefore, the figure shows that goods priced in terms of the German, Japanese, U.K., Italian, or French currencies have become more expensive to U.S. consumers in the last decade but that goods priced in Canadian dollars have become slightly cheaper. Conversely, goods priced in U.S. dollars have become more affordable to Japanese consumers, but more expensive to Canadian consumers.

12.2 THE DOMESTIC MACROECONOMY

The macroeconomy is the environment in which all firms operate. The importance of the macroeconomy in determining investment performance is illustrated in Figure 12.2, which compares the level of the S&P 500 stock price index to estimates of earnings per share of the S&P 500 companies. The graph shows that stock prices tend to rise along with earnings.

FIGURE 12.1
Change in Real Exchange Rate: Dollar versus Major Currencies, 1986–1995

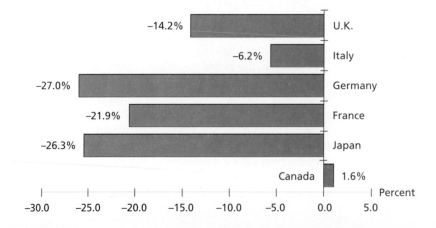

FIGURE 12.2

S&P 500 Index versus Earnings per Share Estimate

Source: *U.S. Comments*, March 27, 1996, Institutional Brokers Estimate System (I/B/E/S).

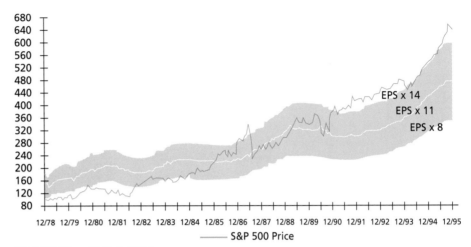

*S&P 500 Price: 638.55 (3-13-96).

While the exact ratio of stock price to earnings per share varies with factors such as interest rates, risk, inflation rates, and other variables, the graph does illustrate that, as a general rule, the ratio has tended to be in the range of 8 to 14. Given "normal" price-to-earnings ratios, we would expect the S&P 500 index to fall within these boundaries. While the earnings-multiplier rule clearly is not perfect, it also seems clear that the level of the broad market and aggregate earnings do trend together. Thus, the first step in forecasting the performance of the broad market is to assess the status of the economy as a whole.

The ability to forecast the macroeconomy can translate into spectacular investment performance. But it is not enough to forecast the macroeconomy well. One must forecast it *better* than one's competitors to earn abnormal profits.

In this section, we will review some of the key economic statistics used to describe the state of the macroeconomy.

Gross Domestic Product

gross domestic product
The market value of goods and services produced over a period of time.

Gross domestic product, or GDP, is the measure of the economy's total production of goods and services. Rapidly growing GDP indicates an expanding economy with ample opportunity for a firm to increase sales. Another popular measure of the economy's output is *industrial production*. This statistic provides a measure of economic activity more narrowly focused on the manufacturing side of the economy.

Employment

unemployment rate
The ratio of the number of people classified as unemployed to the total labor force.

The **unemployment rate** is the percentage of the total labor force (i.e., those who are either working or actively seeking employment) yet to find work. The unemployment rate measures the extent to which the economy is operating at full capacity. The unemployment rate is a factor related to workers only, but further insight into the strength of the economy can be gleaned from the employment rate of other factors of production. Analysts also look at the factory *capacity utilization rate*, which is the ratio of actual output from factories to potential output.

Inflation

inflation
The rate at which the general level of prices for goods and services is rising.

Inflation is the rate at which the general level of prices is rising. High rates of inflation often are associated with "overheated" economies, that is, economies where the demand for goods and services is outstripping productive capacity, which leads to an upward pressure on prices. Most governments walk a fine line in their economic policies. They hope to stimulate their economies enough to maintain nearly full employment, but not so much as to bring on inflationary pressures. The perceived trade-off between inflation and unemployment is at the heart of many macroeconomic policy disputes. There is considerable room for disagreement as to the relative costs of these policies as well as the economy's relative vulnerability to these pressures at any particular time.

Interest Rates

High interest rates reduce the present value of future cash flows, thereby reducing the attractiveness of investment opportunities. For this reason, real interest rates are key determinants of business investment expenditures. Demand for housing and high-priced consumer durables such as automobiles, which are commonly financed, also is highly sensitive to interest rates because interest rates affect interest payments. In Section 12.3, we will examine the determinants of real interest rates.

Budget Deficit

budget deficit
The amount by which government spending exceeds government revenues.

The **budget deficit** of the federal government is the difference between government spending and revenues. Any budgetary shortfall must be offset by government borrowing. Large amounts of government borrowing can force up interest rates by increasing the total demand for credit in the economy. Economists generally believe excessive government borrowing will "crowd out" private borrowing and investing by forcing up interest rates and choking off business investment.

Sentiment

Consumers' and producers' optimism or pessimism concerning the economy are important determinants of economic performance. If consumers have confidence in their future income levels, for example, they will be more willing to spend on big-ticket items. Similarly, businesses will increase production and inventory levels if they anticipate higher demand for their products. In this way, beliefs influence how much consumption and investment will be pursued and affect the aggregate demand for goods and services.

Concept Check

1. Consider an economy where the dominant industry is automobile production for domestic consumption as well as export. Now suppose the auto market is hurt by an increase in the length of time people use their cars before replacing them. Describe the probable effects of this change on (*a*) GDP, (*b*) unemployment, (*c*) the government budget deficit, and (*d*) interest rates.

12.3 INTEREST RATES

The level of interest rates is perhaps the most important macroeconomic factor to consider in one's investment analysis. Forecasts of interest rates directly affect the forecast of returns in the fixed-income market. If your expectation is that rates will increase by more than the consensus view, you will want to shy away from longer term fixed-income securities. Similarly, increases in interest rates tend to be bad news for the stock market. Unanticipated increases in rates generally are associated with stock market declines. Thus, a superior technique to forecast rates would be of immense value to an investor attempting to determine the best asset allocation for his or her portfolio.

Unfortunately, forecasting interest rates is one of the most notoriously difficult parts of applied macroeconomics. Nonetheless, we do have a good understanding of the fundamental factors that determine the level of interest rates:

1. The supply of funds from savers, primarily households.
2. The demand for funds from businesses to be used to finance physical investments in plant, equipment, and inventories.

3. The government's net supply and/or demand for funds as modified by actions of the Federal Reserve Bank.

4. The expected rate of inflation.

Although there are many different interest rates economywide (as many as there are types of securities), economists frequently talk as though there were a single representative rate. We can use this abstraction to gain some insights into determining the real rate of interest if we consider the supply and demand curves for funds.

Figure 12.3 shows a downward-sloping demand curve and an upward-sloping supply curve. On the horizontal axis, we measure the quantity of funds, and on the vertical axis, we measure the real rate of interest.

The supply curve slopes up from left to right because the higher the real interest rate, the greater the supply of household savings. The assumption is that at higher real interest rates, households will choose to postpone some current consumption and set aside or invest more of their disposable income for future use.

The demand curve slopes down from left to right because the lower the real interest rate, the more businesses will want to invest in physical capital. Assuming that businesses rank projects by the expected real return on invested capital, firms will undertake more projects the lower the real interest rate on the funds needed to finance those projects.

Equilibrium is at the point of intersection of the supply and demand curves, point *E* in Figure 12.3.

The government and the central bank (the Federal Reserve) can shift these supply and demand curves either to the right or to the left through fiscal and monetary policies. For example, consider an increase in the government's budget deficit. This increases the government's borrowing demand and shifts the demand curve to the right, which causes the equilibrium real interest rate to rise to point *E'*. That is, a forecast that indicates higher than previously expected government borrowing increases expectations of future interest rates. The Fed can offset such a rise through an increase in the money supply, which will increase the supply of loanable funds, and shift the supply curve to the right.

Thus, while the fundamental determinants of the real interest rate are the propensity of households to save and the expected productivity (or we could say profitability) of firms' investment in physical capital, the real rate can be affected as well by government fiscal and monetary policies.

The supply and demand framework illustrated in Figure 12.3 is a reasonable first approximation to the determination of the real interest rate. To obtain the *nominal* interest rate, one needs to add the expected inflation rate to the equilibrium real rate. As we discussed in Section 6.4, the inflation premium is necessary for investors to maintain a given real rate of return on their investments.

While monetary policy can clearly affect nominal interest rates, there is considerable controversy concerning its ability to affect real rates. There is widespread agreement that, in the long run, the ultimate impact of an increase in the money supply is an increase in prices with no permanent impact on real economic activity. A rapid rate of growth in the money supply,

FIGURE 12.3

Determination of the Equilibrium Real Rate of Interest

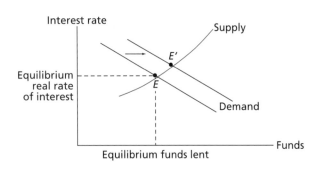

therefore, ultimately would result in a correspondingly high inflation rate and nominal interest rate, but it would have no sustained impact on the real interest rate. However, in the shorter run, changes in the money supply may well have an effect on the real interest rate.

12.4 DEMAND AND SUPPLY SHOCKS

demand shock
An event that affects the demand for goods and services in the economy.

supply shock
An event that influences production capacity and costs in the economy.

A useful way to organize your analysis of the factors that might influence the macroeconomy is to classify any impact as a supply or demand shock. A **demand shock** is an event that affects the demand for goods and services in the economy. Examples of positive demand shocks are reductions in tax rates, increases in the money supply, increases in government spending, or increases in foreign export demand. A **supply shock** is an event that influences production capacity and costs. Examples of supply shocks are changes in the price of imported oil; freezes, floods, or droughts that might destroy large quantities of agricultural crops; changes in the educational level of an economy's work force; or changes in the wage rates at which the labor force is willing to work.

Demand shocks usually are characterized by aggregate output moving in the same direction as interest rates and inflation. For example, a big increase in government spending will tend to stimulate the economy and increase GDP. It also might increase interest rates by increasing the demand for borrowed funds by the government as well as by businesses that might desire to borrow to finance new ventures. Finally, it could increase the inflation rate if the demand for goods and services is raised to a level at or beyond the total productive capacity of the economy.

Supply shocks usually are characterized by aggregate output moving in the opposite direction as inflation and interest rates. For example, a big increase in the price of imported oil will be inflationary because costs of production will rise, which eventually will lead to increases in prices of finished goods. The increase in inflation rates over the near term can lead to higher nominal interest rates. Against this background, aggregate output will be falling. With raw materials more expensive, the productive capacity of the economy is reduced, as is the ability of individuals to purchase goods at now-higher prices. GDP, therefore, tends to fall.

How can we relate this framework to investment analysis? You want to identify the industries that will be most helped or hurt in any macroeconomic scenario you envision. For example, if you forecast a tightening of the money supply, you might want to avoid industries such as automobile producers that might be hurt by the likely increase in interest rates. We caution you again that these forecasts are no easy task. Macroeconomic predictions are notoriously unreliable. And again, you must be aware that in all likelihood your forecast will be made using only publicly available information. Any investment advantage you have will be a result only of better analysis—not better information.

An example of investment advice pegged to macroeconomic forecasts is given in the box on page 335. The analysis is based on the forecast that the economy is about to slow down. As a result, industries with below-average sensitivity to macroeconomic conditions are expected to be the better performers. Such recession-resistant or "defensive" investments include food and health care stocks, both of which are expected to outperform the rest of the market as investors become aware of the slowdown in growth. Similarly, the forecast for low interest rates, which is predicted to help bank stocks, is consistent with a slow-growing economy.

12.5 FEDERAL GOVERNMENT POLICY

As the previous section would suggest, the government has two broad classes of macroeconomic tools—those that affect the demand for goods and services and those that affect their supply. For most of postwar history, demand-side policy has been of primary interest. The focus has been on government spending, tax levels, and monetary policy. Since the 1980s, however, increasing

Industries with Superior Potential

BANKS REMAIN ATTRACTIVE

Bank stocks, one of the strongest groups in 1995, should continue to turn in a stellar performance in 1996. The group's earnings should remain in an uptrend, helped by an expected healthy demand for loans; low interest rates that will widen the spread between the banks' cost of funds and the rate they charge for loans; high credit quality that will keep loan charge-offs modest; and ongoing cost reduction.

FOOD AND BEVERAGE STOCKS GOOD DEFENSIVE PLAYS

Food issues have trailed the broad market's hefty advance. We expect the group to start to outperform soon as investors become more defensive in the face of high stock valuations and a slow-growing economy.

Soft drink stocks have outperformed the market, driven primarily by good earnings and increased investor demand for companies with significant overseas growth potential. We expect earnings to remain in an uptrend,

owing to increased unit case volume growth and higher selling prices. In addition, the industry should continue to benefit from increasing demand in rapidly growing international markets.

PROMISING PROGNOSIS FOR HEALTH CARE STOCKS

Vital signs for the medical industries remain healthy, and earnings of most leading providers of health care goods and services are likely to continue trending higher. Recession-resistant health care issues also offer investors some protection against cyclical fluctuations. While growth in Medicare and Medicaid will probably be slowed under government budget balancing initiatives, the eventual cutbacks should be considerably less than those originally proposed by GOP legislative leaders.

Source: "Industries with Superior Potential," *The Outlook*, December 20, 1995, Standard & Poor's Corporation.

attention has been focused on supply-side economics. Broadly interpreted, supply-side concerns have to do with enhancing the productive capacity of the economy, rather than increasing the demand for the goods and services the economy can produce. In practice, supply-side economists have focused on the appropriateness of the incentives to work, innovate, and take risks that result from our system of taxation. However, issues such as national policies on education, infrastructure (such as communication and transportation systems), and research and development also are properly regarded as part of supply-side macroeconomic policy.

Fiscal Policy

fiscal policy
The use of government spending and taxing for the specific purpose of stabilizing the economy.

Fiscal policy refers to the government's spending and tax actions and is part of "demand-side management." Fiscal policy is probably the most direct way either to stimulate or to slow the economy. Decreases in government spending directly deflate the demand for goods and services. Similarly, increases in tax rates immediately siphon income from consumers and result in fairly rapid decreases in consumption.

Ironically, although fiscal policy has the most immediate impact on the economy, the formulation and implementation of such policy is usually painfully slow and involved. This is because fiscal policy requires enormous amounts of compromise between the executive and legislative branches. Tax and spending policy must be initiated and voted on by Congress, which requires considerable political negotiations, and any legislation passed must be signed by the president, requiring more negotiation. Thus, while the impact of fiscal policy is relatively immediate, its formulation is so cumbersome that fiscal policy cannot in practice be used to fine-tune the economy.

Moreover, much of government spending, such as that for Medicare or social security, is nondiscretionary, meaning that it is determined by formula rather than policy and cannot be changed in response to economic conditions. This places even more rigidity into the formulation of fiscal policy.

A common way to summarize the net impact of government fiscal policy is to look at the government's budget deficit or surplus, which is simply the difference between revenues and expenditures. A large deficit means the government is spending considerably more than it is taking in by way of taxes. The net effect is to increase the demand for goods (via spending) by more than it reduces the demand for goods (via taxes), therefore, stimulating the economy.

Monetary Policy

monetary policy
Actions taken by the Board of Governors of the Federal Reserve System to influence the money supply or interest rates.

Monetary policy refers to the manipulation of the money supply to affect the macroeconomy and is the other main leg of demand-side policy. Monetary policy works largely through its impact on interest rates. Increases in the money supply lower short-term interest rates, ultimately encouraging investment and consumption demand. Over longer periods, however, most economists believe a higher money supply leads only to a higher price level and does not have a permanent effect on economic activity. Thus, the monetary authorities face a difficult balancing act. Expansionary monetary policy probably will lower interest rates and thereby stimulate investment and some consumption demand in the short run, but these circumstances ultimately will lead only to higher prices. The stimulation/ inflation trade-off is implicit in all debate over proper monetary policy.

Fiscal policy is cumbersome to implement but has a fairly direct impact on the economy, while monetary policy is easily formulated and implemented but has a less direct impact. Monetary policy is determined by the Board of Governors of the Federal Reserve System. Board members are appointed by the president for 14-year terms and are reasonably insulated from political pressure. The board is small enough, and often sufficiently dominated by its chairperson, that policy can be formulated and modulated relatively easily.

Implementation of monetary policy also is quite direct. The most widely used tool is the open market operation, in which the Fed buys or sells bonds for its own account. When the Fed buys securities, it simply writes a check, thereby increasing the money supply. (Unlike us, the Fed can pay for the securities without drawing down funds at a bank account.) Conversely, when the Fed sells a security, the money paid for it leaves the money supply. Open market operations occur daily, allowing the Fed to fine-tune its monetary policy.

Other tools at the Fed's disposal are the *discount rate*, which is the interest rate it charges banks on short-term loans, and the *reserve requirement*, which is the fraction of deposits that banks must hold as cash on hand or as deposits with the Fed. Reductions in the discount rate signal a more expansionary monetary policy. Lowering reserve requirements allows banks to make more loans with each dollar of deposits and stimulates the economy by increasing the effective money supply.

Monetary policy affects the economy in a more roundabout way than fiscal policy. While fiscal policy directly stimulates or dampens the economy, monetary policy works largely through its impact on interest rates. Increases in the money supply lower interest rates, which stimulate investment demand. As the quantity of money in the economy increases, investors will find that their portfolios of assets include too much money. They will rebalance their portfolios by buying securities such as bonds, forcing bond prices up and interest rates down. In the longer run, individuals may increase their holdings of stocks as well and ultimately buy real assets, which stimulates consumption demand directly. The ultimate effect of monetary policy on investment and consumption demand, however, is less immediate than that of fiscal policy.

Concept Check

2. Suppose the government wants to stimulate the economy without increasing interest rates. What combination of fiscal and monetary policy might accomplish this goal?

Supply-Side Policies

Fiscal and monetary policy are demand-oriented tools that affect the economy by stimulating the total demand for goods and services. The implicit belief is that the economy will not by itself arrive at a full employment equilibrium, and that macroeconomic policy can push the economy toward this goal. In contrast, supply-side policies treat the issue of the productive capacity of the economy. The goal is to create an environment in which workers and owners of capital have the maximum incentive and ability to produce and develop goods.

Supply-side economists also pay considerable attention to tax policy. While demand siders look at the effect of taxes on consumption demand, supply siders focus on incentives and marginal tax rates. They argue that lowering tax rates will elicit more investment and improve incentives to work, thereby enhancing economic growth. Some go so far as to claim that reductions in tax rates can lead to increases in tax revenues because the lower tax rates will cause the economy and the revenue tax base to grow by more than the tax rate is reduced.

Concept Check

3. Large tax cuts in the 1980s were followed by rapid growth in GDP. How would demand-side and supply-side economists differ in their interpretations of this phenomenon?

12.6 BUSINESS CYCLES

We've looked at the tools the government uses to fine-tune the economy, attempting to maintain low unemployment and low inflation. Despite these efforts, economies repeatedly seem to pass through good and bad times. One determinant of the broad asset allocation decision of many analysts is a forecast of whether the macroeconomy is improving or deteriorating. A forecast that differs from the market consensus can have a major impact on investment strategy.

The Business Cycle

business cycle
Repetitive cycles of recession and recovery.

The economy recurrently experiences periods of expansion and contraction, although the length and depth of these cycles can be irregular. This recurring pattern of recession and recovery is called the **business cycle.** Figure 12.4 presents graphs of several measures of production and output for the years 1967–1995. The production series all show clear variation around a generally rising trend. The bottom graph of capacity utilization also evidences a clear cyclical (although irregular) pattern.

peak
The transition from the end of an expansion to the start of a contraction.

The transition points across cycles are called peaks and troughs, labeled P and T at the top of the graph. A **peak** is the transition from the end of an expansion to the start of a contraction. A **trough** occurs at the bottom of a recession just as the economy enters a recovery. The shaded areas in Figure 12.4 all represent periods of recession. The National Bureau of Economic Research (NBER) is the official designator of peak and trough points.

trough
The transition point between recession and recovery.

As the economy passes through different stages of the business cycle, the relative profitability of different industry groups might be expected to vary. For example, at a trough, just before the economy begins to recover from a recession, one would expect that **cyclical industries,** those with above-average sensitivity to the state of the economy, would tend to outperform other industries. Examples of cyclical industries are producers of durable goods, such as automobiles or washing machines. Because purchases of these goods can be deferred during a recession, sales are particularly sensitive to macroeconomic conditions. Other cyclical industries are producers of capital goods, that is, goods used by other firms to produce their own products. When demand is slack, few companies will be expanding and purchasing capital goods. Therefore, the capital goods industry bears the brunt of a slowdown but does well in an expansion.

cyclical industries
Industries with above-average sensitivity to the state of the economy.

defensive industries
Industries with below-average sensitivity to the state of the economy.

In contrast to cyclical firms, **defensive industries** have little sensitivity to the business cycle. These are industries that produce goods for which sales and profits are least sensitive to the state of the economy. Defensive industries include food producers and processors, pharmaceutical firms, and public utilities. These industries will outperform others when the economy enters a recession.

FIGURE 12.4   Cyclical Indicators, 1967–1995

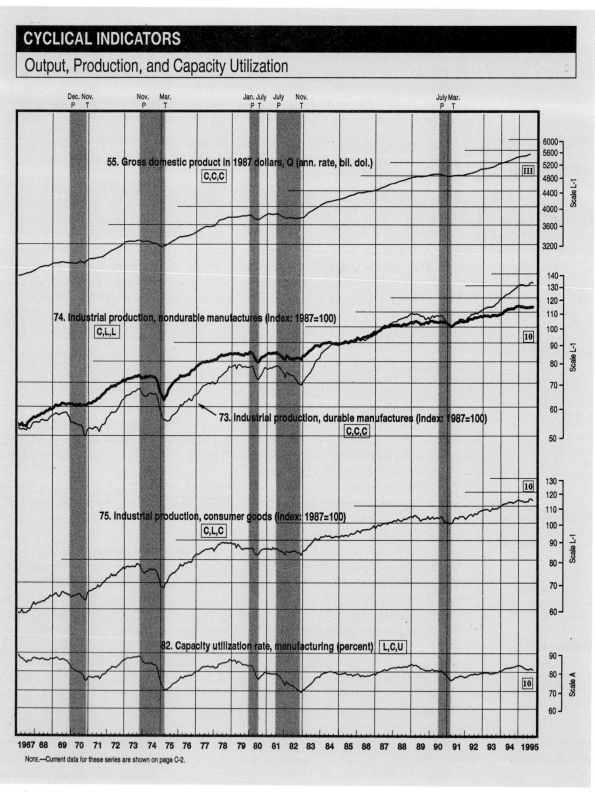

Source: *Survey of Current Business*, U.S. Department of Commerce, November/December 1995.

Recycling Old Myths

RUMOURS OF THE DEATH OF THE BUSINESS CYCLE ARE MUCH EXAGGERATED

The rich industrial economies are heading for another recession. But before businessmen and bankers fling themselves out of windows, note that this forecast, though undoubtedly correct, comes without a date attached. Economic growth has in fact slowed this year, stoking fears that the next recession is looming. At the same time, the usual clutch of optimists has emerged to predict that, thanks to a technological revolution—or even, perish the thought, to better economic management—there will instead be uninterrupted growth forever. Both views are wrong. As far as can be told, the present expansion has some way to go before it hits the buffers. But the buffers will still be hit.

Few economic issues grab more misguided attention, from experts and laymen alike, than the business cycle. Their obsession is almost always founded on misconceptions about the powers of economists and politicians. Ordinary mortals often judge the value of economists on their ability to forecast accurately the next recession. Governments, in turn, are judged by voters on their ability to avoid it. And on both tests, economists and governments seem repeatedly to have failed.

In fact the ability to forecast (or, still better, to prevent) recessions is a bad test of the worth of anybody. True, the experts themselves are often to blame for encouraging its use, by boasting of powers they do not have. Economists are more likely to attract publicity if they can pull forecasts out of their hats. And politicians have for years promised voters steady, recession-free growth—leading the voters to believe that this is not just desirable but feasible. In an ideal world, it would indeed be nice if output grew steadily rather than in a painfully volatile way. But this goal will always be unattainable.

WOULD THAT THEY COULD

Many Keynesian economists hoped that business cycles could be flattened by macroeconomic policies. They were wrong, although—partly thanks to the expansion of government that they encouraged—economic activity has become a bit less bumpy in recent decades, with longer expansions and shorter recessions. The main reason why the business cycle cannot be completely eliminated, however, is that nobody can predict economic turning points sufficiently far in advance. Economists' models, heavily influenced by the recent past, usually fail to spot a recession until it has actually begun—by which time it is too late for any countermeasures to take effect. This is hardly the fault of the boffins: Recessions are often triggered by unpredictable external factors, such as an oil-price shock, or by sudden changes in consumer or business confidence.

Nor is poor prediction the only problem. For governments to eliminate the business cycle would require not only that they could accurately predict activity at least two years ahead (it can take that long for interest rate changes to affect the economy); they would also need to know precisely how their monetary and fiscal levers steered demand. These links will always be uncertain. Only if they had perfect knowledge, and also exercised their powers with perfect prudence (e.g., promptly moving budgets back into surplus during an upswing) could governments have even a theoretical hope of ending recessions. But until perfect pigs are spotted flying in the sky, they would be wise to stop promising things they cannot deliver.

Source: "Recycling Old Myths," *The Economist*, October 28, 1995.

The cyclical/defensive classification corresponds well to the notion of systematic or market risk introduced in our discussion of portfolio theory. When perceptions about the health of the economy become more optimistic, for example, the prices of most stocks will increase as forecasts of profitability rise. Because the cyclical firms are most sensitive to such developments, their stock prices will rise the most. Thus, firms in cyclical industries will tend to have high-beta stocks. In general then, stocks of cyclical firms will show the best results when economic news is positive, but they will also show the worst results when that news is bad. Conversely, defensive firms will have low betas and performance that is relatively unaffected by overall market conditions.

If your assessments of the state of the business cycle were reliably more accurate than those of other investors, choosing between cyclical and defensive industries would be easy. You would choose cyclical industries when you were relatively more optimistic about the economy, and you would choose defensive firms when you were relatively more pessimistic. As we know from our discussion of efficient markets, however, attractive investment choices will rarely be obvious. It usually is not apparent that a recession or expansion has started or ended until several months after the fact. With hindsight, the transitions from expansion to recession and back might be apparent, but it is often quite difficult to say whether the economy is heating up or slowing down at any moment.

This point is emphasized in the box on page 339. The article suggests that one reason why government policymakers cannot eliminate business cycles using fiscal or monetary policy is that nobody, policymakers included, "can predict turning points sufficiently far in advance." Given the lags in both the formulation and implementation of macroeconomic policy, by the time the start of a recession is confirmed, "it is too late for any countermeasures to take effect." Of course, the difficulty in spotting the onset of a recession or recovery is not unique to government economists—it is a challenge for investors as well.

Economic Indicators

leading economic indicators
Economic series that tend to rise or fall in advance of the rest of the economy.

Given the cyclical nature of the business cycle, it is not surprising that to some extent the cycle can be predicted. The NBER has developed a set of cyclical indicators to help forecast, measure, and interpret short-term fluctuations in economic activity. **Leading economic indicators** are those economic series that tend to rise or fall in advance of the rest of the economy. Coincident and lagging indicators, as their names suggest, move in tandem with or somewhat after the broad economy.

Eleven series are grouped into a widely followed composite index of leading economic indicators. Similarly, four coincident and seven lagging indicators form separate indexes. The composition of these indexes appears in Table 12.2.

Figure 12.5 graphs these three series over the period 1958–1995. The numbers on the charts near the turning points of each series indicate the length of the lead time or lag time (in months) from the turning point to the designated peak or trough of the corresponding business cycle. While the index of leading indicators consistently turns before the rest of the economy, the lead time is somewhat erratic. Moreover, the lead time for peaks is consistently longer than that for troughs.

TABLE 12.2
Indexes of Economic Indicators

Source: From *Survey of Current Business*, U.S. Department of Commerce, July 1996.

A. **Leading Indicators**
1. Average weekly hours of production workers (manufacturing).
2. Average weekly initial claims for unemployment insurance.
3. Manufacturers' new orders (consumer goods and materials industries).
4. Vendor performance—slower deliveries diffusion index.
5. Contracts and orders for plant and equipment.
6. New private housing units authorized by local building permits.
7. Change in manufacturers' unfilled orders (durable goods industries).
8. Change in sensitive materials prices.
9. Stock prices, 500 common stocks.
10. Money supply (M2).
11. Index of consumer expectations.

B. **Coincident Indicators**
1. Employees on nonagricultural payrolls.
2. Personal income less transfer payments.
3. Industrial production.
4. Manufacturing and trade sales.

C. **Lagging Indicators**
1. Average duration of unemployment.
2. Ratio of trade inventories to sales.
3. Change in index of labor cost per unit of output.
4. Average prime rate charged by banks.
5. Commercial and industrial loans outstanding.
6. Ratio of consumer installment credit outstanding to personal income.
7. Change in consumer price index for services.

The stock market price index is a leading indicator. This is as it should be, as stock prices are forward-looking predictors of future profitability. Unfortunately, this makes the series of leading indicators much less useful for investment policy—by the time the series predicts an upturn, the market has already made its move. While the business cycle may be somewhat predictable, the stock market may not be. This is just one more manifestation of the efficient market hypothesis.

The money supply is another leading indicator. This makes sense in light of our earlier discussion concerning the lags surrounding the effects of monetary policy on the economy. An expansionary monetary policy can be observed fairly quickly, but it might not affect the economy for several months. Therefore, today's monetary policy might well predict future economic activity.

Other leading indicators focus directly on decisions made today that will affect production in the near future. For example, manufacturers' new orders for goods, contracts and orders for plant and equipment, and housing starts all signal a coming expansion in the economy.

12.7 INDUSTRY ANALYSIS

Industry analysis is important for the same reason that macroeconomic analysis is: Just as it is difficult for an industry to perform well when the macroeconomy is ailing, it is unusual for a firm in a troubled industry to perform well. Similarly, just as we have seen that economic performance can vary widely across countries, performance also can vary widely across industries. Figure 12.6 illustrates the dispersion of industry earnings growth. It shows projected growth in earnings per share in 1996 and 1997 for several major industry groups. The forecasts for 1997, which come from a survey of industry analysts, range from 7.8% for basic industries to 25.1% for technology firms.

Industry groups show even more dispersion in their stock market performance. Figure 12.7 illustrates the stock price performance of the 10 best and 10 worst performing industries in 1995. The spread in annual returns is remarkable, ranging from an 80.48% return for the biotechnology industry to a 14.99% loss in the trucking industry.

Defining an Industry

While we know what we mean by an industry, it can be difficult in practice to decide where to draw the line between one industry and another. Consider, for example, the health care industry. Figure 12.6 shows that the forecast for 1997 growth in industry earnings per share was 20.4%. But the health care "industry" contains firms with widely differing products and prospects. Figure 12.8 breaks down the industry into six subgroups. The forecasted performance of these more narrowly defined groups differs widely, suggesting that they are not members of a homogeneous industry. Similarly, most of these subgroups in Figure 12.8 could be divided into even smaller and more homogeneous groups.

SIC codes
Classification of firms into industry groups using numerical codes to identify industries.

A useful way to define industry groups in practice is given by *Standard Industry Classification* or **SIC codes.** These are codes assigned by the U.S. government for the purpose of grouping firms for statistical analysis. The first two digits of the SIC codes denote very broad industry classifications. For example, the SIC codes assigned to any type of building contractor all start with 15. The third and fourth digits define the industry grouping more narrowly. For example, codes starting with 152 denote *residential* building contractors, and group 1521 contains *single family* building contractors. Firms with the same four-digit SIC code therefore are commonly taken to be in the same industry. Many statistics are computed for even more narrowly defined five-digit SIC groups.

SIC industry classifications are not perfect. For example, both J.C. Penney and Neiman Marcus might be classified as Department Stores. Yet the former is a high-volume "value"

FIGURE 12.5   Indexes of Leading, Coincident, and Lagging Indicators

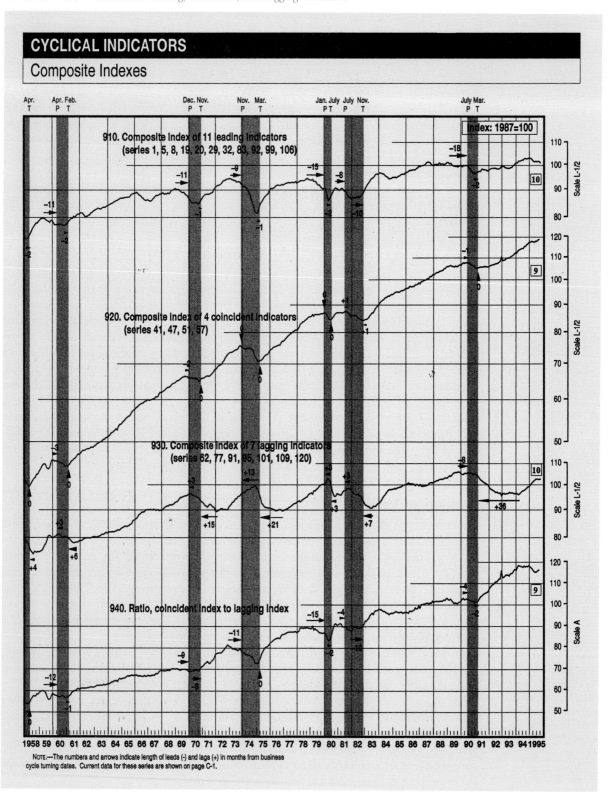

FIGURE 12.6

Estimates of Earnings Growth Rates in Several Industries

Source: *U.S. Comments*, March 27, 1996, Institutional Brokers Estimate System (I/B/E/S).

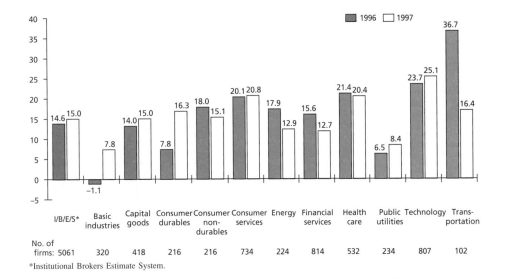

| No. of firms: | 5061 | 320 | 418 | 216 | 216 | 734 | 224 | 814 | 532 | 234 | 807 | 102 |

*Institutional Brokers Estimate System.

FIGURE 12.7

Industry Stock Price Performance, 1995

Source: *The Wall Street Journal*, January 2, 1996. Reprinted by permission of *The Wall Street Journal*, © 1995 Dow Jones & Company. All rights reserved worldwide.

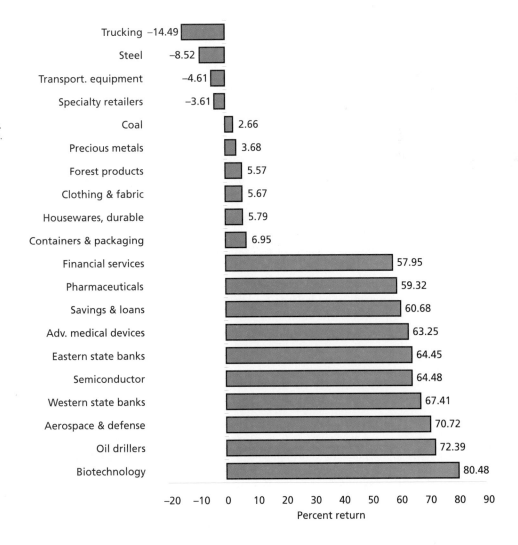

FIGURE 12.8

Estimates of Earnings
Growth for Health Care
Industries

Source: *U.S. Comments*, March
27, 1996, Institutional Brokers
Estimate System (I/B/E/S).

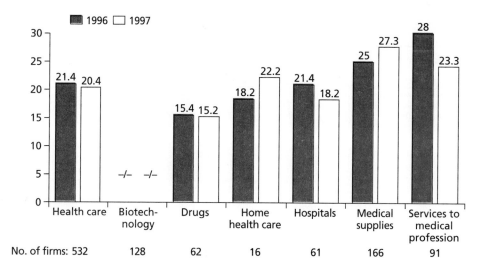

FIGURE 12.9

Industry Cyclicality

Source: Passenger car sales:
Ward's Automobile Yearbook,
1994. Cigarette sales:
Department of Alcohol,
Tobacco, and Firearms
Statistical Releases.

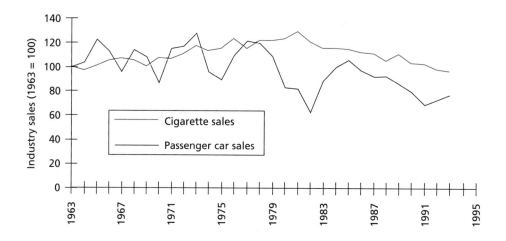

store, while the latter is a high-margin elite retailer. Are they really in the same industry? Still, SIC classifications are a tremendous aid in conducting industry analysis since they provide a means of focusing on very broadly or fairly narrowly defined groups of firms.

Several other industry classifications are provided by other analysts, for example, Standard & Poor's reports on the performance of about 100 industry groups. S&P computes stock price indexes for each group, which is useful in assessing past investment performance. The *Value Line Investment Survey* reports on the conditions and prospects of about 1,700 firms, grouped into about 90 industries. Value Line's analysts prepare forecasts of the performance of industry groups as well as of each firm.

Sensitivity to the Business Cycle

Once the analyst forecasts the state of the macroeconomy, it is necessary to determine the implication of that forecast for specific industries. Not all industries are equally sensitive to the business cycle. For example, consider Figure 12.9, which is a graph of automobile production and shipments of tobacco products, both scaled so that 1963 has a value of 100.

Clearly, the tobacco industry is virtually independent of the business cycle. Demand for tobacco products does not seem to be affected by the state of the macroeconomy in any meaningful way: This is not surprising. Tobacco consumption is determined largely by habit and is a small enough part of most budgets that it will not be given up in hard times.

TABLE 12.3
Operating Leverage

Scenario:	Recession		Normal		Expansion	
Firm:	***A***	***B***	***A***	***B***	***A***	***B***
Sales (million units)	5	5	6	6	7	7
Price per unit	$ 2	$ 2	$ 2	$ 2	$ 2	$ 2
Revenue ($ million)	10	10	12	12	14	14
Fixed costs ($ million)	5	8	5	8	5	8
Variable costs ($ million)	5	2.5	6	3	7	3.5
Total costs ($ million)	$10	$10.5	$11	$11	$12	$11.5
Profits	$ 0	$(0.5)	$ 1	$ 1	$ 2	$ 2.5

Auto production by contrast is highly volatile. In recessions, consumers can try to prolong the lives of their cars until their income is higher. For example, the worst year for auto production, according to Figure 12.9, was 1982. This was also a year of deep recession, with the unemployment rate at 9.5%.

Three factors will determine the sensitivity of a firm's earnings to the business cycle. First is the sensitivity of sales. Necessities will show little sensitivity to business conditions. Examples of industries in this group are food, drugs, and medical services. Other industries with low sensitivity are those for which income is not a crucial determinant of demand. As we noted, tobacco products are examples of this type of industry. Another industry in this group is movies, because consumers tend to substitute movies for more expensive sources of entertainment when income levels are low. In contrast, firms in industries such as machine tools, steel, autos, and transportation are highly sensitive to the state of the economy.

The second factor determining business cycle sensitivity is operating leverage, which refers to the division between fixed and variable costs. (Fixed costs are those the firm incurs regardless of its production levels. Variable costs are those that rise or fall as the firm produces more or less product.) Firms with greater amounts of variable as opposed to fixed costs will be less sensitive to business conditions. This is because, in economic downturns, these firms can reduce costs as output falls in response to falling sales. Profits for firms with high fixed costs will swing more widely with sales because costs do not move to offset revenue variability. Firms with high fixed costs are said to have high operating leverage, as small swings in business conditions can have large impacts on profitability.

An example might help illustrate this concept. Consider two firms operating in the same industry with identical revenues in all phases of the business cycle: recession, normal, and expansion. Firm *A* has short-term rentals on most of its equipment and can reduce its rental expenditures when production slackens. It has fixed costs of $5 million and variable costs of $1 per unit of output. Firm *B* has long-term leases on most of its equipment and must make lease payments regardless of economic conditions. Its fixed costs are higher, $8 million, but its variable costs are only $0.50 per unit. Table 12.3 shows that firm *A* will do better in recessions than firm *B* but not as well in expansions. *A*'s costs move in conjunction with its revenues to help performance in downturns and impede performance in upturns.

degree of operating leverage
Percentage change in profits given a 1% change in sales.

We can quantify operating leverage by measuring how sensitive profits are to changes in sales. The **degree of operating leverage,** or DOL, is defined as:

$$DOL = \frac{\text{Percentage change in profits}}{\text{Percentage change in sales}}$$

DOL greater than 1 indicates some operating leverage. For example, if DOL equals 2, then for every 1% change in sales, profits will change by 2% in the same direction, either up or down.

We have seen that the degree of operating leverage increases with a firm's exposure to fixed costs. In fact, one can show that DOL depends on fixed costs in the following manner:[1]

$$\text{DOL} = 1 + \frac{\text{Fixed costs}}{\text{Profits}}$$

EXAMPLE 12.1
Operating
Leverage

Return to the two firms illustrated in Table 12.3 and compare profits and sales in the normal and recession scenarios. The profits of firm A fall by 100% (from $1 million to $0) when sales fall by 16.7% (from $6 million to $5 million):

$$\text{DOL (firm } A) = \frac{\text{Percentage change in profits}}{\text{Percentage change in sales}} = \frac{-100\%}{-16.7\%} = 6$$

Moreover, we can confirm the relationship between DOL and fixed costs as follows:

$$\text{DOL (firm } A) = 1 + \frac{\text{Fixed costs}}{\text{Profits}} = 1 + \frac{\$5 \text{ million}}{\$1 \text{ million}} = 6$$

Firm B has higher fixed costs, and its operating leverage is higher. Again, compare the data for the normal scenarios and recession. Profits for firm B fall by 150%, from $1 million to $-$$0.5 million. Operating leverage for firm B is therefore

$$\text{DOL (firm } B) = \frac{\text{Percentage change in profits}}{\text{Percentage change in sales}} = \frac{-150\%}{-16.7\%} = 9$$

which reflects its higher level of fixed costs:

$$\text{DOL (firm } B) = 1 + \frac{\text{Fixed costs}}{\text{Profits}} = 1 + \frac{\$8 \text{ million}}{\$1 \text{ million}} = 9$$

The third factor influencing business cycle sensitivity is financial leverage, which is the use of borrowing. Interest payments on debt must be paid regardless of sales. They are fixed costs that also increase the sensitivity of profits to business conditions. We will have more to say about financial leverage in Chapter 14.

Investors should not always prefer industries with lower sensitivity to the business cycle. Firms in sensitive industries will have high-beta stocks and are riskier. But while they swing lower in downturns, they also swing higher in upturns. As always, the issue you need to address is whether the expected return on the investment is fair compensation for the risks borne.

Concept Check

4. Firm C has the same sales as Firms A and B in Table 12.3, but it has fixed costs of $2 million and variable costs of $1.50 per unit. What are its profits in each scenario? What is its DOL?

Industry Life Cycles

Examine the biotechnology industry and you will find many firms with high rates of investment, high rates of return on investment, and very low dividends as a percentage of profits. Do the same for the electric utility industry and you will find lower rates of return, lower investment rates, and higher dividend payout rates. Why should this be?

The biotech industry is still new. Recently, available technologies have created opportunities for the highly profitable investment of resources. New products are protected by patents,

---

[1]Operating leverage and DOL are treated in more detail in most introductory corporate finance texts.

FIGURE 12.10
The Industry Life Cycle

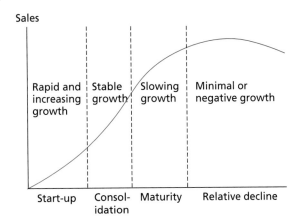

and profit margins are high. With such lucrative investment opportunities, firms find it advantageous to put all profits back into the firm. The companies grow rapidly on average.

Eventually, however, growth must slow. The high profit rates will induce new firms to enter the industry. Increasing competition will hold down prices and profit margins. New technologies become proven and more predictable, risk levels fall, and entry becomes even easier. As internal investment opportunities become less attractive, a lower fraction of profits are reinvested in the firm. Cash dividends increase.

Ultimately, in a mature industry, we observe "cash cows," firms with stable dividends and cash flows and little risk. Their growth rates might be similar to that of the overall economy. Industries in early stages of their life cycles offer high-risk/high-potential-return investments. Mature industries offer lower risk, lower return combinations.

This analysis suggests that a typical **industry life cycle** might be described by four stages: a start-up stage characterized by extremely rapid growth; a consolidation stage characterized by growth that is less rapid but still faster than that of the general economy; a maturity stage characterized by growth no faster than the general economy; and a stage of relative decline, in which the industry grows less rapidly than the rest of the economy, or actually shrinks. This industry life cycle is illustrated in Figure 12.10. Let us turn to an elaboration of each of these stages.

industry life cycle
Stages through which firms typically pass as they mature.

Start-Up Stage   The early stages of an industry often are characterized by a new technology or product such as VCRs or personal computers in the 1980s, or bioengineering in the 1990s. At this stage, it is difficult to predict which firms will emerge as industry leaders. Some firms will turn out to be wildly successful, and others will fail altogether. Therefore, there is considerable risk in selecting one particular firm within the industry.

At the industry level, however, sales and earnings will grow at an extremely rapid rate since the new product has not yet saturated its market. For example, in 1980 very few households had VCRs. The potential market for the product therefore was the entire set of television-watching households. In contrast to this situation, consider the market for a mature product like refrigerators. Almost all households in the U.S. already have refrigerators, so the market for this good is primarily composed of households replacing old refrigerators. Obviously, the growth rate in this market will be far less than for VCRs.

Consolidation Stage   After a product becomes established, industry leaders begin to emerge. The survivors from the start-up stage are more stable, and market share is easier to predict. Therefore, the performance of the surviving firms will more closely track the performance of the overall industry. The industry still grows faster than the rest of the economy as the product penetrates the marketplace and becomes more commonly used.

Maturity Stage   At this point, the product has reached its full potential for use by consumers. Further growth might merely track growth in the general economy. The product has become far more standardized, and producers are forced to compete to a greater extent on the basis of price. This leads to narrower profit margins and further pressure on profits. Firms at this stage sometimes are characterized as "cash cows," firms with reasonably stable cash flow but offering little opportunity for profitable expansion. The cash flow is best "milked from" rather than reinvested in the company.

Relative Decline   In this stage, the industry might grow at less than the rate of the overall economy, or it might even shrink. This could be due to obsolescence of the product, competition from new products, or competition from new low-cost suppliers.

At which stage in the life cycle are investments in an industry most attractive? Conventional wisdom is that investors should seek firms in high-growth industries. This recipe for success is simplistic, however. If the security prices already reflect the likelihood for high growth, then it is too late to make money from that knowledge. Moreover, high growth and fat profits encourage competition from other producers. The exploitation of profit opportunities brings about new sources of supply that eventually reduce prices, profits, investment returns, and finally, growth. This is the dynamic behind the progression from one stage of the industry life cycle to another. The famous portfolio manager Peter Lynch makes this point in *One Up on Wall Street*. He says that

> Many people prefer to invest in a high-growth industry, where there's a lot of sound and fury. Not me. I prefer to invest in a low-growth industry . . . In a low-growth industry, especially one that's boring and upsets people [such as funeral homes or the oil-drum retrieval business], there's no problem with competition. You don't have to protect your flanks from potential rivals . . . and this gives you the leeway to continue to grow (page 131).

In fact, Lynch uses an industry classification system in a very similar spirit to the life-cycle approach we have described. He places firms in the following six groups:

1. *Slow Growers.* Large and aging companies that will grow only slightly faster than the broad economy. These firms have matured from their earlier fast-growth phase. They usually have steady cash flow and pay a generous dividend, indicating that the firm is generating more cash than can be profitably reinvested in the firm.
2. *Stalwarts.* Large, well-known firms like Coca-Cola, Hershey's, or Colgate-Palmolive. They grow faster than the slow growers, but are not in the very rapid growth start-up stage. They also tend to be in noncyclical industries that are relatively unaffected by recessions.
3. *Fast Growers.* Small and aggressive new firms with annual growth rates in the neighborhood of 20 to 25%. Company growth can be due to broad industry growth or to an increase in market share in a more mature industry.
4. *Cyclicals.* These are firms with sales and profits that regularly expand and contract along with the business cycle. Examples are auto companies (see Figure 12.9 again), steel companies, or the construction industry.
5. *Turnarounds.* These are firms that are in bankruptcy or soon might be. If they can recover from what might appear to be imminent disaster, they can offer tremendous investment returns. A good example of this type of firm would be Chrysler in 1982, when it required a government guarantee on its debt to avoid bankruptcy. The stock price rose fifteenfold in the next five years.
6. *Asset Plays.* These are firms that have valuable assets not currently reflected in the stock price. For example, a company may own or be located on valuable real estate that is worth as much or more than the company's business enterprises. Sometimes the hidden asset can be tax-loss carryforwards. Other times the assets may be intangible.

For example, a cable company might have a valuable list of cable subscribers. These assets do not immediately generate cash flow and so may be more easily overlooked by other analysts attempting to value the firm.

Industry Structure and Performance

The maturation of an industry involves regular changes in the firm's competitive environment. As a final topic, we examine the relationship between industry structure, competitive strategy, and profitability. Michael Porter (1980, 1985) has highlighted these five determinants of competition: threat of entry from new competitors, rivalry between existing competitors, price pressure from substitute products, the bargaining power of suppliers, and the bargaining power of buyers.

Threat of Entry   New entrants to an industry put pressure on price and profits. Even if a firm has not yet entered an industry, the potential for it to do so places pressure on prices, since high prices and profit margins will encourage entry by new competitors. Therefore, barriers to entry can be a key determinant of industry profitability. Barriers can take many forms. For example, existing firms may already have secure distribution channels for their products based on long-standing relationships with customers or suppliers that would be costly for a new entrant to duplicate. Brand loyalty also makes it difficult for new entrants to penetrate a market and gives firms more pricing discretion. Proprietary knowledge or patent protection also may give firms advantages in serving a market. Finally, an existing firm's experience in a market may give it cost advantages due to the learning that takes place over time.

Rivalry Between Existing Competitors   When there are several competitors in an industry, there will generally be more price competition and lower profit margins as competitors seek to expand their share of the market. Slow industry growth contributes to this competition since expansion must come at the expense of a rival's market share. High fixed costs also create pressure to reduce prices since fixed costs put greater pressure on firms to operate near full capacity. Industries producing relatively homogeneous goods also are subject to considerable price pressure since firms cannot compete on the basis of product differentiation.

Pressure from Substitute Products   Substitute products means that the industry faces competition from firms in related industries. For example, sugar producers compete with corn syrup producers. Wool producers compete with synthetic fiber producers. The availability of substitutes limits the prices that can be charged to customers.

Bargaining Power of Buyers   If a buyer purchases a large fraction of an industry's output, it will have considerable bargaining power and can demand price concessions. For example, auto producers can put pressure on suppliers of auto parts. This reduces the profitability of the auto parts industry.

Bargaining Power of Suppliers   If a supplier of a key input has monopolistic control over the product, it can demand higher prices for the good and squeeze profits out of the industry. One special case of this issue pertains to organized labor as a supplier of a key input to the production process. Labor unions engage in collective bargaining to increase the wages paid to workers. When the labor market is highly unionized, a significant share of the potential profits in the industry can be captured by the work force.

The key factor determining the bargaining power of suppliers is the availability of substitute products. If substitutes are available, the supplier has little clout and cannot extract higher prices.

Summary

- Macroeconomic policy aims to maintain the economy near full employment without aggravating inflationary pressures. The proper trade-off between these two goals is a source of ongoing debate.
- The traditional tools of macropolicy are government spending and tax collection, which comprise fiscal policy, and manipulation of the money supply via monetary policy. Expansionary fiscal policy can stimulate the economy and increase GDP but tends to increase interest rates. Expansionary monetary policy works by lowering interest rates.
- The business cycle is the economy's recurring pattern of expansions and recessions. Leading economic indicators can be used to anticipate the evolution of the business cycle because their values tend to change before those of other key economic variables.
- Industries differ in their sensitivity to the business cycle. More sensitive industries tend to be those producing high-priced durable goods for which the consumer has considerable discretion as to the timing of purchase. Examples are automobiles or consumer durables. Other sensitive industries are those that produce capital equipment for other firms. Operating leverage and financial leverage increase sensitivity to the business cycle.

Key Terms

budget deficit, *332*	fiscal policy, *335*	monetary policy, *336*
business cycle, *337*	fundamental analysis, *328*	peak, *337*
cyclical industries, *337*	gross domestic product, *331*	SIC codes, *341*
defensive industries, *337*	industry life cycle, *347*	supply shock, *334*
degree of operating leverage, *345*	inflation, *331*	trough, *337*
demand shock, *334*	leading economic indicators, *340*	unemployment rate, *331*
exchange rate, *330*		

Problem Sets

1. What monetary and fiscal policies might be prescribed for an economy in a deep recession?

2. Unlike other investors, you believe the Fed is going to dramatically loosen monetary policy. What would be your recommendations about investments in the following industries?
   a. Gold mining
   b. Construction

3. If you believe the U.S. dollar is about to depreciate more dramatically than do other investors, what will be your stance on investments in U.S. auto producers?

4. According to supply-side economists, what will be the long-run impact on prices of a reduction in income tax rates?

5. Consider two firms producing videocassette recorders. One uses a highly automated robotics process, while the other uses human workers on an assembly line and pays overtime when there is heavy production demand.
   a. Which firm will have higher profits in a recession? In a boom?
   b. Which firm's stock will have a higher beta?

6. Here are four industries and four forecasts for the macroeconomy. Choose the industry that you would expect to perform best in each scenario.
   Industries: Housing construction, health care, gold mining, steel production.
   Economic Forecasts
   Deep recession: Falling inflation, falling interest rates, falling GDP.
   Superheated economy: Rapidly rising GDP, increasing inflation and interest rates.
   Healthy expansion: Rising GDP, mild inflation, low unemployment.
   Stagflation: Falling GDP, high inflation.

7. In which stage of the industry life cycle would you place the following industries? (Warning: There is often considerable room for disagreement concerning the "correct" answers to this question.)

   a. Oil well equipment
   b. Computer hardware
   c. Computer software
   d. Genetic engineering
   e. Railroads

8. For each pair of firms, choose the one that you think would be more sensitive to the business cycle.
   a. General Autos or General Pharmaceuticals.
   b. Friendly Airlines or Happy Cinemas.

9. Choose an industry and identify the factors that will determine its performance in the next three years. What is your forecast for performance in that time period?

10. Why do you think the index of consumer expectations is a useful leading indicator of the macroeconomy? (See Table 12.2.)

11. Why do you think the change in the index of labor cost per unit of output is a useful lagging indicator of the macroeconomy? (See Table 12.2.)

12. You have $5,000 to invest for the next year and are considering three alternatives:
    a. A money market fund with an average maturity of 30 days offering a current yield of 6% per year.
    b. A one-year savings deposit at a bank offering an interest rate of 7.5%.
    c. A 20-year U.S. Treasury bond offering a yield to maturity of 9% per year. What role does your forecast of future interest rates play in your decisions?

13. Universal Auto is a large multinational corporation headquartered in the United States. For segment reporting purposes, the company is engaged in two businesses: production of motor vehicles and information processing services.

    The motor vehicle business is by far the larger of Universal's two segments. It consists mainly of domestic United States passenger car production, but it also includes small truck manufacturing operations in the United States and passenger car production in other countries. This segment of Universal has had weak operating results for the past several years, including a large loss in 1992. Although the company does not reveal the operating results of its domestic passenger car segments, that part of Universal's business is generally believed to be primarily responsible for the weak performance of its motor vehicle segment.

    Idata, the information processing services segment of Universal, was started by Universal about 15 years ago. This business has shown strong, steady growth that has been entirely internal: No acquisitions have been made.

    An excerpt from a research report on Universal prepared by Paul Adams, a CFA candidate, states: Based on our assumption that Universal will be able to increase prices significantly on U.S. passenger cars in 1993, we project a multibillion dollar profit improvement . . .

    a. Discuss the concept of an industrial life cycle by describing each of its four phases.
    b. Identify where each of Universal's two primary businesses—passenger cars and information processing—is in such a cycle.
    c. Discuss how product pricing should differ between Universal's two businesses, based on the location of each in the industrial life cycle.

14. Adams's research report (see problem 13) continued as follows: "With a business recovery already underway, the expected profit surge should lead to a much higher price for Universal Auto stock. We strongly recommend purchase."
    a. Discuss the business cycle approach to investment timing. (Your answer should describe actions to be taken on both stocks and bonds at different points over a typical business cycle.)
    b. Assuming Adams's assertion is correct (that a business recovery is already underway), evaluate the timeliness of his recommendation to purchase Universal Auto, a cyclical stock, based on the business cycle approach to investment timing.

15. Your business plan for your proposed start-up firm envisions first year revenues of $120,000, fixed costs of $30,000, and variable costs equal to one-third of revenue.
    a. What are expected profits based on these expectations?
    b. What is the degree of operating leverage based on the estimate of fixed costs and expected profits?
    c. If sales are 10% below expectation, what will be the decrease in profits?
    d. Show that the percentage decrease in profits equals DOL times the 10% drop in sales.
    e. Based on the DOL, what is the largest percentage shortfall in sales relative to original expectations that the firm can sustain before profits turn negative? What are break-even sales at this point?
    f. Confirm that your answer to (e) is correct by calculating profits at the break-even level of sales.

16. General Weedkillers dominates the chemical weed control market with its patented product Weed-ex. The patent is about to expire, however. What are your forecasts for changes in the industry? Specifically, what will happen to industry prices, sales, the profit prospects of General Weedkillers, and the profit prospects of its competitors? What stage of the industry life cycle do you think is relevant for the analysis of this market?

17. The following questions appeared on recent CFA examinations.
    a. Which one of the following statements *best* expresses the central idea of countercyclical fiscal policy?
       (1) Planned government deficits are appropriate during economic booms, and planned surpluses are appropriate during economic recessions.
       (2) The balanced budget approach is the proper criterion for determining annual budget policy.
       (3) Actual deficits should equal actual surpluses during a period of deflation.
       (4) Government deficits are planned during economic recessions, and surpluses are utilized to restrain inflationary booms.
    b. The supply-side view stresses that:
       (1) Aggregate demand is the major determinant of real output and aggregate employment.
       (2) An increase in government expenditures and tax rates will cause real income to rise.
       (3) Tax rates are a major determinant of real output and aggregate employment.
       (4) Expansionary monetary policy will cause real output to expand without causing the rate of inflation to accelerate.
    c. Which *one* of the following propositions would a strong proponent of supply-side economics be *most* likely to stress?
       (1) Higher marginal tax rates will lead to a reduction in the size of the budget deficit and lower interest rates because they expand government revenues.
       (2) Higher marginal tax rates promote economic inefficiency and thereby retard aggregate output because they encourage investors to undertake low productivity projects with substantial tax-shelter benefits.

      (3) Income redistribution payments will exert little impact on real aggregate supply because they do not consume resources directly.

      (4) A tax reduction will increase the disposable income of households. Thus, the primary impact of a tax reduction on aggregate supply will stem from the influence of the tax change on the size of the budget deficit or surplus.

   d. Which one of the following series is *not* included in the index of leading economic indicators?

      (1) New building permits; private housing units.

      (2) Net business formulation.

      (3) Stock prices.

      (4) Inventories on hand.

   e. How would an economist who believes in crowding out complete the following sentence? "The increase in the budget deficit causes real interest rates to rise and, therefore, private spending and investment

      (1) Increase."

      (2) Stay the same."

      (3) Decrease."

      (4) Initially increase but eventually will decrease."

   f. If the central monetary authorities want to reduce the supply of money to slow the rate of inflation, the central bank should:

      (1) Sell government bonds, which will reduce the money supply; this will cause interest rates to rise and aggregate demand to fall.

      (2) Buy government bonds, which will reduce the money supply; this will cause interest rates to rise and aggregate demand to fall.

      (3) Decrease the discount rate, which will lower the market rate of interest; this will cause both costs and prices to fall.

      (4) Increase taxes, which will reduce costs and cause prices to fall.

18. The corporate life-cycle theory predicts that firms with ample investment opportunities will maintain high investment rates while more mature industries in which attractive investment opportunities are scarce will have higher dividend payout rates. Use MarketBase-E to test this prediction. Compare the dividend payout rates for a sample of industries. For example, consider electric utilities versus telecommunications equipment; tobacco versus home health care; etc. Comment on your findings.

IEM
Applications

1. Suppose you conduct an extensive macroeconomic analysis and complete it just before trade opens for a month in new IEM contracts on the Computer Industry Returns and MSFT (Microsoft) Price Level Markets. In what ways would this analysis help you in predicting what will happen on the IEM in these two markets?

Solutions to
Concept Checks

1. The downturn in the auto industry will reduce the demand for the product in this economy. The economy will, at least in the short term, enter a recession. This would suggest that:

   a. GDP will fall.

   b. The unemployment rate will rise.

   c. The government deficit will increase. Income tax receipts will fall, and government expenditures on social welfare programs probably will increase.

   d. Interest rates should fall. The contraction in the economy will reduce the demand for credit. Moreover, the lower inflation rate will reduce nominal interest rates.

2. Expansionary fiscal policy coupled with expansionary monetary policy will stimulate the economy, with the loose monetary policy keeping down interest rates.

3. A traditional demand-side interpretation of the tax cuts is that the resulting increase in after-tax income increased consumption demand and stimulated the economy. A supply-side interpretation is

that the reduction in marginal tax rates made it more attractive for businesses to invest and for individuals to work, thereby increasing economic output.

4. Firm *C* has the lowest fixed cost and highest variable costs. It should be least sensitive to the business cycle. In fact, it is. Its profits are highest of the three firms in recessions but lowest in expansions.

	Recession	**Normal**	**Expansion**
Revenue	$10	$12	$14
Fixed cost	2	2	2
Variable cost	7.5	9	10.5
Profits	$ 0.5	$ 1	$ 1.5

$$DOL = \frac{\text{Percentage change profits}}{\text{Percentage change sales}} = \frac{50\%}{16.6\%} = 3$$

$$DOL = 1 + \frac{\text{Fixed cost}}{\text{Profits}} = 1 + \frac{\$2}{\$1} = 3$$

Chapter 13

EQUITY VALUATION

AFTER STUDYING THIS CHAPTER, YOU SHOULD BE ABLE TO:

- Calculate the intrinsic value of a firm using either a constant growth or multistage dividend discount model.

- Calculate the intrinsic value of a stock using a dividend discount model in conjunction with a price/earnings ratio.

- Assess the growth prospects of a firm from its P/E ratio.

You saw in our discussion of market efficiency that finding undervalued securities is hardly easy. At the same time, there are enough chinks in the armor of the efficient market hypothesis that the search for such securities should not be dismissed out of hand. Moreover, it is the ongoing search for mispriced securities that maintains a nearly efficient market. Even infrequent discoveries of minor mispricing justify the salary of a stock market analyst.

This chapter describes the ways stock market analysts try to uncover mispriced securities. The models presented are those used by *fundamental analysts*, those analysts who use information concerning the current and prospective profitability of a company to assess its fair market value. Fundamental analysts are different from *technical analysts*, who essentially use trend analysis to uncover trading opportunities. We discuss technical analysis in Chapter 15.

We start with a discussion of alternative measures of the value of a company. From there, we progress to quantitative tools called dividend discount models that security analysts commonly use to measure the value of a firm as an ongoing concern. Next, we turn to price/earnings, or P/E, ratios, explaining why they are of such interest to analysts but also highlighting some of their shortcomings. We explain how P/E ratios are tied to dividend valuation models and, more generally, to the growth prospects of the firm.

13.1 BALANCE SHEET VALUATION METHODS

book value
The net worth of common equity according to a firm's balance sheet.

A common valuation measure is **book value,** which is the net worth of a company as shown on the balance sheet. Table 13.1 gives the balance sheet totals for Ford Motor Co. to illustrate how to calculate book value per share.

TABLE 13.1
Ford's Balance Sheet,
December 31, 1995
($ Million)

Assets	Liabilities and Owners' Equity	
$243,283	Liabilities	$219,736
	Common equity	$23,547
	1,169 million shares outstanding	

Book value of Ford stock on December 31, 1995, was $20.14 per share ($23,547 million divided by 1,169 million shares). On that same date, Ford stock had a market price of $28.875. Would it be fair to say Ford stock was overpriced?

The book value is the result of applying a set of arbitrary accounting rules to spread the acquisition cost of assets over a specified number of years; in contrast, the market price of a stock takes account of the firm's value as a going concern. In other words, the price reflects the market consensus estimate of the present value of the firm's expected future cash flows. It would be unusual if the market price of Ford stock were exactly equal to its book value.

Can book value represent a "floor" for the stock's price, below which level the market price can never fall? Although Ford's book value per share was less than its market price, other evidence disproves this notion. On December 31, 1995, Digital Equipment Corp. stock had a book value of $36.19 per share and a market price of $34.25. Clearly, book value cannot always be a floor for the stock's price.

liquidation value
Net amount that can be realized by selling the assets of a firm and paying off the debt.

A better measure of a floor for the stock price is the firm's **liquidation value** per share. This represents the amount of money that could be realized by breaking up the firm, selling its assets, repaying its debt, and distributing the remainder to the shareholders. The reasoning behind this concept is that if the market price of equity drops below the liquidation value of the firm, the firm becomes attractive as a takeover target. A corporate raider would find it profitable to buy enough shares to gain control and then actually liquidate because the liquidation value exceeds the value of the business as a going concern.

replacement cost
Cost to replace a firm's assets.

Another balance sheet concept that is of interest in valuing a firm is the **replacement cost** of its assets less its liabilities. Some analysts believe the market value of the firm cannot get too far above its replacement cost because, if it did, competitors would try to replicate the firm. The competitive pressure of other similar firms entering the same industry would drive down the market value of all firms until they came into equality with replacement cost.

Tobin's q
Ratio of market value of the firm to replacement cost.

This idea is popular among economists, and the ratio of market price to replacement cost is known as **Tobin's q,** after the Nobel Prize–winning economist James Tobin. In the long run, according to this view, the ratio of market price to replacement cost will tend toward 1, but the evidence is that this ratio can differ significantly from 1 for very long periods of time.

Although focusing on the balance sheet can give some useful information about a firm's liquidation value or its replacement cost, the analyst usually must turn to the expected future cash flows for a better estimate of the firm's value as a going concern. We now examine the quantitative models that analysts use to value common stock in terms of the future earnings and dividends the firm will yield.

13.2 INTRINSIC VALUE VERSUS MARKET PRICE

The most popular model for assessing the value of a firm as a going concern takes off from the observation that an investor in stock expects a return consisting of cash dividends and capital gains or losses. We begin by assuming a one-year holding period and supposing that ABC stock has an expected dividend per share, $E(D_1)$, of $4; that the current price of a share, P_0, is $48; and that the expected price at the end of a year, $E(P_1)$, is $52.

The holding-period return the investor expects is $E(D_1)$ plus the expected price appreciation, $E(P_1) - P_0$, all divided by the current price P_0

$$\text{Expected HPR} = E(r)$$

$$= \frac{E(D_1) + [E(P_1) - P_0]}{P_0}$$

$$= \frac{4 + (52 - 48)}{48} = 0.167 = 16.7\%$$

Note that $E(\ )$ denotes an expected future value. Thus, $E(P_1)$ represents the expectation today of the stock price one year from now. $E(r)$ is referred to as the stock's expected holding-period return. It is the sum of the expected dividend yield, $E(D_1)/P_0$, and the expected rate of price appreciation, the capital gains yield, $[E(P_1) - P_0]/P_0$.

But what is the appropriate discount rate for ABC stock? We know from the capital asset pricing model (CAPM) that when stock market prices are at equilibrium levels, the rate of return that investors can expect to earn on a security is $r_f + \beta[E(r_M) - r_f]$. Thus, the CAPM may be viewed as providing the rate of return an investor can expect to earn on a security given its risk as measured by beta. This is the return that investors will require of any other investment with equivalent risk. We will denote this required rate of return as k. If a stock is priced "correctly," its expected return will equal the required return. Of course, the goal of a security analyst is to find stocks that are mispriced. For example, an underpriced stock will provide an expected return greater than the "fair" or required return.

Suppose that $r_f = 6\%$, $E[(r_M) - r_f] = 5\%$, and the beta of ABC is 1.2. Then the value of k is

$$k = 6\% + 1.2 \times 5\%$$

$$= 12\%$$

The rate of return the investor expects exceeds the required rate based on ABC's risk by a margin of 4.7%. Naturally, the investor will want to include more of ABC stock in the portfolio than a passive strategy would dictate.

Another way to see this is to compare the intrinsic value of a share of stock to its market price. The **intrinsic value,** denoted V_0, of a share of stock is defined as the present value of all cash payments to the investor in the stock, including dividends as well as the proceeds from the ultimate sale of the stock, discounted at the appropriate risk-adjusted interest rate, k. Whenever the intrinsic value, or the investor's own estimate of what the stock is really worth, exceeds the market price, the stock is considered undervalued and a good investment. In the case of ABC, using a one-year investment horizon and a forecast that the stock can be sold at the end of the year at price $P_1 = \$52$, the intrinsic value is

intrinsic value
The present value of a firm's expected future net cash flows discounted by the required rate of return.

$$V_0 = \frac{E(D_1) + E(P_1)}{1 + k}$$

$$= \frac{\$4 + \$52}{1.12}$$

$$= \$50$$

Because intrinsic value, $50, exceeds current price, $48, we conclude that the stock is undervalued in the market. We again conclude investors will want to buy more ABC than they would following a passive strategy.

If the intrinsic value turns out to be lower than the current market price, investors should buy less of it than under the passive strategy. It might even pay to go short on ABC stock, as we discussed in Chapter 3.

In market equilibrium, the current market price will reflect the intrinsic value estimates of all market participants. This means the individual investor whose V_0 estimate differs from the market price, P_0, in effect must disagree with some or all of the market consensus estimates of $E(D_1)$, $E(P_1)$, or k. A common term for the market consensus value of the required rate of return, k, is the **market capitalization rate,** which we use often throughout this chapter.

market capitalization rate
The market-consensus estimate of the appropriate discount rate for a firm's cash flows.

1. You expect the price of IBX stock to be $59.77 per share a year from now. Its current market price is $50, and you expect it to pay a dividend one year from now of $2.15 per share.

   a. What is the stock's expected dividend yield, rate of price appreciation, and holding-period return?

   b. If the stock has a beta of 1.15, the risk-free rate is 6% per year, and the expected rate of return on the market portfolio is 14% per year, what is the required rate of return on IBX stock?

   c. What is the intrinsic value of IBX stock, and how does it compare to the current market price?

13.3 DIVIDEND DISCOUNT MODELS

Consider an investor who buys a share of Steady State Electronics stock, planning to hold it for one year. The intrinsic value of the share is the present value of the dividend to be received at the end of the first year, D_1, and the expected sales price, P_1. We will henceforth use the simpler notation P_1 instead of $E(P_1)$ to avoid clutter. Keep in mind, though, that future prices and dividends are unknown, and we are dealing with expected values, not certain values. We've already established that

$$V_0 = \frac{D_1 + P_1}{1 + k} \tag{13.1}$$

While this year's dividend is fairly predictable given a company's history, you might ask how we can estimate P_1, the year-end price. According to Equation 13.1, V_1 (the year-end value) will be

$$V_1 = \frac{D_2 + P_2}{1 + k}$$

If we assume the stock will be selling for its intrinsic value next year, then $V_1 = P_1$, and we can substitute this value for P_1 into Equation 13.1 to find

$$V_0 = \frac{D_1}{1 + k} + \frac{D_2 + P_2}{(1 + k)^2}$$

This equation may be interpreted as the present value of dividends plus sales price for a two-year holding period. Of course, now we need to come up with a forecast of P_2. Continuing in the same way, we can replace P_2 by $(D_3 + P_3)/(1 + k)$, which relates P_0 to the value of dividends plus the expected sales price for a three-year holding period.

More generally, for a holding period of H years, we can write the stock value as the present value of dividends over the H years, plus the ultimate sales price, P_H.

$$V_0 = \frac{D_1}{1 + k} + \frac{D_2}{(1 + k)^2} + \ldots + \frac{D_H + P_H}{(1 + k)^H} \tag{13.2}$$

Note the similarity between this formula and the bond valuation formula developed in Chapter 10. Each relates price to the present value of a stream of payments (coupons in the case of bonds, dividends in the case of stocks) and a final payment (the face value of the bond or the sales price of the stock). The key differences in the case of stocks are the uncertainty of dividends, the lack of a fixed maturity date, and the unknown sales price at the horizon date. Indeed, one can continue to substitute for price indefinitely to conclude

$$V_0 = \frac{D_1}{1 + k} + \frac{D_2}{(1 + k)^2} + \frac{D_3}{(1 + k)^3} + \ldots \tag{13.3}$$

dividend discount model (DDM)
A formula for the intrinsic value of a firm equal to the present value of all expected future dividends.

Equation 13.3 states the stock price should equal the present value of all expected future dividends into perpetuity. This formula is called the **dividend discount model (DDM)** of stock prices.

It is tempting, but incorrect, to conclude from Equation 13.3 that the DDM focuses exclusively on dividends and ignores capital gains as a motive for investing in stock. Indeed, we assume explicitly in Equation 13.1 that capital gains (as reflected in the expected sales price, P_1) are part of the stock's value. At the same time, the price at which you can sell a stock in the future depends on dividend forecasts at that time.

The reason only dividends appear in Equation 13.3 is not that investors ignore capital gains. It is instead that those capital gains will be determined by dividend forecasts at the time the stock is sold. That is why in Equation 13.2 we can write the stock price as the present value of dividends plus sales price for *any* horizon date. P_H is the present value at time H of all dividends expected to be paid after the horizon date. That value is then discounted back to today, time 0. The DDM asserts that stock prices are determined ultimately by the cash flows accruing to stockholders, and those are dividends.

The Constant Growth DDM

Equation 13.3 as it stands is still not very useful in valuing a stock because it requires dividend forecasts for every year into the indefinite future. To make the DDM practical, we need to introduce some simplifying assumptions. A useful and common first pass at the problem is to assume that dividends are trending upward at a stable growth rate that we will call g. Then if $g = 0.05$, and the most recently paid dividend was $D_0 = 3.81$, expected future dividends are

$$D_1 = D_0(1 + g) = 3.81 \times 1.05 = 4.00$$
$$D_2 = D_0(1 + g)^2 = 3.81 \times (1.05)^2 = 4.20$$
$$D_3 = D_0(1 + g)^3 = 3.81 \times (1.05)^3 = 4.41 \text{ etc.}$$

Using these dividend forecasts in Equation 13.3, we solve for intrinsic value as

$$V_0 = \frac{D_0(1 + g)}{1 + k} + \frac{D_0(1 + g)^2}{(1 + k)^2} + \frac{D_0(1 + g)^3}{(1 + k)^3} + \cdots$$

This equation can be simplified to

$$V_0 = \frac{D_0(1 + g)}{k - g} = \frac{D_1}{k - g} \tag{13.4}$$

Note in Equation 13.4 that we divide D_1 (not D_0) by $k - g$ to calculate intrinsic value. If the market capitalization rate for Steady State is 12%, we can use Equation 13.4 to show that the intrinsic value of a share of Steady State stock is

$$\frac{\$4.00}{0.12 - 0.05} = \$57.14$$

constant growth DDM
A form of the dividend discount model that assumes dividends will grow at a constant rate.

Equation 13.4 is called the **constant growth DDM** or the Gordon model, after Myron J. Gordon, who popularized the model. It should remind you of the formula for the present value of a perpetuity. If dividends were expected not to grow, then the dividend stream would be a simple perpetuity, and the valuation formula for such a nongrowth stock would be $P_0 = D_1/k$.[1] Equation 13.4 is a generalization of the perpetuity formula to cover the case of a *growing* perpetuity. As g increases, the stock price also rises.

---

[1]Recall from introductory finance that the present value of a $1 per year perpetuity is $1/k$. For example, if $k = 10\%$, the value of the perpetuity is $\$1/0.10 = \$10$. Notice that if $g = 0$ in Equation 13.4, the constant growth DDM formula is the same as the perpetuity formula.

**EXAMPLE 13.1
Preferred Stock
and the DDM**

Preferred stock that pays a fixed dividend can be valued using the constant growth dividend discount model. The constant growth rate of dividends is simply zero. For example, to value a preferred stock paying a fixed dividend of $2 per share when the discount rate is 8%, we compute

$$V_0 = \frac{\$2}{0.08 - 0} = \$25$$

**EXAMPLE 13.2
The Constant
Growth DDM**

High Flyer Industries has just paid its annual dividend of $3 per share. The dividend is expected to grow at a constant rate of 8% indefinitely. The risk of High Flyer stock is consistent with a market capitalization rate of 14%. What is the intrinsic value of the stock? What would be your estimate of intrinsic value if you believed that the stock was riskier and warranted a discount rate of 16%?

Because a $3 dividend has just been paid and the growth rate of dividends is 8%, the forecast for the year-end dividend is $3 \times 1.08 = \$3.24$. Using the market capitalization rate of 14%, the value of the stock is

$$V_0 = \frac{D_1}{k - g} = \frac{\$3.24}{0.14 - 0.08} = \$54$$

If the stock is perceived to be riskier, its value must be lower. At the higher market capitalization rate of 16%, the stock is worth only

$$\frac{\$3.24}{0.16 - 0.08} = \$40.50$$

The constant growth DDM is valid only when g is less than k. If dividends were expected to grow forever at a rate faster than k, the value of the stock would be infinite. If an analyst derives an estimate of g that is greater than k, that growth rate must be unsustainable in the long run. The appropriate valuation model to use in this case is a multistage DDM such as that discussed below.

The constant growth DDM is so widely used by stock market analysts that it is worth exploring some of its implications and limitations. The constant growth rate DDM implies that a stock's value will be greater:

1. The larger its expected dividend per share.
2. The lower the market capitalization rate, k.
3. The higher the expected growth rate of dividends.

Another implication of the constant growth model is that the stock price is expected to grow at the same rate as dividends. To see this, suppose Steady State stock is selling at its intrinsic value of $57.14, so that $V_0 = P_0$. Then

$$P_0 = \frac{D_1}{k - g}$$

Note that price is proportional to dividends. Therefore, next year, when the dividends paid to Steady State stockholders are expected to be higher by $g = 5\%$, price also should increase by 5%. To confirm this, note

$$D_2 = \$4(1.05) = \$4.20$$

$$P_1 = D_2/(k - g) = \$4.20/(0.12 - 0.05) = \$60.00$$

which is 5% higher than the current price of $57.14. To generalize

$$P_1 = \frac{D_2}{k - g} = \frac{D_1(1 + g)}{k - g} = \frac{D_1}{k - g}(1 + g)$$

$$= P_0(1 + g)$$

Therefore, the DDM implies that, in the case of constant expected growth of dividends, the expected rate of price appreciation in any year will equal that constant growth rate, g. Note that for a stock whose market price equals its intrinsic value ($V_0 = P_0$) the expected holding-period return will be

$$E(r) = \text{Dividend yield} + \text{Capital gains yield}$$

$$= \frac{D_1}{P_0} + \frac{P_1 - P_0}{P_0} \tag{13.5}$$

$$= \frac{D_1}{P_0} + g$$

This formula offers a means to infer the market capitalization rate of a stock, for if the stock is selling at its intrinsic value, then $E(r) = k$, implying that $k = D_1/P_0 + g$. By observing the dividend yield, D_1/P_0, and estimating the growth rate of dividends, we can compute k. This equation also is known as the *discounted cash flow (DCF) formula*.

This is an approach often used in rate hearings for regulated public utilities. The regulatory agency responsible for approving utility pricing decisions is mandated to allow the firms to charge just enough to cover costs plus a "fair" profit, that is, one that allows a competitive return on the investment the firm has made in its productive capacity. In turn, that return is taken to be the expected return investors require on the stock of the firm. The $D_1/P_0 + g$ formula provides a means to infer that required return.

EXAMPLE 13.3
The Constant Growth Model

Suppose that Steady State Electronics wins a major contract for its revolutionary computer chip. The very profitable contract will enable it to increase the growth rate of dividends from 5% to 6% without reducing the current dividend from the projected value of $4.00 per share. What will happen to the stock price? What will happen to future expected rates of return on the stock?

The stock price ought to increase in response to the good news about the contract, and indeed it does. The stock price rises from its original value of $57.14 to a postannouncement price of

$$\frac{D_1}{k - g} = \frac{\$4.00}{0.12 - 0.06} = \$66.67$$

Investors who are holding the stock when the good news about the contract is announced will receive a substantial windfall.

On the other hand, at the new price the expected rate of return on the stock is 12%, just as it was before the new contract was announced.

$$E(r) = \frac{D_1}{P_0} + g = \frac{\$4.00}{\$66.67} + 0.06 = 0.12, \text{ or } 12\%$$

This result makes sense, of course. Once the news about the contract is reflected in the stock price, the expected rate of return will be consistent with the risk of the stock. Since the risk of the stock has not changed, neither should the expected rate of return.

Concept Check

2. *a.* IBX's stock dividend at the end of this year is expected to be $2.15, and it is expected to grow at 11.2% per year forever. If the required rate of return on IBX stock is 15.2% per year, what is its intrinsic value?
   b. If IBX's current market price is equal to this intrinsic value, what is next year's expected price?
   c. If an investor were to buy IBX stock now and sell it after receiving the $2.15 dividend a year from now, what is the expected capital gain (i.e., price appreciation) in percentage terms? What is the dividend yield, and what would be the holding-period return?

Stock Prices and Investment Opportunities

Consider two companies, Cash Cow, Inc., and Growth Prospects, each with expected earnings in the coming year of $5 per share. Both companies could in principle pay out all of these earnings as dividends, maintaining a perpetual dividend flow of $5 per share. If the market capitalization rate were $k = 12.5\%$, both companies would then be valued at $D_1/k = \$5/0.125 = \$40$ per share. Neither firm would grow in value, because with all earnings paid out as dividends, and no earnings reinvested in the firm, both companies' capital stock and earnings capacity would remain unchanged over time; earnings and dividends would not grow.

Actually, we are referring here to earnings net of the funds necessary to maintain the productivity of the firm's capital, that is, earnings net of "economic depreciation." In other words, the earnings figure should be interpreted as the maximum amount of money the firm could pay out each year in perpetuity without depleting its productive capacity. For this reason, the net earnings number may be quite different from the accounting earnings figure that the firm reports in its financial statements. (We explore this further in the next chapter.)

Now suppose one of the firms, Growth Prospects, engages in projects that generate a return on investment of 15%, which is greater than the required rate of return, $k = 12.5\%$. It would be foolish for such a company to pay out all of its earnings as dividends. If Growth Prospects retains or plows back some of its earnings into its highly profitable projects, it can earn a 15% rate of return for its shareholders, while if it pays out all earnings as dividends, it forgoes the projects, leaving shareholders to invest the dividends in other opportunities at a fair market rate of only 12.5%. Suppose, therefore, Growth Prospects lowers its **dividend payout ratio** (the fraction of earnings paid out as dividends) from 100% to 40%, maintaining a **plowback ratio** (the fraction of earnings reinvested in the firm) of 60%. The plowback ratio also is referred to as the **earnings retention ratio.**

The dividend of the company, therefore, will be $2 (40% of $5 earnings) instead of $5. Will share price fall? No—It will rise! Although dividends initially fall under the earnings reinvestment policy, subsequent growth in the assets of the firm because of reinvested profits will generate growth in future dividends, which will be reflected in today's share price.

Figure 13.1 illustrates the dividend streams generated by Growth Prospects under two dividend policies. A low reinvestment rate plan allows the firm to pay higher initial dividends but results in a lower dividend growth rate. Eventually, a high reinvestment rate plan will provide higher dividends. If the dividend growth generated by the reinvested earnings is high enough, the stock will be worth more under the high reinvestment strategy.

How much growth will be generated? Suppose Growth Prospects starts with plant and equipment of $100 million and is all equity financed. With a return on investment or equity (ROE) of 15%, total earnings are ROE × $100 million = 0.15 × $100 million = $15 million. There are 3 million shares of stock outstanding, so earnings per share are $5, as posited

dividend payout ratio
Percentage of earnings paid out as dividends.

plowback ratio or earnings retention ratio
The proportion of the firm's earnings that is reinvested in the business (and not paid out as dividends).

FIGURE 13.1
Dividend Growth for Two Earnings Reinvestment Policies

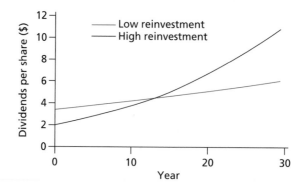

above. If 60% of the $15 million in this year's earnings is reinvested, then the value of the firm's capital stock will increase by $0.60 \times \$15$ million = $9 million, or by 9%. The percentage increase in the capital stock is the rate at which income was generated (ROE) times the plowback ratio (the fraction of earnings reinvested in more capital), which we will denote as b.

Now endowed with 9% more capital, the company earns 9% more income and pays out 9% higher dividends. The growth rate of the dividends, therefore, is

$$g = \text{ROE} \times b$$
$$= 0.15 \times 0.60 = 0.09$$

If the stock price equals its intrinsic value, and this growth rate can be sustained (i.e., if the ROE and payout ratios are consistent with the long-run capabilities of the firm), then the stock should sell at

$$P_0 = \frac{D_1}{k - g} = \frac{\$2}{0.125 - 0.09} = \$57.14$$

When Growth Prospects pursued a no-growth policy and paid out all earnings as dividends, the stock price was only $40. When it reduced current dividends and plowed funds back into the company, the growth rate increased enough to cause the stock price to increase.

The difference between the no-growth price of $40 and the actual price of $57.14 can be ascribed to the present value of the company's excellent investment opportunities. One way to think of the company's value is to describe its stock price as the sum of the no-growth value (the value of current earnings per share, E_1, in perpetuity) plus the present value of these growth opportunities, which we will denote as PVGO. In terms of the example we have been following, PVGO = $17.14

$$\text{Price} = \text{No-growth value per share} + \text{PVGO}$$

$$P_0 = \frac{E_1}{k} + \text{PVGO} \tag{13.6}$$

$$\$57.14 = \$40 + \$17.14$$

It is important to recognize that growth per se is not what investors desire. Growth enhances company value only if it is achieved by investment in projects with attractive profit opportunities (i.e., with ROE > k). To see why, let's now consider Growth Prospects' unfortunate sister company, Cash Cow. Cash Cow's ROE is only 12.5%, just equal to the required rate of return, k. The NPV of its investment opportunities is zero. We've seen that following a zero-growth strategy with $b = 0$ and $g = 0$, the value of Cash Cow will be $E_1/k = \$5/0.125 = \$40$ per share. Now suppose Cash Cow chooses a plowback ratio of $b = 0.60$, the same as Growth Prospects' plowback. Then g would be

$$g = \text{ROE} \times b = 0.125 \times 0.60 = 0.075$$

and the stock price becomes

$$P_0 = \frac{D_1}{k - g} = \frac{\$2}{0.125 - 0.075} = \$40$$

no different from the no-growth strategy.

In the case of Cash Cow, the dividend reduction that frees funds for reinvestment in the firm generates only enough growth to maintain the stock price at the current level. This is as it should be: If the firm's projects yield only what investors can earn on their own, shareholders cannot be made better off by a high reinvestment rate policy. This demonstrates that "growth" is not the same as growth opportunities. To justify reinvestment, the firm must engage in projects with better prospective returns than those shareholders can find elsewhere. Notice also that the PVGO of Cash Cow is zero: PVGO $= P_0 - E_1/k = 40 - 40 = 0$. With ROE $= k$, there is no advantage to plowing funds back into the firm; this shows up as PVGO of zero. In fact, this is why firms with considerable cash flow, but limited investment prospects, are called "cash cows." The cash these firms generate is best taken out of or "milked from" the firm.

EXAMPLE 13.4
Growth
Opportunities

Takeover Target is run by entrenched and incompetent management that insists on reinvesting 60% of its earnings in projects that provide an ROE of 10%, despite the fact that the firm's capitalization rate is $k = 15\%$. The firm's year-end dividend will be $2 per share, paid out of earnings of $5 per share. At what price will the stock sell? What is the present value of growth opportunities? Why would such a firm be a takeover target for another firm?

Given current management's investment policy, the dividend growth rate will be

$$g = \text{ROE} \times b = 10\% \times 0.6 = 6\%$$

and the stock price should be

$$P_0 = \frac{\$2}{0.15 - 0.06} = \$22.22$$

The present value of growth opportunities is

$$
\begin{aligned}
\text{PVGO} &= \text{Price per share} - \text{No-growth value per share} \\
&= \$22.22 - E_1/k \\
&= \$22.22 - \$5/0.15 \\
&= -\$11.11
\end{aligned}
$$

PVGO is *negative*. This is because the net present value of the firm's projects is negative: The rate of return on those assets is less than the opportunity cost of capital.

Such a firm would be subject to takeover, because another firm could buy the firm for the market price of $22.22 per share and increase the value of the firm by changing its investment policy. For example, if the new management simply paid out all earnings as dividends, the value of the firm would increase to its no-growth value, $E_1/k = \$5/0.15 = \$33.33$.

Concept Check

3. *a.* Calculate the price of a firm with a plowback ratio of 0.60 if its ROE is 20%. Current earnings, E_1, will be $5 per share, and $k = 12.5\%$.
   b. What if ROE is 10%, less than the market capitalization rate? Compare the firm's price in this instance to that of a firm with the same ROE and E_1, but a plowback ratio of $b = 0$.

Life Cycles and Multistage Growth Models

As useful as the constant growth DDM formula is, you need to remember that it is based on a simplifying assumption, namely, that the dividend growth rate will be constant forever. In fact, firms typically pass through life cycles with very different dividend profiles in different phases. In early years, there are ample opportunities for profitable reinvestment in the company. Payout ratios are low, and growth is correspondingly rapid. In later years, the firm matures, production capacity is sufficient to meet market demand, competitors enter the market, and attractive opportunities for reinvestment may become harder to find. In this mature phase, the firm may choose to increase the dividend payout ratio, rather than retain earnings. The dividend level increases, but thereafter it grows at a slower rate because of fewer company growth opportunities.

Table 13.2 demonstrates this profile. It gives Value Line's forecasts of return on assets, dividend payout ratio, and three-year growth rate in earnings per share of a sample of the firms included in the semiconductor industry versus those in the northeast region electric

TABLE 13.2

Financial Ratios in
Two Industries

Source: Value Line Investment
Survey, 1995.

	Return on Assets (%)	Payout Ratio (%)	Growth Rate 1995–1998 (%)
Semiconductors			
Analog Devices	16.5%	0.0%	11.6%
Cirrus Logic	18.0	0.0	7.7
Intel	24.0	4.0	9.8
Micron Technologies	22.5	5.0	9.7
Motorola	15.5	13.0	12.6
National Semiconductor	14.0	2.0	13.4
Novellus	16.0	0.0	11.3
Teradyne	19.0	0.0	3.1
Texas Instruments	18.5	13.0	3.4
Average	18.2%	4.1%	9.2%
Electric Utilities			
Boston Edison	8.0%	76.0%	1.9%
Central Maine Power	6.5	67.0	7.2
Central Vermont	8.0	55.0	6.1
Commonwealth Energy	8.0	70.0	0.7
Consolidated Edison	8.0	75.0	1.1
Eastern Utilities	8.0	69.0	4.2
Long Island Lighting	6.5	82.0	2.3
New England Electric	7.5	76.0	1.5
Northeastern Utilities	8.0	70.0	4.7
Average	7.6%	71.1%	3.3%

utility group. (We compare return on assets rather than return on equity because the latter is affected by leverage, which tends to be far greater in the electric utility industry than in the semiconductor industry. Return on assets measures operating income per dollar of total assets, regardless of whether the source of the capital supplied is debt or equity. We will return to this issue in the next chapter.)

The semiconductor firms as a group have had attractive investment opportunities. The average return on assets of these firms is forecast to be 18.2%, and the firms have responded with quite high plowback ratios. Many of these firms pay no dividends at all. The high returns on assets and high plowback ratios result in rapid growth. The average growth rate of earnings per share in this group is projected at 9.2%.

In contrast, the electric utilities are more representative of mature firms. For this industry, return on assets is lower, 7.6%; dividend payout is higher, 71.1%; and average growth is lower, 3.3%.

To value companies with temporarily high growth, analysts use a multistage version of the dividend discount model. Dividends in the early high-growth period are forecast and their combined present value is calculated. Then, once the firm is projected to settle down to a steady growth phase, the constant growth DDM is applied to value the remaining stream of dividends.

two-stage DDM
Dividend discount model in which dividend growth is assumed to level off only at some future date.

We can illustrate this with a real-life example using a **two-stage DDM.** Figure 13.2 is a Value Line Investment Survey report on Motorola, a designer and manufacturer of electronic equipment and components. Some of the relevant information in mid-1996 is highlighted.

Motorola's beta appears at the circled A, its recent stock price at the B, the per share dividend payments at the C, the ROE (referred to as percent earned on net worth) at the D, and the dividend payout ratio (referred to as percent of all dividends to net profits) at the E. The rows ending at C, D, and E are historical time series. The boldfaced italicized entries under 1997 are estimates for that year. Similarly, the entries in the far right column (labeled 99–01) are forecasts for some time between 1999 and 2001, which we will take to be 2000.

FIGURE 13.2   Value Line Investment Survey Report on Motorola

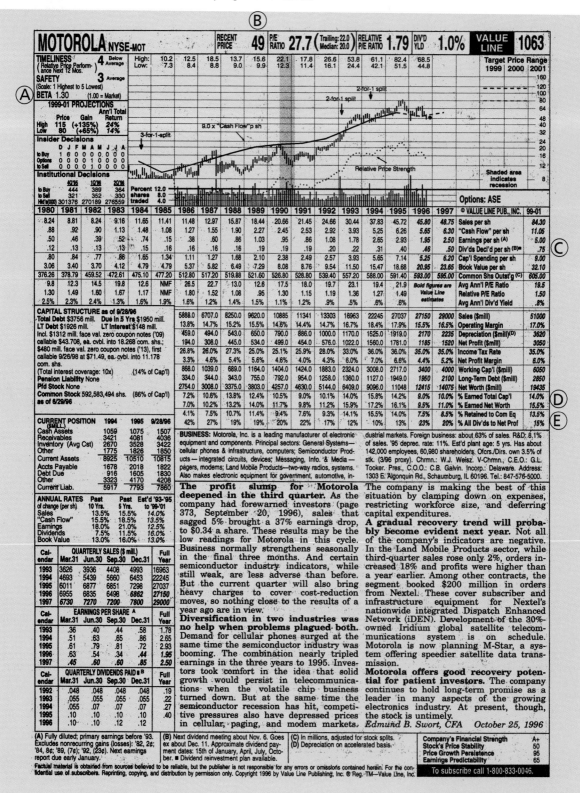

Note that while dividends are $0.50 per share for 1997, dividends forecast for 2000 are $0.75. If we use linear interpolation between 1997 and 2000, we obtain dividend forecasts as follows:

1997	$0.50
1998	$0.58
1999	$0.67
2000	$0.75

Now let us assume the dividend growth rate levels off in 2000. What is a good guess for that steady-state growth rate? Value Line forecasts a dividend payout ratio of 0.15 and an ROE of 15.5%, implying long-term growth will be

$$g = \text{ROE} \times b = 15.5\% \times (1 - 0.15) = 13.2\%$$

Our estimate of Motorola's intrinsic value using an investment horizon of 2000 is therefore obtained from Equation 13.2, which we restate here

$$V_{1996} = \frac{D_{1997}}{(1 + k)} + \frac{D_{1998}}{(1 + k)^2} + \frac{D_{1999}}{(1 + k)^3} + \frac{D_{2000} + P_{2000}}{(1 + k)^4}$$

$$= \frac{0.50}{1 + k} + \frac{0.58}{(1 + k)^2} + \frac{0.67}{(1 + k)^3} + \frac{0.75 + P_{2000}}{(1 + k)^4}$$

Here, P_{2000} represents the forecasted price at which we can sell our shares of Motorola at the end of 2000, when dividends enter their constant growth phase. That price, according to the constant growth DDM, should be

$$P_{2000} = \frac{D_{2001}}{k - g} = \frac{D_{2000}(1 + g)}{k - g} = \frac{0.75 \times 1.132}{k - 0.132}$$

The only variable remaining to be determined in order to calculate intrinsic value is the market capitalization rate, k.

One way to obtain k is from the CAPM. Observe from the Value Line data that Motorola's beta is 1.30. The risk-free rate in 1996 was about 5%. Suppose that the market risk premium were forecast at 7.5%.[2] This would imply that the forecast for the market return was

$$\text{Risk-free rate} + \text{Market risk premium} = 5\% + 7.5\% = 12.5\%$$

Therefore, we can solve for the market capitalization rate for Motorola as

$$k = r_f + \beta[E(r_M) - r_f]$$
$$= 5\% + 1.30(12.5\% - 5\%)$$
$$= 14.8\%$$

Our forecast for the stock price in 2000 is thus

$$P_{2000} = \frac{\$0.75 \times 1.132}{0.148 - 0.132} = \$53.06$$

and today's estimate of intrinsic value is

$$V_{1996} = \frac{0.50}{(1.148)} + \frac{0.58}{(1.148)^2} + \frac{0.67}{(1.148)^3} + \frac{0.75 + 53.06}{(1.148)^4} = \$32.30$$

---

[2]The historical risk premium on the market portfolio has been closer to 8.5%. However, stock analysts in 1996 were relatively pessimistic about market performance over the near term. While the historical risk premium is a guide as to the typical risk premium one might expect from the market, there is no reason that the risk premium cannot vary somewhat from period to period.

We know from the Value Line report that Motorola's actual price was $49 (at the circled B). Our intrinsic value analysis indicates Motorola was overpriced. Should we sell our holdings of Motorola or even sell Motorola short?

Perhaps. But before betting the farm, stop to consider how firm our estimate is. We've had to guess at dividends in the near future, the ultimate growth rate of those dividends, and the appropriate discount rate. Moreover, we've assumed Motorola will follow a relatively simple two-stage growth process. In practice, the growth of dividends can follow more complicated patterns. Even small errors in these approximations could upset a conclusion.

For example, suppose Motorola's true beta is slightly lower than our estimate, 1.20 rather than 1.30. This seemingly minor change will reduce the discount rate to 14.0%. At this lower rate, the intrinsic value of the stock based on the two-stage growth model rises to $64.62, which actually is greater than the stock price at the time. Therefore, our conclusion regarding intrinsic value versus price is reversed.

This exercise shows that finding bargains is not as easy as it seems. While the DDM is easy to apply, establishing its inputs is more of a challenge. This should not be surprising. In even a moderately efficient market, finding profit opportunities has to be more involved than sitting down with Value Line for a half hour.

The exercise also highlights the importance of assessing the sensitivity of your analysis to changes in underlying assumptions when you attempt to value stocks. Your estimates of stock values are no better than your assumptions. Sensitivity analysis will highlight the inputs that need to be most carefully examined. For example, we just found that very small changes in the estimated risk of the stock result in big changes in intrinsic value. Similarly, small changes in the assumed growth rate change intrinsic value substantially. On the other hand, reasonable changes in the dividends forecast between 1997 and 2000 have a small impact on intrinsic value.

Concept Check

4. Confirm that the intrinsic value of Motorola using $\beta = 1.20$ is $64.62. (Hint: First calculate the discount rate and stock price in 2000. Then calculate the present value of all interim dividends plus the present value of the 2000 sales price.)

13.4 PRICE/EARNINGS RATIOS

The Price/Earnings Ratio and Growth Opportunities

price/earnings multiple
The ratio of a stock's price to its earnings per share.

Much of the real-world discussion of stock market valuation concentrates on the firm's **price/earnings multiple,** the ratio of price per share to earnings per share. In fact, one common approach to valuing a firm is to use an earnings multiplier. The value of the stock is obtained by multiplying projected earnings per share by a forecast of the price/earnings ratio. This procedure seems simple, but its apparent simplicity is deceptive. First, forecasting earnings is challenging. As we saw in the previous chapter, earnings will depend on international, macroeconomic, and industry as well as firm-specific factors, many of which are highly unpredictable. Second, forecasting the P/E multiple is even more difficult. P/E ratios vary across industries and over time. Nevertheless, our discussion of stock valuation provides some insight into the factors that ought to determine a firm's P/E ratio.

Recall our discussion of growth opportunities, in which we compared two firms, Growth Prospects and Cash Cow, each of which had earnings per share of $5. Growth Prospects reinvested 60% of its earnings in prospects with an ROE of 15%, while Cash Cow paid out all of its earnings as dividends. Cash Cow had a price of $40, giving it a P/E multiple of 40/5 = 8.0, while Growth Prospects sold for $57.14, giving it a multiple of 57.14/5 = 11.4. This observation suggests the P/E ratio might serve as a useful indicator of expectations of growth opportunities. We can see this explicitly by rearranging Equation 13.6 to

$$\frac{P_0}{E_1} = \frac{1}{k}\left[1 + \frac{PVGO}{E/k}\right] \tag{13.7}$$

When PVGO = 0, Equation 13.7 shows that $P_0 = E_1/k$. The stock is valued like a nongrowing perpetuity of EPS_1. The P/E ratio is just $1/k$. However, as PVGO becomes an increasingly dominant contributor to price, the P/E ratio can rise dramatically. The ratio of PVGO to E/k has a simple interpretation. It is the ratio of the component of firm value reflecting growth opportunities to the component of value reflecting assets already in place (i.e., the no-growth value of the firm, E/k). When future growth opportunities dominate the estimate of total value, the firm will command a high price relative to current earnings. Thus, a high P/E multiple appears to indicate that a firm is endowed with ample growth opportunities.

EXAMPLE 13.5 **P/E Ratios and** **Growth** **Opportunities**

Return again to Takeover Target, the firm we first encountered in Example 13.4. Earnings are $5 per share, and the capitalization rate is 15%, implying that the no-growth value of the firm is $E_1/k = \$5/0.15 = \$33.33$. The stock price actually is $22.22, implying that the present value of growth opportunities equals − $11.11. This implies that the P/E ratio should be

$$\frac{P_0}{E_1} = \frac{1}{k} \left[1 + \frac{PVGO}{E/k} \right] = \frac{1}{0.15} \left[1 + \frac{-\$11.11}{\$33.33} \right] = 4.44$$

In fact, the stock price is $22.22 and earnings are $5 per share, so the P/E ratio is $22.22/$5 = 4.44.

Let's see if P/E multiples do vary with growth prospects. In mid-1996, Motorola's P/E ratio was 19 while Boston Edison's was 10. These numbers do not necessarily imply that Motorola was overpriced compared to Boston Edison. If investors believed at the time that Motorola would grow faster than Boston Edison, the higher P/E multiple would be justified. That is, an investor might well pay a higher price per dollar of *current* earnings if he or she expects that earnings stream to grow rapidly. In fact, Motorola's growth rate has been consistent with its higher P/E multiple. Its earnings per share grew sixfold between 1980 and 1996, while Boston Edison's earnings grew only 3%. Figure 13.4, page 373, shows the EPS history of the two companies.

Clearly, it is differences in expected growth opportunities that justify particular differentials in P/E ratios across firms. The P/E ratio actually is a reflection of the market's optimism concerning a firm's growth prospects. In their use of a P/E ratio, analysts must decide whether they are more or less optimistic than the market. If they are more optimistic, they will recommend buying the stock.

There is a way to make these insights more precise. Look again at the constant growth DDM formula, $P_0 = D_1/(k - g)$. Now recall that dividends equal the earnings that are *not* reinvested in the firm: $D_1 = E_1(1 - b)$. Recall also that $g = ROE \times b$. Hence, substituting for D_1 and g, we find that

$$P_0 = \frac{E_1(1 - b)}{k - (ROE \times b)}$$

implying that the P/E ratio for a firm growing at a long-run sustainable pace is

$$\frac{P_0}{E_1} = \frac{1 - b}{k - (ROE \times b)} \tag{13.8}$$

It is easy to verify that the P/E ratio increases with ROE. This makes sense, because high ROE projects give the firm good opportunities for growth.[3] We also can verify that the P/E ratio increases for higher b as long as ROE exceeds k. This too makes sense. When a firm has good investment opportunities, the market will reward it with a higher P/E multiple if it exploits those opportunities more aggressively by plowing back more earnings into those opportunities.

Remember we noted, however, that growth is not desirable for its own sake. Examine Table 13.3, where we use Equation 13.8 to compute both growth rates and P/E ratios for

---

[3]Note that Equation 13.8 is a simple rearrangement of the DDM formula, with $ROE \times b = g$. Because that formula requires that $g < k$, Equation 13.8 is valid only when $ROE \times b < k$.

TABLE 13.3

Effect of ROE and Plowback on Growth and the P/E Ratio

	Plowback Ratio (b)			
	0	**0.25**	**0.50**	**0.75**
A. Growth Rate, g				
ROE				
10%	0%	2.5%	5.0%	7.5%
12	0	3.0	6.0	9.0
14	0	3.5	7.0	10.5
B. P/E Ratio				
ROE				
10%	8.33	7.89	7.14	5.56
12	8.33	8.33	8.33	8.33
14	8.33	8.82	10.00	16.67

Note: Assumption: k = 12% per year.

different combinations of ROE and b. While growth always increases with the plowback ratio (move across the rows in Panel A of Table 13.3), the P/E ratio does not (move across the rows in Panel B). In the top row of Table 13.3B, the P/E falls as the plowback rate increases. In the middle row, it is unaffected by plowback. In the third row, it increases.

This pattern has a simple interpretation. When the expected ROE is less than the required return, k, investors prefer that the firm pay out earnings as dividends rather than reinvest earnings in the firm at an inadequate rate of return. That is, for ROE lower than k, the value of the firm falls as plowback increases. Conversely, when ROE exceeds k, the firm offers superior investment opportunities, so the value of the firm is enhanced as those opportunities are more fully exploited by increasing the plowback ratio.

Finally, where ROE just equals k, the firm offers "break-even" investment opportunities with a fair rate of return. In this case, investors are indifferent between reinvestment of earnings in the firm or elsewhere at the market capitalization rate, because the rate of return in either case is 12%. Therefore, the stock price is unaffected by the plowback ratio.

One way to summarize these relationships is to say the higher the plowback ratio, the higher the growth rate, but a higher plowback ratio does not necessarily mean a higher P/E ratio. A higher plowback ratio increases P/E only if investments undertaken by the firm offer an expected rate of return higher than the market capitalization rate. Otherwise, higher plowback hurts investors because it means more money is sunk into prospects with inadequate rates of return.

Notwithstanding these fine points, P/E ratios commonly are taken as proxies for the expected growth in dividends or earnings. In fact, a common Wall Street rule of thumb is that the growth rate ought to be roughly equal to the P/E ratio. Peter Lynch, the famous portfolio manager, puts it this way in his book *One Up on Wall Street*:

> The P/E ratio of any company that's fairly priced will equal its growth rate. I'm talking here about growth rate of earnings . . . If the P/E ratio of Coca-Cola is 15, you'd expect the company to be growing at about 15% per year, etc. But if the P/E ratio is less than the growth rate, you may have found yourself a bargain (p. 198).

Let's try his rule of thumb.

EXAMPLE 13.6
P/E Ratio versus Growth Rate

Assume: r_f = 8% (about the value when Peter Lynch was writing)

$r_M - r_f$ = 8% (about the historical average market risk premium)

b = 0.4 (a typical value for the plowback ratio in the U.S.)

Therefore, $r_M = r_f$ + Market risk premium = 8% + 8% = 16%, and k = 16% for an average (β = 1) company. If we also accept as reasonable that ROE = 16% (the same value as the expected return on the stock) we conclude that

$$g = \text{ROE} \times b = 16\% \times 0.4 = 6.4\%$$

and

$$P/E = \frac{1 - 0.4}{0.16 - 0.064} = 6.26$$

Thus the P/E ratio and g are about equal using these assumptions, consistent with the rule of thumb. However, note that this rule of thumb, like almost all others, will not work in all circumstances. For example, the value of r_f today is more like 5%, so a comparable forecast of r_M today would be:

$$r_f + \text{Market risk premium} = 5\% + 8\% = 13\%$$

If we continue to focus on a firm with $\beta = 1$, and ROE still is about the same as k, then

$$g = 13\% \times 0.4 = 5.2\%$$

while

$$P/E = \frac{1 - 0.4}{0.13 - 0.052} = 7.69$$

The P/E ratio and g now diverge. Nevertheless, it still is the case that high P/E stocks are almost invariably expected to show rapid earnings growth, even if the expected growth rate does not precisely equal the P/E ratio.

Concept Check

5. ABC stock has an expected ROE of 12% per year, expected earnings per share of $2, and expected dividends of $1.50 per share. Its market capitalization rate is 10% per year.
   a. What are its expected growth rate, its price, and its P/E ratio?
   b. If the plowback rate were 0.4, what would be the firm's expected dividend per share, growth rate, price, and P/E ratio?

P/E Ratios and Stock Risk

One important implication of any stock valuation model is that (holding all else equal) riskier stocks will have lower P/E multiples. We can see this quite easily in the context of the constant growth model by examining the formula for the P/E ratio (Equation 13.8):

$$\frac{P}{E} = \frac{1 - b}{k - g}$$

Riskier firms will have higher required rates of return (i.e., higher values of k). Therefore, their P/E multiples will be lower. This is true even outside the context of the constant growth model. For *any* expected earnings and dividend stream, the present value of those cash flows will be lower when the stream is perceived to be riskier. Hence the stock price and the ratio of price to earnings will be lower.

Of course, if you scan *The Wall Street Journal*, you will observe many small, risky, start-up companies with very high P/E multiples. This does not contradict our claim that P/E multiples should fall with risk: Instead, it is evidence of the market's expectations of high growth rates for those companies. This is why we said that high risk firms will have lower P/E ratios *holding all else equal*. Holding the projection of growth fixed, the P/E multiple will be lower when risk is perceived to be higher.

Pitfalls in P/E Analysis

No description of P/E analysis is complete without mentioning some of its pitfalls. First, consider that the denominator in the P/E ratio is accounting earnings, which are influenced by somewhat arbitrary accounting rules such as the use of historical cost in depreciation and

FIGURE 13.3

P/E Ratios and Inflation

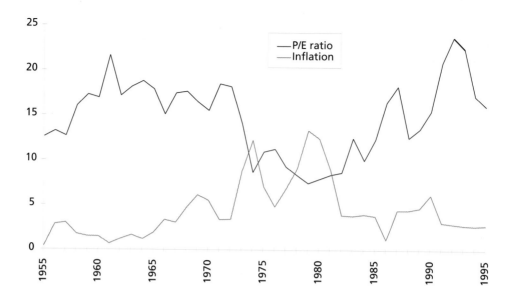

inventory valuation. In times of high inflation, historic cost depreciation and inventory costs will tend to underrepresent true economic values because the replacement cost of both goods and capital equipment will rise with the general level of prices. As Figure 13.3 demonstrates, P/E ratios have tended to be lower when inflation has been higher. This reflects the market's assessment that earnings in these periods are of "lower quality," artificially distorted by inflation, and warranting lower P/E ratios.

Another confounding factor in the use of P/E ratios is related to the business cycle. We were careful in deriving the DDM to define earnings as being net of *economic* depreciation, that is, the maximum flow of income that the firm could pay out without depleting its productive capacity. And reported earnings, as we note above, are computed in accordance with generally accepted accounting principles and need not correspond to economic earnings. Beyond this, however, notions of a normal or justified P/E ratio, as in Equations 13.7 or 13.8, assume implicitly that earnings rise at a constant rate, or, put another way, on a smooth trend line. In contrast, reported earnings can fluctuate dramatically around a trend line over the course of the business cycle.

Another way to make this point is to note that the "normal" P/E ratio predicted by Equation 13.8 is the ratio of today's price to the trend value of future earnings, E_1. The P/E ratio reported in the financial pages of the newspaper, by contrast, is the ratio of price to the most recent *past* accounting earnings. Current accounting earnings can differ considerably from future economic earnings. Because ownership of stock conveys the right to future as well as current earnings, the ratio of price to most recent earnings can vary substantially over the business cycle, as accounting earnings and the trend value of economic earnings diverge by greater and lesser amounts.

As an example, Figure 13.4 graphs the earnings per share of Motorola and Boston Edison since 1980. Note that Motorola's EPS fluctuate considerably. This reflects the company's relatively high degree of sensitivity to the business cycle. Value Line estimates its beta at 1.30. Boston Edison, by contrast, shows much less variation in earnings per share around a smoother and flatter trend line. Its beta was only 0.75.

Because the market values the entire stream of future dividends generated by the company, when earnings are temporarily depressed, the P/E ratio should tend to be high—that is, the denominator of the ratio responds more sensitively to the business cycle than the numerator. This pattern is borne out well.

Figure 13.5 graphs the Motorola and Boston Edison P/E ratios. Motorola, with the more volatile earnings profile, also has a more volatile P/E profile. For example, in 1985, when

FIGURE 13.4

Earnings Growth for Two Companies

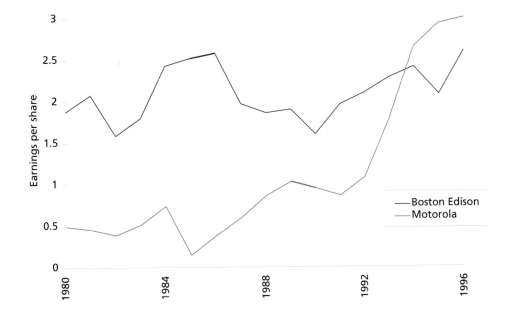

FIGURE 13.5

Price/Earnings Ratios

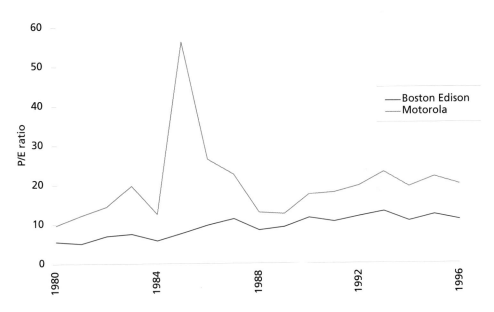

EPS fell to a far-below-trend value of $0.15, the P/E rose to 56.3. The market clearly recognized that earnings were depressed only temporarily.

This example shows why analysts must be careful in using P/E ratios. There is no way to say a P/E ratio is overly high or low without referring to the company's long-run growth prospects, as well as to current earnings per share relative to the long-run trend line.

Nevertheless, Figures 13.4 and 13.5 demonstrate a clear relationship between P/E ratios and growth. Despite considerable short-run fluctuations, Motorola's EPS clearly trended upward over the period. Its compound rate of growth between 1980 and 1996 was 11.8%. Boston Edison's earnings grew far less rapidly, with a 15-year average growth rate of 2.0%. The growth prospects of Motorola are reflected in its consistently higher P/E multiple.

This analysis suggests that P/E ratios should vary across industries and, in fact, they do. Figure 13.6 shows P/E ratios in early 1996 for a sample of industries. P/E ratios for each industry are computed in two ways: by taking the ratio of price to previous year earnings,

FIGURE 13.6

P/E Ratios Based on
1996 and 1997 EPS

Source: Institutional Brokers
Estimate System (I/B/E/S),
U.S. Comments, March 27,
1996.

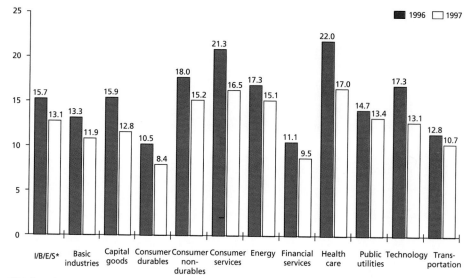

*Data for entire sector.

and projected next-year earnings. Notice that while the ratios based on 1996 earnings appear quite high, the ratios are far more moderate when prices are compared to 1997 earnings. This should not surprise you, since stock market prices are based on firms' future earnings prospects.

Combining P/E Analysis and the DDM

Some analysts use P/E ratios in conjunction with earnings forecasts to estimate the price of stock at an investor's horizon date. The Motorola analysis in Figure 13.2 shows that Value Line forecasted a P/E ratio for 2000 of 19.5. EPS for 2000 were forecast at $5.25, implying a price in 2000 of 19.5 × $5.25 = $102.38. Given an estimate of $102.38 for the 2000 sales price, we would compute Motorola's intrinsic value as

$$V_{1996} = \frac{\$0.44}{(1.141)} + \frac{\$0.50}{(1.141)^2} + \frac{\$0.58}{(1.141)^3} + \frac{\$0.65 + \$102.38}{(1.141)^4} = \$61.96$$

The box on page 375 discusses the relative merits and shortcomings of some of the indicators of stock market valuation that we have discussed in this chapter: the price-to-book ratio, dividend yield, and the price/earnings ratio. The article points out that the "justifiable" P/E ratio depends on the levels of both interest and inflation rates. In fact, the "rule of 20" discussed in the article is consistent with the relationship between P/E ratios and inflation depicted above in Figure 13.3.

13.5 THE AGGREGATE STOCK MARKET

The most popular approach to forecasting the overall stock market is the earnings multiplier approach applied at the aggregate level. The first step is to forecast corporate profits for the coming period. Then we derive an estimate of the earnings multiplier, the aggregate P/E ratio, based on a forecast of long-term interest rates. The product of the two forecasts is the estimate of the end-of-period level of the market.

The forecast of the P/E ratio of the market is sometimes derived from a graph similar to that in Figure 13.7, which plots the *earnings yield* (earnings per share divided by price per share, the reciprocal of the P/E ratio) of the S&P 500 and the yield to maturity on 10-year

Flaws in Market Gauges Make Stocks Seem Expensive

Even before last week's impressive rally, the stock market was outrageously expensive. At least that's what some key market yardsticks show.

But hold on to your sell orders. Many investment experts reckon the fault lies not with the market, but with the measuring sticks. In particular, these experts see serious shortcomings in three popular stock market gauges: the price-to-book value ratio, dividend yield, and the price-to-earnings multiple.

The three standard measures "are all flawed in some way," says Frazier Evans, senior economist at Colonial Group, the Boston mutual fund company. "You have to look under the surface. I'd say that the market is not as expensive as it looks."

DWINDLING DIVIDENDS

Consider, for instance, the market's dividend yield. The companies in the Standard & Poor's 500 stock index are paying annual dividends amounting to 2.8% of their current stock prices. That's well below the historical average dividend yield of 4.7%.

A danger signal? Maybe not. The reason is that corporations seem to be paying out far less of their earnings as dividends these days. Instead, companies are using profits to expand their businesses and buy their own shares—actions designed to boost stock prices.

EFFECT ON BOOK VALUE

At first blush, the market's price-to-book value also suggests shares are richly priced. Bargain hunters often look for stocks that are trading below book value, which is the difference between a company's assets and its liabilities expressed on a per-share basis.

But these days, precious few stocks trade below book value. But once again, the measuring gauge may be faulty. Book value has been distorted by share repurchases, special charges due to corporate restructurings, and the adoption of a new accounting rule concerning retiree health benefits.

What about price-to-earnings multiples? Right now, the market is trading at about 15 times expected 1995 earnings, a tad above the historical average. "There are fewer problems with P/E ratios than with the other two measures," says Kathleen Crowley, a senior vice president with Chicago's Stratford Advisory Group.

Even so, earnings multiples also can mislead. In recent years, reported earnings have been depressed by special charges. In addition, experts say the market's earnings multiple shouldn't be viewed in isolation, but instead should be considered in the context of items like interest rates and inflation.

Colonial's Mr. Evans thinks the inflation rate is especially important. "When inflation has been high, price/earnings ratios have been low," he says. "And when inflation is low, price/earnings ratios have been high."

THE RULE OF 20

Mr. Evans says, "this relationship can be summed up in the rule of 20," which states that "you take 20, subtract the consumer price index, and you have the P/E for the market."

With inflation expected to run between 3 and 3.5% this year, the rule of 20 indicates the market would be fairly priced at a P/E as high as 17.

Source: Jonathan Clements, *The Wall Street Journal*, February 7, 1995. Reprinted by permission of *The Wall Street Journal.* © 1995 Dow Jones & Company, Inc. All Rights Reserved Worldwide.

Treasury bonds. The figure shows that both yields rose dramatically in the 1970s. In the case of Treasury bonds, this was because of an increase in the inflationary expectations built into interest rates. The earnings yield on the S&P 500, however, probably rose because of inflationary distortions that artificially increased reported earnings. We have already seen that P/E ratios tend to fall when inflation rates increase. For most of the 1980s, the earnings yield ran about one percentage point below the T-bond rate.

One might use this relationship and the current yield on 10-year Treasury bonds to forecast the earnings yield on the S&P 500. Given that earnings yield, a forecast of earnings could be used to predict the level of the S&P in some future period. Let's consider a simple example of this procedure.

FIGURE 13.7
Earnings Yield of S&P
500 versus Treasury
Bond Yield

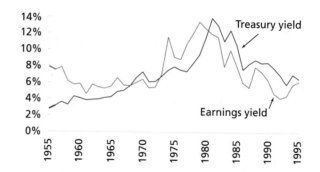

TABLE 13.4
S&P 500 Price
Forecasts under
Various Scenarios

	Most Likely Scenario	Pessimistic Scenario	Optimistic Scenario
Treasury bond yield	6.5%	7.0%	6.0%
Earnings yield	5.5%	6.0%	5.0%
Resulting P/E ratio	18.2	16.7	20.0
EPS forecast	$ 38.09	$ 38.09	$ 38.09
Forecast for S&P 500	693	636	762

Note: The forecast for the earnings yield on the S&P 500 equals the Treasury bond yield minus 1%. The P/E ratio is the reciprocal of the forecasted earnings yield.

EXAMPLE 13.7
Forecasting the
Aggregate Stock
Market

The mid-1996 forecast for 1996 earnings per share for the S&P 500 portfolio was about $38.09.[4] The 10-year Treasury bond yield in mid-1996 was about 6.5%. Since the earnings yield on the S&P 500 has been about one percentage point below the 10-year Treasury yield, a first guess for the earnings yield on the S&P 500 might be 5.5%. This would imply a P/E ratio of 1/0.055 = 18.2. Our forecast for the P/E of the S&P 500 portfolio would then be 18.2 × 38.09 = 693.

Of course, there is uncertainty regarding all three inputs into this analysis: the actual earnings on the S&P 500 stocks, the level of Treasury yields at year end, and the spread between the Treasury yield and the earnings yield. One would wish to perform sensitivity or scenario analysis to examine the impact of changes in all of these variables. To illustrate, consider Table 13.4, which shows a simple scenario analysis treating possible effects of variation in the Treasury bond yield. The scenario analysis shows that the forecasted level of the stock market varies inversely and with dramatic sensitivity to interest rate changes.

Some analysts use an aggregate version of the dividend discount model rather than an earnings multiplier approach. All of these models, however, rely heavily on forecasts of such macroeconomic variables as GDP, interest rates, and the rate of inflation, which are difficult to predict accurately.

Because stock prices reflect expectations of future dividends, which are tied to the economic fortunes of firms, it is not surprising that the performance of a broad-based stock index like the S&P 500 is taken as a leading economic indicator, that is, a predictor of the performance of the aggregate economy. Stock prices are viewed as embodying consensus forecasts of economic activity and are assumed to move up or down in anticipation of movements in the economy. The government's index of leading economic indicators, which is taken to predict the progress of the business cycle, is made up in part of recent stock market performance. However, the predictive value of the market is far from perfect. A well-known joke, often attributed to Paul Samuelson, is that the market has forecast eight of the last five recessions.

---

[4]According to Institutional Brokers Estimate System (I/B/E/S), as of March 1996, I/B/E/S surveys a large sample of stock analysts and reports several analyses of their forecasts for both the economy and individual stocks.

Summary

- One approach to firm valuation is to focus on the firm's book value, either as it appears on the balance sheet or adjusted to reflect the current replacement cost of assets or the liquidation value. Another approach is to focus on the present value of expected future dividends.
- The dividend discount model holds that the price of a share of stock should equal the present value of all future dividends per share, discounted at an interest rate commensurate with the risk of the stock.
- The constant growth version of the DDM asserts that, if dividends are expected to grow at a constant rate forever, then the intrinsic value of the stock is determined by the formula

$$V_0 = \frac{D_1}{k - g}$$

This version of the DDM is simplistic in its assumption of a constant value of g. There are more sophisticated multistage versions of the model for more complex environments. When the constant growth assumption is reasonably satisfied, the formula can be inverted to infer the market capitalization rate for the stock

$$k = \frac{D_1}{P_0} + g$$

- Stock market analysts devote considerable attention to a company's price/earnings ratio. The P/E ratio is a useful measure of the market's assessment of the firm's growth opportunities. Firms with no growth opportunities should have a P/E ratio that is just the reciprocal of the capitalization rate, k. As growth opportunities become a progressively more important component of the total value of the firm, the P/E ratio will increase.
- The models presented in this chapter can be used to explain or to forecast the behavior of the aggregate stock market. The key macroeconomic variables that determine the level of stock prices in the aggregate are interest rates and corporate profits.

Key Terms

book value, *355*
constant growth DDM, *359*
dividend discount model (DDM), *359*
dividend payout ratio, *362*

earnings retention ratio, *362*
intrinsic value, *357*
liquidation value, *356*
market capitalization rate, *357*

plowback ratio, *362*
price/earnings multiple, *368*
replacement cost, *356*
Tobin's *q*, *356*
two-stage DDM, *365*

Problem Sets

1. *a.* Computer stocks currently provide an expected rate of return of 16%. MBI, a large computer company, will pay a year-end dividend of $2 per share. If the stock is selling at $50 per share, what must be the market's expectation of the growth rate of MBI dividends?

   b. If dividend growth forecasts for MBI are revised downward to 5% per year, what will happen to the price of MBI stock? What (qualitatively) will happen to the company's price/earnings ratio?

2. Explain why the following statements are true/false/uncertain.

   a. Holding all else constant, a firm will have a higher P/E if its beta is higher.

   b. P/E will tend to be higher when ROE is higher (assuming plowback is positive).

   c. P/E will tend to be higher when the plowback rate is higher.

3. Even Better Products has come out with a new and improved product. As a result, the firm projects an ROE of 20%, and it will maintain a plowback ratio of 0.30. Its earnings this year will be $2 per share. Investors expect a 12% rate of return on the stock.
   a. At what price and P/E ratio would you expect the firm to sell?
   b. What is the present value of growth opportunities?
   c. What would be the P/E ratio and the present value of growth opportunities if the firm planned to reinvest only 20% of its earnings?

4. a. MF Corp. has an ROE of 16% and a plowback ratio of 50%. If the coming year's earnings are expected to be $2 per share, at what price will the stock sell? The market capitalization rate is 12%.
   b. What price do you expect MF shares to sell for in three years?

5. The constant growth dividend discount model can be used both for the valuation of companies and for the estimation of the long-term total return of a stock.

   Assume:

   > $20 = Price of a stock today

   > 8% = Expected growth rate of dividends

   > $0.60 = Annual dividend one year forward

   a. Using *only* the above data, compute the expected long-term total return on the stock using the constant growth dividend discount model. Show calculations.
   b. Briefly discuss two disadvantages of the constant growth dividend discount model in its application to investment analysis.
   c. Identify two alternative methods to the dividend discount model for the valuation of companies.

6. The market consensus is that Analog Electronic Corporation has an ROE = 9% and a beta of 1.25. It plans to maintain indefinitely its traditional plowback ratio of 2/3. This year's earnings were $3 per share. The annual dividend was just paid. The consensus estimate of the coming year's market return is 14%, and T-bills currently offer a 6% return.
   a. Find the price at which Analog stock should sell.
   b. Calculate the P/E ratio.
   c. Calculate the present value of growth opportunities.
   d. Suppose your research convinces you Analog will announce momentarily that it will immediately reduce its plowback ratio to 1/3. Find the intrinsic value of the stock. The market is still unaware of this decision. Explain why V_0 no longer equals P_0 and why V_0 is greater or less than P_0.

7. If the expected rate of return of the market portfolio is 15% and a stock with a beta of 1.0 pays a dividend yield of 4%, what must the market believe is the expected rate of price appreciation on that stock?

8. The FI Corporation's dividends per share are expected to grow indefinitely by 5% per year.
   a. If this year's year-end dividend is $8 and the market capitalization rate is 10% per year, what must the current stock price be according to the DDM?
   b. If the expected earnings per share are $12, what is the implied value of the ROE on future investment opportunities?
   c. How much is the market paying per share for growth opportunities (that is, for an ROE on future investments that exceeds the market capitalization rate)?

9. Using the data provided, discuss whether the common stock of United States Tobacco Company is attractively priced based on at least three different valuation approaches. (Hint: Use the asset value, DDM, and earnings multiplier approaches.)

	U.S. Tobacco	S&P 500
Recent price	$27.00	$ 290
Book value per share	$ 6.42	
Liquidation value per share	$ 4.90	
Replacement costs of assets per share	$ 9.15	
Anticipated next year's dividend	$ 1.20	$ 8.75
Estimated annual growth in dividends and earnings	10.0%	7.0%
Required return	13.0%	
Estimated next year's EPS	$ 2.40	$ 16.50
P/E ratio based on next year's earnings	11.3	17.6
Dividend yield	4.4%	3.0%

10. The risk-free rate of return is 10%, the required rate of return on the market is 15%, and High-Flyer stock has a beta coefficient of 1.5. If the dividend per share expected during the coming year, D_1, is $2.50 and $g = 5\%$, at what price should a share sell?

11. Your preliminary analysis of two stocks has yielded the information set forth below. The market capitalization rate for both stock A and stock B is 10% per year.

	Stock A	Stock B
Expected return on equity, ROE	14%	12%
Estimated earnings per share, E_1	$ 2.00	$ 1.65
Estimated dividends per share, D_1	$ 1.00	$ 1.00
Current market price per share, P_0	$27.00	$25.00

a. What are the expected dividend payout ratios for the two stocks?
b. What are the expected dividend growth rates of each?
c. What is the intrinsic value of each stock?
d. In which, if either, of the two stocks would you choose to invest?

12. The Tennant Company, founded in 1870, has evolved into the leading producer of large-sized floor sweepers and scrubbers, which are ridden by their operators. Some of the firm's financial data are presented in the following table:

Tennant Company
Selected Historic Operating and Balance Sheet Data (000s Omitted)
As of December 31

	1985	1990	1995
Net sales	$47,909	$109,333	$166,924
Cost of goods sold	27,395	62,373	95,015
Gross profits	20,514	46,960	71,909
Selling, general, and administrative expenses	11,895	29,649	54,151
Earnings before interest and taxes	8,619	17,311	17,758
Interest on long-term debt	0	53	248
Pretax income	8,619	17,258	17,510
Income taxes	4,190	7,655	7,692
After-tax income	$ 4,429	$ 9,603	$ 9,818
Total assets	$33,848	$ 63,555	$106,098
Total common stockholders' equity	25,722	46,593	69,516
Long-term debt	6	532	2,480
Total common shares outstanding	5,654	5,402	5,320
Earnings per share	$ .78	$ 1.78	$ 1.85
Dividends per share	.28	.72	.96
Book value per share	4.55	8.63	13.07

a. Based on these data, calculate a value for Tennant common stock by applying the constant growth dividend discount model. Assume an investor's required rate of return is a five percentage point premium over the current risk-free rate of return of 7%.

b. To your disappointment, the calculation you completed in part (a) results in a value below the stock's current market price. Consequently, you apply the constant growth DDM using the same required rate of return as in your calculation for part (a), but using the company's stated goal of earning 20% per year on stockholders' equity and maintaining a 35% dividend payout ratio. However, you find you are unable to calculate a meaningful answer. Explain why you cannot calculate a meaningful answer, and identify an alternative DDM that may provide a meaningful answer.

13. You are a portfolio manager considering the purchase of Nucor common stock. Nucor is the preeminent "minimill" steel producer in the United States. Minimills use scrap steel as their raw material and produce a limited number of products, primarily for the construction market. You are provided the following information:

Nucor Corporation	
Stock price (Dec. 30, 1997)	$ 53.00
1998 estimated earnings	$ 4.25
1998 estimated book value	$ 25.00
Indicated dividend	$ 0.40
Beta	1.10
Risk-free return	7.0%
High grade corporate bond yield	9.0%
Risk premium—stocks over bonds	5.0%

a. Calculate the expected stock market return. Show your calculations.
b. Calculate the implied total return of Nucor stock.
c. Calculate the required return of Nucor stock using the security market line model (see Chapter 8).
d. Briefly discuss the attractiveness of Nucor based on these data.

14. The stock of Nogro Corporation is currently selling for $10 per share. Earnings per share in the coming year are expected to be $2. The company has a policy of paying out 50% of its earnings each year in dividends. The rest is retained and invested in projects that earn a 20% rate of return per year. This situation is expected to continue indefinitely.

a. Assuming the current market price of the stock reflects its intrinsic value as computed using the constant growth rate DDM, what rate of return do Nogro's investors require?
b. By how much does its value exceed what it would be if all earnings were paid as dividends and nothing were reinvested?
c. If Nogro were to cut its dividend payout ratio to 25%, what would happen to its stock price? What if Nogro eliminated the dividend?

15. The risk-free rate of return is 8%, the expected rate of return on the market portfolio is 15%, and the stock of Xyrong Corporation has a beta coefficient of 1.2. Xyrong pays out 40% of its earnings in dividends, and the latest earnings announced were $10 per share. Dividends were just paid and are expected to be paid annually. You expect that Xyrong will earn an ROE of 20% per year on all reinvested earnings forever.

a. What is the intrinsic value of a share of Xyrong stock?
b. If the market price of a share is currently $100, and you expect the market price to be equal to the intrinsic value one year from now, what is your expected one-year holding-period return on Xyrong stock?

◆IEM
Applications

1. Fixed Dividend Model. Find the most recent quarterly dividend for one of the companies (AAPL, IBM, or MSFT). (The IEM news sections will contain recent dividend information for each contract.) Given this, use the CAPM required returns from Question 4 of Chapter 8 to calculate prices according to the following assumptions:
   a. The company pays fixed, quarterly dividends equal to the last dividend paid.
   b. The next dividend will be paid in exactly one quarter.
   Explain why the stock prices calculated here might differ from those found in *The Wall Street Journal*.

2. Historical Growth Model. Look up the five year historical growth rate in dividends (using Bloomberg, ValueScreen, or company annual reports). Use this as the growth rate along with last quarter's dividend and the CAPM required return to find the price of the company's stock using the Gordon growth model.

3. A Simple Projected Growth Model. To get an alternative estimate of the company's stock price, look up the company's ROE and retention rate (using Bloomberg, ValueScreen, or company annual reports). Determine the projected growth rate in dividends from these numbers and find the price of the company's stock using the Gordon growth model, the CAPM required return and this projected growth rate.

4. The Implied Growth Rate. As an alternative way of determining growth rates, use the current dividend, the CAPM required return, and the current stock price to solve for the growth rate according to the Gordon growth model.

Solutions to Concept Checks

1. a. Dividend yield = $2.15/$50 = 4.3%
   Capital gains yield = (59.77 − 50)/50 = 19.54%
   Total return = 4.3% + 19.54% = 23.84%
   b. $k = 6\% + 1.15(14\% − 6\%) = 15.2\%$
   c. $V_0 = (\$2.15 + \$59.77)/1.152 = \$53.75$, which exceeds the market price. This would indicate a "buy" opportunity.

2. a. $D_1/(k − g) = \$2.15/(0.152 − 0.112) = \$53.75$
   b. $P_1 = P_0(1 + g) = \$53.75(1.112) = \$59.77$
   c. The expected capital gain equals $59.77 − $53.75 = $6.02, for a percentage gain of 11.2%. The dividend yield is $D_1/P_0 = 2.15/53.75 = 4\%$, for a holding-period return of 4% + 11.2% = 15.2%.

3. a. $g = \text{ROE} \times b = 0.20 \times .60 = 0.12$
   $P_0 = 2/(0.125 − 0.12) = 400$
   b. When the firm invests in projects with ROE less than k, its stock price falls.
   If $b = 0.60$, then
   $g = 0.10 \times 0.60 = 0.06$ and
   $P_0 = \$2/(0.125 − 0.06) = \$30.77$
   In contrast, if $b = 0$, then
   $P_0 = \$5/0.125 = \$40$

4. Because $\beta = 1.20$, $k = 5\% + 1.20 [12.5\% − 5\%] = 14\%$

$$V_{1996} = \frac{0.50}{(1.14)} + \frac{0.58}{(1.14)^2} + \frac{0.67}{(1.14)^3} + \frac{0.75 + P_{2000}}{(1.14)^4}$$

Now compute the sales price in 2000 using the constant growth dividend discount model.

$$P_{2000} = \frac{0.75 \times (1 + g)}{k − g} = \frac{0.75 \times 1.132}{0.140 − 0.132} = \$106.13$$

Therefore, $V_{1996} = \$64.62$

5. a. ROE = 12%
   $b = \$0.50/\$2.00 = 0.25$
   $g = \text{ROE} \times b = 12\% \times 0.25 = 3\%$

$P_0 = D_1/(k - g) = \$1.50/(0.10 - 0.03) = \$21.43$

$P_0/E_1 = 21.43/\$2.00 = 10.71$

b. If $b = 0.4$, then $0.4 \times \$2 = \$0.80$ would be reinvested and the remainder of earnings, or $1.20, would be paid as dividends

$g = 12\% \times 0.4 = 4.8\%$

$P_0 = D_1/(k - g) = \$1.20/(0.10 - 0.048) = \$23.08$

$P_0/E_1 = \$23.08/\$2.00 = 11.54$

Chapter 14

FINANCIAL STATEMENT ANALYSIS

AFTER STUDYING THIS CHAPTER YOU SHOULD BE ABLE TO:

- Use a firm's income statement, balance sheet, and statement of cash flows to calculate standard financial ratios.
- Calculate the impact of taxes and leverage on a firm's return on equity using ratio decomposition analysis.
- Measure a firm's operating efficiency using various asset utilization ratios.
- Identify likely sources of biases in conventional accounting data.

In the previous chapter, we explored equity valuation techniques. These techniques take as inputs the firm's dividends and earnings prospects. While the valuation analyst is interested in economic earnings streams, only financial accounting data are readily available. What can we learn from a company's accounting data that can help us estimate the intrinsic value of its common stock?

In this chapter, we show how investors can use financial data as inputs into stock valuation analysis. We start by reviewing the basic sources of such data: the income statement, the balance sheet, and the statement of cash flows. We next discuss the difference between economic and accounting earnings. While economic earnings are more important for issues of valuation, whatever their shortcomings, accounting data still are useful in assessing the economic prospects of the firm. We show how analysts use financial ratios to explore the sources of a firm's profitability and evaluate the "quality" of its earnings in a systematic fashion. We also examine the impact of debt policy on various financial ratios. Finally, we conclude with a discussion of the limitations of financial statement analysis as a tool in uncovering mispriced securities. Some of these limitations are due to differences in firms' accounting procedures. Others arise from inflation-induced distortions in accounting numbers.

14.1 THE MAJOR FINANCIAL STATEMENTS

The Income Statement

income statement
A financial statement showing a firm's revenues and expenses during a specified period.

The **income statement** is a summary of the profitability of the firm over a period of time, such as a year. It presents revenues generated during the operating period, the expenses incurred during that same period, and the company's net earnings or profits, which are simply the difference between revenues and expenses.

It is useful to distinguish four broad classes of expenses: cost of goods sold, which is the direct cost attributable to producing the product sold by the firm; general and administrative expenses, which correspond to overhead expenses, salaries, advertising, and other costs of operating the firm that are not directly attributable to production; interest expense on the firm's debt; and taxes on earnings owed to federal and local governments.

Table 14.1 presents a 1995 income statement for The Gillette Company. At the top are revenues from standard operations. Next come operating expenses, the costs incurred in the course of generating these revenues, including a depreciation allowance. The difference between operating revenues and operating costs is called operating income. Income from other, primarily nonrecurring, sources is then added to obtain earnings before interest and taxes (EBIT), which is what the firm would have earned if not for obligations to its creditors and the tax authorities. EBIT is a measure of the profitability of the firm's operations abstracting from any interest burden attributable to debt financing. The income statement then goes on to subtract net interest expense from EBIT to arrive at taxable income. Finally, the income tax due the government is subtracted to arrive at net income, the "bottom line" of the income statement.

The Balance Sheet

balance sheet
An accounting statement of a firm's financial position at a specified time.

While the income statement provides a measure of profitability over a period of time, the **balance sheet** provides a "snapshot" of the financial condition of the firm at a particular time. The balance sheet is a list of the firm's assets and liabilities at that moment. The difference in assets and liabilities is the net worth of the firm, also called *stockholders' equity*. Like income statements, balance sheets are reasonably standardized in presentation. Table 14.2 is the balance sheet of Gillette for year-end 1995.

The first section of the balance sheet gives a listing of the assets of the firm. Current assets are presented first. These are cash and other items such as accounts receivable or inventories that will be converted into cash within one year. Next comes a listing of long-term assets, which generally corresponds to the company's property, plant, and equipment. The sum of current and long-term assets is total assets, the last line of the assets section of the balance sheet.

TABLE 14.1

Consolidated Statement of Income for The Gillette Company for the Year Ended December 31, 1995 (figures in millions)

Source: Moody's Industrial Manual, 1996.

Operating Revenues	
Net sales	$6,795
Operating Expenses	
Cost of sales	$2,540
Selling, general and administrative expenses	2,635
Depreciation and amortization	248
Total operating expenses	$5,423
Operating income	$1,372
Nonoperating income (expenses)	(25)
Earnings before interest and income taxes	$1,347
Net interest expense	49
Earnings before income taxes	$1,297
Income taxes	473
Net income	$ 824

Note: Column sums subject to rounding error.

TABLE 14.2

Consolidated Balance Sheet for The Gillette Company December 31, 1995

Source: Moody's Industrial Manual, 1996.

	Dollars (millions)	Percent of Total Assets
Assets		
Current assets		
Cash and cash equivalents	$ 49	0.8%
Receivables	1,660	26.2
Inventories	1,035	16.3
Prepaid taxes and other expenses	360	5.7
Total current assets	$ 3,105	49.0%
Property, plant and equipment (net of depreciation)	$ 1,637	25.8%
Net intangible assets	1,221	19.3
Other assets	378	6.0
Total assets	$ 6,340	100.0%
Liabilities and Stockholders' Equity		
Current liabilities		
Loans payable	$ 576	9.1%
Current portion of long-term debt	27	0.4
Accounts payable	1,273	20.1
Income taxes due	248	3.9
Total current liabilities	$ 2,124	33.5%
Long-term debt	$ 691	10.9%
Deferred income taxes	73	1.2
Other long-term liabilities	939	14.8
Total liabilities	$ 3,827	60.4%
Stockholders' equity		
Preferred stock	$ 97	1.5%
Common stock, par value	560	8.8
Additional paid-in capital	31	0.5
Retained earnings	3,383	53.4
Cumulative foreign currency adjustments	(477)	(7.5)
Treasury stock	(1,046)	(16.5)
Other	(34)	(0.5)
Total stockholders' equity	$ 2,514	39.7%
Total liabilities and stockholders' equity	$ 6,340	100.0%

Note: Column sums subject to rounding error.

The liability and stockholders' equity section is arranged similarly. First come short-term or "current" liabilities, such as accounts payable, accrued taxes, and debts that are due within one year. Following this is long-term debt and other liabilities due in more than a year. The difference between total assets and total liabilities is stockholders' equity. This is the net worth or book value of the firm. Stockholders' equity is divided into par value of stock, capital surplus (additional paid-in capital), and retained earnings, although this division is usually unimportant. Briefly, par value plus capital surplus represents the proceeds realized from the sale of stock to the public, while retained earnings represent the buildup of equity from profits plowed back into the firm. Even if the firm issues no new equity, book value will increase each year by the retained earnings of the firm.

The first column of numbers in the balance sheet in Table 14.2 presents the dollar value of each asset. To make it easier to compare firms of different sizes, analysts sometimes present each item on the balance sheet as a percentage of total assets. This is called a *common-size balance sheet* and is presented in the last column of the table.

statement of cash flows
A financial statement showing a firm's cash receipts and cash payments during a specified period.

The Statement of Cash Flows

The **statement of cash flows** replaces what used to be called the statement of changes in financial position or flow of funds statement. It is a report of the cash flow generated by the firm's operations, investments, and financial activities. This statement was mandated by the

TABLE 14.3

Consolidated Statement of Cash Flows for The Gillette Company for the Year Ended December 31, 1995 (figures in millions of dollars)

Source: Moody's Industrial Manual, 1996.

Cash Flows from Operating Activities	
Net income	$ 824
Adjustments to reconcile net income to net cash provided by operating activities:	
Depreciation and amortization	$ 248
Other	(3)
Changes in operating assets and liabilities:	
Decrease (increase) in accounts receivable	(286)
Decrease (increase) in inventories	(94)
Increase (decrease) in accounts payable	67
Decrease (increase) in other current assets	61
Decrease (increase) in noncurrent assets	4
Total adjustments	(3)
Net cash provided by operating activities	$ 821
Cash Flows from Investing Activities	
Cash provided (used) for additions to (disposal of) property, plant, and equipment	$(441)
Acquisitions of businesses	(277)
Other	12
Net cash provided (used) in investing activities	$(706)
Cash Flows from Financing Activities	
Proceeds from exercise of stock option and purchase plans	$ 31
Proceeds from issuance of long-term debt	0
Repayment of long-term debt	(20)
Increase (decrease) in loans payable	134
Dividends paid	(260)
Net cash provided by (used in) financing activities	$(114)
Effect of exchange rate changes on cash	3
Net increase (decrease) in cash and cash equivalents	4

Note: Column sums subject to rounding error.

Financial Accounting Standards Board in 1987 and is sometimes called the FASB Statement No. 95.

While the income statement and balance sheets are based on accrual methods of accounting, which means revenues and expenses are recognized when incurred even if no cash has yet been exchanged, the statement of cash flows recognizes only transactions in which cash changes hands. For example, if goods are sold now, with payment due in 60 days, the income statement will treat the revenue as generated when the sale occurs, and the balance sheet will be immediately augmented by accounts receivable, but the statement of cash flows will not recognize the transaction until the bill is paid and the cash is in hand.

Table 14.3 is the 1995 statement of cash flows for The Gillette Company. The first entry listed under cash flows from operations is net income. The entries that follow modify that figure by components of income that have been recognized but for which cash has not yet changed hands. Increases in accounts receivable, for example, mean income has been claimed on the income statement, but cash has not yet been collected. Hence, increases in accounts receivable reduce the cash flows realized from operations in this period. Similarly, increases in accounts payable mean expenses have been incurred, but cash has not yet left the firm. Any payment delay increases the company's net cash flows in this period.

Another major difference between the income statement and the statement of cash flows involves depreciation, which accounts for a substantial addition to income in the adjustment section of the statement of cash flows in Table 14.3. The income statement attempts to "smooth" large capital expenditures over time to reflect a measure of profitability not distorted by large, infrequent expenditures. The depreciation expense on the income statement is a way of doing this by recognizing capital expenditures over a period of many years rather than at the specific time of those expenditures.

The statement of cash flows, however, recognizes the cash implication of a capital expenditure when it occurs. It will ignore the depreciation "expense" over time but will account for the full capital expenditure when it is paid.

Rather than smooth or allocate expenses over time, as in the income statement, the statement of cash flows reports cash flows separately for operations, investing, and financing activities. This way, any large cash flows such as those for big investments can be recognized explicitly as nonrecurring without affecting the measure of cash flow generated by operating activities.

The second section of the statement of cash flows is the accounting of cash flows from investing activities. These entries are investments in the capital stock necessary for the firm to maintain or enhance its productive capacity.

Finally, the last section of the statement lists the cash flows realized from financing activities. Issuance of securities will contribute positive cash flows, and redemption of outstanding securities will use up cash. For example, Gillette repaid $20 million of outstanding debt during 1995, which was a use of cash. However, it increased its amount of outstanding loans by $134 million, which was a major source of cash flow. The $260 million it paid in dividends reduced net cash flow. Notice that while dividends paid are included in the cash flows from financing, interest payments on debt are included with operating activities, presumably because, unlike dividends, interest payments are not discretionary.

The statement of cash flows provides evidence on the well-being of a firm. If a company cannot pay its dividends and maintain the productivity of its capital stock out of cash flow from operations, for example, and it must resort to borrowing to meet these demands, this is a serious warning that the firm cannot maintain payout at its current level in the long run. The statement of cash flows will reveal this developing problem when it shows that cash flow from operations is inadequate and that borrowing is being used to maintain dividend payments at unsustainable levels.

14.2 ACCOUNTING VERSUS ECONOMIC EARNINGS

accounting earnings
Earnings of a firm as reported on its income statement.

economic earnings
The real flow of cash that a firm could pay out forever in the absence of any change in the firm's productive capacity.

We've seen that stock valuation models require a measure of economic earnings or sustainable cash flow that can be paid out to stockholders without impairing the productive capacity of the firm. In contrast, **accounting earnings** are affected by several conventions regarding the valuation of assets such as inventories (e.g., LIFO versus FIFO treatment) and by the way some expenditures such as capital investments are recognized over time (as depreciation expenses). We will discuss problems with some of these accounting conventions in greater detail later in the chapter. In addition to these accounting issues, as the firm makes its way through the business cycle, its earnings will rise above or fall below the trend line that might more accurately reflect sustainable **economic earnings.** This introduces an added complication in interpreting net income figures. One might wonder how closely accounting earnings approximate economic earnings and, correspondingly, how useful accounting data might be to investors attempting to value the firm.

In fact, the net income figure on the firm's income statement does convey considerable information concerning a firm's products. We see this in the fact that stock prices tend to increase when firms announce earnings greater than market analysis or investors had anticipated. There are several studies to this effect. We showed you one such study in Chapter 9, Figure 9.4, which documented that firms that announced accounting earnings in excess of market expectations enjoyed increases in stock prices, while share of firms that announced below-expected earnings fell in price.

14.3 RETURN ON EQUITY

Past versus Future ROE

return on equity (ROE)
The ratio of net profits to common equity.

We noted in Chapter 13 that **return on equity (ROE)** is one of the two basic factors in determining a firm's growth rate of earnings. There are two sides to using ROE. Sometimes it is reasonable to assume that future ROE will approximate its past value, but a high ROE in the past does not necessarily imply a firm's future ROE will be high.

A declining ROE, on the other hand, is evidence that the firm's new investments have offered a lower ROE than its past investments. The best forecast of future ROE in this case may be lower than the most recent ROE. The vital point for an analyst is not to accept historical values as indicators of future values. Data from the recent past may provide information regarding future performance, but the analyst should always keep an eye on the future. It is expectations of future dividends and earnings that determine the intrinsic value of the company's stock.

Financial Leverage and ROE

An analyst interpreting the past behavior of a firm's ROE or forecasting its future value must pay careful attention to the firm's debt–equity mix and to the interest rate on its debt. An example will show why. Suppose Nodett is a firm that is all-equity financed and has total assets of $100 million. Assume it pays corporate taxes at the rate of 40% of taxable earnings.

return on assets (ROA)
Earnings before interest and taxes divided by total assets.

Table 14.4 shows the behavior of sales, earnings before interest and taxes, and net profits under three scenarios representing phases of the business cycle. It also shows the behavior of two of the most commonly used profitability measures: operating **return on assets (ROA)**, which equals EBIT/total assets, and ROE, which equals net profits/equity.

Somdett is an otherwise identical firm to Nodett, but $40 million of its $100 million of assets are financed with debt bearing an interest rate of 8%. It pays annual interest expenses of $3.2 million. Table 14.5 shows how Somdett's ROE differs from Nodett's.

Note that annual sales, EBIT, and therefore ROA for both firms are the same in each of the three scenarios, that is, business risk for the two companies is identical. It is their financial risk that differs. Although Nodett and Somdett have the same ROA in each scenario, Somdett's ROE exceeds that of Nodett in normal and good years and is lower in bad years.

TABLE 14.4
Nodett's Profitability over the Business Cycle

Scenario	Sales ($ millions)	EBIT ($ millions)	ROA (% per year)	Net Profit ($ millions)	ROE (% per year)
Bad year	$ 80	$ 5	5%	$3	3%
Normal year	100	10	10	6	6
Good year	120	15	15	9	9

TABLE 14.5
Impact of Financial Leverage on ROE

		Nodett		Somdett	
Scenario	EBIT ($ millions)	Net Profits ($ millions)	ROE (%)	Net Profits* ($ millions)	ROE† (%)
Bad year	$ 5	$3	3%	$1.08	1.8%
Normal year	10	6	6	4.08	6.8
Good year	15	9	9	7.08	11.8

*Somdett's after-tax profits are given by 0.6(EBIT − $3.2 million).
†Somdett's equity is only $60 million.

We can summarize the exact relationship among ROE, ROA, and leverage in the following equation[1]

$$ROE = (1 - \text{Tax rate})\left[ROA + (ROA - \text{Interest rate})\frac{\text{Debt}}{\text{Equity}}\right] \quad (14.1)$$

The relationship has the following implications. If there is no debt or if the firm's ROA equals the interest rate on its debt, its ROE will simply equal (1 minus the tax rate) times ROA. If its ROA exceeds the interest rate, then its ROE will exceed (1 minus the tax rate) times ROA by an amount that will be greater the higher the debt/equity ratio.

This result makes intuitive sense: If ROA exceeds the borrowing rate, the firm earns more on its money than it pays out to creditors. The surplus earnings are available to the firm's owners, the equity holders, which raises ROE. If, on the other hand, ROA is less than the interest rate, then ROE will decline by an amount that depends on the debt/equity ratio.

To illustrate the application of Equation 14.1, we can use the numerical example in Table 14.5. In a normal year, Nodett has an ROE of 6%, which is 0.6 (1 minus the tax rate) times its ROA of 10%. However, Somdett, which borrows at an interest rate of 8% and maintains a debt/equity ratio of ⅔, has an ROE of 6.8%. The calculation using Equation 14.1 is

$$ROE = 0.6[10\% + (10\% - 8\%)⅔]$$
$$= 0.6(10\% + ⅘\%)$$
$$= 6.8\%$$

The important point to remember is that increased debt will make a positive contribution to a firm's ROE only if the firm's ROA exceeds the interest rate on the debt.

Note also that financial leverage increases the risk of the equity holder returns. Table 14.5 shows that ROE on Somdett is worse than that of Nodett in bad years. Conversely, in good years, Somdett outperforms Nodett because the excess of ROA over ROE provides additional funds for equity holders. The presence of debt makes Somdett more sensitive to the business cycle than Nodett. Even though the two companies have equal business risk (reflected in their identical EBIT in all three scenarios), Somdett carries greater financial risk than Nodett.

Even if financial leverage increases the expected ROE of Somdett relative to Nodett (as it seems to in Table 14.5), this does not imply the market value of Somdett's equity will be higher. Financial leverage increases the risk of the firm's equity as surely as it raises the expected ROE.

Concept Check

1. Mordett is a company with the same assets as Nodett and Somdett but a debt/equity ratio of 1.0 and an interest rate of 9%. What would its net profit and ROE be in a bad year, a normal year, and a good year?

---

[1]The derivation of Equation 14.1 is as follows:

$$ROE = \frac{\text{Net profit}}{\text{Equity}}$$
$$= \frac{\text{EBIT} - \text{Interest} - \text{Taxes}}{\text{Equity}}$$
$$= \frac{(1 - \text{Tax rate})(\text{EBIT} - \text{Interest})}{\text{Equity}}$$
$$= (1 - \text{Tax rate})\frac{(\text{ROA} \times \text{Assets} - \text{Interest rate} \times \text{Debt})}{\text{Equity}}$$
$$= (1 - \text{Tax rate})\left[\text{ROA} \times \frac{(\text{Equity} + \text{Debt})}{\text{Equity}} - \text{Interest rate} \times \frac{\text{Debt}}{\text{Equity}}\right]$$
$$= (1 - \text{Tax rate})\left[\text{ROA} + (\text{ROA} - \text{Interest rate})\frac{\text{Debt}}{\text{Equity}}\right]$$

14.4 RATIO ANALYSIS

Decomposition of ROE

To understand the factors affecting a firm's ROE, including its trend over time and its performance relative to competitors, analysts often "decompose" ROE into the product of a series of ratios. Each component ratio is in itself meaningful, and the process serves to focus the analyst's attention on the separate factors influencing performance. This kind of decomposition of ROE is often called the Du Pont system.

One useful decomposition of ROE is

$$ROE = \frac{\text{Net profit}}{\text{Pretax profit}} \times \frac{\text{Pretax profit}}{\text{EBIT}} \times \frac{\text{EBIT}}{\text{Sales}} \times \frac{\text{Sales}}{\text{Assets}} \times \frac{\text{Assets}}{\text{Equity}}$$

$$(1) \quad \times \quad (2) \quad \times \ (3) \ \times \ (4) \ \times \quad (5)$$

Table 14.6 shows all these ratios for Nodett and Somdett under the three different economic scenarios.

Let us first focus on factors 3 and 4. Notice that their product, gives us the firm's ROA EBIT/assets.

profit margin or return on sales (ROS)
The ratio of operating profits per dollar of sales (EBIT divided by sales).

Factor 3 is known as the firm's operating **profit margin** or **return on sales (ROS)**. ROS shows operating profit per dollar of sales. In an average year, Nodett's ROS is 0.10, or 10%; in a bad year, it is 0.0625, or 6.25%, and in a good year, 0.125, or 12.5%.

asset turnover (ATO)
The annual sales generated by each dollar of assets (sales/assets).

Factor 4, the ratio of sales to assets, is known as **asset turnover (ATO)**. It indicates the efficiency of the firm's use of assets in the sense that it measures the annual sales generated by each dollar of assets. In a normal year, Nodett's ATO is 1.0 per year, meaning that sales of $1 per year were generated per dollar of assets. In a bad year, this ratio declines to 0.8 per year, and in a good year, it rises to 1.2 per year.

Comparing Nodett and Somdett, we see that factors 3 and 4 do not depend on a firm's financial leverage. The firms' ratios are equal to each other in all three scenarios.

Similarly, factor 1, the ratio of net income after taxes to pretax profit, is the same for both firms. We call this the tax-burden ratio. Its value reflects both the government's tax code and the policies pursued by the firm in trying to minimize its tax burden. In our example, it does not change over the business cycle, remaining a constant 0.6.

While factors 1, 3, and 4 are not affected by a firm's capital structure, factors 2 and 5 are. Factor 2 is the ratio of pretax profits to EBIT. The firm's pretax profits will be greatest when

TABLE 14.6   Ratio Decomposition Analysis for Nodett and Somdett

	ROE	(1) Net Profit / Pretax Profit	(2) Pretax Profit / EBIT	(3) EBIT / Sales (ROS)	(4) Sales / Assets (ATO)	(5) Assets / Equity	(6) Compound Leverage Factor (2) × (5)
Bad Year							
Nodett	0.030	0.6	1.000	0.0625	0.800	1.000	1.000
Somdett	0.018	0.6	0.360	0.0625	0.800	1.667	0.600
Normal Year							
Nodett	0.060	0.6	1.000	0.100	1.000	1.000	1.000
Somdett	0.068	0.6	0.680	0.100	1.000	1.667	1.134
Good Year							
Nodett	0.090	0.6	1.000	0.125	1.200	1.000	1.000
Somdett	0.118	0.6	0.787	0.125	1.200	1.667	1.311

there are no interest payments to be made to debtholders. In fact, another way to express this ratio is

$$\frac{\text{Pretax profits}}{\text{EBIT}} = \frac{\text{EBIT} - \text{Interest expense}}{\text{EBIT}}$$

We will call this factor the *interest-burden (IB) ratio*. It takes on its highest possible value, 1, for Nodett, which has no financial leverage. The higher the degree of financial leverage, the lower the IB ratio. Nodett's IB ratio does not vary over the business cycle. It is fixed at 1.0, reflecting the total absence of interest payments. For Somdett, however, because interest expense is fixed in dollar amount while EBIT varies, the IB ratio varies from a low of 0.36 in a bad year to a high of 0.787 in a good year.

Factor 5, the ratio of assets to equity, is a measure of the firm's degree of financial leverage. It is called the **leverage ratio** and is equal to 1 plus the debt/equity ratio.[2] In our numerical example in Table 14.6, Nodett has a leverage ratio of 1, while Somdett's is 1.667.

leverage ratio
Measure of debt to total capitalization of a firm.

From our discussion in Section 14.2, we know that financial leverage helps boost ROE only if ROA is greater than the interest rate on the firm's debt. How is this fact reflected in the ratios of Table 14.6?

The answer is that to measure the full impact of leverage in this framework, the analyst must take the product of the IB and leverage ratios (that is, factors 2 and 5, shown in Table 14.6 as column 6). For Nodett, factor 6, which we call the compound leverage factor, remains a constant 1.0 under all three scenarios. But for Somdett, we see that the compound leverage factor is greater than 1 in normal years (1.134) and in good years (1.311), indicating the positive contribution of financial leverage to ROE. It is less than 1 in bad years, reflecting the fact that when ROA falls below the interest rate, ROE falls with increased use of debt.

We can summarize all of these relationships as follows

$$\text{ROE} = \text{Tax burden} \times \text{Interest burden} \times \text{Margin} \times \text{Turnover} \times \text{Leverage}$$

Because

$$\text{ROA} = \text{Margin} \times \text{Turnover}$$

and

$$\text{Compound leverage factor} = \text{Interest burden} \times \text{Leverage}$$

We can decompose ROE equivalently as follows

$$\text{ROE} = \text{Tax burden} \times \text{ROA} \times \text{Compound leverage factor}$$

Table 14.6 compares firms with the same ROS and ATO but different degrees of financial leverage. Comparison of ROS and ATO usually is meaningful only in evaluating firms in the same industry. Cross-industry comparisons of these two ratios are often meaningless and can even be misleading.

For example, let us take two firms with the same ROA of 10% per year. The first is a supermarket chain and the second is a gas and electric utility.

As Table 14.7 shows, the supermarket chain has a "low" ROS of 2% and achieves a 10% ROA by "turning over" its assets five times per year. The capital-intensive utility, on the other hand, has a "low" ATO of only 0.5 times per year and achieves its 10% ROA by having an ROS of 20%. The point here is that a "low" ROS or ATO ratio need not indicate a troubled firm. Each ratio must be interpreted in light of industry norms.

---

[2] $\dfrac{\text{Assets}}{\text{Equity}} = \dfrac{\text{Equity} + \text{Debt}}{\text{Equity}} = 1 + \dfrac{\text{Debt}}{\text{Equity}}$

TABLE 14.7

Differences between
ROS and ATO across
Industries

	ROS	×	ATO	=	ROA
Supermarket chain	0.02		5.0		0.10
Utility	0.20		0.5		0.10

TABLE 14.8   Growth Industries Financial Statements, 19X1–19X3 ($ thousands)

	19X0	19X1	19X2	19X3
Income Statements				
Sales revenue		$100,000	$120,000	$144,000
Cost of goods sold (including depreciation)		55,000	66,000	79,200
Depreciation		15,000	18,000	21,600
Selling and administrative expenses		15,000	18,000	21,600
Operating income		30,000	36,000	43,200
Interest expense		10,500	19,095	34,391
Taxable income		19,500	16,905	8,809
Income tax (40% rate)		7,800	6,762	3,524
Net income		11,700	10,143	5,285
Balance Sheets (end of year)				
Cash and marketable securities	$ 50,000	$ 60,000	$ 72,000	$ 86,400
Accounts receivable	25,000	30,000	36,000	43,200
Inventories	75,000	90,000	108,000	129,600
Net plant and equipment	150,000	180,000	216,000	259,200
Total assets	$300,000	$360,000	$432,000	$518,400
Accounts payable	$ 30,000	$ 36,000	$ 43,200	$ 51,840
Short-term debt	45,000	87,300	141,957	214,432
Long-term debt (8% bonds maturing in 19X7)	75,000	75,000	$ 75,000	75,000
Total liabilities	$150,000	$198,300	$260,157	$341,272
Shareholders' equity (1 million shares outstanding)	$150,000	$161,700	$171,843	$177,128
Other data				
Market price per common share at year-end		$ 93.60	$ 61.00	$ 21.00

Even within an industry, ROS and ATO sometimes can differ markedly among firms pursuing different marketing strategies. In the retailing industry, for example, Neiman-Marcus pursues a high-margin, low-ATO policy compared to Wal-Mart, which pursues a low-margin, high-ATO policy.

Concept Check

2. Do a ratio decomposition analysis for the Mordett corporation of Question 1, preparing a table similar to Table 14.6.

Turnover and Other Asset Utilization Ratios

It is often helpful in understanding a firm's ratio of sales to assets to compute comparable efficiency-of-utilization, or turnover, ratios for subcategories of assets. For example, fixed-asset turnover would be

$$\frac{\text{Sales}}{\text{Fixed assets}}$$

This ratio measures sales per dollar of the firm's money tied up in fixed assets.

To illustrate how you can compute this and other ratios from a firm's financial statements, consider Growth Industries, Inc. (GI). GI's income statement and opening and closing balance sheets for the years 19X1, 19X2, and 19X3 appear in Table 14.8.

GI's total asset turnover in 19X3 was 0.303, which was below the industry average of 0.4. To understand better why GI underperformed, we compute asset utilization ratios separately for fixed assets, inventories, and accounts receivable.

GI's sales in 19X3 were $144 million. Its only fixed assets were plant and equipment, which were $216 million at the beginning of the year and $259.2 million at year's end. Average fixed assets for the year were, therefore, $237.6 million [($216 million + $259.2 million)/2]. GI's fixed-asset turnover for 19X3 was $144 million per year/$237.6 million = 0.606 per year. In other words, for every dollar of fixed assets, there were $0.606 in sales during the year 19X3.

Comparable figures for the fixed-asset turnover ratio for 19X1 and 19X2 and the 19X3 industry average are

19X1	19X2	19X3	19X3 Industry Average
0.606	0.606	0.606	0.700

GI's fixed-asset turnover has been stable over time and below the industry average.

Whenever a financial ratio includes one item from the income statement, which covers a period of time, and another from the balance sheet, which is a "snapshot" at a particular time, the practice is to take the average of the beginning and end-of-year balance sheet figures. Thus, in computing the fixed-asset turnover ratio you divide sales (from the income statement) by average fixed assets (from the balance sheet).

Another widely followed turnover ratio is the inventory turnover ratio, which is the ratio of cost of goods sold per dollar of inventory. It is usually expressed as cost of goods sold (instead of sales revenue) divided by average inventory. It measures the speed with which inventory is turned over.

In 19X1, GI's cost of goods sold (less depreciation) was $40 million, and its average inventory was $82.5 million [($75 million + $90 million)/2]. Its inventory turnover was 0.485 per year ($40 million/$82.5 million). In 19X2 and 19X3, inventory turnover remained the same and continued below the industry average of 0.5 per year.

Another measure of efficiency is the ratio of accounts receivable to sales. The accounts receivable ratio usually is computed as average accounts receivable/sales × 365. The result is a number called the **average collection period,** or **days receivables,** which equals the total credit extended to customers per dollar of daily sales. It is the number of days' worth of sales tied up in accounts receivable. You can also think of it as the average lag between the date of sale and the date payment is received.

For GI in 19X3, this number was 100.4 days

$$\frac{(\$36 \text{ million} + \$43.2 \text{ million})/2}{\$144 \text{ million}} \times 365 = 100.4 \text{ days}$$

average collection period, or days receivables
The ratio of accounts receivables to daily sales, or the total amount of credit extended per dollar of daily sales.

The industry average was 60 days.

In summary, use of these ratios lets us see that GI's poor total asset turnover relative to the industry is in part caused by lower than average fixed-asset turnover and inventory turnover, and higher than average days receivables. This suggests GI may be having problems with excess plant capacity along with poor inventory and receivables management procedures.

Liquidity and Coverage Ratios

Liquidity and interest coverage ratios are of great importance in evaluating the riskiness of a firm's securities. They aid in assessing the financial strength of the firm.

Liquidity ratios include the current ratio, quick ratio, and interest coverage ratio.

current ratio
A ratio representing the ability of the firm to pay off its current liabilities by liquidating current assets (current assets/current liabilities).

1. **Current ratio:** current assets/current liabilities. This ratio measures the ability of the firm to pay off its current liabilities by liquidating its current assets (that is, turning them into cash). It indicates the firm's ability to avoid insolvency in the short run. GI's current ratio in 19X1, for example, was $(60 + 30 + 90)/(36 + 87.3) = 1.46$. In other years, it was

19X1	19X2	19X3	19X3 Industry Average
1.46	1.17	0.97	2.0

This represents an unfavorable time trend and poor standing relative to the industry.

quick ratio or acid test ratio
A measure of liquidity similar to the current ratio except for exclusion of inventories (cash plus receivables divided by current liabilities).

2. **Quick ratio:** (cash + receivables)/current liabilities. This ratio is also called the **acid test ratio.** It has the same denominator as the current ratio, but its numerator includes only cash, cash equivalents such as marketable securities, and receivables. The quick ratio is a better measure of liquidity than the current ratio for firms whose inventory is not readily convertible into cash. GI's quick ratio shows the same disturbing trends as its current ratio:

19X1	19X2	19X3	19X3 Industry Average
0.73	0.58	0.49	1.0

interest coverage ratio or times interest earned
A financial leverage measure arrived at by dividing earnings before interest and taxes by interest expense.

3. **Interest coverage ratio:** EBIT/interest expense. This ratio is often called **times interest earned.** It is closely related to the interest-burden ratio discussed in the previous section. A high coverage ratio tells the firm's shareholders and lenders that the likelihood of bankruptcy is low because annual earnings are significantly greater than annual interest obligations. It is widely used by both lenders and borrowers in determining the firm's debt capacity and is a major determinant of the firm's bond rating.

GI's interest coverage ratios are

19X1	19X2	19X3	19X3 Industry Average
2.86	1.89	1.26	5

GI's interest coverage ratio has fallen dramatically over this three-year period, and by 19X3 it is far below the industry average. Probably its credit rating has been declining as well, and no doubt GI is considered a relatively poor credit risk in 19X3.

Market Price Ratios

There are two important market price ratios: the market-to-book-value ratio and the price/earnings ratio.

market-to-book-value ratio
Market price of a share divided by book value per share.

The **market-to-book-value ratio** (P/B) equals the market price of a share of the firm's common stock divided by its *book value*, that is, shareholders' equity per share. Analysts sometimes consider the stock of a firm with a low market-to-book value to be a "safer" investment, seeing the book value as a "floor" supporting the market price.

Analysts presumably view book value as the level below which market price will not fall because the firm always has the option to liquidate, or sell, its assets for their book values. However, this view is questionable. In fact, some firms, such as Digital (see Chapter 13), do sometimes sell for less than book value. Nevertheless, a low market-to-book-value ratio is seen by some as providing a "margin of safety," and some analysts will screen out or reject high P/B firms in their stock selection process.

Proponents of the P/B screen would argue that, if all other relevant attributes are the same for two stocks, the one with the lower P/B ratio is safer. Nevertheless, book value does not necessarily represent liquidation value, which renders the margin of safety notion unreliable.

TABLE 14.9
Effect of ROE and
Plowback Ratio on P/B

ROE	Plowback Ratio (b)			
	0	**25%**	**50%**	**75%**
10%	1.00%	0.95%	0.86%	0.67%
12	1.00	1.00	1.00	1.00
14	1.00	1.06	1.20	2.00

Note: The assumptions and formulas underlying this table are: $E_1 = \$1$; book
value per share = $\$8.33$; $k = 12\%$ per year.

$$g = b \times ROE$$
$$P_0 = \frac{(1 - b)E}{k - g}$$
$$P/B = P_0/\$8.33$$

The theory of equity valuation offers some insight into the significance of the P/B ratio. A high P/B ratio is an indication that investors think a firm has opportunities of earning a rate of return on their investment in excess of the market capitalization rate, k.

To illustrate this point, we can return to the numerical example in Chapter 13, Section 13.4 and Table 13.3. That example assumes the market capitalization rate is 12% per year. Now add the assumptions that the book value per share is $8.33 and that the coming year's expected EPS is $1, so that in the case for which the expected ROE on future investments also is 12%, the stock will sell at $1/0.12 = $8.33, and the P/B ratio will be 1.

Table 14.9 shows the P/B ratio for alternative assumptions about future ROE and plowback ratio.

Reading down any column, you can see how the P/B ratio changes with ROE. The numbers reveal that, for a given plowback ratio, the P/B ratio is higher, the higher the expected ROE. This makes sense, because the greater the expected profitability of the firm's future investment opportunities, the greater its market value as an ongoing enterprise compared with the cost of acquiring its assets.

price/earnings ratio
The ratio of a stock's price to its earnings per share. Also referred to as the P/E multiple.

We've noted that the **price/earnings ratio** that is based on the firm's financial statements and reported in newspaper stock listings is not the same as the price/earnings multiple that emerges from a discounted dividend model. The numerator is the same (the market price of the stock), but the denominator is different. The P/E ratio uses the most recent past accounting earnings, while the P/E multiple predicted by valuation models uses expected future economic earnings.

Many security analysts pay careful attention to the accounting P/E ratio in the belief that among low P/E stocks they are more likely to find bargains than with high P/E stocks. The idea is that you can acquire a claim on a dollar of earnings more cheaply if the P/E ratio is low. For example, if the P/E ratio is 8, you pay $8 per share per $1 of *current* earnings, while if the P/E ratio is 12, you must pay $12 for a claim on $1 of current earnings.

Note, however, that current earnings may differ substantially from future earnings. The higher P/E stock still may be a bargain relative to the low P/E stock if its earnings and dividends are expected to grow at a faster rate. Our point is that ownership of the stock conveys the right to future earnings as well as to current earnings. An exclusive focus on the commonly reported accounting P/E ratio can be shortsighted because by its nature it ignores future growth in earnings.

An efficient markets adherent will be skeptical of the notion that a strategy of investing in low P/E stocks will result in an expected rate of return greater than that of investing in high or medium P/E stocks having the same risk. The empirical evidence on this question is mixed, but if the strategy has worked in the past, it surely should not work in the future because too many investors will be following it. This is the lesson of market efficiency.

Before leaving the P/B and P/E ratios, it is worth pointing out the relationship among these ratios and ROE.

$$ROE = \frac{Earnings}{Book\ value}$$

$$= \frac{Market\ price}{Book\ value} \div \frac{Market\ price}{Earnings}$$

$$= P/B\ ratio \div P/E\ ratio$$

earnings yield
The ratio of earnings to price, E/P.

By rearranging the terms, we find that a firm's **earnings yield,** the ratio of earnings to price, is equal to its ROE divided by the market-for-book-value ratio.

$$\frac{E}{P} = \frac{ROE}{P/B}$$

Thus, a company with a high ROE can have a relatively low earnings yield because its P/B ratio is high. This indicates that a high ROE does not in and of itself imply the stock is a good buy. The price of the stock already may be bid up to reflect an attractive ROE. If so, the P/B ratio will be above 1.0, and the earnings yield to stockholders will be below the ROE, as the equation demonstrates. The relationship shows that a strategy of investing in the stock of high ROE firms may produce a lower holding-period return than investing in the stock of firms with a low ROE.

Clayman (1987) has found that investing in the stocks of 29 "excellent" companies, with mean reported ROE of 19.05% during the period 1976 to 1980, produced results much inferior to investing in 39 "unexcellent" companies, those with a mean ROE of 7.09% during the period. An investor putting equal dollar amounts in the stock of the unexcellent companies would have earned a portfolio rate of return over the 1981 to 1985 period that was 11.3% higher per year than the rate of return on a comparable portfolio of excellent company stocks.

Concept Check

3. What were GI's ROE, P/E, and P/B ratios in the year 19X3? How do they compare to the industry average ratios, which were:

$$ROE = 8.64\%$$
$$P/E = 8$$
$$P/B = 0.69$$

How does GI's earnings yield in 19X3 compare to the industry average?

14.5 AN ILLUSTRATION OF FINANCIAL STATEMENT ANALYSIS

In her 19X3 annual report to the shareholders of Growth Industries, Inc., the president wrote: "19X3 was another successful year for Growth Industries. As in 19X2, sales, assets, and operating income all continued to grow at a rate of 20%."

Is she right?

We can evaluate her statement by conducting a full-scale ratio analysis of Growth Industries. Our purpose is to assess GI's performance in the recent past, to evaluate its future prospects, and to determine whether its market price reflects its intrinsic value.

Table 14.10 shows the key financial ratios we can compute from GI's financial statements. The president is certainly right about the growth in sales, assets, and operating income. Inspection of GI's key financial ratios, however, contradicts her first sentence: 19X3 was not another successful year for GI—it appears to have been another miserable one.

ROE has been declining steadily from 7.51% in 19X1 to 3.03% in 19X3. A comparison of GI's 19X3 ROE to the 19X3 industry average of 8.64% makes the deteriorating time trend especially alarming. The low and falling market-to-book-value ratio and the falling price/earnings ratio indicate that investors are less and less optimistic about the firm's future profitability.

The fact that ROA has not been declining, however, tells us that the source of the declining time trend in GI's ROE must be an inappropriate use of financial leverage. And we see that, while GI's leverage ratio climbed from 2.117 in 19X1 to 2.723 in 19X3, its interest-

TABLE 14.10 Key Financial Ratios of Growth Industries, Inc.

Year	ROE	(1) Net Profit Pretax Profit	(2) Pretax Profit EBIT	(3) EBIT Sales (ROS)	(4) Sales Assets (ATO)	(5) Assets Equity	(6) Compound Leverage Factor (2) × (5)	(7) ROA (3) × (4)	P/E	P/B
19X1	7.51%	0.6	0.650	30%	0.303	2.117	1.376	9.09%	8	0.58
19X2	6.08	0.6	0.470	30	0.303	2.375	1.116	9.09	6	0.35
19X3	3.03	0.6	0.204	30	0.303	2.723	0.556	9.09	4	0.12
Industry average	8.64	0.6	0.800	30	0.400	1.500	1.200	12.00	8	0.69

TABLE 14.11
Growth Industries
Statement of Cash
Flows ($ thousands)

	19X1	19X2	19X3
Cash Flow from Operating Activities			
Net income	$ 11,700	$ 10,143	$ 5,285
+ Depreciation	15,000	18,000	21,600
+ Decrease (increase) in accounts receivable	(5,000)	(6,000)	(7,200)
+ Decrease (increase) in inventories	(15,000)	(18,000)	(21,600)
+ Increase in accounts payable	6,000	7,200	8,640
	$ 12,700	$ 11,343	$ 6,725
Cash Flow from Investing Activities			
Investment in plant and equipment*	$ (45,000)	$ (54,000)	$ (64,800)
Cash Flow from Financing Activities			
Dividends paid†	$ 0	$ 0	$ 0
Short-term debt issued	42,300	54,657	72,475
Change in cash and marketable securities‡	$ 10,000	$ 12,000	$ 14,400

*Gross investment equals increase in net plant and equipment plus depreciation.

†We can conclude that no dividends are paid because stockholders' equity increases each year by the full amount of net income, implying a plowback ratio of 1.0.

‡Equals cash flow from operations plus cash flow from investment activities plus cash flow from financing activities. Note that this equals the yearly change in cash and marketable securities on the balance sheet.

burden ratio fell from 0.650 to 0.204—with the net result that the compound leverage factor fell from 1.376 to 0.556.

The rapid increase in short-term debt from year to year and the concurrent increase in interest expense make it clear that, to finance its 20% growth rate in sales, GI has incurred sizable amounts of short-term debt at high interest rates. The firm is paying rates of interest greater than the ROA it is earning on the investment financed with the new borrowing. As the firm has expanded, its situation has become ever more precarious.

In 19X3, for example, the average interest rate on short-term debt was 20% versus an ROA of 9.09%. (We compute the average interest rate on short-term debt by taking the total interest expense of $34,391,000, subtracting the $6 million in interest on the long-term bonds, and dividing by the beginning-of-year short-term debt of $141,957,000.)

GI's problems become clear when we examine its statement of cash flows in Table 14.11. The statement is derived from the income statement and balance sheet in Table 14.8. GI's cash flow from operations is falling steadily, from $12,700,000 in 19X1 to $6,725,000 in 19X3. The firm's investment in plant and equipment, by contrast, has increased greatly. Net plant and equipment (i.e., net of depreciation) rose from $150,000,000 in 19X0 to $259,200,000 in 19X3. This near doubling of the capital assets makes the decrease in cash flow from operations all the more troubling.

The source of the difficulty is GI's enormous amount of short-term borrowing. In a sense, the company is being run as a pyramid scheme. It borrows more and more each year to maintain its 20% growth rate in assets and income. However, the new assets are not generating enough cash flow to support the extra interest burden of the debt, as the falling cash flow from operations indicates. Eventually, when the firm loses its ability to borrow further, its growth will be at an end.

At this point, GI stock might be an attractive investment. Its market price is only 12% of its book value, and with a P/E ratio of 4, its earnings yield is 25% per year. GI is a likely candidate for a takeover by another firm that might replace GI's management and build shareholder value through a radical change in policy.

Concept Check

4. You have the following information for IBX Corporation for the years 1994 and 1997 (all figures are in $ millions):

	1997	1994
Net income	$ 253.7	$ 239.0
Pretax income	411.9	375.6
EBIT	517.6	403.1
Average assets	4,857.9	3,459.7
Sales	6,679.3	4,537.0
Shareholders' equity	2,233.3	2,347.3

What is the trend in IBX's ROE, and how can you account for it in terms of tax burden, margin, turnover, and financial leverage?

14.6   COMPARABILITY PROBLEMS

Financial statement analysis gives us a good amount of ammunition for evaluating a company's performance and future prospects. But comparing financial results of different companies is not so simple. There is more than one acceptable way to represent various items of revenue and expense according to generally accepted accounting principles (GAAP). This means two firms may have exactly the same economic income yet very different accounting incomes.

Furthermore, interpreting a single firm's performance over time is complicated when inflation distorts the dollar measuring rod. Comparability problems are especially acute in this case because the impact of inflation on reported results often depends on the particular method the firm adopts to account for inventories and depreciation. The security analyst must adjust the earnings and the financial ratio figures to a uniform standard before attempting to compare financial results across firms and over time.

Comparability problems can arise out of the flexibility of GAAP guidelines in accounting for inventories and depreciation and in adjusting for the effects of inflation. Other important potential sources of noncomparability include the capitalization of leases and other expenses and the treatment of pension costs, but they are beyond the scope of this book. The box on page 399 illustrates the types of problems an analyst must be aware of in using financial statements to identify bargain stocks.

Inventory Valuation

LIFO
The last-in first-out accounting method of valuing inventories.

There are two commonly used ways to value inventories: **LIFO** (last-in, first-out) and **FIFO** (first-in, first-out). We can explain the difference using a numerical example.

Suppose Generic Products, Inc., (GPI) has a constant inventory of 1 million units of generic goods. The inventory turns over once per year, meaning the ratio of cost of goods sold to inventory is 1.

FIFO
The first-in first-out accounting method of valuing inventories.

The LIFO system calls for valuing the million units used up during the year at the current cost of production, so that the last goods produced are considered the first ones to be sold. They are valued at today's cost.

The Many Ways of Figuring Financial Results

An investor in First Boston Corp. might have had a pleasant surprise while reading the investment banking company's 1987 financial statement. Despite taking heavy hits in the volatile bond markets and October's stock crash, First Boston reported earnings of $3.12 per share—down 40% from the heights of 1986, but about the same as profits in 1984.

But hold on. Looking through Value Line's *Investment Survey*, the same investor would be dismayed to find that First Boston's earnings for last year were only 59¢ a share. What gives? In this case the explanation is fairly simple. Value Line doesn't take into account the profits First Boston made in selling its Park Avenue headquarters, while the company and other reporting services such as Standard & Poor's do.

This type of discrepancy in reported financial figures is very common (table) and points to a general rule: Where the bottom line falls depends on who's drawing it. S&P's *Stock Report* generally follows the company's accounting in regard to nonrecurring items, but Value Line doesn't. For example, Union Carbide's reserve for Bhopal litigation amounted to 40¢ per share. S&P and Carbide subtracted it from earnings, but Value Line left it in.

The Bottom Line: Take Your Choice

	1987 Earnings per Share	
	S&P	**Value Line**
Alcoa	$2.52	$4.14
Affiliated Publ.	4.08	0.61
First Boston	3.12	0.59
Merrill Lynch	3.58	1.52
Union Carbide	1.76	2.17

Source: Data from Standard & Poor's Corp., Value Line Inc.

FORECAST TOOL

With the rash of mergers, acquisitions, and divestitures in recent years, the varying approaches of reporting services

can result in enormous differences. In 1985, for example, when Warner-Lambert cut its losses by selling three hospital-supply units, S&P showed the company losing $4.05 per share for the year, while Value Line reported a gain of $3.05 per share.

To try to get a "clear-cut number," Value Line will remove from earnings such items as gains or losses from discontinued operations and other special items, says a senior analyst at the firm. He says such a number is more useful to investors looking at the future earning power of a company. Similarly, *Business Week's* Corporate Scoreboard shows earnings from continuing operations, excluding special, nonrecurring, or extraordinary items. Dan Mayper at S&P says S&P's philosophy is to reflect all the special items in the figures and explain their significance in the narrative of the report.

There are also wide variations when it comes to computing a company's book value. That's basically what's left over when you subtract liabilities from assets. Unlike Value Line, S&P gives no credit to such intangible assets as customer lists, patents, trademarks, or franchises. Companies with many intangibles on their books, such as broadcasters and publishers, are bound to look a lot worse in S&P's calculations. For example, Capital Cities/ABC had a 1986 per-share book value of $120.82, said Value Line, while S&P showed a negative net worth of $24.26 per share.

Value Line analyst Marc Gerstein believes that including the intangibles on the balance sheet gives the best idea of a company's value as an ongoing concern. S&P regards its approach as more conservative, designed to approximate the company's liquidation value.

Source: "The Many Ways of Figuring Financial Results," by David Zigas, *Business Week* magazine, 11 April 1988, p. 131.

The FIFO system assumes that the units used up or sold are the ones that were added to inventory first, and goods sold should be valued at original cost.

If the price of generic goods were constant, at the level of $1, say, the book value of inventory and the cost of goods sold would be the same, $1 million under both systems. But suppose the price of generic goods rises by 10 cents per unit during the year as a result of general inflation.

LIFO accounting would result in a cost of goods sold of $1.1 million, while the end-of-year balance sheet value of the 1 million units in inventory remains $1 million. The balance sheet value of inventories is given as the cost of the goods still in inventory. Under LIFO, the last goods produced are assumed to be sold at the current cost of $1.10; the goods remaining are the previously produced goods, at a cost of only $1. You can see that, although LIFO accounting accurately measures the cost of goods sold today, it understates the current value of the remaining inventory in an inflationary environment.

In contrast, under FIFO accounting, the cost of goods sold would be $1 million, and the end-of-year balance sheet value of the inventory is $1.1 million. The result is that the LIFO firm has both a lower reported profit and a lower balance sheet value of inventories than the FIFO firm.

LIFO is preferred over FIFO in computing economics earnings (that is, real sustainable cash flow), because it uses up-to-date prices to evaluate the cost of goods sold. A disadvantage is that LIFO accounting induces balance sheet distortions when it values investment in inventories at original cost. This practice results in an upward bias in ROE because the investment base on which return is earned is undervalued.

In computing the gross national product, the U.S. Department of Commerce has to make an inventory valuation adjustment (IVA) to eliminate the effects of FIFO accounting on the cost of goods sold. In effect, it puts all firms in the aggregate onto a LIFO basis.

Depreciation

Another source of problems is the measurement of depreciation, which is a key factor in computing true earnings. The accounting and economic measures of depreciation can differ markedly. According to the *economic* definition, depreciation is the amount of a firm's operating cash flow that must be reinvested in the firm to sustain its real cash flow at the current level.

The *accounting* measurement is quite different. Accounting depreciation is the amount of the original acquisition cost of an asset that is allocated to each accounting period over an arbitrarily specified life of the asset. This is the figure reported in financial statements.

Assume, for example, that a firm buys machines with a useful economic life of 20 years at $100,000 apiece. In its financial statements, however, the firm can depreciate the machines over 10 years using the straight-line method, for $10,000 per year in depreciation. Thus, after 10 years, a machine will be fully depreciated on the books, even though it remains a productive asset that will not need replacement for another 10 years.

In computing accounting earnings, this firm will overestimate depreciation in the first 10 years of the machine's economic life and underestimate it in the last 10 years. This will cause reported earnings to be understated compared with economic earnings in the first 10 years and overstated in the last 10 years.

If the management of the firm had a zero plowback policy and distributed as cash dividends its accounting earnings, it would pay out too little in the first 10 years relative to the sustainable cash flow. Similarly, a security analyst who relied on the (unadjusted) reported earnings figure during the first few years would see understated economic earnings and would underestimate the firm's intrinsic value.

Depreciation comparability problems add one more wrinkle. A firm can use different depreciation methods for tax purposes than for other reporting purposes. Most firms use accelerated depreciation methods for tax purposes and straight-line depreciation in published financial statements. There also are differences across firms in their estimates of the depreciable life of plant, equipment, and other depreciable assets.

The major problem related to depreciation, however, is caused by inflation. Because conventional depreciation is based on historical costs rather than on the current replacement cost of assets, measured depreciation in periods of inflation is understated relative to replacement cost, and *real* economic income (sustainable cash flow) is correspondingly overstated.

The situation is similar to what happens in FIFO inventory accounting. Conventional depreciation and FIFO both result in an inflation-induced overstatement of real income because both use original cost instead of current cost to calculate net income.

For example, suppose Generic Products, Inc., has a machine with a three-year useful life that originally cost $3 million. Annual straight-line depreciation is $1 million, regardless of what happens to the replacement cost of the machine. Suppose inflation in the first year turns out to be 10%. Then the true annual depreciation expense is $1.1 million in current terms, while conventionally measured depreciation remains fixed at $1 million per year. Accounting income therefore overstates *real* economic income.

As it does in the case of inventory valuation, the Commerce Department in its computation of GDP tries to adjust aggregate depreciation. It does this by applying "capital consumption allowances" (CCA), to account for the distorting effects of conventional depreciation techniques.

Inflation and Interest Expense

While inflation can cause distortions in the measurement of a firm's inventory and depreciation costs, it has perhaps an even greater effect on the calculation of *real* interest expense. Nominal interest rates include an inflation premium that compensates the lender for inflation-induced erosion in the real value of principal. From the perspective of both lender and borrower, therefore, part of what is conventionally measured as interest expense should be treated more properly as repayment of principal.

For example, suppose Generic Products has debt outstanding with a face value of $10 million at an interest rate of 10% per year. Interest expense as conventionally measured is $1 million per year. However, suppose inflation during the year is 6%, so that the real interest rate is 4%. Then $0.6 million of what appears as interest expense on the income statement is really an inflation premium, or compensation for the anticipated reduction in the real value of the $10 million principal; only $0.4 million is *real* interest expense. The $0.6 million reduction in the purchasing power of the outstanding principal may be thought of as repayment of principal, rather than as an interest expense. Real income of the firm is, therefore, understated by $0.6 million.

This mismeasurement of real interest means that inflation results in an underestimate of real income. The effects of inflation on the reported values of inventories and depreciation that we have discussed work in the opposite direction.

Concept Check

5. In a period of rapid inflation, companies ABC and XYZ have the same *reported* earnings. ABC uses LIFO inventory accounting, has relatively fewer depreciable assets, and has more debt than XYZ. XYZ uses FIFO inventory accounting. Which company has the higher *real* income and why?

International Accounting Conventions

The examples cited above illustrate some of the problems that analysts can encounter when attempting to interpret financial data. Even greater problems arise in the interpretation of the financial statements of foreign firms. This is because these firms do not follow GAAP guidelines. Accounting practices in various countries differ to greater or lesser extents from U.S. standards. Here are some of the major issues that you should be aware of when using the financial statements of foreign firms.

Reserving Practices   Many countries allow firms considerably more discretion in setting aside reserves for future contingencies than is typical in the United States. Because additions to reserves result in a charge against income, reported earnings are far more subject to managerial discretion than in the United States.

Germany is a country that allows particularly wide discretion in reserve practice. When Daimler-Benz AG (producer of the Mercedes Benz) decided to issue shares on the New York Stock Exchange in 1993, it had to revise its accounting statements in accordance with U.S. standards. The revisions transformed a $370 million profit for 1993 using German accounting rules into a $1 million *loss* under more stringent U.S. rules.

Depreciation   In the United States, firms typically maintain separate sets of accounts for tax and reporting purposes. For example, accelerated depreciation is typically used for tax purposes, while straight-line depreciation is used for reporting purposes. In contrast, most

FIGURE 14.1

Adjusted versus
Reported Price/
Earnings Ratios

Source: Lawrence S. Speidell
and Vinod Bavishi, "GAAP
Arbitrage: Valuation
Opportunities in International
Accounting Standards,"
Financial Analysts Journal,
November–December 1992,
pp. 58–66.

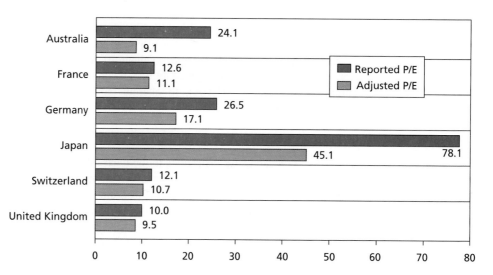

other countries do not allow dual sets of accounts, and most firms in foreign countries use accelerated depreciation to minimize taxes despite the fact that it results in lower reported earnings. This makes reported earnings of foreign firms lower than they would be if the firms were allowed to follow the U.S. practice.

Intangibles   Treatment of intangibles such as goodwill can vary widely. Are they amortized or expensed? If amortized, over what period? Such issues can have a large impact on reported profits.

The effect of different accounting practices can be substantial. A study by Speidell and Bavishi (1992) recalculated the financial statements of firms in several countries using common accounting rules. Figure 14.1, from their study, compares P/E ratios as reported and restated on a common basis. The variation is considerable.

Such differences in international accounting standards have become more of a problem as the drive to globally integrate capital markets progresses. For example, many foreign firms would like to list their shares on the New York Stock Exchange in order to more easily tap the U.S. equity markets, and the NYSE would like to have those firms listed. But the Securities and Exchange Commission (SEC) will not allow such shares to be listed unless the firms prepare their financial statements in accordance with U.S. GAAP standards. This has limited the listing of non-U.S. companies dramatically.

In contrast to the U.S., most large non-U.S. national stock exchanges allow foreign firms to be listed if their financial statements conform to International Accounting Standards (IAS) rules. IAS disclosure requirements tend to be far more rigorous than those of most countries, and they impose greater uniformity in accounting practices. Many argue that IAS rules are already fairly similar to GAAP rules and provide nearly the same quality financial information about the firm. While the SEC does not yet deem IAS standards acceptable for listing in U.S. markets, negotiations are currently underway to change that situation. The box on page 403 reports on the various initiatives being undertaken to enhance global standardization of accounting rules.

Inflation Accounting

In recognition of the need to adjust for the effects of inflation, the Financial Accounting Standards Board in 1980 issued Rule No. 33 (FASB 33). It required large public corporations to supplement their customary financial statements with data pertaining to the effect of inflation.

All Accountants Soon May Speak the Same Language

The major roadblock to foreign companies listing their overseas stock on U.S. exchanges has long been the big difference between accounting standards in the U.S. and abroad. For decades, leading accounting theorists have advocated the harmonization of accounting principles worldwide to end the confusion and lack of comparability. But major foreign companies have resisted the move because they've felt that the tougher U.S. accounting rules would likely prevail in formulating global standards.

Suddenly what seemed like an impossible dream appears a bit closer to reality with new moves by key accounting rulemakers—all with the goal of harmonizing disparate accounting rules worldwide.

The boards of the International Accounting Standards Committee, or IASC, which makes international rules, and the International Organization of Securities Commissions, have just agreed to develop accounting standards by mid-1999 for companies seeking stock lists in global markets to raise cross-border capital. And the Financial Accounting Standards Board, the chief rule-making body for U.S. accountants, has joined with standards setters in Canada, Mexico, and Chile to explore areas in which the four countries can harmonize their accounting standards.

Even the Securities and Exchange Commission, which has long fought to maintain tough U.S. accounting standards, is easing the barriers somewhat. Last year for the first time the SEC accepted three international accounting standards on cash-flow data, the effects of hyperinflation, and business combinations for cross-border stock filings.

But Linda Quinn, who heads the SEC's corporation finance division, is adamant that U.S. accounting standards still won't be dropped for domestic companies—a move that would cause a torrent of opposition from financial analysts and academics who feel that U.S. accounting standards should still be the rule rather than the exception.

Whatever the outcome, the stakes are enormous for both U.S. capital markets and the investment community. Big Board officials note that 55 million shares of non-registered foreign stocks already trade in the U.S. over-the-counter. And they believe the U.S. stock market may lose world

prominence to London and other European exchanges if foreign stocks aren't listed in New York. But financial analysts and accountants say that permitting foreign stocks to be listed here under non-U.S. accounting rules would only confuse and penalize U.S. investors.

Currently, only 204 non-U.S. companies list on the New York Stock Exchange. To the Big Board, this seems like a pittance because there are 2,000 other major foreign companies out there that could qualify for listing. So the exchange has been working quietly to get regulators and rulemakers to permit another 200 or more big foreign companies to list here under international standards. This would almost double the Big Board's capitalization to close to $10 trillion from the current $5.4 trillion—enough to make a ticker-tape parade for whoever could push through these proposals.

But some U.S. stock market analysts fear that these benefits wouldn't be worth the price, which is lack of comparable disclosure among U.S. and foreign stocks. Pat McConnell, Bear Stearns & Co.'s accounting guru, frets that it would prevent U.S. investors from making meaningful comparisons of U.S. and foreign stocks.

Before any meaningful progress can be made in harmonization, international standard setters need a lot more resources and clout. Consider that IASC, which sets international standards, has only three or four full-time staff members, while the FASB has 45 staff members. And IASC has an annual budget of only $1.7 million compared with $15.8 million for FASB.

With such meager resources, IASC needs more money and staff to help cope with the sizable workload it has undertaken. If it cannot get this support from industry, government, and accounting organizations, it will be difficult if not impossible to topple the long-standing Tower of Babel in accounting and produce a lingua franca to dispel the clouds over worldwide financial disclosure.

Source: Lee Berton, "All Accountants Soon May Speak the Same Language," *The Wall Street Journal*, August 29, 1995.

A survey reported by Norby (1983), however, indicated that security analysts, by and large, were ignoring the inflation-adjusted data. One possible reason is that analysts believed FASB 33 just added a other element of noncomparability. In other words, analysts may have judged the inflation-adjusted earnings to be poorer estimates of real economic earnings than the original unadjusted figures.

In 1987, after a lengthy evaluation of the effects of FASB 33, the FASB decided to discontinue it. Today, analysts interested in adjusting reported financial statements for inflation are on their own.

14.7 VALUE INVESTING: THE GRAHAM TECHNIQUE

No presentation of fundamental security analysis would be complete without a discussion of the ideas of Benjamin Graham, the greatest of the investment "gurus." Until the evolution of modern portfolio theory in the latter half of this century, Graham was the single most important thinker, writer, and teacher in the field of investment analysis. His influence on investment professionals remains very strong.

Graham's magnum opus is *Security Analysis*, written with Columbia Professor David Dodd in 1934. Its message is similar to the ideas presented in this chapter. Graham believed careful analysis of a firm's financial statements could turn up bargain stocks. Over the years, he developed many different rules for determining the most important financial ratios and the critical values for judging a stock to be undervalued. Through many editions, his book has had a profound influence on investment professionals. It has been so influential and successful, in fact, that widespread adoption of Graham's techniques has led to elimination of the very bargains they are designed to identify.

In a 1976 seminar Graham said[3]

> I am no longer an advocate of elaborate techniques of security analysis in order to find superior value opportunities. This was a rewarding activity, say, forty years ago, when our textbook "Graham and Dodd" was first published; but the situation has changed a good deal since then. In the old days any well-trained security analyst could do a good professional job of selecting undervalued issues through detailed studies; but in the light of the enormous amount of research now being carried on, I doubt whether in most cases such extensive efforts will generate sufficiently superior selections to justify their cost. To that very limited extent I'm on the side of the "efficient market" school of thought now generally accepted by the professors.

Nonetheless, in that same seminar, Graham suggested a simplified approach to identify bargain stocks:

> My first, more limited, technique confines itself to the purchase of common stocks at less than their working-capital value, or net current-asset value, giving no weight to the plant and other fixed assets, and deducting all liabilities in full from the current assets. We used this approach extensively in managing investment funds, and over a thirty-odd-year period we must have earned an average of some 20% per year from this source. For awhile, however, after the mid-1950s, this brand of buying opportunity became very scarce because of the pervasive bull market. But it has returned in quantity since the 1973–1974 decline. In January 1976 we counted over 100 such issues in the Standard & Poor's *Stock Guide*—about 10% of the total. I consider it a foolproof method of systematic investment—once again, not on the basis of individual results but in terms of the expectable group outcome.

There are two convenient sources of information for those interested in trying out the Graham technique. Both Standard & Poor's *Outlook* and *The Value Line Investment Survey* carry lists of stocks selling below net working capital value.

Summary

- The primary focus of the security analyst should be the firm's real economic earnings rather than its reported earnings. Accounting earnings as reported in financial statements can be a biased estimate of real economic earnings, although empirical studies reveal that reported earnings convey considerable information concerning a firm's prospects.
- A firm's ROE is a key determinant of the growth rate of its earnings. ROE is affected profoundly by the firm's degree of financial leverage. An increase in a firm's debt/equity

---

[3]As cited by John Train in *Money Masters* (New York: Harper & Row, Publishers, Inc., 1987).

ratio will raise its ROE and hence its growth rate only if the interest rate on the debt is less than the firm's return on assets.

- It is often helpful to the analyst to decompose a firm's ROE ratio into the product of several accounting ratios and to analyze their separate behavior over time and across companies within an industry. A useful breakdown is

$$\text{ROE} = \frac{\text{Net profits}}{\text{Pretax profits}} \times \frac{\text{Pretax profits}}{\text{EBIT}} \times \frac{\text{EBIT}}{\text{Sales}} \times \frac{\text{Sales}}{\text{Assets}} \times \frac{\text{Assets}}{\text{Equity}}$$

- Other accounting ratios that have a bearing on a firm's profitability and/or risk are fixed-asset turnover, inventory turnover, days receivable, and the current, quick, and interest coverage ratios.
- Two ratios that make use of the market price of the firm's common stock in addition to its financial statements are the ratios of market to book value and price to earnings. Analysts sometimes take low values for these ratios as a margin of safety or a sign that the stock is a bargain.
- A major problem in the use of data obtained from a firm's financial statements is comparability. Firms have a great deal of latitude in how they choose to compute various items of revenue and expense. It is, therefore, necessary for the security analyst to adjust accounting earnings and financial ratios to a uniform standard before attempting to compare financial results across firms.
- Comparability problems can be acute in a period of inflation. Inflation can create distortions in accounting for inventories, depreciation, and interest expense.

Key Terms

accounting earnings, *387*
acid test ratio, *394*
asset turnover, *390*
average collection
 period, *393*
balance sheet, *384*
current ratio, *394*
days receivables, *393*
earnings yield, *396*

economic earnings, *387*
FIFO, *398*
income statement, *384*
interest coverage ratio, *394*
leverage ratio, *391*
LIFO, *398*
market-to-book-value
 ratio, *394*
price/earnings ratio, *395*

profit margin, *390*
quick ratio, *394*
return on assets, *388*
return on equity, *388*
return on sales, *390*
statement of cash
 flows, *385*
times interest earned, *394*

Problem Set

1. The Crusty Pie Co., which specializes in apple turnovers, has a return on sales higher than the industry average, yet its ROA is the same as the industry average. How can you explain this?
2. The ABC Corporation has a profit margin on sales below the industry average, yet its ROA is above the industry average. What does this imply about its asset turnover?
3. Firm *A* and firm *B* have the same ROA, yet firm *A*'s ROE is higher. How can you explain this?
 (Problems 4–17 are from past Level I CFA examinations.)

4. Which of the following *best* explains a ratio of "net sales to average net fixed assets" that *exceeds* the industry average?
 a. The firm added to its plant and equipment in the past few years.
 b. The firm makes less efficient use of its assets than other firms.
 c. The firm has a lot of old plant and equipment.
 d. The firm uses straight-line depreciation.
5. The rate of return on assets is equivalent to:
 a. Profit margin × Total asset turnover
 b. Profit margin × Total asset turnover × Leverage ratio/Interest expense

      c. (Net income + Interest expense net of income tax + Minority interest in earnings)/
         Average total assets
      d. (Net income + Minority interest in earnings)/Average total assets
         (1) *a* only
         (2) *a* and *c*
         (3) *b* only
         (4) *b* and *d*

6. The financial statements for Seattle Manufacturing Corporation are to be used to com-
    pute the following ratios for 1997 (Tables 14A and 14B).
    a. Return on total assets.
    b. Earnings per share of common stock.
    c. Acid test ratio.
    d. Interest coverage ratio.
    e. Receivables collection period.
    f. Leverage ratio.

TABLE 14A
Seattle Manufacturing
Corp. Consolidated
Balance Sheet, as
of December 31
($ million)

	1996	1997
Assets		
Current assets		
Cash	$ 6.2	$ 6.6
Short-term investment in commercial paper	20.8	15.0
Accounts receivable	77.0	93.2
Inventory	251.2	286.0
Prepaid manufacturing expense	1.4	1.8
Total current assets	$356.6	$402.6
Leased property under capital leases net of accumulated amortization	181.4	215.6
Other	6.2	9.8
Total assets	$544.2	$628.0
Liabilities		
Current liabilities		
Accounts payable	$143.2	$161.0
Dividends payable	13.0	14.4
Current portion of long-term debt	12.0	16.6
Current portion of obligations under capital leases	18.8	22.6
Estimated taxes on income	10.8	9.8
Total current liabilities	$197.8	$224.4
Long-term debt	86.4	107.0
Obligations under capital leases	140.8	165.8
Total liabilities	$425.0	$497.2
Shareholders' Equity		
Common stock, $10 par value 4,000,000 shares authorized; 3,000,000 and 2,680,000 outstanding, respectively	$ 26.8	$ 30.0
Cumulative preferred stock, Series A 8%; $25 par value; 1,000,000 authorized; 600,000 outstanding	15.0	15.0
Additional paid-in capital	26.4	27.0
Retained earnings	51.0	58.8
Total shareholders' equity	$119.2	$130.8
Total liabilities and shareholders' equity	$544.2	$628.0

TABLE 14B

Seattle Manufacturing Corp. Income Statement, Years Ending December 31 ($ millions)

	1996	1997
Sales	$1,166.6	$1,207.6
Other income, net	12.8	15.6
Total revenues	$1,179.4	$1,223.2
Cost of sales	$ 912.0	$ 961.2
Amortization of leased property	43.6	48.6
Selling and administrative expenses	118.4	128.8
Interest expense	16.2	19.8
Total costs and expenses	$1,090.2	$1,158.4
Income before income tax	$ 89.2	$ 64.8
Income tax	19.2	10.4
Net income	$ 70.0	$ 54.4

7. The financial statements for Chicago Refrigerator Inc. are to be used to compute the ratios *a* through *h* on page 408 for 1997 (Tables 14C and 14D).

TABLE 14C

Chicago Refrigerator Inc. Balance Sheet, as of December 31 ($ thousands)

	1996	1997
Assets		
Current assets		
Cash	$ 683	$ 325
Accounts receivable	1,490	3,599
Inventories	1,415	2,423
Prepaid expenses	15	13
Total current assets	$3,603	$6,360
Property, plant, equipment, net	1,066	1,541
Other	123	157
Total assets	$4,792	$8,058
Liabilities		
Current liabilities		
Notes payable to bank	$ —	$ 875
Current portion of long-term debt	38	115
Accounts payable	485	933
Estimated income tax	588	472
Accrued expenses	576	586
Customer advance payment	34	963
Total current liabilities	$1,721	$3,945
Long-term debt	122	179
Other liabilities	81	131
Total liabilities	$1,924	$4,255
Shareholders' equity		
Common stock, $1 par value 1,000,000 shares authorized; 550,000 and 829,000 outstanding, respectively	$ 550	$ 829
Preferred stock, Series A 10%; $25.00 par value; 25,000 authorized; 20,000 and 18,000 outstanding, respectively	500	450
Additional paid-in capital	450	575
Retained earnings	1,368	1,949
Total shareholders' equity	$2,868	$3,803
Total liabilities and shareholders' equity	$4,792	$8,058

TABLE 14D

Chicago Refrigerator Inc. Income Statement, Years Ending December 31 ($ thousands)

	1996	1997
Net sales	$ 7,570	$ 12,065
Other income, net	261	345
Total revenues	$ 7,831	$ 12,410
Cost of goods sold	$ 4,850	$ 8,048
General administrative and marketing expenses	1,531	2,025
Interest expense	22	78
Total costs and expenses	$ 6,403	$ 10,151
Net income before tax	$ 1,428	$ 2,259
Income tax	628	994
Net income	$ 800	$ 1,265

   a. Quick ratio.
   b. Return on assets.
   c. Return on common shareholders' equity.
   d. Earnings per share of common stock.
   e. Profit margin.
   f. Times interest earned.
   g. Inventory turnover.
   h. Leverage ratio.

8. The financial statements for Atlas Corporation are to be used to compute the ratios *a* through *e* on page 409 for 1997 (Tables 14E and 14F).

TABLE 14E

Atlas Corporation Consolidated Balance Sheet, as of December 31 ($ millions)

	1996	1997
Assets		
Current assets		
Cash	$ 3.1	$ 3.3
Short-term investment in commercial paper	2.9	—
Accounts receivable	38.5	46.6
Inventory	125.6	143.0
Prepaid manufacturing expense	0.7	0.9
Total current assets	$170.8	$193.8
Leased property under capital leases net of accumulated amortization	$ 90.7	$107.8
Other	3.1	4.9
Total assets	$264.6	$306.5
Liabilities		
Current liabilities		
Accounts payable	$ 71.6	$ 81.7
Dividends payable	6.5	6.0
Current portion of long-term debt	6.0	8.3
Current portion of obligation under capital leases	9.4	11.3
Estimated taxes on income	5.4	4.9
Total current liabilities	$ 98.9	$112.2
Long-term debt	$ 43.2	$ 53.5
Obligations under capital leases	70.4	82.9
Total liabilities	$212.5	$248.6
Shareholders' equity		
Common stock, $10 par value 2,000,000 shares authorized; 1,340,000 and 1,500,000 outstanding, respectively	$ 13.4	$ 15.0
Additional paid-in capital	13.2	13.5
Retained earnings	25.5	29.4
Total shareholders' equity	$ 52.1	$ 57.9
Total liabilities and shareholders' equity	$264.6	$306.5

TABLE 14F
Atlas Corporation
Income Statement,
Years Ending
December 31,
($ millions)

	1996	1997
Sales	$583.3	$603.8
Other income, net	6.4	2.8
Main revenues	$589.7	$606.6
Cost of sales	$456.0	$475.6
Amortization of leased property	21.8	24.3
Selling and administrative expenses	59.2	64.4
Interest expense	8.1	9.9
Total costs and expenses	$545.1	$574.2
Income before income tax	$ 44.6	$ 32.4
Income tax	9.6	5.2
Net income	$ 35.0	$ 27.2

   a. Acid-test ratio
   b. Inventory turnover
   c. Earnings per share
   d. Interest coverage
   e. Leverage

9. Just before the onset of inflation, a firm switched from FIFO to LIFO. If nothing else changed, the inventory turnover for the next year would be:
   a. Higher.
   b. Lower.
   c. Unchanged.
   d. Unpredictable from the information given.

10. In an inflationary period, the use of FIFO will make which *one* of the following more realistic than the use of LIFO?
   a. Balance sheet
   b. Income statement
   c. Cash flow statement
   d. None of the above

11. A company acquires a machine with an estimated 10-year service life. If the company uses the Accelerated Cost Recovery System depreciation method instead of the straight-line method:
   a. Income will be higher in the 10th year.
   b. Total depreciation expense for the 10 years will be lower.
   c. Depreciation expense will be lower in the first year.
   d. Scrapping the machine after eight years will result in a larger loss.

12. Why might a firm's ratio of long-term debt to long-term capital be lower than the industry average, but its ratio of income-before-interest-and-taxes to debt-interest charges be lower than the industry average?
   a. The firm has higher profitability than average.
   b. The firm has more short-term debt than average.
   c. The firm has a high ratio of current assets to current liabilities.
   d. The firm has a high ratio of total cash flow to total long-term debt.

13. Assuming continued inflation, a firm that uses LIFO will tend to have a _____ current ratio than a firm using FIFO, and the difference will tend to _____ as time passes.
   a. Higher, increase
   b. Higher, decrease
   c. Lower, decrease
   d. Lower, increase

14. In a cash flow statement prepared in accordance with FASB 95, cash flow from investing activities *excludes*:
   a. Cash paid for acquisitions.
   b. Cash received from the sale of fixed assets.
   c. Inventory increases due to a new (internally developed) product line.
   d. All of the above.

15. Cash flow from operating activities *includes*:
   a. Inventory increases resulting from acquisitions.
   b. Inventory changes due to changing exchange rates.
   c. Interest paid to bondholders.
   d. Dividends paid to stockholders.

16. All other things being equal, what effect will the payment of a cash dividend have on the following ratios:

Times Interest Earned	Debt/Equity Ratio
a. Increase	Increase
b. No effect	Increase
c. No effect	No effect
d. Decrease	Decrease

17. The Du Pont formula defines the net return on shareholders' equity as a function of the following components:
   - Operating margin
   - Asset turnover
   - Interest burden
   - Financial leverage
   - Income tax rate

   Using *only* the data in Table 14G:
   a. Calculate each of the five components listed above for 1993 and 1997, and calculate the return on equity (ROE) for 1993 and 1997, using all of the five components.
   b. Briefly discuss the impact of the changes in asset turnover and financial leverage on the change in ROE from 1993 to 1997.

TABLE 14G
Income Statements and
Balance Sheets

	1993	1997
Income Statement Data		
Revenues	$542	$979
Operating income	38	76
Depreciation and amortization	3	9
Interest expense	3	0
Pretax income	32	67
Income taxes	13	37
Net income after tax	$ 19	$ 30
Bargain Sheet Data		
Fixed assets	$ 41	$ 70
Total assets	245	291
Working capital	123	157
Total debt	16	0
Total shareholders' equity	$159	$220

18. Use MarketBase-E to find the profit margin, or return on sales, and the asset turnover of several nonfinancial industry groups (e.g., Home Furniture & Furnishing [SIC = 571]

and Grocery Stores [SIC = 541]). What seems to be the relationship between return on sales and turnover? Is this result expected or unexpected? Why?

19. Examine the Grocery Stores industry using MarketBase-E. Compare the return on assets of several firms in that industry to the industry average. Why does the firm do better or worse than the industry average? Use the Du Pont formula to guide your analysis. Compare the debt ratios, asset turnover, and return on sales of your firms to the industry average.

◼ IEM
Applications

1. Obtain last year's balance sheets and cash flow statements for the companies traded on the IEM Computer Industry Returns Market using the annual report, Edgar, Bloomberg, ValueScreen, or some other source. Conduct a financial analysis as discussed in this chapter. Based on your analysis which stocks do you think are undervalued and overvalued? What does your analysis imply for prices of the IEM contracts that are currently trading in the Computer Industry Returns Market?

Solutions to
Concept Checks

1. A debt/equity ratio of 1 implies that Mordett will have $50 million of debt and $50 million of equity. Interest expense will be 0.09 × $50 million, or $4.5 million per year. Mordett's net profits and ROE over the business cycle will therefore be

		Nodett			Mordett	
Scenario	EBIT	Net Profits	ROE		Net Profits[a]	ROE[b]
Bad year	$5M	$3M	3%		$0.3M	0.6%
Normal year	10	6	6		3.3	6.6
Good year	15	9	9		6.3	12.6

[a]Mordett's after-tax profits are given by: 0.6(EBIT − $4.5 million).
[b]Mordett's equity is only $50 million.

2. Ratio Decomposition Analysis for Mordett Corporation

	ROE	(1) Net Profit Pretax Profit	(2) Pretax Profit EBIT	(3) EBIT Sales (ROS)	(4) Sales Assets (ATO)	(5) Assets Equity	(6) Compound Leverage Factor (2) × (5)
a. Bad Year							
Nodett	0.030	0.6	1.000	0.0625	0.800	1.000	1.000
Somdett	0.018	0.6	0.360	0.0625	0.800	1.667	0.600
Mordett	0.006	0.6	0.100	0.0625	0.800	2.000	0.200
b. Normal Year							
Nodett	0.060	0.6	1.000	0.100	1.000	1.000	1.000
Somdett	0.068	0.6	0.680	0.100	1.000	1.667	1.134
Mordett	0.066	0.6	0.550	0.100	1.000	2.000	1.100
c. Good Year							
Nodett	0.090	0.6	1.000	0.125	1.200	1.000	1.000
Somdett	0.118	0.6	0.787	0.125	1.200	1.667	1.311
Mordett	0.126	0.6	0.700	0.125	1.200	2.000	1.400

3. GI's ROE in 19X3 was 3.03%, computed as follows

$$ROE = \frac{\$5,285}{0.5(\$171,843 + \$177,128)} = 0.0303, \text{ or } 3.03\%$$

Its P/E ratio was $4.0 = \dfrac{\$21}{\$5.285}$

and its P/B ratio was $0.12 = \dfrac{\$21}{\$177}$

Its earnings yield was 25% compared with an industry average of 12.5%.

Note that in our calculations the earnings yield will not equal ROE/(P/B) because we have computed ROE with average shareholders' equity in the denominator and P/B with end-of-year shareholders' equity in the denominator.

4. IBX Ratio Analysis

		(1)	(2)	(3)	(4)	(5)	(6)	(7)
		Net Profit Pretax Profit	Pretax Profit	EBIT	Sales		Combined Leverage	
Year	ROE	$\frac{\text{Net Profit}}{\text{Pretax Profit}}$	$\frac{\text{Pretax Profit}}{\text{EBIT}}$	$\frac{\text{EBIT}}{\text{Sales}}$ (ROS)	$\frac{\text{Sales}}{\text{Assets}}$ (ATO)	$\frac{\text{Assets}}{\text{Equity}}$	Factor (2) × (5)	ROA (3) × (4)
1997	11.4%	0.616	0.796	7.75%	1.375	2.175	1.731	10.65%
1994	10.2	0.636	0.932	8.88	1.311	1.474	1.374	11.65

ROE went up despite a decline in operating margin and a decline in the tax burden ratio because of increased leverage and turnover. Note that ROA declined from 11.65% in 1994 to 10.65% in 1997.

5. LIFO accounting results in lower reported earnings than does FIFO. Fewer assets to depreciate results in lower reported earnings because there is less bias associated with the use of historic cost. More debt results in lower reported earnings because the inflation premium in the interest rate is treated as part of interest.

Chapter 15

TECHNICAL ANALYSIS

AFTER STUDYING THIS CHAPTER YOU SHOULD BE ABLE TO:

- Use the Dow theory to identify situations that technicians would characterize as buy or sell opportunities.

- Use indicators such as volume, put/call ratios, breadth, short interest, or confidence indexes to measure the "technical condition" of the market.

- Explain why most of technical analysis is at odds with an efficiently functioning stock market.

In the three previous chapters, we examined the fundamental analysis of equity, considering how the general macroeconomic environment and the specific prospects of the firm or industry might affect the present value of the dividend stream the firm can be expected to generate. In this chapter, we examine technical analysis. Technical analysis focuses more on the past price movements of a company than on the underlying fundamental determinants of future profitability. Technicians believe the past price and volume data signal future price movements.

Such a view is diametrically opposed to that of the efficient market hypothesis, which holds that all historical data must be reflected in stock prices already. As we lay out the basics of technical analysis in this chapter, we will point out the contradiction between the assumptions on which these strategies are based and the notion of well-functioning capital markets with rational and informed traders.

15.1 TECHNICAL ANALYSIS

Technical analysis is in most instances an attempt to exploit recurring and predictable patterns in stock prices to generate abnormal trading profits. In the words of one of its leading practitioners,

> the technical approach to investment is essentially a reflection of the idea that the stock market moves in trends which are determined by the changing attitudes of investors to a variety of

economic, monetary, political, and psychological forces. The art of technical analysis, for it is an art, is to identify changes in such trends at an early stage and to maintain an investment posture until a reversal of that trend is indicated.[1]

Technicians do not necessarily deny the value of fundamental information, such as we have discussed in the three past chapters. Many technical analysts believe stock prices eventually "close in on" their fundamental values. Technicians believe, nevertheless, that shifts in market fundamentals can be discerned before the impact of those shifts is fully reflected in prices. As the market adjusts to a new equilibrium, astute traders can exploit these price trends.

Technicians also believe that market fundamentals can be perturbed by irrational factors. More or less random fluctuations in price will accompany any underlying trend. If these fluctuations dissipate slowly, they can be taken advantage of for abnormal profits.

These presumptions, of course, clash head-on with those of the efficient market hypothesis (EMH) and with the logic of well-functioning capital markets. According to the EMH, a shift in market fundamentals should be reflected in prices immediately. According to technicians, though, that shift will lead to a gradual price change that can be recognized as a trend. Such exploitable trends in stock market prices would be damning evidence against the EMH, as they would indicate profit opportunities that market participants had left unexploited.

A more subtle version of technical analysis holds that there are patterns in stock prices that can be explained, but that once investors identify and attempt to profit from these patterns, their trading activity affects prices, thereby altering price patterns. This means the patterns that characterize market prices will be constantly evolving, and only the best analysts who can identify new patterns earliest will be rewarded. We call this phenomenon *self-destructing* patterns and explore it in some depth in the chapter.

The notion of evolving patterns is consistent with almost but not-quite efficient markets. It allows for the possibility of temporarily unexploited profit opportunities, but it also views market participants as aggressively exploiting those opportunities once they are uncovered. The market is continually groping toward full efficiency, but it is never quite there.

This is in some ways an appealing middle position in the ongoing debate between technicians and proponents of the EMH. Ultimately, however, it is an untestable hypothesis. Technicians will always be able to identify trading rules that would have worked in the past but need not work any longer. Is this evidence of a once viable trading rule that has now been eliminated by competition? Perhaps. But it is far more likely the trading rule could have been identified only after the fact.

Until technicians can offer rigorous evidence that their trading rules provide *consistent* trading profits, we must doubt the viability of those rules. As you saw in the chapter on the efficient market hypothesis, the evidence on the performance of professionally managed funds generally does not support the efficacy of technical analysis.

15.2 CHARTING

Technical analysts are sometimes called *chartists* because they study records or charts of past stock prices and trading volume, hoping to find patterns they can exploit to make a profit. In this section, we examine several specific charting strategies.

The Dow Theory

Dow theory
A technique that attempts to discern long- and short-term trends in stock market prices.

The Dow theory, named after its creator Charles Dow (who established *The Wall Street Journal*), is the grandfather of most technical analysis. While most technicians today would view the theory as somewhat dated, the approach of many more statistically sophisticated

---

[1]Martin J. Pring, *Technical Analysis Explained*, 2nd ed. (New York: McGraw-Hill Book Company, 1985), p. 2.

FIGURE 15.1

Dow Theory Trends

Source: From Melanie F. Bowman and Thom Hartle, "Dow Theory," *Technical Analysis of Stocks and Commodities*. September 1990, p. 690.

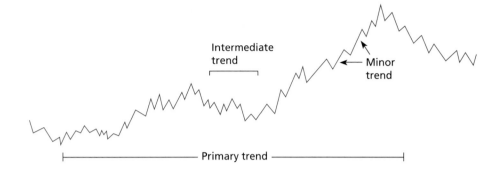

FIGURE 15.2

Dow Jones Industrial Average in 1988

Source: From Melanie F. Bowman and Thom Hartle, "Dow Theory," *Technical Analysis of Stocks and Commodities*. September 1990, p. 690.

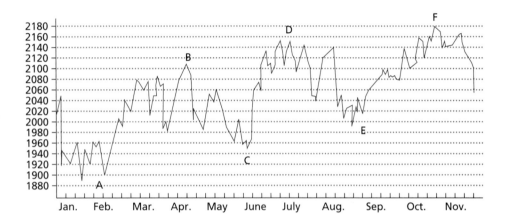

methods are essentially variants of Dow's approach. The aim of the Dow theory is to identify long-term trends in stock market prices. The two indicators used are the Dow Jones Industrial Average (DJIA) and the Dow Jones Transportation Average (DJTA). The DJIA is the key indicator of underlying trends, while the DJTA usually serves as a check to confirm or reject that signal.

The Dow theory posits three forces simultaneously affecting stock prices:

1. The *primary trend* is the long-term movement of prices, lasting from several months to several years.

2. *Secondary* or *intermediate trends* are caused by short-term deviations of prices from the underlying trend line. These deviations are eliminated via *corrections* when prices revert back to trend values.

3. *Tertiary* or *minor trends* are daily fluctuations of little importance.

Figure 15.1 represents these three components of stock price movements. In this figure, the primary trend is upward, but intermediate trends result in short-lived market declines lasting a few weeks. The intraday minor trends have no long-run impact on price.

Figure 15.2 depicts the course of the DJIA during 1988. The primary trend is upward, as evidenced by the fact that each market peak is higher than the previous peak (point F versus D versus B). Similarly, each low is higher than the previous low (E versus C versus A). This pattern of upward-moving "tops" and "bottoms" is one of the key ways to identify the underlying primary trend. Notice in Figure 15.2 that, despite the upward primary trend, intermediate trends still can lead to short periods of declining prices (points B through C, or D through E).

FIGURE 15.3
Dow Theory Signals

Source: From Melanie F.
Bowman and Thom Hartle,
"Dow Theory," *Technical
Analysis of Stocks and
Commodities*. September 1990,
p. 690.

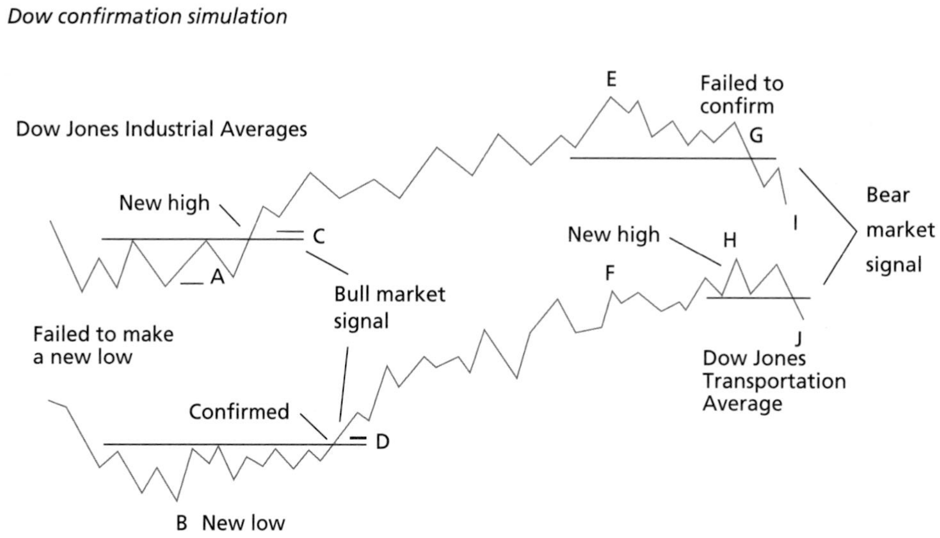

Dow confirmation simulation

Note: A simulated example of confirmation and nonconfirmation by the DJIA and the DJTA.

support level
A price level below which
it is supposedly unlikely
for a stock or stock index
to fall.

resistance level
A price level above which
it is supposedly unlikely
for a stock or stock index
to rise.

The Dow theory incorporates notions of support and resistance levels in stock prices. A **support level** is a value below which the market is relatively unlikely to fall. A **resistance level** is a level above which it is difficult to rise. Support and resistance levels are determined by the recent history of prices. In Figure 15.3, the price at point C would be viewed as a resistance level because the recent intermediate-trend high price was unable to rise above C. Hence, piercing the resistance point is a bullish signal. The fact that the transportation index also pierces its resistance level at point D confirms the bull market signal.

Technicians see resistance and support levels as resulting from common psychological investor traits. Consider, for example, stock XYZ, which traded for several months at a price of $72 and then declined to $65. If the stock eventually begins to increase in price, $72 will be a natural resistance level because the many investors who originally bought at $72 will be eager to sell their shares as soon as they can break even on their investment. Therefore, whenever prices near $72, a wave of selling pressure will develop. Such activity imparts to the market a type of "memory" that allows past price history to influence current stock prospects.

Concept Check

1. Describe how technicians might explain support levels.

At point G in Figure 15.3, the DJIA fails to move to a higher high when the DJTA reaches a higher high at point H. This contradictory signal, called a *nonconfirmation*, is a warning sign. At points I and J, both indexes fall below the low points of the previous trading range, which is taken as a signal of the end of the primary bull market.

In evaluating the Dow theory, don't forget the lessons of the efficient market hypothesis. The Dow theory is based on a notion of predictably recurring price patterns. Yet the EMH holds that if any pattern is exploitable, many investors would attempt to profit from such predictability, which would ultimately move stock prices and cause the trading strategy to self-destruct. While Figure 15.2 certainly appears to describe a classic upward primary trend, one always must wonder whether we can see that trend only *after* the fact. Recognizing patterns as they emerge is far more difficult.

Recent variations on the Dow theory are the Elliott wave theory and the theory of Kondratieff waves. Like the Dow theory, the idea behind Elliott waves is that stock prices can be described by a set of wave patterns. Long-term and short-term wave cycles are superimposed and result in a complicated pattern of price movements, but by interpreting the cycles, one can, according to the theory, predict broad movements. Similarly, Kondratieff waves are named after a Russian economist who asserted that the macroeconomy (and therefore the stock market) moves in broad waves lasting between 48 and 60 years. The Kondratieff waves are therefore analogous to Dow's primary trend, although they are of far longer duration. Kondratieff's assertion is hard to evaluate empirically, however, because cycles that last about 50 years provide only two full data points per century, which is hardly enough data to test the predictive power of the theory.

Other Charting Techniques

The Dow theory posits a particular, and fairly simple, type of pattern in stock market prices: long-lasting trends with short-run deviations around those trends. Not surprisingly, several more involved patterns have been identified in stock market prices. Figure 15.4 illustrates several of these patterns. If stock prices were to actually follow any of these patterns, profit opportunities would result. The patterns are reasonably straightforward to discern, meaning future prices can be extrapolated from current prices.

A variant on pure trend analysis is the *point and figure chart* depicted in Figure 15.5. This figure has no time dimension. It simply traces significant upward or downward movements in stock prices without regard to their timing. The data for Figure 15.5 come from Table 15.1.

Suppose, as in Table 15.1, that a stock's price is currently $40. If the price rises by at least $2, you put an X in the first column at $42 in Figure 15.5. Another increase of at least $2 calls for placement of another X in the first column, this time at the $44 level. If the stock then falls by at least $2, you start a new column and put an O next to $42. Each subsequent $2 price fall results in another O in the second column. When prices reverse yet again and head upward, you begin the third column with an X denoting each consecutive $2 price increase.

The single asterisks in Table 15.1 mark an event resulting in the placement of a new X or O in the chart. The daggers denote price movements that result in the start of a new column of Xs or Os.

Sell signals are generated when the stock price *penetrates* previous lows, and buy signals occur when previous high prices are penetrated. A *congestion area* is a horizontal band of Xs and Os created by several price reversals. These three regions are indicated in Figure 15.6.

One can devise point and figure charts using price increments other than $2, but it is customary in setting up a chart to require reasonably substantial price changes before marking pluses or minuses.

Concept Check

2. Draw a point and figure chart using the history in Table 15.1 with price increments of $3.

Another graphical technique used to summarize price data and aid in the identification of trends is the so-called *candlestick chart*, illustrated in Figure 15.7. The box with the vertical line drawn through it allows the chartist to ascertain the open and close price for the day, as well as the high and low price. The top and bottom of each vertical line represent the high and low price, respectively. If the price increases during the day (e.g., Monday in Figure 15.7), the box is shaded, so the analyst knows that the closing price is at the top of the box and the opening price is at the bottom. If the box is left unshaded (e.g., Tuesday), the stock price is understood to have fallen, and the closing price is at the bottom of the box. The

FIGURE 15.4

Chart Representation of Market Bottoms and Tops

Source: From Irwin Shishko, "Techniques of Forecasting Commodity Prices." *Commodity Yearbook* (New York: Commodity Research Bureau, 1965), p. 4.

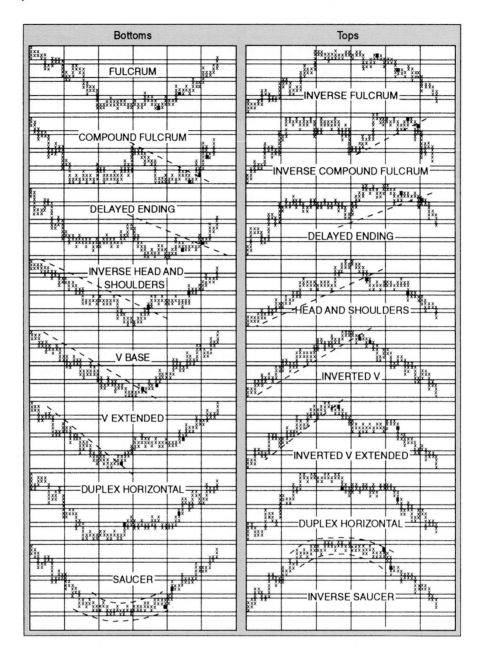

vertical lines extend from the daily high to the daily low price. The chart thus conveys a considerable amount of information about recent stock price history. Obviously, candlestick charts can be drawn using either shorter or longer time periods than one-day returns, for example, using intraday or weekly prices.

A Warning

The search for patterns in stock market prices is nearly irresistible, and the ability of the human eye to discern apparent patterns is remarkable. Unfortunately, it is possible to perceive patterns that really don't exist. Consider Figure 15.8, which presents simulated and actual values of the Dow Jones Industrial Average during 1956 taken from a famous study by Harry Roberts (1959). In Figure 15.8B, it appears as though the market presents a classic

FIGURE 15.5

Point and Figure Chart
for Table 15.1

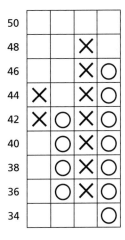

TABLE 15.1

Stock Price History

Date	Price	Date	Price
January 2	$40	February 1	$40*
January 3	40-1/2	February 2	41
January 4	41	February 5	40-1/2
January 5	42*	February 6	42*
January 8	41-1/2	February 7	45*
January 9	42-1/2	February 8	44-1/2
January 10	43	February 9	46*
January 11	43-3/4	February 12	47
January 12	44*	February 13	48*
January 15	45	February 14	47-1/2
January 16	44	February 15	46†
January 17	41-1/2†	February 16	45
January 18	41	February 19	44*
January 19	40*	February 20	42*
January 22	39	February 21	41
January 23	39-1/2	February 22	40*
January 24	39-3/4	February 23	41
January 25	38*	February 26	40-1/2
January 26	35*	February 27	38*
January 29	36†	February 28	39
January 30	37	March 1	36*
January 31	39*	March 2	34*

*Indicates an event that has resulted in a stock price increase or decrease of at least $2.

†Denotes a price movement that has resulted in either an upward or downward reversal in the stock price.

head-and-shoulders pattern where the middle hump (the head) is flanked by two shoulders. When the price index "pierces the right shoulder"—a technical trigger point—it is believed to be heading lower, and it is time to sell your stocks. Figure 15.8A also looks like a "typical" stock market pattern.

Can you tell which of the two graphs is constructed from the real value of the Dow and which from the simulated data? Figure 15.8A is based on the real data. The graph in B was generated using "returns" created by a random number generator. These returns *by construction* were patternless, but the simulated price path that is plotted appears to follow a pattern much like that of A.

Figure 15.9 shows the weekly price changes behind the two panels in Figure 15.8. Here the randomness in both series—the stock price as well as the simulated sequence—is obvious.

A problem related to the tendency to perceive patterns where they don't exist is data mining. After the fact, you can always find patterns and trading rules that would have

FIGURE 15.6

Point and Figure Chart
with Sell Signal, Buy
Signal, and Congestion
Areas

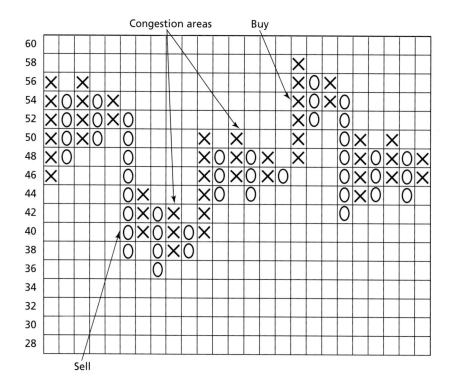

FIGURE 15.7

Candlestick Chart

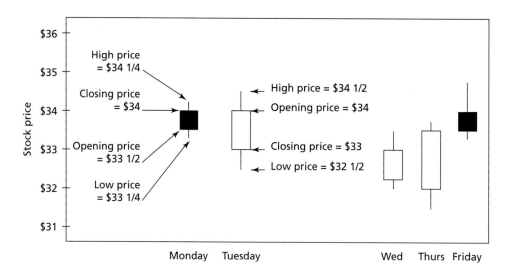

generated enormous profits. If you test enough rules, some will have worked in the past. Unfortunately, picking a theory that would have worked after the fact carries no guarantee of future success.

In this regard, consider a curious investment rule that has worked with uncanny precision since 1967. In years that an original National Football League team wins the Super Bowl (played in January), bet on the stock market rising for the rest of the year. In years that a team from the American Football Conference that was not originally an NFL team wins, bet on a market decline.

Between 1967 and 1996, the NYSE index rose in the year following the Super Bowl 20 of the 23 times that an NFC or original NFL team won. The market fell in six out of seven years that an AFC team won. Despite the overwhelming past success of this rule, would you

FIGURE 15.8 Actual and Simulated Levels for Stock Market Prices of 52 Weeks

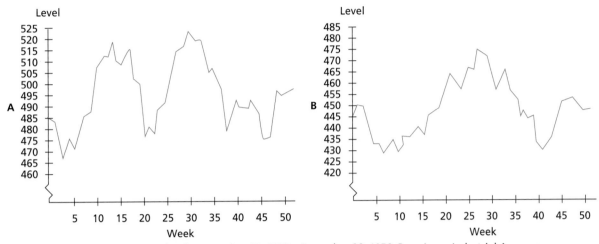

Friday closing levels, December 30, 1955—December 28, 1956, Dow Jones Industrial Average

Source: From Harry Roberts, "Stock Market Patterns and Financial Analysis: Methodological Suggestions," *Journal of Finance*, March 1959, pp. 5–6.
Note: Friday closing levels, December 30, 1955–December 28, 1956, Dow Jones Industrial Average.

FIGURE 15.9 Actual and Simulated Changes in Weekly Stock Prices for 52 Weeks

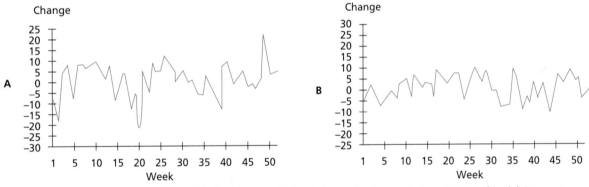

Changes from Friday to Friday (closing) January 6, 1956—December 28, 1956, Dow Jones Industrial Average

Source: From Harry Roberts, "Stock Market Patterns and Financial Analysis: Methodological Suggestions," *Journal of Finance*, March 1959, pp. 5–6.
Note: Changes from Friday to Friday (closing) January 6, 1956–December 28, 1956, Dow Jones Industrial Average.

use it to invest your money? We suspect not. See the box on page 422 for a discussion of the link between the Super Bowl and stock market history.

In evaluating trading rules, you should always ask whether the rule would have seemed reasonable *before* you looked at the data. If not, you might be buying into the one arbitrary rule among many that happened to have worked in the recent past. The hard but crucial question is whether there is reason to believe that what worked in the past should continue to work in the future.

15.3 TECHNICAL INDICATORS

Technical analysts use technical indicators besides charts to assess prospects for market declines or advances. There are three types of technical indicators: sentiment indicators, flow of funds indicators, and market structure indicators. *Sentiment indicators* are intended to measure the expectations of various groups of investors, for example, mutual fund inves-

The Super Bowl Predicts the Market, and Vice Versa

The New England Patriots are distant underdogs to the Green Bay Packers in this Sunday's Super Bowl game, according to the bookies and the commentators in sports pages across the country. But they are favored by the stock market. And if that forecast comes true, the stock market could be in for trouble this year.

Those forecasts are based on observed—and irrelevant—correlations between stock market performance and the results of the Super Bowl. Anyone foolish enough to bet on a game based on the stock market, or credulous enough to believe a football game can forecast the stock market, probably should hire a money manager, or a psychiatrist, or both. But that doesn't stop Wall Street from paying attention.

The first Super Bowl theory, which has been around for decades, holds that if a team from the old National Football League wins the game, the stock market will rise in the following year. On the other hand, if a team from the old American Football League wins, share prices will fall.

That theory had a widespread following in the 1980s, and has kept performing in recent years, albeit with a smaller following. That is because it has become accepted that the stock market always goes up. So, who needs an indicator to forecast such an obvious thing?

As it happens, a team from the old National Football League has won every Super Bowl since 1984, when the (then) Los Angeles Raiders defeated the Washington Redskins. Sure enough, measured from Super Bowl to Super Bowl, the Dow Jones Industrial Average suffered a small decline over the following 12 months.

Since then, Wall Street has seen one of the greatest bull markets ever, and old AFL teams have routinely gone down to defeat in the Super Bowl. And the common wisdom is that such a thing will happen again on Sunday, when Green Bay, an original NFL team, meets the New England Patriots, an old AFL team.

The newer theory attempts to use the stock market to forecast the game. It holds that if the Dow rises from the end of November until game day, the team whose full name appears later in the alphabet will win. This year, the Dow has zoomed after ending November at 6,521.70. Barring a crash today, that means New England would be favored over Green Bay.

Such a theory makes exactly as much sense as the one that holds that football can forecast a market. But when the theory was first discussed in this column eight years ago, it had worked in 12 of 14 years. Since then, it has worked in six of eight years, bringing its record to 18 of 22. That is better than the bookies have done over the same stretch.

Source: Floyd Norris, "The Super Bowl Predicts the Market, and Vice Versa, *The New York Times*, January 24, 1997, p. D6.

tors, corporate insiders, or NYSE specialists. *Flow of funds indicators* are intended to measure the potential for various investor groups to buy or sell stocks in order to predict the price pressure from those actions. Finally, *market structure indicators* monitor price trends and cycles. The charting techniques described in the last section are examples of market structure indicators. We will examine a few more market structure indicators in this section.

Sentiment Indicators

Trin Statistic   Market volume is sometimes used to measure the strength of a market rise or fall. Increased investor participation in a market advance or retreat is viewed as a measure of the significance of the movement. Technicians consider market advances to be a more favorable omen of continued price increases when they are associated with increased trading volume. Similarly, market reversals are considered more bearish when associated with higher volume. The *trin statistic* is the ratio of the number of advancing to declining issues divided by the ratio of volume in advancing versus declining issues.

$$\text{Trin} = \frac{\text{Number advancing/Number declining}}{\text{Volume advancing/Volume declining}}$$

This expression can be rearranged as

$$\text{Trin} = \frac{\text{Volume declining/Number declining}}{\text{Volume advancing/Number advancing}}$$

FIGURE 15.10

Market Diary

Source: From *The Wall Street Journal*, August 2, 1996. Reprinted by permission of *The Wall Street Journal*, © 1996 Dow Jones & Company, Inc. All Rights Reserved Worldwide.

DIARIES			
NYSE	**THUR**	**WED**	**WEEK AGO**
Issues traded	3,197	3,162	3,148
Advances	1,985	1,565	1,549
Declines	550	889	814
Unchanged	662	708	785
New highs	68	33	20
New lows	43	50	65
zAdv vol (000)	338,194	227,425	255,791
zDecl vol (000)	65,291	137,462	107,542
zTotal vol (000)	438,943	402,588	403,618
Closing tick[1]	+647	+377	+4
Closing Arms[2] (trin)	.70	1.06	.80
zBlock trades	10,340	8,993	9,599

Therefore, trin is the ratio of average volume in declining issues to average volume in advancing issues. Ratios above 1.0 are considered bearish because the falling stocks would then have higher average volume than the advancing stocks, indicating net selling pressure. *The Wall Street Journal* reports trin every day in the market diary section, as in Figure 15.10.

Note, however, that for every buyer, there must be a seller of stock. Rising volume in a rising market should not necessarily indicate a larger imbalance of buyers versus sellers. For example, a trin statistic above 1.0, which is considered bearish, could equally well be interpreted as indicating that there is more *buying* activity in declining issues.

odd-lot theory
The theory that net buying of small investors is a bearish signal for a stock.

Odd-Lot Trading   Just as short-sellers tend to be larger institutional traders, odd-lot traders are almost always small individual traders. (An odd lot is a transaction of fewer than 100 shares; 100 shares is one round lot.) The **odd-lot theory** holds that these small investors tend to miss key market turning points, typically buying stock after a bull market has already run its course and selling too late into a bear market. Therefore, the theory suggests that when odd-lot traders are widely buying, you should sell, and vice versa.

The Wall Street Journal publishes odd-lot trading data every day. You can construct an index of odd-lot trading by computing the ratio of odd-lot purchases to sales. A ratio substantially above 1.0 is bearish because it implies small traders are net buyers.

confidence index
Ratio of the yield of top-rated corporate bonds to the yield on intermediate-grade bonds.

Confidence Index   *Barron's* computes a confidence index using data from the bond market. The presumption is that actions of bond traders reveal trends that will emerge soon in the stock market.

The **confidence index** is the ratio of the average yield on 10 top-rated corporate bonds divided by the average yield on 10 intermediate-grade corporate bonds. The ratio will always be below 100% because higher rated bonds will offer lower promised yields to maturity. When bond traders are optimistic about the economy, however, they might require smaller default premiums on lower rated debt. Hence, the yield spread will narrow, and the confidence index will approach 100%. Therefore, higher values of the confidence index are bullish signals.

Concept Check

3. Yields on lower rated debt will rise after fears of recession have spread through the economy. This will reduce the confidence index. Should the stock market now be expected to fall or will it already have fallen?

Put/Call Ratio   Call options give investors the right to buy a stock at a fixed "exercise" price and therefore are a way of betting on stock price increases. Put options give the right to

put/call ratio
Ratio of put options to call options outstanding on a stock.

sell a stock at a fixed price and therefore are a way of betting on stock price decreases.[2] The ratio of outstanding put options to outstanding call options is called the **put/call ratio.** Typically, the put/call ratio hovers around 65%. Because put options do well in falling markets while call options do well in rising markets, deviations of the ratio from historical norms are considered to be a signal of market sentiment and therefore predictive of market movements.

Interestingly, however, a change in the ratio can be given a bullish or a bearish interpretation. Many technicians see an increase in the ratio as bearish, as it indicates growing interest in put options as a hedge against market declines. Thus, a rising ratio is taken as a sign of broad investor pessimism and a coming market decline. Contrarian investors, however, believe that a good time to buy is when the rest of the market is bearish because stock prices are then unduly depressed. Therefore, they would take an increase in the put/call ratio as a signal of a buy opportunity.

Mutual Fund Cash Positions   Technical traders view mutual fund investors as being poor market timers. Specifically, the belief is that mutual fund investors become more bullish after a market advance has already run its course. In this view, investor optimism peaks as the market is nearing its peak. Given the belief that the consensus opinion is incorrect at market turning points, a technical trader will use an indicator of market sentiment to form a contrary trading strategy. The percentage of cash held in mutual fund portfolios is one common measure of sentiment. This percentage is viewed as moving in the opposite direction of the stock market, since funds will tend to hold high cash positions when they are concerned about a falling market and the threat that investors will redeem shares.

Flow of Funds

short interest
The total number of shares currently sold short in the market.

Short Interest   **Short interest** is the total number of shares of stock currently sold short in the market. Some technicians interpret high levels of short interest as bullish, some as bearish. The bullish perspective is that, because all short sales must be covered (i.e., short-sellers eventually must purchase shares to return the ones they have borrowed), short interest represents latent future demand for the stocks. As short sales are covered, the demand created by the share purchase will force prices up.

The bearish interpretation of short interest is based on the fact that short-sellers tend to be larger, more sophisticated investors. Accordingly, increased short interest reflects bearish sentiment by those investors "in the know," which would be a negative signal of the market's prospects.

Credit Balances in Brokerage Accounts   Investors with brokerage accounts will often leave credit balances in those accounts when they plan to invest in the near future. Thus, credit balances may be viewed as measuring the potential for new stock purchases. As a result, a buildup of balances is viewed as a bullish indicator for the market.

Market Structure

Moving Averages   The moving average of a stock index is the average level of the index over a given interval of time. For example, a 52-week moving average tracks the average index value over the most recent 52 weeks. Each week, the moving average is recomputed by dropping the oldest observation and adding the latest. After a period in which prices have generally been falling, the moving average will be above the current price (because the

---

[2]Puts and calls were defined in Chapter 2, Section 2.5.

moving average "averages in" the older and higher prices). When prices have been rising, the moving average will be below the current price.

When the market price breaks through the moving average line from below, it is taken as a bullish signal because it signifies a shift from a falling trend (with prices below the moving average) to a rising trend (with prices above the moving average). Conversely, when prices fall below the moving average, it's considered time to sell.

There is some variation in the length of the moving average considered most predictive of market movements. Two popular measures are 200-day and 53-week moving averages.

EXAMPLE 15.1
Moving Averages

Consider the following price data. Each observation represents the closing level of the Dow Jones Industrial Average (DJIA) on the last trading day of the week. The five-week moving average for each week is the average of the DJIA over the previous five weeks. For example, the first entry, for week 5, is the average of the index value between weeks 1 and 5: 6,290, 6,380, 6,399, 6,379, and 6,450. The next entry is the average of the index values between weeks 2 and 6, and so on.

Week	DJIA	5-Week Moving Average	Week	DJIA	5-Week Moving Average
1	6,290		11	6,590	6,555
2	6,380		12	6,652	6,586
3	6,399		13	6,625	6,598
4	6,379		14	6,657	6,624
5	6,450	6,380	15	6,699	6,645
6	6,513	6,424	16	6,647	6,656
7	6,500	6,448	17	6,610	6,648
8	6,565	6,481	18	6,595	6,642
9	6,524	6,510	19	6,499	6,610
10	6,597	6,540	20	6,466	6,563

Figure 15.11 plots the level of the index and the five-week moving average. Notice that while the index itself moves up and down rather abruptly, the moving average is a relatively smooth series, since the impact of each week's price movement is averaged with that of the previous weeks. Week 16 is a bearish point according to the moving average rule. The price series crosses from above the moving average to below it, signifying the beginning of a downward trend in stock prices.

breadth
The extent to which movements in broad market indexes are reflected widely in movements of individual stock prices.

Breadth   The **breadth** of the market is a measure of the extent to which movement in a market index is reflected widely in the price movements of all the stocks in the market. The most common measure of breadth is the spread between the number of stocks that advance and decline in price. If advances outnumber declines by a wide margin, then the market is

FIGURE 15.11
Moving Averages

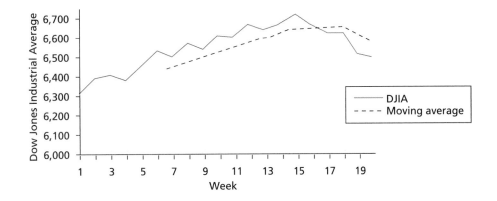

viewed as being stronger because the rally is widespread. These breadth numbers also are reported daily in *The Wall Street Journal* (see Figure 15.10).

Some analysts cumulate breadth data each day as in Table 15.2. The cumulative breadth for each day is obtained by adding that day's net advances (or declines) to the previous day's total. The direction of the cumulated series is then used to discern broad market trends. Analysts might use a moving average of cumulative breadth to gauge broad trends.

relative strength
Recent performance of a given stock or industry compared to that of a broader market index.

Relative Strength   **Relative strength** measures the extent to which a security has outperformed or underperformed either the market as a whole or its particular industry. Relative strength is computed by calculating the ratio of the price of the security to a price index for the industry. For example, the relative strength of Ford versus the auto industry would be measured by movements in the ratio of the price of Ford divided by the level of an auto industry index. A rising ratio implies Ford has been outperforming the rest of the industry. If relative strength can be assumed to persist over time, then this would be a signal to buy Ford.

Similarly, the relative strength of an industry relative to the whole market can be computed by tracking the ratio of the industry price index to the market price index.

Some evidence in support of the relative strength strategy is provided in a study by Jegadeesh and Titman (1993). They ranked firms according to stock market performance in a six-month base period and then examined returns in various follow-up periods ranging from 1 to 36 months. They found that the best performers in the base period continued to outperform other stocks for several months. This pattern is consistent with the notion of persistent relative strength. Ultimately, however, the pattern reverses, with the best base-period performers giving up their initial superior returns. Figure 15.12 illustrates this pattern. The graph shows the cumulative difference in return between the 10% of the sample of stocks with the best base-period returns and the 10% with the worst base-period returns. Initially, the curve trends upward, indicating that the best performers continue to outperform

TABLE 15.2
Breadth

Day	Advances	Declines	Net Advances	Cumulative Breadth
1	802	748	54	54
2	917	640	277	331
3	703	772	−69	262
4	512	1122	−610	−348
5	633	1004	−371	−719

Note: The sum of advances plus declines varies across days because some stock prices are unchanged.

FIGURE 15.12
Cumulative Difference in Returns of Previously Best-Performing and Worst-Performing Stocks in Subsequent Months

Source: Jegadeesh and Titman (1993).

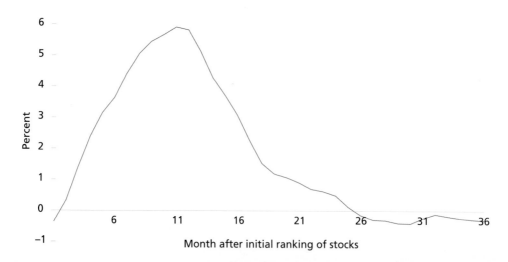

the initial laggards. After about a year, however, the curve turns down, suggesting that abnormal returns on stocks with momentum are ultimately reversed.

**EXAMPLE 15.2
Relative Strength**

The middle two columns of the following table present data on the levels of an auto industry index and a broad market index. Does the auto industry exhibit relative strength? That can be determined by examining the last column, which presents the ratio of the two indexes. Despite the fact that the auto industry as a whole has exhibited positive returns, reflected in the rising level of the industry index, the industry has *not* shown relative strength. The falling ratio of the auto industry index to the market index shows that the auto industry has underperformed the broad market.

Week	Auto Industry	Market Index	Ratio
1	165.6	447.0	0.370
2	166.7	450.1	0.370
3	168.0	455.0	0.369
4	166.9	459.9	0.363
5	170.2	459.1	0.371
6	169.2	463.0	0.365
7	171.0	469.0	0.365
8	174.1	473.2	0.368
9	173.9	478.8	0.363
10	174.2	481.0	0.362

15.4 THE VALUE LINE SYSTEM

The Value Line ranking system may be the most celebrated and well-documented example of successful stock analysis. Value Line is the largest investment advisory service in the world. Besides publishing the *Value Line Investment Survey*, which provides information on investment fundamentals for approximately 1,700 publicly traded companies, Value Line also ranks each of these stocks according to their anticipated price appreciation over the next 12 months. Stocks ranked in group 1 are expected to perform the best, while those in group 5 are expected to perform the worst. Value Line calls this "ranking for timeliness."

Figure 15.13 shows the performance of the Value Line ranking system over the 25 years from 1965 to March 1990. Over the total period, the different groups performed just as the rankings predicted, and the differences were quite large. The total 25-year price appreciation for the group 1 stocks was 3,083% (or 14.8% per year) compared to 15% (or 0.5% per year) for group 5.

How does the Value Line ranking system work? As Bernhard (1979) explains it, the ranking procedure has three components: (1) relative earnings momentum, (2) earnings surprise, and (3) a value index. Most (though not all) of the Value Line criteria are technically oriented, relying on either price momentum or relative strength. Points assigned for each factor determine the stock's overall ranking.

The relative earnings momentum factor is calculated as each company's year-to-year change in quarterly earnings divided by the average change for all stocks.

The earnings surprise factor has to do with the difference between actual reported quarterly earnings and Value Line's estimate. The points assigned to each stock increase with the percentage difference between reported and estimated earnings.

The value index is calculated from the following regression equation

$$V = a + b_1 x_1 + b_2 x_2 + b_3 x_3$$

where

x_1 = A score from 1 to 10 depending on the relative earnings momentum ranking, compared with the company's rank for the last 10 years;

Paying the Piper

ON PAPER, VALUE LINE'S PERFORMANCE IN PICKING STOCKS IS NOTHING SHORT OF DAZZLING . . . FOR AN INVESTOR TO CAPITALIZE ON THAT PERFORMANCE IS A DIFFERENT MATTER

Value Line, Inc., publishes the *Value Line Investment Survey*, that handy review of 1,652 companies. Each week the survey rates stocks from I (best buys) to V (worst). Can you beat the market following these rankings? Value Line tracks the performance of group I from April 1965, when a new ranking formula went into effect. If you bought group I then and updated your list every week, you would have a gain of 15,391% by June 30. That means $10,000 would have grown to about $1.5 million, dividends excluded. The market is up only 245% since 1965, dividends excluded.

Quite an impressive record. There is only one flaw: It ignores transaction costs. Do transaction costs much matter against a performance like that? What does the investor lose in transaction costs? A percentage point a year? Two percent?

None other than Value Line provides an answer to this question, and the answer is almost as startling as the paper performance. Since late 1983, Value Line has run a mutual fund that attempts to track group I precisely. Its return has averaged a dismal 11 percentage points a year worse than the hypothetical results in group I. The fund hasn't even kept up with the market (*see chart*).

What went wrong? "Inefficiencies and costs of implementation," says Mark Tavel, manager of the fund, Value Line Centurion.

The Value Line Centurion Fund's turnover is 200% a year. That's quite a bit of turnover—although by no means

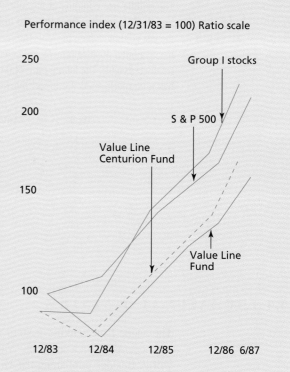

the highest in the business. The turnover is high because in a typical week, 4 of the 100 group I stocks drop down in rank and have to be replaced with new group I stocks. It's not impossible for traders like Centurion to beat the market, but they start out with a handicap.

x_2 = A score from 1 to 10 based on the stock's relative price, with ratios calculated in a similar way to the earnings ratio;

x_3 = The ratio of the stock's latest 10-week average relative price (stock price divided by the average price for all stocks) to its 52-week average relative price; and a, b_1, b_2, and b_3 are the coefficients from the regression estimated on 12 years of data.

Finally, the points for each of the three factors are added, and the stocks are classified into five groups according to the total score.

Investing according to this system does seem to produce superior results on paper, as Figure 15.13 shows. Yet, as the accompanying box points out, in practice, things are not so simple—Value Line's own mutual funds have not kept up even with the broad market averages. The box illustrates that even apparently successful trading rules can be difficult to implement in the market.

concluded

All of which means that paper performance can be pretty fanciful. "Anytime hypothetical returns are offered as proof of a particular investing style, one should also swallow a large grain of salt," says Cam Schmidt of Potomac Investment Management, a money manager in Bethesda, Md., that brought the Value Line discrepancy to *Forbes'* attention.

What are these inefficiencies and costs? And what do they tell investors about the perils of in-and-out trading?

Fund overhead is not a big item. At the $244 million Centurion, which is available only through variable life and annuity policies sold by Guardian Life, the annual expense ratio averages 0.6%. Nor are brokerage commissions large. Funneled at about 5 cents a share mostly to a captive Value Line broker, commissions eat up 0.4% of Centurion's assets per year.

So far we have 1%. Where's the other 10% of the shortfall? Bid-ask spreads, for one. A stock quoted at 39 to sellers might cost a buyer 39½—or even 41 or 42 if the buyer wants a lot of it. With about 95 of the 100 group I stocks at any given time in the Centurion portfolio, Tavel needs to amass an average $2.5 million position in each. Some of these companies have $150 million or less in outstanding shares. The very smallest Tavel doesn't even try to buy.

Timing explains some of the gulf between hypothetical and actual results. The hypothetical performance assumes a purchase at the Wednesday close before publication of the new rankings. Most subscribers get their surveys on Friday morning, however, and buy at the Friday opening—if they are lucky. An internal Value Line rule forbids the funds to act on rank changes before Friday morning.

Why, then, are Wednesday prices used in the performance claims? Because, says Samuel Eisenstadt, Value Line's chief of statistics, until recently that was all Value Line had in its database. Wednesday prices were gathered because it takes nine days to compute, print, and mail the results. The hypothetical buy, then, would come a week after the closing prices used to calculate the rankings, and a day and a half before a real buyer could act on the advice. Eisenstadt says a conversion to Friday night scoring is under way and will no doubt depress reported performance.

A day makes all the difference. A 1985 study by Scott Stickel, now an assistant professor at Wharton, showed that almost all of the excess return on a group I stock is concentrated on three days, almost evenly divided: the Friday when subscribers read about the stock's being promoted into group I, the Thursday before, and the Monday following. Wait until Tuesday to buy and you might as well not subscribe.

Why are prices moving up on Thursday, the day before publication? Eisenstadt suspects the Postal Service of acting with uncharacteristic efficiency in some parts of the country, giving a few subscribers an early start. Another reason for an uptick: Enough is known about the Value Line formula for smart investors to anticipate a rank change by a few days. The trick is to watch group II (near-top) stocks closely. If a quarterly earnings report comes in far better than the forecast published in *Value Line*, grab the stock. "What happens if you're wrong? You're stuck with a group II stock with terrific earnings," says Eisenstadt.

Source: Reprinted by permission of *Forbes* magazine. October 19, 1987. © Forbes, Inc. 1987.

15.5 CAN TECHNICAL ANALYSIS WORK IN EFFICIENT MARKETS?

Self-Destructing Patterns

It should be abundantly clear from our presentations that most of technical analysis is based on ideas totally at odds with the foundations of the efficient market hypothesis. The EMH follows from the idea that rational profit-seeking investors will act on new information so quickly that prices will nearly always reflect all publicly available information. Technical analysis, on the other hand, posits the existence of long-lived trends that play out slowly and predictably. Such patterns, if they exist, would violate the EMH notion of essentially unpredictable stock price changes.

An interesting question is whether a technical rule that seems to work will continue to work in the future once it becomes widely recognized. A clever analyst may occasionally uncover a profitable trading rule, but the real test of efficient markets is whether the rule itself becomes reflected in stock prices once its value is discovered.

Suppose, for example, the Dow theory predicts an upward primary trend. If the theory is widely accepted, it follows that many investors will attempt to buy stocks immediately in

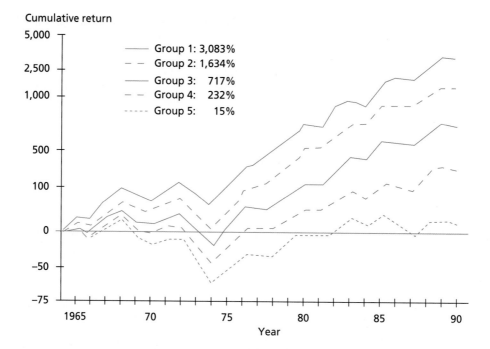

anticipation of the price increase; the effect would be to bid up prices sharply and immediately rather than at the gradual, long-lived pace initially expected. The Dow theory's predicted trend would be replaced by a sharp jump in prices. It is in this sense that price patterns ought to be *self-destructing*. Once a useful technical rule (or price pattern) is discovered, it ought to be invalidated once the mass of traders attempt to exploit it.

An instructive example of this phenomenon is the evidence by Jegadeesh (1990) and Lehmann (1990) that stock prices seem to obey a reversal effect; specifically, the best-performing stocks in one week or month tend to fare poorly in the following period, while the worst performers follow up with good performance. Such a phenomenon can be used to form a straightforward technically based trading strategy: Buy shares that recently have done poorly and sell shares that recently have done well. Lehmann shows such a strategy would have been extremely profitable in the past.

The reversal effect is at odds with market efficiency and at the same time consistent with the viability of technical analysis. The real test of a trading rule, however, comes after the potential of the strategy has been uncovered. Lehmann notes that some professionally managed equity funds now use return reversal strategies in their actively managed portfolios. These activities presumably should eliminate existing profit opportunities by forcing prices to their "correct" levels.

Thus, the market dynamic is one of a continual search for profitable trading rules, followed by destruction by overuse of those rules found to be successful, followed by yet another search for yet-undiscovered rules.

A New View of Technical Analysis

Two writers offer a rigorous foundation for the potential efficacy of technical analysis (Brown and Jennings, 1990). They envision an economy where many investors have private information regarding the ultimate value of a stock. Moreover, as time passes, each investor acquires additional information. Each investor can infer something of the information possessed by other traders by observing the price at which securities trade. The entire sequence of past prices can turn out to be useful in the inference of the information held by other traders. In this sense, technical analysis can be useful to traders even if all traders rationally use all information available to them.

Most discussions of the EMH envision public information commonly available to all traders and ask only if prices reflect that information. In this sense, the Brown and Jennings framework is more complex. Here, different individuals receive different private signals regarding the value of a firm. As prices unfold, each trader infers the good-news or bad-news nature of the signals received by other traders and updates assessments of the firm accordingly. Prices *reveal* as well as *reflect* information and become useful data to traders. Without addressing specific technical trading rules, the Brown and Jennings model is an interesting and innovative attempt to reconcile technical analysis with the usual assumption of rational traders participating in efficient markets.

Summary

- Technical analysis is the search for recurring patterns in stock market prices. It is based essentially on the notion that market prices adjust slowly to new information and, thus, is at odds with the efficient market hypothesis.
- The Dow theory is the earliest chart-based version of technical analysis. The theory posits the existence of primary, intermediate, and minor trends that can be identified on a chart and acted on by an analyst before the trends fully dissipate. Other trend-based theories are based on relative strength, the point and figures chart, and the candlestick diagram.
- Technicians believe high volume and market breadth accompanying market trends add weight to the significance of a trend.
- Odd-lot traders are viewed as uninformed, which suggests informed traders should pursue trading strategies in opposition to their activity. In contrast, short-sellers are viewed as informed traders, lending credence to their activity.
- Value Line's ranking system uses technically based data and has shown great ability to discriminate between stocks with good and poor prospects, but the Value Line mutual fund that uses this system most closely has been only a mediocre performer, suggesting that implementation of the Value Line timing system is difficult.
- New theories of information dissemination in the market suggest there may be a role for the examination of past prices in formulating investment strategies. They do not, however, support the specific charting patterns currently relied on by technical analysts.

Key Terms

breadth, *425*	odd-lot theory, *423*	resistance level, *416*
confidence index, *423*	put/call ratio, *424*	short interest, *424*
Dow theory, *414*	relative strength, *426*	support level, *416*

Problem Sets

1. Consider the graph of stock prices over a two-year period in Figure 15A. Identify likely support and resistance levels.

FIGURE 15A

Simulated Stock Price over Time

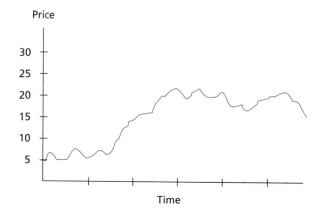

2. Use the data from *The Wall Street Journal* in Figure 15B to construct the trin ratio for the market. Is the trin ratio bullish or bearish?

FIGURE 15B

Market Diary

Source: From *The Wall Street Journal*, August 5, 1996. Reprinted by permission of *The Wall Street Journal*, © 1996 Dow Jones & Company, Inc. All Rights Reserved Worldwide.

DIARIES

NYSE		FRI	THUR	WK 8/2
Issues traded		3,222	3,197	3,321
Advances		2,105	1,985	2,430
Declines		539	550	595
Unchanged		578	662	296
New highs		128	68	163
New lows		25	43	172
zAdv vol	(000)	355,270	338,194	1,194,721
zDecl vol	(000)	50,804	65,291	531,656
zTotal vol	(000)	441,670	438,943	1,901,848

3. Calculate market breadth using the same data as in problem 2. Is the signal bullish or bearish?

4. Collect data on the DJIA for a period covering a few months. Try to identify primary trends. Can you tell whether the market currently is in an upward or downward trend?

5. Using Figure 15C from *The Wall Street Journal*, determine whether market price movements and volume patterns were bullish or bearish around the following dates: September 17, November 5, and January 5. In each instance, compare your prediction to the subsequent behavior of the DJIA in the following few weeks.

FIGURE 15C

Dow Jones Industrial Average and Market Volume

Source: From *The Wall Street Journal*, February 7, 1994, p. C3. Reprinted by permission of *The Wall Street Journal*, © 1994 Dow Jones & Company, Inc. All Rights Reserved Worldwide.

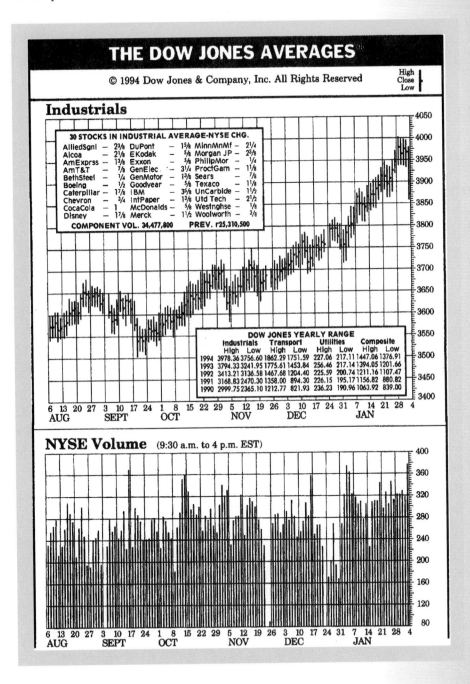

6. Table 15A presents price data for Computers, Inc., and a computer industry index. Does Computers, Inc., show relative strength over this period?

TABLE 15A

Computers, Inc., Stock Price History

Trading Day	Computers, Inc.	Industry Index
1	19 5/8	50.0
2	20	50.1
3	20 1/2	50.5
4	22	50.4
5	21 1/8	51.0
6	22	50.7
7	21 7/8	50.5
8	22 1/2	51.1
9	23 1/8	51.5
10	23 7/8	51.7
11	24 1/2	51.4
12	23 1/4	51.7
13	22 1/8	52.2
14	22	52.0
15	20 5/8	53.1
16	20 1/4	53.5
17	19 3/4	53.9
18	18 3/4	53.6
19	17 1/2	52.9
20	19	53.4
21	19 5/8	54.1
22	21 1/2	54.0
23	22	53.9
24	23 1/8	53.7
25	24	54.8
26	25 1/4	54.5
27	26 1/4	54.6
28	27	54.1
29	27 1/2	54.2
30	28	54.8
31	28 1/2	54.2
32	28	54.8
33	27 1/2	54.9
34	29	55.2
35	29 1/4	55.7
36	29 1/2	56.1
37	30	56.7
38	28 1/2	56.7
39	27 3/4	56.5
40	28	56.1

7. Use the data in Table 15A to compute a five-day moving average for Computers, Inc. Can you identify any buy or sell signals?

8. Construct a point and figure chart for Computers, Inc., using the data in Table 15A. Use $2 increments for your chart. Do the buy or sell signals derived from your chart correspond to those derived from the moving average rule (see problem 7)?

9. Table 15B contains data on market advances and declines. Calculate cumulative breadth and decide whether this technical signal is bullish or bearish.

TABLE 15B
Market Advances and Declines

Day	Advances	Declines
1	906	704
2	653	986
3	721	789
4	503	968
5	497	1095
6	970	702
7	1002	609
8	903	722
9	850	748
10	766	766

10. Is the confidence index rising or falling?

	This Year	Last Year
Yield on top-rated corporate bonds	8%	9%
Yield on intermediate-grade corporate bonds	9	10

▲IEM
Applications

1. Chart the IEM prices for contracts in the Computer Industry Returns Markets for a month of trading. (Daily price summaries can be found on the IEM from the "C"ontract Daily Prices section under the Market "I"nformation screen. They can also be found from the IEM web pages http://www.biz.uiowa.edu/iem under the Computer Industry Returns Market.) Identify any trends, turning points, and patterns that you see based on this analysis. Do you think this is a valuable exercise in helping you predict what will happen during future IEM markets?

Solutions to Concept Checks

1. Suppose a stock had been selling in a narrow trading range around $50 for a substantial period and later increased in price. Now the stock falls back to a price near $50. Potential buyers might recall the price history of the stock and remember that the last time the stock fell so low, they missed an opportunity for large gains when it later advanced. They might then view $50 as a good opportunity to buy. Therefore, buying pressure will materialize as the stock price falls to $50, which will create a support level.

2.

3. By the time the news of recession affects bond yields, it also ought to affect stock prices. The market should fall *before* the confidence index signals that the time is ripe to sell.

Part Five

DERIVATIVE ASSETS: OPTIONS AND FUTURES

Horror stories about large losses incurred by high-flying traders in derivatives markets such as those for futures and options have seemingly become a staple of the evening news in the last decade. Indeed, there have been some amazing losses to report: several totaling hundreds of millions of dollars, and a few amounting to more than a billion dollars. In the wake of these debacles, some venerable institutions have gone under, notable among them, Barings Bank, which once helped the U.S. finance the Louisiana Purchase and the British Empire finance the Napoleonic Wars.

These stories, while important, fascinating, and even occasionally scandalous, often miss the point. Derivatives, when misused, can indeed provide a quick path to insolvency. Used properly, however, they are potent tools for risk management and control. In fact, you will discover in these chapters that one firm was sued for *failing* to use derivatives to hedge price risk. A recent headline in *The Wall Street Journal* on hedging applications using derivatives was entitled "Index Options Touted as Providing Peace of Mind." Hardly material for bankruptcy court or the *National Inquirer*.

Derivatives provide a means to control risk that is qualitatively different from the techniques traditionally considered in portfolio theory. In contrast to the mean-variance analysis we discussed in Parts two and three, derivatives allow investors to change the *shape* of the probability distribution of investment returns. An entirely new approach to risk management follows from this insight.

The following chapters will explore how derivatives can be used as parts of a well-designed portfolio strategy. We will examine some popular portfolio strategies utilizing these securities and take a look at how derivatives are valued.

Chapter 16

OPTIONS MARKETS

AFTER STUDYING THIS CHAPTER YOU SHOULD BE ABLE TO:

- Calculate the profit to various option positions as a function of ultimate security prices.
- Formulate option strategies to modify portfolio risk-return attributes.
- Compute the proper relationship between call and put prices.
- Identify embedded options in various securities and determine how option characteristics affect the prices of those securities.

A relatively recent, but extremely important class of financial assets is derivative securities, or simply *derivatives*. These are securities whose prices are determined by, or "derive from," the prices of other securities. These assets also are called *contingent claims* because their payoffs are contingent on the prices of other securities.

Options and futures contracts are both derivative securities. We will see that their payoffs depend on the value of other securities. Swaps, which we discussed in Chapter 11, also are derivatives. Because the value of derivatives depends on the value of other securities, they can be powerful tools for both hedging and speculation. We will investigate these applications in the next three chapters, beginning in this chapter with options.

Trading of standardized options on a national exchange started in 1973 when the Chicago Board Options Exchange (CBOE) began listing call options. These contracts were almost immediately a great success, crowding out the previously existing over-the-counter trading in stock options. Figure 16.1 documents the incredible growth in trading on the CBOE. Trading volume rose rapidly and steadily between 1973 and 1987. While volume fell off considerably in the wake of the 1987 stock market crash, it has since recovered, and trading volume in 1995 was the highest in the history of the exchange.

Options contracts now are traded on several exchanges. They are written on common stock, stock indexes, foreign exchange, agricultural commodities, precious metals, and interest rate futures. In addition, the over-the-counter market also has enjoyed a tremendous resurgence in recent years as trading in custom-tailored options has exploded. Popular and

FIGURE 16.1

CBOE Fiscal Year Average Daily Volume (Contracts) 1974–1995

Source: 1995 *Annual Report, Chicago Board Options Exchange.*

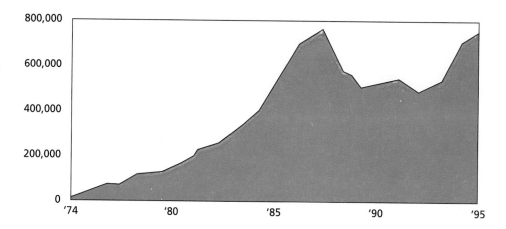

potent for modifying portfolio characteristics, options have become essential tools that every portfolio manager must understand.

This chapter is an introduction to options markets. It explains how puts and calls work and examines their investment characteristics. Popular option strategies are considered next. Finally, we examine a range of securities with embedded options such as callable or convertible bonds.

16.1 THE OPTION CONTRACT

call option
The right to buy an asset at a specified exercise price on or before a specified expiration date.

exercise or strike price
Price set for calling (buying) an asset or putting (selling) an asset.

A **call option** gives its holder the right to purchase an asset for a specified price, called the **exercise** or **strike price,** on or before some specified expiration date. For example, a July call option on Motorola stock with exercise price $50 entitles its owner to purchase Motorola stock for a price of $50 at any time up to and including the expiration date in July. The holder of the call is not required to exercise the option. It is profitable for the holder to exercise the call only if the market value of the asset to be purchased exceeds the exercise price. When the market price does exceed the exercise price, the option holder either may sell the option or "call away" the asset for the exercise price and reap a profit. Otherwise, the option may be left unexercised. If it is not exercised before the expiration date of the contract, a call option simply expires and no longer has value.

The purchase price of the option is called the *premium*. It represents the compensation the purchaser of the call must pay for the ability to exercise the option if exercise becomes profitable. Sellers of call options, who are said to *write* calls, receive premium income now as payment against the possibility they will be required at some later date to deliver the asset in return for an exercise price lower than the market value of the asset. If the option is left to expire worthless because the market price of the asset remains below the exercise price, then the writer of the call clears a profit equal to the premium income derived from the sale of the option.

**EXAMPLE 16.1
Profit and Loss from a Call Option on Motorola**

An October 1996 maturity call option on a share of Motorola stock with an exercise price of $50 per share sells on September 9, 1996, for $2.75. Exchange-traded options expire on the third Friday of the expiration month, which for this option is October 18, 1996. Until the expiration day, the purchaser of a call is entitled to buy shares of Motorola for $50. On October 18, Motorola stock sells for $50.625. This means that immediate exercise would provide net proceeds of $50.625 − $50 = $0.625. Obviously, an investor who pays $2.75 for the call has no intention of exercising it immediately. If, on the other hand, Motorola sells for $55 on October 18, the option will turn out to be a profitable investment since it will give its holder the right to pay $50 for a stock worth $55. The proceeds from the exercise will be

$$\text{Proceeds} = \text{Stock price} - \text{Exercise price} = \$55 - \$50 = \$5$$

and the profit to the investor will be

$$\text{Profit} = \text{Proceeds} - \text{Original investment} = \$5 - \$2.75 = \$2.25$$

This is a holding-period return of $2.25/$2.75 = 0.82 or 82%—over only 40 days! Obviously, option sellers on September 9 did not consider this outcome very likely.

put option
The right to sell an asset at a specified exercise price on or before a specified expiration date.

A **put option** gives its holder the right to *sell* an asset for a specified exercise or strike price on or before some expiration date. An October put on Motorola with exercise price $50 entitles its owner to sell Motorola stock to the put writer at a price of $50 at any time before expiration in October, even if the market price of Motorola is less than $50. While profits on call options increase when the asset increases in value, profits on put options increase when the asset value falls. A put will be exercised only if the exercise price is greater than the price of the underlying asset, that is, only if its holder can deliver for the exercise price an asset with market value less than the exercise price. (One doesn't need to own the shares of Motorola to exercise the Motorola put option. Upon exercise, the investor's broker purchases the necessary shares of Motorola at the market price and immediately delivers or "puts them" to an option writer for the exercise price. The owner of the put profits by the difference between the exercise price and market price.)

**EXAMPLE 16.2
Profit and Loss from a Put Option on Motorola**

An October 1996 maturity put option on Motorola with an exercise price of $50 sells on September 9, 1996, for $2.125. It entitles its owner to sell a share of Motorola for $50 at any time until October 18. Because the stock price is currently a bit more than $50 a share, it would not make sense at the moment to exercise the option to sell at $50. Indeed, if Motorola stock remains above $50 by the expiration date, the put will be left to expire worthless. If, on the other hand, Motorola is selling below $50 at expiration, the put holder will find it optimal to exercise. For example, if the stock price is only $48, the payoff from exercising will be

$$\text{Proceeds} = \text{Exercise price} - \text{Stock price} = \$50 - \$48 = \$2$$

Despite the $2 payoff at maturity, the investor still realizes a loss of $0.125 on the put, because it cost $2.125 to purchase. Nevertheless, exercise of the put will be optimal at maturity if the stock price is below the exercise price because the exercise proceeds will offset at least part of the investment in the option. The investor in the put will clear a profit on the investment if Motorola is selling below $47.875 at the maturity date. At that price, the proceeds from exercise will just cover the original cost of the put.

in the money
An option where exercise would be profitable.

out of the money
An option where exercise would not be profitable.

at the money
An option where the exercise price and asset price are equal.

An option is described as **in the money** when its exercise would produce a positive payoff for its holder. An option is **out of the money** when exercise would be unprofitable. A call option is in the money when the exercise price is below the asset value because purchase at the exercise price would be profitable. It is out of the money when the exercise price exceeds the asset value; no one would exercise the right to purchase for the exercise price an asset worth less than that price. Conversely, put options are in the money when the exercise price exceeds the asset's value, because delivery of the lower valued asset in exchange for the exercise price is profitable for the holder. Options are **at the money** when the exercise price and asset price are equal.

Options Trading

Some options trade on over-the-counter (OTC) markets. The OTC market offers the advantage that the terms of the option contract—the exercise price, maturity date, and number of shares committed—can be tailored to the needs of the traders. The costs of establishing an OTC option contract, however, are relatively high. Today, most option trading occurs on organized exchanges.

Options contracts traded on exchanges are standardized by allowable maturity dates and exercise prices for each listed option. Each stock option contract provides for the right to

FIGURE 16.2
Listing of Stock Option Quotations

Source: From *The Wall Street Journal,* September 10, 1996. Reprinted by permission of *The Wall Street Journal,* © 1996 Dow Jones & Company, Inc. All Rights Reserved Worldwide.

LISTED OPTIONS QUOTATIONS

Option/Strike		Exp.	–Call– Vol.	–Call– Last	–Put– Vol.	–Put– Last
117 5/8	110	Sep	618	7 7/8	869	1/4
117 5/8	110	Oct	205	9 5/8	778	1 3/8
117 5/8	110	Jan	1901	13 5/8	362	3 7/8
117 5/8	110	Apr	...	...	413	5 5/8
117 5/8	115	Sep	4490	3 1/2	2007	7/8
117 5/8	115	Oct	1614	6	847	2 7/8
117 5/8	115	Jan	398	10 1/8	93	5 5/8
117 5/8	120	Sep	3486	1	127	3 1/4
117 5/8	120	Oct	2143	3 3/8	68	5 1/2
117 5/8	120	Jan	545	7 1/2	16	8 1/4
117 5/8	120	Apr	69	10 1/8	1	9 7/8
117 5/8	125	Oct	602	1 11/16	...	...
117 5/8	125	Jan	314	5 3/8	1	11 1/2
117 5/8	125	Apr	250	8	...	...
117 5/8	130	Oct	100	3/4	33	13 1/8
117 5/8	130	Jan	304	3 5/8	1	15
117 5/8	135	Oct	35	5/16	...	...
117 5/8	135	Jan	98	2 3/8	...	...
117 5/8	140	Jan	194	1 11/16	...	...
IGame	15	Oct	33	5 5/8	...	...
20 3/8	20	Sep	35	11/16	10	1/4
20 3/8	20	Oct	78	1 1/8	...	...
20 3/8	22 1/2	Oct	40	3/8	...	...
In Pap	35	Jan	...	...	81	3/8
41	40	Sep	38	1	...	...
41	40	Oct	39	1 15/16	20	1
InfRec	12 1/2	Oct	65	1 3/4	20	11/16
13 1/2	15	Sep	88	1/4	25	1 1/2
13 1/2	15	Oct	114	3/4	...	...
13 1/2	15	Dec	35	1 5/16	...	...
13 1/2	15	Mar	84	2 1/2	...	...
13 1/2	17 1/2	Oct	50	3/8	...	...
13 1/2	20	Dec	50	3/8	...	...
Infrnu	30	Sep	35	5/8	...	...
28 3/8	35	Dec	112	2 1/2	...	...
Intuit	30	Sep	...	...	35	1/2
32 1/2	35	Sep	67	1/2	35	2 5/8
32 1/2	50	Apr	...	...	39	18 1/8
Iomega	8 3/4	Nov	...	...	170	7/16
13 5/16	10	Oct	12	3 3/4	148	3/8
13 5/16	10	Nov	51	4 1/4	61	3/4
13 5/16	10	Feb	65	5	120	1 1/4
13 5/16	12 1/2	Sep	461	1 5/16	269	7/16
13 5/16	12 1/2	Oct	333	2 3/16	165	1 3/16

Option/Strike		Exp.	–Call– Vol.	–Call– Last	–Put– Vol.	–Put– Last
124 7/8	130	Sep	727	3/8	9	5 3/4
124 7/8	130	Oct	485	2 5/8	12	7 3/8
124 7/8	130	Jan	173	7	1	10 1/4
124 7/8	135	Oct	78	1 1/8	20	10 7/8
124 7/8	135	Jan	67	5	...	...
MictchS	12 1/2	Dec	10	3 3/4	40	13/16
15 1/4	15	Sep	35	15/16	...	...
MidAtl	15	Mar	75	1 7/8	6	2 9/16
Millerln	35	Feb	45	8 1/4	...	...
MMM	70	Sep	81	1/2	...	...
Mobil	115	Sep	63	3 3/8	20	5/8
117 3/4	115	Oct	15	4 1/2	54	1 1/8
117 3/4	115	Nov	40	5 1/8	10	2 3/4
MblTel	12 1/2	Oct	50	2 3/16	...	...
14	15	Sep	50	5/16	...	...
14	17 1/2	Sep	...	...	64	3 5/8
MoneySt	25	Nov	37	1 1/2	...	...
Monsan	30	Oct	115	2 7/16	...	...
32	31	Oct	45	2	...	...
32	32	Oct	73	1 3/8	2	1 9/16
Morgan	90	Oct	46	1 5/8	...	...
89	95	Oct	54	7/16	100	7 5/8
Motrla	40	Jan	55	12 1/4	120	3/4
50 5/8	50	Sep	42	1 3/4	639	1
50 5/8	50	Oct	284	2 3/4	1963	2 1/8
50 5/8	50	Jan	85	5	312	3 3/8
50 5/8	50	Apr	...	...	57	4 1/8
50 5/8	55	Sep	319	1/8	33	4 1/8
50 5/8	55	Oct	383	15/16	390	5 1/4
50 5/8	55	Jan	386	2 5/8	27	6 1/8
50 5/8	55	Apr	81	3 7/8	...	...
50 5/8	60	Oct	343	1/4	145	8 3/8
50 5/8	60	Jan	252	1 1/4	10	8 5/8
50 5/8	65	Oct	35	1/8	15	13 1/2
50 5/8	65	Jan	74	5/8	...	...
50 5/8	70	Jan	62	1/4	20	18 1/2
MusicLd	5	Oct	...	...	500	3 1/4
Mylex	12 1/2	Feb	37	3 3/8	...	...
14 1/4	15	Nov	45	1 1/16	40	2
NABI Inc	10	Sep	...	...	50	1/4
10 3/8	10	Dec	...	...	140	3/4
NBTY	12 1/2	Sep	50	3 1/2	...	...
16 1/8	15	Oct	85	1 3/4	...	...
16 1/8	17 1/2	Dec	440	1	...	...

Note: Prices are for September 9, 1996.

buy or sell 100 shares of stock (except when stock splits occur after the contract is listed and the contract is adjusted for the terms of the split).

Standardization of the terms of listed option contracts means all market participants trade in a limited and uniform set of securities. This increases the depth of trading in any particular option, which lowers trading costs and results in a more competitive market. Exchanges, therefore, offer two important benefits: ease of trading, which flows from a central marketplace where buyers and sellers or their representatives congregate, and a liquid secondary market where buyers and sellers of options can transact quickly and cheaply.

Figure 16.2 is a reproduction of listed stock option quotations from *The Wall Street Journal.* The circled options are for shares of Motorola. The numbers in the column below the company name represent the last recorded price on the New York Stock Exchange for Motorola stock, \$50.625 per share.[1] The first column shows that options are traded on Motorola at exercise prices of \$40 through \$70 in \$5 increments. These values also are called the *strike prices.*

The exercise or strike prices bracket the stock price. While exercise prices generally are set at five-point intervals for stocks, larger intervals may be set for stocks selling above \$100, and intervals of \$2½ may be used for stocks selling below \$30. If the stock price moves outside the range of exercise prices of the existing set of options, new options with appropriate exercise prices may be offered. Therefore, at any time, both in-the-money and out-of-the-money options will be listed, as in the Motorola example.

[1]Occasionally, this price may not match the closing price listed for the stock on the stock market page. This is because some NYSE stocks also trade on the Pacific Stock Exchange, which closes after the NYSE, and the stock pages may reflect the more recent Pacific Exchange closing price. The options exchanges, however, close with the NYSE, so the closing NYSE stock price is appropriate for comparison with the closing option price.

The next column in Figure 16.2 gives the maturity month of each contract, followed by two pairs of columns showing the number of contracts traded on that day and the closing price for the call and put, respectively.

When we compare the prices of call options with the same maturity date but different exercise prices in Figure 16.2 we see that the value of the call is lower when the exercise price is higher. This makes sense, for the right to purchase a share at a given exercise price is not as valuable when the purchase price is higher. Thus, the October maturity Motorola call option with strike price $50 sells for $2.75, while the $55 exercise price October call sells for less than a dollar. Conversely, put options are worth *more* when the exercise price is higher: You would rather have the right to sell Motorola shares for $55 than for $50, and this is reflected in the prices of the puts. The October maturity put option with strike price $55 sells for $5.25, while the $50 exercise price October put sells for only $2.125.

Throughout Figure 16.2, you will see that many options may go an entire day without trading. A lack of trading is denoted by three dots in the volume and price columns. Because trading is infrequent, it is not unusual to find option prices that appear out of line with other prices. You might see, for example, two calls with different exercise prices that seem to sell for the same price. This discrepancy arises because the last trades for these options may have occurred at different times during the day. At any moment, the call with the lower exercise price must be worth more, and the put less, than an otherwise-identical call or put with a higher exercise price.

Figure 16.2 illustrates that the maturities of most exchange-traded options tend to be fairly short, ranging up to only several months. For larger firms and some stock indexes, however, longer-term options are traded with maturities ranging up to three years. These options are called LEAPS (for Long-term Equity AnticiPation Securities).

Concept Check

1. *a.* What will be the proceeds and net profits to an investor who purchases the October maturity Motorola calls with exercise price $50 if the stock price at maturity is $45? What if the stock price at maturity is $55?
   b. Now answer part (*a*) for an investor who purchases an October maturity Motorola put option with exercise price $50.

American and European Options

American option
Can be exercised on or before its expiration.

An **American option** allows its holder to exercise the right to purchase (if a call) or sell (if a put) the underlying asset on *or before* the expiration date. **European options** allow for exercise of the option only on the expiration date. American options, because they allow more leeway than their European counterparts, generally will be more valuable. Virtually all traded options in this country are American. Foreign currency options and stock index options traded on the Chicago Board Options Exchange are notable exceptions to this rule, however.

European option
Can be exercised only at expiration.

The Option Clearing Corporation

The Option Clearing Corporation (OCC), the clearinghouse for options trading, is jointly owned by the exchanges on which stock options are traded. The OCC places itself between options traders, becoming the effective buyer of the option from the writer and the effective writer of the option to the buyer. All individuals, therefore, deal only with the OCC, which effectively guarantees contract performance.

When an option holder exercises an option, the OCC arranges for a member firm with clients who have written that option to make good on the option obligation. The member firm selects from among its clients who have written that option to fulfill the contract. The selected client must deliver 100 shares of stock at a price equal to the exercise price for each call option contract written or must purchase 100 shares at the exercise price for each put option contract written.

Because the OCC guarantees contract performance, option writers are required to post margin to guarantee that they can fulfill their contract obligations. The margin required is determined in part by the amount by which the option is in the money, because that value is an indicator of the potential obligation of the option writer upon exercise of the option. When the required margin exceeds the posted margin, the writer will receive a margin call. The *holder* of the option need not post margin because the holder will exercise the option only if it is profitable to do so. After purchasing the option, no further money is at risk.

Margin requirements also depend on whether the underlying asset is held in portfolio. For example, a call option writer owning the stock against which the option is written can satisfy the margin requirement simply by allowing a broker to hold that stock in the brokerage account. The stock is then guaranteed to be available for delivery should the call option be exercised. If the underlying security is not owned, however, the margin requirement is determined by the value of the underlying security as well as by the amount by which the option is in or out of the money. Out-of-the-money options require less margin from the writer, for expected payouts are lower.

Other Listed Options

Options on assets other than stocks also are widely traded. These include options on market indexes and industry indexes, on foreign currency, and even on the futures prices of agricultural products, gold, silver, fixed-income securities, and stock indexes. We will discuss these in turn.

Index Options   An index option is a call or put based on a stock market index such as the S&P 500 or the New York Stock Exchange index. Index options are traded on several broad-based indexes as well as on several industry-specific indexes. We discussed many of these indexes in Chapter 2.

The construction of the indexes can vary across contracts or exchanges. For example, the S&P 100 index is a value-weighted average of the 100 stocks in the Standard & Poor's 100 stock group. The weights are proportional to the market value of outstanding equity for each stock. The Major Market Index, by contrast, is a price-weighted average of 20 stocks, most of which are in the Dow Jones Industrial Average group, while the Value Line index is an equally weighted average of roughly 1,700 stocks.

More recently, options contracts on foreign stock indexes have been introduced. For example, options on the Nikkei 225 Index of Japanese stocks trade on the Chicago Mercantile Exchange and options on the Japan Index trade on the American Stock exchange. Options on the Financial Times Share Exchange (FTSE) 100 Index of large firms in the United Kingdom, and Eurotrak 200 Index of both the FTSE 100 and Eurotrak 100 stock trade on the Chicago Board Options Exchange (CBOE).

In contrast to stock options, index options do not require that the call writer actually "deliver the index" upon exercise or that the put writer "purchase the index." Instead, a cash settlement procedure is used. The payoff that would accrue upon exercise of the option is calculated, and the option writer simply pays that amount to the option holder. The payoff is equal to the difference between the exercise price of the option and the value of the index. For example, if the S&P index is at $840 when a call option on the index with exercise price $830 is exercised, the holder of the call receives a cash payment of the $10 difference times the contract multiplier of 100, or $1,000 per contract.

Figure 16.3 is a reproduction of the listings of index options from *The Wall Street Journal.* The top of the listing shows recent price ranges for over 30 stock indexes. The option listings are similar to those of stock options. However, instead of supplying separate columns for put and calls, the index options are all listed in one column, and the letters *p* or *c* are used to denote puts or calls. The index listings also report the "open interest" for each contract, which

FIGURE 16.3
Index Options

Source: From *The Wall Street Journal.* September 10, 1996. Reprinted by permission of *The Wall Street Journal,* © 1996 Dow Jones & Company, Inc. All Rights Reserved Worldwide.

INDEX OPTIONS TRADING

Oct	655 c	323	6 3/4	+ 1 1/4	1,492
Oct	655 p	2	23 7/8	− 2 5/8	123
Nov	655 c	21	10 3/4	+ 2 1/8	144
Sep	660 c	4,339	13/16	+ 3/8	14,217
Sep	660 p	15	20 1/4	− 7 1/2	121
Oct	660 c	382	4 7/8	+ 1 3/8	2,728
Oct	660 p	8	23 1/4	− 6	127
Dec	660 c	1,000	12 1/2	+ 1	716
Dec	660 p	2	31	− 3 3/8	120
Sep	665 c	1,924	3/8	+ 1/16	11,703
Sep	665 p	1	29 1/2	− 3 1/2	26
Oct	665 c	280	3 1/8	+ 5/8	2,567
Nov	665 c	10	6	+ 5/8	2
Nov	665 p	1	33 3/8	...	...
Sep	670 c	472	3/16	+ 1/16	11,556
Oct	670 c	288	2 1/4	+ 5/8	2,518
Nov	670 c	613	5 1/2	+ 2 5/8	867
Dec	670 c	5	9 1/4	+ 1 1/4	3,030
Dec	670 p	10	35 1/2	− 6 7/8	8
Sep	675 c	58	1/8	...	10,121
Oct	675 c	1,392	1 5/8	+ 1/2	2,883
Nov	675 c	5	4	+ 7/8	2,277
Sep	680 c	1,820	1/16	− 1/16	7,709
Oct	680 c	262	7/8	+ 1/8	4,786
Nov	680 c	4	3	+ 1/2	1,046
Dec	680 c	7	6	+ 2	133
Call Vol.		**76,401**	**Open Int.**		**287,573**
Put Vol.		**87,148**	**Open Int.**		**322,891**

S & P 500 INDEX-AM(SPX)

Sep	400 c	300	259	− 5 7/8	7,310
Sep	400 p	700	1/16	...	3,160
Oct	400 c	300	260	+ 5	200
Oct	400 p	300	1/8	− 1/16	200
Dec	450 p	70	5/16	− 3/16	11,290
Dec	500 p	76	3/4	− 1/8	9,251
Oct	525 p	60	1/4	− 3/8	585
Dec	525 p	30	1 1/4	− 7/16	9,076
Oct	550 p	16	7/16	− 3/16	1,378
Dec	550 p	110	1 13/16	− 15/16	14,003
Oct	575 p	10	13/16	− 15/16	3,390
Nov	575 p	100	1 3/4	− 1 3/4	26
Dec	575 p	2	3 1/2	− 5/8	24,254
Sep	580 p	50	1/8	− 1/16	7,259
Sep	585 p	225	3/16	− 1/16	11,495
Oct	590 p	4	1 1/4	− 1	4,076
Sep	595 c	9,634	68 5/8	− 12 1/8	35,000

Strike		Vol.	Last	Net Chg.	Open Int.
Dec	670 c	30	21	+ 4 7/8	4,494
Dec	670 p	116	21	− 7	1,622
Sep	675 c	743	1 7/8	+ 3/4	21,788
Sep	675 p	36	12 3/4	− 7 1/4	16,029
Oct	675 c	227	7 3/4	+ 2	80
Oct	675 p	17	19 3/8	− 2 5/8	3
Dec	675 c	456	18	+ 4 3/4	20,521
Dec	675 p	40	22 7/8	− 9 3/4	18,042
Sep	680 c	947	7/8	+ 5/16	14,140
Sep	680 p	90	22	− 3	4,888
Oct	680 c	1,696	6	+ 1 5/8	2,837
Oct	680 p	1	19 5/8	− 9 7/8	243
Nov	680 p	14	23 1/4	− 5 3/4	114
Sep	685 c	40	1/2	+ 1/4	9,768
Oct	685 c	70	4 1/4	+ 3/4	5,454
Oct	685 p	100	27 1/4	...	...
Dec	685 c	1	12	+ 1/2	5,760
Dec	685 p	2	29	− 5 3/4	162
Sep	690 c	266	1/4	+ 1/8	12,454
Oct	690 c	426	2 3/4	+ 3/8	5,452
Nov	690 c	1	5 3/4	+ 3/4	1,181
Oct	695 c	35	1 5/8	+ 3/8	85
Sep	700 c	98	1/8	...	25,517
Oct	700 c	155	1 1/8	+ 1/8	8,487
Oct	700 p	2	35	− 20	511
Nov	700 c	500	3 3/4	+ 13/16	2,977
Dec	700 c	43	7	+ 1 1/2	21,701
Dec	700 p	106	36 1/2	− 6 1/8	10,230
Sep	705 c	10	1/16	...	4,494
Oct	710 c	605	7/16	− 1/16	1,000
Sep	725 c	200	1/16	...	7,304
Sep	725 p	210	60 3/4	− 11	2,465
Call Vol.		**42,347**	**Open Int.**		**611,178**
Put Vol.		**64,544**	**Open Int.**		**1,107,476**

S & P BANKS(BIX)

Sep	365 c	10	20 3/8	+ 1 1/2	20
Oct	385 p	20	8	− 1 1/2	20
Call Vol.		**10**	**Open Int.**		**2,707**
Put Vol.		**20**	**Open Int.**		**2,510**

RANGES FOR UNDERLYING INDEXES

Monday, September 9, 1996

	High	Low	Close	Net Chg.	From Dec. 31	% Chg.
S&P 100 (OEX)	640.57	632.77	640.53	+ 7.76	+ 54.61	+ 9.3
S&P 500 -A.M.(SPX)	663.77	655.68	663.77	+ 8.09	+ 47.84	+ 7.8
S&P Banks (BIX)	388.93	383.50	388.38	+ 4.83	+ 57.88	+ 17.5
CB-Tech (TXX)	165.15	162.73	164.76	+ 2.03	+ 8.23	+ 5.3
CB-Mexico (MEX)	89.03	87.83	89.03	+ 1.10	+ 17.29	+ 24.1
CB-Lps Mex (VEX)	8.97	8.76	8.95	0.00	+ 1.78	+ 24.8
Nasdaq 100 (NDX)	672.09	663.53	671.98	+ 7.76	+ 95.75	+ 16.6
Russell 2000 (RUT)	335.62	334.09	335.62	+ 1.52	+ 19.65	+ 6.2
Lps S&P 100 (OEX)	64.06	63.28	64.05	+ 0.77	+ 5.46	+ 9.3
Lps S&P 500 (SPX)	66.38	65.57	66.38	+ 0,81	+ 4.79	+ 7.8
S&P Midcap (MID)	232.71	231.85	232.60	+ 0.75	+ 14.76	+ 6.8
Major Mkt (XMI)	587.17	580.26	586.45	+ 6.19	+ 50.85	+ 9.5
Leaps MMkt (XLT)	58.72	58.03	58.65	+ 0.62	+ 5.09	+ 9.5
Hong Kong (HKO)			226.90	+ 3.79	+ 23.99	+ 11.8
Leaps HK (HKL)			22.69	+ 0.38	+ 2.40	+ 11.8
IW Internet (IIX)	225.29	221.73	225.15	+ 3.42	− 8.05	− 3.5
AM-Mexico (MXY)	100.62	99.38	100.53	+ 0.68	+ 16.91	+ 20.2
Institutl -A.M.(XII)	701.35	692.61	701.19	+ 8.56	+ 64.47	+ 10.1
Japan (JPN)			205.26	+ 1.26	+ 3.42	+ 1.7
MS Cyclical (CYC)	369.29	365.25	369.07	+ 3.82	+ 28.85	+ 8.5
MS Consumr (CMR)	309.30	305.33	309.27	+ 3.94	+ 24.52	+ 8.6
MS Hi Tech (MSH)	318.29	314.71	317.31	+ 1.61	+ 1.54	+ 0.5
Pharma (DRG)	326.81	322.95	326.76	+ 3.81	+ 30.81	+ 10.4
Biotech (BTK)	128.85	126.94	128.70	+ 1.33	− 5.07	− 3.8
Comp Tech (XCI)	269.41	265.39	268.96	+ 3.57	+ 40.34	+ 17.7
NYSE (NYA)	356.29	352.67	356.28	+ 3.61	+ 26.77	+ 8.1
Gold/Silver (XAU)	125.22	120.66	121.26	− 3.68	+ 0.84	+ 0.7
OTC (XOC)	481.61	476.27	481.61	+ 5.19	+ 56.91	+ 13.4
Utility (UTY)	244.92	243.45	244.92	+ 2.09	− 32.68	− 11.8
Value Line (VLE)	622.24	619.12	622.23	+ 3.09	+ 52.33	+ 9.2
Bank (BKX)	460.34	455.16	459.61	+ 5.22	+ 65.76	+ 16.7
Semicond (SOX)	163.61	160.91	161.39	− 0.50	− 39.27	− 19.6
Top 100 (TPX)	603.79	597.82	603.70	+ 7.56	+ 50.68	+ 9.2

AMERICAN

COMP TECH(XCI)

Sep	235 p	10	1/8	− 15/16	102
Sep	260 p	3	2 9/16	− 15/16	58
Oct	260 p	1	5 1/2	− 1 5/8	6
Sep	265 c	10	7	+ 3/4	10
Sep	265 p	2	3 5/8	− 1 1/4	85
Oct	270 p	5	9 7/8	− 1/8	10
Call Vol.		**10**	**Open Int.**		**1,405**
Put Vol.		**21**	**Open Int.**		**1,176**

HONG KONG INDEX(HKO)

Sep	215 p	5	5/16	− 7/8	48
Oct	215 c	235	13 3/4	− 1 5/8	298
Sep	225 c	3	3 3/4	+ 1/2	54
Sep	225 p	47	1 5/8	− 2 1/2	204
Oct	230 c	169	4 1/2	+ 7/8	334
Sep	235 p	3	7 5/8	− 3	10
Call Vol.		**411**	**Open Int.**		**6,210**
Put Vol.		**55**	**Open Int.**		**1,875**

INSTITUTIONAL-AM(XII)

Sep	625 p	50	3/16	− 5/8	200
Sep	655 p	5	13/16	− 2 3/16	35
Oct	665 p	1	4 3/4	− 1	30
Sep	680 p	1	2 5/16	− 6 3/16	32
Nov	680 p	20	11	− 3 1/2	...
Sep	690 c	25	11 7/8	+ 1 1/4	6,050
Sep	690 p	2	3	− 8 7/8	6,050
Sep	695 p	2	4 3/4	− 5 3/4	30
Sep	700 c	7	7	+ 2 1/4	110
Sep	710 c	2	2 3/8	− 4 1/8	230
Call Vol.		**34**	**Open Int.**		**39,164**
Put Vol.		**81**	**Open Int.**		**47,131**

INTERNET(IIX)

Oct	210 p	10	3 3/4	− 1 1/8	154
Oct	215 p	20	5 1/2	− 2 1/8	53
Sep	220 c	1	7	+ 2 1/8	1
Oct	230 c	20	7 7/8	+ 1 3/8	20
Oct	240 c	10	4 1/2	+ 5/8	19
Call Vol.		**35**	**Open Int.**		**2,004**
Put Vol.		**30**	**Open Int.**		**7,008**

JAPAN INDEX(JPN)

Sep	200 c	10	6 3/8	− 3/4	965
Dec	200 c	25	11 1/2	+ 1/2	1,089
Oct	205 p	2	4 1/4	− 1	7
Sep	210 p	15	4 1/2	− 1/2	272
Oct	210 c	24	3 3/8	+ 5/8	424
Dec	210 c	5	5 5/8	...	92
Sep	220 p	90	13 1/2	− 1 7/8	415
Call Vol.		**66**	**Open Int.**		**49,498**
Put Vol.		**107**	**Open Int.**		**10,989**

MAJOR MARKET(XMI)

Sep	525 p	20	1/4	− 1/8	6,460
Dec	550 p	10	7 1/2	− 3 1/8	93
Sep	560 p	2	1 1/4	− 2 1/2	86
Oct	565 p	3	5 1/4	− 2 5/8	20
Nov	565 p	2	9 1/8	...	...
Sep	570 c	5	18 3/4	+ 4 3/4	76
Sep	570 p	9	1 9/16	− 2 3/16	153
Sep	575 p	7	2 11/16	− 1 15/16	213
Oct	575 c	1	18 1/8	...	...
Sep	580 p	11	3 3/4	− 2 1/8	192
Oct	580 c	2	14 7/8	+ 3 1/2	217
Oct	580 p	2	9 3/4	− 5 3/4	23
Sep	585 c	33	6 3/4	+ 2 1/4	369

Note: Prices are for September 9, 1996.

is the number of contracts currently outstanding. Notice from the trading volume and open interest columns that the S&P 100 options contract, often called the OEX after its ticker symbol, is the most actively traded contract on the CBOE, although volume on the S&P 500 index contracts is also quite high. Together, these contracts dominate CBOE volume.

Futures Options Futures options give their holders the right to buy or sell a specified futures contract, using as a futures price the exercise price of the option. Although the delivery process is slightly complicated, the terms of futures options contracts are designed in effect to allow the option to be written on the future price itself. The option holder receives upon exercise net proceeds equal to the difference between the current futures price on the specified asset and the exercise price of the option. Thus, if the futures price is, say, \$37, and the call has an exercise price of \$35, the holder who exercises the call option on the futures gets a payoff of \$2. Many of the futures options in Figure 16.4 are foreign exchange futures options; they are written on the futures price of foreign exchange rather than on the actual or spot exchange rate.

Foreign Currency Options A currency option offers the right to buy or sell a quantity of foreign currency for a specified amount of domestic currency. Foreign currency options have traded on the Philadelphia Stock Exchange since December 1982. Since then, both the Chicago Board Options Exchange and the Chicago Mercantile Exchange have listed foreign currency options. Currency option contracts call for purchase or sale of the currency in

FIGURE 16.4

Futures Options

From *The Wall Street Journal*, September 10, 1996. Reprinted by permission of *The Wall Street Journal*, © 1996 Dow Jones & Company, Inc. All Rights Reserved Worldwide.

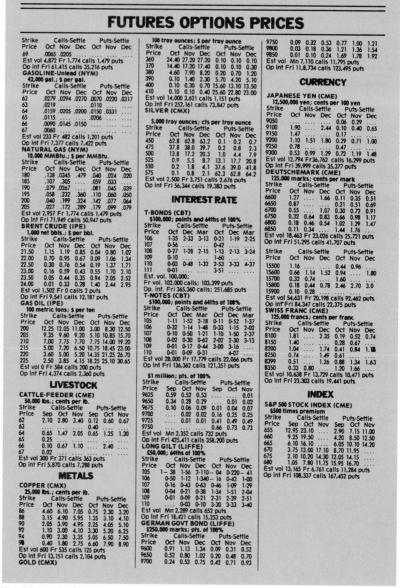

Note: Prices are for September 9, 1996.

exchange for a specified number of U.S. dollars. Contracts are quoted in cents or fractions of a cent per unit of foreign currency.

Figure 16.5 shows a *Wall Street Journal* listing of some of these contracts. The size of each option contract is specified for each listing. The call option on the British pound on the Philadelphia exchange, for example, entitles its holder to purchase 31,250 pounds for a specified number of cents per pound on or before the expiration date. The September 1996 call option with strike price of 154 cents sells for 1.80 cents, which means each contract costs $0.018 × 31,250 = $562.50. The current exchange rate is 155.67 cents per pound. Therefore, the option is in the money by 1.67 cents, the difference between the current exchange rate and the exercise price.

There is an important difference between currency options such as those traded on the Philadelphia exchange (Figure 16.5) and currency *futures* options (Figure 16.4). The former

FIGURE 16.5
Foreign Currency
Options

Source: From *The Wall Street Journal*, September 10, 1996. Reprinted by permission of *The Wall Street Journal*, © 1996 Dow Jones & Company, Inc. All Rights Reserved Worldwide.

OPTIONS — PHILADELPHIA EXCHANGE

	Calls Vol.	Last	Puts Vol.	Last
JYen				91.51
6,250,000 Japanese Yen-100ths of a cent per unit.				
92 Sep	...	...	15	0.47
DMark				66.72
62,500 German Mark EOM-European style.				
67 Oct	25	0.70	...	...
68 Oct	50	0.33	...	...
62,500 German Marks EOM-European style.				
67½ Oct	75	0.50	...	...
Australian Dollar				80.07
50,000 Australian Dollar EOM-cents per unit.				
80 Sep	...	...	19	0.52
50,000 Australian Dollars-cents per unit.				
78½ Oct	3	1.52	...	...
50,000 Australian Dollars-cents per unit.				
78 Oct	...	...	50	0.06
79 Oct	...	...	50	0.20
80 Sep	...	...	40	0.21
81 Oct	50	0.22	...	...
81 Dec	15	0.59	...	...
British Pound				155.65
31,250 British Pounds-European style.				
155 Oct	...	...	26	0.50
156 Oct	...	...	20	1.00
31,250 British Pounds-cents per unit.				
154 Sep	30	1.80	...	...
156 Sep	64	0.35	...	...
156 Dec	...	...	11	1.96
French Franc				195.64
250,000 French Francs-European style.				

	Calls Vol.	Last	Puts Vol.	Last
19 Sep	8	6.40	...	...
19¼ Oct	12	4.32	...	...
GMark-JYen				72.92
62,500 GMark-JYen cross EOM.				
72½ Sep	...	...	6	0.25
62,500 German Mark-Japanese Yen cross.				
73 Sep	4	0.19	...	...
German Mark				66.72
62,500 German Marks EOM-cents per unit.				
66½ Sep	...	...	50	0.22
62,500 German Marks-European style.				
67 Dec	23	1.20	...	...
68 Dec	23	0.72	...	...
62,500 German Marks-cents per unit.				
66 Sep	3	0.96	...	...
66 Dec	...	...	10	0.61
66½ Sep	...	...	400	0.13
67 Sep	...	...	141	0.36
67 Oct	...	...	40	0.69
67½ Sep	100	0.06	...	...
68 Sep	25	0.05	2	0.90
68 Dec	20	0.83	...	...
68½ Oct	100	0.12	...	...
69 Sep	10	0.03	...	...
70 Sep	...	...	10	2.93
75 Sep	...	...	2	7.90

	Calls Vol.	Last	Puts Vol.	Last
Japanese Yen				91.51
113½ Sep	...	...	200	0.03
114½ Sep	...	...	10	0.29
6,250,000 Japanese Yen EOM-100ths of a cent per unit.				
94 Oct	20	0.34	...	...
Swiss Franc				81.85
62,500 Swiss Franc EOM-cents per unit.				
82 Sep	...	...	30	0.48
62,500 Swiss Francs EOM.				
84½ Oct	30	0.34	...	...
62,500 Swiss Francs-European Style.				
78 Sep	10	4.28	...	...
78 Dec	10	5.06	...	...
79 Sep	35	3.28	...	...
79 Oct	25	3.60	...	...
79 Oct	10	4.20	...	...
79½ Sep	40	2.82	...	...
80 Sep	40	2.38	...	...
80 Oct	40	2.66	...	...
81 Oct	...	...	70	0.27
83 Dec	1	0.11	1	0.71
85 Dec	480	0.76	...	...
62,500 Swiss Francs-cents per unit.				
81 Oct	...	...	40	0.27
81 Dec	...	...	12	0.91
82 Sep	31	0.45	...	...
82½ Sep	...	...	30	0.70
83 Sep	20	0.09	...	...
Call Vol 4,742			Open Int ...	164,013
Put Vol 2,791			Open Int ...	151,036

Note: Prices are for September 9, 1996.

provide payoffs that depend on the difference between the exercise price and the exchange rate at maturity. The latter are foreign exchange futures options that provide payoffs that depend on the difference between the exercise price and the exchange rate *futures price* at maturity. Because exchange rates and exchange rate futures prices generally are not equal, the options and futures-options contracts will have different values, even with identical expiration dates and exercise prices. For example, in Figure 16.5, the call option on the German mark on the Philadelphia exchange with strike price 68 ½ cents and October maturity is quoted at 0.12. The corresponding futures option from Figure 16.4 with the same strike price and maturity is quoted at 0.11.

Interest Rate Options   Options on particular U.S. Treasury notes and bonds are listed on the Amex and CBOE. Options also are traded on Treasury bills, certificates of deposit, GNMA pass-through certificates, and yields on Treasury securities of various maturities. Options on several interest rate futures also are traded. Among them are contracts on Treasury bond, Treasury note, municipal bond, LIBOR, Eurodollar, and Euromark futures.

16.2 VALUES OF OPTIONS AT EXPIRATION

Call Options

Recall that a call option gives the right to purchase a security at the exercise price. If you hold a call option on Motorola stock with an exercise price of $40, and Motorola is now selling at $50, you can exercise your option to purchase the stock at $40 and simultaneously sell the shares at the market price of $50, clearing $10 per share. Yet if the shares sell below $40, you can sit on the option and do nothing, realizing no further gain or loss. The value of the call option at expiration equals

$$\text{Payoff to call holder} = S_T - X \text{ if } S_T > X$$
$$0 \quad \text{if } S_T \leq X$$

where S_T is the value of the stock at expiration, and X is the exercise price. This formula emphasizes the option property because the payoff cannot be negative. That is, the option is exercised only if S_T exceeds X. If S_T is less than X, exercise does not occur, and the option expires with zero value. The loss to the option holder in this case equals the price originally paid for the right to buy at the exercise price. More generally, the *profit* to the option holder is the payoff to the option minus the original purchase price.

FIGURE 16.6

Payoff and Profit to
Call Option at
Expiration

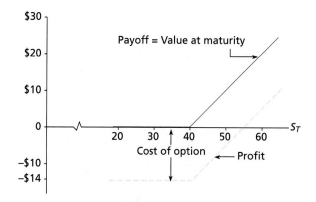

The value at expiration of the call on Motorola with exercise price $40 is given by the following schedule.

Motorola value	$30	$40	$50	$60	$70
Option value	0	0	10	20	30

For Motorola prices at or below $40, the option expires worthless. Above $40, the option is worth the excess of Motorola's price over $40. The option's value increases by one dollar for each dollar increase in the Motorola stock price. This relationship can be depicted graphically, as in Figure 16.6.

The solid line in Figure 16.6 depicts the value of the call at maturity. The net *profit* to the holder of the call equals the gross payoff less the initial investment in the call. Suppose the call cost $14. Then the profit to the call holder would be as given in the dashed (bottom) line of Figure 16.6. At option expiration, the investor has suffered a loss of $14 if the stock price is less than or equal to $40.

Profits do not become positive unless the stock price at expiration exceeds $54. The break-even point is $54, because at that price the payoff to the call, $S_T - X = \$54 - \$40 = \$14$, equals the cost paid to acquire the call. Hence, the call holder shows a profit only if the stock price is higher.

Conversely, the writer of the call incurs losses if the stock price is high. In that scenario, the writer will receive a call and will be obligated to deliver a stock worth S_T for only X dollars.

$$\text{Payoff to call writer} = -(S_T - X) \text{ if } S_T > X$$
$$0 \text{ if } S_T \leq X$$

The call writer, who is exposed to losses if Motorola increases in price, is willing to bear this risk in return for the option premium.

Figure 16.7 depicts the payoff and profit diagrams for the call writer. These are the mirror images of the corresponding diagrams for call holders. The break-even point for the option writer also is $54. The (negative) payoff at that point just offsets the premium originally received when the option was written.

Put Options

A put option conveys the right to sell an asset at the exercise price. In this case, the holder will not exercise the option unless the asset sells for *less* than the exercise price. For example, if Motorola shares were to fall to $40, a put option with exercise price $50 could be exercised to give a $10 payoff to its holder. The holder would purchase a share of Motorola for $40 and simultaneously deliver it to the put option writer for the exercise price of $50.

FIGURE 16.7
Payoff and Profit to
Call Writers at
Expiration

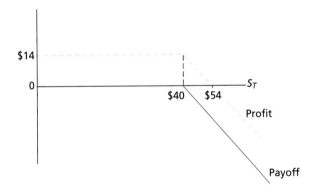

FIGURE 16.8
Payoff and Profit to Put
Option at Expiration

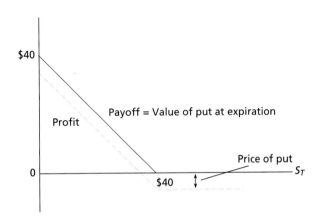

The value of a put option at expiration is

$$\text{Payoff to put holder} = 0 \qquad \text{if } S_T \geq X$$
$$X - S_T \text{ if } S_T < X$$

The solid line in Figure 16.8 illustrates the payoff at maturity to the holder of a put option on Motorola stock with an exercise price of $40. If the stock price at option maturity is above $40, the put has no value, as the right to sell the shares at $40 would not be exercised. Below a price of $40, the put value at expiration increases by $1 for each dollar the stock price falls. The dashed line in Figure 16.8 is a graph of the put option owner's profit at expiration, net of the initial cost of the put.

2. Analyze the strategy of put writing.
   a. What is the payoff to a put writer as a function of the stock price?
   b. What is the profit?
   c. Draw the payoff and profit graphs.
   d. When do put writers do well? When do they do poorly?

Writing puts *naked* (i.e., writing a put without an offsetting short position in the stock for hedging purposes) exposes the writer to losses if the market falls. Writing naked out-of-the-money puts was once considered an attractive way to generate income, as it was believed that as long as the market did not fall sharply before the option expiration, the option premium could be collected without the put holder ever exercising the option against the writer. Because only sharp drops in the market could result in losses to the writer of the put, the strategy was not viewed as overly risky. However, the accompanying box (page 448)

The Black Hole: How Some Investors Lost All Their Money in the Market Crash

THEIR SALES OF "NAKED PUTS" QUICKLY COME TO GRIEF, DAMAGE SUITS ARE FILED

When Robert O'Connor got involved in stock-index options, he hoped his trading profits would help put his children through college. His broker, Mr. O'Connor explains, "said we would make about $1,000 a month, and if our losses got to $2,000 to $3,000, he would close out the account."

Instead, Mr. O'Connor, the 46-year-old owner of a small medical X-ray printing concern in Grand Rapids, Michigan, got caught in one of the worst investor blowouts in history. In a few minutes on October 19, he lost everything in his account plus an *additional* $91,000—a total loss of 175% of his original investment.

SCENE OF DISASTER

For Mr. O'Connor and hundreds of other investors, a little-known corner of the Chicago Board Options Exchange was the "black hole" of Black Monday's market crash. In a strategy marketed by brokers nationwide as a sure thing, these customers had sunk hundreds of millions of dollars into "naked puts"—unhedged, highly leveraged bets that the stock market was in no danger of plunging. Most of these naked puts seem to have been options on the Standard & Poor's 100 stock index, which are traded on the CBOE. When stocks crashed, many traders with unhedged positions got margin calls for several times their original investment.

THE 'PUT' STRATEGY

The losses were especially sharp in "naked, out-of-the-money puts." A seller of puts agrees to buy stock or stock-index contracts at a set price before the put expires. These contracts are usually sold "out of the money"—priced at a level below current market prices that makes it unprofitable to exercise the option so long as the market rises or stays flat. The seller pockets a small amount per contract.

But if the market plunges, as it did October 19, the option swings into the money. The seller, in effect, has to pay pre-plunge stock prices to make good on his contract—and he takes a big loss.

"You have to recognize that there is unlimited potential for disaster" in selling naked options, says Peter Thayer, executive vice president of Gateway Investment Advisors Inc., a Cincinnati-based investment firm that trades options to hedge its stock portfolios. Last September, Gateway bought out-of-the-money put options on the S&P 100 stock index on the CBOE at $2 to $3 a contract as "insurance" against a plunging market. By October 20, the day after the crash, the value of those contracts had soared to $130. Although Gateway profited handsomely, the parties on the other side of the trade were clobbered.

FIRM SUED

Brokers who were pushing naked options assumed that the stock market wouldn't plunge into uncharted territory. Frank VanderHoff, one of the two main brokers who put 50 to 70 H.B. Shaine clients into stock-index options, says he told clients that the strategy's risk was "moderate barring a nuclear attack or a crash like 1929." It wasn't speculative. The market could go up or down, but not *substantially* up or down. If the crash had only been as bad as '29, he adds, "we would have made it."

notes that in the wake of the market crash of October 1987, such put writers suffered huge losses. Participants now perceive much greater risk to this strategy.

Options versus Stock Investments

Purchasing call options is a bullish strategy; that is, the calls provide profits when stock prices increase. Purchasing puts, in contrast, is a bearish strategy. Symmetrically, writing calls is bearish, while writing puts is bullish. Because option values depend on the price of the underlying stock, the purchase of options may be viewed as a substitute for direct purchase or sale of a stock. Why might an option strategy be preferable to direct stock transactions? We can begin to answer this question by comparing the values of option versus stock positions in Motorola.

Suppose you believe Motorola stock will increase in value from its current level, which we will assume is $50. You know your analysis could be incorrect, however, and that

Motorola could fall in price. Suppose a six-month maturity call option with exercise price of $40 sells for $15, and the semiannual interest rate is 2%. Consider the following three strategies for investing a sum of $15,000. For simplicity, suppose Motorola will not pay any dividends until after the six-month period.

Strategy *A:* Purchase 300 shares of Motorola

Strategy *B:* Purchase 1,000 call options on Motorola with exercise price $40. (This would require 10 contracts, each for 100 shares.)

Strategy *C:* Purchase 300 call options for $4,500. Invest the remaining $10,500 in six-month T-bills, to earn 2% interest.

Let us trace the possible values of these three portfolios when the options expire in six months as a function of Motorola stock price at that time.

Portfolio	Motorola Price					
	$30	**$40**	**$50**	**$60**	**$70**	**$80**
A: All stock	$9,000	$12,000	$15,000	$18,000	$21,000	$24,000
B: All options	0	0	10,000	20,000	30,000	40,000
C: Call plus bills	10,710	10,710	13,710	16,710	19,710	22,710

Portfolio *A* will be worth 300 times the share value of Motorola. Portfolio *B* is worthless unless Motorola sells for more than the exercise price of the call. Once that point is reached, the portfolio is worth 1,000 times the excess of the stock price over the exercise price. Finally, portfolio *C* is worth $10,710 from the investment in T-bills ($10,500 × 1.02 = $10,710) plus any profits from the 300 call options. Remember that each of these portfolios involves the same $15,000 initial investment. The rates of return on these three portfolios are as follows:

Portfolio	Motorola Price					
	$30	**$40**	**$50**	**$60**	**$70**	**$80**
A: All stock	−40.0%	−20.0%	0.0%	20.0%	40.0%	60.0%
B: All options	−100.0	−100.0	−33.3	33.3	100.0	166.7
C: Call plus bills	−28.6	−28.6	−8.6	11.4	31.4	51.4

These rates of return are graphed in Figure 16.9.

FIGURE 16.9

Rate of Return to Three Strategies

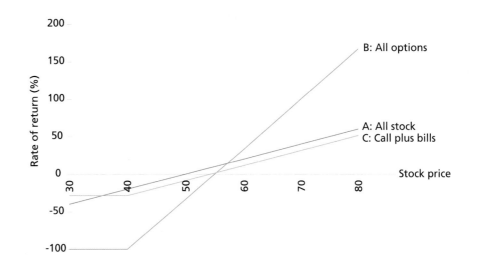

Comparing the returns of portfolios B and C to those of the simple investment in Motorola stock represented by portfolio A, we see that options offer two interesting features. First, an option offers leverage. Compare the returns of portfolios B and A. When Motorola stock falls in price even moderately, to $40, the value of portfolio B falls precipitously to zero—a rate of return of negative 100%. Conversely, modest increases in the rate of return on the stock result in disproportionate increases in the option rate of return. For example, a 14% increase in the stock price from $60 to $70 would increase the rate of return on the call from 33% to 100%. In this sense, calls are a levered investment on the stock. Their values respond more than proportionately to changes in the stock value.

Figure 16.9 vividly illustrates this point. The slope of the all-option portfolio is far steeper than that of the all-stock portfolio, reflecting its greater proportional sensitivity to the value of the underlying security. The leverage factor is the reason that investors (illegally) exploiting inside information commonly choose options as their investment vehicle.

The potential insurance value of options is the second interesting feature, as portfolio C shows. The T-bill plus option portfolio cannot be worth less than $10,710 after six months, as the option can always be left to expire worthless. The worst possible rate of return on portfolio C is −28.6%, compared to a (theoretically) worst possible rate of return of Motorola stock of −100% if the company were to go bankrupt. Of course, this insurance comes at a price: When Motorola does well, portfolio C does not perform as well as portfolio A, the all-stock portfolio. For stock prices above $50, portfolio C underperforms portfolio A by 8.6 percentage points.

This simple example makes an important point. While options can be used by speculators as effectively leveraged stock positions, as in portfolio B, they also can be used by investors who desire to tailor their risk exposures in creative ways, as in portfolio C. For example, the call plus T-bills strategy of portfolio C provides a rate of return profile quite unlike that of the stock alone. The absolute limitation on downside risk is a novel and attractive feature of this strategy. We will discuss below several option strategies that provide other novel risk profiles that might be attractive to hedgers and other investors.

The Put-Call Parity Relationship

Say you buy a call option and write a put option, each with the same exercise price, X, and the same expiration date, T. At expiration, the payoff on your investment will equal the payoff to the call, minus the payoff that must be made on the put. The payoff for each option will depend on whether the ultimate stock price, S_T, exceeds the exercise price at contract expiration.

	$S_T \leq X$	$S_T > X$
Payoff of call held	0	$S_T - X$
−Payoff of put written	$-(X - S_T)$	0
Total	$S_T - X$	$S_T - X$

Figure 16.10 illustrates this payoff pattern. Compare the payoff to that of a portfolio made up of the stock plus a borrowing position, where the money to be paid back will grow, with interest, to X dollars at the maturity of the loan. Such a position is a *levered* equity position in which $X/(1 + r_f)^T$ dollars is borrowed today (so that X will be repaid at maturity), and S_0 dollars is invested in the stock. The total payoff of the levered equity position is $S_T - X$, the same as that of the option strategy. Thus, the long call–short put position replicates the levered equity position. Again, we see that option trading provides leverage.

Because the option portfolio has a payoff identical to that of the levered equity position, the costs of establishing them must be equal. The net cash outlay necessary to establish the option position is $C - P$: The call is purchased for C, while the written put generates income

FIGURE 16.10

The Payoff Pattern of a Long Call–Short Put Position

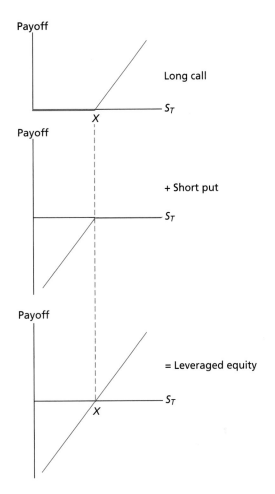

of P. Likewise, the levered equity position requires a net cash outlay of $S_0 - X/(1 + r_f)^T$, the cost of the stock less the proceeds from borrowing. Equating these costs, we conclude

$$C - P = S_0 - X/(1 + r_f)^T \tag{16.1}$$

put-call parity theorem
An equation representing the proper relationship between put and call prices.

Equation 16.1 is called the **put-call parity theorem** because it represents the proper relationship between put and call prices. If the parity relationship is ever violated, an arbitrage opportunity arises.

Suppose you confront the following data for a certain stock.

EXAMPLE 16.3
Put-Call Parity

Stock price	$110
Call price (six-month maturity, $X = \$105$)	17
Put price (six-month maturity, $X = \$105$)	5
Risk-free interest rate	10.25% effective annual yield (5% per 6 months)

We use these data in the put-call parity theorem to see if parity is violated.

$$C - P \overset{?}{=} S_0 - X/(1 + r_f)^T$$
$$17 - 5 \overset{?}{=} 110 - 105/1.05$$
$$12 \overset{?}{=} 10$$

TABLE 16.1

Arbitrage Strategy

Position	Immediate Cash Flow	Cash Flow in Six Months	
		$S_T < 105$	$S_T \geq 105$
Buy stock	−110	S_T	S_T
Borrow $X/(1 + r_f)^T = \$100$	+100	−105	−105
Sell call	+17	0	$-(S_T - 105)$
Buy put	−5	$105 - S_T$	0
Total	2	0	0

This result, a violation of parity (12 does not equal 10) indicates mispricing and leads to an arbitrage opportunity. You can buy the relatively cheap portfolio (the stock plus borrowing position represented on the right-hand side of the equation) and sell the relatively expensive portfolio (the long call–short put position corresponding to the left-hand side, that is, write a call and buy a put).

Let's examine the payoff to this strategy. In six months, the stock will be worth S_T. The $100 borrowed will be paid back with interest, resulting in a cash flow of $105. The written call will result in a cash outflow of S_T − $105 if S_T exceeds $105. The purchased put pays off $105 − S_T if the stock price is below $105.

Table 16.1 summarizes the outcome. The immediate cash inflow is $2. In six months, the various positions provide exactly offsetting cash flows: The $2 inflow is realized risklessly without any offsetting outflows. This is an arbitrage opportunity that investors will pursue on a large scale until buying and selling pressure restores the parity condition expressed in Equation 16.1.

Equation 16.1 actually applies only to options on stocks that pay no dividends before the maturity date of the option. It also applies only to European options, as the cash flow streams from the two portfolios represented by the two sides of Equation 16.1 will match only if each position is held until maturity. If a call and a put may be optimally exercised at different times before their common expiration date, then the equality of payoffs cannot be assured, or even expected, and the portfolios will have different values.

The extension of the parity condition for European call options on dividend-paying stocks is, however, straightforward. Problem 13 at the end of the chapter leads you through the extension of the parity relationship. The more general formulation of the put-call parity condition is

$$P = C - S_0 + PV(X) + PV(\text{dividends}) \tag{16.2}$$

where $PV(\text{dividends})$ is the present value of the dividends that will be paid by the stock during the life of the option. If the stock does not pay dividends, Equation 16.2 becomes identical to Equation 16.1.

Notice that this generalization would apply as well to European options on assets other than stocks. Instead of using dividend income per se in Equation 16.2, we would let any income paid out by the underlying asset play the role of the stock dividends. For example, European put and call options on bonds would satisfy the same parity relationship, except that the bond's coupon income would replace the stock's dividend payments in the parity formula.

Let's see how well parity works using real data on the Motorola options in Figure 16.2. The October maturity call with exercise price $50 and time to expiration of 40 days cost $2.75 while the corresponding put option cost $2.125. Motorola was selling for $50.625, and the annualized short-term interest rate on this date was 4.5%. There are no dividends to be paid to a stock purchaser between the date of the listing, September 9, and the option maturity date. According to parity, we should find that

$$P = C + PV(X) - S_0 + PV \text{ (dividends)}$$

$$2.125 = 2.75 + \frac{50}{(1.045)^{40/365}} - 50.625 + 0$$

$$2.125 = 2.75 + 49.759 - 50.625$$

$$2.125 = 1.884$$

So, parity is violated by about $0.24 per share. Is this a big enough difference to exploit? Probably not. You have to weigh the potential profit against the trading costs of the call, put, and stock. More important, given the fact that options trade relatively infrequently, this deviation from parity might not be "real" but may instead be attributable to "stale" price quotes at which you cannot actually trade.

Option Strategies

An unlimited variety of payoff patterns can be achieved by combining puts and calls with various exercise prices. Below we explain the motivation and structure of some of the more popular ones.

Protective Put   Imagine you would like to invest in a stock, but you are unwilling to bear potential losses beyond some given level. Investing in the stock alone seems risky to you because in principle you could lose all the money you invest. You might consider instead investing in stock and purchasing a put option on the stock.

Table 16.2 shows the total value of your portfolio at option expiration. Whatever happens to the stock price, you are guaranteed a payoff equal to the put option's exercise price because the put gives you the right to sell Motorola for the exercise price even if the stock price is below that value.

<table>
<tr><td>

EXAMPLE 16.4
Protective Put

</td><td>

Suppose the strike price is $X = \$55$ and Motorola is selling for $52 at option expiration. Then the value of your total portfolio is $55: The stock is worth $52 and the value of the expiring put option is

$$X - S_T = \$55 - \$52 = \$3$$

Another way to look at it is that you are holding the stock and a put contract giving you the right to sell the stock for $55. If $S < \$55$, you can still sell the stock for $55 by exercising the put. On the other hand, if the stock price is above $55, say $59, then the right to sell a share at $55 is worthless. You allow the put to expire unexercised, ending up with a share of stock worth $S_T = \$59$.

</td></tr>
</table>

protective put
An asset combined with a put option that guarantees minimum proceeds equal to the put's exercise price.

Figure 16.11 illustrates the payoff and profit to this **protective put** strategy. The solid line in Figure 16.11C is the total payoff. The dashed line is displaced downward by the cost of establishing the position, $S_0 + P$. Notice that potential losses are limited.

It is instructive to compare the profit on the protective put strategy with that of the stock investment. For simplicity, consider an at-the-money protective put, so that $X = S_0$. Figure 16.12 compares the profits for the two strategies. The profit on the stock is zero if the stock price remains unchanged, and $S_T = S_0$. It rises or falls by $1 for every dollar swing in the ultimate stock price. The profit on the protective put is negative and equal to the cost of the put if S_T is below S_0. The profit on the protective put increases one for one with increases in the stock price.

Figure 16.12 makes it clear that the protective put offers some insurance against stock price declines in that it limits losses. As we shall see in the next chapter, protective put strategies are the conceptual basis for the portfolio insurance industry. The cost of the protection is that, in the case of stock price increases, your profit is reduced by the cost of the put, which turned out to be unneeded.

This example also shows that despite the common perception that "derivatives mean risk," derivative securities can be used effectively for *risk management*. In fact, such risk management is becoming accepted as part of the fiduciary responsibility of financial managers. The nearby box (page 455) discusses the recent court case *Brane v. Roth* in which a company's board of directors was successfully sued for failing to use derivatives to hedge the price risk of grain held in storage. Such hedging might have been accomplished using either protective puts, or, as suggested in the box, futures contracts. Many observers believe that this case will soon lead to a broad legal obligation for firms to use derivatives and other techniques to manage risk.

TABLE 16.2

Payoff to Protective Put
Strategy

	$S_T \leq X$	$S_T > X$
Stock	S_T	S_T
Put	$X - S_T$	0
Total	X	S_T

FIGURE 16.11

Value of a Protective
Put Position at
Expiration

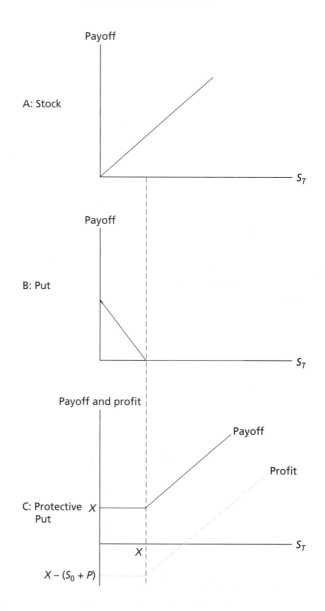

Covered Calls A **covered call** position is the purchase of a share of stock with the simultaneous sale of a call on that stock. The position is "covered" because the potential obligation to deliver the stock is covered by the stock held in the portfolio. Writing an option without an offsetting stock position is called by contrast *naked option writing*. The payoff to a covered call, presented in Table 16.3, equals the stock value minus the payoff of the call. The call payoff is subtracted because the covered call position involves issuing a call to another investor who can choose to exercise it to profit at your expense.

The solid line in Figure 16.13C illustrates the payoff pattern. You see that the total position is worth S_T when the stock price at time T is below X and rises to a maximum of X

covered call

Writing a call on an asset
together with buying the
asset.

Future Shock

A company's board of directors is successfully sued by its shareholders for not using derivatives to hedge its risks? It sounds far-fetched. But, after a court decision in America last year, the day when directors have a legal duty to hedge could be coming closer.

The cast of *Brane v. Roth* involved no Wall Street investment bank or securities house, but a humble grain co-operative in Indiana. America has thousands of agricultural co-ops, which buy and sell produce on behalf of their shareholders (local farmers who entrust their annual harvests to co-ops in the hope of getting the best price). When the manager of the Indiana co-op finished selling his farmers' crops in 1980—a year in which the price of gain collapsed—the co-op had made a gross loss of $424,000

He might have avoided the loss by using grain futures on the Chicago Board of Trade to hedge against falling prices. The co-op's worried accountant had, in fact, advised the board the previous year that it should be hedging against this risk. The directors authorized the manager to do so. As a result, the manager did hedge—but only a paltry $20,050 of the co-op's $7.3m of grain sales. Losses mounted as the price of grain tumbled.

"Negligence," cried shareholders, and promptly sued the co-op's manager and four directors. After long proceedings, the Indiana courts agreed, citing the failure to hedge as the manager's central sin. As for the directors, they had a duty to understand hedging techniques and should have watched over the manager more carefully. In June 1992 the co-op's directors lost their final appeal.

The case, believed to be the first ruling of its kind, was spotted recently by Philip Johnson, a partner of a New York law firm, Skadden, Arps, Slate, Meagher & Flom (and a former chairman of the Commodities and Futures Trading Commission). He reckons the ruling, though it has no legal force outside Indiana, will prove an irresistible precedent for lawyers elsewhere: ignorance of derivatives is no excuse for not using them. And that applies to ordinary businesses as well as to the financial institutions which most obviously must manage financial risk. If Mr. Johnson is right in his assessment, the next case will not be long in coming.

© 1993 *The Economist Newspaper Group, Inc.* Reprinted with permission. Further reproduction prohibited.

FIGURE 16.12

Protective Put versus Stock Investment

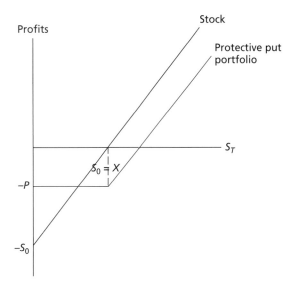

when S_T exceeds X. In essence, the sale of the call option means the call writer has sold the claim to any stock value above X in return for the initial premium (the call price). Therefore, at expiration, the position is worth at most X. The dashed line of Figure 16.13C is the net profit to the covered call.

Writing covered call options has been a popular investment strategy among institutional investors. Consider the managers of a fund invested largely in stocks. They might find it appealing to write calls on some or all of the stock in order to boost income by the premiums collected. Although they thereby forfeit potential capital gains should the stock price rise above the exercise price, if they view X as the price at which they plan to sell the stock anyway, then the call may be viewed as enforcing a kind of "sell discipline." The written call guarantees the stock sale will occur as planned.

**EXAMPLE 16.5
Covered Call**

Assume a pension fund holds 1,000 shares of GXX stock, with a current price of $130 per share. Suppose management intends to sell all 1,000 shares if the share price hits $140, and a call expiring in 90 days with an exercise price of $140 currently sells for $5. By writing 10 GXX call contracts (100 shares each) the fund can pick up $5,000 in extra income. The fund would lose its share of profits from any movement of GXX stock above $140 per share, but given that it would have sold its shares at $140, it would not have realized those profits anyway.

straddle

A combination of a call and a put, each with the same exercise price and expiration date.

Straddle   A long **straddle** is established by buying both a call and a put on a stock, each with the same exercise price, X, and the same expiration date, T. Straddles are useful strategies for investors who believe a stock will move a lot in price but are uncertain about the direction of the move. For example, suppose you believe an important court case that will make or break a company is about to be settled, and the market is not yet aware of the situation. The stock will either double in value if the case is settled favorably or will drop by half if the settlement goes against the company. The straddle position will do well regardless of the outcome because its value is highest when the stock price makes extreme upward or downward moves from X.

The worst-case scenario for a straddle is no movement in the stock price. If S_T equals X, both the call and the put expire worthless, and the investor's outlay for the purchase of both options is lost. Straddle positions basically are bets on volatility. An investor who establishes a straddle must view the stock as more volatile than the market does. Conversely, investors who *write* straddles—selling both a call and a put—must believe the market is less volatile. They accept the option premiums now, hoping the stock price will not change much before option expiration.

The payoff to a straddle is presented in Table 16.4. The solid line of Figure 16.14C illustrates this payoff. Notice the portfolio payoff is always positive, except at the one point where the portfolio has zero value, $S_T = X$. You might wonder why all investors don't pursue such a no-lose strategy. The straddle requires that both the put and call be purchased. The value of the portfolio at expiration, while never negative, still must exceed the initial cash outlay for a straddle investor to clear a profit.

The dashed line of Figure 16.14C is the profit to the straddle. The profit line lies below the payoff line by the cost of purchasing the straddle, $P + C$. It is clear from the diagram that the straddle position generates a loss unless the stock price deviates substantially from X. The stock price must depart from X by the total amount expended to purchase the call *and* the put in order for the purchaser of the straddle to clear a profit.

Strips and *straps* are variations of straddles. A strip is two puts and one call on a security with the same exercise price and maturity date. A strap is two calls and one put.

Concept Check

3. Graph the profit and payoff diagrams for strips and straps.

spread

A combination of two or more call options or put options on the same asset with differing exercise prices or times to expiration.

Spreads   A **spread** is a combination of two or more call options (or two or more puts) on the same stock with differing exercise prices or times to maturity. Some options are bought, while others are sold, or written. A *vertical* or *money spread* involves the purchase of one option and the simultaneous sale of another with a different exercise price. A *horizontal* or *time spread* refers to the sale and purchase of options with differing expiration dates.

Consider a vertical spread in which one call option is bought at an exercise price X_1, while another call with identical expiration date, but higher exercise price, X_2, is written. The

TABLE 16.3

Payoff to a Covered Call

	$S_T \leq X$	$S_T > X$
Payoff of stock	S_T	S_T
−Payoff of call	−0	$-(S_T - X)$
Total	S_T	X

FIGURE 16.13

Value of a Covered Call Position at Expiration

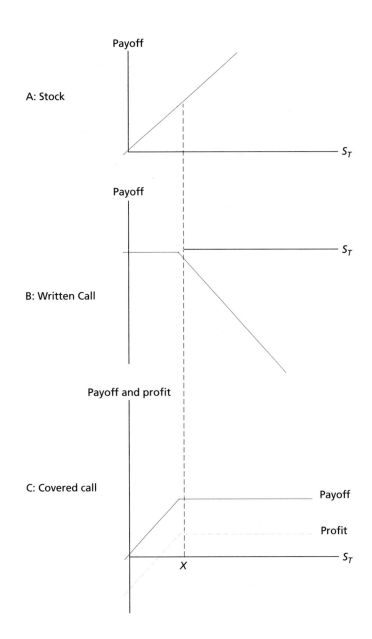

payoff to this position will be the difference in the value of the call held and the value of the call written, as in Table 16.5.

There are now three instead of two outcomes to distinguish: the lowest-price region, where S_T is below both exercise prices; a middle region, where S_T is between the two exercise prices; and a high-price region, where S_T exceeds both exercise prices. Figure 16.15 illustrates the payoff and profit to this strategy, which is called a *bullish spread* because the

TABLE 16.4
Payoff to a Straddle

	$S_T < X$	$S_T \geq X$
Payoff of call	0	$S_T - X$
+Payoff of put	$+(X - S_T)$	$+0$
Total	$X - S_T$	$S_T - X$

FIGURE 16.14
Payoff and Profit to a
Straddle at Expiration

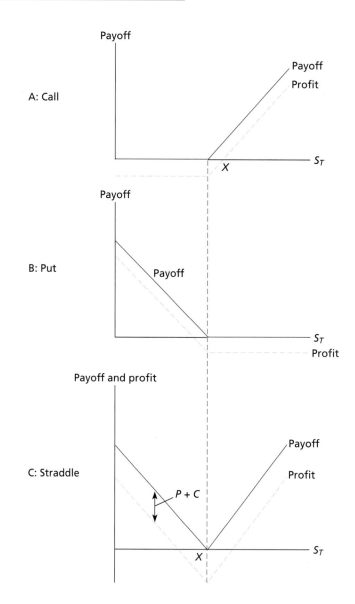

payoff either increases or is unaffected by stock price increases. Holders of bullish spreads benefit from stock price increases.

EXAMPLE 16.6
Bullish Spread

A bullish spread would be appropriate for an investor who has a target wealth goal in mind but is unwilling to risk losses beyond a certain level.

Suppose you are contemplating buying a house for $150,000. You might set this figure as your goal. Your current wealth may be $145,000, and you are unwilling to risk losing more than $10,000. A call with exercise price $135 sells for $15, while a call with exercise price $150 sells for $5. A bullish spread on 1,000 shares (10 option contracts) with $X_1 = \$135$ and $X_2 = \$150$ would give you a good chance to realize a $5,000 profit (if S_T exceeds $150) without risking loss of more than $10,000.

TABLE 16.5
Payoff to a Bullish
Vertical Spread

	$S_T \leq X_1$	$X_1 < S_T \leq X_2$	$S_T > X_2$
Payoff of call, exercise price = X_1	0	$S_T - X_1$	$S_T - X_1$
−Payoff of call, exercise price = X_2	−0	−0	$-(S_T - X_2)$
Total	0	$S_T - X_1$	$X_2 - X_1$

FIGURE 16.15
Value of a Bullish
Spread Position at
Expiration

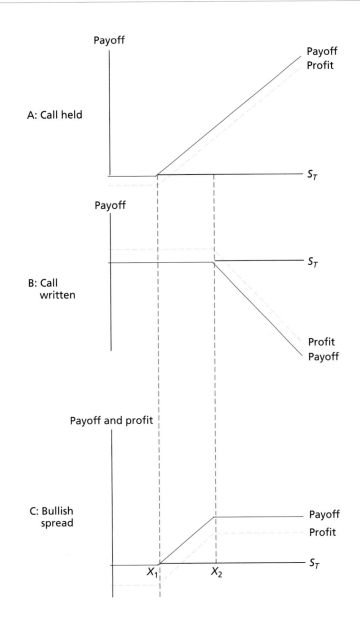

Another motivation for a bullish spread might be that the investor thinks one option is overpriced relative to another. For example, an investor who believes the $X = \$135$ call is cheap compared to the $X = \$150$ call might establish the spread, even without a strong desire to take a bullish position in the stock.

16.3 OPTION-LIKE SECURITIES

Suppose you never intend to trade an option directly. Why do you need to appreciate the properties of options in formulating an investment plan? Many financial instruments and

FIGURE 16.16
Values of Callable
Bonds Compared with
Straight Bonds

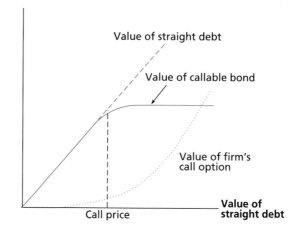

agreements have features that convey implicit or explicit options to one or more parties. If you are to value and use these securities correctly, you must understand these embedded option attributes.

Callable Bonds

You know from Chapter 10 that most corporate bonds are issued with call provisions entitling the issuer to buy bonds back from bondholders at some time in the future at a specified call price. A call provision conveys a call option to the issuer, where the exercise price is equal to the price at which the bond can be repurchased. A callable bond arrangement is essentially a sale of a *straight bond* (a bond with no option features such as callability or convertibility) to the investor and the concurrent sale of a call option by the investor to the bond-issuing firm.

There must be some compensation for offering this implicit call option to the firm. If the callable bond were issued with the same coupon rate as a straight bond, we would expect it to sell at a discount to the straight bond equal to the value of the call. To sell callable bonds at par, firms must issue them with coupon rates higher than the coupons on straight debt. The higher coupons are the investor's compensation for the call option retained by the issuer. Coupon rates usually are selected so that the newly issued bond will sell at par value.

Figure 16.16 illustrates this option-like property. The horizontal axis is the value of a straight bond with otherwise identical terms as the callable bond. The dashed 45-degree line represents the value of straight debt. The solid line is the value of the callable bond, and the dotted line is the value of the call option retained by the firm. A callable bond's potential for capital gains is limited by the firm's option to repurchase at the call price.

Concept Check

4. How is a callable bond similar to a covered call strategy on a straight bond?

The option inherent in callable bonds actually is more complex than an ordinary call option because usually it may be exercised only after some initial period of call protection. The price at which the bond is callable may change over time also. Unlike exchange-listed options, these features are defined in the initial bond covenants and will depend on the needs of the issuing firm and its perception of the market's tastes.

Concept Check

5. Suppose the period of call protection is extended. How will the coupon rate the company needs to offer on its bonds change to enable the issuer to sell the bonds at par value?

Convertible Securities

Convertible bonds and convertible preferred stock convey options to the holder of the security rather than to the issuing firm. A convertible security typically gives its holder the right to exchange each bond or share of preferred stock for a fixed number of shares of common stock, regardless of the market prices of the securities at the time.

Concept Check

6. Should a convertible bond issued at par value have a higher or lower coupon rate than a nonconvertible bond at par?

For example, a bond with a conversion ratio of 10 allows its holder to convert one bond of par value $1,000 into 10 shares of common stock. Alternatively, we say the conversion price in this case is $100: To receive 10 shares of stock, the investor sacrifices bonds with face value $1,000 or $100 of face value per share. If the present value of the bond's scheduled payments is less than 10 times the value of one share of stock, it may pay to convert; that is, the conversion option is in the money. A bond worth $950 with a conversion ratio of 10 could be converted profitably if the stock were selling above $95, as the value of the 10 shares received for each bond surrendered would exceed $950. Most convertible bonds are issued "deep out of the money." That is, the issuer sets the conversion ratio so that conversion will not be profitable unless there is a substantial increase in stock prices and/or decrease in bond prices from the time of issue.

A bond's conversion value equals the value it would have if you converted it into stock immediately. Clearly, a bond must sell for at least its conversion value. If it did not, you could purchase the bond, convert it immediately, and clear a riskless profit. This condition could never persist, for all investors would pursue such a strategy and ultimately would bid up the price of the bond.

The straight bond value or "bond floor" is the value the bond would have if it were not convertible into stock. The bond must sell for more than its straight bond value because a convertible bond has more value; it is in fact a straight bond plus a valuable call option. Therefore, the convertible bond has two lower bounds on its market price: the conversion value and the straight bond value.

Figure 16.17 illustrates the option-like properties of the convertible bond. Figure 16.17A shows the value of the straight debt as a function of the stock price of the issuing firm. For healthy firms, the straight debt value is almost independent of the value of the stock because default risk is small. However, if the firm is close to bankruptcy (stock prices are low), default risk increases, and the straight bond value falls. Panel B shows the conversion value of the bond. Panel C compares the value of the convertible bond to these two lower bounds.

When stock prices are low, the straight bond value is the effective lower bound, and the conversion option is nearly irrelevant. The convertible will trade like straight debt. When stock prices are high, the bond's price is determined by its conversion value. With conversion all but guaranteed, the bond is essentially equity in disguise.

We can illustrate with two examples.

	Bond *A*	Bond *B*
Annual coupon	$80	$80
Maturity date	10 years	10 years
Quality rating	Baa	Baa
Conversion ratio	20	25
Stock price	$30	$50
Conversion value	$600	$1,250
Market yield on 10-year Baa-rated bonds	8.5%	8.5%
Value as straight debt	$967	$967
Actual bond price	$972	$1,255
Reported yield to maturity	8.42%	4.76%

FIGURE 16.17

Value of a Convertible
Bond as a Function of
Stock Price

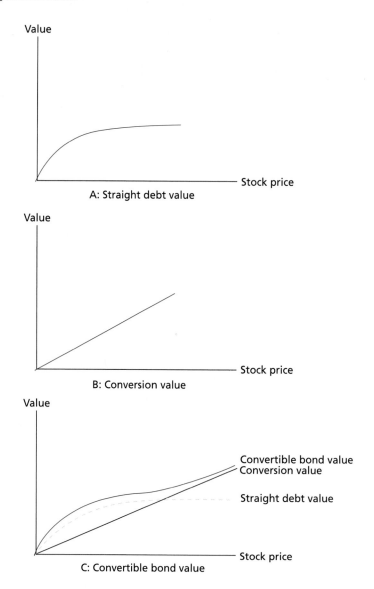

A: Straight debt value

B: Conversion value

C: Convertible bond value

Bond *A* has a conversion value of only $600. Its value as straight debt, in contrast, is $967. This is the present value of the coupon and principal payments at a market rate for straight debt of 8.5%. The bond's price is $972, so the premium over straight bond value is only $5, reflecting the low probability of conversion. Its reported yield to maturity based on scheduled coupon payments and the market price of $972 is 8.42%, close to that of straight debt.

The conversion option on bond *B* is in the money. Conversion value is $1,250, and the bond's price, $1,255, reflects its value as equity (plus $5 for the protection the bond offers against stock price declines). The bond's reported yield is 4.76%, far below the comparable yield on straight debt. The big yield sacrifice is attributable to the far greater value of the conversion option.

In theory, we could value convertible bonds by treating them as straight debt plus call options. In practice, however, this approach is often impractical for several reasons:

1. The conversion price frequently increases over time, which means the exercise price for the option changes.
2. Stocks may pay several dividends over the life of the bond, further complicating the option value analysis.

3. Most convertibles also are callable at the discretion of the firm. In essence, both the investor and the issuer hold options on each other. If the issuer exercises its call option to repurchase the bond, the bondholders typically have a month during which they still can convert. When issuers use a call option, knowing that bondholders will choose to convert, the issuer is said to have *forced a conversion.* These conditions together mean the actual maturity of the bond is indeterminate.

Warrants

warrant

An option issued by the firm to purchase shares of the firm's stock.

Warrants are essentially call options issued by a firm. One important difference between calls and warrants is that exercise of a warrant requires the firm to issue a new share of stock to satisfy its obligation—the total number of shares outstanding increases. Exercise of a call option requires only that the writer of the call deliver an already-issued share of stock to discharge the obligation. In this case, the number of shares outstanding remains fixed. Also unlike call options, warrants result in a cash flow to the firm when the warrant holder pays the exercise price. These differences mean warrant values will differ somewhat from the values of call options with identical terms.

Like convertible debt, warrant terms may be tailored to meet the needs of the firm. Also like convertible debt, warrants generally are protected against stock splits and dividends in that the exercise price and the number of warrants held are adjusted to offset the effects of the split.

Warrants often are issued in conjunction with another security. Bonds, for example, may be packaged together with a warrant "sweetener," frequently a warrant that may be sold separately. This is called a *detachable warrant.*

Issue of warrants and convertible securities creates the potential for an increase in outstanding shares of stock if exercise occurs. Exercise obviously would affect financial statistics that are computed on a per share basis, so annual reports must provide earnings per share figures under the assumption that all convertible securities and warrants are exercised. These figures are called *fully diluted earnings per share.*[2]

Collateralized Loans

Many loan arrangements require that the borrower put up collateral to guarantee the loan will be paid back. In the event of default, the lender takes possession of the collateral. A nonrecourse loan gives the lender no recourse beyond the right to the collateral. That is, the lender may not sue the borrower for further payment if the collateral turns out not to be valuable enough to repay the loan.

This arrangement gives an implicit call option to the borrower. Assume the borrower is obligated to pay back L dollars at the maturity of the loan. The collateral will be worth S_T dollars at maturity. (Its value today is S_0.) The borrower has the option to wait until loan maturity and repay the loan only if the collateral is worth more than the L dollars necessary to satisfy the loan. If the collateral is worth less than L, the borrower can default on the loan, discharging the obligation by forfeiting the collateral, which is worth only S_T.

Another way of describing such a loan is to view the borrower as turning over collateral to the lender but retaining the right to reclaim it by paying off the loan. The transfer of the collateral with the right to reclaim it is equivalent to a payment of S_0 dollars, less a simultaneous recovery of a sum that resembles a call option with exercise price L. Basically, the borrower turns over collateral and keeps an option to "repurchase" it for L dollars at the maturity of the loan if L turns out to be less than S_T. This is a call option.

---

[2]We should note that the exercise of a convertible bond need not reduce earnings per share (EPS). Diluted EPS will be less than undiluted EPS only if interest saved (per share) on the converted bonds is less than the prior EPS.

A third way to look at a collaterized loan is to assume the borrower will repay the L dollars with certainty but also retain the option to sell the collateral to the lender for L dollars, even if S_T is less than L. In this case, the sale of the collateral would generate the cash necessary to satisfy the loan. The ability to "sell" the collateral for a price of L dollars represents a put option, which guarantees the borrower can raise enough money to satisfy the loan simply by turning over the collateral.

It may seem strange to think we can describe the same loan as involving either a put option or a call option, as the payoffs to calls and puts are so different. Yet the equivalence of the two approaches is nothing more than a reflection of the put-call parity relationship. In our call-option description of the loan, the value of the borrower's liability is $S_0 - C$: The borrower turns over the asset, which is a transfer of S_0 dollars, but retains a call that is worth C dollars. In the put-option description, the borrower is obligated to pay L dollars but retains the put, which is worth P: The present value of this net obligation is $L/(1 + r_f)^T - P$. Because these alternative descriptions are equivalent ways of viewing the same loan, the value of the obligations must be equal

$$S_0 - C = L/(1 + r_f)^T - P \tag{16.3}$$

Treating L as the exercise price of the option, equation 16.3 is simply the put-call parity relationship.

Figure 16.18 illustrates this fact. Figure 16.18A is the value of the payment to be received by the lender, which equals the minimum of S_T or L. Panel B shows that this amount can be expressed as S_T minus the payoff of the call implicitly written by the lender and held by the borrower. Panel C shows it also can be viewed as a receipt of L dollars minus the proceeds of a put option.

Levered Equity and Risky Debt

Investors holding stock in incorporated firms are protected by limited liability, which means that if the firm cannot pay its debts, the firm's creditors may attach only the firm's assets and may not sue the corporation's equity holders for further payment. In effect, any time the corporation borrows money, the maximum possible collateral for the loan is the total of the firm's assets. If the firm declares bankruptcy, we can interpret this as an admission that the assets of the firm are insufficient to satisfy the claims against it. The corporation may discharge its obligations by transferring ownership of the firm's assets to the creditors.

Just as is true for nonrecourse collateralized loans, the required payment to the creditors represents the exercise price of the implicit option, while the value of the firm is the underlying asset. The equity holders have a put option to transfer their ownership claims on the firm to the creditors in return for the face value of the firm's debt.

Alternatively, we may view the equity holders as retaining a call option. They have, in effect, already transferred their ownership claim to the firm to the creditors but have retained the right to reacquire the ownership claim by paying off the loan. Hence, the equity holders have the option to "buy back" the firm for a specified price, or they have a call option.

The significance of this observation is that analysts can value corporate bonds using option pricing techniques. The default premium required of risky debt in principle can be estimated using option valuation models. We will consider some of these models in the next chapter.

16.4 EXOTIC OPTIONS

Investors clearly value the portfolio strategies made possible by trading options; this is reflected in the heavy trading volume in these markets and their tremendous success. Success breeds imitation, and in recent years we have witnessed tremendous innovation in the

FIGURE 16.18

Collateralized Loan

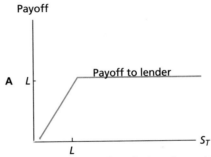

Payoff

A L

Payoff to lender

L

S_T

When S_T exceeds L, the loan is repaid and the collateral is reclaimed. Otherwise, the collateral is forfeited and the total loan repayment is worth only S_T.

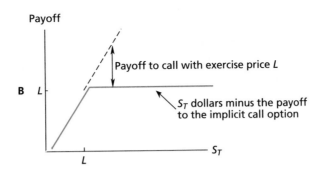

Payoff

B L

Payoff to call with exercise price L

S_T dollars minus the payoff to the implicit call option

L

S_T

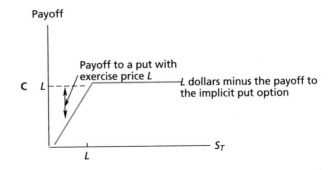

Payoff

C L

Payoff to a put with exercise price L

L dollars minus the payoff to the implicit put option

L

S_T

range of option instruments available to investors. Part of this innovation has occurred in the market for customized options, which now trade in active over-the-counter markets. Many of these options have terms that would have been highly unusual even a few years ago; they therefore are called "exotic options." In this section, we will survey some of the more interesting variants of these new instruments.

Asian Options

You already have been introduced to American and European options. *Asian options* are options with payoffs that depend on the average price of the underlying asset during at least some portion of the life of the option. For example, an Asian call option may have a payoff that is either equal to the average stock price over the last three months minus the strike price, if that value is positive, or zero. These options may be of interest to firms that wish to hedge a profit stream that depends on the average price of a commodity over some period of time.

Barrier Options

Barrier options have payoffs that depend not only on some asset price at option expiration, but also on whether the underlying asset price has crossed through some "barrier." For example, a *down-and-out option* is one type of barrier option that automatically expires worthless if and when the stock price falls below some barrier price. Similarly, *down-and-in options* will not provide a payoff unless the stock price *does* fall below some barrier at least once during the life of the option. These options also are referred to as knock-out and knock-in options.

Lookback Options

Lookback options have payoffs that depend in part on the minimum or maximum price of the underlying asset during the life of the option. For example, a lookback call option might provide a payoff equal to the maximum stock price during the life of the option minus the exercise price, as opposed to the *closing* stock price minus the exercise price. Such an option provides (for a fee, of course) a form of perfect market timing, providing the call holder with a payoff equal to the one that would accrue if the asset were purchased for X dollars and later sold at what turns out to be its highest price.

Currency-Translated Options

Currency-translated options have either asset or exercise prices denominated in a foreign currency. A good example of such an option is the *quanto,* which allows an investor to fix in advance the exchange rate at which an investment in a foreign currency can be converted back into dollars. The right to translate a fixed amount of foreign currency into dollars at a given exchange rate is a simple foreign exchange option. Quantos are more interesting, however, because the amount of currency that will be translated into dollars depends on the investment performance of the foreign security. Therefore, a quanto in effect provides a *random number* of options.

Binary Options

Binary options (also called "bet" options) have fixed payoffs that depend on whether a condition is satisfied by the price of the underlying asset. For example, a binary call option might pay off a fixed amount of $100 if the stock price at maturity exceeds the exercise price.

There are many more exotic options that we do not have room to discuss, and new ones are continually being created. For a comprehensive review of these options and their valuation (which is far more complex than the valuation of the simple options emphasized in this chapter), we refer you to the compilation of articles complied by *RISK Magazine* included in the list of References in Appendix B of the text.

Summary

- A call option is the right to buy an asset at an agreed-upon exercise price. A put option is the right to sell an asset at a given exercise price.
- American options allow exercise on or before the exercise date. European options allow exercise only on the expiration date. Most traded options are American in nature.
- Options are traded on stocks, stock indexes, foreign currencies, fixed-income securities, and several futures contracts.

- Options can be used either to lever up an investor's exposure to an asset price or to provide insurance against volatility of asset prices. Popular option strategies include covered calls, protective puts, straddles, and spreads.
- The put-call parity theorem relates the prices of put and call options. If the relationship is violated, arbitrage opportunities will result. Specifically, the relationship that must be satisfied is

$$P = C - S_0 + PV(X) + PV(\text{dividends})$$

where X is the exercise price of both the call and the put options, and $PV(X)$ is the present value of the claim to X dollars to be paid at the expiration date of the options.
- Many commonly traded securities embody option characteristics. Examples of these securities are callable bonds, convertible bonds, and warrants. Other arrangements, such as collateralized loans and limited-liability borrowing, can be analyzed as conveying implicit options to one or more parties.

Key Terms

American option, *441*	exercise price, *438*	put option, *439*
at the money, *439*	in the money, *439*	spread, *457*
call option, *438*	out of the money, *439*	straddle, *456*
covered call, *454*	protective put, *453*	strike price, *438*
European option, *441*	put-call parity theorem, *451*	warrant, *463*

Problem Set

1. Turn back to Figure 16.2, which lists the prices of various Motorola options. Use the data in the figure to calculate the payoff and the profits for investments in each of the following October maturity options, assuming that the stock price on the maturity date is $55.
   a. Call option, $X = 50$
   b. Put option, $X = 50$
   c. Call option, $X = 55$
   d. Put option, $X = 55$
   e. Call option, $X = 60$
   f. Put option, $X = 60$

2. Suppose you think Wal-Mart stock is going to appreciate substantially in value in the next six months. Say the stock's current price, S_0, is $100, and the call option expiring in six months has an exercise price, X, of $100 and is selling at a price, C, of $10. With $10,000 to invest, you are considering three alternatives:
   a. Invest all $10,000 in the stock, buying 100 shares.
   b. Invest all $10,000 in 1,000 options (10 contracts).
   c. Buy 100 options (one contract) for $1,000 and invest the remaining $9,000 in a money market fund paying 4% interest over six months (8% per year).
   What is your rate of return for each alternative for four stock prices six months from now? Summarize your results in the table and diagram below.

Rate of Return on Investment

	Price of Stock Six Months from Now			
	$80	$100	$110	$120
a. All stocks (100 shares)				
b. All options (1,000 shares)				
c. Bills + 100 options				

3. The common stock of the P.U.T.T. Corporation has been trading in a narrow price range for the past month, and you are convinced it is going to break far out of that range in the next three months. You do not know whether it will go up or down, however. The current price of the stock is $100 per share, and the price of a three-month call option with an exercise price of $100 is $10.

   a. If the risk-free interest rate is 10% per year, what must be the price of a three-month put option on P.U.T.T. stock with an exercise price of $100?

   b. What would be a simple options strategy to exploit your conviction about the stock price's future movements? How far would the price have to move in either direction for you to make a profit on your initial investment?

4. The common stock of the C.A.L.L. Corporation has been trading in a narrow range around $50 per share for months, and you believe it is going to stay in that range for the next three months. The price of a three-month put option with an exercise price of $50 is $4.

   a. If the risk-free interest rate is 10% per year, what must be the price of a three-month call option on C.A.L.L. stock with an exercise price of $50 if the option is at the money?

   b. What would be a simple options strategy using a put and a call to exploit your conviction about the stock price's future movement? What is the most money you can make on this position? How far can the stock price move in either direction before you lose money?

   c. How can you create a position involving a put, a call, and riskless lending that would have the same payoff structure as the stock at expiration? The stock will pay no dividends in the next three months. What is the net cost of establishing that position now?

5. On the death of his grandmother several years ago, Bill Melody received as a bequest from her estate 2,000 shares of General Motors common stock. The price of the stock at time of distribution from the estate was $75 a share, and this became the cost basis of Melody's holding. Late in 1997, Melody agreed to purchase a new condominium for his parents at a total cost of $160,000, payable in full upon its completion in March 1998. Melody planned to sell the General Motors stock in order to raise funds to purchase the condominium.

   At year-end 1997, GM's market price was around $75 a share, but it looked to be weakening. This concerned Melody, for if the price of the stock were to drop by a significant amount before he sold, the proceeds would not be sufficient to cover the purchase of the condominium in March 1998.

   Melody visited with three investment counseling firms to seek advice in developing a strategy that, at a minimum, would protect the value of his principal at or near $150,000 ($75 a share). Ideally, the strategy would enhance the value to $160,000, so Melody would have the total cost of the condominium. Four alternatives were discussed:

   a. Melody's own opinion was to sell the General Motors stock at $75 a share and invest the proceeds in a 10% certificate of deposit maturing in three months.

    b. Anderson Investment Advisors suggested Melody write a March 1998 call option on his General Motors stock at a strike price of $80. The March 1998 calls were quoted at $2.

    c. Cole Capital Management suggested Melody purchase March 1998 at-the-money put options on General Motors, now quoted at $2.

    d. MBA Associates suggested Melody keep the stock, purchase March 1998 at-the-money put options on GM, and finance the purchase by selling March calls with a strike price of $80.

Disregarding transaction costs, dividend income, and margin requirements, rank order the four alternatives in terms of their ability to fulfill the strategy of at least preserving the value of Melody's principal at $150,000 and preferably increasing the value to $160,000 by March 1998. Support your conclusions by showing the payoff structure of each alternative.

6. *a.* A butterfly spread is the purchase of one call at exercise price X_1, the sale of two calls at exercise price X_2, and the purchase of one call at exercise price X_3. X_1 is less than X_2, and X_2 is less than X_3 by equal amounts, and all calls have the same expiration date. Graph the payoff diagram to this strategy.

    b. A vertical combination is the purchase of a call with exercise price X_2 and a put with exercise price X_1, with X_2 greater than X_1. Graph the payoff to this strategy.

7. A bearish spread is the purchase of a call with exercise price X_2 and the sale of a call with exercise price X_1, with X_2 greater than X_1. Graph the payoff to this strategy and compare it to Figure 16.15.

8. You are attempting to formulate an investment strategy. On the one hand, you think there is great upward potential in the stock market and would like to participate in the upward move if it materializes. However, you are not able to afford substantial stock market losses and so cannot run the risk of a stock market collapse, which you also think is a possibility. Your investment advisor suggests a protective put position: Buy both shares in a market index stock fund and put options on those shares with three-month maturity and exercise price of $260. The stock index is currently selling for $300. However, your uncle suggests you instead buy a three-month call option on the index fund with exercise price $280 and buy three-month T-bills with face value $280.

    a. On the same graph, draw the *payoffs* to each of these strategies as a function of the stock fund value in three months. (Hint: Think of the options as being on one "share" of the stock index fund, with the current price of each share of the index equal to $300.)

    b. Which portfolio must require a greater initial outlay to establish? (Hint: Does either portfolio provide a final payoff that is always at least as great as the payoff of the other portfolio?)

    c. Suppose the market prices of the securities are as follows.

Stock fund	$300
T-bill (face value $280)	270
Call (exercise price $280)	40
Put (exercise price $260)	2

      Make a table of profits realized for each portfolio for the following values of the stock price in three months: $S_T = 0, 260, 280, 300, and 320. Graph the profits to each portfolio as a function of S_T on a single graph.

    d. Which strategy is riskier? Which should have a higher beta?

    e. Explain why the data for the securities given in part (*c*) do *not* violate the put-call parity relationship.

9. The agricultural price support system guarantees farmers a minimum price for their output. Describe the program provisions as an option. What is the asset? The exercise price?

10. In what ways is owning a corporate bond similar to writing a put option? A call option?

11. An executive compensation scheme might provide a manager a bonus of $1,000 for every dollar by which the company's stock price exceeds some cutoff level. In what way is this arrangement equivalent to issuing the manager call options on the firm's stock?

12. Consider the following options portfolio. You write an October maturity call option on Motorola with exercise price $55. You write an October maturity Motorola put option with exercise price $50.

    a. Graph the payoff of this portfolio at option expiration as a function of Motorola's stock price at that time.

    b. What will be the profit/loss on this position if Motorola is selling at $52 on the option maturity date? What if Motorola is selling at $60? Use *The Wall Street Journal* listing from Figure 16.2 to answer this question.

    c. At what two stock prices will you just break even on your investment?

    d. What kind of "bet" is this investor making; that is, what must this investor believe about Motorola's stock price in order to justify this position?

13. In this problem, we derive the put-call parity relationship for European options on stocks that pay dividends before option expiration. For simplicity, assume that the stock makes one dividend payment of $D per share at the expiration date of the option.

    a. What is the value of the stock-plus-put position on the expiration date of the option?

    b. Now consider a portfolio comprised of a call option and a zero-coupon bond with the same maturity date as the option and with face value $(X + D)$. What is the value of this portfolio on the option expiration date? You should find that its value equals that of the stock-plus-put portfolio, regardless of the stock price.

    c. What is the cost of establishing the two portfolios in parts (a) and (b)? Equate the cost of these portfolios, and you will derive the put-call parity relationship, Equation 16.2.

14. Consider the following portfolio. You *write* a put option with exercise price $90 and *buy* a put with the same maturity date with exercise price $95.

    a. Plot the value of the portfolio at the maturity date of the options.

    b. On the same graph, plot the profit of the portfolio. Which option must cost more?

15. A Ford put option with strike price $60 trading on the Acme options exchange sells for $2. To your amazement, a Ford put with the same maturity selling on the Apex options exchange but with strike price $62 also sells for $2. If you plan to hold the options position to maturity, devise a zero-net-investment arbitrage strategy to exploit the pricing anomaly. Draw the profit diagram at maturity for your position.

16. You buy a share of stock, write a one-year call option with $X = \$10$, and buy a one-year put option with $X = \$10$. Your net outlay to establish the entire portfolio is $9.50. What is the risk-free interest rate? The stock pays no dividends.

17. Demonstrate that an at-the-money call option on a given stock must cost more than an at-the-money put option with the same maturity. (Hint: Use put-call parity.)

18. You write a call option with $X = \$50$ and buy a call with $X = \$60$. The options are on the same stock and have the same maturity date. One of the calls sells for $3; the other sells for $9.

    a. Draw the *payoff* graph for this strategy at the option maturity date.

    b. Draw the *profit* graph for this strategy.

c. What is the break-even point for this strategy? Is the investor bullish or bearish on the stock?

19. Devise a portfolio using only call options and shares of stock with the following value (payoff) at the option maturity date. If the stock price is currently $53, what kind of bet is the investor making?

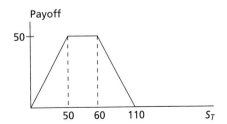

◼IEM
Applications

IEM Computer Industry Returns and MSFT (Microsoft) Price Level Market contracts are actually specialized options contracts called "Binary Options" (because they have payoffs of either $0 or $1 depending on the underlying securities).

1. Are IEM options:
   a. American Style
   b. European Style
   c. Both
   d. Neither

2. Plot the payoff and profit function for the currently traded MSxxxmH and MSxxxmL contracts in the MSFT (Microsoft) Price Level Market on the IEM. Base your diagrams on the last trade price. In what ways do these functions differ from the exchange traded options?

3. Notice that the value of holding one share of each contract MSxxxmH and MSxxxmL always equals $1. Explain how this is equivalent to "put-call parity" as described in the chapter.

Solutions to Concept Checks

1. *a.* Proceeds $= S_T - X = S_T - \$50$ if this value is positive; otherwise, the call expires worthless.
   Profit = Proceeds − Price of call option = Proceeds − $2.75

	$S_T = \$45$	$S_T = \$55$
Proceeds	$0	$5
Profits	−2.75	2.25

   b. Proceeds $= X - S_T = \$50 - S_T$ if this value is positive; otherwise, the put expires worthless.
   Profit = Proceeds − Price of put option = Proceeds − $2.125.

	$S_T = \$45$	$S_T = \$55$
Proceeds	$5	$0
Profits	2.875	−2.125

2. *a.* Payoff to put writer $= 0$ if $S_T \geq X$
   $\qquad\qquad\qquad\quad -(X - S_T)$ if $S_T < X$

   b. Profit =   Initial premium realized + Ultimate payoff
   $\qquad\quad = P$ if $S_T \geq X$
   $\qquad\quad P - (X - S_T)$ if $S_T < X$

c.

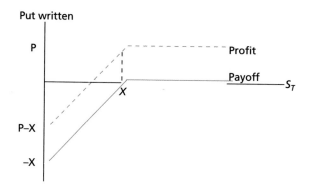

d. Put writers do well when the stock price increases; they do poorly when it falls.

3.

Payoff to a Strip

	$S_T \leq X$	$S_T > X$
2 Puts	$2(X - S_T)$	0
1 Call	0	$S_T - X$

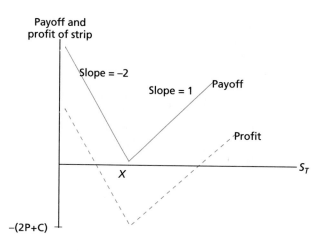

Payoff to a Strap

	$S_T \leq X$	$S_T > X$
1 Put	$X - S_T$	0
2 Calls	0	$2(S_T - X)$

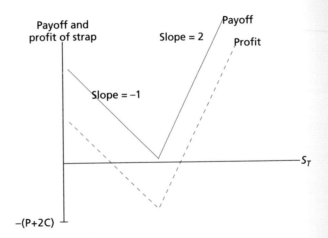

4. The covered call strategy would consist of a straight bond with a call written on the bond. The value of the strategy at option expiration as a function of the value of the straight bond is given in the figure following, which is virtually identical to Figure 16.16.

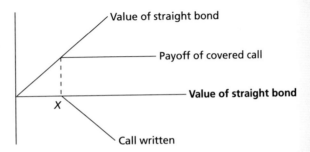

5. The call option is worth less as call protection is expanded. Therefore, the coupon rate need not be as high.

6. Lower. Investors will accept a lower coupon rate in return for the conversion option.

Chapter 17

OPTION VALUATION

AFTER STUDYING THIS CHAPTER YOU SHOULD BE ABLE TO:

- Identify the features of an option that affect its market value.
- Compute an option value in a two-scenario model of the economy.
- Compute the Black-Scholes value of an option.
- Compute the hedge ratio of an option.
- Formulate a portfolio insurance plan using option hedge ratios.

In the previous chapter, we examined option markets and strategies. We ended by noting that many securities contain embedded options that affect both their values and their risk-return characteristics. In this chapter, we turn our attention to option valuation issues. Understanding most option valuation models requires considerable mathematical and statistical background. Still, many of the ideas and insights of these models can be demonstrated in simple examples, and we will concentrate on these.

We start with a discussion of the factors that ought to affect option prices. After this qualitative discussion, we present a simple "two-state" quantitative option valuation model and show how we can generalize it into a useful and accurate pricing tool. Next, we move on to one particular valuation formula, the famous Black-Scholes model, one of the most significant breakthroughs in finance theory in the past three decades.

Finally, we look at some of the more important applications of option pricing theory in portfolio management and control. One of its most controversial applications has been in the provision of portfolio insurance.

17.1 OPTION VALUATION: INTRODUCTION

Intrinsic and Time Values

Consider a call option that is out of the money at the moment, with the stock price below the exercise price. This does not mean the option is valueless. Even though immediate exercise today would be unprofitable, the call retains a positive value because there is always a chance the stock price will increase sufficiently by the expiration date to allow for profitable exercise. If not, the worst that can happen is that the option will expire with zero value.

intrinsic value
Stock price minus exercise price, or the profit that could be attained by immediate exercise of an in-the-money call option.

The value $S_0 - X$ is sometimes called the **intrinsic value** of in-the-money call options because it gives the payoff that could be obtained by immediate exercise. Intrinsic value is set equal to zero for out-of-the-money or at-the-money options. The difference between the actual call price and the intrinsic value is commonly called the *time value* of the option.

"Time value" is an unfortunate choice of terminology because it may confuse the option's time value with the time value of money. Time value in the options context simply refers to the difference between the option's price and the value the option would have if it were expiring immediately. It is the part of the option's value that may be attributed to the fact that it still has positive time to expiration.

Most of an option's time value typically is a type of "volatility value." As long as the option holder can choose not to exercise, the payoff cannot be worse than zero. Even if a call option is out of the money now, it still will sell for a positive price because it offers the potential for a profit if the stock price increases, while imposing no risk of additional loss should the stock price fall. The volatility value lies in the right not to exercise the option if that action would be unprofitable. The option to exercise, as opposed to the obligation to exercise, provides insurance against poor stock price performance.

As the stock price increases substantially, it becomes more likely that the call option will be exercised by expiration. In this case, with exercise all but assured, the volatility value becomes minimal. As the stock price gets even larger, the option value approaches the "adjusted" intrinsic value, the stock price minus the present value of the exercise price, $S_0 - PV(X)$.

Why should this be? If you *know* the option will be exercised and the stock purchased for X dollars, it is as though you own the stock already. The stock certificate might as well be sitting in your safe-deposit box now, as it will be there in only a few months. You just haven't paid for it yet. The present value of your obligation is the present value of X, so the present value of the net payoff of the call option is $S_0 - PV(X)$.[1]

Figure 17.1 illustrates the call option valuation function. The value curve shows that when the stock price is low, the option is nearly worthless because there is almost no chance that it will be exercised. When the stock price is very high, the option value approaches adjusted intrinsic value. In the midrange case, where the option is approximately at the money, the option curve diverges from the straight lines corresponding to adjusted intrinsic value. This is because, while exercise today would have a negligible (or negative) payoff, the volatility value of the option is quite high in this region. The option always increases in value with the stock price. The slope is greatest, however, when the option is deep in the money. In this case, exercise is all but assured, and the option increases in price one for one with the stock price.

Determinants of Option Values

We can identify at least six factors that should affect the value of a call option: the stock price, the exercise price, the volatility of the stock price, the time to expiration, the interest rate, and the dividend rate of the stock. The call option should increase in value with the stock price and decrease in value with the exercise price because the payoff to a call, if

---

[1]This discussion presumes the stock pays no dividends until after option expiration. If the stock does pay dividends before maturity, then there *is* a reason you would care about getting the stock now rather than at expiration—getting it now entitles you to the interim dividend payments. In this case, the adjusted intrinsic value of the option must subtract the value of the dividends the stock will pay out before the call is exercised. Adjusted intrinsic value would more generally be defined as $S_0 - PV(X) - PV(D)$, where D is the dividend to be paid before option expiration.

FIGURE 17.1
Call Option Value
Before Expiration

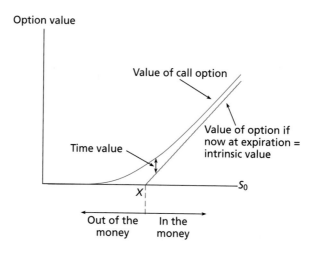

exercised, equals $S_T - X$. The magnitude of the expected payoff from the call increases with the difference $S_0 - X$.

Call option value also increases with the volatility of the underlying stock price. To see why, consider circumstances where possible stock prices at expiration may range from $10 to $50 compared to a situation where stock prices may range only from $20 to $40. In both cases, the expected, or average, stock price will be $30. Suppose the exercise price on a call option is also $30. What are the option payoffs?

High-Volatility Scenario

Stock price	$10	$20	$30	$40	$50
Option payoff	0	0	0	10	20

Low-Volatility Scenario

Stock price	$20	$25	$30	$35	$40
Option payoff	0	0	0	5	10

If each outcome is equally likely, with probability 0.2, the expected payoff to the option under high-volatility conditions will be $6, but under the low-volatility conditions, the expected payoff to the call option is half as much, only $3.

Despite the fact that the average stock price in each scenario is $30, the average option payoff is greater in the high-volatility scenario. The source of this extra value is the limited loss an option holder can suffer, or the volatility value of the call. No matter how far below $30 the stock price drops, the option holder will get zero. Obviously, extremely poor stock price performance is no worse for the call option holder than moderately poor performance.

In the case of good stock performance, however, the call option will expire in the money, and it will be more profitable the higher the stock price. Thus, extremely good stock outcomes can improve the option payoff without limit, but extremely poor outcomes cannot worsen the payoff below zero. This asymmetry means volatility in the underlying stock price increases the expected payoff to the option, thereby enhancing its value.

Concept Check

1. Should a put option increase in value with the volatility of the stock?

Similarly, longer time to expiration increases the value of a call option. For more distant expiration dates, there is more time for unpredictable future events to affect prices, and the

TABLE 17.1
Determinants of Call
Option Values

If This Variable Increases	The Value of a Call Option
Stock price, S	Increases
Exercise price, X	Decreases
Volatility, σ	Increases
Time to expiration, T	Increases
Interest rate, r_f	Increases
Dividend payouts	Decreases

range of likely stock prices increases. This has an effect similar to that of increased volatility. Moreover, as time to expiration lengthens, the present value of the exercise price falls, thereby benefiting the call option holder and increasing the option value. As a corollary to this issue, call option values are higher when interest rates rise (holding the stock price constant), because higher interest rates also reduce the present value of the exercise price.

Finally, the dividend payout policy of the firm affects option values. A high dividend payout policy puts a drag on the rate of growth of the stock price. For any expected total rate of return on the stock, a higher dividend yield must imply a lower expected rate of capital gain. This drag on stock appreciation decreases the potential payoff from the call option, thereby lowering the call value. Table 17.1 summarizes these relationships.

Concept Check

2. How should the value of a put option respond to the firm's dividend payout policy?

17.2 BINOMIAL OPTION PRICING

Two-State Option Pricing

A complete understanding of commonly used option valuation formulas is difficult without a substantial mathematics background. Nevertheless, we can develop valuable insight into option valuation by considering a simple special case. Assume a stock price can take only two possible values at option expiration: The stock will either increase to a given higher price or decrease to a given lower price. Although this may seem an extreme simplification, it allows us to come closer to understanding more complicated and realistic models. Moreover, we can extend this approach to describe far more reasonable specifications of stock price behavior. In fact, several major financial firms employ variants of this simple model to value options and securities with option-like features.

Suppose the stock now sells at $100, and the price will either double to $200 or fall in half to $50 by year end. A call option on the stock might specify an exercise price of $125 and a time to expiration of one year. The interest rate is 8%. At year end, the payoff to the holder of the call option will be either zero, if the stock falls, or $75, if the stock price goes to $200.

These possibilities are illustrated by the following "trees."

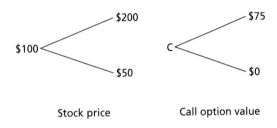

Stock price   Call option value

Compare this payoff to that of a portfolio consisting of one share of the stock and borrowing of $46.30 at the interest rate of 8%. The payoff of this portfolio also depends on the stock price at year end.

Value of stock at year end	$50	$200
−Repayment of loan with interest	−50	−50
Total	$ 0	$150

We know the cash outlay to establish the portfolio is $53.70: $100 for the stock, less the $46.30 proceeds from borrowing. Therefore, the portfolio's value tree is

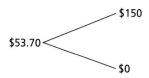

The payoff of this portfolio is exactly twice that of the call option for either value of the stock price. In other words, two call options will exactly replicate the payoff to the portfolio; it follows that two call options should have the same price as the cost of establishing the portfolio. Hence, the two calls should sell for the same price as the "replicating portfolio." Therefore

$$2C = \$53.70$$

or each call should sell at $C = \$26.85$. Thus, given the stock price, exercise price, interest rate, and volatility of the stock price (as represented by the magnitude of the up or down movements), we can derive the fair value for the call option.

This valuation approach relies heavily on the notion of *replication*. With only two possible end-of-year values of the stock, the payoffs to the levered stock portfolio replicate the payoffs to two call options and so need to command the same market price. This notion of replication is behind most option pricing formulas. For more complex price distributions for stocks, the replication technique is correspondingly more complex, but the principles remain the same.

One way to view the role of replication is to note that, using the numbers assumed for this example, a portfolio made up of one share of stock and two call options written is perfectly hedged. Its year-end value is independent of the ultimate stock price.

Stock value	$50	$200
−Obligations from 2 calls written	−0	−150
Net payoff	$50	$ 50

The investor has formed a riskless portfolio with a payout of $50. Its value must be the present value of $50, or $50/1.08 = $46.30. The value of the portfolio, which equals $100 from the stock held long, minus $2C$ from the two calls written, should equal $46.30. Hence, $100 − 2C = \$46.30$, or $C = \$26.85$.

The ability to create a perfect hedge is the key to this argument. The hedge locks in the end-of-year payout, which can be discounted using the risk-free interest rate. To find the value of the option in terms of the value of the stock, we do not need to know either the option's or the stock's beta or expected rate of return. The perfect hedging, or replication, approach enables us to express the value of the option in terms of the current value of the stock without this information. With a hedge position, the final stock price does not affect the investor's payoff, so the stock's risk and return parameters have no bearing.

The hedge ratio of this example is one share of stock to two calls, or one-half. For every call option written, one-half share of stock must be held in the portfolio to hedge away risk. This ratio has an easy interpretation in this context: It is the ratio of the range of the values of the option to those of the stock across the two possible outcomes. The option is worth either zero or $75, for a range of $75. The stock is worth either $50 or $200, for a range of $150. The ratio of ranges, $75/$150, is one-half, which is the hedge ratio we have established.

The hedge ratio equals the ratio of ranges because the option and stock are perfectly correlated in this two-state example. When the returns of the option and stock are perfectly correlated, a perfect hedge requires that the option and stock be held in a fraction determined only by relative volatility.

We can generalize the hedge ratio for other two-state option problems as

$$H = \frac{C^+ - C^-}{S^+ - S^-}$$

where C^+ or C^- refers to the call option's value when the stock goes up or down respectively, and S^+ and S^- are the stock prices in the two states. The hedge ratio, H, is the ratio of the swings in the possible end-of-period values of the option and the stock. If the investor writes one option and holds H shares of stock, the value of the portfolio will be unaffected by the stock price. In this case, option pricing is easy: Simply set the value of the hedged portfolio equal to the present value of the known payoff.

Using our example, the option pricing technique would proceed as follows:

1. Given the possible end-of-year stock prices, $S^+ = \$200$ and $S^- = \$50$, and the exercise price of $125, calculate that $C^+ = \$75$ and $C^- = \$0$. The stock price range is $150, while the option price range is $75.

2. Find that the hedge ratio is $75/$150 = 0.5.

3. Find that a portfolio made up of 0.5 shares with one written option would have an end-of-year value of $25 with certainty.

4. Show that the present value of $25 with a one-year interest rate of 8% is $23.15.

5. Set the value of the hedged position equal to the present value of the certain payoff

$$0.5S_0 - C_0 = \$23.15$$
$$\$50 - C_0 = \$23.15$$

6. Solve for the call's value, $C_0 = \$26.85$.

What if the option were overpriced, perhaps selling for $30? Then you can make arbitrage profits. Here is how.

	Initial Cash Flow	Cash Flow in 1 Year for Each Possible Stock Price	
		S = $50	S = $200
1. Write 2 options.	$ 60	$ 0	$–150
2. Purchase 1 share.	–100	50	200
3. Borrow $40 at 8% interest and repay in 1 year.	40	–43.20	–43.20
Total	$ 0	$ 6.80	$ 6.80

Although the net initial investment is zero, the payoff in one year is positive and riskless. If the option were underpriced, one would simply reverse this arbitrage strategy: Buy the option, and sell the stock short to eliminate price risk. Note, by the way, that the present value of the profit to the above arbitrage strategy equals twice the amount by which the option is overpriced. The present value of the risk-free profit of $6.80 at an 8% interest rate is $6.30. With two options written in the strategy above, this translates to a profit of $3.15 per option, exactly the amount by which the option was overpriced: $30 versus the "fair value" of $26.85.

3. Suppose the call option had been underpriced, selling at $24. Formulate the arbitrage strategy to exploit the mispricing, and show that it provides riskless cash flow in one year of $3.08 per option purchased.

Concept Check

Generalizing the Two-State Approach

Although the two-state stock price model seems simplistic, we can generalize it to incorporate more realistic assumptions. To start, suppose we were to break up the year into two six-month segments and then assert that over each half-year segment the stock price could take on two values. Here we will say it can increase 10% or decrease 5%. A stock initially selling at $100 could follow the following possible paths over the course of the year:

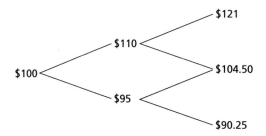

The midrange value of $104.50 can be attained by two paths: an increase of 10% followed by a decrease of 5%, or a decrease of 5% followed by an increase of 10%.

There are now three possible end-of-year values for the stock and three for the option:

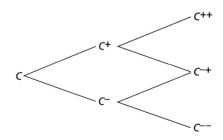

Using methods similar to those we followed above, we could value C^+ from knowledge of C^{++} and C^{+-}, then value C^- from knowledge of C^{-+} and C^{--}, and finally value C from knowledge of C^+ and C^-. And there is no reason to stop at six-month intervals. We could next break the year into four three-month units, or 12 one-month units, or 365 one-day units, each of which would be posited to have a two-state process. Although the calculations become quite numerous and correspondingly tedious, they are easy to program into a computer, and such computer programs are used widely by participants in the options market.

As we break the year into progressively finer subintervals, the range of possible year-end stock prices expands and, in fact, will ultimately take on a familiar bell-shaped distribution. This can be seen from an analysis of the event tree for the stock for a period with three subintervals.

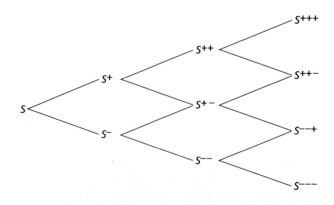

First, notice that as the number of subintervals increases, the number of possible stock prices also increases. Second, notice that extreme events such as S^{+++} or S^{---} are relatively rare, as they require either three consecutive increases or decreases in the three subintervals. More moderate, or midrange, results such as S^{++-} can be arrived at by more than one path; any combination of two price increases and one decrease will result in stock price S^{++-}. Thus, the midrange values will be more likely. The probability of each outcome is described by the binomial distribution, and this multiperiod approach to option pricing is called the **binomial model.**

binomial model
An option valuation model predicated on the assumption that stock prices can move to only two values over any short time period.

For example, using our initial stock price of $100, equal probability of stock price increases or decreases, and three intervals for which the possible price increase is 5% and the decrease is 3%, we can obtain the probability distribution of stock prices from the following calculations. There are eight possible combinations for the stock price movement in the three periods: $+ + +, + + -, + - +, - + +, + - -, - + -, - - +, - - -$. Each has probability of $\frac{1}{8}$. Therefore, the probability distribution of stock prices at the end of the last interval would be as follows.

Event	Probability	Stock Price	
3 up movements	1/8	100×1.05^3	= $115.76
2 up and 1 down	3/8	$100 \times 1.05^2 \times 0.97$	= $106.94
1 up and 2 down	3/8	$100 \times 1.05 \times 0.97^2$	= $98.79
3 down movements	1/8	100×0.97^3	= $91.27

The midrange values are three times as likely to occur as the extreme values. Figure 17.2A is a graph of the frequency distribution for this example. The graph approaches the appearance of the familiar bell-shaped curve. In fact, as the number of intervals increases, as in Figure 17.2B, the frequency distribution progressively approaches the lognormal distribution rather than the normal distribution.[2]

Suppose we were to continue subdividing the interval in which stock prices are posited to move up or down. Eventually, each node of the event tree would correspond to an infinitesimally small time interval. The possible stock price movement within that time interval would be correspondingly small. As those many intervals passed, the end-of-period stock price would more and more closely resemble a lognormal distribution. Thus, the apparent oversimplification of the two-state model can be overcome by progressively subdividing any period into many subperiods.

At any node, one still could set up a portfolio that would be perfectly hedged over the next tiny time interval. Then, at the end of that interval, on reaching the next node, a new hedge ratio could be computed and the portfolio composition could be revised to remain hedged over the coming small interval. By continuously revising the hedge position, the portfolio would remain hedged and would earn a riskless rate of return over each interval. This is called *dynamic hedging,* the continued updating of the hedge ratio as time passes. As the dynamic hedge becomes ever finer, the resulting option valuation procedure becomes more precise.

Concept Check

4. Would you expect the hedge ratio to be higher or lower when the call option is more in the money?

---

[2]Actually, more complex considerations enter here. The limit of this process is lognormal only if we assume also that stock prices move continuously, by which we mean that over small time intervals only small price movements can occur. This rules out rare events such as sudden, extreme price moves in response to dramatic information (like a takeover attempt). For a treatment of this type of "jump process," see John C. Cox and Stephen A. Ross, "The Valuation of Options for Alternative Stochastic Processes," *Journal of Financial Economics* 3 (January–March 1976), pp. 145–66, or Robert C. Merton, "Option Pricing When Underlying Stock Returns Are Discontinuous," *Journal of Financial Economics* 3 (January–March 1976), pp. 125–44.

FIGURE 17.2
Probability
Distributions

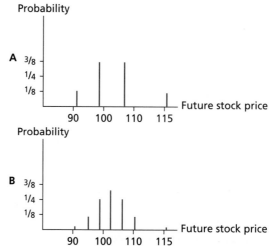

A. Possible outcomes and associated probabilities for stock prices after three periods. The stock price starts at $100, and in each period it can increase by 5% or decrease by 3%.

B. Each period is subdivided into two smaller subperiods. Now there are six periods, and in each of these the stock price can increase by 2.5% or fall by 1.5%. As the number of periods increases, the stock price distribution approaches the familiar bell-shaped curve.

17.3 BLACK-SCHOLES OPTION VALUATION

While the binomial model we have described is extremely flexible, it requires a computer to be useful in actual trading. An option pricing *formula* would be far easier to use than the tedious algorithm involved in the binomial model. It turns out that such a formula can be derived if one is willing to make just two more assumptions: that both the risk-free interest rate and stock price volatility are constant over the life of the option.

The Black-Scholes Formula

Financial economists searched for years for a workable option pricing model before Black and Scholes (1973) and Merton (1973) derived a formula for the value of a call option. Now widely used by options market participants, the **Black-Scholes pricing formula** for a call option is

Black-Scholes pricing formula
A formula to value an option that uses the stock price, the risk-free interest rate, the time to maturity, and the standard deviation of the stock return.

$$C_0 = S_0 N(d_1) - Xe^{-rT}N(d_2) \tag{17.1}$$

where

$$d_1 = \frac{ln(S_0/X) + (r + \sigma^2/2)T}{\sigma\sqrt{T}}$$

$$d_2 = d_1 - \sigma\sqrt{T}$$

and where

C_0 = Current call option value.

S_0 = Current stock price.

$N(d)$ = The probability that a random draw from a standard normal distribution will be less than d. This equals the area under the normal curve up to d, as in the shaded area of Figure 17.3.

X = Exercise price.

$e = 2.71828$, the base of the natural log function.

r = Risk-free interest rate (the annualized continuously compounded rate on a safe asset with the same maturity as the expiration date of the option, which is to be distinguished from r_f, the discrete period interest rate).

T = Time to maturity of option in years.

ln = Natural logarithm function.

σ = Standard deviation of the annualized continuously compounded rate of return of the stock.

The option value does not depend on the expected rate of return on the stock. In a sense, this information is already built into the formula with inclusion of the stock price, which itself depends on the stock's risk and return characteristics. This version of the Black-Scholes formula is predicated on the assumption that the stock pays no dividends.

Although you may find the Black-Scholes formula intimidating, we can explain it at a somewhat intuitive level. The trick is to view the $N(d)$ terms (loosely) as risk-adjusted probabilities that the call option will expire in the money. First, look at Equation 17.1 assuming both $N(d)$ terms are close to 1.0; that is, when there is a very high probability that the option will be exercised. Then the call option value is equal to $S_0 - Xe^{-rT}$, which is what we called earlier the adjusted intrinsic value, $S_0 - PV(X)$. This makes sense; if exercise is certain, we have a claim on a stock with current value S_0 and an obligation with present value $PV(X)$ or with continuous compounding, Xe^{-rT}.

Now look at Equation 17.1, assuming the $N(d)$ terms are close to zero, meaning the option almost certainly will not be exercised. Then the equation confirms that the call is worth nothing. For middle-range values of $N(d)$ between 0 and 1, Equation 17.1 tells us that the call value can be viewed as the present value of the call's potential payoff adjusting for the probability of in-the-money expiration.

How do the $N(d)$ terms serve as risk-adjusted probabilities? This question quickly leads us into advanced statistics. Notice, however, that d_1 and d_2 both increase as the stock price increases. Therefore, $N(d_1)$ and $N(d_2)$ also increase with higher stock prices. This is the property we would desire of our "probabilities." For higher stock prices relative to exercise prices, future exercise is more likely.

FIGURE 17.3
A Standard Normal
Curve

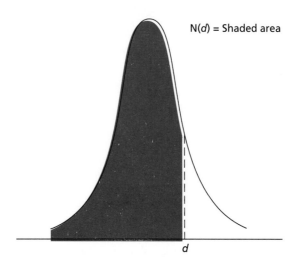

N(*d*) = Shaded area

d

TABLE 17.2
Cumulative Normal Distribution

d	N(d)	d	N(d)	d	N(d)
−3.00	0.0013	−1.58	0.0571	−0.76	0.2236
−2.95	0.0016	−1.56	0.0594	−0.74	0.2297
−2.90	0.0019	−1.54	0.0618	−0.72	0.2358
−2.85	0.0022	−1.52	0.0643	−0.70	0.2420
−2.80	0.0026	−1.50	0.0668	−0.68	0.2483
−2.75	0.0030	−1.48	0.0694	−0.66	0.2546
−2.70	0.0035	−1.46	0.0721	−0.64	0.2611
−2.65	0.0040	−1.44	0.0749	−0.62	0.2676
−2.60	0.0047	−1.42	0.0778	−0.60	0.2743
−2.55	0.0054	−1.40	0.0808	−0.58	0.2810
−2.50	0.0062	−1.38	0.0838	−0.56	0.2877
−2.45	0.0071	−1.36	0.0869	−0.54	0.2946
−2.40	0.0082	−1.34	0.0901	−0.52	0.3015
−2.35	0.0094	−1.32	0.0934	−0.50	0.3085
−2.30	0.0107	−1.30	0.0968	−0.48	0.3156
−2.25	0.0122	−1.28	0.1003	−0.46	0.3228
−2.20	0.0139	−1.26	0.1038	−0.44	0.3300
−2.15	0.0158	−1.24	0.1075	−0.42	0.3373
−2.10	0.0179	−1.22	0.1112	−0.40	0.3446
−2.05	0.0202	−1.20	0.1151	−0.38	0.3520
−2.00	0.0228	−1.18	0.1190	−0.36	0.3594
−1.98	0.0239	−1.16	0.1230	−0.34	0.3669
−1.96	0.0250	−1.14	0.1271	−0.32	0.3745
−1.94	0.0262	−1.12	0.1314	−0.30	0.3821
−1.92	0.0274	−1.10	0.1357	−0.28	0.3897
−1.90	0.0287	−1.08	0.1401	−0.26	0.3974
−1.88	0.0301	−1.06	0.1446	−0.24	0.4052
−1.86	0.0314	−1.04	0.1492	−0.22	0.4129
−1.84	0.0329	−1.02	0.1539	−0.20	0.4207
−1.82	0.0344	−1.00	0.1587	−0.18	0.4286
−1.80	0.0359	−0.98	0.1635	−0.16	0.4365
−1.78	0.0375	−0.96	0.1685	−0.14	0.4443
−1.76	0.0392	−0.94	0.1736	−0.12	0.4523
−1.74	0.0409	−0.92	0.1788	−0.10	0.4602
−1.72	0.0427	−0.90	0.1841	−0.08	0.4681
−1.70	0.0446	−0.88	0.1894	−0.06	0.4761
−1.68	0.0465	−0.86	0.1949	−0.04	0.4841
−1.66	0.0485	−0.84	0.2005	−0.02	0.4920
−1.64	0.0505	−0.82	0.2061	0.00	0.5000
−1.62	0.0526	−0.80	0.2119	0.02	0.5080
−1.60	0.0548	−0.78	0.2177	0.04	0.5160

EXAMPLE 17.1
Black-Scholes Call Option Valuation

You can use the Black-Scholes formula fairly easily. Suppose you want to value a call option under the following circumstances:

Stock price $S_0 = 100$
Exercise price $X = 95$
Interest rate $r = 0.10$
Time to expiration $T = 0.25$ (one-quarter year)
Standard deviation $\sigma = 0.50$

First calculate

$$d_1 = \frac{\ln(100/95) + (0.10 + 0.5^2/2)0.25}{0.5\sqrt{0.25}} = 0.43$$

$$d_2 = 0.43 - 0.5\sqrt{0.25} = 0.18$$

Next find $N(d_1)$ and $N(d_2)$. The normal distribution function is available on most computer spreadsheets. The values of the function also are tabulated and many be found in many statistics textbooks. A table of $N(d)$ is provided here as Table 17.2. The table reveals (using interpolation for 0.43) that

TABLE 17.2
Concluded

d	N(d)	d	N(d)	d	N(d)
0.06	0.5239	0.86	0.8051	1.66	0.9515
0.08	0.5319	0.88	0.8106	1.68	0.9535
0.10	0.5398	0.90	0.8159	1.70	0.9554
0.12	0.5478	0.92	0.8212	1.72	0.9573
0.14	0.5557	0.94	0.8264	1.74	0.9591
0.16	0.5636	0.96	0.8315	1.76	0.9608
0.18	0.5714	0.98	0.8365	1.78	0.9625
0.20	0.5793	1.00	0.8414	1.80	0.9641
0.22	0.5871	1.02	0.8461	1.82	0.9656
0.24	0.5948	1.04	0.8508	1.84	0.9671
0.26	0.6026	1.06	0.8554	1.86	0.9686
0.28	0.6103	1.08	0.8599	1.88	0.9699
0.30	0.6179	1.10	0.8643	1.90	0.9713
0.32	0.6255	1.12	0.8686	1.92	0.9726
0.34	0.6331	1.14	0.8729	1.94	0.9738
0.36	0.6406	1.16	0.8770	1.96	0.9750
0.38	0.6480	1.18	0.8810	1.98	0.9761
0.40	0.6554	1.20	0.8849	2.00	0.9772
0.42	0.6628	1.22	0.8888	2.05	0.9798
0.44	0.6700	1.24	0.8925	2.10	0.9821
0.46	0.6773	1.26	0.8962	2.15	0.9842
0.48	0.6844	1.28	0.8997	2.20	0.9861
0.50	0.6915	1.30	0.9032	2.25	0.9878
0.52	0.6985	1.32	0.9066	2.30	0.9893
0.54	0.7054	1.34	0.9099	2.35	0.9906
0.56	0.7123	1.36	0.9131	2.40	0.9918
0.58	0.7191	1.38	0.9162	2.45	0.9929
0.60	0.7258	1.40	0.9192	2.50	0.9938
0.62	0.7324	1.42	0.9222	2.55	0.9946
0.64	0.7389	1.44	0.9251	2.60	0.9953
0.66	0.7454	1.46	0.9279	2.65	0.9960
0.68	0.7518	1.48	0.9306	2.70	0.9965
0.70	0.7580	1.50	0.9332	2.75	0.9970
0.72	0.7642	1.52	0.9357	2.80	0.9974
0.74	0.7704	1.54	0.9382	2.85	0.9978
0.76	0.7764	1.56	0.9406	2.90	0.9981
0.78	0.7823	1.58	0.9429	2.95	0.9984
0.80	0.7882	1.60	0.9452	3.00	0.9986
0.82	0.7939	1.62	0.9474	3.05	0.9989
0.84	0.7996	1.64	0.9495		

$$N(0.43) = 0.6664$$
$$N(0.18) = 0.5714$$

Thus, the value of the call option is

$$C = 100 \times 0.6664 - 95\ e^{-0.10 \times 0.25} \times 0.5714$$
$$= 66.64 - 52.94 = \$13.70$$

Concept Check

5. Calculate the call option value if the standard deviation on the stock is 0.6 instead of 0.5. Confirm that the option is worth more using this higher volatility.

What if the option price in Example 17.1 were $15 rather than $13.70? Is the option mispriced? Maybe, but before betting your career on that, you may want to reconsider the valuation analysis. First, like all models, the Black-Scholes formula is based on some simplifying abstractions that make the formula only approximately valid.

Some of the important assumptions underlying the formula are the following:

1. The stock will pay no dividends until after the option expiration date.
2. Both the interest rate, r, and variance rate, σ^2, of the stock are constant (or in slightly more general versions of the formula, both are *known* functions of time—any changes are perfectly predictable).
3. Stock prices are continuous, meaning that sudden extreme jumps, such as those in the aftermath of an announcement of a takeover attempt, are ruled out.

Variants of the Black-Scholes formula have been developed to deal with some of these limitations.

Second, even within the context of the Black-Scholes model, you must be sure of the accuracy of the parameters used in the formula. Four of these—S_0, X, T, and r—are straightforward. The stock price, exercise price, and time to maturity are readily determined. The interest rate used is the money market rate for a maturity equal to that of the option.

The last input, though, the standard deviation of the stock return, is not directly observable. It must be estimated from historical data, from scenario analysis, or from the prices of other options, as we will describe momentarily. Because the standard deviation must be estimated, it is always possible that discrepancies between an option price and its Black-Scholes value are simply artifacts of error in the estimation of the stock's volatility.

In fact, market participants often give the option valuation problem a different twist. Rather than calculating a Black-Scholes option value for a given stock standard deviation, they ask instead: "What standard deviation would be necessary for the option price that I can observe to be consistent with the Black-Scholes formula?" This is called the **implied volatility** of the option, the volatility level for the stock that the option price implies. Investors can then judge whether they think the actual stock standard deviation exceeds the implied volatility. If it does, the option is considered a good buy; if actual volatility seems greater than the implied volatility, the option's fair price would exceed the observed price.

Another variation is to compare two options on the same stock with equal expiration dates but different exercise prices. The option with the higher implied volatility would be considered relatively expensive because a higher standard deviation is required to justify its price. The analyst might consider buying the option with the lower implied volatility and writing the option with the higher implied volatility.

implied volatility
The standard deviation of stock returns that is consistent with an option's market value.

▬▬▬▬▬▬

Concept Check

6. Consider the option in the example selling for $15 with Black-Scholes value of $13.70. Is its implied volatility more or less than 0.5?

Put Option Valuation

We have concentrated so far on call option valuation. We can derive Black-Scholes European put option values from call option values using the put-call parity theorem. To value the put option, we simply calculate the value of the corresponding call option in Equation 17.1 from the Black-Scholes formula, and solve for the put option value as

$$
\begin{aligned}
P &= C + PV(X) - S_0 \\
&= C + Xe^{-rT} - S_0
\end{aligned}
\tag{17.2}
$$

We must calculate the present value of the exercise price using continuous compounding to be consistent with the Black-Scholes formula.

**EXAMPLE 17.2
Black-Scholes Put
Option Valuation**

Using data from the Black-Scholes call option example ($C = \$13.70$, $X = \$95$, $S = \$100$, $r = 0.10$, and $T = 0.25$), we find that a European put option on that stock with identical exercise price and time to maturity is worth

$$P = \$13.70 + \$95e^{-0.10 \times 0.25} - \$100 = \$6.35$$

As we noted traders can do, we might then compare this formula value to the actual put price as one step in formulating a trading strategy.

Equation 17.2 is valid for European puts on nondividend-paying stocks. Listed put options are American options that offer the opportunity of early exercise, however. Because an American option allows its owner to exercise at any time before the expiration date, it must be worth at least as much as the corresponding European option. However, while Equation 17.2 describes only the lower bound on the true value of the American put, in many applications the approximation is very accurate.

17.4 USING THE BLACK-SCHOLES FORMULA

Hedge Ratios and the Black-Scholes Formula

hedge ratio or delta
The number of shares of stock required to hedge the price risk of holding one option.

In the last chapter, we considered two investments in Motorola: 300 shares of Motorola stock or 1000 call options on Motorola. We saw that the call option position was more sensitive to swings in Motorola's stock price than the all-stock position. To analyze the overall exposure to a stock price more precisely, however, it is necessary to quantify these relative sensitivities. A tool that enables us to summarize the overall exposure of portfolios of options with various exercise prices and times to maturity is the hedge ratio. An option's **hedge ratio** is the change in the price of an option for a $1 increase in the stock price. A call option, therefore, has a positive hedge ratio, and a put option has a negative hedge ratio. The hedge ratio is commonly called the option's **delta.**

If you were to graph the option value as a function of the stock value as we have done for a call option in Figure 17.4, the hedge ratio is simple the slope of the value function evaluated at the current stock price. For example, suppose the slope of the curve at $S_0 = \$120$ equals 0.60. As the stock increases in value by $1, the option increases by approximately $0.60, as the figure shows.

For every call option written, 0.60 shares of stock would be needed to hedge the investor's portfolio. For example, if one writes 10 options and holds six shares of stock, according to the hedge ratio of 0.6, a $1 increase in stock price will result in a gain of $6 on the stock holdings, while the loss on the 10 options written will be $10 \times \$0.60$, an equivalent $6. The stock price movement leaves total wealth unaltered, which is what a hedged position is

FIGURE 17.4

Call Option Value and
Hedge Ratio

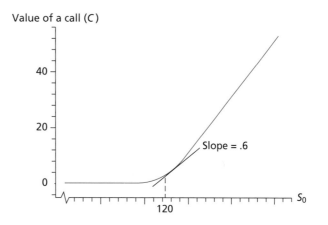

intended to do. The investor holding both the stock and options in proportions dictated by their relative price movements hedges the portfolio.

Black-Scholes hedge ratios are particularly easy to compute. The hedge ratio for a call is $N(d_1)$, while the hedge ratio for a put is $N(d_1) - 1$. We defined $N(d_1)$ as part of the Black-Scholes formula in Equation 17.1. Recall that $N(d)$ stands for the area under the standard normal curve up to d. Therefore, the call option hedge ratio must be positive and less than 1.0, while the put option hedge ratio is negative and of smaller absolute value than 1.0.

Figure 17.4 verifies the insight that the slope of the call option valuation function is less than 1.0, approaching 1.0 only as the stock price becomes extremely large. This tells us that option values change less than one for one with changes in stock prices. Why should this be? Suppose an option is so far in the money that you are absolutely certain it will be exercised. In that case, every $1 increase in the stock price would increase the option value by $1. But if there is a reasonable chance the call option will expire out of the money, even after a moderate stock price gain, a $1 increase in the stock price will not necessarily increase the ultimate payoff to the call; therefore, the call price will not respond by a full $1.

The fact that hedge ratios are less than 1.0 does not contradict our earlier observation that options offer leverage and are sensitive to stock price movements. Although *dollar* movements in option prices are slighter than dollar movements in the stock price, the *rate of return* volatility of options remains greater than stock return volatility because options sell at lower prices. In our example, with the stock selling at $120, and a hedge ratio of 0.6, an option with exercise price $120 may sell for $5. If the stock price increases to $121, the call price would be expected to increase by only $0.60, to $5.60. The percentage increase in the option value is $0.60/$5.00 = 12%, however, while the stock price increase is only $1/$120 = 0.83%. The ratio of the percent changes is 12%/0.83% = 14.4. For every 1% increase in the stock price, the option price increases by 14.4%. This ratio, the percent change in option price per percent change in stock price, is called the **option elasticity.**

option elasticity
The percentage increase in an option's value given a 1% increase in the value of the underlying security.

The hedge ratio is an essential tool in portfolio management and control. An example will show why.

**EXAMPLE 17.3
Portfolio Hedge Ratios**

Consider two portfolios, one holding 750 IBM calls and 200 shares of IBM and the other holding 800 shares of IBM. Which portfolio has greater dollar exposure to IBM price movements? You can answer this question easily using the hedge ratio.

Each option changes in value by H dollars for each dollar change in stock price, where H stands for the hedge ratio. Thus, if H equals 0.6, the 750 options are equivalent to 450 ($= 0.6 \times 750$) shares in terms of the response of their market value to IBM stock price movements. The first portfolio has less dollar sensitivity to stock price change because the 450 share-equivalents of the options plus the 200 shares actually held are less than the 800 shares held in the second portfolio.

This is not to say, however, that the first portfolio is less sensitive to the stock's rate of return. As we noted in discussing option elasticities, the first portfolio may be of lower total value than the second, so despite its lower sensitivity in terms of total market value, it might have greater rate of return sensitivity. Because a call option has a lower market value than the stock, its price changes more than proportionally with stock price changes, even though its hedge ratio is less than 1.0.

Concept Check

7. What is the elasticity of a put option currently selling for $4 with exercise price $120, and hedge ratio −0.4 if the stock price is currently $122?

Portfolio Insurance

In Chapter 16, we showed that protective put strategies offer a sort of insurance policy on an asset. The protective put has proven to be extremely popular with investors. Even if the asset price falls, the put conveys the right to sell the asset for the exercise price, which is a way to lock in a minimum portfolio value. With an at-the-money put ($X = S_0$), the maximum loss

FIGURE 17.5
Return Characteristics
for a Portfolio with a
Protective Put

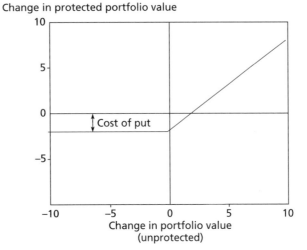

that can be realized is the cost of the put. The asset can be sold for *X,* which equals its original value, so even if the asset price falls, the investor's net loss over the period is just the cost of the put. If the asset value increases, however, upside potential is unlimited. Figure 17.5 graphs the profit or loss on a protective put position as a function of the change in the value of the underlying asset.

portfolio insurance
Portfolio strategies that limit investment losses while maintaining upside potential.

While the protective put is a simple and convenient way to achieve **portfolio insurance,** that is, to limit the worst-case portfolio rate of return, there are practical difficulties in trying to insure a portfolio of stocks. First, unless the investor's portfolio corresponds to a standard market index for which puts are traded, a put option on the portfolio will not be available for purchase. And if index puts are used to protect a nonindexed portfolio, tracking error can result. For example, if the portfolio falls in value while the market index rises, the put will fail to provide the intended protection. Tracking error limits the investor's freedom to pursue active stock selection because such error will be greater as the managed portfolio departs more substantially from the market index.

Moreover, the desired horizon of the insurance program must match the maturity of a traded put option in order to establish the appropriate protective put position. Today, long-term index options called LEAPS (for Long-Term Equity AnticiPation Securities) trade on the Chicago Board Options Exchange with maturities of several years. However, this market has been active only for a few years. In the mid-1980s, while most investors pursuing insurance programs had horizons of several years, actively traded puts were limited to maturities of less than a year. Rolling over a sequence of short-term puts, which might be viewed as a response to this problem, introduces new risks because the prices at which successive puts will be available in the future are not known today.

Providers of portfolio insurance with horizons of several years, therefore, cannot rely on the simple expedient of purchasing protective puts for their clients' portfolios. Instead, they follow trading strategies that replicate the payoffs to the protective put position.

Here is the general idea. Even if a put option on the desired portfolio with the desired expiration date does not exist, a theoretical option pricing model (such as the Black-Scholes model) can be used to determine how that option's price would respond to the portfolio's value if the option did trade. For example, if stock prices were to fall, the put option would increase in value. The option model could quantify this relationship. The net exposure of the (hypothetical) protective put portfolio to swings in stock prices is the sum of the exposures of the two components of the portfolio: the stock and the put. The net exposure of the portfolio equals the equity exposure less the (offsetting) put option exposure.

We can create "synthetic" protective put positions by holding a quantity of stocks with the same net exposure to market swings as the hypothetical protective put position. The key

FIGURE 17.6
Hedge Ratios Change
as the Stock Price
Fluctuates

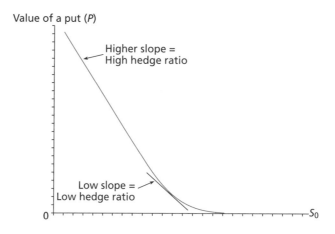

to this strategy is the option delta, or hedge ratio, that is, the change in the price of the protective put option per change in the value of the underlying stock portfolio.

**EXAMPLE 17.4
Synthetic
Protective Puts**

Suppose a portfolio is currently valued at $100 million. An at-the-money put option on the portfolio might have a hedge ratio or delta of −0.6, meaning the option's value swings $0.60 for every dollar change in portfolio value, but in an opposite direction. Suppose the stock portfolio falls in value by 2%. The profit on a hypothetical protective put position (if the put existed) would be as follows (in millions of dollars):

Loss on stocks	2% of $100 = $2.00
+Gain on put:	0.6 × $2.00 = 1.20
Net loss	$0.80

We create the synthetic option position by selling a proportion of shares equal to the put option's delta (i.e., selling 60% of the shares) and placing the proceeds in risk-free T-bills. The rationale is that the hypothetical put option would have offset 60% of any change in the stock portfolio's value, so one must reduce portfolio risk directly by selling 60% of the equity and putting the proceeds into a risk-free asset. Total return on a synthetic protective put position with $60 million in risk-free investments such as T-bills and $40 million in equity is

Loss on stocks:	2% of $40 = $0.80
+Loss on bills:	= 0
Net loss	= $0.80

The synthetic and actual protective put positions have equal returns. We conclude that if you sell a proportion of shares equal to the put option's delta and place the proceeds in cash equivalents, your exposure to the stock market will equal that of the desired protective put position.

dynamic hedging
Constant updating of
hedge positions as market
conditions change.

The difficulty with synthetic positions is that deltas constantly change. Figure 17.6 shows that as the stock price falls, the magnitude of the appropriate hedge ratio increases. Therefore, market declines require extra hedging, that is, additional conversion of equity into cash. This constant updating of the hedge ratio is called **dynamic hedging,** as discussed in Section 17.2 Another term for such hedging is *delta hedging,* because the option delta is used to determine the number of shares that need to be bought or sold.

Dynamic hedging is one reason portfolio insurance has been said to contribute to market volatility. Market declines trigger additional sales of stock as portfolio insurers strive to increase their hedging. These additional sales are seen as reinforcing or exaggerating market downturns.

Delta-Hedging: The New Name in Portfolio Insurance

Portfolio insurance, the high-tech hedging strategy that helped grease the slide in the 1987 stock market crash, is alive and well.

And just as in 1987, it doesn't always work out as planned, as some financial institutions found out in the recent European bond market turmoil.

Banks, securities firms, and other big traders rely heavily on portfolio insurance to contain their potential losses when they buy and sell options. But since portfolio insurance got a bad name after it backfired on investors in 1987, it goes by an alias these days—the sexier, Star Trek moniker of "delta-hedging."

Whatever you call it, the recent turmoil in European bond markets taught some practitioners—including banks and securities firms that were hedging options sales to hedge funds and other investors—the same painful lessons of earlier portfolio insurers: Delta-hedging can break down in volatile markets, just when it is needed most.

What's more, at such times, it can actually feed volatility. The complexities of hedging certain hot-selling "exotic" options may only compound such glitches.

"The tried-and-true strategies for hedging [these products] work fine when the markets aren't subject to sharp moves or large shocks," says Victor S. Filatov, president of Smith Barney Global Capital Management in London. But turbulent times can start "causing problems for people who normally have these risks under control."

Options are financial arrangements that give buyers the right to buy, or sell, securities or other assets at prearranged prices over some future period. An option can gyrate wildly in value with even modest changes in the underlying security's price; the relationship between the two is known as the option's "delta." Thus, dealers in these instruments need some way to hedge their delta to contain the risk.

How you delta-hedge depends on the bets you're trying to hedge. For instance, delta-hedging would prompt options sellers to sell into falling markets and buy into rallies. It would give the opposite directions to options buyers, such as dealers who might hold big options inventories.

In theory, delta-hedging takes place with computer-timed precision, and there aren't any snags. But in real life, it doesn't always work so smoothly.

"When volatility ends up being much greater than anticipated, you can't get your delta trades off at the right points," says an executive at one big derivatives dealer.

A SCENARIO IN TREASURYS

How does this happen? Take the relatively simple case of dealers who sell "call" options on long-term Treasury bonds. Such options give buyers the right to buy bonds at a fixed price over a specific time period. And compared with buying bonds outright, these options are much more sensitive to market moves.

Because selling the calls made those dealers vulnerable to a rally, they delta-hedged by buying bonds. As bond prices turned south [and option deltas fell], the dealers shed their hedges by selling bonds, adding to the selling orgy. The plunging markets forced them to sell at lower prices than expected, causing unexpected losses on their hedges.

To be sure, traders say delta-hedging wasn't the main source of selling in the markets' fall. That dubious honor goes to the huge dumping by speculators of bond and stock holdings that were purchased with borrowed money. While experts may agree that delta-hedging doesn't actually cause crashes, in some cases it can speed the decline once prices slip.

By the same token, delta-hedging also tends to buoy prices once they turn up—which may be one reason why markets correct so suddenly these days.

Source: Abridged from Barbara Donnelly Granito, "Delta-Hedging: The New Name in Portfolio Insurance," *The Wall Street Journal*, March 17, 1994, p. C1. Reprinted by permission of *The Wall Street Journal,* © 1994 Dow Jones & Company, Inc. All Rights Reserved Worldwide.

In practice, portfolio insurers do not actually buy or sell stocks directly when they update their hedge positions. Instead, they minimize trading costs by buying or selling stock index futures as a substitute for sale of the stocks themselves. As you will see in the next chapter, stock prices and index future prices usually are very tightly linked by cross-market arbitrageurs so that futures transactions can be used as reliable proxies for stock transactions. Instead of selling equities based on the put option's delta, insurers will sell an equivalent number of futures contracts.[3]

---

[3]Notice, however, that the use of index futures reintroduces the problem of tracking error between the portfolio and the market index.

FIGURE 17.7

S&P 500 Cash-to-Futures Spread in Points at 15-Minute Intervals

Source: From *The Wall Street Journal.* Reprinted by permission of *The Wall Street Journal,* © 1987 Dow Jones & Company, Inc. All Rights Reserved Worldwide.

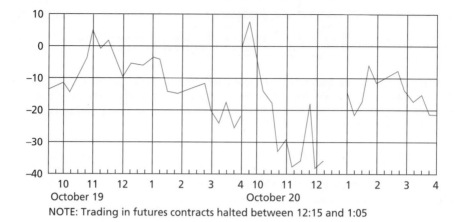

NOTE: Trading in futures contracts halted between 12:15 and 1:05

Several portfolio insurers suffered great setbacks during the market "crash" of October 19, 1987, when the Dow Jones Industrial Average fell more than 500 points. A description of what happened then should help you appreciate the complexities of applying a seemingly straightforward hedging concept.

1. Market volatility at the crash was much greater than ever encountered before. Put option deltas based on historical experience were too low; insurers underhedged, held too much equity, and suffered excessive losses.

2. Prices moved so fast that insurers could not keep up with the necessary rebalancing. They were "chasing deltas" that kept getting away from them. The futures market saw a "gap" opening, where the opening price was nearly 10% below the previous day's close. The price dropped before insurers could update their hedge ratios.

3. Execution problems were severe. First, current market prices were unavailable, with trade execution and the price quotation system hours behind, which made computation of correct hedge ratios impossible. Moreover, trading in stocks and stock futures ceased during some periods. The continuous rebalancing capability that is essential for a viable insurance program vanished during the precipitous market collapse.

4. Futures prices traded at steep discounts to their proper levels compared to reported stock prices, thereby making the sale of futures (as a proxy for equity sales) to increase hedging seem expensive. While you will see in the next chapter that stock index futures prices normally exceed the value of the stock index, Figure 17.7 shows that on October 19, futures sold far below the stock index level. The so-called cash-to-futures spread was negative most of the day. When some insurers gambled that the futures price would recover to its usual premium over the stock index and chose to defer sales, they remained underhedged. As the market fell farther, their portfolios experienced substantial losses.

While most observers believe that the portfolio insurance industry will never recover from the market crash, the nearby box (page 491) points out that delta hedging is still alive and well on Wall Street. Dynamic hedges are widely used by large firms to hedge potential losses from the options they write. The article also points out, however, that these traders are increasingly aware of the practical difficulties in implementing dynamic hedges in very volatile markets.

17.5 EMPIRICAL EVIDENCE

There have been an enormous number of empirical tests of the Black-Scholes option pricing model. For the most part, the results of the studies have been positive in that the Black-Scholes model generates option values fairly close to the actual prices at which options trade. At the same time, some regular empirical failures of the model have been noted.

Geske and Roll (1984) have argued that these empirical results can be attributed to the failure of the Black-Scholes model to account for the possible early exercise of American calls on stocks that pay dividends. They show that the theoretical bias induced by this failure corresponds closely to the actual "mispricing" observed empirically.

Whaley (1982) examines the performance of the Black-Scholes formula relative to that of more complicated option formulas that allow for early exercise. His findings indicate that formulas that allow for the possibility of early exercise do better at pricing than the Black-Scholes formula. The Black-Scholes formula seems to perform worst for options on stocks with high dividend payouts. The true American call option formula, on the other hand, seems to fare equally well in the prediction of option prices on stocks with high or low dividend payouts.

In a recent paper, Rubinstein (1994) points out that the performance of the Black-Scholes model has deteriorated in recent years in the sense that options on the same stock with the same expiration date, which *should* have the same implied volatility, actually exhibit progressively different implied volatilities as strike prices vary. He attributes this to an increasing fear of another market crash like that experienced in 1987, and he notes that, consistent with this hypothesis, out-of-the-money put options are priced higher (that is, with higher implied volatilities) than other puts. He suggests a method to extend the option valuation framework to allow for these issues.

Summary

- Option values may be viewed as the sum of intrinsic value plus time or "volatility" value. The volatility value is the right to choose not to exercise if the stock price moves against the holder. Thus, option holders cannot lose more than the cost of the option regardless of stock price performance.
- Call options are more valuable when the exercise price is lower, when the stock price is higher, when the interest rate is higher, when the time to maturity is greater, when the stock's volatility is greater, and when dividends are lower.
- European put option values can be derived using call option values and the put-call parity theorem.
- Options may be priced relative to the underlying stock price using a simple two-period, two-state pricing model. As the number of periods increases, the model can approximate more realistic stock price distributions. The Black-Scholes formula may be seen as a limiting case of the binomial option model, as the holding period is divided into progressively smaller subperiods.
- The hedge ratio is the number of shares of stock required to hedge the price risk involved in writing one option. Hedge ratios are near zero for deep out-of-the-money call options and approach 1.0 for deep in-the-money calls.
- Although hedge ratios are less than 1.0, call options have elasticities greater than 1.0. The rate of return on a call (as opposed to the dollar return) responds more than one for one with stock price movements.
- Portfolio insurance can be obtained by purchasing a protective put option on an equity position. When the appropriate put is not traded, portfolio insurance entails a dynamic hedge strategy where a fraction of the equity portfolio equal to the desired put option's delta is sold, with proceeds placed in risk-free securities.

Key Terms

binomial model, *481*
Black-Scholes pricing
  formula, *482*
delta, *487*

dynamic hedging, *490*
hedge ratio, *487*
implied volatility, *486*

intrinsic value, *475*
option elasticity, *488*
portfolio insurance, *489*

Problem Sets

1. We showed in the text that the value of a call option increases with the volatility of the stock. Is this also true of put option values? Use the put-call parity theorem as well as a numerical example to prove your answer.

2. In each of the following questions, you are asked to compare two options with parameters as given. The risk-free interest rate for *all* cases should be assumed to be 6%. Assume the stocks on which these options are written pay no dividends.

   a.

Put	*T*	*X*	σ	Price of Option
A	0.5	50	0.20	10
B	0.5	50	0.25	10

   Which put option is written on the stock with the lower price?
   (1) A
   (2) B
   (3) Not enough information

   b.

Put	*T*	*X*	σ	Price of Option
A	0.5	50	0.2	10
B	0.5	50	0.2	12

   Which put option must be written on the stock with the lower price?
   (1) A
   (2) B
   (3) Not enough information

   c.

Call	*S*	*X*	σ	Price of Option
A	50	50	0.20	12
B	55	50	0.20	10

   Which call option must have the lower time to maturity?
   (1) A
   (2) B
   (3) Not enough information

   d.

Call	*T*	*X*	*S*	Price of Option
A	0.5	50	55	10
B	0.5	50	55	12

   Which call option is written on the stock with higher volatility?
   (1) A
   (2) B
   (3) Not enough information

   e.

Call	*T*	*X*	*S*	Price of Option
A	0.5	50	55	10
B	0.5	55	55	7

Which call option is written on the stock with higher volatility?
   (1) A
   (2) B
   (3) Not enough information

3. Reconsider the determination of the hedge ratio in the two-state model (p. 478), where we showed that one-half share of stock would hedge one option. What is the hedge ratio at the following exercise prices: $115, $100, $75, $50, $25, and $10? What do you conclude about the hedge ratio as the option becomes progressively more in the money?

4. Show that Black-Scholes call option hedge ratios also increase as the stock price increases. Consider a one-year option with exercise price $50 on a stock with annual standard deviation 20%. The T-bill rate is 8% per year. Find $N(d_1)$ for stock prices $45, $50, and $55.

5. We will derive a two-state put option value in this problem. Data: $S_0 = 100$; $X = 110$; $1 + r = 1.1$. The two possibilities for S_T are 130 and 80.
   a. Show that the range of S is 50 while that of P is 30 across the two states. What is the hedge ratio of the put?
   b. Form a portfolio of three shares of stock and five puts. What is the (nonrandom) payoff to this portfolio? What is the present value of the portfolio?
   c. Given that the stock currently is selling at 100, show that the value of the put must be 10.91.

6. Calculate the value of a *call* option on the stock in problem 5 with an exercise price of 110. Verify that the put-call parity theorem is satisfied by your answers to problems 5 and 6. (Do not use continuous compounding to calculate the present value of X in this example, because the interest rate is quoted as an effective annual yield.)

7. Use the Black-Scholes formula to find the value of a call option on the following stock:
   Time to maturity   = 6 months
   Standard deviation = 50% per year
   Exercise price   = $50
   Stock price   = $50
   Interest rate   = 10%

8. Recalculate the value of the option in problem 7, successively substituting one of the changes below while keeping the other parameters as in problem 7:
   a. Time to maturity = 3 months
   b. Standard deviation = 25% per year
   c. Exercise price = $55
   d. Stock price = $55
   e. Interest rate = 15%
   Consider each scenario independently. Confirm that the option value changes in accordance with the prediction of Table 17.1.

9. Would you expect a $1 increase in a call option's exercise price to lead to a decrease in the option's value of more or less than $1?

10. All else being equal, is a put option on a high beta stock worth more than one on a low beta stock? The firms have identical firm-specific risk.

11. All else being equal, is a call option on a stock with a lot of firm-specific risk worth more than one on a stock with little firm-specific risk? The betas of the stocks are equal.

12. All else being equal, will a call option with a high exercise price have a higher or lower hedge ratio than one with a low exercise price?

13. Should the rate of return of a call option on a long-term Treasury bond be more or less sensitive to changes in interest rates than the rate of return of the underlying bond?

14. If the stock price falls and the call price rises, then what has happened to the call option's implied volatility?

15. If the time to maturity falls and the put price rises, then what has happened to the put option's implied volatility?

16. According to the Black-Scholes formula, what will be the value of the hedge ratio of a call option as the stock price becomes infinitely large? Explain briefly.

17. According to the Black-Scholes formula, what will be the value of the hedge ratio of a put option for a very small exercise price?

18. The hedge ratio of an at-the-money call option on IBM is 0.4. The hedge ratio of an at-the-money put option is −0.6. What is the hedge ratio of an at-the-money straddle position on IBM?

19. These three put options all are written on the same stock. One has a delta of −0.9, one a delta of −0.5, and one a delta of −0.1. Assign deltas to the three puts by filling in the table below.

Put	X	Delta
A	10	
B	20	
C	30	

20. You are *very* bullish (optimistic) on stock EFG, much more so than the rest of the market. In each question, choose the portfolio strategy that will give you the biggest dollar profit if your bullish forecast turns out to be correct. Explain your answer.
    a. *Choice A:* $100,000 invested in calls with $X = 50$.
       Choice B: $100,000 invested in EFG stock.
    b. *Choice A:* 10 call options contracts (for 100 shares each), with $X = 50$.
       Choice B: 1,000 shares of EFG stock.

21. Imagine you are a provider of portfolio insurance. You are establishing a four-year program. The portfolio you manage is currently worth $100 million, and you hope to provide a minimum return of 0%. The equity portfolio has a standard deviation of 25% per year, and T-bills pay 5% per year. Assume for simplicity that the portfolio pays no dividends (or that all dividends are reinvested).
    a. What fraction of the portfolio should be placed in bills? What fraction in equity?
    b. What should the manager do if the stock portfolio falls by 3% on the first day of trading?

22. You would like to be holding a protective put position on the stock of XYZ Co. to lock in a guaranteed minimum value of $100 at year end. XYZ currently sells for $100. Over the next year, the stock price will increase by 10% or decrease by 10%. The T-bill rate is 5%. Unfortunately, no put options are traded on XYZ Co.
    a. Suppose the desired put option were traded. How much would it cost to purchase?
    b. What would have been the cost of the protective put portfolio?
    c. What portfolio position in stock and T-bills will ensure you a payoff equal to the payoff that would be provided by a protective put with $X = \$100$? Show that the payoff to this portfolio and the cost of establishing the portfolio matches that of the desired protective put.

IEM
Applications

IEM Computer Industry Returns and MSFT (Microsoft) Price Level Market contracts are actually specialized options contracts called "Binary Options" (because they have payoffs of either $0 or $1 depending on the underlying securities).

1. Plot the payoff and profit function for the currently traded MSxxxmH and MSxxxmL contracts based on the last trade price. In what ways does these functions differ from the exchange traded options?

2. If risk-neutral pricing holds for MSxxxmH, what must the probabilities of paying off $1 and $0 be for this contract? (Recall that the risk free rate in the IEM is zero.)

3. If you knew the probabilities that MSFT stock would finish a particular month at a price above or below the cutoff level for the MSFT (Microsoft) Price Level Market on the IEM, how would you value the contracts traded on the IEM (MSxxxmH and MSxxxmL)?

4. Given today's price of MSFT stock on the stock market and its variance, how would you go about determining what the prices of MSxxxmH and MSxxxmL on the IEM should be?

Solutions to Concept Checks

1. Yes. Consider the same scenarios as for the call.

Stock price	$10	$20	$30	$40	$50
Put payoff	20	10	0	0	0
Stock price	20	25	30	35	40
Put payoff	10	5	0	0	0

The low volatility scenario yields a lower expected payoff.

2. Puts should be more valuable for higher dividend payout policies. These policies reduce future stock prices, which will increase the expected payout from the put.

3. Because the option now is underpriced, we want to reverse our previous strategy.

	Initial Cash Flow	Cash Flow in 1 Year for Each Possible Stock Price	
		$S = \$50$	$S = \$200$
Buy 2 options	$-48	$ 0	$ 150
Short-sell 1 share	100	-50	-200
Lend $52 at 8% interest rate	52	56.16	56.16
Total	$ 0	$ 6.16	$ 6.16

4. Higher. For deep out-of-the-money options, an increase in the stock price still leaves the option unlikely to be exercised. Its value increases only fractionally. For deep in-the-money options, exercise is likely, and option holders benefit by a full dollar for each dollar increase in the stock, as though they already own the stock.

5. Because $\sigma = 0.6$, $\sigma^2 = 0.36$.

$$d_1 = \frac{ln(100/95) + (0.10 + 0.36/2)0.25}{0.6 \sqrt{0.25}} = 0.4043$$

$$d_2 = d_1 - 0.6 \sqrt{0.25} = 0.1043$$

Using Table 17.2 and interpolation,

$$N(d_1) = 0.6570$$
$$N(d_2) = 0.5415$$
$$C = 100 \times 0.6570 - 95 \, e^{-0.10 \times 0.25} \times 0.5415$$
$$= 15.53$$

6. Implied volatility exceeds 0.5. Given a standard deviation of 0.5, the option value is $13.70. A higher volatility is needed to justify the actual $15 price.

7. A $1 increase in stock price is a percentage increase of $1/122 = 0.82\%$. The put option will fall by $(0.4 \times \$1) = \$0.40$, a percentage decrease of $\$0.40/\$4 = 10\%$. Elasticity is $-10/0.82 = -12.2$.

Chapter 18

FUTURES MARKETS

AFTER STUDYING THIS CHAPTER YOU SHOULD BE ABLE TO:

- Calculate the profit on futures positions as a function of current and eventual futures prices.
- Formulate futures market strategies for hedging or speculative purposes.
- Compute the futures price appropriate to a given price on the underlying asset.
- Design arbitrage strategies to exploit futures market mispricing.

Futures and forward contracts are like options in that they specify the purchase or sale of some underlying security at some future date. The key difference is that the holder of an option to buy is not compelled to buy and will not do so if the trade is unprofitable. A futures or forward contract, however, carries the obligation to go through with the agreed-upon transaction.

A forward contract is not an investment in the strict sense the funds are paid for an asset. It is only a commitment today to transact in the future. Forward arrangements are part of our study of investments, however, because they offer a powerful means to hedge other investments and generally modify portfolio characteristics.

Forward markets for future delivery of various commodities go back at least to ancient Greece. Organized *futures markets,* though, are a relatively modern development, dating only to the 19th century. Futures markets replace informal forward contracts with highly standardized, exchange-traded securities.

Figure 18.1 documents the tremendous growth of trading activity in futures markets since 1976. The figure shows that trading in financial futures has grown particularly rapidly and that financial futures now dominate the entire futures market. We will concentrate on financial futures in this chapter.

This chapter describes the workings of futures markets and the mechanics of trading in these markets. We show how futures contracts are useful investment vehicles for both hedgers and speculators and how the futures price relates to the spot price of an asset.

FIGURE 18.1 Futures and Options on Futures Trading Volume: 1976–1995

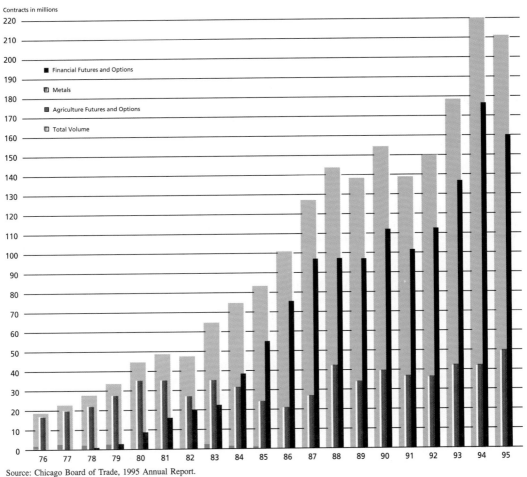

Chicago Board of Trade
Futures and Options on Futures Trading Volume: The Last 20 Years

Contracts in millions

■ Financial Futures and Options

▨ Metals

■ Agriculture Futures and Options

☐ Total Volume

Source: Chicago Board of Trade, 1995 Annual Report.

Finally, we take a look at some specific financial futures contracts—those written on stock indexes, foreign exchange, and fixed-income securities.

18.1 THE FUTURES CONTRACT

To see how futures and forwards work and how they might be useful, consider the portfolio diversification problem facing a farmer growing a single crop, let us say wheat. The entire planting season's revenue depends critically on the highly volatile crop price. The farmer can't easily diversify his position because virtually his entire wealth is tied up in the crop.

The miller who must purchase wheat for processing faces a portfolio problem that is the mirror image of the farmer's. He is subject to profit uncertainty because of the unpredictable future cost of the wheat.

Both parties can reduce this source of risk if they enter into a **forward contract** requiring the farmer to deliver the wheat when harvested at a price agreed upon now, regardless of the market price at harvest time. No money need change hands at this time. A forward contract is simply a deferred-delivery sale of some asset with the sales price agreed upon now. All that is required is that each party be willing to lock in the ultimate price to be paid or

forward contract
An arrangement calling for future delivery of an asset at an agreed-upon price.

received for delivery of the commodity. A forward contract protects each party from future price fluctuations.

Futures markets formalize and standardize forward contracting. Buyers and sellers do not have to rely on a chance matching of their interests; they can trade in a centralized futures market. The futures exchange also standardizes the types of contracts that may be traded: It establishes contract size, the acceptable grade of commodity, contract delivery dates, and so forth. While standardization eliminates much of the flexibility available in informal forward contracting, it has the offsetting advantage of liquidity because many traders will concentrate on the same small set of contracts. Futures contracts also differ from forward contracts in that they call for a daily settling up of any gains or losses on the contract. In contrast, in the case of forward contracts, no money changes hands until the delivery date.

In a centralized market, buyers and sellers can trade through brokers without personally searching for trading partners. The standardization of contracts and the depth of trading in each contract allows futures positions to be liquidated easily through a broker rather than personally renegotiated with the other party to the contract. Because the exchange guarantees the performance of each party to the contract, costly credit checks on other traders are not necessary. Instead, each trader simply posts a good faith deposit, called the *margin,* in order to guarantee contract performance.

The Basics of Futures Contracts

futures price
The agreed-upon price to be paid on a futures contract at maturity.

The futures contract calls for delivery of a commodity at a specified delivery or maturity date, for an agreed-upon price, called the **futures price,** to be paid at contract maturity. The contract specifies precise requirements for the commodity. For agricultural commodities, the exchange sets allowable grades (e.g., No. 2 hard winter wheat or No. 1 soft red wheat). The place or means of delivery of the commodity is specified as well. Delivery of agricultural commodities is made by transfer of warehouse receipts issued by approved warehouses. In the case of financial futures, delivery may be made by wire transfer; in the case of index futures, delivery may be accomplished by a cash settlement procedure such as those used for index options. (Although the futures contract technically calls for delivery of an asset, delivery rarely occurs. Instead, parties to the contract much more commonly close out their positions before contract maturity, taking gains or losses in cash.)[1]

long position
The futures trader who commits to purchasing the asset.

Because the futures exchange specifies all the terms of the contract, the traders need bargain only over the futures price. The trader taking the **long position** commits to purchasing the commodity on the delivery date. The trader who takes the **short position** commits to delivering the commodity at contract maturity. The trader in the long position is said to "buy" a contract; the short-side trader "sells" a contract. The words *buy* and *sell* are figurative only, because a contract is not really bought or sold like a stock or bond; it is entered into by mutual agreement. At the time the contract is entered into, no money changes hands.

short position
The futures trader who commits to delivering the asset.

Figure 18.2 shows prices for futures contracts as they appear in *The Wall Street Journal.* The boldface heading lists in each case the commodity, the exchange where the futures contract is traded in parentheses, the contract size, and the pricing unit. The first contract listed is for corn, traded on the Chicago Board of Trade (CBT). Each contract calls for delivery of 5,000 bushels, and prices in the entry are quoted in cents per bushel.

The next several rows detail price data for contracts expiring on various dates. The September 1996 maturity corn contract, for example, opened during the day at a futures price of 377¾ cents per bushel. The highest futures price during the day was 381¾, the lowest was 374, and the settlement price (a representative trading price during the last few minutes of trading) was 375½. The settlement price decreased by 2¼ cents from the previous

[1]We will show you how this is done later in the chapter.

trading day. The highest futures price over the contract's life to date was 439, the lowest 260 cents. Finally, open interest, or the number of outstanding contracts, was 56,043. Similar information is given for each maturity date.

The trader holding the long position, that is, the person who will purchase the good, profits from price increases. Suppose that when the contract matures in September, the price of corn turns out to be 380½ cents per bushel. The long position trader who entered the contract at the futures price of 375½ cents on August 15 earns a profit of 5 cents per bushel: The eventual price is 5 cents higher than the originally agreed-upon futures price. As each contract calls for delivery of 5,000 bushels (ignoring brokerage fees), the profit to the long position equals 5,000 × $0.05 = $250 per contract. Conversely, the short position loses 5 cents per bushel. The short position's loss equals the long position's gain.

To summarize, at maturity

$$\text{Profit to long} = \text{Spot price at maturity} - \text{Original futures price}$$

$$\text{Profit to short} = \text{Original futures price} - \text{Spot price at maturity}$$

where the spot price is the actual market price of the commodity at the time of the delivery.

The futures contract is, therefore, a zero sum game, with losses and gains to all positions netting out to zero. Every long position is offset by a short position. The aggregate profits to futures trading, summing over all investors, also must be zero, as is the net exposure to changes in the commodity price.

Concept Check

1. Graph the profit realized by an investor who enters the long side of a futures contract as a function of the price of the asset on the maturity date. Compare this graph to a graph of the profits realized by the purchaser of the asset itself. Next, try the same exercise for a short futures position and a short sale of the asset.

Existing Contracts

Futures and forward contracts are traded on a wide variety of goods in four broad categories: agricultural commodities, metals and minerals (including energy commodities), foreign currencies, and financial futures (fixed-income securities and stock market indexes). The financial futures contracts are a relatively recent innovation, for which trading was introduced in 1975. Innovation in financial futures has been rapid and is ongoing. Table 18.1 lists various contracts trading in the United States in 1996.

Outside the futures markets, a well-developed network of banks and brokers has established a forward market in foreign exchange. This forward market is not a formal exchange in the sense that the exchange specifies the terms of the traded contract. Instead, participants in a forward contract may negotiate for delivery of any quantity of goods, whereas, in the formal futures markets, contract size is set by the exchange. In forward arrangements, banks and brokers simply negotiate contracts for clients (or themselves) as needed.

18.2 MECHANICS OF TRADING IN FUTURES MARKETS

The Clearinghouse and Open Interest

Trading in futures contracts is more complex than making ordinary stock transactions. If you want to make a stock purchase, your broker simply acts as an intermediary to enable you to buy shares from or sell shares to another individual through the stock exchange. In futures trading, however, the clearinghouse plays a more active role.

When an investor contacts a broker to establish a futures position, the brokerage firm wires the order to the firm's trader on the floor of the futures exchange. In contrast to stock trading, which involves specialists or market makers in each security, most futures trades in the United States occur among floor traders in the "trading pit" for each contract. Traders

FIGURE 18.2   Futures Listings

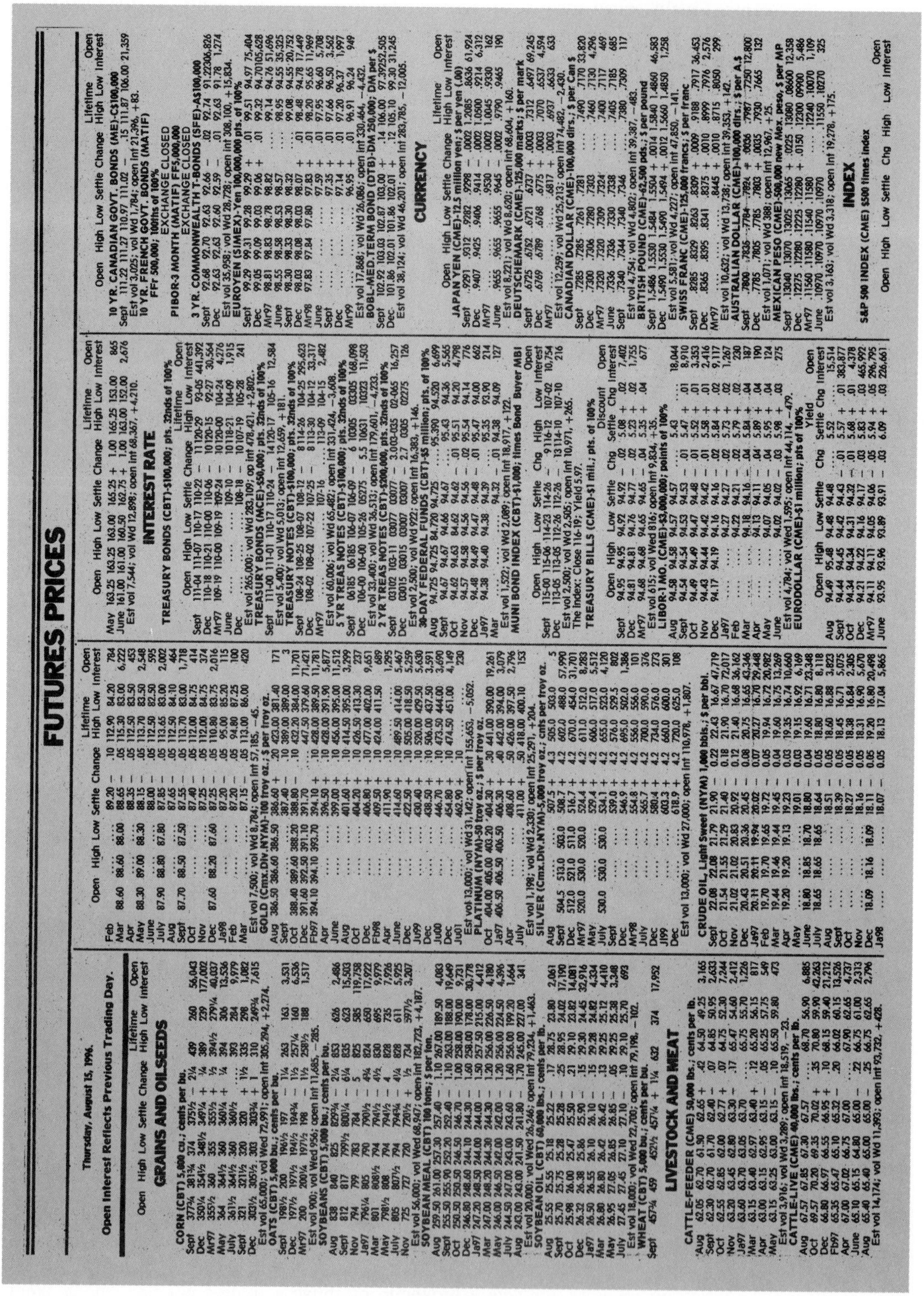

$e = 2.71828$, the base of the natural log function.

r = Risk-free interest rate (the annualized continuously compounded rate on a safe asset with the same maturity as the expiration date of the option, which is to be distinguished from r_f, the discrete period interest rate).

T = Time to maturity of option in years.

ln = Natural logarithm function.

σ = Standard deviation of the annualized continuously compounded rate of return of the stock.

The option value does not depend on the expected rate of return on the stock. In a sense, this information is already built into the formula with inclusion of the stock price, which itself depends on the stock's risk and return characteristics. This version of the Black-Scholes formula is predicated on the assumption that the stock pays no dividends.

Although you may find the Black-Scholes formula intimidating, we can explain it at a somewhat intuitive level. The trick is to view the $N(d)$ terms (loosely) as risk-adjusted probabilities that the call option will expire in the money. First, look at Equation 17.1 assuming both $N(d)$ terms are close to 1.0; that is, when there is a very high probability that the option will be exercised. Then the call option value is equal to $S_0 - Xe^{-rT}$, which is what we called earlier the adjusted intrinsic value, $S_0 - PV(X)$. This makes sense; if exercise is certain, we have a claim on a stock with current value S_0 and an obligation with present value $PV(X)$ or with continuous compounding, Xe^{-rT}.

Now look at Equation 17.1, assuming the $N(d)$ terms are close to zero, meaning the option almost certainly will not be exercised. Then the equation confirms that the call is worth nothing. For middle-range values of $N(d)$ between 0 and 1, Equation 17.1 tells us that the call value can be viewed as the present value of the call's potential payoff adjusting for the probability of in-the-money expiration.

How do the $N(d)$ terms serve as risk-adjusted probabilities? This question quickly leads us into advanced statistics. Notice, however, that d_1 and d_2 both increase as the stock price increases. Therefore, $N(d_1)$ and $N(d_2)$ also increase with higher stock prices. This is the property we would desire of our "probabilities." For higher stock prices relative to exercise prices, future exercise is more likely.

FIGURE 17.3
A Standard Normal Curve

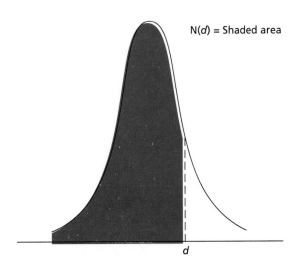

TABLE 17.2
Cumulative Normal
Distribution

d	N(d)	d	N(d)	d	N(d)
−3.00	0.0013	−1.58	0.0571	−0.76	0.2236
−2.95	0.0016	−1.56	0.0594	−0.74	0.2297
−2.90	0.0019	−1.54	0.0618	−0.72	0.2358
−2.85	0.0022	−1.52	0.0643	−0.70	0.2420
−2.80	0.0026	−1.50	0.0668	−0.68	0.2483
−2.75	0.0030	−1.48	0.0694	−0.66	0.2546
−2.70	0.0035	−1.46	0.0721	−0.64	0.2611
−2.65	0.0040	−1.44	0.0749	−0.62	0.2676
−2.60	0.0047	−1.42	0.0778	−0.60	0.2743
−2.55	0.0054	−1.40	0.0808	−0.58	0.2810
−2.50	0.0062	−1.38	0.0838	−0.56	0.2877
−2.45	0.0071	−1.36	0.0869	−0.54	0.2946
−2.40	0.0082	−1.34	0.0901	−0.52	0.3015
−2.35	0.0094	−1.32	0.0934	−0.50	0.3085
−2.30	0.0107	−1.30	0.0968	−0.48	0.3156
−2.25	0.0122	−1.28	0.1003	−0.46	0.3228
−2.20	0.0139	−1.26	0.1038	−0.44	0.3300
−2.15	0.0158	−1.24	0.1075	−0.42	0.3373
−2.10	0.0179	−1.22	0.1112	−0.40	0.3446
−2.05	0.0202	−1.20	0.1151	−0.38	0.3520
−2.00	0.0228	−1.18	0.1190	−0.36	0.3594
−1.98	0.0239	−1.16	0.1230	−0.34	0.3669
−1.96	0.0250	−1.14	0.1271	−0.32	0.3745
−1.94	0.0262	−1.12	0.1314	−0.30	0.3821
−1.92	0.0274	−1.10	0.1357	−0.28	0.3897
−1.90	0.0287	−1.08	0.1401	−0.26	0.3974
−1.88	0.0301	−1.06	0.1446	−0.24	0.4052
−1.86	0.0314	−1.04	0.1492	−0.22	0.4129
−1.84	0.0329	−1.02	0.1539	−0.20	0.4207
−1.82	0.0344	−1.00	0.1587	−0.18	0.4286
−1.80	0.0359	−0.98	0.1635	−0.16	0.4365
−1.78	0.0375	−0.96	0.1685	−0.14	0.4443
−1.76	0.0392	−0.94	0.1736	−0.12	0.4523
−1.74	0.0409	−0.92	0.1788	−0.10	0.4602
−1.72	0.0427	−0.90	0.1841	−0.08	0.4681
−1.70	0.0446	−0.88	0.1894	−0.06	0.4761
−1.68	0.0465	−0.86	0.1949	−0.04	0.4841
−1.66	0.0485	−0.84	0.2005	−0.02	0.4920
−1.64	0.0505	−0.82	0.2061	0.00	0.5000
−1.62	0.0526	−0.80	0.2119	0.02	0.5080
−1.60	0.0548	−0.78	0.2177	0.04	0.5160

EXAMPLE 17.1
Black-Scholes
Call Option
Valuation

You can use the Black-Scholes formula fairly easily. Suppose you want to value a call option under the following circumstances:

Stock price $S_0 = 100$

Exercise price $X = 95$

Interest rate $r = 0.10$

Time to expiration $T = 0.25$ (one-quarter year)

Standard deviation $\sigma = 0.50$

First calculate

$$d_1 = \frac{ln(100/95) + (0.10 + 0.5^2/2)0.25}{0.5\sqrt{0.25}} = 0.43$$

$$d_2 = 0.43 - 0.5\sqrt{0.25} = 0.18$$

Next find $N(d_1)$ and $N(d_2)$. The normal distribution function is available on most computer spreedsheets. The values of the function also are tabulated and many be found in many statistics textbooks. A table of $N(d)$ is provided here as Table 17.2. The table reveals (using interpolation for 0.43) that

FIGURE 18.2 Concluded

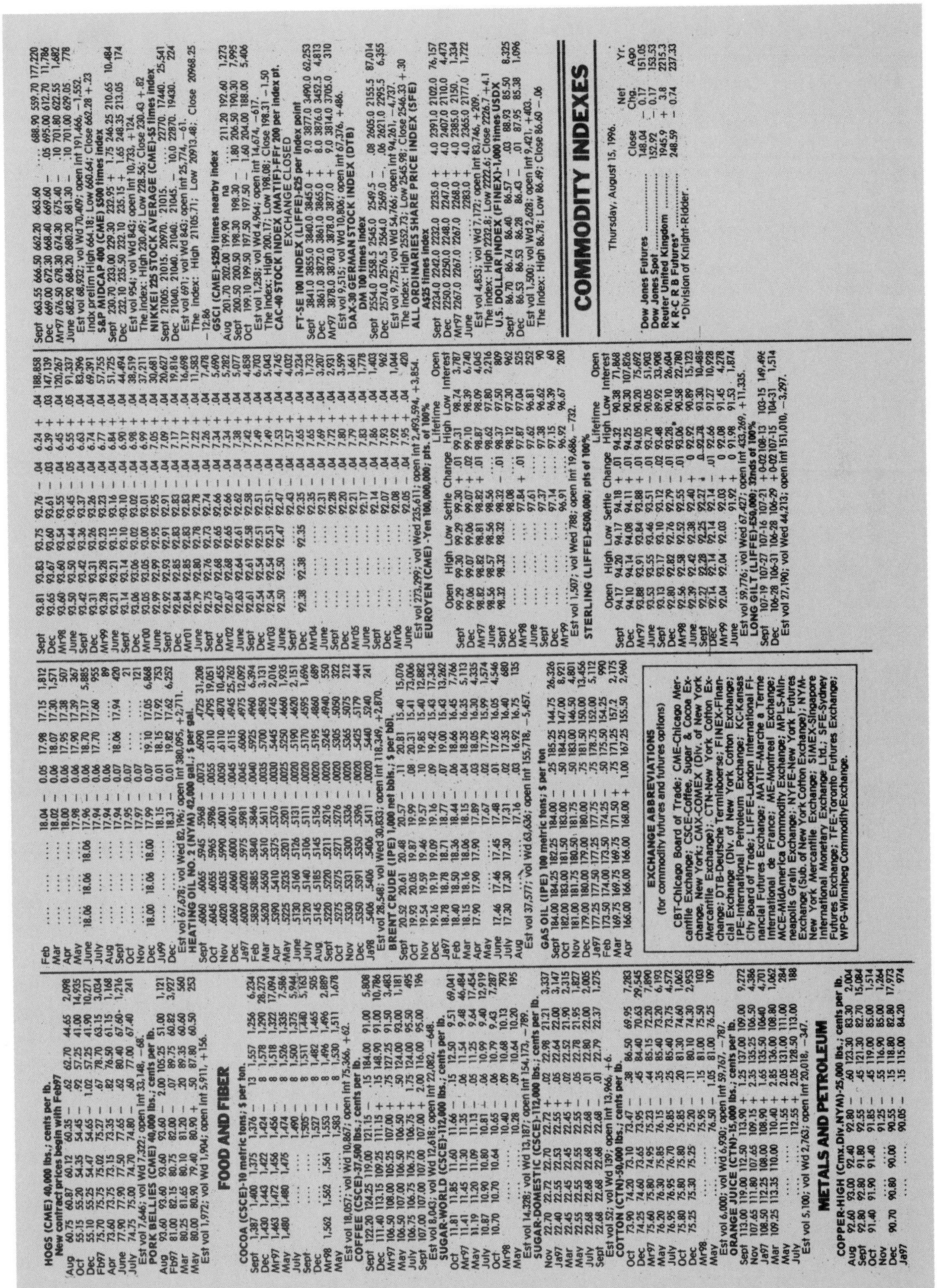

FOOD AND FIBER

METALS AND PETROLEUM

COMMODITY INDEXES

Thursday, August 15, 1996.

	Close	Net Chg.	Yr. Ago
Dow Jones Futures	148.04	−0.17	151.05
Dow Jones Spot	152.92	−0.17	153.53
Reuter United Kingdom	—	—	2215.3
K R C R B Futures*	248.59	+ 0.74	237.33

*Division of Knight-Ridder.

EXCHANGE ABBREVIATIONS
(for commodity futures and futures options)

CBT-Chicago Board of Trade; CME-Chicago Mercantile Exchange; CSCE-Coffee, Sugar & Cocoa Exchange, New York; CMX-COMEX (Div. of New York Mercantile Exchange); CTN-New York Cotton Exchange; DTB-Deutsche Terminboerse; FINEX-Financial Futures Exchange (Div. of New York Cotton Exchange); IPE-International Petroleum Exchange; KC-Kansas City Board of Trade; LIFFE-London International Financial Futures Exchange; MATIF-Marche a Terme International de France; MCE-MidAmerica Commodity Exchange; MPLS-Minneapolis Grain Exchange; NYFE-New York Futures Exchange (Sub. of New York Cotton Exchange); NYM-New York Mercantile Exchange; SIMEX-Singapore International Monetary Exchange Ltd.; SFE-Sydney Futures Exchange; TFE-Toronto Futures Exchange; WPG-Winnipeg CommodityExchange.

Source: From *The Wall Street Journal*, August 16, 1996. Reprinted by permission of *THE WALL STREET JOURNAL*, © 1996 Dow Jones & Company, Inc. All Rights Reserved Worldwide.

TABLE 18.1 Futures Contracts

Foreign Currencies	Agricultural	Metals and Energy	Interest Rate Futures	Equity Indexes
British pound	Corn	Copper	Eurodollars	S&P 500 index
Canadian dollar	Oats	Aluminum	Euroyen	S&P Midcap 400
Japanese yen	Soybeans	Gold	Euromark	Major Market Index
Swiss franc	Soybean meal	Platinum	Eurolira	Nasdaq 100
French franc	Soybean oil	Palladium	Euroswiss	NYSE index
Deutsche mark	Wheat	Silver	Sterling	Russell 2000 index
U.S. dollar index	Barley	Crude oil	Long gilt†	Eurotop 100
European currency unit	Flaxseed	Heating oil	Short gilt†	FTSE index (British)
Australian dollar	Canola	Gas oil	German government bond	CAC-40 (French)
Mexican peso	Rye	Natural gas	Italian government bond	DAX-30 (German)
Brazilian real	Cattle (feeder)	Gasoline	Canadian government bond	All ordinary (British)
Mark/yen cross rate	Cattle (live)	Propane	Treasury bonds	Toronto 35
Mark/franc cross rate	Hogs	CRB index*	Treasury notes	(Canadian)
Mark/sterling cross rate	Pork bellies		Treasury bills	
	Cocoa		LIBOR	
	Coffee		Municipal bond index	
	Cotton		Federal funds rate	
	Orange juice		Bankers' acceptance	
	Sugar		PIBOR (Paris)	
	Lumber			
	Rice			

*The Commodity Research Bureau's index of futures prices of agricultural as well as metal and energy prices.
†Gilts are British government bonds.

use voice or hand signals to signify their desire to buy or sell. Once a trader willing to accept the opposite side of a trade is located, the trade is recorded and the investor is notified.

clearinghouse
Established by exchanges to facilitate trading. The clearinghouse may interpose itself as an intermediary between two traders.

At this point, just as is true for options contracts, the **clearinghouse** enters the picture. Rather than having the long and short traders hold contracts with each other, the clearinghouse becomes the seller of the contract for the long position and the buyer of the contract for the short position. The clearinghouse is obligated to deliver the commodity to the long position and to pay for delivery from the short; consequently, the clearinghouse's position nets to zero. This arrangement makes the clearinghouse the trading partner of each trader, both long and short. The clearinghouse, bound to perform on its side of each contract, is the only party that can be hurt by the failure of any trader to observe the obligations of the futures contract. This arrangement is necessary because a futures contract calls for future performance, which cannot be as easily guaranteed as an immediate stock transaction.

Figure 18.3 illustrates the role of the clearinghouse. Panel A shows what would happen in the absence of the clearinghouse. The trader in the long position would be obligated to pay the futures price to the short position trader, and the trader in the short position would be obligated to deliver the commodity. Panel B shows how the clearinghouse becomes an intermediary, acting as the trading partner for each side of the contract. The clearinghouse's position is neutral, as it takes a long and a short position for each transaction.

The clearinghouse makes it possible for traders to liquidate positions easily. If you are currently long in a contract and want to undo your position, you simply instruct your broker to enter the short side of a contract to close out your position. This is called a *reversing trade*. The exchange nets out your long and short positions, reducing your net position to zero. Your zero net position with the clearinghouse eliminates the need to fulfill at maturity either the original long or reversing short position.

The *open interest* on the contract is the number of contracts outstanding. (Long and short positions are not counted separately, meaning that open interest can be defined as either the number of long or short contracts outstanding.) The clearinghouse's position nets out to zero, and so it is not counted in the computation of open interest. When contracts begin trading, open interest is zero. As time passes, open interest increases as progressively more

FIGURE 18.3

A. Trading without the Clearinghouse **B.** Trading with a Clearinghouse

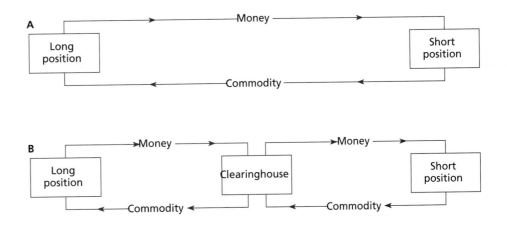

contracts are entered. Almost all traders, however, liquidate their positions before the contract maturity date.

Instead of actually taking or making delivery of the commodity, market participants virtually all enter reversing trades to cancel their original positions, thereby realizing the profits or losses on the contract. The fraction of contracts that result in actual delivery is estimated to range from less than 1% to 3%, depending on the commodity and the activity in the contract. The image of a trader awakening one delivery date with a mountain of wheat in the front yard is amusing, but unlikely.

You can see the typical pattern of open interest in Figure 18.2. In the soybean contract, for example, the August delivery contract is close to maturity, and the open interest is relatively small; most contracts have been reversed already. The next few maturities have significantly greater open interest. Finally, the most distant maturity contracts have little open interest, as they have been available only recently, and few participants have yet traded.

Marking to Market and the Margin Account

Anyone who saw the film "Trading Places" knows that Eddie Murphy as a trader in orange juice futures had no intention of purchasing or delivering orange juice. Traders simply bet on the futures price of juice. The total profit or loss realized by the long trader who buys a contract at time 0 and closes, or reverses, it at time t is just the change in the futures price over the period, $F_t - F_0$. Symmetrically, the short trader earns $F_0 - F_t$.

marking to market
The daily settlement of obligations on futures positions.

The process by which profits or losses accrue to traders is called **marking to market.** At initial execution of a trade, each trader establishes a margin account. The margin is a security account consisting of cash or near-cash securities, such as Treasury bills, that ensures the trader will be able to satisfy the obligations of the futures contract. Because both parties to the futures contract are exposed to losses, both must post margin. If the initial margin on corn, for example, is 10%, the trader must post $1877.50 per contract for the margin account. This is 10% of the value of the contract ($3.755 per bushel × 5,000 bushels per contract).

Because the initial margin may be satisfied by posting interest-earning securities, the requirement does not impose a significant opportunity cost of funds on the trader. The initial margin is usually set between 5% and 15% of the total value of the contract. Contracts written on assets with more volatile prices require higher margins.

On any day that futures contracts trade, futures prices may rise or fall. Instead of waiting until the maturity date for traders to realize all gains and losses, the clearinghouse requires all positions to recognize profits as they accrue daily. If the future price of corn rises from 375½ to 377½ cents per bushel, for example, the clearinghouse credits the margin account of the long position for 5,000 bushels times 2 cents per bushel, or $100 per contract. Conversely, for the short position, the clearinghouse takes this amount from the margin account for each contract held. Although the price of corn has changed by only 0.53% (2/375.5), the percentage return on the long corn position on that day is 10 times greater: The $100 gain on the position is 5.3% of the $1,877.50 posted as margin. The 10-to-1 ratio of percentage changes reflects the leverage inherent in the futures position, since the corn contract was established with an initial margin of 1/10th the value of the underlying asset.

This daily settling is called *marking to market*. It means the maturity date of the contract does not govern realization of profit or loss. Marking to market ensures that, as futures prices change, the proceeds accrue to the trader's margin account immediately. We will provide a more detailed example of this process shortly.

Concept Check

2. What must be the net inflow or outlay from marking to market for the clearinghouse?

maintenance, or variation, margin
An established value below which a trader's margin may not fall. Reaching the maintenance margin triggers a margin call.

If a trader accrues sustained losses from daily marking to market, the margin account may fall below a critical value called the **maintenance, or variation, margin.** Once the value of the account falls below this value, the trader receives a margin call. For example, if the maintenance margin on corn is 5%, then the margin call will go out when the 10% margin initially posted has fallen about in half, to $939 per contract. (This requires that the futures price fall only about 19 cents, as each 1 cent drop in the futures price results in a loss of $50 to the long position.) Either new funds must be transferred into the margin account, or the broker will close out enough of the trader's position to meet the required margin for that position. This procedure safeguards the position of the clearinghouse. Positions are closed out before the margin account is exhausted—the trader's losses are covered, and the clearinghouse is not affected.

Marking to market is the major way in which futures and forward contracts differ, besides contract standardization. Futures follow this pay- (or receive-) as-you-go method. Forward contracts are simply held until maturity, and no funds are transferred until that date, although the contracts may be traded.

It is important to note that the futures price on the delivery date will equal the spot price of the commodity on that date. As a maturing contract calls for immediately delivery, the futures price on that day must equal the spot price—the cost of the commodity from the two competing sources is equalized in a competitive market.[2] You may obtain delivery of the commodity either by purchasing it directly in the spot market or by entering the long side of a futures contract.

A commodity available from two sources (the spot and futures markets) must be priced identically, or else investors will rush to purchase it from the cheap source in order to sell it in the high-priced market. Such arbitrage activity could not persist without prices adjusting to eliminate the arbitrage opportunity. Therefore, the futures price and the spot price must converge at maturity. This is called the **convergence property.**

convergence property
The convergence of futures prices and spot prices at the maturity of the futures contract.

For an investor who establishes a long position in a contract now (time 0) and holds that position until maturity (time T), the sum of all daily settlements will equal $F_T - F_0$, where F_T stands for the futures price at contract maturity. Because of convergence, however, the futures price at maturity, F_T, equals the spot price, P_T, so total futures profits also may be expressed as $P_T - F_0$. Thus, we see that profits on a futures contract held to maturity perfectly track changes in the value of the underlying asset.

---

[2]Small differences between the spot and futures price at maturity may persist because of transportation costs, but this is a minor factor.

**EXAMPLE 18.1
Marking to
Market and
Futures Contract
Profits**

Assume the current futures price for silver for delivery five days from today is $5.10 per ounce. Suppose that over the next five days, the futures price evolves as follows:

Day	Futures Price
0 (today)	$5.10
1	5.20
2	5.25
3	5.18
4	5.18
5 (delivery)	5.21

The spot price of silver on the delivery date is $5.21: The convergence property implies that the price of silver in the spot market must equal the futures price on the delivery day.

The daily mark-to-market settlements for each contract held by the long positions will be as follows:

Day	Profit (Loss) per Ounce	× 5,000 Ounces/Contract = Daily Proceeds
1	$5.20 − $5.10 = $0.10	$500
2	$5.25 − $5.20 = $0.05	250
3	$5.18 − $5.25 = −$0.07	−350
4	$5.18 − $5.18 = $0	0
5	$5.21 − $5.18 = $0.03	150
		Sum = $550

The profit on day 1 is the increase in the futures price from the previous day, or ($5.20 − $5.10) per ounce. Because each silver contract on the Commodity Exchange calls for purchase and delivery of 5,000 ounces, the total profit per contract is 5,000 times $0.10, or $500. On day 3, when the futures price falls, the long position's margin account will be debited by $350. By day 5, the sum of all daily proceeds is $550. This is exactly equal to 5,000 times the difference between the final futures price of $5.21 and the original futures price of $5.10. Thus, the sum of all the daily proceeds (per ounce of silver held long) equals $P_T − F_0$.

Cash versus Actual Delivery

Most futures markets call for delivery of an actual commodity, such as a particular grade of wheat or a specified amount of foreign currency, if the contract is not reversed before maturity. For agricultural commodities, where quality of the delivered good may vary, the exchange sets quality standards as part of the futures contract. In some cases, contracts may be settled with higher or lower grade commodities. In these cases, a premium or discount is applied to the delivered commodity to adjust for the quality differences.

cash delivery
The cash value of the underlying asset (rather than the asset itself) is delivered to satisfy the contract.

Some futures contracts call for **cash delivery.** An example is a stock index futures contract where the underlying asset is an index such as the Standard & Poor's 500 or the New York Stock Exchange index. Delivery of every stock in the index clearly would be impractical. Hence, the contract calls for "delivery" of a cash amount equal to the value that the index attains on the maturity date of the contract. The sum of all the daily settlements from marking to market results in the long position realizing total profits or losses of $S_T − F_0$, where S_T is the value of the stock index on the maturity date T, and F_0 is the original futures price. Cash settlement closely mimics actual delivery, except the cash value of the asset rather than the asset itself is delivered by the short position in exchange for the futures price.

More concretely, the S&P 500 index contract calls for delivery of $500 times the value of the index. At maturity, the index might list at 775, a market value-weighted index of the prices of all 500 stocks in the index. The cash settlement contract calls for delivery of $500 × 775, or $387,500 cash in return for 500 times the futures price. This yields exactly the same profit as would result from directly purchasing 500 units of the index for $387,500 and then delivering it for 500 times the original futures price.

Regulations

Futures markets are regulated by the Commodities Futures Trading Commission (CFTC), a federal agency. The CFTC sets capital requirements for member firms of the futures exchanges, authorizes trading in new contracts, and oversees maintenance of daily trading records.

The futures exchange may set limits on the amount by which future prices may change from one day to the next. For example, the price limit on silver contracts traded on the Chicago Board of Trade is $1, which means that if silver futures close today at $5.10 per ounce, trades in silver tomorrow may vary only between $6.10 and $4.10 per ounce. The exchange may increase or reduce these price limits in response to perceived changes in the price volatility of the contract. Price limits often are eliminated as contracts approach maturity, usually in the last month of trading.

Price limits traditionally are viewed as a means to limit violent price fluctuations. This reasoning seems dubious. Suppose an international monetary crisis overnight drives up the spot price of silver to $8.00. No one would sell silver futures at prices for future delivery as low as $5.10. Instead, the futures price would rise each day by the $1 limit, although the quoted price would represent only an unfilled bid order—no contracts would trade at the low quoted price. After several days of limit moves of $1 per day, the futures price would finally reach its equilibrium level, and trading would occur again. This process means no one could unload a position until the price reached its equilibrium level. This example shows that price limits offer no real protection against fluctuations in equilibrium prices.

Taxation

Because of the mark-to-market procedure, investors do not have control over the tax year in which they realize gains or losses. Instead, price changes are realized gradually, with each daily settlement. Therefore, taxes are paid at year end on cumulated profits or losses regardless of whether the position has been closed out.

18.3 FUTURES MARKET STRATEGIES

Hedging and Speculation

Hedging and speculating are two polar uses of futures markets. A speculator uses a futures contract to profit from movements in futures prices, a hedger to protect against price movements.

If speculators believe prices will increase, they will take a long position for expected profits. Conversely, they exploit expected price declines by taking a short position.

EXAMPLE 18.2
Speculating with T-Bond Futures

Let's consider the use of the T-bond futures contract, the listings for which appear in Figure 18.2. Each T-bond contract on the Chicago Board of Trade (CBT) calls for delivery of $100,000 par value of bonds. The listed futures price of 110-22 (that is, 110 and 22/32) means the market price of the underlying bonds is 110.6875% of par, or $110,687.50. Therefore, for every increase of one point in the T-bond futures price (e.g., to 111-22), the long position gains $1,000, and the short loses that amount. Therefore, if you are bullish on bond prices, you might speculate by buying T-bond futures contracts.

If the T-bond futures price increases by one point to 111-22, you profit by your speculation by $1,000 per contract. If the forecast is incorrect, and T-bond futures prices decline, you lose $1,000 times the decrease in the futures price for each contract purchased. Speculators bet on the direction of futures price movements.

Why would a speculator buy a T-bond futures contract? Why not buy T-bonds directly? One reason lies in transaction costs, which are far smaller in futures markets.

Another reason is the leverage futures trading provides. Recall that each T-bond contract calls for delivery of $100,000 par value, worth about $110,688 in our example. The initial margin required for this account might be only $15,000. The $1,000 per contract gain translates into a 6.67% ($1,000/$15,000) return on the money put up, despite the fact that the T-bond futures price increases only 0.90% (1/110.6875). Future margins, therefore, allow speculators to achieve much greater leverage than is available from direct trading in a commodity.

Hedgers, by contrast, use futures markets to insulate themselves against price movements. An investor holding a T-bond portfolio, for example, might anticipate a period of interest rate volatility and want to protect the value of the portfolio against price fluctuations. In this case, the investor has no desire to bet on price movements in either direction. To achieve such protection, a hedger takes a short position in T-bond futures, which obligates the hedger to deliver T-bonds at the contract maturity date for the current futures price. This locks in the sales price for the bonds and guarantees that the total value of the bond-plus-futures position at the maturity date is the futures price.[3]

<table>
<tr><td>

EXAMPLE 18.3
Hedging with
T-Bond Futures

</td><td>

Suppose as in Figure 18.2 that the T-bond futures price for September 1996 delivery is $110.6875 (per $100 par value), which we will round off to $110.69, and that the only three possible T-bond prices in September are $109.69, $110.69, and $111.69. If investors currently hold 200 bonds, each with par value $1,000, they would take short positions in two contracts, each for $100,000 value. Protecting the value of a portfolio with short futures positions is called *short hedging*.

</td></tr>
</table>

The profits in September from each of the two short futures contracts will be 1,000 times any decrease in the futures price. At maturity, the convergence property ensures that the final futures price will equal the spot price of the T-bonds. Hence, the futures profit will be 2,000 times $(F_0 - P_T)$, where P_T is the price of the bonds on the delivery date, and F_0 is the original futures price, $110.69.

Now consider the hedged portfolio consisting of the bonds and the short futures positions. The portfolio value as a function of the bond price in September can be computed as follows:

	T-Bond Price in September 1996		
	$109.69	**$110.69**	**$111.69**
Bond holdings (Value = 2,000 P_T)	$219,380	$221,380	$223,380
Futures profits or losses	+2,000	0	−2,000
Total	$221,380	$221,380	$221,380

The total portfolio value is unaffected by the eventual bond price, which is what the hedger wants. The gains or losses on the bond holdings are exactly offset by those on the two contracts held short.

For example, if bond prices fall to $109.69, the losses on the bond portfolio are offset by the $2,000 gain on the futures contracts. That profit equals the difference between the futures price on the maturity date (which equals the spot price on that date, $109.69) and the originally contracted futures price of $110.69. For short contracts, a profit of $1 per $100 par value is realized from the fall in the spot price. Because two contracts call for delivery of $200,000 par value, this results in a $2,000 gain that offsets the decline in the value of the bonds held in the portfolio. In contrast to a speculator, a hedger is indifferent to the ultimate price of the asset. The short hedger, who has in essence arranged to sell the asset for an agreed-upon price, need not be concerned about further developments in the market price.

To generalize the example, note that the bond will be worth P_T at the maturity of the futures contract, while the profit on the futures contract is $F_0 - P_T$. The sum of the two positions is F_0 dollars, which is independent of the eventual bond price.

A *long hedge* is the analogue to a short hedge for a purchaser of an asset. Consider, for example, a pension fund manager who anticipates a cash inflow in two months that will be invested in fixed-income securities. The manager views T-bonds as very attractively priced now

---

[3]To keep things simple, we will assume that the T-bond futures contract calls for delivery of a bond with the same coupon and maturity as that in the investor's portfolio. In practice, a variety of bonds may be delivered to satisfy the contract, and a "conversion factor" is used to adjust for the relative values of the eligible delivery bonds. We will ignore this complication.

and would like to lock in current prices and yields until the investment actually can be made two months hence. The manager can lock in the effective cost of the purchase by entering the long side of a contract, which commits her to purchasing at the current futures price.

Concept Check

3. Suppose that T-bonds will be selling in September at $109.69, $110.69, or $111.69. Show that the cost in September of purchasing $200,000 par value of T-bonds net of the profit/loss on two long T-bond contracts will be $221,380 regardless of the eventual bond price.

Exact futures hedging may be impossible for some goods because the necessary futures contract is not traded. For example, miners of bauxite, the ore from which aluminum is made, might like to trade in bauxite futures, but they cannot because such contracts are not listed. Because bauxite and aluminum prices are highly correlated, however, a close hedge may be established by shorting aluminum futures. Hedging a position using futures on another commodity is called *cross-hedging*.

Concept Check

4. What are the sources of risk to an investor who uses aluminum futures to hedge an inventory of bauxite?

Basis Risk and Hedging

basis

The difference between the futures price and the spot price.

The **basis** is the difference between the futures price and the spot price.[4] As we have noted, on the maturity date of a contract, the basis must be zero: The convergence property implies that $F_T - P_T = 0$. Before maturity, however, the futures price for later delivery may differ substantially from the current spot price.

We discussed the case of a short hedger who holds an asset (T-bonds, in our example) and a short position to deliver that asset in the future. If the asset and futures contract are held until maturity, the hedger bears no risk, as the ultimate value of the portfolio on the delivery date is determined by the current futures price. Risk is eliminated because the futures price and spot price at contract maturity must be equal: Gains and losses on the futures and the commodity position will exactly cancel. If the contract and asset are to be liquidated early, before contract maturity, however, the hedger bears **basis risk,** because the futures price and spot price need not move in perfect lockstep at all times before the delivery date. In this case, gains and losses on the contract and the asset need not exactly offset each other.

Some speculators try to profit from movements in the basis. Rather than betting on the direction of the futures or spot prices per se, they bet on the changes in the difference between the two. A long spot–short futures position will profit when the basis narrows.

basis risk

Risk attributable to uncertain movements in the spread between a futures price and a spot price.

EXAMPLE 18.4
Speculating on the Basis

Consider an investor holding 100 ounces of gold, who is short one gold futures contract. Gold today sells for $391 an ounce, and the futures price for June delivery is $396 an ounce. Therefore, the basis is currently $5. Tomorrow, the spot price might increase to $394, while the futures price increases to $398.50, so the basis narrows to $4.50. The investor's gains and losses are as follows:

Gain on holdings of gold (per ounce): $394 − $391   = $3.00

Loss on gold futures position (per ounce): $398.50 − $396 = $2.50

The investor gains $3 per ounce on the gold holdings, but loses $2.50 an ounce on the short futures position. The net gain is the decrease in the basis, or $0.50 an ounce.

---

[4]Usage of the word *basis* is somewhat loose. It sometimes is used to refer to the futures-spot difference, $F - P$, and other times it is used to refer to the spot-futures difference, $P - F$. We will consistently call the basis $F - P$.

spread (futures)
Taking a long position in a futures contract of one maturity and a short position in a contract of different maturity, both on the same commodity.

A related strategy is a **spread** position, where the investor takes a long position in a futures contract of one maturity and a short position in a contract on the same commodity, but with a different maturity. Profits accrue if the difference in futures prices between the two contracts changes in the hoped-for direction; that is, if the futures price on the contract held long increases by more (or decreases by less) than the futures price on the contract held short. Like basis strategies, spread positions aim to exploit movements in relative price structures rather than to profit from movements in the general level of prices.

EXAMPLE 18.5
Speculating on the Spread

Consider an investor who holds a September maturity contract long and a June contract short. If the September futures price increases by 5 cents while the June futures price increases by 4 cents, the net gain will be 5 cents − 4 cents, or 1 cent.

18.4 THE DETERMINATION OF FUTURES PRICES

The Spot-Futures Parity Theorem

There are at least two ways to obtain an asset at some date in the future. One way is to purchase the asset now and store it until the targeted date. The other way is to take a long futures position that calls for purchase of the asset on the date in question. As each strategy leads to an equivalent result, namely, the ultimate acquisition of the asset, you would expect the market-determined cost of pursuing these strategies to be equal. There should be a predictable relationship between the current price of the asset, including the costs of holding and storing it, and the futures price.

To make the discussion more concrete, consider a futures contract on gold. This is a particularly simple case: Explicit storage costs for gold are minimal, gold provides no income flow for its owners (in contrast to stocks or bonds that make dividend or coupon payments), and gold is not subject to the seasonal price patterns that characterize most agricultural commodities. Instead, in market equilibrium, the price of gold will be at a level such that the expected rate of capital gains will equal the fair expected rate of return given gold's investment risk. Two strategies that will assure possession of the gold at some future date T are:

Strategy A: Buy the gold now, paying the current or "spot" price, S_0, and hold it until time T, when its spot price will be S_T.

Strategy B: Initiate a long futures position, and invest enough money now in order to pay the futures price when the contract matures.

Strategy B will require an immediate investment of the *present value* of the futures price in a riskless security such as Treasury bills, that is, an investment of $F_0/(1 + r_f)^T$ dollars, where r_f is the rate paid on T-bills. Examine the cash flow streams of the following two strategies.[5]

Strategy A:	Action	Initial Cash Flow	Cash Flow at Time T
	Buy gold	$-S_0$	S_T
Strategy B:	Action	**Initial Cash Flow**	**Cash Flow at Time T**
	Enter long position	0	$S_T - F_0$
	Invest $F_0/(1 + r_f)^T$ in bills	$-F_0/(1 + r_f)^T$	F_0
	Total for strategy B	$-F_0/(1 + r_f)^T$	S_T

---

[5]We ignore the margin requirement on the futures contract and treat the cash flow involved in establishing the futures position as zero for the two reasons mentioned above: First, the margin is small relative to the amount of gold controlled by one contract; and second, and more importantly, the margin requirement may be satisfied with interest-bearing securities. For example, the investor merely needs to transfer Treasury bills already owned into the brokerage account. There is no time-value-of-money cost.

The initial cash flow of strategy A is negative, reflecting the cash outflow necessary to purchase the gold at the current spot price, S_0. At time T, the gold will be worth S_T.

Strategy B involves an initial investment equal to the present value of the futures price that will be paid at the maturity of the futures contract. By time T, the investment will grow to F_0. In addition, the profits to the long position at time T will be $S_T - F_0$. The sum of the two components of strategy B will be S_T dollars, exactly enough to purchase the gold at time T regardless of its price at that time.

Each strategy results in an identical value of S_T dollars at T. Therefore, the cost, or initial cash outflow, required by these strategies also must be equal; it follows that

$$F_0/(1 + r_f)^T = S_0$$

or,

$$F_0 = S_0(1 + r_f)^T \tag{18.1}$$

This gives us a relationship between the current price and the futures price of the gold. The interest rate in this case may be viewed as the "cost of carrying" the gold from the present to time T. The cost in this case represents the time-value-of-money opportunity cost—instead of investing in the gold, you could have invested risklessly in Treasury bills to earn interest income.

EXAMPLE 18.6
Futures Pricing

Suppose that gold currently sells for $360 an ounce. If the risk-free interest rate is 1% per month, a six-month maturity futures contract should have a futures price of

$$F_0 = S_0(1 + r_f)^T = \$360(1.01)^6 = \$382.15$$

If the contract has a 12-month maturity, the futures price should be

$$F_0 = \$360(1.01)^{12} = \$405.66$$

If Equation 18.1 does not hold, investors can earn arbitrage profits. For example, suppose the six-month maturity futures price in Example 18.6 were $383 rather than the "appropriate" value of $382.15 that we just derived. An investor could realize arbitrage profits by pursuing a strategy involving a long position in strategy A (buy the gold) and a short position in strategy B (sell the futures contract and borrow enough to pay for the gold purchase).

Action	Initial Cash Flow	Cash Flow at Time T (6 Months)
Borrow $360, repay with interest at time T	+$360	$-\$360(1.01)^6 = -\$382.15$
Buy gold for $360	−360	S_T
Enter short futures position ($F_0 = \$383$)	0	$383 - S_T$
Total	$0	$0.85

The net initial investment of this strategy is zero. Moreover, its cash flow at time T is positive and riskless: The total payoff at time T will be $0.85 regardless of the price of gold. (The profit is equal to the mispricing of the futures contract, $383 rather than $382.15.) Risk has been eliminated because profits and losses on the futures and gold positions exactly offset each other. The portfolio is perfectly hedged.

Such a strategy produces an arbitrage profit—a riskless profit requiring no initial net investment. If such an opportunity existed, all market participants would rush to take advantage of it. The results? The price of gold would be bid up, and/or the futures price offered down, until Equation 18.1 is satisfied. A similar analysis applies to the possibility that F_0 is less than $382.15. In this case, you simply reverse the above strategy to earn riskless profits. We conclude, therefore, that in a well-functioning market in which arbitrage opportunities are competed away, $F_0 = S_0(1 + r_f)^T$.

5. Return to the arbitrage strategy just laid out. What would be the three steps of the strategy if F_0 were too low, say \$381? Work out the cash flows of the strategy now and at time T in a table like the one above.

The arbitrage strategy can be represented more generally as follows:

Action	Initial Cash Flow	Cash Flow at Time T
1. Borrow S_0	S_0	$-S_0(1 + r_f)^T$
2. Buy gold for S_0	$-S_0$	S_T
3. Enter short futures position	0	$F_0 - S_T$
Total	0	$F_0 - S_0(1 + r_f)^T$

The initial cash flow is zero by construction: The money necessary to purchase the stock in step 2 is borrowed in step 1, and the futures position in step 3, which is used to hedge the value of the stock position, does not require an initial outlay. Moreover, the total cash flow to the strategy at time T is riskless because it involves only terms that are already known when the contract is entered. This situation could not persist, as all investors would try to cash in on the arbitrage opportunity. Ultimately prices would change until the time T cash flow was reduced to zero, at which point F_0 would once again equal $S_0(1 + r_f)^T$. This result is called the **spot-futures parity theorem** or **cost-of-carry relationship;** it gives the normal or theoretically correct relationship between spot and futures prices.

We can easily extend the parity theorem to the case where the underlying asset provides a flow of income to its owner. For example, consider a futures contract on a stock index such as the S&P 500. In this case, the underlying asset (i.e., the stock portfolio indexed to the S&P 500 index), pays a dividend yield to the investor. If we denote the dividend yield as d, then the net cost of carry is only $r_f - d$; the time value cost of the wealth that is tied up in the stock is offset by the flow of dividends from the stock. The net opportunity cost of holding the stock is the foregone interest less the dividends received. Therefore, in the dividend-paying case, the spot-futures parity relationship is[6]

spot-futures parity theorem, or cost-of-carry relationship
Describes the theoretically correct relationship between spot and futures prices. Violation of the parity relationship gives rise to arbitrage opportunities.

$$F_0 = S_0(1 + r_f - d)^T \qquad (18.2)$$

where d is the dividend yield on the stock. Problem 5 at the end of the chapter leads you through a derivation of this result.

The arbitrage strategy just described should convince you that these parity relationships are more than just theoretical results. Any violations of the parity relationship give rise to arbitrage opportunities that can provide large profits to traders. We will see shortly that index arbitrage in the stock market is a tool used to exploit violations of the parity relationship for stock index futures contracts.

EXAMPLE 18.7
Stock Index
Futures Pricing

Suppose that the risk-free interest rate is 1% per month, the dividend yield on the stock index is 0.2% per month, and the stock index is currently at 700. The net cost of carry is therefore 1% − 0.2% = 0.8% per month. Given this, a three-month contract should have a futures price of $700(1.008)^3 = 716.93$, while a six-month contract should have a futures price of $700(1.008)^6 = 734.28$. If the index rises to 704, both futures prices will rise commensurately: The three-month futures price will rise to $704(1.008)^3 = 721.03$, while the six-month futures price will rise to $704(1.008)^6 = 738.48$.

Spreads

Just as we can predict the relationship between spot and futures prices, there are similar ways to determine the proper relationships among futures prices for contracts of different

---

[6]This relationship is only approximate in that it assumes the dividend is paid just before the maturity of the contract.

FIGURE 18.4

Futures Prices in
January 1996 for Gold
Contracts Maturing in
February, April, and
June 1996

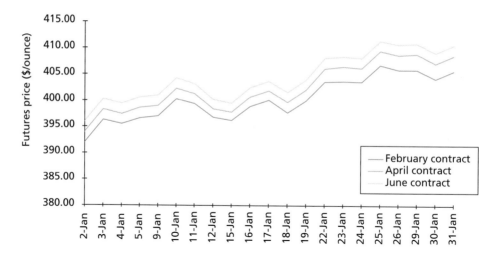

maturity dates. Equation 18.2 shows that the futures price is in part determined by time to maturity. If $r_f > d$, as is usually the case for stock index futures, then the futures price will be higher on longer-maturity contracts. You can easily verify this by examining Figure 18.2, which includes *Wall Street Journal* listings of several stock index futures contracts. For futures on assets like gold, which pay no "dividend yield," we can set $d = 0$ and conclude that F must increase as time to maturity increases.

Equation 18.2 shows that futures prices should all move together. It is not surprising that futures prices for different maturity dates move in unison, for all are linked to the same spot price through the parity relationship. Figure 18.4 plots futures prices on gold for three maturity dates. It is apparent that the prices move in virtual lockstep and that the more distant delivery dates require higher futures prices, as Equation 18.2 predicts.

18.5 FINANCIAL FUTURES

Although futures markets have their origins in agricultural commodities, today's market is dominated by contracts on financial assets, as we saw in Figure 18.1.

Stock Index Futures

Currently, there are no stock futures on individual shares; futures trade instead on stock market indexes such as the Standard & Poor's 500. In contrast to most futures contracts, which call for delivery of a specified commodity, these contracts are settled by a cash amount equal to the value of the stock index in question on the contract maturity date times a multiplier that scales the size of the contract. This cash settlement duplicates the profits that would arise with actual delivery.

There are several stock index futures contracts currently traded. Table 18.2 lists some contracts on major indexes, showing under contract size the multiplier used to calculate contract settlements. An S&P 500 contract with a futures price of 770 and a final index value of 775, for example, would result in a profit for the long side of $500 \times (775 - 770) =$ $2,500. The S&P contract by far dominates the market in stock index futures.

Most futures contracts such as the S&P 500 or NYSE are written explicitly on a particular stock index. This gives investors the ability to hedge against or speculate on the performance of the given index. The Major Market Index is a bit of an exception. Because the Chicago Board of Trade was not given permission by Dow Jones to create a contract explicitly tied to the Dow Jones Industrial Average, it chose to create its own index designed to track the DJIA as closely as possible. However, Dow Jones seems to have changed its position. In June 1997, it was in negotiations to license its name for several derivative contracts.

TABLE 18.2   Stock Index Futures

Contract	Underlying Market Index	Contract Size	Exchange
S&P 500	Standard & Poor's 500 index. A value-weighted arithmetic average of 500 stocks.	$500 times the S&P 500 index.	Chicago Mercantile Exchange
Major Market Index	Price-weighted arithmetic average of 20 blue-chip stocks. Index is designed to track the Dow Jones Industrial Average.	$250 times the Major Market Index.	Chicago Board of Trade
S&P Midcap	Index of 400 firms of mid-range market value.	$500 times index.	Chicago Mercantile Exchange
National Over-the-Counter	Value-weighted arithmetic average of 100 of the largest over-the-counter stocks.	$500 times the OTC index.	Philadelphia Board of Trade
Nikkei	Nikkei 225 stock average.	$5 times the Nikkei index.	Chicago Mercantile Exchange
FT-SE 100	Financial Times-Share Exchange Index of 100 U.K. firms.	£25 times the FT-SE Index.	London International Financial Futures Exchange
FT-SE Eurotrack 100	Index of 100 non-U.K. European firms.	50 deutsche marks times the index.	London International Financial Futures Exchange
CAC 40	Index of 40 of the largest French firms.	200 French francs times the index.	MATIF (Marche a Terme International de France)
DAX 30	Index of 30 of the largest German firms.	100 deutsche marks times the index.	DTB (Deutsche Terminboerse)

TABLE 18.3

Correlations Among U.S. Stock Market Indexes

Source: *Futures and Options: Theories and Applications* by Stoll and Whaley. Copyright 1993. By permission of South-Western College Publishing, a division of International Thomson Publishing, Inc., Cincinnati, OH 45227.

Index	DJIA	MMI	S&P 500	Value Line	NYSE
DJIA	1.0000	0.9779	0.9774	0.8880	0.9750
MMI	0.9779	1.0000	0.9497	0.8104	0.9403
S&P 500	0.9774	0.9497	1.0000	0.9137	0.9972
Value Line	0.8880	0.8104	0.9137	1.0000	0.9337
NYSE	0.9750	0.9403	0.9972	0.9337	1.0000

Note: Correlations were computed from weekly percentage rates of price appreciation during calendar year 1989.

The broad-based U.S. stock market indexes are all highly correlated. Table 18.3 presents a correlation matrix for five U.S. indexes. The highest correlation, 0.9972, is between the S&P 500 and the NYSE indexes. This near-perfect correlation reflects the fact that both indexes are value-weighted and that the S&P 500 firms account for about two-thirds of the market capitalization of the NYSE. However, even the DJIA, with only 30 stocks, exhibits a correlation above 0.97 with both the S&P and NYSE. This is testament to the power of even moderate diversification.

Creating Synthetic Stock Positions

One reason stock index futures are so popular is that they substitute for holdings in the underlying stocks themselves. Index futures let investors participate in broad market movements without actually buying or selling large numbers of stocks.

Because of this, we say futures represent "synthetic" holdings of the market position. Instead of holding the market directly, the investor takes a long futures position in the index. Such a strategy is attractive because the transaction costs involved in establishing and liquidating futures positions are much lower than what would be required to take actual spot positions. Investors who wish to buy and sell market positions frequently find it much cheaper and easier to play the futures market. Market timers who speculate on broad market moves rather than individual securities are large players in stock index futures for this reason.

One way to market time is to shift between Treasury bills and broad-based stock market holdings. Times attempt to shift from bills into the market before market upturns and to shift back into bills to avoid market downturns, thereby profiting from broad market movements. Market timing of this sort, however, can result in huge trading costs with the frequent purchase and sale of many stocks. An attractive alternative is to invest in Treasury bills and hold varying amounts of market index futures contracts.

The strategy works like this. When timers are bullish, they will establish many long futures positions that they can liquidate quickly and cheaply when expectations turn bearish. Rather than shifting back and forth between T-bills and stocks, traders buy and hold T-bills and adjust only the futures position. (Recall strategies A and B of the preceding section where we showed that a T-bill plus futures position resulted in a payoff equal to the stock price.) This strategy minimizes transaction costs. An advantage of this technique for timing is that investors can implicitly buy or sell the market index in its entirety, whereas market timing in the spot market would require the simultaneous purchase or sale of all the stocks in the index. This is technically difficult to coordinate and can lead to slippage in the execution of a timing strategy.

The nearby box (page 517) illustrates that it is now commonplace for money managers to use futures contracts to create synthetic equity positions in stock markets. The article notes that futures positions can be particularly helpful in establishing synthetic positions in foreign equities, where trading costs tend to be greater and markets tend to be less liquid.

Index Arbitrage and the Triple-Witching Hour

Whenever the actual futures price differs from its parity value, there is an opportunity for profit. This is why the parity relationships are so important. One of the most notable developments in trading activity has been the advent of **index arbitrage,** an investment strategy that exploits divergences between the actual futures price on a stock market index and its theoretically correct parity value.

In principle, index arbitrage is simple. If the futures price is too high, short the futures contract and buy the stocks in the index. If it is too low, go long in futures and short the stocks. You can perfectly hedge your position and should earn arbitrage profits equal to the mispricing of the contract.

In practice, however, index arbitrage can be difficult to implement. The problem lies in buying the stocks in the index. Selling or purchasing shares in all 500 stocks in the S&P 500 is difficult for two reasons. The first is transaction costs, which may outweigh any profits to be made from the arbitrage. Second, it is extremely difficult to buy or sell the stock of 500 different firms simultaneously—and any lags in the execution of such a strategy can destroy the effectiveness of a plan to exploit short-lived price discrepancies.

Arbitrageurs need to trade an entire portfolio of stocks quickly and simultaneously if they hope to exploit temporary disparities between the futures price and its corresponding stock index. For this they need a coordinated trading program; hence the term **program trading,** which refers to coordinated purchases or sales of entire portfolios of stocks. Such strategies can be executed using the NYSE SuperDot (designated order turnaround) system, which enables traders to send coordinated buy or sell programs to the floor of the stock exchange over computer lines. (We discussed the SuperDot system in Chapter 3.)

In each year, there are four maturing S&P 500 futures contracts. On these four Fridays, which occur simultaneously with the expiration of S&P index options and options on some individual stocks, the market has tended to exhibit above-average volatility. These dates have been dubbed the **triple-witching hour** because of the volatility associated with the expirations in the three types of contracts, although it appears that only the futures contract expiration actually affects the market.

Expiration-day volatility can be explained by program trading to exploit arbitrage opportunities. Suppose that some time before a stock index futures contract matures, the futures price is a little above its parity value. Arbitrageurs will attempt to lock in superior profits by

index arbitrage
Strategy that exploits divergences between actual futures prices and their theoretically correct parity values to make a riskless profit.

program trading
Coordinated buy orders and sell orders of entire portfolios, usually with the aid of computers, often to achieve index arbitrage objectives.

triple-witching hour
The four times a year that the S&P 500 futures contract expires at the same time as the S&P 100 index option contract and option contracts on individual stocks.

Got a Bundle to Invest Fast? Think Stock-Index Futures

As investors go increasingly global and market turbulence grows, stock-index futures are emerging as the favorite way for nimble money managers to deploy their funds.

Indeed, research from Goldman, Sachs & Co. shows that, in most major markets, trading in stock futures now exceeds the buying and selling of actual shares. In the U.S., for instance, average daily trading volume of futures based on the Standard & Poor's 500 stock index was a whopping $16.8 billion in 1994. By contrast, New York Stock Exchange trading averaged only $10.56 billion a day.

What's the big appeal? Speed, ease, and cheapness. For most major markets, stock futures not only boast greater liquidity but also lower transaction costs than traditional trading methods.

Portfolio managers stress that in today's fast-moving markets, it's critical to implement decisions quickly. For giant mutual and pension funds eager to keep assets fully invested, shifting billions around through stock-index futures is much easier than trying to identify individual stocks to buy and sell.

"When I decide it's time to move into France, Germany, or Britain, I don't necessarily want to wait around until I find exactly the right stocks," says Fabrizio Pierallini, manager of New York-based Vontobel Ltd.'s Euro Pacific Fund.

Mr. Pierallini, who has $120 million invested in stocks in Europe, Asia, and Latin America, says he later finetunes his market picks by gradually shifting out of futures into favorite stocks. To the extent Mr. Pierallini's stocks outperform the market, futures provide a means to preserve those gains, even while hedging against market declines.

For instance, by selling futures equal to the value of the underlying portfolio, a manager can almost completely insulate a portfolio from market moves. Say a manager succeeds in outperforming the market, but still loses 3% while the market as a whole falls 10%. Hedging with futures would capture that margin of outperformance, transforming the loss into a profit of roughly 7%. Demand for such protection helped account for stock futures' surging popularity in last year's difficult markets, Goldman said in its report.

"You can get all the value your mangers are going to add" relative to the market, "and you don't need to worry about the costs of trading" actual securities, said David Leinweber, director of research at First Quadrant Corp., a Pasadena, Calif., investment firm that traded some $59 billion of futures in 1994.

Among First Quadrant's futures-intensive strategies is "global tactical asset allocation," which involves trading whole markets worldwide as traditional managers might trade stocks. The growing popularity of such asset-allocation strategies has given futures a big boost in recent years.

To capitalize on global market swings, "futures do the job for us better than stocks, and they're cheaper," said Jarrod Wilcox, director of global investments at PanAgora Asset Management, a Boston-based asset allocator. Even when PanAgora does take positions in individual stocks, it often employs futures to modify its position, such as by hedging part of its exposure to that particular stock market.

When it comes to investing overseas, Mr. Wilcox noted, futures are often the only vehicle that makes sense from a cost standpoint. Abroad, transaction taxes and sky-high commissions can wipe out more than 1% of the money deployed on each trade. By contrast, a comparable trade in futures costs as little as 0.05%.

"Futures allow us to convert [even] modest opportunities into profits for our clients," Mr. Wilcox said. If trading actual stocks "costs 1% in fees to get in and another 1% to get out, it's too costly to do."

Source: Suzanne McGee, *The Wall Street Journal*, February 21, 1995. Reprinted by permission of *The Wall Street Journal*, © 1995 Dow Jones & Company, Inc. All Rights Reserved Worldwide.

buying the stocks in the index (the program trading buy order) and taking an offsetting short futures position. If and when the pricing disparity reverses, the position can be unwound at a profit. Alternatively, arbitrageurs can wait until contract maturity day and realize a profit by simultaneously closing out of the offsetting stock and futures positions. By waiting until contract maturity, arbitrageurs can be assured that the futures price and stock index price will be aligned—they rely on the convergence property.

Obviously, when many program traders follow such a strategy at contract expiration, a wave of program selling passes over the market. The result? Prices go down. This is the expiration-day effect. If execution of the arbitrage strategy calls for an initial sale (or short sale) of stocks, unwinding on expiration day requires repurchase of the stocks, with the opposite effect: Prices increase.

FIGURE 18.5
Program Trading
Activity

From *The Wall Street Journal,*
September 13, 1996. Reprinted
by permission of *The Wall
Street Journal,* © 1996 Dow
Jones & Company, inc. All
Rights Reserved Worldwide.

PROGRAM TRADING

NEW YORK—Program trading in the week ended Friday accounted for 15.6%, or an average of 54.8 million shares daily of New York Stock Exchange volume.

Brokerage firms executed an additional 15.3 million daily shares of program trading away from the Big Board, mostly on foreign markets. Program trading is the simultaneous purchase or sale of at least 15 different stocks with a total value of $1 million or more.

Of the program total on the Big Board, 31.8% involved stock index arbitrage, down from 33.2% in the prior week. In this strategy, traders dart between stocks and stock-index options and futures to capture fleeting price differences.

Some 52% of program trading was executed by firms for their customers, while 46.5% was done for their own accounts, or principal trading. Another 1.5% was designated as customer facilitation, in which firms use principal positions to facilitate customer trades.

The New York Stock Exchange's program trading report includes profiles of trading whenever the Dow Jones Industrial Average moves 50 points or more in a single direction during any one-hour period. There was one such period this week.

The period occurred on Tuesday when the industrial average moved down more than 50 points during the first hour of trading. The following firms reported making program trades during 9:30-10:30 a.m.: First Options, Nomura Securities, Merrill Lynch, Deutsche Bank and Lehman Brothers.

Of the five most-active firms, Nomura Securities, Morgan Stanley, First Boston and Lehman Brothers executed most of their program trading for their own accounts, while First Options executed all or most of its program activity for customers, as agent.

NYSE PROGRAM TRADING

Volume (in millions of shares) for the week ending Sept. 6, 1996

Top 15 Firms	Index Arbitrage	Derivative-Related*	Other Strategies	Total
First Options	....	37.1	8.4	45.5
Nomura Securities	10.6	....	18.3	28.9
Morgan Stanley	1.4	2.6	14.1	18.1
First Boston	8.7	....	4.8	13.5
Lehman Brothers	8.4	....	3.2	11.6
Deutsche Bank	11.6	....	....	11.6
Interactive Brokers	....	....	11.6	11.6
Salomon Brothers	....	1.4	9.6	11.0
Susquehanna Bkrg. Srvs.	6.5	....	1.2	7.7
Merrill Lynch	....	....	7.6	7.6
Bear Stearns	1.2	....	6.0	7.2
RBC Dominion	6.2	....	0.2	6.4
UBS Securities	5.9	....	....	5.9
Paine Webber	....	1.1	2.9	4.0
Thomas Williams	0.7	....	2.9	3.6
OVERALL TOTAL	**69.7**	**42.3**	**107.2**	**219.2**

*Other derivative-related strategies besides index arbitrage
Source: New York Stock Exchange

The program trading associated with index arbitrage commonly accounts for 10–20% of NYSE daily volume. *The Wall Street Journal* regularly reports on program trading, both in aggregate and for the largest traders. Figure 18.5 is a reproduction of one such report.

Foreign Exchange Futures

Exchange rates between currencies vary continually and often substantially. This variability can be a source of concern for anyone involved in international business. A U.S. exporter who sells goods in England, for example, will be paid in British pounds, and the dollar value of those pounds depends on the exchange rate at the time payment is made. Until that date, the U.S. exporter is exposed to foreign exchange rate risk. This risk can be hedged through currency futures or forward markets. For example, if you know you will receive £100,000 in 60 days, you can sell those pounds forward today in the forward market and lock in an exchange rate equal to today's forward price.

The forward market in foreign exchange is relatively informal. It is simply a network of banks and brokers that allows customers to enter forward contracts to purchase or sell currency in the future at a currently agreed-upon rate of exchange. The bank market in currencies is among the largest in the world, and most large traders with sufficient credit-

FIGURE 18.6

Spot and Forward Prices in Foreign Exchange

Source: From *The Wall Street Journal*, September 13, 1996. Reprinted by permission of *The Wall Street Journal*, © 1996 Dow Jones & Company, Inc. All Rights Reserved Worldwide.

CURRENCY TRADING

EXCHANGE RATES

Thursday, September 12, 1996

The New York foreign exchange selling rates below apply to trading among banks in amounts of $1 million and more, as quoted at 3 p.m. Eastern time by Dow Jones Telerate Inc. and other sources. Retail transactions provide fewer units of foreign currency per dollar.

Country	U.S. $ equiv. Thu	U.S. $ equiv. Wed	Currency per U.S. $ Thu	Currency per U.S. $ Wed
Argentina (Peso)	1.0012	1.0012	.9988	.9988
Australia (Dollar)	.7972	.7993	1.2544	1.2511
Austria (Schilling)	.09403	.09422	10.635	10.613
Bahrain (Dinar)	2.6525	2.6525	.3770	.3770
Belgium (Franc)	.03210	.03220	31.155	31.055
Brazil (Real)	.9833	.9833	1.0170	1.0170
Britain (Pound)	1.5557	1.5551	.6428	.6430
30-Day Forward	1.5553	1.5548	.6430	.6432
90-Day Forward	1.5551	1.5548	.6430	.6432
180-Day Forward	1.5561	1.5558	.6427	.6428
Canada (Dollar)	.7288	.7291	1.3721	1.3715
30-Day Forward	.7297	.7300	1.3704	1.3698
90-Day Forward	.7316	.7319	1.3669	1.3664
180-Day Forward	.7344	.7345	1.3617	1.3614
Chile (Peso)	.002430	.002427	411.55	412.05
China (Renminbi)	.1200	.1200	8.3352	8.3353
Colombia (Peso)	.0009634	.0009643	1038.00	1037.00
Czech. Rep. (Koruna)				
Commercial rate	.03770	.03749	26.527	26.675
Denmark (Krone)	.1714	.1720	5.8343	5.8123
Ecuador (Sucre)				
Floating rate	.0003057	.0003055	3271.00	3273.00
Finland (Markka)	.2186	.2192	4.5738	4.5627
France (Franc)	.1936	.1939	5.1650	5.1565
30-Day Forward	.1939	.1943	5.1571	5.1480
90-Day Forward	.1945	.1948	5.1414	5.1333
180-Day Forward	.1955	.1958	5.1154	5.1077
Germany (Mark)	.6611	.6619	1.5126	1.5108
30-Day Forward	.6624	.6633	1.5097	1.5077
90-Day Forward	.6652	.6660	1.5033	1.5015
180-Day Forward	.6699	.6706	1.4928	1.4912
Greece (Drachma)	.004149	.004158	241.00	240.50
Hong Kong (Dollar)	.1293	.1293	7.7322	7.7320
Hungary (Forint)	.006368	.006367	157.04	157.05
India (Rupee)	.02798	.02793	35.735	35.810
Indonesia (Rupiah)	.0004299	.0004291	2326.00	2330.50
Ireland (Punt)	1.6088	1.6093	.6216	.6214
Israel (Shekel)	.3155	.3156	3.1692	3.1688
Italy (Lira)	.0006573	.0006550	1521.45	1526.75
Japan (Yen)	.009083	.009065	110.10	110.31

Country	U.S. $ equiv. Thu	U.S. $ equiv. Wed	Currency per U.S. $ Thu	Currency per U.S. $ Wed
30-Day Forward	.009121	.009106	109.64	109.82
90-Day Forward	.009201	.009183	108.69	108.90
180-Day Forward	.009324	.009309	107.25	107.43
Jordan (Dinar)	1.4065	1.4065	.7110	.7110
Kuwait (Dinar)	3.3434	3.3322	.2991	.3001
Lebanon (Pound)	.0006410	.0006408	1560.00	1560.50
Malaysia (Ringgit)	.3998	.3999	2.5010	2.5008
Malta (Lira)	2.7778	2.7778	.3600	.3600
Mexico (Peso)				
Floating rate	.1326	.1326	7.5440	7.5425
Netherland (Guilder)	.5897	c.5905	1.6958	c1.6936
New Zealand (Dollar)	.6936	.6965	1.4418	1.4358
Norway (Krone)	.1541	.1546	6.4872	6.4665
Pakistan (Rupee)	.02735	.02735	36.560	36.560
Peru (new Sol)	.4046	.4046	2.4716	2.4716
Philippines (Peso)	.03814	.03813	26.222	26.227
Poland (Zloty)	.3607	.3593	2.7725	2.7830
Portugal (Escudo)	.006455	.006475	154.92	154.45
Russia (Ruble) (a)	.0001859	.0001860	5379.00	5375.00
Saudi Arabia (Riyal)	.2666	.2666	3.7506	3.7505
Singapore (Dollar)	.7092	.7097	1.4100	1.4090
Slovak Rep. (Koruna)	.03263	.03263	30.650	30.650
South Africa (Rand)	.2221	.2234	4.5015	4.4760
South Korea (Won)	.001215	.001217	822.80	821.40
Spain (Peseta)	.007826	.007855	127.78	127.30
Sweden (Krona)	.1495	.1494	6.6877	6.6915
Switzerland (Franc)	.8081	.8095	1.2375	1.2354
30-Day Forward	.8104	.8120	1.2339	1.2316
90-Day Forward	.8152	.8165	1.2267	1.2248
180-Day Forward	.8230	.8243	1.2151	1.2132
Taiwan (Dollar)	.03637	.03638	27.492	27.491
Thailand (Baht)	.03940	.03939	25.383	25.385
Turkey (Lira)	.00001126	.00001128	88813.50	88614.00
United Arab (Dirham)	.2723	.2723	3.6720	3.6720
Uruguay (New Peso)				
Financial	.1209	c.1209	8.2700	c8.2700
Venezuela (Bolivar) b	.002098	.002098	476.63	476.63
Brady Rate	.002095	.002095	477.25	477.25
SDR	1.4446	1.4445	.6922	.6923
ECU	1.2514	1.2558		

Special Drawing Rights (SDR) are based on exchange rates for the U.S., German, British, French, and Japanese currencies. Source: International Monetary Fund.

European Currency Unit (ECU) is based on a basket of community currencies. c-Corrected.

a-fixing, Moscow Interbank Currency Exchange.

b-Changed to market rate effective Apr. 22.

worthiness execute their trades here rather than in futures markets. Contracts in these markets are not standardized in a formal market setting. Instead, each is negotiated separately. Moreover, there is no marking to market as would occur in futures markets. Currency forward contracts call for execution only at the maturity date.

For currency futures, however, there are formal markets established by the Chicago Mercantile Exchange (International Monetary Market), the London International Financial Futures Exchange, and the MidAmerica Commodity Exchange. Here, contracts are standardized by size, and daily marking to market is observed. Moreover, there are standard clearing arrangements that allow traders to enter or reverse positions easily.

Figure 18.6 reproduces a *Wall Street Journal* listing of foreign exchange spot and forward rates. The listing gives the number of U.S. dollars required to purchase a unit of foreign currency and then the amount of foreign currency needed to purchase $1.

The forward quotations in Figure 18.6 always apply to rolling delivery in 30, 90, or 180 days. Thus, tomorrow's forward listings will apply to a maturity date one day later than today's listing. In contrast, foreign exchange futures contracts mature at specified dates in March, June, September, and December (see Figure 18.2); these four maturity days are the only dates each year when futures contracts settle.

Interest Rate Futures

The late 1970s and 1980s saw a dramatic increase in the volatility of interest rates, leading to investor desire to hedge returns on fixed-income securities against changes in interest rates. As one example, thrift institutions that had loaned money on home mortgages before 1975 suffered substantial capital losses on those loans when interest rates later increased. An interest rate futures contract could have protected banks against such large swings in yields. The significance of these losses has spurred trading in interest rate futures.

The major U.S. interest rate contracts currently traded are on Eurodollars, Treasury bills, Treasury notes, Treasury bonds, and a municipal bond index. The range of these securities provides an opportunity to hedge against a wide spectrum of maturities from very short (T-bills) to long term (T-bonds). In addition, futures contracts tied to interest rates in Germany, Japan, the United Kingdom, and several other countries trade and are listed in *The Wall Street Journal*. Figure 18.2 shows listings of some of these contracts in *The Wall Street Journal*.

The Treasury contracts call for delivery of a Treasury bond, bill, or note. Should interest rates rise, the market value of the security at delivery will be less than the original futures price, and the deliverer will profit. Hence, the short position in the interest rate futures contract gains when interest rates rise and bond prices fall.

Similarly, Treasury bond futures can be useful hedging vehicles for bond dealers or underwriters. We saw earlier, for example, how the T-bond contract could be used by an investor to hedge the value of a T-bond portfolio or by a pension fund manager who anticipates the purchase of a Treasury bond. The newer contract on the municipal bond index allows for more direct hedging of long-term bonds other than Treasury issues.

An episode that occurred in October 1979 illustrates the potential hedging value offered by T-bond contracts. Salomon Brothers, Merrill Lynch, and other underwriters brought out a $1 billion issue of IBM bonds. As is typical, the underwriting syndicate quoted an interest rate at which it guaranteed the bonds could be sold. This underwriting arrangement is called a "firm commitment," and is discussed in more detail in Chapter 3. (In essence, the syndicate buys the company's bonds at an agreed-upon price and then takes the responsibility of reselling them in the open market. If interest rates increase before the bonds can be sold to the public, the syndicate, not the issuer, bears the capital loss from the fall in the value of the bonds.)

In this case, the syndicate led by Salomon Brothers and Merrill Lynch brought out the IBM debt to sell at yields of 9.62% for $500 million of 7-year notes and 9.41% for $500 million of 25-year bonds. These yields were only about four basis points above comparable maturity U.S. government bond yields, reflecting IBM's excellent credit rating. The debt issue was brought to market on Thursday, October 4, when the underwriters began placing the bonds with customers. Interest rates, however, rose slightly that Thursday, making the IBM yields less attractive, and only about 70% of the issue had been placed by Friday afternoon, leaving the syndicate still holding between $250 million and $300 million of bonds.

Then on Saturday, October 6, the Federal Reserve Board announced a major credit-tightening policy. Interest rates jumped by almost a full percentage point. The underwriting syndicate realized the balance of the IBM bonds could not be placed to its regular customers at the original offering price and decided to sell them in the open bond market. By that time, the bonds had fallen nearly 5% in value, so that the underwriter's loss was about $12 million on the unsold bonds. The net loss on the underwriting operation came to about $7 million, after the profit of $5 million that had been realized on the bonds that were placed.

As the major underwriter with the lion's share of the bonds, Salomon lost about $3.5 million on the bond issue. Yet, while most of the other underwriters were vulnerable to the interest rate movement, Salomon had hedged its bond holdings by shorting about $100 million in Government National Mortgage Association (GNMA) and Treasury bond futures. Holding a short position, Salomon Brothers realized profits on the contract when interest rates increased. The profits on the short futures position resulted because the value of the bonds required to be delivered to satisfy the contract decreased when interest rates rose. Salomon Brothers probably about broke even on the entire transaction, making estimated gains on the futures position of about $3.5 million, which largely offset the capital loss on the bonds it was holding.

How could Salomon Brothers have constructed the proper hedge ratio, that is, the proper number of futures contracts per bond held in its inventory? The T-bond futures contract nominally calls for delivery of an 8% coupon, 20-year maturity government bond in return for the futures price. (In practice, other bonds may be substituted for this standard bond to settle the contract, but we will use the 8% bond for illustration.) Suppose the market interest rate is 10% and Salomon is holding $100 million worth of bonds, with a coupon rate of 10% and 20 years to maturity. The bonds currently sell at 100% of par value. If the interest rate were to jump to 11%, the bonds would fall in value to a market value of $91.98 per $100 of par value, a loss of $8.02 million. (We use semiannual compounding in this calculation.)

To hedge this risk, Salomon would need to short enough futures so that the profits on the futures position would offset the loss on the bonds. The 8%, 20-year bond of the futures contract would sell for $82.84 at an interest rate of 10%. If the interest rate were to jump to 11%, the bond price would fall to $75.93, and the fall in the price of the 8% bond, $6.91, would approximately equal the profit on the short futures position per $100 par value.[7] Because each contract calls for delivery of $100,000 par value of bonds, the gain on each short position would equal $6,910. Thus, to offset the $8.02 million loss on the value of the bonds, Salomon theoretically would need to hold $8.02 million/$6,910 = 1,161 contracts short. The total gain on the contracts would offset the loss on the bonds and leave Salomon unaffected by interest rate swings.

The actual hedging problem is more difficult for several reasons, most of which are due to the fact that this is really a cross-hedge: Salomon is hedging its IBM bonds by selling contracts on Treasury bonds and, to a lesser extent, GNMA bonds. Some of the complications in this hedging strategy are: (1) Salomon probably would hold more than one issue of bonds in its inventory; (2) interest rates on government and corporate bonds will not be equal and need not move in lockstep; (3) the T-bond contract may be settled with any of several bonds instead of the 8% benchmark bond; and (4) taxes could complicate the picture. Nevertheless, the principles illustrated here underlie all hedging activity.

Summary

- Forward contracts are arrangements that call for the future delivery of an asset at a currently agreed-upon price. The long trader is obligated to purchase the good, and the short trader is obligated to deliver it. If the price at the maturity of the contract exceeds the forward price, the long side benefits by virtue of acquiring the good at the contract price.
- A futures contract is similar to a forward contract, differing most importantly in the aspects of standardization and marking to market, which is the process by which gains and losses on futures contract positions are settled daily. In contrast, forward contracts call for no cash transfers until contract maturity.
- Futures contracts are traded on organized exchanges that standardize the size of the contract, the grade of the deliverable asset, the delivery date, and the delivery location. Traders negotiate only the contract price. This standardization creates increased liquidity in the marketplace and means buyers and sellers can easily find many traders for a desired purchase or sale.
- The clearinghouse acts as an intermediary between each pair of traders, acting as the short position for each long, and as the long position for each short, so traders need not be concerned about the performance of the trader on the opposite side of the contract. Traders are required to post margins in order to guarantee their own performance on the contracts.
- The gain or loss to the long side for a futures contract held between time 0 and t is $F_t - F_0$. Because $F_T = P_T$ at maturity, the long's profit if the contract is held until maturity is $P_T - F_0$, where P_T is the spot price at time T and F_0 is the original futures price. The gain or loss to the short position is $F_0 - P_T$.

[7]We say approximately because the exact figure depends on the time to maturity of the contract. We assume here that the maturity date is less than a month away so that the futures price and the bond price move in virtual lockstep.

- Futures contracts may be used for hedging or speculating. Speculators use the contracts to take a stand on the ultimate price of an asset. Short hedgers take short positions in contracts to offset any gains or losses on the value of an asset already held in inventory. Long hedgers take long positions in futures contracts to offset gains or losses in the purchase price of a good.
- The spot-futures parity relationship states that the equilibrium futures price on an asset providing no service or payments (such as dividends) is $F_0 = P_0(1 + r_f)^T$. If the futures price deviates from this value, then market participants can earn arbitrage profits.
- If the asset provides services or payments with yield d, the parity relationship becomes $F_0 = P_0(1 + r_f - d)^T$. This model is also called the cost-of-carry model, because it states that the futures price must exceed the spot price by the net cost of carrying the asset until maturity date T.
- Futures contracts calling for cash settlement are traded on various stock market indexes. The contracts may be mixed with Treasury bills to construct artificial equity positions, which makes them potentially valuable tools for market timers. Market index contracts also are used by arbitrageurs who attempt to profit from violations of the parity relationship.
- Interest rate futures allow for hedging against interest rate fluctuations in several different markets. The most actively traded contract is for Treasury bonds.

Key Terms

basis, *510*	forward contract, *499*	short position, *500*
basis risk, *510*	futures price, *500*	spot-futures parity
cash delivery, *507*	index arbitrage, *516*	theorem, *513*
clearinghouse, *504*	long position, *500*	spread, *511*
convergence property, *506*	maintenance margin, *506*	triple-witching hour, *516*
cost-of-carry	marking to market, *506*	variation margin, *506*
relationship, *513*	program trading, *516*	

Problem Set

1. *a.* Using Figure 18A, compute the dollar value of the stocks traded on one contract on the Standard & Poor's 500 index. The closing spot price of the S&P index is given in the last line of the figure. If the margin requirement is 10% of the futures price times the multiplier of 500, how much must you deposit with your broker to trade the September contract?

    b. If the September futures price were to increase to $675, what rate of return would you earn on your net investment if you entered the long side of the contract at the price shown in the figure?

    c. If the September futures price falls by 1%, what is the percentage gain or loss on your net investment?

FIGURE 18A

Source: From *The Wall Street Journal*, September 13, 1996. Reprinted by permission of *The Wall Street Journal*, © 1996 Dow Jones & Company, Inc. All Rights Reserved Worldwide.

INDEX

S&P 500 INDEX (CME) $500 times index

	Open	High	Low	Settle	Chg	High	Low	Open Interest
Sept	666.80	674.30	665.50	672.15	+ 5.15	688.90	559.70	119,951
Dec	676.00	680.15	674.85	678.10	+ 5.10	695.00	612.70	89,267
Mr97	682.00	686.45	681.80	684.50	+ 5.05	701.80	622.55	2,896
June	689.50	693.15	688.45	690.99	+ 4.85	701.00	629.05	1,252

Est vol 147,029; vol Wd 118,123; open int 213,366, +970.
Indx prelim High 673.07; Low 667.34; Close 671.13 +3.85

2. Why is there no futures market in cement?

3. Why might individuals purchase futures contracts rather than the underlying asset?

4. What is the difference in cash flow between short-selling an asset and entering a short futures position?

5. Consider a stock that will pay a dividend of D dollars in one year, which is when a futures contract matures. Consider the following strategy: Buy the stock, short a futures contract on the stock, and borrow S_0 dollars, where S_0 is the current price of the stock.
   a. What are the cash flows now and in one year? (Remember the dividend the stock will pay.)
   b. Show that the equilibrium futures price must be $F_0 = S_0(1 + r) - D$ to avoid arbitrage.
   c. Call the dividend yield $d = D/S_0$, and conclude that $F_0 = S_0(1 + r - d)$.

6. a. A hypothetical futures contract on a nondividend-paying stock with current price $150 has a maturity of one year. If the T-bill rate is 8%, what should the futures price be?
   b. What should the futures price be if the maturity of the contract is three years?
   c. What if the interest rate is 12% and the maturity of the contract is three years?

7. Your analysis leads you to believe the stock market is about to rise substantially. The market is unaware of this situation. What should you do?

8. In each of the following cases, discuss how you, as a portfolio manager, could use financial futures to protect a portfolio.
   a. You own a large position in a relatively illiquid bond that you want to sell.
   b. You have a large gain on one of your long Treasuries and want to sell it, but you would like to defer the gain until the next accounting period, which begins in four weeks.
   c. You will receive a large contribution next month that you hope to invest in long-term corporate bonds on a yield basis as favorable as is now available.

9. Suppose the value of the S&P 500 stock index is currently $660. If the one-year T-bill rate is 5% and the expected dividend yield on the S&P 500 is 2%, what should the one-year maturity futures price be?

10. It is now January. The current interest rate is 8%. The June futures price for gold is $346.30, while the December futures price is $360.00. Is there an arbitrage opportunity here? If so, how would you exploit it?

11. The Chicago Board of Trade has just introduced a new futures contract on Brandex stock, a company that currently pays no dividends. Each contract calls for delivery of 1,000 shares of stock in one year. The T-bill rate is 6% per year.
    a. If Brandex stock now sells at $120 per share, what should the futures price be?
    b. If the Brandex stock price drops by 3%, what will be the change in the futures price and the change in the investor's margin account?
    c. If the margin on the contract is $12,000, what is the percentage return on the investor's position?

12. Your client, for whom you are underwriting a $400 million bond issue, is concerned that market conditions will change before the issue is brought to market. He has heard it may be possible to reduce the risk exposure by hedging in the Government National Mortgage Association (GNMA) futures market. Specifically, he asks you to:
    a. Briefly explain how the hedge works.
    b. Describe practical problems that would limit the effectiveness of the hedge.

13. Futures contracts and options on a futures contract can be used to modify risk. Identify the fundamental distinction between a futures contract and an option on a futures contract, and briefly explain the difference in the manner that futures and options modify *portfolio* risk.

14. Suppose an S&P index portfolio pays a dividend yield of 2% annually. The index currently is 700. The T-bill rate is 5%, and the S&P futures price for delivery in one year is $725. Construct an arbitrage strategy to exploit the mispricing and show that your profits one year hence will equal the mispricing in the futures market.

15. *a.* How should the parity condition (Equation 18.2) for stocks be modified for futures contracts on Treasury bonds? What should play the role of the dividend yield in that equation?

    b. In an environment with an upward-sloping yield curve, should T-bond futures prices on more distant contracts be higher or lower than those on near-term contracts?

    c. Confirm your intuition by examining Figure 18.2

16. The one-year futures price on a particular stock-index portfolio is 406, the stock index currently is 400, the one-year risk-free interest rate is 3%, and the year-end dividend that will be paid on a $400 investment in the index portfolio is $5.

    a. By how much is the contract mispriced?

    b. Formulate a zero-net-investment arbitrage portfolio and show that you can lock in riskless profits equal to the futures mispricing.

    c. Now assume (as is true for small investors) that if you short-sell the stocks in the market index, the proceeds of the short-sale are kept with the broker, and you do not receive any interest income on the funds. Is there still an arbitrage opportunity (assuming you don't already own the shares in the index)? Explain.

    d. Given the short-sale rules, what is the no-arbitrage *band* for the stock-futures price relationship? That is, given a stock index of 400, how high and how low can the futures price be without giving rise to arbitrage opportunities?

17. The S&P 500 index is currently at 700. You manage a $7 million indexed equity portfolio. The S&P 500 futures contract has a multiplier of $500.

    a. If you are temporarily bearish on the stock market, how many contracts should you sell to fully eliminate your exposure over the next six months?

    b. If T-bills pay 2% per six months and the semiannual dividend yield is 1%, what is the parity value of the futures price? Show that if the contract is fairly priced, the total risk-free proceeds on the hedged strategy in part (*a*) provide a return equal to the T-bill rate.

    c. How would your hedging strategy change if, instead of holding an indexed portfolio, you hold a portfolio of only one stock with a beta of 0.6? How many contracts would you now choose to sell? Would your hedged position be riskless? What would be the beta of the hedged position?

18. The margin requirement on the S&P 500 futures contract is 10%, and the stock index is currently 750. Each contract has a multiplier of $500. How much margin must be put up for each contract sold? If the futures price falls by 1% to 742.50, what will happen to the margin account of an investor who holds one contract? What will be the investor's percentage return based on the amount put up as margin?

19. The multiplier for a futures contract on a certain stock market index is $500. The maturity of the contract is one year, the current level of the index is 400, and the risk-free interest rate is 0.5% per *month*. The dividend yield on the index is 0.2% per month. Suppose that *after one month,* the stock index is at 410.

    a. Find the cash flow from the mark-to-market proceeds on the contract. Assume that the parity condition always holds exactly.

    b. Find the holding-period return if the initial margin on the contract is $15,000.

20. You are a corporate treasurer who will purchase $1 million of bonds for the sinking fund in three months. You believe rates soon will fall and would like to repurchase the company's sinking fund bonds, which currently are selling below par, in advance of requirements. Unfortunately, you must obtain approval from the board of directors for

such a purchase, and this can take up to two months. What action can you take in the futures market to hedge any adverse movements in bond yields and prices until you actually can buy the bonds? Will you be long or short? Why?

Solutions to Concept Checks

1.

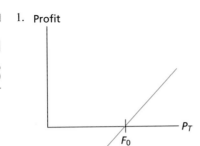

Long futures profit = $P_T - F_0$

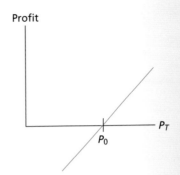

Asset profit = $P_T - P_0$

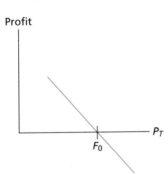

Short futures profit = $F_0 - P_T$

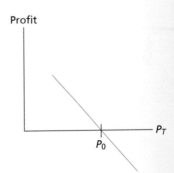

Short sale profit = $P_0 - P_T$

2. The clearinghouse has a zero net position in all contracts. Its long and short positions are offsetting, so that net cash flow from marking to market must be zero.

3.

	T-Bond Price in September		
	$109.69	**$110.69**	**$111.69**
Cash flow to purchase bonds (= −2,000 P_T)	−$219,380	−$221,380	−223,380
Profits on long futures position	−2,000	$0	2,000
Total cash flow	−$221,380	−$221,380	−$221,380

4. The risk would be that aluminum and bauxite prices do not move perfectly together. Thus, basis risk involving the spread between the futures price and bauxite spot prices could persist even if the aluminum futures price were set perfectly relative to aluminum itself.

5.

Action	Initial Cash Flow	Time-T Cash Flow
Lend S_0	−$360	$360(1.01)^6 = 382.15
Short gold	+360	−S_T
Long futures	0	$S_T - \$381$
Total	$0	$1.15 risklessly

Part Six

ACTIVE INVESTMENT MANAGEMENT

Active managers take it on faith that markets are not *always* efficient and that, at least occasionally, bargains are to be found in security markets. But how should mispriced securities be handled? Even if you believe that a stock has an incredible expected rate of return, you still will want to take advantage of the benefits of diversification and include other securities in your portfolio. But achieving efficient diversification in this context can be next to impossible, since you obviously cannot analyze every stock in the universe of securities and perform a full-blown portfolio optimization.

Chapters 19–21 deal in part with some important issues that arise in the context of active investment management. For example, how heavily should active managers plunge into stocks that they believe are mispriced? Is there a role for index funds even in the portfolios of active managers? How should the performance of active managers be evaluated?

Stock selection is not the only focus of active management, of course. Considerable effort also goes into asset allocation or market timing, and these activities also give rise to interesting questions. How valuable is the ability to time markets? How might one test whether a portfolio manager actually has the ability to time markets? More generally, how can one evaluate the performance of managers who engage in both market timing and security selection? You will find answers to all of these questions in the chapters that follow.

Chapter 19

PERFORMANCE EVALUATION

AFTER STUDYING THIS CHAPTER YOU SHOULD BE ABLE TO:

- Compute risk-adjusted rates of return, and use these rates to evaluate investment performance.

- Decompose excess returns into components attributable to asset allocation choices versus security selection choices.

- Assess the performance of portfolio managers.

In previous chapters, we derived predictions for expected return as a function of risk. In this chapter, we ask how we can evaluate the performance of a portfolio manager given the risk of his or her portfolio. Even measuring average portfolio returns is not as straightforward as it might seem. There also are difficulties in adjusting average returns for risk, which presents a host of other problems.

We begin with conventional approaches to risk adjustment. These use the risk measures developed in Part Two of the text to compare investment results. We show the problems with these approaches when you apply them in a real and complex world. Finally, we examine evaluation procedures used in the field. We show how overall investment results can be decomposed and attributed to the underlying asset allocation and security selection decisions of the portfolio manager.

19.1 RISK-ADJUSTED RETURNS

Comparison Groups

The major difficulty in portfolio performance evaluation is that average portfolio returns must be adjusted for risk before we can compare them meaningfully.

The fact that common stocks have offered higher average returns than Treasury bonds (as demonstrated in Table 19.1) does not prove that stocks are superior investment vehicles. One must consider the fact that stocks also have been more volatile investments. For the same reason, the fact that a mutual fund outperforms the S&P 500 over a long period is not necessarily evidence of superior stock selection ability. If the mutual fund has a higher beta

TABLE 19.1

Average Annual Returns
by Investment Class,
1926–1996

Source: Prepared from data in
Table 6.2

	Arithmetic Average	Geometric Average	Standard Deviation
Common stocks of small firms*	19.0	12.6	40.4
Common stocks of large firms	12.5	10.5	20.4
Long-term Treasury bonds	5.3	5.0	8.0
U.S. Treasury bills	3.8	3.7	3.3

*These are firms with relatively low market values of equity. Market capitalization is computed as price per share times shares outstanding.

than the index, it *should* outperform the index (on average) to compensate investors in the fund for the higher nondiversifiable risk they bear. Thus, performance evaluation must involve risk as well as return comparisons.

The simplest and most popular way to adjust returns for portfolio risk is to compare rates of return with those of other investment funds with similar risk characteristics. For example, high-yield bond portfolios are grouped into one "universe," growth stock equity funds are grouped into another universe, and so on. Then the average returns of each fund within the universe are ordered, and each portfolio manager receives a percentile ranking depending on relative performance within the **comparison universe,** the collection of funds to which performance is compared. For example, the manager with the ninth-best performance in a universe of 100 funds would be the 90th percentile manager: Her performance was better than 90% of all competing funds over the evaluation period.

comparison universe
The set of portfolio managers with similar investment styles that is used in assessing the relative performance of an individual portfolio manager.

These relative rankings usually are displayed in a chart like that shown in Figure 19.1. The chart summarizes performance rankings over four periods: one quarter, one year, three years, and five years. The top and bottom lines of each box are drawn at the rate of return of the 95th and 5th percentile managers. The three dotted lines correspond to the rates of return of the 75th, 50th (median), and 25th percentile managers. The diamond is drawn at the average return of a particular fund, the Markowill Group, and the square is drawn at the return of a benchmark index such as the S&P 500. This format provides an easy-to-read representation of the performance of the fund relative to the comparison universe.

FIGURE 19.1

Universe Comparison:
Periods Ending
December 31, 1997.

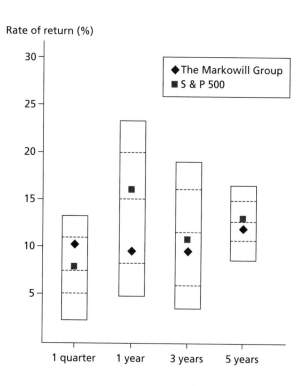

This comparison with other managers of similar investment groups is a useful first step in evaluating performance. Even so, such rankings can be misleading. Consider that within a particular universe some managers may concentrate on particular subgroups, so that portfolio characteristics are not truly comparable. For example, within the equity universe, one manager may concentrate on high beta stocks. Similarly, within fixed-income universes, interest rate risk can vary across managers. These considerations show that we need a more precise means for risk adjustment.

Risk Adjustments

Methods of risk-adjusted performance using mean-variance criteria developed simultaneously with the capital asset pricing model (CAPM). Jack Treynor (1966), William Sharpe (1966), and Michael Jensen (1969) were quick to recognize the implications of the CAPM for rating the performance of managers. Within a short time, academicians were in command of a battery of performance measures, and a bounty of scholarly investigation of mutual fund performance was pouring from the ivory tower. Soon after, agents emerged who were willing to supply rating services to portfolio managers eager for regular feedback. This trend has since lost some of its force.

One explanation for the lagging popularity of risk-adjusted performance measures is the generally negative cast of the resulting performance statistics. In nearly efficient markets, it is extremely difficult for analysts to perform well enough to overcome research and transaction costs. We saw in Chapter 9 that most professionally managed equity funds have generally underperformed the S&P 500 index on both risk-adjusted and raw return measures.

For now, however, we can catalogue some possible risk-adjusted performance measures and examine the circumstances in which each measure might be most relevant. To illustrate these measures, we will use a hypothetical portfolio for which monthly returns in the past five years resulted in the following statistics. We also present comparable data for the market portfolio for the same period.

	Portfolio	Market
Beta	0.8	1.0
Average return	16%	14%
Standard deviation	20%	24%

Finally, suppose the average return on risk-free assets during the five-year period was 6%.

Three risk-adjusted performance statistics are the Sharpe measure, the Treynor measure, and the Jensen measure. The Sharpe measure is presented as follows:

$$\frac{\bar{r}_p - \bar{r}_f}{\sigma_p}$$

Sharpe measure
Reward-to-volatility ratio; ratio of portfolio excess return to standard deviation.

The **Sharpe measure** divides average portfolio excess return over the sample period by the standard deviation of returns over that period. The numerator is the incremental return the portfolio earned in comparison with an alternative investment in the risk-free asset, and the denominator is the increment in portfolio volatility compared with the risk-free alternative. Therefore, the ratio measures the reward to (total) volatility trade-off. (The bars over r_p as well as r_f denote the fact that, because the risk-free rate may not be constant over the measurement period, we are taking a sample average of both.) Using our numbers, the Sharpe measure for the portfolio is $(16 - 6)/20 = 0.5$, while for the market it is $(14 - 6)/24 = 0.33$.

In contrast, the Treynor measure is given as follows:

$$\frac{\bar{r}_p - \bar{r}_f}{\beta_p}$$

Treynor measure
Ratio of portfolio excess return to beta.

Like Sharpe's, the **Treynor measure** gives average excess return per unit of risk incurred, but it uses systematic risk instead of total risk. The Treynor measure for the portfolio over this period is $(16 - 6)/0.8 = 12.5$, while for the market portfolio it is $(14 - 6)/1.0 = 8$.

In contrast to these two methods, the Jensen measure is as follows:

$$\alpha_p = \bar{r}_p - [\bar{r}_f + \beta_p(\bar{r}_M - \bar{r}_f)]$$

Jensen measure
The alpha of an investment.

The **Jensen measure** is the average return on the portfolio over and above that predicted by the CAPM, given the portfolio's beta and the average market return. The Jensen measure is the portfolio's alpha value. Using our numbers, the Jensen measure is $16 - [6 + 0.8(14 - 6)] = 3.6\%$.

Each measure has its own appeal. In this instance, all three measures are consistent in revealing that the portfolio outperformed the market benchmark on a risk-adjusted basis. However, this need not be the case. As the following Concept Check illustrates, the three measures do not necessarily provide consistent assessments of relative performance, as the risk measures used to adjust returns differ substantially.

Concept Check

1. Consider the following data for a particular sample period:

	Portfolio P	Market M
Average return	35%	28%
Beta	1.2	1.0
Standard deviation	42%	30%

Calculate the following performance measures for portfolio P and the market: Sharpe, Jensen (alpha), and Treynor. The T-bill rate during the period was 6%. By which measures did portfolio P outperform the market?

A variant of these risk-adjusted return measures has recently been introduced by Leah Modigliani of Morgan Stanley and her grandfather Franco Modigliani, past winner of the Nobel Prize for economics.[1] Their approach has been dubbed the M^2 measure (for Modigliani-squared). Like the Sharpe ratio, it focuses on total volatility as a measure of risk, but, like the Jensen measure, its risk-adjusted measure of performance has the easy interpretation of a differential return relative to the benchmark index. The nearby box (page 531) discusses the approach of the M^2 measure. Morgan Stanley reports that *Money* magazine has begun using the M^2 measure as a way to evaluate mutual fund performance.

Because different risk adjustment procedures can yield different implications for performance evaluation, it is essential that you choose the appropriate measure for the task. For example, suppose you are a pension fund manager who is selecting potential portfolio managers to oversee investment of the fund's assets. If you envision hiring one investment manager to manage all the fund's assets, then you must be concerned with the total variability of investment performance. Both the systematic and firm-specific risk remaining in the portfolio will affect total risk because the pension fund is not diversified across managers. The manager's portfolio will be the entire portfolio, with no further opportunities for diversification. In this case, the Sharpe measure is the appropriate basis on which to evaluate the portfolio manager. Because that manager is in charge of the entire portfolio, she must be attentive to diversification of firm-specific risk and should be judged on her achievement of excess return to *total* portfolio volatility.

In contrast, suppose your pension fund is large, and you envision hiring many managers, giving each a fraction of the total assets of the plan. You hope that hiring a set of managers,

---

[1]Franco Modigliani and Leah Modigliani, "Risk-Adjusted Performance," *Journal of Portfolio Management*, Winter 1997, pp. 45–54.

Top Funds: Where to Earn without Getting Burned

So your stock fund streaked to a market-beating 25% return over the past 12 months. Congratulations. But before you uncork the Korbel, ask yourself this: Just how much risk did you incur to achieve that lofty return?

"Total returns in the absolute are not too meaningful, since they don't tell you how far you stuck your neck out to get them," says noted financial planner Harold Evensky. To help investors identify which funds are rewarding them for the risks they take, Leah Modigliani, a U.S. equity strategist at Morgan Stanley, and her grandfather, Franco Modigliani, a Nobel-Prizewinning economist, have devised a new measure of risk-adjusted return that Morgan Stanley has labeled the Modigliani^2, or M^2.

First, we imagine that each fund's portfolio is mixed with a position in T-bills so that the complete or "adjusted" portfolio matches the volatility of a benchmark such as the S&P 500 or Russell 2000. For example, if the benchmark is the S&P 500, and the fund has 1.5 times the standard deviation of the index, the adjusted portfolio would be two-thirds invested in the managed portfolio and one-third invested in bills. The adjusted or M^2 portfolio would then have the same standard deviation as the index. If the managed portfolio had *lower* standard deviation than the index, it would be leveraged by borrowing money and investing the pro-

ceeds in the portfolio. "The goal is to put each fund on the same risk scale," says Leah Modigliani.

The "M^2 return" is the return on this adjusted portfolio. Because the M^2 portfolio has the same risk as its benchmark, the two portfolios can be compared on the basis of return alone. By comparing the M^2 return to the performance of the fund's benchmark, you can determine whether you have been rewarded for the risks it took.

The results can be enlightening. For example, AIM Constellation, an aggressive growth fund, posted a 16.6% total return during the past five years, topping the S&P 500's 15.2%. But because its raw returns varied so widely from quarter to quarter, Constellation's M^2 return equals a more modest 10.6%. By contrast, Fidelity Puritan, a staid balanced fund that gained only 14.8%, beat both Constellation and the S&P with a risk-adjusted return of 19.7%. "With this measure, investors can more easily see in real return figures how funds performed given the risk they took," says Leah Modigliani.

Source: Adapted from Penelope Wang and Derek Gordon, "Top Funds: Where to Earn without Getting Burned," *Money* 26, no. 3 (March 1997), pp. 49–52.

each with an investment specialty, will enhance returns. This means the pension plan effectively ends up with a portfolio of portfolio managers. Each manager can pursue his or her specialty without paying much attention to issues of diversification because the plan as a whole will have diversified returns across the several managed portfolios. With assets spread across many portfolio managers, the residual firm-specific risks of each portfolio become irrelevant because of diversification across portfolios. In this case, only nondiversifiable risk should matter. Such circumstances call for the use of a beta-based risk adjustment, and either the Treynor or Jensen measure would be appropriate.

To distinguish between the Treynor and Jensen measures, consider Table 19.2, which details the performance of two portfolios, P and Q, as well as the market portfolio. Portfolio P has the lower alpha, or Jensen's measure, but it also has the lower beta. Its excess risk-adjusted return per unit of systematic risk incurred is actually higher than that of portfolio Q. This is reflected in P's higher Treynor measure.

If we were to set a goal of a portfolio beta of 0.9 as an appropriate level of systematic risk, then portfolio P would be the better choice. Portfolio P offers an excess return of 11%, with a beta of 0.9. To achieve an overall beta of 0.9 using portfolio Q (which has a beta of 1.60), we would need to mix the portfolio with Treasury bills. Weights of $7/16$ in bills and $9/16$ in portfolio Q would result in an overall beta of 0.9 but would reduce excess return to $9/16 \times 19\% = 10^{11}/_{16}\%$, which is less than portfolio P's excess return.

Figure 19.2 illustrates these differences. Although Q has the higher alpha, the line from the origin to Q, which represents the achievable combinations of excess return and beta, lies *below* portfolio P's line, meaning it offers less attractive opportunities.

TABLE 19.2

Portfolio Performance

	Portfolio P	Portfolio Q	Market
Beta	0.90	1.60	1.0
Excess return, $r - r_f$	11%	19%	10%
Alpha*	2%	3%	0
Treynor measure	12.2	11.9	10

*Alpha = Excess return − (Beta × Market excess return)
= $(r - r_f) - \beta(r_M - r_f)$
= $r - [r_f + \beta(r_M - r_f)]$

The Treynor measure tells us the ratio of excess return earned per unit of systematic risk incurred. As our comparison of portfolios P and Q suggests, Treynor would argue that it is appropriate to measure performance as excess return divided by beta because we would want to standardize all portfolios to an appropriate level of systematic risk before choosing among them. Because the ratio of excess return to beta is the slope of the line from the origin to points P or Q in Figure 19.2, the portfolio with the higher Treynor measure will be the one with the steeper line in the figure.

It is important to use the performance measure that fits the relevant scenario. Evaluating portfolios by different performance measures may yield quite different results.

It is clear that we must adjust portfolio returns for risk before evaluating performance. The nearby box (page 533) shows how important such adjustments can be. It reports on the results of a series of investment "contests" between investment professionals and randomly chosen stocks (the dartboard portfolio) sponsored by *The Wall Street Journal*. While the professionals have tended to win the contest, the box shows that risk-adjustment nearly wipes out the differential.

Risk Adjustments with Changing Portfolio Composition

One potential problem with risk-adjustment techniques is that they all assume that portfolio risk, whether it is measured by standard deviation or beta, is constant over the relevant time period. This isn't necessarily so. If a manager attempts to increase portfolio beta when she thinks the market is about to go up and to decrease beta when she is pessimistic, both the standard deviation and the beta of the portfolio will change over time, by design. This can wreak havoc with our performance measures.

FIGURE 19.2

Treynor Measure

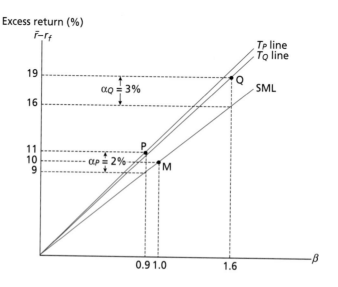

Luck or Logic? Debate Rages on Over "Efficient-Market" Theory

For just over five years now, the Investment Dartboard column has pitted investment pros against the forces of chance, in the form of darts heaved at the stock listings. One aim has been to provide a lighthearted test of the "efficient-market theory."

The theory, hated on Wall Street but accepted by many academics, states that stock-picking success is basically a "random walk," or a matter of luck. The notion is that, since all publicly known information is instantaneously factored into stock prices, an uninformed person—or a chimp throwing darts—can do as well as a knowledgeable professional.

Theorists allow for a couple of exceptions. People who possess nonpublic "inside information" can beat the market, they say. Some efficient-market theorists also say people who pick riskier, more volatile stocks can beat the market. Such stocks exaggerate the overall market's up and down moves. In the average year, most stocks have more ups than downs, so the odds are with the risk-taker. Another way of looking at it is that investors demand to be compensated for the extra risk of holding a volatile stock.

Five years of Investment Dartboard columns have simply thrown gasoline on the flames of the debate. There's fuel for both sides of the argument.

On the surface, the results clearly favor the professionals and go against the theory. Since the contest adopted its current rules in 1990, the pros have won 24 times, the darts 17 times. The average six-month gain for the pros, 8.4%, has been much better than the 3.3% gain achieved by the darts. (Those figures are price changes only, without dividends.)

But Burton Malkiel, an economics professor at Princeton University and a leading exponent of the efficient-market theory, says there's less than meets the eye in the pros' apparent success in the contest.

According to Professor Malkiel, the pros' favorable showing can be explained by two factors. First, they are picking riskier, more volatile, stocks than the darts are. Second, they benefit from a favorable publicity effect on the day the article is published.

With Professor Malkiel, Gilbert E. Metcalf, an assistant professor of economics at Princeton, recently wrote a paper analyzing the Dartboard contests from 1990 through 1992. The professors found that the pros' picks were about 40% more volatile—and therefore riskier—than the overall market. The dart stocks were only about 6% more volatile than the market.

In other words, the pros' selections tend to move up or down 14% for every 10% the overall market moves. Once you adjust for risk, the researchers say, the pros' margin shrinks to 0.4%, which is not statistically significant.

But that's not all. The researchers say the pros are riding the coattails of a strong "announcement effect" that causes the pros' picks to surge on the day they appear in this newspaper. Take away the announcement effect, they say, and the pros' superiority vanishes altogether.

In the contest, the starting price is the price at 4 PM Eastern time the day before the article appears. But Messrs. Metcalf and Malkiel found that if results were measured from 4 PM on the day the article appears, the pros' average gain in 1990–1992 would have been nearly a percentage point behind that of the darts.

Partisans of the pros would reply that starting the clock at 4 PM on publication day would unfairly penalize the pros. Their buy recommendations would have an artificially high starting point, having already been pushed up by several hours of column-inspired trading. Also, the six-month contest period allows plenty of time for the pros' picks to come back to earth.

So, the great debate remains unsettled. Which, of course, allows the fun to continue. Professor Malkiel, incidentally, was the honorary thrower of the first dart in the Investment Dartboard column, back in October 1988.

FIGURE 19.3
Portfolio Returns

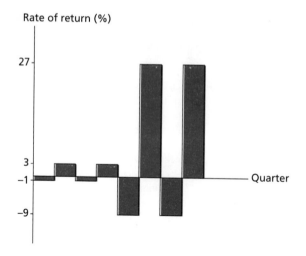

Rate of return (%)

EXAMPLE 19.1
Risk
Measurement
with Changing
Portfolio
Composition

Suppose the Sharpe measure of the passive strategy (investing in a market index fund) is 0.4. A portfolio manager is in search of a better, active strategy. Over an initial period of, say, 52 weeks, he executes a low-risk or defensive strategy with an annualized mean excess return of 1% and a standard deviation of 2%. This makes for a Sharpe measure of 0.5, which beats the passive strategy.

Over the next period of another 52 weeks, this manager finds that a high-risk strategy is optimal, with an annual mean excess return of 9% and standard deviation of 18%. Here again the Sharpe measure is 0.5. Over the two years, our manager maintains a better-than-passive Sharpe measure.

Figure 19.3 shows a pattern of (annualized) quarterly returns that is consistent with our description of the manager's strategy over two years. In the first four quarters, the excess returns are −1%, 3%, −1%, and 3%, making for an average of 1% and standard deviation of 2%. In the next four quarters, the returns are −9%, 27%, −9%, and 27%, making for an average of 9% and standard deviation of 18%. Thus, *each* year undoubtedly exhibits a Sharpe measure of 0.5.

But if we take the eight-quarter sequence as a single measurement period, instead of two independent periods, and measure the portfolio's mean and standard deviation over that full period, we get an average excess return of 5% and standard deviation of 13.42%, resulting in a Sharpe measure of only 0.37, apparently inferior to the passive strategy!

What happened? Sharpe's measure does not recognize the shift in the mean from the first four quarters to the next as a result of a strategy change. Instead, the difference in mean returns in the two years adds to the *appearance* of volatility in portfolio returns. The change in mean returns across time periods contributed to the variability of returns over the same period. But in this case, variability per se should not be interpreted as volatility or riskiness in returns. Part of the variability in returns is due to intentional choices that shift the expected or mean return. This part should not be ascribed to uncertainty in returns. Unfortunately, an outside observer might not realize that policy changes within the sample period are the source of some of the return variability. Therefore, the active strategy with shifting means appears riskier than it really is, which biases the estimate of the Sharpe measure downward.

For actively managed portfolios, therefore, it is crucial to keep track of portfolio composition and changes in portfolio mean return and risk. We will see another example of this problem when we talk about market timing.

19.2 MARKET TIMING

In its pure form, market timing involves shifting funds between a market index portfolio and a safe asset, such as T-bills or a money market fund, depending on whether the market as a whole is expected to outperform the safe asset. In practice, most managers do not shift fully

FIGURE 19.4

Characteristic Lines A:
No Market Timing,
Beta Is Constant
B: Market Timing, Beta
Increases with
Expected Market
Excess Return

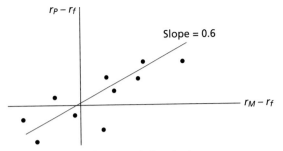

A. No Market Timing, Beta Is Constant

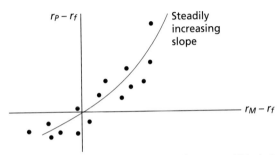

B. Market Timing, Beta Increases with Expected Market
Excess Return

between bills and the market. How might we measure partial shifts into the market when it is expected to perform well?

To simplify, suppose the investor holds only the market index portfolio and T-bills. If the weight on the market were constant, say 0.6, then the portfolio beta would also be constant, and the portfolio characteristic line would plot as a straight line with a slope 0.6, as in Figure 19.4A. If, however, the investor could correctly time the market and shift funds into it in periods when the market does well, the characteristic line would plot as in Figure 19.4B. The idea is that if the timer can predict bull and bear markets, more will be shifted into the market when the market is about to go up. The portfolio beta and the slope of the characteristic line will be higher when r_M is higher, resulting in the curved line that appears in 19.4B.

Treynor and Mazuy (1966) tested to see whether portfolio betas did in fact increase prior to market advances, but they found little evidence of timing ability. A similar test was implemented by Henriksson (1984). His examination of market timing ability for 116 funds in 1968–1980 found that, on average, portfolio betas actually *fell* slightly during the market advances, although in most cases the response of portfolio beta to the market was not statistically significant. Eleven funds had statistically positive values of market timing, while eight had significantly negative values. Overall, 62% of the funds had negative point estimates of timing ability.

In sum, empirical tests show little evidence of market timing ability. Perhaps this should be expected; given the tremendous values to be reaped by a successful market timer, it would be surprising to uncover clear-cut evidence of such skills in nearly efficient markets.

19.3 PERFORMANCE ATTRIBUTION PROCEDURES

Rather than focus on risk-adjusted returns, practitioners often want simply to ascertain which decisions resulted in superior or inferior performance. Superior investment performance depends on an ability to be in the "right" securities at the right time. Such timing and selection ability may be considered broadly, such as being in equities as opposed to fixed-income securities when the stock market is performing well. Or it may be defined at a more detailed level, such as choosing the relatively better-performing stocks within a particular industry.

Portfolio managers constantly make both broad-brush asset market allocation decisions as well as more detailed sector and security allocation decisions within markets. Performance attribution studies attempt to decompose overall performance into discrete components that may be identified with a particular level of the portfolio selection process.

Attribution analysis starts from the broadest asset allocation choices and progressively focuses on ever-finer details of portfolio choice. The difference between a managed portfolio's performance and that of a benchmark portfolio then may be expressed as the sum of the contributions to performance of a series of decisions made at the various levels of the portfolio construction process. For example, one common attribution system decomposes performance into three components: (1) broad asset market allocation choices *across* equity, fixed-income, and money markets; (2) industry (sector) choice *within* each market; and (3) security choice within each sector.

To illustrate this method, consider the attribution results for a hypothetical portfolio. The portfolio invests in stocks, bonds, and money market securities. An attribution analysis appears in Tables 19.3 through 19.6. The portfolio return over the month is 5.34%.

The first step is to establish a benchmark level of performance against which performance ought to be compared. This benchmark is called the **bogey.** It is designed to measure the returns the portfolio manager would earn if she were to follow a completely passive strategy. "Passive" in this context has two attributes. First, it means the allocation of funds across broad asset classes is set in accord with a notion of "usual" or neutral allocation across sectors. This would be considered a passive asset market allocation. Second, it means that, within each asset class, the portfolio manager holds an indexed portfolio, for example, the S&P 500 index for the equity sector. The passive strategy used as a performance benchmark rules out both asset allocation and security selection decisions. Any departure of the manager's return from the passive benchmark must be due to either asset allocation bets (departures from the neutral allocation across markets) or security selection bets (departures from the passive index within asset classes).

While we've already discussed in earlier chapters the justification for indexing within sectors, it is worth briefly explaining the determination of the neutral allocation of funds across the broad asset classes. Weights that are designated as "neutral" will depend on the risk tolerance of the investor and must be determined in consultation with the client. For example, risk-tolerant clients may place a large fraction of their portfolio in the equity market, perhaps directing the fund manager to set neutral weights of 75% equity, 15% bonds, and 10% cash equivalents. Any deviation from these weights must be justified by a belief that one or another market will either over- or underperform its usual risk-return profile. In contrast, more risk-averse clients may set neutral weights of 45%/35%/20% for the three markets. Therefore, their portfolios in normal circumstances will be exposed to less risk than that of the risk-tolerant client. Only intentional bets on market performance will result in departures from this profile.

In Table 19.3, the neutral weights have been set at 60% equity, 30% fixed-income, and 10% cash equivalents (money market securities). The bogey portfolio, comprised of investments in each index with the 60/30/10 weights, returned 3.97%. The managed portfolio's measure of performance is positive and equal to its actual return less the return of the bogey: 5.34 − 3.97 = 1.37%. The next step is to allocate the 1.37% excess return to the separate decisions that contributed to it.

Asset Allocation Decisions

The managed portfolio is actually invested in the equity, fixed-income, and money markets with weights of 70%, 7%, and 23%, respectively. The portfolio's performance could be due to the departure of this weighting scheme from the benchmark 60/30/10 weights and/or to superior or inferior results *within* each of the three broad markets.

TABLE 19.3
Performance of the
Managed Portfolio

	Bogey Performance and Excess Return	
Component	**Benchmark Weight**	**Return of Index during Month (%)**
Equity (S&P 500)	0.60	5.81
Bonds (Lehman Bros. Index)	0.30	1.45
Cash (money market)	0.10	0.48
Bogey = (0.60 × 5.81) + (0.30 × 1.45) + (0.10 × 0.48) = 3.97%		
Return of managed portfolio		5.34%
− Return of bogey portfolio		3.97
Excess return of managed portfolio		1.37%

TABLE 19.4
Performance
Attribution

	A. Contribution of Asset Allocation to Performance				
Market	**(1) Actual Weight in Market**	**(2) Benchmark Weight in Market**	**(3) Excess Weight**	**(4) Market Return Minus Bogey (%)**	**(5) = (3) × (4) Contribution to Performance (%)**
Equity	0.70	0.60	0.10	1.84	0.1840
Fixed-income	0.07	0.30	−0.23	−2.52	0.5796
Cash	0.23	0.10	0.13	−3.49	−0.4537
Contribution of asset allocation					0.3099

	B. Contribution of Selection to Total Performance				
Market	**(1) Portfolio Performance (%)**	**(2) Index Performance (%)**	**(3) Excess Performance (%)**	**(4) Portfolio Weight**	**(5) = (3) × (4) Contribution (%)**
Equity	7.28	5.81	1.47	0.70	1.03
Fixed-income	1.89	1.45	0.44	0.07	0.03
Contribution of selection within markets					1.06

To isolate the effect of the manager's asset allocation choice, we measure the performance of a hypothetical portfolio that would have been invested in the indexes for each market with weights 70/7/23. This return measures the effect of the shift away from the benchmark 60/30/10 weights without allowing for any effects attributable to active management of the securities selected within each market.

Superior performance relative to the bogey is achieved by overweighting investments in markets that turn out to perform better than the bogey and by underweighting those in poorly performing markets. The contribution of asset allocation to superior performance equals the sum over all markets of the excess weight in each market times the return of the market index in excess of the bogey.

Table 19.4A demonstrates that asset allocation contributed 31 basis points to the portfolio's overall excess return of 137 basis points. The major factor contributing to superior performance in this month is the heavy weighting of the equity market in a month when the equity market has an excellent return of 5.81%.

Sector and Security Selection Decisions

If 0.31% of the excess performance can be attributed to advantageous asset allocation across markets, the remaining 1.06% then must be attributable to sector selection and security selection within each market. Table 19.4B details the contribution of the managed portfolio's sector and security selection to total performance.

Panel B shows that the equity component of the managed portfolio has a return of 7.28% versus a return of 5.81% for the S&P 500. The fixed-income return is 1.89% versus 1.45%

TABLE 19.5   Sector Selection within the Equity Market

Sector	(1) (2) Beginning of Month Weights (%)		(3) Difference in Weights	(4) Sector Return	(5) Sector Over/Under Performance*	(6) = (3) × (5) Sector Allocation Contribution (basis points)
	Portfolio	S&P 500				
Basic materials	1.96	8.3	−6.34	6.4	0.9	−5.7
Business services	7.84	4.1	3.74	6.5	1.0	3.7
Capital goods	1.87	7.8	−5.93	3.7	−1.8	10.7
Consumer cyclical	8.47	12.5	−4.03	8.4	2.9	−11.7
Consumer noncyclical	40.37	20.4	19.97	9.4	3.9	77.9
Credit sensitive	24.01	21.8	2.21	4.6	0.9	2.0
Energy	13.53	14.2	−0.67	2.1	−3.4	2.3
Technology	1.95	10.9	−8.95	−0.1	−5.6	50.1
Total						129.3

*S&P 500 performance net of dividends was 5.5%. Returns were compared net of dividends.

TABLE 19.6

Portfolio Attribution: Summary

		Contribution (Basis Points)
1. Asset allocation		31.0
2. Selection		
a. Equity excess return		
i. Sector allocation	129	
ii. Security allocation	18	
	147 × 0.70 (portfolio weight) =	102.9
b. Fixed-income excess return	44 × 0.07 (portfolio weight) =	3.1
Total excess return of portfolio		137.0

for the Lehman Brothers Index. The superior performance in both equity and fixed-income markets weighted by the portfolio proportions invested in each market sums to the 1.06% contribution to performance attributable to sector and security selection.

Table 19.5 documents the sources of the equity market performance by each sector within the market. The first three columns detail the allocation of funds within the equity market compared to their representation in the S&P 500. Column (4) shows the rate of return of each sector, and column (5) documents the performance of each sector relative to the return of the S&P 500. The contribution of each sector's allocation presented in column (6) equals the product of the difference in the sector weight and the sector's relative performance.

Note that good performance (a positive contribution) derives from overweighting well-performing sectors such as consumer nondurables, as well as underweighting poorly performing sectors such as capital goods. The excess return of the equity component of the portfolio attributable to sector allocation alone is 129 basis poinits, or 1.29%. As the equity component of the portfolio outperformed the S&P 500 by 1.47%, we conclude that the effect of security selection within sectors must have contributed an additional 1.47 − 1.29, or 0.18%, to the performance of the equity component of the portfolio.

A similar sector analysis can be applied to the fixed-income portion of the portfolio, but we do not show those results here.

Summing Up Component Contributions

In this particular month, all facets of the portfolio selection process were successful. Table 19.6 details the contribution of each aspect of performance. Asset allocation across the major security markets contributes 31 basis points. Sector and security allocation within those markets contributes 106 basis points, for total excess portfolio performance of 137 basis points.

The sector and security allocation of 106 basis points can be partitioned further. Sector allocation within the equity market results in excess performance of 129.3 basis points, and security selection within sectors contributes 18 basis points. (The total equity excess performance of 147 basis points is multiplied by the 70% weight in equity to obtain contribution to portfolio performance.) Similar partitioning could be done for the fixed-income sector.

Concept Check

2. *a.* Suppose the benchmark weights had been set at 70% equity, 25% fixed-income, and 5% cash equivalents. What then would be the contributions of the manager's asset allocation choices?

   b. Suppose the S&P 500 return had been 5%. Recompute the contribution of the manager's security selection choices.

Summary

- The appropriate performance measure depends on the role to be evaluated. The Sharpe measure is most appropriate when the portfolio represents the entire investment fund. The Treynor measure or Jensen measure is appropriate when the portfolio is to be mixed with several other assets, allowing for diversification of firm-specific risk outside of the portfolio.
- The shifting mean and variance of actively managed portfolios make it even harder to assess performance. A typical example is the attempt of portfolio managers to time the market, resulting in ever-changing portfolio betas and standard deviations.
- Common attribution procedures partition performance improvements to asset allocation, sector selection, and security selection. Performance is assessed by calculating departures of portfolio composition from a benchmark or neutral portfolio.

Key Terms

bogey, *536*
comparison universe, *528*

Jensen measure, *530*
Sharpe measure, *529*

Treynor measure, *530*

Problem Sets

Questions 1–3 appeared in past CFA examinations.

1. A plan sponsor with a portfolio manager who invests in small-capitalization, high-growth stocks should have the plan sponsor's performance measured against which *one* of the following?

   a. S&P 500 index.
   b. Wilshire 5000 index.
   c. Dow Jones Industrial Average.
   d. S&P 400 index.

2. Assume you purchased a rental property for $50,000 and sold it one year later for $55,000 (there was no mortgage on the property). At the time of the sale, you paid $2,000 in commissions and $600 in taxes. If you received $6,000 in rental income (all of it received at the end of the year), what annual rate of return did you earn?

   a. 15.3%
   b. 15.9%
   c. 16.8%
   d. 17.1%

3. A two-year investment of $2,000 results in a return of $150 at the end of the first year and a return of $150 at the end of the second year, in addition to the return of the original investment. The internal rate of return on the investment is:

   a. 6.4%
   b. 7.5%
   c. 15.0%
   d. None of the above

4. Based on current dividend yields and expected capital gains, the expected rates of return on portfolios A and B are 11% and 14%, respectively. The beta of A is 0.8 while that of B is 1.5. The T-bill rate is currently 6%, while the expected rate of return of the S&P 500 index is 12%. The standard deviation of portfolio A is 10% annually, while that of B is 31%, and that of the index is 20%.

   a. If you currently hold a market index portfolio, would you choose to add either of these portfolios to your holdings? Explain.

   b. If instead you could invest *only* in bills and *one* of these portfolios, which would you choose?

5. Evaluate the timing and selection abilities of four managers whose performances are plotted in the following four scatter diagrams.

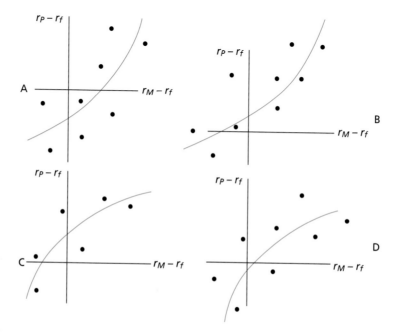

6. Consider the following information regarding the performance of a money manager in a recent month. The table presents the actual return of each sector of the manager's portfolio in column (1), the fraction of the portfolio allocated to each sector in column (2), the benchmark or neutral sector allocations in column (3), and the returns of sector indexes in column (4).

	(1) Actual Return	(2) Actual Weight	(3) Benchmark Weight	(4) Index Return
Equity	2.0%	0.70	0.60	2.5% (S&P 500)
Bonds	1.0	0.20	0.30	1.2 (Salomon Brothers Index)
Cash	0.5	0.10	0.10	0.5

   a. What was the manager's return in the month? What was her over- or underperformance?

   b. What was the contribution of security selection to relative performance?

   c. What was the contribution of asset allocation to relative performance? Confirm that the sum of selection and allocation contributions equals her total "excess" return relative to the bogey.

7. Conventional wisdom says one should measure a manager's investment performance over an entire market cycle. What arguments support this contention? What arguments contradict it?

8. Does the use of universes of managers with similar investment styles to evaluate relative investment performance overcome the statistical problems associated with instability of beta or total variability?

9. During a particular year, the T-bill rate was 6%, the market return was 14%, and a portfolio manager with beta of 0.5 realized a return of 10%. Evaluate the manager based on the portfolio alpha.

10. The chairman provides you with the following data, covering one year, concerning the portfolios of two of the fund's equity managers (firm *A* and firm *B*). Although the portfolios consist primarily of common stocks, cash reserves are included in the calculation of both portfolio betas and performance. By way of perspective, selected data for the financial markets are included in the following table.

	Total Return	Beta
Firm *A*	24.0%	1.0
Firm *B*	30.0	1.5
S&P 500	21.0	
Lehman Bond Index	31.0	
91-day Treasury bills	12.0	

a. Calculate and compare the risk-adjusted performance of the two firms relative to each other and to the S&P 500.

b. Explain *two* reasons the conclusions drawn from this calculation may be misleading.

11. Carl Karl, a portfolio manager for the Alpine Trust Company, has been responsible since 1985 for the City of Alpine's Employee Retirement Plan, a municipal pension fund. Alpine is a growing community, and city services and employee payrolls have expanded in each of the past 10 years. Contributions to the plan in fiscal 1990 exceeded benefit payments by a three-to-one ratio.

The plan's Board of Trustees directed Karl five years ago to invest for total return over the long term. However, as trustees of this highly visible public fund, they cautioned him that volatile or erratic results could cause them embarrassment. They also noted a state statute that mandated that not more than 25% of the plan's assets (at cost) be invested in common stocks.

At the annual meeting of the trustees in November 1990, Karl presented the following portfolio and performance report to the Board.

Alpine Employee Retirement Plan

Asset Mix as of 9/30/90	At Cost (Millions)		At Market (Millions)	
Fixed-income assets:				
Short-term securities	$ 4.5	11.0%	$ 4.5	11.4%
Long-term bonds and mortgages	26.5	64.7	23.5	59.5
Common stocks	10.0	24.3	11.5	29.1
	$41.0	100.0%	$39.5	100.0%

Investment Performance

	Annual Rates of Return for Periods Ending 9/30/90	
	5 Years	1 Year
Total Alpine Fund:		
Time-weighted	8.2%	5.2%
Dollar-weighted (Internal)	7.7%	4.8%
Assumed actuarial return	6.0%	6.0%
U. S. Treasury bills	7.5%	11.3%
Large sample of pension funds (average 60% equities, 40% fixed income)	10.1%	14.3%
Common stocks—Alpine Fund	13.3%	14.3%
Average portfolio beta coefficient	0.90	0.89
Standard & Poor's 500 stock index	13.8%	21.1%
Fixed-income securities—Alpine Fund	6.7%	1.0%
Salomon Brothers' Bond Index	4.0%	−11.4%

Karl was proud of his performance and was chagrined when a trustee made the following critical observations:

a. "Our one-year results were terrible, and it's what you've done for us lately that counts most."

b. "Our total fund performance was clearly inferior compared to the large sample of other pension funds for the last five years. What else could this reflect except poor management judgment?"

c. "Our common stock performance was especially poor for the five-year period."

d. "Why bother to compare your returns to the return from Treasury bills and the actuarial assumption rate? What your competition could have earned for us or how we would have fared if invested in a passive index (which doesn't charge a fee) are the only relevant measures of performance."

e. "Who cares about time-weighted return? If it can't pay pensions, what good is it!"

Appraise the merits of each of these statements and give counter arguments that Mr. Karl can use.

◼IEM Applications

1. Have you tried active portfolio management with your IEM portfolio in the form of market timing? Have you tried security selection? How have you done this and why?

2. How is your IEM portfolio doing relative to the risks you have undertaken?

Solutions to Concept Checks

1. Sharpe: $(\bar{r} - \bar{r}_f)/\sigma$

   $S_P = (35 - 6)/42 = 0.69$

   $S_M = (28 - 6)/30 = 0.733$

   Jensen: $\bar{r} - [\bar{r}_f + \beta(\bar{r}_M - \bar{r}_f)]$

   $\alpha_P = 35 - [6 + 1.2(28 - 6)] = 2.6\%$

   $\alpha_M = 0$

   Treynor: $(\bar{r} - \bar{r}_f)/\beta$

   $T_P = (35 - 6)/1.2 = 24.2$

   $T_M = (28 - 6)/1.0 = 22$

2. Performance Attribution

   First compute the new bogey performance as

   $(0.70 \times 5.81) + (0.25 \times 1.45) + (0.05 \times 0.48) = 4.45\%$

a. Contribution of Asset Allocation to Performance

Market	(1) Actual Weight in Market	(2) Benchmark Weight in Market	(3) Excess Weight	(4) Market Return Minus Bogey (%)	(5) = (3) × (4) Contribution to Performance (%)
Equity	0.70	0.70	0.00	1.36	0.00
Fixed-income	0.07	0.25	−0.18	−3.00	0.54
Cash	0.23	0.05	0.18	−3.97	−0.71
Contribution of asset allocation					−0.17

b. Contribution of Selection to Total Performance

Market	(1) Portfolio Performance (%)	(2) Index Performance (%)	(3) Excess Performance (%)	(4) Portfolio Weight	(5) = (3) × (4) Contribution (%)
Equity	7.28	5.00	2.28	0.70	1.60
Fixed-income	1.89	1.45	0.44	0.07	0.03
Contribution of selection within markets					1.63

Chapter 20

INTERNATIONAL DIVERSIFICATION

AFTER STUDYING THIS CHAPTER YOU SHOULD BE ABLE TO:

- Demonstrate the advantages of international diversification.

- Formulate hedge strategies to offset the currency risk involved in international investments.

- Decompose investment returns into contributing factors such as country, currency, and stock selection.

- Show why investments in precious metals and real estate have been useful additions to traditional portfolios in the last two decades.

- Assess the advantages and disadvantages of adding nontraditional assets such as art or rare coins to portfolios comprised of more traditional investment vehicles.

Although we in the United States customarily treat the S&P 500 as the market index portfolio, this practice is increasingly inappropriate. Equities represent less than 25% of total U.S. wealth and a much smaller proportion than that of world wealth. In this chapter, we look beyond domestic markets to survey issues of extended diversification.

In one sense, international investing may be viewed as no more than a straightforward generalization of our earlier treatment of portfolio selection with a larger menu of assets from which to construct a portfolio. One faces similar issues of diversification, security analysis, security selection, and asset allocation. On the other hand, international investments pose some problems not encountered in domestic markets. Among these are the presence of exchange rate risk, restrictions on capital flows across national boundaries, an added dimension of political risk and country-specific regulations, and differing accounting practices in different countries.

We begin by demonstrating that international diversification can improve portfolio performance. Next, we examine exchange rate risk and how such risk can be mitigated using foreign exchange futures and forward contracts. We look at investment strategies in an international context and show how performance attribution studies may be adapted to an international setting. Finally, in an appendix, we expand on the theme of extended diversification by showing that "nontraditional" asset groups such as real estate and precious metals can play important roles in investor portfolios.

20.1 INTERNATIONAL INVESTMENTS

The World Market Portfolio

world investable wealth
The part of world wealth that is traded and therefore accessible to investors.

To appreciate the myopia of an exclusive investment focus on U.S. stocks and bonds, consider in Figure 20.1 the components of **world investable wealth**. The pie chart shows the investable part of world wealth, that is, the part of world wealth that is traded and is accessible to investors. According to these estimates, U.S. equity makes up less than 20% of the world portfolio, while U.S. stocks and bonds together comprise less than 35% of the world capital market. The figure excludes direct investment in durables and foreign real estate.

Figure 20.2 shows another view of the relative share of the U.S. in the world economy. Here, the breakdown is by gross domestic product rather than the size of the capital market, but the message is the same: The United States does not comprise the majority of the world economy. International diversification is worth exploring.

This is clear evidence that "traditional" U.S. assets—stocks, bonds, and bills—are but a small fraction of the potential universe of investments. If you confine a portfolio exclusively to U.S. asset classes, clearly you will pass up important opportunities for diversification.

FIGURE 20.1
Wealth of the World, 1993

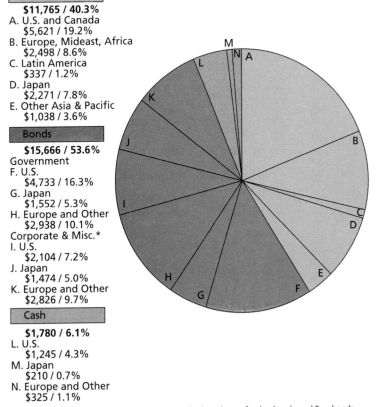

All values are in billions of U.S. dollars

Equity
$11,765 / 40.3%
A. U.S. and Canada
  $5,621 / 19.2%
B. Europe, Mideast, Africa
  $2,498 / 8.6%
C. Latin America
  $337 / 1.2%
D. Japan
  $2,271 / 7.8%
E. Other Asia & Pacific
  $1,038 / 3.6%

Bonds
$15,666 / 53.6%
Government
F. U.S.
  $4,733 / 16.3%
G. Japan
  $1,552 / 5.3%
H. Europe and Other
  $2,938 / 10.1%
Corporate & Misc.*
I. U.S.
  $2,104 / 7.2%
J. Japan
  $1,474 / 5.0%
K. Europe and Other
  $2,826 / 9.7%

Cash
$1,780 / 6.1%
L. U.S.
  $1,245 / 4.3%
M. Japan
  $210 / 0.7%
N. Europe and Other
  $325 / 1.1%

*Miscellaneous bonds include domestic public and private issues, foreign bonds, and Eurobonds.

FIGURE 20.2

Estimates of the Gross Domestic Product of Major Economies, 1993 (Data in Billions of Dollars)

Source: *Global Outlook*, March 1993.

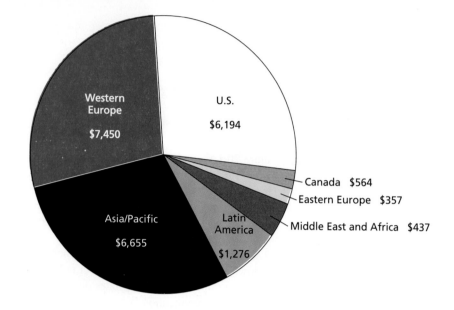

International Diversification

Table 20.1 presents some evidence on the risk and return characteristics of stock and bond investments in various countries. The first pair of columns are average returns in both local currencies as well as dollars, and the second pair are standard deviations of returns in both local currencies and dollars. The data show that the risk-return profiles across countries are reasonably similar. However, because returns across countries are only imperfectly correlated, there are great opportunities for gains from diversification internationally.

From the discussion of diversification in Chapter 7, you know that adding to a portfolio assets that are not perfectly correlated will enhance the reward-to-volatility ratio. Increasing globalization lets us take advantage of foreign securities as a feasible way to extend diversification.

The evidence in Figure 20.3 is clear. The figure presents the standard deviation of equally weighted portfolios of various sizes as a percent of the average standard deviation of a one-

TABLE 20.1

Average Annualized Risk and Return from International Stocks and Bonds, 1980–1993

Source: Roger G. Clarke and Mark P. Kritzman, *Currency Management: Concepts and Practices*, Charlottesville, VA, Research Foundation of the Institute of Chartered Financial Analysts, 1996.

Asset/Country	Average Returns		Standard Deviations	
	Asset Return (Local currency)	Asset Return (in U.S. dollars)	Asset Risk (Local currency)	Asset Risk ($ returns)
Stocks				
United States	15.7%	na	21.1%	na
United Kingdom	20.4	18.3%	21.9	23.5%
Germany	20.9	21.7	23.4	25.0
France	19.2	17.2	25.2	26.6
Japan	11.1	17.3	23.7	26.6
Australia	17.8	14.8	24.9	27.6
Canada	11.3	10.5	22.1	23.4
Bonds				
United States	12.6%	na	19.0%	na
United Kingdom	15.5	13.4%	17.1	22.4%
Germany	12.9	13.7	13.2	21.2
France	13.2	11.1	13.7	20.0
Japan	9.4	15.6	13.8	21.4
Australia	21.3	18.4	16.8	21.6
Canada	13.0	12.2	17.3	19.2

Note: Data represent the perspective of a U.S.-based investor.

FIGURE 20.3

International
Diversification

Source: Modified from B.
Solnik, "Lessons for Internal
Asset Allocation," *Financial
Analysis Journal,* July–August,
1994.

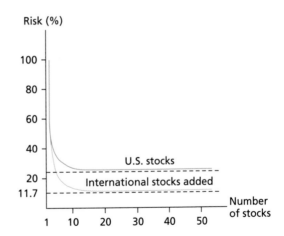

stock portfolio. That is, a value of 20 means the diversified portfolio has only 20% the standard deviation of a typical stock.

There is a marked reduction in risk for a portfolio that includes foreign as well as U.S. stocks, so rational investors should invest across borders. Adding international to national investments enhances the power of portfolio diversification.

Table 20.2 presents results from a study of stock and bond returns showing that although the correlation coefficients between the U.S. stock index and stock and bond index portfolios of other large industrialized economies are typically positive, they are much smaller than 1.0. Most correlations are below 0.5. In contrast, correlation coefficients between diversified U.S. portfolios, say, with 40 to 50 securities, typically exceed 0.9. This imperfect correlation across national boundaries allows for the improvement in diversification potential that shows up in Figure 20.3.

Concept Check

1. What would Figure 20.3 look like if we allowed the possibility of diversifying into real estate investments in addition to foreign equity?

TABLE 20.2 Correlations of Unhedged Asset Returns, 1980–1993

Asset/Country	Stocks							Bonds						
	U.S.	Ger.	U.K.	Jap.	Aus.	Can.	Fra.	U.S.	Ger.	U.K.	Jap.	Aus.	Can.	Fra.
Stocks														
United States	1.00													
Germany	0.37	1.00												
United Kingdom	0.53	0.47	1.00											
Japan	0.26	0.36	0.43	1.00										
Australia	0.43	0.29	0.50	0.26	1.00									
Canada	0.73	0.36	0.54	0.29	0.56	1.00								
France	0.44	0.63	0.51	0.42	0.34	0.39	1.00							
Bonds														
United States	0.35	0.28	0.17	0.15	0.00	0.27	0.19	1.00						
Germany	0.08	0.56	0.30	0.35	0.05	0.13	0.46	0.40	1.00					
United Kingdom	0.13	0.34	0.61	0.36	0.19	0.27	0.33	0.34	0.60	1.00				
Japan	0.03	0.31	0.27	0.63	0.10	0.11	0.36	0.33	0.67	0.54	1.00			
Australia	0.19	0.20	0.31	0.12	0.67	0.32	0.16	0.13	0.17	0.25	0.17	1.00		
Canada	0.31	0.26	0.21	0.19	0.18	0.52	0.23	0.69	0.36	0.41	0.35	0.25	1.00	
France	0.12	0.53	0.33	0.37	0.10	0.16	0.58	0.36	0.90	0.57	0.65	0.21	0.33	1.00

Note: Data represent the U.S. dollar perspective.

Source: Roger G. Clarke and Mark P. Kritzman, *Currency Management: Concepts and Practices,* Charlottesville, VA, Research Foundation of the Institute of Chartered Financial Analysts, 1996.

FIGURE 20.4

The Minimum Variance Frontier

Source: From Campbell R. Harvey, "The World Price of Covariance Risk," *Journal of Finance* 46 (March 1991), pp. 111–58.

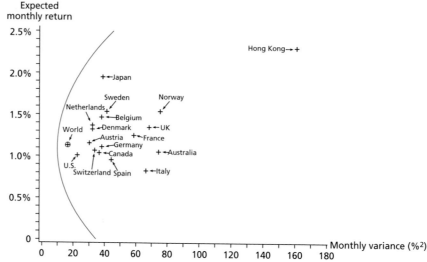

The minimum variance frontier is calculated from the unconditional means, variances, and covariances of 17 country returns. The returns are in U.S. dollars and are from Morgan Stanley Capital International. The data are from 1970:2–1989:5 (232 observations).

FIGURE 20.5

Passive Efficient Frontier versus EAFE (return based on country risk)

Source: Jarrod W. Wilcox, "EAFE Is for Wimps," *Journal of Portfolio Management*, Spring 1994.

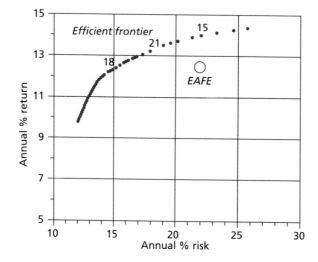

Figure 20.4 offers yet a different perspective on opportunities for international diversification. It shows risk-return opportunities offered by several asset classes, alone and combined into portfolios. (All returns here are calculated in terms of U.S. dollars.) The efficient frontiers generated from the full set of assets including foreign stocks and bonds offer the best possible risk-return pairs; they are vastly superior to the risk-return profile of U.S. stocks alone.

Lest you think that mean-variance analysis is too "academic," consider Figure 20.5, which is reproduced from a paper in the *Journal of Portfolio Management* written by a portfolio manager at Batterymarch Financial Management.[1] The article is devoted to the management of "risk for international portfolios." The entire analysis of risk management is performed in terms of efficient frontiers that exploit international diversification. In this figure, the author examines the efficiency of one index of non-U.S. stocks, the EAFE index (which we will describe in detail below).

---

[1] Jarrod W. Wilcox, "EAFE Is for Wimps," *Journal of Portfolio Management*, Spring 1994.

New Funds That Track Foreign Markets

LOW-COST FOREIGN INDEX FUNDS CALLED WEBS AND COUNTRYBASKETS ELIMINATE SOME OF THE GUESSWORK AND COSTS OF INVESTING ABROAD.

With foreign markets generally stronger this year, a new way to invest abroad has appeared at a good time. Two competing products, WEBS and CountryBaskets, are shares of open-end mutual funds that replicate the price and yield performance of foreign stock market indexes and trade on a stock exchange like stocks. You sell these shares rather than redeeming them, but there the similarity to closed-end country funds ends. The new funds create and redeem shares in large blocks as needed, thus preventing the big premiums or discounts to net asset value typical of closed-end country funds. As index funds, foreign index baskets are passively managed, so their expenses run much lower than for current open- or closed-end country funds.

Both products are continuously priced, an advantage over open-end international funds, which are priced once a day. They can be bought on margin and sold short even in a falling market. Like any listed stock, they can be used as part of a hedging strategy. While these features make them useful to traders, they offer conservative, long-term investors a convenient and relatively economical means of diversifying into foreign markets.

The two products track their foreign indexes differently. WEBS portfolio managers use a mix of stocks and derivative investments such as listed futures, options, and swaps on OTC equity derivatives to maintain performance close to their underlying foreign indexes. CountryBaskets achieve more precise tracking by holding nearly all the equities in each of the underlying indexes and making minor adjustments with listed futures and options. WEBS trade at $1/16$ of a point increments and CountryBaskets at eighths of a point.

As diversified portfolios representing foreign markets as a whole, WEBS and CountryBaskets are less volatile than many of the equities they hold, and, by investing in the market, you avoid the problems ADR investors often have in getting information and evaluating shares subject to different accounting rules. WEBS and CountryBaskets are also useful to investors who want to target specific countries as part of portfolio balancing.

Investors may prefer the active management, diversity, and flexibility of open-end international equity index funds as a way to limit currency and political risks of investing in foreign markets. As conventional open-end funds, however, the international funds are sometimes forced by net redemptions to sell stocks at inopportune times, which can be a particular problem in foreign markets with highly volatile stocks.

Foreign index baskets pay dividends at least annually on realized capital gains and the accumulated cash dividends of the underlying stocks less accumulated fund expenses. As index funds, they can be expected to have low turnover, so their taxable capital gains distributions are expected to be minimal.

You pay brokerage commissions on purchase and sale of WEBS and CountryBasket shares, but since their portfolios are passively managed, their management and administrative fees are relatively low and they eliminate most of the transaction charges typical of managed funds. WEBS and CountryBaskets average annual expenses are expected to be around 0.8% versus 1.8% for open-end international funds and 1.6% for closed-end funds.

Foreign Index Baskets					
WEBS	**Symbol (Amex)**	**WEBS**	**Symbol (Amex)**	**Country Baskets**	**Symbol (NYSE)**
Australia	EWA	Malyasia	EWM	Australia	GXA
Austria	EWO	Mexico	EWW	France	GXF
Belgium	EWK	Netherlands	EWN	Germany	GXG
Canada	EWC	Singapore	EWS	Hong Kong	GXH
France	EWQ	Spain	EWP	Italy	GXI
Germany	EWG	Sweden	EWD	Japan	GXJ
Hong Kong	EWH	Switzerland	EWL	South Africa	GXR
Italy	EWI	U.K.	EWU	U.K.	GXK
Japan	EWJ			U.S.	GXU

Source: From *The Outlook*, May 22, 1996.

TABLE 20.3
Sampling of Emerging
Country Funds, 1997

Source: *The Wall Street
Journal*, January 9, 1997.

Closed-End Funds		Closed-End Funds	
Fund Name	**Symbol**	**Fund Name**	**Symbol**
Europe/Middle East		**Pacific/Asia**	
First Israel	ISL	Indonesia	IF
Portugal	PGF	Jakarta Growth	JGF
Turkish Inv.	TKF	Jardine Fleming China	JFC
Latin America		Korea	KF
		Korean Inv.	KIF
Argentina	AF	Malaysia	MF
Brazil	BZF	R.O.C. Taiwan	ROC
Brazilian Eqty.	BZL	Scudder New Asia	SAF
Chile	CH	Taiwan	TWN
Emerging Mexico	MEF	Thai	TTF
Latin Amer. Eqty.	LAQ	Thai Capital	TC
Latin Amer. Inv.	LAM	**Global**	
Latin Amer. Disc.	LDF		
Mexico Equity & Income	MXF	Emerging Markets Tele.	ETF
Pacific/Asia		Morgan Stanley EM	MSF
		Templeton Emerging	EMF
Asia Pacific	APB	**Income**	
China	CHN		
First Philippine	FPF	Alliance World	AWG
Greater China	GCH	Emerging Markets Income	EMD
India Growth	IGF	Latin Amer. Dollar	LBF

Open-End Funds	
Fund Name	**Assets (millions), 1997**
Fidelity Emerging Markets	$1,283
G.T. Global Emerging Market A	197
G.T. Latin Amer. Growth A	166
Govett Emerging Markets	60
Lexington Worldwide EM	265
Merrill Develop Cap. Market	309
Merrill Latin Amer. A	519
Montgomery Emerging Mkt.	907
Morgan Stanley EM	1,292
Scudder Emerging Market Income	324
Templeton Dev. Mkts.	3,206
Vanguard Int'l Index: Emerging	622

Individuals, too, can now easily invest internationally. Many mutual funds cater to the demand for international diversification. For example, Fidelity offers funds with investments concentrated overseas generally, in Europe, in the Pacific Basin, and in developing economies in an emerging opportunities fund. Vanguard, consistent with its indexing philosophy, offers separate index funds for Europe, the Pacific Basin and emerging markets. In addition, several firms sponsor single-country mutual and closed-end funds.

There are now mutual funds that specialize in the stock markets of the so-called emerging economies. The nearby box (page 549) discusses a wide range of single-country index funds, and Table 20.3 presents a list of funds that focus on emerging markets.

Exchange Rate Risk

political risk
Possibility of the expropriation of assets, changes in tax policy, restrictions on the exchange of foreign currency for domestic currency, or other changes in the business climate of a country.

exchange rate risk
The uncertainty in asset returns due to movements in the exchange rates between the dollar and foreign currencies.

International investing poses unique challenges and a variety of new risks for U.S. investors. Information in foreign markets may be less timely and more difficult to come by. In smaller economies with correspondingly smaller securities markets, there may be higher transaction costs and liquidity problems. Investment advisors need special expertise concerning **political risk,** by which we mean the possibility of the expropriation of assets, changes in tax policy, the institution of restrictions on the exchange of foreign currency for domestic currency, or other changes in the business climate of a country.

FIGURE 20.6

Stock Market Returns in Dollars and Local Currencies

Source: *The Economist*, March 8–14, 1997.

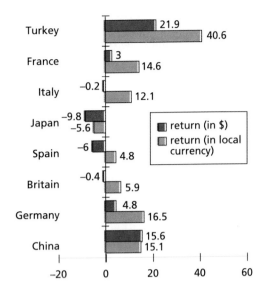

Beyond these risks, international investing entails **exchange rate risk.** The dollar return from a foreign investment depends not only on the returns in the foreign currency, but also on the exchange rate between the dollar and that currency.

EXAMPLE 20.1 Investment in the U.K.

Consider an investment in England in risk-free British government bills paying 10% annual interest in British pounds. While these U.K. bills would be the risk-free asset to a British investor, this is not the case for a U.S. investor. Suppose, for example, the current exchange rate is $2 per pound, and the U.S. investor starts with $20,000. That amount can be exchanged for £10,000 and invested at a riskless 10% rate in the United Kingdom to provide £11,000 in one year.

What happens if the dollar–pound exchange rate varies over the year? Say that during the year, the pound depreciates relative to the dollar, so that by year end only $1.80 is required to purchase £1. The £11,000 can be exchanged at the year-end exchange rate for only $19,800 (= £11,000 × $1.80/ £), resulting in a loss of $200 relative to the initial $20,000 investment. Despite the positive 10% pound-denominated return, the dollar-denominated return is a negative 1%.

We can generalize from Example 20.1. The $20,000 is exchanged for $20,000/$E_0$ pounds, where E_0 denotes the original exchange rate ($2/ £). The U.K. investment grows to $(20,000/E_0)[1 + r_f(\text{UK})]$ British pounds, where $r_f(\text{UK})$ is the risk-free rate in the United Kingdom. The pound proceeds ultimately are converted back to dollars at the subsequent exchange rate E_1, for total dollar proceeds of $20,000(E_1/E_0)[1 + r_f(\text{UK})]$. The dollar-denominated return on the investment in British bills, therefore, is

$$1 + r(\text{US}) = [1 + r_f(\text{UK})]E_1/E_0 \tag{20.1}$$

We see in Equation 20.1 that the dollar-denominated return for a U.S. investor equals the pound-denominated return times the exchange rate "return." For a U.S. investor, the investment in the British bill is a combination of a safe investment in the United Kingdom and a risky investment in the performance of the pound relative to the dollar. Here, the pound fared poorly, falling from a value of $2.00 to only $1.80. The loss on the pound more than offsets the earnings on the British bill.

Figure 20.6 illustrates this point. It presents rates of returns on stock and bond market indexes in several countries for the first 10 weeks of 1997. The light boxes depict returns in local currencies, while the dark boxes depict returns in dollars, adjusting for exchange rate movements. It's clear that exchange rate fluctuations over this period had large effects on dollar-denominated returns in several countries.

2. Using the data in Example 20.1, calculate the rate of return in dollars to a U.S. investor holding the British bill if the year-end exchange rate is: (*a*) $E_1 = \$2.00/\pounds$; (*b*) $E_1 = \$2.20/\pounds$.

The investor in our example could have hedged the exchange rate risk using a forward or futures contract in foreign exchange. Recall that a forward or futures contract on foreign exchange calls for delivery or acceptance of one currency for another at a stipulated exchange rate. Here, the U.S. investor would agree to deliver pounds for dollars at a fixed exchange rate, thereby eliminating the future risk involved with conversion of the pound investment back into dollars.

EXAMPLE 20.2
Hedging Exchange Rate Risk

If the futures exchange rate had been $F_0 = \$1.93/\pounds$ when the investment was made, the U.S. investor could have assured a riskless dollar-denominated return by locking in the year-end exchange rate at $\$1.93/\pounds$. In this case, the riskless U.S. return would have been 6.15%.

$$[1 + r_f(\text{UK})]F_0/E_0$$
$$= (1.10) \ 1.93/2.00$$
$$= 1.0615$$

Here are the steps to take to lock in the dollar-denominated returns. The futures contract entered in the second step exactly offsets the exchange rate risk incurred in step 1.

Initial Transaction	End-of-Year Proceeds in Dollars
Exchange $20,000 for £10,000 and invest at 10% in the United Kingdom.	£11,000 × E_1
Enter a contract to deliver £11,000 for dollars at the (forward) exchange rate $1.93/£.	£11,000(1.93 − E_1)
Total	£11,000 × $1.93/£ = $21,230

You may recall that the futures hedge in Example 20.2 is the same type of hedging strategy at the heart of the spot-futures parity relationship discussed in Chapter 18. In both instances, futures markets are used to eliminate the risk of holding another asset. The U.S. investor can lock in a riskless dollar-denominated return either by investing in the United Kingdom and hedging exchange rate risk or by investing in riskless U.S. assets. Because the returns on two riskless strategies must provide equal returns, we conclude

$$\frac{F_0}{E_0} = \frac{1 + r_f(\text{US})}{1 + r_f(\text{UK})} \tag{20.2}$$

interest rate parity relationship, or covered interest arbitrage relationship
The spot-futures exchange rate relationship that precludes arbitrage opportunities.

This relationship is called the **interest rate parity relationship** or **covered interest arbitrage relationship.**

Consider the intuition behind this result. If $r_f(\text{US})$ is greater than $r_f(\text{UK})$, money invested in the United States will grow at a faster rate than money invested in the United Kingdom. If this is so, why wouldn't all investors decide to invest their money in the United States? One important reason is that the dollar may be depreciating relative to the pound. Although dollar investments in the United States grow faster than pound investments in the United Kingdom, each dollar is worth progressively fewer pounds as time passes. Such an effect will exactly offset the advantage of the higher U.S. interest rate.

To complete the argument, we need only determine how a depreciating dollar will affect Equation 20.2. If the dollar is depreciating, meaning that progressively more dollars are required to purchase each pound, then the forward exchange rate, F_0 (which equals the dollars required to purchase one pound for delivery in the future), must exceed E_0, the current exchange rate.

That is exactly what Equation 20.2 tells us: When $r_f(US)$ exceeds $r_f(UK)$, F_0 must exceed E_0. The depreciation of the dollar embodied in the ratio of F_0 to E_0 exactly compensates for the difference in interest rates available in the two countries. Of course, the argument also works in reverse: If $r_f(US)$ is less than $r_f(UK)$, then F_0 will be less than E_0.

**EXAMPLE 20.3
Covered Interest
Arbitrage**

What if the interest rate parity relationship were violated? Suppose $r_f(US)$ is 6.15%, but the futures price is $1.90/£ instead of $1.93/£. You could adopt a strategy to reap arbitrage profits. In this example, let E_1 denote the exchange rate that will prevail in one year. E_1 is, of course, a random variable from the perspective of today's investors.

Action	Initial Cash Flow (in $)	Cash Flow in One Year (in $)
1. Borrow 1 UK pound in London. Repay in one year.	$ 2.00	$-E_1(1.10)$
2. Convert the pound to $2 and lend in the United States.	−2.00	2.00(1.0615)
3. Enter a contract to purchase 1.10 pounds at a (futures) price of $F_0 = \$1.90/£$	0	$1.10(E_1 - 1.90)$
Total	$ 0	$0.033

In step 1, you borrow one pound in the United Kingdom (worth $2 at the current exchange rate) and, after one year, repay the pound borrowed with interest. Because the loan is made in the United Kingdom at the U.K. interest rate, you would repay 1.10 pounds, which would be worth $E_1(1.10)$ dollars. The U.S. loan in step 2 is made at the U.S. interest rate of 6.15%. The futures position in step 3 results in receipt of 1.10 pounds, for which you would first pay F_0 dollars each and then trade into dollars at exchange rate E_1.

The exchange rate risk here is exactly offset between the pound obligation in step 1 and the futures position in step 3. The profit from the strategy is, therefore, riskless and requires no net investment. This is an arbitrage opportunity.

Concept Check

3. What are the arbitrage strategy and associated profits if the initial future price is $F_0 = \$1.95/pound$?

Ample empirical evidence bears out this theoretical relationship. For example, on May 18, 1994, the interest rate on U.S. Treasury securities with maturity of one-half year was 4.85%, while the comparable rate in the United Kingdom was 5.19%. The spot exchange rate was $1.5095/ £. Substituting these values into Equation 20.2, we find that interest rate parity implies that the forward exchange rate for delivery in one-half year should have been $1.5095 \times (1.0485/1.0519)^{1/2} = \$1.5071/£$. The actual forward rate was $1.5073/£, which was so close to the parity value that transaction costs would have prevented arbitrageurs from profiting from the discrepancy.

Unfortunately, such perfect exchange rate hedging usually is not so easy. In our example, we knew exactly how many pounds to sell in the forward or futures market because the pound-denominated proceeds in the United Kingdom were riskless. If the U.K. investment had not been in bills, but instead had been in risky U.K. equity, we would know neither the ultimate value in pounds of our U.K. investment nor how many pounds to sell forward. That is, the hedging opportunity offered by foreign exchange forward contracts would be imperfect.

To summarize, the generalization of Equation 20.1 is that

$$1 + r(US) = [1 + r(foreign)] \, E_1/E_0 \qquad (20.3)$$

where $r(foreign)$ is the possibly risky return earned in the currency of the foreign investment. You can set up a perfect hedge only in the special case that $r(foreign)$ is itself a known number. In that case, you know you must sell in the forward or futures market an amount of foreign currency equal to $[1 + r(\text{foreign})]$ for each unit of that currency you purchase today.

4. How many pounds would the investor in Example 20.2 need to sell forward to hedge exchange rate risk if: (a) $r(\text{UK}) = 20\%$; and (b) $r(\text{UK}) = 30\%$?

Passive and Active International Investing

When we discussed investment strategies in the purely domestic context, we used a market index portfolio like the S&P 500 as a benchmark passive equity investment. This suggests a world market index might be a useful starting point for a passive international strategy.

European, Australian, Far East (EAFE) index
A widely used index of non-U.S. stocks computed by Morgan Stanley.

One widely used index of non-U.S. stocks is the **European, Australian, Far East (EAFE) index** computed by Morgan Stanley. Additional indexes of world equity performance are published by Capital International Indices, Salomon Brothers, First Boston, and Goldman Sachs. Portfolios designed to mirror or even replicate the country, currency, and company representation of these indexes would be the obvious generalization of the purely domestic passive equity strategy.

An issue that sometimes arises in the international context is the appropriateness of market-capitalization weighting schemes in the construction of international indexes. Capitalization weighting is far and away the most common approach. However, some argue that it might not be the best weighting scheme in an international context. This is in part because different countries have differing proportions of their corporate sector organized as publicly traded firms. For example, in 1994, U.K. firms received a total weighting of 16.7% of the EAFE index in terms of market value of equity, but accounted for only 8.0% of the gross domestic product (GDP) of the EAFE countries. In contrast, French firms represented 5.8% of the market-value weighted index despite that fact that France accounted for fully 11.4% of EAFE GDP.

Some argue that it is more appropriate to weight international indexes by GDP rather than market capitalization because an internationally diversified portfolio should purchase shares in proportion to the broad asset base of each country, and GDP might be a better measure of the importance of a country in the international economy than the value of its outstanding stocks. Others have even suggested weights proportional to the import share of various countries. The argument is that investors who wish to hedge the price of imported goods might choose to hold securities in foreign firms in proportion to the goods imported from those countries.

Table 20.4 uses data from the second quarter of 1994 to illustrate the different weightings that would emerge for the EAFE countries using market capitalization, GDP, and U.S. import shares. The differing methodologies result in substantially different weights for some countries. In particular, Japan had a market-value weight of just under 50% despite the fact that its GDP was only 33.4% of the EAFE total. This disproportionate weight was due primarily to much higher price/earnings ratios in Japan in 1994.

Active portfolio management in an international context also may be viewed as an extension of active domestic management. In principle, one would form an efficient frontier from the full menu of world securities and determine the optimal risky portfolio. In the context of international investing, however, we more often take a broader asset-allocation perspective toward active management. We focus mainly on potential sources of abnormal returns: currency selection, country selection, stock selection within countries, and cash-bond selection within countries.

currency selection
Asset allocation in which the investor chooses among investments denominated in different currencies.

We can measure the contribution of each of these factors following a manner similar to the performance attribution techniques introduced in Chapter 19.

1. **Currency selection** measures the contribution to total portfolio performance attributable to exchange rate fluctuations relative to the investor's benchmark currency, which we will take to be the U.S. dollar. We might use a benchmark like the EAFE index to compare a

TABLE 20.4

Weighting Schemes for EAFE Countries

Source: Bruce Clarke and Anthony W. Ryan, "Proper Overseas Benchmark a Critical Choice," *Pensions and Investments*, May 30, 1994, p. 28. Reprinted by permission.

Country	Market Capitalization	Gross Domestic Product (GDP)
Australia	2.4%	2.4%
Austria	0.4	1.6
Belgium	1.1	1.9
Denmark	0.6	1.2
Finland	0.3	0.8
France	5.8	11.4
Germany	6.7	15.4
Hong Kong	3.3	0.9
Italy	1.9	9.2
Ireland	0.2	0.4
Japan	48.3	33.4
Malaysia	1.6	0.5
New Zealand	0.3	0.3
Netherlands	2.9	2.8
Norway	0.3	0.9
Singapore	0.9	1.4
Spain	1.8	4.6
Sweden	1.3	1.8
Switzerland	4.2	2.1
U.K.	16.7	8.0

portfolio's currency selection for a particular period to a passive benchmark. EAFE currency selection would be computed as the weighted average of the currency appreciation of the currencies represented in the EAFE portfolio using as weights the fraction of the EAFE portfolio invested in each currency.

country selection
Asset allocation in which the investor chooses among investments in different countries.

2. **Country selection** measures the contribution to performance attributable to investing in the better-performing stock markets of the world. It can be measured as the weighted average of the equity *index* returns of each country using as weights the share of the manager's portfolio in each country. We use index returns to abstract from the effect of security selection within countries. To measure a manager's contribution relative to a passive strategy, we might compare country selection to the weighted average across countries of equity index returns using as weights the share of the EAFE portfolio in each country.

stock selection
Choice of specific stocks within a country's equity market.

3. **Stock selection** ability may, as in Chapter 19, be measured as the weighted average of equity returns *in excess of the equity index* in each country. Here, we would use local currency returns and use as weights the investments in each country.

cash/bond selection
Choice between money market versus longer-term bonds.

4. **Cash/bond selection** may be measured as the excess return derived from weighting bonds and bills differently from some benchmark weights.

Table 20.5 gives an example of how to measure the contribution of the decisions an international portfolio manager might make.

Concept Check

5. Using the data in Table 20.5, compute the manager's country and currency selection if portfolio weights had been 40% in Europe, 20% in Australia, and 40% in the Far East.

Factor Models and International Investing

International investing presents a good opportunity to demonstrate an application of multifactor models of security returns such as those considered in connection with the arbitrage pricing model. Natural factors might include the following:

1. A world stock index.
2. A national (domestic) stock index.
3. Industrial-sector indexes.
4. Currency movements.

TABLE 20.5

Example of
Performance
Attribution:
International

	EAFE Weight	Return on Equity Index	Currency Appreciation $E_1/E_0 - 1$	Manager's Weight	Manager's Return
Europe	0.30	10%	10%	0.35	8%
Australia	0.10	5	−10	0.10	7
Far East	0.60	15	30	0.55	18

Currency Selection

EAFE: $(0.30 \times 10\%) + (0.10 \times -10\%) + (0.60 \times 30\%) = 20\%$ appreciation
Manager: $(0.35 \times 10\%) + (0.10 \times -10\%) + (0.55 \times 30\%) = 19\%$ appreciation
Loss of 1% relative to EAFE

Country Selection

EAFE: $(0.30 \times 10\%) + (0.10 \times 5\%) + (0.60 \times 15\%) = 12.5\%$
Manager: $(0.35 \times 10\%) + (0.10 \times 5\%) + (0.55 \times 15\%) = 12.25\%$
Loss of 0.25% relative to EAFE

Stock Selection

$(8\% - 10\%)0.35 + (7\% - 5\%)0.10 + (18\% - 15\%)0.55 = 1.15\%$
Contribution of 1.15% relative to EAFE

TABLE 20.6

Relative Importance of
World, Industrial,
Currency, and
Domestic Factors in
Explaining Return of a
Stock

Source: Modified from Bruno
Solnik, *International
Investments*, 3rd Edition,
Exhibit 7.6 © 1966 Addison-
Wesley Publishing Company,
Inc. Reprinted by permission
of Addison-Wesley Longman
Publishing Company, Inc.

	Average R-SQR of Regression on Factors				
	Single-Factor Tests				Joint Test
Locality	World	Industrial	Currency	Domestic	All Four Factors
Switzerland	0.18	0.17	0.00	0.38	0.39
West Germany	0.08	0.10	0.00	0.41	0.42
Australia	0.24	0.26	0.01	0.72	0.72
Belgium	0.07	0.08	0.00	0.42	0.43
Canada	0.27	0.24	0.07	0.45	0.48
Spain	0.22	0.03	0.00	0.45	0.45
United States	0.26	0.47	0.01	0.35	0.55
France	0.13	0.08	0.01	0.45	0.60
United Kingdom	0.20	0.17	0.01	0.53	0.55
Hong Kong	0.06	0.25	0.17	0.79	0.81
Italy	0.05	0.03	0.00	0.35	0.35
Japan	0.09	0.16	0.01	0.26	0.33
Norway	0.17	0.28	0.00	0.84	0.85
Netherlands	0.12	0.07	0.01	0.34	0.31
Singapore	0.16	0.15	0.02	0.32	0.33
Sweden	0.19	0.06	0.01	0.42	0.43
All countries	0.18	0.23	0.01	0.42	0.46

Solnik and de Freitas (1988) use such a framework, and Table 20.6 shows some of their results for several countries. The first four columns of numbers present the R-square of various one-factor regressions. Recall that the R-square, or R^2, measures the percentage of return volatility of a company's stock that can be explained by the particular factor treated as the independent or explanatory variable. Solnik and de Freitas estimate the factor regressions for many firms in a given country and report the average R-square across the firms in that country.

In this case, the table reveals that the domestic factor seems to be the dominant influence on stock returns. While the domestic index alone generates an average R-square of 0.42 across all countries, adding the three additional factors (in the last column of the table) increases the average R-square only to 0.46. This is consistent with the low cross-country correlation coefficients in Table 20.2.

At the same time, there is clear evidence of a world market factor in results of the market crash of October 1987. Even though we have said equity returns across borders show only

FIGURE 20.7

Regional Indexes Around the Crash, October 14–October 26, 1987

Source: From Richard Roll, "The International Crash of October 1987," *Financial Analysis Journal*, September–October 1988.

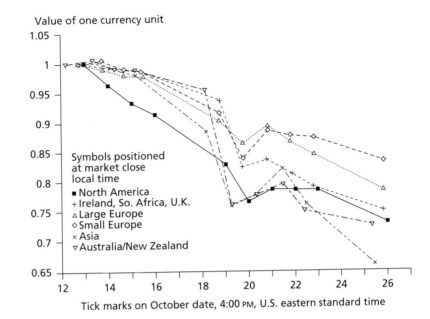

moderate correlation, a study by Richard Roll (1988) shows negative October 1987 equity index returns in all 23 countries considered. Figure 20.7, reproduced from Roll's study, shows the values he found for regional equity indexes during that month. The obvious correlation among returns suggests some underlying world factor common to all economies. Roll found that the beta of a country's equity index on a world index (estimated through September 1987) was the best predictor of that index's response to the October 1987 crash, which lends further support to the presence of a world factor.

Equilibrium in International Capital Markets

We can use the capital asset pricing model (CAPM) or the arbitrage pricing theory (APT) to predict expected rates of return in an international capital market equilibrium, just as we can for domestic assets. The models need some adaptation for international use, however.

For example, one might expect that a world CAPM would result simply by replacing a narrow domestic market portfolio with a broad world market portfolio and measuring betas relative to the world portfolio. This approach was pursued in part of a paper by Ibbotson, Carr, and Robinson (1982), who calculated betas of equity indexes of several countries against a world equity index. Their results appear in Table 20.7. The betas for different countries show surprising variability.

While such a straightforward generalization of the simple CAPM seems like a reasonable first step, it is subject to some problems:

1. Taxes, transaction costs, and capital barriers across countries make it difficult and not always attractive for investors to hold a world index portfolio. Some assets are simply unavailable to foreign investors.

2. Investors in different countries view exchange rate risk from the perspective of their different domestic currencies. Thus, they will not agree on the risk characteristics of various securities and, therefore, will not derive identical efficient frontiers.

3. Investors in different countries tend to consume different baskets of goods, either because of differing tastes or because of tariffs, transportation costs, or taxes. If relative prices of goods vary over time, the inflation risk perceived by investors in different countries also will differ.

TABLE 20.7
Equity Returns,
1960–1980

Source: From Roger G.
Ibbotson, Richard C. Carr, and
Anthony W. Robinson,
"International Equity and
Bond Returns," *Financial
Analysts Journal*, July–August
1982.

	Average Return	Standard Deviation of Return	Beta	Alpha
Australia	12.20	22.80	1.02	1.52
Austria	10.30	16.90	.01	4.86
Belgium	10.10	13.80	.45	2.44
Canada	12.10	17.50	.77	2.75
Denmark	11.40	24.20	.60	2.91
France	8.10	21.40	.50	.17
Germany	10.10	19.90	.45	2.41
Italy	5.60	27.20	.41	−1.92
Japan	19.00	31.40	.81	9.49
Netherlands	10.70	17.80	.90	.65
Norway	17.40	49.00	−.27	13.39
Spain	10.40	19.80	.04	4.73
Sweden	9.70	16.70	.51	1.69
Switzerland	12.50	22.90	.87	2.66
United Kingdom	14.70	33.60	1.47	1.76
United States	10.20	17.70	1.08	−.69

These problems suggest that the simple CAPM will not work as well in an international context as it would if all markets were fully integrated. Some evidence suggests that assets that are less accessible to foreign investors carry higher risk premiums than a simple CAPM would predict (Errunza and Losq, 1985).

The APT seems better designed for use in an international context than the CAPM, as the special risk factors that arise in international investing can be treated much like any other risk factor. World economic activity and currency movements might simply be included in a list of factors already used in a domestic APT model.

Summary

- U.S. assets are only a small fraction of the world wealth portfolio. International capital markets offer important opportunities for portfolio diversification with enhanced risk-return characteristics.
- Exchange rate risk imparts an extra source of uncertainty to investments denominated in foreign currencies. Much of that risk can be hedged in foreign exchange futures or forward markets, but a perfect hedge is not feasible unless the foreign currency rate of return is known.
- Several world market indexes can form a basis for passive international investing. Active international management can be partitioned into currency selection, country selection, stock selection, and cash/bond selection.
- A factor model applied to international investing would include a world factor as well as the usual domestic factors. While some evidence suggests domestic factors dominate stock returns, effects of the October 1987 crash demonstrate the existence of an important international factor.

Key Terms

cash/bond selection, 555
country selection, 555
covered interest arbitrage
    relationship, 552
currency selection, 555

European, Australian, Far
    East (EAFE) index, 554
exchange rate risk, 550
interest rate parity
    relationship, 552

political risk, 550
stock selection, 555
world investable
    wealth, 545

Problem Sets

1. Suppose a U.S. investor wishes to invest in a British firm currently selling for £40 per share. The investor has $10,000 to invest, and the current exchange rate is $2/£.
   a. How many shares can the investor purchase?

b. Fill in the table below for rates of return after one year in each of the nine scenarios (three possible prices per share in pounds times three possible exchange rates).

Price per Share (£)	Pound-Denominated Return (%)	Dollar-Denominated Return for Year-End Exchange Rate		
		$1.80/£	$2/£	$2.20/£
£35				
£40				
£45				

c. When is the dollar-denominated return equal to the pound-denominated return?

2. If each of the nine outcomes in problem 1 is equally likely, find the standard deviation of both the pound- and dollar-denominated rates of return.

3. Now suppose the investor in problem 1 also sells forward £5,000 at a forward exchange rate of $2.10/£.
   a. Recalculate the dollar-denominated returns for each scenario.
   b. What happens to the standard deviation of the dollar-denominated return? Compare it to both its old value and the standard deviation of the pound-denominated return.

4. Calculate the contribution to total performance from currency, country, and stock selection for the manager in the example below:

	EAFE Weight	Return on Equity Index	E_1/E_0	Manager's Weight	Manager's Return
Europe	0.30	20%	0.9	0.35	18%
Australia	0.10	15	1.0	0.15	20
Far East	0.60	25	1.1	0.50	20

5. If the current exchange rate is $1.75/£, the one-year forward exchange rate is $1.85/£, and the interest rate on British government bills is 8% per year, what risk-free dollar-denominated return can be locked in by investing in the British bills?

6. If you were to invest $10,000 in the British bills of problem 5, how would you lock in the dollar-denominated return?

7. Renée Michaels, CFA, plans to invest $1 million in U.S. government cash equivalents for the next 90 days. Michaels's client has authorized her to use non-U.S. government cash equivalents, but only if the currency risk is hedged to U.S. dollars by using forward currency contracts.
   a. Calculate the U.S. dollar value of the hedged investment at the end of 90 days for *each* of the two cash equivalents in the table below. Show all calculations.
   b. Briefly explain the theory that best accounts for your results.
   c. Based upon this theory, estimate the implied interest rate for a 90-day U.S. government cash equivalent.

Interest Rates 90-Day Cash Equivalents	
Japanese government	7.6%
German government	8.6

Exchange Rates Currency Units per U.S. Dollar		
	Spot	90-Day Forward
Japanese yen	133.05	133.47
German deutsche mark	1.5260	1.5348

8. Suppose that the spot price of the Swiss franc is currently 40 cents. The 1-year futures price is 44 cents. Is the interest rate higher in the United States or Switzerland?

9. *a.* The spot price of the British pound is currently $1.50. If the risk-free interest rate on one-year government bonds is 10% in the United States and 15% in the United Kingdom, what must the forward price of the pound be for delivery one year from now?

   b. How could an investor make risk-free arbitrage profits if the forward price were higher than the price you gave in answer to (*a*)? Give a numerical example.

10. Consider the following information:

$$r_{US} = 5\%$$

$$r_{UK} = 7\%$$

$$E_0 = 2.0 \text{ dollars per pound}$$

$$F_0 = 1.97 \text{ (one-year delivery)}$$

where the interest rates are annual yields on U.S. or U.K. bills. Given this information:
   a. Where would you lend?
   b. Where would you borrow?
   c. How could you arbitrage?

11. John Irish, CFA, is an independent investment advisor who is assisting Alfred Darwin, the head of the Investment Committee of General Technology Corporation, to establish a new pension fund. Darwin asks Irish about international equities and whether the Investment Committee should consider them as an additional asset for the pension fund.
   a. Explain the rationale for including international equities in General's equity portfolio. Identify and describe three relevant considerations in formulating your answer.
   b. List three possible arguments against international equity investment and briefly discuss the significance of each.
   c. To illustrate several aspects of the performance of international securities over time, Irish shows Darwin the accompanying graph of investment results experienced

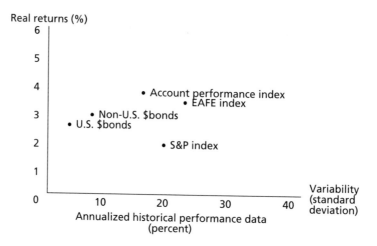

by a U.S. pension fund in the recent past. Compare the performance of the U.S. dollar and non-U.S. dollar equity and fixed-income asset categories, and explain the significance of the result of the account performance index relative to the results of the four individual asset class indexes.

Solutions to Concept Checks

1. The graph would asymptote to a lower level, as shown in the figure below, reflecting the improved opportunities for diversification. There still would be a positive level of nondiversifiable risk.

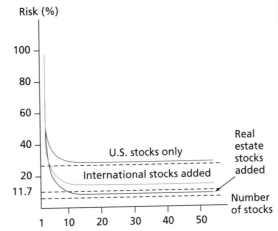

2. $1 + r(US) = [(1 + r_f(UK)] \times (E_1/E_0)$
   a. $1 + r(US) = 1.1 \times 1.0 = 1.10$. Therefore, $r(US) = 10\%$.
   b. $1 + r(US) = 1.1 \times 1.1 = 1.21$. Therefore, $r(US) = 21\%$.

3. According to interest rate parity, F_0 should be $1.93. As the futures price is too high, we should reverse the arbitrage strategy just considered.

Action	Cash Flow Now ($)	Cash Flow in One Year ($)
Borrow $2 in the United States.	$ 2.00	−2.00(1.0615)
Convert the borrowed dollars to pounds, and lend in the United Kingdom at a 10% interest rate.	−2.00	$1.10E_1$
Enter a contract to sell 1.10 pounds at a futures price of $1.95/£.	0.00	$1.10(1.95 − E_1)$
Total	$ 0.00	$0.022

4. You must sell forward the number of pounds you will end up with at the end of the year. This value cannot be known with certainty, however, unless the rate of return of the pound-denominated investment is known.
   a. $10,000 \times 1.20 = 12,000$ pounds
   b. $10,000 \times 1.30 = 13,000$ pounds

5. *Country selection:*

$$(0.40 \times 10\%) + (0.20 \times 5\%) + (0.40 \times 15\%) = 11\%$$

This is a loss of 1.5% (11% versus 12.5%) relative to the EAFE passive benchmark.
Currency selection:

$$(0.40 \times 10\%) + (0.20 \times -10\%)) + (0.40 \times 30\%) = 14\%$$

This is a loss of 6% (14% versus 20%) relative to the EAFE benchmark.

Appendix A

INVESTMENTS IN NONTRADITIONAL ASSET GROUPS

REAL ESTATE

Like international investments, real estate can play an important role in diversified portfolios. Table 20A.1 shows low or negative correlation of returns on real estate investments (measured from returns on real estate investment trusts) with those of stocks, bonds, and bills, indicating enhanced opportunity for portfolio risk reduction.

Another view of some attractive characteristics of real estate investments emerges from a study by Ibbotson, Siegel, and Love (1985). Index model regressions for several asset classes over 1959–1984 show that U.S. real estate had a beta of only 0.31 when regressed on the world market portfolio and an annual alpha (abnormal risk-adjusted return) of 2.52%. This indicates low risk and high return, at least for this historical period. Regression of U.S. real estate returns on the U.S. inflation rate yielded a slope coefficient of 0.80, confirming the effectiveness of real estate as an effective inflation hedge. When the rate of inflation rose faster than expected, so did the nominal return on real estate investments.

PRECIOUS METALS

Table 20A.2 from a study by Jaffe (1989) documents the performance of gold and silver relative to U.S. equities in the 1971–1987 period. While metals clearly were more volatile, their average returns also outran those of equity. However, since 1987, gold and silver have been poor investments. The rates of return on gold in 1988 and 1989 were 3.1% and −20.5%, respectively; the returns for silver in these two years were −7.4% and −23.2%. The return history (1975–1992) of gold and silver are shown in Figure 20A.1.

One feature often attributed to metals is an ability to serve as an inflation hedge. Jaffe (1989) found that a regression of gold returns on U.S. inflation produced a slope coefficient of 2.95, indicating that a 1% increase in inflation was associated with an increased nominal return to metals of almost 3%. He warns, however, that the relationship is quite noisy, meaning the hedging value of gold can be unreliable.

An open issue concerns the best way to invest in metals. That is, should one buy metals, futures contracts on metals, or stock in companies that mine and refine metals? Although there is no single correct answer to this question, each approach has certain advantages as well as drawbacks. Buying metals (in the form of gold or silver coins, for example) offers the advantage of small-scale transactions but might entail relatively large storage or insur-

TABLE 20A.1   Correlation Analysis

Below are the Pearson correlation coefficients for 252 monthly returns on the general stock market (large stocks), U.S. Treasury bonds (T-bonds), investment-grade corporate bonds (corporate bonds), U.S. Treasury bills (T-bills), inflation, small-capitalization stocks (small stocks), and REITs for the period January 1972 to December 1992. *** indicates significance at the 0.01% level, ** indicates significance at the 1% level, and * indicates significance at the 5% level.

	Large Stocks	Small Stocks	T-Bills	T-Bonds	Corp Bonds	Inflation	REITs
Large stocks	1.000	0.782***	−0.082	.358***	0.388***	−0.215**	0.633***
Small stocks		1.000	−0.083	0.196**	0.233**	−0.162*	0.731***
T-bills			1.000	0.069	0.036	0.384***	−0.087
T-bonds				1.000	0.933***	−0.200**	0.205**
Corporate bonds					1.000	−0.208**	0.240***
Inflation						1.000	−0.178**
REITs							1.000

Source: Michael A. Goldstein and Edward F. Nelling, "Equity versus Mortgage REITs: Stocks or Bonds?" Georgia Institute of Technology working paper, 1997.

TABLE 20.A2

Precious Metal Returns, 1971–1987

Source: From Jeffrey F. Jaffe, "Gold and Gold Stocks as Investments for Institutional Portfolios," *Financial Analysts Journal* 45 (March–April 1989), pp. 53–59.

	Average Return (Arithmetic mean)	Standard Deviation of Annual Return
Gold	18.7	27.3
Silver	18.1	40.1
Equity (U.S.)	12.7	15.6

FIGURE 20A.1

Gold and Silver Price Indexes

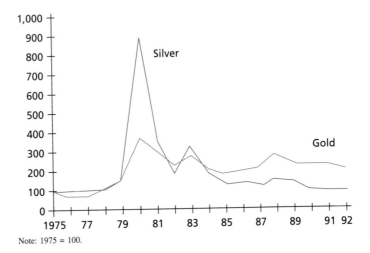

Note: 1975 = 100.

ance costs. Futures contracts offer a low-cost way to bet on prices of traded metals but require a large minimum investment. Futures also allow no opportunity for tax timing because of the mark-to-market provision, and they require frequent monitoring as contracts mature and must be rolled over. Finally, investments in stocks of particular companies that mine or refine metals involve issues of firm-specific risk, quality of management, and particular dividend policies that might have beneficial or deleterious tax or cash flow implications for the investor.

TABLE 20A.3

Returns on
Nontraditional Asset
Classes

Source: Salomon Bros. From
The Wall Street Journal, June
11, 1991, p C1. Reprinted by
permission of *The Wall Street
Journal*, © 1991 Dow Jones &
Company, Inc. All Rights
Reserved Worldwide.

The Asset Derby
Old-master paintings were the best performing investment asset over the past 20 years, a tally by Salomon Bros. shows. But stocks were best for the past 10 years, and oil was tops in 1990.

Asset Category	Investment Performance[a]			
	20 Years	**10 Years**	**5 Years**	**1 Year**
Old master paintings	12.3%	15.8%	23.4%	6.5%
Stocks	11.6	16.0	13.3	11.8
Chinese ceramics	11.6	8.1	15.1	3.6
Gold	11.5	−2.9	1.0	−0.7
Diamonds	10.5	6.4	10.2	0.0
Stamps	10.0	−0.7	−2.4	−7.7
Bonds	9.4	15.2	9.7	13.2
Oil	8.9	−5.9	8.5	20.7
Treasury bills (3-month)	8.6	8.8	7.0	7.1
House prices	7.3	4.4	4.6	4.7
Farmland (U.S.)	6.3	−1.8	1.3	2.1
Silver	5.0	−9.3	−4.8	−18.9
Foreign exchange	4.5	3.8	5.4	0.2
Consumer Price Index	**6.3%**	**4.3%**	**4.5%**	**5.0%**

[a]Compound annual return (including dividend or interest income, if any) for periods ended June 1, 1991.

OTHER NONTRADITIONAL ASSETS

Table 20A.3 presents returns on a wide range of assets for various periods ending in 1990. We see here that over the 20 years ending in June 1990, nontraditional assets such as coins, Chinese ceramics, or old masters actually outperformed stocks, bonds, and bills. A few words of warning are warranted, however. First, these data do not rank risk along with return, and investment risk in these nontraditionals can be considerable. In the year between May 1990 and May 1991, the best-performing asset in Table 20A.3, coins, turned in a rate of return of −43%[1] wiping out nearly half the gains of the previous two decades. Similarly, 1991 was a very poor year for investments in works of art. In addition, these assets do not trade in liquid markets. If you try to sell an old master, for example, you will need to pay either an auction fee or a bid-ask spread to an art dealer. These costs of buying and selling mean frequent transactions can swiftly wipe out any capital appreciation. Finally, these assets are difficult for amateurs to evaluate in terms of quality and can be expensive to store safely or to insure. While they may have valid places in well-diversified portfolios, they are hardly a free lunch.

[1]This is according to an index complied by *Numismatic News* and reported in *USA Today*, May 30, 1991, p. B1.

Chapter 21

ACTIVE PORTFOLIO MANAGEMENT

AFTER STUDYING THIS CHAPTER YOU SHOULD BE ABLE TO:

- Assess the value of market timing ability.
- Use the Treynor-Black model of efficient security analysis.
- Perform security analysis in multifactor security markets.

So far, we have alluded to active portfolio management in only three contexts: determining the optimal risky portfolio (Chapter 7), security analysis that generates input to the optimization (Part Four), and fixed-income portfolio management (Part Three). In this chapter, we go further in applying portfolio principles to security analysis.

Anyone who studies the principles of modern finance must wonder about what seems like a contradiction between equilibrium analysis—in particular the theory of efficient markets—and the real-world environment where we all know that profit-seeking investment managers use active strategies to exploit perceived market inefficiencies.

Even if you accept the efficient market hypothesis, there are reasons to believe active management can be effective, and we discuss these at the outset. Next, we consider the objectives of active portfolio management. We analyze two forms of active management: market timing, which is based solely on macroeconomic factors, and security selection, which includes microeconomic forecasting. At the end of the chapter, we show how multifactor models are used in active portfolio management.

21.1 THE LURE OF ACTIVE MANAGEMENT

How can a theory of active portfolio management make sense if we accept the notion that markets are in equilibrium? Chapter 9 on market efficiency gives a thorough analysis of efficient market theory; here we summarize how the theory fits with active management strategy.

Market efficiency prevails when many investors are willing to depart from a passive strategy of efficient diversification, so that they can add mispriced securities to their portfolio. Their objective is to realize "abnormal" returns.

The competition for such returns ensures that prices will be near their "fair" values. This means most managers will not beat the passive strategy *if we take risk into account with reward.* Exceptional managers, however, might beat the average forecasts that are built into market prices and consequently construct portfolios that will earn abnormal returns.

How can this happen? There is economic logic behind the result, as well as some empirical evidence indicating that exceptional portfolio managers can beat the average forecast. First, the economic logic. We must assume that if no analyst can beat the passive strategy, investors will be smart enough not to pay for expensive analysis; they will adopt less-expensive, passive strategies. In that case, funds under active management will dry up, and prices will no longer reflect sophisticated forecasts. The resulting profit opportunities will lure back active managers who once again will become successful.[1] The critical assumption here is that investors make wise decisions on how to manage their money. Direct evidence on that has yet to be produced.

As for empirical evidence, consider the following: (1) some portfolio managers experience streaks of abnormal returns that are hard to label as lucky outcomes; (2) the "noise" in realized rates of return is enough that we cannot reject outright the hypothesis that some investment managers can beat the passive strategy by a statistically small, yet economically significant, margin; and (3) some anomalies in realized returns—such as the turn-of-the-year effects—have been sufficiently persistent to suggest that managers who identified them, and acted on them in a timely fashion, could have beaten the passive strategy over prolonged periods.

These observations are enough to convince us that there is a role for active portfolio management. Active management offers an inevitable lure, even if investors agree that security markets are *nearly* efficient.

At the extreme, suppose capital markets are perfectly efficient, an easily accessible market index portfolio is available, and this portfolio is the efficient risky portfolio. In this case, security selection would be futile. You would do best following a passive strategy of allocating funds to a money market fund (the safe asset) and the market index portfolio. Under these simplifying assumptions, the optimal investment strategy seems to require no effort or know-how.

But this is too hasty a conclusion. To allocate investment funds to the risk-free and risky portfolios requires some analysis. You need to decide the fraction, y, to be invested in the risky market portfolio, M, so you must know the reward-to-variability ratio

$$S_M = \frac{E(r_M) - r_f}{\sigma_M}$$

where $E(r_M) - r_f$ is the risk premium on M and σ_M^2 the variance of M. To make a rational allocation of funds requires an estimate of σ_M and $E(r_M)$, so even a passive investor needs to do some forecasting.

Forecasting $E(r_M)$ and σ_M is complicated further because security classes are affected by different environment factors. Long-term bond returns, for example, are driven largely by changes in the term structure of interest rates, while returns on equity depend also on changes in the broader economic environment, including macroeconomic factors besides interest rates. Once you begin considering how economic conditions influence separate sorts of investments, you might as well use a sophisticated asset allocation program to determine the proper mix for the portfolio. It is easy to see how investors get lured away from a purely passive strategy.

Even the definition of a "pure" passive strategy is not very clear-cut, as simple strategies involving only the market index portfolio and risk-free assets now seem to call for market

---

[1]This point is worked out fully in Sanford J. Grossman and Joseph E. Stiglitz, "On the Impossibility of Informationally Efficient Markets," *American Economic Review* 70 (June 1980), pp 393–408.

analysis. Our strict definition of a pure passive strategy is one that invests only in index funds and weights those funds by fixed proportions that do not change in response to market conditions. A portfolio strategy that always places 60% in a stock market index fund, 30% in a bond index fund, and 10% in a money market fund, regardless of expectations.

Active management is attractive because the potential profit is enormous, even though competition among managers is bound to drive market prices to near-efficient levels. For prices to remain efficient to some degree, decent profits to diligent analysts must be the rule rather than the exception, although large profits may be difficult to earn. Absence of profits would drive people out of the investment management industry, resulting in prices moving away from informationally efficient levels.

21.2 OBJECTIVES OF ACTIVE PORTFOLIOS

What does an investor expect from a professional portfolio manager, and how do these expectations affect the manager's response? If all clients were risk neutral (indifferent to risk), the answer would be straightforward: The investment manager should construct a portfolio with the highest possible expected rate of return, and the manager should then be judged by the realized *average* rate of return.

When the client is risk averse, the answer is more difficult. Lacking standards to proceed by, the manager would have to consult with each client before making any portfolio decision in order to ascertain that the prospective reward (average return) matched the client's attitude toward risk. Massive, continuous client input would be needed, and the economic value of professional management would be questionable.

Fortunately, the theory of mean-variance efficiency allows us to separate the "product decision," which is how to construct a mean-variance efficient risky portfolio, from the "consumption decision," which describes the investor's allocation of funds between the efficient risky portfolio and the safe asset. You have learned already that construction of the optimal risky portfolio is purely a technical problem and that there is a single optimal risky portfolio appropriate for all investors. Investors differ only in how they apportion investment between that risky portfolio and the safe asset.

The theory of efficient frontiers is not without practitioner adherents. For example, the accompanying box (page 568), presents an advertisement by J.P. Morgan Investment that focuses on efficient frontier analysis.

The mean-variance theory also speaks to performance in offering a criterion for judging managers on their choice of risky portfolios. In Chapter 7, we established that the optimal risky portfolio is the one that maximizes the reward-to-variability ratio, that is, the expected excess return divided by the standard deviation. A manager who maximizes this ratio will satisfy all clients regardless of risk aversion.

Clients can evaluate managers using statistical methods to draw inferences from realized rates of return about prospective, or ex ante, reward-to-variability ratios. The Sharpe measure, as this ratio is called, is now a widely accepted way to track performance of professionally managed portfolios.

$$S_P = \frac{E(r_P) - r_f}{\sigma_P}$$

The most able manager will be the one who consistently obtains the highest Sharpe measure, implying that the manager has real forecasting ability. A client's judgment of a manager's ability will affect the fraction of investment funds allocated to this manager; the client can invest the remainder with competing managers and in a safe fund.

If managers' Sharpe measures were reasonably constant over time, and clients could reliably estimate them, allocating funds to managers would be an easy decision.

How J.P. Morgan Investment Sponsors in International

International fixed-income securities account for nearly half the world's $5.4 trillion bond market—and offer plan sponsors increasingly attractive opportunities. J.P. Morgan Investment, the leader in this field, manages more than $3 billion of international fixed-income securities. We believe you should consider including international bonds in your pension portfolio.

Estimated market value $5.4 trillion
(publicly issued securities)

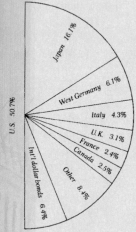

U.S. 50.7%
Japan 16.1%
West Germany 6.1%
Italy 4.3%
U.K. 3.1%
France 2.4%
Canada 2.5%
Other 8.4%
Int'l dollar bonds 6.4%

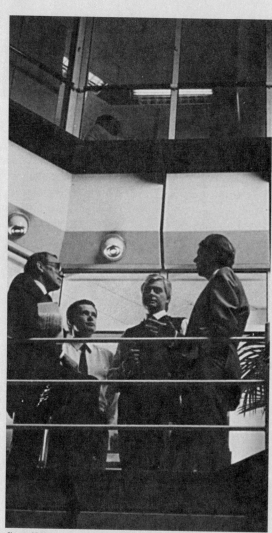

Shown at J.P. Morgan Investment's London headquarters are international fixed income team members (left to right) Anthony G. Bird, Hans K-E Danielsson, Bernard A. Wagenmann, and Adrian F. Lee

Finds Opportunities for Plan Fixed-Income Markets

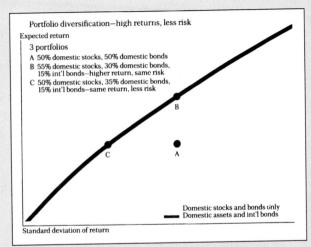

Portfolio diversification—high returns, less risk

Expected return

3 portfolios
A 50% domestic stocks, 50% domestic bonds
B 55% domestic stocks, 30% domestic bonds,
   15% int'l bonds—higher return, same risk
C 50% domestic stocks, 35% domestic bonds,
   15% int'l bonds—same return, less risk

Domestic stocks and bonds only
—— Domestic assets and int'l bonds

Standard deviation of return

The graph above shows that international fixed income investments can reduce you portfolio's risk and improve its return. Even if your pension plan already includes international equities, bonds will provide an effective way to further diversify your portfolio at lower levels of risk. In addition, the immediate outlook for international bonds is particularly favorable due to government fiscal and monetary policies now taking effect in many non-U.S. economies.

Managing Markets and Currencies

At J.P. Morgan Investment we seek to maximize long-term benefits for our clients, as well as to capitalize on short-term market movements. We select the markets most likely to offer the best return. At the same time we ensure maximum control of currency risk through active hedging.

Using this approach, J.P. Morgan Investment has outperformed return indexes in both rising an falling markets.

Active Management, Global Strength

Our strength in international fixed-income management is our global network of portfolio managers, analysts, and traders, and the worldwide resources of The Morgan Bank. Professionals in New York, London, Singapore, and Tokyo, continuously monitor and assess market developments to find the opportunities that will produce the best returns for our clients.

To learn more about our ideas and strengths in international fixed income management, write or call: Adrian F. Lee, Vice President, J.P. Morgan Investment Management Inc., 83 Pall Mall, London SW1Y5ES; telephone 01-930 9444. Or Anthony P. Wilson, Vice President, 522 Fifth Avenue, New York, NY 10036; telephone (212)837-2300.

J.P. Morgan Investment—An active investor in world capital markets. J.P. Morgan Investments has managed international bonds since 1977. We participate actively in both U.S. and international fixed income markets. Our International Investment Group, headquartered in London since 1974, serves clients all over the world, and specializes in managing single and multicurrency portfolios for corporations and governments diversifying into other markets.

J.P. Morgan Investment

Actually, the use of the Sharpe measure as the prime measure of a manager's ability requires some qualification. We know from the previous chapter on performance evaluation (Chapter 19) that the Sharpe ratio is the appropriate measure of performance only when the client's entire wealth is managed by the professional investor. Moreover, clients may impose additional restrictions on portfolio choice that further complicate the performance evaluation problem. These complications, however, can be addressed once the methodology described below is understood.

21.3 MARKET TIMING

Consider the results of two different investment strategies:

1. Investor X, who put $1,000 in 30-day commercial paper on January 1, 1927, and rolled over all proceeds into 30-day paper (or into 30-day T-bills after they were introduced), would have ended on December 31, 1978, 52 years later, with $3,600.
2. Investor Y, who put $1,000 in the NYSE index on January 1, 1927, and reinvested all dividends in that portfolio, would have ended on December 31, 1978, with $67,500.

market timing
Asset allocation in which the investment in the market is increased if one forecasts that the market will out perform T-bills.

Suppose we define perfect **market timing** as the ability to tell (with certainty) at the beginning of each month whether the NYSE will outperform 30-day commercial paper. The perfect market timer would shift all funds at the beginning of each month into either cash equivalents (30-day paper) or equities (the NYSE portfolio), whichever is predicted to do better. Beginning with $1,000 on the same date, how would the perfect timer have ended up 52 years later?

This is how Professor Robert Merton began a seminar with finance professors several years ago. The boldest guess of the responses was a few million dollars. The actual result: $5.36 billion.

Concept Check

1. What are the monthly and annually compounded rates of return for the X, Y, and perfect-timing strategies over the period 1927–1978?

These results have some lessons for us. The first has to do with the power of compounding. Its effect is particularly important as more and more of the funds under management represent pension savings. The horizons of pension investments may not be as long as 52 years, but they are measured in decades, making compounding a significant factor.

The second is a huge difference between the end value of the all-safe asset strategy ($3,600) and of the all-equity strategy ($67,500). Why would anyone invest in safe assets given this historical record? If you have absorbed all the lessons of this book, you know the reason: risk. The averages of the annualized monthly rates of return and the standard deviations on the all-bills and all-equity strategies were

	Arithmetic Mean	Standard Deviation
Bills	2.55	2.10
Equities	10.70	22.14

The significantly higher standard deviation of the rate of return on the equity portfolio is commensurate with its significantly higher average return. The higher average return reflects the risk premium.

Is the return premium on the perfect-timing strategy a risk premium? Because the perfect timer never does worse than either bills or the market, the extra return cannot be compensation for the possibility of poor returns; instead it is attributable to superior analysis. The value of superior information is reflected in the tremendous ending value of the portfolio. This value does not reflect compensation for risk.

The monthly results for the all-equity and the perfect-timing portfolios were

Portfolio: Monthly Statistics	(1) All Equity	(2) Perfect Timer Who Does Not Charge	(3) Perfect Timer Who Imposes a Fair Charge
Average rate of return	0.85	2.58	0.55
Average excess return	0.64	2.37	0.34
Standard deviation	5.89	3.82	3.55
Highest return	38.55	38.55	30.14
Lowest return	−29.12	0.06	−7.06
Coefficient of skewness	0.42	4.28	2.84

Ignore for the moment column 3. The first two rows of results are self-explanatory. The third line, "standard deviation," requires some discussion. The standard deviation of the rate of return earned by the perfect market timer (who does not charge) was 3.82%, far higher than the volatility of T-bills. This does not imply that perfect timing is a riskier strategy than bills. Here, standard deviation is a misleading measure of risk.

To see why, consider how you might choose between two hypothetical strategies. Strategy 1 offers a sure rate of return of 5%; strategy 2 offers an uncertain return that is given by 5% *plus* a random number that is zero with a probability of 0.5 and 5% with a probability of 0.5. The results for each strategy are

	Strategy 1 (%)	Strategy 2 (%)
Expected return	5	7.5
Standard deviation	0	2.5
Highest return	5	10
Lowest return	5	5

Clearly, strategy 2 dominates strategy 1, as its rate of return is *at least* equal to that of strategy 1 and sometimes greater. No matter how risk averse you are, you will always prefer strategy 2 to strategy 1, even though strategy 2 has a significant standard deviation. Compared to strategy 1, strategy 2 provides only good surprises, so the standard deviation in this case cannot be a measure of risk.

You can look at these strategies as analogous to the case of the perfect timer compared with an all-equity or all-bills strategy. In every period, the perfect timer obtains at least as good a return, in some cases better. Therefore, the timer's standard deviation is a misleading measure of risk when you compare perfect timing to an all-equity or all-bills strategy.

Returning to the empirical results, you can see that the highest rate of return is identical for the all-equity and the timing–no charge strategies, while the lowest rate of return is positive for the same perfect timer and disastrous for the all-equity portfolio. Another reflection of this is seen in the coefficient of skewness, which measures the asymmetry of the distribution of returns. Because the equity portfolio is almost (but not exactly) normally distributed, its coefficient of skewness is very low at 0.42. In contrast, the perfect-timing strategy effectively eliminates the negative tail of the distribution of portfolio returns (the part below the risk-free rate). Its returns are "skewed to the right," and its coefficient of skewness is quite large, 4.28.

The third column is perhaps the most interesting of the three. If you were a perfect timer, you would charge clients for your valuable service (saintly benevolence not being one of your otherworldly characteristics). Subtracting a fair fee from the monthly rate of return of the timer's portfolio makes the average rate of return lower than that of the passive, all-equity strategy.

Yet because the fee is set to be fair, the two portfolios (the all-equity and the market-timing-with-fee portfolios) must be equally attractive after risk adjustment. Here again, the

FIGURE 21.1

Rate of Return of a
Perfect Market Timer

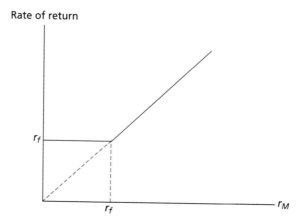

standard deviation of the market timing strategy (with fee) is of no help in adjusting for risk because the coefficient of skewness remains high, 2.84. In other words, standard mean-variance analysis presents complications when we use it for valuing market timing. We need an alternative approach.

Valuing Market Timing as an Option

The key to analyzing the pattern of returns of a perfect market timer is to compare the returns of a perfect foresight investor with those of another investor who holds a call option on the equity portfolio. Investing 100% in bills plus holding a call option on the equity portfolio will yield returns identical to those of the portfolio of the perfect timer who invests 100% in either the safe asset or the equity portfolio, whichever will yield the higher return. The perfect timer's return is shown in Figure 21.1. The rate of return is bounded from below by the risk-free rate, r_f.

To see how the value of information can be treated as an option, suppose the market index currently is at S_0, and a call option on the index has exercise price of $X = S_0 (1 + r_f)$. If the market outperforms bills over the coming period, S_T will exceed X; it will be less than X otherwise. Now look at the payoff to a portfolio consisting of this option and S_0 dollars invested in bills.

	Payoff to Portfolio	
Outcome:	$S_T \leq X$	$S_T > X$
Bills	$S_0(1 + r_f)$	$S_0(1 + r_f)$
Option	0	$S_T - X$
Total	$S_0(1 + r_f)$	S_T

The portfolio returns the risk-free rate when the market is bearish (that is, when the market return is less than the risk-free rate) and pays the market return when the market is bullish and beats bills. This represents perfect market timing. Consequently, the value of perfect timing ability is equivalent to the value of the call option, for a call enables the investor to earn the market return only when it exceeds r_f.

This insight let Robert Merton (1981) value timing ability according to the theory of option valuation; it also allows calculation of a fair charge for timing, which is subtracted in column 3.

The Value of Imperfect Forecasting

But managers are not perfect forecasters. While managers who are right most of the time presumably do very well, "right most of the time" does not mean merely the *percentage* of the time a manager is right. For example, a Tucson, Arizona, weather forecaster who *always* predicts "no rain" may be right 90% of the time, but this "stopped clock" strategy does not require any forecasting ability.

Neither is the overall proportion of correct forecasts an appropriate measure of market forecasting ability. If the market is up two days out of three, and a forecaster always predicts a market advance, the two-thirds success rate is not a measure of forecasting ability. We need to examine the proportion of bull markets ($r_M > r_f$) correctly forecast *and* the proportion of bear markets ($r_M < r_f$) correctly forecast.

If we call P_1 the proportion of the correct forecasts of bull markets and P_2 the proportion for bear markets, then $P_1 + P_2 - 1$ is the correct measure of timing ability. For example, a forecaster who always guesses correctly will have $P_1 = P_2 = 1$ and will show ability of 1 (100%). An analyst who always bets on a bear market will mispredict all bull markets ($P_1 = 0$), will correctly "predict" all bear markets ($P_2 = 1$), and will end up with timing ability of $P_1 + P_2 - 1 = 0$. If C denotes the (call option) value of a perfect market timer, then $P_1 + P_2 - 1)C$ measures the value of imperfect forecasting ability.

The incredible potential payoff to accurate timing documented by Merton versus the relative scarcity of billionaires should suggest to you that market timing is far from a trivial exercise and that very imperfect timing is the most that we can hope for. The nearby box (page 574) confirms this conclusion.

Concept Check

2. What is the market timing score of someone who flips a fair coin to predict the market?

21.4 SECURITY SELECTION: THE TREYNOR-BLACK MODEL

Overview of the Treynor-Black Model

Security analysis is the other dimension of active investment besides timing the overall market and asset allocation. Suppose you are an analyst studying individual securities. Quite likely, you will turn up several securities that appear to be mispriced and offer positive alphas. But how do you exploit your analysis? Concentrating a portfolio on these securities entails a cost, namely, the firm-specific risk you could shed by more fully diversifying. As an active manager, you must strike a balance between aggressive exploitation of security mispricing and diversification considerations that dictate against concentrating a portfolio in a few stocks.

Jack Treynor and Fischer Black (1973) have developed a portfolio construction model for managers who use security analysis. It assumes security markets are nearly efficient. The essence of the model is this:

1. Security analysts in an active investment management organization can analyze in depth only a relatively small number of stocks out of the entire universe of securities. The securities not analyzed are assumed to be fairly priced.
2. For the purpose of efficient diversification, the market index portfolio is the baseline portfolio, which the model treats as the passive portfolio.
3. The macro forecasting unit of the investment management firm provides forecasts of the expected rate of return and variance of the passive (market index) portfolio.
4. The objective of security analysis is to form an active portfolio of a necessarily limited number of securities. Perceived mispricing of the analyzed securities is the determining principle in the composition of this active portfolio.
5. Analysts follow several steps to make up the active portfolio and forecast its performance:
   a. Estimate the characteristic line of each analyzed security and obtain its beta and residual variance. From the beta and the macro forecast, $E(r_M) - r_f$, determine the *required* rate of return of the security.

Market Timing Also Stumps Many Pros

Individual investors often imagine that the Wall Street pros must know how to dart between stocks, bonds, and cash—in other words, to time the markets so they profit when prices soar and hang on to gains when prices dive.

Don't bet on it.

For 10 years now, *The Wall Street Journal*—with help from Wilshire Associates of Santa Monica, Calif., and Carpenter Analytical Services of Hanover, N.H.—has studied the asset-allocation advice of strategists at the nation's biggest brokerage houses. Asset allocation is the art of dividing an investment portfolio among stocks, bonds, cash, and other alternatives.

A decade of results throws cold water on the notion that the strategists exhibit any special ability to time the markets. According to Robin Carpenter, president of Carpenter Analytical, the strategists' average annual gain from market timing is a mere 0.18%. That's the extra return above what each would have earned by sticking with his or her own average recommended blend for the entire period.

Who Has the Best Blend?

Performance of asset-allocation blends recommended by 14 major brokerage houses in periods ended Dec. 31, 1996. Figures do not include transaction costs. Houses are ranked by 12-month performance. Also shown is the mix each house now recommends.

Brokerage Houses	Performance			Recommended Blend		
	Three-Month	One Year	Five Year	Stocks	Bonds	Cash
Lehman Brothers	7.1%	17.8%	76.1%	65%	35%	0%
Goldman Sachs	6.6	17.4	80.9	60	25	10[1]
Paine Webber	6.4	15.8	75.5	54	35	11
First Boston	6.4	15.7	N.A.	60	30	10
Raymond James	6.5	15.6	64.2	60	15	15[2]
Prudential	6.2	15.3	74.3	70	25	5
Dean Witter	6.3	15.0	76.1	65	20	15
Bear Stearns	6.2	15.0	N.A.	55	35	10
Edward Jones	5.8	15.0	N.A.	65	25	10[3]
Smith Barney	5.8	14.3	71.1	50	40	10
Salomon Brothers	5.9	13.9	66.0	45	35	20
A.G. Edwards	5.7	13.8	67.3	60	30	10
Everen	5.1	13.1	67.5	62	33	5[4]
Merrill Lynch	4.7	11.5	67.8	40	50	10[5]
Average	6.1%	14.9%	71.5%	58%	31%	10%

By Comparison:

	Three-Month	One Year	Five Year
Robot blend[6]	6.2%	15.0%	73.2%
Stocks	8.1	23.6	104.8
Bonds	4.7	4.9	44.4
Cash	1.3	5.4	25.1

[1]Recommends 5% in commodities.
[2]45% in U.S. stocks, 15% international, 10% in real estate.
[3]55% in U.S. stocks, 10% international.
[4]47% in U.S. stocks, 15% international.
[5]26% in U.S. stocks, 14% international.
[6]Always 55% stocks, 35% bonds, 10% cash.

NA = Not applicable (not in study for full period).
Sources: Company documents, Wilshire Associates, Carpenter Analytical Services.

And almost all of that meager edge comes from timing the bond market, not the stock market. (The study covers 14 brokerage houses, 8 of which have been included for the full 10-year period.)

Over the past 10 years, the *Journal's* trusty "asset allocation robot," which always keeps 55% in stocks, 35% in bonds, and 10% in cash, has achieved an estimated return of 12.3% a year. Returns for the flesh-and-blood strategists have ranged from 11.4% at A.G. Edwards Inc. in St. Louis to 13.5% at Prudential Securities, a unit of Prudential Insurance Co. of America.

Strategists at six of the eight firms beat the robot over the 10-year period, but not by a great deal. By and large, they did so not by market timing but by habitually recommending more stocks than the robot does.

Source: John R. Dorfman, "Market Timing Also Stumps Many Pros," *The Wall Street Journal*, January 30, 1997.

b. Determine the expected return. Subtracting the required return yields the expected *abnormal* return (alpha) of the security.

c. Use the estimates for the values of alpha, beta, and residual risk to determine the optimal weight of each security in the active portfolio.

d. Estimate the alpha, beta, and residual variance for the active portfolio according to the weights of the securities in the portfolio.

6. The macroeconomic forecasts for the passive index portfolio and the composite forecast for the active portfolio are used to determine the optimal risky portfolio, which will be a combination of the passive and active portfolios.

Treynor-Black model
An optimizing model for portfolio managers who use security analysis in a nearly efficient market.

Although some sophisticated investment managers use the **Treynor-Black model,** it has not taken the industry by storm. This is unfortunate for several reasons:

1. Just as even imperfect market-timing ability has enormous value, security analysis of the sort Treynor and Black propose has similar potential value. Even with far-from-perfect security analysis, active management can add value.

2. The Treynor-Black model is easy to implement. Moreover, it is useful even relaxing some of its simplifying assumptions.

3. The model lends itself to use with decentralized decision making, which is essential to efficiency in complex organizations.

Portfolio Construction

Assuming all securities are fairly priced and using the index model as a guideline for the rate of return on securities, the rate of return security *i* is given by

$$r_i = r_f + \beta_i (r_M - r_f) + e_i \tag{21.1}$$

where e_i is the zero mean, firm-specific (nonsystematic) component.

Absent security analysis, Treynor and Black take Equation 21.1 to represent the rate of return on all securities and assume the index portfolio (*M*) is efficient. For simplicity, they also assume the nonsystematic components of returns, e_i, are independent across securities. Market timing is incorporated in the terms r_M and σ_M, representing index portfolio forecasts. The overall investment in the risky portfolio will be affected by the optimism or pessimism reflected in these numbers.

Assume a team of security analysts investigates a subset of the universe of available securities, with the objective of forming an active portfolio. That portfolio will then be mixed with the index portfolio to improve diversification. For each security, *k*, that is researched, we write the rate of return as

$$r_k = r_f + \beta_k (r_M - r_f) + e_k + \alpha_k \tag{21.2}$$

where α_k represents the extra (abnormal) expected return attributable to the mispricing of the security. Thus, for each security analyzed, the research team estimates the parameters

$$\alpha_k, \beta_k, \sigma^2(e_k)$$

active portfolio
In the context of the Treynor-Black model, the portfolio formed by mixing analyzed stocks of perceived nonzero alpha values. This portfolio is ultimately mixed with the passive market index portfolio.

If all the α_k turn out to be zero, there would be no reason to depart from the passive strategy, and the index portfolio would remain the manager's choice. But this is a remote possibility. In general, there will be a significant number of nonzero α values, some positive and some negative.

Consider first how you would use the active portfolio once you found it. Suppose the **active portfolio** *(A)* has been constructed somehow and has the parameters

$$\alpha_A, \beta_A, \sigma^2(e_A)$$

FIGURE 21.2

The Optimization Process with Active and Passive Portfolios

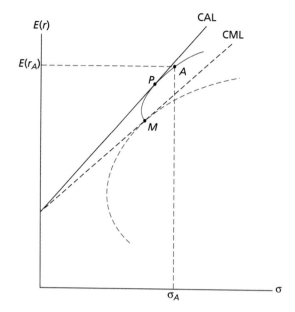

The total variance of the active portfolio is the sum of its systematic variance, $\beta_A^2\sigma_M^2$, plus the nonsystematic variance, $\sigma^2(e_A)$. These three parameters, plus the mean and variance of the index portfolio, are sufficient to identify the opportunity set generated by the active and passive portfolios.

Figure 21.2 shows the optimization process with active and passive portfolios. The dashed efficient frontier line represents the universe of all securities, assuming they are all fairly priced, that is, that all alphas are zero. By definition, the market index (M) is on this efficient frontier and is tangent to the (dashed) capital market line (CML). In practice, our analysts do not need to (indeed cannot) know this frontier, but they need to forecast the index portfolio and construct the optimal risky portfolio using the index and active (A) portfolios. The optimal portfolio (P) will lie on the capital allocation line (CAL) that lies above the CML.

From the viewpoint of an investor with superior analysis, the index portfolio will be inefficient; that is, the active portfolio (A) constructed from mispriced securities will lie above the CML.

The optimal combination of the active portfolio with the passive portfolio takes off from the construction of an optimal risky portfolio from two risky assets that we first encountered in Chapter 7. As the active portfolio is not perfectly correlated with the index, further diversification—that is, mixing it with the index—is likely to be beneficial.

We can judge the success of the active management, and the contribution of the active portfolio (A), by the Sharpe measure (ratio of reward to variability) of the resultant risky portfolio (P), compared with that of the index portfolio (M).

The mathematics of the efficient frontier reveal that the Sharpe measure of the risky portfolio is

$$S(P) = [S^2(M) + \alpha_A^2/\sigma^2(e_A)]^{1/2}$$

Thus, the critical variable in determining the success of the active portfolio is its ratio of alpha to nonsystematic risk, $\alpha_A/\sigma(e_A)$.

The intuition here is straightforward. You mix the active portfolio with the index for the benefit of diversification. The position to take in the active portfolio relative to the market portfolio depends on the strength of the active portfolio's abnormal return, α_A, relative to its weakness given by its diversifiable risk, $\sigma^2(e_A)$, sometimes referred to as the *adjusted alpha*.

The contribution of individual securities (say, k) to the active portfolio (A) is analogous to that of the active portfolio to the risky portfolio (P). It is measured by the adjusted alpha, $\alpha_k/\sigma(e_k)$.

21.5 MULTIFACTOR MODELS AND ACTIVE PORTFOLIO MANAGEMENT

Sophisticated investment management organizations often prefer a multifactor versus a single-factor structure of security returns. Yet, so far, our analytical framework for active portfolio management seems to rest on the validity of the index model, that is, on a single-factor security model.

To move from a single-factor to a multifactor structure, we begin with the *residuals* (nonsystematic components) of the rate of return of the multifactor model. We continue to form the active portfolio by calculating each security's alpha relative to its fair return (given its betas on *all* factors), and then we combine the active portfolio with the portfolio that would be formed in the absence of security analysis. The multifactor framework does, however, raise the issue of the configuration of an efficient passive portfolio from candidate factor portfolios.

To simplify, let us consider a two-factor world, and let the two factor portfolios be called M and H. Then we generalize the index model to

$$r_i - r_f = \beta_{iM}(r_M - r_f) + \beta_{iH}(r_H - r_f) + \alpha_i + e_i$$
$$= r_\beta + \alpha_i + e_i$$

(21.3)

β_{iM} and β_{iH} are the betas of the security relative to portfolios M and H. Given return forecasts on the factor portfolios, r_M and r_H, the fair excess return on a security is denoted r_β and its abnormal return is α_i.

How can we use Equation 21.3 to form an optimal passive portfolio—that is, a portfolio that does not require security analysis? Absent security analysis (assuming all alphas to be zero), we would use the asset allocation program discussed in Chapter 7 to construct the optimal index portfolio. In the two-factor case, as in Equation 21.3, asset allocation is reduced to a universe of two risky assets and a risk-free asset.

Adding security analysis for an active management strategy, we can apply the Treynor-Black model. We proceed as follows:

1. For each security, we estimate the betas (two in this case) and the residual variance.
2. The alpha is determined from security analysis.
3. An active portfolio is constructed on the basis of the ratio of alpha to residual variance.
4. The active portfolio (A) betas and residual variance are computed.
5. We apply the asset allocation program to the three portfolios ($M, H,$ and A) and obtain the optimal risky portfolio.

The only departure from the single-factor case is in step 5. The estimation of two or more betas in step 1 simply implies that a multiple regression has to be used instead of a single-variable one.

It is possible, however, that the factor structure of the market has hedging implications. This means certain clients prefer a certain correlation of their portfolios with one or more of the factors. These investors may be willing to accept an inferior Sharpe measure in order to maintain a risky portfolio that has the desired hedge qualities. Portfolio optimization for these investors is more complicated, requiring specific information on client preferences. The portfolio manager will not be able to satisfy diverse clients with one portfolio.

Summary

- Active portfolio managers attempt to construct a risky portfolio that improves on the reward-to-variability (Sharpe) ratio of a passive strategy.
- Active management has two components: market timing (or, in a multifactor market, asset allocation) and security analysis.
- The value of perfect market-timing ability is enormous. The rate of return to a perfect market timer will be uncertain, but its risk cannot be measured by standard deviation, because perfect timing dominates a passive strategy, providing only "good" surprises.
- Perfect-timing ability is equivalent to having a call option on the market portfolio. The value of the option can be determined using valuation techniques such as the Black-Scholes formula.
- The value of *imperfect* timing, such as whether stocks will outperform bills, is given by the sum of the probabilities of the true outcome conditional on the forecast: $P_1 + P_2 - 1$. If perfect timing is equivalent to call option C, then imperfect timing can be valued by: $(P_1 + P_2 - 1)C$.
- The Treynor-Black model is based on an index model that takes market-timing forecasts as given. The investment manager uses security analysis and statistics to construct an active portfolio. The active portfolio is mixed with the index portfolio to maximize the Sharpe measure of the optimal risky portfolio.
- In the Treynor-Black model, the weight of each analyzed security is proportional to the ratio of its alpha to its residual variance.

Key Terms

market timing, *570*   Treynor-Black model, *575*   active portfolio, *575*

Problem Sets

1. Historical data suggest the standard deviation of an all-equity strategy is about 5.5% per month. Suppose the risk-free rate is now 1% per month and market volatility is at its historical level. What would be a fair monthly fee to a perfect market timer, according to the Black-Scholes formula?

2. A fund manager scrutinizing the record of two market timers comes up with this information:

Number of months that $r_M > r_f$	135
Correctly predicted by timer A	78
Correctly predicted by timer B	86
Number of months that $r_M < r_f$	92
Correctly predicted by timer A	57
Correctly predicted by timer B	50

   a. What are the conditional probabilities, P_1 and P_2, and the total ability parameters for timers A and B?

   b. Using the historical data of problem 1, what is a fair monthly fee for the two timers?

■IEM Applications

1. Over a one-month IEM market period, determine what would happen to the value of your portfolio if you engaged in market timing and always purchased securities that subsequently went up in value and sold securities that went down in value. Determine what would happen if you selected securities perfectly (i.e., invested your entire portfolio in the security that ultimately paid off $1 when its price was at its historical low.)

2. Why are the possible IEM profits from Problem 1 mostly illusionary?

1. We show the answer for the annual compounded rate of return for each strategy and leave you to compute the monthly rate:
   Beginning-of-period fund: $F_0 = \$1,000$
   End-of-period fund for each strategy:

$$F_1 = \begin{cases} 3,600 & \text{Strategy = Bills only} \\ 67,500 & \text{Strategy = Market only} \\ 5,360,000,000 & \text{Strategy = Perfect timing} \end{cases}$$

Number of periods: $N = 52$ years
Annual compounded rate:

$$(1 + r_A)^N = \frac{F_1}{F_0}$$

$$r_A = \left(\frac{F_1}{F_0}\right)^{1/N} - 1$$

$$r_A = \begin{cases} 2.49\% & \text{Strategy = Bills only} \\ 8.44\% & \text{Strategy = Market only} \\ 34.71\% & \text{Strategy = Perfect timing} \end{cases}$$

2. The timer will guess bear or bull markets randomly. One-half of all bull markets will be preceded by a correct forecast, and, similarly, one-half of all bear markets will be preceded by a correct forecast. Hence, $P_1 + P_2 - 1 = 1/2 + 1/2 - 1 = 0$.

Appendixes

Appendix A

SOURCES OF FINANCIAL AND ECONOMIC INFORMATION

Information is crucial in successful investing. In many cases, however, the biggest challenge facing investors is not a scarcity of information. For most investors, processing and interpreting the vast amount of information available is an even more daunting task than uncovering information. In this appendix, we provide a guided tour of some of the more important sources of information. We will progress from coverage of more general to more specific topics.

GENERAL INTEREST PUBLICATIONS

The Wall Street Journal is the most widely read source of financial and economic news. It has the highest circulation of any daily newspaper. The *Journal* reports on international, national, industry, and firm-specific news. It provides an extensive daily listing of security prices and interest rates, and it reports firms' earnings and dividend announcements as they are made.

Barrons is a weekly publication with even more extensive reporting of financial market prices, especially foreign security listings. It also contains regular features on various aspects of the securities market.

Investor's Daily began in 1984 in competition with *The Wall Street Journal*. It provides more price data than *The Wall Street Journal* but contains less descriptive reporting.

Business Week is oriented toward ongoing and complete business news reporting. In contrast, *Forbes* and *Fortune* are both biweekly publications and are oriented toward more lengthy feature stories on particular companies, individuals, or issues. *Forbes* is known in part for its annual report on American industry, where it reports performance of several industries for the past five years. It also assesses performance of mutual funds annually.

Other financial and business-oriented general periodicals are *Dun's Review* and *Financial World*. Two good publications with an institutional focus are *Institutional Investor* and *Pensions and Investments Age*.

MACROECONOMIC DATA

The U.S. government offers an extensive set of publications.

The *Federal Reserve Bulletin* is published monthly by the Board of Governors of the Federal Reserve System. It provides extensive data on the banking system and the money supply. The *Bulletin* is the primary source for most information on the monetary system. It also contains other macroeconomic data such as figures on GNP, interest rates, corporate profits, and employment.

The *Survey of Current Business* is published monthly by the U.S. Commerce Department. It provides detailed data on national income and production accounts, which are essentially breakdowns of GNP. The survey also provides considerable data on the labor market. It also provides production data for individual industries as well as employment, interest rates, prices, and foreign economic data.

The *Economic Report of the President* is an annual publication with over 100 tables on national income and expenditure, employment and wages, business activity, consumer and producer prices, government finance and budgets, corporate profits, interest rates, and international statistics.

The *Statistical Abstract of the United States* is prepared annually by the U.S. Bureau of the Census. It includes statistics on the social, demographic, economic, and political makeup of the United States in its approximately 1,000 pages of tables.

INDUSTRY DATA

As noted, the *Survey of Current Business* contains considerable industry data. Other government publications from the Census Bureau are the *Censuses of: Manufacturers; Retail Trade; Service Industries;* and *Wholesale Trade.* The Census Bureau also publishes an *Annual Survey of Manufacturers* and *Current Industrial Reports.*

Private companies also publish industry data and outlooks. Among these are *Moody's Investor Services,* which publishes *Industry Review,* and Standard & Poor's Corporation, which publishes *Industry Survey.* S&P covers about 70 industries, providing current and historical information as well as prospects for each. Value Line also provides industry analysis in its weekly *Investment Survey.* Each week a different industry is highlighted. Sample excerpts from these publications appear below with the discussion of company data.

COMPANY DATA

The original sources for most company data are annual reports, which are published every year by publicly held corporations. The annual report contains financial statements for the current and recent years and management's assessment of the company's past and future performance. Most firms also issue quarterly financial reports with more sketchy information. More detailed information is provided in the Form 10-K and Form 10-Q, which all firms with publicly traded securities must file with the Securities and Exchange Commission. Company prospectuses also contain considerable information. The prospectus, which is prepared for investors when the company issues new securities, contains financial statements, as well as considerable data on the company's operations and management. The data in the prospectus are more detailed than those in the annual report.

Value Line publishes a wealth of data on about 1,700 firms in its *Investment Survey.* A sample page from the survey appears in Figure A.1. The page contains 15 years of historical and forecast balance sheet and income statement data, stock price history, dividend data, capital structure information, a short description of the company's line of business and prospects, stock beta, and projected stock performance. Value Line's performance forecast, called timeliness, was discussed in Chapter 18. The *Survey* is published weekly. Each week, 6 to 10 industries are analyzed. Over the year, all 1,700 firms are evaluated once.

Moody's Manuals also provide a wealth of company data. Moody's contains recent and historical balance sheets and income statements, information on outstanding securities issued by the firm, and useful descriptive material on the company. Moody's Manuals are arranged as follows: *Bank and Finance; Industrial; International; Municipal & Government; OTC Industrials; OTC Unlisted; Public Utility;* and *Transportation.* Moody's also

FIGURE A.1 Value Line *Investment Survey*, Sample Report

Ratings & Reports   A   B   BB   C   D

PHILIP MORRIS NYSE-MO | RECENT PRICE **85** | P/E RATIO **8.4** (TRAILING: 9.6 / MEDIAN: 9.5) | RELATIVE P/E RATIO **0.73** | DIV'D YLD **5.1%** | 343

	1970	1971	1972	1973	1974	1975	1976	1977	1978	1979	1980	1981	1982	1983	1984	1985	1986	1987	© Value Line, Inc.	88-90E
High	17.8	29.6	34.2	30.7	29.6	31.6	32.4	38.4	38.6	48.5	55.1	67.8	72.4	83.3	95.1					
Low	11.7	16.9	24.4	17.0	20.4	24.9	25.8	27.9	31.1	29.1	42.0	44.1	54.0	62.1	79.0					
Sales per sh	15.62	17.70	19.57	23.50	26.29	30.68	36.09	43.41	53.37	66.67	78.73	86.81	93.06	103.82	113.79	*123.30*	*133.50*			178.00
"Cash Flow" per sh	.99	1.18	1.40	1.63	1.88	2.22	2.80	3.47	4.22	5.28	6.17	7.18	8.46	9.85	11.61	*13.40*	*15.60*			26.50
Earnings per sh	.84	1.01	1.17	1.36	1.58	1.81	2.24	2.80	3.39	4.08	4.63	5.28	6.23	7.17	8.43	*10.10*	*12.00*			16.00
Div'ds Decl'd per sh	.26	.30	.32	.34	.38	.44	.58	.78	1.03	1.25	1.60	2.00	2.40	2.90	3.40	*4.00*	*4.60*			6.50
Cap'l Spending per sh	.39	.57	1.10	1.61	1.88	2.06	1.85	2.34	4.56	5.07	6.06	8.15	7.31	4.53	2.46	*2.70*	*2.75*			4.00
Book Value per sh	4.47	5.36	6.28	7.33	8.43	10.32	12.00	14.08	17.00	19.84	22.87	26.35	29.09	32.27	33.72	*38.30*	*44.75*			68.65
Common Shs Outst'g	96.64	104.68	108.89	110.76	114.53	118.71	118.97	119.84	124.27	124.54	124.75	125.40	125.90	124.98	121.40	*120.00*	*118.00*			118.00
Avg Ann'l P/E Ratio	11.3	15.4	21.0	22.1	15.5	13.7	12.7	10.4	9.8	8.4	8.6	9.3	8.4	8.8	7.5	Bold figures are Value Line estimates				11.0
Relative P/E Ratio	.81	.98	1.44	2.18	2.17	1.83	1.63	1.36	1.34	1.22	1.14	1.13	.93	.74	.69					.90
Avg Ann'l Div'd Yield	2.8%	2.0%	1.3%	1.1%	1.5%	1.8%	2.0%	2.7%	3.1%	3.7%	4.0%	4.1%	4.6%	4.6%	4.7%					3.7%

100 x Cash Flow psh

2 for 1 split   **2 for 1 split**

Options Trade On ASE

Relative Price Strength

Percent shares traded: 9.0 / 6.0 / 3.0

Insider Decisions

	F	M	A	M	J	J	A	S	O	N	D	J	F	M	A
to Buy	3	3	4	1	0	3	2	1	3	1	0	1	3	4	2
to Sell	1	3	1	2	2	4	3	3	6	1	0	3	3	3	5

Institutional Decisions

	1Q'84	2Q'84	3Q'84	4Q'84	1Q'85
to Buy	152	158	142	128	147
to Sell	146	130	141	172	183
Hdg's (000)	73666	75144	74487	74356	74952

Target Price Range 1988 1989 1990

July 5, 1985 — Value Line

TIMELINESS **2** (Relative Price Perform-ance Next 12 Mos) — Above Average

SAFETY **1** (Scale: 1 Highest to 5 Lowest) — Highest

BETA **.90** (1.00 = Market)

1988-90 PROJECTIONS

	Price	Gain	Ann'l Total Return
High	190	(+125%)	26%
Low	155	(+80%)	20%

Figure	1982	1983	1984	1985	1986	...	1988
Sales ($ mill)	4293.8	5202.0	6632.5	8302.9	9822.3	10886	11716	12976	13814	*14800*	*5750*		21000
Operating Margin	18.2%	18.4%	18.3%	18.7%	14.9%	18.2%	16.6%	12.0%	18.1%	*19.8%*	*19.8%*		18.8%
Depreciation ($ mill)	67.7	81.6	116.2	149.6	192.9	240.4	283.7	327.0	375.5	*390*	*415*		5.25
Net Profit ($ mill)	265.7	334.9	408.6	507.9	576.8	659.7	781.8	903.5	1034.1	*1220*	*1425*		1890
Income Tax Rate	43.7%	56.5%	45.2%	43.9%	40.5%	38.9%	40.0%	43.0%	45.2%	*45.0%*	*45.0%*		44.0%
Net Profit Margin	6.2%	6.4%	6.2%	6.1%	5.9%	6.1%	6.7%	7.0%	7.5%	*8.2%*	*9.0%*		9.0%
Working Cap'l ($ mill)	1202.3	1415.8	1585.1	1833.2	1849.3	2053.0	2236.5	1116.5	1288.6	*1500*	*1900*		4200
Long-Term Debt ($ mill)	1247.8	1426.6	2147.0	2447.8	2598.1	3499.0	3749.3	2514.7	2059.5	*1800*	*1600*		1800
Net Worth ($ mill)	1430.0	1690.1	2114.7	2471.0	2853.0	3304.6	3662.9	4033.7	4092.9	*4600*	*5275*		8100
% Earned Total Cap'l	11.7%	12.3%	11.1%	11.8%	12.0%	11.2%	12.3%	15.8%	18.6%	*20.5%*	*22.0%*		20.0%
% Earned Net Worth	18.6%	19.8%	19.3%	20.6%	20.2%	20.0%	21.3%	22.4%	25.3%	*26.5%*	*27.0%*		23.5%
% Retained to Comm Eq	13.8%	14.3%	13.4%	14.3%	13.2%	12.4%	13.1%	13.3%	15.1%	*16.0%*	*16.5%*		14.0%
% All div'ds to Net Prof	26%	28%	31%	31%	35%	38%	39%	40%	40%	*40%*	*38%*		41%

CAPITAL STRUCTURE as of 12/31/84
Total Debt $2588.6 mill Due in Yrs $1161.8 mill.
LT Debt $2059.5 mill. LT interest $210.0 mill.
(LT interest earned: 8.0x; total interest coverage: 7.0x) (33% of Cap'l)

Pension Liability None in '84 vs. None in '83

Pfd Stock None

Common Stock 121,395,290 shs. (67% of Cap'l)

CURRENT POSITION $ MILL.

	1982	1983	12/31/84
Cash Assets	53.9	29.8	93.7
Receivables	691.1	781.8	854.3
Inventory(LIFO)	3068.5	2599.2	2653.5
Other	36.8	42.0	38.6
Current Assets	3850.3	3452.8	3640.1
Accts Payable	423.7	437.3	471.9
Debt Due	—	560.2	529.1
Other	1190.1	1338.8	1350.5
Current Liab.	1613.8	2336.3	2351.5

ANNUAL RATES of change (per sh)

	Past 10 Yrs	Past 5 Yrs	Est '82-'84 to '88-'90
Sales	16.0%	13.5%	9.5%
"Cash Flow"	20.0%	18.0%	13.0%
Earnings	19.0%	17.5%	15.0%
Dividends	24.0%	23.5%	14.5%
Book Value	15.5%	13.5%	13.5%

QUARTERLY SALES ($ mill.)

Calendar	Mar. 31	June 30	Sept. 30	Dec. 31	Full Year
1982	2795	3065	3065	2721	11716
1983	3021	3400	3464	3091	12976
1984	3249	3609	3666	3290	13814
1985	3315	*3900*	*3950*	*3635*	*14800*
1986	*3675*	*4100*	*4150*	*3825*	*15750*

EARNINGS PER SHARE

Calendar	Mar. 31	June 30	Sept. 30	Dec. 31	Full Year
1982	1.34	1.51	1.99	1.39	6.23
1983	1.47	1.75	2.27	1.68	7.17
1984	1.67	2.10	2.62	2.04	8.43
1985	2.12	*2.50*	*3.05*	*2.43*	*10.10*
1986	*2.50*	*3.00*	*3.68*	*2.90*	*12.00*

QUARTERLY DIVIDENDS PAID

Calendar	Mar. 31	June 30	Sept. 30	Dec. 31	Full Year
1981	.40	.50	.50	.50	1.90
1982	.50	.60	.60	.60	2.30
1983	.60	.725	.725	.725	2.78
1984	.725	.85	.85	.85	3.28
1985	.85	1.00	1.00		

BUSINESS: Philip Morris Inc. is the nation's largest cigarette producer (estimated 35% of domestic consumption) and exporter. Major brands: *Marlboro, Benson & Hedges, Parliament, Merit, Virginia Slims, Players.* Acquired Miller, second largest beer manufacturer in U.S., in 1970. Sells *High Life, Lite and Lowenbrau.* Acquired Seven-Up, third leading soft drink co. in '78. Owns Mission Viejo, West Coast real estate developer. '84 depreciation rate: 6.7%. Estimated plant age: 5 yrs. Insiders own about 1.5% of common stock. Has 60,000 employees, 30,300 common stockholders. Chairman & C.E.O.: H. Maxwell, President: & C.O.O.: J.A. Murphy Inc. Virginia. Address: 120 Park Avenue, New York, NY 10017.

We look for Philip Morris to generate a huge amount of excess cash over the next three to five years. The company's core domestic tobacco business throws off an awesome level of profits—$1.7 billion in 1984 and an estimated $2.0 billion this year. Since capital requirements for this operation are relatively modest (and declining), much of these funds are available for other investment purposes. Indeed, our cash flow analysis suggests that through the end of this decade, PM's "free" cash flow will average about $1 billion annually and could be much more if the company decides to scuttle the Miller and/or Seven-Up divisions, neither of which have lived up to expectations.

How will management utilize these monies? Completion of an announced share buyback program, coupled with a steady paring of the debt load and regular, double-digit dividend increases through the 1988-90 period, seem all but assured; such moves, however, would "sop up" only a portion of the excess cash flow. Further share repurchases could be undertaken, but we think the acquisition of a major consumer products outfit remains an intriguing possibility. Though we won't factor the

benefits from acquisitions into our estimates and projections until any deals are finalized, success in this regard could greatly enhance PM's earnings growth prospects—and stock price appreciation potential—to the 1988-90 period. As it is, based on current operations alone, we look for PM's share profits to grow at about a 15% rate, compounded annually over the next three to five years. **These timely shares have been under pressure of late,** as Wall Street struggled to determine the possible effect of pending product liability litigation against cigarette manufacturers, a very complicated and difficult to assess situation. Though PM does not expect any cases in which it is directly involved to go to trial this year and although to date the tobacco industry has never lost a

(Continued on page 389)

Projected Sales (and Operating Margins) by Company's Use

	1982	1983	1984	1985
Philip Morris, the	4330.0(25.5%)	5520.0(24.2%)	6134.0(26.5%)	*3000(21.8%)*
Philip Morris, the	3584.0(12.5%)	3647.0(10.0%)	3741.0(11.5%)	*4100(11.4%)*
Miller Brewing	2929.8(5.4%)	2922.0(7.8%)	2928.0(4.0%)	*3000(8.3%)*
Seven Up	531.0(0.1%)	650.0(0.6%)	734.0(0.7%)	*200(1.8%)*
Philip Morris, the	233.0(3.3%)	237.0(6.7%)	277.0(16.6%)	*3000(10.3%)*
Mission Viejo	130.0(4.6%)	—	—	*—(—)*
Company Total	**11718.1(14.7%)**	**12976.0(14.9%)**	**13814.0(16.8%)**	**13300(18.8%)**

After depreciation, before interest exp. & equity income

(A) Includes Seven-Up from 6/78. **(B)** Based on avg. shs. outst'g. Next earnings report due late July. Est'd current cost eqs./sh.: '84, $5.93. **(C)** Next div'd meeting about | Aug. 29. Goes ex about Sept. 10. Approx. div'd payment dates: Jan. 10, Apr. 10, July 10, Oct. 10. ■ Div'd reinvestment plan available. **(D)** Incl. intangibles. In '84 $547 | mill., $4.50/sh. **(E)** in mill, adj. for stock splits & div'ds. **(F)** Mission Viejo rept'd on equity basis from 1983. **(G)** Excl. nonrecur writeoff of $1.19/sh. in 4th qtr. of '84.

Company's Financial Strength	A
Stock's Price Stability	90
Price Growth Persistence	60
Earnings Predictability	100

FIGURE A.1   (concluded)

Sample Value Line Report

A Recent price—nine days prior to delivery date.

AA Here is the core of Value Line's advice—the rank for Timeliness; the rank for Safety; Beta—the stock's sensitivity to fluctuations of the market as a whole.

B P/E ratio—the most recent price divided by the latest six months' earnings per share plus earnings estimated for the next six months.

BB P/E median—a rounded average of four middle values of the range of average annual price-earnings ratios over the past 10 years.

C Relative P/E ratio—the stock's current P/E divided by the median P/E for all stocks under Value Line review.

D Dividend yield—cash dividends *estimated to be declared in the next 12 months* divided by the recent price.

E The 3-5 year target price range, estimated. The range is placed in proper position on the price chart and is shown numerically in the "1988–90 Projections" box in the lower right-hand corner of the price chart.

F The date of delivery to the subscribers. The survey is mailed on a schedule that aims for delivery to every subscriber on Friday afternoon.

G Annual total return—the estimated future average annual growth plus current dividend yield—plus possible annualized change in the trend of the price-earnings ratio.

H The stock's **highest and lowest price** of the year.

I The value line—reported earnings plus depreciation ("cash flow") multiplied by a number selected to correlate the stock's 3- to 5-year projected target price with "cash flow" projected out to 1988–90.

J Monthly price ranges of the stock—plotted on a ratio (logarithmic) grid to show percentage changes in true proportion. For example, a ratio chart equalizes the move of a $10 stock that rises to $11 with a $100 stock that rises to $110. Both have advanced 10% and over the same space on a ratio grid.

K Relative price strength—describes the stock's past price performance relative to the Value Line Composite Average of 1,700 stocks. The Timeliness rank usually predicts the future direction of this line.

L The number of shares traded monthly as a percentage of the total shares outstanding.

M Statistical milestones that reveal significant long-term trends. The statistics are presented in two ways: 1) The upper series records results on a per-share basis; 2) the lower series records results on a company basis. On other pages, you will find conclusions that might be drawn from an inspection of these milestones.

Note that the statistics for the year 1985 are estimated, as are the figures for the average of the years 1988–90. The estimates would be revised, if necessary, should future evidence require. The weekly *Summary & Index* would promptly call attention to such revisions.

N A condensed summary of the **business**.

O A 400-word report on **recent developments and prospects**—issued once every three months on a preset schedule.

P Most large corporations engage in several lines of business. Hence sales and profit margins are shown by **lines of business**.

Q Value Line indexes of **financial strength, price stability, price growth persistence, and earnings predictability**.

R Footnotes explain a number of things, such as the way earnings are reported, whether "fully diluted," on a "primary" basis, or on an "average shares outstanding" basis.

S Quarterly dividends paid are actual payments. The total of dividends paid in four quarters may not equal the figure shown in the annual series on dividends declared. (Sometimes a dividend declared at the end of the year will be paid in the first quarter of the following year.)

T Quarterly earnings are shown on a per-share basis (estimates in bold type). Quarterly sales are shown on a gross basis.

U Annual rates of change (on a per-share basis). Actual past, estimated future.

V Current position—current assets, current liabilities, and other components of working capital.

W The capital structure as of recent date showing the percentage of capital in long-term debt (33%), and in common stock (67%); the number of times that total interest charges were earned (7.0 in 1984).

X A record of **the decisions taken by the biggest institutions** (over $70 million in equity holdings)—including banks, insurance companies, mutual funds, investment advisors, internally managed endowments, and pension funds—to buy or sell during the past five quarters and how many shares were involved, and the total number of shares they hold.

Y The record of insider decisions—decisions by officers and directors to buy or sell as reported to the SEC a month or more after execution.

Z Options patch—indicates listed options are available on the stock and on what exchange they are most actively traded.

---

publishes the monthly *Bond Record*, with data on thousands of bonds; the weekly *Bond Survey* of new offerings and current conditions; the *Dividend Record;* the *International Bond Review;* and the *Handbook of Common Stocks*, with financial data on hundreds of firms. The *Handbook* contains brief sketches on each firm with limited financial data, earnings and dividend information, and short descriptions of the firm and its prospects (see Figure A.2).

Standard & Poor's *Corporation Records* are similar to Moody's *Manuals*. They provide data on publicly traded securities. Each volume is updated throughout the year. In addition, S&P's *Stock Reports* provide current and historical financial data on firms traded on the NYSE, Amex, and Nasdaq markets. These short reports also contain a description of the firm, its current outlook, and important developments. S&P's *Stock Guide* contains short

FIGURE A.2   Moody's Handbook of Common Stocks, Sample Report

INTERNATIONAL BUSINESS MACHINES CORPORATION

LISTED	SYM.	LTPS♦	STPS♦	IND. DIV.	REC. PRICE	RANGE (52 -WEEKS)	YLD
NYSE	IBM	71.4	83.5	$4.84*	101	140 –96	4.8%

HIGH GRADE. WEAK DOMESTIC DEMAND WILL PRESSURE RESULTS DESPITE STRONG OPERATING MARGINS.

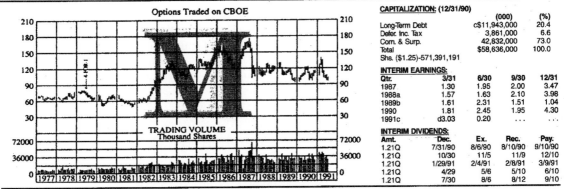

CAPITALIZATION: (12/31/90)

	(000)	(%)
Long-Term Debt	c$11,943,000	20.4
Defer. Inc. Tax	3,861,000	6.6
Com. & Surp.	42,832,000	73.0
Total	$58,636,000	100.0
Shs. ($1.25)-571,391,191		

INTERIM EARNINGS:

Qtr.	3/31	6/30	9/30	12/31
1987	1.30	1.95	2.00	3.47
1988a	1.57	1.63	2.10	3.98
1989b	1.61	2.31	1.51	1.04
1990	1.81	2.45	1.95	4.30
1991c	d3.03	0.20	...	...

INTERIM DIVIDENDS:

Amt.	Dec.	Ex.	Rec.	Pay.
1.21Q	7/31/90	8/6/90	8/10/90	9/10/90
1.21Q	10/30	11/5	11/9	12/10
1.21Q	1/29/91	2/4/91	2/8/91	3/9/91
1.21Q	4/29	5/6	5/10	6/10
1.21Q	7/30	8/6	8/12	9/10

BACKGROUND:

IBM is the largest manufacturer of information processing equipment and systems. IBM applies advanced information technology to solve the problems in business, government, science, space, defense, education, medicine and other areas. IBM offers customers solutions that incorporate information processing systems, software, communication systems and other products and services to address specific needs. While most products are sold or leased through IBM worldwide marketing organization. IBM utilizes external distribution channels through IBM Business Partners. In 1990, revenues were derived: sales, 64%; support, 16%; software, 14% and rentals & financing, 6%.

RECENT DEVELOPMENTS:

IBM announced a strategic alliance with Apple Computer to develop a new operating system that makes computing more user-friendly. For the quarter ended 6/30/91, net income plunged 92% to $114 million compared with $1.41 billion a year ago. Revenues fell 11% to $14.73 billion. Poor results were attributed to the drop in sales of computer equipment, unfavorable foreign currency exchange rates and higher charges related to severance packages. However, demand for workstations and midrange mainframes improved and sales form support services rose 16%.

PROSPECTS:

Intense discount pricing within the computer industry accompanied by lower demand from both domestic and European markets clouds the near-term outlook. Meanwhile, long-term prospects are brightened by IBM's new comprehensive product offerings which include the System/390 ES 9000 line of mainframes, entry level models of the AS/400 minicomputers, two high-end models of the PS/2 computer and the PS/1 home computer. In addition. IBM's alliance with Apple to design an operating system centered around an object oriented software bode well for long-term growth. Brisk demand, competitively-priced workstations and the laptop computer will boost sales.

STATISTICS:

YEAR	GROSS REVS. ($mill.)	OPER. PROFIT MARGIN %	RET. ON EQUITY %	NET INCOME ($mill.)	WORK CAP ($mill.)	SENIOR CAPITAL ($mill.)	SHARES (000)	EARN. PER SH.$	DIV PER SH.$	DIV PAY %	PRICE RANGE	P/E RATIO	AVG. YIELD %
81	29,070	20.7	18.2	3,308	2,983	2,669	592,294	5.63	3.44	61	71¹/₂– 48⁵/₈	10.7	6.0
82	34,364	23.4	22.1	4,409	4,805	2,851	602,406	7.39	3.44	47	98 – 55⁵/₈	10.4	4.5
83	40,180	23.9	23.6	5,485	7,763	2,674	610,725	9.04	3.71	41	134¹/₄– 92¹/₄	12.5	3.3
84	45,937	24.5	24.8	6,582	10,735	3,269	612,686	10.77	4.10	38	128¹/₂– 99	10.6	3.6
85	50,056	22.4	20.5	6,555	14,637	3,955	615,418	10.67	4.40	41	158¹/₂–117³/₈	12.9	3.2
86	51,250	15.3	13.9	4,789	15,006	4,169	605,923	7.81	4.40	56	161⁷/₈–119¹/₄	18.0	3.1
87	54,217	14.3	13.7	5,258	17,643	3,858	597,052	8.72	4.40	50	175⁷/₈–102	15.9	3.2
88	59,681	14.7	13.9	a5,491	17,956	8,518	589,741	a9.27	4.40	47	129¹/₈–104¹/₂	12.6	3.8
89	62,710	11.0	9.8	b3,758	14,175	10,825	574,700	b6.47	4.73	73	130⁷/₈– 93³/₄	17.3	4.2
90	69,018	16.0	14.1	6,020	13,644	11,943	571,391	10.51	4.84	46	123¹/₈– 94¹/₂	10.4	4.4

♦Long-Term Price Score—Short-Term Price Score: See page 4a. STATISTICS ARE AS ORIGINALLY REPORTED.a-Excludes $315 million ($0.53 per share) credit for an accounting change. b-Includes $2.4 billion ($4.16 a share) charge for restructuring. c-Includes debentures convertible into common stock. e-Includes a net charge of $2.3 billion ($3.96 a sh.) related to changes in accounting for post-retirement benefits.

INCORPORATED: June 16, 1911—NY	**TRANSFER AGENT(S):** First Chicago Trust Co. of N.Y. New York, NY	**OFFICERS:** Chairman & C.E.O. J. F. Akers
PRINCIPAL OFFICE: Old Orchard Road Armonk, NY 10504 Tel.:(914) 765-7777	**REGISTRAR(S):** First Chicago Trust Company of N.Y. New York, NY	President J. D. Kuehler S.V.P. & C.F.O. F. A. Metz, Jr.
ANNUAL MEETING: Last Mon. in April	**INSTITUTIONAL HOLDINGS:** No. of Institutions: 1,441 Shares Held: 302,584,660	Treasurer R. Ripp Secretary J. E. Hickey
NUMBER OF STOCKHOLDERS: 789,046		

Source: *Moody's Investors Service, 1990.*

sketches of thousands of companies, including: principal business, historic stock price ranges, recent dividend and earnings data, and capital structure data. The *Bond Guide* lists the S&P quality rating for thousands of bonds as well as some key financial ratios pertaining to bond safety. Both guides are published monthly. Sample pages from the *Stock Guide* appear in Figure A.3. S&P also publishes *Dividend Record, Earnings Forecaster*, the weekly *Outlook* with advice on industries and specific securities, as well as several other periodicals.

Dun and Bradstreet's *Industry Norms and Key Business Ratios* is a useful source for evaluating a company's financial strength. This publication offers average financial ratios for 125 industries that can be used as benchmarks for firms in that industry.

In addition to these standard sources, you should be aware that data on firms are available through brokerage reports and investment letters, most of which come with buy or sell recommendations.

SECURITY MARKETS

Extensive daily listings are available in *The Wall Street Journal, Investor's Daily, New York Times*, and several other newspapers. S&P's *Daily Stock Price Record*, which is published each quarter, contains daily price data for that entire quarter. The *Record* has separate volumes for NYSE, Amex, and Nasdaq firms. Security prices are also available from computerized databases. (See discussion below.)

Historical data on price indexes for several asset classes are available from an annual series of publications by Ibbotson Associates titled *Stocks, Bonds, Bills and Inflation. The Wall Street Journal Index* provides historical data on the Dow Jones averages.

Data on the financial marketplace—the stock exchanges, for example—are published annually in the New York Stock Exchange *Fact Book* and the American Stock Exchange *Databook*. These publications contain information on trading activity, membership, and investor characteristics.

The Securities and Exchange Commission (SEC) publishes a monthly *Statistical Bulletin* with data on the security industry. The data provided include trading volume on all exchanges, prices, volatility, and information on new issues. The SEC also publishes an *Annual Report* with a discussion of the year's events, a summary of much of the data that appeared in the *Statistical Bulletin*, and some annual data series.

COMPUTER DATABASES

It is almost impossible to keep up with the rapidly growing collection of computerized databases. Here is a list of some of the more popular and useful sources.

The *Dow Jones News/Retrieval* is an industry leader for computerized investor services. It is an on-line database containing current economic, corporate, industry, financial news, reports, and statistics for the United States. Information provided includes news for the current day as well as some historical information. The database also covers world news, as well as financial and corporate information for Japan, Europe, and Canada. Table A.1 summarizes the data available from the service.

S&P's *Compustat* is another financial database with annual and quarterly balance sheet and income statement data on companies listed on the NYSE, Amex, and OTC, regional, and Canadian stock exchanges. The historical data usually are available for up to 20 years (annual tape) or 48 quarters (quarterly tape).

The *CRSP* (Center for Research in Security Prices) tape from the University of Chicago contains daily and monthly price series on NYSE, Amex, and Nasdaq traded stocks. The center also maintains a government bond tape.

FIGURE A.3 *Standard & Poor's Stock Guide*, Sample Report

Int'l Business Machines 1210

NYSE Symbol IBM Options on CBOE (Jan–Apr–Jul–Oct) In S&P 500

Price	Range	P–E Ratio	Dividend	Yield	S&P Ranking	Beta
Nov. 26'90	1990					
113 7/8	123⅛–94½	16	4.84	4.3%	A	0.74

Summary

IBM is the world's dominant manufacturer of mainframe computers and is also a major supplier of minicomputers, computer peripheral equipment, personal computers, networking products, and system software. The earnings recovery begun in 1990 should continue into 1991, aided by initial sales of a new generation of mainframe computers. In August, 1990 the company announced that it would put its domestic typewriter and small printer products businesses into a new unit to be majority owned by Clayton & Dubilier, Inc.

Current Outlook

Earnings for 1991 are projected at $10.70 a share, compared with the $10.00 estimated for 1990.

The $1.21 quarterly dividend is the minimum expectation.

Gross income for 1991 should advance at a somewhat slower pace than the almost 8% gain expected for 1990. Progress would be limited by slower worldwide economic growth, despite revenues gains from the introduction of new mainframe and work station lines. Profit margins should improve, with benefits from the domestic cost containment program more than offsetting pricing pressures in the mainframe and minicomputer markets.

Revenues (Billion $)

Quarter	1991	1990	1989	1988
Mar	....	14.19	12.73	12.06
Jun	....	16.50	15.21	13.91
Sep	....	15.28	14.31	13.71
Dec	....	....	20.46	20.00
			62.71	59.66

Revenues for the first nine months of 1990 advanced 8.8%, year to year, aided by increased demand for high end files, AS 400 minicomputers and PS/2 personal computers, software and support services, and higher leasing revenues. Profit margins benefited from the greater volume and initial gains from the cost reduction program. Net income increased 12%, to $6.21 a share (on 1.6% fewer shares) from $5.43.

Capital Share Earnings ($)

Quarter	1991	1990	1989	1988
Mar	E1.85	1.81	1.61	1.57
Jun	E2.55	2.45	2.31	1.63
Sep	E2.00	1.95	1.51	2.10
Dec	E4.30	E3.79	1.04	3.97
	E10.70	E10.00	6.47	9.27

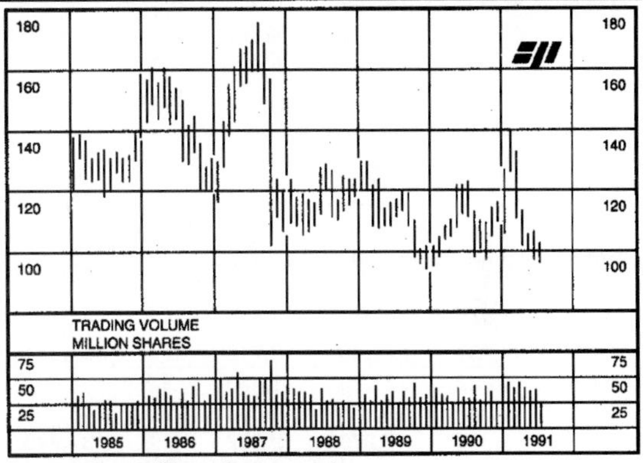

Important Developments

Sep.'90–The company introduced a new generation of mainframe computers, the System/390 line.

Aug. '90–IBM announced that it will consolidate its domestic typewriter, keyboard, personal printers and supplies business into a new unit to be majority owned by Clayton & Dubilier, Inc.

Feb.'90–A new line of high performance technical workstations was introduced.

Jan.'90–The company restructured its domestic operations, resulting in a $2.4 billion pretax charge in the fourth quarter of 1989, equal to $2.58 a share after taxes. Savings from expected capacity reductions and technology investment writedowns could add $1.00 to share earnings by 1991.

Next earnings report expected in mid–January.

Per Share Data ($)

Yr. End Dec. 31	1989	[1]1988	1987	1986	1985	1984	1983	1982	1981	1980
Tangible Bk. Val.	66.33	65.78	62.81	55.40	50.60	41.79	38.02	33.13	30.66	28.18
Cash Flow	13.76	15.80	14.57	13.23	15.64	16.02	15.02	13.36	11.29	10.83
Earnings[2]	6.47	9.27	8.72	7.81	10.67	10.77	9.04	7.39	5.63	6.10
Dividends	4.73	4.40	4.40	4.40	4.40	4.10	3.71	3.44	3.44	3.44
Payout Ratio	72%	47%	50%	56%	41%	38%	41%	47%	62%	56%
Prices–High	130⅞	129½	175⅞	161⅞	158¾	128½	134¼	98	71½	72¾
Low	93⅜	104¼	102	119¼	117⅜	99	92¼	55⅜	48⅜	50⅜
P/E Ratio	20–14	14–11	20–12	21–15	15–11	12–9	15–10	13–8	13–9	12–8

Data as orig. reptd. 1.Reflects acctg. change. 2.Bef. spec. item(s) of +0.53 in 1988. E–Estimated

Standard NYSE Stock Reports
Vol. 57/No. 233/Sec.13

December 4, 1990

Standard & Poor's Corp.
25 Broadway, NY, NY 10004

FIGURE A.3　(concluded)

1210

International Business Machines Corporation

Income Data (Millions $)

Year Ended Dec. 31	Revs.	Oper. Inc.	% Oper. Inc. of Revs.	Cap Exp.	Depr.	Int. Exp.	[2]Net Bef. Taxes	Eff. Tax Rate	[2]Net Inc.	% Net Inc. of Revs.	Cash Flow
1989	62,710	13,553	21.6	6,414	4,240	1,118	6,645	43.4%	3,758	6.0	7,998
[1]1988	59,681	12,617	21.1	5,431	3,871	802	9,033	39.2%	5,491	9.2	9,362
1987	54,217	11,269	20.8	4,304	3,527	619	8,609	38.9%	5,258	9.7	8,785
1986	51,250	11,175	21.8	4,620	3,316	604	8,389	42.9%	4,789	9.3	8,105
1985	50,056	14,281	28.5	6,430	3,051	443	11,619	43.6%	6,555	13.1	9,606
1984	45,937	14,446	31.4	5,473	3,215	408	11,623	43.4%	6,582	14.3	9,797
1983	40,180	13,216	32.9	4,930	3,627	390	9,940	44.8%	5,485	13.7	9,112
1982	34,364	11,618	33.6	6,685	3,562	514	7,930	44.4%	[1]4,409	12.8	7,971
1981	29,070	9,356	32.2	6,845	3,329	480	5,988	44.8%	3,308	11.4	6,637
1980	26,213	8,499	32.4	6,592	2,759	[1]325	5,897	39.6%	3,562	13.6	6,321

Balance Sheet Data (Million $)

Dec. 31	Cash	Assets	Curr. Liab.	Ratio	Total Assets	Ret. On Assets	Long Term Debt	Common Equity	Total Inv. Capital	% LT Debt of Cap.	Ret. On Equity
1989	4,961	35,875	21,700	1.7	77,734	5.0%	10,825	38,509	52,614	20.6	9.8%
1988	6,123	35,343	17,387	2.0	73,037	8.1%	8,518	39,509	52,650	16.2	14.2%
1987	6,967	31,020	13,377	2.3	63,688	8.7%	3,858	38,263	47,271	8.2	14.6%
1986	7,257	27,749	12,743	2.2	57,814	8.7%	4,169	34,374	43,067	9.7	14.5%
1985	5,622	26,070	11,433	2.3	52,634	13.7%	3.955	31,990	39,595	10.0	22.4%
1984	4,362	20,375	9,640	2.1	42,808	16.4%	3,269	26,489	31,815	10.3	26.4%
1983	5,536	17,270	9,507	1.8	37,243	15.6%	2,674	23,219	26,606	10.1	25.2%
1982	3,300	13,014	8,209	1.6	32,541	14.1%	2,851	19,960	23,134	12.3	22.9%
1981	2,029	10,303	7,320	1.4	29,586	11.7%	2,669	18,161	21,082	12.7	19.0%
1980	2,112	9,925	6,526	1.5	26,703	13.9%	2,099	16,453	18,734	11.2	22.7%

Data as orig. reptd.; finance subs. consol aft.1987. 1. Reflects acctg. change. 2. Incl. equity in earns. of nonconsol. subs.
3. Bef. spec. item in 1988.

Business Summary

IBM is the largest manufacturer of data processing equipment and systems. Industry segment contributions to revenues in recent years:

	1989	1988
Processors/peripherals	43%	44%
Workstations	20%	19%
Programs/maint./other	34%	34%
Federal systems	3%	3%

Hardware sales provided 66% of revenues in 1989, software and services 29%, and rentals 5%. Foreign operations contributed 59% of revenues in 1989 and $4.1 billion of net profits.

Processors manipulate data through the operation of a stored program. Peripherals include printers, storage and telecommunication devices. Workstations include small business computers, intelligent workstations and typewriters. Program products include applications and systems software. Maintenance represents separately billed maintenance services. Other revenues are derived from financing revenue, supplies and miscellaneous support services. The Federal systems group serves the U.S. government's defense, space and other agencies.

Dividend Data

Dividends have been paid since 1916. A dividend reinvestment plan is available.

Amt of Divd. $	Date Decl.	Ex-divd. Date	Stock of Record	Payment Date
1.21	Jan. 30	Feb. 5	Feb. 9	Mar. 10'0
1.21	Apr. 30	May 4	May 10	Jun. 9'90
1.21	Jul 31	Aug. 6	Aug. 10	Sep. 10'90
1.21	Oct. 30	Nov. 5	Nov. 9	Dec. 10'90

Next dividend meeting: late Jan.'91.

Finances

Research, development and engineering expense totaled $6.8 billion (11% of gross income) in 1989, versus $5.9 billion (9.9%) in 1988.

Capitalization

Long Term Debt: $11,167,000,000, incl. $1.25 billion of 7⅞% debs. conv. into com. at $153.66 a sh.

Capital Sock: 571,052,736 shs. ($1.25 par).
Institutions hold approximately 51%.
Shareholders of record: 815,580.

Office—Armonk, New York 10504. Tel—(914) 765-1900. Stockholder Relations Dept—690 Madison Ave., NYC 10022. Tel—(212) 735-7000. Chrmn—J. F. Akers. Secy—J. E. Hickey. Treas—D. A. Finley. Investor Contact—H. Park. Dirs—J. F. Akers, S. D. Bechtel, Jr. H. Brown, J. E. Burke, F. T. Cary, W. T. Coleman, Jr, T. F. Frist, Jr, F. Gerber N. deB. Katzenbach, N. O. Keohane. J. D. Kuehler, R. W. Lyman, J. R. Monro, T. S. Murphy, J. R. Opel, H. Sihler, J. B. Slaughter, E. S. Woolard, Jr. Transfer Agent & Registrar—Morgan Shareholder Services Trust Co., NYC. incorporated in New York in 1911. Empl—383.

TABLE A.1

Dow Jones News/
Retrieval Contents

A. News
   1. Press releases
   2. Credit market news
   3. Business and financial news from *The Wall Street Journal,* Dow Jones News Service, and other industry publications, including text search capability
   4. National and world news
   5. News alerts
B. Company Profits and Reports
   1. Comprehensive company reports
   2. Company and industry tracking service
C. Company and Industry Statistics and Forecasts
   1. Dun and Bradstreet reports on 750,000 companies
   2. SEC filing extracts
   3. Canadian news
   4. Earnings forecasts
   5. Insider trading reports
   6. Analysts' reports on companies and industries
D. Quotes and Market Averages
   1. Current quotes on stocks, bonds, futures, and indexes
   2. Historical security prices and index levels
   3. Historical Dow Jones Averages
E. Services
   1. On-line brokerage service (Fidelity)
   2. Travel services
   3. *Wall Street Week* transcripts
   4. Shopping
   5. Sports and weather
   6. Book and movie reviews

The Berkeley *Options Data Base* contains records of option quotes on the Chicago Board Options Exchange from 1976.

The *Disclosure Database* contains financial and textual data extracted from Securities and Exchange Commission filings (in particular, the 10-K) and provides information on over 10,000 American and foreign public companies. More than 200 individual fields, categorized into company résumé, financial information, and textual or management information sections, can be searched and displayed. Information sources include the 10-K, 10-Q, and 8-K reports, as well as annual reports to stockholders.

More general economic databases are:

Citibase (put out by Citicorp) contains 5,000 time series from more than 100 government and private sources.

The International Monetary Fund's *International Financial Statistics* tape contains data on domestic and international finance such as exchange rates, international trade, prices, production, interest rates, and government finance.

The *Flow of Funds Accounts* compiled by the Board of Governors of the Federal Reserve System are available on tape and contain both flows and year-end assets and liabilities of the following sectors: households, businesses, governments, banking, and nonbank finance.

Appendix B

REFERENCES

Alexander, Sidney. "Price Movements in Speculative Markets: Trends or Random Walks, No. 2." In *The Random Character of Stock Market Prices,* ed. Paul Cootner. Cambridge, Mass.: MIT Press, 1964.

Amihud, Yakov, and Haim Mendelson. "Asset Pricing and the Bid-Ask Spread." *Journal of Financial Economics* 17 (December 1986), pp. 223–50; and "Liquidity, Asset Prices, and Financial Policy." *Financial Analysts Journal* 47 (November/December 1991), pp. 56–66.

Arbel, Avner. "Generic Stocks: An Old Product in a New Package." *Journal of Portfolio Management*, Summer 1985, pp. 4–13.

Arbel, Avner, and Paul J. Strebel. "Pay Attention to Neglected Firms." *Journal of Portfolio Management*, Winter 1983, pp. 37–42.

Banz, Rolf. "The Relationship between Return and Market Value of Common Stocks." *Journal of Financial Economics* 9 (March 1981), pp. 3–18.

Basu, Sanjoy. "The Investment Performance of Common Stocks in Relation to Their Price-Earnings Ratios: A Test of the Efficient Market Hypothesis." *Journal of Finance* 32 (June 1977), pp. 663–82.

———. "The Relationship between Earnings Yield, Market Value, and Return for NYSE Common Stocks: Further Evidence." *Journal of Financial Economics* 12 (June 1983), pp. 129–56.

Bernhard, Arnold. *Value Line Methods of Evaluating Common Stocks*. New York: Arnold Bernhard and Co., 1979.

Bernard, Victor L. and Jacob K. Thomas. "Post-Earnings-Announcement Drift: Delayed Price Response or Risk Premium?" *Journal of Accounting Research* 27 (1989), pp. 1–36.

Black, Fischer. "Yes, Virginia, There Is Hope: Tests of the Value Line Ranking System." Graduate School of Business, University of Chicago, 1971.

Black, Fischer; Michael C. Jensen; and Myron Scholes. "The Capital Asset Pricing Model: Some Empirical Tests." *Studies in the Theory of Capital Markets* ed. Michael C. Jensen. Praeger, 1972.

Black, Fischer, and Myron Scholes. "The Pricing of Options and Corporate Liabilities." *Journal of Political Economy* 81 (May–June 1973), pp. 637–59.

From Black-Scholes to Black Holes: New Frontiers in Options. London: *RISK Magazine*, 1992.

Blume, Marshall E., and Robert F. Stambaugh. "Biases in Computed Returns: An Application to the Size Effect." *Journal of Finance Economics*, 1983, pp. 387–404.

Bogle, John C. *Bogle on Mutual Funds*. Burr Ridge, IL: Irwin Professional Publishing, 1994.

Bogle, John C. "Investing in the 1990s: Remembrance of Things Past, and Things Yet to Come." *Journal of Portfolio Management*, Spring 1991, pp. 5–14.

Brennan, Michael. "Taxes, Market Valuation and Corporate Financial Policy." *National Tax Journal*, 1970.

Brinson, Hood, and Bibower. "Components of Portfolio Performance." *Financial Analysts Journal*, July–August 1986.

Brown, David, and Robert H. Jennings. "On Technical Analysis." *Review of Financial Studies* 2 (1989), pp. 527–52.

Brown, Lawrence D., and Michael Rozeff. "The Superiority of Analysts' Forecasts as Measures of Expectations: Evidence from Earnings." *Journal of Finance*, March 1978.

Campbell, John Y., and Robert Shiller. "Stock Prices, Earnings and Expected Dividends." *Journal of Finance* 43 (July 1988), pp. 661–76.

Carhart, Mark M. "Persistence in Mutual Fund Performance Re-examined." University of Chicago, mimeo, 1992; and "On Persistence in Mutual Fund Performance." University of Chicago, mimeo, 1994.

Chopra, Navin; Josef Lakonishok; and Jay R. Ritter. "Measuring Abnormal Performance: Do Stocks Overreact?" *Journal of Financial Economics* 31 (1992), pp. 235–68.

Clarke, Roger, and Mark P. Kritzman, *Currency Management: Concepts and Practices*. Charlottesville: Research Foundation of the Institute of Chartered Financial Analysts, 1996.

Clayman, Michelle. "In Search of Excellence: The Investor's Viewpoint." *Financial Analysts Journal*, May–June 1987.

Connolly, Robert. "An Examination of the Robustness of the Weekend Effect." *Journal of Financial and Quantitative Analysis* 24 (June 1989), pp. 133–69.

Conrad, Jennifer, and Gautam Kaul. "Time-Variation in Expected Returns." *Journal of Business* 61 (October 1988), pp. 409–25.

Copeland, Thomas E., and David Mayers. "The Value Line Enigma (1965–1978): A Case Study of Performance Evaluation Issues." *Journal of Financial Economics*, November 1982.

DeBondt, Werner F. M., and Richard Thaler. "Does the Stock Market Overreact?" *Journal of Finance* 40 (1985), pp. 793–805.

Douglas, George W. "Risk in Equity Markets: An Empirical Appraisal of Market Efficiency." *Yale Economic Essays* IX (Spring 1969).

Dunn, Patricia, and Rolf D. Theisen. "How Consistently Do Active Managers Win?" *Journal of Portfolio Management* 9 (Summer 1983), pp. 47–53.

Elton, E. J.: M. J. Gruber; S. Das; and M. Hlavka. "Efficiency with Costly Information: A Reinterpretation of Evidence from Managed Portfolios." *Review of Financial Studies* 6 (1993), pp. 1–22.

Errunza, Vihang, and Etienne Losq. "International Asset Pricing under Mild Segmentation: Theory and Test." *Journal of Finance* 40 (March 1985), pp. 105–124.

Fama, Eugene. "The Behavior of Stock Market Prices." *Journal of Business* 38 (January 1965), pp. 34–105.

Fama, Eugene, and Marshall Blume. "Filter Rules and Stock Market Trading Profits." *Journal of Business* 39 (Supplement, January 1966), pp. 226–41.

Fama, Eugene F. and Kenneth R. French. "Business Conditions and Expected Returns on Stocks and Bonds." *Journal of Financial Economics* 25 (November 1989), pp. 3–22.

Fama, Eugene F., and Kenneth R. French. "Common Risk Factors in the Returns on Stocks and Bonds." *Journal of Financial Economics* 33 (1993), pp. 3–56.

Fama, Eugene F., and Kenneth French. "The Cross Section of Expected Stock Returns." *Journal of Finance* 47 (June 1992), pp. 427–465.

Fama, Eugene F., and Kenneth R. French. "Dividend Yields and Expected Stock Returns." *Journal of Financial Economics* 22 (October 1988), pp. 3–25.

Fama, Eugene, and Kenneth R. French. "Permanent and Temporary Components of Stock Prices." *Journal of Political Economy* 96 (1987), pp. 246–73.

Fama, Eugene, and James MacBeth. "Risk, Return and Equilibrium: Empirical Tests." *Journal of Political Economy* 81 (March 1973).

Fisher, Irving. *The Theory of Interest: As Determined by Impatience to Spend Income and Opportunity to Invest It*. New York: Augustus M. Kelley, Publishers, 1965, originally published in 1930.

Flannery, Mark J., and Christopher M. James. "The Effect of Interest Rate Changes on the Common Stock Returns of Financial Institutions." *Journal of Finance* 39 (September 1984), pp. 1141–54.

Foster, George; Chris Olsen; and Terry Shevlin. "Earnings Releases, Anomalies, and the Behavior of Security Returns," *The Accounting Review* 59 (October 1984).

French, Kenneth. "Stock Returns and the Weekend Effect." *Journal of Financial Economics* 8 (March 1980), pp. 55–69.

Geske, Robert, and Richard Roll. "On Valuing American Call Options with the Black-Scholes European Formula." *Journal of Finance* 39 (June 1984), pp. 443–56.

Gibbons, Michael, and Patrick Hess. "Day of the Week Effects and Asset Returns." *Journal of Business* 54 (October 1981), pp. 579–98.

Givoly, Dan, and Dan Palmon. "Insider Trading and Exploitation of Inside Information: Some Empirical Evidence." *Journal of Business* 58 (1985), pp. 69–87.

Goetzmann, William N., and Roger G. Ibbotson. "Do Winners Repeat?" *Journal of Portfolio Management*, Winter 1994, pp. 9–18.

Grieves, Robin, and Alan J. Marcus. "Riding the Yield Curve: Reprise." *Journal of Portfolio Management*, Winter 1992.

Grinblatt, Mark, and Sheridan Titman. "Mutual Fund Performance: An Analysis of Quarterly Portfolio Holdings." *Journal of Business* 62 (1989), pp. 393–416.

Grossman, Sanford J., and Joseph E. Stiglitz. "On the Impossibility of Informationally Efficient Markets." *American Economic Review* 70 (June 1980), pp. 393–408.

Henriksson, Roy D. "Market Timing and Mutual Fund Performance: An Empirical Investigation." *Journal of Business* 57 (January 1984).

Homer, Sidney, and Martin L. Leibowitz. *Inside the Yield Book: New Tools for Bond Market Strategy*. Englewood Cliffs, N.J.: Prentice Hall, 1972.

Ibbotson, Roger G. "Price Performance of Common Stock New Issues," *Journal of Financial Economics* 2 (September 1975).

Ibbotson, Roger; Richard C. Carr; and Anthony W. Robinson. "International Equity and Bond Returns." *Financial Analysts Journal*, July–August 1982.

Ibbotson, R. C., and L. B. Siegel. "The World Market Wealth Portfolio." *Journal of Portfolio Management*, Winter 1983.

Ibbotson, R. C.; L. B. Siegel; and K. Love. "World Wealth: Market Values and Returns." *Journal of Portfolio Management*, Fall 1985.

Jaffe, Jeffrey F. "Special Information and Insider Trading." *Journal of Business* 47 (July 1974), pp. 410–28.

————. "Gold and Gold Stocks as Investments for Institutional Portfolios." *Financial Analysts Journal* 45 (March–April 1989), pp. 53–59.

Jagannathan, Ravi, and Zhenyu Wang. "The Conditional CAPM and the Cross-Section of Expected Returns." *Staff Report 208, Federal Reserve Bank of Minneapolis*, 1996.

Jegadeesh, Narasimhan. "Evidence of Predictable Behavior of Security Returns." *Journal of Finance* 45 (September 1990), pp. 881–98.

Jegadeesh, Narasimhan, and Sheridan Titman. "Returns to Buying Winners and Selling Losers: Implications for

Stock Market Efficiency." *Journal of Finance* 48 (March 1993), pp. 65–91.

Jensen, Michael C. "The Performance of Mutual Funds in the Period 1945–1964." *Journal of Finance,* May 1968.

———. "Risk, the Pricing of Capital Assets, and the Evaluation of Investment Portfolios." *Journal of Business* 42 (April 1969), pp. 167–247.

Keim, Donald B. "Size Related Anomalies and Stock Return Seasonality: Further Empirical Evidence." *Journal of Financial Economics* 12 (June 1983), pp. 13–32.

Keim, Donald B., and Robert F. Stambaugh. "Predicting Returns in the Stock and Bond Markets." *Journal of Financial Economics* 17 (1986), pp. 357–90.

Kendall, Maurice. "The Analysis of Economic Time Series, Part I: Prices." *Journal of the Royal Statistical Society* 96 (1953), pp. 11–25.

Kopcke, Richard W., and Geoffrey R. H. Woglom. "Regulation Q and Savings Bank Solvency—The Connecticut Experience." In *The Regulation of Financial Institutions,* Federal Reserve Bank of Boston Conference Series, No. 21, 1979.

Lakonishok, Josef; Andrei Shleifer; and Robert W. Vishney. "Contrarian Investment, Extrapolation, and Risk." *Journal of Finance* 50 (1995), pp. 1541–1578.

La Porta, Raphael. "Expectations and the Cross-Section of Stock Returns." *Journal of Finance* 51 (December 1996), pp. 1715–1742.

Latane, H. A., and C. P. Jones. "Standardized Unexpected Earnings—1971–1977." *Journal of Finance,* June 1979.

Lehmann, Bruce. "Fads, Martingales and Market Efficiency." *Quarterly Journal of Economics* 105 (February 1990), pp. 1–28.

Levy, Robert A. "The Predictive Significance of Five-Point Chart Patterns." *Journal of Business* 44 (July 1971). pp. 316–23.

Lo, Andrew W., and Craig MacKinlay. "Stock Market Prices Do Not Follow Random Walks: Evidence from a Simple Specification Test." *Review of Financial Studies* 1 (Spring 1988), pp. 41–66.

Loeb, T. F. "Trading Cost: The Critical Link between Investment Information and Results." *Financial Analysts Journal,* May–June 1983.

Lynch, Peter, with John Rothchild. *One Up on Wall Street.* New York: Penguin Books, 1989.

Macaulay, Frederick. *Some Theoretical Problems Suggested by the Movements of Interest Rates, Bond Yields, and Stock Prices in the United States Since 1856.* New York: National Bureau of Economic Research, 1938.

Malkiel, Burton G. "Returns from Investing in Equity Mutual Funds: 1971–1991." *Journal of Finance* 50 (June 1995), pp. 549–572.

Marcus, Alan J. "The Magellan Fund and Market Efficiency." *Journal of Portfolio Management* 17 (Fall 1990), pp. 85–88.

Mayers, David. "Nonmarketable Assets and Capital Market Equilibrium under Uncertainty." In *Studies in the Theory of Capital Markets,* ed. M. C. Jensen. New York: Praeger, 1972.

Merton, Robert C. "Theory of Rational Option Pricing." *Bell Journal of Economics and Management Science* 4 (Spring 1973), pp. 141–83.

———. "On Market Timing and Investment Performance: An Equilibrium Theory of Value for Market Forecasts." *Journal of Business* 54 (July 1981).

Miller, Merton H., and Myron Scholes. "Rate of Return in Relation to Risk: A Re-examination of Some Recent Findings." In *Studies in the Theory of Capital Markets,* ed. Michael C. Jensen. Praeger, 1972.

Morrell, John A. "Introduction to International Equity Diversification." In *International Investing for U.S. Pension Funds,* Institute for Fiduciary Education, London/Venice, May 6–13. 1989.

Niederhoffer, Victor, and Patrick Regan. "Earnings Changes, Analysts' Forecasts, and Stock Prices." *Financial Analysts Journal,* May–June 1972.

Norby, W. C. "Applications of Inflation-Adjusted Accounting Data." *Financial Analysts Journal,* March–April 1983.

Perry, Kevin, and Robert A. Taggart. "The Growing Role of Junk Bonds in Corporate Finance." *Continental Bank Journal of Applied Corporate Finance* 1 (Spring 1988).

Porter, Michael E. *Competitive Advantage: Creating and Sustaining Superior Performance.* New York: The Free Press, a Division of Macmillan, Inc., 1985.

Poterba, James M., and Lawrence Summers. "Mean Reversion in Stock Market Prices: Evidence and Implications." *Journal of Financial Economics* 22 (1987), pp. 27–59.

Redington, F. M. "Review of the Principle of Life-Office Valuations." *Journal of the Institute of Actuaries* 78 (1952), pp. 286–340.

Reinganum, Marc R. "The Anatomy of a Stock Market Winner." *Financial Analysts Journal,* March–April 1988, pp. 272–84.

Reinganum, Marc R. "The Anomalous Stock Market Behavior of Small Firms in January: Empirical Tests for Tax-Loss Effects," *Journal of Financial Economics* 12 (June 1983), pp. 89–104.

Ritter, Jay R. "The Buying and Selling Behavior of Individual Investors at the Turn of the Year." *Journal of Finance* 43 (July 1988), pp. 701–17.

Roberts, Harry. "Stock Market 'Patterns' and Financial Analysis: Methodological Suggestions." *Journal of Finance* 14 (March 1959), pp. 11–25.

Roll, Richard. "A Critique of the Capital Asset Theory Tests: Part I: On Past and Potential Testability of the Theory." *Journal of Financial Economics* 4 (1977).

Roll, Richard. "The International Crash of October 1987." *Financial Analysts Journal,* September–October 1988.

Ross, Stephen A. "Return, Risk and Arbitrage." In *Risk and Return in Finance,* eds. I. Friend and J. Bicksler. Cambridge, Mass.: Ballinger, 1976.

Rubinstein, Mark. "Implied Binomial Trees." *Journal of Finance* 49 (July 1994), pp. 771–818.

Samuelson, Paul. "The Judgment of Economic Science on Rational Portfolio Management." *Journal of Portfolio Management* 16 (Fall 1989), pp. 4–12.

Seyhun, H. Nejat. "Insiders' Profits, Costs of Trading and Market Efficiency." *Journal of Financial Economics* 16 (1986), pp. 189–212.

Sharpe, William F. "Mutual Fund Performance." *Journal of Business* 39 (January 1966).

Sharpe, William S. "A Simplified Model for Portfolio Analysis." *Management Science* IX (January 1963), pp. 277–93.

Shiller, Robert. "Do Stock Prices Move Too Much to Be Justified by Subsequent Changes in Dividends?" *American Economic Review* 71 (June 1981).

Solnik, Bruno, and A. De Freitas. "International Factors of Stock Price Behavior." CESA Working Paper, February 1986 (cited in Bruno Solnik. *International Investments*. Reading, Mass.: Addison Wesley Publishing Co., 1988).

Speidell, Lawrence S., and Vinod Bavishi. "GAAP Arbitrage: Valuation Opportunities in International Accounting Standards." *Financial Analysts Journal*, November–December 1992, pp. 58–66.

Stickel, Scott E. "The Effect of Value Line Investment Survey Rank Changes on Common Stock Prices." *Journal of Financial Economics* 14 (1986), pp. 121–44.

Tobin, James. "Liquidity Preference as Behavior toward Risk." *Review of Economic Studies* XXVI (February 1958), pp. 65–86.

Treynor, Jack L. "How to Rate Management Investment Funds." *Harvard Business Review* 43 (January–February 1966).

Treynor, Jack L., and Kay Mazuy. "Can Mutual Funds Outguess the Market?" *Harvard Business Review* 43 (July–August 1966).

Treynor, Jack, and Fischer Black. "How to Use Security Analysis to Improve Portfolio Selection." *Journal of Business* 46 (January 1973).

Trippi, Robert R., and Duane Desieno. "Trading Equity Index Futures with Neural Networks." *Journal of Portfolio Management* 19 (Fall 1992).

_____, and Efraim Turban, eds. *Neural Networks in Finance and Investing*. Chicago: Probus Publishing Co., 1993.

Wallace, A. "Is Beta Dead?" *Institutional Investor* 14 (July 1980), pp. 22–30.

Whaley, Robert E. "Valuation of American Call Options on Dividend-Paying Stocks: Empirical Tests." *Journal of Financial Economics* 10 (1982), pp. 29–58.

Appendix C

MATHEMATICAL TABLES

TABLE C.1 Future Value of $1 at the End of t Periods $= (1 + r)^t$

	Interest Rate																			
Period	**1%**	**2%**	**3%**	**4%**	**5%**	**6%**	**7%**	**8%**	**9%**	**10%**	**12%**	**14%**	**15%**	**16%**	**18%**	**20%**	**24%**	**28%**	**32%**	**36%**
1	1.0100	1.0200	1.0300	1.0400	1.0500	1.0600	1.0700	1.0800	1.0900	1.1000	1.1200	1.1400	1.1500	1.1600	1.1800	1.2000	1.2400	1.2800	1.3200	1.3600
2	1.0201	1.0404	1.0609	1.0816	1.1025	1.1236	1.1449	1.1664	1.1881	1.2100	1.2544	1.2996	1.3225	1.3456	1.3924	1.4400	1.5376	1.6384	1.7424	1.8496
3	1.0303	1.0612	1.0927	1.1249	1.1576	1.1910	1.2250	1.2597	1.2950	1.3310	1.4049	1.4815	1.5209	1.5609	1.6430	1.7280	1.9066	2.0972	2.3000	2.5155
4	1.0406	1.0824	1.1255	1.1699	1.2155	1.2625	1.3108	1.3605	1.4116	1.4641	1.5735	1.6890	1.7490	1.8106	1.9388	2.0736	2.3642	2.6844	3.0360	3.4210
5	1.0510	1.1041	1.1593	1.2167	1.2763	1.3382	1.4026	1.4693	1.5386	1.6105	1.7623	1.9254	2.0114	2.1003	2.2878	2.4883	2.9316	3.4360	4.0075	4.6526
6	1.0615	1.1262	1.1941	1.2653	1.3401	1.4185	1.5007	1.5869	1.6771	1.7716	1.9738	2.1950	2.3131	2.4364	2.6996	2.9860	3.6352	4.3980	5.2899	6.3275
7	1.0721	1.1487	1.2299	1.3159	1.4071	1.5036	1.6058	1.7138	1.8280	1.9487	2.2107	2.5023	2.6600	2.8262	3.1855	3.5832	4.5077	5.6295	6.9826	8.6054
8	1.0829	1.1717	1.2668	1.3686	1.4775	1.5938	1.7182	1.8509	1.9926	2.1436	2.4760	2.8526	3.0590	3.2784	3.7589	4.2998	5.5895	7.2058	9.2170	11.703
9	1.0937	1.1951	1.3048	1.4233	1.5513	1.6895	1.8385	1.9990	2.1719	2.3579	2.7731	3.2519	3.5179	3.8030	4.4355	5.1598	6.9310	9.2234	12.166	15.917
10	1.1046	1.2190	1.3439	1.4802	1.6289	1.7908	1.9672	2.1589	2.3674	2.5937	3.1058	3.7027	4.0456	4.4114	5.2338	6.1917	8.5944	11.806	16.060	21.647
11	1.1157	1.2434	1.3842	1.5395	1.7103	1.8983	2.1049	2.3316	2.5804	2.8531	3.4785	4.2262	4.6524	5.1173	6.1759	7.4301	10.657	15.112	21.199	29.439
12	1.1268	1.2682	1.4258	1.6010	1.7959	2.0122	2.2522	2.5182	2.8127	3.1384	3.8960	4.8179	5.3503	5.9360	7.2876	8.9161	13.215	19.343	27.983	40.037
13	1.1381	1.2936	1.4685	1.6651	1.8856	2.1329	2.4098	2.7196	3.0658	3.4523	4.3635	5.4924	6.1528	6.8858	8.5994	10.699	16.386	24.759	36.937	54.451
14	1.1495	1.3195	1.5126	1.7317	1.9799	2.2609	2.5785	2.9372	3.3417	3.7975	4.8871	6.2613	7.0757	7.9875	10.147	12.839	20.319	31.691	48.757	74.053
15	1.1610	1.3459	1.5580	1.8009	2.0789	2.3966	2.7590	3.1722	3.6425	4.1772	5.4736	7.1379	8.1371	9.2655	11.974	15.407	25.196	40.565	64.359	100.71
16	1.1726	1.3728	1.6047	1.8730	2.1829	2.5404	2.9522	3.4259	3.9703	4.5950	6.1304	8.1372	9.3567	10.748	14.129	18.488	31.243	51.293	84.954	136.97
17	1.1843	1.4002	1.6528	1.9479	2.2920	2.6928	3.1588	3.7000	4.3276	5.0545	6.8660	9.2765	10.761	12.468	16.672	22.186	38.741	66.461	112.14	186.28
18	1.1961	1.4282	1.7024	2.0258	2.4066	2.8543	3.3799	3.9960	4.7171	5.5599	7.6900	10.575	12.375	14.463	19.673	26.623	48.039	85.071	148.02	253.34
19	1.2081	1.4568	1.7535	2.1068	2.5270	3.0256	3.6165	4.3157	5.1417	6.1159	8.6128	12.056	14.232	16.777	23.214	31.948	59.568	108.89	195.39	344.43
20	1.2202	1.4859	1.8061	2.1911	2.6533	3.2071	3.8697	4.6610	5.6044	6.7275	9.6463	13.743	16.367	19.461	27.393	38.338	73.864	139.38	257.92	468.57
21	1.2324	1.5157	1.8603	2.2788	2.7860	3.3996	4.1406	5.0338	6.1088	7.4002	10.804	15.668	18.822	22.574	32.324	46.005	91.592	178.41	340.45	637.26
22	1.2447	1.5460	1.9161	2.3699	2.9253	3.6035	4.4304	5.4365	6.6586	8.1403	12.100	17.861	21.645	26.186	38.142	55.206	113.57	228.36	449.39	866.67
23	1.2572	1.5769	1.9736	2.4647	3.0715	3.8197	4.7405	5.8715	7.2579	8.9543	13.552	20.362	24.891	30.376	45.008	66.247	140.83	292.30	593.20	1178.7
24	1.2697	1.6084	2.0328	2.5633	3.2251	4.0489	5.0724	6.3412	7.9111	9.8497	15.179	23.212	28.625	35.236	53.109	79.497	174.63	374.14	783.02	1603.0
25	1.2824	1.6406	2.0938	2.6658	3.3864	4.2919	5.4274	6.8485	8.6231	10.835	17.000	26.462	32.919	40.874	62.669	95.396	216.54	478.90	1033.6	2180.1
30	1.3478	1.8114	2.4273	3.2434	4.3219	5.7435	7.6123	10.063	13.268	17.449	29.960	50.950	66.212	85.850	143.37	237.38	634.82	1645.5	4142.1	10143.
40	1.4889	2.2080	3.2620	4.8010	7.0400	10.286	14.974	21.725	31.409	45.259	93.051	188.88	267.86	378.72	750.38	1469.8	5455.9	19427.	66521.	*
50	1.6446	2.6916	4.3839	7.1067	11.467	18.420	29.457	46.902	74.358	117.39	289.00	700.23	1083.7	1670.7	3927.4	9100.4	46890.	*	*	*
60	1.8167	3.2810	5.8916	10.520	18.679	32.988	57.946	101.26	176.03	304.48	897.60	2595.9	4384.0	7370.2	20555.	56348.	*	*	*	*

*Future value is greater than 99,999.

TABLE C.2 Present Value of $1 to Be Received after t Periods $= 1/(1 + r)^t$[1]

Period	1%	2%	3%	4%	5%	6%	7%	8%	9%	10%	12%	14%	15%	16%	18%	20%	24%	28%	32%	36%
1	0.9901	0.9804	0.9709	0.9615	0.9524	0.9434	0.9346	0.9259	0.9174	0.9091	0.8929	0.8772	0.8696	0.8621	0.8475	0.8333	0.8065	0.7813	0.7576	0.7353
2	0.9803	0.9612	0.9426	0.9246	0.9070	0.8900	0.8734	0.8573	0.8417	0.8264	0.7972	0.7695	0.7561	0.7432	0.7182	0.6944	0.6504	0.6104	0.5739	0.5407
3	0.9706	0.9423	0.9151	0.8890	0.8638	0.8396	0.8163	0.7938	0.7722	0.7513	0.7118	0.6750	0.6575	0.6407	0.6086	0.5787	0.5245	0.4768	0.4348	0.3975
4	0.9610	0.9238	0.8885	0.8548	0.8227	0.7921	0.7629	0.7350	0.7084	0.6830	0.6355	0.5921	0.5718	0.5523	0.5158	0.4823	0.4230	0.3725	0.3294	0.2923
5	0.9515	0.9057	0.8626	0.8219	0.7835	0.7473	0.7130	0.6806	0.6499	0.6209	0.5674	0.5194	0.4972	0.4761	0.4371	0.4019	0.3411	0.2910	0.2495	0.2149
6	0.9420	0.8880	0.8375	0.7903	0.7462	0.7050	0.6663	0.6302	0.5963	0.5645	0.5066	0.4556	0.4323	0.4104	0.3704	0.3349	0.2751	0.2274	0.1890	0.1580
7	0.9327	0.8706	0.8131	0.7599	0.7107	0.6651	0.6227	0.5835	0.5470	0.5132	0.4523	0.3996	0.3759	0.3538	0.3139	0.2791	0.2218	0.1776	0.1432	0.1162
8	0.9235	0.8535	0.7894	0.7307	0.6768	0.6274	0.5820	0.5403	0.5019	0.4665	0.4039	0.3506	0.3269	0.3050	0.2660	0.2326	0.1789	0.1388	0.1085	0.0854
9	0.9143	0.8368	0.7664	0.7026	0.6446	0.5919	0.5439	0.5002	0.4604	0.4241	0.3606	0.3075	0.2843	0.2630	0.2255	0.1938	0.1443	0.1084	0.0822	0.0628
10	0.9053	0.8203	0.7441	0.6756	0.6139	0.5584	0.5083	0.4632	0.4224	0.3855	0.3220	0.2697	0.2472	0.2267	0.1911	0.1615	0.1164	0.0847	0.0623	0.0462
11	0.8963	0.8043	0.7224	0.6496	0.5847	0.5268	0.4751	0.4289	0.3875	0.3505	0.2875	0.2366	0.2149	0.1954	0.1619	0.1346	0.0938	0.0662	0.0472	0.0340
12	0.8874	0.7885	0.7014	0.6246	0.5568	0.4970	0.4440	0.3971	0.3555	0.3186	0.2567	0.2076	0.1869	0.1685	0.1372	0.1122	0.0757	0.0517	0.0357	0.0250
13	0.8787	0.7730	0.6810	0.6006	0.5303	0.4688	0.4150	0.3677	0.3262	0.2897	0.2292	0.1821	0.1625	0.1452	0.1163	0.0935	0.0610	0.0404	0.0271	0.0184
14	0.8700	0.7579	0.6611	0.5775	0.5051	0.4423	0.3878	0.3405	0.2992	0.2633	0.2046	0.1597	0.1413	0.1252	0.0985	0.0779	0.0492	0.0316	0.0205	0.0135
15	0.8613	0.7430	0.6419	0.5553	0.4810	0.4173	0.3624	0.3152	0.2745	0.2394	0.1827	0.1401	0.1229	0.1079	0.0835	0.0649	0.0397	0.0247	0.0155	0.0099
16	0.8528	0.7284	0.6232	0.5339	0.4581	0.3936	0.3387	0.2919	0.2519	0.2176	0.1631	0.1229	0.1069	0.0930	0.0708	0.0541	0.0320	0.0193	0.0118	0.0073
17	0.8444	0.7142	0.6050	0.5134	0.4363	0.3714	0.3166	0.2703	0.2311	0.1978	0.1456	0.1078	0.0929	0.0802	0.0600	0.0451	0.0258	0.0150	0.0089	0.0054
18	0.8360	0.7002	0.5874	0.4936	0.4155	0.3503	0.2959	0.2502	0.2120	0.1799	0.1300	0.0946	0.0808	0.0691	0.0508	0.0376	0.0208	0.0118	0.0068	0.0039
19	0.8277	0.6864	0.5703	0.4746	0.3957	0.3305	0.2765	0.2317	0.1945	0.1635	0.1161	0.0829	0.0703	0.0596	0.0431	0.0313	0.0168	0.0092	0.0051	0.0029
20	0.8195	0.6730	0.5537	0.4564	0.3769	0.3118	0.2584	0.2145	0.1784	0.1486	0.1037	0.0728	0.0611	0.0514	0.0365	0.0261	0.0135	0.0072	0.0039	0.0021
21	0.8114	0.6598	0.5375	0.4388	0.3589	0.2942	0.2415	0.1987	0.1637	0.1351	0.0926	0.0638	0.0531	0.0443	0.0309	0.0217	0.0109	0.0056	0.0029	0.0016
22	0.8034	0.6468	0.5219	0.4220	0.3418	0.2775	0.2257	0.1839	0.1502	0.1228	0.0826	0.0560	0.0462	0.0382	0.0262	0.0181	0.0088	0.0044	0.0022	0.0012
23	0.7954	0.6342	0.5067	0.4057	0.3256	0.2618	0.2109	0.1703	0.1378	0.1117	0.0738	0.0491	0.0402	0.0329	0.0222	0.0151	0.0071	0.0034	0.0017	0.0008
24	0.7876	0.6217	0.4919	0.3901	0.3101	0.2470	0.1971	0.1577	0.1264	0.1015	0.0659	0.0431	0.0349	0.0284	0.0188	0.0126	0.0057	0.0027	0.0013	0.0006
25	0.7798	0.6095	0.4776	0.3751	0.2953	0.2330	0.1842	0.1460	0.1160	0.0923	0.0588	0.0378	0.0304	0.0245	0.0160	0.0105	0.0046	0.0021	0.0010	0.0005
30	0.7419	0.5521	0.4120	0.3083	0.2314	0.1741	0.1314	0.0994	0.0754	0.0573	0.0334	0.0196	0.0151	0.0116	0.0070	0.0042	0.0016	0.0006	0.0002	0.0001
40	0.6717	0.4529	0.3066	0.2083	0.1420	0.0972	0.0668	0.0460	0.0318	0.0221	0.0107	0.0053	0.0037	0.0026	0.0013	0.0007	0.0002	0.0001	*	*
50	0.6080	0.3715	0.2281	0.1407	0.0872	0.0543	0.0339	0.0213	0.0134	0.0085	0.0035	0.0014	0.0009	0.0006	0.0003	0.0001	*	*	*	*

*The present value factor is zero to four decimal places.

TABLE C.3 Present Value of an Annuity of \$1 per Period for t Periods $= [1 - 1/(1 + r)^t]/r$

Number of Periods	1%	2%	3%	4%	5%	6%	7%	8%	9%	10%	12%	14%	15%	16%	18%	20%	24%	28%	32%
1	0.9901	0.9804	0.9709	0.9615	0.9524	0.9434	0.9346	0.9259	0.9174	0.9091	0.8929	0.8772	0.8696	0.8621	0.8475	0.8333	0.8065	0.7813	0.7576
2	1.9704	1.9416	1.9135	1.8861	1.8594	1.8334	1.8080	1.7833	1.7591	1.7355	1.6901	1.6467	1.6257	1.6052	1.5656	1.5278	1.4568	1.3916	1.3315
3	2.9410	2.8839	2.8286	2.7751	2.7232	2.6730	2.6243	2.5771	2.5313	2.4869	2.4018	2.3216	2.2832	2.2459	2.1743	2.1065	1.9813	1.8684	1.7663
4	3.9020	3.8077	3.7171	3.6299	3.5460	3.4651	3.3872	3.3121	3.2397	3.1699	3.0373	2.9137	2.8550	2.7982	2.6901	2.5887	2.4043	2.2410	2.0957
5	4.8534	4.7135	4.5797	4.4518	4.3295	4.2124	4.1002	3.9927	3.8897	3.7908	3.6048	3.4331	3.3522	3.2743	3.1272	2.9906	2.7454	2.5320	2.3452
6	5.7955	5.6014	5.4172	5.2421	5.0757	4.9173	4.7665	4.6229	4.4859	4.3553	4.1114	3.8887	3.7845	3.6847	3.4976	3.3255	3.0205	2.7594	2.5342
7	6.7282	6.4720	6.2303	6.0021	5.7864	5.5824	5.3893	5.2064	5.0330	4.8684	4.5638	4.2883	4.1604	4.0386	3.8115	3.6046	3.2423	2.9370	2.6775
8	7.6517	7.3255	7.0197	6.7327	6.4632	6.2098	5.9713	5.7466	5.5348	5.3349	4.9676	4.6389	4.4873	4.3436	4.0776	3.8372	3.4212	3.0758	2.7860
9	8.5660	8.1622	7.7861	7.4353	7.1078	6.8017	6.5152	6.2469	5.9952	5.7590	5.3282	4.9464	4.7716	4.6065	4.3030	4.0310	3.5655	3.1842	2.8681
10	9.4713	8.9826	8.5302	8.1109	7.7217	7.3601	7.0236	6.7101	6.4177	6.1446	5.6502	5.2161	5.0188	4.8332	4.4941	4.1925	3.6819	3.2689	2.9304
11	10.3676	9.7868	9.2526	8.7605	8.3064	7.8869	7.4987	7.1390	6.8052	6.4951	5.9377	5.4527	5.2337	5.0286	4.6560	4.3271	3.7757	3.3351	2.9776
12	11.2551	10.5753	9.9540	9.3851	8.8633	8.3838	7.9427	7.5361	7.1607	6.8137	6.1944	5.6603	5.4206	5.1971	4.7932	4.4392	3.8514	3.3868	3.0133
13	12.1337	11.3484	10.6350	9.9856	9.3936	8.8527	8.3577	7.9038	7.4869	7.1034	6.4235	5.8424	5.5831	5.3423	4.9095	4.5327	3.9124	3.4272	3.0404
14	13.0037	12.1062	11.2961	10.5631	9.8986	9.2950	8.7455	8.2442	7.7862	7.3667	6.6282	6.0021	5.7245	5.4675	5.0081	4.6106	3.9616	3.4587	3.0609
15	13.8651	12.8493	11.9379	11.1184	10.3797	9.7122	9.1079	8.5595	8.0607	7.6061	6.8109	6.1422	5.8474	5.5755	5.0916	4.6755	4.0013	3.4834	3.0764
16	14.7179	13.5777	12.5611	11.6523	10.8378	10.1059	9.4466	8.8514	8.3126	7.8237	6.9740	6.2651	5.9542	5.6685	5.1624	4.7296	4.0333	3.5026	3.0882
17	15.5623	14.2919	13.1661	12.1657	11.2741	10.4773	9.7632	9.1216	8.5436	8.0216	7.1196	6.3729	6.0472	5.7487	5.2223	4.7746	4.0591	3.5177	3.0971
18	16.3983	14.9920	13.7535	12.6593	11.6896	10.8276	10.0591	9.3719	8.7556	8.2014	7.2497	6.4674	6.1280	5.8178	5.2732	4.8122	4.0799	3.5294	3.1039
19	17.2260	15.6785	14.3238	13.1339	12.0853	11.1581	10.3356	9.6036	8.9501	8.3649	7.3658	6.5504	6.1982	5.8775	5.3162	4.8435	4.0967	3.5386	3.1090
20	18.0456	16.3514	14.8775	13.5903	12.4622	11.4699	10.5940	9.8181	9.1285	8.5136	7.4694	6.6231	6.2593	5.9288	5.3527	4.8696	4.1103	3.5458	3.1129
21	18.8570	17.0112	15.4150	14.0292	12.8212	11.7641	10.8355	10.0168	9.2922	8.6487	7.5620	6.6870	6.3125	5.9731	5.3837	4.8913	4.1212	3.5514	3.1158
22	19.6604	17.6580	15.9369	14.4511	13.1630	12.0416	11.0612	10.2007	9.4424	8.7715	7.6446	6.7429	6.3587	6.0113	5.4099	4.9094	4.1300	3.5558	3.1180
23	20.4558	18.2922	16.4436	14.8568	13.4886	12.3034	11.2722	10.3741	9.5802	8.8832	7.7184	6.7921	6.3988	6.0442	5.4321	4.9245	4.1371	3.5592	3.1197
24	21.2434	18.9139	16.9355	15.2470	13.7986	12.5504	11.4693	10.5288	9.7066	8.9847	7.7843	6.8351	6.4338	6.0726	5.4509	4.9371	4.1428	3.5619	3.1210
25	22.0232	19.5235	17.4131	15.6221	14.0939	12.7834	11.6536	10.6748	9.8226	9.0770	7.8431	6.8729	6.4641	6.0971	5.4669	4.9476	4.1474	3.5640	3.1220
30	25.8077	22.3965	19.6004	17.2920	15.3725	13.7648	12.4090	11.2578	10.2737	9.4269	8.0552	7.0027	6.5660	6.1772	5.5168	4.9789	4.1601	3.5693	3.1242
40	32.8347	27.3555	23.1148	19.7928	17.1591	15.0463	13.3317	11.9246	10.7574	9.7791	8.2438	7.1050	6.6418	6.2335	5.5482	4.9966	4.1659	3.5712	3.1250
50	39.1961	31.4236	25.7298	21.4822	18.2559	15.7619	13.8007	12.2335	10.9617	9.9148	8.3045	7.1327	6.6605	6.2463	5.5541	4.9995	4.1666	3.5714	3.1250

TABLE C.4 Future Value of an Annuity of $1 per Period for t Periods $= [(1 + r)^t - 1]/r$

Number of Periods	1%	2%	3%	4%	5%	6%	7%	8%	9%	10%	12%	14%	15%	16%	18%	20%	24%	28%	32%	36%
1	1.0000	1.0000	1.0000	1.0000	1.0000	1.0000	1.0000	1.0000	1.0000	1.0000	1.0000	1.0000	1.0000	1.0000	1.0000	1.0000	1.0000	1.0000	1.0000	1.0000
2	2.0100	2.0200	2.0300	2.0400	2.0500	2.0600	2.0700	2.0800	2.0900	2.1000	2.1200	2.1400	2.1500	2.1600	2.1800	2.2000	2.2400	2.2800	2.3200	2.3600
3	3.0301	3.0604	3.0909	3.1216	3.1525	3.1836	3.2149	3.2464	3.2781	3.3100	3.3744	3.4396	3.4725	3.5056	3.5724	3.6400	3.7776	3.9184	4.0624	4.2096
4	4.0604	4.1216	4.1836	4.2465	4.3101	4.3746	4.4399	4.5061	4.5731	4.6410	4.7793	4.9211	4.9934	5.0665	5.2154	5.3680	5.6842	6.0156	6.3624	6.7251
5	5.1010	5.2040	5.3091	5.4163	5.5256	5.6371	5.7507	5.8666	5.9847	6.1051	6.3528	6.6101	6.7424	6.8771	7.1542	7.4416	8.0484	8.6999	9.3983	10.146
6	6.1520	6.3081	6.4684	6.6330	6.8019	6.9753	7.1533	7.3359	7.5233	7.7156	8.1152	8.5355	8.7537	8.9775	9.4420	9.9299	10.980	12.136	13.406	14.799
7	7.2135	7.4343	7.6625	7.8983	8.1420	8.3938	8.6540	8.9228	9.2004	9.4872	10.089	10.730	11.067	11.414	12.142	12.916	14.615	16.534	18.696	21.126
8	8.2857	8.5830	8.8932	9.2142	9.5491	9.8975	10.260	10.637	11.028	11.436	12.300	13.233	13.727	14.240	15.327	16.499	19.123	22.163	25.678	29.732
9	9.3685	9.7546	10.159	10.583	11.027	11.491	11.978	12.488	13.021	13.579	14.776	16.085	16.786	17.519	19.086	20.799	24.712	29.369	34.895	41.435
10	10.462	10.950	11.464	12.006	12.578	13.181	13.816	14.487	15.193	15.937	17.549	19.337	20.304	21.321	23.521	25.959	31.643	38.593	47.062	57.352
11	11.567	12.169	12.808	13.486	14.207	14.972	15.784	16.645	17.560	18.531	20.655	23.045	24.349	25.733	28.755	32.150	40.238	50.398	63.122	78.998
12	12.683	13.412	14.192	15.026	15.917	16.870	17.888	18.977	20.141	21.384	24.133	27.271	29.002	30.850	34.931	39.581	50.895	65.510	84.320	108.44
13	13.809	14.680	15.618	16.627	17.713	18.882	20.141	21.495	22.953	24.523	28.029	32.089	34.352	36.786	42.219	48.497	64.110	84.853	112.30	148.47
14	14.947	15.974	17.086	18.292	19.599	21.015	22.550	24.215	26.019	27.975	32.393	37.581	40.505	43.672	50.818	59.196	80.496	109.61	149.24	202.93
15	16.097	17.293	18.599	20.024	21.579	23.276	25.129	27.152	29.361	31.772	37.280	43.842	47.580	51.660	60.965	72.035	100.82	141.30	198.00	276.98
16	17.258	18.639	20.157	21.825	23.657	25.673	27.888	30.324	33.003	35.950	42.753	50.980	55.717	60.925	72.939	87.442	126.01	181.87	262.36	377.69
17	18.430	20.012	21.762	23.698	25.840	28.213	30.840	33.750	36.974	40.545	48.884	59.118	65.075	71.673	87.068	105.93	157.25	233.79	347.31	514.66
18	19.615	21.412	23.414	25.645	28.132	30.906	33.999	37.450	41.301	45.599	55.750	68.394	75.836	84.141	103.74	128.12	195.99	300.25	459.45	700.94
19	20.811	22.841	25.117	27.671	30.539	33.760	37.379	41.446	46.018	51.159	63.440	78.969	88.212	98.603	123.41	154.74	244.03	385.32	607.47	954.28
20	22.019	24.297	26.870	29.778	33.066	36.786	40.995	45.762	51.160	57.275	72.052	91.025	102.44	115.38	146.63	186.69	303.60	494.21	802.86	1298.8
21	23.239	25.783	28.676	31.969	35.719	39.993	44.865	50.423	56.765	64.002	81.699	104.77	118.81	134.84	174.02	225.03	377.46	633.59	1060.8	1767.4
22	24.472	27.299	30.537	34.248	38.505	43.392	49.006	55.457	62.873	71.403	92.503	120.44	137.63	157.41	206.34	271.03	469.06	812.00	1401.2	2404.7
23	25.716	28.845	32.453	36.618	41.430	46.996	53.436	60.893	69.532	79.543	104.60	138.30	159.28	183.60	244.49	326.24	582.63	1040.4	1850.6	3271.3
24	26.973	30.422	34.426	39.083	44.502	50.816	58.177	66.765	76.790	88.497	118.16	158.66	184.17	213.98	289.49	392.48	723.46	1332.7	2443.8	4450.0
25	28.243	32.030	36.459	41.646	47.727	54.865	63.249	73.106	84.701	98.347	133.33	181.87	212.79	249.21	342.60	471.98	898.09	1706.8	3226.8	6053.0
30	34.785	40.568	47.575	56.085	66.439	79.058	94.461	113.28	136.31	164.49	241.33	356.79	434.75	530.31	790.95	1181.9	2640.9	5873.2	12941	28172.3
40	48.886	60.402	75.401	95.026	120.80	154.76	199.64	259.06	337.88	442.59	767.09	1342.0	1779.1	2360.8	4163.2	7343.9	22729.	69377.	*	*
50	64.463	84.579	112.80	152.67	209.35	290.34	406.53	573.77	815.08	1163.9	2400.0	4994.5	7217.7	10436.	21813.	45497.	*	*	*	*
60	81.670	114.05	163.05	237.99	353.58	533.13	813.52	1253.2	1944.8	3034.8	7471.6	18535.	29220.	46058.	*	*	*	*	*	*

*Future value is greater than 99,999.

598

Appendix D

REFERENCES TO CFA QUESTIONS

Each end-of-chapter CFA question is reprinted with permission from the Association for Investment Management and Research (AIMR), Charlottesville, VA. Following is a list of the CFA questions in the end-of-chapter material and the exams/study guides from which they were taken and updated.

Chapter 2

1. 1986 Level II CFA Study Guide, © 1986.
2. 1986 Level II CFA Study Guide, © 1986.

Chapter 3

19. 1986 Level I CFA Study Guide, © 1986.
20. 1986 Level I CFA Study Guide, © 1986.
21. 1986 Level I CFA Study Guide, © 1986.

Chapter 5

1. 1988 Level I CFA Study Guide, © 1988.
2. 1988 Level I CFA Study Guide, © 1988.
3. From various CFA exams.
4. From various CFA exams.
5. 1981 Level II CFA Study Guide, © 1981.
6. 1985 Level III CFA Study Guide, © 1985.
7. 1988 Level I CFA Study Guide, © 1988.
8. 1982 Level III CFA Study Guide, © 1982.

Chapter 7

16. 1982 Level III CFA Study Guide, © 1982.
17. 1982 Level III CFA Study Guide, © 1982.
18. 1982 Level III CFA Study Guide, © 1982.

Chapter 9

13. 1981 Level I CFA Study Guide, © 1981.
14. 1989 Level III CFA Study Guide, © 1989.

18. 1985 Level III CFA Study Guide, © 1985.
19. 1985 Level III CFA Study Guide, © 1985.
20. 1985 Level III CFA Study Guide, © 1985.

Chapter 10

24. 1993 Level I CFA Study Guide, © 1993.
25. 1993 Level I CFA Study Guide, © 1993.
26. 1993 Level I CFA Study Guide, © 1993.
27. 1986 Level I CFA Study Guide, © 1986.
28. 1986 Level I CFA Study Guide, © 1986.

Chapter 11

7. 1985 Level I CFA Study Guide, © 1985.
13. From various CFA exams.
14. From various CFA exams.
15. 1983 Level III CFA Study Guide, © 1983.
16. 1981 Level I CFA Study Guide, © 1981.
17. 1983 Level III CFA Study Guide, © 1983.

Chapter 12

13. 1993 Level II CFA Study Guide, © 1993.
14. 1993 Level II CFA Study Guide, © 1993.
15. From various CFA exams.

Chapter 13

5. 1987 Level I CFA Study Guide, © 1987.
9. 1987 Level I CFA Study Guide, © 1987.
12. 1988 Level I CFA Study Guide, © 1988.
13. 1986 Level I CFA Study Guide, © 1986.

Chapter 14

4. 1988 Level I CFA Study Guide, © 1988.
5. 1988 Level I CFA Study Guide, © 1988.
6. 1987 Level I CFA Study Guide, © 1987.
7. 1986 Level I CFA Study Guide, © 1986.
8. 1985 Level I CFA Study Guide, © 1985.
9.–17. From various CFA exams.

Chapter 16

5. 1984 Level III CFA Study Guide, © 1984.

Chapter 18

8. 1982 Level III CFA Study Guide, © 1982.
12. 1986 Level III CFA Study Guide, © 1986.
13. 1986 Level III CFA Study Guide, © 1986.

Chapter 19

1.–3. From various CFA exams.

10. 1983 Level III Study Guide, © 1983.

11. 1981 Level III Study Guide, © 1981.

Chapter 20

7. 1986 Level III Study Guide, © 1986.

11. 1986 Level III Study Guide, © 1986.

Name Index

Subject Index